# Computer Concepts with Microcomputer Applications

## Lotus Version


**GARY B. SHELLY**

**THOMAS J. CASHMAN**

**GLORIA A. WAGGONER**


Lynn Ransome

The Shelly and Cashman Series
Boyd & Fraser Publishing Company

## SHELLY AND CASHMAN TITLES FROM BOYD & FRASER

Computer Concepts
Computer Concepts with BASIC
    ClassNotes and Study Guide to Accompany Computer Concepts and Computer Concepts with BASIC
Computer Concepts with Microcomputer Applications (Lotus® version)
Computer Concepts with Microcomputer Applications (VP-Planner Plus® version)
    ClassNotes and Study Guide to Accompany Computer Concepts with Microcomputer Applications (VP-Planner Plus® and Lotus® versions)
Learning to Use WordPerfect® Lotus 1-2-3® and dBASE III PLUS®
    ClassNotes and Study Guide to Accompany Learning to Use WordPerfect® Lotus 1-2-3® and dBASE III PLUS®
Learning to Use WordPerfect® VP-Planner Plus® and dBASE III PLUS®
    ClassNotes and Study Guide to Accompany Learning to Use WordPerfect® VP-Planner Plus® and dBASE III PLUS®
Learning to Use WordPerfect®
    ClassNotes and Study Guide to Accompany Learning to Use WordPerfect®
Learning to Use VP-Planner Plus®
    ClassNotes and Study Guide to Accompany Learning to Use VP-Planner Plus®
Learning to Use Lotus 1-2-3®
    ClassNotes and Study Guide to Accompany Learning to Use Lotus 1-2-3®
Learning to Use dBASE III PLUS®
    ClassNotes and Study Guide to Accompany Learning to Use dBASE III PLUS®
Computer Fundamentals with Application Software
    Workbook and Study Guide to Accompany Computer Fundamentals with Application Software
Learning to Use SuperCalc®3 dBASE III® and WordStar® 3.3: An Introduction
Learning to Use SuperCalc®3: An Introduction
Learning to Use dBASE III®: An Introduction
Learning to Use WordStar® 3.3: An Introduction
BASIC Programming for the IBM Personal Computer
Turbo Pascal Programming

## FORTHCOMING SHELLY AND CASHMAN TITLES

RPG II and III    Systems Analysis and Design



Developed and produced by Solomon & Douglas
Manufactured in the United States of America

Credits for photos and illustrations appear on page I-1, which constitutes a continuation of the copyright page.



Library of Congress Cataloging-in-Publication Data

Shelly, Gary B.
Computer concepts with microcomputer applications / Gary Shelly, Thomas J. Cashman, Gloria Waggoner. -- Lotus 1-2-3 ed.
p. cm. -- (Shelly and Cashman series)
Include index.
ISBN 0-87835-359-3
1. Computers. 2. Microcomputers--Programming. 3. Lotus 1-2-3 (Computer program) I. Cashman, Thomas J. II. Waggoner, Gloria, 1947- . III. Title. IV. Series: Shelly, Gary B. Shelly and Cashman series.
QA76.S5113 1989
005.36'9--dc19    88-38291
CIP

5 6 7 8 9 10 W 6 5 4 3 2 1 0

# CONTENTS

## CHAPTER 1 AN INTRODUCTION TO COMPUTERS 1.1



## CHAPTER 2 MICROCOMPUTER APPLICATIONS: USER TOOLS 2.1



## CHAPTER 3 PROCESSING DATA INTO INFORMATION 3.1

## CHAPTER 4 INPUT TO THE COMPUTER 4.1



## CHAPTER 5 THE PROCESSOR UNIT 5.1



## MAKING A CHIP 5.17

## CHAPTER 6 OUTPUT FROM THE COMPUTER 6.1

## CHAPTER 7 AUXILIARY STORAGE 7.1



## CHAPTER 8 FILE ORGANIZATION AND DATABASES 8.1



## CHAPTER 9 DATA COMMUNICATIONS 9.1



## CHAPTER 10 OPERATING SYSTEMS AND SYSTEM SOFTWARE 10.1

## CHAPTER 11 COMMERCIAL APPLICATION SOFTWARE 11.1



## CHAPTER 12 THE INFORMATION SYSTEM DEVELOPMENT LIFE CYCLE 12.1



## CHAPTER 13 PROGRAM DEVELOPMENT 13.1

## CHAPTER 14 CAREER OPPORTUNITIES 14.1



## CHAPTER 15 TRENDS AND ISSUES IN THE INFORMATION AGE 15.1



## INTRODUCTION TO DOS DOS 1



# Word Processing Using WordPerfect

## PROJECT 1 TYPING, SAVING, AND PRINTING A SIMPLE LETTER WP 2

## PROJECT 5 FORMATTING FUNCTIONS, FILE MANAGEMENT, AND MACROS WP 125



## PROJECT 6 ADVANCED WORDPERFECT FUNCTIONS WP 150



# Spreadsheets Using Lotus 1-2-3

## PROJECT 1 BUILDING A WORKSHEET L 2



## PROJECT 2 FORMATTING AND PRINTING A WORKSHEET L 48

## PROJECT 6 SORTING AND QUERYING A WORKSHEET DATABASE L 210



# Database Management Using dBASE III PLUS

## PROJECT 1 CREATING AND DISPLAYING A DATABASE dB 5



## PROJECT 2 DISPLAYING RECORDS IN A DATABASE dB 41



## PROJECT 3 SORTING AND REPORT PREPARATION dB 78



## PROJECT 4 ADDING, CHANGING, AND DELETING dB 116

## PROJECT 5 ADDITIONAL TOPICS dB 142



## PROJECT 6 THE DOT PROMPT dB 178



## For More Information about the Shelly and Cashman Series

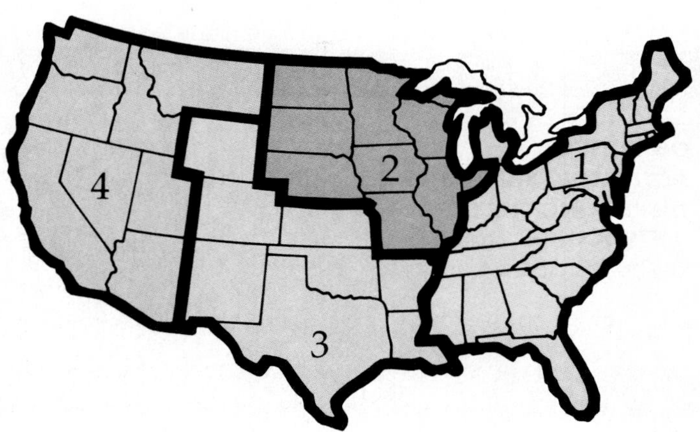


1 ORDER INFORMATION
5101 Madison Road
Cincinnati, OH 45227-1490
General Telephone–513-527-6945
Telephone: 1-800-543-8440
FAX: 513-527-6979
Telex: 214371

FACULTY SUPPORT INFORMATION
5101 Madison Road
Cincinnati, OH 45227-1490
General Telephone–513-527-6950
Telephone: 1-800-543-8444

Alabama, Connecticut, Delaware, Florida, Georgia, Indiana*, Kentucky, Maine, Maryland, Massachusetts, Michigan (Lower)**, Mississippi, New Hampshire, New Jersey, New York, North Carolina, Ohio, Pennsylvania, Rhode Island, South Carolina, Tennessee, Vermont, Virginia, West Virginia, District of Columbia

*Except for ZIP Code Areas 463, 464. These areas contact Region 2 Office.
**Except for the Upper Peninsula. This area contacts Region 2 Office.

2 ORDER INFORMATION and FACULTY SUPPORT INFORMATION
355 Conde Street
West Chicago, IL 60185
General Telephone–312-231-6000
Telephone: 1-800-543-7972

Illinois, Indiana*, Iowa, Michigan (Upper)**, Minnesota, Missouri, Nebraska, North Dakota, South Dakota, Wisconsin

*Only for ZIP Code Areas 463, 464. Other areas contact Region 1 office.
**Only for Upper Peninsula. Other areas contact Region 1 office.

3 ORDER INFORMATION
13800 Senlac Drive
Suite 100
Dallas, TX 75234
General Telephone–214-241-8541
Telephone: 1-800-543-7972

FACULTY SUPPORT INFORMATION
5101 Madison Road
Cincinnati, OH 45227-1490
General Telephone–513-527-6950
Telephone: 1-800-543-8444

Arkansas, Colorado, Kansas, Louisiana, New Mexico, Oklahoma, Texas, Wyoming

4 ORDER INFORMATION and FACULTY SUPPORT INFORMATION
6185 Industrial Way
Livermore, CA 94550
General Telephone–415-449-2280
Telephone: 1-800-543-7972

Alaska, Arizona, California, Hawaii, Idaho, Montana, Nevada, Oregon, Utah, Washington

# PREFACE

This textbook presents fundamental computer concepts in a manner that emphasizes their importance from the user's point of view. These concepts are reinforced by appendices on the most widely used microcomputer applications—word processing, spreadsheet, and database. No previous experience with computers is required for this text.

## ORGANIZATION OF THE TEXTBOOK

This textbook consists of fifteen concepts chapters and four appendices—an introduction to DOS, and three microcomputer applications.

**The Concepts** Fifteen chapters cover a full range of computer and processing concepts. The concept of the information system is introduced in Chapter 1 and used throughout the text. The impact of microcomputers is also addressed throughout. Chapter 2 presents a unique overview of microcomputer applications early in the text. Up-to-date topics such as disk cartridges, relational database systems, computer viruses, SQL and fourth generation languages, and desktop publishing are included where relevant.

**The Applications** After an introduction to the most commonly used DOS commands, students are presented six problem-oriented projects for each software application.

Each project uses the unique Shelly and Cashman problem-oriented approach, in which various problems are presented and then *thoroughly* explained in a step-by-step manner. Numerous, carefully labeled screens and keystroke sequences illustrate the exact steps necessary to solve the problems. Using this approach, students are visually guided as they enter the various commands and quickly learn how to use the software.

Project Summaries list key concepts covered in the project, and keystroke summaries provide a list of each keystroke used to solve the project's problem. Numerous and varied Student Assignments appear at the end of each project and include the following: true/false and multiple choice questions; assignments to explain various commands; realistic problems for students to analyze and solve by applying what they have learned in the project, and minicases for the dBASE projects.

## SUPPLEMENTS TO ACCOMPANY THIS TEXT

Nine teaching and learning materials supplement this textbook. They are the Companion Software, Instructor's Manual, Test Bank, ProTest, Transparency Masters, Data Diskette, HyperGraphics, and *Instructor's Manual to Accompany HyperGraphics*, and *ClassNotes and Study Guide*.

**Companion Software** Free educational versions of WordPerfect, VP-Planner Plus, and dBASE III PLUS are available to adopters of this text. Note that these versions are *not* tutorials but *actual* applications software packages in their commercial form. The software is available for IBM Personal Computers and PS/2 series, and for IBM compatibles. For more information on how adopters can receive this free software, refer to the bottom of the previous page.

**WordPerfect** This educational version contains most of the WordPerfect package. It was developed to help students *learn* the features of WordPerfect, not to be a fully usable tool for professional documents. The limitations of the training version are as follows:

- Documents on the screen can be as large as you desire, but saved documents must be 4K (about 4,000 characters).
- Data files created with the educational version can be imported to the commercial version and vice versa.
- Data files of any size can be printed through parallel printer port 1 without defining a printer.
- One font (excluding extended ASCII characters) can be supported.
- The characters *WPC appear randomly throughout printed documents.

- The educational version of the speller and thesaurus permits training on all the functions of these tools; but these tools cannot be used with any of your own documents due to diskette memory limitations.
- The Help function of the educational version presents the function-key template; as with the speller and thesaurus, memory limitations do not allow the complete help menus to be included on the educational version.
- Data files created with the educational version can be imported to the commercial version and vice versa.

Except for these changes this educational version has the same functionality as the commercial version of WordPerfect 4.2. (Note that WordPerfect Corporation does not publish an educational version of WordPerfect 5.0.)

**Lotus 1-2-3** A free educational version of VP-Planner Plus, a popular spreadsheet package that works like Lotus 1-2-3, is available to adopters of this text. Every sequence of Lotus 1-2-3 keystrokes in this textbook is exactly the same for VP-Planner Plus and the VP-Planner Plus screen can be changed to resemble the Lotus 1-2-3 screen.

The educational version of VP-Planner Plus provides a worksheet of 64 columns by 256 rows and does not allow creation of multidimensional arrays, but otherwise has the same capabilities as the commercial version of VP-Planner Plus.

**dBASE III PLUS** This educational version is limited to 31 records per database file, but otherwise has the same capabilities as the commercial version of dBASE.

**Instructor's Manual** This manual includes Lesson Plans, and Answers and Solutions. The Lesson Plans include: chapter or project objectives, chapter or project overviews, chapter or project outlines that are annotated with textbook page numbers on which the outlined material is covered, notes, teaching tips, additional activities, and a key for using the Transparency Masters. Complete answers and solutions for all exercises, projects, controversial issues, Student Assignments, and Minicases are included.

**Test Bank** This book contains test questions with answers and is a hard copy version of ProTest (see below). It is comprised of three types of questions—true/false, multiple choice, and fill-in. Each chapter or project has approximately 50 true/false, 25 multiple choice, and 35 fill-ins.

**ProTest** This easy-to-use, computerized test generating system is available free to adopters of this textbook. ProTest is menu-driven and allows the creation of custom testing documents plus answer keys. It includes all of the questions from the Test Bank including true/false, multiple choice, and fill-in. ProTest will run on the IBM PC, IBM PS/2, or compatible systems with two diskette drives or a hard disk.

**Transparency Masters** A Transparency Master is included for *every* figure in the textbook.

**Data Diskette** This free supplement contains the documents (letters and memos) used to teach the WordPerfect projects, the Lotus 1-2-3 project worksheets, Student Assignment solutions for WordPerfect and Lotus 1-2-3, the databases that students will create and use in the dBASE minicases, and the data for the dBASE employee database example.

**HyperGraphics** HyperGraphics is an instructional delivery system; it is a piece of software that presents the entire text's content by using graphics, color, animation, and interactivity. It is a state-of-the-art, computer-based teaching and learning environment that enhances classroom instruction and promotes interactive learning and self-study.

**What Hardware Do You Need for HyperGraphics?** You need three pieces of hardware to run HyperGraphics; two additional pieces are optional.

1. An IBM Personal Computer or PS/2 Series computer (or compatible) with a standard CGA graphics card.
2. A standard overhead projector and projection screen.
3. A standard projection device, such as a color projector or a liquid crystal display (LCD), that fits on the projection area of the overhead projector. The projection device is connected to the personal computer, resulting in the projection of the computer's screen.
4. A hand-held remote control device (*optional*) that allows the instructor to navigate throughout the presentation materials and still move freely around the classroom.
5. A set of response pads (*optional*), small pads consisting of 10 digit keys, that can be pressed to indicate a student's response. (These pads are linked to the microcomputer by a controller device.)

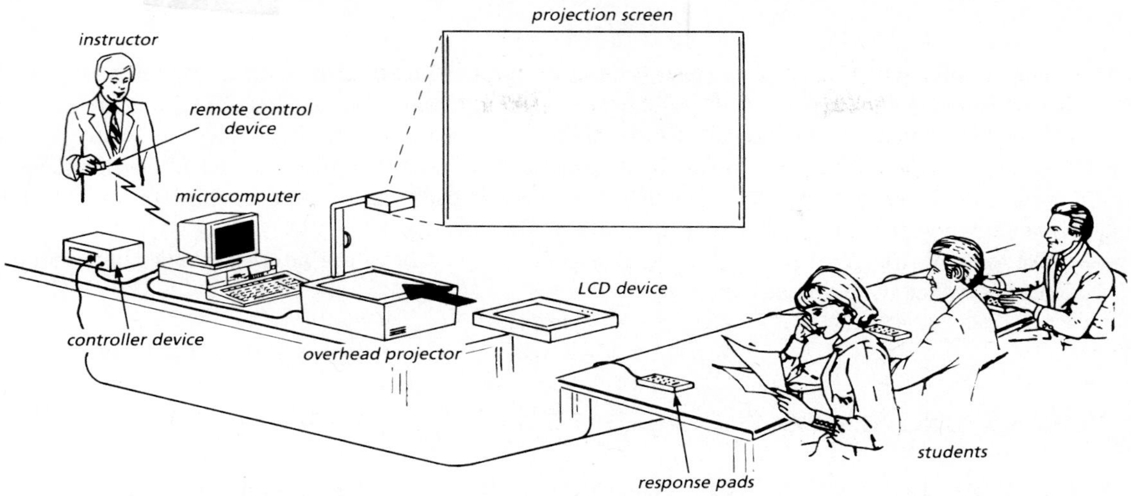

**How Does the Instructor Use HyperGraphics?** HyperGraphics is very easy to use. The instructor presses the appropriate keys on the hand-held remote control device or the keyboard and thereby controls the screen display. This display is projected through the LCD to the overhead projector. The instructor has complete control over the order and pacing of how the lessons are taught. By pushing one or more keys he or she can do such things as:

- View and select from the lesson menu
- Deliver the lesson's instructional materials in sequence
- Repeat any portion of a lesson to reinforce or review material
- Move ahead to specific portions of the lesson
- View the chapter objectives at any time
- View one or more questions about the lesson at any time
- Have students respond to one or more questions via the response pads
- Log students' responses to questions
- Randomly select students to respond to a question
- End a lesson
- Return directly to that point in the lesson where he or she stopped in the previous class meeting

**What Are the Benefits of Using the Student Response Pads?** Instructors can assess student comprehension and retention of class instruction immediately and accurately if they use HyperGraphics with the student response pads. Suppose the instructor presents a multiple choice question on the screen at the end of a segment of a lesson. Students see an indication light illuminate on their response pads, and they have a period of time (controlled by the instructor) to press the button corresponding to the answer of their choice. Answers are tabulated by the microcomputer, and an optional aggregate bar chart of the answers selected is immediately available for viewing by the entire class. Each student's answer is also available on disk for later analysis or review. Thus, the progress of the entire class as well as each student can be tracked throughout the course.

**What Does HyperGraphics Cost?** HyperGraphics is *free* to adopters of this textbook. The only cost is for the computer and the projection device and screen, equipment that most educational institutions already possess. (Student response pads and the controller device are available at an extra charge.)

**Instructor's Manual to Accompany HyperGraphics** This manual contains teaching tips and guidelines for enhancing your classroom instruction using HyperGraphics and easy to implement installation instructions.

**ClassNotes and Study Guide** The *ClassNotes and Study Guide* provides a chance for students to review and study independently. If used with HyperGraphics, this supplement relieves students from laborious and tedious notetaking responsibilities, freeing them to concentrate on the instruction.

## ACKNOWLEDGMENTS

We would like to express our gratitude to the individuals whose efforts made the completion of this project possible and whose talents are reflected in the final results.

Special thanks to Bill Waggoner, whose years of computer industry experience contributed significantly to the content and quality of the concepts chapters.

Thanks also to Jeanne Huntington, typesetter; Michael Broussard and Ken Russo, artists; Becky Herrington, production and art coordinator; Sheryl Rose, manuscript editor; Gerald Swaim, Debbie Moore, and Harriette Treadwell, research assistants; Scott Alkire and Martha Simmons, production assistants; and Marion Hansen, photo researcher.

We are especially grateful to Mary Douglas, director of production, and Susan Solomon, director of development, whose expertise in the field of publishing and commitment to quality is reflected on each page of the text. Our sincere thanks for your encouragement; you truly deserve your reputation as the "best in the business."

Finally we would like to thank Tom Walker, Vice President and Publisher of Boyd & Fraser. His belief in the project and commitment to excellence motivated us to do our best.

**RESEARCH AND PHOTO ACKNOWLEDGMENTS:** The following organizations donated materials used for research and photographs in this book. We thank them.

3Com Corp.; 3M Company; ACCO International, Inc.; Accurex Corp.; Acme Visible Records; ADAC Laboratories; Adage, Inc.; Addisk, Inc.; Adobe Systems, Inc.; Advanced Computer Communications; Advanced Matrix Technology, Inc.; Agricultural Software Consultants; Aim Technology; Aldus Corp.; All Easy Software Corp.; Allied Corp.; Amdahl Corp.; Amdek Corp.; American Laser Systems, Inc.; American Software; AMP, Inc.; Analog Devices; Anderson Jacobsen; Apollo Computer, Inc.; Apple Computer, Inc.; Applicon, Inc.; Applied Data Research, Inc.; Armor Systems, Inc.; Ashton-Tate; Ask Computer Systems, Inc.; AST Research, Inc.; AT&T Bell Laboratories; Atchison, Topeka and Santa Fe Railway Co.; Atek Information Services, Inc.; Auto-Trol Technology Corp.; Autodesk, Inc.; Automated Insurance Resource Systems, Inc.; Aydin Corp.; BancTec, Inc.; Bank of America; BASF Corp. Information Systems; Bates Manufacturing Co.; BBN Software Products; BDT Products, Inc.; Beagle Bros.; Beehive International; Bell & Howell Co.; Bishop Graphic, Inc.; BR Intec Corp.; Broderbund Software, Inc.; Brother International Corp.; Bruning Computer Graphics; Buttonware, Inc.; CADAM, Inc.; Cadlogic Systems Corp.; Career Corp.; CalComp; Camwil, Inc.; Canon USA, Inc.; Century Analysis, Inc.; Chrislin Industries, Inc.; Chromatics, Inc.; Chrysler Motors, Inc.; Cincinnati Milacron, Inc.; Cincom Systems, Inc.; Cipher Data Products, Inc.; Claris Corp.; Cognotronics Corp.; Coin Financial Systems, Inc.; Cole, Layer, Trumble Co.; Command Technology Corp.; Compaq Computer Corp.; CompuScan, Inc.; Computer Associates; Compute Methods Corp.; Computer Museum, Boston; Computer Power Products; Computer Power, Inc.; Computer Support Group; ComputerLand; Computervision Corp.; ComputerEdge Magazine; Control Applications; Control Data Corp.; Convergent Technologies, Inc.; Corning Glass Works; CPT Corp.; Cray Research, Inc.; Cullinet Softwear; Cummins-Allison Corp.; Cylix Communications Corporation; Dartmouth College News Service; Data General Corp.; Datacopy Corp.; Datagram Corp.; Datapoint Corp.; Dataproducts Corp.; Daytronic Corp.; DBX; Delco Associates, Inc.; Dest Corp.; Develcon, Inc.; Diebold, Inc.; Digital Equipment Corp.; Dorf & Stanton Communications, Inc.; Drexler Technology Corp.; Eastman Kodak Company; ElectroCom Automation, Inc.; Electrohome Ltd.; Electronic Arts; Electronic Form Systems; Emerson Electric Co.; Emulex Corp.; Engineered Data Products; Epson America, Inc.; Esprit Systems, Inc.; Evans & Sutherland; Everex Systems, Inc.; Eye Communication Systems, Inc.; Fellowes Manufacturing Co.; Firestone Tire & Rubber Co.; Forney Engineering Co.; Fortune Systems Corp.; Fujitsu of America, Inc.; Gandalf Technologies, Inc.; General Electric Co.; General Meters Corp.; General Motors Corp.; General Robotics Corp.; GenRad, Inc.; Geber Systems Technology, Inc.; Gould, Inc.; GRiD Systems Corp.; Harris Corp.; Harris/3M; Haworth, Inc.; Hayes Microcomputer Products, Inc.; HEI, Inc.; Heidelberg West; Hercules Computer Technology; Hewlett-Packard Co.; Hitachi America Ltd.; Honeywell Bull, Inc.; Hughes Aircraft Co.; Hunt Manufacturing Co.; ICS Computer Products; Imunelec, Inc.; Index Technology; Industrial Data Terminals Corp.; Information Builders; Information Design, Inc.; Infotron Systems Corp.; InfoWorld Publishing, Inc.; Intecolor Corp.; Integrated Marketing Corp.; Integrated Software Systems Corp.; Intel Corp.; Interface Group, Inc.; Intermec Corp.; Internal Revenue Service; International Business Machines Corp.; International Mailing Systems; International Power Machines; Intertec Diversified Systems, Inc.; Ioline Corp.; ITT Information Systems; Jax International; Jet Propulsion Laboratory/California Institute of Technology; John Fluke Manufacturing Co., Inc.; Kao Corp. of America; Kaypro Corp.; Krueger, Inc.; Kurta Corp.; L/F Technologies, Inc.; Lear Siegler, Inc.; Liberty Electronics; Lockheed Corp.; Logical Business Machines; Logitech, Inc.; Lotus Development Corp.; LXE Division of Electromagnetic Sciences, Inc.; Management Science America, Inc.; Maxell Corp. of America; Maxtor Corp.; MBI, Inc.; McDonnell Douglas Computer Systems, Inc.; MDS Qantel, Inc.; Mead Data Central; Memorex Corp.; Mentor Graphics Corp.; Message Processing Systems, Inc.; MICOM Systems, Inc.; Micro Display Systems, Inc.; Microcomputer Accessories, Inc.; Micrografx, Inc.; Micron Technology, Inc.; MicroPro International Corp.; Microsoft Corp.; Microtek; Mini-Computer Business Applications, Inc.; Minolta Corp.; Modular Computer Systems, Inc.; Moore Business Forms, Inc.; Motorola, Inc.; Mountain Computer, Inc.; MSI Data Corp.; NASA; National Semiconductor Corp.; NCR Corp.; NEC America, Inc.; NEC Home Electronics; NEC Information Systems, Inc.; Neuron Data, Inc.; Norman Magnetics, Inc.; Norsk Data; Northern Telecom, Inc.; Novation, Inc.; Okidata; Olivetti USA; Oracle Corp.; Packard Bell; Panafax Corp.; Panasonic Industrial Co.; Panel Concepts, Inc.; Paperback Software; Paradyne Corp.; Penril DataComm; Perception Technology; Pertec Peripherals Corp.; Photo & Sound Co.; Pitney Bowes; Plus Development Corp.; Polariod Corp.; Prentice Corp.; Princeton Graphics Systems; Princeton University; Printronix; Promethus Products, Inc.; Pyramid Technology; Quadram Corp.; Quality Micro Systems; Questronics, Inc.; Quicksoft, Inc.; Racal-Milgo; Racal-Vadic; Radio Shack, A Division of Tandy Corp.; RB Graphic Supply Co.; RCA; Reliance Plastics & Packaging Division; Ring King Visibles, Inc.; Rockwell International; Royal Seating Corp.; Sato Corp.; Schlage Electronics; Scientific Atlanta; Scientific Calculations, Inc.; Scotland Rack, Ltd.; Seagate Technology Shaffstall Corp.; Sharp Electronics Corp.; Siecor Corp. of America; Siemens Information Systems, Inc.; Silicon Graphics; Sony Corp. of America; Soricon Corp.; Spectra Physics; Spectragraphics Corp.; SRI International; STB Systems, Inc.; Steelcase, Inc.; Storage Technology Corp.; Summagraphics Corp.; Sun Microsystems, Inc.; Sunol Systems; Symbolics, Inc.; Synergistics, Inc.; Syntrex, Inc.; T/Maker Co.; TAB Products Co.; Talaris Systems, Inc.; Tallgrass Technologies; Tandem Computers, Inc.; Tandon Corp.; Tangent Technologies; TDA, Inc.; Tecmar, Inc.; Telematics; Telenet Communications Corp.; Telenova, Inc.; TeleVideo Systems, Inc.; Telex Communications, Inc.; Telex Computer Products, Inc.; Teltone Corp.; Texas Instruments, Inc.; Thomson Information Systems Corp.; Thunderware, Inc.; Toor Furniture Corp.; Topaz, Inc.; TOPS, a division of Sun Microsystems, Inc.; Toshiba America, Inc.; Totec Co. Ltd.; U.S. Department of the Navy; U.S. Postal Service; UIS, Inc.; Ungermann-Bass, Inc.; Unisys Corp.; Universal Data Systems; Varityper; Ven-Tel, Inc.; Vermont Microsystems; Versatec; Verticom, Inc.; Video-7, Inc.; Viking; Votan; Voxtron Systems, Inc.; Wandel & Goltermann, Inc.; Wang Laboratories, Inc.; Weber Marking Systems, Inc.; Western Digital Corp.; Western Graphtec, Inc.; Westinghouse Furniture Systems; WordPerfect Corp.; Wyse Technology; Xerox Corp.; Xtra Business Systems; Z-Soft Corp.; Zehntel, Inc.; Zenith Data Systems; Ziff-Davis Publishing Co.

CHAPTER 1

# An Introduction to Computers

CHAPTER 1

# An Introduction to Computers

## OBJECTIVES

- Explain what a computer is and how it processes data to produce information.
- Identify the four operations of the information processing cycle: input, process, output, and storage.
- Explain how the operations of the information processing cycle are performed by computer hardware and software.
- Identify the major categories of computers.
- Describe the six elements of an information system: equipment, software, data, personnel, users and procedures.
- Identify the qualities of information.
- Describe the evolution of the computer industry.

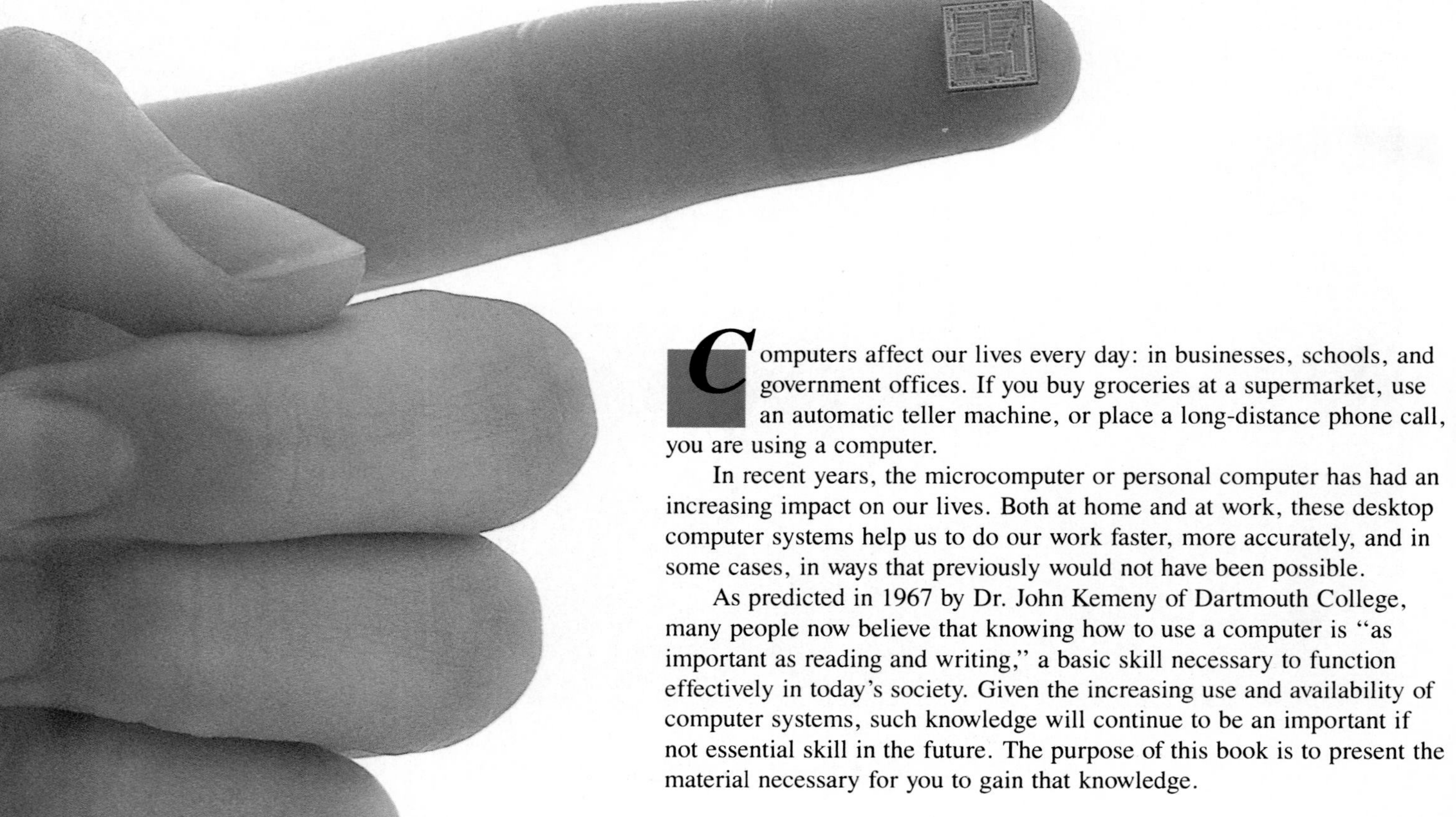

**FIGURE 1-1**
**This microcomputer chip contains the electronic circuits that perform the operations of a computer.**

Computers affect our lives every day: in businesses, schools, and government offices. If you buy groceries at a supermarket, use an automatic teller machine, or place a long-distance phone call, you are using a computer.

In recent years, the microcomputer or personal computer has had an increasing impact on our lives. Both at home and at work, these desktop computer systems help us to do our work faster, more accurately, and in some cases, in ways that previously would not have been possible.

As predicted in 1967 by Dr. John Kemeny of Dartmouth College, many people now believe that knowing how to use a computer is "as important as reading and writing," a basic skill necessary to function effectively in today's society. Given the increasing use and availability of computer systems, such knowledge will continue to be an important if not essential skill in the future. The purpose of this book is to present the material necessary for you to gain that knowledge.

## WHAT IS A COMPUTER?

The most obvious question related to understanding computers and their impact on our lives is, "What is a computer?" A **computer** is an electronic device, operating under the control of instructions stored in its own memory unit, that can accept data (input), process data arithmetically and logically, produce output from the processing, and store the results for future use. This definition of a computer encompasses devices of many different sizes and capabilities. While a microcomputer chip such as the one shown in Figure 1-1 may fulfill the definition of a computer, the term is generally used to describe a collection of devices that function together to process data. An example of the devices that make up a computer is shown in Figure 1-2.

## WHAT DOES A COMPUTER DO?

Whether they are small or large, computers are capable of performing four general operations. These operations comprise the **information processing cycle**. They are input, process, output, and storage. Collectively, these operations describe the storage capabilities of a computer and the procedures that a computer performs in order to process data into information.

**Data** is required for all computer processing. It refers to the raw facts, including numbers and words, given to a computer during the input operation. In the processing phase, the computer manipulates the data in a predetermined manner to create information. **Information** refers to data that has been processed into a form that has meaning and is useful. The production of information by processing data on a computer is called **information processing**, or sometimes **electronic data processing**. During the output operation, the information that has been created is put into some form, such as a printed report, that people can use. The information can also be stored in an electronic format for future use.

The people who either use the computer directly or utilize the information it provides are called **computer users, end users**, or sometimes just simply **users**. Figure 1-3 shows a computer user and demonstrates how the four operations of the information processing cycle can take place on a personal computer. (1) The computer user inputs data by pressing the keys on the keyboard. (2) The data is then processed or manipulated by the unit called the processor.

**FIGURE 1-3**
**The use of this personal computer illustrates the four operations of the information processing cycle: input, process, output, and storage. ▼**

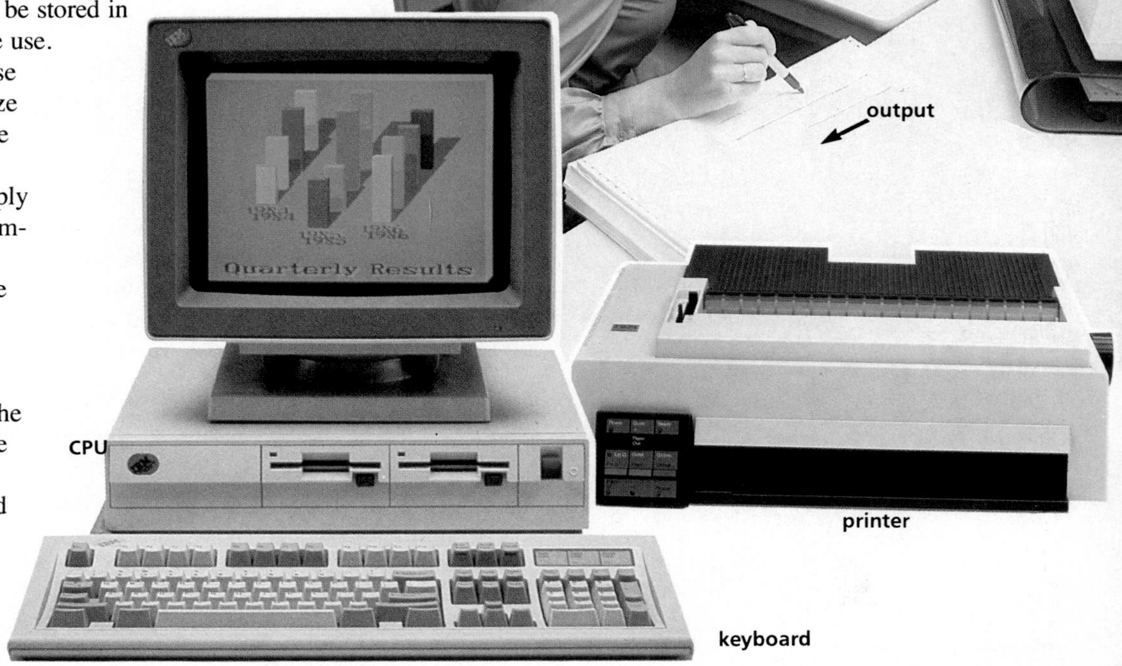

**FIGURE 1-2**
**The devices that comprise a microcomputer. ▶**

(3) The output or results from the processing are displayed on the screen or printed on the printer, providing information to the user. (4) Finally, the output may be stored on a disk for future reference.

## WHY IS A COMPUTER SO POWERFUL?

The input, process, output, and storage operations that a computer performs may seem very basic and simple. However, the computer's power derives from its ability to perform these operations very quickly, accurately, and reliably. In a computer, operations occur through the use of electronic circuits contained on small chips as shown in Figure 1-4. When data flows along these circuits it travels at close to the speed of light. This allows processing to be accomplished in billionths of a second. The electronic circuits in modern computers are very reliable and seldom fail.

Storage capability is another reason why computers are so powerful. They can store enormous amounts of data and keep that data readily available for processing. This capability combined with the factors of speed, accuracy, and reliability are why a computer is considered to be such a powerful tool for information processing.

## HOW DOES A COMPUTER KNOW WHAT TO DO?

For a computer to perform the operations in the information processing cycle, it must be given a detailed set of instructions or steps that tell it exactly what to do. These instructions can be called a **computer program**, **program instructions**, or **software**.

Before the information processing cycle for a specific job begins, the computer program corresponding to that job is stored in the computer. Once it is stored, the computer can begin to process data by executing the program's first instruction. The computer proceeds to execute one program instruction after another until the job is complete.

**FIGURE 1-4**
**Inside a computer are boards containing the chips and other electronic components that process data in billionths of a second.**

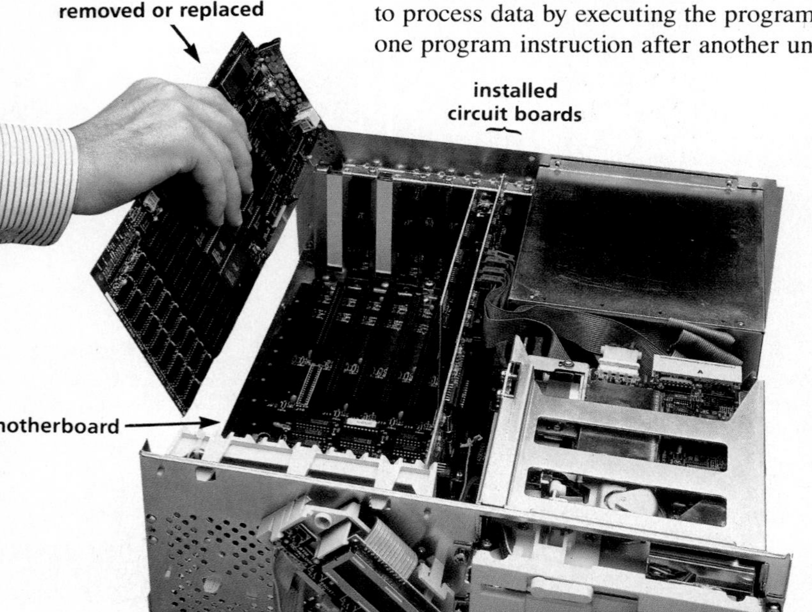


## INFORMATION PROCESSING: A BUSINESS APPLICATION

The example in Figure 1-5 illustrates the use of a computer to produce varied information from data contained on a sales invoice. Once the appropriate computer program has been loaded into the computer, processing occurs as follows:

1. The computer user enters data on the sales invoice into the computer.
2. The data entered into the computer is processed to create information.

3. Output from the processing is generated in three forms:
   a. A bar chart illustrates the daily sales, using a different color to represent each day of the week.
   b. A monthly sales report shows the monthly sales. The report displays the total sales for each week, together with the total sales for the month.
   c. The screen displays the name of the salesperson who generated the most sales during the month. In this example, Joan Rice had total sales of $1,250.00, which was the highest for the month.
4. The data entered and information created are stored for future use.

A key point of this example is that several different forms of information can be produced from a single set of data. Without the computer's ability to manipulate the data, the information produced would be difficult, costly, and time consuming to obtain.

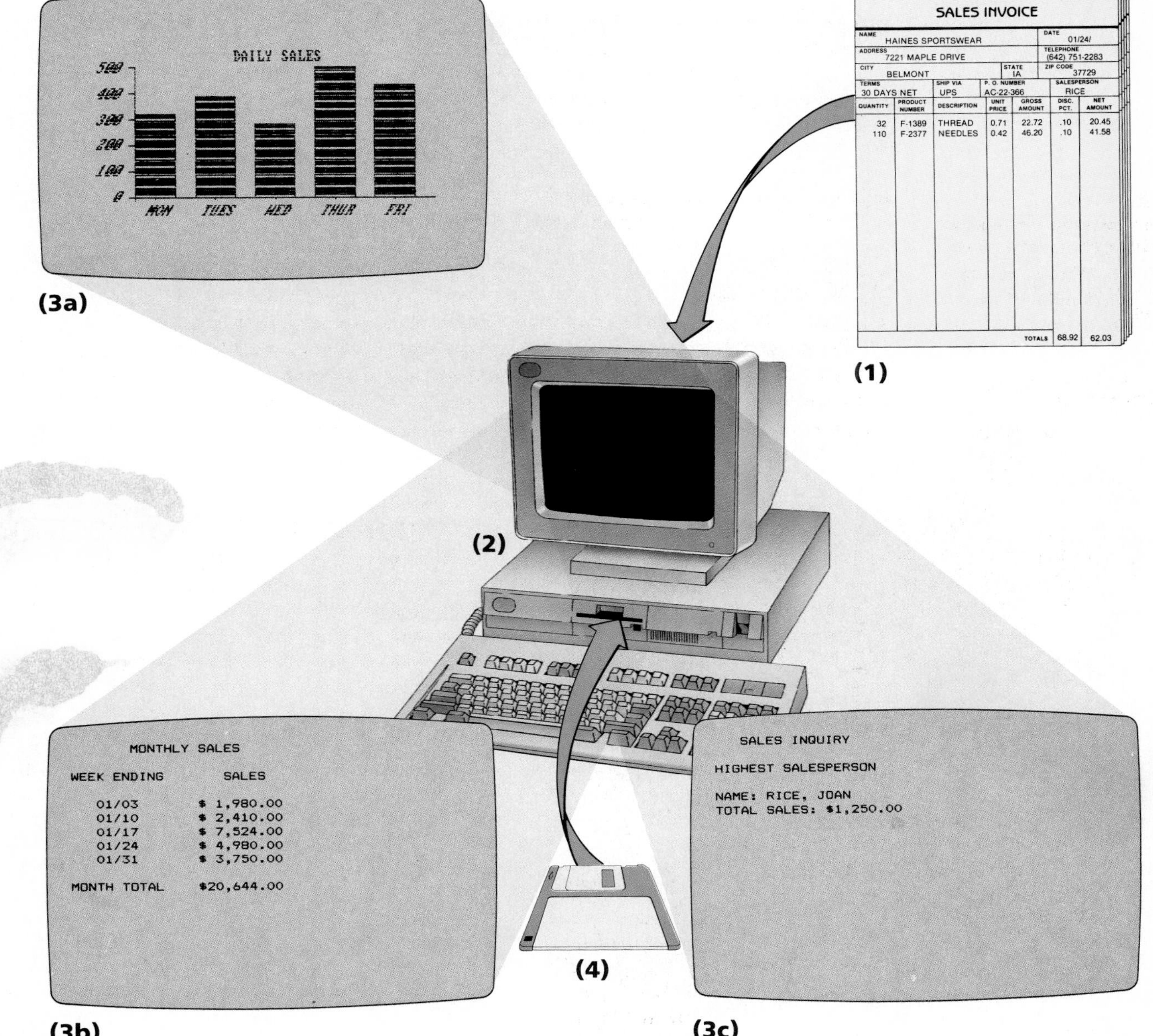


**FIGURE 1-5**
**The data contained on the sales invoices is entered into the computer. After the data is processed, information in the form of a graph, a report, and a screen display is produced.**

## THE INFORMATION PROCESSING CYCLE

Your understanding of the information processing cycle introduced in this chapter is fundamental to understanding computers and how they process data into information. To review, the information processing cycle consists of four operations. They are: input, process, output, storage.

The first three of these operations, **input**, **process**, and **output**, describe the procedures that a computer performs in order to process data into information. The fourth operation, **storage**, describes a computer's electronic storage capability. As you learn more about computers you will see that these four operations apply to both the computer equipment and the computer software. The equipment or devices of a computer are classified according to the operations that they perform. Computer software is made up of instructions that describe how the operations are to be performed.

## WHAT ARE THE COMPONENTS OF A COMPUTER?

Processing data on a computer is performed by specific equipment that is often referred to as computer **hardware** (Figure 1-6). This equipment consists of: input devices, processor unit, output devices, auxiliary storage units.

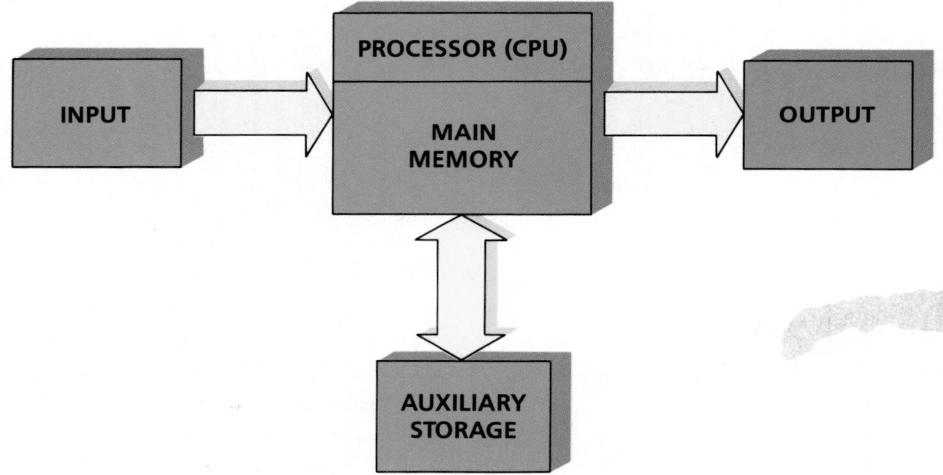


**FIGURE 1-6**
**A computer is composed of input devices through which data is entered into the computer; the processor that processes data stored in main memory; output devices on which the results of the processing are made available; and auxiliary storage units that store data for future processing.**

### Input Devices

**Input devices** are used to enter data into a computer. A common input device is the **keyboard** (Figure 1-7a). As the data is entered or **keyed**, it is displayed on a screen and stored in the computer.

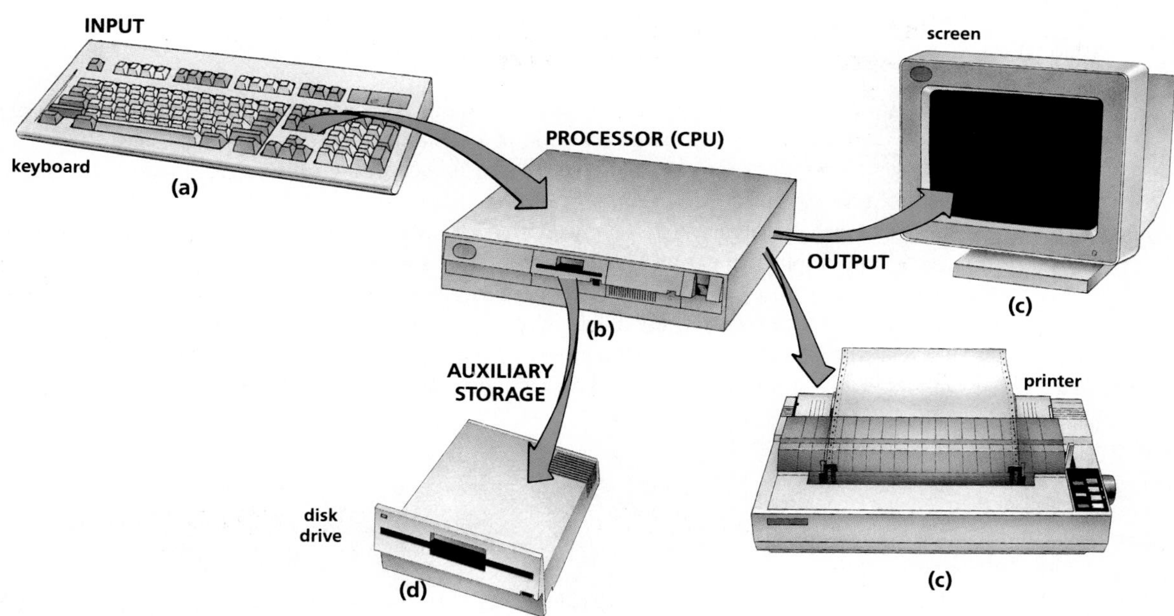


**FIGURE 1-7**
**This figure illustrates the components of a computer that perform the four operations of the information processing cycle.**

## Processor Unit

The **processor unit** (Figure 1-7b) of a computer contains the electronic circuits that actually cause the processing of data to occur. All arithmetic and logical data processing takes place in the processor. Numeric calculations such as addition, subtraction, multiplication, and division are called **arithmetic operations**. Comparisons of data to see if one value is greater than, equal to, or less than another are called **logical operations**. The processor is sometimes called the **central processing unit** or **CPU**.

**Main memory**, also called **primary storage**, is a part of the processor unit. Main memory electronically stores data and program instructions when they are being processed.

## Output Devices

Output from a computer can be presented in many forms. Where the computer is used for business applications or business-related personal applications, the two most commonly used **output devices** are the **printer** and the computer **screen** (Figure 1-7c). Other frequently used names for the screen are the **monitor** or the **CRT**, which stands for **cathode ray tube**.

## Auxiliary Storage Units

**Auxiliary storage units** store instructions and data when they are not being used by the processor unit. A common auxiliary storage device on personal computers is a disk drive (Figure 1-7d), which stores data as magnetic spots on a small plastic disk called a **diskette** or **floppy disk**. Another auxiliary storage device is called a **hard disk drive**. Hard disk drives contain nonremovable metal disks and provide larger storage capacities than floppy disk drives.

Each computer component plays an important role. The processing unit is where the actual processing of data occurs. The input devices, output devices, and auxiliary storage units that surround the processing unit are sometimes referred to as **peripheral devices**.

## CATEGORIES OF COMPUTERS

Figure 1-8 shows the following four major categories of computers: microcomputers, minicomputers, mainframe computers, and supercomputers.

Computers are generally classified according to their size, speed, processing capabilities, and price. However, because of rapid changes in technology, firm definitions of these categories do not exist. This year's speed, performance, and price classification of a mainframe might fit next year's classification of a minicomputer. Even though they are not firmly defined, the categories are frequently referred to and should be generally understood.

**Microcomputers** (Figure 1-8a), also called **personal computers** or **micros**, are the small desktop-size systems that have become so widely used in recent years. These machines are generally priced under $10,000. This category also includes laptop, portable, and supermicro computers.

**FIGURE 1-8**
**(a) Microcomputers are small desktop-sized computers. These machines have become so widely used that they are sometimes called ''desktop appliances.''**

**(b) Minicomputers can perform many of the functions of a mainframe computer, but on a smaller scale.**

**(c) Mainframe computers are large, powerful machines that can handle many users concurrently and process large volumes of data.**

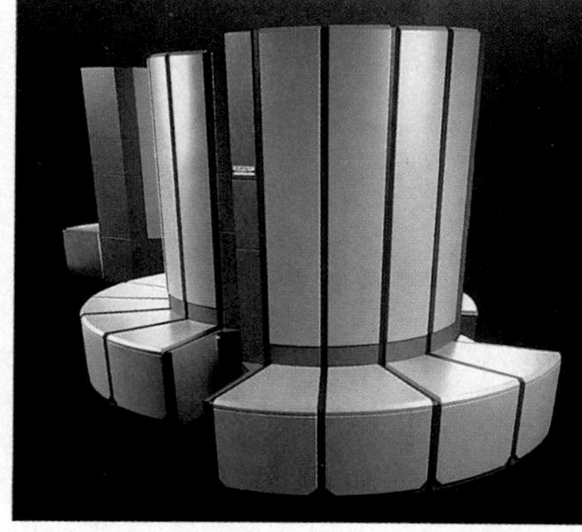

**(d) Supercomputers are the most powerful and expensive computers.**

**Minicomputers** (Figure 1-8b) are more powerful than microcomputers and can support a number of users performing different tasks. Originally developed to perform specific tasks such as engineering calculations, their use grew rapidly as their performance and capabilities increased. These systems can cost from approximately $25,000 up to several hundred thousand dollars. The most powerful "minis" are called superminicomputers.

**Mainframe** computers (Figure 1-8c) are large systems that can handle numerous users, store large amounts of data, and process transactions at a very high rate. Mainframes usually require a specialized environment including separate air conditioning and electrical power. Raised flooring is often built to accommodate the many cables connecting the system components underneath. The price range for mainframes is from several hundred thousand dollars to several million dollars.

**Supercomputers** (Figure 1-8d) are the most powerful category of computers and, accordingly, the most expensive. The ability of these systems to process hundreds of millions of instructions per second is used for such applications as weather forecasting, space exploration, and other jobs requiring long, complex calculations. These machines cost several million dollars.

## COMPUTER SOFTWARE

As previously mentioned, a computer is directed by a series of instructions called a computer program (see Figure 1-9), which specifies the sequence of operations to be performed. To do this, the program must be stored in the main memory of the computer. Computer programs are commonly referred to as **computer software**.

COMPUTER PROGRAM LISTING

```
100 REM TELLIST                SEPTEMBER 22              SHELLY/CASHMAN
110                                                                 REM
120 REM THIS PROGRAM DISPLAYS THE NAME, TELEPHONE AREA CODE
130 REM AND PHONE NUMBER OF INDIVIDUALS.
140                                                                 REM
150 REM VARIABLE NAMES:
160 REM    A.....AREA CODE
170 REM    T$....TELEPHONE NUMBER
180 REM    N$....NAME
190                                                                 REM
200 REM ***** DATA TO BE PROCESSED *****
210                                                                 REM
220 DATA 714, "749-2138", "SAM HORN"
230 DATA 213, "663-1271", "SUE NUNN"
240 DATA 212, "999-1193", "BOB PELE"
250 DATA 312, "979-4418", "ANN SITZ"
260 DATA 999, "999-9999", "END OF FILE"
270                                                                 REM
280 REM ***** PROCESSING *****
290                                                                 REM
300 READ A, T$, N$
310                                                                 REM
320 WHILE N$<> "END OF FILE"
330   PRINT N$, A, T$
340   READ A, T$, N$
350 WEND
360                                                                 REM
370 PRINT " "
380 PRINT "END OF TELEPHONE LISTING"
390 END
```

**FIGURE 1-9**
**A computer program contains instructions that specify the sequence of operations to be performed. This program is written in a language called BASIC. It allows the user to generate a telephone directory of names, area codes, and telephone numbers.**

Many instructions can be used to direct a computer to perform a specific task. For example, some instructions allow data to be entered from a keyboard and stored in main computer memory; some instructions allow data in main memory to be used in calculations, such as adding a series of numbers to obtain a total; some instructions compare two values stored in main memory and direct the computer to perform alternative operations based on the results of the comparison; and some instructions direct the computer to print a report, display information on the screen, draw a color graph on a screen, or store data on a disk.

Computer programs are written by people with specialized training. They determine the instructions necessary to process the data and place the instructions in the correct sequence so that the desired results will occur. Complex programs may require hundreds or even thousands of program instructions.

Computer software is the key to productive use of computers. Without the proper software, a computer cannot perform the desired tasks. With the correct software, a computer can become a valuable tool.

## Application Software Packages

Most end users do not write their own programs. In large corporations, the information processing department develops programs for unique company applications. In addition, programs required for common business and personal applications can be purchased from software vendors or stores that sell computer products (Figure 1-10). Purchased programs are often referred to as **application software packages** or simply **software packages**.

## Microcomputer Applications Software Packages

Personal computer users often use application software packages. The four most commonly used packages, shown in Figure 1-11, are: word processing software, electronic spreadsheet software, computer graphics software, and database software.

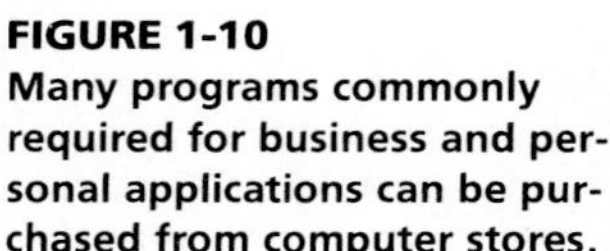
**FIGURE 1-10**
**Many programs commonly required for business and personal applications can be purchased from computer stores.**

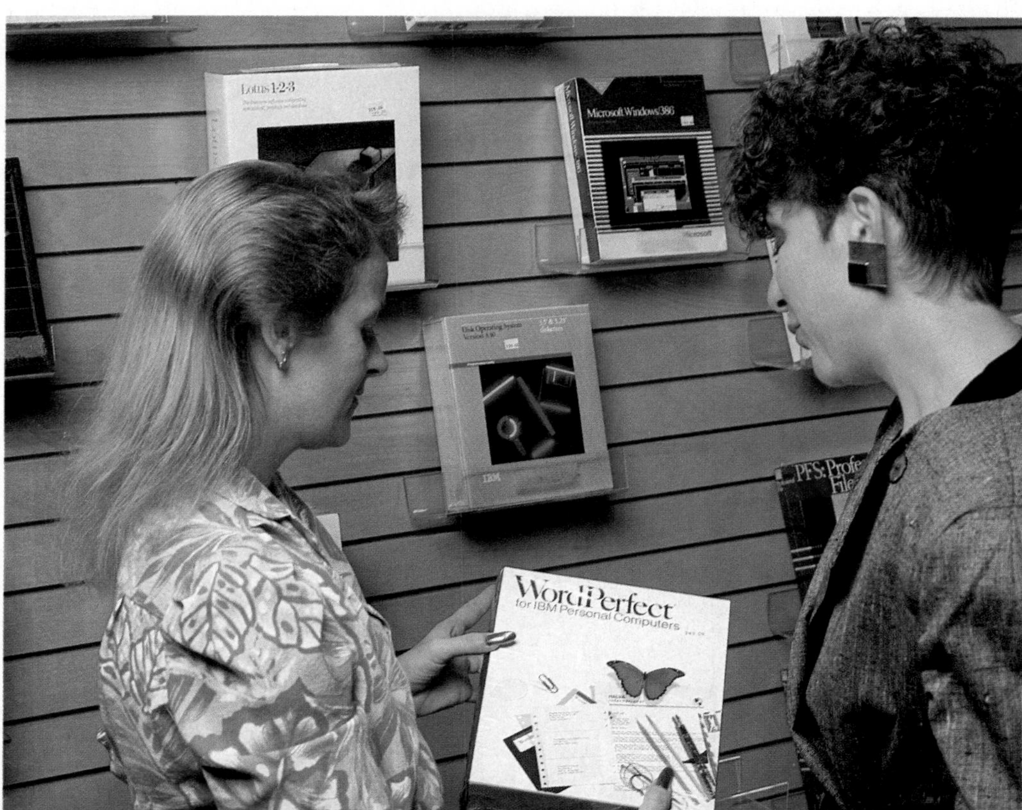

**FIGURE 1-11**
Commonly used microcomputer applications software packages.

```
LETTER                                          01/14
Space 01   Line 07  Page 01      Letter to Johnson
.........1.........2.........3.........4.........5
January 14

Harold A. Johnson
Yonnet Mfg. Co.
3342 Halliard Ave.
Hillsboro, UT 77531

Dear Mr. Johnson:

     I have received your letter concerning the
YT-9975 metal fasteners. We are interested in
testing the part. Would you please send one dozen
of the YT-9975 fasteners. Upon receipt, we shall
begin testing and let you know our decision in
two weeks.

             Sincerely,


             James L. Honnecut
             Vice President, Manufacturing
```

(a) word processing

(a) **Word processing** is used to write letters, memos, and other documents. As the user keys in words and letters, they display on the screen. The user can easily add, delete, and change any text entered until the document is exactly as desired. When the text is correct, the user can save the document on auxiliary storage and can also print it on a printer.

JOHNSON MANUFACTURING CORPORATION
BUDGET FORECAST

FOR THE PERIOD 01/01 THRU 03/31

| ITEM | JAN | FEB | MAR | TOTAL |
|---|---|---|---|---|
| SALES | 112560 | 213450 | 211347 | 537357 |
| RETURNS | 1778 | 331 | 2381 | 4490 |
| NET SALES | 110782 | 213119 | 208966 | 532867 |
| PROD COST | 42773 | 85380 | 71858 | 200011 |
| MARKETING | 13507 | 36287 | 38042 | 87836 |
| PLANT | 21889 | 22229 | 23492 | 67610 |
| G.A. | 31227 | 41783 | 42139 | 115149 |
| TOTAL COSTS | 109396 | 185679 | 175531 | 470606 |
| GROSS PROFIT | 1386 | 27440 | 33435 | 62261 |
| PROFIT % | .013 | .129 | .160 | .117 |

(b) electronic spreadsheet

(b) **Electronic spreadsheet** software is frequently used by people who work with numbers. The user enters the data and the formulas to be used on the data; then the program applies the formulas to the data and calculates the results. A powerful feature of electronic spreadsheet software is the ability to ask "what if" questions by changing the data and quickly recalculating the new results. For example, the user could direct the software to recalculate the profits based on a percentage increase in sales and a percentage decrease in costs.

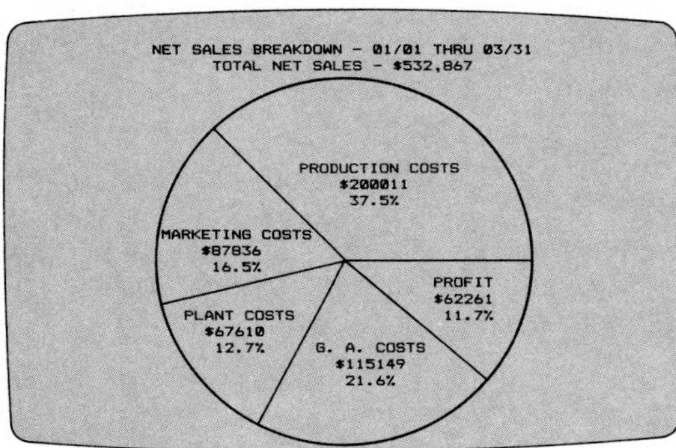


(c) computer graphics

(c) **Computer graphics** software provides the ability to transform a series of numeric values into graphic form for easier analysis and interpretation. In this example, the cost values from the electronic spreadsheet have been transformed into a pie chart. The chart makes it easier to see the various cost elements. Using graphics software, these graphs can be produced in seconds instead of the days that were required for a graphic artist to hand draw each graph.

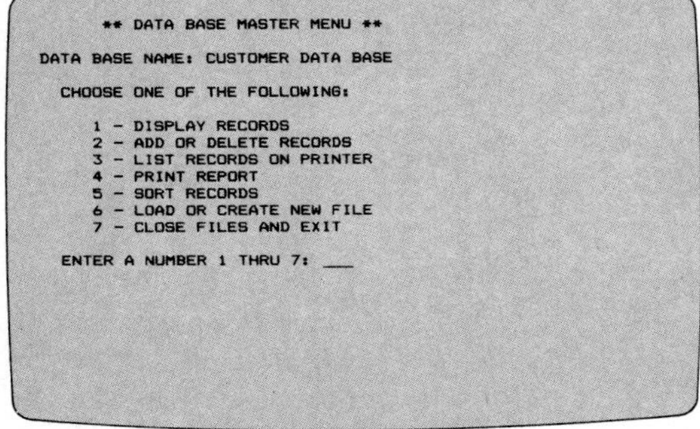

** DATA BASE MASTER MENU **
DATA BASE NAME: CUSTOMER DATA BASE
CHOOSE ONE OF THE FOLLOWING:
1 - DISPLAY RECORDS
2 - ADD OR DELETE RECORDS
3 - LIST RECORDS ON PRINTER
4 - PRINT REPORT
5 - SORT RECORDS
6 - LOAD OR CREATE NEW FILE
7 - CLOSE FILES AND EXIT
ENTER A NUMBER 1 THRU 7: ___


(d) database

(d) **Database** software allows the user to enter, retrieve, and update data in an organized and efficient manner. This screen shows a menu created with a database package. A menu is a list of processes that can be selected by the user and then performed by the program. The user chooses the number corresponding to the processing desired. In this example, the user can display records from the database, add or delete records, list and print data on a printer, sort records, and perform other database maintenance functions.

**Word processing software** (Figure 1-11a) is used to create and print documents that would otherwise be prepared on a typewriter. A key advantage of word processing software is its ability to make changes easily in documents, such as correcting spelling, changing margins, and adding, deleting, or relocating entire paragraphs. These changes would be difficult and time consuming to make on a typewriter. Once created, the documents can be printed quickly and accurately.

**Electronic spreadsheet software** (Figure 1-11b) allows the user to add, subtract, and perform user-defined calculations on rows and columns of numbers. These numbers can be changed and the **spreadsheet** quickly recalculates the new results. Electronic spreadsheet software eliminates the tedious recalculations required with manual methods.

**Graphics software** (Figure 1-11c) converts numbers and text into graphic output that visually conveys the relationships of the data. Some graphics software allows the use of color to further enhance the visual presentation. Line, bar, and pie charts are the most frequent forms of graphics output. Spreadsheet information is frequently converted into a graphic form, such as these charts. In fact, graphics capabilities are included in many spreadsheet packages.

**Database software** (Figure 1-11d) allows the user to enter, retrieve, and update data in an organized and efficient manner. These software packages have flexible inquiry and reporting capabilities that allow users to access the data in different ways.

## A Typical Application: Budget Spreadsheet

Electronic spreadsheets are one of the most widely used software applications. In the following example, a user develops a budget spreadsheet for the first quarter of a year. The user enters the revenues and the costs for the first three months of the year. Then the spreadsheet program calculates the total revenues and total costs, the profit for each month (calculated by subtracting costs from revenues), and the profit percentage (obtained by dividing the profit by the revenues). In addition, the spreadsheet program calculates the total profit and the total profit percentage.

The diagrams in Figures 1-12, 1-13, and 1-14 show the steps that occur in order to obtain the spreadsheet output. A more complete description of these steps follows.

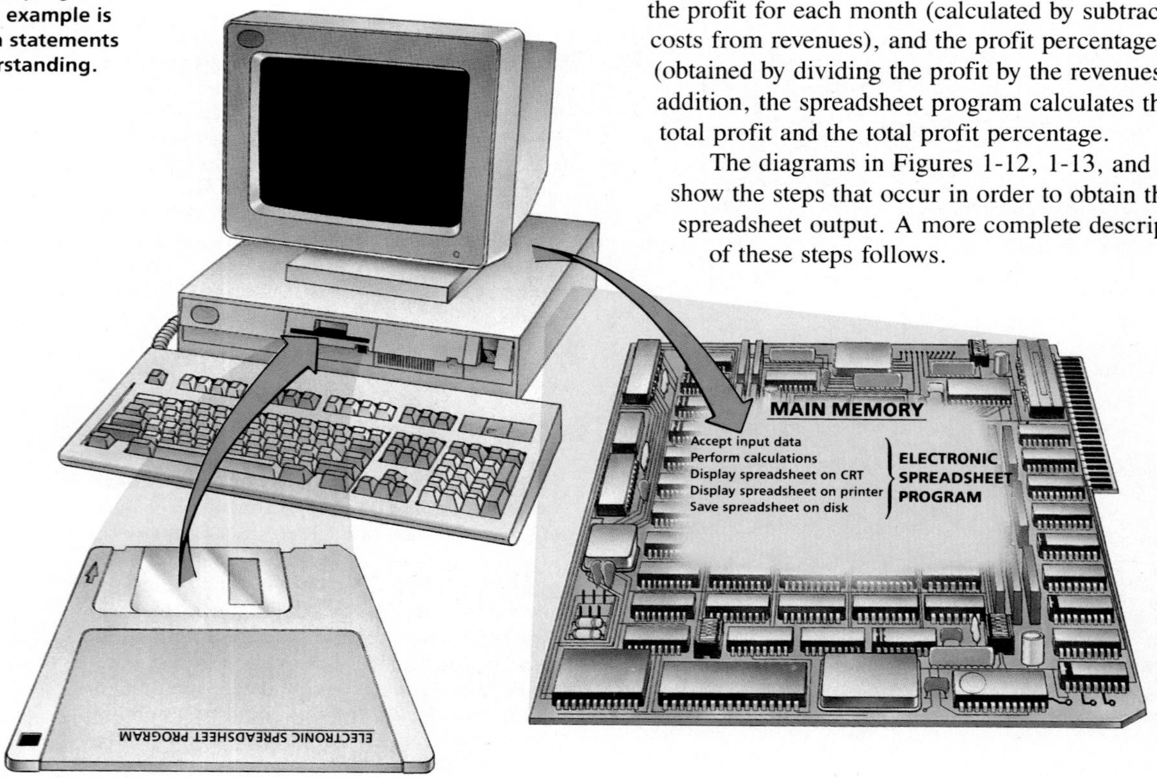

**FIGURE 1-12**
**After the floppy disk is inserted in the disk drive, the spreadsheet program is copied into main memory. The program illustrated in this example is shown as English statements for ease of understanding.**

**Loading the Program** For processing to occur, a computer program must first be stored in the main memory of the computer. The process of getting the program into memory is called loading the program. The spreadsheet program in this example is stored on a floppy disk. To load the program into the main memory of the computer, a copy of the spreadsheet program is transferred from the floppy disk into main memory.

In Figure 1-12, the floppy disk on which the program is stored is inserted into the floppy disk drive. The user then issues the command to load the program from the floppy disk into main memory. After the program is loaded into main memory, the user directs the computer to begin executing the program.

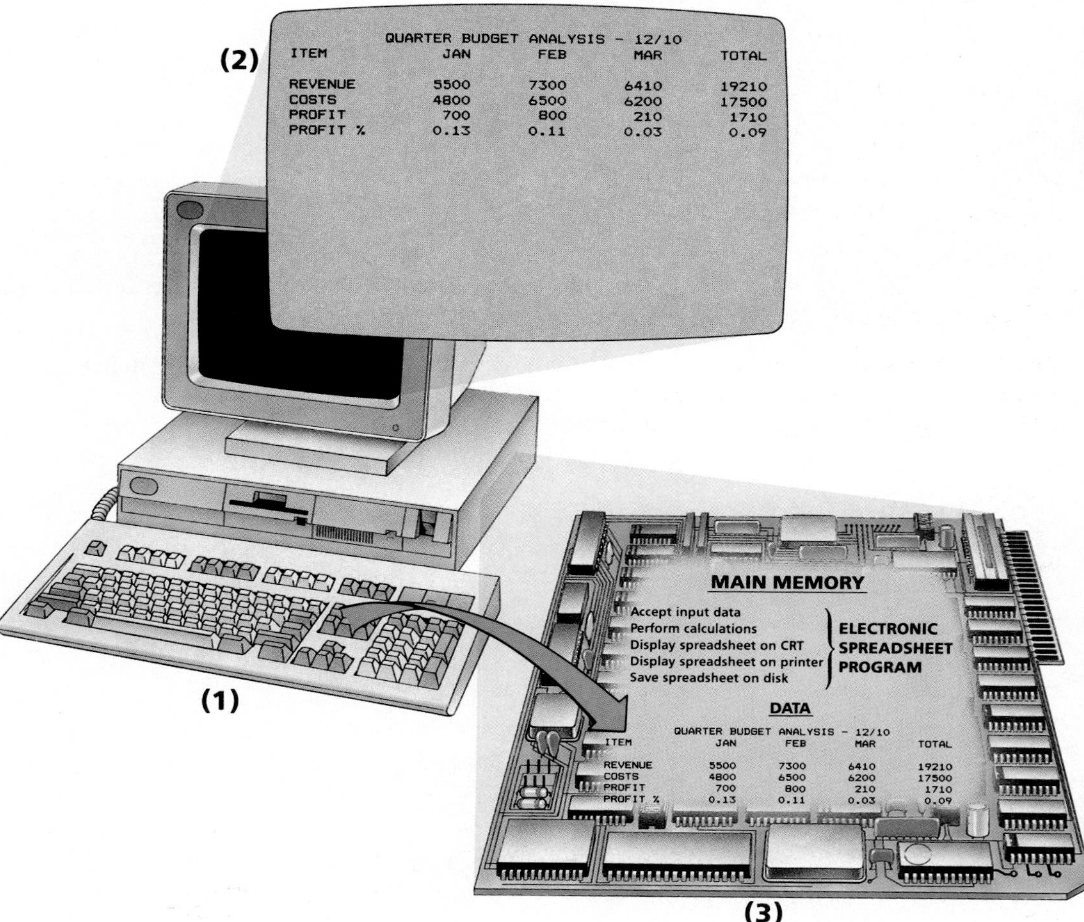


**FIGURE 1-13**
**In this example, the user enters a report heading, column and row headings, the revenues for January, February, and March, and the costs for the three months.**

**Step 1—Input: Enter the Data** The first step in the program is to input the data (Figure 1-13). This is accomplished by using a keyboard. As the data is entered on the keyboard (1), it is displayed on the screen (2) and stored in main memory (3).

The data for this application consists of not only the numbers on which calculations are to be performed, but also some words indicating the contents of each of the columns and rows on the screen.

**Step 2—Process: Perform the Calculations** As Figure 1-14 shows, the user has entered the data (1) and the program will direct the processor to perform the required calculations (2). In this example, the program calculates the profit for each month, the total revenue, costs, and profit for the quarter, the profit percent for each month, and the total profit percent.

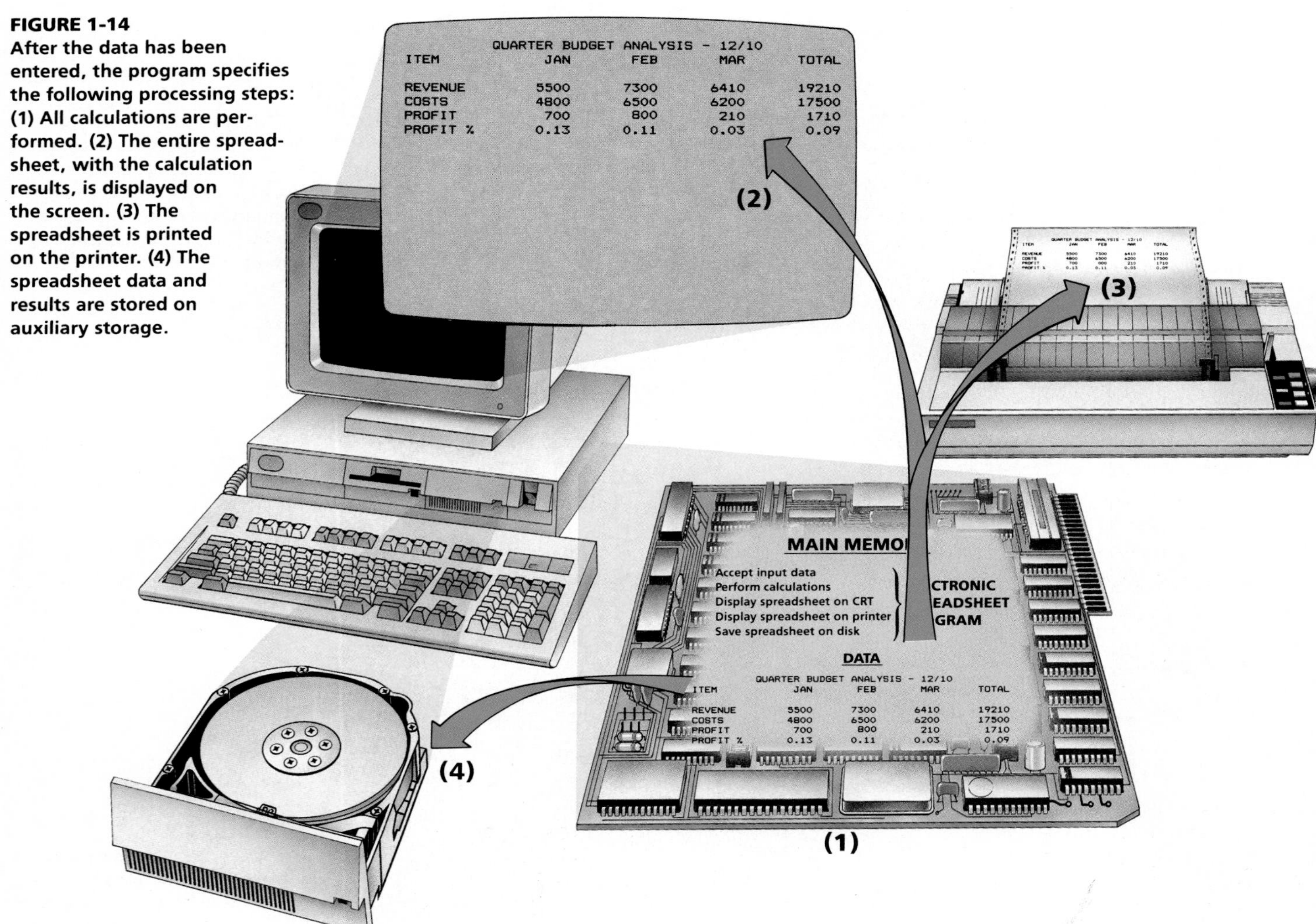


**FIGURE 1-14**
**After the data has been entered, the program specifies the following processing steps: (1) All calculations are performed. (2) The entire spreadsheet, with the calculation results, is displayed on the screen. (3) The spreadsheet is printed on the printer. (4) The spreadsheet data and results are stored on auxiliary storage.**

The preceding operations illustrate the calculating ability of computers. Whenever any calculations are performed on data, the data must be stored in main memory. The results of the calculations are also stored in main memory. If desired, the program can issue instructions to store the results on an auxiliary storage device, such as a hard or floppy disk.

**Step 3—Output: Display the Results** After the calculations have been completed, the program specifies that the spreadsheet, with the results of the calculations, is to be displayed on the screen. The program also specifies that the results are to be printed on the printer (3). When this instruction is executed, the spreadsheet is printed on paper so that the results of the processing can be used by someone other than the computer user.

**Step 4—Storage: Save the Program and Data** The spreadsheet is also stored on a disk, in this example a hard disk, so that at a later time it can be retrieved and utilized again (4).

## WHAT ARE THE ELEMENTS OF AN INFORMATION SYSTEM?

Obtaining useful and timely information from computer processing requires more than just the equipment and software described so far. Other elements required for successful information processing include accurate data, trained information systems personnel, knowledgeable users, and documented procedures.

The equipment must be reliable and capable of handling the expected work load. The software must have been carefully developed and tested, and the data entered to be processed must be accurate. If the data is incorrect, the resulting information produced from it will be incorrect. Properly trained data processing personnel are required to run most medium and large computer systems. Users are sometimes overlooked as an important element of an information system, but with expanding computer use, users are taking increasing responsibility for the successful operation of information systems. This includes responsibility for the accuracy of both input and output information. In addition, users are taking a more active role in the development of computer applications. They work closely with information systems department personnel in the development of computer applications that relate to their areas of expertise. Finally, all information processing applications should have documented procedures covering not only the computer operations but any other related procedures as well.

To summarize, the six elements of an information system are: equipment, software, data, personnel, users, and procedures.

Figure 1-15 shows an example of each of the elements. The following section illustrates the elements as they occur in a large multiuser computer environment.

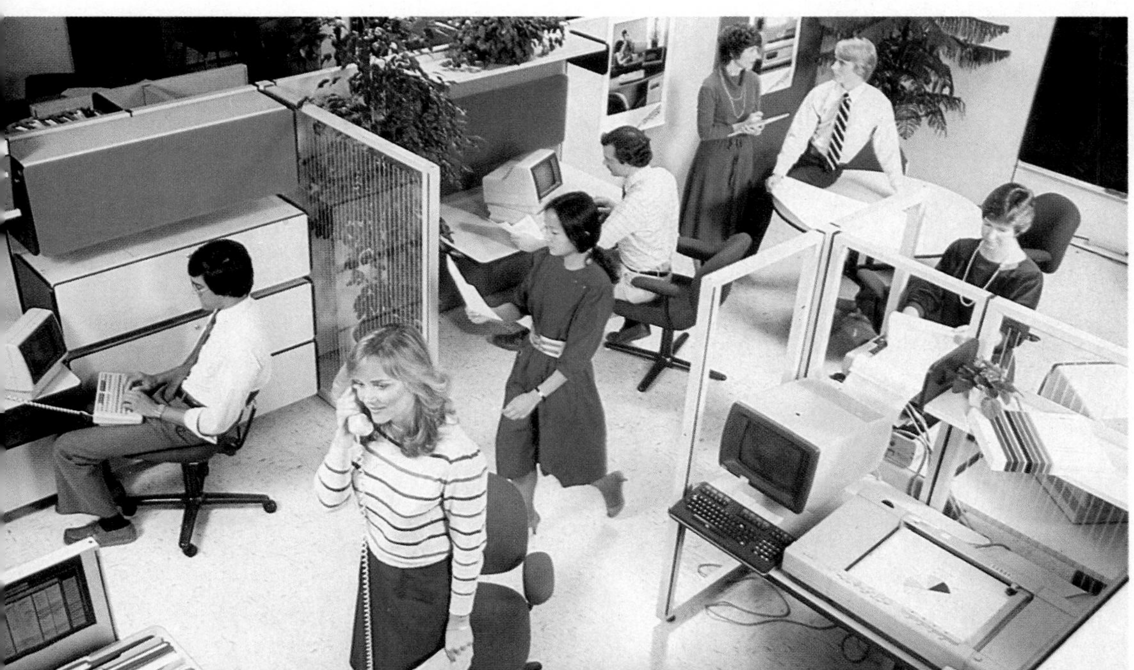

**FIGURE 1-15**
**An information system requires (1) computer equipment; (2) software, which runs the equipment; (3) data, which the computer manipulates; people, including both (4) computer personnel who manage the equipment and (5) users who use the information that the equipment produces; and finally (6) procedures, which help the entire system run efficiently.**

# A TOUR OF AN INFORMATION SYSTEMS DEPARTMENT

Many organizations use computers that concurrently process requests from more than one user. For example, one or more accounts receivable clerks could be entering cash receipts at the same time that one or more accounts payable clerks are entering invoices. Such systems are usually referred to as **multiuser computers**. Multiuser computers are generally under the control of a separate department of the company called the **information systems department**, the **data processing department**, or sometimes just the **computer department**.

The discussion that follows illustrates the elements of an information system by touring a typical information systems department.

## Equipment

We identified the hardware components of a computer system as input devices, processor, output devices, and auxiliary storage. These general classifications apply to the multiuser computer system discussed in this example.

**Input Devices** The primary input device on a multiuser system is a terminal (Figure 1-16). A **terminal** is a device consisting of a keyboard and a screen, which is connected through a communication line or cable to a computer.

**FIGURE 1-16**
**A terminal contains a keyboard and a screen. The screen displays the data entered via the keyboard. ▼**

**Processor** The processor unit of a multiuser computer (Figure 1-17) allocates computer resources to the programs that are being processed. Modern computer processors are so fast that they can usually handle numerous users and still provide very quick response time.

**Output Devices** The most commonly used output devices for a multiuser computer are a printer (Figure 1-18) and a terminal (Figure 1-19). When large volumes of printed output must be produced, high-speed printers are used. The terminal can display both text material and graphics in either monochrome or color.

**◀ FIGURE 1-17**
**This mainframe computer processes data for numerous users. Such a computer is usually placed in a room designed specifically for the machine. Special air conditioning, humidity control, electrical wiring, and flooring are required for many of these installations.**

**Auxiliary Storage** The two major types of auxiliary storage for a multiuser computer are magnetic disk and magnetic tape.

**Magnetic disk** is the most widely used auxiliary storage on multiuser computers. When using magnetic disk, data is recorded on an oxide-coated metal platter (the disk) as a series of magnetic spots. Disk drives can store data on either removable disks or fixed disks. **Removable disks** refer to disk packs that can be taken out of the disk drive. In Figure 1-20, the blue containers for the removable disk packs can be seen sitting on the disk drives. **Fixed disk** drives utilize nonremovable disk packs enclosed in sealed units that prevent contamination of the disk surface.

**Magnetic tape** (Figure 1-21) stores data as magnetic spots on one-quarter to one-half-inch tape on cassettes or reels. On systems with disk drives, tape is most often used to store data that does not have to be accessed frequently. Another common use of tape is for backup storage. The contents of the disk drives are regularly copied to tape to protect against data loss such as in the case of disk drive failure.

◄ **FIGURE 1-18**
**High-speed printers are necessary to print the large volume of reports generated by a multiuser computer system.**

**FIGURE 1-19**
**A terminal is both an input and an output device. In this picture, the user is viewing a color graphics display. ▼**

◄ **FIGURE 1-20**
**Removable disk packs are mounted on the disk drives in this picture. The multiple disk drives shown here are common in large computer installations.**

**FIGURE 1-21**
**This photo shows a magnetic tape drive that uses reels of half-inch tape. Tape is often used to back up the data stored on disk drives. ▼**

When a disk pack or tape is not in use, it is stored in a **data library** (Figure 1-22). These disk packs and tapes must be catalogued so that when they are required, they can be located quickly and taken to the computer room for use.

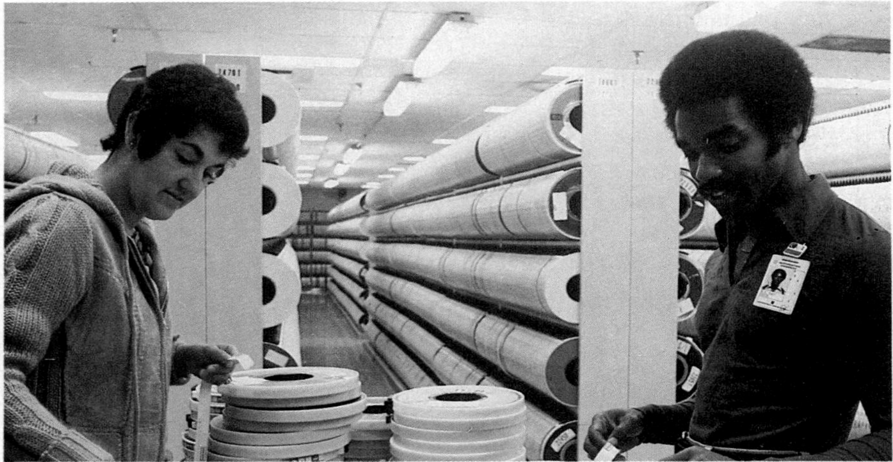

**FIGURE 1-22**
**The data library stores disk packs and tapes when they are not in use.**

## Software

The information systems department keeps its software on either disks or tapes. Once the disk or tape containing the software is mounted on the disk or tape drive, the processor can run the software by reading it into main memory and executing the program instructions. Depending on the amount of disk storage available and how frequently a program is used, some software applications are always available for processing. An example would be order processing software that enters orders into the computer while the sales clerk is on the phone with the customer. Because a phone call can come in at any time, this software application must always be available for processing.

## Data

Data exists throughout an organization and comes to the information systems department in many forms. Often data is in the form of **source documents**, which are original documents such as sales invoices. Sometimes there are no source documents. Then data can be entered directly into the system by users or it can be entered by machines that read special codes or labels. In all cases, the accuracy of the data is important because it will affect the usefulness of the resulting information.

## Personnel

In order to implement applications on a computer, the information systems department usually employs people who have specialized training in computers and information processing. These employees may include data entry personnel to prepare and enter data into the computer; computer operators to run the computer; programmers to write specialized programs; systems analysts to design the software applications; a database administrator to control and manage data; and management to oversee the use of the computer.

**Data Entry Personnel** **Data entry personnel** (Figure 1-23) are responsible for entering large volumes of data into the computer system. Data is usually entered on terminals from source documents.

### Computer Operators

The **computer operator** is responsible for a number of different tasks. When the computer is running, messages are displayed on the **operator's console** (Figure 1-24) indicating the status of the system. For example, a message may indicate that a special form, such as a check, must be placed in a printer. The operator responds to these messages in order to keep the computer running. In many instances, more than one operator is required to run a large computer.

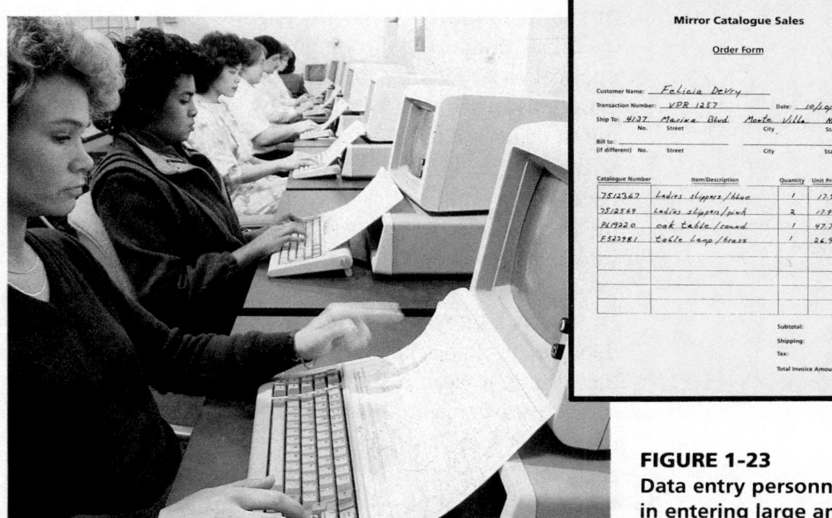

**Mirror Catalogue Sales**

Order Form

Customer Name: Felicia DeVry
Transaction Number: VPR 1257 Date: 10/10/90
Ship To: 4137 (No.) Marina Blvd. (Street) Monte Villa (City) NM (State) 88100 (Zip.)
Bill to: (if different) No. Street City State Zip.

| Catalogue Number | Item/Description | Quantity | Unit Price | Total Price |
|---|---|---|---|---|
| 7512367 | Ladies slippers/blue | 1 | 17.90 | 17.90 |
| 7512569 | Ladies slippers/pink | 2 | 17.90 | 35.80 |
| P619220 | oak table/round | 1 | 47.70 | 47.70 |
| F523981 | table lamp/brass | 1 | 26.90 | 26.90 |
| | | | | |
| | | | | |
| | | | | |
| | | | | |
| | | | | |

Subtotal: 128.30
Shipping: 9.50
Tax: 7.70
Total Invoice Amount: 145.50

**FIGURE 1-23**
**Data entry personnel specialize in entering large amounts of data from source documents.**

**Computer Programmers** **Computer programmers** design, write, test, and implement specialized programs that process data on a computer. The design specifications from the systems analyst tell the programmer what processing needs to be accomplished. It is the programmer's job to develop the specific programs of computer instructions that process the data and create the required information. The analyst specifies "what" is to be done; the programmer decides "how" to do it.

**FIGURE 1-24**
**The console allows the computer operator to monitor the processing.**

**Systems Analysts** Systems **analysts** are called upon to review current or proposed applications within a company to determine if the applications should be implemented using a computer. Applications are considered for computer implementation if, among other things, productivity can be increased or more timely information can be generated to aid in the management of the company. If an application is to be "computerized," the analyst studies the application to identify the data used, how the data is processed, and other aspects of the application that are pertinent to the new system. The analyst then designs the new system by defining the data required for the computer application, developing the manner in which the data will be processed in the new system, and specifying the associated activities and procedures necessary to implement the application using the computer. Analysts work closely with both the people who will be using and benefiting from the new system and the programmers in the information systems department who will be writing the computer programs (Figure 1-25).

**Database Administrator** An important function within the information systems department is the management of data. In many companies, this task is the responsibility of the **database administrator**. Among other things, the database administrator must develop procedures to ensure that correct data is entered into the system, that confidential company data is not lost or stolen, that access to company data is restricted to those who need the data, and that data is available when needed. This function is very important to most companies where billions of pieces of data are processed on the computer, and the loss or misappropriation of that data could be detrimental to business.

**Information Systems Department Management** Management within an information systems department is found at varying levels, depending on the size and complexity of the department. Most information systems departments have operations management, systems management, programming management, and a manager of the entire department. The **systems manager** oversees the activities in the systems analysis and design area of the department. The **programming manager** is in charge of all programmers within the department. Each of the previously mentioned managers may also have **project managers** within their area. The **operations manager** oversees the operational aspects of the department, including the scheduling, maintenance, and operation of the equipment. The information systems department manager is in charge of the entire department and may have the title **vice president of information systems** or **chief information officer**.

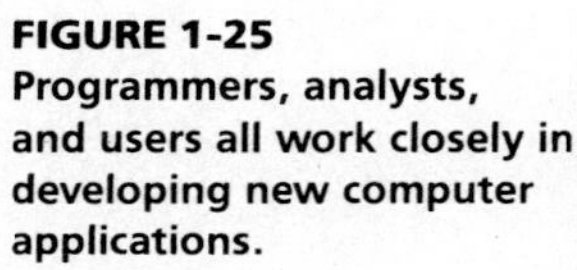

**FIGURE 1-25**
**Programmers, analysts, and users all work closely in developing new computer applications.**

## Users

Users interact with the information systems department in several ways. They are often the first to request that a specific application be computerized. When a systems analyst is assigned to study the application, the analyst will rely on the users' knowledge of the requirements to determine if computerization is feasible. Once an application is implemented, users usually maintain an ongoing relationship with the information systems department. They may request special reports or processing and make suggestions about improving the application.

## Procedures

Written procedures are an important part of any information system. Procedures should be documented for all steps in the processing cycle, including those steps that are not computerized. Accurate, up-to-date procedures minimize processing errors, reduce training time for new employees, and serve as a guide for future changes to the application.

## Summary of the Tour of an Information Systems Department

During the tour of the information systems department we have seen the six elements of an information system: equipment, software, data, personnel, users, and procedures. Each of these elements directly affects an organization's ability to successfully process data into useful information.

# SUMMARY OF AN INTRODUCTION TO COMPUTERS

This chapter presented a broad introduction to concepts and terminology that are related to computers. You now have an understanding of what a computer is, how it processes data into information, and which elements are necessary for a successful information system. The following photo essay is a time line that shows the evolution of modern computers.

# CHAPTER SUMMARY

1. A **computer** is an electronic device, operating under the control of instructions stored in its own memory unit, that can accept data (input), process data arithmetically and logically, produce output from the processing, and store the results for future use.
2. A computer can perform **input**, **process**, **output**, and **storage** operations. These operations are called the **information processing cycle**.
3. **Data** refers to the raw facts, including numbers and words, that are processed on a computer.
4. **Information** is data that has been processed into a form that has meaning and is useful.
5. The production of information by processing data on a computer is called **information processing**.
6. **Computer users** are the people who either directly use the computer or utilize the information it provides.
7. A computer is a powerful tool because it is reliable and can process data quickly and accurately.
8. A **computer program** is a detailed set of instructions that tells the computer exactly what to do.

9. Computer processing can produce many different forms of information from a single set of data.
10. Processing data on a computer is performed by computer equipment including input devices, the processor unit, output devices, and auxiliary storage units. Computer equipment is often referred to as **hardware**.
11. **Input devices** are used to enter data into a computer.
12. The **processor unit** contains the electronic circuits that cause processing to take place.
13. **Arithmetic operations** are numeric calculations such as addition, subtraction, multiplication and division that take place in the processor.
14. **Logical operations** are comparisons of data in the processor to see if one value is greater than, equal to, or less than another value.
15. The processor is sometimes called the **central processing unit (CPU)**.
16. **Main memory** consists of components that electronically store data and program instructions.
17. **Output devices** are used to print or display data and information.
18. **Auxiliary storage units** are used to store program instructions and data when they are not being used in the main memory of the computer.
19. The four major categories of computers are microcomputers, minicomputers, mainframes, and supercomputers.
20. Types of **microcomputers** include laptop, portable, desktop, and supermicro computers.
21. **Minicomputers** address the needs of users who want more processing power than a microcomputer but do not need the power of a mainframe. Minicomputers can support a number of users performing different tasks.
22. **Mainframe** computers are large systems that can handle numerous users, store large amounts of data, and process transactions at a very high rate.
23. **Supercomputers**, the most powerful and expensive category of computers, can process hundreds of millions of instructions per second and perform long, complex calculations.
24. **Computer software** is another name for computer programs.
25. A computer program must first be loaded into main memory before it can be executed.
26. Programs purchased from computer stores or software vendors are called **application software packages**.
27. Four commonly used personal computer software packages are word processing, electronic spreadsheet, graphics, and database software.
28. **Word processing software** is used to create and print documents.
29. **Electronic spreadsheet software** performs calculations on rows and columns of numeric data based on formulas entered by the user.
30. **Graphics software** provides the ability to transform numbers and text into a graphic format.
31. **Database software** allows the user to enter, retrieve, and update data efficiently.
32. The elements of an information system are equipment, software, data, personnel, users and procedures.
33. **Multiuser computers** can concurrently process requests from more than one user.
34. A **terminal**, consisting of a keyboard and screen, is the most commonly used input device for a large computer.
35. Modern computer processors are so fast that they can usually handle numerous users and still provide very quick response time.
36. The most commonly used output devices for large computers are terminals and high-speed printers.
37. Auxiliary storage devices used on a large computer include **magnetic disk** and **magnetic tape**.
38. A **data library** stores disk packs and tapes when they are not in use.
39. Data can be entered directly into the computer by users or by machines.
40. **Source documents** are original documents, such as sales invoices, from which data can be entered.
41. **Data entry personnel** prepare and enter data into the computer.
42. **Computer operators** run the computer equipment and monitor processing operations.
43. **Computer programmers** design, write, test, and implement programs that process data on a computer.
44. **Systems analysts** review and design computer applications. Analysts work closely with users and programmers.
45. A **database administrator** is responsible for managing a company's data.
46. Management within an information systems department includes a **systems manager**, **programming manager**, **operations manager**, and a department manager, sometimes called the **vice president of information systems** or **chief information officer**.
47. **Users** play an important role in the development of computer applications.
48. Procedures should be documented for all steps in the processing cycle, including those steps that are not computerized.

## KEY TERMS

Application software packages *1.10*
Arithmetic operations *1.7*
Auxiliary storage units *1.7*
Cathode ray tube (CRT) *1.7*
Central processing unit (CPU) *1.7*
Chief information officer *1.20*
Computer *1.3*
Computer department *1.16*
Computer operator *1.19*
Computer program *1.4*
Computer programmers *1.19*
Computer software *1.9*
Computer users *1.3*
CPU (central processing unit) *1.7*
CRT (cathode ray tube) *1.7*
Data *1.3*
Data entry personnel *1.19*
Data library *1.18*
Data processing department *1.16*
Database administrator *1.20*
Database software *1.12*
Diskette *1.7*
Electronic data processing *1.3*
Electronic spreadsheet software *1.12*
End users *1.3*
Fixed disk *1.17*
Floppy disk *1.7*
Graphics software *1.12*
Hard disk drive *1.7*
Hardware *1.6*
Information *1.3*
Information processing *1.3*
Information processing cycle *1.3*
Information systems department *1.16*
Input *1.6*
Input devices *1.6*
Keyboard *1.6*
Keyed *1.6*
Logical operations *1.7*
Magnetic disk *1.17*
Magnetic tape *1.17*
Main memory *1.7*
Mainframe *1.9*
Micro *1.8*
Microcomputers *1.8*
Minicomputer *1.9*
Monitor *1.7*
Multiuser computers *1.16*
Operations manager *1.20*
Operator's console *1.19*
Output *1.6*
Output devices *1.7*
Peripheral devices *1.7*
Personal computers *1.8*
Primary storage *1.7*
Printer *1.7*
Process *1.6*
Processor unit *1.7*
Program instructions *1.4*
Programming manager *1.20*
Project managers *1.20*
Removable disks *1.17*
Screen *1.7*
Software *1.4*
Software packages *1.10*
Source documents *1.18*
Spreadsheet *1.12*
Storage *1.6*
Supercomputers *1.9*
Systems analysts *1.20*
Systems manager *1.20*
Terminal *1.16*
Users *1.3*
Vice president of information systems *1.20*
Word processing software *1.12*

## REVIEW QUESTIONS

1. What is the definition of a computer?
2. Identify the four operations a computer can perform, and explain operation.
3. What is data? What is information? How is information derived from data?
4. What is the information processing cycle?
5. What are the four specific hardware units found on a computer? Describe each of them.
6. What is the difference between main memory and auxiliary storage? Why are both necessary?
7. What is computer software? Why is it critical to the operation of a computer?
8. Identify the four software packages most often used with personal computers.
9. Describe the processing of a typical application on a personal computer.
10. What are the six elements of an information system?
11. Identify some of the differences among microcomputers, minicomputers, mainframe computers, and supercomputers.
12. Who are some of the personnel who work in an information systems department?
13. What is the role of a systems analyst? How does that position differ from the job of a computer programmer?
14. What is the user's role in an information system?
15. List the key developments in the evolution of the modern computer.

## CONTROVERSIAL ISSUES

1. When Dr. Kemeny made his prediction in 1967 that learning how to use a computer would be as important as learning how to read and write, few people had access to computers. Since that time, millions of computers have been sold. Do you feel that it is necessary for all students to study computers and their uses? If so, at what grade levels: elementary school, high school, or college?
2. Some people believe that the computer is replacing people in the workforce. Based on what you have learned about computers in Chapter 1, do you think this is a valid statement, or do you think that computers help people do a better job?
3. You learned in this chapter that accurate data is required in order to provide meaningful information. What are some of the consequences if management decisions are based on incorrect data? What obligation does management have to ensure that decisions are based on correct data?

## RESEARCH PROJECTS

1. Write or call a manufacturer of a mini or mainframe computer (IBM, Honeywell, DEC, HP, etc.) and ask for a brochure describing one of their popular models. Prepare a report for your class based on what you learned.
2. Prepare a report for your class describing the use of computers at your school. You may focus on a single department or prepare a general report about computer use throughout the school.
3. Prepare a detailed report on an individual who made a contribution to the history of the computer industry.

# The Evolution of the Computer Industry

The electronic computer industry began about fifty years ago. This time line summarizes the major events in the evolution of the computer industry.

During the years 1943 to 1946, Dr. John W. Mauchly and J. Presper Eckert, Jr., completed the ENIAC (Electronic Numerical Integrator and Computer), the first large-scale electronic digital computer. The ENIAC weighed thirty tons, contained 18,000 vacuum tubes, and occupied a thirty by fifty foot space.

In 1952, the public awareness of computers increased when the UNIVAC I correctly predicted that Dwight D. Eisenhower would win the presidential election after analyzing only 5% of the tallied vote.

1930 1937 1940 1945 1950 1952

Dr. John V. Atanasoff and his assistant, Clifford Berry, designed and began to build the first electronic digital computer during the winter of 1937-38. Their machine, the Atanasoff-Berry-Computer or ABC, provided the foundation for the next advances in electronic digital computers.

Dr. John von Neumann is credited with writing a report in 1945 describing a number of new hardware concepts and how to use stored programs. This brilliant breakthrough laid the foundation for the digital computers that have been built since then.

In 1951-52, after much discussion, IBM made the decision to add computers to their line of business equipment products. This led IBM to become a dominant force in the computer industry.

In 1952, Dr. Grace Hopper, a mathematician and commodore in the U.S. Navy, wrote a paper describing how to program a computer with symbolic notation instead of the detailed machine language that had been used.

FORTRAN (FORmula TRANslator) was introduced in 1957. This programming language proved that efficient, easy-to-use computer languages could be developed. FORTRAN is still in use.

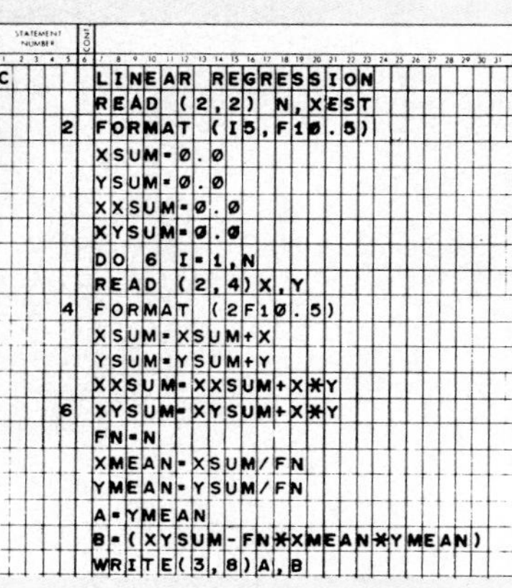

```
C     LINEAR REGRESSION
      READ (2,2) N,XEST
    2 FORMAT (I5,F1Ø.5)
      XSUM=Ø.Ø
      YSUM=Ø.Ø
      XXSUM=Ø.Ø
      XYSUM=Ø.Ø
      DO 6 I=1,N
      READ (2,4)X,Y
    4 FORMAT (2F1Ø.5)
      XSUM=XSUM+X
      YSUM=YSUM+Y
      XXSUM=XXSUM+X*Y
    6 XYSUM=XYSUM+X*Y
      FN=N
      XMEAN=XSUM/FN
      YMEAN=YSUM/FN
      A=YMEAN
      B=(XYSUM-FN*XMEAN*YMEAN)
      WRITE(3,8)A,B
```

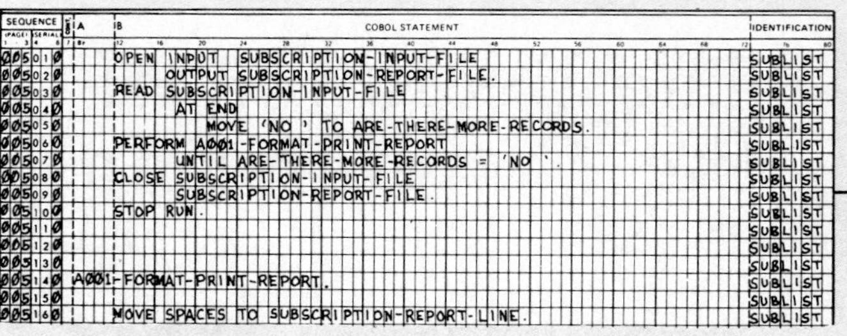

```
SEQUENCE  A   B                 COBOL STATEMENT                            IDENTIFICATION
ØØ5Ø1Ø        OPEN INPUT  SUBSCRIPTION-INPUT-FILE                          SUBLIST
ØØ5Ø2Ø             OUTPUT SUBSCRIPTION-REPORT-FILE.                        SUBLIST
ØØ5Ø3Ø        READ SUBSCRIPTION-INPUT-FILE                                 SUBLIST
ØØ5Ø4Ø               AT END                                                SUBLIST
ØØ5Ø5Ø                  MOVE 'NO ' TO ARE-THERE-MORE-RECORDS.              SUBLIST
ØØ5Ø6Ø        PERFORM AØØ1-FORMAT-PRINT-REPORT                             SUBLIST
ØØ5Ø7Ø              UNTIL ARE-THERE-MORE-RECORDS = 'NO '.                  SUBLIST
ØØ5Ø8Ø        CLOSE SUBSCRIPTION-INPUT-FILE                                SUBLIST
ØØ5Ø9Ø              SUBSCRIPTION-REPORT-FILE.                              SUBLIST
ØØ51ØØ        STOP RUN.                                                    SUBLIST
ØØ511Ø                                                                     SUBLIST
ØØ512Ø                                                                     SUBLIST
ØØ513Ø                                                                     SUBLIST
ØØ514Ø    AØØ1-FORMAT-PRINT-REPORT.                                        SUBLIST
ØØ515Ø                                                                     SUBLIST
ØØ516Ø        MOVE SPACES TO SUBSCRIPTION-REPORT-LINE.                     SUBLIST
```

Dr. Hopper became instrumental in developing high-level languages such as COBOL, a business applications language that was introduced in 1960. COBOL uses English-like phrases and can be run on most brands of computers, making it one of the most widely used languages in the world.

By 1959, over 200 programming languages had been created.

1952 | 1955 | 1957 | 1958 | 1959 | 1960

In 1958, computers built with transistors (above) marked the beginning of the second generation of computer hardware. Previous computers built with vacuum tubes (left) are called first-generation machines.

Third-generation computers were introduced in 1964. Their controlling circuitry is stored on chips. The family of IBM System/360 computers were the first third-generation machines.

Dr. Ted Hoff of Intel Corporation is credited with developing the first microprocessor or microprogrammable computer chip, the Intel 4004, in 1969.

1964 1965 1968 1969

From 1958 to 1964, it is estimated, the number of computers in the U.S. grew from 2,500 to 18,000.

The 1960s saw the birth of the software industry. In 1968, Computer Science Corporation became the first software company to be listed on the New York Stock Exchange.

In 1969, under pressure from the industry, IBM announced that some of its software would be priced separately from the computer hardware. This "unbundling" opened up the industry to emerging software firms.

In 1965, Dr. John Kemeny of Dartmouth led the development of the BASIC programming language. BASIC is the most commonly used language on microcomputers. More people know how to program in BASIC than any other language.

Digital Equipment Corporation (DEC) introduced the first minicomputer in 1965.

Fourth-generation computers emerged in 1970. These machines were built with chips that utilized LSI (large-scale integration). The chips used in 1965 could contain as many as 1,000 circuits. By 1970, the LSI chip could contain as many as 15,000.

The VisiCalc spreadsheet program written by Dan Bricklin and Bob Frankston was introduced in 1979. This product was originally written to run on Apple II computers. Together, VisiCalc and Apple II computers became rapidly successful in the business community. Most people consider VisiCalc to be the single most important reason why microcomputers gained acceptance in the business world.

1970 1975 1980

The MITS, Inc., Altair computer was the first commercially successful microcomputer. It sold in kit form for less than $500.

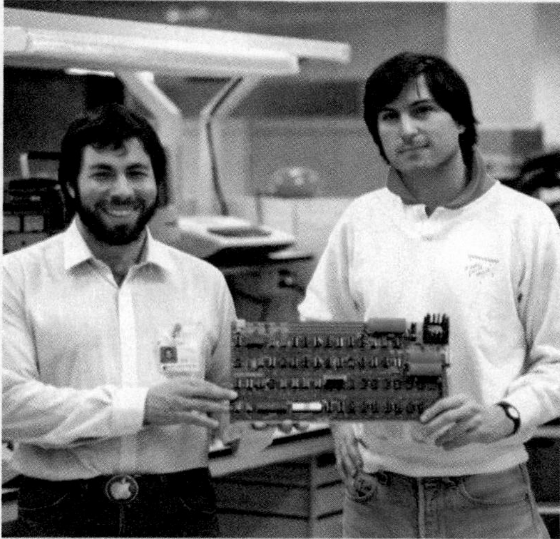

In 1976, Steve Jobs and Steve Wozniak built the first Apple computer.

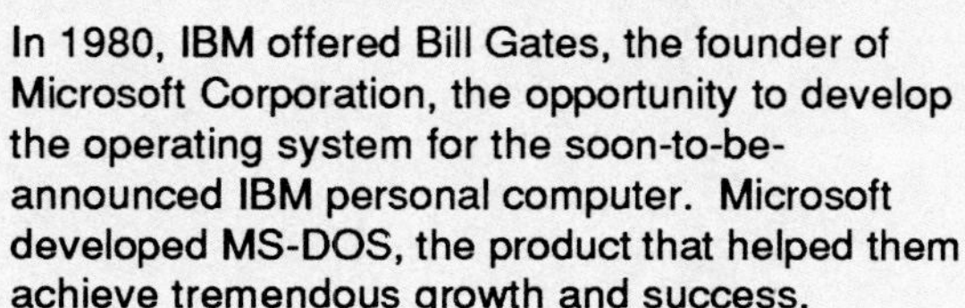

In 1980, IBM offered Bill Gates, the founder of Microsoft Corporation, the opportunity to develop the operating system for the soon-to-be-announced IBM personal computer. Microsoft developed MS-DOS, the product that helped them achieve tremendous growth and success.

The Lotus 1-2-3 integrated software package, developed by Mitch Kapor, was introduced in 1983. It combined spread-sheet, graphics, and database programs in one package.

1981 1982 1983 1985

It is estimated that 313,000 microcomputers were sold in 1981. In 1982, the number jumped to 3,275,000.

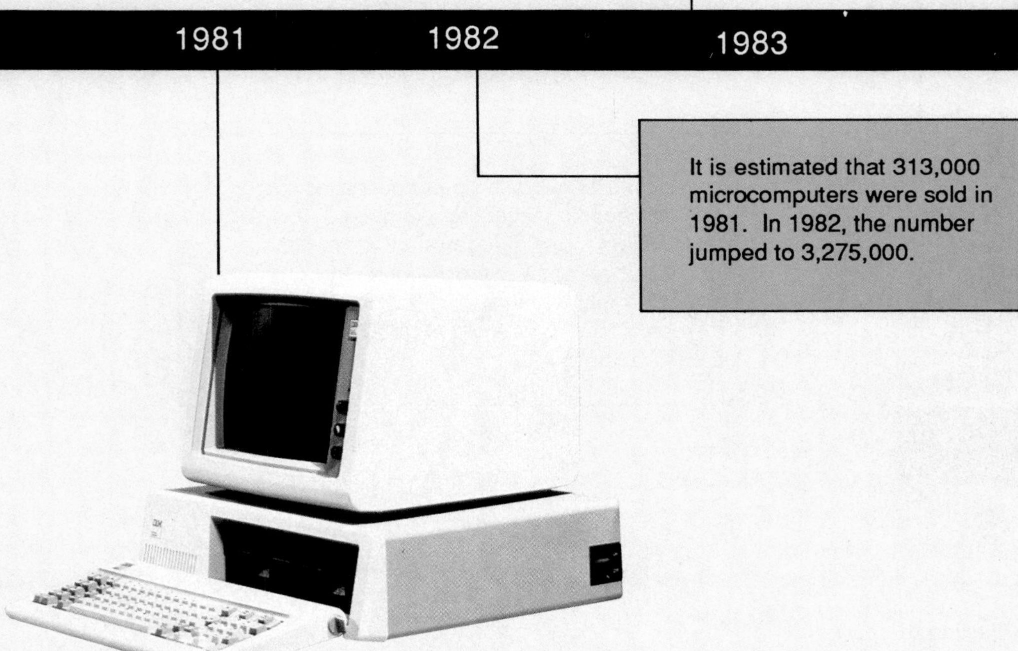

The IBM PC was introduced in 1981, signaling IBM's entrance in the microcomputer market-place. The IBM PC quickly garnered the largest share of the personal computer market and became the personal computer most often used in business.

The IBM Application System 400, introduced in 1988, made a significant impact on the minicomputer and mainframe market, allowing users to expand their computing capabilities more easily.

1987 1988 1990

Several microcomputers utilizing the powerful Intel 80386 microprocessor were introduced in 1987. These machines can handle processing that previously only large systems could perform.

OS/2, an IBM microcomputer operating system, will enable microcomputers to be as powerful as many of today's minicomputers. Further, it will allow microcomputers to become multiuser systems, that is, multiple keyboards and screens can be attached to the same computer.

The computer industry will continue to evolve as improved technology and innovation lead to a variety of new computer applications.

## CHAPTER 2

# Microcomputer Applications: User Tools

CHAPTER 2

# Microcomputer Applications: User Tools

## OBJECTIVES

- Identify the four most widely used general microcomputer software applications.
- Describe how each of the four applications can help users.
- Explain the key features of each of the four major microcomputer applications.
- Describe the key features of data communications and desktop publishing software.
- Explain integrated software and its advantages.
- List and describe five guidelines for purchasing software application packages.
- Discuss tips for using each of the four major microcomputer applications.

---

**Computer literate** is a term you might have heard used to describe people who have an understanding of computers and how they are used in our modern world. Today, understanding the common applications used on microcomputers is often considered a part of being computer literate. In fact, a knowledge of these applications is now considered by many educators and employers to be more important than a knowledge of programming. Because of this, we place an introduction to microcomputer applications focusing on the four most widely used applications early in this book. Learning the features of each application will help you understand how microcomputers are used by people in our modern world and provide a foundation to help you learn.

## AN INTRODUCTION TO GENERAL MICROCOMPUTER APPLICATIONS

The applications discussed in this chapter are sometimes referred to as **general microcomputer applications**. This software is called "general" because it is useful to a broad range of users. Word processing is a good example of a general application. Regardless of the type of business a company does, word processing can be used as a tool to help employees generate documents.

An important advantage of general applications is that you don't need any special technical skills or ability to use them. These programs are designed to be **user friendly**, in other words, easy to use. You do not need detailed computer instructions as you would if you were programming. Instead, you operate the software through simple commands. **Commands** are the instructions that you use to operate the software. For example, when you are finished using an application and you want to save your work, you issue an instruction called a "save" command. To use this command you might type SAVE WORKFILE. The word SAVE is the command and WORKFILE is the name under which your work will be stored.

**User interfaces** (Figure 2-1) are methods and techniques that make using an application simpler. They include function keys, screen prompts, menus, and icons. The **function keys** that are included on computer keyboards are a type of user interface. Pressing a function key in an applications program is a shortcut that takes the place of entering a command. The software defines exactly what the function key causes to happen. If you used a function key to perform the SAVE command described above, pressing one key instead of several could generate the entire command SAVE WORKFILE.

**FIGURE 2-1**
**User interfaces.**

**(a) Function keys are programmed to execute commonly used instructions.**

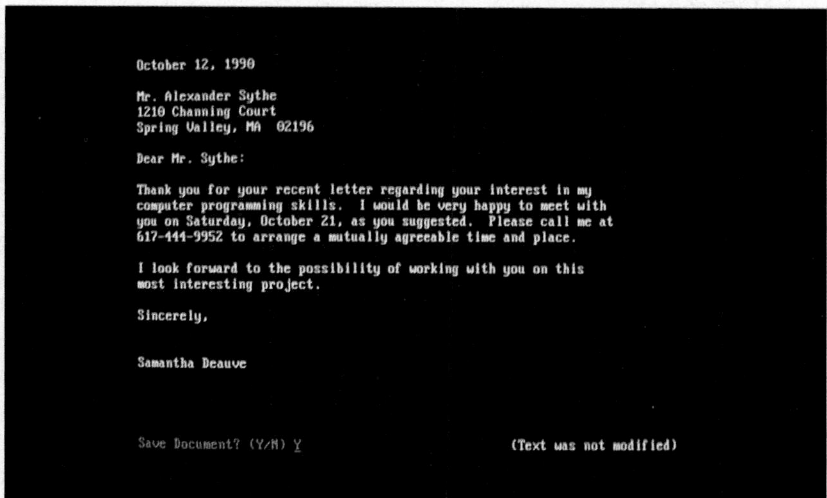


**(b) Screen prompts, such as the red question in the lower left of this screen, indicate that the software is waiting for the user to respond.**

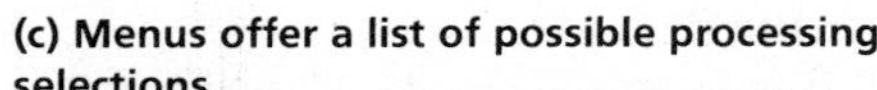

**(c) Menus offer a list of possible processing selections.**

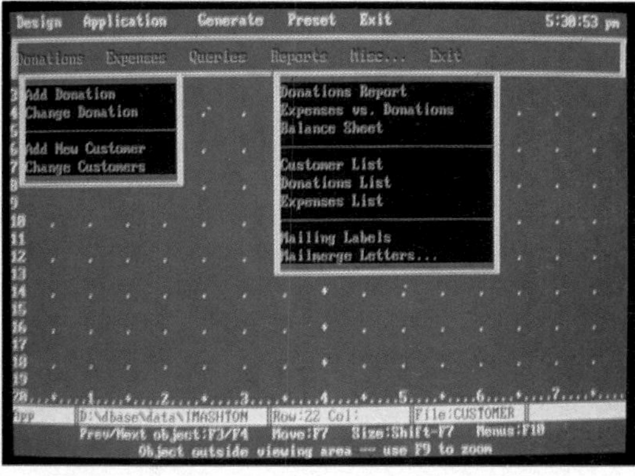


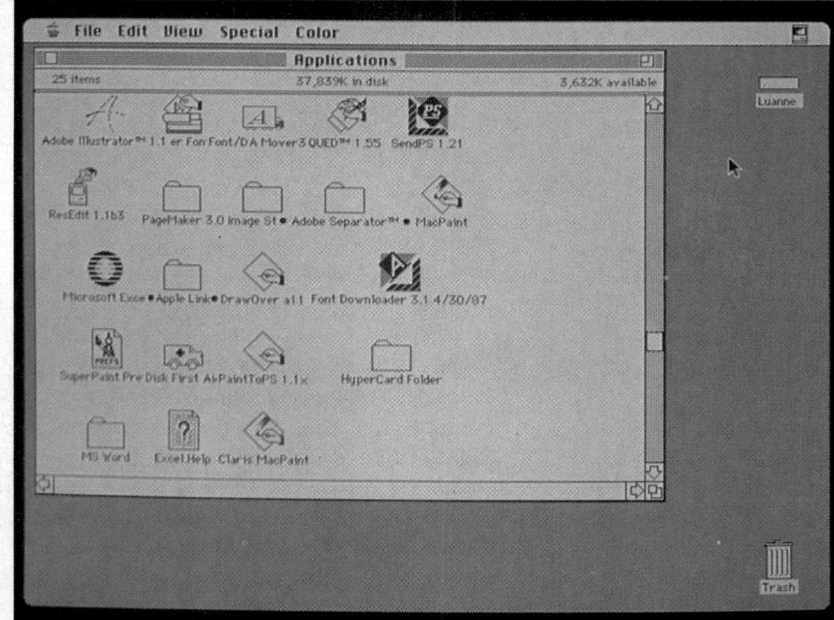


**(d) Icons are symbols that represent a computer activity.**

Screen **prompts** are the messages that the program displays to help you while you are using an application. **Menus**, a special kind of screen prompt, are used in applications to provide a list of processing options. You make a selection from the menu by pressing the number or letter key that corresponds with the desired option. **Icons** refer to pictures instead of words that are displayed on the screen to show you various program options.

These are some of the features included in general applications packages that help to make them user friendly. These aids minimize the need for technical computer knowledge when you are using general applications packages.

## THE FOUR MOST COMMON GENERAL APPLICATIONS

While there are many kinds of general applications available, four software applications packages are the most widely used. They are:

1. word processing software
2. electronic spreadsheet software
3. database software
4. graphics software

Although we will discuss these four applications on microcomputers, they are actually available on computers of all sizes. The concepts you will learn about each application package on microcomputers will also apply if you are working on a larger system.

## WORD PROCESSING SOFTWARE: A DOCUMENT PRODUCTIVITY TOOL

Probably the most widely used general application is word processing. If you need to create **documents**, such as letters or memos, you can increase your productivity by learning to use this software tool. Some of the popular packages used today include WordPerfect, WordStar, and Microsoft Word. This section discusses using a word processor to create a document.

**Word processing software** is used to prepare documents electronically (Figure 2-2). It allows you to enter text on the computer keyboard in the same manner as documents are created on a typewriter. As you enter the characters, they are displayed on the screen and stored in the computer's main memory. Because this is an electronic format, it is easy to **edit** the document by making changes and corrections to the text. Errors may be corrected and words, sentences, paragraphs, or pages may be added or deleted. When the document is complete, you enter a command and have the computer send the document to the printer. The document's format is also under your control. You can specify the margins, define the page length, and select the print style. The document can be printed as many times as you like. Each copy is an original and looks the same as the other copies. The computer's storage capability allows you to store your documents so that they can be used again. It is an efficient way to file documents because many documents can fit on one disk. If you wish, previously stored documents can be combined to make new documents, and you do not have to reenter the text as you would on a typewriter.

The value of word processing is that it reduces the time required to prepare and produce written documents. Any editing you wish to do in the document is easy because the software allows you to make changes quickly and efficiently. In addition, the tedious task of typing a final draft is eliminated.

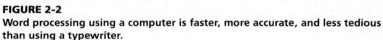

**FIGURE 2-2**
**Word processing using a computer is faster, more accurate, and less tedious than using a typewriter.**

Most word processing packages include additional support features such as spelling checkers, a thesaurus, and some limited grammar checking.

## Spelling Checkers

**Spelling checker software** allows you to check individual words or the entire document for correct spelling. To check individual words, you position the cursor at the start of the word and press a key defined by the software to indicate that the spelling is to be checked. The word in the text will then be checked against an electronic dictionary stored on a disk that is part of the spelling checker software. Some spelling checker dictionaries contain over 100,000 words.

When the entire document is checked for spelling, each word is compared against entries in the dictionary. If an exact match is not found, the word is highlighted. A menu is then superimposed on the screen, giving you a list of similar words that may be the correct spelling. You may select one of the words displayed on the menu, edit the highlighted word, leave the word unchanged, or add the word to the dictionary. Many users customize their software dictionaries by adding company, street, city, and personal names to the dictionary so that the software can check the correct spelling of those words.

## Thesaurus

**Thesaurus software** allows you to look up synonyms for words in a document while you are using your word processor. Using a thesaurus is similar to using a spelling checker. When you want to look up a synonym for a word, you place the cursor on the word that you want to check, enter a command through the keyboard, and the thesaurus software displays a menu of possible synonyms. If you find a word you want to use, you select the desired word from the list and the software automatically incorporates it in the document by replacing the previous word.

## Grammar Checkers

**Grammar checker software** can be used to check for certain grammar, writing style, and sentence structure errors. These programs can check documents for excessive usage of a word or phrase and can identify sentences that are too long. They can also show you words that have been repeated such as "and and" or words used out of context such as "four example."

## A Word Processing Example

Figures 2-3 through 2-10 illustrate the following word processing example. Let's say the vice president of sales of a company wants to send a memo announcing a meeting of all sales personnel. She remembers that last month she sent a similar memo to just the sales managers. Thus, the first thing she does is load last month's memo into main memory so it will appear on the screen (Figure 2-3). This memo might be stored on a hard disk or on a floppy diskette.

**FIGURE 2-3**
**Last month's memo that will be changed for this month's meeting.**

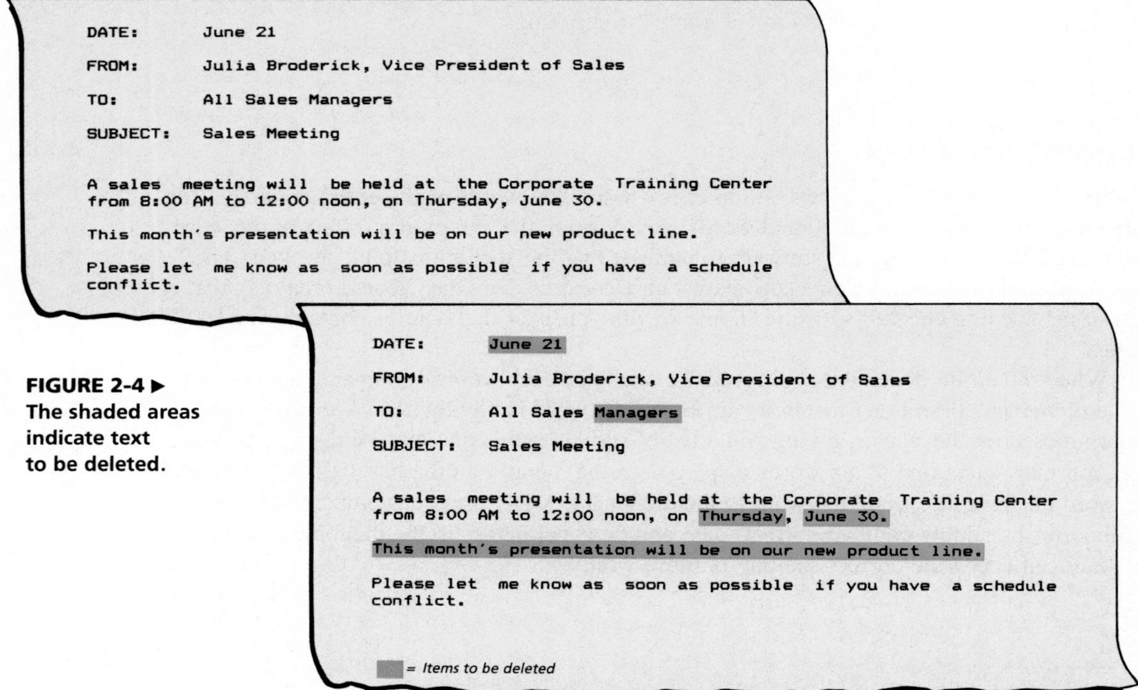

DATE: June 21

FROM: Julia Broderick, Vice President of Sales

TO: All Sales Managers

SUBJECT: Sales Meeting

A sales meeting will be held at the Corporate Training Center from 8:00 AM to 12:00 noon, on Thursday, June 30.

This month's presentation will be on our new product line.

Please let me know as soon as possible if you have a schedule conflict.

DATE: June 21

FROM: Julia Broderick, Vice President of Sales

TO: All Sales Managers

SUBJECT: Sales Meeting

A sales meeting will be held at the Corporate Training Center from 8:00 AM to 12:00 noon, on Thursday, June 30.

This month's presentation will be on our new product line.

Please let me know as soon as possible if you have a schedule conflict.



**FIGURE 2-4 ▶**
**The shaded areas indicate text to be deleted.**

Word processing changes are usually of three types: to **insert** data, **delete** data, or **move** data. Often it makes sense to do your insertions and deletions at the same time; as you edit your document, you delete the existing word or phrase and insert the new one. **Replace** is a combination of the delete and insert commands. With replace, you can scan a document for a single or multiple occurrence of a word or phrase and replace it with another or delete it entirely. Figure 2-4 shows the document with the text to be deleted. Figure 2-5 shows the document after the new text has been inserted.

The **move** command allows you to either cut (remove) or copy a sentence, paragraph, page, or block of text. In our example, the VP of sales, Julia Broderick, decided she wanted to move the existing paragraph 3 in front of the existing paragraph 2 (Figure 2-6). First she would highlight or somehow signify the text to be moved. Next she would indicate that she wants to "cut" and not "copy" the marked text. With a **cut**, you are removing text from an area. With a **copy**, the word processor makes a copy of the marked text but leaves the marked text where it was. After you perform either the cut or the copy, the word processor needs to know where you want to place or **paste** the text. This is usually done by moving the cursor to the point where you want the moved text to begin. You then give a command to execute the move. Figure 2-7 shows the cut text "pasted" into a position that now makes it the second paragraph.

After the text changes are made, Julia runs a spelling checker. The spelling checker matches each word in the document against its spelling dictionary and discovers an unrecognized word: "personel." Figure 2-8 shows how a spelling checker might present two alternatives for the correct spelling of the word. Julia merely has to enter the letter B and the word processor will change "personel" to "personnel" (Figure 2-9).

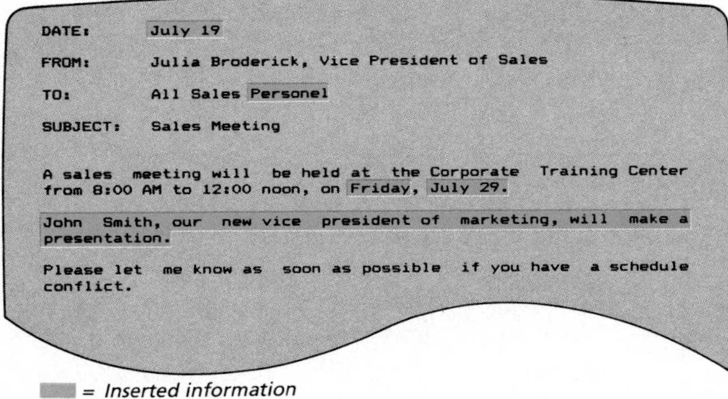


= *Inserted information*

▲
**FIGURE 2-5**
**The shading on the computer screen shows the new text inserted into last month's memo.**

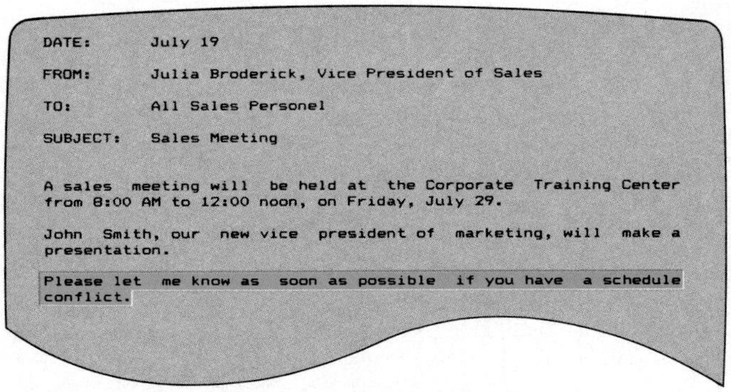

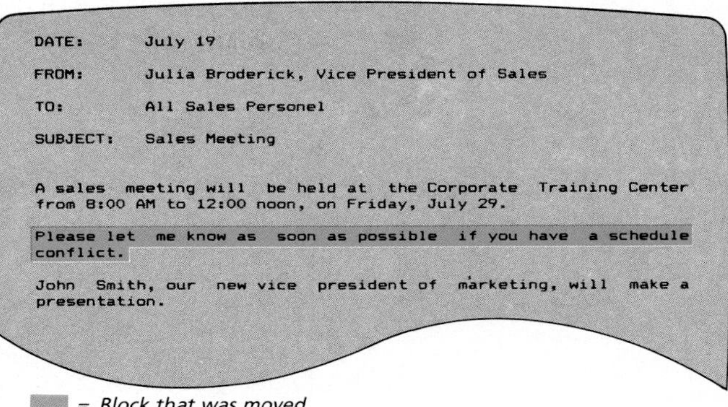


= *Block that was moved*

▲
**FIGURE 2-7**
**Memo after third paragraph was moved to second paragraph.**

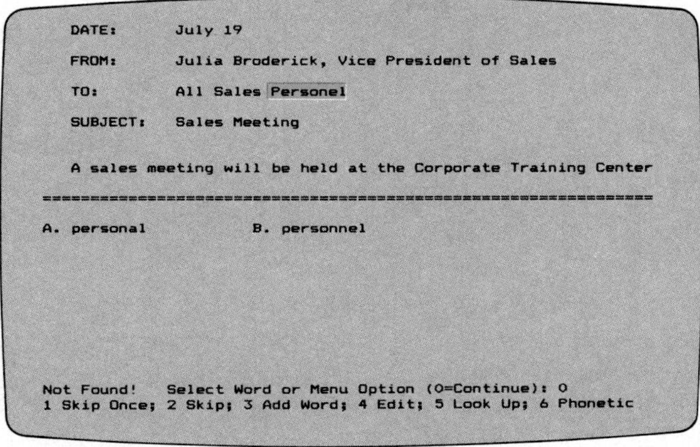


= *Block that was moved*

▲
**FIGURE 2-8**
**Spelling checker highlighting unrecognized word and showing two possible spellings.**

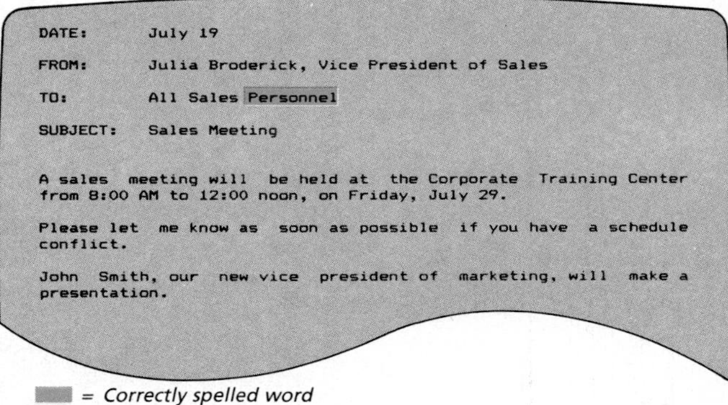


= *Correctly spelled word*

▲
**FIGURE 2-9**
**Correct spelling of "personnel" inserted into text by spelling checker.**

DATE: July 19
FROM: Julia Broderick, Vice President of Sales
TO: All Sales Personel
SUBJECT: Sales Meeting
A sales meeting will be held at the Corporate Training Center from 8:00 AM to 12:00 noon, on Friday, July 29.
John Smith, our new vice president of marketing, will make a presentation.
Please let me know as soon as possible if you have a schedule conflict.

= *Block to be moved to second paragraph*

▲
**FIGURE 2-6**
**The shading shows the text to be moved from third to second paragraph.**

Before printing the memo, Julia reviews its format. She decides that the document is too wide and increases the margins. Figure 2-10 shows the document with the wider, 1 1/2-inch, margins.

**FIGURE 2-10**
**Memo after margins are changed.**

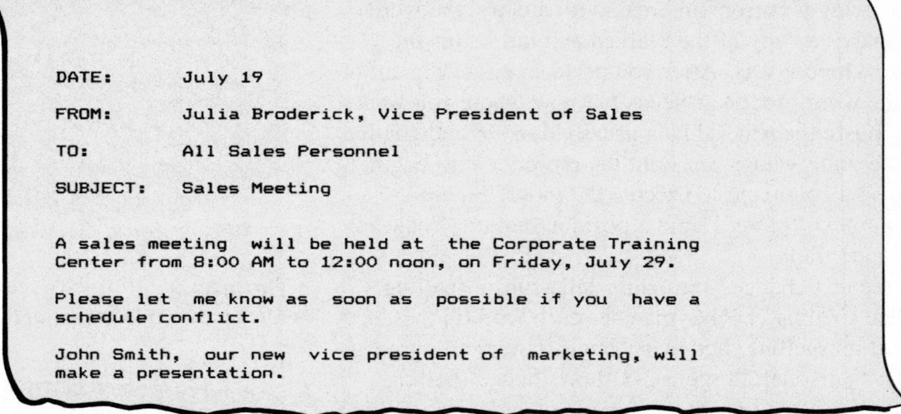

DATE: July 19

FROM: Julia Broderick, Vice President of Sales

TO: All Sales Personnel

SUBJECT: Sales Meeting

A sales meeting will be held at the Corporate Training Center from 8:00 AM to 12:00 noon, on Friday, July 29.

Please let me know as soon as possible if you have a schedule conflict.

John Smith, our new vice president of marketing, will make a presentation.

Now that the text and format are correct, Julia will save the document before printing it in case a system or power failure occurs during printing. Once saved, the document can be printed as often as necessary and is available for use or modification at a later date.

Word processing software is a productivity tool that allows you to create, edit, format, print, and store documents. Each of the many word processing packages available may have slightly different capabilities, but most have the features summarized in Figure 2-11.

**FIGURE 2-11**
**Common features of word processing software.**

**WORD PROCESSING FEATURES**

**INSERTION AND MOVING**
- Insert character
- Insert word
- Insert line
- Move sentences
- Move paragraphs
- Move blocks
- Merge text

**DELETE FEATURES**
- Delete character
- Delete word
- Delete sentence
- Delete paragraph
- Delete entire text

**SCREEN CONTROL**
- Scroll up and down by line
- Scroll by page
- Word wrap
- Uppercase and lowercase display
- Underline display
- Screen display according to defined format
- Bold display
- Superscript display
- Subscript display

**SEARCH AND REPLACE**
- Search and replace word
- Search and replace character strings

**PRINTING**
- Set top and bottom margins
- Set left and right margins
- Set tab stops
- Print columns
- Single, double, triple space control
- Variable space control within text
- Right justify
- Center lines
- Subscripts
- Superscripts
- Underline
- Boldface
- Condensed print
- Enlarged print
- Special type fonts
- Proportional spacing
- Headers
- Footers
- Page numbering
- Print any page from file

FIGURE 2-12
The electronic spreadsheet on the right still uses the row and column format of the manual spreadsheet on the left.

## ELECTRONIC SPREADSHEET SOFTWARE: A NUMBER PRODUCTIVITY TOOL

Electronic spreadsheet software allows you to organize numeric data in a worksheet or table format called an **electronic spreadsheet** or **spreadsheet**. Manual methods have long been used to organize numeric data in this manner (Figure 2-12). You will see that the data in an electronic spreadsheet is organized in the same manner as it is in a manual spreadsheet, one that is done by hand. Within a spreadsheet, data is organized horizontally in **rows** and vertically in **columns**. The intersection where a row and column meet is called a **cell** (Figure 2-13).

Cells may contain three types of data: labels (text), values (numbers), and formulas. The text, or **labels** as they are sometimes called, are used to identify the data and to document the worksheet. Good spreadsheets are well documented and contain descriptive titles. The rest of the cells in a spreadsheet may appear to contain numbers or **values**. However, some of the cells actually contain formulas. The **formulas** perform calculations on the data in the spreadsheet and display the resulting value in the cell containing the formula.

In a manual spreadsheet, each of the totals would have to be calculated by hand. In an electronic spreadsheet, the user enters a formula into a cell. Then the result for that cell is calculated and displayed automatically. Once a formula is entered into a cell, it can be copied to any other cell that requires a similar formula. As the formula is copied, the formula calculations are performed automatically.

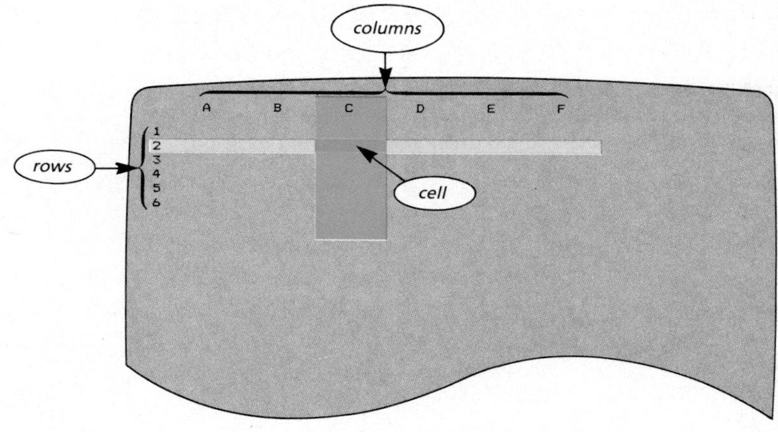


FIGURE 2-13
In a spreadsheet, rows refer to the horizontal lines of data and columns refer to the vertical lines of data. Note that rows are identified by numbers and columns are identified by letters. The intersection of a row and column is called a cell. The highlighted cell is the cursor. You can move the cursor by pressing the arrow keys on the keyboard.

One of the most powerful features of the electronic spreadsheet occurs when the data in a spreadsheet changes. To appreciate the capabilities of spreadsheet software, let's discuss how a change is handled in a manual system. When a value in a manual spreadsheet changes, it must be erased and a new value written into the cell. All cells that contain formulas referring to the value that changed must also be erased, recalculated, and the result reentered. For example, the row totals and column totals would be updated to reflect changes to any values within their areas. In large manual spreadsheets, accurately posting changes and updating the values affected can be time consuming. But posting changes on an electronic spreadsheet is

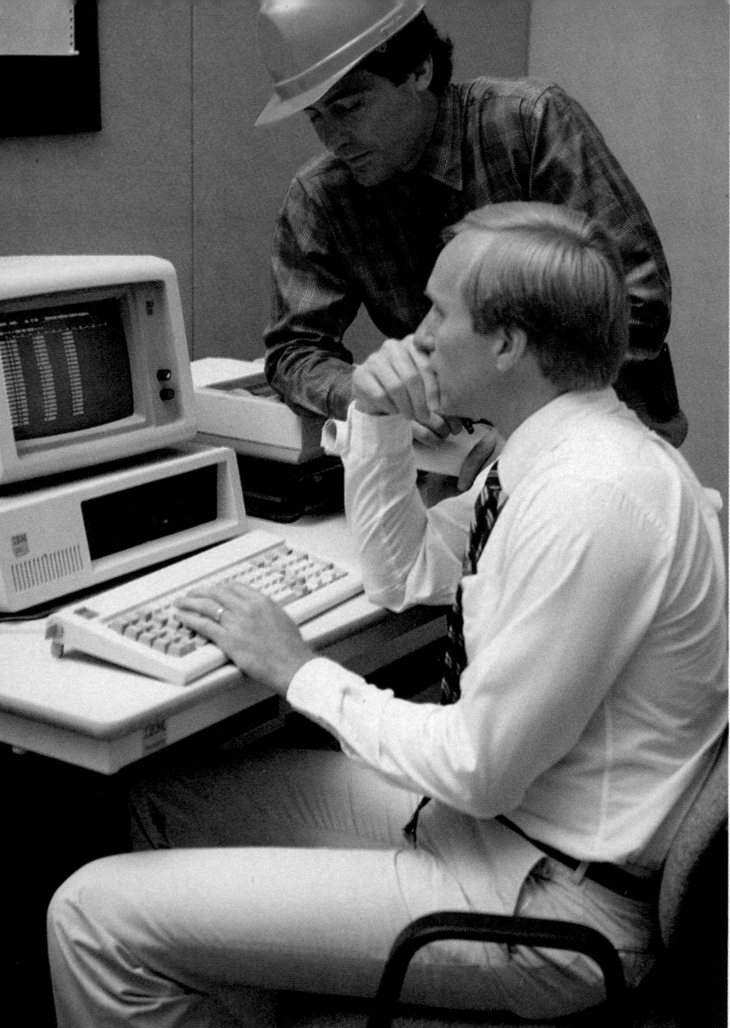

**FIGURE 2-14**
**The "what if" testing capability of electronic spreadsheets is a powerful tool used to aid managers in making decisions.**

easy. You change data in a cell by simply typing in the new value. All other values that are affected are updated *automatically*. While the updating happens very quickly, if you watch the screen closely you can sometimes see the values change. As row and column totals are updated, the changes are said to *ripple* through the spreadsheet.

An electronic spreadsheet's ability to recalculate when data is changed makes it a valuable tool for management personnel. This capability allows managers to perform "what if" testing by changing the numbers in a spreadsheet (Figure 2-14). The resulting values that are calculated by the spreadsheet software provide management with valuable decision support information based on the alternatives tested.

To illustrate this powerful tool, we will show you how to develop the spreadsheet that was used as an example in Chapter 1. You may remember that the completed spreadsheet contains revenues, costs, profit, and profit percentage for three months and the totals for the three months. By following Figures 2-15 through 2-19, you can see that the first step in creating the spreadsheet is to enter the labels or titles. These should be short but descriptive, to help you organize the layout of the data in your spreadsheet. The next step is to enter the data or numbers in the body of the spreadsheet, and finally the formulas. At this point you can give commands to print the spreadsheet and to store it on a disk.

An electronic spreadsheet is a productivity tool that organizes and performs calculations on numeric data. Spreadsheets are one of the most popular software applications. They have been adapted to a wide range of business and nonbusiness applications. Some of the popular packages used today are Lotus 1-2-3, Excel, SuperCalc, and VP-Planner. Most of the packages available will have the features shown in Figure 2-20.

prompt line
CELL: B4
VALUE:
A B C D E
1
2 ITEM JAN FEB MAR TOTAL
3
4 REVENUE
5 COSTS
6 PROFIT
7 PROFIT %
cursor in cell B4

**FIGURE 2-15**
**Labels identify rows and columns in a spreadsheet. The prompt line at the top left of the screen has two parts: CELL, which identifies the column and row being referenced; and VALUE, which identifies the value in the cell. The cursor, is located in cell B4, the intersection of column B and row 4. No value has been entered into B4.**

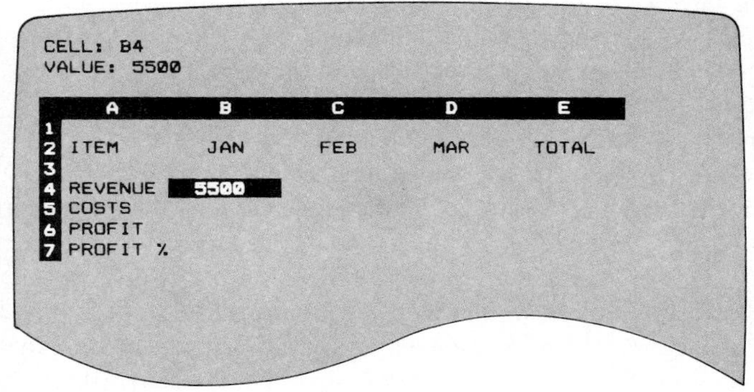


**FIGURE 2-16**
**The value 5500 is entered and stored at cell B4. Note the entries in the display at the top left corner of the screen, identifying which value (in this case a number) has been entered into which cell.**

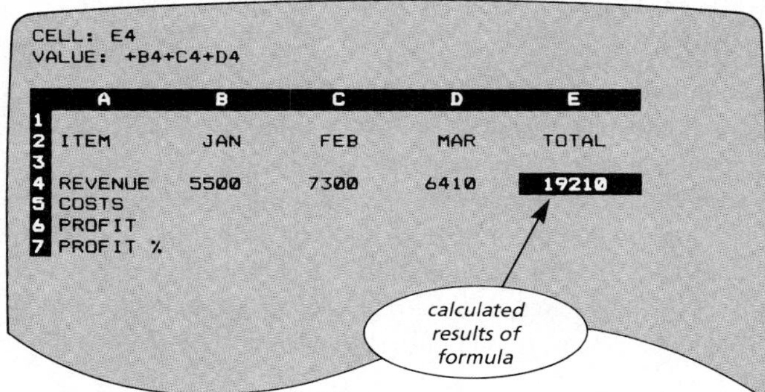


**FIGURE 2-17**
The arrow keys are used to move the cursor to cells in the spreadsheet. The values 7300 and 6410 are entered in cells C4 and D4. A formula is entered in cell E4. The formula specifies that the content of cell E4 is to be the sum of the values in cells B4, C4, and D4. The spreadsheet itself displays the numeric sum. The prompt line at the top of the screen, however, shows the formula used to calculate the value.

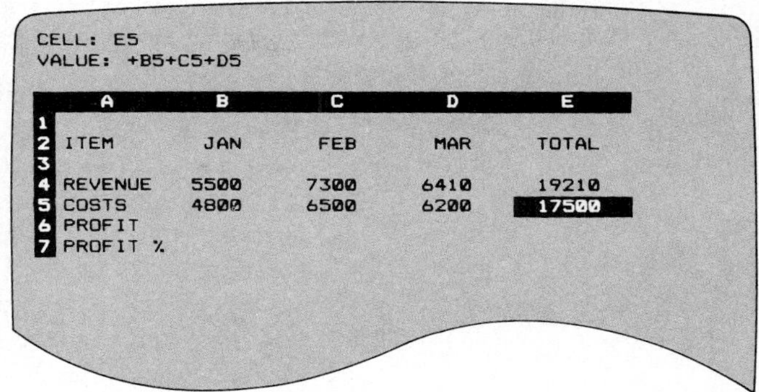


**FIGURE 2-18**
The formula required for cell E5 is similar to the one entered for cell E4; it totals the amounts in the three previous columns. When we copy the formula from E4 into E5, the software automatically changes the cell references from B4, C4, and D4 to B5, C5, and D5.

CELL: E7
VALUE: +E6/E4

| | A | B | C | D | E |
|---|---|---|---|---|---|
| 1 | | | | | |
| 2 | ITEM | JAN | FEB | MAR | TOTAL |
| 3 | | | | | |
| 4 | REVENUE | 5500 | 7300 | 6410 | 19210 |
| 5 | COSTS | 4800 | 6500 | 6200 | 17500 |
| 6 | PROFIT | 700 | 800 | 210 | 1710 |
| 7 | PROFIT % | 0.13 | 0.11 | 0.03 | 0.09 |

**FIGURE 2-19**
This screen shows the completed spreadsheet. The value in cell E7 is derived from the formula illustrated on the prompt line, which specifies that the value in cell E6 is to be divided by the value in cell E4. (The slash character indicates division.) Since the value in E6 is the total profit and the value in E4 is the total revenue, the result of the division operation is the profit percentage.

**SPREADSHEET FEATURES**

| | |
|---|---|
| **WORKSHEET**<br>Global format<br>Insert column<br>Insert row<br>Delete column<br>Delete row<br>Set up titles<br>Set up windows<br>**RANGE**<br>Format range of data<br>Erase cells<br>**COPY**<br>Copy from cells<br>Copy to cells | **MOVE**<br>Move from cells<br>Move to cells<br>**FILE**<br>Save<br>Retrieve<br>Erase<br>List<br>**PRINT**<br>Set up margins<br>Define header<br>Define footer<br>Specify range to print<br>Define page length<br>Condensed print |

**FIGURE 2-20**
Common features of spreadsheet software

# DATABASE SOFTWARE: A DATA MANAGEMENT TOOL

**Database software** allows you to create electronic files on your computer and to retrieve, manipulate, and update the data you store in the files. Just as in a manual system, a **file** is a collection of related data. For example, a file might consist of customer's names and addresses. In a manual system (Figure 2-21), the data might be recorded on paper and stored in a filing cabinet. On the computer, the data will be stored in an electronic format on an auxiliary storage device such as a disk. Another term that is used to reference data is record. A **record** is a collection of related facts or data items. In our name and address file example, all the information that relates to one person would be considered a record. Each of the facts or data items within a record is called a **field**.

Sometimes the word database is used interchangeably with the word file. However, the term **database** usually refers to a collection of data that is organized in multiple files. Understanding the difference between the terms file and database will help you to understand the difference between file management software and database software. In general, **file management software** allows you to work with one file at a time, while database software allows you to work with multiple files.

The screens in Figures 2-22 through 2-26 present the development of a personal checking account file and inquiry system using a file management system. The file management main menu (Figure 2-22) presents 5 choices: to create a file, enter data, update the file, display data, and terminate the processing of the file management system. To begin, you would select option 1, CREATE FILE.

When you select option 1, the FILE MANAGEMENT CREATE FILE information shown in Figure 2-23 is displayed. A prompt asks you to enter a file name, the name under which the file being created will be stored on disk. In this example, you would enter the name CHECKING.

You are then asked to enter descriptions for each field in the records to be stored in the file. A field description consists of a field name, the type of data to be stored in the field (A for alphanumeric, N for numeric data), and the number of characters in the field. In a numeric field, if digits are to appear to the right of the decimal point, you must specify the number of digits to the right. Thus, for the amount field, the designation 6.2 means there are six numeric digits in the field with two of those digits to the right of the decimal point.

Once you have defined the fields in the records, you enter data into the records. Therefore, you would choose main menu entry 2, ENTER DATA and Figure 2-24 would appear. The file management system prompts you to enter data for each record by typing the data to be stored in the field. Thus, after the field name NUMBER, you enter the check number. You complete each field in the same manner, and continue to enter data until all data is entered for the checking account file.

After the file has been defined and data has been stored in it, you can use the file to produce information. Therefore you would choose option 4, DISPLAY DATA, from the main menu. You are then asked to enter the commands that specify what should be displayed and how the data should be processed prior to being displayed. As Figure 2-25 shows, you stated that the data should be sorted on the field called NUMBER, and that all fields in the record should be displayed.

**FIGURE 2-21**
**An electronic database is similar to a manual system; related data items are stored in files.**

In Figure 2-26, you direct the system to display only those records where the class is equal to UTILITY and to print a total for the field AMOUNT. As a result, the report shows only those records for which the classification is UTILITY. The values in the amount field are totalled and printed after all records have been processed.

In addition to creating, retrieving, and storing data, most database and file management software provide for the manipulation of the data. This includes sorting the data in ascending or descending sequence by specifying a few simple English-like commands. Figure 2-27 lists some features of popular database software, such as dBASE III PLUS.

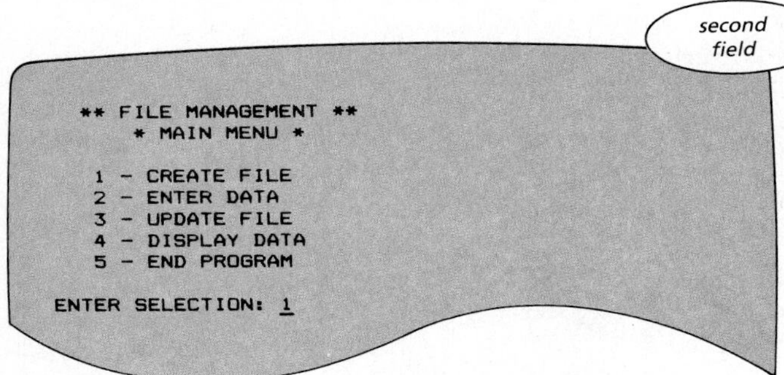


**FIGURE 2-22**
**A typical main menu of file management software.**

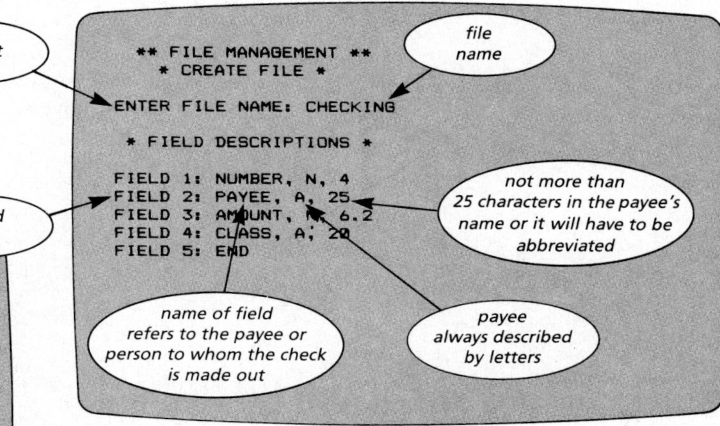


**FIGURE 2-23**
**CREATE FILE screen showing definition of fields for records in the CHECKING file.**

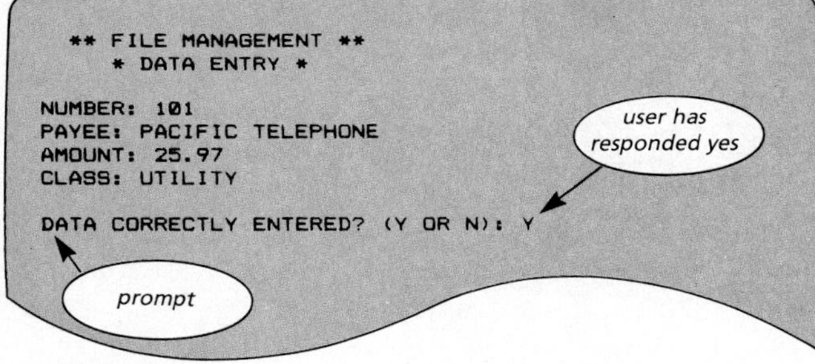


**FIGURE 2-24**
**Data entry screen.**

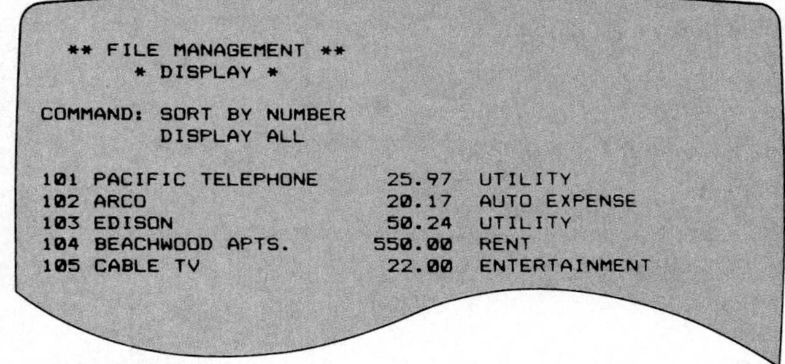


**FIGURE 2-25**
**Display of all records sorted by record number.**

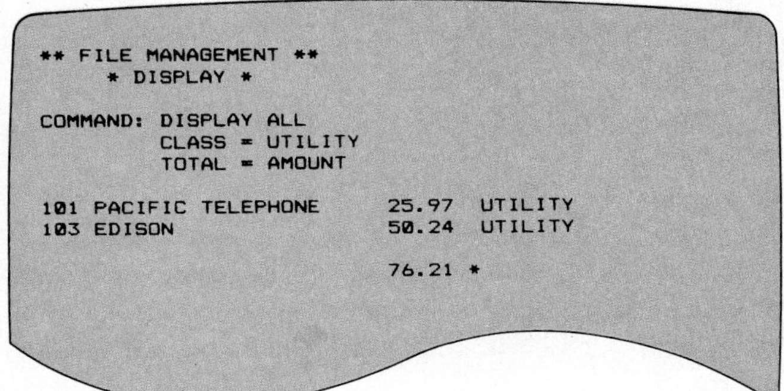


**FIGURE 2-26**
**Display of only the UTILITY class records with a total calculated on the amount.**

| DATABASE FEATURES | |
|---|---|
| **OPERATIONS**<br>Create database<br>Copy data<br>Delete data<br>Sort data<br>**EDITING**<br>Display data<br>Update data | **ARITHMETIC**<br>Compute the average<br>Count the records<br>Sum data fields<br>**OUTPUT**<br>Retrieve data<br>Produce a report |

**FIGURE 2-27**
**Common features of database software.**

Note again that when using this microcomputer application, you do not need to have any special technical knowledge. Database software and file managers are general application tools that are designed to help you easily and efficiently manage data electronically.

## GRAPHICS SOFTWARE: A DATA PRESENTATION TOOL

Information presented in the form of a graph or a chart is commonly referred to as **graphics**. Studies have shown that information presented in graphic form can be understood much faster than information presented in writing. Three common forms of graphics are **pie charts**, **bar charts**, and **line diagrams** (Figure 2-28).

**FIGURE 2-28**

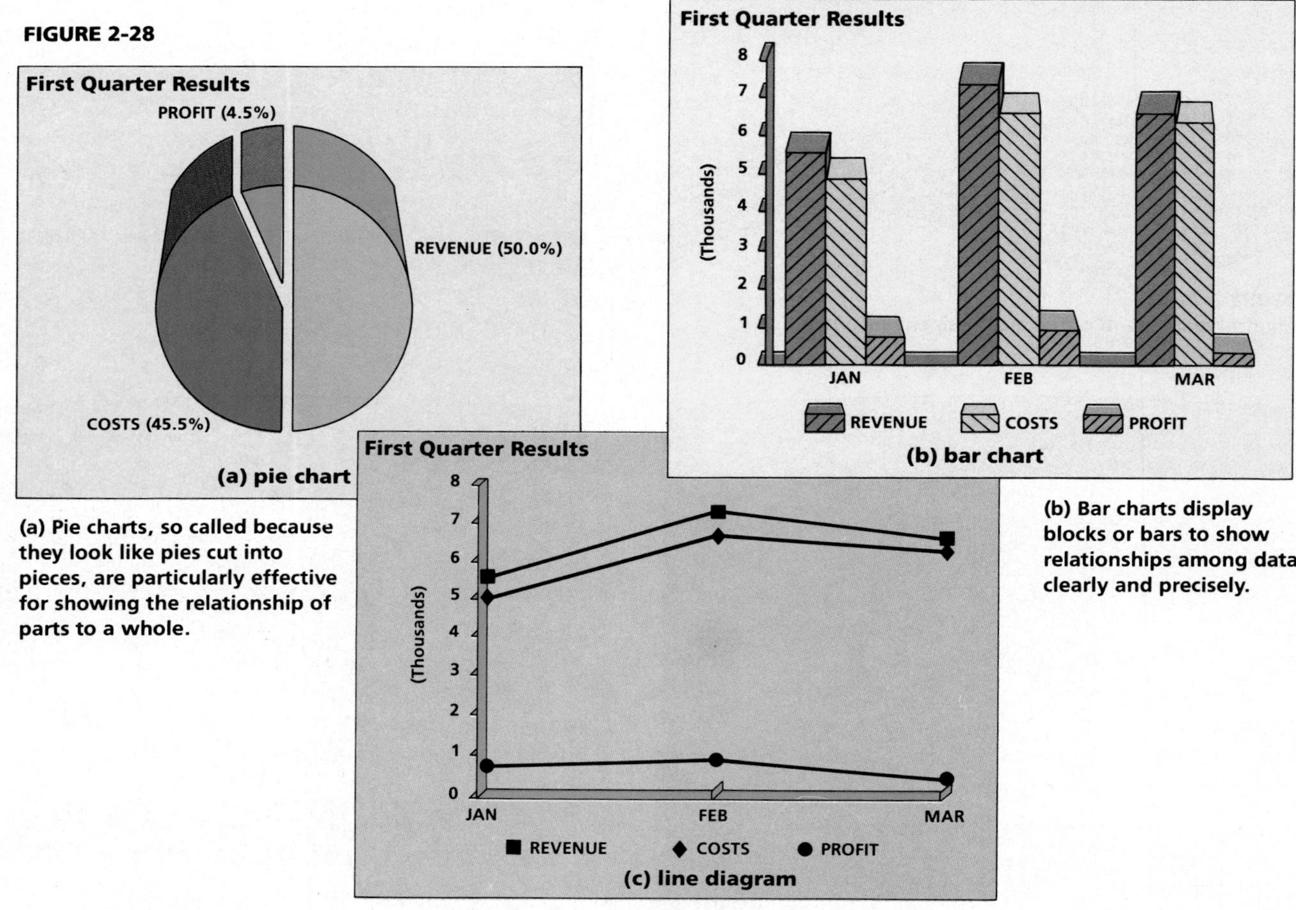


**(a) Pie charts, so called because they look like pies cut into pieces, are particularly effective for showing the relationship of parts to a whole.**

**(b) Bar charts display blocks or bars to show relationships among data clearly and precisely.**

**(c) Line diagrams are particularly effective for showing movement or a change in the condition of the data.**

Today, there are many software packages of different capabilities that can create graphics, including most spreadsheet packages. The graphics capabilities of these packages can be grouped into two categories: analytical graphics and presentation graphics. Both kinds can transform numeric data into graphic form.

**Analytical graphics** is widely used by management personnel when reviewing information and when communicating information to others within their organization (Figure 2-29).

For example, a production manager who is planning a meeting with the president of the company may use color graphics to depict the expenditures of the production department. This graphic display would have more impact and lead to better understanding than would a printed column of production figures.

As its name implies, **presentation graphics** goes beyond analytical graphics by offering the user a wide choice of presentation effects. These include three-dimensional displays, background patterns, multiple text fonts, and image libraries that contain illustrations of factories, people, coins, dollar signs and other symbols that can be incorporated into the graphic (Figure 2-30). Figure 2-31 shows an example of presentation graphics projected in front of an audience and one of the devices that can be used to project presentation graphics.

To create graphics on your computer, you must follow the directions that apply to your graphics software package. Most packages will prompt you to enter the data the graph will represent, and then ask you to select the type of graph you would like. After entering the data, you can select several different graphic forms to see which one will best convey your message. When you decide on a graph, you can print it and also store it for future reference.

Using graphics software as a presentation tool allows you to efficiently create professional-quality graphics that can help you communicate information more effectively.

**▲ FIGURE 2-29**
**Color can enhance the presentation of graphic information.**

**FIGURE 2-30**
**An example of presentation graphics. ▼**

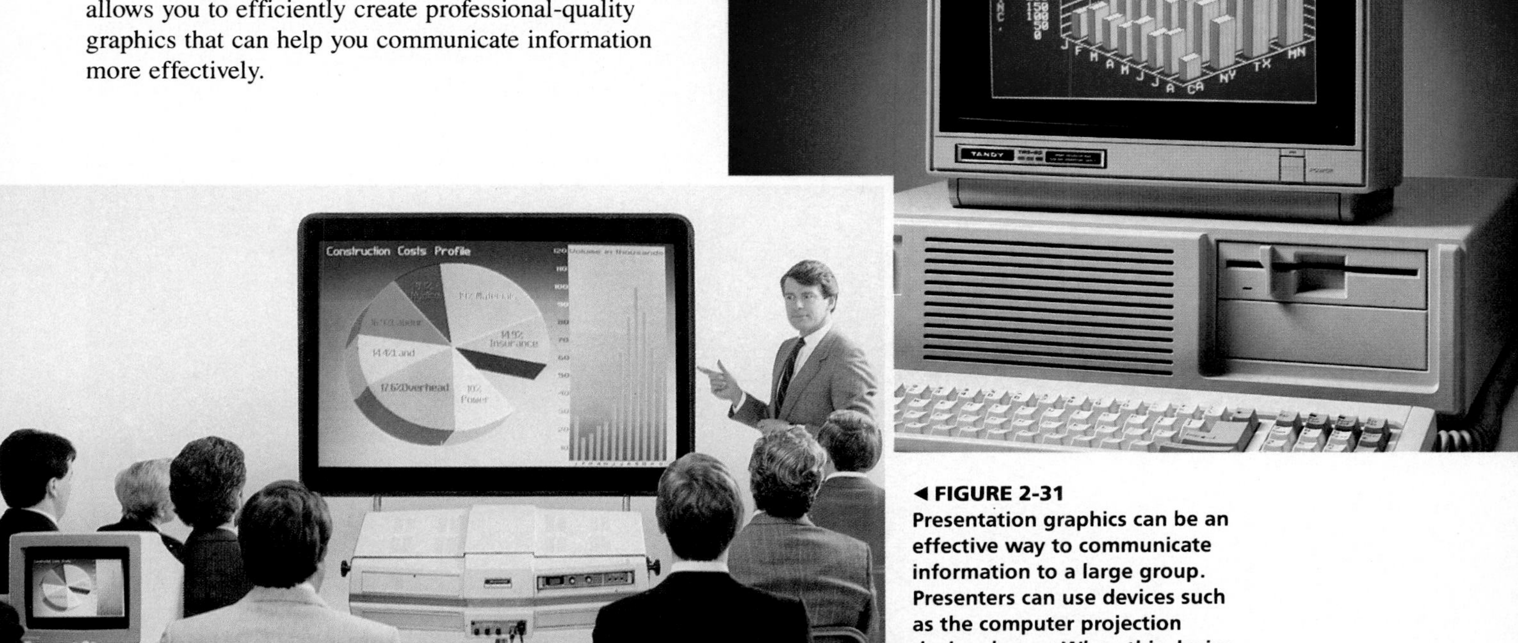


**◄ FIGURE 2-31**
**Presentation graphics can be an effective way to communicate information to a large group. Presenters can use devices such as the computer projection device shown. When this device is connected to a microcomputer and placed over a standard projector, it can project everything on the microcomputer screen onto a large screen.**

# OTHER POPULAR MICROCOMPUTER APPLICATIONS

The four applications discussed so far, word processing, spreadsheet, database, and graphics, are the most widely used microcomputer applications. Two other packages that are finding increasing use are data communications and desktop publishing.

## Data Communications

**Data communications software** is used to transmit data from one computer to another. It gives users access to online databases such as stock prices and airline schedules, and services such as home banking and shopping.

Microcomputer data communications software often involves using a telephone line connected to special communication equipment either inside or attached to the computer. Similar equipment must be present at the other computer that will be accessed. The data communications software is used to dial the other system and establish the communication connection. Once the connection is established, the user enters commands and responses that control the transmission of data from one computer to the other.

## Desktop Publishing

**Desktop publishing software** allows the user to combine text and graphics to produce high-quality printed documents. Desktop publishing systems go far beyond the capabilities of typical word processing systems by providing many different type sizes and styles and the ability to merge charts, pictures, and illustrations with the text. Numerous special effects such as borders and backgrounds can also be used to enhance the appearance of a document. Businesses of all sizes are increasingly using desktop publishing systems to produce better-looking brochures and communications and to control the production of work that previously could only be done by graphic artists. Figure 2-32 is an example of a document produced on a desktop publishing system.

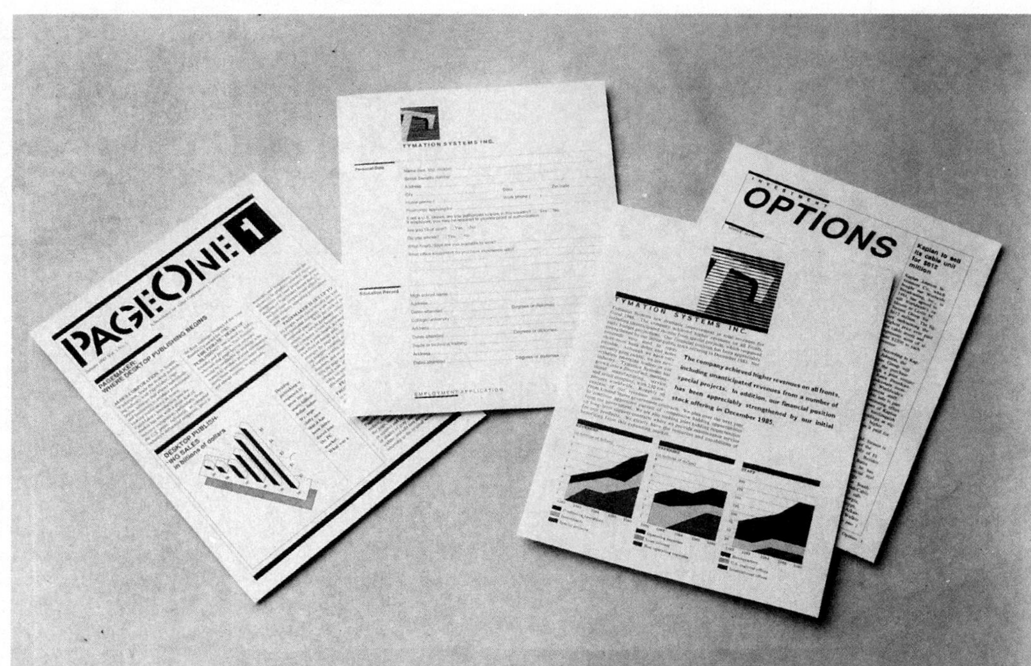


**FIGURE 2-32**
**High-quality printed documents can be produced with desktop publishing software.**

# INTEGRATED SOFTWARE

Software packages such as electronic spreadsheet and word processing are generally used independently of each other. But what if you wanted to place information from a spreadsheet into a word processing document? The spreadsheet data would have to be reentered in the word processing document. This would be time consuming and errors could be introduced as you reentered the data. The inability of separate programs to communicate with one another and use a common set of data has been overcome through the use of integrated software.

**Integrated software** refers to packages that combine applications such as word processing, electronic spreadsheet, database, graphics, and data communications into a single, easy-to-use set of programs. Application packages that are included in integrated packages are designed to have a consistent command structure; that is, common commands such as those used to SAVE or LOAD files are the same for all the applications in the package. Besides the consistent presentation, a key feature of integrated packages is their ability to pass data quickly and easily from one application to another. For example, revenue and cost information from a database on daily sales could be quickly loaded into a spreadsheet. The spreadsheet could be used to calculate gross profits. Once the calculations are completed, all or a portion of the spreadsheet data can be passed to the graphics program to create pie, bar, line, or other graphs. Finally, the graphic (or the spreadsheet) can be transferred to a word processing document. A possible disadvantage of an integrated package is that individual integrated programs may not have all the features that are available in nonintegrated packages.

Integrated programs frequently use windows. A **window** is a rectangular portion of the screen that is used to display information. Windows can display help information about the commands of the program you are using or, with integrated packages, they can actually display data from another application. Many programs today can display multiple windows on the screen (Figure 2-33) and allow the user to move from one application window to another. Although they are called "windows" because of their ability to "see" into another part of the program, many people consider windows to be more like multiple sheets of paper on top of a desk. The papers can be shuffled, placed side by side, or moved entirely off the desk until needed again.

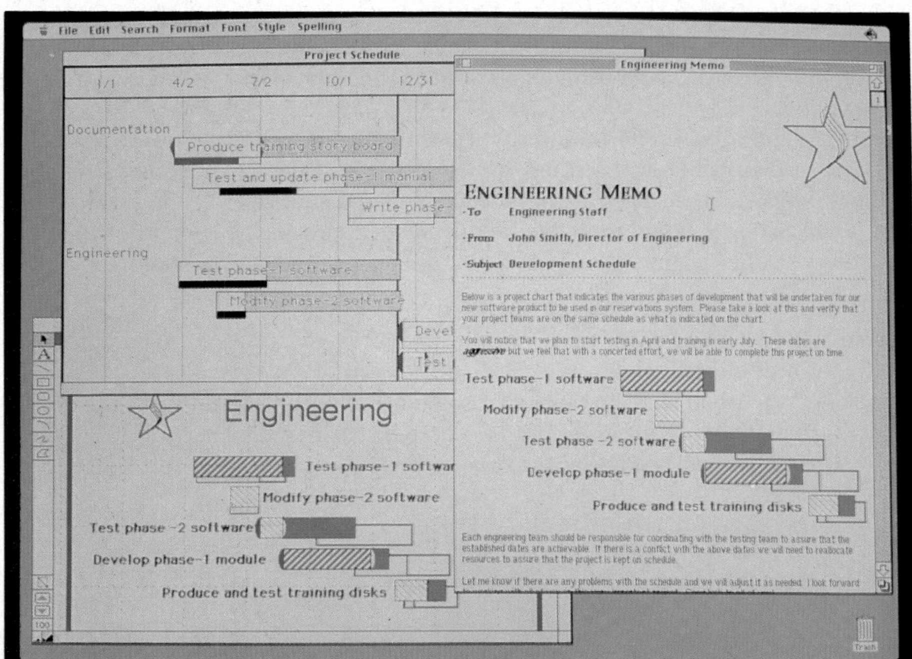


**FIGURE 2-33**
Windows on the Macintosh computer let you see several applications at one time. In this example the user can plan projects using project management software (top left), pictorially present the plan using graphics software (bottom left), and write about the plan using word processing software (right).

## GUIDELINES FOR PURCHASING MICROCOMPUTER APPLICATIONS SOFTWARE

Whenever you purchase applications software (Figure 2-34), you should make sure that the software will meet your needs. Do this by following these five steps:

**FIGURE 2-34**
**Shop carefully for software, evaluating the available packages and suppliers. Many people spend more on software than they do on their computer equipment.**

1. **Verify that the software performs the task you desire.** In some cases, software that is supposed to perform particular functions either does not perform the functions or performs them in a manner that will be unacceptable to you. The best method of verifying that the software performs satisfactorily is to try it out prior to purchase. Many computer stores and software vendors will allow you to try software to see if it meets your needs before you purchase it. Some software developers even have special demonstration versions that allow you to try package features on a limited-use basis.
2. **Verify that the software will run on your computer.** The best way to verify this is to run the software on a computer that is the same as yours. Such factors as the number of disk drives, whether the software can run on a computer without a hard disk, main memory requirements, and graphics capabilities or requirements must be evaluated before you buy. For example, it would be unwise to purchase a package that is incompatible with your printer or one with graphics capabilities that your computer cannot handle.
3. **Make sure that the software is adequately documented.** The written material that accompanies the software is known as **documentation**. Even the best software may be unusable if the documentation does not clearly and completely describe what the software does, how it does it, how to recover from errors, and how to back up data.
4. **Purchase the software from a reputable store, distributor, or vendor.** Regardless of the care taken, software often contains errors. A reputable store or vendor will do everything possible to correct those errors. Admittedly, it can be hard to check on a company's reputation. Asking for references is probably the best method if you are not familiar with the prospective supplier.
5. **Obtain the best value, but keep in mind that that might not mean the lowest price.** Different stores or distributors will sell the same software package for different prices. Be sure to compare prices, but also ask about product support. Sometimes a store will offer training on products that you buy from them; other vendors provide no support or training. Also, some vendors offer telephone service so that you can call to ask questions about the software.

If you keep these factors in mind when buying application software packages, you are likely to be pleased with the software you buy.

A good place to look when shopping for microcomputer applications software is in computer magazines such as *InforWorld* and *PC World*. These magazines regularly review applications packages and publish articles and charts to help you choose the package best suited to your needs.

# LEARNING AIDS AND SUPPORT TOOLS FOR APPLICATION USERS

Learning to use an application software package involves time and practice. Fortunately, several support tools are available to help you: tutorials, online help, trade books, and keyboard templates (Figure 2-35).

**Tutorials** are step-by-step instructions using real examples that show you how to use an application. Some tutorials are written manuals, but more and more, tutorials are in the software form, allowing you to use your computer to learn about a package.

**Online help** refers to additional instructions that are available within the application. In most packages, a function key or special combination of keys are reserved for the help feature. When you are using an application and have a question, pressing the designated "help" key will temporarily overlay your work on the screen with information on how to use the package. When you are finished using the help feature, pressing another key allows you to return to your work.

The documentation that accompanies software packages is frequently organized as reference material. This makes it very useful once you know how to use a package but difficult to

**FIGURE 2-35**
This figure shows four ways to learn application software packages.

Software **tutorials** help you learn an application while using the actual software on your computer.

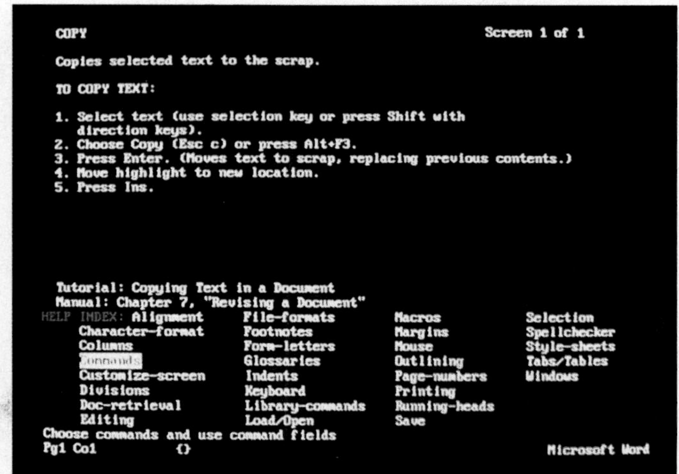


**Online help** gives you assistance without your having to leave the application.

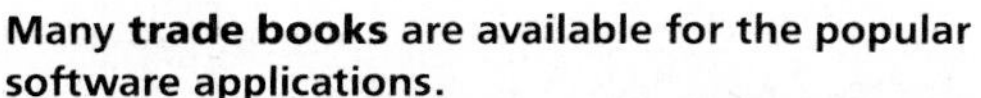

Many **trade books** are available for the popular software applications.

**Keyboard templates** give you quick reference to software commands.

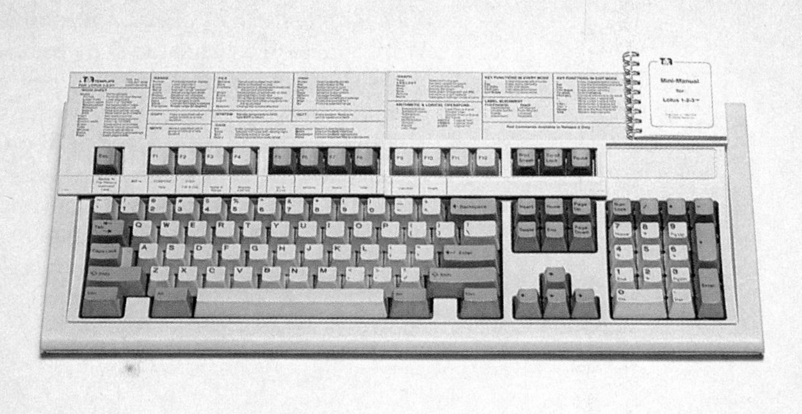

use when you are first learning it. For this reason, many **trade books** are available to help users learn to use the features of microcomputer application packages. These books can usually be found where software is sold and are frequently carried in regular bookstores.

**Keyboard templates** are plastic sheets that fit around a portion of your keyboard. The keyboard commands to select the various features of the application programs are printed on the template. Having these prompts readily available is helpful for both beginners and experienced users.

## TIPS FOR USING MICROCOMPUTER APPLICATIONS

The following tips are listed under specific applications. Some of them will make sense now and will be useful to new users. Others may not be clear now but will be useful as you increase your proficiency with each application. Using this section for reference will help you develop good techniques as you learn microcomputer applications. Remember, it may take up to twenty hours or more of use before you become familiar with a package's capabilities. Don't expect to be an "instant expert."

### Tips for Using Word Processing

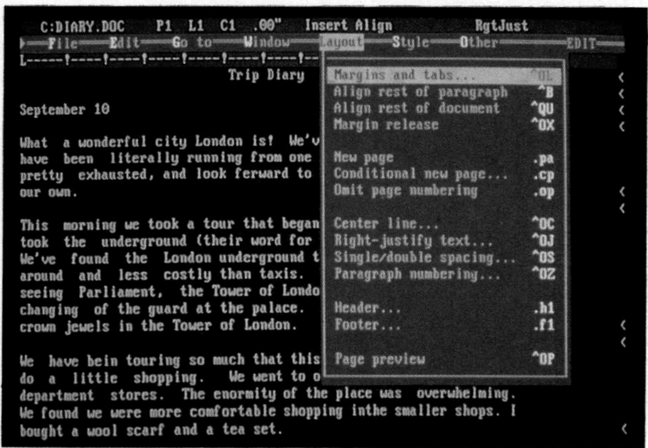


1. **Learn how to move the cursor.** Some people only learn the simplest methods of moving around inside a document: one character at a time sideways, and one line at a time up or down. But most word processors have a number of methods to move faster, such as a word at a time, to the end of a line, to the end of a sentence, to the top or bottom of the screen, to the top or bottom of a page, to a specific page, etc. Learn these movement commands and you'll save yourself a lot of editing time.
2. **Think about how your document "looks" as well as what it "says."** The use of underlining, boldface, indentation, borders, titles, and other stylistic features can enhance your document and help get your message across. After you get your words right, review your document one more time just to improve the visual presentation.
3. **Use a spelling checker.** Even if you're a champion speller, you still probably make a typo every once in a while. Get in the habit of running the spelling checker on all documents you create after every time you've added text.
4. **File your document under a meaningful name.** The main reason for a meaningful name is so you can recognize the document at a later date. If possible, place the name on the document itself. You've probably noticed document name or number references on letters from attorneys, accountants, and others who generate large volumes of correspondence.
5. **Create document templates for frequently used documents.** A **document template** is a document with the title, headings, footings, spacing, and other features that you want to have in frequently generated documents. The template usually contains everything except the text of the document. An example would be an interoffice memo template that contains the title (Interoffice Memorandum) and the TO:, FROM:, SUBJECT:, and DATE: headings. Using a document template reduces the time to prepare a document and results in a consistent format.

6. **When working on a document, save it frequently.** Nothing is more frustrating than entering a large amount of text and then losing it because of a system or power failure or an accidental mistake. Get in the habit of saving your document frequently, say every ten minutes or so, to minimize any data loss.

## Tips for Using Electronic Spreadsheets

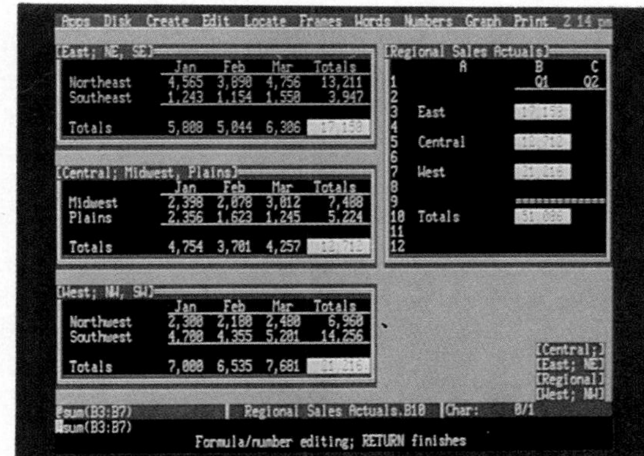


1. **State your assumptions explicitly in the upper portion of your spreadsheet. Assumptions** are data elements such as the unit selling price or an interest rate that are used in spreadsheet calculations. Instead of placing these items in formulas, put them in a separate cell and reference the cell in your formula. This not only makes your calculations more obvious but makes subsequent changes and "what if" testing easier.
2. **Use range names for key cells.** Rather than referring to the cell that contains the unit price assumption by its cell number, use the option to give that cell a name, such as PRICE. Using named cells minimizes reference errors and makes your formulas more meaningful.
3. **Use meaningful names for your row and column descriptions.** Give some thought to the text you use to label rows and columns, especially if your spreadsheet will be used by others. A few extra characters can go a long way to helping someone understand the data being presented.
4. **Leave room for expansion.** Even the best designed spreadsheets can grow as you add additional data elements, rows, or columns. Anticipate the areas of your spreadsheet that may expand and structure them accordingly by providing blank rows and columns.
5. **Highlight your results.** Remember that your spreadsheet is also a visual document. If the main purpose of the spreadsheet is to calculate a single number such as net profit, try to highlight the result by using underlines, asterisks, or white space to set it apart from the other data.
6. **Document your spreadsheet in your spreadsheet.** A description of the spreadsheet and the assumptions helps other users understand the spreadsheet's purpose and can help you if you haven't worked with it for a while.

## Tips for Using Database Software

1. **Before you start, take time to design your file.** Although data elements can be added later, it's desirable to have all necessary elements provided for at the beginning.
2. **Use meaningful names for the files and data fields.** Meaningful names are a good practice for all applications but especially in a database, where it's likely that you'll be working with multiple files and a large number of data fields.
3. **Avoid the use of significant identification numbers (IDs).** A significant ID is the identifying field or key field of a record in which two or more data elements are combined, thus building "significance" into the ID. An example would be an inventory parts file ID in which the ID is the part number plus a code indicating the part type. The problem with significant ID schemes is that they grow increasingly more

complicated and eventually break down; sooner or later you'll encounter an item that won't fit the scheme. Avoid this confusion by establishing separate fields for each data item.

4. **Have the system generate IDs whenever possible.** This tip is closely related to the last tip discussing significant IDs. Obviously the system shouldn't generate the ID for files where the ID is something like a social security number. But when the ID is merely an identifier to be used to distinguish between the records, such as a transaction number, have the system generate it.
5. **Create an index file if you frequently access a file by something other than the file ID field.** Let's say you have an employee file that you normally access by its ID, the employee number. Occasionally, however, you need to access records by employee name. You could sort the file by name each time but a faster way would be to create and maintain an index to the file based on employee name.

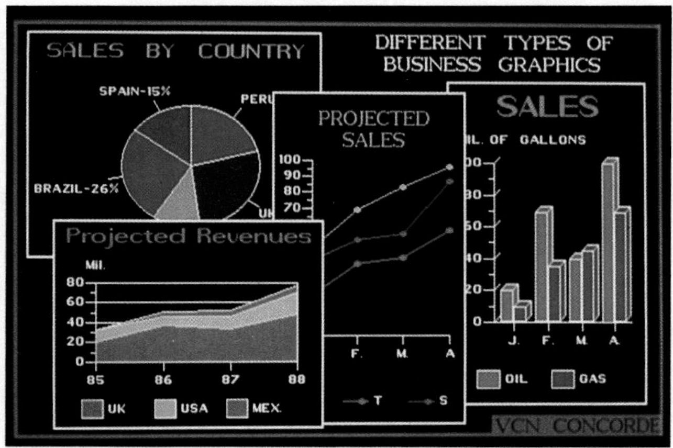


## Tips for Using Graphics

1. **Keep in mind that a graphic is a visual presentation.** Before you start, give some thought to the arrangement ("composition") of the information to be presented.
2. **Don't try to present too much information.** If you do, you'll wind up with a cluttered look that will make the information difficult to understand.
3. **Choose the most appropriate type of graphic.**
   a. Bar charts show the relationship between variables such as the amount of sales (variable 1) for each month (variable 2).
   b. Pie charts are excellent for showing the relationship between individual variables (the pie slices) and the total of all variables (the whole pie). The effectiveness of pie charts is lessened if some of the variables are too small in relation to the others (resulting in pie slices too thin) or if there are too many variables.
   c. Line diagrams link a set of variables with a connecting line and are excellent for showing a trend as indicated by a rising or falling line.
4. **Use words sparingly.** Use text to title the graphic and identify the variables but don't overdo the use of words. If you have a choice of type styles, choose one that's simple and easy to read. Leave space around text so that it will stand out and can be easily read.
5. **Use colors carefully.** If you have a choice of colors, choose them carefully. The right colors can enhance the presentation while the wrong ones can confuse and distract. Lighter colors should be on top of darker, "heavier" colors.
6. **Be consistent.** If you're making a series of graphics, the type style, graphic size, headings, borders, use of colors, etc., should be the same for all items.
7. **Projected graphics should be simple.** If your graphic is going to be projected in front of an audience, you can't display as much information as you can if the graphic is going to be read by an individual. Remember, the audience can't see the projected graphic as well as someone holding a printed copy and they will only have a limited amount of time to look at it.

## CHAPTER SUMMARY

1. **Computer literate** is a term used to describe people who have an understanding of computers and how they are used in our modern world.
2. Software that is useful to a broad range of users is sometimes referred to as **general microcomputer applications software**.
3. The four most widely used microcomputer software applications are word processing, electronic spreadsheet, database, and graphics.
4. **Word processing software** is used to prepare documents electronically.
5. Additional support features for a word processing application can include a spelling checker, thesaurus, and grammar checker.
6. **Spelling checker software** allows you to check individual words or an entire document for correct spelling.
7. **Thesaurus software** allows you to look up synonyms for words in a document while you are using your word processor.
8. **Grammar checker software** identifies possible grammar, writing style, and sentence structure errors.
9. Word processing software is a document productivity tool that allows you to create, edit, format, print, and store documents.
10. **Electronic spreadsheet software** allows you to organize numeric data in a worksheet or table format.
11. A spreadsheet is composed of **rows** and **columns**. Each intersection of a row and column is a **cell**.
12. A spreadsheet cell can contain one of the following: a **label**, a **value**, or a **formula**.
13. The "what if" capability of electronic spreadsheet software is a powerful tool that is widely used by management personnel for decision support information.
14. **Database software** and **file management software** are used to organize, retrieve, manipulate, and update data that is stored in files.
15. In general, database software can work with data that is stored in multiple files. File management software is designed to work with one data file at a time.
16. Information presented in the form of a graph or a chart is commonly referred to as **graphics**. Three popular graphics used to present information include **pie, bar, and line charts**.
17. **Data communications software** allows you to transmit data from one computer to another.
18. **Desktop publishing software** can combine text and graphics to produce high-quality printed documents.
19. **Integrated software** packages combine several applications in one package and allow data to be shared between the applications.
20. When you purchase software, you should perform the following steps: (1) Verify that the software performs the task desired. (2) Verify that the software runs on your computer. (3) Make sure the software documentation is adequate. (4) Purchase the software from a reputable store, distributor, or vendor. (5) Obtain the best value.
21. Aids such as tutorials, online help, trade books, and keyboard templates are useful in learning and using microcomputer applications.

## KEY TERMS

Analytical graphics *2.14*
Assumptions *2.21*
Bar chart *2.14*
Cell *2.9*
Columns *2.9*
Commands *2.2*
Computer literate *2.2*
Copy *2.7*
Cut *2.7*
Database *2.12*
Database software *2.12*
Data communications software *2.16*
Delete *2.6*
Desktop publishing software *2.16*
Document *2.4*
Document template *2.20*
Edit *2.4*
Electronic spreadsheet *2.9*
Electronic spreadsheet software *2.9*
Field *2.12*
File *2.12*
File management software *2.12*
Formula *2.9*
Function keys *2.3*
General microcomputer applications *2.2*
Grammar checker software *2.6*
Graphics *2.14*
Icons *2.4*
Insert *2.6*
Integrated software *2.17*

## REVIEW QUESTIONS

1. Define the term computer literate.
2. What is general microcomputer applications software?
3. List the four most widely used microcomputer application packages and describe how each application helps users.
4. What is a spelling checker? Describe a typical procedure when a misspelled word is found.
5. Explain how management personnel use the "what if" capability of electronic spreadsheets. Why is this capability useful for decision support?
6. What is the difference between database software and file management software?
7. List the three most commonly used charts. Draw an example of each.
8. Describe the advantage of using integrated software. What is a possible disadvantage? What are windows and how are they used in integrated software packages?
9. List the five steps that should be performed when purchasing software. Describe each of them.
10. List and describe four learning aids that can help you use general microcomputer application packages.

## CONTROVERSIAL ISSUES

1. Some organizations insist that their employees use an integrated package so that data can be easily transferred between users. Other organizations let their users make individual decisions on which package they want to use for a particular application. Discuss the advantages and disadvantages of both policies.
2. Spreadsheets are increasingly used to support and justify management decisions. Sometimes these spreadsheets are very complex and are based on hundreds of calculations and assumptions. Discuss the responsibility of the person presenting the spreadsheet to document and explain the assumptions used by the spreadsheet.

## RESEARCH PROJECTS

1. Interview a person who uses a word processing package on a regular basis. Write a report on the types of documents he or she prepares. Include the person's comments on the different word processing features.
2. Find someone who has developed an electronic spreadsheet no larger than a single page. Make a manual (hand-prepared) copy of the spreadsheet. Change one value in each data row and record the time it takes you to recalculate the spreadsheet totals. Report your findings.
3. Assume that you have decided to use a database package to record all the things you own. Define the fields that would make up your database record.

CHAPTER 3

# Processing Data Into Information

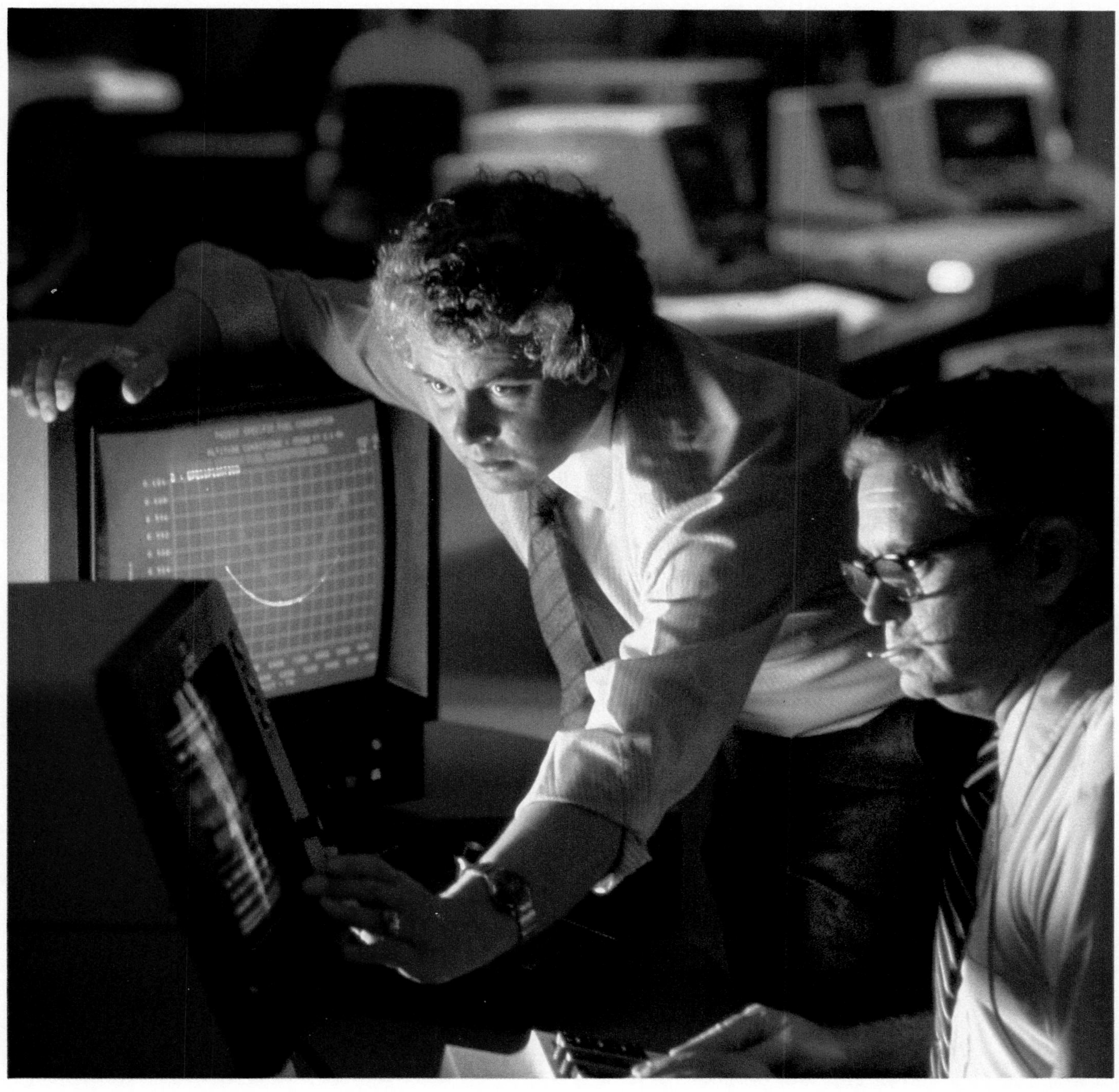

CHAPTER 3

# Processing Data Into Information

## OBJECTIVES

- Explain the four operations of the information processing cycle: input, process, output, and storage.
- Define data and explain the terms used to organize data in an information processing system: field, record, file, database.
- Discuss data management and explain why it is needed.
- Explain arithmetic and logical processing.
- Describe interactive processing and batch processing.
- List and explain the qualities of information.

---

The information processing cycle is basic to all computers, large or small. It is important that you understand this cycle, for much of your success in understanding computers and what they do depends on having an understanding or "feeling" for the movement of data as it flows through the information processing cycle and becomes information. This chapter discusses the information processing cycle, examines the nature of data—how it is organized for processing on a computer and how it is managed—and describes the qualities of information. Reading this chapter will give you a more detailed understanding of the input, processing, output, and storage operations that a computer performs to process data into information.

Also, this chapter summarizes the general types of processing that computers perform and discusses interactive and batch processing methods. Each processing method has advantages and is appropriate for certain types of applications. Business examples demonstrate the use of each processing method.

## OVERVIEW OF THE INFORMATION PROCESSING CYCLE

As seen in Chapter 1, the **information processing cycle** consists of four operations: input, processing, output, and storage. Regardless of the size and type of computer, these operations are used to process data into a meaningful form called information.

The operations in the information processing cycle are carried out through the combined use of computer equipment, also called computer hardware, and computer software. The computer software, or programs, contain instructions that direct the computer equipment to perform the tasks necessary to process data into information.

The diagram in Figure 3-1 illustrates some of the various devices used in conjunction with computer software to carry out the information processing cycle. Input devices are used to enter both the computer programs and the data into main memory. The primary input devices are keyboards on microcomputers and terminals on larger machines. Disk drives and tape drives can also be used to input data that has been stored on these auxiliary storage devices. The function of the input devices is to place into the main memory of the computer the program that is to be executed and the data that is to be processed. Both the program that is to control the processing and the data that is to be processed must be in main memory for processing to occur. Once the computer program is stored in main memory, the person using the computer gives a command to start the program. The processor executes each instruction in the program. These instructions direct the computer to perform the input, processing, output, and storage operations that will process the data into information.

The primary output devices on computers are printers and screens. The format of a report on a printer or a screen is under the control of the program stored in main memory. The program will format the data to be printed or displayed and then issue the commands that cause the output to occur.

Auxiliary storage devices, also called secondary storage devices, commonly used with computers are magnetic disk and magnetic tape. The programs and data not being used by the computer are stored on auxiliary storage until they are needed. Then they are loaded from auxiliary storage into main memory.

Note that some input and output devices can be used for more than one type of operation in the information processing cycle. For example, disk and tape units are used as auxiliary storage devices to store data, but when a disk or tape is receiving data from the main memory of the computer, it is operating as an output device. This process is described as writing or sending data to the auxiliary storage. When data is copied from disk or tape to the main memory of the computer, the disk or tape is operating as an input device. This process is described as reading data into the main memory of the computer. Terminals are also used as both input and output devices. Thus, to understand what is occurring in the information processing cycle, it is important for you to focus on the type of operation being performed rather than the device that is being used.

As we have discussed, the purpose of an information processing system is to process data into information. Data is the prime ingredient in this cycle. Without data, the computer hardware and software have nothing to manipulate. Because data is such an important part of the information cycle, it is important for you to understand what data is, how it is organized, and how it is managed.

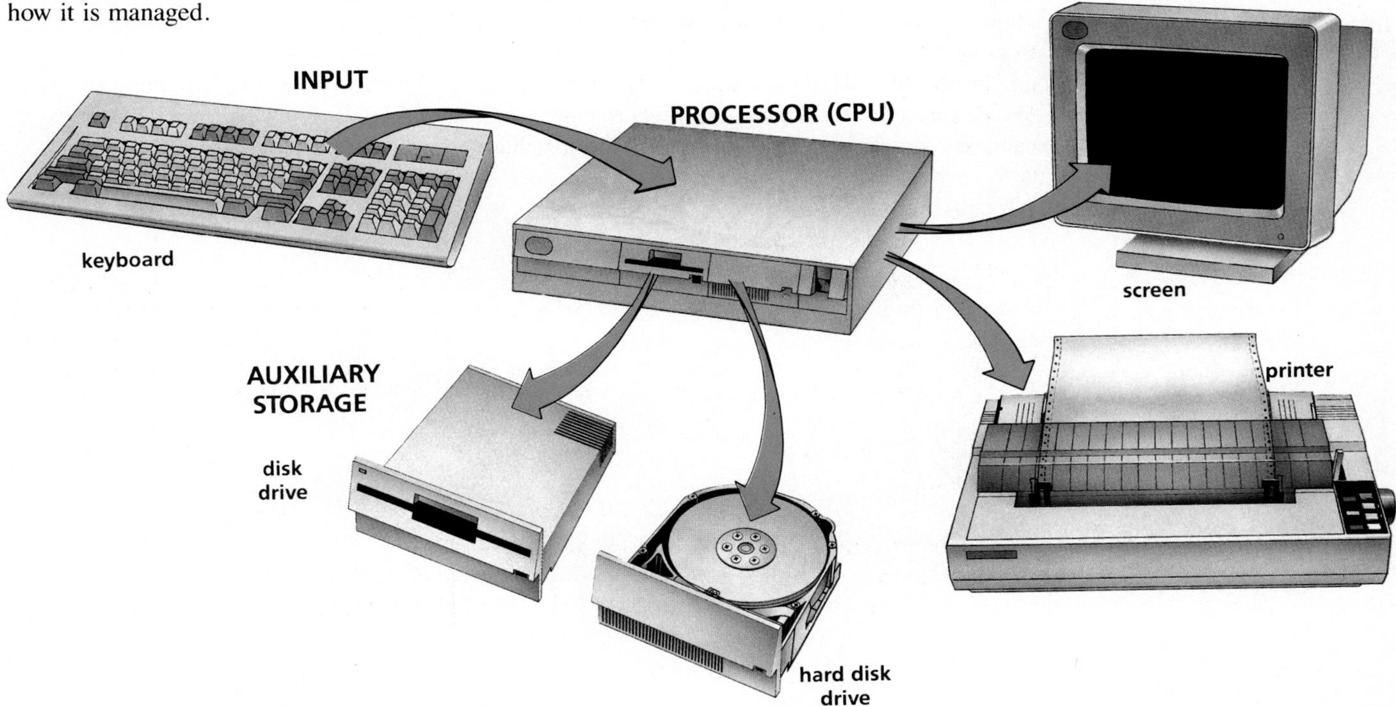


**FIGURE 3-1**
**A computer consists of input devices, the processor, output devices, and auxiliary storage units. This equipment or hardware is used to perform the operations of the information processing cycle.**

## WHAT IS DATA AND HOW IS IT ORGANIZED?

**Data** is the raw facts, including numbers and words, that a computer receives during the input operation and processes to produce information. For example, in a monthly sales application (Figure 3-2), the value 01/31, identifying a month and day, is data. In a payroll application (Figure 3-3), the social security number 332-98-8776 is data. The name HAYNES is data.

Data is comprised of **characters**. These characters are classified as **alphabetic** (A–Z), **numeric** (0–9) or **special** (all characters other than A–Z and 0–9, such as , ? / ! % & : ;). The raw facts that we refer to as data are made up of a combination of these three kinds of characters. In the previous example, the date 01/31 is made up of the numeric characters 0 1 3 and the special character /. The social security number contains numeric characters and the special character -. The name Haynes contains only alphabetic characters.

Each fact or unique piece of data is referred to as a **data item**, **data field**, or just a **field**. Fields are classified by the characters that they contain. For example, a field that contains only alphabetic characters, such as the name field containing Haynes, is called an **alphabetic field**. A field that contains numeric characters is called a **numeric field**. Numeric fields may also contain some special characters that are commonly used with numbers, such as a decimal point (.) and the plus ( + ) and minus (–) signs. Even with the plus sign ( + ) and decimal point (.) the number +500.00 is still called a numeric field. Fields that contain a combination of character types, such as the date 01/31 (numeric and special characters), are called **alphanumeric** fields. Even though the word "alphanumeric" implies only alphabetic and numeric characters, it also includes fields that contain special characters. The term alphanumeric is used to describe all fields that do not fall into the alphabetic or numeric classifications.

A field is normally most meaningful when combined with related fields. To illustrate, the month and day 01/31 by itself is not as useful as when it is related to monthly sales (Figure 3-2). Also, the social security number 332-98-8776 is more useful when it is related to the name HAYNES and to the paycheck amount $327.00 (Figure 3-3). Because related fields are more meaningful if they are together, fields are organized into groups called records.

A **record** is a collection of related fields. Each record normally corresponds to a specific unit of information. For example, a record that could be used to produce the payroll report in Figure 3-3 is illustrated in Figure 3-4. The fields in the record are the social security number, employee name, and paycheck amount. This example shows that the data in each record is used to produce a line on the payroll report. The first record contains all the data concerning the employee named Haynes. The second record contains all the data concerning the employee named Johnston. Each subsequent record contains all the data for a given employee. Thus, you can see how related data items are grouped together to form a record.

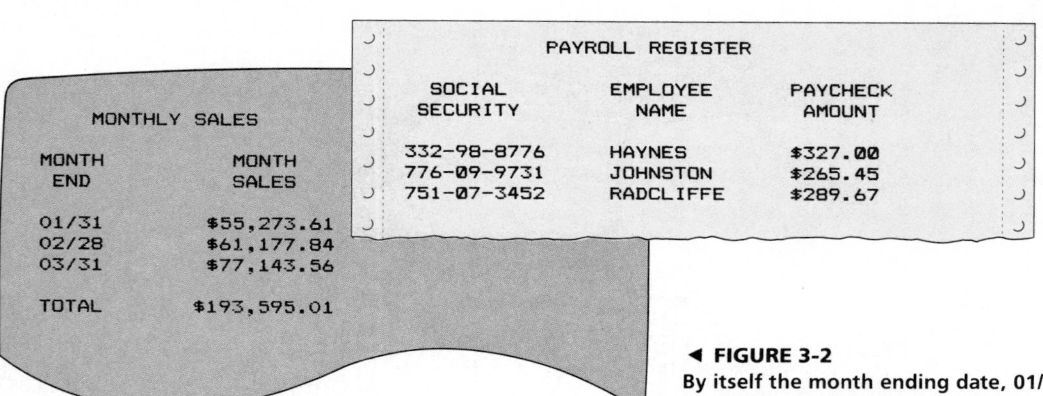

PAYROLL REGISTER

| SOCIAL SECURITY | EMPLOYEE NAME | PAYCHECK AMOUNT |
|---|---|---|
| 332-98-8776 | HAYNES | $327.00 |
| 776-09-9731 | JOHNSTON | $265.45 |
| 751-07-3452 | RADCLIFFE | $289.67 |

MONTHLY SALES

| MONTH END | MONTH SALES |
|---|---|
| 01/31 | $55,273.61 |
| 02/28 | $61,177.84 |
| 03/31 | $77,143.56 |
| TOTAL | $193,595.01 |

◄ **FIGURE 3-3**
**The social security number becomes more meaningful when it is related to an employee name and pay rate.**

◄ **FIGURE 3-2**
**By itself the month ending date, 01/31, is not as useful as when it is related to the monthly sales amount.**

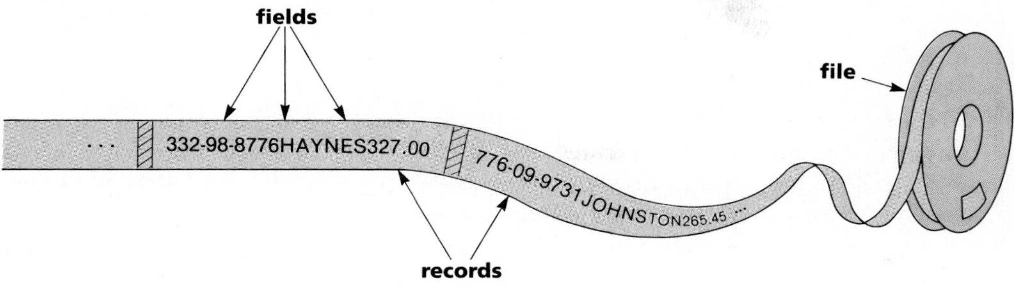


**FIGURE 3-4**
**The records of this payroll file are sequentially stored on magnetic tape. The file contains the social security number, name, and paycheck amount for all employees.**

A collection of records is called a **file**. The payroll file in Figure 3-4, for example, contains all the records required to produce the payroll register report. Files are stored on some medium, such as magnetic tape or magnetic disk. Records on tape are usually arranged in a **sequential** manner. This means that the records in the file are arranged in some sequence such as employee number order or product number order. In the payroll file, for example, records could be arranged alphabetically by employee name or numerically by employee number. The field that is used to arrange the records in a specific order is called the **key field**. The records in files stored on disk can be arranged sequentially or randomly. In a **random** file, records are not arranged in any sequence or specific order.

Data is frequently organized in a **database**. As we discussed in Chapter 2, a database provides an efficient way to establish a relationship between data items and implies that a relationship has been established between multiple files. Data that has been organized in a database can be efficiently manipulated and retrieved by a computer.

### Summary of Data Organization

In this section we have defined data as the raw facts that are processed by a computer system. We have also defined the terms used to describe how data is organized. We have seen that the smallest elements of data are alphabetic, numeric, and special characters and that these characters are used to build the fields, records, files, and databases that are manipulated by an information system to create information.

## DATA MANAGEMENT

For data to be useful in the processing cycle, it must have certain attributes such as accuracy. **Data management** refers to techniques, methods, and procedures that are used to manage these attributes and provide for the security and maintenance of data. The purpose of data management is to ensure that data required for an application will be available in the correct form and at the proper time for processing.

To illustrate data management, we use an example of a credit checking bureau (Figure 3-5). A summary of the application follows:

1. Data entered into the database of the credit bureau is acquired from numerous sources such as banks and stores. The data relates to people's credit ratings and includes facts such as income, history of paying debts, bankruptcies, and certain personal information.
2. The database is stored on auxiliary storage.

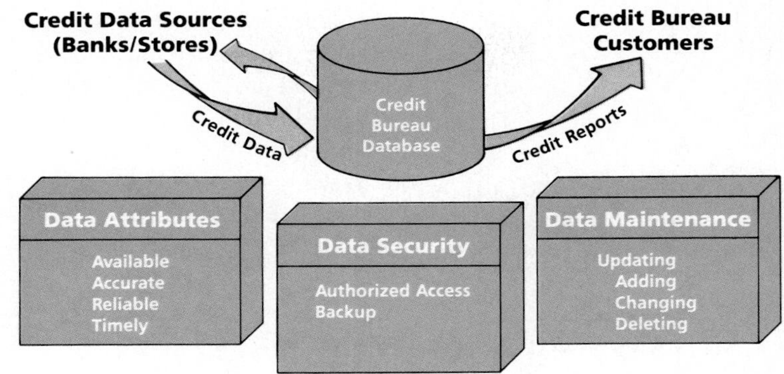


**FIGURE 3-5**
**Data management is concerned with the attributes, security, and maintenance of data. If well managed, data will be available to users when they want it and in a form they can use to create information.**

3. Customers of the credit bureau can call the bureau and request an individual's credit rating. The credit bureau employee uses a terminal to retrieve information concerning the credit rating from the database and gives the caller a brief credit history of the person in question. The system also generates a record that causes a complete credit history to be printed that night. The report will be mailed to the customer the following day.

## Data Attributes

One attribute of data is that it must be *available*. In the credit bureau application, it would not be possible to implement the system if banks, stores, and other organizations were not willing to provide information about account holders. Therefore, prior to implementing an application on a computer, there must be assurance that the data required will be available.

Another important attribute of data in this application or any other is its integrity. **Data integrity** affects the confidence a user has in processing that data. The three primary elements of data integrity are: (1) data accuracy, (2) reliable data entry, and (3) timeliness.

For a user to have confidence in the information provided by a computer system, he or she first must be confident that the data used to create the information is *accurate*. This means that the source of the data is reliable and the data is correctly reported. For example, if someone incorrectly reports to the credit bureau that an individual did not pay a bill and this information becomes part of the database, a responsible customer could be denied credit unjustly. Users must be confident that the people and organizations providing data to the credit bureau provide accurate data.

A second element of data integrity is *reliable data entry*. Data entered for processing must be entered correctly. In the credit bureau example, if a bank reports that the balance on a credit card account is $200.00, but the balance is incorrectly entered as $20,000.00, the information generated would be invalid.

The third element of data integrity is timeliness. *Timeliness* means that data to be processed has not lost its usefulness or accuracy because time has passed. For example, assume that two years ago a salary of $15,000.00 was entered for an individual. Today, that data is not timely because two years have passed and the person may be earning either less or more.

Data integrity is critical. Before an application is implemented on a computer, all the criteria for valid data must be defined and checks for valid data should be placed in the programs.

## Data Security

Data management also includes managing data security. **Data security** refers to protecting data to keep it from being misused or lost. This is an important issue because misuse or loss of data can have serious consequences. In the credit bureau example, a person's credit rating and history of financial transactions are confidential. People do not want their credit information made available to unauthorized organizations. Therefore, the credit bureau must develop systems and procedures that allow only authorized personnel to access the data stored in the database. In addition, if the data in the database should be tampered with or lost, the credit bureau must have some method for recovering the correct data. Therefore, data in an information system is periodically copied or backed up. **Backup** refers to making copies of data files so that if data is lost or destroyed, a timely recovery can be made and processing can continue.

## Data Maintenance

**Data maintenance**, another aspect of data management, refers to the procedures used to maintain data accuracy by keeping data current. These procedures are called **updating** and include **adding** new data, such as creating a record for a new person to include in the credit bureau database; **changing** existing information, such as posting a change of address to an existing record; and **deleting** obsolete information, such as removing inactive records after some designated period of time.

## Summary of Data Management

Management of data is critical if an application is to be successfully processed on a computer. Data management includes managing data attributes, data security, and data maintenance. If inadequate attention is given to managing data, the information processing system will not perform as intended and the output will have little value.

# HOW THE INFORMATION PROCESSING CYCLE WORKS

Now that you have learned about data, and how it is organized and managed, we can discuss the input, process, output and storage operations of the information processing cycle and show the role that data plays in each of the four operations.

## Input Operations

**Input operations** transfer data from an input device to main memory. We have already identified many input devices—including keyboards, terminals, magnetic disk, and magnetic tape. There are many other specialized types of input devices. Some of these devices can interpret special bar codes on products, numbers on checks, and handwritten characters. Some input devices even understand the human voice.

Regardless of the input device used, the principle is the same: data entered from the input device is electronically stored in main memory. Once in main computer memory, the data can be processed under the control of a computer program.

Figure 3-6 on the next page shows the input operation required to build employee files on a personal computer. Such files are common to all companies. The user enters, or inputs, the employee's name and social security number into the main memory by pressing the appropriate keys on the keyboard.

The steps involved in entering the data into main memory and forming the employee identification number are as follows:

1. A computer program is stored in main memory. When the program begins to process, it displays a message on the screen directing the user to enter the employee's name. When the user types the name on the keyboard of the computer, the name is stored in the NAME field in main memory.
2. The program then displays a message requesting that the user enter the employee's social security number. As the digits in the social security number are entered, they are stored in main memory in a SOCIAL SECURITY field that has been defined by the program. After both the name and the social security number have been entered and stored in main memory, the input operations are complete.

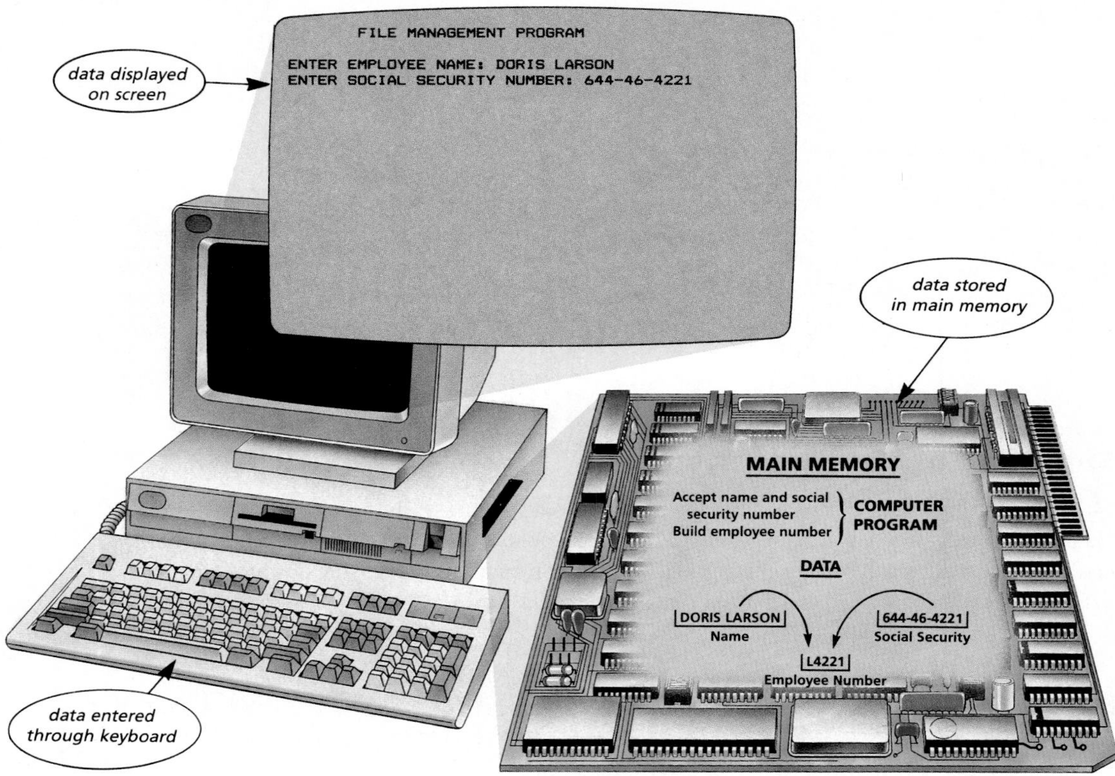


**FIGURE 3-6**
**In this example of an input operation, the software directs the user to enter the employee's name and social security number. When the user enters this data on the keyboard, the data is electronically stored in main computer memory. The program then builds the employee number by moving the first letter of the last name and the last four digits of the social security number to the EMPLOYEE NUMBER field.**

Important points illustrated by this portion of the example are: (1) Operations that occur on a computer are under the control of a program stored in the main memory of the computer. (2) The data entered from the input device (in this example, a keyboard) is electronically stored in main computer memory.

The input operation is important, because data must first be entered into main computer memory before it can be processed.

## Processing Operations

**Processing operations** define how the data will be manipulated into a usable form. In the employee file example, the user wants to process data in order to build an employee identification number. The employee identification number consists of the first letter of the employee's last name and the last four digits of the social security number.

The processing operations are directed by instructions within the program. These instructions specify that the first letter of the last name and the last digits of the social security number are to be moved to the EMPLOYEE NUMBER field that has been defined by the program.

When data is moved from one location to another in main memory, the data in the sending location is copied or duplicated to the receiving location. Thus, in Figure 3-6, when the first letter of the last name is moved to the EMPLOYEE NUMBER field, the last name in the NAME field is not affected. Similarly, when the last four digits of the social security number are moved to the EMPLOYEE NUMBER field, the social security number in that field is not affected. The data is now located in both the sending and receiving memory locations.

As shown in the previous example, moving data from one location to another in main memory is considered a processing operation. Two other types of processing that are performed with computers include arithmetic and logical processing. The next two sections discuss these operations.

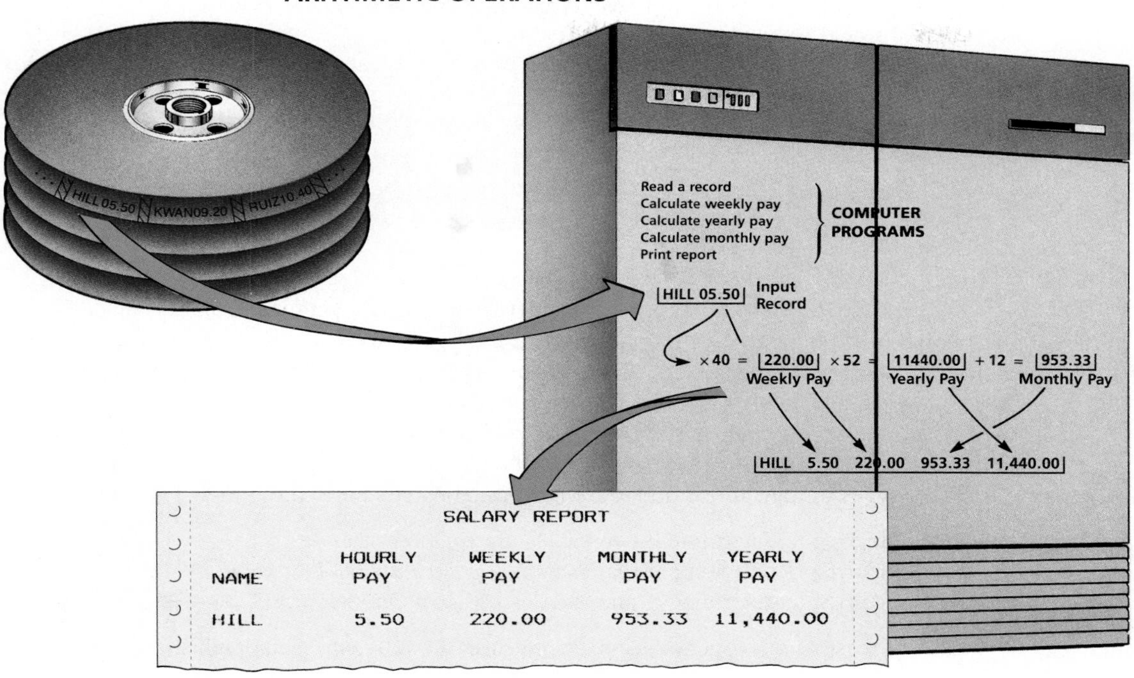


**FIGURE 3-7**
**In this example of arithmetic processing, the program first reads an input record containing an employee name and hourly pay rate. The program then calculates the weekly, monthly, and yearly pay. The results of the calculations are printed in the salary report.**

**Arithmetic Operations** Business and scientific applications frequently require that **arithmetic operations** such as addition, subtraction, multiplication, and division be performed. On many computers, millions of arithmetic operations can be performed in one second. The ability to perform arithmetic operations rapidly and accurately is an important characteristic of all computers.

To illustrate the arithmetic capabilities of the computer, Figure 3-7 shows an application developed to determine a person's weekly, monthly, and yearly pay, based on hourly pay.

The first program instruction reads a record from the disk into main memory. The record contains the employee name and the hourly pay rate. These two data fields are contained in each employee's record. The file stored on disk contains a record for each of the employees.

When the record is read into main memory, program instructions direct that the weekly, yearly, and monthly pay are to be calculated. The weekly pay is determined by multiplying the hourly rate times 40 hours. The yearly pay is obtained by multiplying the weekly rate by 52 weeks. The monthly pay is calculated by dividing the yearly pay by 12. Note that when the yearly and monthly pay are calculated, answers from the previous calculations are used. Any numeric data stored in main memory, including results of previous calculations, can be used in arithmetic operations. After the calculations are completed, instructions in the program describe the output operations that will print a report.

In Figure 3-7, the first record in the file for the employee Hill has been processed. The file contains subsequent records for Kwan, Ruiz, and others. The same operations that were performed to calculate the weekly, yearly, and monthly pay for Hill are required for each subsequent employee. Thus, the program instructions will be repeated for each employee record. The computer will input the data from each record one at a time and then repeat the instructions "Read a Record, Calculate Weekly Pay, Calculate Yearly Pay, Calculate Monthly Pay, Print Report" for each record so long as there are more records in the file to be processed.

The ability to repeat the instructions in a program is very important because it allows a computer to process any number of records with a single set of instructions. It is similar to the method you would use if you were computing the weekly pay for each employee by hand. You would compute the weekly pay for each employee one at a time and write the result in the report. You would follow the same steps for each employee. In a similar manner, the computer processes one employee, or record, at a time and repeats the same steps, or instructions, for each employee.

Important points illustrated by this example are: (1) The program stored in main memory can perform arithmetic operations on numeric data. (2) Answers derived from arithmetic operations can be used in other calculations and can also be used as output from a program. (3) The computer is processing one record at a time. (4) One set of program instructions can be repeated any number of times.

**Logical Operations** The **logical operations** are the computer's ability to *compare* data stored in main memory. All computers have instructions that can compare numeric, alphabetic, and special characters. Based on the results of the comparison, different types of processing can be performed. It is this logical ability of computers that allows them to compute overtime pay, play games such as chess, perform medical diagnoses, make hotel reservations, and perform any other task that is based on comparing data.

Three types of logical operations are performed by computer programs. They are:

1. Comparing to determine if two values are *equal to* each other.
2. Comparing to determine if one value is *greater than* another value.
3. Comparing to determine if one value is *less than* another value.

Each of these logical operations is explained in the following paragraphs.

**FIGURE 3-8**
**The program that creates the grade report uses the computer's ability to compare values. It compares a student's GPA (grade point average) to the value 4.0. If the GPA is equal to 4.0, the message HONOR STUDENT is printed on the report, along with the student's name and grade point average. If the comparison is not equal, no message is printed.**

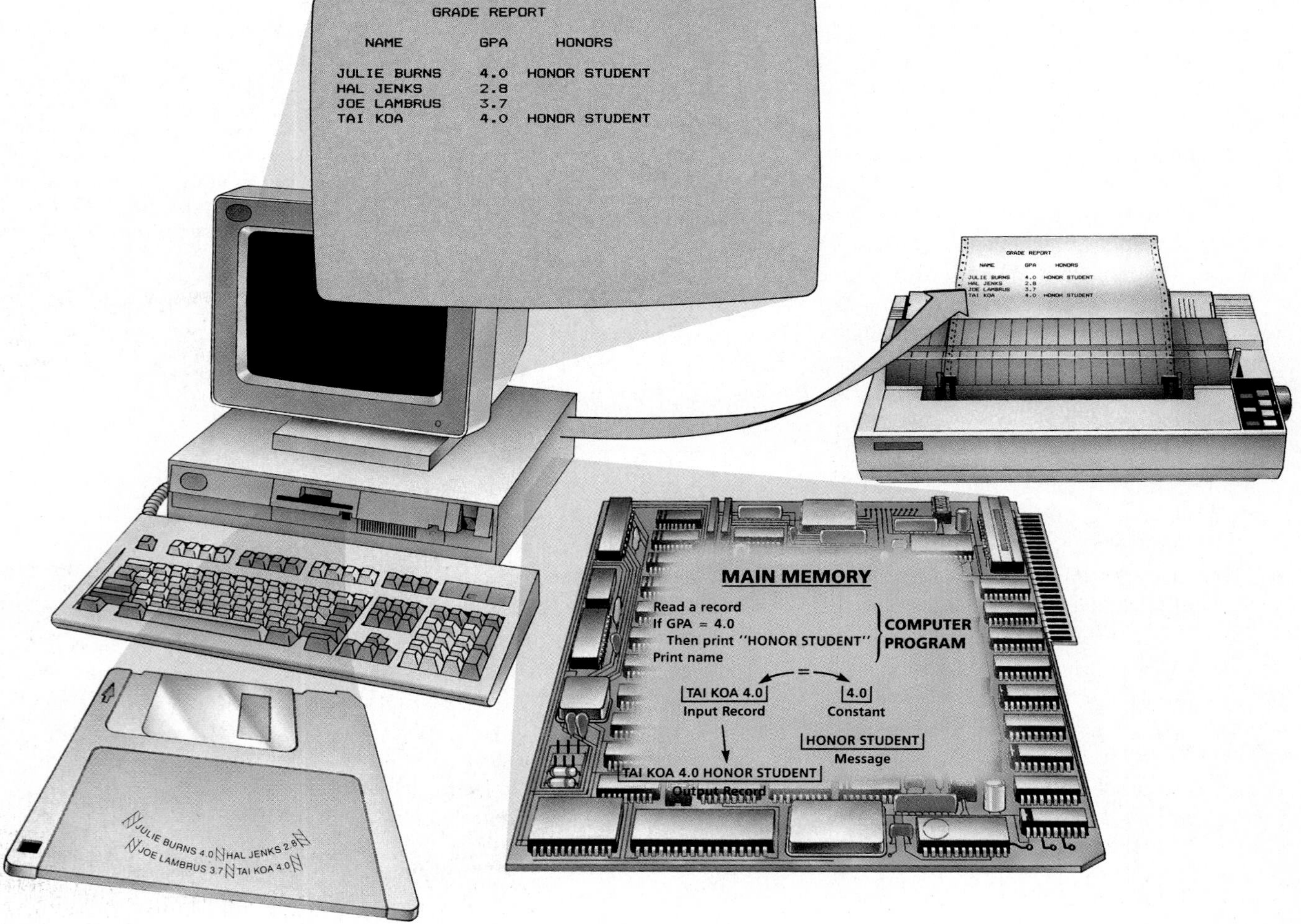

The example in Figure 3-8 illustrates the computer's ability to compare two values to determine if they are equal. This example shows a program whose function is to create a grade report. In order to make this report, an input record containing the student's name and grade point average is read. The grade point average is then compared to the value 4.0. If the grade point average is equal to 4.0, the message HONOR STUDENT is printed on the report. If the grade point average is not equal to 4.0, the message is not printed on the report.

When comparing two values, the program will specify what processing should occur when the condition tested is true and when it is false. In this example, when the condition is true (the grade point average is equal to 4.0), the processing is to print the message on the report together with the student name and average. When the condition is false (the grade point average is not equal to 4.0), the processing is not to print the message. Note that when comparing for an equal condition, the program essentially compares for an unequal condition as well.

A second type of comparison is to determine if one value is greater than another value. In the example in Figure 3-9, a database menu is displayed and the user is asked to enter a choice specifying which of the five functions is to be performed. The user should enter a value from 1 to 5. If, however, the value entered is greater than 5, an entry error has been made and the user is directed by the program to reenter the menu choice. How does the program cause the processing to occur? The program stored in main memory first displays the menu on the screen for the user. It then accepts the menu choice that the user enters. Next, the value entered by the user is compared to the value 5. If the choice entered by the user is greater than 5, the program displays the message, "Please reenter a value from 1 to 5." If the value entered by the user is not greater than five, processing will continue with another comparison to determine if the value is from 1 to 5.

The third type of comparison that is commonly performed on a computer is to determine if one value is less than another value. To illustrate this, the example in Figure 3-9 continues in Figure 3-10 on the next page, to check if the menu choice entered by the user is less than 1. If so, the user has entered an invalid value. The program will display an error message asking the user to reenter the choice and then will accept the new choice. If the value entered by the user is not less than 1, the program will continue with its processing.

An important point to note in each of the three comparison operations is that the program must specify the different types of processing that the computer is to perform. In other words, the program must specify what to do for both true and false comparison conditions. The ability of a computer to compare data and then select one of two processing paths is a simple but powerful feature that is used in programs of all levels of complexity.

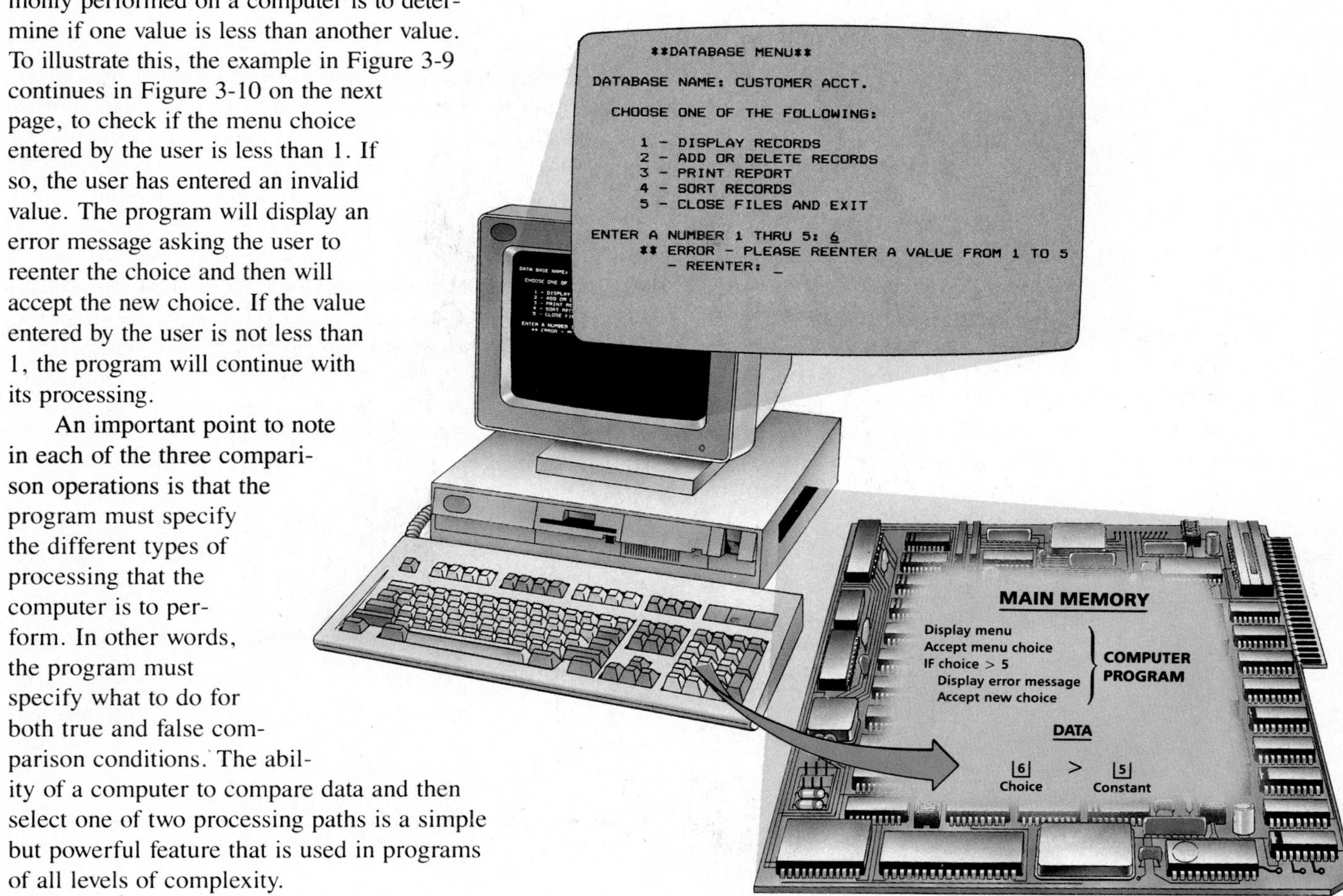


**FIGURE 3-9**
**When the user enters a menu choice, the program compares the value entered to 5, the number of valid selections. If the value entered is greater than 5, an error message is displayed and the user must reenter the choice. In this example, the user entered the value 6, the program displayed an error message, and the user was asked to reenter the choice.**

**FIGURE 3-10**
**The value entered by the user is compared to the value 1. Because the value entered is less than 1, an error message is displayed and the user was asked to reenter a choice.**

## Output Operations

The purpose of the input operations is to provide data and of the processing operations is to produce information. **Output operations** refer to the operations that take the information produced and put it in a form that can be used by a person or a machine. Reports are a common form of output that are often used by business people. Reports may be printed on the printer or displayed on a screen (Figure 3-11). There are many other types of output, including graphics and sound.

The type of output produced by an application depends on several factors. Some of these factors include the intended use of the output, the speed with which output delivery must take place (i.e., does the user need it right now or can it wait until later), and whether the output is to be permanently kept or used only at the moment. Whenever an application is designed for implementation on a computer, the format of the output and the way it will be presented must be defined. Users work closely with information processing personnel during the development of applications to define the best method and format of presentation.

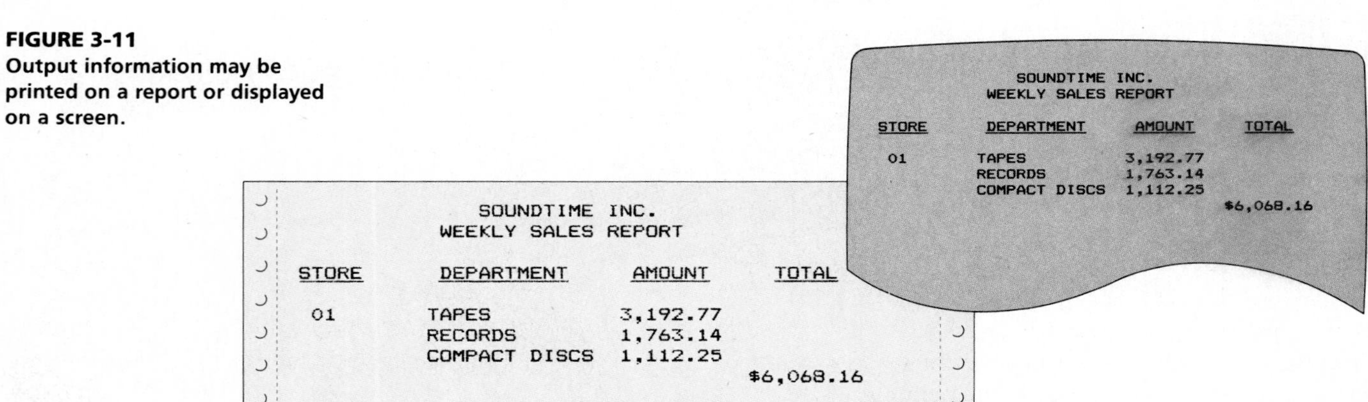

SOUNDTIME INC.
WEEKLY SALES REPORT

| STORE | DEPARTMENT | AMOUNT | TOTAL |
|---|---|---|---|
| 01 | TAPES | 3,192.77 | |
| | RECORDS | 1,763.14 | |
| | COMPACT DISCS | 1,112.25 | |
| | | | $6,068.16 |

**FIGURE 3-11**
**Output information may be printed on a report or displayed on a screen.**

## Storage Operations

The first three operations of the information processing cycle, input, process, and output, describe the procedures that a computer performs in order to process data into information. The fourth operation, storage, refers to the electronic storage capability of a computer. To be more specific, **storage operations** refer to the transfer of programs, data, and information from main memory to an auxiliary storage device such as magnetic disk and magnetic tape (Figure 3-12 on the next page). Storage operations allow programs, data, and information that are not currently needed in main memory to be saved in an electronic format for future use. Programs and data are usually stored in this manner. Sometimes information, or the result of processing, is stored on auxiliary storage. An example of information storage would be storing on disk or tape a copy of a report that is to be printed at a later time.

## Summary of the Information Processing Cycle

As you have seen, the information processing cycle consists of input, processing, output, and storage operations. These operations are controlled by a computer program. When a program begins to execute, it first directs the input operation by specifying how the data that is to be processed should be entered into main memory. Both the program directing the processing and the data to be processed must be in main memory for processing to occur. Next, the computer program directs the processing operation. Processing consists of arithmetic and logical operations and includes moving data from one location to another in main memory. As the program continues executing, it directs the output operation. This phase of the information processing cycle organizes the information produced into some form that can be used by people or other machines. Finally, program instructions direct the storage operation. Programs, data, and information that may be needed for future use are stored on auxiliary storage devices for subsequent retrieval.

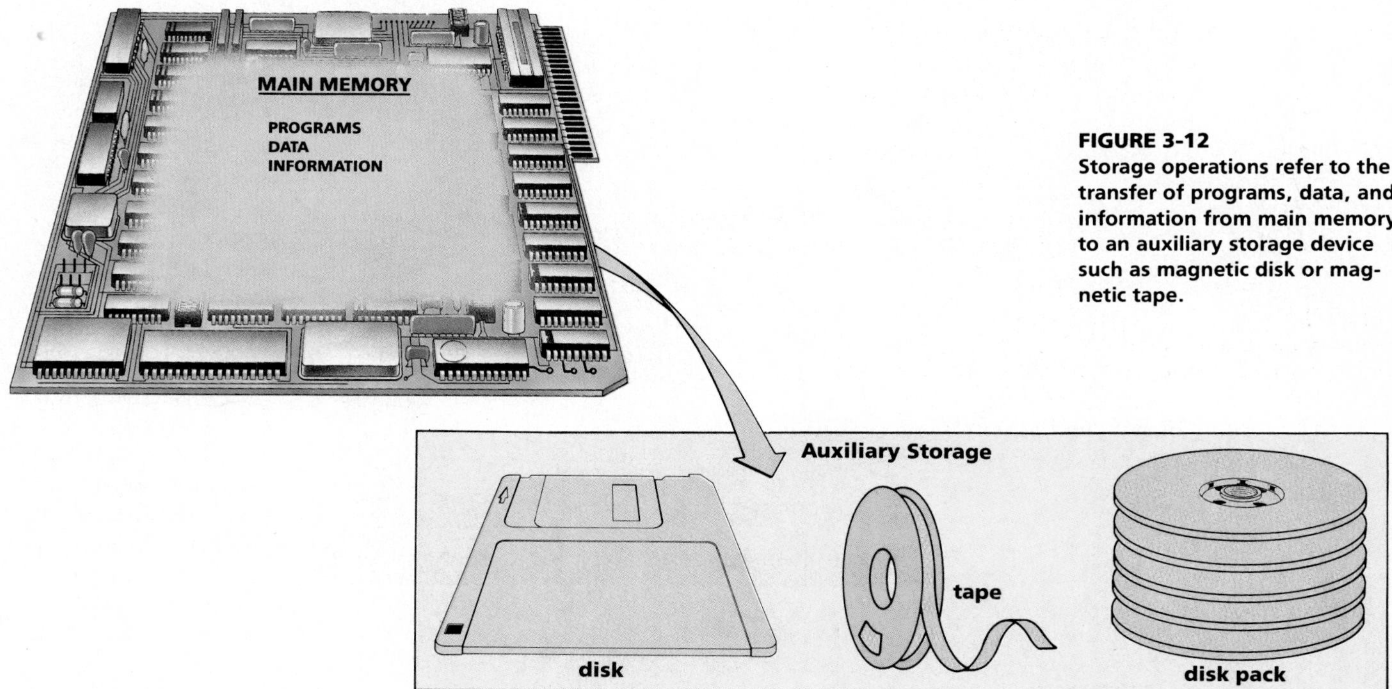


**FIGURE 3-12**
**Storage operations refer to the transfer of programs, data, and information from main memory to an auxiliary storage device such as magnetic disk or magnetic tape.**

# METHODS OF PROCESSING DATA INTO INFORMATION

The information processing cycle is usually implemented on a computer in one of two ways. These two methods are called interactive processing and batch processing. **Interactive processing** means that data is processed upon entry and output is produced immediately. In **batch processing**, data is collected and at some later time, all the data that has been gathered is processed as a group or "batch." Examples of these methods are given in the following sections.

## Interactive Processing

The example in Figure 3-13 illustrates interactive processing. The program used in a bank accepts a beginning year, a yearly deposit amount, and an interest rate. It then calculates and displays the annual value of the savings account. This program is interactive because after the user enters the year, deposit amount, and interest rate, the program immediately performs the calculations and produces output for the user. This example illustrates the use of a personal computer for interactive processing. But large computers, such as minicomputers and mainframes, can also be used for interactive processing.

One type of interactive processing is called transaction processing. In **transaction processing**, the computer user enters all the data pertaining to a complete transaction. After all the data is entered, the program performs the processing required for that particular transaction.

The example in Figure 3-14 illustrates transaction processing as it could be used in a car rental agency. When a car is returned, the rental clerk enters on the terminal all the data required to prepare the final auto rental agreement. The program immediately retrieves the car's record from the disk (based on the license number), performs the necessary calculations, and writes the final rental agreement on the printer. The clerk then gives a copy to the customer. In addition to printing the final rental agreement, the program changes the car's record on disk by placing the ending mileage in the record. After this processing is done, the entire auto rental transaction is completed.

**FIGURE 3-13**
**This is an example of interactive processing to calculate the value of a savings account. After the user enters the beginning year, yearly deposit amount, and the interest rate, the program calculates and displays what the value of the account would be for the next 20 years.**

INTERACTIVE PROCESSING

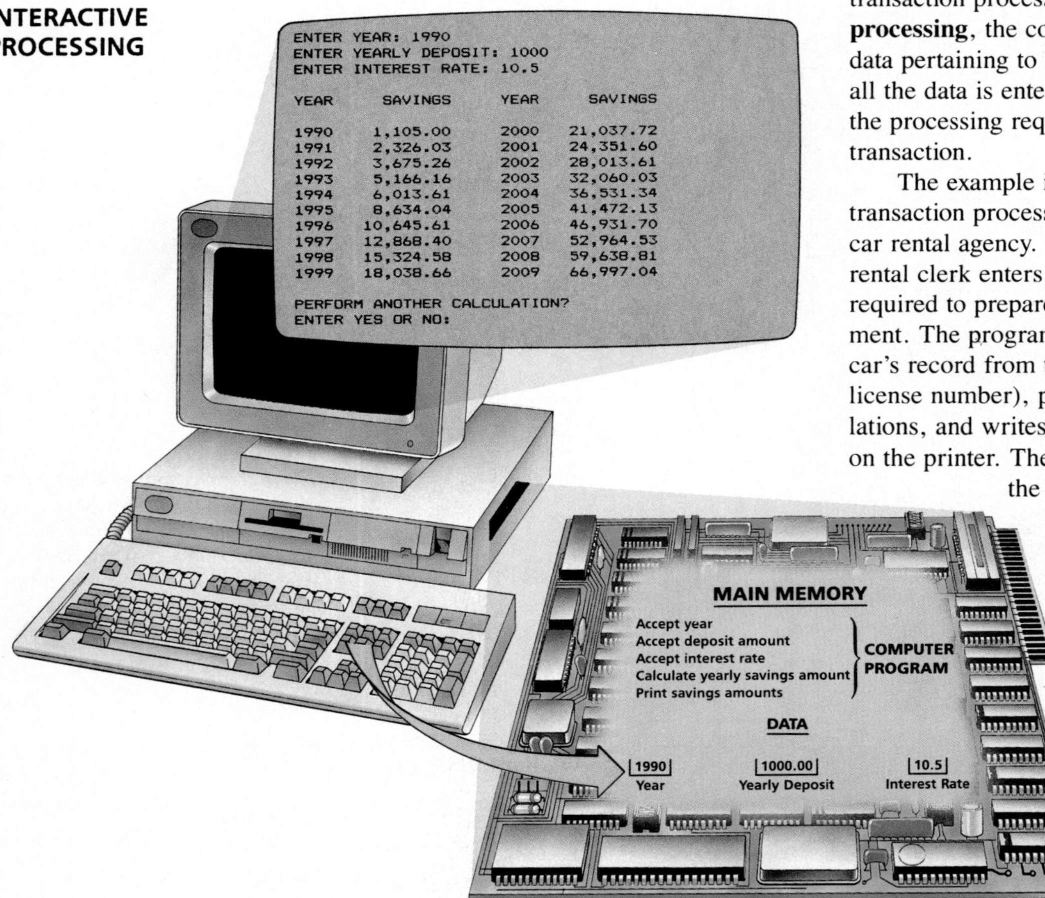

Note that the entire transaction was completed immediately after the user entered the input data. The key to understanding interactive processing is to realize that as soon as the required input data has been entered, the program performs the processing and generates output.

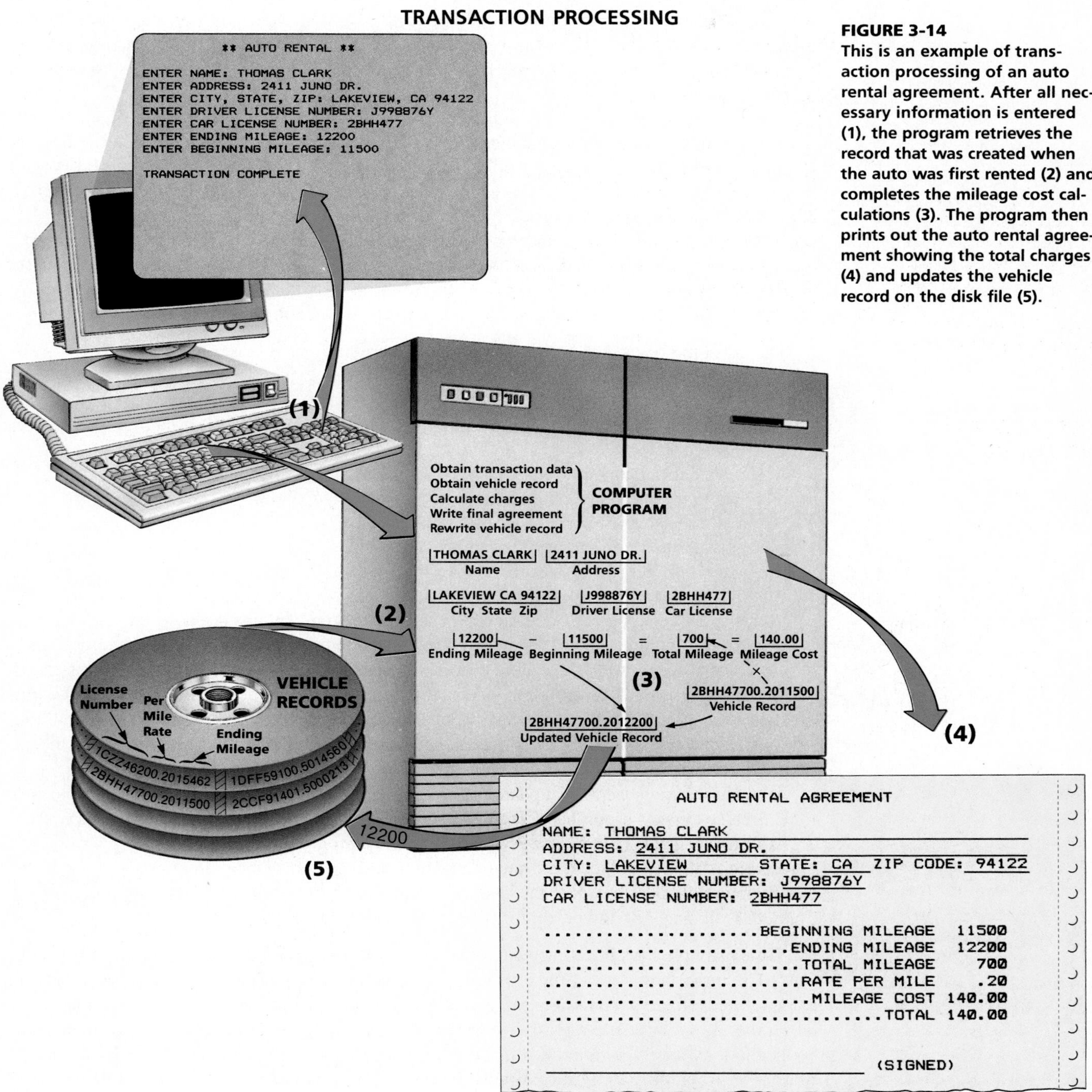


**FIGURE 3-14**
**This is an example of transaction processing of an auto rental agreement. After all necessary information is entered (1), the program retrieves the record that was created when the auto was first rented (2) and completes the mileage cost calculations (3). The program then prints out the auto rental agreement showing the total charges (4) and updates the vehicle record on the disk file (5).**

**After the updated record is rewritten, the ending mileage (12200) would be in the record. This is not shown in the record stored on disk.**

## Batch Processing

Batch processing was used extensively when computers were first used in business. In many cases, source documents containing the data to be processed were brought to a central location where the data was punched on cards or placed on magnetic tape. All the data, in one single group or batch, was then read into the computer for processing. Many of the early applications implemented on computers, such as payroll or billing operations, were best processed in a batch environment.

Today, interactive processing is the most prominent method of processing because it provides immediate results and keeps data current. However, batch processing is still the best way to implement some applications. Applications that require periodic processing of a large number of records are good possibilities for batch processing. Payroll applications that create paychecks periodically, such as every other week, normally operate using a batch method of processing. Other users of batch processing include utility companies, which must send out thousands of bills each month, and credit card companies, which process thousands of charges and payments each month.

As shown in Figure 3-15, the following steps take place in batch processing.

1. The consumer uses a credit card to purchase an item from a store. A sales receipt is produced and becomes the source document.
2. The sales receipt is transmitted to the data entry section of the information systems department at the bank or company processing the credit card purchase. In this example, it is the First Federal Bank.
3. At a terminal, a data entry clerk enters the data from the sales receipt into a disk file. Several data entry personnel could be entering sales receipts at the same time.
4. When all the sales receipts for a given day have been entered, the file of data stored on disk is read into main memory and processed one record at a time. This is batch processing, where all records have been batched into one input file and then processed together.
5. When the input record is read from the batch input file, the corresponding customer record from the account file is also retrieved. The account file contains a record for each cardholder. The record contains the account number, the cardholder's name and address, and the account balance. In the example, the customer's name is Hal Dukes, the address is 613 Acorn Drive, Plain, Wyoming 83742, and the account balance prior to processing the purchase record is $265.40. When the account record is retrieved, it is updated to reflect the latest status of the account by adding the purchase amount from the input record to the account balance found in the account record.
6. After the account record is updated, it is rewritten in the account file. Thus, the next time Hal Dukes makes a purchase, the new balance, $309.39, will be in his account record.
7. After all the sales receipts are processed, another program might be run to prepare the account statements. Account statements are usually sent out once a month and contain the previous statement balance, the current charges, the current balance, the minimum payment (calculated by the program), and the payment due date.

This example illustrated each step that could occur when a purchase is made with a credit card. The important point of the example is that the input records are all batched together into a single input file. They are then processed as a group, updating the account file. At some later time, all account file records are processed as a batch to provide account statements. In applications of this type, hundreds or even thousands of records would be processed in one run of the program. Batch processing is the most appropriate method for processing this application because it provides the information when it is needed and it is cheaper than interactive processing.

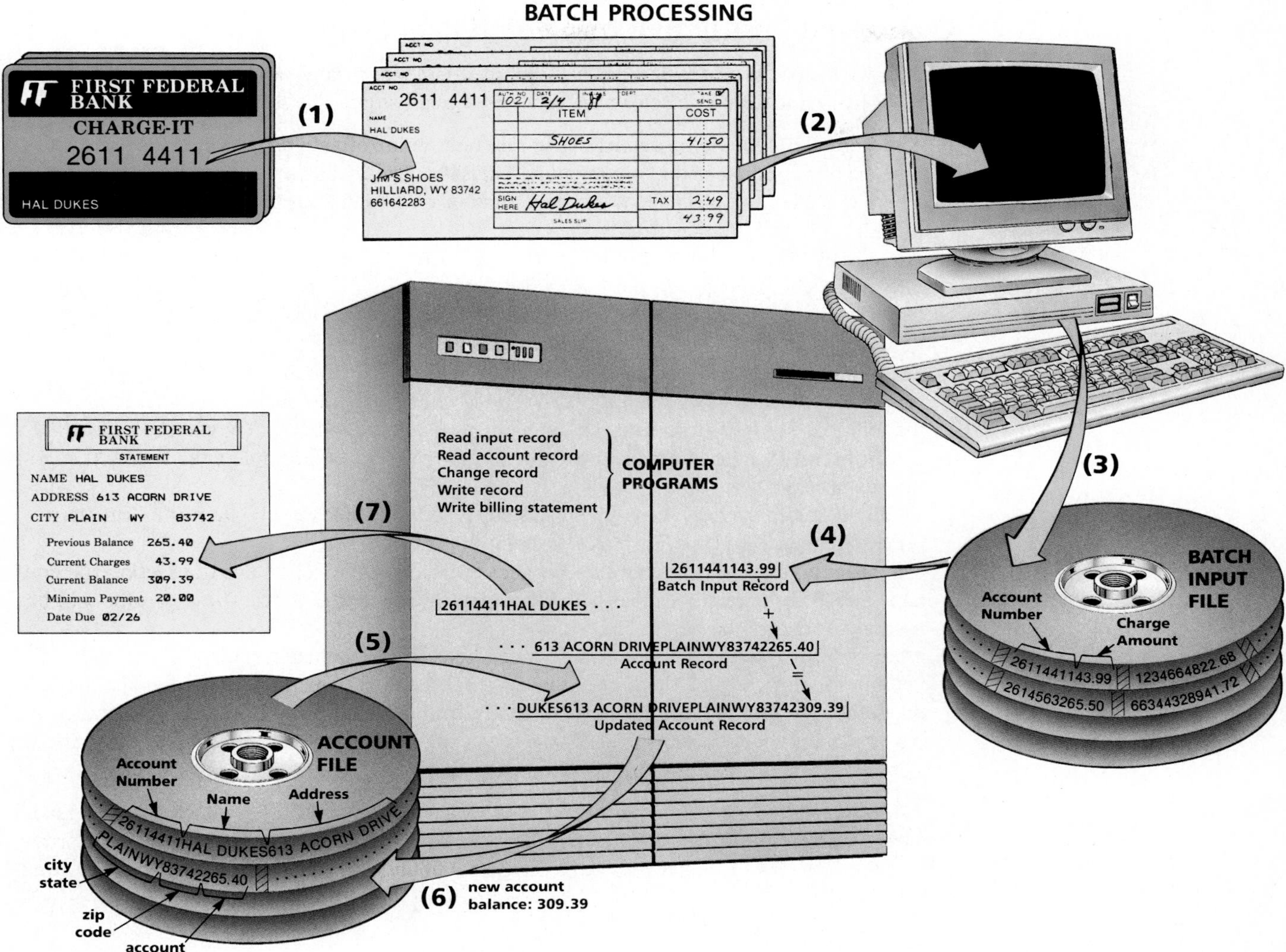


**FIGURE 3-15**
In this example of batch processing, a customer uses a credit card to make a purchase (1). A copy of the sales receipt is entered into the computer system (2) and recorded in a batch input file with charges for other customers (3). At the end of the day, when all charges have been entered into the file, the file is read by a program (4) and processed in a batch mode to update customer account balances stored on another file (5). New account balance amounts are written on the account file (6). At a later time, another program is run to produce customer account statements (7).

## Combined Interactive and Batch Processing

Interactive and batch processing can be combined in a single application. This is illustrated in Figure 3-16, which shows a sales transaction in a retail store. The following steps occur:

1. The store clerk enters the details of the sale on a **point of sale terminal**, a special cash register that is connected to a computer. The sales data includes the department number where the sale took place (14), the item number of the item purchased (A437), and the quantity of items purchased (01).
2. As soon as the sales information (input data) is stored in main memory, the program directs the computer to retrieve the record corresponding to the item number (A437) from the item file. The record retrieved contains the item number (A437), the quantity of the item in inventory (0527), and the unit price for the item (14.95).
3. The program reduces the quantity in the item record (527) by the quantity purchased (1), giving the new inventory quantity (526). It also multiplies the quantity purchased (1) by the unit price (14.95) to determine the total sales amount (14.95). The total sales amount is sent back to the point of sale terminal, where the clerk can complete the transaction with the customer.
4. The item record with the new quantity (526) is written back into the item file. Interactive processing has been used in steps 1 through 4.
5. The program also adds a record to the sales transaction file. The sales transaction file contains a record for each sale that is made during the day at the store. These records will be used at the end of the day in batch processing.
6. After the store is closed and all transactions have been completed, the sales transaction file is input to a program that produces the daily sales report. This report contains the department and sales amount for each sale, the total dollar sales amount for each department of the store, and the total sales in the store for the day. Batch processing has been used in steps 5 and 6.

This application illustrates both interactive processing and batch processing of data generated from a single transaction. When the sales clerk enters the sale on the point of sale terminal and the program responds with the total sales amount, interactive processing has occurred. As soon as the data was entered, the program processed the data by performing the calculations, updating the item file, and producing output on the point of sale terminal. At the same time, input data for batch processing was created when the program wrote a record in the sales transaction file. When these transactions were used to produce the daily sales report, batch processing occurred. All the transaction records were batched together to be processed at one time. It would make little sense to produce the daily sales report until all the sales transactions for the day had been completed. Thus, batch processing is the appropriate method to use to prepare the daily sales report. Because each sale must be processed as it occurs, interactive processing is the appropriate method for the sales and item record processing.

## Summary of Processing Methods

Interactive and batch processing are the two main methods for processing data on a computer. Generally, most processing that is performed on personal computers is interactive processing. On larger computers, the trend is toward more interactive processing, although batch processing is still appropriate for some applications. In addition, some processing involves a combination of both interactive and batch processing.

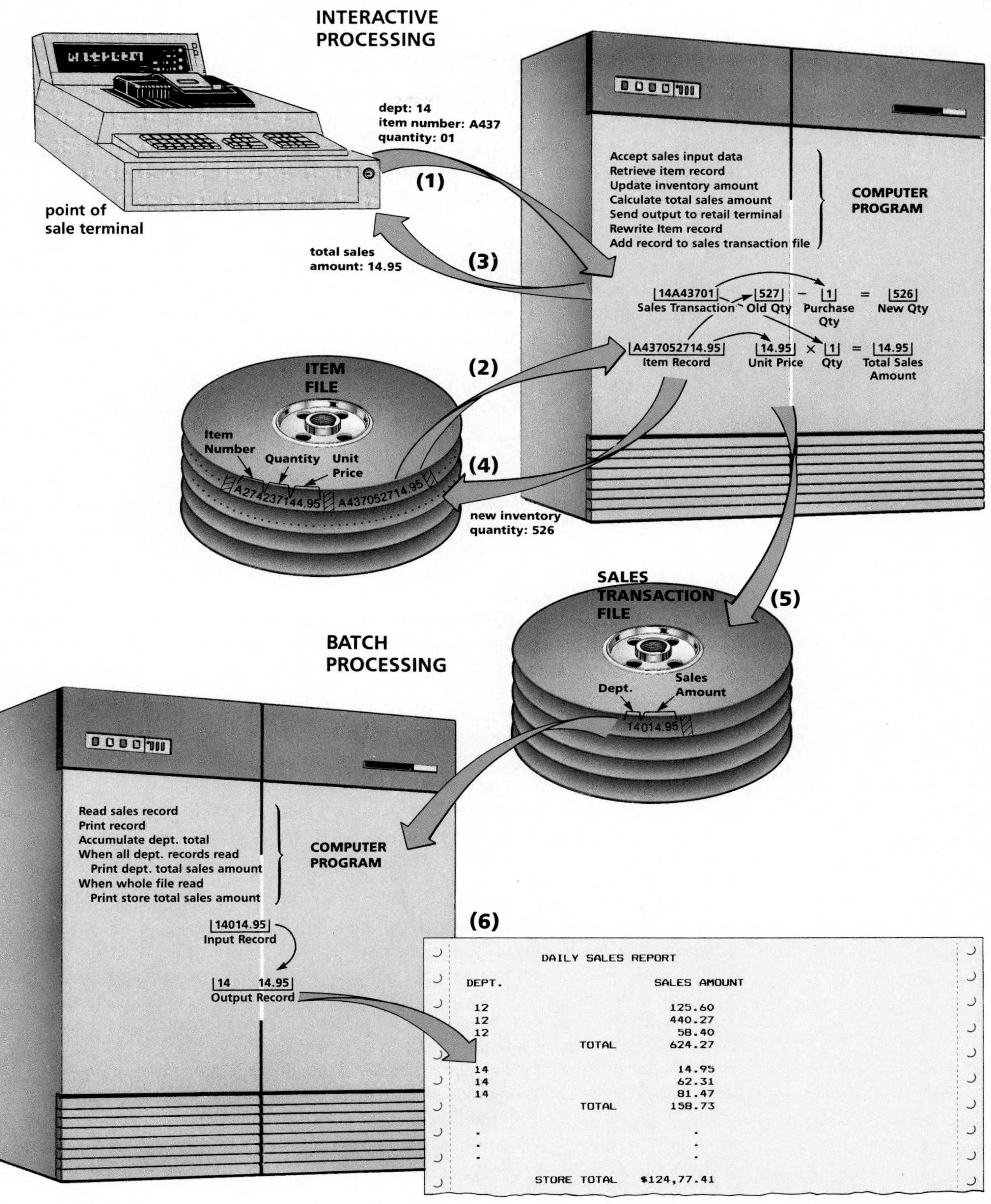


**FIGURE 3-16**
This example illustrates both interactive and batch processing resulting from a single sales transaction. The inventory balance is updated interactively but the sales report is prepared by batch processing at the end of the day.

## QUALITIES OF INFORMATION

As we have discussed, the purpose of processing data is to create information. Just as data should have certain characteristics, so too should information. These characteristics are often called the "qualities of information." Terms used to describe these qualities include the following: accurate, verifiable, timely, organized, meaningful, useful, and cost effective.

Although it may seem obvious, the first quality of information is that it should be *accurate*. Inaccurate information is often worse than no information at all. As you may recall, accuracy was also a characteristic of data. And although accurate data does not guarantee accurate information, it is impossible to produce accurate information from erroneous data. The computer jargon term **GIGO** states this point very well; it stands for "Garbage In, Garbage Out."

Closely related to accuracy is the quality of information being *verifiable*. This means that if necessary, the user can confirm the information. For example, before relying on the amounts in a summary report, an accountant would want to know that the totals could be supported by details of transactions.

Another quality of information is that it must be *timely*. Although most information loses its value with time, some information, such as trends, becomes more valuable as time passes and more information is obtained. The important point here is that the timeliness must be appropriate for any decisions that will be made based on the information. Up-to-the-minute information may be required for some decisions while older information may be satisfactory or more appropriate for others.

To be of the most value, information should be *organized* to suit users' requirements. For example, a sales representative assigned to sell only to companies in a specific area would prefer to have a prospect list organized by zip code rather than a list that was only in alphabetical order.

**Meaningful** information means that the information is relevant to the person who receives it. Much information is only meaningful to specific individuals or groups within an organization. Extraneous and unnecessary information should be eliminated and the "audience" of the information should always be kept in mind.

To be *useful*, information should result in an action being taken or specifically not taken, as the case may be. Often, this quality can be improved through **exception reporting**, which focuses only on the information that exceeds certain limits. An example of exception reporting would be an inventory report showing items whose balance on hand is less than a predetermined minimum quantity. Rather than looking through an entire inventory report to find such items, the exception report would quickly bring these items to the attention of the persons responsible for inventory management.

Last, but not least, information must be *cost effective*. In other words, the cost to produce the information must be less than the "value" of the information. This can sometimes be hard to determine. If the value of the information cannot be determined, perhaps the information should only be produced as required instead of regularly. Many organizations periodically review the information they produce in reports to determine if the reports still have the qualities discussed above and their production cost can still be justified or possibly reduced.

Although the qualities of information have been discussed in conjunction with computer systems, these qualities apply to all information regardless of how it is produced. Knowing these qualities will help you evaluate the information you receive and provide every day.

## SUMMARY OF PROCESSING DATA INTO INFORMATION

The concepts presented in this chapter concerning data, the information processing cycle, interactive and batch processing, and the qualities of information apply to all information processing systems. By now you have developed an understanding and a "feeling" for the way a computer processes data into information. Your increased understanding should help you to feel more comfortable with computers and how they can be used.

## CHAPTER SUMMARY

1. The **information processing cycle** consists of input, processing, output, and storage operations.
2. Regardless of the size and type of computer, the information processing cycle is used to process data into information.
3. The operations in the information processing cycle are carried out through the combined use of computer equipment, also called computer hardware, and computer software.
4. Computer software, or programs, contain the instructions that direct the computer equipment to perform the four types of operations.
5. The primary input devices are keyboards on microcomputers and terminals on larger machines.
6. Input devices are used to enter both computer programs and data into main memory.
7. Both the program that is to control the processing and the data to be processed must be in main memory for processing to occur.
8. Program instructions are executed by the processor.
9. The primary output devices on computers are printers and screens.
10. Auxiliary storage devices commonly used with computers are magnetic tape and magnetic disk.
11. Some devices are used for more than one purpose in the information processing cycle. For example, disks can be used for both input and output.
12. Data is the prime ingredient of an information processing system.
13. **Data** is defined as raw facts and consists of the numbers and words that a computer receives and processes to produce information.
14. Data is composed of **characters**. These include **alphabetic** (A–Z), **numeric** (0–9), and **special** characters, such as ( ) * & % # @ , .
15. Individual facts are referred to as **data items**, **data fields**, or **fields**.
16. Fields may be classified as **numeric**, **alphabetic**, or **alphanumeric**.
17. A field is often more useful when it is combined with other related fields.
18. A **record** is a collection of related fields.
19. A collection of related records is called a **file**.
20. Files are stored on some medium, such as magnetic tape or magnetic disk.
21. In a **sequential** file, records are arranged in alphabetical or numerical order by a **key field**.
22. The records in a **random** file are not arranged in any sequence or order.
23. A **database** provides an efficient way to establish a relationship between data items and implies that a relationship has been established between multiple files.
24. Data is organized into fields, records, files, and databases for processing on a computer.
25. **Data management** refers to techniques and procedures that ensure that the data required for an application will be available in the correct form and at the proper time for processing.
26. Data management includes the management of data attributes, data security, and data maintenance.
27. Data attributes include data availability and data integrity.
28. Data that is required for input must be available.
29. **Data integrity** determines the confidence a user can have in the processing of that data. The three elements of data integrity are data accuracy, reliable data entry, and timeliness.

30. Accurate data depends on a reliable source.
31. Reliable data entry must occur for the information generated to be valid.
32. Timeliness means that data has not lost its usefulness or accuracy because time has passed.
33. **Data security** is an important issue because misuse or loss of data can have serious consequences.
34. **Backup** procedures provide for maintaining copies of data so that in the event of loss data can be recovered.
35. **Data maintenance** refers to **updating** data. This includes **adding**, **changing** and **deleting** data in order to keep it current.
36. **Input operations** cause the data that is to be processed to be stored in main memory.
37. Once data is stored in main memory, it can be processed under the control of a computer program.
38. **Processing operations** define how the data will be manipulated into a usable form.
39. When data is moved from one location in memory to another, it is not destroyed but is duplicated in the new location.
40. Two main types of processing operations include arithmetic and logical processing of data.
41. Many computers are able to perform millions of **arithmetic operations** in one second, including addition, subtraction, multiplication, and division.
42. The results of arithmetic operations can be used in subsequent arithmetic operations, moved to other locations in main memory, and used for output.
43. **Logical operations** allow a computer to compare two data fields to determine if one is **equal to**, **greater than**, or **less than** the other.
44. Logical operations are performed on a computer by the execution of program instructions that direct the computer to compare data fields that are currently stored in main memory.
45. The result of a logical operation determines which of the processing paths of a program will be performed.
46. The ability of a computer to compare data and then select one of two processing paths is a powerful feature that is used in programs of all levels of complexity.
47. The process of repeating the instructions in a program allows a single set of program instructions to process any number of records.
48. **Output operations** take the information produced and put it in a form that can be used by a person or a machine. A common form of output are reports that are displayed on the screen or printed on the printer.
49. **Storage operations** refer to the transfer of programs, data, and information from main memory to an auxiliary storage device such as magnetic disk and magnetic tape.
50. The two methods used for processing data on a computer are interactive processing and batch processing.
51. **Interactive processing** means that data is processed upon entry and output is produced immediately.
52. **Transaction processing** is a type of interactive processing in which the user enters all the data pertaining to a complete transaction and the program immediately performs all the processing required for that particular transaction.
53. In **batch processing**, data is collected and at some later time, all the data that has been gathered is processed as a group or batch.
54. Batch and interactive processing can be combined in a single application.
55. The terms used to describe the qualities of information include accurate, verifiable, timely, organized, meaningful, useful, and cost effective.
56. **GIGO** is an acronym that stands for "Garbage In, Garbage Out."

## KEY TERMS

Adding (data) *3.7*
Alphabetic (characters) *3.4*
Alphabetic field *3.4*
Alphanumeric field *3.4*
Arithmetic operations *3.9*
Backup *3.6*
Batch processing *3.14*
Changing (data) *3.7*
Characters *3.4*
Data *3.4*
Database *3.5*
Data field *3.4*
Data integrity *3.6*
Data item *3.4*
Data maintenance *3.7*
Data management *3.5*
Data security *3.6*
Deleting (data) *3.7*
Exception reporting *3.20*
Field *3.4*
File *3.5*
GIGO *3.20*
Information processing cycle *3.2*
Input operations *3.7*
Interactive processing *3.14*
Key field *3.5*
Logical operations *3.10*
Meaningful *3.20*
Numeric (characters) *3.4*
Numeric field *3.4*
Output operations *3.12*
Point of sale terminal *3.18*
Processing operations *3.8*
Random *3.5*
Record *3.4*
Sequential *3.5*
Special (characters) *3.4*
Storage operations *3.13*
Transaction processing *3.14*
Updating *3.7*

## REVIEW QUESTIONS

1. What are the four elements of the information processing cycle? What types and sizes of computers can be used to implement the information processing cycle?
2. What is the definition of data? What terms are used to describe how data is organized for processing?
3. Why is data management important?
4. What is data integrity? What are the three elements of data integrity?
5. What is meant by data security? How does it relate to the privacy of an individual?
6. What is the input operation on a computer? What happens when the input operation takes place?
7. Why is the ability to repeat instructions in a program important?
8. Name three logical operations that can be performed on data.
9. Describe the purpose of the output operations. What is the most common form of output used by people?
10. Why are storage operations necessary? What are the primary devices used for auxiliary storage?
11. What is interactive processing? Give an example.
12. What is transaction processing?
13. What is batch processing? When is its use appropriate?
14. Is it possible to have batch processing and interactive processing in the same application? Why wouldn't just one processing method be used?
15. Describe the qualities of information.

## CONTROVERSIAL ISSUES

1. In this chapter, we noted that computers can perform millions of arithmetic operations in a single second. Some people claim that much greater speed is needed for computers so that applications such as weather prediction and space flight simulation can be accurately performed within a reasonable time period. These people think research money should be spent to find ways to develop faster computers. Other people argue that computers process data fast enough and that research money should be spent in other areas, such as developing privacy safeguards. Take a side in this debate and defend your position.

2. Software is currently available that lets medical patients inform a computer of their symptoms by answering a series of questions. The program then compares the answers to symptoms retrieved from auxiliary storage. When equal conditions are found, a possible diagnosis will be given and, perhaps, a treatment suggested. Is the computer doing the same type of "thinking" that a doctor does when analyzing symptoms? Take a position and defend it.
3. In the past few years, some have advocated that all applications placed on a computer should use the interactive processing method. These people state that such features as the inherent delays when processing data in a batch method make batch processing obsolete. Other experts dispute this, saying that for some applications, batch is the best means for processing data. Take a position on this disagreement and defend your position.

## RESEARCH PROJECTS

1. A banking application was described in this chapter. Visit a bank or savings and loan in your area. Determine the techniques they use to enter a new customer, make changes in account records for deposits and withdrawals, and close an account. Write a report for your class.
2. Obtain a manual for a programming language such as BASIC or COBOL. List and describe all the instructions that are used to compare data and the comparisons they can make. Include in your report the rules for comparing numeric data to numeric data and alphabetic data to alphabetic data.

CHAPTER 4

# Input to the Computer

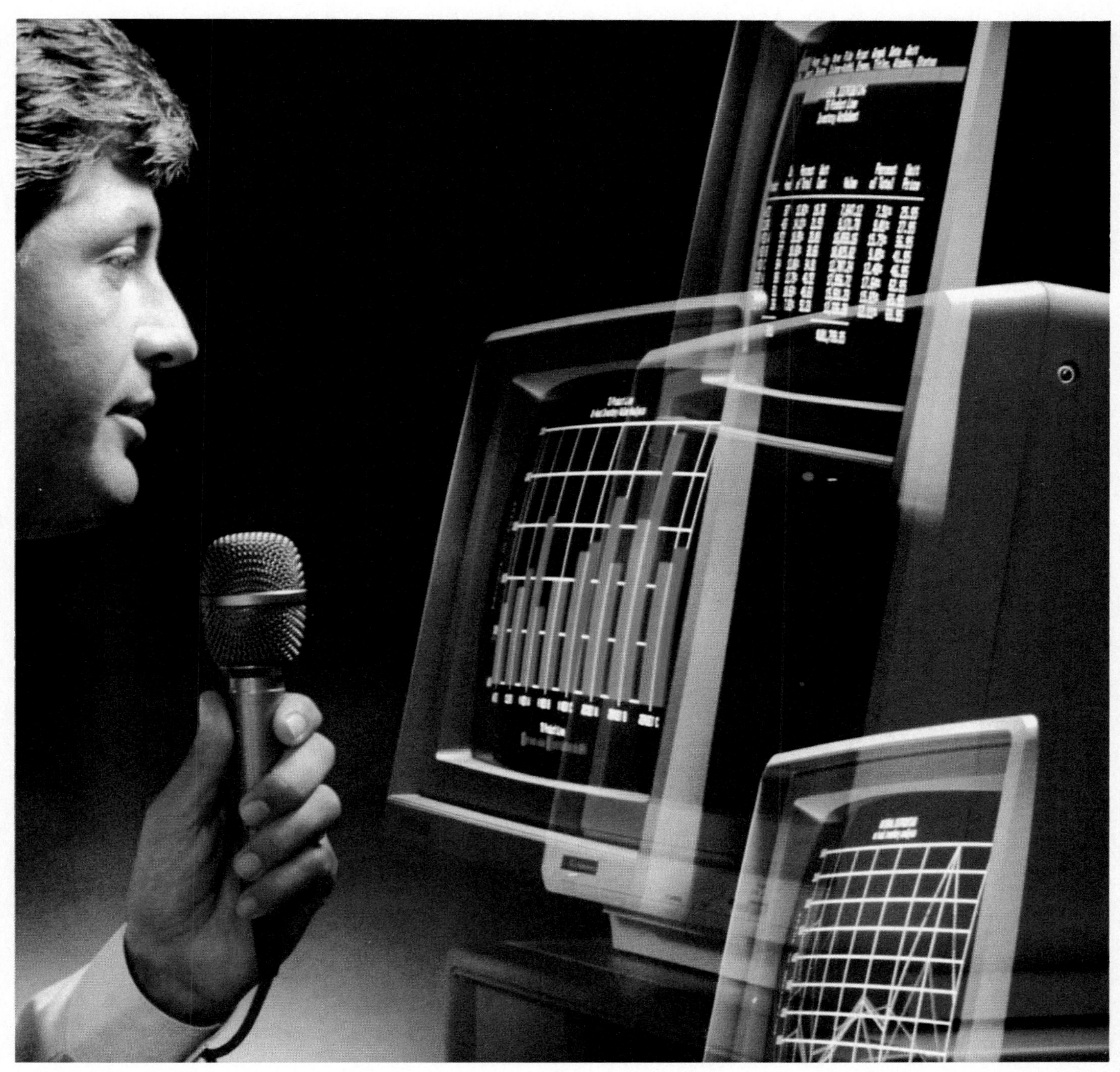

CHAPTER 4

# Input to the Computer

## OBJECTIVES

- Define the four types of input and how the computer uses each type.
- Describe the standard features of keyboards and explain how to use the cursor control and function keys.
- Identify the two types of terminals and how to use each type.
- Describe several input devices other than the keyboard and terminal.
- Define user interface and explain how it has evolved.
- Define the term menu and describe various forms of menus.
- Discuss some of the features that should be included in a good user interface.
- Discuss the differences between interactive and batch processing data entry.
- Describe online and offline data entry and the uses for each.
- List and explain the systems and procedures associated with data entry.
- Explain the term ergonomics and describe some of the changes that have occurred in equipment design.

---

In the information processing cycle, the input operation must take place before any data can be processed and any information produced. Without valid input data, a computer is not capable of producing any useful information.

When they were first utilized for business applications, nearly all computers used punched cards as input. The data was recorded on cards using a device called a keypunch. A keypunch is a machine that contains a keyboard and a punching mechanism. As the operator presses the keys, holes representing numbers, letters of the alphabet, or special characters are punched into the card. The cards are then collected together and read into main memory by a card reader.

Today, punched cards are not as often used as input to a computer. In addition, the user has more choices concerning the type of input device or devices to be used for an application. This chapter examines some of the devices used for input, the ways that both hardware and software are designed to make input operations easier for the user, and the various methods of entering data into the computer.

# WHAT IS INPUT?

**Input** refers to the process of entering programs, commands, user responses, and data into main memory. Input can also refer to the media (e.g., tapes, cards, documents, etc.) that contain these input types. These four types of input are used by a computer in the following ways:

- **Programs** are the sets of instructions that direct the computer to perform the necessary operations to process data into information. The program that is loaded and stored in main memory determines the processing that the computer will perform. When a program is first entered into a computer it is input by way of a keyboard. Once the program has been entered and stored on auxiliary storage, it can be transferred to main memory by a command.
- **Commands** are key words and phrases that the user inputs to direct the computer to perform certain activities. For example, if you wanted to use a payroll program, you might issue a command such as LOAD "PAYROLL" to load the program named PAYROLL into main memory from auxiliary storage. To begin the execution of the program you would enter another command such as RUN (Figure 4-1).
- **User responses** refer to the data that a user inputs in response to a question or message from the software. Usually these messages display on a screen and the user responds through a keyboard. One of the most common responses is to answer "Yes" or "No" to a question. Based on the answer, the computer program will perform specific actions. For example, in a spreadsheet program, typing the letter Y in response to the message "Do you want to save this file?" will result in the spreadsheet file being saved (written) to the auxiliary storage device.
- **Data** is raw facts; it is the source from which information is produced. It must be entered and stored in main computer memory for processing to occur. For example, data entered from sales orders can be processed by a computer program to produce sales reports useful to management. Data is the most common type of input.

Regardless of the type, input will be entered through some kind of input device. The next section of this chapter discusses the various types of available input devices.

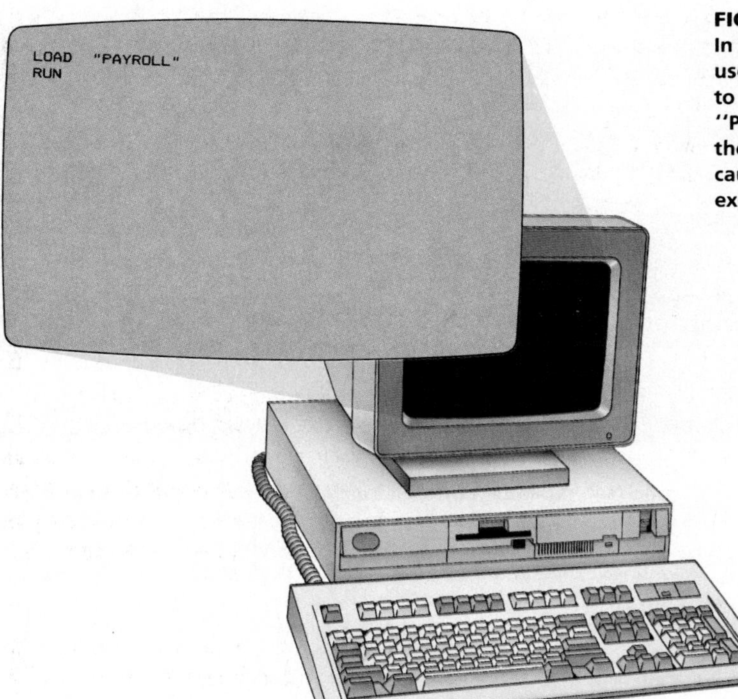


**FIGURE 4-1**
**In this example, the computer user first entered a command to load the program called "PAYROLL" and then issued the command RUN, which will cause the program to be executed.**

## THE KEYBOARD

**Keyboards** are the most commonly used input devices. Users input data to a computer by pressing the keys on the keyboard. Keyboards are connected to other devices, such as a personal computer or a terminal, that have screens. As the user enters data on the keyboard, it displays on the screen.

The keyboards used for computer input are very similar to the keyboards used on the familiar office machine, the typewriter (Figure 4-2). They contain numbers, letters of the alphabet, and some special characters. In addition, many computer keyboards are equipped with a special **numeric keypad** on the right-hand side of the keyboard. These numeric keys are arranged in an adding machine or calculator format and aid the user with data entry.

**FIGURE 4-2**
**The IBM PS/Model 30 keyboard shown in the picture contains a numeric keypad, cursor control keys, and function keys. The keys on the numeric keypad are arranged in the same order as the keys on an adding machine or a calculator. This arrangement allows those skilled in entering numbers to input numeric data at a much faster rate than if the number keys were across the top of the keyboard as they are on a typewriter. The four cursor control keys are identified by up ↑, down ↓, left ←, and right → arrows. When the user presses one of these keys, the cursor moves one position in the direction indicated by the arrow. Function keys are used for specific commands that are either programmed by the user or determined by the application software. Function keys can be located in different places, but on most keyboards they are either on the left side or along the top.**

Keyboards also contain keys that can be used to position the cursor on the screen. A **cursor** is a symbol, such as a highlighted rectangle or an underline character, that indicates where on the screen the next character entered will be displayed. The keys that move the cursor are called **arrow keys** or **cursor control keys**. When pressed, the keys move the cursor in the direction where the arrow points. Cursor control keys have an up arrow, a down arrow, a left arrow, and a right arrow. When you press any of these keys, the cursor moves one space in the direction specified by the arrow. In addition, many keyboards contain other cursor control keys such as the HOME key, which when pressed sends the cursor to the upper left position of the screen or document.

Some computer keyboards also contain keys that are used to alter or edit the text displayed on the screen. For example, the INSERT and DELETE keys allow characters to be inserted into or deleted from data that appears on the screen.

**Function keys** are keys that can be programmed to accomplish certain tasks that will assist the user. For example, a function key might be programmed for use as a help key when a terminal is used for word processing. Whenever the key is pressed, messages will appear that give instructions pertaining to the word processor. Another use of function keys is to save keystrokes. Sometimes several keystrokes are required to accomplish a certain task, for example, printing a document. Some application software packages are written so that the user can either enter the individual keystrokes or press a function key and obtain the same result.

The disadvantage of using a keyboard as an input device is that training is required to use it efficiently. Users who do not know how to type are at a disadvantage because of the time they spend looking for the appropriate keys. While there are other input devices that are appropriate in some situations, users should be encouraged to develop their keyboard skills.

## TERMINALS

Terminals, sometimes called **display terminals** or **video display terminals (VDTs)**, consist of a keyboard and a screen. They fall into two basic categories: dumb terminals and intelligent terminals (sometimes called programmable terminals). We explain the features of each type in the following paragraphs. Figure 4-3 shows an example of each type of terminal.

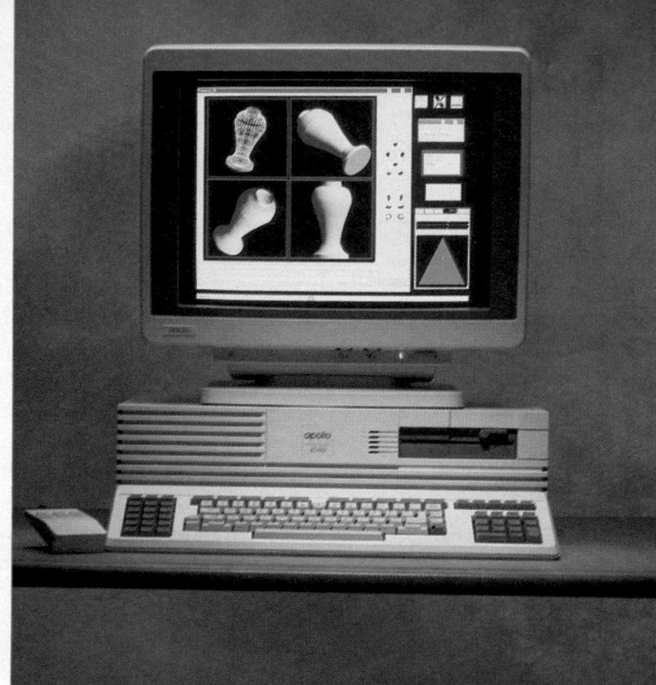

**FIGURE 4-3**
Terminals can be classified into two broad categories: dumb terminals and intelligent terminals. From appearance alone, it is often difficult to tell in which category a terminal belongs. In these photos the dumb terminal on the left lacks a CPU.

## Dumb Terminals

A **dumb terminal** consists of a keyboard and a display screen that can be used to enter and transmit data to or receive and display data from a computer to which it is connected. A dumb terminal has no independent processing capability or auxiliary storage and cannot function as a stand-alone device.

## Intelligent Terminals

**Intelligent terminals** are terminals whose processing capabilities are built in. These terminals are also known as **programmable terminals** because they can be programmed by the user to perform many basic tasks, including both arithmetic and logic operations. Personal computers are frequently used as intelligent terminals (Figure 4-4).

Intelligent terminals often contain not only the keyboard and screen associated with other terminals, but also are supported with disk drives and printers, so they can perform limited processing tasks when not communicating directly with the central computer. In some instances, when the user enters data, the data will be checked for errors and some type of report will be produced. In addition, the valid data that is entered will be stored on the disk connected to the terminal. After the data has been entered and stored on disk, it will be transmitted over communication lines to the central computer. This operation is sometimes called **uploading**, because the data is loaded from the smaller terminal "up" to the bigger main computer. Uploading is used most often when the data entered is to be processed in a batch processing mode.

As the amount of processing power that is incorporated into intelligent terminals increases, more processing can occur at the site of the terminal prior to sending the data to the central computer. This means that the large minicomputer or mainframe at the central site can perform the main processing and serve multiple users faster, rather than having to use its resources to perform tasks that can be performed by the intelligent terminal.

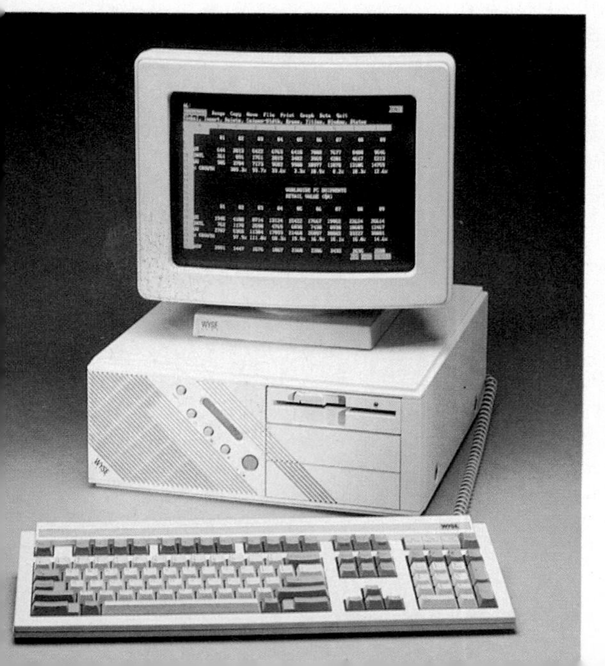

**FIGURE 4-4**
This WYSE pc 286 personal computer can function as both a stand-alone computer or as a terminal when it is connected to another computer system.

## Special Purpose Terminals

FIGURE 4-5
This point of sale terminal is specially designed for grocery store item entry. The checker can press separate keys to process the prices of produce, meat, and other items.

Terminals are found in virtually every environment that generates data for processing on a computer. While many are standard terminals like those previously described, others are designed to perform specific jobs and contain features uniquely designed for use in a particular industry.

The terminal shown in Figure 4-5 is called a point of sale terminal. **Point of sale terminals** allow data to be entered at the time and place where the transaction with a customer occurs, such as in fast-food restaurants or hotels, for example. Point of sale terminals serve as input to either minicomputers located at the place of business or larger computers located elsewhere. The data entered is used to maintain sales records, update inventory, make automatic calculations such as sales tax, verify credit, and perform other activities associated with the sales transactions and critical to running the business. Point of sale terminals are designed to be easy to operate, requiring little technical knowledge.

# OTHER INPUT DEVICES

Besides keyboards and terminals, there is an increasing variety of other input devices. This section describes some of the devices used for general purpose applications.

## The Mouse

The mouse, initially designed by Xerox, is a unique device used with personal computers and some computer terminals. A **mouse** is a small, lightweight device that easily fits in the palm of your hand. You move it across a flat surface such as a desktop (Figure 4-6) to control the movement of the cursor on a screen. The mouse is attached to the computer by a cable. On the bottom of the mouse are one or more wheels or balls. As the mouse moves across the flat surface, the computer electronically senses the movement of the wheels. The movement of the cursor on the screen corresponds to the movement of the mouse (Figure 4-7). When you move the mouse left on the surface of the table or desk, the cursor moves left on the screen. When you move the mouse right, the cursor moves right, and so on.

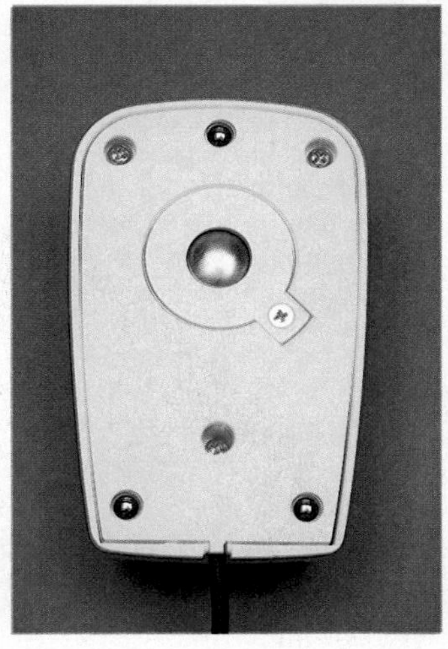

FIGURE 4-6 ►
The mouse can be moved to control the cursor on the screen. Press the button at the top of the mouse to make selections or perform functions, depending on the software being used. The ball on the underside of the mouse moves as the user pushes the mouse around on a hard, flat surface. The movement of the ball causes the cursor to move correspondingly on the screen.

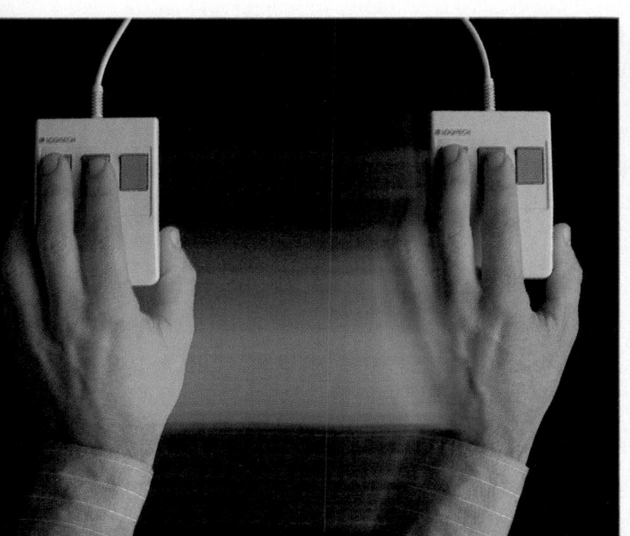

◄ FIGURE 4-7
This drawing illustrates using a mouse. The index finger, which rests on the top of the mouse, acts as a pointer to guide the movement of the mouse and the related movement of the cursor on the screen.

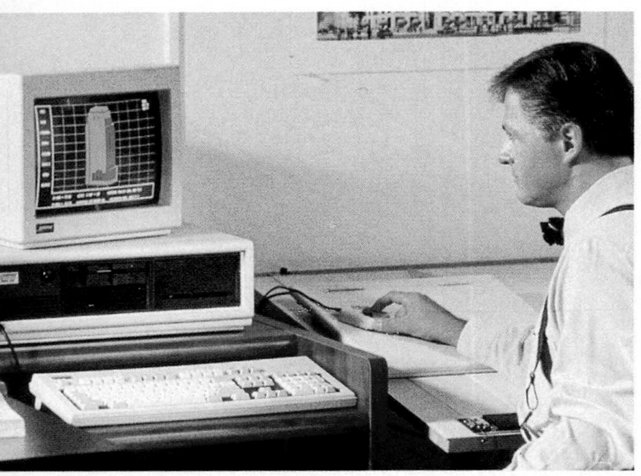

FIGURE 4-8
Notice that some amount of clear desk space is required for moving the mouse.

On top of the mouse are one or more buttons. By moving the cursor on the screen and pressing the buttons, you can make menu choices, choose letters or words in a word processing application for addition or deletion, move data from one point on the screen to another, and perform many other actions that move and rearrange information displayed on the screen.

The primary advantage of a mouse is that it is easy to use. Proponents of the mouse say that with a little practice, a person can use a mouse to point to locations on the screen just as easily as using a finger. For some applications such as desktop publishing, a mouse is indispensable.

There are two major disadvantages of the mouse. The first is that it requires empty desk space where it can be moved about (Figure 4-8). The second disadvantage is that the user must remove a hand from the keyboard and place it on the mouse whenever the cursor is to be moved or a command is to be given. Some keyboard experts have noted that taking hands from the keyboard slows the effective data entry speed considerably. Thus, some people have said the mouse is not an effective tool in those environments where keying must be performed rapidly, such as in word processing applications. Others, however, say that using a mouse is far superior to using the cursor control keys on a keyboard.

## Touch Screens

**Touch screens** allow users to merely touch areas of the screen to enter data. They let the user interact with a computer by the touch of a finger, rather than typing on a keyboard or moving a mouse. The user enters data by touching words or numbers, or locations identified on the screen (Figure 4-9).

Several electronic techniques change a touch on the screen into electronic impulses that can be interpreted by the computer software. One of the most common techniques utilizes beams of infrared light, that are projected across the surface of the screen. A finger or other utensil touching the screen interrupts the beams, generating an electronic signal. This signal identifies the location on the screen where the touch occurred. The software interprets the signal and performs the required function.

Touch screens are not used to enter large amounts of data. They are used, however, for applications in which the user must issue a command to the software to perform a particular task or must choose from a list of options to be performed.

There are both advantages and disadvantages of touch screens. A significant advantage is that they are very "natural" to use; that is, people are used to pointing to things. With touch screens, they can point to indicate the processing they want performed by the computer. In addition, touch screens are usually easy for the user to learn. As quickly as pointing a finger, the user's request is processed. Finally, touch screens allow absolute cursor movement; that is, the user can point a finger at the location where the cursor is to appear and it will. This can be considerably faster than repeatedly pressing arrow keys to move the cursor from one location on the screen to another.

Two major complaints are lodged against touch screens. First, the resolution of the touching area is not precise. Thus, while a user can point to a box or a fairly large area on the screen and the electronics can determine the location of the touch, it is difficult to point to a single character in a word processing application, for example, and indicate that the character should be deleted. In cases such as these, a keyboard is easier to use. A second complaint is that after a period of reaching for the screen, the user's arm may become tired.

FIGURE 4-9
Touch screens allow the user to make choices and execute commands by actually touching areas of the screen. Touch screens require special software that determines where the user touched the screen and what action should be taken.

## Graphic Input Devices

**Graphic input devices** are used to translate graphic input data, such as photos or drawings, into a form that can be processed on a computer. Three major devices that are used for graphic input are light pens, digitizers, and graphics tablets. A **light pen** is used by touching it on the display screen to create or modify graphics (Figure 4-10). A **digitizer** converts points, lines, and curves from a sketch, drawing, or photograph to digital impulses and transmits them to a computer (Figures 4-11 and 4-12). A **graphics tablet** works in a manner similar to a digitizer, but it also contains unique characters and commands that can be automatically generated by the person using the tablet (Figure 4-13).

**FIGURE 4-10**
**Placing the light pen at a point on the screen activates a sensing device within the pen. The activated pen transmits the location of the light to the computer, where the program can perform the desired tasks. ▼**

**FIGURE 4-11**
**The device in this aerospace engineer's hand reads and translates the coordinates on the printed wiring board layout into coordinates that can be stored in the computer and later used to reproduce the drawing on a screen or a printer. ▼**

**FIGURE 4-12**
**Digitizers are used in business to create original art or to trace and reproduce existing art quickly and accurately. ▼**

**◄ FIGURE 4-13**
**The graphics tablet in this picture is used by an automotive design engineer for the development and definition of a car body. The stylus, held in the engineer's right hand, is used to input commands by touching specific sections of the tablet.**

FIGURE 4-14
This manager has just used his voice input system to request that sales data be presented in a bar graph. Often such systems have to be "trained" to recognize a particular user's voice.

## Voice Input

One of the more exciting developments is the use of voice input, sometimes referred to as voice or speech recognition. As the name implies, **voice input** allows the user to enter data and issue commands to the computer with spoken words (Figure 4-14).

Most systems require the user to "train" the system first by speaking the words that will be used a number of times. As the words are spoken, they are digitized by the system; that is, they are broken down into digital components that the computer can recognize. After each word has been spoken several times, the system has developed a digital pattern for the word that can be stored on auxiliary storage. When the user later speaks a word to the system to request a particular action, the system compares the word to words that were previously entered and that it can "understand." When it finds a match, the software performs the activity associated with the word. For example, in voice-controlled word processing systems, spoken words can be used to control such functions as single and double spacing, choosing type styles, and centering text.

The major advantage of voice input is that the user does not have to key, move, or touch anything in order to enter data into the computer. It is expected that voice input will be a significant factor in the years to come.

# INPUT DEVICES DESIGNED FOR SPECIFIC PURPOSES

Some input devices have been designed to perform specific tasks. Here we illustrate a few of these devices.

## Magnetic Ink Character Recognition

**Magnetic ink character recognition** or **MICR** is a type of machine-readable data. This type of data is read into the computer by input devices called **MICR readers**. MICR is found almost exclusively in the banking industry. In the 1950s, the industry chose MICR as the method to be used to encode and read the billions of checks written each year.

When MICR is used, special characters encoded on checks identify such items as the bank number and the account number. When a check is processed, the amount is also encoded on it by a bank operator. The items are encoded in special MICR characters (Figure 4-15) using a special ink that can be magnetized during processing. MICR readers interpret the electronic signals generated from the magnetized characters so checks can be sorted and processed to prepare bank statements for customers. MICR devices can process over 1,000 checks per minute (Figure 4-16). MICR also is used in utility companies, credit card companies, and other industries that must process large volumes of data.

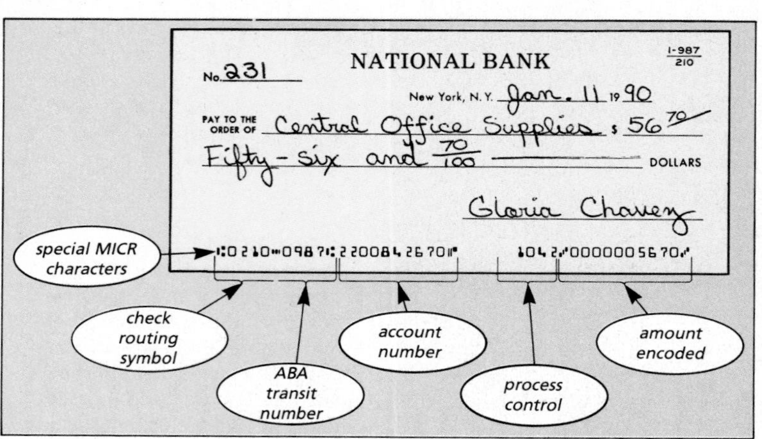


FIGURE 4-15
The characters at the bottom of a check can be read by MICR devices. All the banks in the United States and in many foreign countries use these codes for checks.

## Scanners

**Scanners** include a variety of devices that "read" printed codes, characters, or images and convert them into a form that can be processed by the computer. This section describes several different types of scanning devices.

**Optical Character Readers** **Optical character recognition (OCR)** devices are scanners that read typewritten, computer-printed, and in some cases hand-printed characters from ordinary documents. OCR devices range from large machines that can automatically read thousands of documents per minute to hand-held wands (Figure 4-17).

An OCR device scans the shape of a character on a document, compares it with a predefined shape stored in its memory, and converts the character read into a corresponding bit pattern for storing in main memory. The standard OCR typeface, called OCR-A, is illustrated in Figure 4-18 on the next page. The characters can be read easily by both humans and machines. OCR-B is a set of standard characters widely used in Europe and Japan.

**FIGURE 4-16 ▲**
**This MICR reader-sorter can process up to 1,200 documents per minute. After the documents are read, they are sorted into the vertical bins shown in the top center portion of the machine. This device can be connected directly to a computer to allow the documents to be processed as they are read.**

**◀ FIGURE 4-17**
**This hand-held optical character recognition device is being used to read a typed document. Such wands can be used for both interactive and batch data entry.**

ABCDEFGHIJKLMNOPQRSTUVWXYZ
abcdefghijklmnopqrstuvwxyz

⑂⑀⑁$%|&*{}—+■:",.?
1234567890-=■;',./

**FIGURE 4-18**
**In the full OCR-A standard character set shown above. Characters such as B and 8, S and 5, and zero and the letter O are designed so the reading device can easily distinguish between them.**

**FIGURE 4-19**
**These hand-printed characters can be read by some types of OCR devices. The two small dots in each square identify where certain portions of each numeric digit must be placed.**

Some optical character readers can read hand-printed characters. Building a machine able to read and interpret hand-printed characters is a challenging task even in this era of high technology. The characters must be carefully printed according to a strict set of rules regarding their shapes. The example in Figure 4-19 illustrates the shape of hand-printed characters that can be read with an OCR device.

The most widespread application for OCR devices is for reading turn-around documents prepared by computer printers. A **turn-around document** is designed to be returned to the organization that originally issued it. When the document is returned ("turned around"), the data on it is read by an OCR device. For example, many utility bills, department store bills, insurance premium statements, and so on request that the consumer return the statement with a payment (Figure 4-20). The statement is printed with characters that can be read by OCR devices. When the customer returns it, the machine reads it to give proper credit for the payment received. Some OCR devices, such as the one shown in Figure 4-20, are small enough to fit on top of a desk.

**Optical Mark Readers** An **Optical mark reader (OMR)** is a scanning device that can read carefully placed pencil marks on specially designed documents. The pencil marks on the form usually indicate responses to questions and can be read and interpreted by a computer program. Optical mark readers are frequently used to score tests.

**FIGURE 4-20**
**In this picture, utility company payment receipts are being read by an OCR device. These receipts are examples of turn-around documents because they were designed to be returned to the utility with the customer's payment.**

**FIGURE 4-21**
**Most modern grocery stores use optical scanning devices such as the one shown here. A laser beam, emitted from the opening on the counter, reads the bar code on the product package. Most retail products have the Universal Product Code (UPC) imprinted somewhere on the label or package. The UPC code uniquely identifies both the manufacturer and the product. The scanning device is connected to a computer system that uses the UPC code to look up the price of the product and add the price into the total sale. A keyboard above the scanner is used to code the numbers for items such as fruit, which do not have UPC labels.**

**Laser Scanners** A scanning device often used by modern grocery stores at checkout counters is a **laser scanner** (Figure 4-21). These devices use a laser beam to scan and read the special bar code printed on the products.

**Page Scanners** A **page scanner** is a type of scanner that can convert an entire page of printed material into the individual characters and words that can be processed by a word processing program. Other types of scanners can convert images such as photos and art work for eventual use with desktop publishing systems (Figure 4-22).

**Image Processing** As we've previously discussed, much of the information input to the computer is taken from source documents. Usually, only a portion of the information on the source document is input. But sometimes the entire source document is needed for data, such as a signature or a drawing. In these situations, organizations often implement image processing systems. **Image processing systems** use software and special equipment, including scanners, to input and store an actual image of the source document. These systems are like giant electronic filing cabinets that allow users to rapidly access and review exact reproductions of the original documents (Figure 4-23).

**FIGURE 4-22**
**The scanner at the left can input text, graphics, or photographs for use in word processing or desktop publishing applications.**

**FIGURE 4-23**
**Image processing systems record and store an exact copy of a document. These systems are often used by insurance companies that may need to refer to any of hundreds of thousands of documents.**

FIGURE 4-24
This portable data collection device is being used to take an inventory in a warehouse. The data is stored in memory and can later be transferred to a computer system for processing.

## Data Collection Devices

Data entry is not confined to office environments or restricted to dedicated data entry personnel. **Data collection devices** are designed and used for obtaining data at the site where the transaction or event being reported takes place. For example, in Figure 4-24 a man is taking inventory in a warehouse. Rather than write down the number and type of items and then enter this data, he uses a portable data collection device to record the inventory count in the device's memory. After he takes the inventory, the data can be transmitted to a computer for processing.

Unlike most terminals, data collection equipment is designed to be used in environments where heat, humidity, and cleanliness are difficult or impossible to control (Figure 4-25). In addition, data collection devices are often used by people whose primary task is not to enter the data. Entering the data is only a small portion of their job duties. Therefore, the terminals must be easy to operate in any environment.

Using data collection devices can provide important advantages over alternative methods of input preparation. Because the data is entered as it is collected, clerical costs and transcription errors are reduced or eliminated. If the data collection devices are directly connected to the computer, the data is immediately available for processing.

Data collection devices range from portable devices that can be carried throughout a store or factory (such as in Figure 4-24) to sophisticated terminal systems with multiple input stations that feed directly into a central computer. These devices will continue to improve and find increased use in data entry applications.

Figure 4-26 summarizes the most commonly used input devices. While each device has advantages and disadvantages, each is appropriate for specific applications. Several of these devices incorporate a user interface to be more efficient.

FIGURE 4-25
This photograph illustrates a data collection terminal that has been designed to accommodate the user. Data collection devices should be simple and quick to operate, so that entering the data does not interfere with the main job of the person using the terminal.

| DEVICE | DESCRIPTION |
|---|---|
| Keyboard | Most commonly used input device. Special keys may include numeric keypad, cursor control keys, and function keys. |
| Terminal | Video display terminals are dumb or intelligent. |
| Mouse | Small input device used to move the cursor on a screen and select options. |
| Touch screens | User interacts with the computer by touching the screen. |
| Graphic input | Light pens, digitizers, and graphics tablets translate graphic data into a form that can be processed by a computer. |
| Voice input | User enters data and issues commands with spoken words. |
| MICR reader | Used primarily in banking to read the magnetic ink characters printed on checks. |
| Scanner | A variety of devices that read printed codes, characters, or images. |
| Data collection | Used to input data where it is generated. |

**FIGURE 4-26** This table summarizes some of the more common data input devices.

## USER INTERFACES

With the widespread use of terminals and personal computers, input operations are performed by many types of users whose computer knowledge and experience varies greatly. Some users have a limited knowledge of computers and others have many years of experience. In addition, some users interact with computers daily, while others use them only occasionally. Information systems need to provide all users with a means of interacting with the computer efficiently. This is done through user interfaces.

A **user interface** is the combination of hardware and software that allows a user to communicate with a computer system. Through a user interface, users are able to input values that will: (1) respond to messages presented by the computer; (2) control the computer; and (3) request information from the computer. Thus, a user interface provides the means for communication between an information system and the user.

Both the hardware and software working together form a user interface. A terminal is an example of hardware that is frequently part of a user interface. The screen on the terminal displays messages to the user. The devices used for responding to the messages and controlling the computer include the keyboard, the mouse, and other types of input devices. The software associated with an interface are the programs. These programs determine the messages that are given to the user, the manner in which the user can respond, and the actions that will take place based on the user's responses.

## EVOLUTION OF USER INTERFACE SOFTWARE

In most instances, the software determines the quality of the user interface. To help you understand user interfaces we examine how user interface software has evolved and where the user interface software technology is today.

When computers were first used for business processing, users did not interact with the computer. Programmers and computer operators were the only people allowed to control the computer processing. While some programmers were also users (for example, scientists who wrote programs so they could use the results in their own work), there was generally little need to worry about the interface with nontechnical users. All that was required was a means for technicians such as operators and programmers, who were familiar with the computer and its operations, to communicate with the software.

In addition, during the early years of computer usage, computers executed programs much more slowly than they do today and memory was very expensive. Therefore, when software was developed, the ease of using a program was secondary to the fact that software had to execute quickly and use as little memory as possible. This dictated that commands and messages be as brief as possible.

When terminals first became available and gave users direct access to the central computer, most software was still difficult to use. Frequently, users had to learn detailed commands to direct the computer to perform the desired tasks. These commands normally consisted of special characters, words, and cryptic abbreviations that made them difficult to learn and remember. Infrequent users often had to retrain themselves each time they wanted to use the machine.

The example in Figure 4-27 illustrates a typical procedure and commands that a user might have used in the 1960s to communicate with the computer. First, users had to "log on" to the computer by identifying themselves. The software would determine if the person was an authorized user and if access to the computer should be allowed. While this is still common today, the procedures for logging on are much easier now than in earlier years. Note that the user had to begin the message with a single slash (/) followed by the word LOGON. This entry was followed immediately by a comma, open quotation marks, a name, and closed quotation marks. A comma was entered next and then the date. This format and spacing had to be followed exactly. A missing comma, quotation mark, slash, or even any one of these in the wrong position would cause the software to issue an error message. Thus, the user needed to know not only the data to be entered, but also the exact format to be followed.

The example in Figure 4-27 shows the additional lines that were required. The entry /T.1 means that terminal 1 was being used. The next entry designated the program to be executed, and the last entry informed the software that the user had entered all the commands. When the /END command was entered, the software would begin performing the processing requested by the user.

/LOGON, "JACOB" ,12/15/67
/T.1
/EXEC.TXT.EDT
/END

**FIGURE 4-27**
**The entries illustrated here represent the type of commands that were required when users first began to have access to computers. Spacing and punctuation also had to be correct for the commands to be accepted. Understandably, many users found it difficult and frustrating to use the computer.**

The entries illustrated in this example were acceptable for computer specialists, but such commands were not easy for the general user to master. Both users and computer professionals recognized that there was considerable room for improvement in the software that communicated with users.

The following sections discuss some of the user interface techniques that have been developed, such as prompts and menus, and how they have improved communication between the user and the computer.

## Prompts

One of the first steps in improving user interface software was to display prompts on the screen. A **prompt** is a message to the user that displays on the screen and provides helpful information or instructions regarding some entry to be made or action to be taken.

The example in Figure 4-28 illustrates the use of prompts. On the first line, the prompt ENTER LAST NAME: appears on the screen. This message tells the user to enter his or her last name.

After the user enters his or her last name, a second prompt displays. This prompt, ENTER DATE (MM/DD/YY), indicates not only what is to be entered but also the exact format it should have. MM/DD/YY means to enter the date as a two-digit month number followed by a slash (/), a two-digit day number followed by a slash, and a two-digit year number. Thus, the entry 04/05/90 is valid, but 4/5/90 is not.

To help ensure that the user inputs valid data, the software should use **data editing**, the ability to check the data for proper format and acceptable values. When data is entered incorrectly, a message should be displayed so that the user becomes aware of the error and can reenter the data. The example in Figure 4-29 illustrates what might occur when the data is not entered in the correct format. Note that an error message displays and requests the user to reenter the date.

Prompts, combined with data editing, were a great stride forward in developing user interfaces. Today, prompts are widely used to assist users in entering valid input and communicating with computer systems.

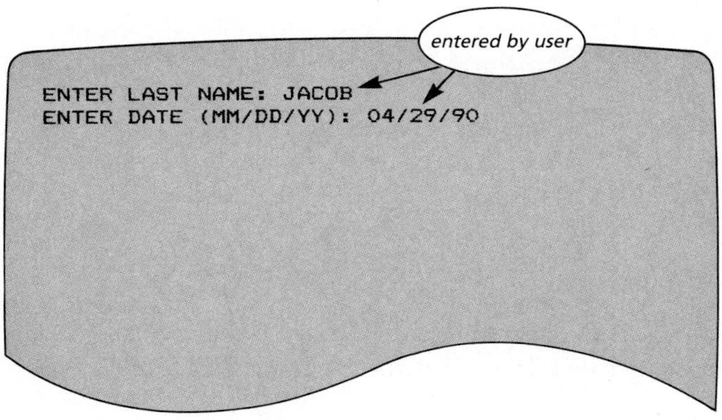


**FIGURE 4-28**
**Prompts aid the user in entering data. They can tell the user what data to enter as well as the required format (as shown for the date entry). Prompts were one of the first types of interfaces designed to assist the user in utilizing the computer.**

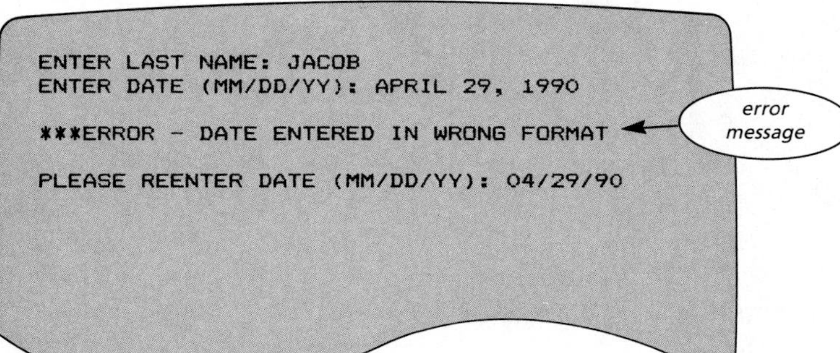


**FIGURE 4-29**
**The software used for this screen checks the date entered and gives an error message if the date is entered in the wrong format.**

## Menus

As user interfaces continued to develop, people who wrote software recognized that much of the data entry users required was involved with choosing alternatives. For example, the user might have to choose which of four software programs to execute, which of five documents to use during word processing, or which function to perform in an electronic spreadsheet application. To allow the user to make an easy choice from various alternatives, menus were developed.

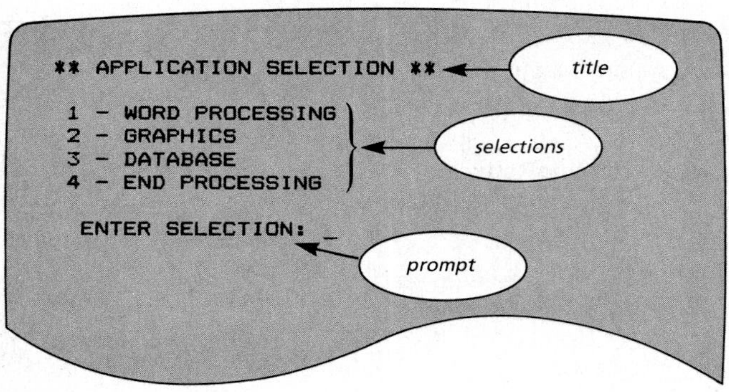


**FIGURE 4-30**
**A menu consists of a title, the selections that can be made, and a prompt for the user to make an entry.**

A **menu** is a display on a screen that allows a user to make a selection from multiple alternatives. A menu generally consists of three parts (Figure 4-30): a title, the selections, and a prompt. The title identifies the menu and orients the user to the choices that can be made. The selections consist of both a means for identifying the choices and the words that describe them. The prompt asks the user to enter one of the selections.

The screens in Figure 4-31 illustrate several ways in which a user can choose word processing from menus.

**Sequential Number** In Example 1, each of the selections is identified by a number. The user enters the numbers 1, 2, 3, or 4 to select the desired processing operation. Entering a 1 means that the word processing program will be retrieved from auxiliary storage and brought into main memory for execution. Entering a 2 executes the graphics program, and entering a 3, the database program. Menus should always contain an entry that lets the user exit. In Example 1, this is entry 4.

**Alphabetic Selection** In Example 2 letters of the alphabet identify the various processing options. The user makes a selection by entering the letter next to the processing description. Sometimes the letters used are simply A, B, C, and D but the person who designed this menu chose to make the letters significant. Thus, entering W will select word processing; entering G selects graphics; D, database; and E ends the processing.

**Cursor Positioning** Example 3 illustrates a menu in which the choice is made by using the arrow or cursor control keys to position the cursor adjacent to the desired selection. Then the Enter key is pressed to make the choice.

**Reverse Video** Example 4 illustrates using reverse video to highlight the selection. **Reverse video** means that the normal screen display pattern, such as amber on black, is reversed to highlight and draw attention to a certain character, word, or section of the screen. In the example, the directions instruct the user to move the reverse video from one selection to another by pressing the space bar. Pressing the space bar once moves the reverse video from the word processing option to graphics; pressing it again highlights the database option. If the space bar was pressed when reverse video was highlighting the end processing option, the reverse video would move to word processing. This is called **wraparound**. It is a shortcut that allows users to go quickly from the bottom to the top or from the top to the bottom of a menu. To make a selection in reverse video, the user highlights the desired procedure and presses the Return key.

**Icon Selection** In Example 5, the same reverse video method is used to highlight the choices, but the choices are also identified by graphic images or icons. An **icon** is a pictorial representation of a function to be performed on the computer. Pressing the space bar highlights each of the words under the graphic in reverse video. Pressing the Return key executes the chosen function.

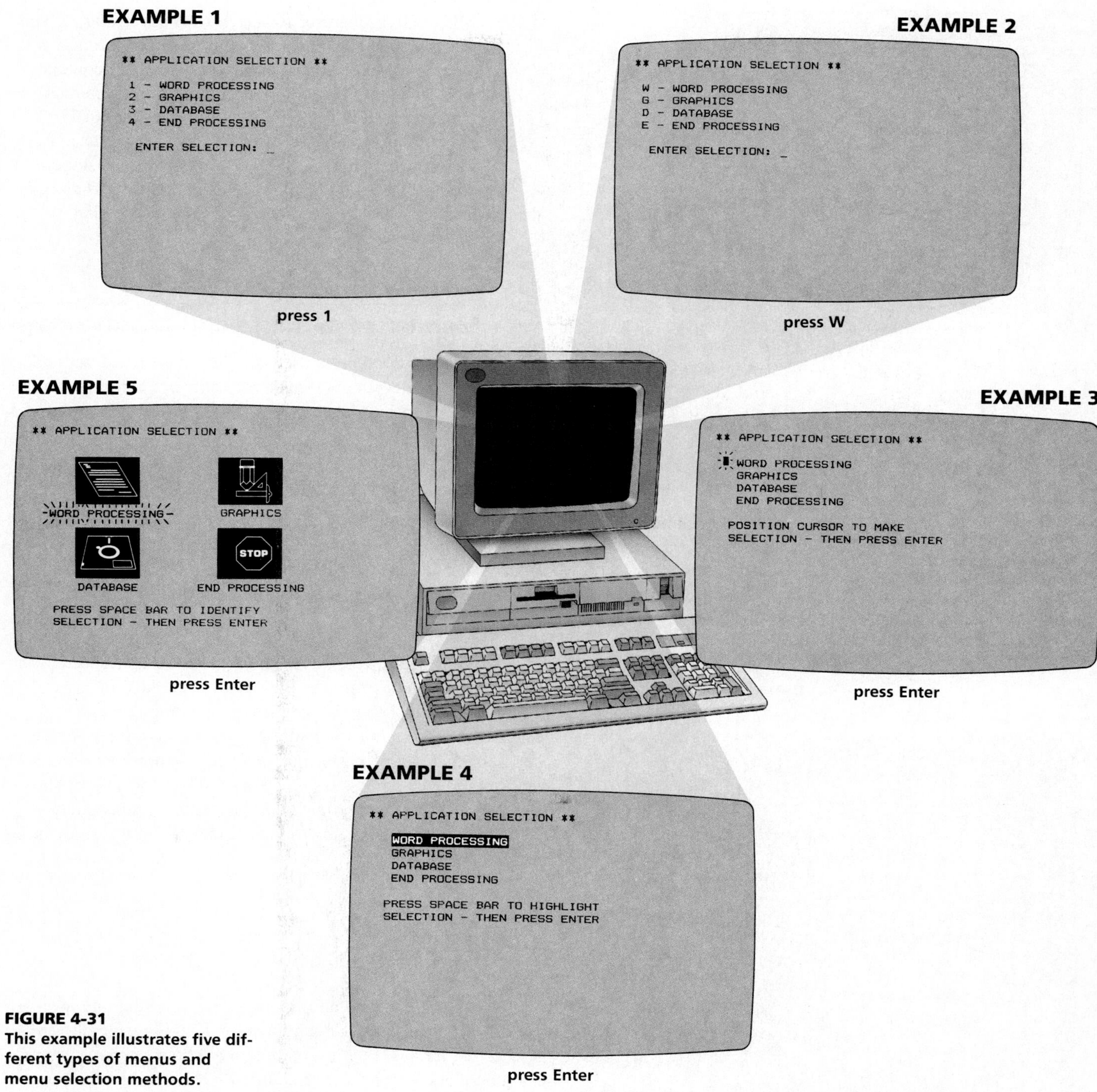


**FIGURE 4-31**
**This example illustrates five different types of menus and menu selection methods.**

From these examples, it is clear that a variety of methods can be used to identify and choose the selections in a menu.

## Submenus

Some applications require the use of several related menus. Menus that further define the operations that can be performed are called **submenus**.

The example in Figure 4-32 illustrates the main menu from Example 1 in Figure 4-31,

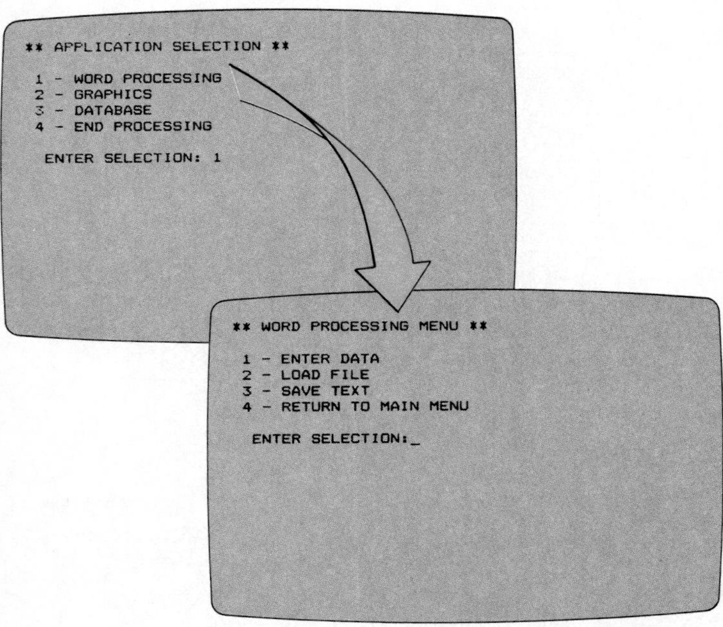


**FIGURE 4-32**
**A submenu is used when additional selections can be made within an application. In this example, the submenu displays additional word processing selections.**

which allows the user to select word processing, graphics, or database. When the word processing function is selected, a submenu appears. This submenu contains more detailed functions. Depending on the submenu selection, additional menus could be displayed. For example, if the user selected option 1, enter data, from the submenu shown in Figure 4-32, a third menu could appear that would display selections relative to margin settings, page length, and other word processing functions.

## Menus: Advantages and Disadvantages

Menus are a type of user interface that is used with all sizes and types of computers. There are both advantages and disadvantages to menus. Some of the advantages are:

1. The user does not have to remember special commands. He or she merely chooses a selection from a list of possible operations or functions.
2. The user can become productive with a minimum of training. Instead of having to learn a lot of technical computer information, he or she merely needs to understand the application and the results of choosing a particular option from the menu.
3. The user is guided through the application because only the options that are available are presented.

The disadvantage most often associated with menus, according to some experienced users, is that they can be slow and restrictive. For example, the menus illustrated in Figure 4-32 are good for the novice or infrequent computer user because they take him or her step-by-step through the possible operations that can be performed. The experienced user, however, knows what processing is required. Therefore, he or she may prefer to enter a few quick commands and immediately begin work instead of having to view and respond to two or more menus.

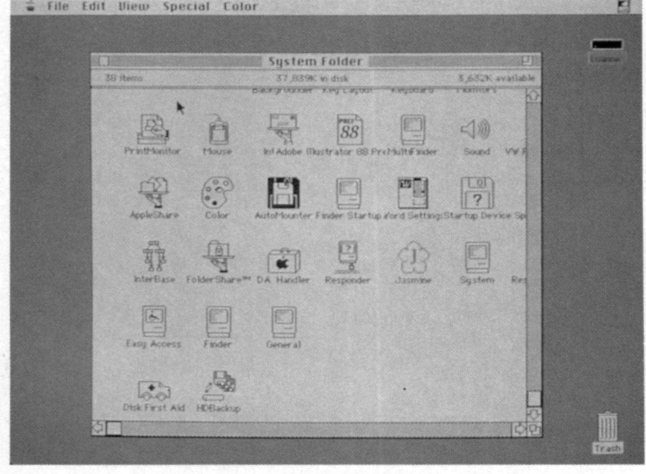


**FIGURE 4-33**
**This screen illustrates icons representing functions or data that the user can select. In the upper right corner, for example, the icon of a speaker refers to the turning off or turning on of sounds the computer can make to signal errors and other messages to the user. Icons allow the user to quickly identify the processing options available.**

## GRAPHICS

Graphics can play an important role in aiding the user to effectively interact with a computer. For example, in Figure 4-33, the user's option to choose color is represented by the icon (picture) of an artist's palette. An icon representing functions to be performed on a computer is helpful because people not familiar with computer terminology can still use the machine.

## FEATURES OF A USER INTERFACE

The following list identifies some features that should be included in a good user interface.

1. System responses to the user—**System responses** are those messages and actions taken by the computer when a user enters data into the computer. In a well-designed system, the user receives a response for every action taken. A response can be shown in two ways. First, a message can be displayed that tells the user something is happening. For example, when a large program is being loaded into main memory from auxiliary storage, the message "Program Loading" would appear on the screen. A second type of feedback occurs when the screen changes based on an entry by the user. For example, in Figure 4-32, when the user chose selection 1 from the main menu, a submenu immediately displayed on the screen. This action told the user that the data had been accepted by the computer and was being operated on. Without a response from the computer, the user does not know if the input was accepted. A response from the system avoids user confusion.

   A second issue with respect to user response is response time. **Response time** is the elapsed time between the instant a user enters data and the instant the computer responds. A common guideline for response time is that it should never be greater than two seconds. When the activity requested by the user will require more than two seconds for the computer to accomplish, a message such as "Processing—Please Wait" should be displayed.
2. Screen design—The design of the messages and pictures that appear on the screen can have a significant impact on the usability of the system. The most important rule is to keep the screen uncluttered and simple. Each message and each action that a user must take should be clear and easily understood. All messages, menus, and prompts within a system should follow a consistent format. This reduces the time needed for users to learn how to use a system and increases ease of use for experienced users.
3. User responses—In general, the simpler the entry required from the user, the better the user interface. Users are seldom skilled typists. Thus, if the user does not have to enter a large number of characters, data entry will be faster and fewer errors will occur.
4. Error recovery—Because errors are inevitable, it should be as easy as possible for a user to recover from one. Whenever the user makes an error, three user interface activities should take place: (1) the user should be alerted that an error has been made; (2) the error should be identified as specifically as possible; and (3) the user should be told how to recover from the error. In general, error recovery can take place in three ways: (1) the user can reenter the data that caused the error; (2) the user can "back up" to a previous operation; or (3) the user can exit from the operation where the error was made.
5. Control and security—Many multiuser computer systems require users to "sign on" to the computer by entering an identification, such as a name or account number followed by a password. A **password** is a value, such as a word or number, which identifies the user. Unless the user enters the password, the computer will not allow access to the machine. These procedures help to ensure that only authorized users obtain access to the computer.

The systems and procedures listed on the previous page should be kept in mind by computer professionals when designing and developing user interfaces, and by users when they are evaluating software or hardware for purchase.

The question that must be asked when designing or deciding on a user interface is, Who will be using it and what is their level of computer experience? A good user interface must be appropriate for the people who are going to be using it.

## DATA ENTRY FOR INTERACTIVE AND BATCH PROCESSING

As discussed in Chapter 3, computer applications use either interactive or batch processing methods to process data into information. The methods used to enter data for interactive and batch processing differ. We explain them in the following paragraphs.

### Data Entry for Interactive Processing

Data entered in the interactive processing mode generates immediate output. In most interactive data entry, the person entering the data is communicating directly with the computer that will process the data. Therefore, data entry for interactive processing is said to be **online data entry**, meaning that the device from which the data is being entered is connected directly to the computer.

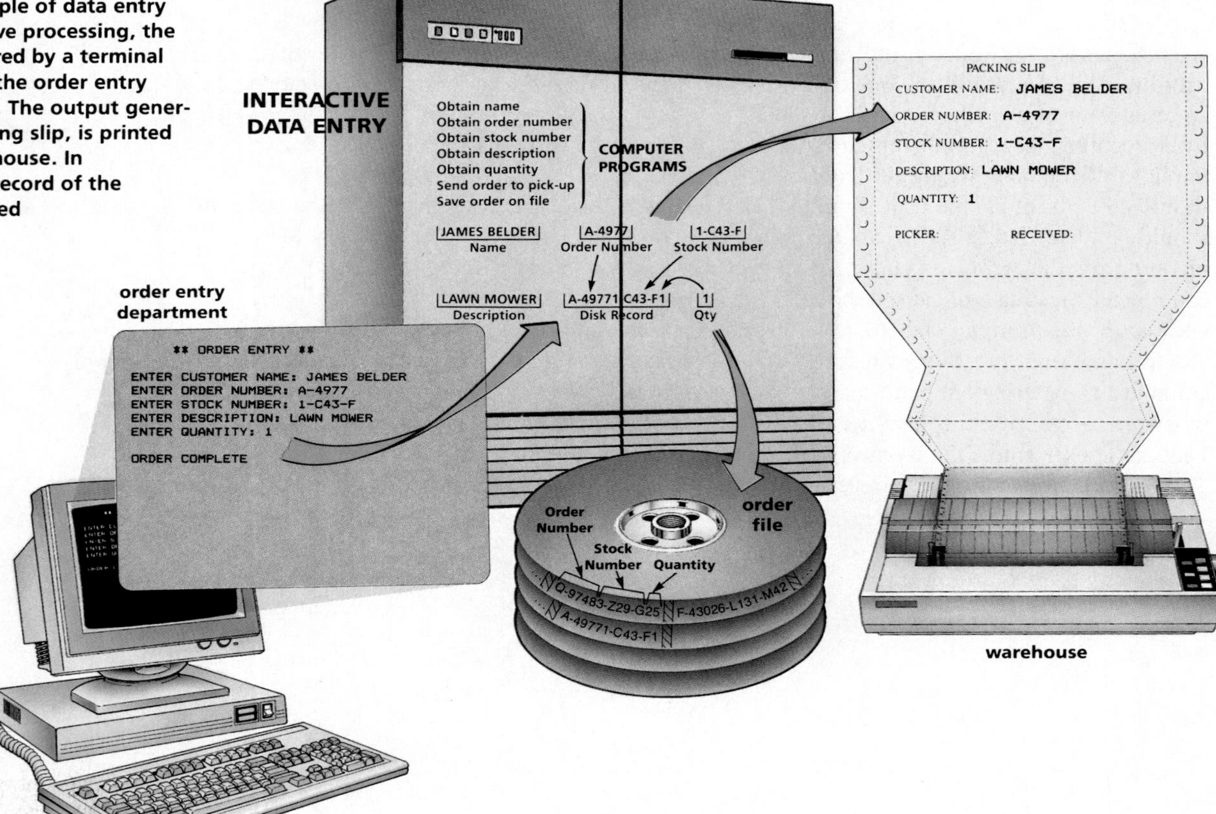


**FIGURE 4-34**
**In this example of data entry for interactive processing, the data is entered by a terminal operator in the order entry department. The output generated, a picking slip, is printed in the warehouse. In addition, a record of the order is stored on disk.**

The output generated from interactive data entry processing is not always produced at the location where the data was entered. In Figure 4-34, for example, the data is entered from a terminal located in the order entry department. The data entered concerns a purchase by a customer. After the data is entered, a picking slip is printed in the warehouse. The worker in the warehouse would then retrieve the item purchased (in this case, a lawn mower) and package it for shipping. The terminal operator in the order entry department never sees the output generated, yet this is interactive processing because the data entered is processed immediately.

The person entering the order in the order entry department may enter hundreds of such orders each day. When large amounts of data are entered by a terminal operator whose only job is to enter the data, the data entry function is said to be **production data entry**.

## Data Entry for Batch Processing

When data is entered for processing in the batch processing mode, it is stored on a storage medium (usually tape or disk) for processing at a later time. Data for batch processing can be entered in either an online or offline manner. As noted previously, online data entry means that the device from which the data is being entered is connected directly to the computer that will process it (Figure 4-35).

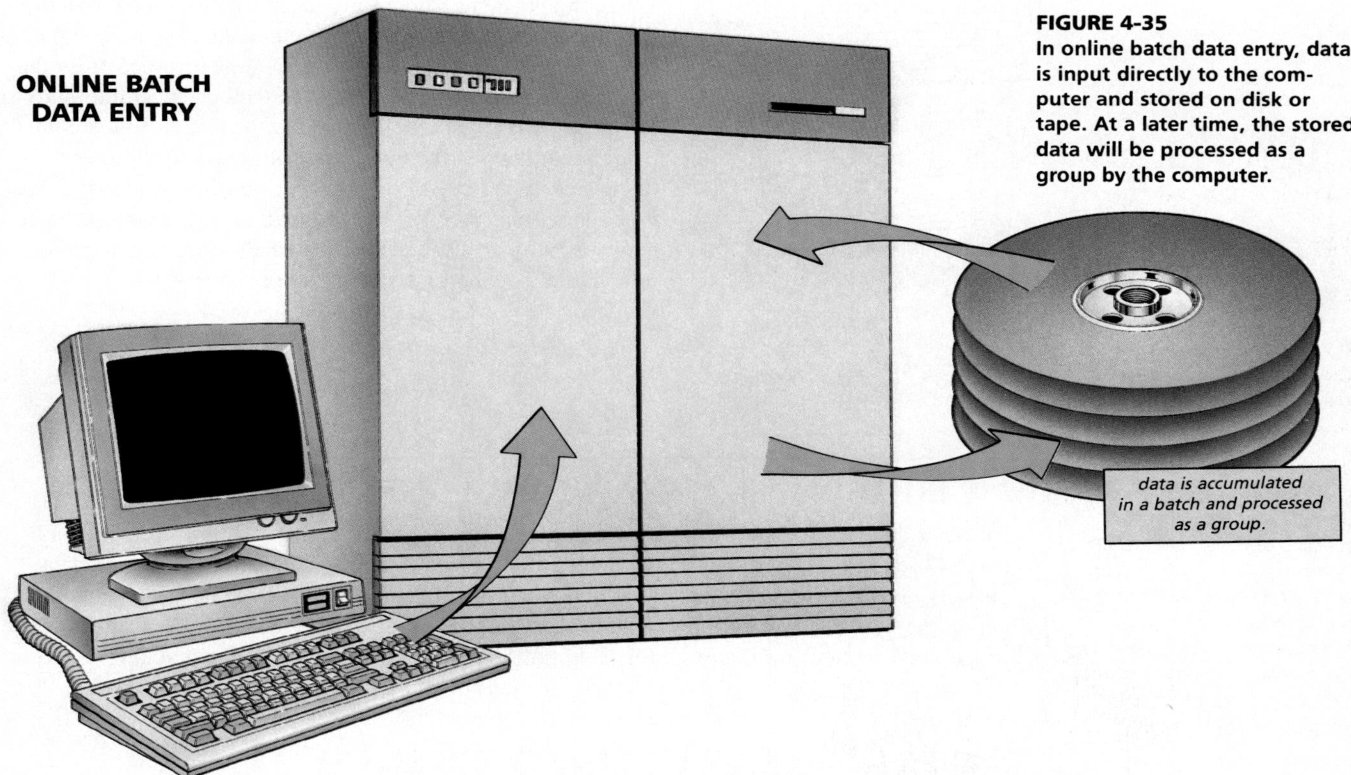
ONLINE BATCH DATA ENTRY
data is accumulated in a batch and processed as a group.

**FIGURE 4-35**
**In online batch data entry, data is input directly to the computer and stored on disk or tape. At a later time, the stored data will be processed as a group by the computer.**

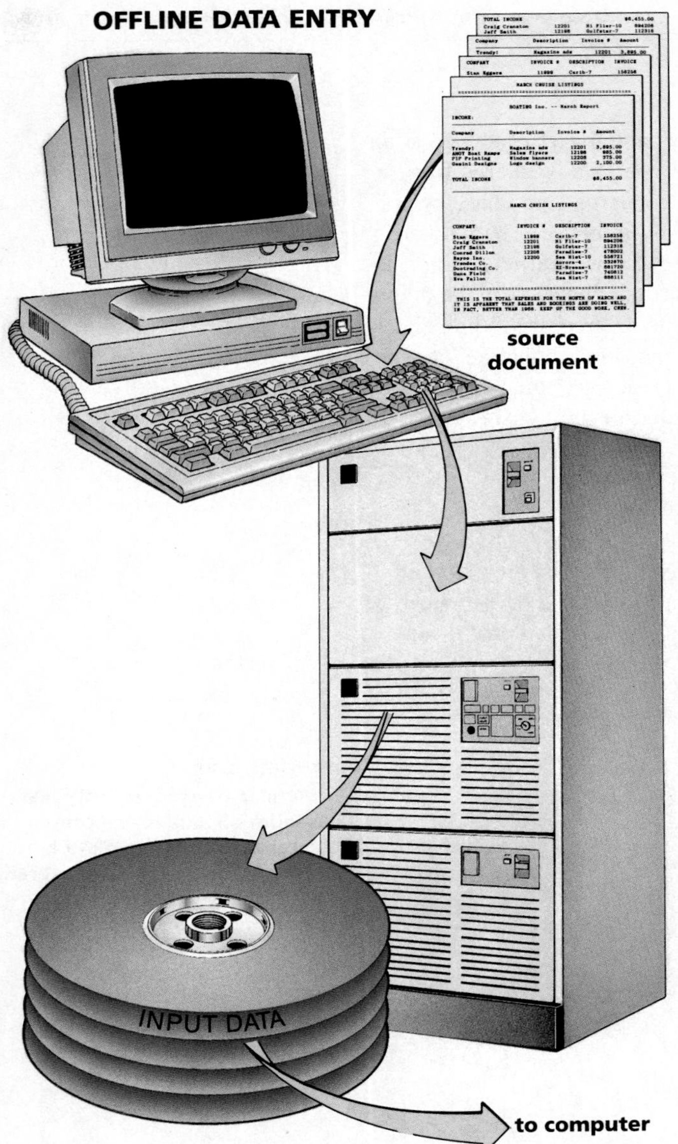


**FIGURE 4-36**
**In offline data entry, the data is input to a computer other than the one that will eventually process it. Often computers used for offline data entry are dedicated to data input functions and perform little if any processing. The data entered is later transferred to another computer for processing.**

**Offline data entry** means that the device from which the data is being entered is not connected to the computer that will process it (Figure 4-36). Instead, the data is entered using a dedicated computer or other device devoted to the data entry function. This computer or special device accepts the input data and stores it on disk or tape. At a later time, the disk or tape can be transported to the site where the data will be entered for processing in a batch mode to produce information. An example of such a system is the key-to-disk shared processor system shown in Figure 4-37.

When offline data entry is used, source documents must be accumulated prior to entering the data. For example, in a payroll application, timecards for hourly employees would be the source documents from which the hours worked would be entered by the data entry operators.

In many applications, controls are established to ensure that data is entered and processed accurately. In a credit card payment application, for example, payments are usually divided into batches for processing. The payments for each batch are added manually and recorded prior to data entry. When the payment batches are processed on the computer, the total amount of the payments calculated by the computer for each batch is compared to the total determined from the manual addition performed prior to data entry. If the totals are the same, it is evidence that the data was input to the computer accurately. If the totals are not the same, however, then further checking must be performed to determine if the data was entered incorrectly or if the manually determined batch total was wrong. This technique of balancing to a predetermined total is called a **batch control**.

## Summary of Interactive and Batch Data Entry

Entering data to produce information can take place online or offline. Online data entry is always used for interactive processing and often for batch processing as well. Offline data entry is used for batch processing. When using offline data entry, source documents from which the data is obtained must be gathered prior to the data being entered. Regardless of the processing method, producing information often requires a large amount of data entry.

# AN EXAMPLE OF ONLINE DATA ENTRY

Many types of devices can be used to enter data but by far the most common device is the terminal. We illustrate using terminals for online data entry with an order entry example. Order entry is the process followed when an order is received from a customer. An order entry application usually proceeds in the following manner:

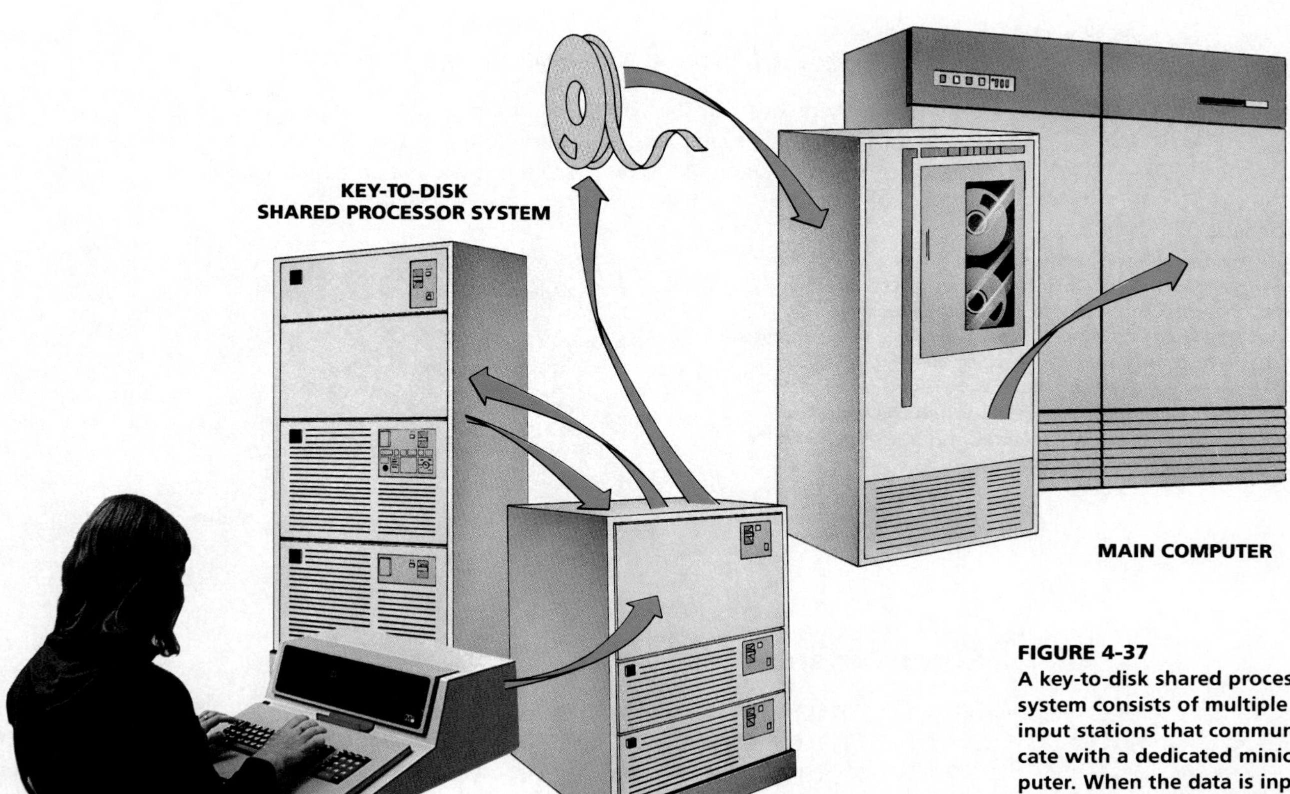


**FIGURE 4-37**
**A key-to-disk shared processor system consists of multiple input stations that communicate with a dedicated minicomputer. When the data is input, it is stored in a disk file. When the data entry is completed, the disk file is output to tape. The tape is then physically transferred to another computer that will process the data.**

1. The order is received from the customer, either through the mail or over the telephone, and the data concerning the customer and the order is entered into the computer by the data entry operator.
2. When the order is entered, the order entry program performs a credit check by retrieving credit data from a credit file stored on disk. The order is stored in the open order disk file so that a record of it is retained.
3. In addition, when the order is entered, the order entry program controlling the data entry operation determines if the item ordered is in inventory by reading a record from an inventory file or database. If the item ordered is in inventory, a picking slip is printed in the warehouse. A picking slip alerts warehouse personnel that an order has been received and specifies who the customer is and what items are to be shipped. Then, or at a later time, the warehouse personnel retrieve the item and package it for shipping. When the item is shipped, they will enter that information into the computer. Then the record for the order will be removed from the open order file and placed in the shipped file.
4. If the item ordered is not in the warehouse inventory, the order record will be placed in the backorder file and the customer will be notified that the item is not available. A backorder is an order for an item that is not currently in inventory. The order will be held until the item is available, at which time the order will be filled.

The following sections explain the data entry procedure that could be followed by a person entering orders using an online entry system.

## Order Entry Menu

The data entry process for the sample order entry system begins with the Order Entry menu (Figure 4-38). In this example, the function to be performed is entering orders. Therefore, the data entry operator enters the value 1 to choose the option ENTER ORDERS.

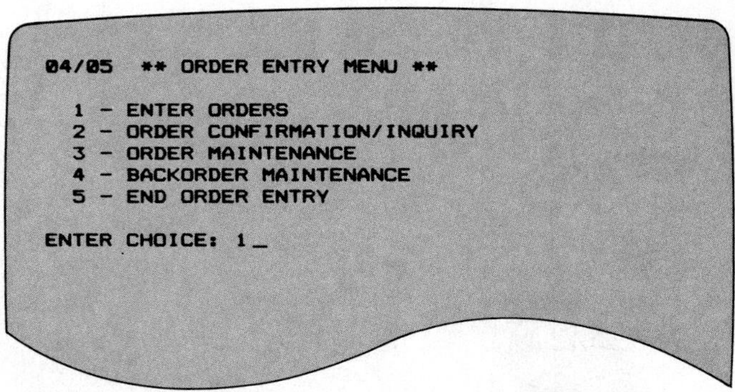


**FIGURE 4-38**
**The Order Entry menu specifies the options available for processing sales orders. Option 1 allows orders to be entered. Option 2 provides for order confirmations and inquiries into the order file. Option 3 allows certain changes to be made to orders, such as revising the ship to address. Option 4 provides for changes to backorders, orders for products that were not in inventory when the order was entered. Option 5 would be selected if the user wanted to end the order processing function.**

## Enter Orders

The following six steps are illustrated in Figure 4-39.

In Step 1, when the data entry operator chooses option 1 on the main menu, the first of two screens required to enter orders displays. The screen contains colors to designate different types of information. The blue characters are either headings or prompts that identify the fields to be processed. Each area where data will be displayed or entered is shown in reverse video. The white areas indicate fields that must be entered by the data entry operator. The red areas will contain fixed data based on the operator's entries. These fixed areas cannot be changed by the data entry operator. The yellow areas indicate **default values**, data that will be automatically displayed but which can be changed by the operator if needed.

In Step 2, the operator enters the data for the first field, the customer number. Here the value AE-1073 is the number for the customer ordering items. Note that instead of reverse video when the data is entered, the actual characters display in the same color as the reverse video; that is, the customer number displays in white because the reverse video was in white. The process of entering the data is shown in Figure 4-40 on the next page, where the first character (A) has been entered. The character is white but the rest of the input area on the screen where data has not yet been entered retains the reverse video. This technique is commonly used on terminals where reverse video identifies input fields.

Step 3 shows what the screen would look like after the operator enters the customer number. The order number is generated by the order entry computer program. It displays in red because the terminal operator cannot reference or change the order number. The bill to data also displays in red because it will not be changed. The bill to data, which is the name of the company and the address to which the bill for the items will be sent, was obtained from a customer file based on the customer number that was entered. The ship to data identifies the place to which the items will be sent. The company name displays in red because it will not be changed. The ship to address, however, displays reversed on a yellow background because the data is default data. It is used in data entry so that the operator does not have to spend time entering data that normally does not change. In this case, the address shown is the same as the bill to address because most of the time, items ordered by Hinkle Ltd. are shipped to the same address. This is the default address, so the operator would merely press the Enter key and continue to the next field. In this example, however, the ship to address is to be changed. Therefore, the operator must key in the new ship to address. Step 4 shows how the new ship to address displays.

**FIGURE 4-39**
**These six steps show how data would be entered in the first screen of a sample order entry application.**

**STEP 1**

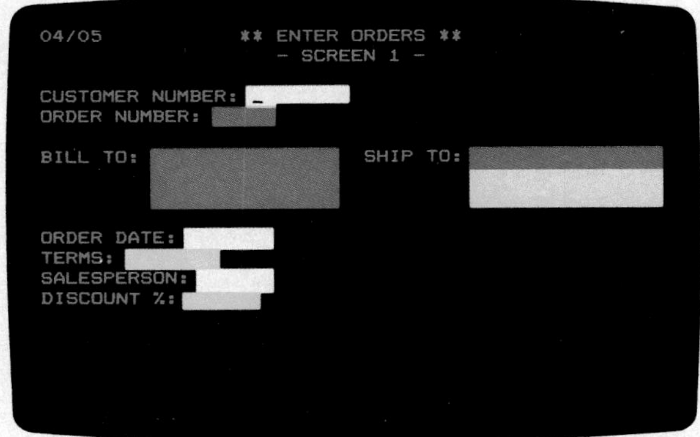


**Step 1: Each field is identified by color. The blue fields are titles and prompts. The red fields will contain data that cannot be changed. The white fields must be entered by the operator. The yellow fields are default fields.**

**STEP 2**

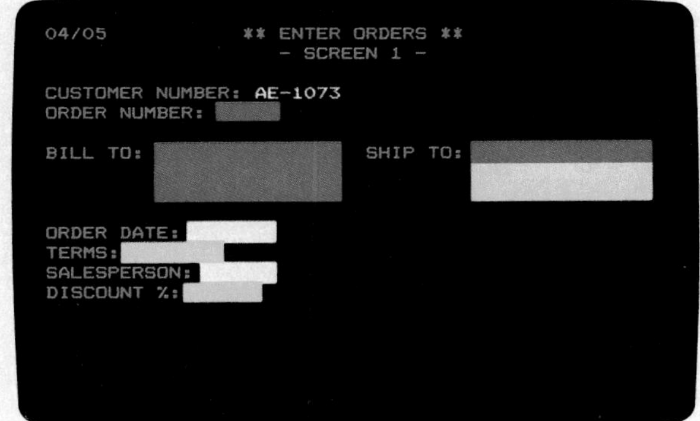


**Step 2: In this step, the data entry operator has entered the customer number. The customer number is displayed in white letters because the operator had to enter the data. The operator would then press the Enter key to continue.**

**STEP 3**

04/05
** ENTER ORDERS **
- SCREEN 1 -
CUSTOMER NUMBER: AE-1073
ORDER NUMBER: 1372
BILL TO: HINKLE LTD.
721 AVERY WAY
LONGO, CO 74113
SHIP TO: HINKLE LTD.
721 AVERY WAY
LONGO, CO 74113
ORDER DATE:
TERMS: NET 30
SALESPERSON:
DISCOUNT %: .055

**Step 3: Data retrieved from a customer file based on the customer number is displayed on the screen. The cursor is placed on the ship to address. The operator can enter data here if it is different from the default values.**

**STEP 4**

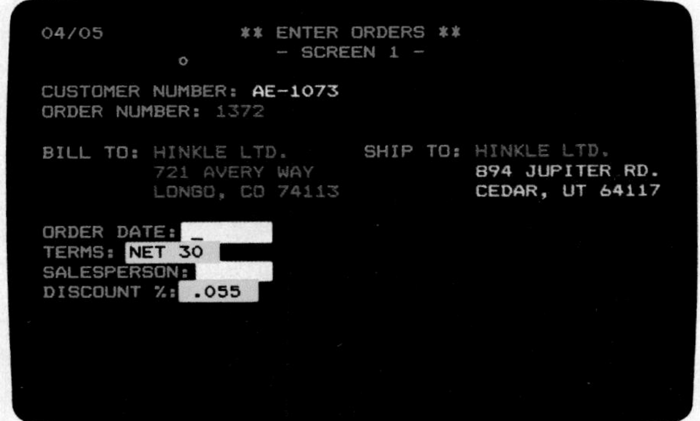


**Step 4: The order date must be entered by the operator. Therefore, it is displayed in white. The default values in the ship to field have been changed to yellow characters because they have now been entered.**

**STEP 5**

04/05
** ENTER ORDERS **
- SCREEN 1 -
CUSTOMER NUMBER: AE-1073
ORDER NUMBER: 1372
BILL TO: HINKLE LTD.
721 AVERY WAY
LONGO, CO 74113
SHIP TO: HINKLE LTD.
894 JUPITER RD.
CEDAR, UT 64117
ORDER DATE: 03/31
TERMS: NET 30
SALESPERSON: _
DISCOUNT %: .055

**Step 5: The salesperson must be entered by the data entry operator. The default value in the terms field specified net 30. The operator accepted the default value by pressing the Enter key instead of entering new data.**

**STEP 6**

04/05
** ENTER ORDERS **
- SCREEN 1 -
CUSTOMER NUMBER: AE-1073
ORDER NUMBER: 1372
BILL TO: HINKLE LTD.
721 AVERY WAY
LONGO, CO 74113
SHIP TO: HINKLE LTD.
894 JUPITER RD.
CEDAR, UT 64117
ORDER DATE: 03/31
TERMS: NET 30
SALESPERSON: B-49
DISCOUNT %: .055
PRESS ENTER KEY TO CONTINUE_

**Step 6: After the data entry operation for the first screen has been completed, all data is displayed as color characters on a black screen. The reverse video is not necessary because no data remains to be entered.**

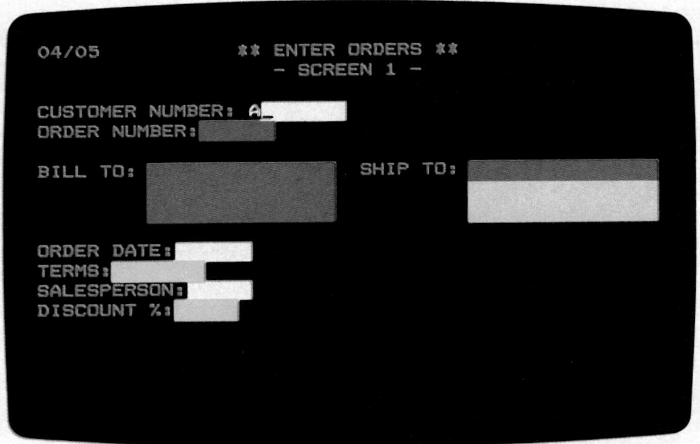


**FIGURE 4-40**
**When a value is entered in a reverse video field, the normal technique is to display the character in the color of the reverse video field and to remove the reverse video field for that character. Here, the letter A has been entered into a white field; therefore, the letter is displayed in white on a black background.**

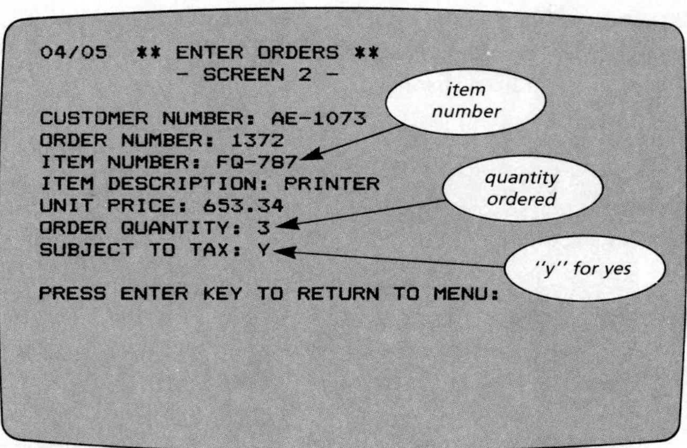


**FIGURE 4-41**
**On the second order entry screen, the operator enters the item number and the quantity ordered. The program uses the item number to look up and display the item description and the unit price. The subject to tax default value is Y, but the operator can change it.**

Next, the controlling program places the cursor at the order date field (Step 5) and the operator enters the order date (03/31). The order date field is white because the operator must always enter the order date.

In Step 5, by pressing the Enter key, the operator has accepted the default terms that the program displayed. The salesperson data, however, must be entered by the operator because it is in white. The default value for the discount percent is also accepted by the operator.

Step 6 shows how the screen would look after all data entry has been completed for the first order entry screen.

Next, the operator presses the Enter key to display the second screen required for the order entry operation (Figure 4-41). On this screen, the operator must enter the number of the item purchased and the order quantity. The item description and unit price are displayed by the order entry program. The single default value on this screen is the subject to tax field. Here, the operator can change the Y (signifying yes to the question, Is this purchase subject to tax?) to N. In this example, the default value was accepted. After entering all the data, the operator can press the Enter key to return to the main menu (Figure 4-38) and enter another order.

This example is a composite of many different order entry systems and illustrates some of the features of these systems.

## DATA ENTRY PROCEDURES

The procedures developed for the data entry function are important because accurate data must be entered into a computer to ensure data integrity. In addition, since users are interacting directly with the computer during the data entry function, procedures and documentation must be quite clear. The following issues must be addressed in order to implement a data entry application successfully:

1. Origination of data—Data entered for processing on a computer is generated from many sources throughout a company. It is important to identify which people and operations will generate the data so that appropriate procedures can be written to specify what data is to be gathered, how it is to be gathered, and who is to gather it.
2. Location of the data entry function—Data is generally entered either from the centralized data entry section of the information systems department or from various locations throughout an organization. The hardware, software and personnel needs vary depending upon which of these two locations is used. In a **centralized data entry** operation, the data is keyed by trained operators from source documents. When data is entered in the centralized data entry section, it is usually processed in a batch processing mode.

   Entering data from various locations in an organization is called **distributed data entry**. Quite often the data entry takes place at the site where the data is generated, for example, sales orders being entered by the sales department. Often, data entered using distributed data entry is processed in an interactive processing mode.
3. Timing requirements for acquiring the data—In some applications, the time of day or the day of the week when the data becomes available is important. For example, if all timecards for employees must be received by Monday at 4 p.m. for employees to be paid Friday, timing is important and must be identified in the documentation for the data entry.
4. Timing requirements for entering the data—The amount of time that can elapse between when the event being reported takes place and when the data about that event must be entered should be specified. In some applications, an event can occur but the data need not be entered until hours or even days later. For example, in the payroll application mentioned above, timecards are retrieved Monday at 4 p.m. These timecards record the workers' time for the previous week. The data may not be entered until Tuesday. Therefore, more than a week might elapse between when the event occurred and when the data about the event was entered.

   In most cases when entry time is not a critical factor, the data is recorded on source documents and given to data entry personnel in either a centralized or distributed location to enter. In other applications, however, the data must be entered as the event or transaction is occurring and at the location where it is occurring. This process is sometimes called **source data collection**. For example, when a retail sale is made using a point of sale terminal, the data must be entered at the moment the sale is made so that the sale can be completed with the customer. Therefore, it is important that the documentation for the data entry system specify the timing requirements for entering data.
5. Flow of the input data—The documentation must specify the flow of the data from the point where it originates to the point where it is entered for processing on the computer. Any handling required, any recording on source documents, and any changes in format from source to data entry must be documented.
6. Transaction volume—The amount of data entered for a given time period and location must be estimated. Any particularly high or low volumes may require special procedures.
7. Manner of entering the data—Based on many of the factors specified in items 1–6, the procedures must specify how the data is to be entered, identifying devices and methods. For example, it could be specified that data is to be entered from source documents using terminals in an online, centralized environment.
8. Editing and error handling—The documentation must specify the editing for the entered data and the steps to take if the data is not valid. Although different applications will have specific criteria for validating input data, there are a number of tests that are performed on input data before the data is processed in a computer. Some of these tests are:

   a. Tests for numeric or alphabetic data (Figure 4-42)—For example, in the United States a zip code must always be numeric. Therefore, the program performing the editing can check the values in the zip code field. If they are not numeric, the data is incorrect.

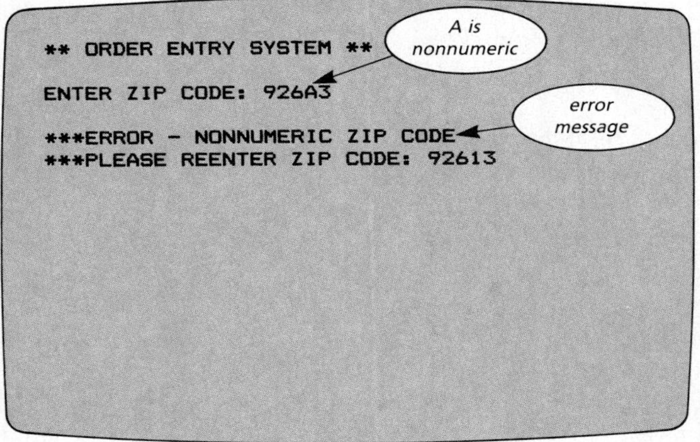


**FIGURE 4-42**
**In this example, a nonnumeric zip code is entered and an error message displays. When a numeric zip code is entered, the data is accepted and no error message displays.**

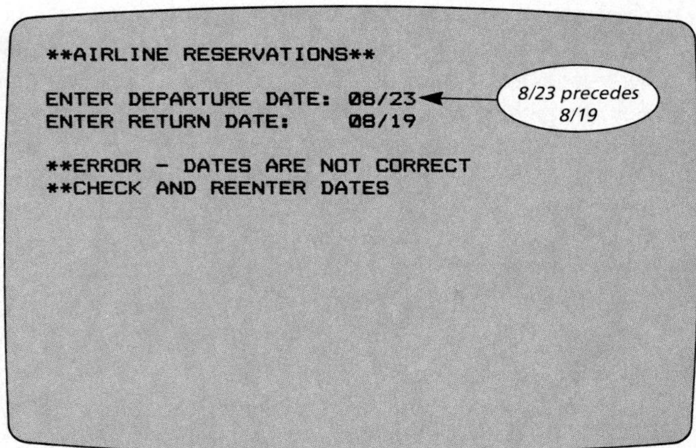


**FIGURE 4-43**
**On this airline reservation screen, the user entered a return date earlier than the departure date and the system displayed an error message.**

b. Tests for data reasonableness—A reasonableness check ensures that the data entered is within normal or accepted boundaries. For example, suppose no employee within a company is authorized to work more than 80 hours per week. If the value entered in the hours worked field is greater than 80, the value in the field would be indicated as a probable error.

c. Tests for data consistency—In some cases, data entered cannot, by itself, be found to be invalid. If, however, the data is examined in the context of other data entered for the same record or group of fields, discrepancies might be found. For example, in an airline reservation system, round-trip tickets are often purchased (Figure 4-43). If the terminal operator enters the date on which the passenger is leaving, the editing program can only check whether the date entered is valid. Similarly, when the return date is entered, the program can again make sure it is a valid date. In addition, however, the return date can be compared to the departure date. If the return date is earlier than the departure date, it is likely that an error has been made when entering one of the dates.

d. Tests for transcription and transposition errors—There is always a possibility that an operator will make an error when entering data. A **transcription error** occurs when an error is made in copying the values from a source document. For example, if the operator keys the customer number 7165 when the proper number is 7765, a transcription error has been made. A **transposition error** happens when the operator switches two numbers. Such an error has occurred when the number 7765 is entered as 7756.

9. Data controls and security—The controls and security that will be applied to the data must be defined. This includes what the controls and security measures are, how they are to be implemented, and what action is to be taken if the security of the data is compromised in any way.

10. Personnel requirements—Specifying personnel requirements includes defining who will gather the data, who will enter it, and how many people will be required to enter the data for the application. Personnel must be educated about gathering and entering the data. They must be trained in using the equipment and software, ensuring reliable data entry, entering the data according to specified procedures, and interpreting any output received from the computer during interactive processing.

## ERGONOMICS

To be efficient when you are using a computer, it is important that you be comfortable. Being comfortable results in less fatigue, better accuracy, and higher input rates, factors that are important to all users, but particularly to data entry personnel. **Ergonomics** is the study of the design and arrangement of equipment so that people will interact with the equipment in a healthy, comfortable, and efficient manner. As related to computer equipment, ergonomics is concerned with such factors as the physical design of the keyboard, screens, and related hardware, and the manner in which people interact with these hardware devices.

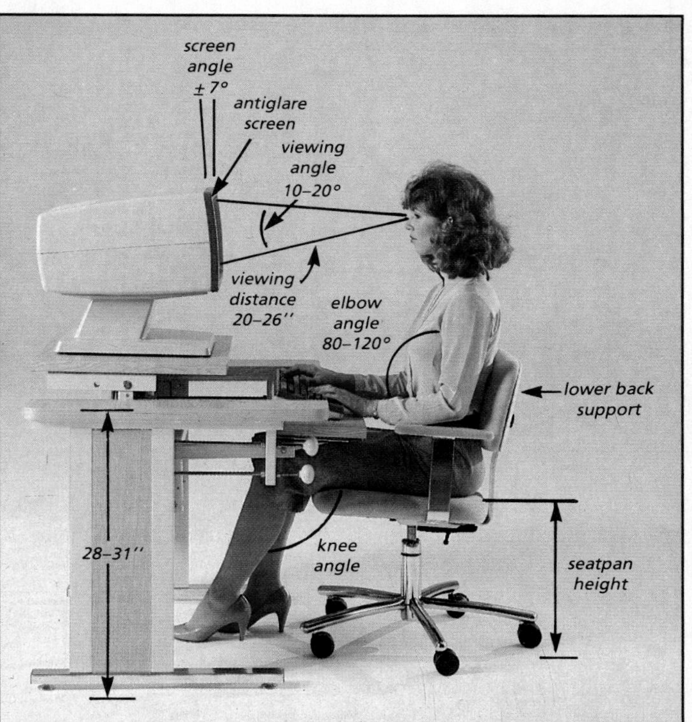


**FIGURE 4-44**
**This illustration shows some of the ergonomic factors that should be considered when using a terminal for a long or repeated length of time.**

The first computer terminals contained the keyboard and screen as a single unit. The screen frequently displayed white characters on a black background. Early studies found significant user dissatisfaction with the terminals. One study reported that 90% of the personnel who used these terminals complained of health problems, including eye fatigue, blurred vision, itching and burning eyes, and back problems. As a result of these studies, a number of design recommendations for terminals were made. These recommendations included the following:

1. Computer keyboards should be detached from the screen so that they can be positioned on a desk for the convenience and comfort of the user.
2. The screen should be movable, and the angle at which the user views the contents of the screen should be adjustable.
3. Amber or green text on a black background is preferable to black characters on a white background or white characters on a black background.
4. The screen should be of high quality to eliminate any flickering of the image and characters on the screen. The characters displayed on the screen should appear as solid as possible.
5. The images on the screen should be in sharp focus over the entire screen area.
6. The screen should have an antiglare coating. Screen glare has been a common complaint of many terminal users, and it is known that glare can be harmful to eyes. A flat screen, now used on some terminals, can also reduce glare.
7. Screens that will display multiple elements of information should use color to distinguish the different elements, thus cutting down on the strain of looking for and identifying information displayed on the screen.

Figure 4-44 illustrates some of the above recommendations. The keyboard is detachable, the visual display unit is adjustable, and the screen has an antiglare coating. The illustration also shows the use of a lower back support. Note the position of the user's body in relation to the terminal.

As more and more workers use terminals and personal computers, the importance of ergonomically designed equipment increases. Manufacturers are now aware of the importance of ergonomic design and, as a result, are designing and building terminals and personal computers that incorporate ergonomic design for the health and comfort of users.

## SUMMARY OF INPUT TO THE COMPUTER

This chapter covered various aspects of input to the computer. We discussed the four types of input and how they are used, input devices, user interfaces, and data entry. After reading this chapter you should have a better overall understanding of computer input.

## CHAPTER SUMMARY

1. **Input** refers to the process of entering programs, commands, user responses, and data into the computer memory.
2. The **keyboard** is the most commonly used input device. Special keys may include the **numeric keypads**, **cursor control keys**, and **function keys**.
3. **Video display terminals** fall into two basic categories: **dumb terminals** and **intelligent terminals**.
4. A **mouse** is a small input device used to control the movement of the cursor and to select options displayed on the screen.
5. **Touch screens** allow the user to interact with a computer by merely touching the screen.
6. **Light pens**, **digitizers**, and **graphics tablets** are graphic input devices used to translate graphic input data into a form that can be processed by the computer.
7. **Voice input** allows the user to enter data and issue commands to a computer with spoken words.
8. **Magnetic ink character recognition (MICR)** is a type of machine-readable data used almost exclusively in the banking industry.
9. **Scanners** are devices that read printed codes, characters, or images and convert them into a form that can be processed by the computer.
10. **Optical character recognition (OCR)** devices are scanners that read typewritten, computer-printed, and in some cases hand-printed characters from ordinary documents.
11. An **Optical mark reader** is a scanning device that can read carefully placed pencil marks on a specially designed form.
12. **Data collection devices** are designed and used for obtaining data at the site where the transaction or event being reported takes place.
13. A **user interface** is the combination of hardware and software that allows a user to communicate with a computer system.
14. User interfaces have evolved from technical commands to techniques such as prompts and menus.
15. A **prompt** is a message to the user that is displayed on the screen and provides information or instructions regarding some entry to be made or action to be taken.
16. **Data editing** is used to check input data for proper format and acceptable values. It helps to ensure that valid data is entered by the user.
17. A **menu** is a display on a screen that allows the user to select from multiple alternatives. There are several types of menu selection techniques including sequential and alphabetic selection, cursor positioning, reverse video, and icon selection.
18. An **icon** is a pictorial representation of a function to be performed on the computer.
19. Graphics can play an important role in aiding the user to interact effectively with a computer.
20. Features that relate to good interfaces include: system responses, screen design, user responses, error recovery, and control and security.
21. When a user enters data into a computer, the messages and action taken by the computer are referred to as **system responses**.
22. The elapsed time between the instant a user enters data and the instant the computer responds is called the **response time**.
23. Screen design should provide messages and pictures in an uncluttered, simple format.
24. All messages, menus, and prompts within a system should follow a consistent format.
25. Input will be faster and fewer errors will be made if the operator response or input from users is as simple as possible.
26. When user input errors occur, a good interface will tell the user, identify the error, and explain how to correct it.
27. **Passwords** are unique user identification codes that are used on multiuser systems to allow only authorized users access to the computer.

28. Data entry for interactive processing is said to be **online**, meaning that the device from which the data is being entered is connected directly to the computer.
29. Data entry for batch processing is said to be **offline**, meaning that the device from which the data is being entered is not connected to the computer that will process it.
30. In many applications, controls are established to ensure that the data entered is processed accurately. For example, balancing to a predetermined total is called a **batch control**.
31. The procedures developed for the data entry function are important because accurate data must be entered into a computer to ensure data integrity.
32. Within an organization, it is important to identify which people and operations will generate the data.
33. **Centralized data entry** is performed by trained operators from **source documents**.
34. **Distributed data entry** often takes place at the site where the data is generated and is input to the computer by a variety of users.
35. In most applications, timing requirements for acquiring and entering data are important and should be identified.
36. Data documentation should specify the flow of the data from the point where it originates to the point where it is entered for processing.
37. Transaction volume refers to the amount of data that must be entered for a given time period and a given location.
38. Data entry procedures should identify the devices and the methods for entering data.
39. Data editing and error handling procedures include a number of distinct tests that can be performed on the data prior to processing. Some of these are numeric and alphabetic testing, tests for reasonableness and consistency, and transcription and transposition tests.
40. **Transcription errors** refer to operator errors made at the time of input, such as entering 7165 instead of 7665.
41. **Transposition errors** refer to operator errors where two characters are switched, such as entering 7756 instead of 7765.
42. Data controls and security procedures should be defined.
43. Data entry procedures should specify the personnel requirements for both gathering and entering input data.
44. **Ergonomics** is the study of the design and arrangement of equipment so that people will interact with the equipment in a healthy, comfortable, and efficient manner.
45. Manufacturers are now designing equipment that incorporates ergonomic design features.

## KEY TERMS

## REVIEW QUESTIONS

1. What are the four types of input and how are they used?
2. Describe the features available on a computer keyboard.
3. Name two types of display terminals. Describe each type.
4. Describe a mouse and list its advantages and disadvantages.
5. Describe three different types of graphic input devices.
6. What are data collection devices? How do they differ from other input devices?
7. What is a user interface? Why is it important?
8. Describe the evolution of user interface software.
9. What is a prompt? What are the attributes of a good prompt?
10. What is a menu? Describe the five types of menu selection.
11. What is an icon? Why is an icon used?
12. Name and briefly describe the five features that apply to good user interfaces.
13. What are the differences between data entry for interactive and for batch processing?
14. List ten procedures associated with data entry.
15. What is ergonomics? List and describe six ergonomic features that a terminal should have.

## CONTROVERSIAL ISSUES

1. Manufacturers of computer hardware and software that use the mouse as an input device and icons on the screen claim that the majority of people who use computers will prefer this method. They claim that most people are not familiar with computers and the easier computers are to use, the more people who will use them. Some of their competitors claim that these devices are useful when people are learning to use a computer but that users quickly tire of the "cuteness" and prefer a device on which more productive work can be done. Which argument do you think is correct? Could they both be correct?
2. Proponents of touch screen technology claim that the touch screen is the answer to user interface problems because all a user must do is touch the screen to input data. Opponents claim it is much too limited as an input device. Take a position in this dispute.
3. The use of display terminals has increased significantly in recent years. With the increased use has come claims that using terminals is harmful to health. It has been claimed that long use of video display terminals has caused such problems as miscarriages and back ailments. Some unions have questioned the advisability of sitting in front of a terminal for eight hours. Terminal manufacturers have argued that ergonomically designed terminals present no danger to health. Research the arguments and take a position on this controversy.

## RESEARCH PROJECTS

1. Visit a local computer store that sells a computer that uses a mouse and icons. Use the machine for a period of time and report back to your class concerning its good points and bad points.
2. Visit a retail or grocery store in your area and prepare a report on the point of sale terminals in use. Be sure to identify the type of terminal used, the manner in which data is entered, the computer to which the terminal is connected, and any problems or difficulties employees have had using the terminals.
3. Visit a local bank or retail store that has terminals communicating with a large computer. Ask a person at the establishment to show you how they interface with the computer. Pay particular attention to the screen formats, the data that the user must enter, and the response times. Prepare a report on your experiences for your class.
4. Bring a turn-around document that you have received in the mail and explain it to the class.
5. The data entry function has changed significantly during the history of business data processing. Research the history of the data entry function and prepare an oral or written report. Include in your report the hardware devices used, the manner in which data was entered, the location from which data was entered, and the different procedures used for data entry over the years.

CHAPTER 5

# The Processor Unit

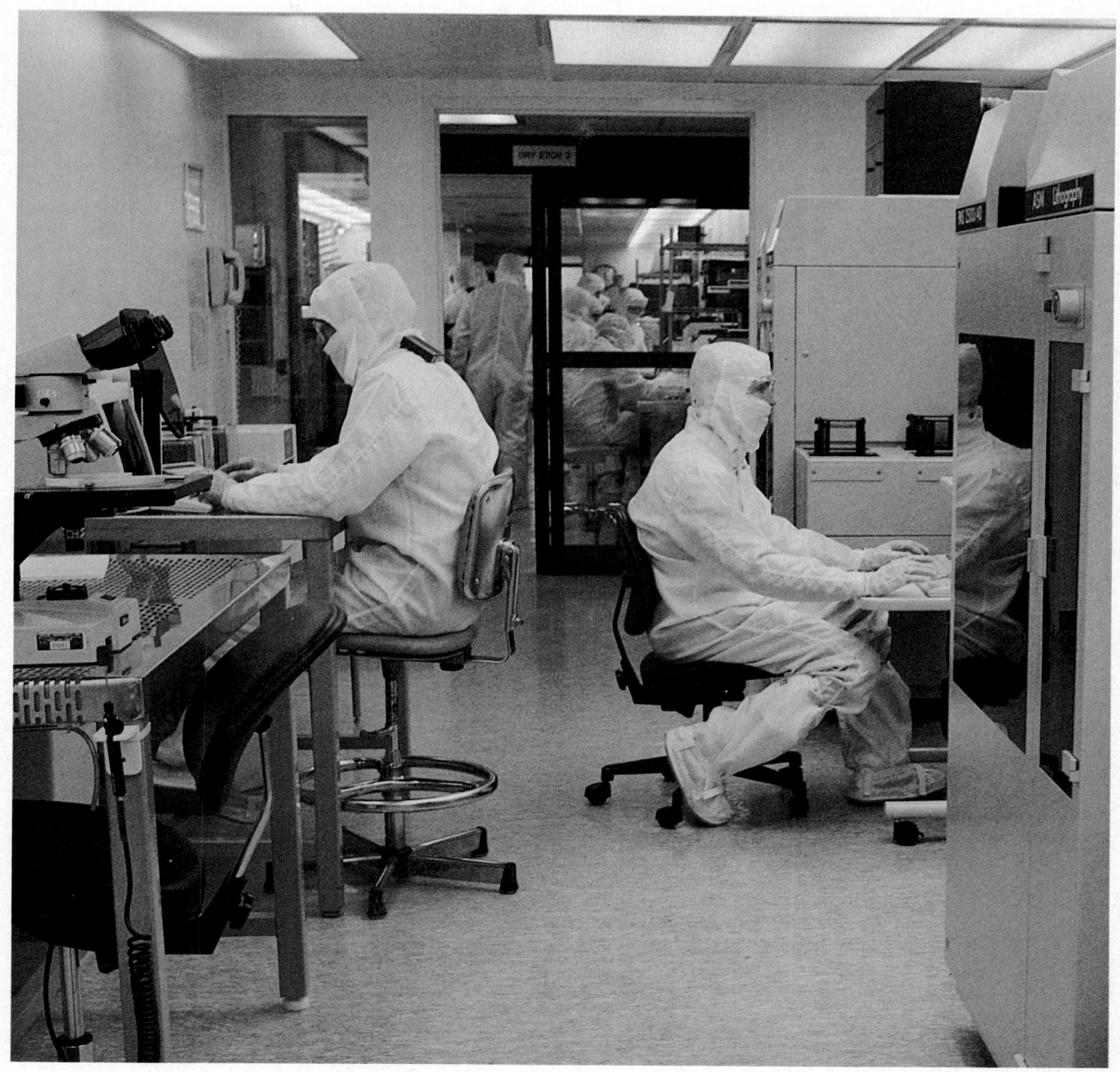

CHAPTER 5

# The Processor Unit

## OBJECTIVES

- Identify the components of the processor unit and describe their use.
- Define a bit and describe how a series of bits in a byte is used to represent characters.
- Discuss how the ASCII and EBCDIC codes represent characters.
- Describe why the binary and hexadecimal numbering systems are used with computer systems.
- List and describe the four steps in a machine cycle.
- Discuss the three primary factors that affect the speed of the processor unit.
- Describe the characteristics of RAM and ROM memory. List several other types of memory.
- Describe the process of manufacturing integrated circuits.

The information processing cycle consists of input, processing, output, and storage operations. When an input operation is completed and both a program and data are stored in main memory, processing operations can begin. During these operations, the processor unit executes, or performs, the program instructions and processes the data into information.

This chapter examines the components of the processor unit, describes how main memory stores programs and data, and discusses the sequence of operations that occurs when instructions are executed on a computer.

## WHAT IS THE PROCESSOR UNIT?

While the term computer is used to describe the collection of devices that perform the information processing cycle, it is sometimes used more specifically to describe the processor unit. It is in the processor unit that the execution of computer programs and the manipulation of data takes place. The main components of the processor unit are the central processing unit or CPU and the main memory of the computer (Figure 5-1).

## The Central Processing Unit

The central processing unit (CPU) contains the control unit and the arithmetic/logic unit. These two components work together using the program and data stored in main memory to perform the processing operations.

The control unit can be thought of as the "brain" of the computer. Just as the human brain controls the body, the control unit "controls" the computer. The **control unit** operates by repeating the following four operations: fetching, decoding, executing, and storing. **Fetching** means obtaining the next program instruction from main memory. **Decoding** is translating the program instruction into the commands that the computer can process. **Executing** refers to the actual processing of the computer commands, and **storing** takes place when the result of the instruction is written to main memory.

The second part of the CPU is the **arithmetic/logic unit**. This unit contains the electronic circuitry necessary to perform arithmetic and logical operations on data. Arithmetic operations include addition, subtraction, multiplication, and division. Logical operations consist of comparing one data item to another to determine if the first data item is greater than, equal to, or less than the other.

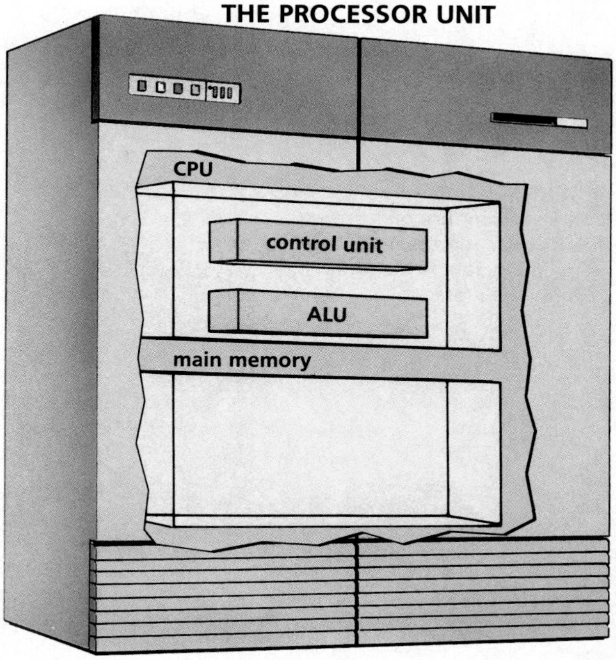

THE PROCESSOR UNIT

CPU

control unit

ALU

main memory

**FIGURE 5-1**
**The processor unit of a computer contains two main components: the central processing unit (CPU), which includes the control unit and the arithmetic/logic unit, and main memory.**

## Main Memory

In addition to the CPU, **main memory** or **primary storage** is also contained in the processor unit of the computer. (Figure 5-2) Main memory stores three items: (1) the *operating system* or software that directs and coordinates the computer equipment; (2) an *application program* containing the instructions that will direct the work to be done; and (3) the *data* currently being processed by the application program. Data is stored in areas of main memory referred to as input and output areas. These areas receive and send data to the input and output devices. Another area of main memory called working storage is used to store any other data that is needed for processing.

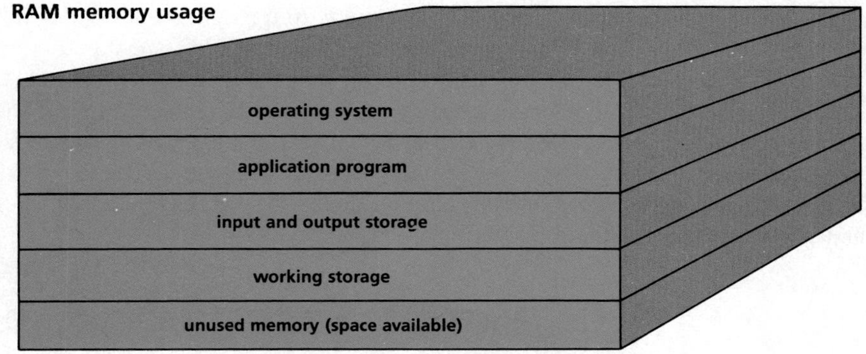


**FIGURE 5-2**
**Main memory is used to store several types of data and programs. As program instructions are executed and new data and programs are input and output, the allocation of memory space changes.**

Within main memory, each storage location is called a **byte**. Just as a house on a street has a unique address that indicates its location on the street, each byte in the main memory of a computer has an address that indicates its location in memory (Figure 5-3). The number that indicates the location of a byte in memory is called a **memory address**. Whenever the computer references a byte, it does so by using the memory address of that location.

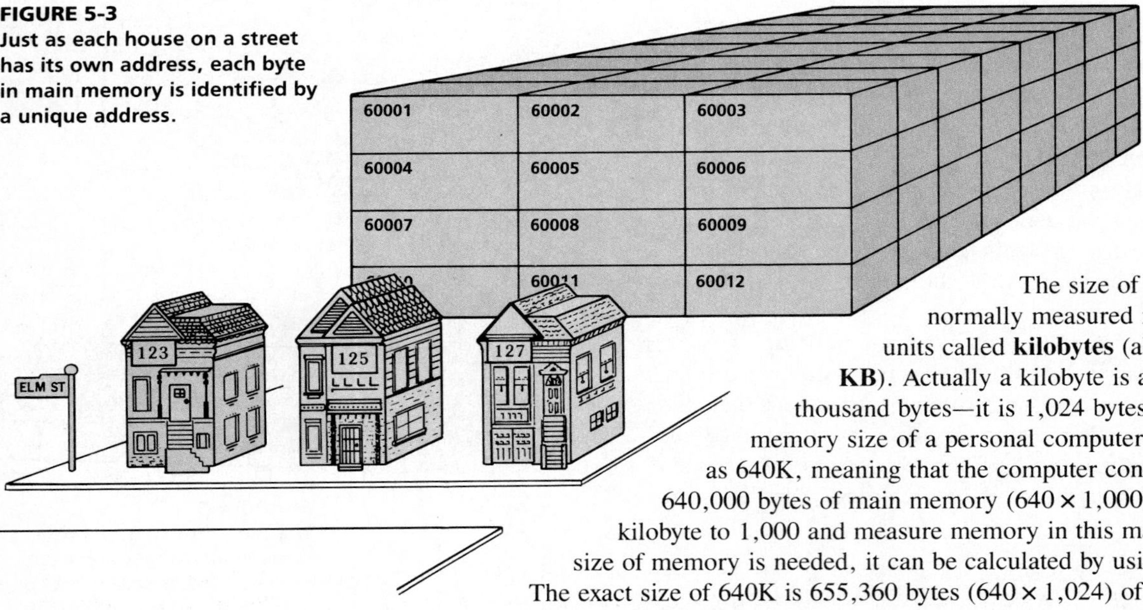

**FIGURE 5-3**
**Just as each house on a street has its own address, each byte in main memory is identified by a unique address.**

The size of main memory is normally measured in thousand-byte units called **kilobytes** (abbreviated as **K** or **KB**). Actually a kilobyte is a little larger than a thousand bytes—it is 1,024 bytes. For example, the memory size of a personal computer could be expressed as 640K, meaning that the computer contains approximately 640,000 bytes of main memory (640 × 1,000). Most users round kilobyte to 1,000 and measure memory in this manner. If the exact size of memory is needed, it can be calculated by using the value 1,024. The exact size of 640K is 655,360 bytes (640 × 1,024) of main memory.

Several other terms are used to describe memory size. When memory exceeds 1,000K or one million bytes, it is measured in **megabytes**, abbreviated **MB**. A billion bytes of memory, available on some large computers, is called a **gigabyte** or **GB**.

## HOW PROGRAMS AND DATA ARE REPRESENTED IN MEMORY

Program instructions and data are made up of a combination of the three types of characters: alphabetic (A through Z), numeric (0 through 9) and special (all other characters). To understand how program instructions and data are stored in main memory, it is sometimes helpful to think of them as being stored character by character. Generally speaking, when we think of characters being stored in main memory, we think of one character being stored in one memory location or byte. Thus, the name TOM would take three memory locations or bytes because there are three letters in that name. The number $157.50 would take seven memory locations or bytes because there are seven characters (including the $ and .) in the number (Figure 5-4).

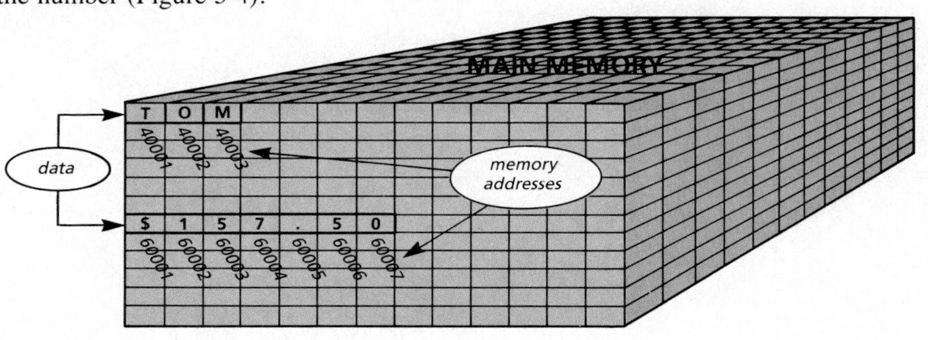


**FIGURE 5-4**
**Each character (alphabetic, numeric, or special) usually requires one memory location (byte) for storage.**

A byte contains eight bits. A **bit** is an element of a byte that can represent only two values. It can either be "off," represented in Figure 5-5 by an open circle, or "on," represented by a filled-in circle. Each alphabetic, numeric, and special character stored in the memory of the computer is represented by a combination of on and off bits. The computer can distinguish between characters because the combination of off and on bits assigned to each character is unique.

A mathematical way of representing the off and on conditions of a bit is to use 0 to represent off and 1 to represent on. The **binary** number system (base 2) represents quantities by using only the two symbols, 0 and 1. For this reason, binary is used to represent the electronic status of the bits inside the processing unit (Figure 5-5). The term bit was derived from the words *b*inary dig*it*.

**FIGURE 5-5**
**A graphic example of an eight-bit byte with two bits on and six bits off. The on bits (filled-in circles) are represented by the binary number 1 and the off bits (open circles) are represented by binary 0. (This combination of bits represents the letter A in ASCII code).**

Two popular codes that use combinations of zeros and ones for representing characters in memory are the ASCII and EBCDIC codes. A chart summarizing these codes is shown in Figure 5-6. Notice how the combination of bits, represented in binary, is unique for each character.

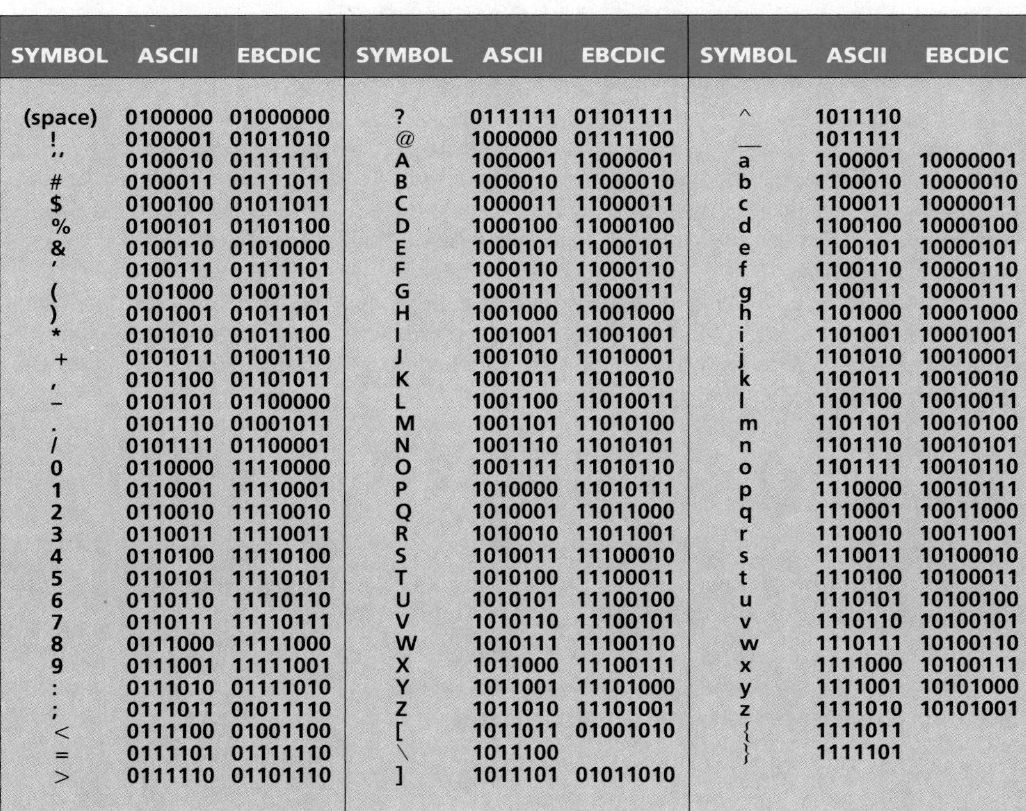

| SYMBOL | ASCII | EBCDIC | SYMBOL | ASCII | EBCDIC | SYMBOL | ASCII | EBCDIC |
|---|---|---|---|---|---|---|---|---|
| (space) | 0100000 | 01000000 | ? | 0111111 | 01101111 | ^ | 1011110 | |
| ! | 0100001 | 01011010 | @ | 1000000 | 01111100 | _ | 1011111 | |
| " | 0100010 | 01111111 | A | 1000001 | 11000001 | a | 1100001 | 10000001 |
| # | 0100011 | 01111011 | B | 1000010 | 11000010 | b | 1100010 | 10000010 |
| $ | 0100100 | 01011011 | C | 1000011 | 11000011 | c | 1100011 | 10000011 |
| % | 0100101 | 01101100 | D | 1000100 | 11000100 | d | 1100100 | 10000100 |
| & | 0100110 | 01010000 | E | 1000101 | 11000101 | e | 1100101 | 10000101 |
| ' | 0100111 | 01111101 | F | 1000110 | 11000110 | f | 1100110 | 10000110 |
| ( | 0101000 | 01001101 | G | 1000111 | 11000111 | g | 1100111 | 10000111 |
| ) | 0101001 | 01011101 | H | 1001000 | 11001000 | h | 1101000 | 10001000 |
| * | 0101010 | 01011100 | I | 1001001 | 11001001 | i | 1101001 | 10001001 |
| + | 0101011 | 01001110 | J | 1001010 | 11010001 | j | 1101010 | 10010001 |
| , | 0101100 | 01101011 | K | 1001011 | 11010010 | k | 1101011 | 10010010 |
| – | 0101101 | 01100000 | L | 1001100 | 11010011 | l | 1101100 | 10010011 |
| . | 0101110 | 01001011 | M | 1001101 | 11010100 | m | 1101101 | 10010100 |
| / | 0101111 | 01100001 | N | 1001110 | 11010101 | n | 1101110 | 10010101 |
| 0 | 0110000 | 11110000 | O | 1001111 | 11010110 | o | 1101111 | 10010110 |
| 1 | 0110001 | 11110001 | P | 1010000 | 11010111 | p | 1110000 | 10010111 |
| 2 | 0110010 | 11110010 | Q | 1010001 | 11011000 | q | 1110001 | 10011000 |
| 3 | 0110011 | 11110011 | R | 1010010 | 11011001 | r | 1110010 | 10011001 |
| 4 | 0110100 | 11110100 | S | 1010011 | 11100010 | s | 1110011 | 10100010 |
| 5 | 0110101 | 11110101 | T | 1010100 | 11100011 | t | 1110100 | 10100011 |
| 6 | 0110110 | 11110110 | U | 1010101 | 11100100 | u | 1110101 | 10100100 |
| 7 | 0110111 | 11110111 | V | 1010110 | 11100101 | v | 1110110 | 10100101 |
| 8 | 0111000 | 11111000 | W | 1010111 | 11100110 | w | 1110111 | 10100110 |
| 9 | 0111001 | 11111001 | X | 1011000 | 11100111 | x | 1111000 | 10100111 |
| : | 0111010 | 01111010 | Y | 1011001 | 11101000 | y | 1111001 | 10101000 |
| ; | 0111011 | 01011110 | Z | 1011010 | 11101001 | z | 1111010 | 10101001 |
| < | 0111100 | 01001100 | [ | 1011011 | 01001010 | { | 1111011 | |
| = | 0111101 | 01111110 | \ | 1011100 | | } | 1111101 | |
| > | 0111110 | 01101110 | ] | 1011101 | 01011010 | | | |

**FIGURE 5-6**
**This chart shows alphabetic, numeric, and special characters as they are represented in the ASCII and EBCDIC codes. Note how each character is represented in binary using zeros and ones.**

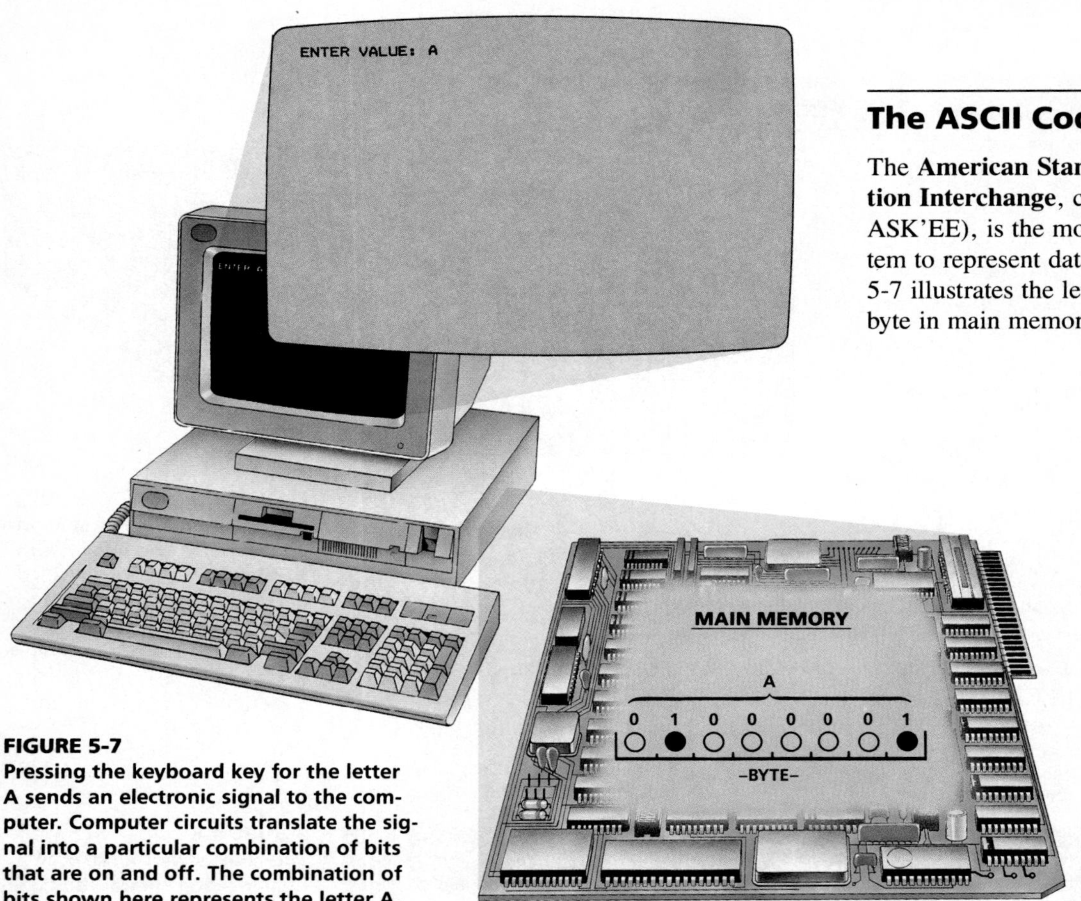


**FIGURE 5-7**
**Pressing the keyboard key for the letter A sends an electronic signal to the computer. Computer circuits translate the signal into a particular combination of bits that are on and off. The combination of bits shown here represents the letter A.**

## The ASCII Code

The **American Standard Code for Information Interchange**, called **ASCII** (pronounced ASK'EE), is the most widely used coding system to represent data. The example in Figure 5-7 illustrates the letter A stored in an eight-bit byte in main memory using the ASCII code.

When you type the letter A on the keyboard, the electronic circuitry of the computer interprets the character and stores it in main memory as a series of on and off bits. In the example, the combination of bits that are on and off represent the letter A in the ASCII code. When the character is displayed on the screen or printed, the ASCII code is translated back into the alphabetic symbol A.

As you can see by looking at the chart in Figure 5-6, the ASCII code uses only the rightmost seven bits of the eight bits in a byte to represent characters. These seven bits provide 128 combinations, enough to represent all the standard characters including numeric, uppercase and lowercase alphabetic, and special.

## The EBCDIC Code

The ASCII code is widely used on personal computers and many minicomputers. Another common coding scheme used primarily on mainframes is called the **Extended Binary Coded Decimal Interchange Code** or **EBCDIC** (pronounced "EB-SEE-DICK").

## Binary Representation of Numbers

When the ASCII or EBCDIC codes are used, each character that is represented is stored in one byte of memory. Note, however, that there are other binary formats of data representation that allow multiple digits to be stored in one byte or memory location.

## PARITY

Regardless of whether ASCII, EBCDIC, or other binary methods are used to represent characters in main memory, it is important that the characters be stored accurately. For each byte of memory, most computers have at least one extra bit, called a **parity bit**, that is used by the computer for error checking. A parity bit can detect if one of the bits in a byte has been inadvertently changed. Such an error could occur because of voltage fluctuations, static electricity, or a memory chip failure.

Computers are either odd or even parity machines. In computers with **odd parity**, the total number of "on" bits in the byte (including the parity bit) must be an odd number (Figure 5-8). In computers with **even parity**, the total number of on bits must be an even number. Parity is checked each time a memory location is used. When data is moved from one location to another in main memory, the parity bits of both the sending and receiving locations are compared to see if they are the same. If the system detects a difference or if the wrong number of bits is on (e.g., an even number in a system with odd parity), an error message displays. Some computers use multiple parity bits that enable them to detect and correct a single bit error and detect multiple bit errors.

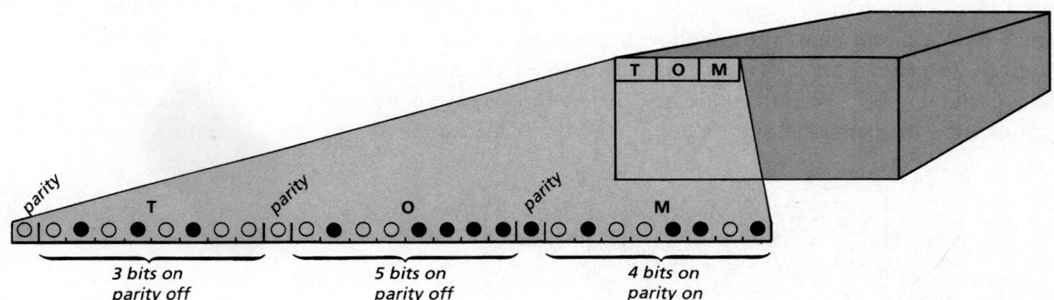


**FIGURE 5-8**
**In a computer with odd parity, the parity bit is turned on or off in order to make the total number of on bits (including the parity bit) an odd number. Here, the letters T and O have an odd number of bits and the parity bit is left off. However, the number of bits for the letter M is even, so in order to achieve odd parity, the parity bit is turned on. Turning on the parity bit makes the total number of bits in the byte an odd number (five).**

## NUMBER SYSTEMS

This section describes the number systems that are used with computers. While thorough knowledge of this subject is required for technical computer personnel, a general understanding of number systems and how they relate to computers is all most users need.

As you have seen, the binary (base 2) number system is used to represent the electronic status of the bits in main memory. It is also used for other purposes, such as addressing the memory locations. Another number system that is commonly used with computers is **hexadecimal** (base 16). Figure 5-9 shows how the decimal values 0 through 15 are represented in binary and hexadecimal.

| DECIMAL | BINARY | HEXADECIMAL |
|---|---|---|
| 0 | 0000 | 0 |
| 1 | 0001 | 1 |
| 2 | 0010 | 2 |
| 3 | 0011 | 3 |
| 4 | 0100 | 4 |
| 5 | 0101 | 5 |
| 6 | 0110 | 6 |
| 7 | 0111 | 7 |
| 8 | 1000 | 8 |
| 9 | 1001 | 9 |
| 10 | 1010 | A |
| 11 | 1011 | B |
| 12 | 1100 | C |
| 13 | 1101 | D |
| 14 | 1110 | E |
| 15 | 1111 | F |

**FIGURE 5-9**
**The chart shows the binary and hexadecimal representation of decimal numbers 0 through 15. Note how letters represent the numbers 10 through 15.**

The mathematical principles that apply to the binary and hexadecimal number systems are the same as those that apply to the decimal number system. To help you better understand these principles we will start with the familiar decimal system, then progress to the binary and hexadecimal number systems.

## The Decimal Number System

The decimal number system is a base 10 number system (note that "deci" means 10). The *base* of a number system indicates how many symbols are used in it. Decimal uses the 10 symbols 0 through 9. Each of the symbols in the number system has a value associated with it. For example, you know that 3 represents a quantity of three and 5 represents a quantity of five. The decimal number system is also a positional number system. This means that in a number such as 143, each position in the number has a value associated with it. When you look at the decimal number 143, you know that the 3 is in the ones, or units, position and represents three ones or (3 × 1); the 4 is in the tens position and represents four tens or (4 × 10); and the 1 is in the hundreds position and represents one hundred or (1 × 100). The number 143 is the sum of the values in each position of the number (100 + 40 + 3 = 143). Figure 5-10 is a power chart showing how the positional values (hundreds, tens, and units) for a number system can be calculated. Starting on the right and working to the left, we raise the base of the number system, in this case 10, to consecutive powers ($10^2$ $10^1$ $10^0$). These calculations are a mathematical way of computing the place values in a number system.

**FIGURE 5-10**
**This chart shows the positional values in the decimal number 143.**

| power of 10 | $10^2$ | $10^1$ | $10^0$ |
|---|---|---|---|
| positional value | 100 | 10 | 1 |
| number | 1 | 4 | 3 |

$$(1 \times 100) + (4 \times 10) + (3 \times 1) = 100 + 40 + 3 = 143$$

When you use number systems other than decimal, the same principles apply. The base of the number system indicates the number of symbols that are used and each position in a number system has a value associated with it. The positional value can be calculated by raising the base of the number system to consecutive powers.

## The Binary Number System

As we have discussed, binary is a base 2 number system ("bi" means two), and the symbols that are used are 0 and 1. Just as each position in a decimal number has a place value associated with it, so does each position in a binary number. In binary, the place values are successive powers of two (such as $2^3$ $2^2$ $2^1$ $2^0$) or (8 4 2 1). To construct a binary number, ones are placed in the positions where the corresponding values add up to the quantity that is to be represented and zeros are placed in the other positions. For example, the binary place values are (8 4 2 1) and the binary number 1001 has ones in the positions for the values 8 and 1 and zeros in the positions for 4 and 2. Therefore, the quantity represented by 1001 is 9 (8 + 0 + 0 + 1) (Figure 5-11).

| power of 2 | $2^3$ | $2^2$ | $2^1$ | $2^0$ |
|---|---|---|---|---|
| positional value | 8 | 4 | 2 | 1 |
| binary | 1 | 0 | 0 | 1 |

$$(1 \times 8) + (0 \times 4) + (0 \times 2) + (1 \times 1) =$$
$$8 + 0 + 0 + 1 = 9$$

**FIGURE 5-11**
This chart shows how to convert the binary number 1001 to the decimal number 9. Each place in the binary number represents a successive power of 2.

## The Hexadecimal Number System

Many computers use a base 16 number system called hexadecimal. The hexadecimal number system uses 16 symbols to represent values. These include the symbols 0 through 9 and A through F (Figure 5-9). The mathematical principles previously discussed also apply to hexadecimal (Figure 5-12).

| power of 16 | $16^1$ | $16^0$ |
|---|---|---|
| positional value | 16 | 1 |
| hexadecimal | A(10) | 5 |

$$(10 \times 16) + (5 \times 1) =$$
$$160 + 5 = 165$$

**FIGURE 5-12**
This chart shows how the hexadecimal number A5 is converted into the decimal number 165. Note that the value 10 is substituted for the A during computations.

The primary reason why the hexadecimal number system is used with computers is because it can represent binary values in a more compact form and because the conversion between the binary and the hexadecimal number systems is very efficient. An eight-digit binary number can be represented by a two-digit hexadecimal number. For example, in the EBCDIC code (used by some computers to represent data), the decimal number 5 is represented as 11110101. This value can be represented in hexadecimal as F5.

One way to convert a binary number to a hexadecimal number is to divide the binary number (from right to left) into groups of four digits; calculate the value of each group; and then change any two-digit values (10 through 15) into the symbols A through F that are used in hexadecimal (Figure 5-13).

## Summary of Number Systems

As mentioned at the beginning of the section on number systems, binary and hexadecimal are used primarily by technical computer personnel. For the general user, a complete understanding of numbering systems is not required. The concepts that you should remember about number systems are that binary is used for purposes such as representing the electronic status of the bits in main memory and also for memory addresses. Hexadecimal is used to represent binary in a more compact form.

| positional value | 8421 | 8421 |
|---|---|---|
| binary | 1111 | 0101 |
| decimal | 15 | 5 |
| hexadecimal | F | 5 |

**FIGURE 5-13**
This chart shows how the EBCDIC code 11110101 for the value 5 is converted into the hexadecimal value F5.

# HOW THE PROCESSOR UNIT EXECUTES PROGRAMS AND MANIPULATES DATA

The program instructions that users write are usually in a form similar to English. Before these instructions can be executed, they must be translated by the computer into a form called machine language instructions. A **machine language instruction** is one that the electronic circuits in the CPU can interpret and convert into one or more of the commands in the computer's instruction set. The **instruction set** contains the commands such as add or move that the computer's circuits can directly perform. To help you understand how the processor unit works, let's look at an example of a machine language instruction.

## Machine Language Instructions

A machine language instruction is usually composed of three parts: an operation code; values indicating the number of characters to be processed by the instruction; and the addresses in main memory of the data to be used in the execution of the instruction (Figure 5-14).

**FIGURE 5-14**
**A machine language instruction consists of an operation code, the lengths of the fields to be processed, and the main memory addresses of the fields.**



The **operation code** is a unique value that is typically stored in the first byte in the instruction. This unique value indicates what operation is to be performed. For example, the letter A stored as the operation code might indicate that an *add*ition operation is to occur. The letter M might mean that a *move* operation is to take place.

The number of characters to be processed is included in the machine language instruction so that the CPU will manipulate the proper number of bytes. For example, if a four-digit field were to be added to another four-digit field, the number of characters specified in the instruction for each field would be four.

The main memory addresses of the fields involved in the operation are also specified in the instruction. This specification of the main memory address enables the CPU to locate where in main memory the data to be processed is stored.

The illustration in Figure 5-15 shows the steps involved in executing a computer instruction. The instruction A44 7000 9000 indicates that the four-digit fields that begin in locations 7000 and 9000 are to be added together. When this instruction is executed, the following steps occur:

1. The instruction is fetched from main memory and placed in an instruction register. An **instruction register** is an area of memory within the control unit of the CPU that can store a single instruction at a time.
2. After the control unit decodes the instruction, it fetches the data specified at the two addresses in the instruction from main memory.
3. The arithmetic/logic unit executes the instruction by adding the two numbers.
4. The control unit then stores the result of the processing by moving the sum to main memory.

This basic sequence of fetch the instruction, decode the instruction, execute the instruction, and store the results is the way most computers process instructions.

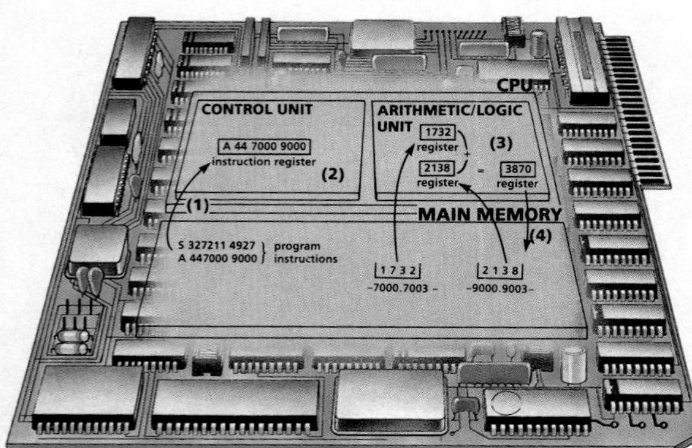


**FIGURE 5-15**
**Executing a program instruction**

## The Machine Cycle

The four steps illustrated above, fetch, decode, execute, and store, are called the **machine cycle**. As shown in Figure 5-16, the machine cycle is made up of the instruction cycle and the execution cycle. The **instruction cycle** refers to the fetching of the next program instruction and the decoding of that instruction. The **execution cycle** includes the execution of the instruction and the storage of the processing results. When the computer is again ready to fetch the next program instruction, one machine cycle is completed.

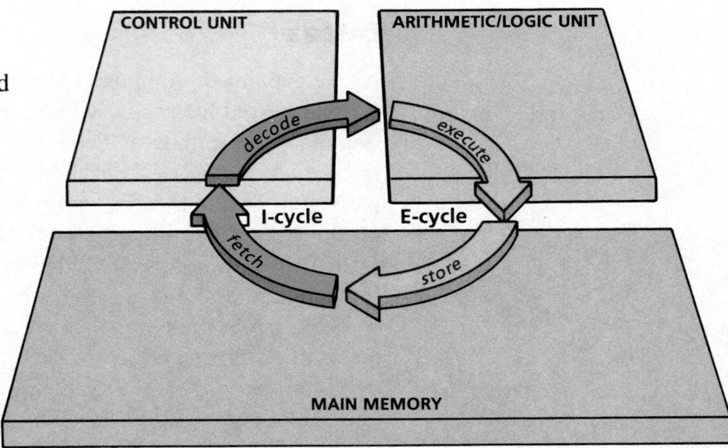


**FIGURE 5-16**
**The machine cycle consists of four steps: fetching the next instruction, decoding the instruction, executing the instruction, and storing the result. Fetching and decoding are considered part of the instruction or I cycle. Executing and storing are considered part of the execution or E cycle.**

# PROCESSOR SPEEDS

Although the machine cycle may appear to be cumbersome and time consuming, computers can perform millions of machine cycles in one second. In fact, the processing speed of computers is often compared in **MIPS**—million instructions per second. A computer with a rating of 1 MIPS could process one million instructions per second. The most powerful personal computers today are rated at between 3 and 4 MIPS. Larger computers can process 75 to 100 MIPS and supercomputers are capable of over 200 MIPS.

The speed in which a computer can execute the machine cycle is influenced by three factors: the system clock, the buses, and the word size (Figure 5-17).

| FACTOR | AFFECT ON SPEED |
|---|---|
| System clock | The clock generates electronic pulses used to synchronize processing. Faster clock speed results in more operations in a given amount of time. |
| Bus width | Bus width determines how much data can be transferred at any one time. A 32-bit bus can transfer twice as much data at one time as a 16-bit bus. |
| Word size | Word size is the number of bits that can be manipulated at any one time. A computer with a 32-bit word size can manipulate twice as much data at one time as a system with a 16-bit word size. |

**FIGURE 5-17**
**Factors affecting computer speed.**

## System Clock

The control unit utilizes the **system clock** to synchronize, or control the timing, of all computer operations. The system clock generates electronic pulses at a fixed rate, measured in **megahertz**. One megahertz equals one million pulses, or cycles, per second. The speed of the system clock varies among computers. Some personal computers can operate at speeds in excess of 30 megahertz.

## Buses

As we explained, computers store and process data as a series of electronic bits. These bits are transferred internally within the circuitry of the computer along paths capable of transmitting electrical impulses. The bits must be transferred from input devices to memory, from memory to the CPU, from the CPU to memory, and from memory to output devices. Any path along which bits are transmitted is called a **bus** or **data bus**. Buses can transfer eight, 16, or 32 bits at a time. An eight-bit bus has eight lines and can transmit eight bits at a time. On a 16-bit bus, bits can be moved from place to place 16 bits at a time and on a 32-bit bus, bits are moved 32 bits at a time.

The larger the number of bits that are handled by a bus, the faster the computer can transfer data. For example, assume a number in memory occupies four eight-bit bytes. With an eight-bit bus four steps would be required to transfer the data from memory to the CPU because on the eight-bit data bus, the data in each eight-bit byte would be transferred in an individual step. A 16-bit bus has 16 lines in the data bus, so only two transfers would be necessary to move the data in four bytes. And on a 32-bit bus, the entire four bytes could be transferred at one time. The fewer number of transfer steps required, the faster the transfer of the data occurs.

## Word Size

Another factor that affects the speed of a computer is the word size. The **word size** is the number of bits that the CPU can process at one time, as opposed to the bus size, which is the number of bits the computer can transmit at one time. Like data buses, the word size of a machine is measured in bit sizes. Processors can have eight-, 16-, 32-, or 64-bit word sizes. A processor with an eight-bit word size can manipulate eight bits at a time. If two four-digit numbers are to be added in the ALU of an eight-bit processor, it will take four operations because a separate operation will be required to add each of the four digits. With a 16-bit processor, the addition will take two operations and with a 32-bit processor, only one operation would be required to add the numbers together. Sometimes the word size of a computer is given in bytes instead of bits. For example, a word size of 16 bits may be expressed as a word size of two bytes because there are eight bits in a byte. The larger the word size of the processor, the faster the computer is able to process data.

In summary, the speed of a computer is influenced by the system clock, the size of the buses, and the word size. When you purchase a computer, the speed requirements you want should be based on your intended use of the computer. Eight-bit computers may be useful and fast enough for personal and educational applications. Sixteen-bit computers are widely used today for applications such as word processing, electronic spreadsheets, or database. Thirty-two-bit computers are considered very powerful and are useful for multiuser systems and applications that require complex and time-consuming calculations, such as graphics. A few personal computers, many minicomputers, and most mainframes are 32-bit computers. Most supercomputers are 64-bit computers.

# ARCHITECTURE OF PROCESSOR UNITS

The processor unit of a computer can be designed and built in many different ways. For example, the processor for a personal computer may be housed on a single printed circuit board while a larger machine may require a number of circuit boards for the CPU, main memory, and the related electronic circuitry.

## Microprocessors

The smallest processor, called a **microprocessor** (Figure 5-18), is a single integrated circuit that contains the CPU and sometimes memory. An **integrated circuit**, also called an **IC**, **chip**, or **microchip**, is a complete electronic circuit that has been etched on a small chip of nonconducting material such as silicon. Microcomputers are built using microprocessors for their CPU. Figure 5-19 lists some of the microprocessors commonly used in personal computers today.

**FIGURE 5-18 ►**
**The Intel 80386 microprocessor has a word size and bus width of 32 bits and can operate at between 16 and 32 megahertz.**

**FIGURE 5-19**
**A comparison of some of the more widely used microprocessor chips. ▼**

| MICROPROCESSOR | MANUFACTURER | WORD SIZE (BITS) | I/O BUS WIDTH (BITS) | CLOCK SPEED MHz) | MICROCOMPUTERS USING THIS CHIP |
|---|---|---|---|---|---|
| 6502 | MOS Technology | 8 | 8 | 4 | Apple IIe<br>Atari 800 |
| 8088 | Intel | 16 | 8 | 8 | IBM PC and XT<br>HP 150<br>Compaq Portable |
| 8086 | Intel | 16 | 16 | 8 | Compaq Deskpro<br>Many IBM compatibles |
| 80286 | Intel | 16 | 16 | 8–12 | IBM PC/AT<br>IBM PS/2 model 50<br>Compaq Deskpro 286 |
| 68000 | Motorola | 32 | 16 | 12.5 | Apple Macintosh SE and<br>Commodore Amiga |
| 68020 | Motorola | 32 | 32 | 12.5–32 | Apple Macintosh II |
| 80386 | Intel | 32 | 32 | 16–32 | Compaq Deskpro 386<br>IBM PS/2 model 80 |

## Coprocessors

One way computers can increase their productivity is through the use of a **coprocessor**, a special microprocessor chip or circuit board designed to perform a specific task. For example, math coprocessors are commonly added to computers to greatly speed up the processing of numeric calculations. Other types of coprocessors extend the capability of a computer by increasing the amount of software that will run on the computer.

## Parallel Processing

Most computers contain one central processing unit (CPU) that processes a single instruction at a time. When one instruction is finished, the CPU begins execution of the next instruction, and so on until the program is completed. This method is known as **serial processing**. **Parallel processing** involves the use of multiple CPUs, each with their own memory. Parallel processors divide up a problem so that multiple CPUs can work on their assigned portion of the problem simultaneously. As you might expect, parallel processors require special software that can recognize how to divide up problems and bring the results back together again.

## RISC Technology

As computers have evolved, more and more commands have been added to hardware instruction sets. In recent years, however, computer designers have reevaluated the need for so many instructions and have developed systems based on RISC technology. **RISC**, which stands for reduced instruction set computing (or computers), involves reducing the instructions to only those that are most frequently used. Without the burden of the occasionally used instructions, the most frequently used instructions operate faster and overall processing capability or *throughput* of the system is increased.

In summary, you can see that there are many different types of processor architecture that are used on computers. Regardless of the architecture used, the important concept to remember is that the processor units on all computers perform essentially the same functions.

**FIGURE 5-20**
**This photograph illustrates 32 transistors on an NCR semiconductor chip that is used for computer memory. The transistors are enlarged 600 times their actual size.**

# TYPES OF MEMORY

As we noted, electronic components are used to store data in computer memory. The actual materials and devices used for memory have changed throughout the years. The first device used for storing data was the vacuum tube. After the vacuum tube, core memory was used. **Core memory** consisted of small, ring-shaped pieces of material that could be magnetized, or polarized, in one of two directions. The polarity indicated whether the core was on or off. Today, semiconductor memory is used in virtually all computers (Figure 5-20). **Semiconductor memory** is an integrated circuit containing thousands of transistors. A **transistor** is an electronic component that can be either on or off and represents a bit in memory.

When core memory was used as main memory, the time required to access data stored in the memory was measured in **microseconds** (millionths of a second). Access to data stored in semiconductor memory is measured in **nanoseconds** (billionths of a second). In addition, the cost of semiconductor memory is just a fraction of the cost for core memory. Today you can buy 64K of semiconductor memory for about $30, whereas 64K of core memory once cost as much as $15,000. Figure 5-21 shows how the storage capacity of semiconductor memory has increased over recent years, while the cost of semiconductor memory has decreased. The trend is expected to continue. It has been predicted that by the end of the century it will be possible to store over a billion components on a chip.

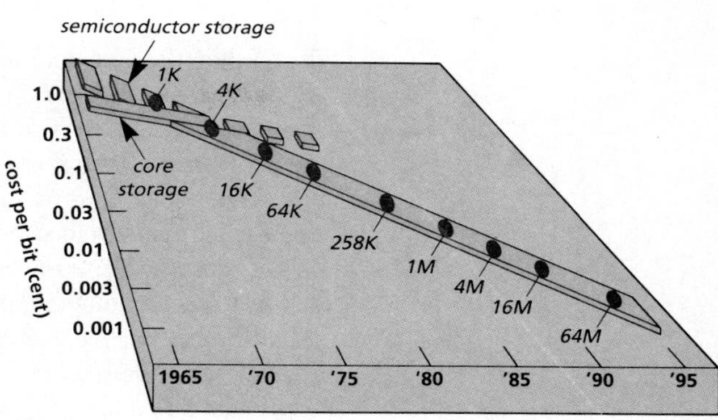


**FIGURE 5-21**
**The chart shows the declining cost and increased storage capacity of semiconductor storage.**

As you can see, semiconductor memory is compact, fast, and inexpensive. Several different types of semiconductor memory chips are used in computers. They are RAM, ROM, PROM, EPROM, and EEPROM chips.

## RAM Memory

**Random access memory**, or **RAM**, is the name given to the integrated circuits or chips that are used for main memory. It is the type of memory that we have discussed so far in this chapter. Data and programs are transferred into and out of RAM and data stored in RAM is manipulated by computer program instructions.

There are two types of RAM memory chips: dynamic RAM and static RAM. **Dynamic RAM** chips are smaller and simpler in design than static RAM chips. With dynamic RAM the current or charge on the chip is periodically refreshed or regenerated by special regenerator circuits in order for the chip to retain the stored data. **Static RAM** chips are larger and more complicated than dynamic RAM and do not require the current to be periodically regenerated. The main memory of most computers uses dynamic RAM chips.

The example in Figure 5-22 illustrates the processing that could occur as a series of area codes are entered into RAM (computer memory) from a terminal. The first area code, 212, is entered from the keyboard and stored at memory locations 66000, 66001, and 66002. Once in memory, this field can be processed as required.

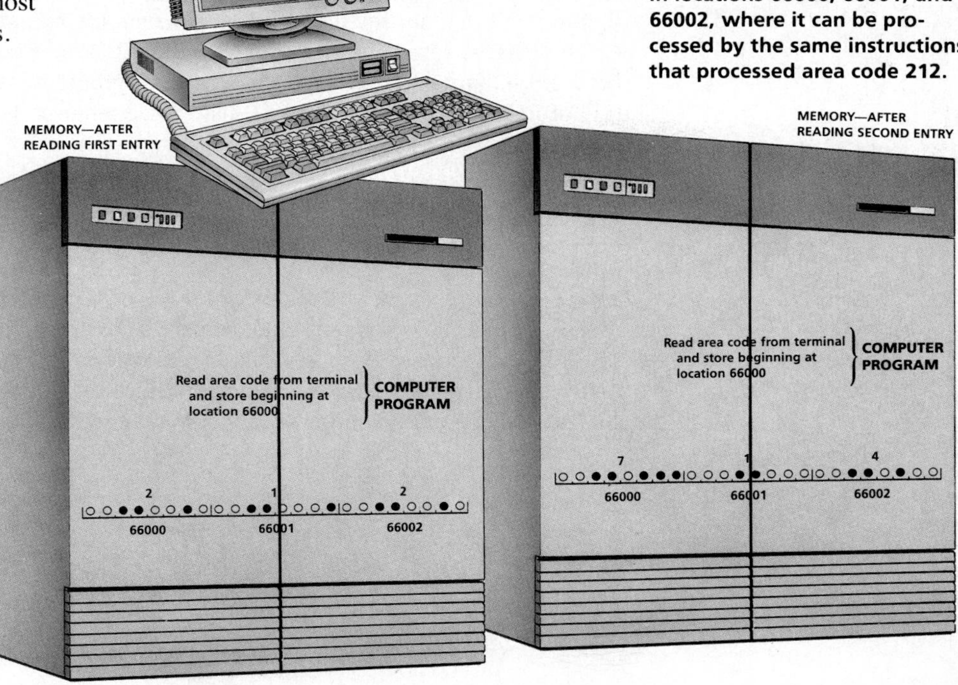


**FIGURE 5-22**
**The instruction in the program specifies that the area code is to be read into adjacent memory locations beginning with location 66000. After the data is placed in these locations, it can be processed by the program. When the same instruction is executed the second time, the value 714 entered by the terminal operator is stored in locations 66000, 66001, and 66002, where it can be processed by the same instructions that processed area code 212.**

When the instruction to read (input) data into memory from the keyboard is executed again, the second area code entered from the keyboard, area code 714, would replace the previous value (212) at locations 66000, 66001, and 66002 in memory. Area code 714 could then be processed by the same instructions that processed area code 212.

When data is moved from one location to another in main memory, the data at the receiving location is replaced by the new data. The data in the sending location remains intact. Data is not removed from one location and placed in another location. Instead, the data remains in the sending location and a copy of the data is transferred to and stored in the new location.

Another aspect of RAM memory is that it is said to be **volatile** because the programs and data stored in RAM are erased when the power to the computer is turned off. Auxiliary storage is used to store programs or data that may be needed for future use.

## ROM Memory

**ROM** stands for **read only memory**. With ROM, data is permanently recorded in the memory when it is manufactured. ROM memory retains its contents even when the power is off. The data or programs that are stored in ROM can be read and used, but cannot be altered, hence the name "read only." ROM is used to store items such as the instruction set of the computer. In addition, many of the special purpose computers used in automobiles, appliances, and so on use small amounts of ROM to store instructions that will be executed repeatedly. Instructions that are stored in ROM memory are called **firmware** or **microcode**.

## Other Types of Memory

**PROM** means **programmable read only memory**. PROM acts the same as ROM when it is part of the computer; that is, it can only be read and its contents cannot be altered. With PROM, however, the data or programs are not stored in the memory when they are manufactured. Instead, PROM can be loaded with specially selected data or programs prior to installing it in a computer. A variation of PROM is **EPROM** (pronounced "EE-PROM"), which means **erasable programmable read only memory**. In addition to being used in the same way as PROM, EPROM allows the user to erase the data stored in the memory and to store new data or programs in the memory. EPROM is erased through the use of special ultraviolet light devices that destroy the bit settings within the memory.

**EEPROM** (pronounced "double-E-PROM"), or **electronically erasable programmable read only memory**, allows the stored data or programs to be erased electrically. The advantage of EEPROM is that it does not have to be removed from the computer to be changed.

# SUMMARY

In this chapter we examined various aspects of the processor unit including its components, how programs and data are stored, and how the processor executes program instructions to process data into information. While a detailed understanding of this material is not a prerequisite for computer literacy, understanding these principles will increase your overall comprehension of how processing occurs on a computer.

# Making a Chip

A chip is made by building layers of electronic pathways and connections by using conducting and nonconducting materials on a surface of silicon. The combination of these materials into specific patterns forms microscopic electronic components such as transistors, diodes, and capacitors that make up the integrated chip circuit. The application of the materials to the silicon is done through a series of technically sophisticated chemical and photographic processes. The following photographs illustrate some of the manufacturing steps.

1

A chip begins with a design developed by an engineer using a computer aided circuit design program. Some circuits only take a month or two to design whereas others may take a year or more. The computer aided design system (1) allows the engineer to rearrange the design of the circuit pathways and then see them displayed on the screen. Most chips have at least four to six layers but some have up to fifteen. A separate design is required for each layer of the chip circuit. To better review the design, greatly enlarged printouts are prepared (2). After the design is finalized, a glass photo mask is prepared for each layer (3). To provide for mass production of the chips, the design is reduced to the actual size of the circuit, approximately 1/4-inch square, and duplicated over one hundred times on the surface of the photo mask. In a process similar to printing a picture from a negative, the photo mask will be used to project the circuit design onto the material used to make the chips.

2

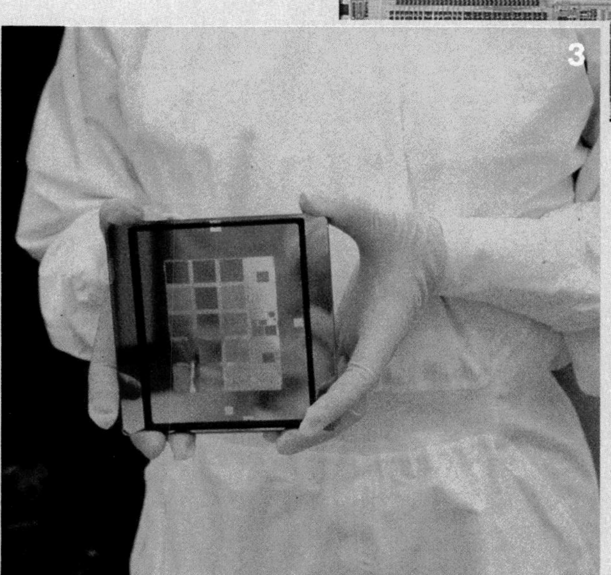

3

Although other materials can be used, the most common raw material used to make chips is silicon crystals (4) that have been refined from quartz rocks. The silicon crystals are melted and "grown" into a cylinder, called an ingot, two to three feet long and six inches in diameter (5). After being smoothed, the silicon ingot is sliced into wafers four to six inches in diameter and 4/1000 of an inch thick. Much of the chip manufacturing process is performed in special laboratories called "clean rooms." Because even the smallest particle of dust can ruin a chip, rooms are kept 1000 times cleaner than a hospital operating room. People who work in these facilities must wear special protective clothing called "bunny suits" (6). After the wafer has been polished and sterilized, it is placed in a diffusion oven where the first layer of material is added to the wafer surface (7). These layers of materials will be etched away to form the circuits. Before etching, a soft, gelatin-like emulsion called photoresist is added to the wafer. During lithography (8), the photoresist is covered by a photo mask and exposed to ultraviolet light. The exposed photoresist becomes hard and the covered photoresist remains soft. The soft photoresist and some of the surface materials are etched away with chemicals or hot gases leaving what will become the circuit pathways. In some facilities, the etching process is done by a robot (9).

4

5

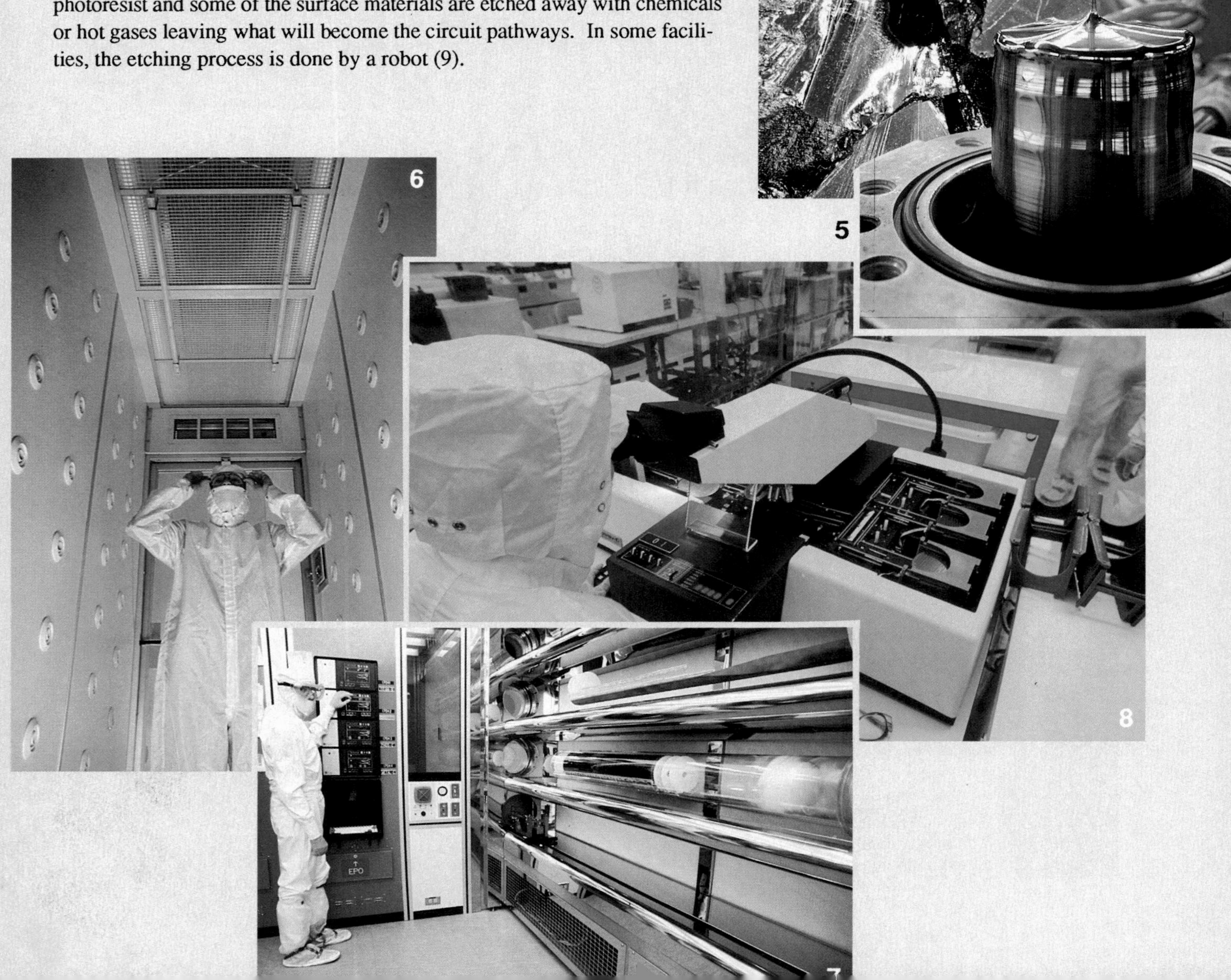

The process of adding material and photoresist to the wafer, exposing it to ultraviolet light, and etching away the unexposed surface, is repeated using a different photo mask for each layer of the circuit. After the circuits are tested on the wafer, they are cut into individual die by the use of a diamond saw (10) or a laser. The individual chip die (11), approximately 1/4-inch square, are packaged in a hard plastic case (12) that contains pins that connect the chip to a socket on a circuit board (13).

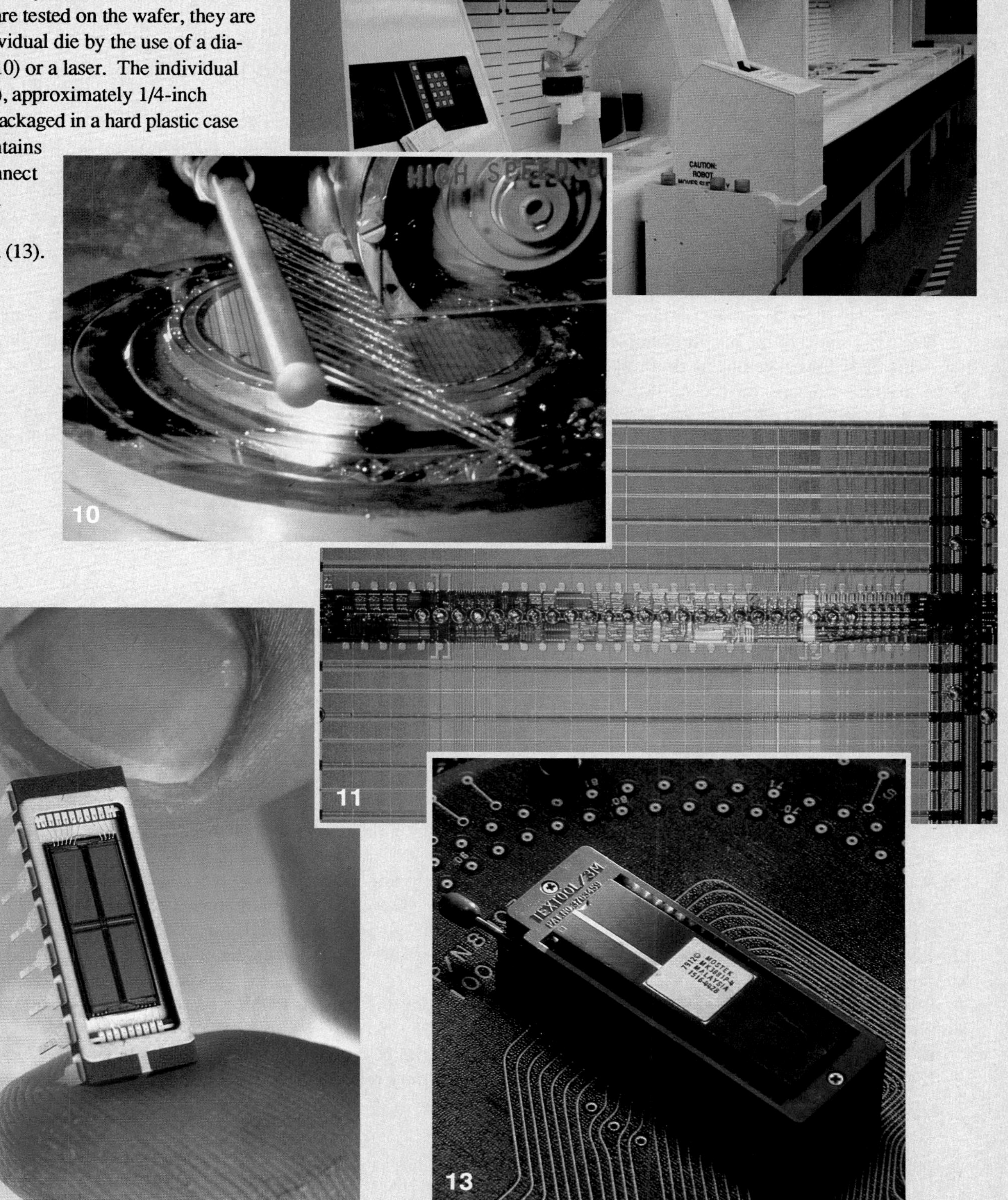

## CHAPTER SUMMARY

1. The central processing unit and the main memory are contained in the processor unit.
2. The central processing unit or CPU contains the **control unit** and the **arithmetic/logic unit**. The control unit directs and coordinates all the activities on the computer. The arithmetic/logic unit performs arithmetic and logic operations.
3. The **main memory**, also called **primary storage** stores programs and data.
4. Each storage location in main memory is called a **byte** and is identified by a **memory address**.
5. The size of main memory is normally expressed in terms of **kilobytes** (approximately 1,000 bytes) of storage. A machine with 640K has approximately 640,000 memory locations.
6. A byte consists of eight **bits**. A bit can represent only two values—off and on.
7. When a letter is entered into main memory from a keyboard, the electronic circuitry interprets the character and stores the character in memory as a series of on and off bits. The computer can distinguish between characters because the combination of off and on bits assigned to each character is unique.
8. One of the most widely used codes to represent characters is the **American Standard Code for Information Interchange**, called the **ASCII code**.
9. A code used for mainframes is the **Extended Binary Coded Decimal Interchange Code (EBCDIC)**.
10. Most computers use **parity bits** for error checking.
11. The **binary** (base 2) number system is used by the computer for purposes such as memory addresses and representing the electronic status of the bits in main memory. **Hexadecimal** (base 16) is used to represent binary in a more compact form.
12. A **machine language instruction** can be decoded and executed by the CPU.
13. A machine language instruction is usually composed of an **operation code**; values indicating the number of characters to be processed; and main memory addresses of the data to be processed.
14. Steps in the **machine cycle** consist of: fetch the next instruction; decode the instruction; execute the instruction; store the results.
15. The speed of a computer is influenced by the system clock, the bus size, and the word size.
16. The **system clock** is used by the control unit to synchronize all computer operations.
17. A **bus** is any line that transmits bits between memory and the input/output devices, and between memory and the CPU.
18. The number of bits that the CPU can process at one time is called the **word size**.
19. Computers can be eight-bit, 16-bit, 32-bit, or 64-bit machines.
20. **Microprocessors** are used for the CPU in microcomputers.
21. **Coprocessors** can be used to enhance and expand the capabilities of a computer.
22. Parallel processors divide up a problem so that multiple CPUs can work on their assigned portion of the problem simultaneously.
23. **RISC** technology involves reducing a computer's instruction set to only those instructions that are most frequently used.
24. **Core memory** consisted of small, ring-shaped pieces of material that could be magnetized, or polarized, in one of two directions.
25. **Semiconductor memory** is now used in most computers. It consists of transistors etched into a semiconductor material such as silicon.
26. A **microsecond** is a millionth of a second. A **nanosecond** is a billionth of a second. Access to data stored in semiconductor memory is measured in nanoseconds.
27. **RAM**, which stands for **random access memory**, is used for main memory.
28. Once a character is stored at a location in RAM memory, it will remain there until another character is placed into the same location. When the electrical power supply is turned off, all programs and data in RAM are erased.
29. **ROM** stands for **read only memory**. Data or programs are stored in ROM when the memory is manufactured, and they cannot be altered.
30. **PROM** means **programmable read only memory**. PROM acts the same as ROM except data can be stored into the PROM memory prior to being installed in the computer.
31. **EPROM**, or **erasable programmable read only memory**, can be erased through the use of special ultraviolet devices.
32. **EEPROM** or **electronically erasable programmable read only memory**, can be electronically erased without being removed from the computer.

## KEY TERMS

American Standard Code for Information Interchange (ASCII) *5.6*
Arithmetic/logic unit *5.3*
ASCII code *5.6*
Binary *5.5*
Bit *5.5*
Bus *5.12*
Byte *5.4*
Chip *5.13*
Control unit *5.3*
Coprocessor *5.14*
Core memory *5.14*
Data bus *5.12*
Decoding *5.3*
Dynamic RAM *5.15*
EBCDIC *5.6*
EEPROM *5.16*
Electronically erasable programmable read only memory (EEPROM) *5.16*
EPROM *5.16*
Erasable programmable read only memory (EPROM) *5.16*
Even parity *5.7*
Executing *5.3*
Execution cycle *5.11*
Extended Binary Coded Decimal Interchange Code (EBCDIC) *5.6*
Fetching *5.3*
Firmware *5.16*
GB *5.4*
Gigabyte (GB) *5.4*
Hexadecimal *5.7*
IC *5.13*
Instruction cycle *5.11*
Instruction register *5.10*
Instruction set *5.10*
Integrated circuit (IC) *5.13*
K *5.4*
KB *5.4*
Kilobyte (K or KB) *5.4*
Machine cycle *5.11*
Machine language instruction *5.10*
Main memory *5.3*
MB *5.4*
Megabyte (MB) *5.4*
Megahertz *5.11*
Memory address *5.4*
Microchip *5.13*
Microcode *5.16*
Microprocessor *5.13*
Microsecond *5.15*
MIPS *5.11*
Nanoseconds *5.15*
Odd parity *5.7*
Operation code *5.10*
Parallel processing *5.14*
Parity bit *5.7*
Primary storage *5.3*
Programmable read only memory (PROM) *5.16*
PROM *5.16*
RAM *5.15*
Random access memory (RAM) *5.15*
Read only memory (ROM) *5.16*
RISC (reduced instruction set computing) *5.14*
ROM *5.16*
Semiconductor memory *5.14*
Serial processing *5.14*
Static RAM *5.15*
Storing *5.3*
System clock *5.11*
Transistor *5.14*
Volatile *5.16*
Word size *5.12*

## REVIEW QUESTIONS

1. Identify the two components of the central processing unit and describe the functions of each.
2. Define the terms bit and byte. Illustrate how the number 14 is represented in binary, hexadecimal, ASCII, and EBCDIC.
3. What does the letter K stand for when referring to main memory?
4. Describe how a group of characters entered into the computer as a field are stored in main memory. Draw a diagram to illustrate how the letters in your first name would be stored using the ASCII code. Begin at main memory address 45663.
5. What is parity and how is it used?
6. What are the two number systems that are used with computers? Why are they used?
7. What are the components of a machine language instruction? Describe the steps that occur in main memory and the CPU when two numbers are added together.
8. What are the three factors that influence the speed of a processor?
9. What is a microprocessor and how is it used?
10. Define each of the following terms: RAM, ROM, PROM, EPROM, EEPROM.
11. Describe the process of manufacturing integrated circuits.

## CONTROVERSIAL ISSUES

1. The lower cost of producing electronic components outside the United States has caused many U.S. companies to become involved in offshore manufacturing. In addition, the importation of computer goods from foreign manufacturers has affected the computer industry in this country. Discuss whether restrictions should be placed on integrated circuits and other computer goods that are imported or manufactured offshore.
2. All microcomputers are not compatible. For example, unless special enhancements are made, software that is written for an IBM personal computer system will not run on an Apple Macintosh computer. Some people feel that industry standards should be set to eliminate the problems caused by incompatibility. Others feel that standards would restrict competition and product development. Write a paper to discuss your opinions on this topic.

## RESEARCH PROJECTS

1. Many different types of devices and methods have been used for main memory. Research the history of main computer memory and prepare a report. Include information on the way the data was stored, the speed of the memory, any limitations of the method, the amount of memory that could be used, and the cost of the memory.
2. The semiconductor industry is very competitive. It develops both the microprocessors and the memory chips used in most computers today. Not only is the industry competitive in the United States, but significant competition is also generated by foreign manufacturers. Prepare a report on the industry as it is today, and include an analysis of its stance with respect to foreign competition.

# CHAPTER 6

# Output from the Computer

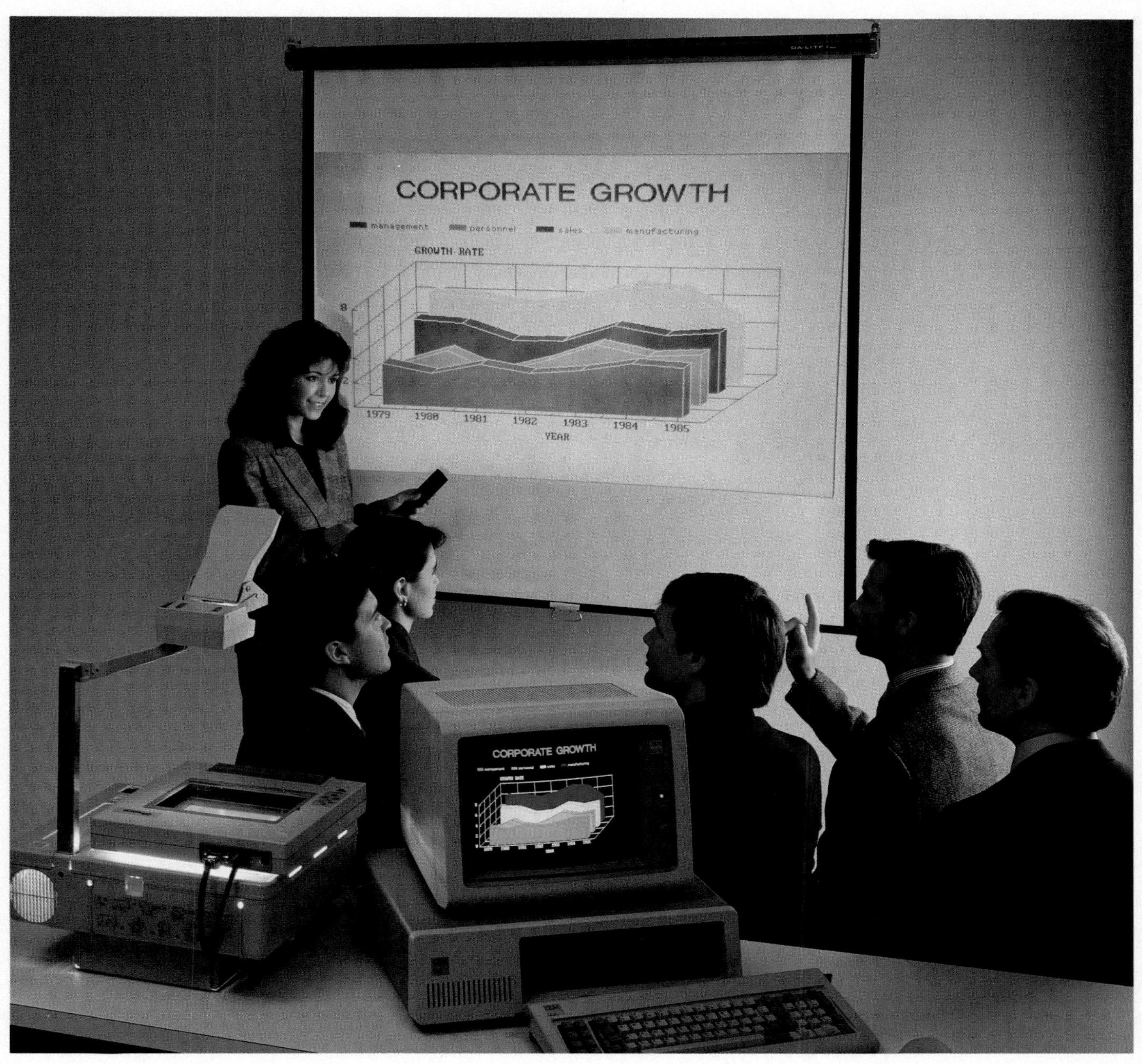

CHAPTER 6

# Output from the Computer

## OBJECTIVES

- Define the term output.
- List the common types of reports and graphs that are used for output.
- Describe the classifications of printers.
- List the types of printers used with personal computers and describe how they work.
- Discuss the quality of output obtainable from various types of printers.
- Describe printers used for large computers.
- Describe the types of screens available and list common screen features.
- List and describe other types of output devices used with computers.

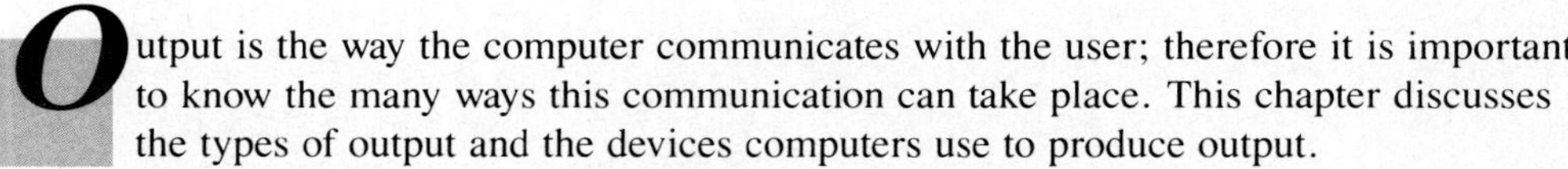

Output is the way the computer communicates with the user; therefore it is important to know the many ways this communication can take place. This chapter discusses the types of output and the devices computers use to produce output.

## WHAT IS OUTPUT?

**Output** is data that has been processed into a useful form called information that can be used by a person or a machine. Output that is used by a machine, such as a disk or tape file, is usually an intermediate result that eventually will be processed into output that can be used by people. Computer output exists in a variety of forms.

## COMMON TYPES OF OUTPUT

The type of output generated from the computer depends on the needs of the user and the hardware and software that are used. The two most common types of output are reports and graphics. These types of output may be printed on a printer or displayed on a screen. Output that is printed is called **hard copy** and output that is displayed is called **soft copy** (Figure 6-1).

## Reports

A **report** is data or information presented in an organized form. Most people think of reports as items printed on paper or displayed on a screen. But information printed on forms such as invoices or payroll checks can also be considered types of reports. One way to classify reports is by who uses them. An **internal report** is used by individuals in the performance of their jobs. For example, a daily sales report that is distributed to sales personnel is an internal report because it is used only by personnel *within* the organization. An **external report** is used outside the organization. Payroll checks that are printed and distributed to employees each week are external reports.

Reports may be classified by the way they present information. Three types of reports are common: detail reports, summary reports, and exception reports.

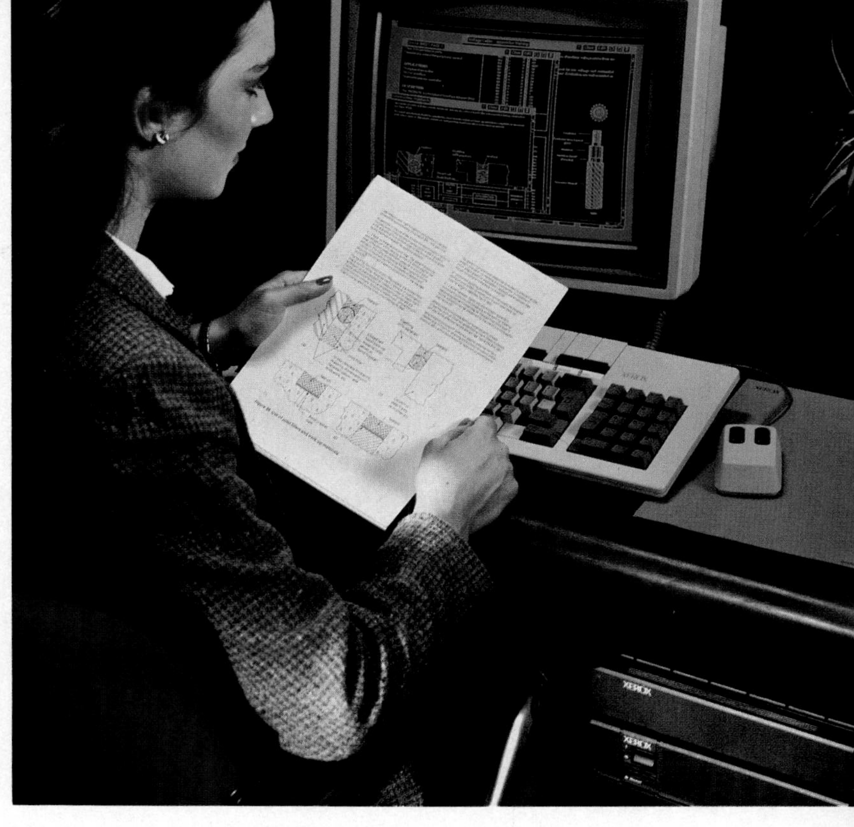

**FIGURE 6-1**
**This photograph shows the same output in hard copy and soft copy form. An advantage of hard copy is that the user can write comments on it and route it to other users.**

In a **detail report**, each line on the report usually corresponds to one input record that has been read and processed. Detail reports contain a great deal of information and can be quite lengthy. They are usually required by individuals who need access to the day-to-day information that reflects the operating status of the organization. For example, people in the sales department of a retail store should have access to the number of units sold of each product. The units sold report in Figure 6-2 contains a line for each item, which corresponds to each input record.

As the name implies, a **summary report** summarizes data. It contains totals for certain values found in the input records. The report illustrated in Figure 6-3 contains a summary of the units sold for each department. The information on the summary report consists of totals from the information contained in the detail report in Figure 6-2. Summary reports are most useful for individuals who do not require a detailed knowledge of each transaction. For example, detail reports contain more information than most managers have time to review. With a summary report, however, a manager can quickly review information in summarized form.

UNITS SOLD REPORT

| DEPT. | DEPT NAME | ITEM | DESCRIPTION | QTY SOLD |
|---|---|---|---|---|
| 10 | MENS FURNISHINGS | 105 | T-SHIRT | 3 |
| 10 | MENS FURNISHINGS | 109 | SOCKS | 127 |
| 12 | SLEEPWEAR | 199 | ROBE | 6 |
| 14 | MENS ACCESSORIES | 266 | HAT | 4 |

**FIGURE 6-2**
**The data for this detail report was obtained from each input record that was read and processed. A line was printed for each record.**

SALES BY DEPARTMENT

| DEPT. NO. | DEPT. NAME | UNITS SOLD | SALES $ |
|---|---|---|---|
| 10 | MENS FURNISHINGS | 130 | 653.35 |
| 12 | SLEEPWEAR | 6 | 189.70 |
| 14 | MENS ACCESSORIES | 4 | 98.00 |

**FIGURE 6-3**
**This summary report contains the sales for each department. The report can be prepared from the same data that prepared the report in Figure 6-2.**

INVENTORY EXCEPTION REPORT

| ITEM NO. | ITEM DESCRIPTION | QUANTITY ON HAND |
|---|---|---|
| 105 | T-SHIRT | 24 |
| 125 | SCARF | 3 |
| 126 | BELT | 17 |

**FIGURE 6-4**
This exception report lists inventory items with a quantity of less than 25. They could have been selected from thousands of inventory records. Only these items met the user's "exception criteria."

An **exception report** contains information that is outside of "normal" user-specified values or conditions and thus is an "exception" to the majority of the data. For example, if an organization with an inventory wanted to have an on-hand quantity of more than 25 of every inventory item at all times, it would design an exception report to tell them if the amount of any inventory items fell below this level. An example of such a report is shown in Figure 6-4.

Exception reports help users to focus on situations that may require immediate decisions or specific actions. The advantage of exception reports is that they save time and money. In a large department store, for example, there may be over 100,000 inventory items. A detail report containing all inventory items could be longer than 2,000 pages. To search through the report to determine the items whose on-hand quantity was less than 25 would be a difficult and time-consuming task. The exception report, however, could extract these items, which might number 100–200, and place them on a two- to four-page report that could be prepared in just a few minutes.

## Graphics

Another common type of output is computer graphics. In business, **computer graphics** are often used to assist in analyzing data. Computer graphics display information in the form of charts, graphs, or pictures so that the information can be understood easily and quickly (Figure 6-5). Facts contained in a lengthy report and data relationships that are difficult to understand in words can often be summarized in a single chart or graph.

In the past, graphics were not widely used in business because each time data was revised, a graphic artist would have to redraw the chart or graph. Today, relatively inexpensive graphics software makes it possible to redraw a chart, graph, or picture within seconds rather than the hours or days that were previously required. Many application software packages, such as spreadsheets, include graphics capabilities. As we discussed in Chapter 2, the three most popular types of charts and graphs are pie charts, bar charts, and line charts.

A **pie chart** is normally used to depict data that may be expressed as a percentage of a whole (Figure 6-6). Pie charts show easy visual comparisons of the relative size of each component within a whole, where the whole represents 100 percent. If used with a color output device, most graphics software allows each component to be displayed in a different color, lets text material be placed on the screen in various colors, and provides shading. Some graphics software even allows certain segments of the chart to be shown with a three-dimensional effect for emphasis.

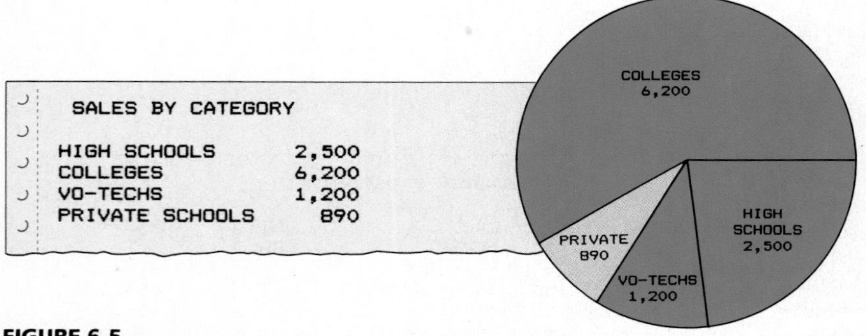

SALES BY CATEGORY

| | |
|---|---|
| HIGH SCHOOLS | 2,500 |
| COLLEGES | 6,200 |
| VO-TECHS | 1,200 |
| PRIVATE SCHOOLS | 890 |



**FIGURE 6-5**
This small report lists sales of magazines by school category. With the addition of the pie chart graphic, however, the manager can easily see that colleges account for more than half the sales and that private schools represent a small percentage of the sales. Both the report and the graphic use the same information, but the graphic helps the manager to understand the information more quickly.

**Bar charts** are among the most versatile and popular types of display charts used for comparing data (Figure 6-7). Bar charts represent data by vertical or horizontal bars. They are useful for comparing data in which sizes or quantities vary and the amount of variance needs to be made clear. Graphics software can display bars of different colors, vertical or horizontal bars, and text material where required.

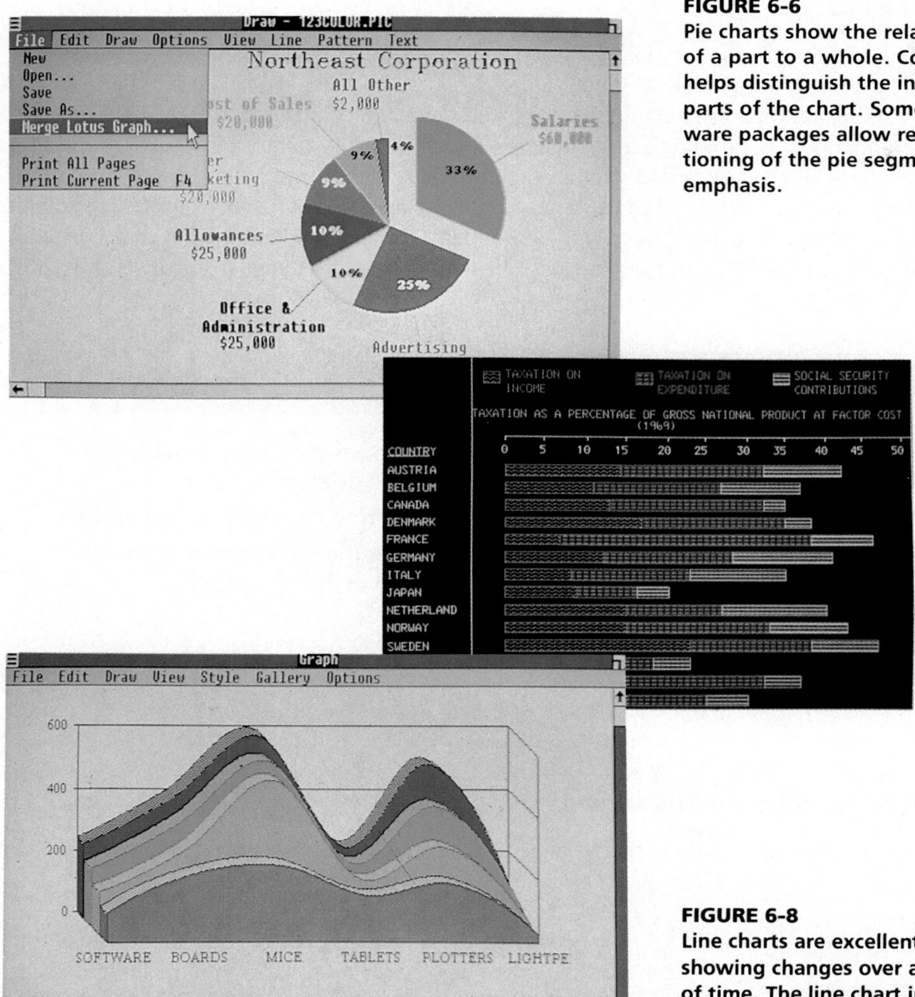


**FIGURE 6-6**
**Pie charts show the relationship of a part to a whole. Color helps distinguish the individual parts of the chart. Some software packages allow repositioning of the pie segments for emphasis.**

**FIGURE 6-7**
**A bar chart (left) can have vertical or horizontal bars. The horizontal bars in this picture depict taxation as a percentage of the gross national product for different countries. The length of the bars represents the total taxation. The colors within the bars represent the different parts of the whole taxation amount.**

**FIGURE 6-8**
**Line charts are excellent for showing changes over a period of time. The line chart in this picture is rendered using three dimensions and color to enhance the data's presentation.**

**Line charts** may also be generated by graphics software. These charts represent data relationships by a continuous line across the chart (Figure 6-8). Line charts are particularly useful for showing a change in a value or quantity over a period of time.

From the examples of the various types of graphs and charts, you can see how computer graphics offers a powerful tool for the business user who must present data in a meaningful manner or for the manager who must review, analyze, and make decisions based on data relationships.

A variety of devices are used to produce the output created in the information processing cycle. The following paragraphs describe the most commonly used output devices.

# PRINTERS

Printing requirements vary greatly among computer users. For example, the user of a personal computer generally uses a printer capable of printing 100 to 200 lines per minute. Users of mainframe computers, such as utility companies that send printed bills to hundreds of thousands of customers each month, need printers that are capable of printing thousands of lines per minute. These different needs have resulted in the development of printers with varying capabilities. Due to the many choices available and because printed output is so widely used, users must be familiar with the factors to consider when choosing a printer (Figure 6-9).

**FIGURE 6-9**
**Factors that affect the choice of a printer**

| QUESTION | EXPLANATION |
|---|---|
| How much output will be produced? | Desktop printers are not designed for continuous use. High volume (more than several hundred pages a day) requires a heavy-duty printer. |
| Who will use the output? | Most organizations want external reports to be prepared on a high-quality printer. |
| Where will the output be produced? | If the output will be produced at the user's desk, a sound enclosure may be required to reduce the noise of some printers to an acceptable level. |
| Are multiple copies required? | Some printers cannot use multipart paper. |

## How Are Printers Classified?

Printers can be classified by how they transfer characters from the printer to the paper, either by impact or nonimpact, and by printer speed.

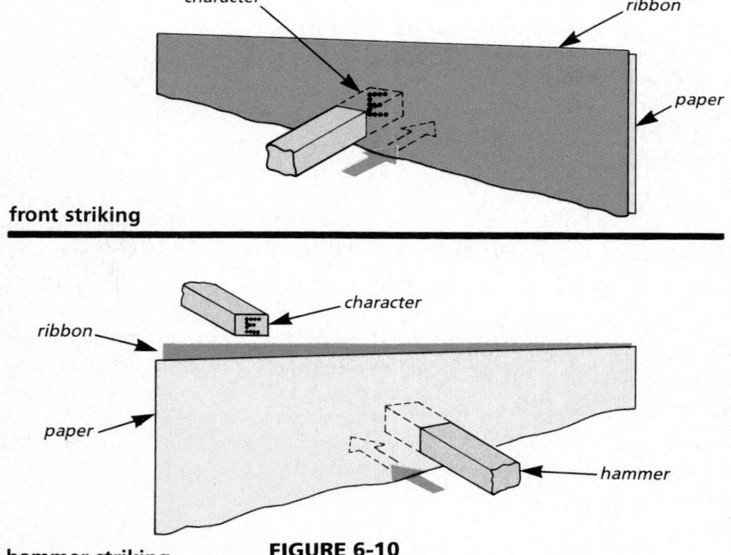


**FIGURE 6-10**
**Impact printers operate in one of two ways: front striking or hammer striking.**

**Impact and Nonimpact** **Impact printers** transfer the image onto paper by some type of printing mechanism striking the paper, ribbon, and character together. One technique is **front striking** in which the printing mechanism that forms the character strikes a ribbon against the paper from the front to form an image. This is similar to the method used on typewriters. The second technique utilizes a **hammer striking** device. The ribbon and paper are struck against the character from the back by a hammer to form the image on the paper (Figure 6-10).

A number of technologies are used to accomplish nonimpact printing. **Nonimpact printing** means that printing occurs without having a mechanism striking against a sheet of paper. For example, ink is sprayed against the paper or heat is used to transfer the character.

Each of these two methods of printing has its advantages and disadvantages. Impact printing can be noisy because the paper is struck when printing occurs. But because the paper is struck, carbon paper can be used to create multiple copies of a report, such as an invoice, that go to different people. Although nonimpact printers cannot create carbon copies, they are very quiet and are ideal for desktop applications where the normal requirements only call for a single printed copy.

**Speed** Another way to classify printers is by the speed at which they print. Printers can be classified as low speed, medium speed, high speed, and very high speed.

**Low-speed printers** print one character at a time. The rate of printing for low-speed printers is expressed in the number of characters that can be printed in one second. Low-speed printers can print from 15 to 600 characters per second.

Medium-speed and high-speed printers are called **line printers** because they can print multiple characters on a line at the same time. The rate of printing for these machines is stated in terms of the number of lines per minute that can be printed. **Medium-speed printers** can print from 300 to 600 lines per minute. Printers that can print from 600 to 3,000 lines per minute are classified as **high-speed printers**.

**Very high-speed printers** can print in excess of 3,000 lines per minute; some, more than 20,000 lines per minute. Very high-speed printers are often called **page printers** because they print an entire page at one time.

## Printer Features

To decide which printer to choose for a particular job, it is important to know the different features that a printer might have. Common feature choices include carriage size, type of paper feed mechanism, and bidirectional printing capability.

**Carriage Size** Most printers are built with either a standard or wide carriage. A **standard carriage** printer can accommodate paper up to 8 1/2 inches wide. A **wide carriage** printer can accommodate paper up to 14 inches wide. Using a normal character size, most printers can print 80 characters per line on a standard carriage and 132 characters per line on a wide carriage.

**Feed Mechanism** The feed mechanism determines how the paper is moved through the printer. Two types of feed mechanisms are found on printers, tractor feed and friction feed. **Tractor feed mechanisms** transport continuous form paper through the printer by using sprockets, small protruding prongs of plastic or metal, which fit into holes on each side of the paper. The pages of **continuous form paper** are connected for continuous flow through the printer (Figure 6-11). Where it is necessary to feed single sheets of paper into the printer, **friction feed mechanisms** are used. As the name implies, paper is moved through friction feed printers by pressure on the paper and the carriage, as it is on a typewriter. As the carriage rotates, the paper is transported through the printer.

**FIGURE 6-11**
Each sheet of continuous form paper is connected with the next. A feed mechanism pulls the paper through the printer using the holes on each side of the form. Perforations between each page allow a printed report to be folded and may be used to separate each page.

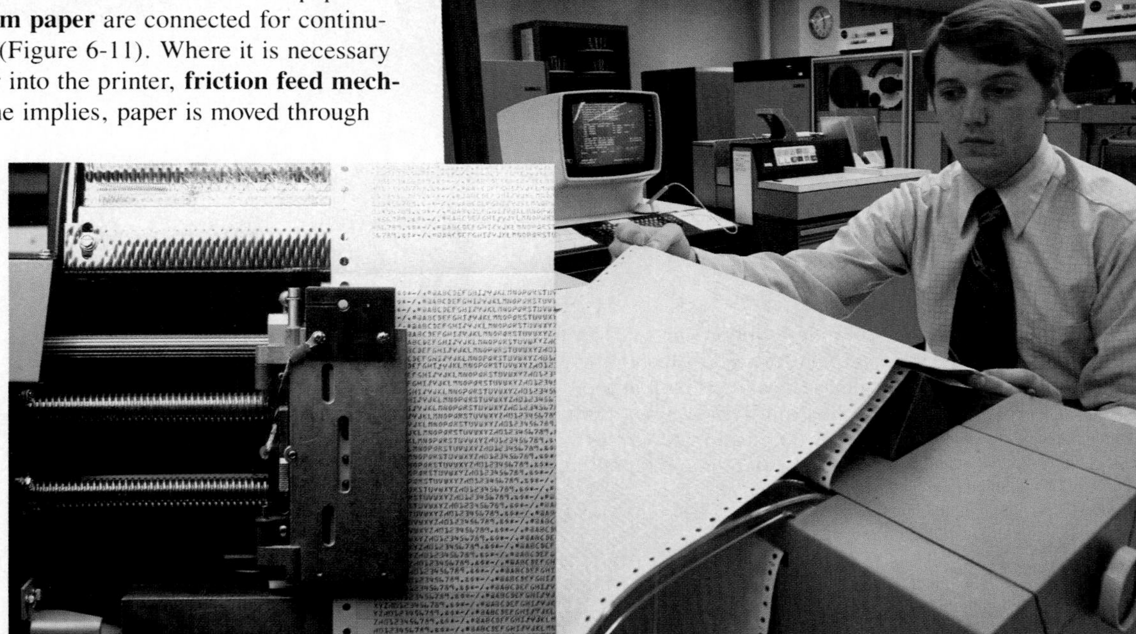

**Bidirectional Printing** Some printers are designed to print in a **bidirectional** manner. That is, the print head, the device that contains the mechanism for transferring the character to the paper, can print as it moves from left to right, and from right to left. The printer does this by storing the next line to be printed in its memory and then printing the line forward or backward as needed. Bidirectional printing can almost double the number of characters that can be printed in a given period of time.

## PRINTERS FOR SMALL AND MEDIUM COMPUTERS

The increased popularity and use of personal computers has resulted in the development of a large number of printers that vary significantly in speed, quality, and price. Some of these printers are also used on larger systems. The following paragraphs describe the print devices most commonly used on small and medium-size computers.

### Dot Matrix Printers

Dot matrix printers are used extensively because they are versatile and relatively inexpensive. The Epson printer shown in Figure 6-12 is a well-known dot matrix printer that is used with personal computers. Figure 6-13 shows a popular Printronix printer that is frequently used with many medium-size computers.

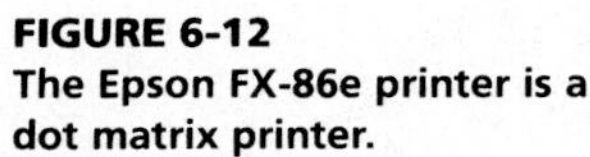

**FIGURE 6-12**
**The Epson FX-86e printer is a dot matrix printer.**

A **dot matrix printer** is an impact printer. Its print head consists of a series of small tubes containing pins that, when pressed against a ribbon and paper, print small dots. The

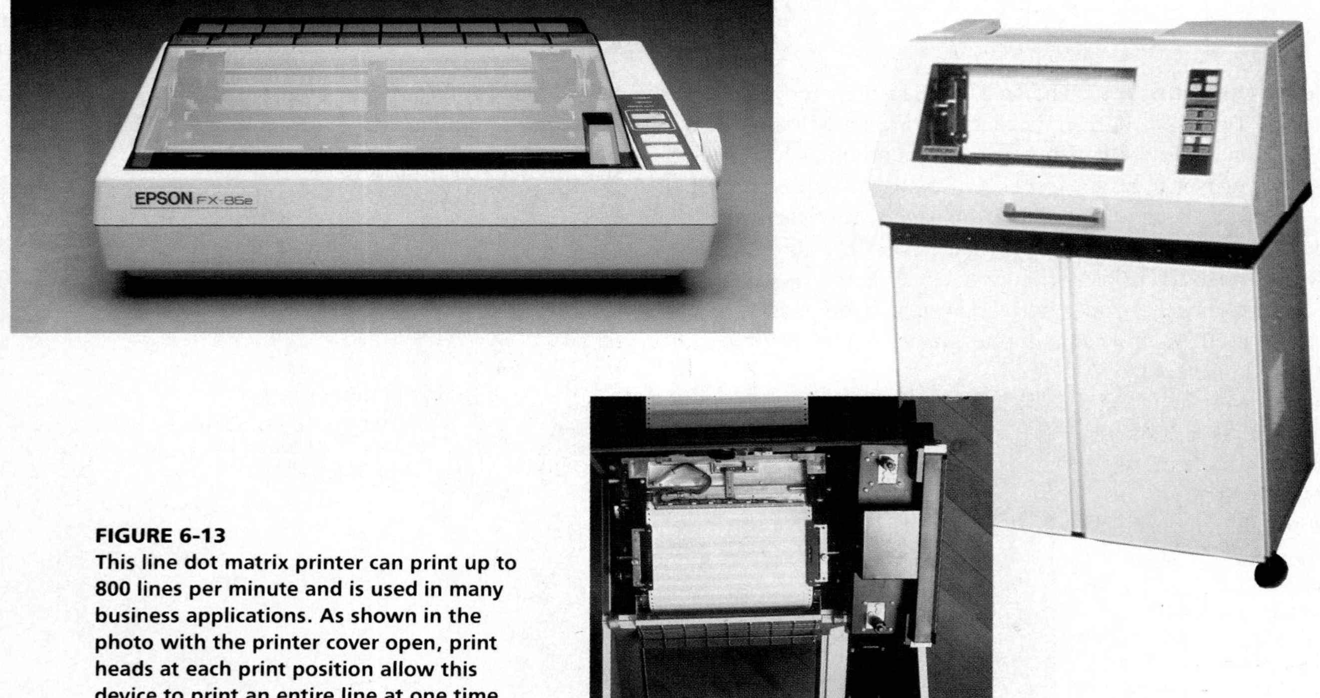


**FIGURE 6-13**
**This line dot matrix printer can print up to 800 lines per minute and is used in many business applications. As shown in the photo with the printer cover open, print heads at each print position allow this device to print an entire line at one time.**

combination of small dots printed closely together forms the character (Figure 6-14).

To print a character using a dot matrix printer, the character stored in main memory is sent to the printer's electronic circuitry. The printer circuitry activates the pins in the print head that correspond to the pattern of the character to be printed. The selected pins strike the ribbon and paper and print the character. Low-speed dot matrix printers utilize a movable print head that prints one character at a time. Medium- and high-speed dot matrix printers have print mechanisms at each print position and are able to print an entire line at one time.

Dot matrix printers can contain a varying number of pins, depending on the manufacturer and the printer model. Print heads consisting of nine and 24 pins are most common. Figure 6-15 illustrates the formation of the letter E using a nine-pin dot matrix printer.

A character produced by a dot matrix printer is made up of a series of dots. The quality of print produced is partly dependent on the number of pins used to form the character. A 24-pin print head produces better-looking characters than a nine-pin print head because the dots are closer together.

Several methods are used to improve the quality of dot matrix printers. On a nine-pin printer, one method is to print a line twice. Using this technique a line is printed, and then the print head is shifted very slightly and the line is printed again. This results in overlapping dots, which give the appearance of solid characters (Figure 6-16). The disadvantage, of course, is that the printing takes longer since each character is printed twice. Twenty-four-pin printers can produce the same print quality in a single pass.

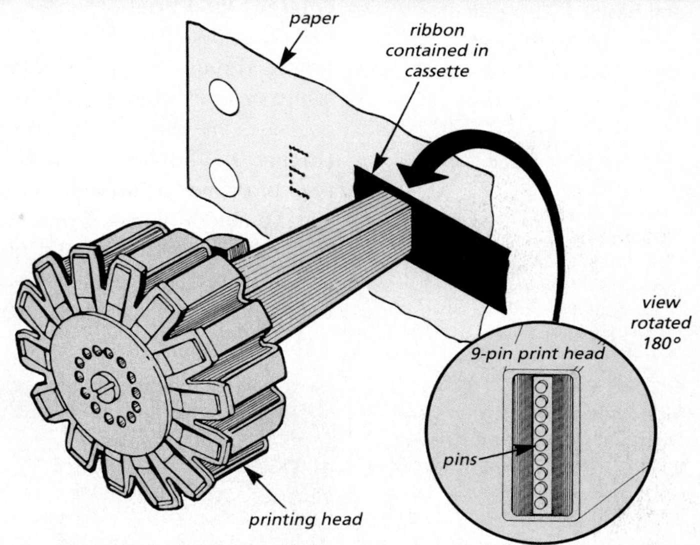


**FIGURE 6-14**
**The print head for a dot matrix printer consists of a series of pins. When activated, the pins strike the ribbon that strikes the paper, creating a dot on the paper.**

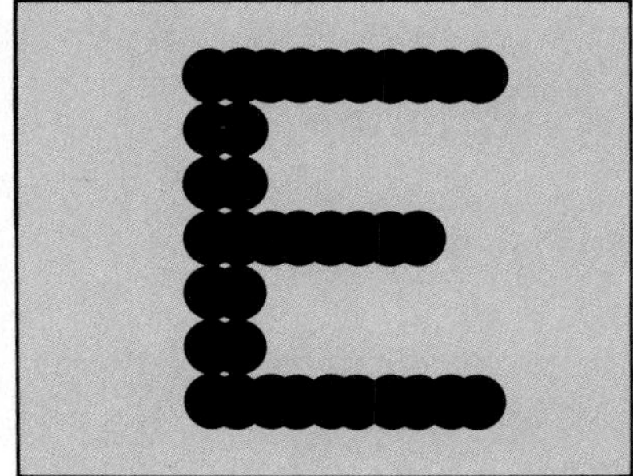

**FIGURE 6-16**
**The letter E in this example is formed by overprinting, or printing the character twice. When it is printed the second time, the print head is slightly offset so that much of the space between the dots is filled in. This gives the character a better appearance and makes it easier to read.**

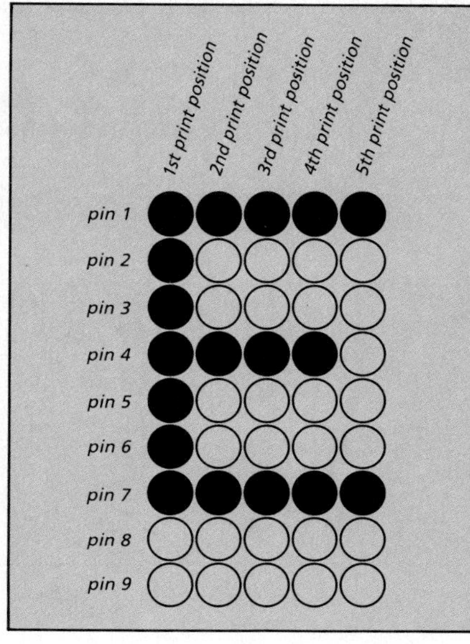


**FIGURE 6-15**
**The letter E is formed with seven vertical and five horizontal dots. As the nine-pin print head moves from left to right, it fires one or more pins into the ribbon, which makes a dot on the paper. At print position 1, it fires pins 1 through 7. At print positions 2 through 4, it fires pins 1, 4, and 7. At print position 5, it fires pins 1 and 7. Pins 8 and 9 are used for lowercase characters such as p, q, y, g, and j that extend below the line.**

CONDENSED PRINT - NORMAL CHARACTERS
**CONDENSED PRINT - EMPHASIZED CHARACTERS**

STANDARD PRINT - NORMAL CHARACTERS
**STANDARD PRINT - EMPHASIZED CHARACTERS**

ENLARGED PRINT - NORMAL CHARACTERS
**ENLARGED PRINT - EMPHASIZED CHARACTERS**

**FIGURE 6-17**
**Three type sizes are shown in this example—condensed, standard, and enlarged. All three are printed using normal and emphasized (also called "bold") print density.**

Many dot matrix printers can also print characters in two or more sizes and densities. Typical sizes include condensed print, standard print, and enlarged print. In addition, each of the three print sizes can be printed with increased density or darkness, called bold print. Figure 6-17 illustrates condensed, condensed bold, standard, standard bold, enlarged, and enlarged bold print.

Most dot matrix printers have a graphics mode that enables them to print pictures and graphs (Figure 6-18). In graphics mode, the individual print head pins can be activated separately or in combination to form unique shapes or continuous lines. When special software packages are used, dot matrix printers can print in many different type styles and sizes (Figure 6-19). The flexibility of the dot matrix printer has resulted in widespread use of this type of printer by all types of computer users.

Some dot matrix printers can print in multiple colors using ribbons that contain the colors red, green, and blue. Color output is obtained by repeated printing and repositioning of the paper, print head, and ribbon. Such printers can be useful in printing graphs and charts, but output quality is not comparable to color produced by other types of printers.

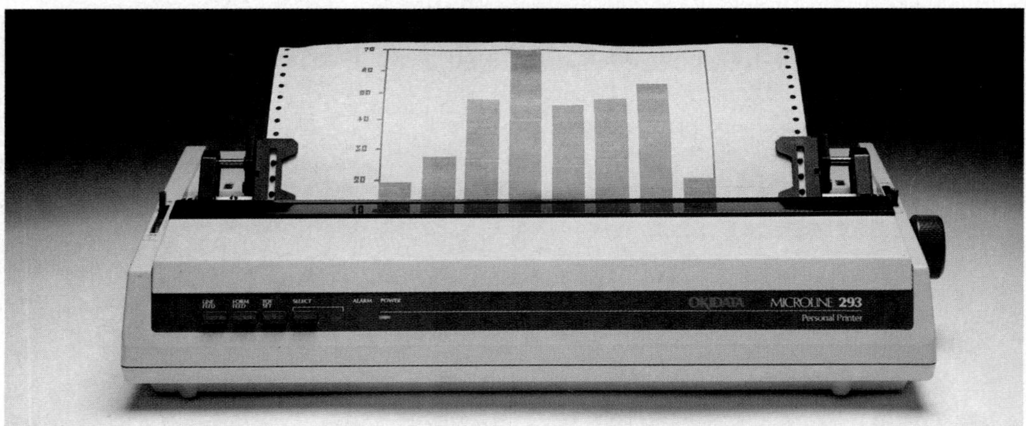


**FIGURE 6-18**
**Many dot matrix printers are capable of producing colored output using special ribbons.**

Monaco Chicago *Los Angeles*
Venice Geneva Helvetica
Athens London San Francisco
Σψμβολ Courier New York

**FIGURE 6-19**
**These letter styles illustrate the abilities of dot matrix printers to print graphics, depending on the software directing the printer.**

## Daisy Wheel Printers

When users require printed output of high quality, such as for business or legal correspondence, a letter-quality printer is often used. The term **letter quality** refers to the quality of the printed character that is suitable for formal or professional business letters. A letter-quality printed character is a fully formed, solid character like those made by typewriters. It is not made up of a combination of dots, as by a dot matrix printer.

The letter-quality printer most often used with personal computers is the daisy wheel printer (Figure 6-20). The **daisy wheel printer** is an impact printer. It consists of a type element containing raised characters that strike the paper through an inked ribbon.

The daisy wheel element somewhat resembles the structure of a flower, with many long, thin petals (Figure 6-21). Each "petal" has a raised character at the tip. When printing occurs, the type element (daisy wheel) rotates so that the character to be printed is in printing position. A hammer extends, striking the selected character against the ribbon and paper, printing the character. Because of the time required to rotate the daisy wheel, the daisy wheel printer is normally slower than a dot matrix printer; however, the print quality is higher. Printing speeds vary from 20 to 80 characters per second.

An additional feature of the daisy wheel printer is that the daisy wheel can be easily replaced. Daisy wheels come in a variety of sizes and fonts. A font, or typeface as they are sometimes called, is a complete set of characters in a particular style such as script, gothic, or roman. Therefore, whenever the user wishes to change fonts, he or she can remove one daisy wheel and put another wheel on the printer.

The disadvantage of a daisy wheel printer is that it is capable of printing only the characters that are on the wheel. It cannot, therefore, print graphic output.

**FIGURE 6-20**
**A daisy wheel printer produces letter-quality output comparable to that produced by a typewriter. Either continuous form or single-sheet paper can be used with most daisy wheel printers.**

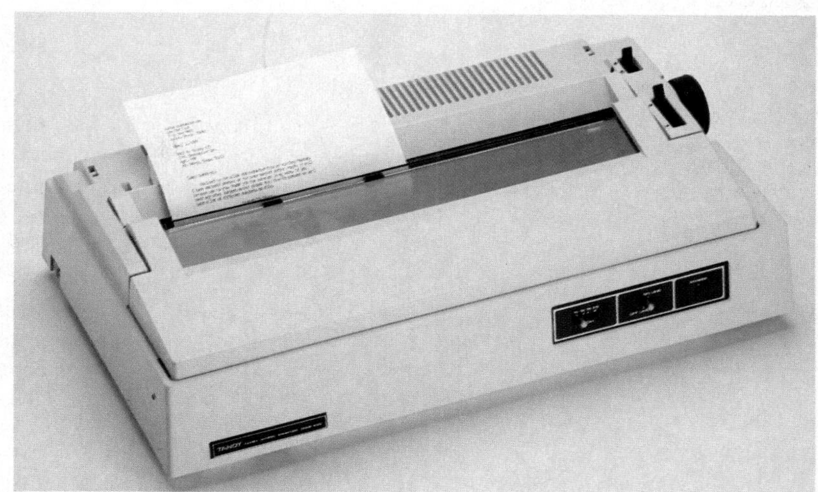

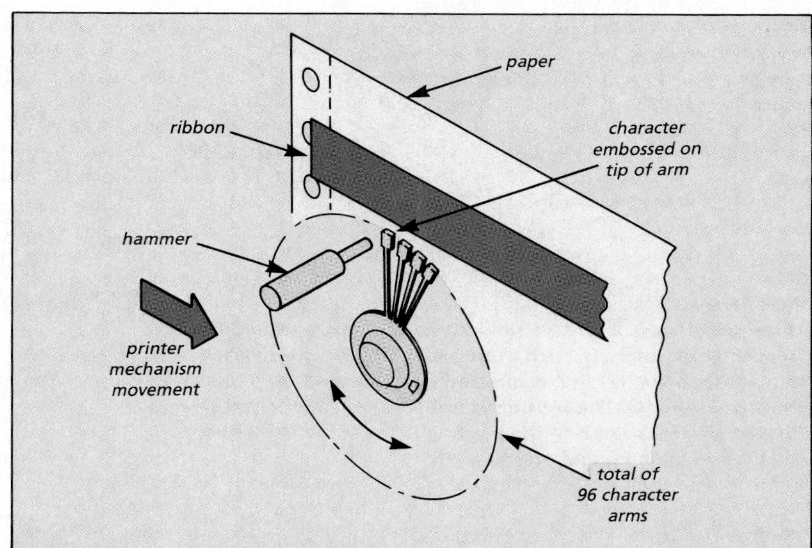


**FIGURE 6-21**
**The daisy wheel print element consists of a number of arms, each with a character at the end. When the printer is running the wheel spins until the desired character is lined up with the hammer. The hammer then strikes against the ribbon and paper, printing the character.**

FIGURE 6-22
A color ink jet printer by IBM.

## Thermal Printers

**Thermal printers** use heat to produce fully formed characters, usually on special chemically treated paper. An advantage of thermal printers is that they are very quiet. Disadvantages are their need for special paper and their relatively slow printing speed. Thermal printers are not as commonly used as they once were.

## Ink Jet Printers

A popular type of nonimpact printer is an **ink jet printer**. To form a character, an ink jet printer uses nozzles that spray ink onto the page. Ink jet printers produce relatively high-quality print and are very quiet because the paper is not struck as it is by dot matrix or daisy wheel printers. Disadvantages are that ink jet printers cannot produce multiple copies, and the ink sometimes smears on soft, porous paper. The ink jet printer in Figure 6-22 is designed for use with personal computers.

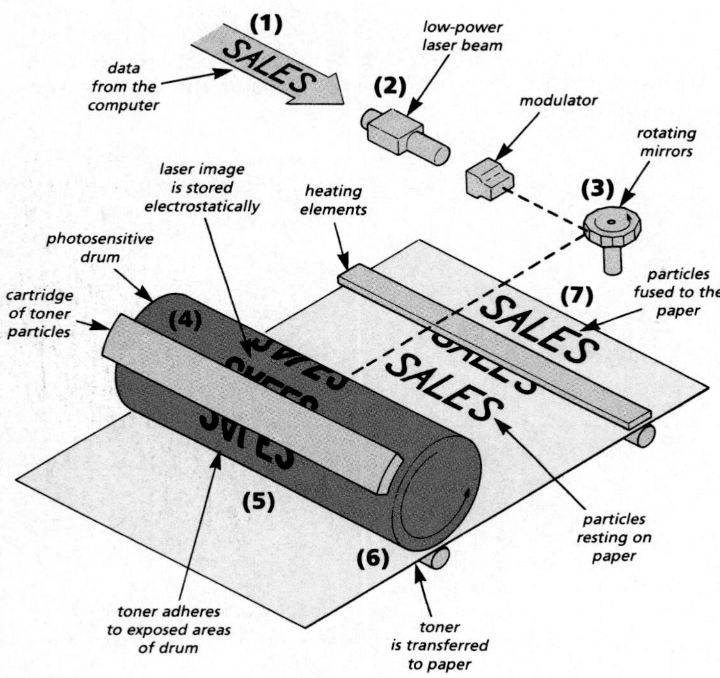



FIGURE 6-23
Laser printers use a process similar to a copying machine. Data from the computer (1), such as the word SALES, is converted into a laser beam (2) that is directed by a mirror (3) to a photosensitive drum (4). The sensitized drum attracts toner particles (5) that are transferred to the paper (6). The toner is fused to the paper with heat and pressure (7).

## Laser Printers

The **laser printer** is a nonimpact printer that operates in a manner similar to a copying machine (Figure 6-23). The laser printer converts data from the computer into a laser beam that is directed by a mirror to a positively charged revolving drum. Each position on the drum touched by the laser beam becomes negatively charged and attracts the toner (powdered ink). The toner is transferred onto the paper and then fused to the paper by heat and pressure. The end result is a high-quality printed image. As shown in Figure 6-24, laser printers can produce a variety of output.

FIGURE 6-24
The output illustrated in this picture was produced by a laser printer. Note that the output contains a mixture of different sizes and styles of print.

# PRINTERS FOR LARGE COMPUTERS

Minicomputers and mainframes are frequently used to process and print large volumes of data. As the demand for printing information from a computer increases, the use of higher speed printers is required. The three types of printers often used on large computers are chain printers, band printers, and high-speed laser printers.

## Chain Printers

The **chain printer** is a widely used high-speed printer. It contains numbers, letters of the alphabet, and selected special characters on a rotating chain (Figure 6-25). The chain consists of a series of type slugs that contain the character set. The character set on the type slugs is repeated two or more times on the chain mechanism. The chain rotates at a very high speed. Each possible print position has a hammer that can fire against the back of the paper, forcing the paper and ribbon against the character on the chain. As the chain rotates, the hammer fires when the character to be printed is in the proper position.

The chain printer has proven to be very reliable. It produces good print quality at up to 3,000 lines per minute. The printers in the large computer installation in Figure 6-26 are chain printers.

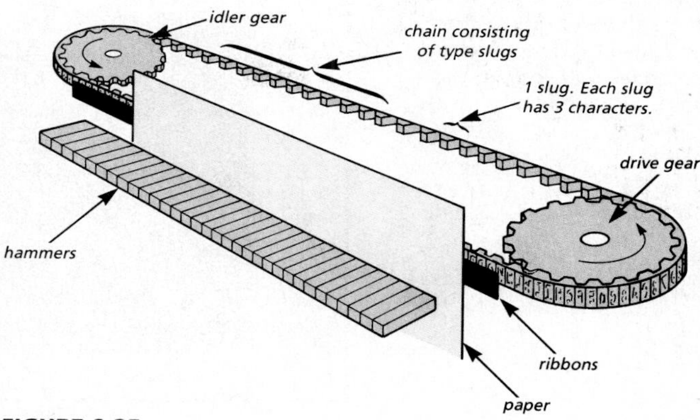


**FIGURE 6-25**
**The chain printer contains a complete set of characters on several sections of a chain that rotates at a high, constant rate of speed. Print hammers are located at each horizontal print position. The paper and ribbon are placed between the hammers and the chain. As the chain rotates, the hammers fire when the proper characters are in front of their print positions.**

**FIGURE 6-26**
**These high-speed chain printers are used in a large computer installation to produce thousands of lines of printed output per minute.**

## Band Printers

**Band printers**, similar to chain printers, utilize a horizontal, rotating band containing characters. The characters are struck by hammers located behind the paper and a ribbon to create a line of print on the paper (Figure 6-27).

Interchangeable type bands can be used on band printers. The different type bands contain many different fonts or print styles. A band printer can produce up to six carbon copies, has good print quality, high reliability, and depending on the manufacturer and model of the printer, can print in the range of 300 to 2,000 lines per minute.

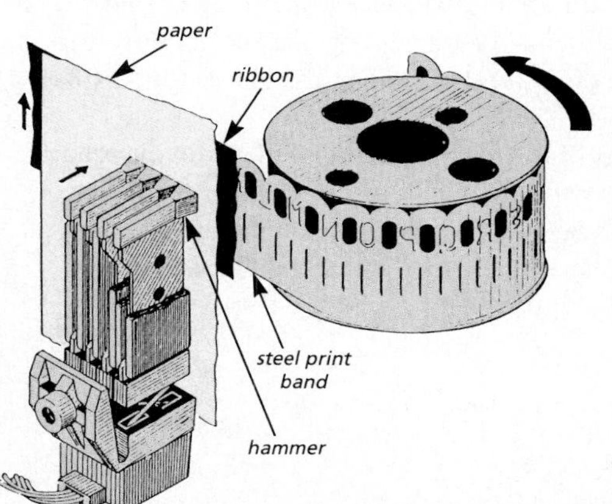


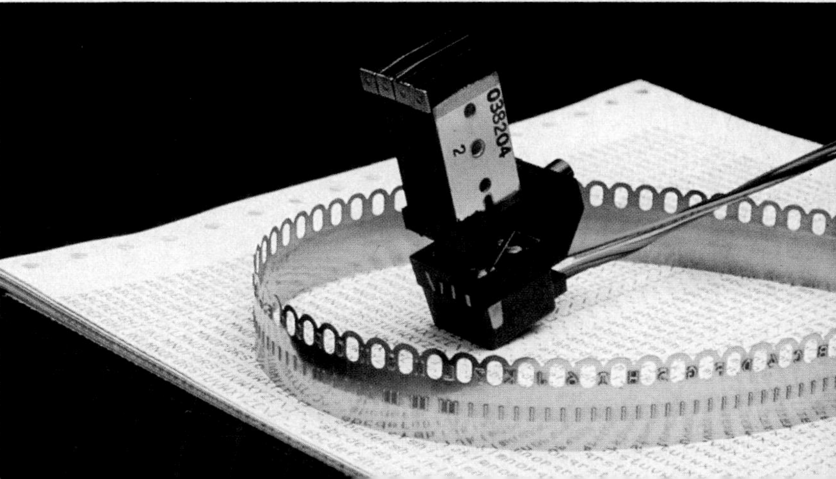

**FIGURE 6-27**
**A band printer uses a metal band that contains solid characters. Print hammers (shown inside the band) at each print location strike the paper and the ribbon, forcing them into the band to print the character.**

FIGURE 6-28
This laser printer can operate at speeds up to 70 pages per minute. As shown in the picture, high-speed printers often use tape drives that contain the data to be printed.

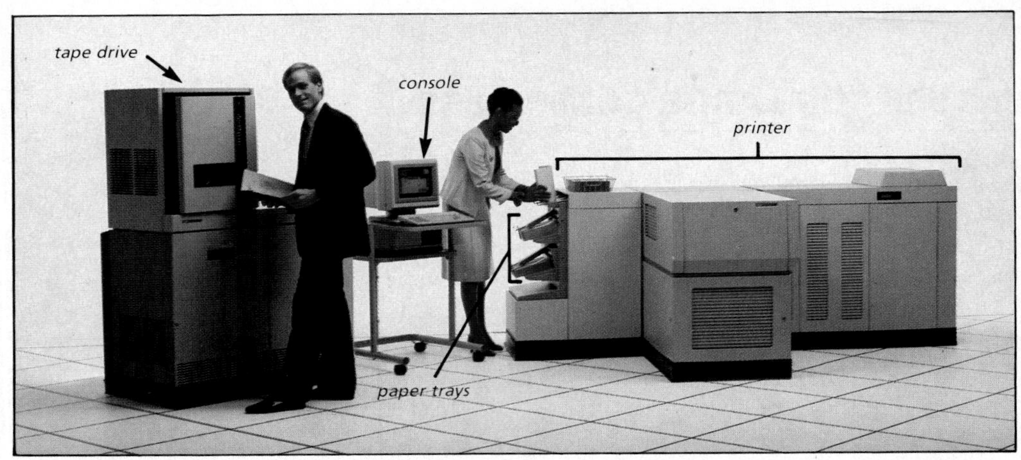


## High-Speed Laser Printers

**High-speed laser printers**, also called **page printers**, can produce printed output at the rate of over 20,000 lines per minute, the equivalent of over 400 pages of 50 lines per page. As shown in Figure 6-28, these high-speed printers usually consist of a dedicated computer and tape drive to maximize the printing speed. When the device is printing, the paper moves so fast that it must be folded and stacked mechanically.

# SCREENS

The **screen**, also called the monitor, CRT (cathode ray tube), or VDT (video display terminal), is another important output device. Screens are used on both personal computers and terminals to display many different types of output. For example, responses obtained from user inquiries to a database are frequently displayed on a screen. A screen can also be used to display electronic spreadsheets, electronic mail, and graphs of various types.

## Screen Features

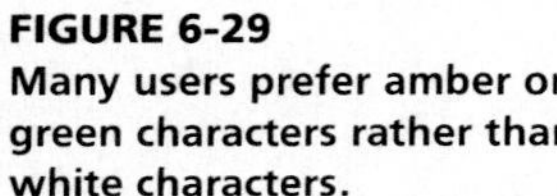

FIGURE 6-29
Many users prefer amber or green characters rather than white characters.

**Size** The most widely used screens are equivalent in size to a 12- to 15-inch television screen. Although there is no standard number of displayed characters, screens are usually designed to display 80 characters on a line with a maximum of 25 lines displayed at one time. The 25th line is often reserved for messages or system status reports, not for data. This provides for a maximum of 2,000 characters on the screen at once. Some terminals can display up to 132 characters on a single horizontal line. The more characters that are displayed on a line, the smaller the size of the characters. Therefore, an important consideration when selecting a terminal is the number of characters displayed on the screen at one time and the *resolution* (clarity) of the characters displayed.

**Color** Most of the early screens displayed white characters on a black background. Research has indicated, however, that other color combinations are easier on the eyes. Today, many screens display either green or amber characters on a black background (Figure 6-29).

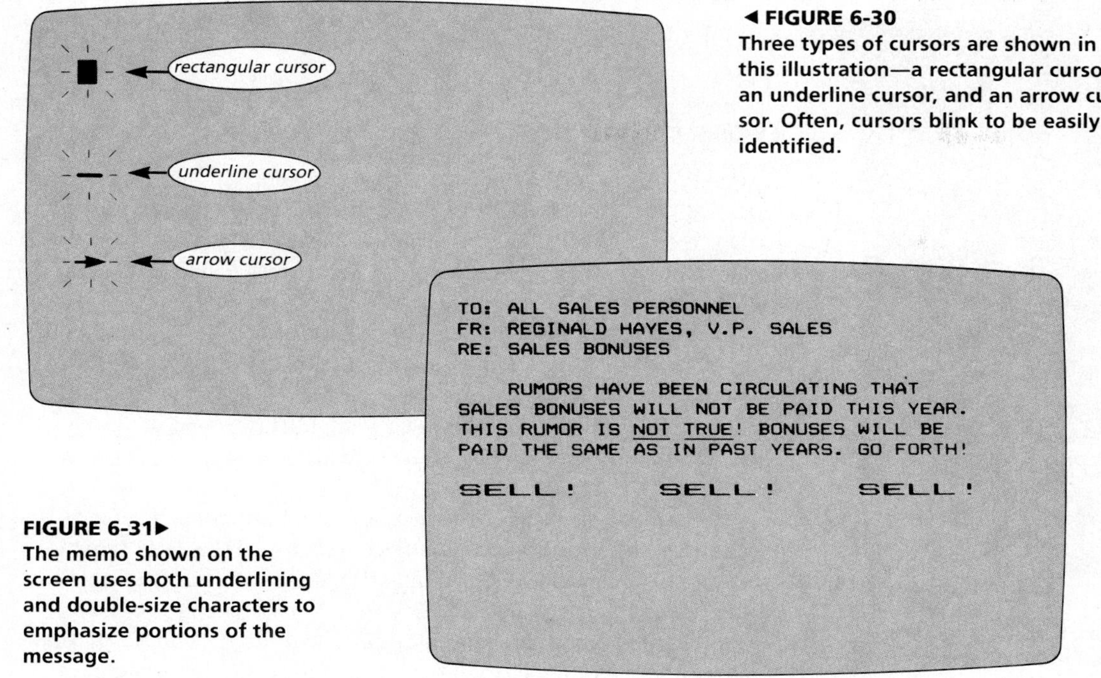


◀ **FIGURE 6-30**
**Three types of cursors are shown in this illustration—a rectangular cursor, an underline cursor, and an arrow cursor. Often, cursors blink to be easily identified.**

**FIGURE 6-31▶**
**The memo shown on the screen uses both underlining and double-size characters to emphasize portions of the message.**

**Cursor** A **cursor** is a symbol that indicates where on the screen the next character entered will be displayed. It can also be used as a marker on a screen to identify the choices a user can make. Some of the symbols used to represent cursors are shown in Figure 6-30. Most cursors blink when they are displayed on the screen so the user can quickly find their location.

**Scrolling** **Scrolling** is a method of moving lines displayed on the screen up or down one line at a time. As a new line is added, for example, to the bottom of the screen, an existing one, from the top of the screen, is removed. The line removed from the screen remains in the computer's memory even though it is no longer displayed. When the screen is scrolled in the opposite direction (in this example, down), the line from the top that was removed reappears on the screen and the line at the bottom is removed.

**Paging** When **paging** is used, an entirely new "page" or screen of data can be displayed. This feature is useful in applications such as word processing when a user wants to use the screen to move quickly through pages of a long document.

**Other Screen Features** Screen features also include several options that can be used to emphasize displayed characters: reverse video, underlining, bold, blinking, and double size. **Reverse video** refers to the process of reversing the normal display on the screen. For example, it is possible to display a dark background with light characters or a light background with dark characters. Thus, if the normal screen had amber characters on a black background, reverse video shows black characters on an amber background. This feature permits single characters, whole words or lines, and even the entire screen to be reversed. The **underlining** feature allows characters, words, lines, or paragraphs to be underlined. Another feature used for emphasis is the ability to display some characters or words as bold. **Bold** means that characters are displayed at a greater brightness level than the surrounding text. The **blinking** feature makes characters or words on a screen blink, thus drawing attention to them. The **double size** feature means that certain characters or words are displayed at twice the size of normal characters and words. Figure 6-31 illustrates how underlining and double-size characters highlight data on the screen.

FIGURE 6-32
The high resolution of this plasma display allows the screen to display any combination of character fonts, line drawings, charts, sketches and letters.

## Types of Screens

Several types of screens are used with computers. The most common types are monochrome screens, color screens, plasma screens, and LCD screens. Plasma and LCD screens, which do not use the conventional cathode ray tube technology, are sometimes called **flat panel display screens** because of their relatively flat screens.

**Monochrome screens** specially designed for use with personal computers or for use as computer terminals usually display a single color, such as white, green, or amber characters on a black background. The characters are displayed without flicker and with very good resolution. Some monochrome screens have graphics capabilities.

The use of **color screens** is increasing in business and science applications, because numerous studies have found that color enables the user to more easily read and understand the information displayed on the screen.

A **plasma screen** produces a bright, clear image with no flicker (Figure 6-32). The screens are flat, so that they can be installed on desks or walls, taking up very little space.

With the development of truly portable computers that could be conveniently carried by hand or in a briefcase came a need for an output display that was equally as portable. Although several technologies have been developed, **liquid crystal displays (LCD)** are used as the output display for a number of laptop computers (Figure 6-33). LCD displays are also used in watches, calculators, and other electronic devices.

FIGURE 6-33
The liquid crystal display (LCD) screen used with this portable computer can display numbers, letters, and special characters, and even has some graphics capabilities.

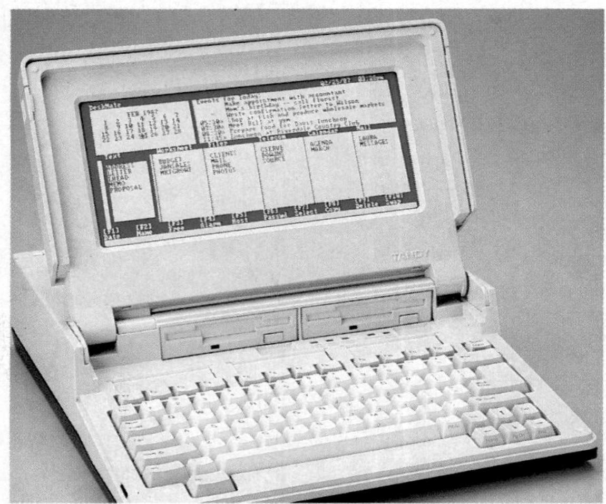

## How Characters Are Displayed on a Screen

Most screens used with personal computers and terminals utilize cathode ray tube (CRT) technology. When these screens produce an image, the following steps occur (Figure 6-34):

1. The image to be displayed on the screen is sent electronically from the CPU to the cathode ray tube.
2. An electron gun generates an electron beam of varying intensity, depending on the electronic data received from the CPU.
3. The yoke, which generates an electromagnetic field, moves the electron beam horizontally across the **phosphor-coated screen**.
4. The electron beam causes the desired phosphors to emit light. The higher the intensity of the beam, the brighter the phosphor glows. It is the phosphor-emitted light that produces an image on the screen.

On most screens, the phosphors that emit the light causing the image on the screen do not stay lit very long. They must be *refreshed* by having the electron beam light them again. If the screen is not scanned enough times per second, the phosphors will begin to lose their light. When this occurs, it appears that the characters on the screen are flickering. To eliminate flicker, a scan rate of 60 times per second is normal when the screen is used for alphanumeric display.

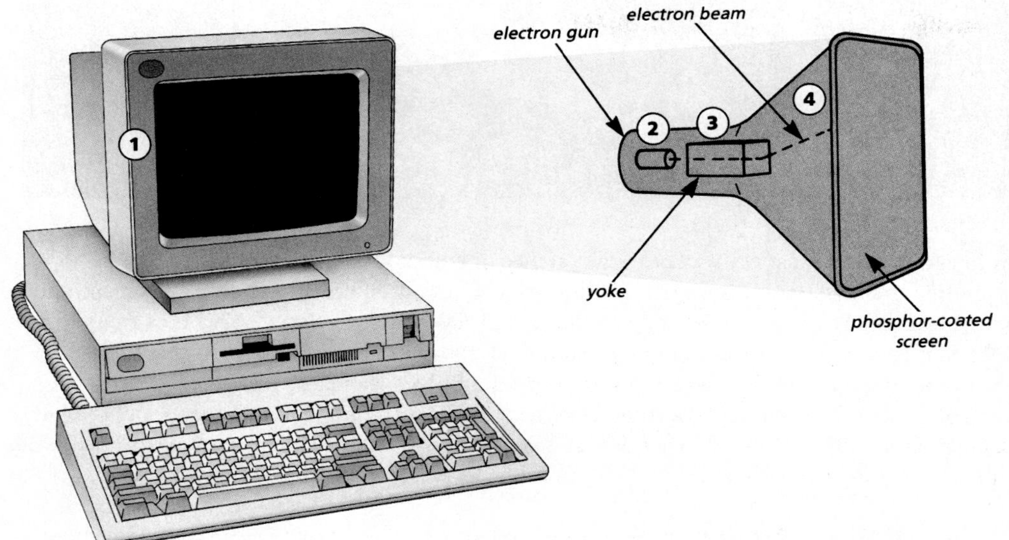


FIGURE 6-34
**When an image is formed on a screen, the information to be displayed is sent to the screen (1). Then the electron gun (2) generates an electron beam. The yoke (3) directs the beam to a specific spot on the screen (4), where the phosphors struck by the electron beam begin to glow and form an image on the screen.**

The brightness of the image on the screen depends on the intensity of the electron beam striking the phosphor, which in turn depends on the voltage applied to the beam. As the beam scans each phosphor dot, the intensity is varied precisely to turn each dot on or off.

Computer screens are divided into addressable locations. The manner of indicating the number of addressable locations varies with the type of screen. On a screen used primarily for characters and alphanumeric displays, the number of locations is usually identified by specifying the number of lines and the number of characters per line that can be displayed (sometimes called the character display addressing scheme).

Screens used for graphics are called **dot-addressable displays**, or sometimes **bit-mapped displays**. On these monitors, the number of addressable locations corresponds to the number of dots that can be illuminated. Each addressable dot that can be illuminated is called a **picture element** or **pixel** (Figure 6-35).

With dot-addressable displays, the resolution or clarity of the characters depends to a great extent on the number of pixels on the screen. The greater the number of pixels, the better the screen resolution. The number of pixels on a screen is determined through a combination of the software in the computer, the connection between the computer and the screen, and the screen itself. Some screens and computers operate in two or more resolution modes. For example, the IBM PS/2 series of personal computers, when operating in graphics mode, can use either medium or high resolution. In medium resolution, the screen contains 64,000 individual pixels arranged in 200 rows, each row containing 320 pixels. When high resolution is used, 480 rows can contain 640 pixels for a total of 307,200 distinct points.

Devices are currently available that offer very high-resolution graphics. The resolution of these devices is high enough to provide

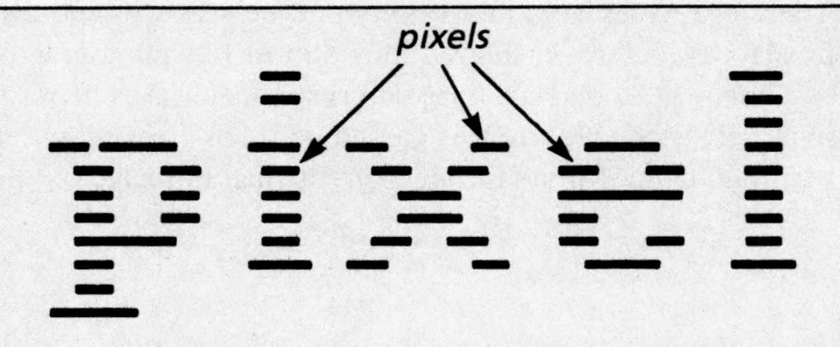

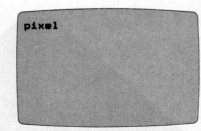

FIGURE 6-35
**The word pixel shown in this drawing is made up of pixels as they would be displayed on a dot-addressable or bit-mapped screen. Each pixel is a small rectangular spot of light that appears on the screen at the point where it is activated by an electron beam. These pixels must be reactivated about 60 times per second to appear as a solid character without screen flicker.**

**FIGURE 6-36**
The picture on the left shows how very high-resolution graphics can depict features such as shading, reflections, and highlights. The picture on the right shows how very high-resolution graphics can be used for simulation exercises; in this case, a flying situation. Through the use of the computer, this picture could be changed quickly to show the plane taking off and landing.

an image that is almost equivalent to the quality of a photograph (Figure 6-36). High-resolution graphics requires a great deal of storage, and it is more difficult electronically to maintain a steady image on the screen. In the past few years, however, there have been great improvements in picture resolutions. In addition, costs have been reduced so that high-resolution graphics are now widely used. Several graphics standards have been developed, including CGA (Color Graphics Adapter), EGA (Enhanced Graphics Adapter), and the latest standard from IBM called VGA (Video Graphics Array). Each standard provides for different numbers of pixels and colors.

**How Color Is Produced** Color is produced on a screen in several ways. Remember that on a monochrome screen, a single electron beam strikes the phosphor-coated screen, causing the chosen phosphor dot to light. If the characters are green on a black background, the phosphors emit a green light when activated. Similarly, if the characters are amber on black, the phosphors emit an amber light.

To show color on a screen, three phosphor dots are required for each pixel. These dots are red, blue, and green (Figure 6-37). The electron beam must turn on the desired color phosphors within the pixel to generate an image. In the simplest configuration, eight colors can be generated—no color (black), red only, blue only, green only, red and blue (magenta), red and green (yellow), blue and green (blue-green), and red, blue, and green together (white). By varying the intensity of the electron beam striking the phosphors, many more colors can be generated.

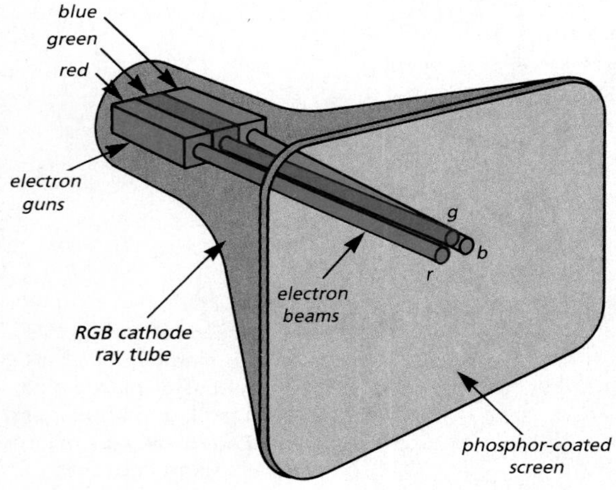


**FIGURE 6-37**
On color monitors, each pixel contains three phosphor dots: one red, one green, and one blue. These dots can be turned on individually or in combinations to display a wide range of colors.

Two common types of color screens are composite video monitors and RGB monitors. Both monitors produce color images, and both monitors can be used for color graphics. A **composite video monitor** uses a single electron signal to turn on the color phosphors within the pixel. An **RGB monitor** uses three signals, one for each color, red, green, and blue, to turn on the required phosphors. The difference is that the RGB monitor produces a much clearer display with much better color and character resolution.

**How Flat Panel Displays Work** Plasma screens use a relatively new display technology. A plasma screen consists of a grid of conductors sealed between two flat plates of glass. The space between the glass is filled with neon/argon gas. When the gas at an intersection in the grid is electronically excited, it creates an image. Each intersection of the grid of wires in a plasma screen is addressable. Therefore, characters in a variety of type styles, line drawings, charts, or even pictures can be displayed. Pictures displayed look almost like photographs.

In an LCD display, a liquid crystal material is deposited between two sheets of polarizing material. When a current is passed between crossing wires, the liquid crystals are aligned so that light cannot shine through, producing an image on the screen.

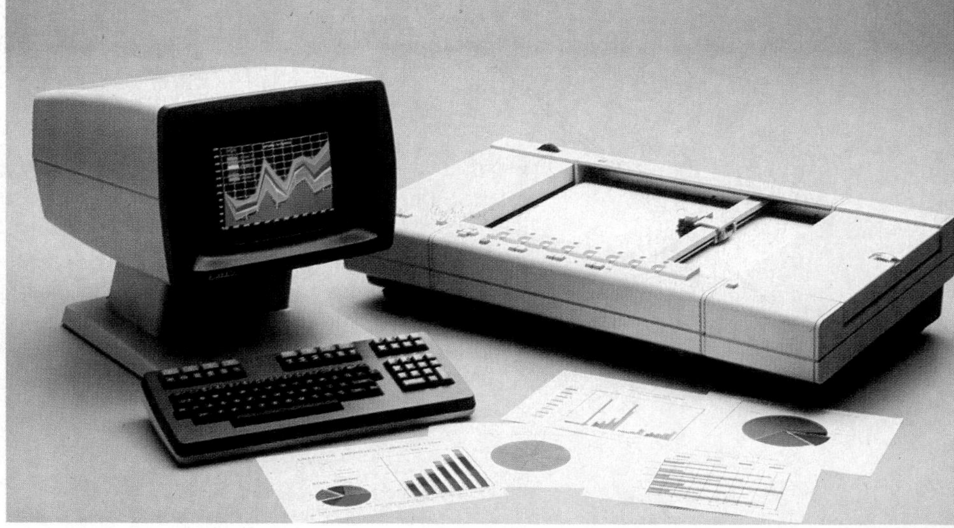

## OTHER OUTPUT DEVICES

Although printers and display devices provide the large majority of computer output, other devices are available for particular uses and applications. These include plotters, computer output microfilm devices, and voice output devices.

### Plotters

FIGURE 6-38
**An example of a flatbed plotter.**

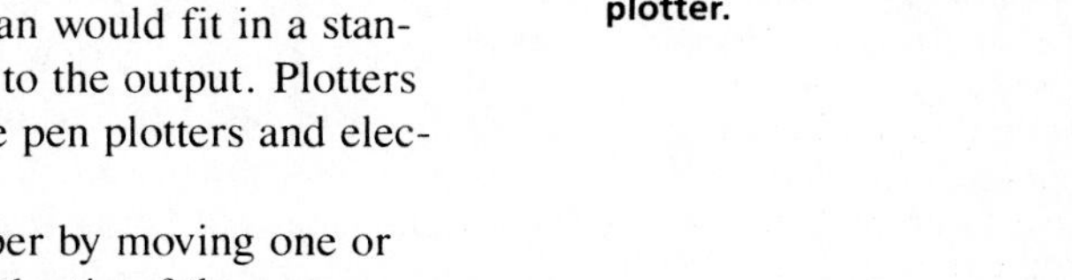

A **plotter** is an output device used to produce high-quality line drawings, such as building plans, charts, or circuit diagrams. These drawings can be quite large; some plotters are designed to handle paper up to 40 inches by 48 inches, much larger than would fit in a standard printer. The plotter can also draw numbers and letters to add text to the output. Plotters can be classified by the way they create the drawing. The two types are pen plotters and electrostatic plotters.

As the name implies, **pen plotters** create images on a sheet of paper by moving one or more pens over the surface of the paper or by moving the paper under the tip of the pens.

Two different kinds of pen plotters are flatbed plotters and drum plotters. When a **flatbed plotter** is used to plot or draw, the pen or pens are instructed by the software to move to the down position so the pen contacts the flat surface of the paper. Further instructions then direct the movement of the pens to create the image. Most flatbed plotters have one or more pens of varying colors or widths. The plotter illustrated in Figure 6-38 is a flatbed plotter that can create color drawings. Another kind of flatbed plotter holds the pen stationary and moves the paper under the pen.

A **drum plotter** uses a rotating drum or cylinder over which drawing pens are mounted. The pens can move to the left and right as the drum rotates, creating an image (Figure 6-39). An advantage of the drum plotter is that the length of the plot is virtually unlimited, since roll paper can be used. The width of the plot is limited by the width of the drum.

With an **electrostatic plotter**, the paper moves under a row of wires (called styli) that can be turned on to create an electrostatic charge on the paper. The paper then passes through a developer and the drawing emerges where the charged wires touched the

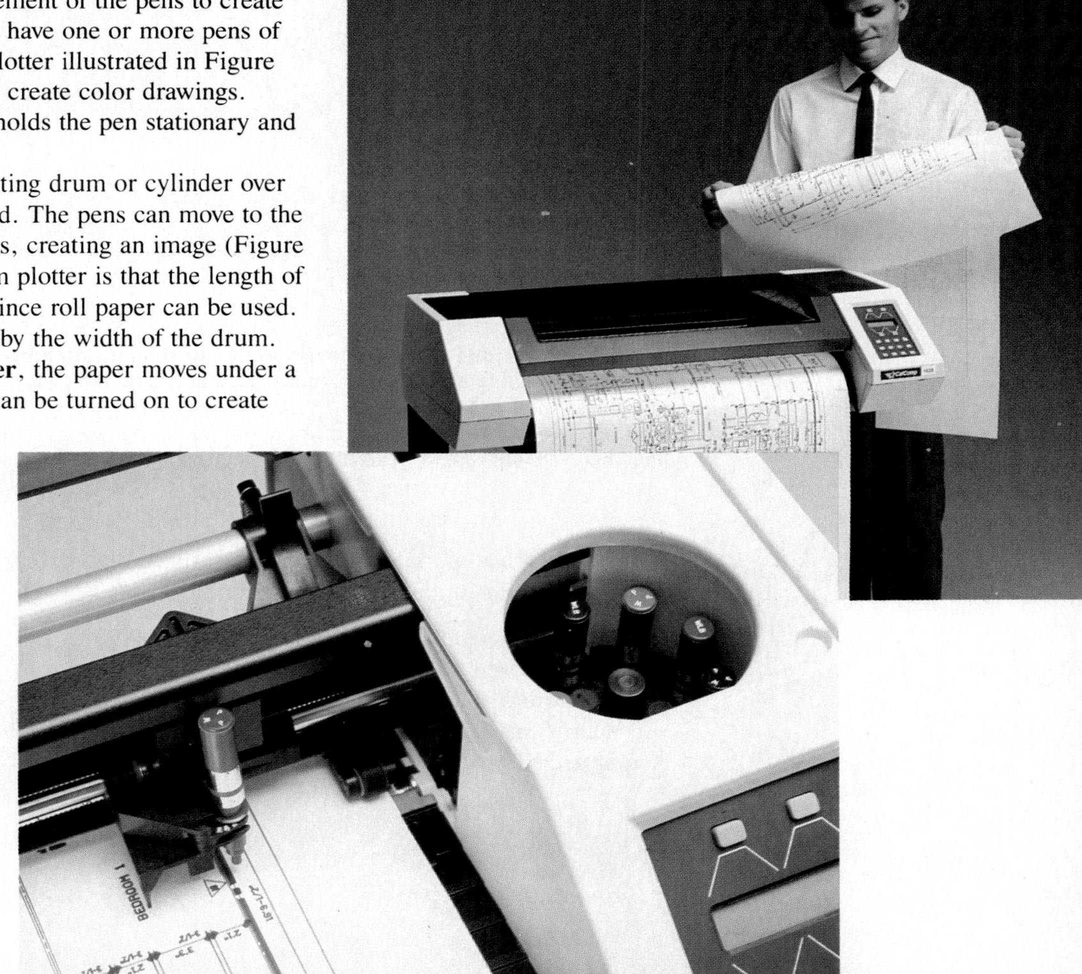


**FIGURE 6-39**
**This drum plotter utilizes eight pens of different colors to create diagrams. As the paper moves forward and back, the pens move left and right and, under software control, draw where instructed.**

paper. The electrostatic printer image is composed of a series of very small dots, resulting in relatively high-quality output. In addition, the speed of plotting is faster than with pen plotters.

Factors affecting the cost of a plotter are based on the resolution of the drawing and the speed of the plotting. Resolution is determined by the smallest movement a pen can make on the paper. Typical plotter movements may vary from .001 to .0005 inch. Plotting speeds of up to 36 inches per second are possible. Costs range from under $1,000 to over $100,000 for very high-speed plotters with extremely fine resolution.

## Computer Output Microfilm

**Computer output microfilm (COM)** is an output technique that records output from a computer as microscopic images on roll or sheet film. The images stored on COM are the same as the images that would be printed on paper. The COM recording process reduces characters 24, 42, or 48 times smaller than would be produced on a printer. The information is then recorded on sheet film called **microfiche** or on 16mm, 35mm, or 105mm roll film.

The data to be recorded by the device can come directly from the computer (online) or from a magnetic tape that was previously produced by the computer (offline) (Figure 6-40). After the COM film is processed, the user can view it.

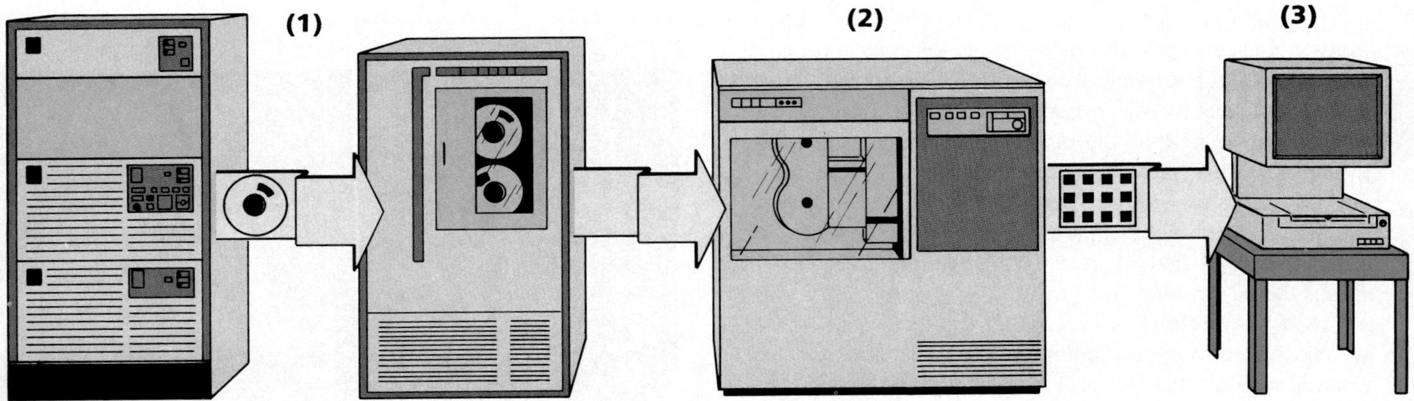


**FIGURE 6-40**
**This drawing illustrates the computer output microfilm (COM) process. The computer generates printed images on an output tape that is transferred to the tape drive attached to the COM machine (1). The COM machine reads the tape and produces reduced images of the printed output on film (2); in this example, microfiche sheet film. Then the film can be viewed using special microfilm reader devices (3).**

Microfilm has several advantages over printed reports or other storage media for certain applications. Some of these advantages are:

1. Data can be recorded on the film at up to 30,000 lines per minute—faster than all except very high-speed printers.
2. Costs for recording the data are lower. The cost of printing a three-part, 1,000-page report is approximately $28, whereas the cost of producing the same report on microfilm is approximately $3.

3. Less space is required to store microfilm than printed materials. A microfiche that weighs one ounce can store the equivalent of 10 pounds of paper.
4. Microfiche provides a less expensive way to store data. For example, the cost per million characters (megabyte) on a disk is approximately $20, while the cost per megabyte on microfilm is approximately $.65.

To access data stored on microfilm, a variety of readers are available. They utilize indexing techniques to provide a quick reference to the data. Some microfilm readers can perform automatic data lookup, called **computer-assisted retrieval**, under the control of an attached minicomputer. With the powerful indexing software and hardware now available for microfilm, a user can usually locate any piece of data in a 200,000,000-character database in less than 10 seconds, at a far lower cost per inquiry than using an online inquiry system consisting of a computer system that stores the data on a hard disk.

## Voice Output

The other important means of generating output from a computer is voice output. **Voice output** consists of spoken words that are conveyed to the user from the computer. Thus, instead of reading words on a printed report or monitor, the user hears the words over earphones, the telephone, or other devices from which sound can be generated.

The data that produces voice output is usually created in one of two ways. First, a person can talk into a device that will encode the words in a digital pattern. For example, the words "The number is" can be spoken into a microphone, and the computer software can assign a digital pattern to the words. The digital data is then stored on a disk. At a later time, the data can be retrieved from the disk and translated back from digital data into voice, so that the person listening will actually hear the words.

A second type of voice generation is new but holds great promise. Called a **voice synthesizer**, it can transform words stored in main memory into speech. The words are analyzed by a program that examines the letters stored in memory and generates sounds for the letter combinations. The software can apply rules of intonation and stress to make it sound as though a person were speaking. The speech is then projected over speakers attached to the computer. computer.

You may have heard voice output used by the telephone company for giving number information. Automobile and vending machine manufacturers are also incorporating voice output into their products. The potential for this type of output is great and it will undoubtedly be used in many products and services in the future.

## SUMMARY OF OUTPUT TO THE COMPUTER

The output step of the information processing cycle uses a variety of devices to provide users with information. Some of the devices that were discussed in this chapter, including printers and screens, are summarized in Figure 6-41.

**FIGURE 6-41**
This table summarizes some of the more common output devices

| OUTPUT DEVICE | DESCRIPTION |
|---|---|
| Printers—Impact | |
| Dot matrix | Prints text and graphics using small dots. |
| Daisy wheel | Prints letter-quality documents—no graphics. |
| Chain | High-speed printer to 3,000 lines per minute—designed to print text. |
| Band | High-speed printer to 2,000 lines per minute—designed to print text. |
| Printers—Nonimpact | |
| Thermal | Uses heat to produce fully formed characters. |
| Ink jet | Sprays ink onto page to form text and graphic output—prints quietly. |
| Laser | Produces high-quality text and graphics. |
| High-speed laser | Can exceed 20,000 lines per minute. |
| Screens | |
| Monochrome | Displays white, green, or amber images on a black background. |
| Color | Uses multiple colors to enhance displayed information. |
| Plasma | A flat screen that produces bright, clear images with no flicker. |
| LCD | A flat screen used on many laptop computers. |
| Plotters | Produces hard copy graphic output. |
| COM | Records reduced-size information on sheet film called microfiche or on roll film. |
| Voice | Conveys information to the user from the computer in the form of speech. |

## CHAPTER SUMMARY

1. **Output** is data that has been processed into a useful form called information that can be used by a person or a machine.
2. An **external report** is used outside the organization.
3. An **internal report** is used within an organization by people performing their jobs.
4. The major consideration for internal reports is that they be clear and easy to use. For external reports, the quality of the printed output may be important.
5. In a **detail report**, each line on the report usually corresponds to one input record.
6. A **summary report** contains summarized data, consisting of totals from detailed input data.
7. An **exception report** contains information that will help users to focus on situations that may require immediate decisions or specific actions.
8. **Computer graphics** are used to present information so it can be quickly and easily understood.
9. A **pie chart** is normally used to depict data that can be expressed as a percentage of a whole.

10. A **bar chart**, is best used for comparing sizes or quantities.
11. **Line charts** are particularly useful when showing changes over a period of time.
12. Computer printers fall into two broad categories: impact printers and nonimpact printers.
13. **Impact printing** devices transfer the image onto paper by some type of printing mechanism striking the paper, ribbon, and character together.
14. Impact printers can be **front striking** or **hammer striking**.
15. A **nonimpact printer** creates an image without having characters strike against a sheet of paper.
16. Impact printing is noisy but multiple copies can be made.
17. Nonimpact printers are quiet and some print very fast.
18. Computer printers may be classified by the speed at which they print: low, medium, high, and very high speed.
19. The printing rate of **low-speed printers** is expressed as the number of characters that can be printed in one second.
20. The printing rate for **medium-speed printers** and **high-speed printers** is stated as the number of lines printed per minute.
21. Medium- and high-speed printers are sometimes called **line printers**.
22. **Very high-speed printers** are sometimes called **page printers**.
23. Features of printers include carriage size, type of paper feed mechanism, and bidirectional printing.
24. The pages of **continuous form paper** are connected for continuous flow through the printer.
25. **Tractor feed mechanisms** transport continuous form paper by using sprokets inserted into holes on the sides of the paper.
26. **Friction feed** mechanisms move paper through a printer by pressure between the paper and the carriage.
27. **Dot matrix printers** can print text and graphics and are used with more personal computers than any other type of printer.
28. Dot matrix printers have small pins that are contained in a print head. The pins strike the paper and ribbon to print a character.
29. Most dot matrix printers print **bidirectionally**, meaning the print head can print while moving in either direction.
30. The quality of a dot matrix printer is partly dependent on the number of pins used to form the character.
31. Most dot matrix printers can print condensed print, standard print, and enlarged print.
32. Some dot matrix printers can print in color.
33. A **letter-quality** printed character is a fully formed character that is easy to read.
34. The most widely used letter-quality printer for personal computers is the **daisy wheel printer**.
35. Speeds of a daisy wheel printer vary from 20 to 60 characters per second.
36. **Thermal printers** use heat to produce fully formed characters, usually on chemically treated paper.
37. An **ink jet printer** uses a nozzle to spray liquid ink drops onto the page. Some ink jet printers print in color.
38. **Chain printers** print up to 3,000 lines per minute.
39. **Band printers** have interchangeable bands with many different styles of fonts.
40. **Laser printer** are nonimpact printers that operate in a manner similar to a copying machine.
41. Types of screens include monochrome screens, color screens, plasma screens, and LCD screens.
42. **Monochrome** monitors usually display green, white, or amber characters on a black background.
43. **Color screens** are being used more because color enables the user to more easily read and understand the information displayed on the screen.
44. A **plasma** display can produce all kinds and sizes of type styles, charts, and drawings.
45. **Liquid crystal displays** use a polarizing material and liquid crystal to form images.
46. Most screens utilize cathode ray tube (CRT) technology.
47. To display color on a color monitor, three separate dots (red, blue, green) are turned on by an electron beam.
48. The two types of color monitors are: **composite video monitors** and **RGB monitors**.
49. A **computer plotter** is an output device that can create drawings, diagrams, and similar types of output.
50. **Computer output microfilm (COM)** is an output technique that records output from a computer as microscopic images on roll or sheet film.
51. COM offers the advantages of faster recording speed, lower costs of recording the data, less space required for storing the data, and lower costs of storing the data.
52. **Voice output** consists of spoken words that are conveyed to the computer user from the computer.
53. A **voice synthesizer** can transform words stored in main memory into human speech.

## KEY TERMS

Band printers *6.13*
Bar charts *6.4*
Bidirectional *6.8*
Bit-mapped displays *6.17*
Blinking *6.15*
Bold *6.15*
Chain printer *6.13*
Color screens *6.16*
COM *6.20*
Composite video monitor *6.18*
Computer-assisted retrieval *6.21*
Computer graphics *6.4*
Computer output microfilm (COM) *6.20*
Continuous form paper *6.7*
Cursor *6.15*
Daisy wheel printer *6.11*
Detail report *6.3*
Dot-addressable displays *6.17*
Dot matrix printer *6.8*
Double size *6.15*
Drum plotter *6.19*
Electrostatic plotter *6.19*
Exception report *6.4*
External report *6.3*
Flatbed plotters *6.19*
Flat panel display screens *6.16*
Friction feed mechanisms *6.7*
Front striking *6.6*
Hammer striking *6.6*
Hard copy *6.2*
High-speed laser printers *6.14*
High-speed printers *6.7*
Impact printers *6.6*
Ink jet printer *6.12*
Internal report *6.3*
Laser printers *6.12*
LCD *6.16*
Letter quality *6.11*
Line charts *6.5*
Line printers *6.7*
Liquid crystal displays (LCD) *6.16*
Low-speed printers *6.7*
Medium-speed printers *6.7*
Microfiche *6.20*
Monochrome screens *6.16*
Nonimpact printing *6.6*
Output *6.2*
Page printers *6.7*
Paging *6.15*
Pen plotters *6.19*
Phosphor-coated screen *6.16*
Picture element *6.17*
Pie charts *6.4*
Pixel *6.17*
Plasma screen *6.16*
Plotter *6.19*
Report *6.3*
Reverse video *6.15*
RGB monitor *6.18*
Screen *6.14*
Scrolling *6.15*
Soft copy *6.2*
Standard carriage *6.7*
Summary report *6.3*
Thermal printers *6.12*
Tractor feed mechanisms *6.7*
Underlining *6.15*
Very high-speed printers *6.7*
Voice output *6.21*
Voice synthesizer *6.21*
Wide carriage *6.7*

## REVIEW QUESTIONS

1. Name and describe three types of commonly used reports.
2. What are the advantages of displaying information in a graphic form? What are the disadvantages? What are the three most commonly used types of charts?
3. What are the two major categories of printers? What are the differences between the two?
4. How does a dot matrix printer produce an image? What effect on the quality of print does this method have? What techniques are used on dot matrix printers to improve the print quality?
5. What does the term "letter quality" mean? What types of printers print with letter quality?
6. Describe some of the print capabilities of dot matrix printers with respect to graphics and character size and style.
7. How does an ink jet printer produce images? What are some advantages of ink jet printers?
8. Explain how a laser printer works. What are some advantages of laser printers?
9. What are the three major types of high-speed printers? List the characteristics such as speed and manner of printing for each one.
10. What types of screens are used with computers? List some screen features.
11. List the steps involved in displaying an image on a CRT screen.
12. Describe some of the different types of plotters and the manner in which they produce drawings.
13. List several advantages of microfilm over printed reports.
14. Describe the two ways of creating voice output.

## CONTROVERSIAL ISSUES

1. Some experts in business management have pointed out that much of the paperwork generated within a business organization is not used. Further, they have noted that managers do not have time to examine the reams of paper they receive in order to gain the information they need to make decisions. These experts have argued that very high-speed printers contribute to the paperwork explosion and, therefore, contribute to rather than help solve the problem. Others argue that in their right place, these printers are invaluable. Take a side in this dispute and prepare an argument.
2. "Automation—The Curse of Modern Society" was the title of a speech given at a meeting of union leaders. The speaker stated that the ability of the computer to develop drawings that are equal to or better than those prepared by graphic artists directly threatens the skilled worker. Others have said that having the computer perform these jobs frees people to do more creative work. What do you think?

## RESEARCH PROJECTS

1. The speed, quality, and prices of printers are constantly changing as new innovations appear. Examine a current issue of a personal computer magazine and clip out four advertisements for printers. Write to the printer manufacturers and obtain detailed information about the printers. Then make a presentation to your class concerning what you found.
2. Visit an installation in your area that uses plotters. Bring back and share with your class the drawings that are produced on the plotters.

**CHAPTER 7**

# Auxiliary Storage

## CHAPTER 7

# Auxiliary Storage

### OBJECTIVES

- Define auxiliary storage.
- Identify the primary devices used for personal computer auxiliary storage.
- Describe the manner in which data is stored on disks.
- Describe the methods used to back up data stored on floppy and hard disks.
- Identify the types of disk storage used with large computers.
- Explain how tape storage is used with large computers.
- List and describe three other forms of auxiliary storage: optical, solid state, and mass storage.

---

Storage, performed by all computers, is the fourth and final operation in the information processing cycle. Upon completion of this chapter you will be able to add the knowledge you acquire about storage operations to what you have learned in previous chapters about input, processing, and output operations. In addition, you will be familiar with the various types and capabilities of auxiliary storage devices that are used with computers.

## WHAT IS AUXILIARY STORAGE?

Computer storage can be classified into two types: main memory and auxiliary storage. As you have seen, main memory temporarily stores programs and data that are being processed. **Auxiliary storage**, or **secondary storage**, stores programs and data when they are not being processed, just as a filing cabinet is used in an office to store records. Records that are not being used are kept in the file cabinet until they are needed. In the same way, data and programs that are not being used on a computer are kept in auxiliary storage until they are needed. Auxiliary storage devices that are used with computers include devices such as magnetic disk and tape (Figure 7-1).

Auxiliary storage devices provide a more permanent form of storage than main memory because they are **nonvolatile**, that is, data and programs that have been placed on auxiliary storage devices are retained when the power is turned off. Main memory is volatile, which means that when power is turned off, whatever is stored in main memory is erased.

Auxiliary storage devices can be used as both input and output devices. When they are used to receive data that has been processed by the computer they are functioning as output devices. When data that they stored is transferred to the computer for processing, they are functioning as input devices.

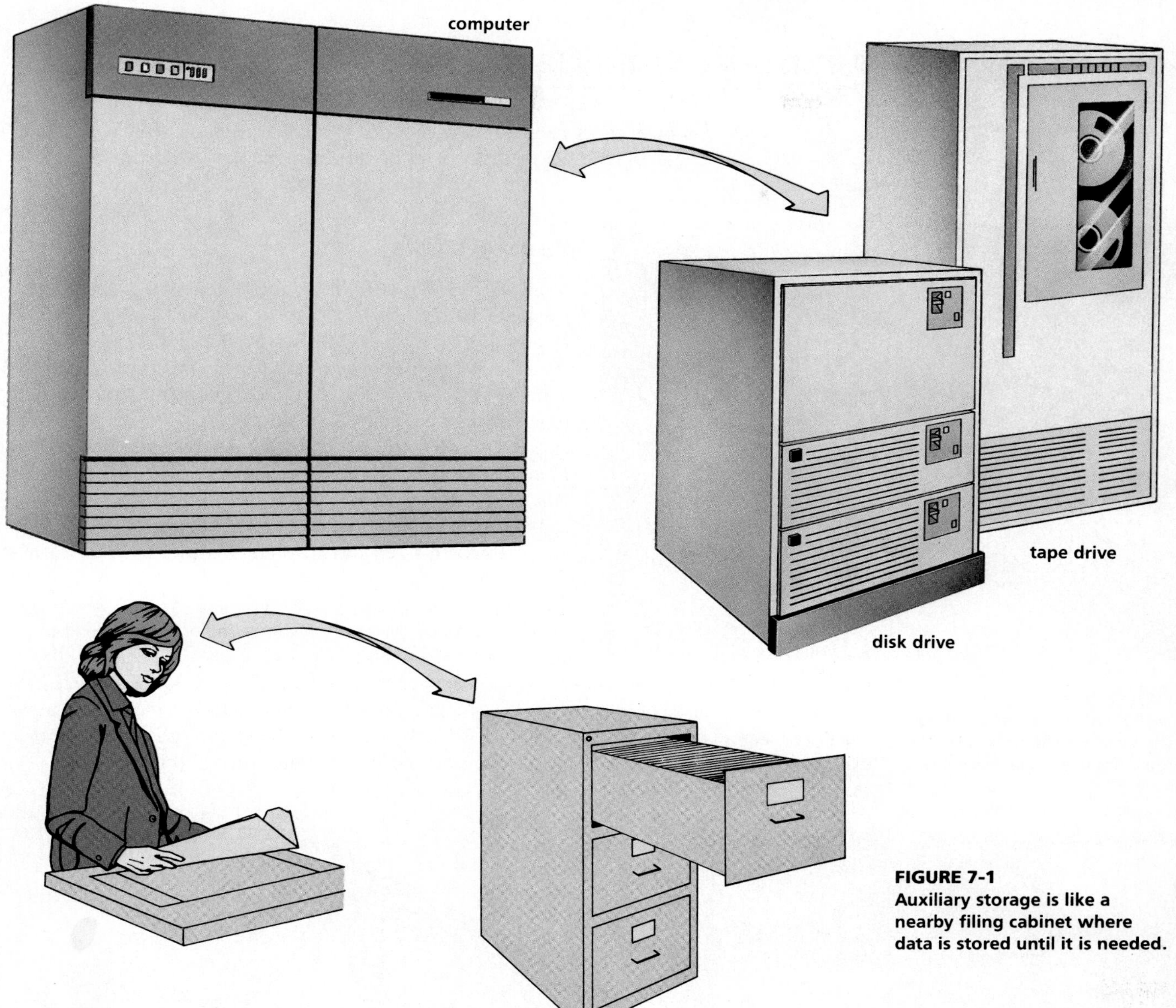


**FIGURE 7-1**
**Auxiliary storage is like a nearby filing cabinet where data is stored until it is needed.**

The auxiliary storage needs of users can vary greatly. Those who use personal computers, may find the amount of data to be stored to be relatively small. For example, the names, addresses, and telephone numbers of several hundred friends or customers of a small business might require only 20,000 bytes of auxiliary storage (200 records × 100 characters per record). Users of large computers such as banks or insurance companies, however, may need auxiliary storage devices that can store billions of characters. To meet the different needs of users, a variety of storage devices are available. In the next section we explain the devices that are designed for users with personal computers. Later in the chapter, we discuss the devices that are used with larger computer systems.

# AUXILIARY STORAGE FOR PERSONAL COMPUTERS

Personal computer users have several categories of auxiliary storage from which to choose. These include floppy disks, hard disks, and removable disk cartridges.

FIGURE 7-2
In this picture, a user is inserting a diskette into the disk drive of an IBM microcomputer.

## Floppy Disks

In the early 1970s IBM introduced the floppy disk and the floppy disk drive as a new type of auxiliary storage. Today, **floppy disks**, also called **diskettes**, **floppies**, or just **disks**, are used as a principal auxiliary storage medium for personal computers (Figure 7-2). This type of storage is convenient, reliable, and relatively low in cost.

Floppy disks are available in a number of different sizes. Many personal computers take disks that are 5 1/4 inches in diameter. Smaller disks, 3 1/2 inches in diameter, are also commonly used and are increasing in popularity (Figure 7-3).

A floppy disk consists of a circular piece of thin mylar plastic (the actual disk), which is coated with an oxide material similar to that used on magnetic tape. On a 5 1/4 inch disk, the circular piece of plastic is enclosed in a flexible square protective jacket. The jacket has an opening so that a portion of the disk's surface is exposed for reading and recording (Figure 7-4). On a 3 1/2 inch disk, the circular piece of plastic is enclosed in a rigid plastic cover and a piece of metal called the shutter covers the reading and recording area. When the 3 1/2 inch disk is inserted into a disk drive, the drive slides the shutter to the side to expose the disk surface (Figure 7-5).

FIGURE 7-3
The most commonly used disks for personal computers are 5 1/4 and 3 1/2 inch disks.

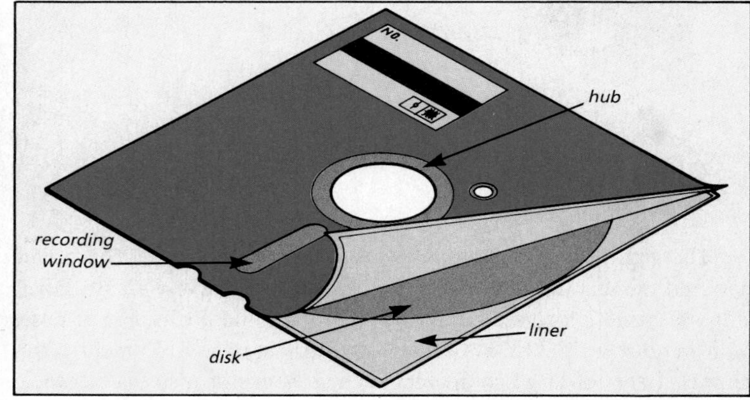


FIGURE 7-4
A 5 1/4 inch floppy disk, or diskette, consists of the disk itself enclosed within a protective jacket, usually made of a vinyl material. The liner of the diskette is essentially friction-free so that the disk can turn freely, but the liner does contact the disk and keep it clean. The magnetic surface of the diskette, which is exposed through the window in the jacket, allows data to be read and stored. The large hole (hub) in the diskette is used to mount the diskette in the disk drive. The small hole is used by some disk drives as an indicator for where to store data.

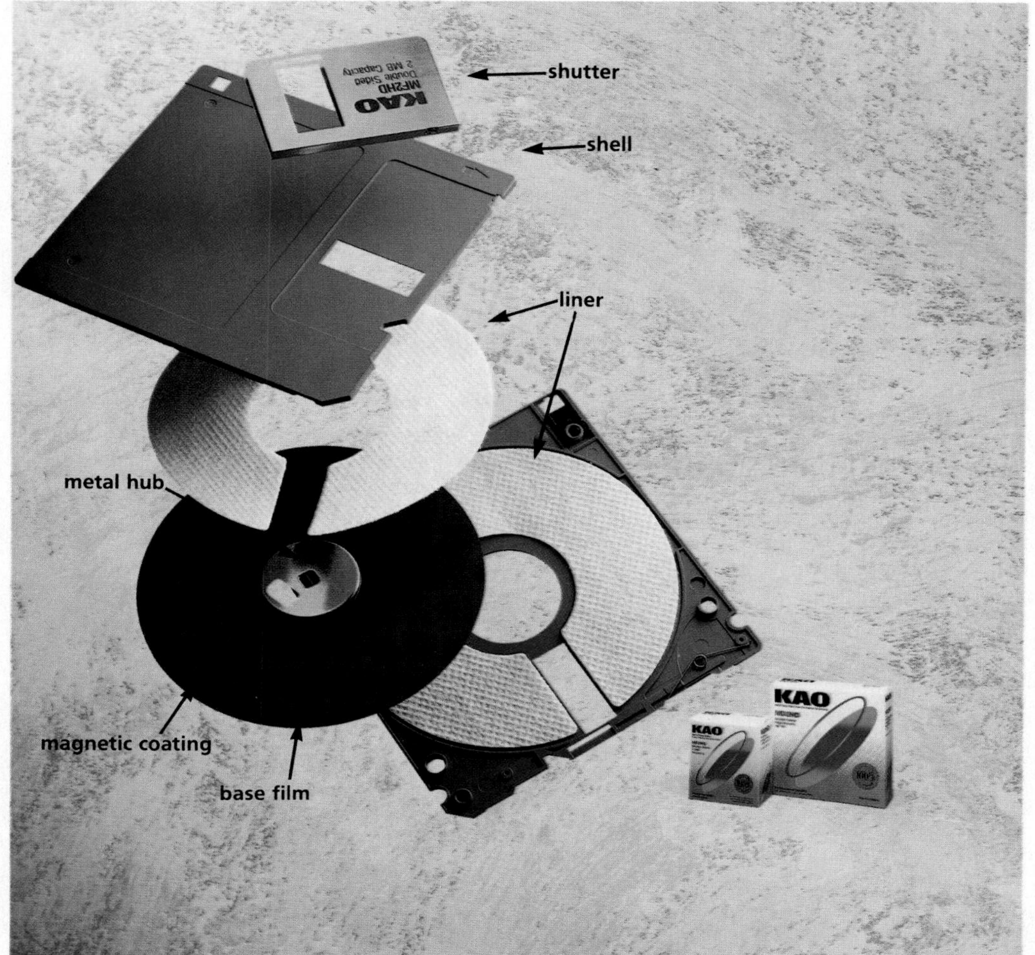


**FIGURE 7-5**
**In a 3 1/2 inch diskette the flexible plastic disk is enclosed between two liners that clean the disk surface of any microscopic debris and help to disperse static electricity. The outside cover is made of a rigid plastic material and the recording window is covered by a metal shutter that slides to the side when the disk is inserted into the disk drive.**

**How Is a Floppy Disk Formatted?** Before a floppy disk can be used on a microcomputer for auxiliary storage, it must be formatted. The **formatting** process includes defining the tracks and sectors on the surface of a disk (Figure 7-6). A **track** is a narrow recording band forming a full circle around the disk. Each track on the disk is divided into sectors. A **sector** is a section of a track. It is the basic storage unit of floppy disks. When data is read from a disk, a minimum of one full sector is read. When data is stored on a disk, at least one full sector is written. The number of tracks and sectors that are placed on a disk when it is formatted varies based on the capacity of the disk, the capabilities of the disk drive being used, and the specifications in the software that does the formatting. Many 5 1/4 inch disks are formatted with 40 tracks and 9 sectors on the surface of the disk. The 3 1/2 inch disks are usually formatted with 80 tracks and 9 sectors on each side. A 3 1/2 inch disk has more tracks than a 5 1/4 inch disk because even though it is smaller in size it has a larger storage capacity. When 40 tracks are recorded on a diskette, the tracks are numbered from 0 to 39. When 80 tracks are used, the tracks are numbered from 0 to 79.

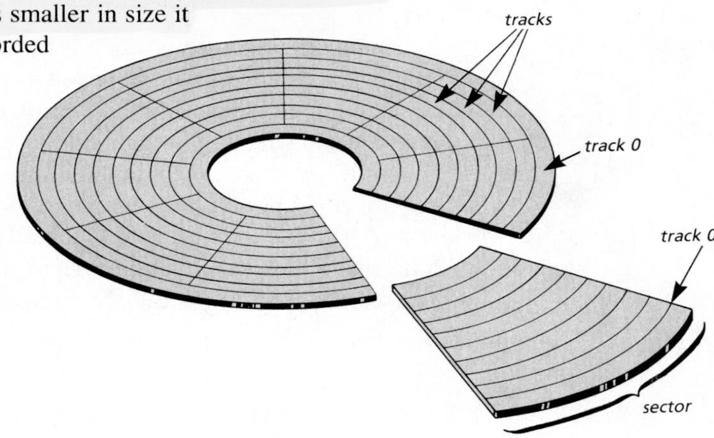

**FIGURE 7-6**
**Each track on a diskette is a narrow, circular band. On a diskette containing 40 tracks, the outside track is called track 0 and the inside track is called track 39. The distance between track 0 and track 39 on a 5 1/4 inch diskette is less than one inch. The disk surface is divided into sectors. This example shows a diskette with nine sectors.**

**Hard- and Soft-Sectored Diskettes** Disks and disk drives are classified as either hard-sectored or soft-sectored. A **hard-sectored disk** has a hole in front of each sector, normally near the center of the disk (Figure 7-7). These holes provide timing information to the drive. Hard-sectored disks will always contain the same number and size of sectors because the sectors are defined by the sector holes. Therefore, the exact storage capacity of a hard-sectored disk can always be determined. For example, a hard-sectored disk that contains 16 sectors with 256 bytes per sector will always be able to store a maximum of 4,096 bytes per track (16 × 256). When the disk is two-sided and contains 40 tracks per side, the total storage capacity of the disk is 327,680 bytes (4,096 × 40 × 2).

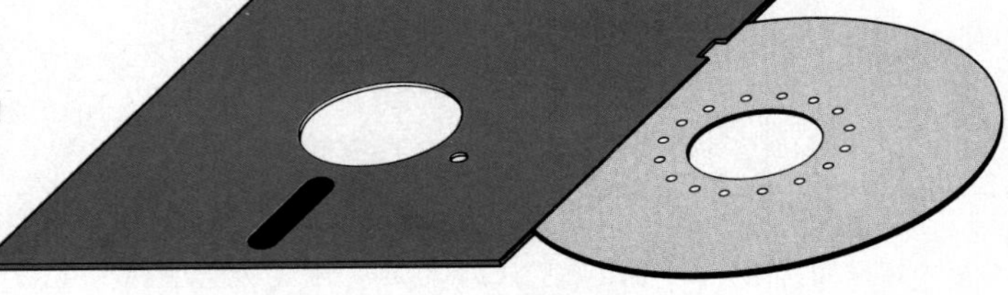

**FIGURE 7-7**
**Within its protective jacket this hard-sectored diskette contains 16 holes, evenly spaced around a circle on the disk. The holes indicate exactly where a sector begins.**

**FIGURE 7-8**
**A soft-sectored disk has only a single index hole. The drive can use the hole to find the beginning of any track. The number of sectors on a track and the number of bytes in each sector are determined by the software that formats the disk.**

A **soft-sectored disk** has a single index hole that indicates the beginning of the track (Figure 7-8). The number of sectors per track and the number of characters that can be stored in each sector are defined by the software when the disk is formatted. For example, a soft-sectored disk can be formatted with 40 tracks on each side, nine sectors per track, and 512 bytes per sector, for a total of 368,640 bytes (characters) stored on the disk.

**What Is the Storage Capacity of a Floppy Disk?** Knowing the storage capacity of a disk gives a user an idea of how much data or how many programs can be stored on the disk. The number of characters that can be stored on a disk depends on three basic factors: (1) the number of sides of the disk used; (2) the recording density of the bits on a track; and (3) the number of tracks on the diskette.

Some disks and drives are designed so that data can be recorded on only one side of the disk. These drives are called **single-sided drives**. Similarly, disks on which data can be recorded on one side only are called **single-sided disks**. Today, most disk drives are designed to record and read data on both sides of the disk. Drives that can read and write data on both sides of the disk are called **double-sided drives** and the disks are called **double-sided disks**. The use of double-sided drives and disks doubles the number of characters that can be stored on the disk. The term cylinder is sometimes used with double-sided disks. A **cylinder** is defined as all tracks of the same number. For example, track 0 on side 1 of the disk and track 0 on side 2 of the disk is called cylinder 0.

Another factor in determining the storage capacity of a disk is the recording density provided by the drive. The **recording density** is the number of bits that can be recorded on one inch of the innermost track on the disk. This measurement is referred to as **bits per inch (bpi)**. The higher the recording density, the higher the storage capacity of the disk.

The third factor that influences the number of characters that can be stored on a disk is the number of tracks onto which data can be recorded. This measurement is referred to as **tracks per inch (tpi)**. As we saw earlier in this chapter, the number of tracks depends on the size of the disk, the drive being used, and how the disk was formatted.

While the capacity of floppy disks can vary, a common capacity for a 5 1/4 inch disk is approximately 360K and for a 3 1/2 inch disk, 720K. On some computers floppy disks can store 2 megabytes (million characters) of data.

**How Is Data Stored on a Floppy Disk?** Regardless of the type of floppy disk or the formatting scheme that is used, the method of storing data on a disk is essentially the same. When a disk is inserted in a disk drive, the center hole fits over a hub mechanism that positions the disk in the unit (Figure 7-9). The circular plastic disk rotates within its cover at approximately 300 revolutions per minute. Data is stored on tracks character by character, using the same code, such as ASCII (American Standard Code for Information Interchange), that is used to store characters in main memory. Electronic impulses are placed along a track to represent the bit pattern for each character. To do this, a recording mechanism in the drive called the **read/write head** rests on the surface of the rotating disk, generating electronic impulses representing the bits to be recorded (Figure 7-10). To access different tracks on the disk, the drive moves the read/write head from track to track.

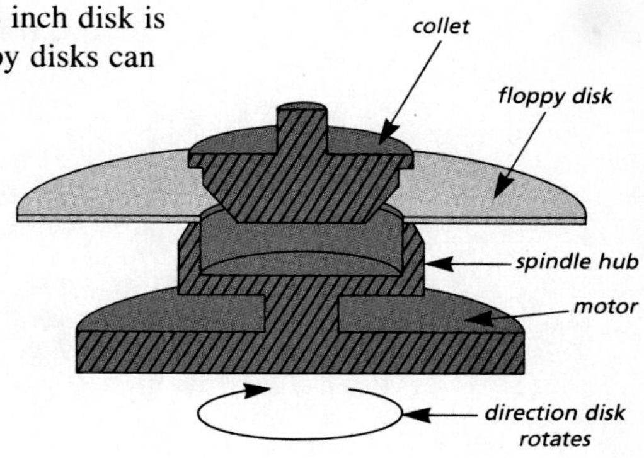

**FIGURE 7-9**
**When a floppy disk is inserted in a drive, the center hole is positioned between the collet and the hub. After the door to the disk drive is closed and the disk is engaged, it begins rotating within the protective jacket at approximately 300 RPM.**

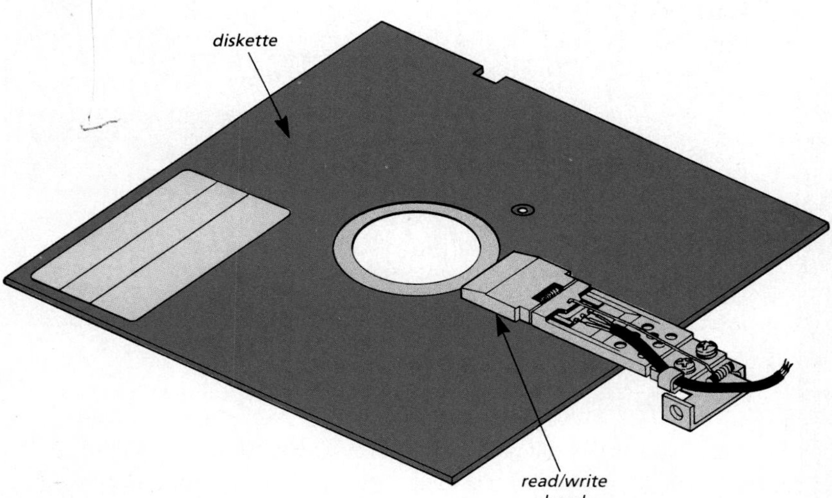


**FIGURE 7-10**
**The read/write head moves back and forth over the opening in the protective jacket to read or write data on the disk.**

**What Is Access Time?** Data stored in sectors on a floppy disk must be retrieved and placed in main memory to be processed. The time required to access and retrieve the data is called the **access time**.

The access time for a floppy disk drive depends on four factors:

1. **Seek time**, the time it takes to position the read/write head over the proper track.
2. **Latency**, the time it takes for the sector containing the data to rotate under the read/write head.

3. **Settling time**, the time required for the read/write head to be placed in contact with the disk.
4. **Data transfer rate**, the time required to transfer the data from the disk to main memory.

The access time for floppy disks varies from about 175 milliseconds (one millisecond equals 1/1000 of a second) to approximately 300 milliseconds. What this means to the user is that, on the average, data stored in a single sector on a diskette can be retrieved in approximately 1/5 to 1/3 of a second.

**The Care of Floppy Disks** With reasonable care, floppy disks provide an inexpensive and reliable form of storage. In handling floppy disks, take care to avoid exposing them to heat, magnetic fields, and contaminated environments. One advantage of the 3 1/2 inch disk is that it has a rigid plastic cover that provides more protection for the data stored on the plastic disk inside than the flexible cover on a 5 1/4 inch disk. Figure 7-11 shows ways to care for floppy disks properly.

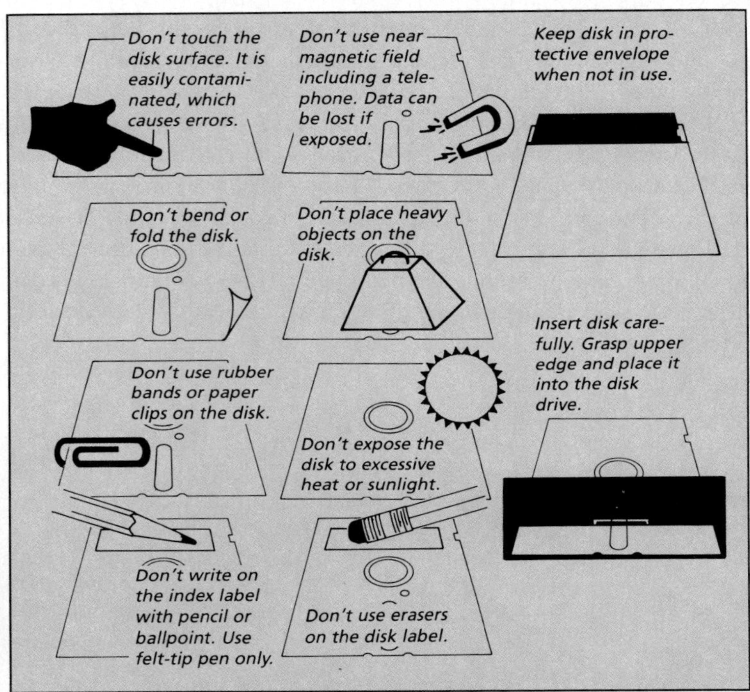

Don't touch the disk surface. It is easily contaminated, which causes errors.
Don't use near magnetic field including a telephone. Data can be lost if exposed.
Keep disk in protective envelope when not in use.
Don't bend or fold the disk.
Don't place heavy objects on the disk.
Insert disk carefully. Grasp upper edge and place it into the disk drive.
Don't use rubber bands or paper clips on the disk.
Don't expose the disk to excessive heat or sunlight.
Don't write on the index label with pencil or ballpoint. Use felt-tip pen only.
Don't use erasers on the disk label.


**FIGURE 7-11**
**Guidelines for the proper care of floppy disks.**

## Hard Disks

Hard disks provide larger and faster auxiliary storage capabilities for personal computers. **Hard disks** consist of one or more rigid metal **platters** coated with a metal oxide material that allows data to be magnetically recorded on the surface of the platters (Figure 7-12). In this section we discuss the two types of hard disks used on personal computers, fixed disks and hard cards.

**FIGURE 7-12**
**A hard disk consists of one or more disk platters. Each side of the platter is coated with a metal oxide substance that allows data to be magnetically stored.**

**FIGURE 7-13**
A hard card is a hard disk on a circuit board that can be mounted in a computer's expansion slot. In the picture below, the protective cover for the disk has been removed.

**What Is a Fixed Disk?** Hard disks used on personal computers are sometimes called **fixed disks** because the platters used to store the data are permanently mounted inside the computer and are not removable like floppy disks. On fixed disks, the metal disks, the read/write heads, and the mechanism for moving the heads across the surface of the disk are enclosed in a sealed case. This helps to ensure a clean environment for the disk.

The **hard card** is a circuit board that has a hard disk built onto it. Hard cards provide an easy way to expand the storage capacity of a personal computer because the board can be installed into an expansion slot of the computer (Figure 7-13).

**FIGURE 7-14**
This picture of a hard disk drive illustrates the access arm and the read/write heads, which are over the surface of the disks. These heads are extremely stable. They can read and write tracks very close together on the surface of the disk.
▼

**How Is Data Stored on a Hard Disk?** Storing data on hard disks is similar to storing data on floppy disks. Hard drives contain a spindle on which one or more disk platters are mounted. The spindle rotates the disk platters at a high rate of speed, usually 3,600 revolutions per minute. In order to read or write data on the surface of the spinning disk platter, the disk drives are designed with **access arms**, or **actuators**. The access arms or actuators contain one or more read/write heads per disk surface (Figure 7-14). These read/write heads "float" on a cushion of air and do not actually touch the surface of the disk. The distance between the head and the surface varies from approximately one-millionth of an inch to 1/2 millionth of an inch. As shown in Figure 7-15, the close tolerance leaves no room for any type of contamination. If some form of contamination is introduced or if the alignment of the read/write heads is altered by something accidentally jarring the computer, the disk head can collide with and damage the disk surface, causing a loss of data. This event is known as a **head crash**. Because of the time needed to repair the disk and to reconstruct the data that was lost, head crashes can be extremely costly for users.

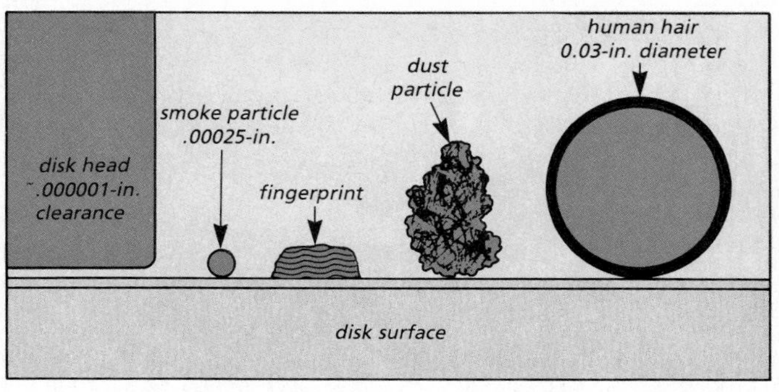


◄ **FIGURE 7-15**
The clearance between a disk head and the disk surface is about 1 millionth of an inch. With these tolerances, contamination such as a smoke particle, fingerprint, dust particle, or human hair could render the drive unusable. Sealed disk drives are designed to minimize contamination.

When reading data from the disk, the read/write head senses the magnetic spots that are recorded on the disk along the various tracks and transfers the data to main memory. When writing, the read/write head transfers data from main memory and stores it as magnetic spots on the tracks on the recording surface of one or more of the disks. As the disk rotates at a high rate of speed, the read/write heads move across its surface.

The number of platters permanently mounted on the spindle in the drive can vary. For 5 1/4 inch drives, the number varies between one and four platters. On many drives, each surface of a platter can be used to store data. Thus, if one platter is used in the drive, two surfaces are available for data. If two platters are used, four surfaces are available for data, and so on. Naturally, the more platters, the more data that can be stored on the drive.

The storage capacity of hard drives is measured in megabytes or millions of bytes (characters) of storage. Common sizes for personal computers range from 10MB to 100MB of storage and even larger sizes are available. As an idea of how much data these storage capacities represent, 10MB of storage is equivalent to approximately 5,000 double-spaced typewritten pages.

In addition to a larger storage capacity, hard disks provide faster access time than floppy disks. The typical access time of a hard disk for a personal computer is between 25 and 80 milliseconds.

The use of a hard disk drive on a personal computer provides many advantages for users. Because of its large storage capacity, a hard disk can store many software application programs and data files. When a user wants to run a particular application or access a particular data file on a hard disk, it is always available. The user does not have to find the appropriate floppy disk and insert it into the drive. In addition, the faster access time of a hard disk reduces the time needed to load programs and access data.

**Disk Cartridges** Another variation of disk storage available for use with personal computers is the removable **disk cartridge**. Disk cartridges, which can be inserted and removed from a computer (Figure 7-16), offer the storage and fast access features of hard disks and the portability of floppy disks. Disk cartridges are often used when data security is an issue. At the end of a work session, the disk cartridge can be removed and locked up, leaving no data on the computer.

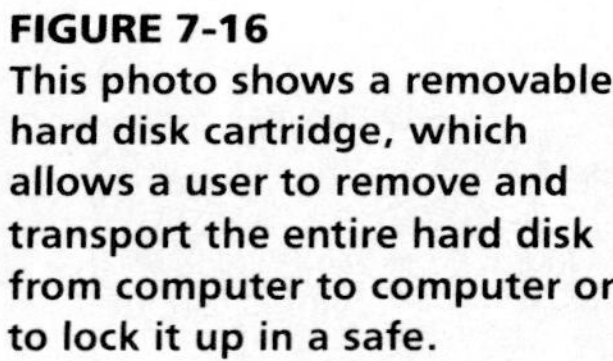

**FIGURE 7-16**
**This photo shows a removable hard disk cartridge, which allows a user to remove and transport the entire hard disk from computer to computer or to lock it up in a safe.**

## Protecting Data Stored on a Disk

Regardless of whether you are using floppy disks, hard disks, or removable disk cartridges on a personal computer, you must protect the data you store on the disk from being lost. Disk storage is reusable and data that is stored on a disk may be overwritten and replaced with new data. This is a desirable feature allowing users to remove or replace unwanted files. However, it also raises the possibility of accidentally removing or replacing a file that you really wanted to keep. To protect programs and data stored on disks, there are several things you can do.

**How Is the Write-Protect Notch Used?** One way to protect the data and programs stored on a floppy disk is to use the write-protect notch. On the 5 1/4 inch disks, this notch is located on the side of the disk. To prevent writing to a disk, a user covers this notch with a small piece of removable tape. Before writing data onto a disk, the disk drive checks the notch. If the notch is open the drive will proceed to write on the disk. If the notch is covered the disk drive will not write on the disk (Figure 7-17).

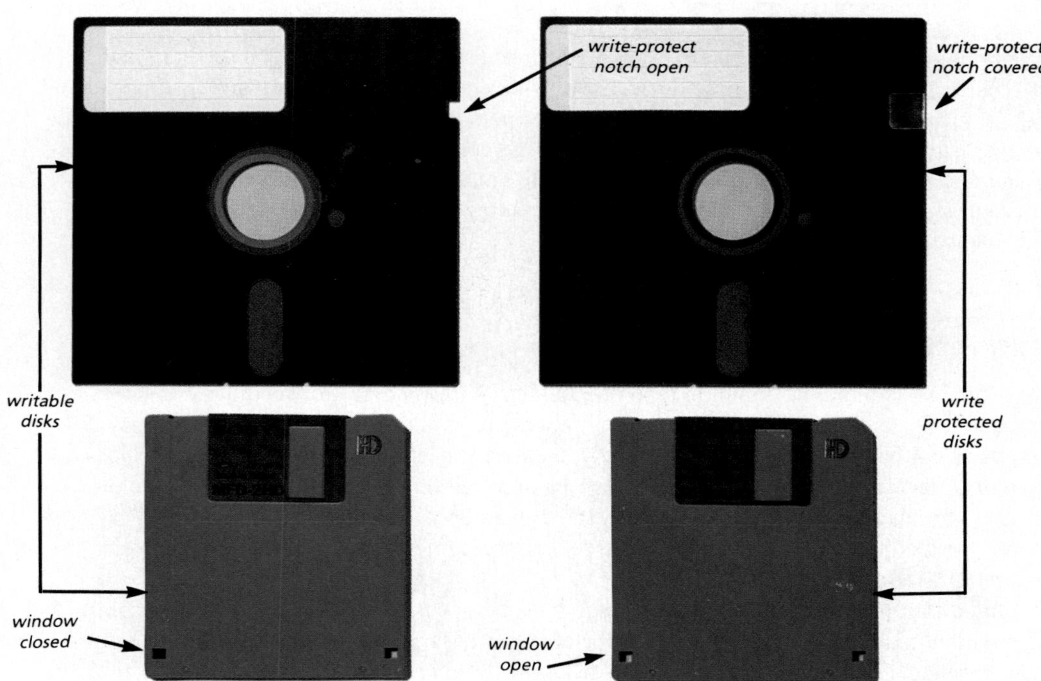


**FIGURE 7-17**
**The write-protect notch of the 5 1/4 inch disk on the left is open and therefore data could be written to the disk. The notch of the 5 1/4 inch disk on the right, however, is covered. Data could not be written to this disk. The reverse situation is true for the 3 1/2 inch disk. Data cannot be written on the 3 1/2 inch disk on the right because the small black piece of plastic is not covering the window in the lower left corner. Plastic covers the window of the 3 1/2 inch disk on the left, so data can be written on this disk.**

On 3 1/2 inch disks, the situation is reversed. The write-protect notch is a small window in the corner of the disk. A piece of plastic in the window can be moved to open and close the window. If the write-protect window is closed, the drive can write on the disk. If the window is open, the drive will not write on the disk.

**Backup Storage** Another way to protect programs and data stored on disks is by creating backup storage. As discussed in Chapter 3, backup storage means creating a duplicate copy of important programs and data on a separate disk. To back up floppy disks, simply copy the data on one disk to another floppy disk. When using hard disks, however, the user is faced with a more difficult problem. The amount of data that can be stored on a hard disk can fill many floppy disks. For example, to back up a hard disk containing 10 million characters, approximately thirty 5 1/4 inch diskettes that could each store 360,000 characters would be required. For this reason, cartridge tape is sometimes used to back up hard disk storage.

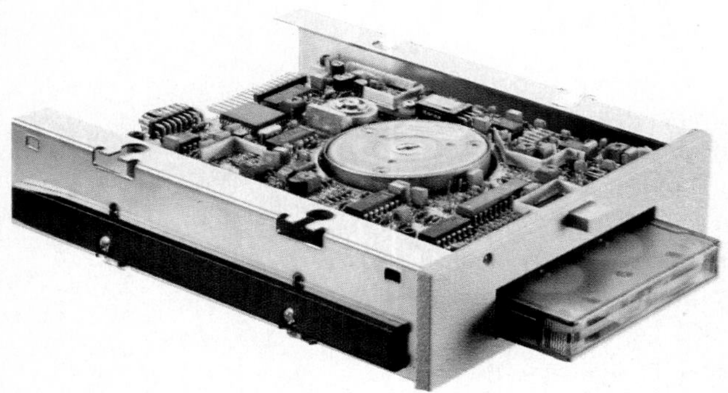

FIGURE 7-18
Cartridge tape drives are an effective way to back up and store data that would otherwise require numerous diskettes.

**Cartridge Tape** A device commonly used to back up hard disks on personal computers is the **cartridge tape drive** (Figure 7-18). When these devices are available on a personal computer, the data and programs that are stored on a hard disk can be copied onto the tape cartridge for backup storage.

Some cartridge tape drives can operate in a **streaming mode**, without the normal stopping and starting usually associated with tape operations. Tape streaming results in more data being recorded in less time. Using the streaming method, a cartridge tape unit can completely copy a 20 million byte hard disk in approximately four minutes.

## AUXILIARY STORAGE FOR MEDIUM AND LARGE COMPUTERS

A wide variety of devices are available for use as auxiliary storage on medium and large computers. Most of these devices use storage techniques that are similar, if not identical, to the devices that we discussed for personal computers. As you would expect, however, storage devices used for medium and large computers provide greater storage capacity and faster retrieval rates than devices used with small systems. For discussion purposes, we group storage devices for medium and large computers into three categories: magnetic disk, magnetic tape, and other storage devices.

### Magnetic Disk

Magnetic disk is the most common type of auxiliary storage device for medium and large computers. Disks for medium and large computers are similar to devices used on personal computers but have larger capacities, usually as a result of having more recording surfaces. Some disk devices used on large computers can store billions of characters of information. Because of their ability to retrieve data directly from a specific location on the disk, disk devices for medium and large computers are sometimes referred to as **direct-access storage devices (DASD)**.

One difference between auxiliary storage for a personal computer and for larger computers is that many more disk devices can be attached to larger computers. While most personal computers are limited to two to four disks, medium computers can support 8 to 16 disk devices and large computers can support over 100 high-speed disk devices. Figure 7-19 shows a large number of disk units attached to a single mainframe computer.

FIGURE 7-19
A mainframe computer can have dozens of fixed disk storage devices attached to it.

Disk devices for medium and large computers fall into two categories: fixed disks and removable disks.

**Fixed Disks** Fixed disks, the most commonly used disks for medium and large computers, can be either mounted in the same cabinet as the computer or enclosed in their own stand-alone cabinet. As with fixed disks in personal computers, fixed disks on medium and large computers contain nonremovable platters that are enclosed in airtight cases to prevent contamination (Figure 7-20).

**FIGURE 7-20**
**A high-speed, high-capacity fixed disk drive in a stand-alone cabinet.**

**Removable Disks** Removable disk units were introduced in the early 1960s and were the most prevalent type of disk storage for nearly 20 years. During the 1980s, however, removable disks began to be replaced by fixed disks that offered larger storage capacities and higher reliability.

Removable disk devices consist of the drive unit, which is usually in its own cabinet, and the removable recording media, called a **disk pack**. Removable disk packs consist of 5 to 11 metal platters that are used on both sides for recording data. The recording capacity of these packs varies from 10 to 300 megabytes of data. One advantage of removable disk packs is that the data on a disk drive can be quickly changed by removing one pack and replacing it with another. This can be accomplished in minutes. When removable disk packs are not mounted in a disk drive they are stored in a protective plastic case. When the packs are being used, the plastic case is usually placed on top of the drive unit. Figure 7-21 shows a large installation of removable disk devices with the empty protective disk pack cases on top of the drives.

**FIGURE 7-21**
**A large installation of removable disk drives showing the protective disk pack cases on top of the drive units.**

**How Is Data Physically Organized on a Disk?** Depending on the type of disk drive, data is physically organized in one of two ways on disks used with medium and large computers. One way is the sector method and the other is the cylinder method.

As with the floppy disks and hard disks used with personal computers, the **sector method** for physically organizing data on disks divides each track on the disk surface into individual storage areas called sectors (Figure 7-22). Each sector can contain a specified number of bytes. Data is referenced by indicating the surface, track, and sector where the data is stored.

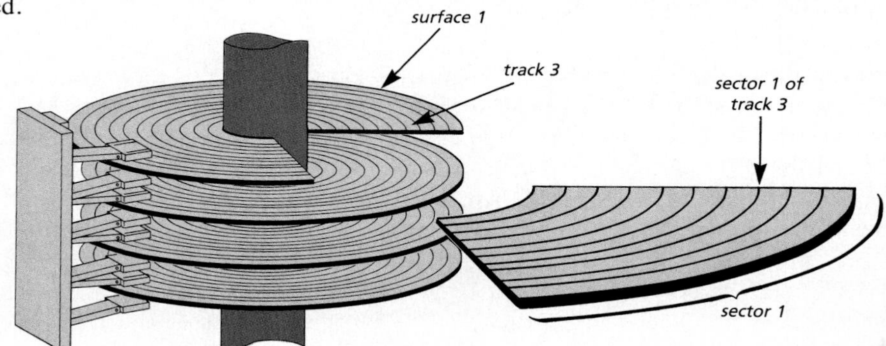


**FIGURE 7-22**
**The sector method of disk addressing divides each track into a number of sectors. To locate data, the surface, track, and sector where the data is stored are specified.**

With the **cylinder method**, all tracks of the same number on each recording surface are considered part of the same cylinder (Figure 7-23). For example, if each platter contained 200 tracks, the tenth track on all surfaces would be considered part of the tenth cylinder. All twentieth tracks would be part of the twentieth cylinder, and so on. When the computer requests data from a disk using the cylinder method, it must specify the cylinder, recording surface, and record number. Because the access arms containing the read/write heads all move together, they are always over the same track on all surfaces. Thus, using the cylinder method to record data "down" the disk surfaces reduces the movement of the read/write head during both reading and writing of data.

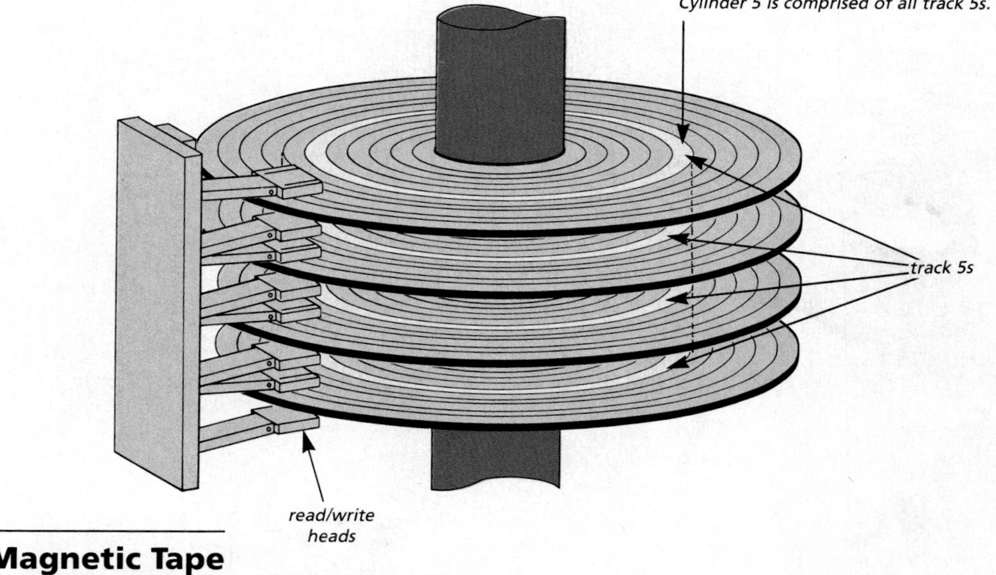


**FIGURE 7-23**
**The cylinder method reduces the movement of the read/write head (thereby saving time) by writing information "down" the disk on the same track of successive surfaces.**

## Magnetic Tape

During the 1950s and early 1960s, prior to the introduction of removable disk pack drives, magnetic tape was the primary method of storing large amounts of data. Today, even though tape is no longer used by medium and large computers as the primary method of auxiliary storage, it still functions as a cost-effective way to store data that does not have to be accessed immediately. In addition, tape serves as the primary means of backup for most medium and large systems and is often used when data is transferred from one system to another.

**Magnetic tape** consists of a thin ribbon of plastic. The tape is coated on one side with a material that can be magnetized to record the bit patterns that represent data. The most common types of magnetic tape devices are reel-to-reel and cartridge. Reel-to-reel tape is usually 1/2 inch wide and cartridge tape is 1/4 inch wide (Figure 7-24).

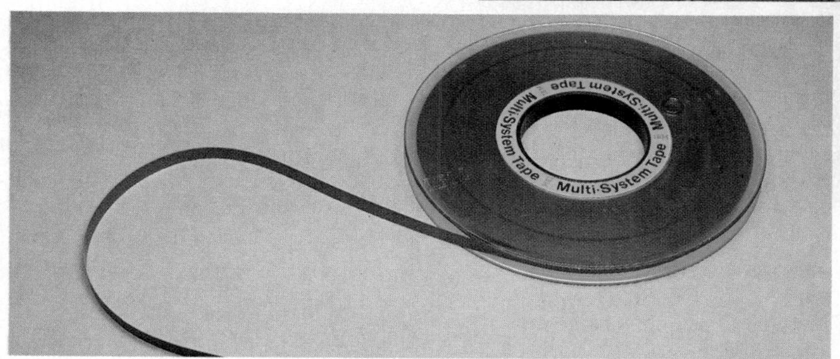


**FIGURE 7-24 ▲**
**In the top picture a computer operator is positioning a reel of magnetic tape on a tape device. Below is a standard 10 1/2-inch reel of magnetic tape.**

### Reel-to-Reel Tape Devices

Reel-to-reel tape devices use two reels: a supply reel to hold the tape that will be read or written on, and the take-up reel to temporarily hold portions of the supply reel tape as it is being processed. At the completion of processing, tape on the take-up reel is wound back onto the supply reel. As the tape moves from one reel to another, it passes over a read/write head (Figure 7-25), an electromagnetic device that can read or write data on the tape.

Older style tape units (Figure 7-26) are vertical cabinets with vacuum columns that hold five or six feet of slack tape to prevent breaking during sudden start or stop operations.

Newer style tape units (Figure 7-27) allow a tape to be inserted through a slot opening similar to the way videotapes are loaded in a videocassette recorder. This front-loading tape drive takes less space and can be cabinet mounted. The drive automatically threads the end of the tape onto an internal take-up reel.

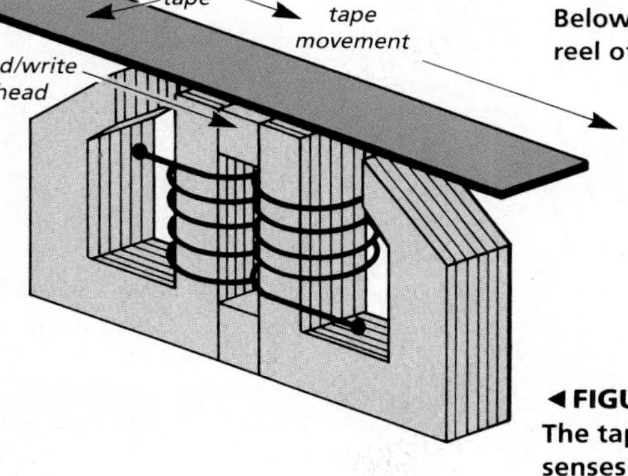


**◄ FIGURE 7-25**
**The tape read/write head senses and records the electronic bits that represent data.**

**FIGURE 7-26 ▲**
**Older style reel-to-reel magnetic tape storage devices.**

**FIGURE 7-27 ►**
**Newer style tape drives allow the user to slide the tape into a slot at the front of the unit. The drive automatically threads the tape.**

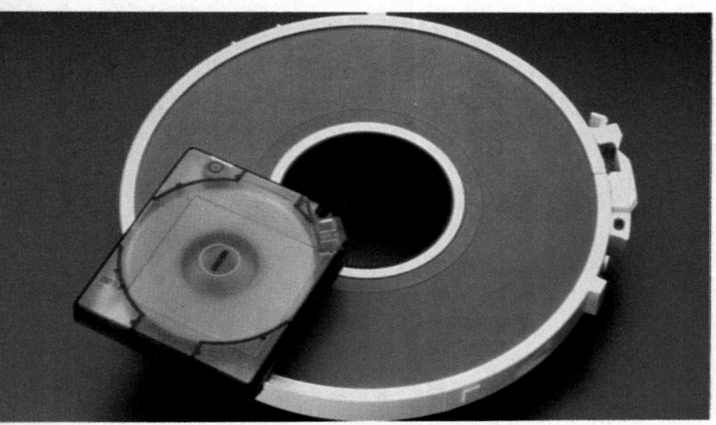

FIGURE 7-28
The four inch by five inch tape cartridge can hold 20% more data than the 10 1/2 inch reel of tape.

Reels of tape usually come in lengths of 300, 1,200, 2,400 and 3,600 feet and can store up to 100 megabytes of data.

**Cartridge Tape Devices** Cartridge tape devices for medium and large computers are identical to units previously discussed for personal computers. They are becoming increasingly popular because they can store more data and take less space than the traditional 10 1/2 inch diameter reels of tape (Figure 7-28).

**How Is Data Stored on Magnetic Tape?** Data is recorded on magnetic tape in the form of magnetic spots that can be read and transferred to main memory. The magnetic spots on the tape are organized into a series of horizontal rows called channels. The presence or absence of magnetic spots representing bits is used to represent a given character on the tape.

Several different coding structures are used with magnetic tape, including both ASCII and EBCDIC. The coding structure for EBCDIC divides half-inch tape into nine horizontal channels. A combination of bits in a vertical column that consists of the nine horizontal channels is used to represent characters and the error-checking parity bit on the tape (Figure 7-29).

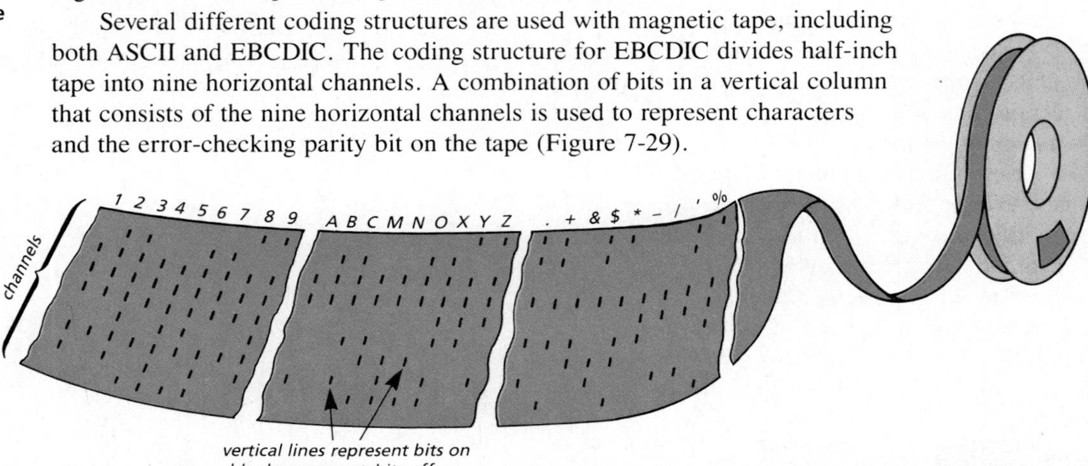


FIGURE 7-29
One of the most common coding structures found on magnetic tape is the EBCDIC code, which is stored in nine channels on the tape. Eight channels are used to store the bits representing a character. The ninth channel is a parity error-checking channel.

**Tape density** is the number of characters or bytes that can be stored on an inch of tape. As on disk drives, tape density is expressed in bytes per inch or bpi. Commonly used tape densities are 800, 1,600, 3,200 and 6,250 bpi. Some of the newer cartridge tape devices can record at densities of over 38,000 bpi. The higher the density, the more data that can be stored on a tape.

Tape is considered a **sequential storage** media because the computer must read tape records one after another until it finds the one it wants. Tapes do not have fixed data storage location addresses like disk drives that allow direct access of a record.

In order to allow some room for starting and stopping, tapes use **interblock gaps (IBG)**, also called **interrecord gaps (IRG)** (Figure 7-30). These spaces are usually about .6 inch long. To increase recording efficiency, **blocked records** are normally used. Blocking refers to placing two or more individual records, called **logical records**, into a block to form a **physical record** (Figure 7-31). A logical record refers to the amount of data that a program uses when it processes one record. A physical record refers to the amount of data that is physically transferred into memory from the tape. For example, there could be three employee payroll (logical) records contained within one block or (physical) record on a tape. Using blocking has two advantages. First, the tape is used more efficiently. More data can be stored because the gap between each logical record is eliminated. Second, because an entire physical record is read into memory each time data is read from the tape, reading data takes place faster. Two or more logical records are read each time data is transferred from the tape to main memory.

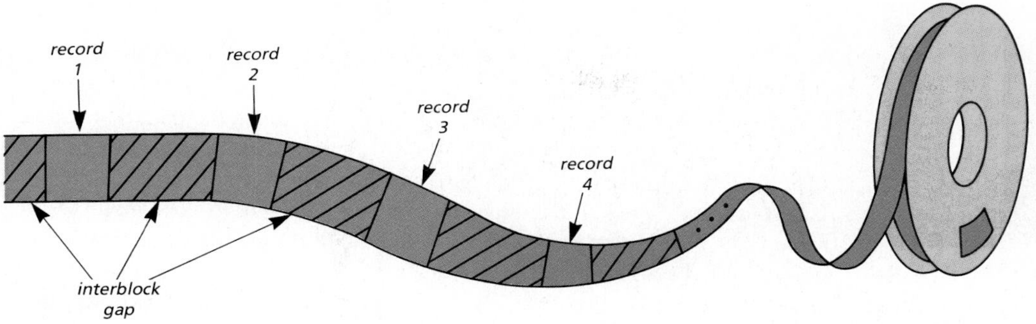


**FIGURE 7-30**
**Records stored on tape are stored sequentially, separated by an interblock gap that allows for the starting and stopping of the tape drive. The interblock gap is typically .6 inch wide.**

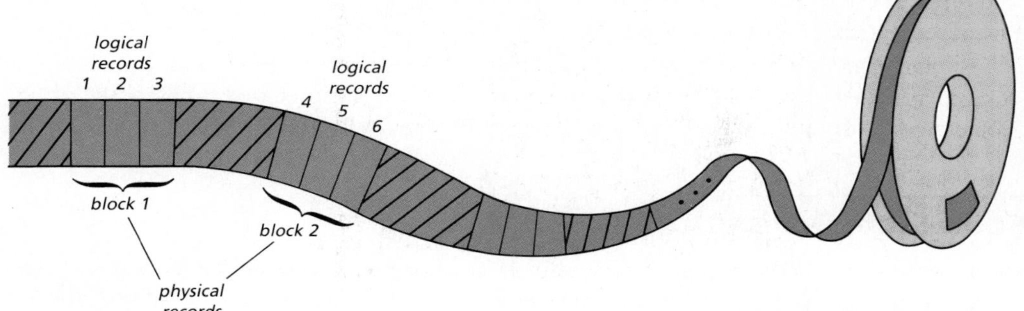


**FIGURE 7-31**
**Three logical records are stored in each block or physical record in this diagram. An entire block of records is brought into main memory each time the tape file is read.**

# OTHER FORMS OF AUXILIARY STORAGE

While the conventional disk and tape devices described above comprise the majority of auxiliary storage devices and media, several other means for storing data are used. These include optical storage technology, solid-state devices, and mass storage devices.

## Optical Storage Technology

Optical storage technology is one of the newest and most promising methods of data storage. Enormous quantities of information can be stored on **optical disks** by using a laser to burn microscopic holes on the surface of a hard plastic disk (Figure 7-32). A lower power laser reads the disk by reflecting light off the disk surface. The reflected light is converted into a series of bits that the computer can process.

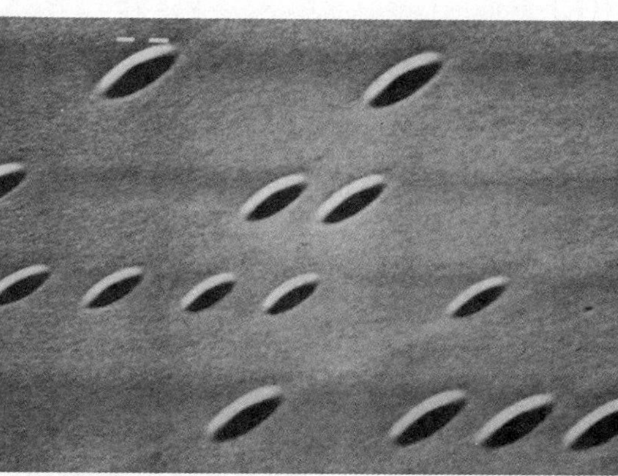

**FIGURE 7-32**
**To record data on an optical disk (left), a laser burns microscopic holes on the surface (right).**

FIGURE 7-33
An optical compact disk can store hundreds of times the data as on a comparable-size floppy disk.

A full-size 12 inch optical disk can store several billion characters of information. The smaller disks, just under five inches in diameter, can store over 800 million characters or approximately 800 times the data that can be stored on a 5 1/4 inch floppy diskette. That's enough space to store approximately 400,000 pages of typed data. The smaller optical disks are called **CDROM**, for compact disk read-only memory (Figure 7-33). They use the same laser technology that is used for the CDROM disks that have become popular for recorded music.

The disadvantage of optical disks now available is that they cannot be modified once the data is recorded. Most optical disks are prerecorded but some devices provide for one-time recording. These units are called **WORM** devices, for write once, read many. Recently announced optical disk devices will be able to erase and rerecord disks.

Even as read-only devices, optical disks have great potential. Because of their tremendous storage capacities, entire catalogs or reference materials can be stored on a single disk. Some people predict that optical disks will soon replace data now stored on film such as microfiche.

## Solid-State Devices

To the computer, solid-state storage devices look and act just like disk drives, only faster. But as their name suggests, they contain no moving parts, only electronic circuits. **Solid-state storage devices** use the latest in random-access memory (RAM) technology to provide high-speed data access and retrieval. Rows of RAM chips (Figure 7-34) provide megabytes of memory that can be accessed much faster than the fastest conventional disk drives. Solid-state storage devices are significantly more expensive than conventional disk drives offering the same storage capacity.

## Mass Storage Devices

**Mass storage devices** provide for the automated retrieval of data from a "library" of storage media such as cartridge tapes or floppy disks. Mass storage is ideal for extremely large databases that require all information to be readily accessible even though any one portion of the database may be infrequently required. Mass storage systems take less room than conventional tape storage and can retrieve and begin accessing records within seconds. Figure 7-35 shows a mass storage system that uses tape cartridges.

FIGURE 7-34
Solid-state storage devices use megabytes of RAM chips to simulate a conventional disk drive. ▼

FIGURE 7-35►
This mass storage system can access any one of thousands of tape cartridges in an average of 11 seconds. Each cartridge is a 4 × 4 inch square and about 1 inch thick.

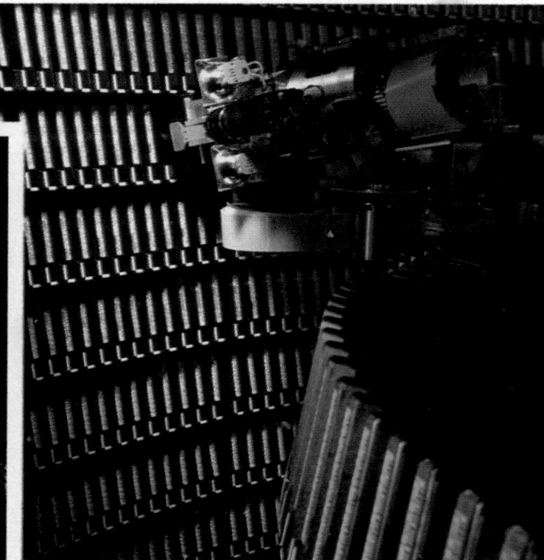

## SUMMARY OF AUXILIARY STORAGE

Auxiliary storage is used to store programs and data that are not currently being processed by the computer. This chapter discussed the various types of auxiliary storage used with computers. The chart in Figure 7-36 provides a summary of the auxiliary storage devices. What you have learned about these devices and storage operations in general can now be added to what you have learned about the input, processing, and output operations of the information processing cycle.

**FIGURE 7-36**
**A summary of some of the more common auxiliary storage devices.**

| DEVICE | DESCRIPTION |
|---|---|
| **Personal Computers** | |
| Floppy disk | Plastic storage media that is reliable and low in cost. |
| Hard disk | Fixed metal storage media that provides large storage capacity and fast access. |
| Hard card | Fixed disk that is built on a circuit board and installed in an expansion slot of a personal computer. |
| Disk cartridge | Combines storage and access features of hard disk and portability of floppy disks. |
| Tape cartridge | Used to back up hard disks on personal computers. |
| **Medium and Large Computers** | |
| Fixed disk | Large multiplatter fixed disk with high storage capacity and fast access. |
| Removable disk | Disk drives with removable disk packs. |
| Reel tape | Magnetic tape device using the reel-to-reel method of moving tape. |
| Tape cartridge | Magnetic tape device using cartridge method of holding tape. |
| **Other Storage Devices** | |
| Optical storage | Uses lasers to record and read data on a hard plastic disk. High quality and large storage capacity. |
| Solid state | Uses RAM chips to provide high-speed data access and retrieval. |
| Mass storage | Automated retrieval of storage media such as tape cartridges and floppy disks. |

## CHAPTER SUMMARY

1. **Auxiliary storage** is used to store data that is not being processed on the computer.
2. The **floppy disk** or **diskette** is used as a primary auxiliary storage medium with personal computers.
3. Most personal computers use a diskette 5 1/4 inches in diameter. Smaller diskettes (approximately 3 1/2 inches in diameter) are also available and are increasing in popularity.
4. A floppy disk consists of a plastic disk enclosed within a square protective jacket. A portion of the surface of the disk is exposed so data can be stored on it.
5. Data is stored on a disk in tracks. A **track** is a narrow recording band forming a full circle around the diskette.
6. The number of tracks most often found are 40 tracks or 80 tracks per diskette.
7. Each track on a disk is divided into **sectors**, the basic unit of disk storage. A minimum of one full sector of data is read from a diskette: a minimum of one sector is written on a diskette.
8. A **hard-sectored disk** contains holes in the diskette indicating where each sector begins.
9. A **soft-sectored disk** contains one hole indicating where the tracks begin. The number of sectors and the number of characters in each sector are determined by the software that formats the disk.

10. The factors affecting disk storage capacity are the number of sides of the disk used; the recording density of the bits; and the number of tracks on the disk.
11. **Single-sided drives** read and record data on only one side of a diskette. **Double-sided drives** read and record data on both sides of the disk.
12. The **recording density** is stated as the number of bits that can be recorded on one inch of the innermost track on a disk. The measurement is referred to as **bits per inch (bpi)**.
13. To read or write data on a disk, the disk is placed in the disk drive. Within its protective covering the disk rotates at about 300 revolutions per minute. The **read/write head** rests on the disk and senses or generates electronic impulses representing bits.
14. The time required to access and retrieve data stored on a diskette is called the **access time**.
15. Access time depends on four factors: (1) **seek time**, the time it takes to position the read/write head on the correct track; (2) **latency time**, the time it takes for the data to rotate under the read/write head; (3) **settling time**, the time required for the head to be placed in contact with the disk; and (4) **data transfer rate**, the amount of data that can be transferred from the disk to main memory.
16. Floppy disks should not be exposed to heat or magnetic fields. With proper care, floppy disks provide an inexpensive and reliable form of storage.
17. A **hard disk** consists of one or more rigid metal **platters** coated with a metal oxide material.
18. On **fixed disks**, the metal disks, read/write heads, and access arm are enclosed in a sealed case. These disks provide high storage capabilities and fast access times.
19. To read and write data on a hard disk, an **access arm** moves read/write heads in and out. The heads float very close to the surface of the disk, generating or sensing electronic impulses that represent bits.
20. The number of platters in a hard disk for a microcomputer can vary from one to four. On many disks, both sides of the platters can be used for storing data.
21. The typical access time for a microcomputer hard disk is between 25 and 85 milliseconds.
22. **Removable disk cartridges** offer the storage and access features of hard disks with the portability of floppy disks.
23. The write-protect notch on floppy disks can be used to protect the data stored on a disk from being overwritten.
24. To backup storage means to create a duplicate copy of important programs and data on a separate disk or tape.
25. The normal method for floppy disk backup is to copy the data onto another disk. For hard disk, the disk is often copied to a **cartridge tape**.
26. Disk drives used with large computers can be categorized as either fixed disks or removable disks.
27. **Fixed disks** are sealed in an enclosure and permanently mounted in the disk drive.
28. **Disk packs** contain between 5 and 11 platters that can be mounted and removed from the disk drive.
29. The **sector method** (identifying the surface, track, and sector number) or the **cylinder method** (identifying the cylinder, recording surface, and record number) can be used to physically organize and address data stored on disk.
30. The tracks that can be referenced at one position of the access arm are called a **cylinder**.
31. **Magnetic tape** is used primarily for backup purposes in large computer installations.
32. Data is recorded on **magnetic tape** as a series of magnetic spots along a horizontal channel. Each spot represents a bit in a coding scheme. Large computers commonly use the EBCDIC coding scheme on nine-track tape.
33. **Tape density** is the number of characters or bytes that can be stored on one inch of tape. Common densities are 800, 1,600, 3,200, and 6,520 bytes per inch.
34. **Sequential organization** means records are stored one after the other on the tape.
35. An **interblock gap** separates records stored on tape.
36. **Blocked records** mean two or more **logical records** are stored in a **physical record** on the tape.
37. **Optical disks** use a laser beam recording and reading method and can store enormous quantities of data.
38. RAM chips are used in **solid-state storage devices**. These devices act just like disk drives but provide faster data access and retrieval.
39. Automated retrieval of storage media is provided by **mass storage devices**.

## KEY TERMS

Access arms *7.9*
Access time *7.7*
Actuators *7.9*
Auxiliary storage *7.2*
Bits per inch (bpi) *7.7*
Blocked records *7.16*
Cartridge tape drive *7.12*
CDROM *7.18*
Cylinder *7.6*
Cylinder method *7.14*
Data transfer rate *7.8*
Direct-access storage devices (DASD) *7.12*
Disk cartridge *7.10*
Diskette *7.4*
Disk pack *7.13*
Disks *7.4*
Double-sided disk *7.6*
Double-sided drive *7.6*
Fixed disk *7.9*
Floppies *7.4*
Floppy disk *7.4*
Formatting *7.5*
Hard card *7.9*
Hard disk *7.8*
Hard-sectored disk *7.6*
Head crash *7.9*
Interblock gap (IBG) *7.16*
Interrecord gap (IRG) *7.16*
Latency *7.7*
Logical records *7.16*
Magnetic tape *7.15*
Mass storage devices *7.18*
Nonvolatile *7.2*
Optical disks *7.17*
Physical record *7.16*
Platters *7.8*
Read/write head *7.7*
Recording density *7.7*
Reel-to-reel *7.15*
Secondary storage *7.2*
Sector *7.5*
Sector method *7.14*
Seek time *7.7*
Sequential storage *7.16*
Settling time *7.8*
Single-sided disk *7.6*
Single-sided drive *7.6*
Soft-sectored disk *7.6*
Solid-state storage devices *7.18*
Streaming mode *7.12*
Tape density *7.16*
Track *7.5*
Tracks per inch (TPI) *7.7*
WORM *7.18*

## REVIEW QUESTIONS

1. Differentiate between the uses of main memory and auxiliary storage.
2. Draw a diagram of a diskette and label the main parts.
3. What does formatting a disk mean?
4. What are the three factors influencing the storage capacity of a disk? Briefly describe each of them.
5. Describe the care and handling of floppy disks.
6. Identify the factors that influence the access time of a disk drive.
7. Describe the characteristics of a fixed disk drive. What sizes are commonly used with personal computers?
8. What is disk backup? How are floppy disks normally backed up? How are hard disks backed up?
9. Describe the differences between fixed disks and removable disks on large computers.
10. Describe the sector method of disk organization and the cylinder method of disk organization.
11. How is data stored on magnetic tape? What are typical tape densities?
12. Describe optical storage technology. Why is it one of the most promising methods of data storage?

## CONTROVERSIAL ISSUES

1. A study of personal computer owners found that less than 10 percent regularly backup the files and databases they use. The consensus of these users was that new auxiliary storage devices, particularly the hard disk drives, are so reliable and error free that backup is a waste of time and storage. Experts who reviewed this study commented that these users were inviting disaster because even a few failures are enough to justify full file and database backup. Who is right? Take a position on this issue.
2. The cost of semiconductor memory has decreased significantly in recent years. In addition, research is being done constantly to find new ways for storing data. As a result, some experts believe magnetic memory such as disk and tape will be obsolete in a few years. Others say this will never happen. What is your opinion?

## RESEARCH PROJECTS

1. The storage capacities of hard disks vary considerably. Obtain the names of five different manufacturers of hard disk drives used with personal computers. Write to each of the manufacturers to obtain literature concerning their drives. Prepare a report summarizing the information you have collected.
2. The storage capacities of optical disks allow complete reference works to be stored on a single compact disk. Write a paper on possible applications of this technology.
3. Data storage requirements vary based on the type of organization. Write a paper on the storage requirements of a bank, a retailer with online cash registers, and the government agency that issues passports. Consider the amount and type of storage required and the necessity of having immediate access to the stored data.

# CHAPTER 8

# File Organization and Databases

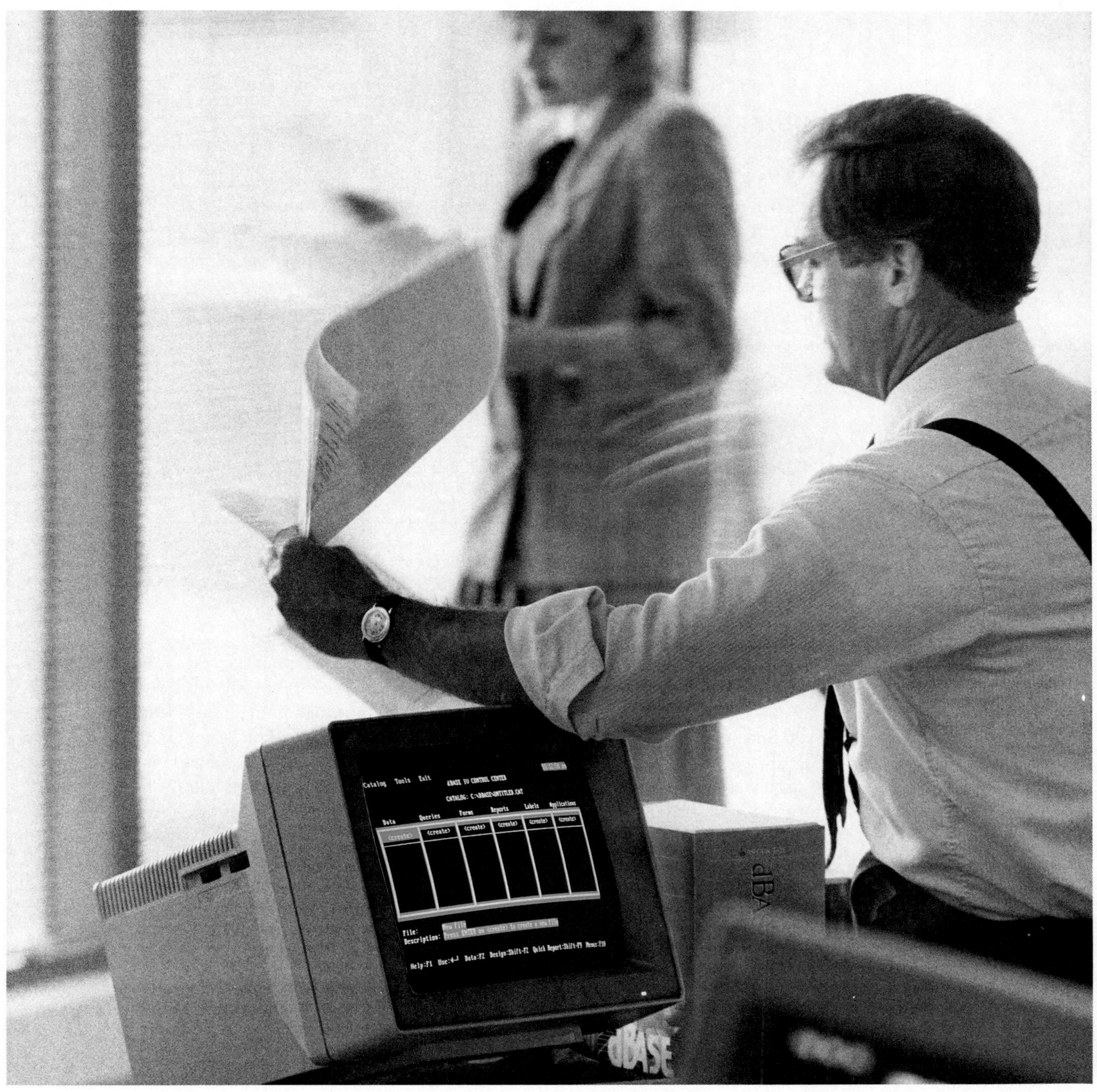

## CHAPTER 8

# File Organization and Databases

### OBJECTIVES

- Describe sequential files, indexed files, and direct (or relative) files.
- Explain the difference between sequential retrieval and random retrieval of records from a file.
- Describe the data maintenance procedures for updating files, including adding, changing, and deleting data in a file or database.
- Discuss the advantages of a database management system (DBMS).
- Describe a relational database system.
- Describe a hierarchical database system.
- Describe a network database system.
- Explain the use of a query language.
- Describe the responsibilities of a database administrator.

---

The data and information that a company has accumulated is usually considered a valuable asset. For data and information to provide maximum benefit to a company, they must be carefully organized, used, and managed. While you are now familiar with the auxiliary storage devices used to store data and information, it is equally important that you understand the various ways in which the data and information stored on these devices is organized, used, and managed. The purpose of this chapter is to explain (1) how files on auxiliary storage are organized, retrieved and maintained (kept current); and (2) the advantages, organization, use, and management of databases.

As you read this chapter, you will notice that several of the file and database concepts that are discussed were introduced earlier in the text. With the computer knowledge that you now have, especially about auxiliary storage devices, you are ready for a more in-depth look at these topics. The first part of this chapter concentrates on how files are organized and used. The second part of this chapter discusses the advantages, organization, and use of databases. Learning this information will help you to better understand how data and information is stored and managed on a computer.

# WHAT IS A FILE?

A *file* is a collection of related records that is usually stored on an auxiliary storage device. A *record* is a collection of related fields and a *field*, also called a *data item* or *data element*, is a fact (Figure 8-1). Files contain data that pertains to one topic. For example, a business can have separate files that contain data related to personnel, inventory, customers, vendors, and so forth. Most companies have hundreds, sometimes thousands of files that store the data pertaining to their business. Files that are stored on auxiliary storage devices can be organized in several different ways and there are advantages and disadvantages to each of these types of file organization.

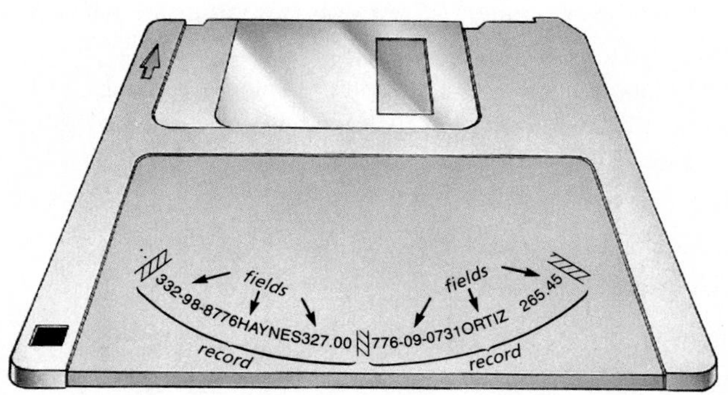


**FIGURE 8-1**
**This payroll file stored on a diskette contains payroll records. Each payroll record contains a social security field, a name field, and a paycheck amount field.**

# TYPES OF FILE ORGANIZATION

Three types of file organization are used on auxiliary storage devices. These are sequential, indexed, and direct, or relative, file organization.

## Sequential File Organization

**Sequential file organization** means that records are stored one after the other, normally in ascending or descending order, based on a value in each record called the key. The **key** is a field that contains data, such as a social security number, that is used to sequence the records in a file (Figure 8-2). Files that are stored on tape are always sequential files. Files on disk may be sequential, indexed, or direct.

**FIGURE 8-2**
**The student records in this file are stored sequentially in ascending order using the social security number as the key field. The records in this file will be retrieved sequentially.**

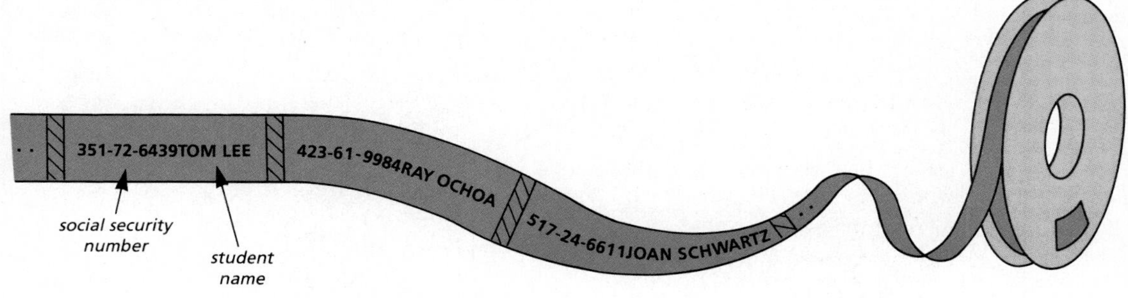

Records that are stored using sequential file organization are also retrieved sequentially. **Sequential retrieval**, also called **sequential access**, means that the records in a file are retrieved one record after another in the same order that the records are stored. For example, in Figure 8-2, the file contains student records stored in sequence by social security number. The data in the file is retrieved one record after another in the same sequence that it is stored in the file.

Sequential retrieval has a major disadvantage—since records must be retrieved one after another in the same sequence as they are stored, the only way to retrieve a record is to read all preceding records first. Therefore, in Figure 8-2, if the record for Joan Schwartz must be retrieved, the records for Tom Lee and for Ray Ochoa must be read before retrieving the Joan Schwartz record. Because of this, sequential retrieval is not used when fast access to a particular record is required. However, sequential retrieval is appropriate when records are processed one after another.

A common use of sequential files in a computer center is as backup files, where data from a disk is copied onto a tape or another disk so that if the original data becomes unusable, the original file can be restored from the backup file.

## Indexed File Organization

A second type of file organization is called **indexed file organization**. Just as in a sequential file, records are stored in an indexed file in an ascending or descending sequence based on the value in the key field of the record.

An indexed file, however, also contains an index. An **index** consists of a list containing the values of the key field and the corresponding disk address for each record in a file (Figure 8-3). In the same way that an index for a book points to the page where a particular topic is covered, the index for a file points to the place on a disk where a particular record is located. The index is usually stored with a file when the file is created. The index is retrieved from the disk and placed in main memory when the file is to be processed.

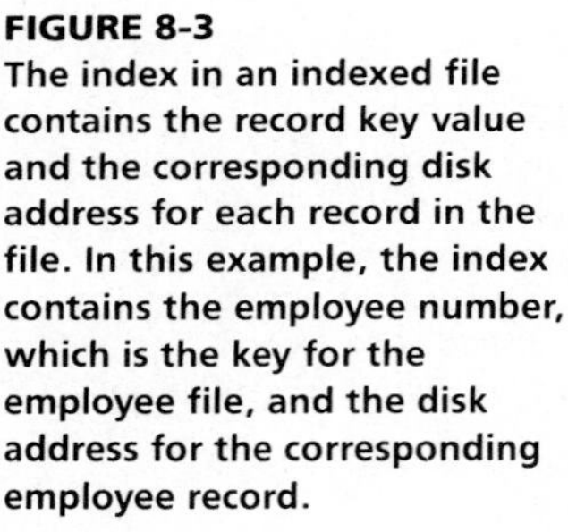

**FIGURE 8-3**
**The index in an indexed file contains the record key value and the corresponding disk address for each record in the file. In this example, the index contains the employee number, which is the key for the employee file, and the disk address for the corresponding employee record.**

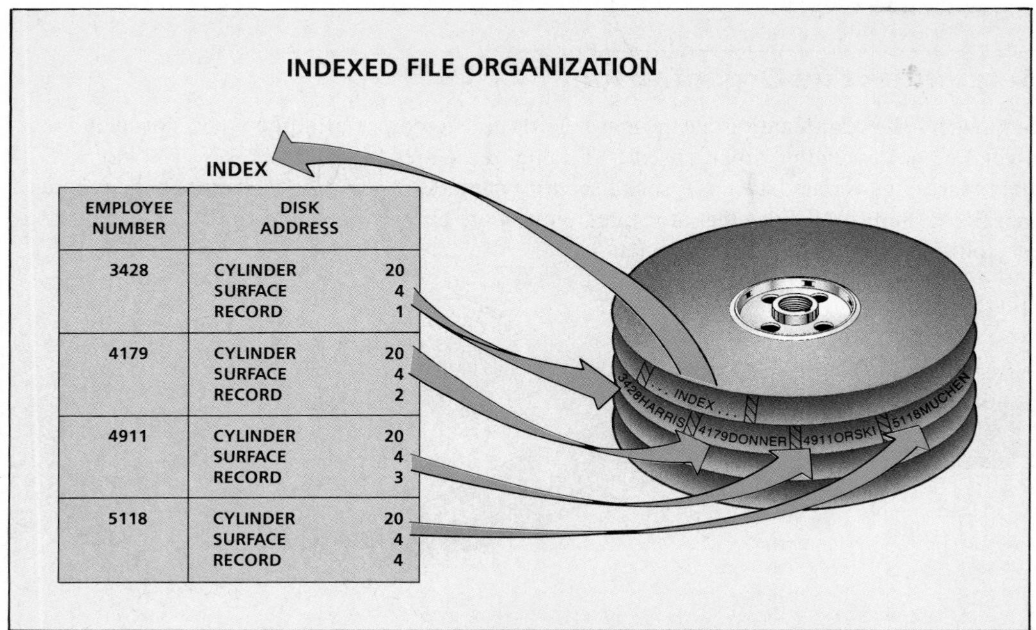

Records can be accessed in an indexed file both sequentially and randomly. As previously discussed, sequential retrieval means that the records in a file are retrieved one record after another in the same order that the records are stored. **Random retrieval**, also called **random access**, means any record in a file can be directly accessed (retrieved) regardless of where it is stored in the file. For example, the 50th record in a file can be retrieved first, followed by the 3rd record, and then the 20th record. Random retrieval is used when fast access to a record is required, as in a reservation system. For random retrieval to be used, files must be stored on disk.

To randomly access a record in an indexed file, the index is searched until the key of the record to be retrieved is found. The address of the record (also stored in the index) is then used to retrieve the record directly from the file without reading any other records. For example, if an inquiry was received from the personnel office asking the name of employee number 5118, the index could be searched until key 5118 was found (Figure 8-4). The corresponding disk address (cylinder 20, surface 4, record 4) would then be used to read the record directly from the disk into main memory.

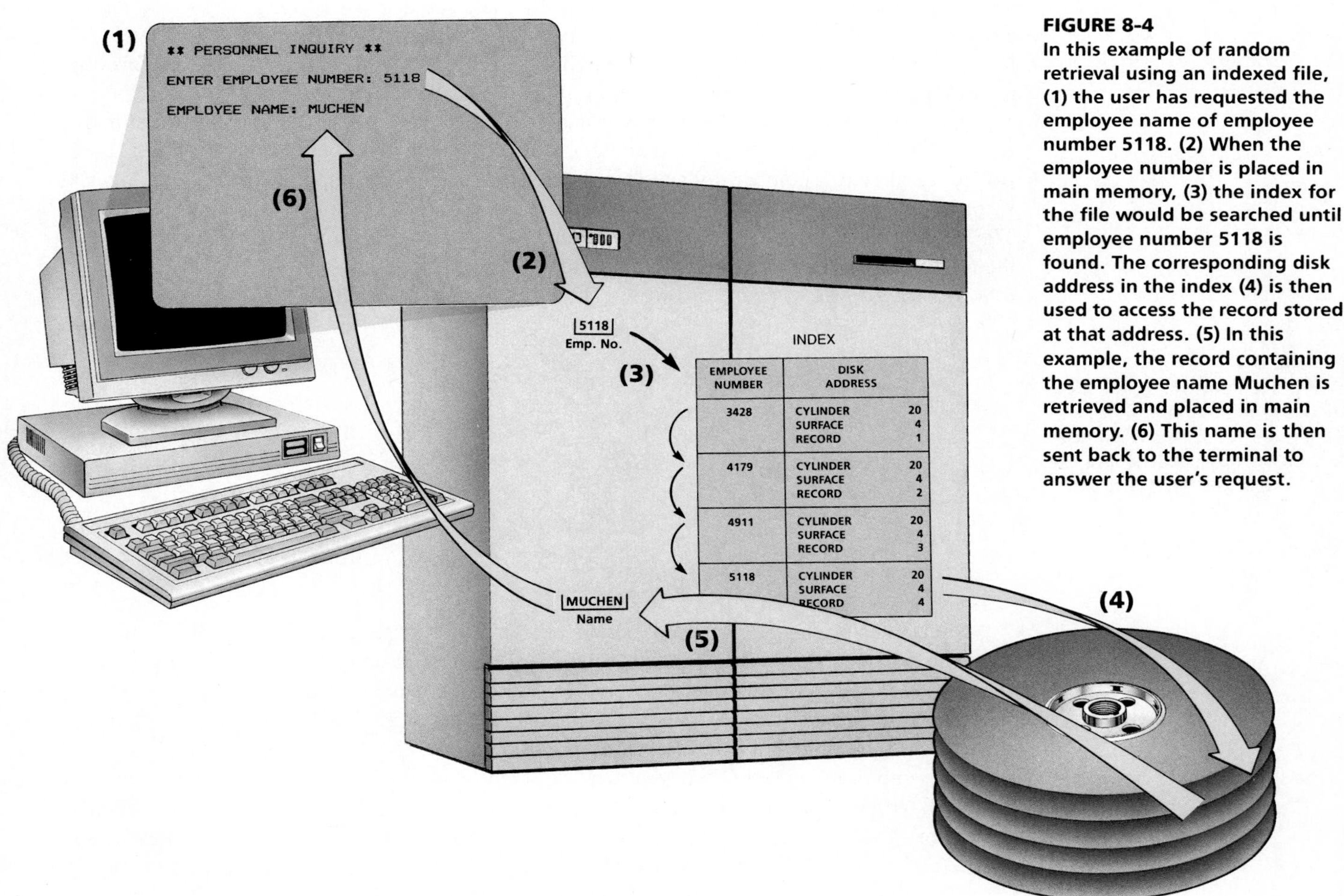


**FIGURE 8-4**
**In this example of random retrieval using an indexed file, (1) the user has requested the employee name of employee number 5118. (2) When the employee number is placed in main memory, (3) the index for the file would be searched until employee number 5118 is found. The corresponding disk address in the index (4) is then used to access the record stored at that address. (5) In this example, the record containing the employee name Muchen is retrieved and placed in main memory. (6) This name is then sent back to the terminal to answer the user's request.**

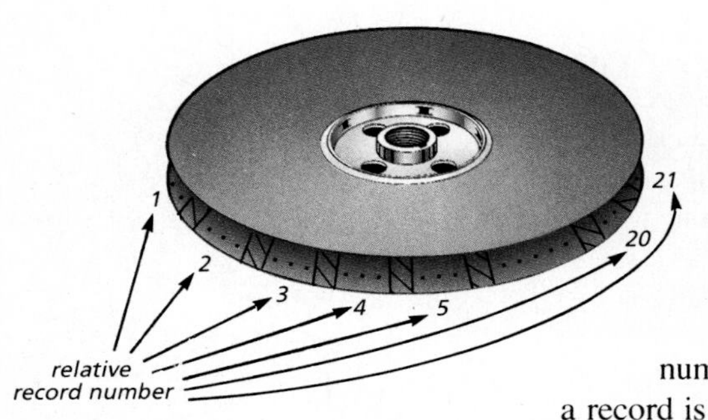


FIGURE 8-5
The relative address of a record is the same as the numeric position of the record in the file. The fifth record has a relative address of 5.

## Direct or Relative File Organization

A **direct file** or **relative file** (occasionally called a random file) contains records that are stored and retrieved according to either their disk address or their position within a file. This means that the program that stores and accesses records in a direct file must specify either the exact physical address of a record in the file (for example, cylinder, surface and track number, or track and sector number), or the relative location (position) where a record is stored in the file, such as the first, tenth, or fiftieth record (Figure 8-5).

The location where a record is stored is based on a key value found in the record. For example, a program could establish a file that has nine locations where records can be stored. These locations are sometimes called **buckets**. A bucket can contain multiple records. If the key in the record is a one-digit value (1–9), then the value in the key would specify the relative location within the file where the record was stored. For example, the record with key 3 would be placed in relative location or bucket 3; the record with key 6 would be placed in relative location 6, and so on.

Usually the storage of records in a file is not so simple. For instance, what if the maximum number of records to be stored in a direct file is 100 and the key for the record is a four-digit number? In this case, the key of the record could not be used to specify the relative or actual location of the record because the four-digit key could result in up to 9,999 records. In cases such as these, an arithmetic formula must be used to calculate the relative or actual location in the file where the record is stored. The process of using a formula and performing the calculation to determine the location of a record is called **hashing**.

One hashing method is the division/remainder method. Using this method, a prime number close to but not greater than the number of records to be stored in the file is chosen. A **prime number** is a number divisible by only itself and 1. For example, suppose you have 100 records. The number 97 is the closest prime number to 100 without being greater than 100. The key of the record is then divided by 97 and the remainder from the division operation is the relative location where the record is stored. For example, if the record key is 3428, the relative location where the record will be stored in the file is location 33 (Figure 8-6).

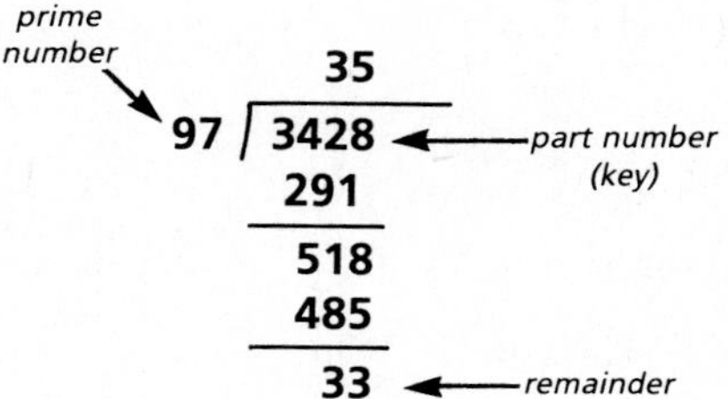


FIGURE 8-6
When the value 3428 is divided by the prime number 97, the remainder is 33. This remainder is used as the bucket where the record with key 3428 is stored in the direct file.

Direct files present one problem not encountered with sequential or indexed files. In all three file organization methods, the key in the record must be unique so that it can uniquely identify the record. For example, the employee number, when acting as the key in an employee file, must be unique. When a hashing technique is used to calculate a disk address, however, it is possible that two different keys could identify the same location on disk. For example, employee number 3331 generates the same relative location (33) as employee number 3428. When the locations generated from the different keys are the same they are called **synonyms**. The occurrence of this event is called a **collision**. A method that is often used to resolve collisions is to place the record that caused the collision in the next available storage location. This location may be in the same bucket (if multiple records are stored in a bucket) or in the next bucket (Figure 8-7).

Once a record is stored in its relative location within a direct file, it can be retrieved either sequentially or randomly. The method normally used with direct files is random retrieval. In order to randomly retrieve a record from a direct file three steps are performed:

1. The program must obtain the key of the record to be retrieved. The value of the key is entered into the computer by a user or as data from an input device.
2. The program determines the location of the record by performing the same hashing process as when the record was initially stored. Thus, to retrieve the record with key 3428, the key value would be divided by the prime number 97. The remainder, 33, specifies the location of the bucket where the record will be found.
3. The software then directs the computer to bucket 33 to retrieve the record.

Sequential retrieval from a direct file can be accomplished by indicating that the record from the first relative location is to be retrieved, followed by the record from the second relative location, and so on. All the records in the file are retrieved based on their relative location in the file.

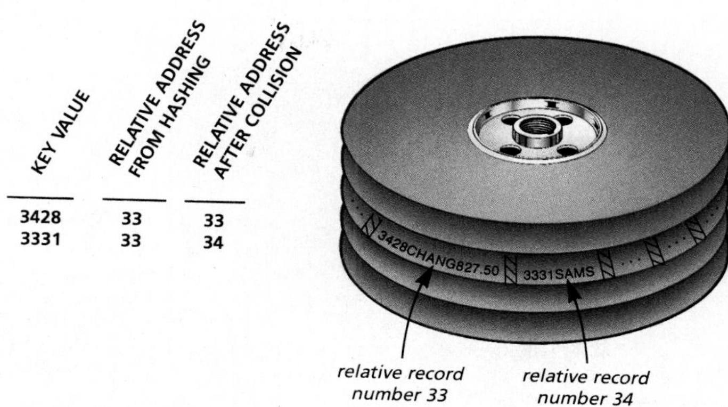


**FIGURE 8-7**
**Sometimes the hashing computation produces synonyms, or records that have the same relative address. In this example, both records have a relative address of 33. When the computer tries to store the second record and finds that location 33 is already full, it stores the second record at the next available location. In this example, record 3331 would be stored in location 34.**

## Summary of File Organization Concepts

Files are organized as either sequential, indexed, or direct files. Sequential file organization can be used on tape or disk and requires that the records in the file be retrieved sequentially. Indexed files must be stored on disk and the records can be accessed either sequentially or randomly. Direct files are stored on disk and are usually accessed randomly (Figure 8-8).

| FILE TYPE | TYPE OF STORAGE | ACCESS METHOD |
|---|---|---|
| Sequential | Tape or Disk | Sequential |
| Indexed | Disk | Random* or Sequential |
| Direct (Relative) | Disk | Random* or Sequential |

* *Primarily accessed as random files*

**FIGURE 8-8**
**The chart shows the type of storage and the access methods that can be used with each of the three file types.**

# HOW IS DATA IN FILES MAINTAINED?

Data stored on auxiliary storage must be kept current to produce accurate results when it is processed. To keep the data current, the records in the files must be updated. **Updating** records within a file consists of adding records to the file, changing records within the file, and deleting records from the file.

## Adding Records

Records are added to a file when additional data is needed to make the file current. For example, if a customer opens a new account at a bank, a record containing the data for the new account must be added to the bank's account file. The process that would take place to *add* this record to the file is shown in Figure 8-9.

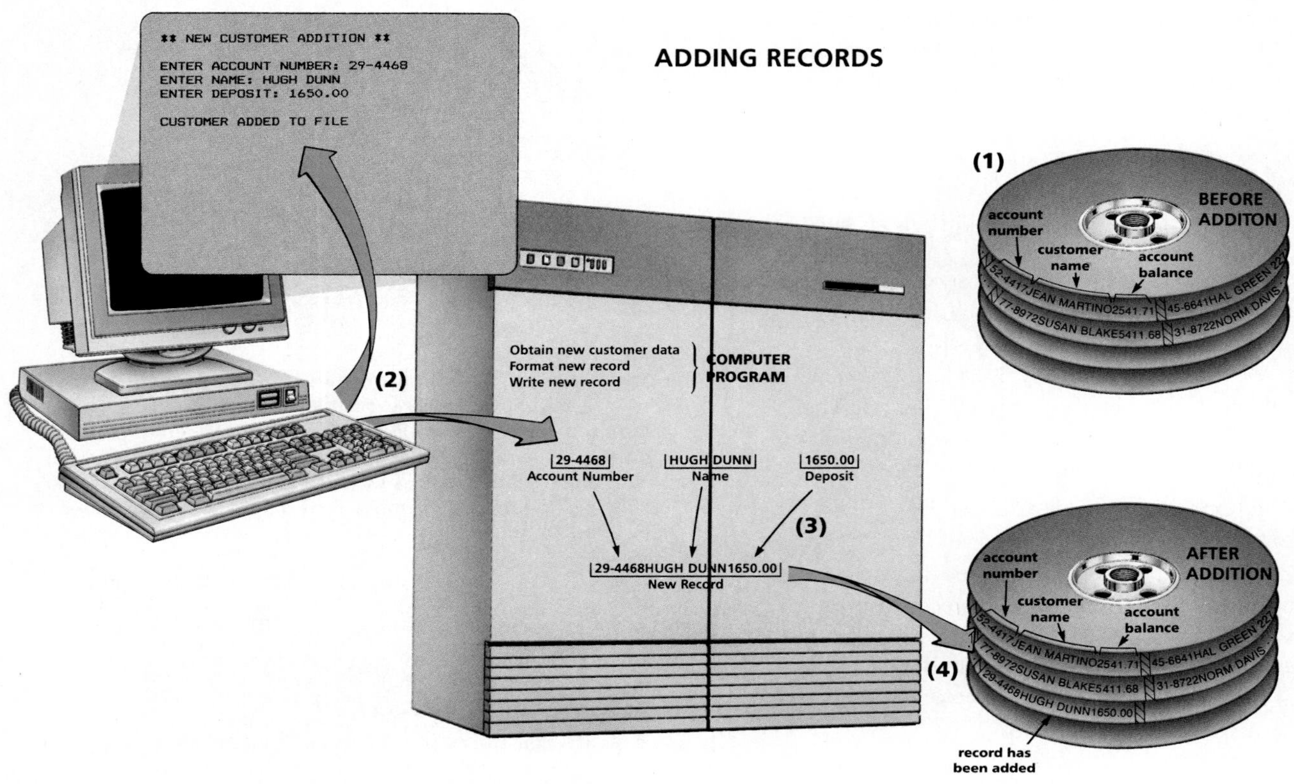


**FIGURE 8-9**
**In this example of adding records, (1) the file first exists without the new account. (2) The teller enters the account number, customer name, and deposit. (3) This data is used to create a record that is then (4) added to the file.**

1. A bank teller enters the new customer data into the computer through a terminal. The data includes the account number, the customer name, and the deposit that will become the account balance.
2. The update program moves the data entered by the user into the new record area in main memory.
3. The update program writes the new record to the file. The location on the disk where the record is written is determined by the program. In some cases, a new record will be written between other records in the file. In other cases, such as illustrated in this example, the added record is added to the end of the file.

Whenever data is stored on auxiliary storage for subsequent use, the ability to add records must be present in order to keep the data current.

## Changing Records

The second task that must be accomplished when updating data is to *change* data that is currently stored in a record. Changes to data stored on auxiliary storage take place for two primary reasons: (1) to correct data that is known to be incorrect, and (2) to update data when new data becomes available.

As an example of the first type of change, assume in Figure 8-9 that instead of entering HUGH DUNN as the name for the customer, the teller enters HUGH DONE. The error is not noticed and the customer leaves the bank. Later in the day, when the customer returns to question the transaction, the name stored in the file must be changed so that it contains the correct spelling. Therefore, the teller would enter HUGH DUNN as a change to the name field in the record. This change is made to replace data known to be incorrect with data known to be correct.

The bank account example also illustrates the second reason for change—to update data when new data becomes available. This type of change is made when a customer deposits or withdraws money. In Figure 8-10, Jean Martino has withdrawn $500.00. The record for Jean Martino must be changed to reflect her withdrawal. The following steps occur:

1. The teller enters Jean Martino's account number 52-4417 and the amount 500.00.
2. The update program retrieves the record for account number 52-4417 and stores the record in main memory.
3. The program subtracts the withdrawal amount from the account balance in the record. This changes the account balance to reflect the correct balance in the account.
4. After the balance has been changed in memory, the record is written back onto the disk. After the change, the account balance has been updated, and the record stored on auxiliary storage contains the correct account balance.

Changing data stored on auxiliary storage to reflect the correct and current data is an important part of the updating process that is required for data.

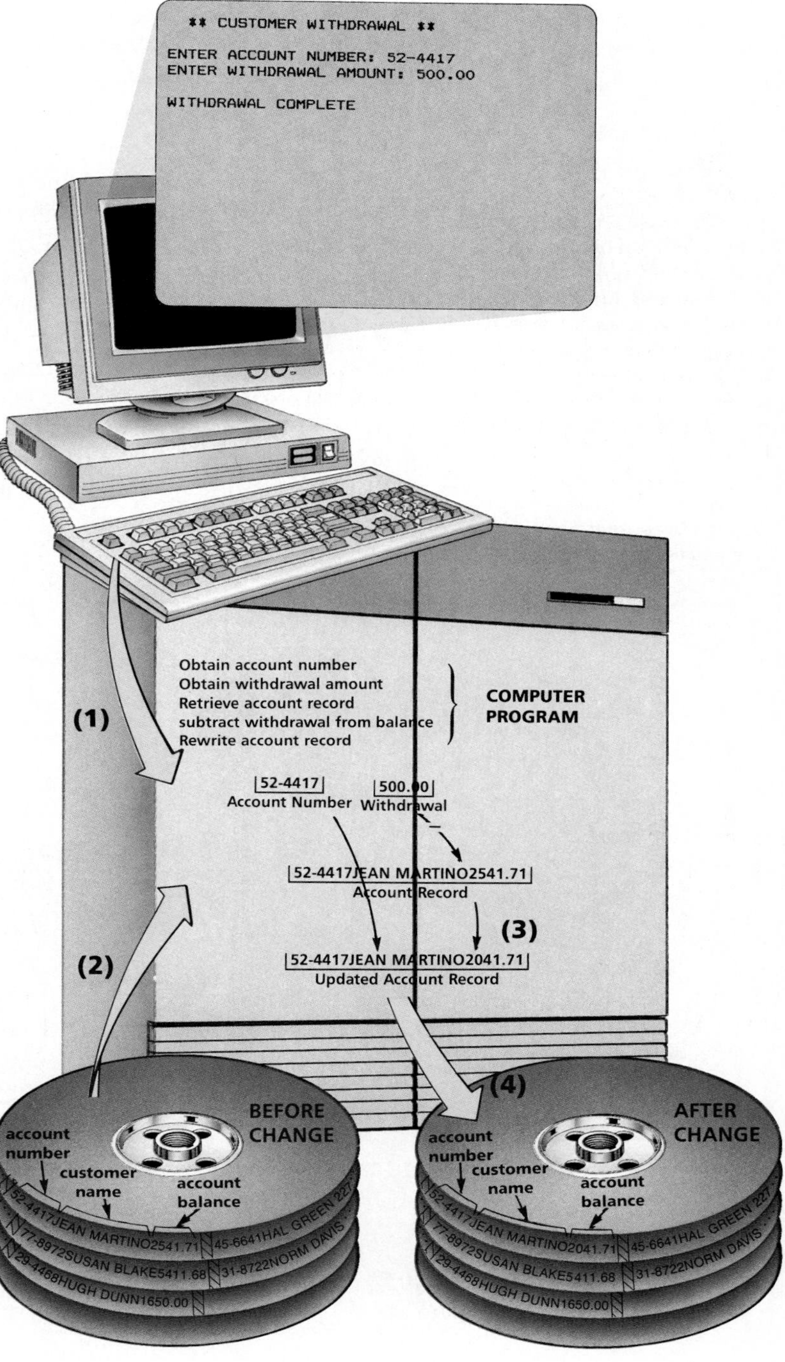


**FIGURE 8-10**
**When Jean Martino withdraws $500.00, the bank's records must be changed to reflect her new account balance. In this example, (1) the teller enters Jean Martino's account number and withdrawal amount, (2) the account number is used to retrieve Jean's account balance record; and (3) the account balance is reduced by the amount of the withdrawal ($500.00). The record is then rewritten back onto the disk (4).**

## Deleting Records

The third major type of activity that must occur when updating data is to delete records stored in a file or database. Records are deleted when they are no longer needed as data. Figure 8-11 shows the updating procedures to *delete* a record for Hal Gruen who has closed his account. The following steps occur:

1. The teller enters Hal Gruen's account number (45-6641).
2. The update program retrieves the record from the disk using the account number as the key. The record is placed in main memory.
3. The actual processing that occurs to delete a record from a file depends on the type of file organization being used and the processing requirements of the application. Sometimes the record is removed from the file. Other times, as in this example, the record is not removed from the file. Instead, the record is *flagged*, or marked, in some manner so that it will not be processed again. In this example, the first three characters of the account number are changed from the actual number to the letters DEL (short for delete).
4. After the letters DEL have been placed in the first three characters of the account number, the record is written back to the file. The application program will not process the record again because it begins with DEL instead of a valid account number. Even though the record is still physically stored on the disk, it is effectively deleted because it will not be retrieved for processing.

**FIGURE 8-11**
**In this example, (1) the account number entered by the teller is used to (2) retrieve Hal Green's account record. (3) The account record is marked as deleted by placing the letters DEL In the first three positions of the account number. The record is then rewritten (4) back to the file. With DEL in the account number, the record will not be retrieved by the application program because it does not have a valid key value.**

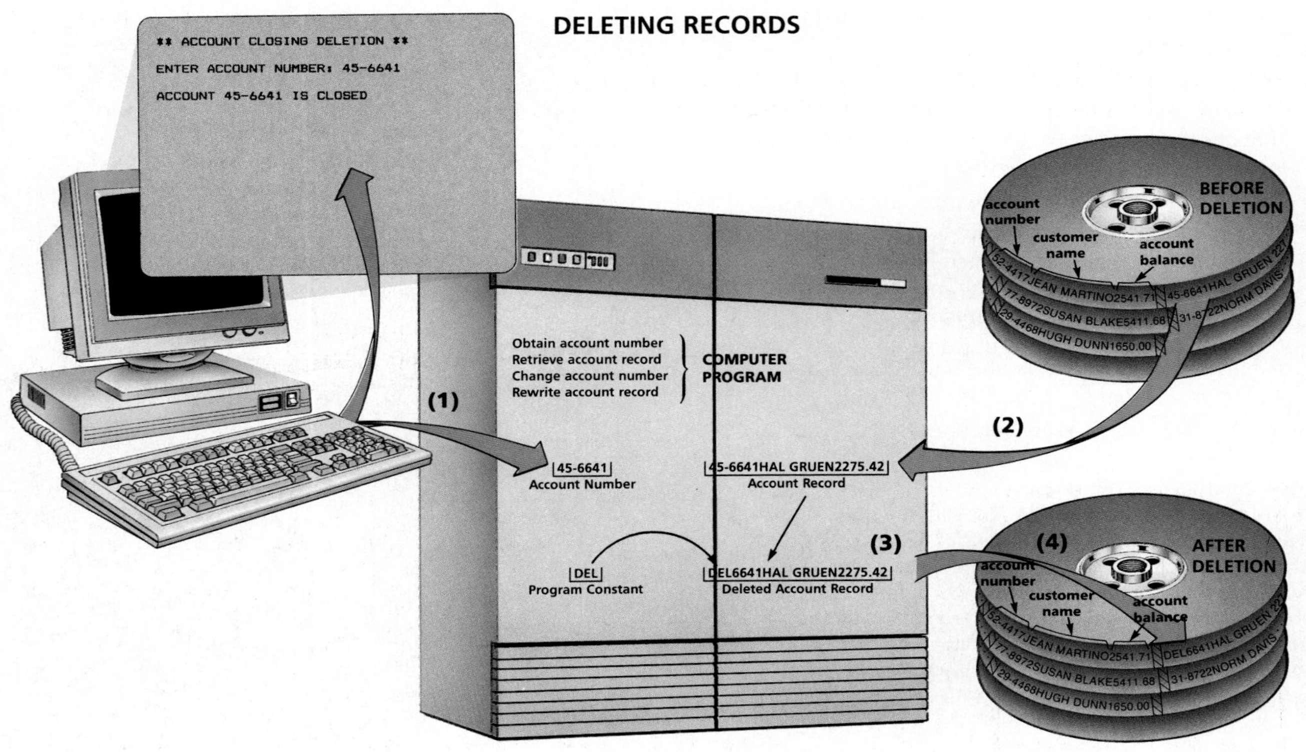

Deleting records from auxiliary storage is important because it provides a way of either removing or flagging records that are no longer needed for processing. This is necessary to keep data accurate.

### Summary of How Data Is Maintained

Data maintenance is updating or adding, changing, and deleting data stored on auxiliary storage. The maintenance of data is critical if information derived from the processing of that data is to be reliable. When updating data, it does not matter if the data is stored as a single file or if it is part of a series of files organized into a database. The concept of adding, changing, and deleting data to keep it current remains the same.

## DATABASES: A BETTER WAY TO MANAGE DATA AND INFORMATION

As stated at the beginning of this chapter, more and more businesspeople realize that next to the skills of their employees, data (and the information it represents) is one of a company's most valuable assets. They recognize that the information that has been accumulated on sales trends, competitors' products and services, employee skills, and production processes is a valuable resource that would be difficult if not impossible to replace.

Unfortunately, in many cases this resource is located in different files in different departments throughout the organization, often known only to the individuals who work with their specific portion of the total information. In these cases, the potential value of the information goes unrealized because it is not known to people in other departments who may need it or it cannot be accessed efficiently. In an attempt to organize their information resources and provide for timely and efficient access, many companies have implemented databases.

## WHAT IS A DATABASE?

Previously in this chapter, we've discussed how data elements (characters, fields, and records) can be organized in files. In file-oriented systems, each file is independent. In a **database**, the data is organized in multiple related files. These related files are not independent of one another and it is possible for them to obtain data from one another. A **database management system (DBMS)** is the software that allows the user to create, maintain, and report the data and file relationships. Note that a **file management system**, sometimes mistakenly referred to as a database management system, is software that only allows the user to create, maintain, and access a single file at a time.

## WHY USE A DATABASE?

The following example (Figure 8-12) illustrates some of the advantages of a database system as compared to a file-oriented system. Assume that a business periodically mails catalogs to its customers. If the business is using a file-oriented system, it would probably have a file used for the catalog mailing application that contains information about the catalog plus customer information, such as customer account number, name, and address. Files that are used in a file-oriented system are independent of one another. Therefore, other applications, such as the sales application, that also need to have customer information would each have files that contain the same customer information stored in the catalog mailing file. Thus in a file-oriented system, the customer data would be duplicated several times in different files. This duplication of data wastes auxiliary storage space. In addition, it makes maintaining the data difficult because when a customer record must be updated, all files containing that data must be individually updated.

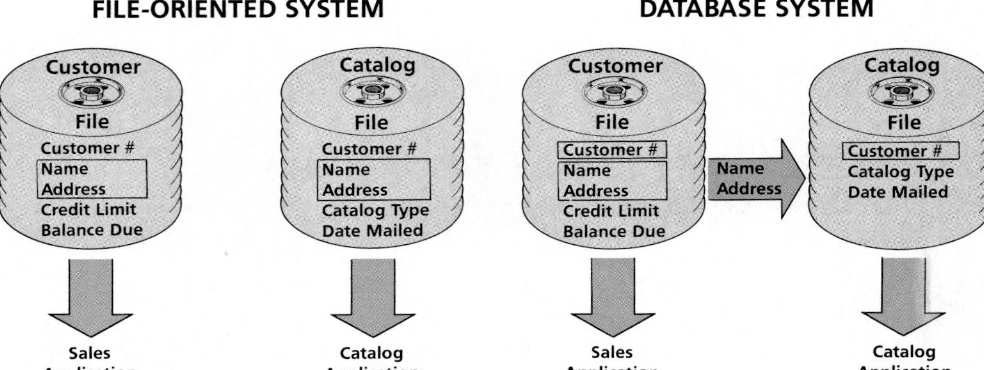


**FIGURE 8-12**
**In a file-oriented system, each file contains the customer name and address. In the database system, only the customer file contains the name and address. Other files, such as the catalog file, use the customer number to retrieve the customer name and address when it is needed for processing.**

In a database system, however, only one of the applications would have a file containing the customer name and address data. That is because in a database system, files are integrated; related files are linked together by the database software either through predefined relationships or through common data fields. In this example, the link could be the customer account number. If the sales file contained the customer account number, name, and address, the catalog mailing file would only need to contain the customer's account number plus the other catalog information. When the catalog application software is executed, the customer's name and address would be obtained from the sales file. The advantage of the database is that because the files are integrated, the customer name and address would only be stored once. This saves auxiliary storage space. It also allows data to be maintained more easily because update information only needs to be entered once.

As the previous example illustrates, a database system offers a number of advantages over a file-oriented system. These advantages and several others are summarized in the following list:

1. **Reduced data redundancy.** Redundant or duplicate data is greatly reduced in a database system. Frequently used data elements such as names, addresses, and descriptions are stored in one location. Having such items in one instead of many locations lowers the cost of maintaining the data.
2. **Improved data integrity.** Closely related to reduced data redundancy is the database advantage of improved data integrity. Because data is only stored in one place, it is more likely to be accurate. When it is updated, all applications that use the data will be using the most current version.
3. **Integrated files.** As demonstrated by the catalog mailing example (Figure 8-12), a key advantage of a database management system is its ability to "integrate" or join together data from more than one file for inquiry or reporting purposes.
4. **Improved data security.** Most database management systems allow the user to establish different levels of security over information in the database. For example, a department manager may have "read only" privileges on certain payroll data: the manager could inquire about the data but not change it. The payroll supervisor would have "full update"

privileges: the supervisor could not only inquire about the data but could also make changes. A nonmanagement employee would probably have no access privileges to the payroll data and could neither inquire about nor change the data.

Now that we've discussed some of their advantages, let's discuss the different types of databases.

## TYPES OF DATABASE ORGANIZATION

There are three major types of database organization: relational, hierarchical, and network. The relational database structure is the most recent of the three methods and is considered a trend for the future. The relational database structure takes advantage of large-capacity direct-access storage devices that were not available when the hierarchical and network methods were developed.

### Relational Database

In a **relational database**, data is organized in tables that in database terminology are called **relations**. The tables are further divided into rows (called **tuples**) and fields (called **attributes**). The tables can be thought of as files and the rows as records. The description or name of a particular attribute is called a **domain**. Figure 8-13 illustrates these terms with a student name and address file.

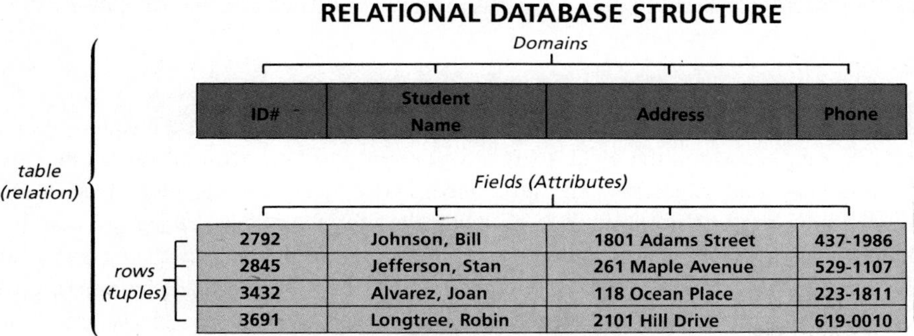


**FIGURE 8-13**
**This example illustrates the terms used to identify the data in a relational database. A relational database is made up of multiple tables that can be thought of as files. In this example, other tables would probably exist for student grades, courses, faculty, and other logical groups of data.**

As previously mentioned, a key advantage of a database is its ability to link multiple files together. A relational database accomplishes this by using a common field, sometimes called a **link**, that exists in each file. For example, in a database for a college, the link between files containing student information could be the student identification number. Hierarchical and network databases can also extract data from multiple files, but in these database structures, the data relationships that will enable the multiple file combination must be defined *when the database is created*. The advantage of a relational database is that the data relationships do not have to be predefined. The relational database only needs a common field in both data files to make a relationship between them. Because it is sometimes difficult to know ahead of time how data will be used, the flexibility provided by a relational database is an important advantage.

Another advantage of a relational database is its ability to add new fields. All that needs to be done is to define the fields in the appropriate table. With hierarchical and network database systems, the entire database has to be "redefined": existing relationships have to be reestablished to include the new fields.

## Hierarchical Database

In a **hierarchical database** (Figure 8-14), data is organized in a series like a family tree or organization chart (the term hierarchy means an organized series). Like a family tree, the hierarchical database has branches made up of parent and child records. Each **parent record** can have multiple child records. However, each **child record** can only have one parent. The parent record at the top of the database is referred to as the **root** record.

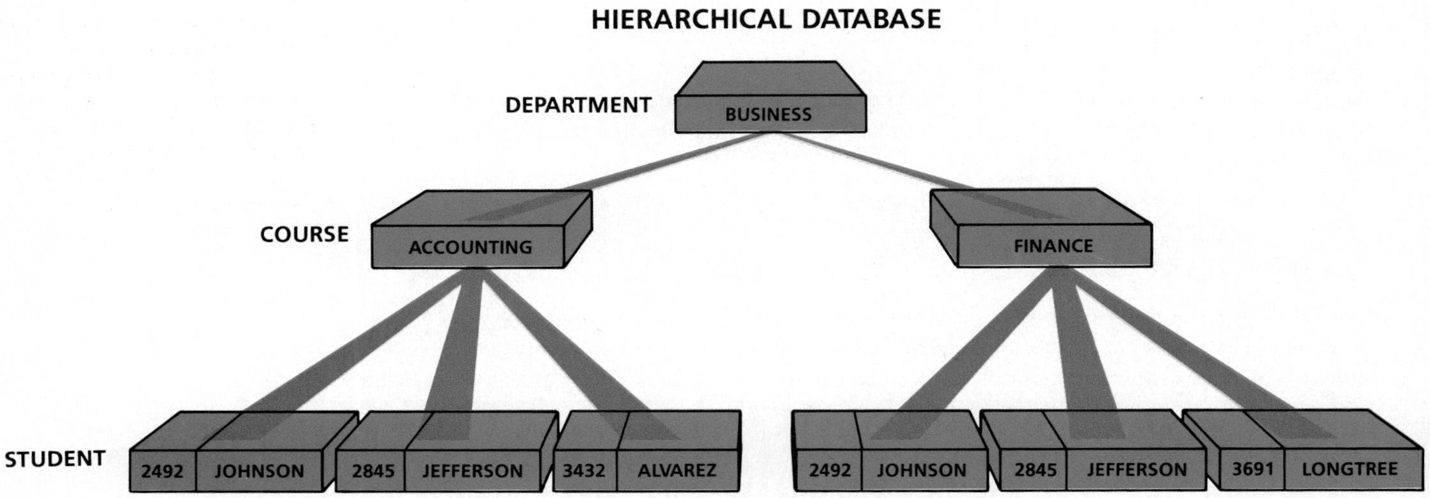

HIERARCHICAL DATABASE

DEPARTMENT
BUSINESS
COURSE
ACCOUNTING
FINANCE
STUDENT
2492 JOHNSON
2845 JEFFERSON
3432 ALVAREZ
2492 JOHNSON
2845 JEFFERSON
3691 LONGTREE

**FIGURE 8-14**
**In this hierarchical database, Johnson, Jefferson, and Longtree are the children of Finance and Finance is their parent. Finance and Accounting are the children of Business and Business is their parent. These relationships must be established before the database can be used.**

Hierarchical databases are the oldest form of database organization and reflect the fact that they were developed when the disk and memory capacity of computers was limited and most processing was done in batch mode. Data access is sequential in the sense that an inquiry begins at the root record and proceeds down the branch until the requested data is found. All parent-child relationships must be established before the user can access the database. These relationships are defined by the person who is responsible for designing the database and are established when the database is created in a separate process that is sometimes called "generating the database."

After the database is created, access must be made through the established relationships. This points out two disadvantages of hierarchical databases. First, records located in separate branches of the database cannot be accessed easily at the same time. Second, adding new fields to database records or modifying existing fields, such as adding the four-digit zip code extension, requires the redefinition of the entire database. Depending on the size of the database, this redefinition process can take a considerable amount of time. The advantage of a hierarchical database is that because the data relationships are predefined, access to and updating of data is very fast.

## Network Database

A **network database** (Figure 8-15) is similar to a hierarchical database except that each child record can have more than one parent. In network database terminology, a child record is referred to as a **member** and a parent record is referred to as an **owner**. Unlike the hierarchical database, the network database is able to establish relationships between different branches of the data and thus offers increased access capability for the user. However, like the hierarchical database, these data relationships must be established prior to the use of the database and must be redefined if fields are added or modified.

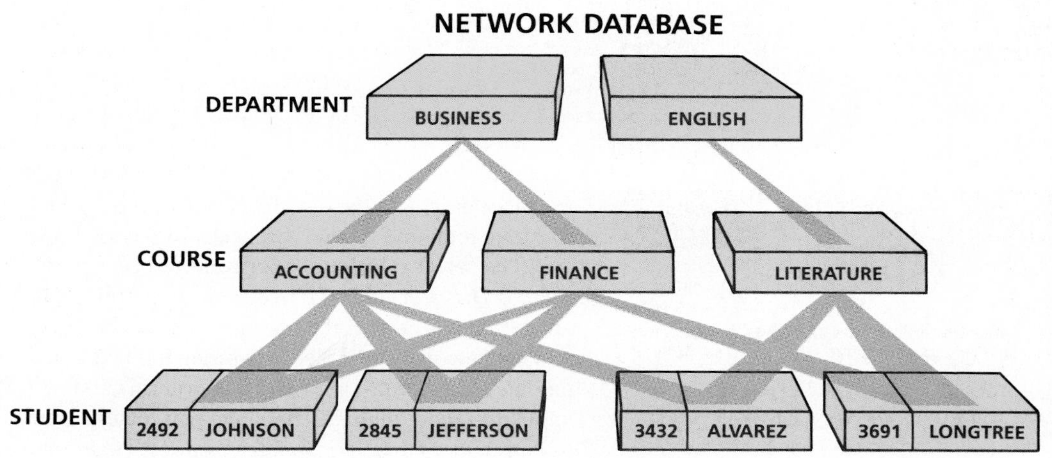


**FIGURE 8-15**
**In a network database, lower level (member) records can be related to more than one higher level (owner) record. For example, Longtree's owners are Finance and Literature. Accounting has three members, Johnson, Jefferson, and Alvarez. As in a hierarchical database, these relationships must be established before the database can be used.**

## DATABASE MANAGEMENT SYSTEMS

Database management systems, the software that manage the creation, maintenance and reporting of database data, have a number of common features. These features include:

1. **Data dictionary.** The **data dictionary** defines each data field that will be contained in the database files. The dictionary is used to record the field name, size, description, type of data (e.g., text, numeric, or date), and relationship to other data elements.
2. **Utilities.** Database management system utility programs provide for a number of maintenance tasks including creating files and dictionaries, monitoring performance, copying data, and deleting unwanted records.
3. **Security.** Most database management systems allow the user to specify different levels of user access privileges. The privileges can be established for each user for each type of access (retrieve, update, and delete) to each data field. Note that without some type of access security, the data in a database is more subject to unauthorized access than in a decentralized system of individual files.
4. **Query language.** The query language is one of the most valuable features of a database management system. It allows the user to retrieve information from the database based on the criteria and in the format specified by the user.

## QUERY LANGUAGES: ACCESS TO THE DATABASE

A **query language** is a simple English-like language that allows users to specify what data they want to see on a report or screen display. Although each query language has its own grammar, syntax, and vocabulary, these languages can generally be learned in a short time by persons without a programming background.

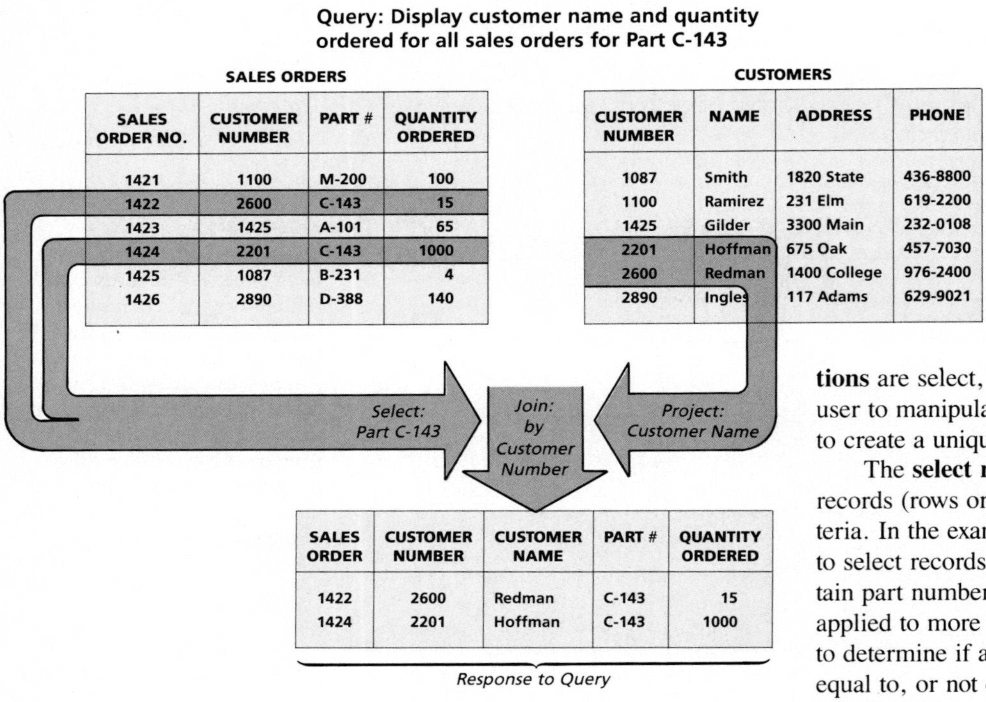

Query: Display customer name and quantity ordered for all sales orders for Part C-143

SALES ORDERS

| SALES ORDER NO. | CUSTOMER NUMBER | PART # | QUANTITY ORDERED |
|---|---|---|---|
| 1421 | 1100 | M-200 | 100 |
| 1422 | 2600 | C-143 | 15 |
| 1423 | 1425 | A-101 | 65 |
| 1424 | 2201 | C-143 | 1000 |
| 1425 | 1087 | B-231 | 4 |
| 1426 | 2890 | D-388 | 140 |

CUSTOMERS

| CUSTOMER NUMBER | NAME | ADDRESS | PHONE |
|---|---|---|---|
| 1087 | Smith | 1820 State | 436-8800 |
| 1100 | Ramirez | 231 Elm | 619-2200 |
| 1425 | Gilder | 3300 Main | 232-0108 |
| 2201 | Hoffman | 675 Oak | 457-7030 |
| 2600 | Redman | 1400 College | 976-2400 |
| 2890 | Ingles | 117 Adams | 629-9021 |

Select: Part C-143

Join: by Customer Number

Project: Customer Name

| SALES ORDER | CUSTOMER NUMBER | CUSTOMER NAME | PART # | QUANTITY ORDERED |
|---|---|---|---|---|
| 1422 | 2600 | Redman | C-143 | 15 |
| 1424 | 2201 | Hoffman | C-143 | 1000 |

Response to Query

**FIGURE 8-16**
**This example illustrates the three relational operations (select, project, and join) that would be used to produce a response to the query.**

## A Query Example

Figure 8-16 shows how a user might query a relational database. This example illustrates the relational operations that may be performed when a relational database inquiry is made. These three **relational operations** are select, project, and join. They allow the user to manipulate the data from one or more files to create a unique "view" or subset of the total data.

The **select relational operation** selects certain records (rows or tuples) based on user-supplied criteria. In the example, the user queries the database to select records from the sales order file that contain part number C-143. Selection criteria can be applied to more than one field and can include tests to determine if a field is greater than, less than, equal to, or not equal to a value specified by the user. Connectors such as AND and OR can also be used.

The **project relational operation** specifies the fields (attributes) that appear on the query output. In the example, the user wants to see the names of the customers who placed orders for part number C-143.

The **join relational operation** is used to combine two files (relations or tables). In the example, the link used to join the two files is the customer number, a field contained in each file.

After the query is executed, most query languages allow the user to give the query a unique name and save it for future use.

## Structured Query Language: An Emerging Standard

One of the most widely used query languages is **Structured Query Language**, often referred to as **SQL**. Originally developed during the 1970s by IBM, SQL has been incorporated into a number of relational database software packages including ORACLE by Oracle Corporation and INGRES by Relational Technology. IBM actively supports SQL and incorporates it into their two major relational database system products, SQL/DS and DB2. SQL received increased support as the emerging relational database management system query language when, in 1985, the American National Standards Institute formed a committee to develop industry standards for SQL. The standards were issued in 1987. Today, it is difficult to pick up a computer industry publication and not read about at least one database software vendor announcing plans to incorporate SQL into its product. The standardization of SQL will further accelerate its implementation on a wide range of computer systems from micros to supercomputers. This fact, coupled with the increasing dominance of relational databases, will mean that SQL will be used by many computer users.

FIGURE 8-17
The database administrator plays a key role in the managing of a company's data. The DBA should possess good technical as well as good management skills.

## DATABASE ADMINISTRATION

The centralization of an organization's data into a database requires a great deal of cooperation and coordination on the part of the database users. In file-oriented systems, if a user wanted to keep track of some data he or she would just create another file, often duplicating some data that was already being tracked by someone else. In a database system, the user must first check to see if some or all of the data is already on file and if not, how it can be added to the system. The role of coordinating the use of the database belongs to the database administrator.

### The Database Administrator

The **database administrator**, or **DBA**, is the person responsible for coordinating all database activities (Figure 8-17). In small organizations, this person usually has other responsibilities such as the overall management of the computer resources. In medium and large organizations, the role of DBA is a full-time job for one or more people. The job of DBA usually includes the following responsibilities:

1. **Database design.** The DBA determines the initial design of the database and specifies where to add additional data files and records when they are needed.
2. **User coordination.** The DBA is responsible for letting users know what data is available in the database and how the users can retrieve it. The DBA also reviews user requests for additions to the database and helps establish priorities for their implementation.
3. **Backup and recovery.** The centralization of data in a database makes an organization particularly vulnerable to a computer system failure. It is often the responsibility of the DBA to minimize this risk, making sure that all data is regularly backed up and that contingency plans are prepared (and periodically tested) for a prolonged equipment or software malfunction.
4. **System security.** It is the DBA's responsibility to establish and monitor system access privileges to prevent the unauthorized use of an organization's data.
5. **Performance monitoring.** The performance of the database, usually measured in terms of response time to a user request, can be affected by a number of factors such as file sizes and the types and frequency of inquiries during the day. Most database management systems have utility programs that enable the DBA to monitor these factors and make adjustments to provide for more efficient database use.

In addition to the DBA, the user also has a role in a database management system.

### The Responsibility of the User in a Database Management System

One of the user's first responsibilities is to become familiar with the data in the existing database. First-time database users are often amazed at the wealth of information available to help them perform their jobs more effectively.

Another responsibility of the user, in organizations of any size, is to play an active part in the specification of additions to the database. The maintenance of an organization's database is an ongoing task that must be constantly measured against the overall goals of the organization. Therefore users must participate in designing the database that will be used to help them achieve those goals and measure their progress.

## MANAGING DATA ON A PERSONAL COMPUTER

A variety of data management systems are available for personal computers, ranging from simple file management programs to full relational database management systems. As with large system packages, many personal computer software vendors are developing or modifying existing packages to support Structured Query Language (SQL). The advantage of SQL packages for personal computers is that they can directly query mainframe databases that support SQL.

The increased computing power of the latest personal computers has also allowed database management packages originally written for mainframe computers to be modified to run on the smaller systems. ORACLE (Oracle Corporation) and INGRES (Relational Technology) are two SQL-based packages that have been adapted to personal computers.

Perhaps the best known and most widely used personal computer-based database management system is the dBASE series from Ashton-Tate Corporation. dBASE III PLUS offers a relational database manager, a programming language, and application development tools. dBASE IV includes a complete implementation of SQL.

With so many data management packages available (a recent survey included 43), it's difficult to decide which one to choose. For those with simple needs, a file management package is probably all that is necessary. For larger databases with multiple files, one of the more popular database management systems will offer increased capability and growth potential. For complex database requirements, the packages originally developed on mainframes should provide all the database resources required. If you need to select a database software package for your personal computer, you may want to refer to the section in Chapter 2 that discusses how to choose software packages for a personal computer.

## SUMMARY OF DATABASES

Databases provide a better way of organizing data by relating items in multiple files. With databases, redundant data is minimized and data integrity improved. Database query languages allow data to be retrieved according to the criteria and in the format specified by the user.

Understanding the database and file concepts that have been presented in this chapter will help you to have a better understanding of how data and information are organized and managed on the auxiliary storage of a computer. Whether you are a home computer user who wants to store personal data on floppy disks or a hard drive, or a mainframe user accessing the database of the company where you are employed, a fundamental knowledge of how data is organized and managed will be useful to you.

## CHAPTER SUMMARY

1. A file is a collection of related records that is usually stored on an auxiliary storage device. The three types of file organization are sequential, indexed, and direct or relative.
2. When **sequential file organization** is used, records are stored one after the other, normally in ascending or descending order by the value in the **key** field.
3. **Sequential retrieval** means that the records on a tape or disk file are retrieved (accessed) one after another in the same order that the records are stored on the tape or disk.

4. With **indexed file organization**, the records are stored on the disk in an indexed file in ascending or descending sequence based on a key field. An index is used to retrieve records.
5. An **index** consists of entries containing the key to the records and the disk addresses of the records.
6. **Random retrieval**, or access, allows the records in a disk file to be accessed in any order based on the value in a key field or on the location of a record in a file. Random retrieval is used when fast access to a record is required.
7. Random access and sequential access can be used with indexed files.
8. A **direct file** or **relative file** contains records that are stored and retrieved according to their disk address or their physical location within the file.
9. The locations on a disk where records in a direct file can be stored are called **buckets**.
10. **Hashing** means using a formula or performing a calculation to determine the location (position) where a record will be placed on a disk.
11. A **collision** occurs when the hashing operation generates the same disk location (called **synonyms**) for records with different key values.
12. Data maintenance refers to the process of **updating** files and databases by adding, changing, or deleting data from a file.
13. A **database** uses multiple related files to organize data.
14. A **database management system (DBMS)** is the software that allows the user to create, maintain, and report the data and file relationships used in a database.
15. By contrast, a **file management system** allows a user to access only one file at a time.
16. **Reduced data redundancy** (data that is duplicated in several different files), **improved data integrity** (data accuracy), **integrated files** (joining data from more than one file), and **improved data security** (ensuring that the data is accessible only to those with the proper authorization) are the major advantages of using a database.
17. A **relational database** is organized into tables called **relations**. The relations are divided into **tuples** (rows) and **attributes** (fields). Each attribute is given a unique name, called the **domain**.
18. In a relational database, a common attribute or **link** is used to connect multiple files.
19. The advantage of a relational database is that the data relationships do not need to be predefined.
20. A **hierarchical database** is organized in a top to bottom series of parent-child relationships. Each **parent record** can have multiple child records. However, each **child record** can have only one parent. The parent record at the top of the hierarchy is called the **root** record.
21. A **network database** is organized similar to a hierarchical database except each child record (called a **member**) may have more than one parent record (called an **owner**).
22. Data relationships in both the hierarchical database and the network database must be established prior to the use of the database.
23. The database management system consists of a **data dictionary** that defines each data field to be used in the database; utility programs (usually referred to as utilities) that provide a number of special functions (such as copying data, creating files, and deleting records); security levels that control access to the data; and a **query language** that allows users to specify what data they wish to view.
24. The **relational operations** of a relational database include the select relational operation, the project relational operation, and the join relational operation.
25. The **select relational operation** selects specific records based on the specifications provided by the user.
26. The **project relational operation** specifies the fields to be displayed.
27. The **join relational operation** is used to combine two files.
28. A widely used query language is **Structured Query Language (SQL)**.
29. The **database administrator (DBA)** is the person who coordinates all use of the database.
30. The database administrator is responsible for database design, user coordination, backup and recovery, database security, and database performance monitoring.
31. Users should become familiar with the data in their organization's database and should actively participate in the specification of additions to the database that will affect their jobs.

## KEY TERMS

Attributes *8.13*
Backup and recovery *8.17*
Buckets *8.6*
Child record *8.14*
Collision *8.6*
Database *8.11*
Database administrator (DBA) *8.17*
Database design *8.17*
Database management system (DBMS) *8.11*
Data dictionary *8.15*
Direct file *8.6*
Domain *8.13*
File management system *8.11*
Hashing *8.6*
Hierarchical database *8.14*
Improved data integrity *8.12*
Improved data security *8.12*
Index *8.4*
Indexed file organization *8.4*
Integrated files *8.12*
Join relational operation *8.16*
Key *8.3*
Link *8.13*
Member *8.15*
Network database *8.15*
Owner *8.15*
Parent record *8.14*
Performance monitoring *8.17*
Prime number *8.6*
Project relational operation *8.16*
Query language *8.16*
Random access *8.5*
Random retrieval *8.5*
Reduced data redundancy *8.12*
Relational database *8.13*
Relational operations *8.16*
Relations *8.13*
Relative file *8.6*
Root *8.14*
Security *8.15*
Select relational operation *8.16*
Sequential access *8.4*
Sequential file organization *8.3*
Sequential retrieval *8.4*
Structured Query Language (SQL) *8.16*
Synonyms *8.6*
System security *8.17*
Tuples *8.13*
Updating *8.7*
User coordination *8.17*
Utilities *8.15*

## REVIEW QUESTIONS

1. Describe sequential file organization. How are records in sequential files retrieved?
2. What is an indexed file? Describe how the index is used to retrieve records from an indexed file.
3. How is the location where a record is stored in a direct file determined?
4. What is a collision? What are synonyms?
5. List the three data maintenance procedures that are used to update files. Give an example of each.
6. Write a definition for the term database.
7. What is the difference between a database management system and a file management system?
8. What are the advantages of a database management system over a file-oriented system?
9. In a relational database, how are different files related to one another?
10. What is the difference between the structures of a hierarchical and a network database?
11. How is a data dictionary used?
12. Why is access security important in a database system?
13. How is a database query used?
14. What are the responsibilities of a database administrator?
15. What are the responsibilities of the user in a database management system?

## CONTROVERSIAL ISSUES

1. Security experts have said that the risk of computer crime increases when a database is used in a company as opposed to when application-related files are used. They theorize that since all the data is accessible in one place, it would be easier to manipulate the data for illegal purposes. Database management system developers maintain that with proper security measures, databases are just as secure as files, if not more secure. What do you think?
2. Government attempts to establish a database on all citizens have been opposed by people who claim that it would be an invasion of privacy. Discuss the possible advantages and possible misuse of such a database.

## RESEARCH PROJECTS

1. Find articles on relational databases in recent journals and magazines. Report on the performance characteristics of relational databases, particularly with respect to the time required to retrieve and display information from more than one file (a joint operation).
2. Prepare a report on various databases available for use on personal computers.
3. Prepare a report on a database management system that supports Structured Query Language (SQL).

CHAPTER 9

# Data Communications

CHAPTER 9

# Data Communications

## OBJECTIVES

- Define data communications.
- Describe the basic components of a data communications system.
- Describe the various transmission media that are used for communication channels.
- Describe the different types of line configurations.
- Describe how data is transmitted.
- Identify and explain the communications equipment that can be used in a data communications system.
- Describe the functions that communications software can perform.
- Explain the two major categories of networks and describe the common network configurations.
- Discuss how personal computers can use data communications.

---

Computers are well recognized as important computing devices. They should also be recognized as important communication devices. It is now possible for a computer to communicate with other computers anywhere in the world. This capability allows users to quickly and directly access data and information that otherwise would have been unavailable or that probably would have taken considerable time to acquire. Banks, retail stores, airlines, hotels, and many others businesses use computers for communication purposes. Personal computer users communicate with other personal computer users and also access special databases available on larger machines to quickly and conveniently obtain information such as weather reports, stock market data, airline schedules, news stories, or even theater and movie reviews.

This chapter provides an overview of data communications and explains some of the terminology, equipment, procedures, and applications that relate to computers and their use as communication devices.

## WHAT IS DATA COMMUNICATIONS?

**Data communications** is the transmission of data over a communication channel, such as a standard telephone line, between one computer (or a terminal) and another computer.

Figure 9-1 shows the basic components of a data communications system. These components include:

1. A computer or a terminal.
2. Data communication equipment that sends (and can usually receive) data.
3. The communication channel over which the data is sent.
4. Data communications equipment that receives (and can usually send) data.
5. Another computer.

As you will see, the basic model of a data communications system illustrated in Figure 9-1 can be applied to virtually all data communications systems.

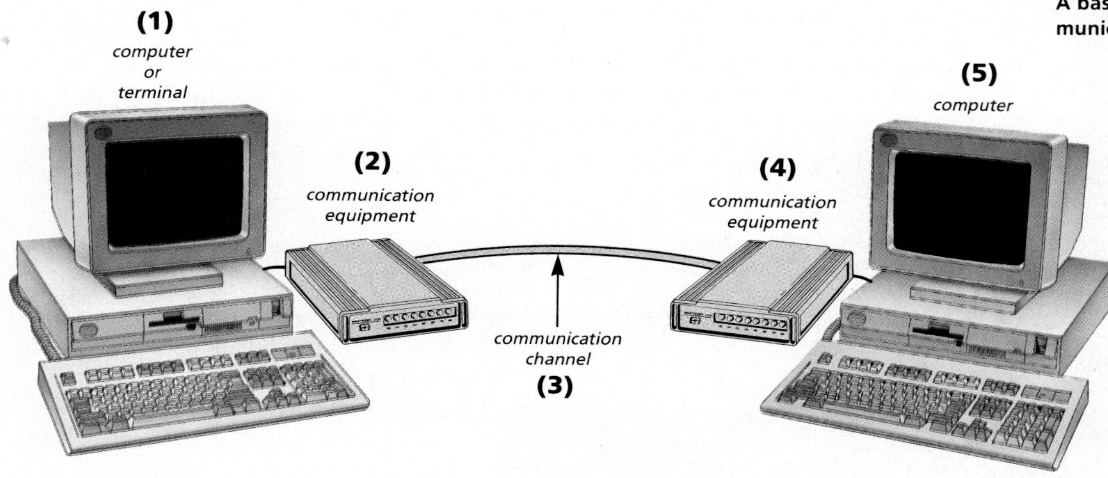


**FIGURE 9-1**
**A basic model of a data communications system.**

## COMMUNICATION CHANNELS

A **communication channel** is the link or path that the data follows as it is transmitted from the sending equipment to the receiving equipment in a data communications system. These channels are made up of one or more **transmission media**, including twisted pair wire, coaxial cable, fiber optics, microwaves, and communication satellites.

### Twisted Pair Wire

**Twisted pair wire** (Figure 9-2) consists of pairs of copper wires that are twisted together. To insulate and identify the wires, each wire is covered with a thin layer of colored plastic. Twisted pair wire is commonly used for telephone lines. It is an inexpensive transmission medium, and it can be easily strung from one location to another. The disadvantage of twisted pair wire is that it is susceptible to outside electrical interference generated by fans or air conditioners. This interference can garble the data as it is sent over the line, causing transmission errors to occur.

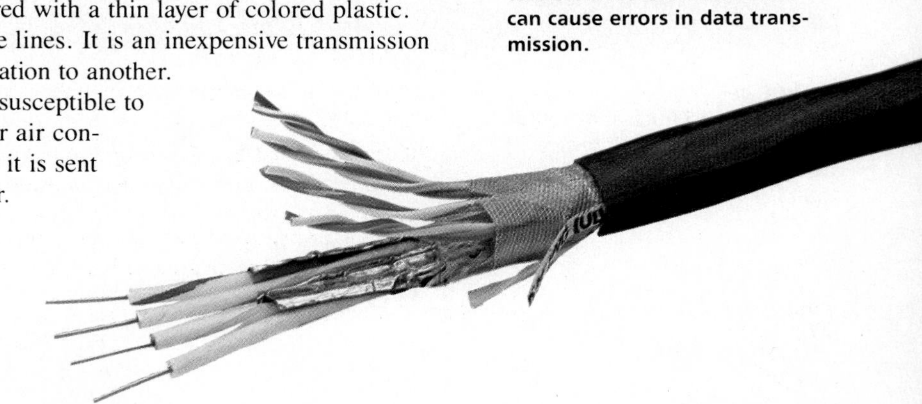

**FIGURE 9-2**
**Twisted pair wire is most commonly used as telephone wire. It is inexpensive but susceptible to electrical interference that can cause errors in data transmission.**

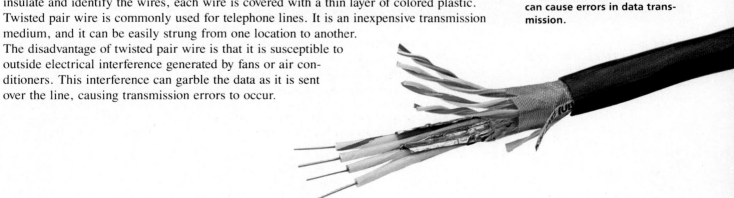

**FIGURE 9-3**
This photograph shows several types of coaxial cable that can be used to transmit data.

## Coaxial Cable

A **coaxial cable** is a high-quality communication line that is used in offices, laid under the ground and under the ocean. Coaxial cable consists of a wire or central conductor surrounded by a nonconducting insulator that is in turn surrounded by a woven metal shielding layer, and finally a plastic outer coating (Figure 9-3). Because of its more heavily insulated construction, coaxial cable is not susceptible to electrical interference and can transmit data at higher data rates over longer distances than twisted pair telephone wire.

There are two types of coaxial cable, named for the transmission techniques they support: baseband and broadband. **Baseband** coaxial cable carries one signal at a time. The signal, however, can travel very fast—in the area of ten million bits per second for the first 1,000 feet. The speed drops off significantly as the length of cable increases and special equipment is needed to amplify (boost) the signal if it is transmitted more than approximately one mile.

**Broadband** coaxial cable can carry multiple signals at one time. It is similar to cable TV where a single cable offers a number of channels to the user. A particular advantage of broadband channels is that data, audio, and video transmission can take place over the same line.

## Fiber Optics

**Fiber optics** (Figure 9-4) is a technology that may eventually replace conventional wire and cable in communication systems. This technology is based on the ability of smooth hair-thin strands of material to conduct light with high efficiency. The major advantages of fiber optics over wire cables include substantial weight and size savings and increased speed of transmission. A single fiber-optic cable can carry several hundred thousand voice communications simultaneously. Although fiber optics is not yet used on a large scale, it is frequently being used in new installations and promises to dramatically increase data communication capabilities.

**FIGURE 9-4**
The two-strand fiber-optic cable can transmit as much information as the 1500-pair copper cable.

## Microwaves

**Microwaves** are a type of radio waves that can be used to provide high-speed transmission of both voice and data. Data is transmitted through the air from one microwave station to another in a manner similar to the way radio signals are transmitted. A disadvantage of microwaves is that they are limited to line-of-sight transmission. This means that microwaves must be transmitted in a straight line and that there can be no obstructions, such as buildings or mountains, between microwave stations. For this reason, microwave stations are characterized by antennas positioned on tops of buildings, towers, or mountains (Figure 9-5). Because of the curvature of the earth, the maximum distance between microwave stations is about thirty miles.

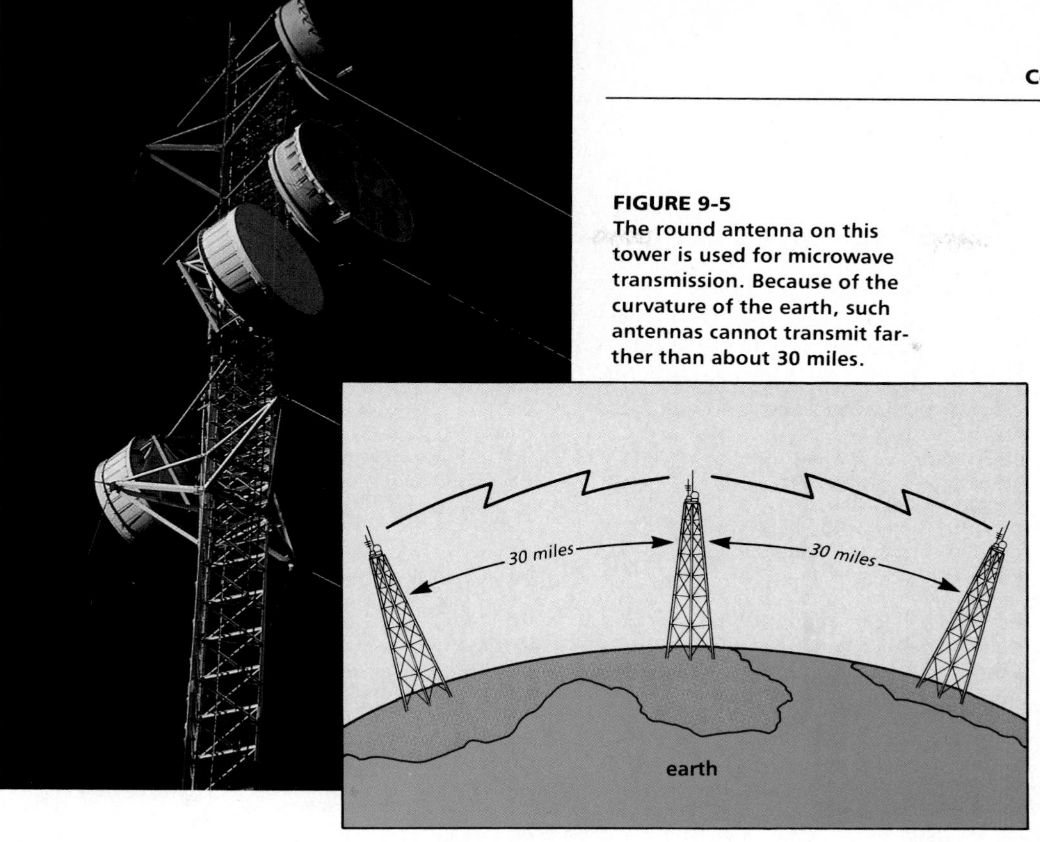


**FIGURE 9-5**
The round antenna on this tower is used for microwave transmission. Because of the curvature of the earth, such antennas cannot transmit farther than about 30 miles.

**FIGURE 9-6**
Earth stations use large dish antennas to communicate with satellites and microwave antennas. ▼

## Communication Satellites

**Communication satellites** have the ability to receive signals from earth, amplify the signals, and retransmit the signals back to the earth. **Earth stations** (Figure 9-6) are communication facilities that use large dish-shaped antennas to transmit and receive data from satellites. The transmission to the satellite is called an **uplink** and the transmission from the satellite to a receiving earth station is called a **downlink**. Communication satellites are normally placed about 22,000 miles above the earth in a geosynchronous orbit (Figure 9-7). This means that the satellite rotates with the earth, so that the same dish antennas on earth that are used to send and receive signals can remain fixed on the satellite at all times.

◀ **FIGURE 9-7**
Communication satellites are placed in geosynchronous orbits approximately 22,000 miles above the earth. This satellite is shown emerging from the cargo bay of a space shuttle.

## An Example of a Communication Channel

When data is transmitted over long distances, it is likely that a number of different types of transmission media will be used to make a complete communication channel. The diagram in Figure 9-8 illustrates some of the various transmission media that could be used to transmit data from a personal computer on the west coast of the United States to a large computer on the east coast. The steps that could occur are:

1. An entry is made on the personal computer. The data is sent over telephone lines from the computer to a microwave station.
2. The data is then transmitted between microwave stations that are usually located no more than thirty miles apart.
3. The data is transmitted from the last microwave station to an earth station.
4. The earth station transmits the data to the communications satellite.
5. The satellite relays the data to another earth station on the other side of the country.
6. The data received at the earth station is transmitted to microwave stations.
7. The data is sent by the telephone lines to the large computer.

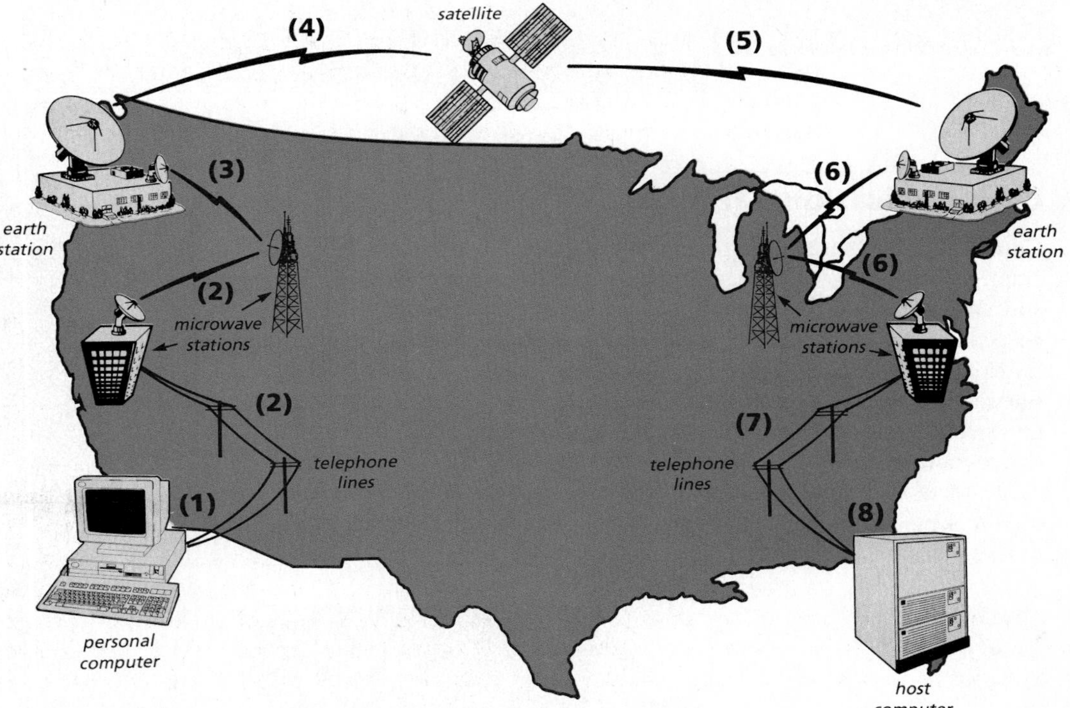


**FIGURE 9-8**
**This diagram illustrates the use of telephone wires, microwave transmission, and a communication satellite to allow a personal computer to communicate with a large host computer.**

The entire transmission process just described would take less than one second.

Not all data transmission is as complex as this example, but such sophisticated communication systems do exist to satisfy the needs of some users.

## LINE CONFIGURATIONS

There are two major **line configurations** (types of line connections) that are commonly used in data communications: point-to-point lines and multidrop or multipoint lines.

## Point-to-Point Lines

A **point-to-point line** is a direct line between a sending and a receiving device. It may be one of two types: a switched line or a dedicated line (Figure 9-9).

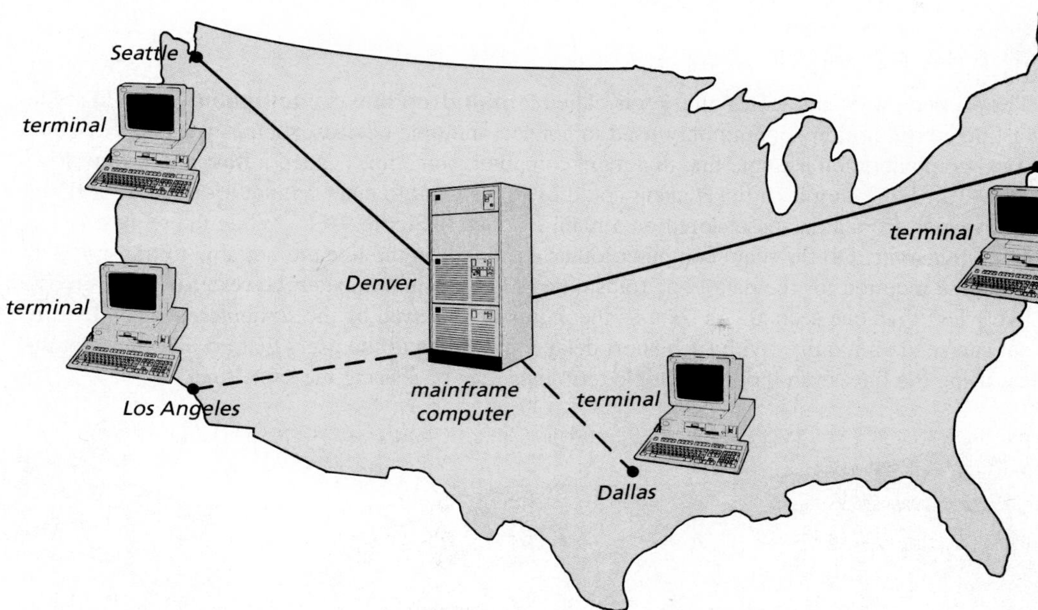


**FIGURE 9-9**
**This diagram illustrates a point-to-point line configuration using both switched phone (dial up) lines (- - - -) and dedicated leased lines (———) connected to a main computer in Denver. The leased lines are always connected whereas the switched lines have to be connected each time they are used.**

**Switched Line** A **switched line** uses a regular telephone line to establish a communication connection. Each time a connection is made, the line to be used for the call is selected by the telephone company switching stations (hence the name switched line). Using a switched line is the same as one person using a phone to call another person. The communication equipment at the sending end dials the phone number of the communication equipment at the other end. When the communication equipment at the receiving end answers the call, a connection is established and data can be transmitted. When the transmission of data is complete, the communication equipment at either end terminates the call by "hanging up" and the line is disconnected.

An advantage of using switched lines is that a connection can be made between any two locations that have phone service and communication equipment. For example, a personal computer could dial one computer to get information about the weather and then hang up and place a second call to another computer to get information about the stock market. A disadvantage of a switched line is that the quality of the line cannot be controlled because the line is chosen at random by the telephone company switching equipment. A switched line used for data communication is charged the same rate as a regular phone call.

**Dedicated Line** A **dedicated line** is a line connection that is always established (unlike the switched line where the line connection is reestablished each time it is used). The communication device at one end is always connected to the device at the other end. A user can create a dedicated line connection by running a wire or cable between two points, such as between two offices or buildings, or the dedicated line can be provided by an outside organization such as the phone company or some other communication service company. If the dedicated line is provided by an outside organization, it is sometimes called a **leased line** or a **private line**. Because a dedicated line is always established, the quality and consistency of the connection is better than on a switched line. Dedicated lines provided by outside organizations are usually charged on a flat fee basis: a fixed amount each month regardless of how much time the line is actually used to transmit data. The cost of dedicated lines varies based on the distance between the two connected points and, sometimes, the speed at which data will be transmitted.

## Multidrop Lines

The second major line configuration is called a **multidrop line** or **multipoint line**. This type of line configuration is commonly used to connect multiple devices, such as terminals or personal computers, on a single line to a main computer, sometimes called a **host computer** (Figure 9-10). For example, a ticket agent could use a terminal to enter an inquiry requesting flight information from a database stored on a main computer (Figure 9-11). While the request is being transmitted to the main computer, other terminals on the line are not able to transmit data. The time required for the data to be transmitted to the main computer, however, is short—most likely less than one second. As soon as the inquiry is received by the computer, a second terminal can send an inquiry. With such short delays, it appears to the users that no other terminals are using the line, even though multiple terminals may be sharing the same line.

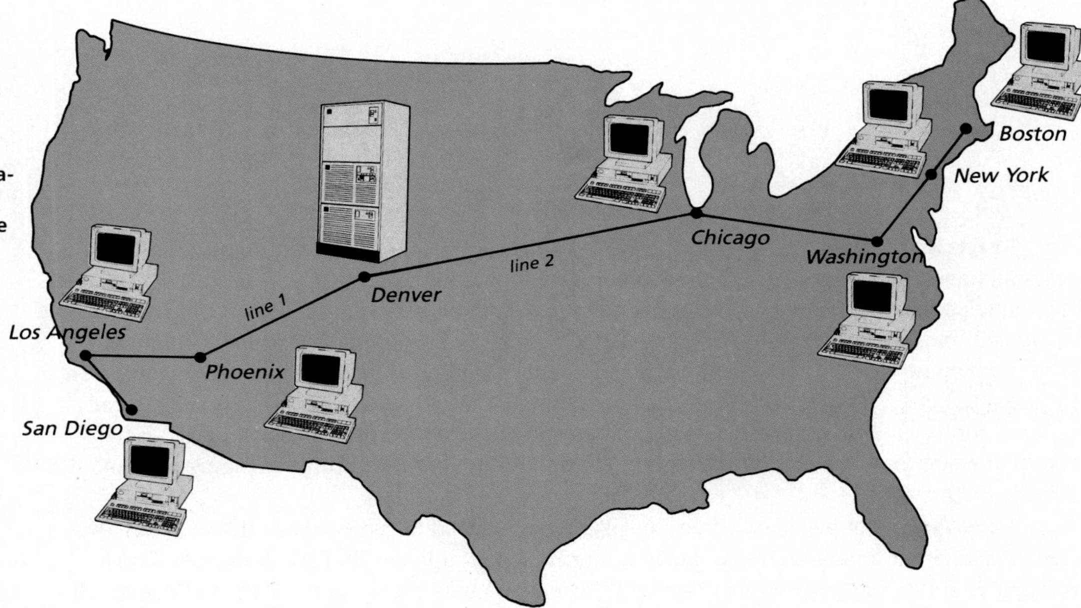


**FIGURE 9-10**
**This diagram illustrates two multidrop lines connecting several cities with a computer in Denver. Each line is shared by terminals at several locations. Multidrop line configurations are less expensive than individual lines to each remote location.**

The number of terminals to be placed on one line is a decision made by the designer of the system based on the amount of traffic that will be found on the line. For example, 100 or more terminals could be contained on a single line, provided each of them was only going to be sending short messages, such as inquiries, and each terminal was going to use the communication line only a few hours per day. But if longer messages such as reports were required and the terminals were to be used almost continuously, the number of terminals on one line would have to be smaller.

A leased line is almost always used for multidrop line configurations. The use of multidrop lines can decrease line costs considerably because one line is used by many terminals.

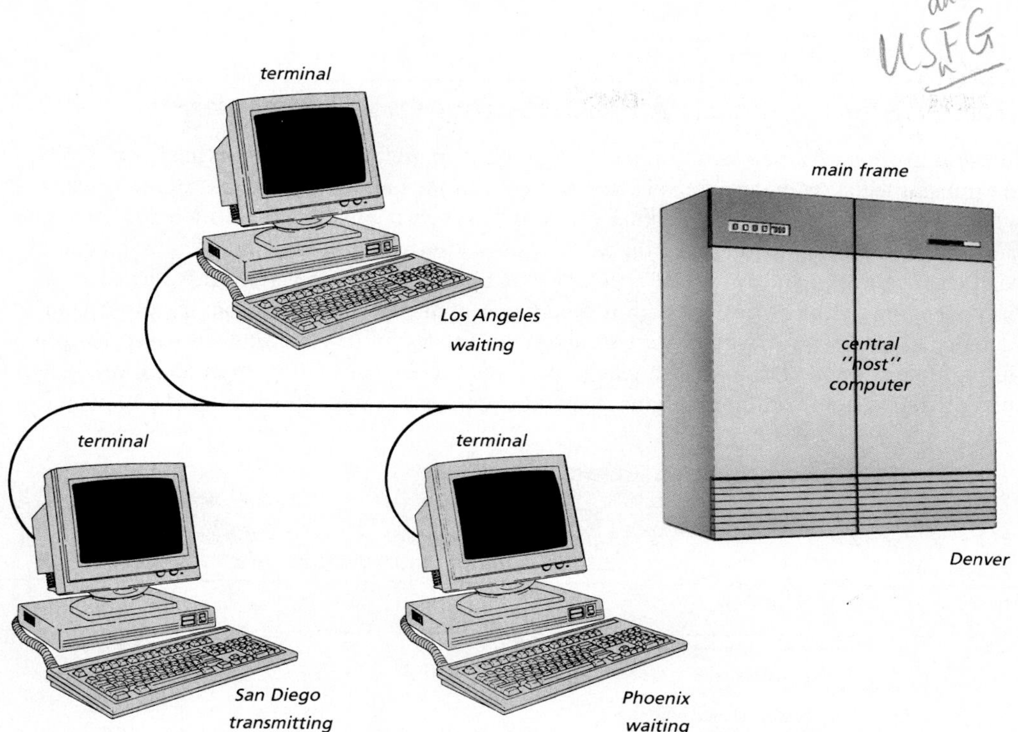


**FIGURE 9-11**
On a multidrop line, several terminals share the same line. Only one terminal at a time can transmit data to the host computer.

# CHARACTERISTICS OF COMMUNICATION CHANNELS

The communication channels we have discussed can be categorized by a number of characteristics, including the type of signal, transmission mode, transmission direction, and transmission rate.

## Types of Signals: Digital and Analog

Computer equipment is designed to process data as **digital signals**, individual electrical pulses that can represent the bits that are grouped together to form characters. However, telephone equipment was originally designed to carry only voice transmission, which is comprised of a continuous electrical wave called an **analog signal** (Figure 9-12). Therefore, in order to use voice phone lines to carry data, a special piece of equipment called a **modem** is used to convert the digital signals into analog signals. We discuss modems in more detail later in this chapter.

**FIGURE 9-12**
Individual electrical pulses of the digital signal are converted into analog (electrical wave) signals for transmission over voice phone lines. At the main computer receiving end, another modem converts the analog signals back into digital signals that can be processed by the computer.

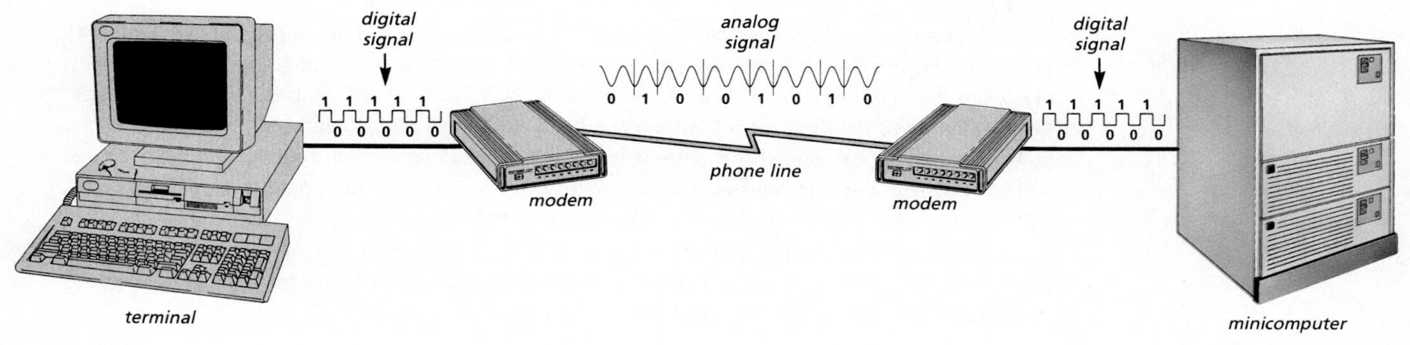

## Transmission Modes: Asynchronous and Synchronous

In **asynchronous transmission mode** (Figure 9-13), individual characters (made up of bits) are transmitted at irregular intervals, for example, as they are entered by a user. To distinguish where one character stops and another starts, the asynchronous communication mode uses a start and a stop bit. An additional bit called a **parity bit** is sometimes included at the end of each character to provide a way of checking against data loss. The parity bit is turned on or off depending on the error detection method being used. As you recall from the discussion on memory in Chapter 5, parity bits are used to detect if one of the data bits has been changed during transmission. The asynchronous transmission mode is used for lower speed data transmission and is used with most communication equipment designed for personal computers.

**FIGURE 9-13**
**In asynchronous transmission mode, individual characters are transmitted. In synchronous transmission mode, multiple characters are sent in a block. Synchronous transmission is faster and more accurate.**

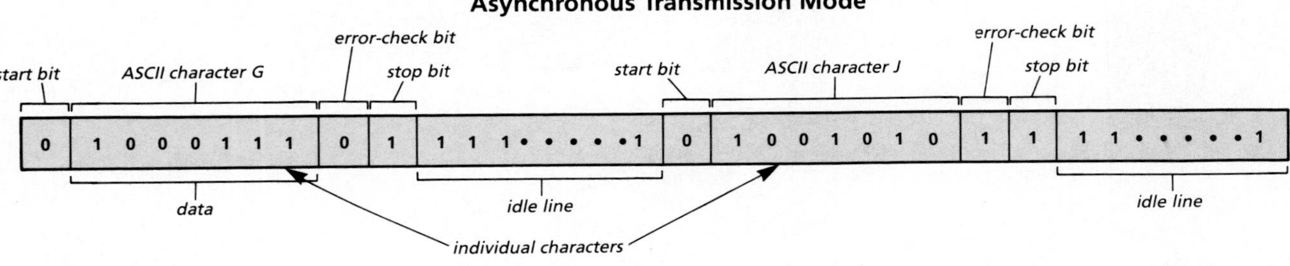


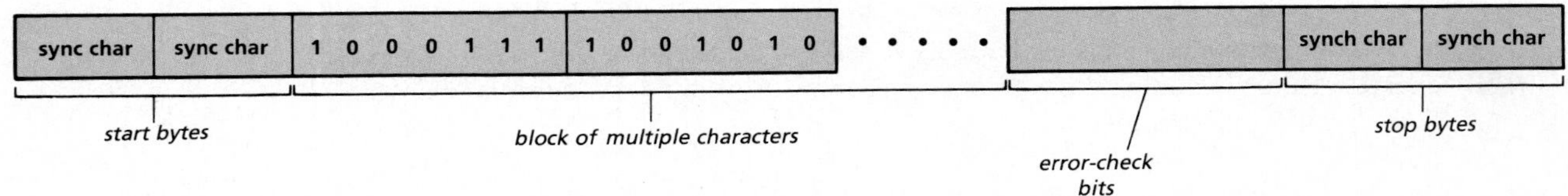


In the **synchronous transmission mode** (also shown in Figure 9-13), large blocks of data are transmitted at regular intervals. Timing signals synchronize the communication equipment at both the sending and receiving ends and eliminate the need for start and stop bits for each character. Error-checking bits and start and end indicators called sync bytes are also transmitted. Synchronous transmission requires more sophisticated and expensive equipment but does give much higher speeds and accuracy than asynchronous transmission.

## Direction of Transmission: Simplex, Half-Duplex, and Full-Duplex

The direction of data transmission is classified as either simplex, half-duplex, or full-duplex (Figure 9-14). In **simplex transmission**, data flows in only one direction. Simplex is used only when the sending device, such as a temperature sensor, never requires a response from the computer. For example, if a computer is used to control the temperature of a building, numerous sensors are placed throughout it. Each sensor is connected to the computer with a simplex transmission line because the computer only needs to receive data from the temperature sensors and does not need to send data back to the sensors.

In **half-duplex transmission**, data can flow in both directions but in only one direction at a time. An example is a citizens band radio. The user can talk or listen but not do both at the same time. Half-duplex is often used between terminals and a central computer.

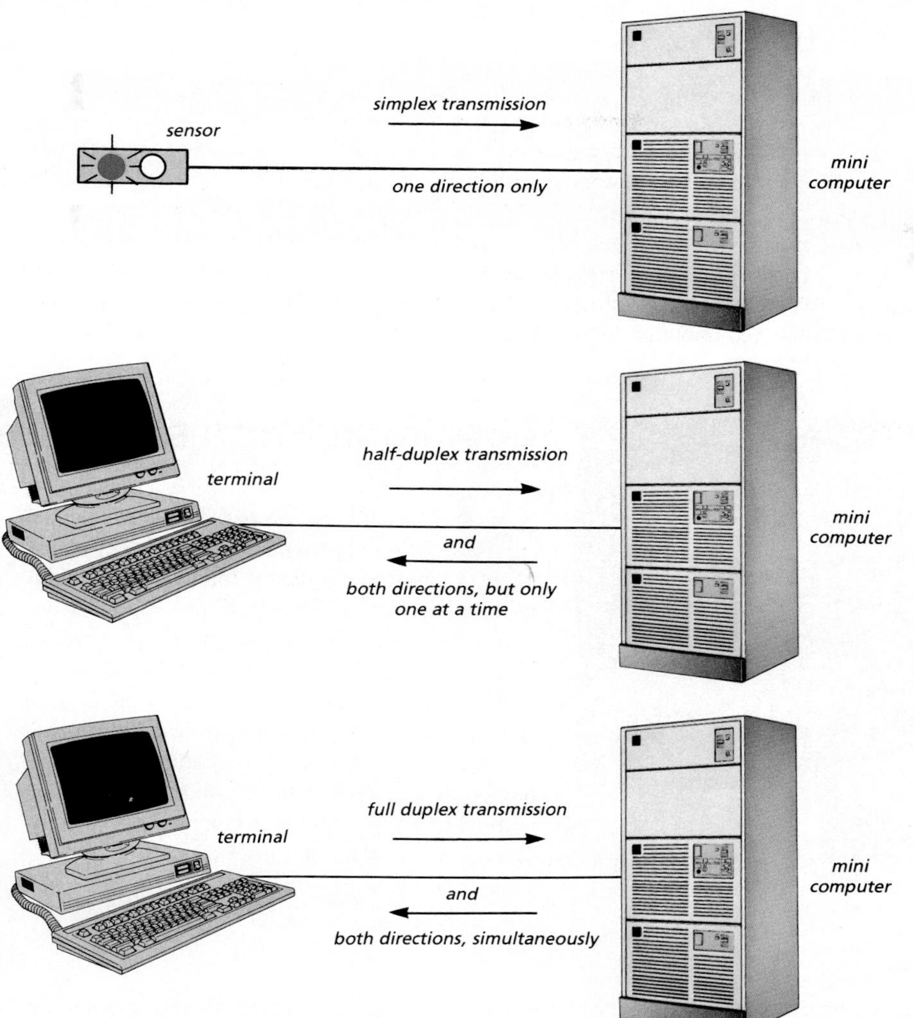


**FIGURE 9-14**
Simplex transmission allows data to flow in only one direction. Half-duplex allows data to flow in both directions but not at the same time. Full-duplex allows data to flow in both directions simultaneously.

In **full-duplex transmission**, data can be sent in both directions at the same time. A normal phone line is an example of full-duplex transmission. Both parties can talk at the same time. Full-duplex transmission is used for most interactive computer applications and for computer-to-computer data transmission.

## Transmission Rate

The transmission rate of a communication channel is determined by its bandwidth and its speed. The **bandwidth** is the range of frequencies that a channel can carry. Since transmitted data can be assigned to different frequencies, the wider the bandwidth, the more frequencies, and the more data that can be transmitted at the same time. Figure 9-15 summarizes the bandwidths of the communication channels we have discussed.

**FIGURE 9-15**
Bandwidth and relative carrying capacity of communication channels. Bandwidth is measured in Hertz or cycles per second. A megahertz is one million cycles per second; a gigahertz is one billion cycles per second; and a terahertz is one trillion cycles per second.

| TRANSMISSION CHANNEL | BANDWIDTH (HERTZ) | RELATIVE CARRYING CAPACITY |
|---|---|---|
| Twisted pair | 10–100,000 | 1 |
| Coaxial cable | 1–1000 megahertz | 1000 |
| Microwave | 1–10 gigahertz | 10,000 |
| Satellite | 2–40 gigahertz | 40,000 |
| Fiber optics | 100–1000 terahertz | 1,000,000,000 |

The speed at which data is transmitted is usually expressed as bits per second or as a baud rate.

**Bits per second (bps)** is the number of bits that can be transmitted in one second. Using a 10-bit byte to represent a character (7 data bits, 1 start, 1 stop, and 1 parity bit), a 2,400 bps transmission would transmit 240 characters per second. At this rate, a 20-page single-spaced report would be transmitted in approximately five minutes.

The **baud rate** is the number of times per second that the signal being transmitted changes. With each change, one or more bits can be transmitted. At speeds up to 2,400 bps, usually only one bit is transmitted per signal change and thus the bits per second and the baud rate are the same. To achieve speeds in excess of 2,400 bps, more than one bit is transmitted with each signal change and thus the bps will exceed the baud rate.

**FIGURE 9-16**
**An external modem is connected to a terminal or computer and to a phone outlet.**

## COMMUNICATION EQUIPMENT

If a terminal or a personal computer is within approximately 1,000 feet of another computer, the two devices can usually be directly connected by a cable. Over 1,000 feet, however, the electrical signal weakens to the point that some type of special communication equipment is required to increase or change the signal to transmit it farther. A variety of complex communication equipment exists to perform this task, but the equipment that a user is most likely to encounter is a modem, a multiplexor, and a front-end processor.

### Modems

A **modem** converts the digital signals of a terminal or computer to analog signals that can be transmitted over phone equipment. The word modem comes from a combination of the words *mo*dulate, which means to change into a sound or analog signal, and *de*modulate, which means to convert an analog signal into a digital signal. A modem must be present at both the sending and receiving ends of a communication channel.

An **external modem** (Figure 9-16) is a separate or stand-alone device that is attached to the computer or terminal by a cable and to the phone outlet by a standard phone cord. An advantage of an external modem is that it may be moved from one terminal or computer to another.

**FIGURE 9-17**
**An internal modem is mounted inside a personal computer.**

An **internal modem** (Figure 9-17) is a circuit board that is installed inside a computer or terminal. Internal modems are generally less expensive than comparable external modems but once installed, they are not as easy to move.

An **acoustic modem**, also called an **acoustic coupler**, is designed to be used with a phone handset (Figure 9-18). The acoustic coupler converts the digital signals generated by the terminal or personal computer into a series of audible tones, which are picked up by the mouthpiece in the headset in the same manner that a telephone picks up a person's voice. The analog signals are then transmitted over the

**FIGURE 9-18**
**The acoustic coupler in the lower left corner of this picture allows a portable computer user to communicate with another computer over telephone lines. Note that the telephone handset is placed in the molded rubber cups on the acoustic coupler.**

communication channel. An acoustic coupler provides portability but is generally less reliable than an internal or external modem, because small outside sounds can be picked up by the acoustic coupler and cause transmission errors. Acoustic couplers are not common and are primarily used for special applications, such as with portable computers.

Modems can tránsmit data at rates from 300 to 38,400 bits per second (bps). Most personal computers would use either a 1,200 or 2,400 bps modem. Business or heavier volume users would use faster and more expensive modems.

## Multiplexors

A **multiplexor** combines more than one input signal into a single stream of data that can be transmitted over a communication channel (Figure 9-19). The multiplexor at the sending end codes each character it receives with an identifier that is used by the multiplexor at the receiving end to separate the combined data stream into its original parts. A multiplexor may be connected to a separate modem or may have a modem built in. By combining the individual data streams into one, a multiplexor increases the efficiency of communications and saves the cost of individual communication channels.

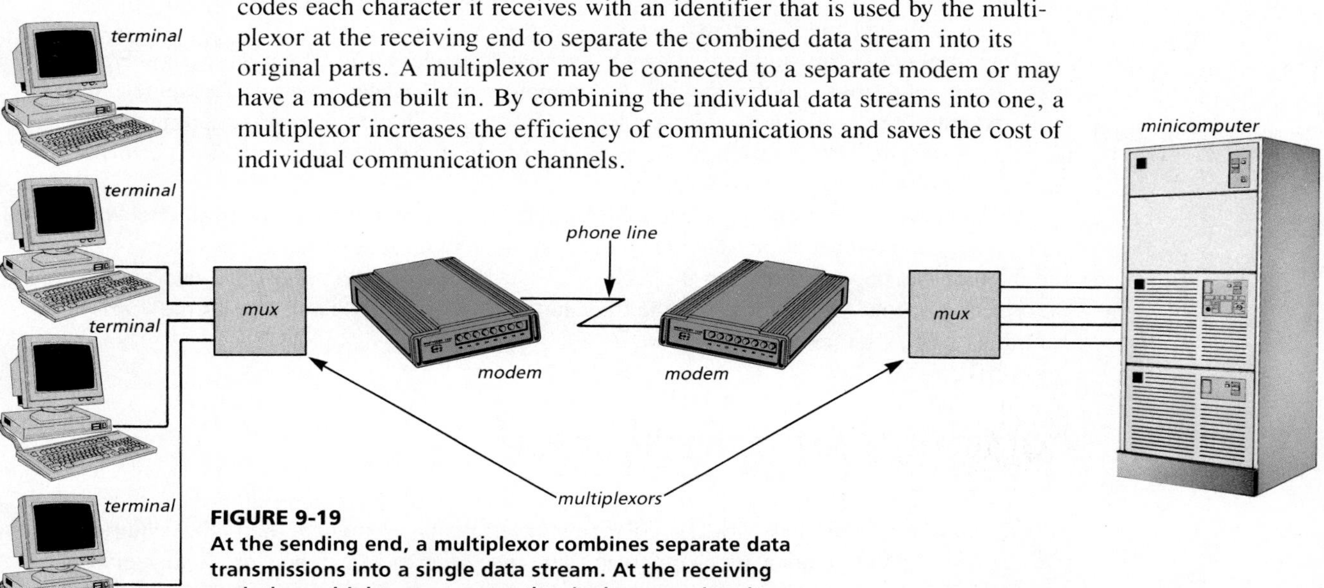


**FIGURE 9-19**
**At the sending end, a multiplexor combines separate data transmissions into a single data stream. At the receiving end, the multiplexor separates the single stream into its original parts.**

## Front-End Processors

A **front-end processor** (Figure 9-20) is a computer that is dedicated to handling the data communication requirements of a larger computer. Relieved of these tasks, the activity of the large computer is dedicated to processing data, while the front-end processor communicates the data. Tasks that the front-end processor would handle include **polling** (checking the connected terminals or computers to see if they have data to send), error checking and correction, and access security to make sure that a connected device or the user of the connected device is authorized to access the computer.

**FIGURE 9-20**
**This IBM Series 1 minicomputer is often used as a front-end processor to relieve the main computer of data communication tasks.**

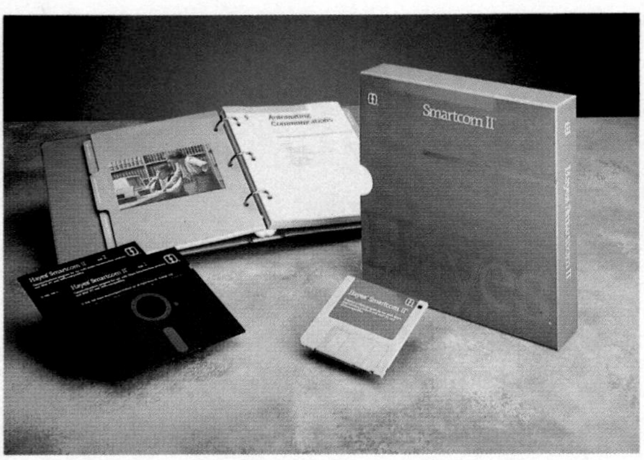


**FIGURE 9-21**
**Communication software performs a variety of tasks that assist the user in using data communications equipment.**

# COMMUNICATION SOFTWARE

Sometimes communications equipment is preprogrammed to accomplish its designed communication tasks. In other cases, the user must load a program before beginning data transmission. These programs, referred to as **communications software**, can perform a number of tasks including dialing (if a switched phone line is used), terminal emulation, and data encryption (Figure 9-21).

Dialing software allows the user to store, review, select and dial phone numbers of computers that can be called. The software provides a variety of meaningful messages to assist the user in establishing a connection before transmitting data. For example, a person who uses a personal computer at home to communicate with a computer at the office could use dialing software to establish the communication connection. The software would display the office computer's phone number on the user's personal computer screen. The user would enter the appropriate command for the dialing software, working with a modem, to begin dialing the office computer and to establish a connection. During the 10 or 15 seconds that this process takes, the software would display messages to indicate specifically what was happening, such as "DIALING," "CARRIER DETECT" (which means that the office computer has "answered"), and "CONNECTED" (to indicate that the communication connection has been established and data transmission can begin).

**Terminal emulation** software allows a personal computer to imitate or appear to be a specific type of terminal so that the personal computer can connect to another computer. Most mini and mainframe computers are designed to work with a limited number of terminals that have specific characteristics such as speed and parity. Terminal emulation software performs the necessary speed and parity conversion.

Data encryption is used to protect confidential data during transmission. **Data encryption** is the conversion of data at the sending end into an unrecognizable string of characters or bits and the reconversion of the data at the receiving end. Without knowing how the data was encrypted, someone who intercepted the transmitted data would have a difficult time determining what the data meant.

# COMMUNICATION NETWORKS

A communication **network** is a collection of terminals, computers, and other equipment that use communication channels to share data. Networks can be classified as either local area networks or wide area networks.

## Local Area Networks (LANs)

A **local area network** or **LAN** is a communications network that is privately owned and that covers a limited geographic area, such as an office, a building, or a group of buildings.

The LAN consists of a communication channel that connects either a series of computer terminals together with a minicomputer or, more commonly, a group of personal computers to one another. Very sophisticated LANs may connect a variety of office devices, such as word processing equipment, computer terminals, video equipment, and personal computers.

Two common applications of local area networks are hardware resource sharing and information resource sharing. **Hardware resource sharing** allows each personal computer in the network to access and use devices that would be too expensive to provide for each user or would not be justified for each user because of only occasional use. For example, when a number of personal computers are used on the network, each may need to use a laser printer. Using a LAN, a laser printer could be purchased and made a part of the network. Whenever a user of a personal computer on the network needed the laser printer, it could be accessed over the network.

To illustrate, the drawing in Figure 9-22 depicts a simple local area network consisting of four personal computers linked together by a cable. Three of the personal computers (computer 1 in the sales and marketing department, computer 2 in the accounting department, and computer 3 in the personnel department) are available for use at all times. Computer 4 is used as a **network control unit**, sometimes called a **server**, which is dedicated to handling the communication needs of the other computers in the network. The users of this LAN have connected the laser printer to the network control unit. Using the LAN, all computers and the network control unit can use the printer.

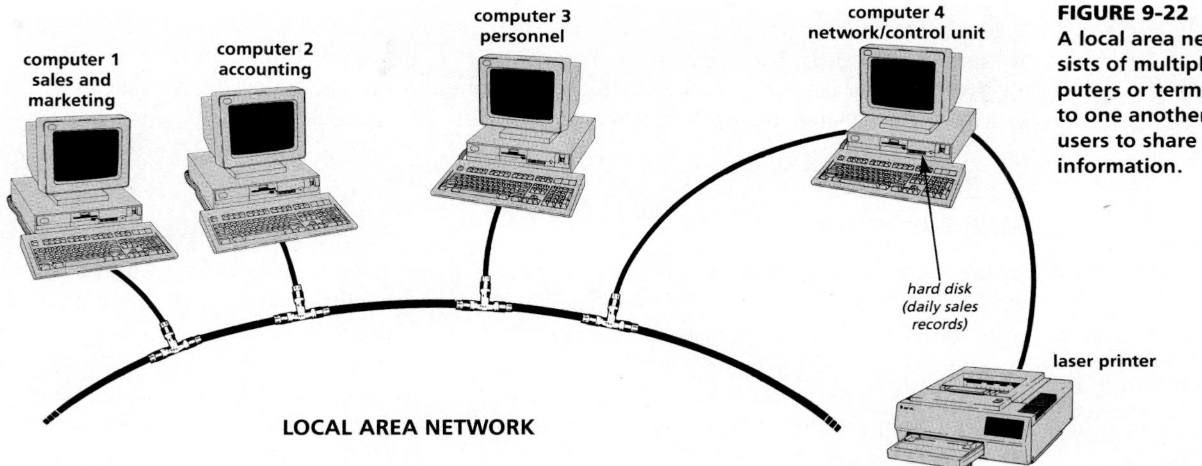


**FIGURE 9-22**
**A local area network (LAN) consists of multiple personal computers or terminals connected to one another. The LAN allows users to share hardware and information.**

**Information resource sharing** allows anyone using a personal computer on the local area network to access data stored on any other computer in the network. In actual practice, hardware resource sharing and information resource sharing are often combined. For example, in Figure 9-22, the daily sales records could be stored on the hard disk associated with the control unit personal computer. Anyone needing access to the sales records could use this information resource. The ability to access and store data on common auxiliary storage is an important feature of many local area networks.

Frequently used software is another type of resource that is often shared on a local area network. For example, if all users need access to word processing software, the software can be stored on the hard disk and accessed by all users as needed. This is much more convenient and faster than having the software stored on a floppy disk and available at each computer. For software written in-house, this is a common approach. Note, however, that the licensing agreement from many software companies does not permit the purchase of a single software package for use by all the computers in a network; therefore, it may be necessary to obtain a special agreement, called a **site license**, if a commercial software package is to be stored on hard disk and accessed by many users. Many software vendors now sell a network version of their packages.

## Wide Area Networks (WANs)

A **wide area network** or **WAN** is one that is geographic in scope (as opposed to local) and uses phone lines, microwaves, satellites, or a combination of communication channels. Public wide area network companies include so-called "common carriers" such as the telephone companies. In recent years, telephone company deregulation has encouraged a number of companies to build their own wide area networks and others, such as MCI, to build WANs to compete with the telephone companies. Some common carriers are now offering **Integrated Services Digital Network (ISDN)** services. ISDN establishes an international standard for the digital transmission of data using different channels and communication companies.

# NETWORK CONFIGURATIONS

Communication networks are usually configured or arranged in one or a combination of three patterns, sometimes called a **topology**. These configurations are star, bus, and ring networks. Although these configurations can also be used with wide area networks, we illustrate them with local area networks.

## Star Network

A **star network** (Figure 9-23) contains a central computer and one or more terminals or personal computers connected to it, forming a star. A pure star network consists of only point-to-point lines between the terminals and the computer, but most star networks, such as the one shown in Figure 9-23, include both point-to-point lines and multidrop lines. A star network configuration is often used when the central computer contains all the data required to process the input from the terminals, such as an airline reservation system. For example, if inquiries are being processed in the star network, all the data to answer the inquiry would be contained in the database stored on the central computer.

A star network can be relatively efficient and close control can be kept over the data processed on the network. Its major disadvantage is that the entire network is dependent on the central computer and the associated hardware and software. If any of these elements fail, the entire network is disabled. Therefore, in most large star networks, backup systems are available in case the primary system fails.

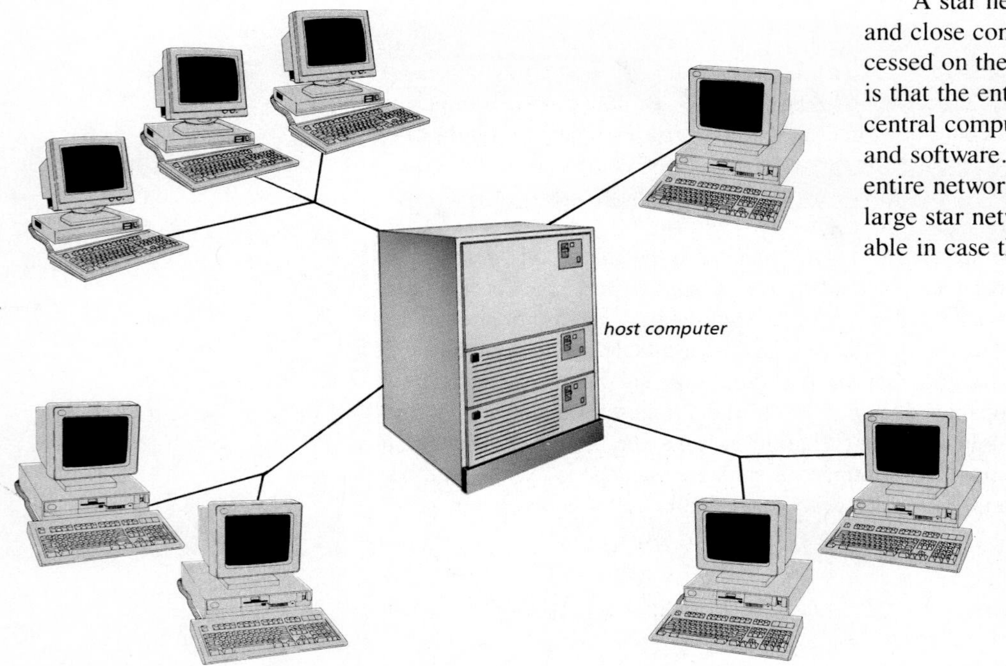

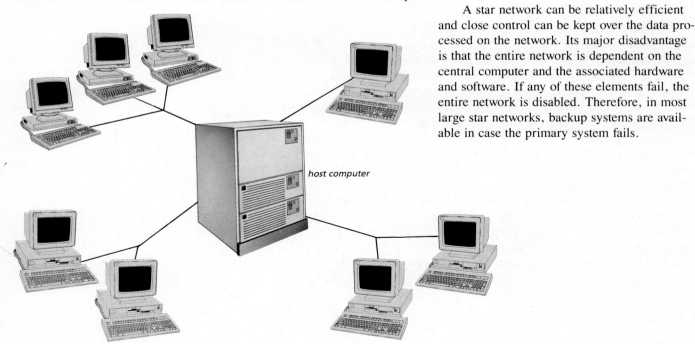

**FIGURE 9-23**
**A star network contains a single, centralized host computer with which all the terminals or personal computers in the network communicate. Both point-to-point and multidrop lines can be used in a star network.**

## Bus Network

When a **bus network** is used, all devices in the network are connected to and share a single cable. Information is transmitted in either direction from any one personal computer to another. Any message can be directed to a specific device. An advantage of the bus network is that devices can be attached or detached from the network at any point without disturbing the rest of the network. In addition, if one computer on the network fails, this does not affect the other users of the network. Figure 9-22 illustrates a simple bus network.

## Ring Network

A **ring network** does not utilize a centralized host computer. Rather, a series of computers communicate with one another (Figure 9-24). A ring network can be useful when all the processing is not done at a central site, but at local sites. For example, computers could be located in three departments: the accounting department, the personnel department, and the shipping and receiving department. The computers in each of these departments could perform the processing required for each of the departments. On occasion, however, the computer in the shipping and receiving department could communicate with the computer in the accounting department to update certain data stored on the accounting department computer. Ring networks have not been extensively implemented for data communications systems that are used for long-distance communication; they are used more for local communications.

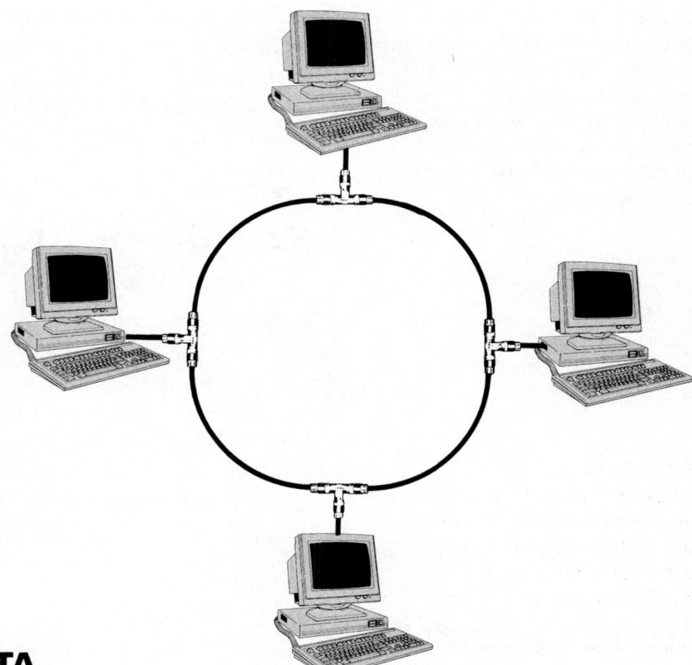

**FIGURE 9-24**
**In a ring network, all computers are connected in a continuous loop. Data flows around the ring in only one direction.**

# THE PERSONAL COMPUTER AND DATA COMMUNICATIONS

The increased use of personal computers and the decreasing cost of communications equipment has resulted in a number of services that are now available to the individual personal computer user. To use these services, all that is required is a personal computer, a modem, communications software, and a phone line (Figure 9-25). These services include home banking, electronic shopping, commercial databases, and electronic bulletin boards.

Home banking, sometimes called electronic banking, allows a user to schedule payments to creditors, make transfers from one account to another, review bank statements and cleared checks, and inquire about current account balances.

Electronic shopping allows a user to select from a catalog of merchandise that the service offers for sale. The catalog is displayed on the user's screen. Theoretically, these items cost no more or cost less than comparable items found in stores because the electronic shopping seller doesn't have to operate a showroom. In addition, an electronic shopper has the added convenience of not having to go out to make the purchase.

Commercial databases offer a wealth of information in hundreds of subject areas. These services are literally electronic libraries containing information on such topics as economics, education, science, law, and a variety of business subjects. One service, NEXIS, offers access

FIGURE 9-25
This person is using a personal computer to schedule checking account payments with a home banking service. This is one of many services that are now available to individual personal computer users.

to the complete text of the *Encyclopaedia Britannica*. CompuServe offers a variety of databases that include information on world and business news, travel, and weather. Dow Jones provides business and financial information including access to the full text of the *Wall Street Journal*. To access commercial databases, users generally pay an initial subscription fee and additional charges based on the amount of use.

Electronic bulletin boards, like their physical counterparts, allow users to post messages on virtually any subject. These bulletin boards are usually maintained by computer clubs or vendors for local users although some have been established for wider use. Some bulletin boards offer members access to public domain software, programs that are available free to anyone who wants to use them. These programs can be **downloaded** or transferred to the user's own personal computer. If the user wants to contribute a program to the public domain software, it is **uploaded** or transferred to the bulletin board system.

## SUMMARY OF DATA COMMUNICATIONS

Data communications will continue to have an increasing impact on the way people work and the way they use computers. Individuals and organizations are no longer limited to local data resources but instead, with communication capabilities, can obtain information from anywhere in the world at electronic speed. With data communications technology rapidly changing, today's businesses are challenged to find ways to adapt the technology to provide better products and services for their customers and make their operations more efficient. For individuals, the new technology offers increased access to worldwide information and services, and provides new opportunities for education.

## CHAPTER SUMMARY

1. The transmission of data from one computer (or terminal) to another computer over communication channels is called **data communications**.
2. The basic components of a data communications system are: (1) a personal computer or terminal; (2) data communications equipment that sends (and can usually receive) data; (3) the communication channel over which data is sent; (4) data communications equipment that receives (and can usually send) data; and (5) a computer.
3. A **communication channel** is the link or path that the data follows as it is transmitted from the sending device to the receiving device in a data communications system.
4. A communication channel can consist of various **transmission media** including twisted pair wire, coaxial cable, fiber optics, microwaves, and communication satellites.
5. **Twisted pair wire** is the color-coded copper wires that are twisted together and commonly used as telephone wire.
6. **Coaxial cable** is high-quality underground or suboceanic communication lines consisting of a central conductor or wire that is surrounded by a nonconducting insulator and encased in a woven metal shield.
7. Coaxial cable can be either **baseband**, carrying one signal at a time at very high rates of speed, or **broadband**, carrying multiple signals at a time.
8. **Fiber optics** uses technology based on the ability of smooth, hair-thin strands of material that conduct light waves to rapidly and efficiently transmit data.
9. **Microwaves** are high-speed radio transmissions sent through the air between microwave stations.

10. **Communication satellites** are man-made space devices that receive, amplify, and retransmit signals from earth.
11. **Earth stations** are communication facilities that contain large dish-shaped antennas used to transmit data to and receive data from communication satellites.
12. **Line configurations** can be either point-to-point lines or multidrop lines.
13. A **point-to-point line** is a direct line between a sending and receiving device. It may be either a **switched line** (a connection established through regular telephone lines) or a **dedicated line** (a line whose connection between devices is always established).
14. A **multidrop line**, also known as a **multipoint line**, uses a single line to connect multiple devices to a main computer.
15. Computer equipment processes data as **digital signals**, which are individual electrical pulses representing the bits that are grouped together to form characters.
16. **Analog signals** are continuous electrical waves that are used to transmit data over standard telephone lines.
17. A **modem** is a special piece of equipment that converts the digital signals used by computer equipment into analog signals that are used by telephone equipment.
18. There are two modes of transmitting data: **asynchronous transmission mode**, which transmits one character at a time at irregular intervals using start and stop bits, and **synchronous transmission mode**, which transmits blocks of data at regular intervals using timing signals to synchronize the sending and receiving equipment.
19. Transmissions may be classified according to the direction in which the data can flow on a line: sending only (**simplex transmission**); sending or receiving, but in only one direction at a time (**half-duplex transmission**); and sending and receiving at the same time (**full-duplex transmission**).
20. The transmission rate of a communication channel depends on the **bandwidth** and its speed. The wider the bandwidth, the greater the number of signals that can be carried on the channel at one time, and the more data that can be transmitted.
21. **Bits per second (bps)** is the number of bits that can be transmitted in one second.
22. There are three basic types of modems: an **external modem**, which is a separate stand-alone device attached to the computer or terminal by a cable and to the phone outlet by a standard phone cable; an **internal modem**, which is a circuit board installed inside a computer or terminal; and an **acoustic modem** or **acoustic coupler**, which is a device used with a phone handset.
23. A **multiplexor** combines more than one input signal into a single stream of data that can be transmitted over a communications channel.
24. A **front-end processor** is a computer dedicated to handling the data communications requirements of a larger computer.
25. **Communication software** consists of programs that perform tasks such as dialing (software that stores, selects, and dials phone numbers); **terminal emulation** (software that allows the personal computer to imitate or appear to be a specific type of terminal so that the personal computer can connect to specific types of computers); and **data encryption** (software that can code and decode transmitted data for security purposes).
26. A **network** is a collection of terminals, computers, and other equipment that use communication channels to share data.
27. A **local area network (LAN)** is a communications network that covers a limited geographic area and is privately owned.
28. Two common uses of local area networks are **hardware resource sharing**, which allows all network users to access a single piece of equipment rather than each user having to be connected to his or her own device, and **information resource sharing**, which allows the network users to access data stored on other computers in the network.
29. A **wide area network** or **WAN** is a network that covers a large geographical area.
30. Network **topology** describes the pathways by which devices in a network are connected to each other.
31. A **star network** contains a central computer and one or more terminals or computers connected to it, forming a star.
32. In a **bus network** all devices in the network are connected to and share a single cable.
33. A **ring network** has a series of computers connected to each other in a ring.
34. For a personal computer to access other computers through data communications, it must have a modem, communications software, and a phone line.
35. Some of the data communication services available to personal computer users are home banking, electronic shopping, commercial databases, and electronic bulletin boards.

## KEY TERMS

Acoustic coupler *9.12*
Acoustic modem *9.12*
Analog signal *9.9*
Asynchronous transmission mode *9.10*
Bandwidth *9.11*
Baseband *9.4*
Baud rate *9.12*
Bits per second (bps) *9.12*
Broadband *9.4*
Bus network *9.17*
Coaxial cable *9.4*
Communication channel *9.3*
Communication satellites *9.5*
Communications software *9.14*
Data communications *9.2*
Data encryption *9.14*
Dedicated line *9.7*
Digital signal *9.8*
Downlink *9.5*
Downloaded *9.18*
Earth stations *9.5*
External modems *9.12*
Fiber optics *9.4*
Front-end processors *9.13*
Full-duplex transmission *9.11*
Half-duplex transmission *9.11*
Hardware resource sharing *9.14*
Host computer *9.8*
Information resource sharing *9.15*
Integrated Services Digital Network (ISDN) *9.16*
Internal modem *9.12*
Leased line *9.7*
Line configuration *9.6*
Local area network (LAN) *9.14*
Microwaves *9.4*
Modem *9.9*
Multidrop line *9.8*
Multiplexor *9.13*
Multipoint line *9.8*
Network *9.14*
Network control unit *9.15*
Parity bit *9.10*
Point-to-point line *9.7*
Polling *9.13*
Private line *9.7*
Ring network *9.17*
Server *9.15*
Simplex transmission *9.10*
Site license *9.15*
Star network *9.16*
Switched line *9.7*
Synchronous transmission mode *9.10*
Terminal emulation *9.14*
Topology *9.16*
Transmission media *9.3*
Twisted pair wire *9.3*
Uplink *9.5*
Uploaded *9.18*
Wide area network (WAN) *9.16*

## REVIEW QUESTIONS

1. Define data communications. What are the basic components of a data communications system?
2. List five kinds of transmission media used for communication channels.
3. Describe the two major types of line configurations. What are the advantages and disadvantages of each?
4. List and describe the three types of data transmission (direction) that are used.
5. Why is a modem used? Describe some of the types of modems available.
6. Describe some of the tasks that communications software can perform.
7. Compare and contrast a local area network and a wide area network.
8. Discuss the reasons for using a local area network.
9. Name three topologies or configurations that are used with networks. Draw a diagram of each.
10. Describe several data communications services that are available to personal computer users.

## CONTROVERSIAL ISSUES

1. Some personal computer users have used communication equipment and software to illegally gain access to private databases. These individuals, known as "hackers," often claim that their illegal access was only a harmless prank. Do you think this type of computer usage is harmless? Explain your position.
2. The use of data communications equipment now allows some individuals to work for their company from their homes. These individuals "commute" electronically and do their work via a computer terminal or personal computer connected by a communication channel to their company's main computer. Discuss the advantages and disadvantages of such a working relationship.

CHAPTER 10

# Operating Systems and System Software

# CHAPTER 10

# Operating Systems and System Software

## OBJECTIVES

- Define the terms operating system and system software.
- Describe the various types of operating systems and explain the differences in their capabilities.
- Describe the functions of an operating system, including allocating system resources, monitoring system activities, and using utilities.
- Explain the difference between proprietary and portable operating systems.
- Name and briefly describe the major operating systems that are being used today.

---

When most people think of software they think of applications software such as the word processing, spreadsheet, and database software that we discuss in this text. However, for application software to run on a computer, another type of software is needed to interface between the user, the applications software, and the equipment. This software consists of programs that are referred to as the operating system. The operating system is part of what is called the system software.

## WHAT IS SYSTEM SOFTWARE?

**System software** consists of all the programs including the operating system that are related to controlling the operations of the computer equipment. System software differs from applications software. Applications software tells the computer how to produce information, such as how to calculate the correct amount to print on a paycheck. In contrast, some of the functions that system software perform are: starting up the computer; loading, executing, and storing application programs; storing and retrieving files; and performing a variety of utility functions such as formatting disks, sorting data files, and translating program instructions into machine language. The most important part of the system software is the operating system.

## WHAT IS AN OPERATING SYSTEM?

All computers utilize an operating system. An **operating system (OS)** consists of one or more programs that manage the operations of a computer. These programs function as an interface between the user, the application programs, and the computer equipment (Figure 10-1).

For a computer to operate, the essential and most frequently used instructions in the operating system must be stored in main memory. This portion of the operating system is called by many different names: the **supervisor**, **monitor**, **executive**, **master program**, **control program** and **kernel**. The remaining part of the operating system is usually stored on disk and can be loaded into main memory whenever it is needed.

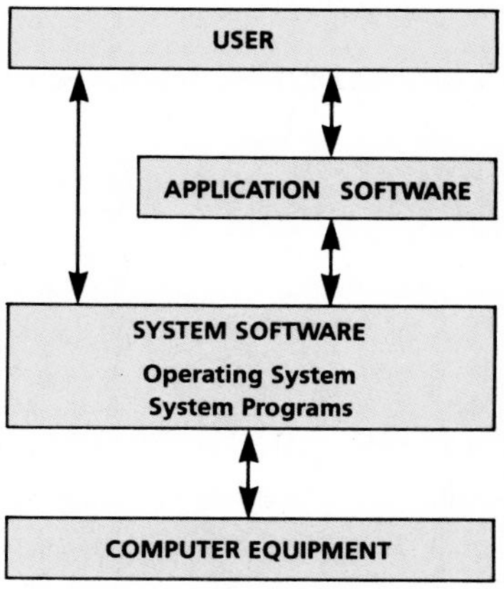

USER

APPLICATION SOFTWARE

SYSTEM SOFTWARE
Operating System
System Programs

COMPUTER EQUIPMENT

**FIGURE 10-1**
**The operating system and other system programs act as an interface between the user, the application software, and the computer equipment.**

## LOADING AN OPERATING SYSTEM

The process of loading an operating system into the main memory of the computer is called **booting** the system. Figure 10-2 shows the steps that occur when an operating system is loaded on a personal computer. While this process is not identical to that used on large computers, the functions performed are similar:

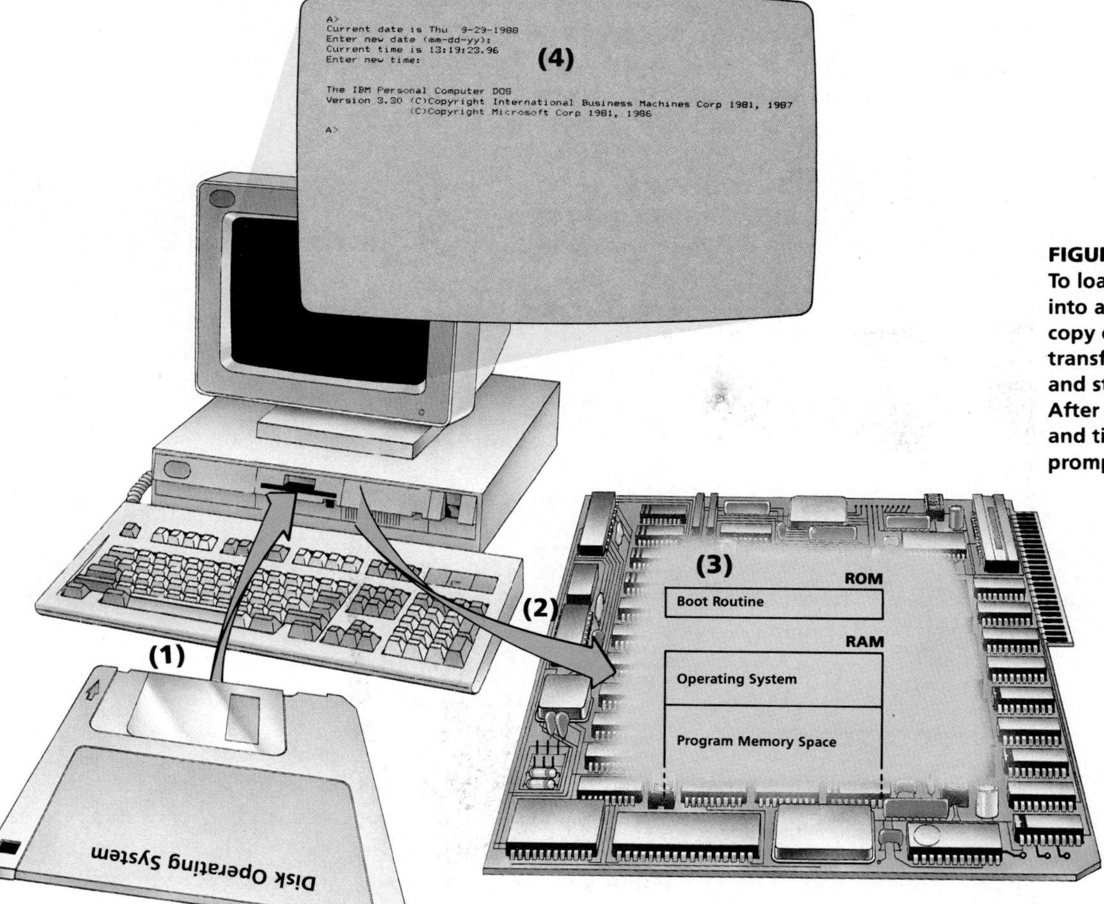


**FIGURE 10-2**
**To load the operating system into a personal computer (1), a copy of the operating system is transferred from the disk (2) and stored in main memory (3). After the user enters the date and time (4), the system prompt (A>) is displayed.**

1. A floppy disk that contains the operating system is placed in the disk drive. Note that if the operating system was stored on a hard disk, the floppy disk would not be used.
2. When the computer is turned on, the boot routine, which is stored in ROM, issues the commands to load the operating system into main memory. To do this, a copy of the operating system is transferred from the floppy disk or hard disk into main memory.
3. The boot instructions that loaded the operating system transfer control of the computer to the operating system. In many cases, the operating system requests that the user enter the correct date and time, after which the **operating system prompt** is displayed. The prompt indicates to the user that the operating system is ready to accept a command such as to run an application program.

Once the operating system is loaded into main memory, it usually remains in memory until the computer is turned off. The operating system controls the loading and manages the execution of each application program that is requested by the user. When an application program completes its task, the operating system queries the user by displaying the system prompt. The prompt indicates that the operating system is ready to receive a command specifying the next program or operation that is to be performed.

## TYPES OF OPERATING SYSTEMS

The various types of operating systems include single program, multiprogramming, multiprocessing, and virtual machine operating systems. These operating systems can be classified by two criteria: (1) whether or not they allow more than one user to use the computer at the same time and (2) whether or not they allow more than one program to run at the same time (Figure 10-3).

| | SINGLE PROGRAM | MULTIPROGRAMMING | MULTIPROCESSING | VIRTUAL MACHINE |
|---|---|---|---|---|
| NUMBER OF PROGRAMS RUNNING | One | More than one | More than one on each CPU | More than one on each operating system |
| NUMBER OF USERS | One | One or more than one (Multiuser) | More than one on each CPU | More than one on each operating system |

**FIGURE 10-3**
**Operating systems can be classified by whether they allow more than one user and more than one program to be operating at one time.**

### Single Program

**Single program** operating systems allow only a single user to run a single program at one time. This was the first type of operating system developed. Today, many personal computers use this type of operating system.

### Multiprogramming

**Multiprogramming** operating systems, also called **multitasking** operating systems, allow more than one program to be run at the same time. Even though the CPU is only able to work on one program instruction at a time, its ability to switch back and forth between programs makes it appear that all programs are running at the same time. For example, with a multiprogramming operating system the computer could be performing a complex spreadsheet calculation and at the same time be downloading a file from another computer while the user is writing a memo with the word processing program.

Multiprogramming operating systems on personal computers can usually support a single user running multiple programs. Multiprogramming operating systems on some personal computers and most mini and mainframe computers can support more than one user running more than one program. This version of a multiprogramming operating system is sometimes called a **multiuser-multiprogramming** operating system. Most of these operating systems also allow more than one user to be running the same program. For example, a wholesale distributor may have dozens of terminal operators entering sales orders using the same order entry program.

### Multiprocessing

Computers that have more than one CPU are called **multiprocessors**. A **multiprocessing** operating system coordinates the operations of multiprocessor computers. Because each CPU in a multiprocessor computer can be executing one program instruction, more than one instruction can be executed simultaneously. Besides providing an increase in performance, most multiprocessors offer another advantage. If one CPU fails, work can be shifted to the remaining CPUs. The ability to continue processing when a major component fails is called **fault tolerance**.

### Virtual Machine

A **virtual machine (VM)** operating system, available on some large computers, allows a single computer to run two or more different operating systems. The VM operating system allocates system resources to each operating system. To users it appears that they are working on separate systems. The advantage of this approach is that an organization can concurrently (at the same time) run different operating systems that are best suited to different tasks. For example, some operating systems are best for interactive processing and others are best for batch processing. With a VM operating system both types of operating systems can be run at the same time.

## FUNCTIONS OF OPERATING SYSTEMS

The operating system performs a number of functions that allow the user and the application software to interact with the computer. These functions apply to all operating systems but become more complex for operating systems that allow more than one program run at a time. The functions can be grouped into three areas: allocating system resources, monitoring system activities, and utilities (Figure 10-4).

| ALLOCATING RESOURCES | MONITORING ACTIVITIES | UTILITIES |
|---|---|---|
| CPU management<br>Memory management<br>Input/output management | System performance<br>System security | File management<br>Sorting |

**FIGURE 10-4**
**Operating system functions.**

## Allocating System Resources

The primary function of the operating system is to allocate the resources of the computer system. These resources include the CPU, main memory, and the input and output devices such as disk and tape drives and printers. Like a police officer directing traffic, the operating system decides what resource will currently be used and for how long.

**CPU Management** Because a CPU can only work on one program instruction at a time, a multiprogramming operating system must keep switching the CPU among the different instructions of the programs that are waiting to be performed. A common way of allocating CPU processing is time slicing. A **time slice** is a fixed amount of CPU processing time, usually measured in milliseconds (thousandths of a second). With this technique, each user in turn receives a time slice. Since some instructions take longer to execute than others, some users may have more instructions completed in their time slice than other users. When a user's time slice has expired, the operating system directs the CPU to work on another user's program instructions and the most recent user moves to the "end of the line" to await the next time slice (Figure 10-5). Unless the system has a heavy workload, however, users may not even be aware that their program has been temporarily set aside. Before they notice a delay, the operating system has allocated them another time slice and their processing continues.

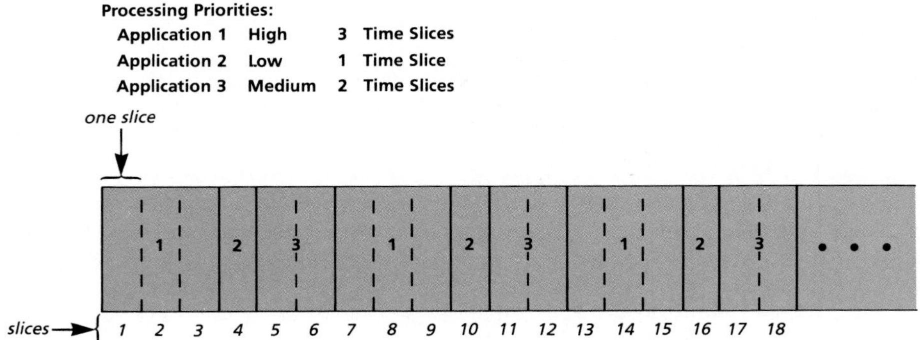


**FIGURE 10-5**
**With the time slice method of CPU management, each application is allocated one or more fixed amounts of time called slices. Higher priority applications receive more consecutive slices than lower priority applications. When its processing time has expired, an application goes to the end of the line until all other applications have received at least one time slice.**

Because some work is more important than other work, most operating systems have ways to adjust the amount of time slices a user receives, either automatically or based on user-specified criteria. One technique for modifying time slices is to have different priorities assigned to each user. The highest priority would receive several consecutive time slices for each time slice received by the lowest priority. For example, it would be logical to assign a higher priority to a program that processes orders and records sales than to an accounting program that could be run at a later time. Another way of allocating time slices is based on the type of work being performed. For example, some operating systems automatically allocate more time slices to interactive processes such as keyboard entry than they do to CPU-only processes such as calculations or batch processing.

**Memory Management** During processing, memory is used to store a variety of items including the operating system, application program instructions for one or more programs, data waiting to be processed, and workspace used for calculations, sorting, and other temporary tasks. Data that has just been read or is waiting to be sent to an output device is stored in reserved areas of memory called **buffers**. It is the operating system's job to keep track of all this data by allocating memory.

All operating systems allocate at least some portion of memory into fixed areas called partitions (Figure 10-6). Some operating systems allocate all memory on this basis while others use partitions only for the operating system instructions and buffers. Another way of allocating memory is called virtual memory management or virtual storage.

**Virtual memory management** increases the effective (or "virtual") limits of memory by expanding the amount of main memory to include disk space (Figure 10-7). Without virtual memory management, an entire program must be loaded into main memory during execution. With virtual memory management, only a portion of the program that is currently being used is required to be in main memory. Virtual memory management is used with multiprogramming operating systems to maximize the number of programs that can be using memory at the same time. The operating system performs virtual memory management by transferring data and instructions to and from memory and the disk by using one or both of the following methods: segmentation and paging.

| OPERATING SYSTEM |
|---|
| Partition 1<br>Program A |
| Partition 2<br>Program B |
| Partition 3<br>Program C<br>Data |
| Partition 4<br>(Available) |

**FIGURE 10-6**
**Some computer systems allocate memory into fixed blocks called partitions. The CPU then keeps track of programs and data by assigning them to a specific partition.**

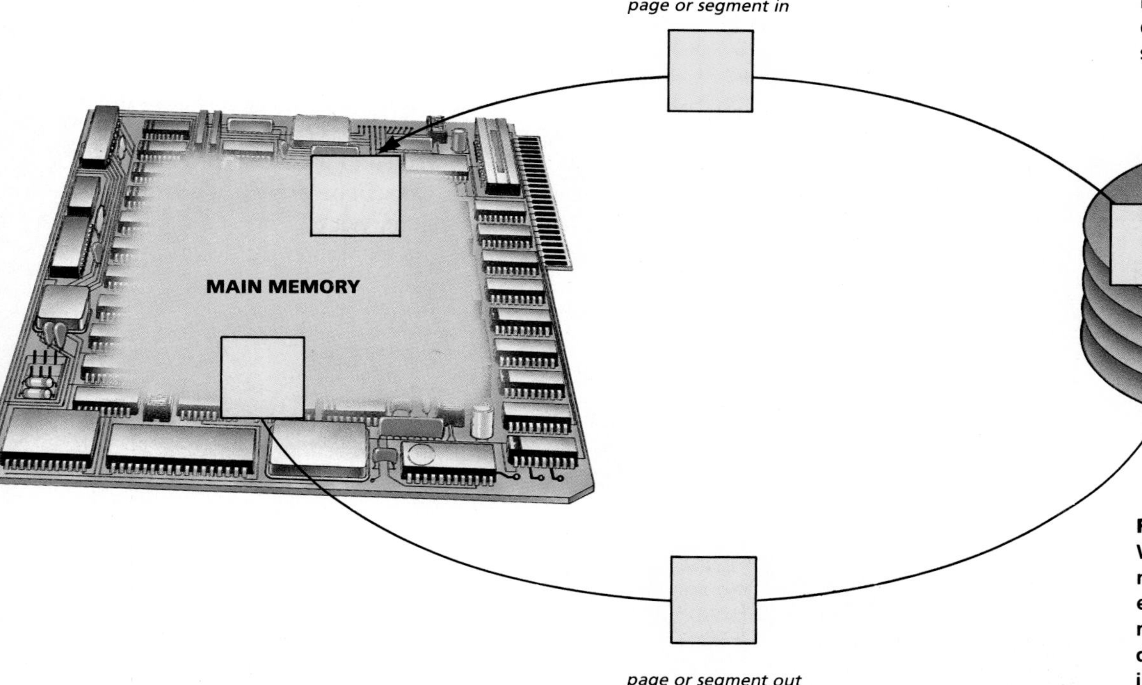


**FIGURE 10-7**
**With virtual memory management, the operating system expands the amount of main memory to include available disk space. Data and program instructions are transferred to and from memory and disk as required. The segmentation technique transfers logical portions of programs that may be of different sizes. The paging technique transfers pages of the same size. To make room for the new page or segment, the least recently used page or segment is "swapped," or written back to the disk.**

In **segmentation**, programs are divided into logical portions called **segments**. Because the segments are based on logical portions of a program, some segments are larger than others. When a particular program instruction is required, the segment containing that instruction is transferred from the disk into main memory.

In **paging**, a fixed amount of space, generally from 512 to 4K bytes, is transferred from the disk each time data is required. This fixed amount of data is called a **page** or a **frame**. Because a page is a fixed amount of space, it may not correspond to a logical division of a program.

In both segmentation and paging, a time comes when memory is full but another page or segment needs to be read into memory. When this occurs, the operating system makes room for the new data by writing back to disk one or more of the pages or segments currently in memory. This process is referred to as **swapping**. The operating system usually chooses the least recently used page or segment to transfer back to disk.

**Input and Output Management** At any one time, a number of different input devices can be trying to send data to the computer. At the same time, the CPU could be ready to send data to an output device such as a terminal or printer or a storage device such as a disk. It is the operating system's responsibility to manage these input and output processes.

Some devices, such as a tape drive, are usually allocated to a specific user or application program. This is because tape is a sequential storage medium and generally it would not make sense to have more than one application writing records to a single tape. Disk drives are usually allocated to all users because the programs and data files that users need are stored on these devices. The operating system keeps track of disk read and write requests, stores these requests in buffers along with the associated data for write requests, and usually processes them sequentially. A printer may be allocated to all users or restricted to a specific user. A printer would be restricted to a specific user, for example, if the printer was going to be used with preprinted forms such as payroll checks.

Because the printer is a relatively slow device compared to other computer system devices, the technique of spooling is used to increase printer efficiency and reduce the number of printers required. With **spooling** (Figure 10-8), a report is first written (saved) to the disk before being printed. Writing to the disk is much faster than writing to the printer. For example, a report that may take half an hour to print (depending on the speed of the printer) may only take one minute to write to the disk. After the report is written to the disk, the CPU is available to process other programs. The report saved on the disk can be printed at a later time or, on a multiprogramming operating system, a print program can be run (at the same time other programs are running) to process the **print spool** (the reports on the disk waiting to be printed).

**FIGURE 10-8**
**Spooling increases both CPU and printer efficiency by writing reports to the disk before they are printed. After the reports are written to disk, the CPU is able to begin processing other programs. Writing to the disk is much faster than writing directly to the printer.**

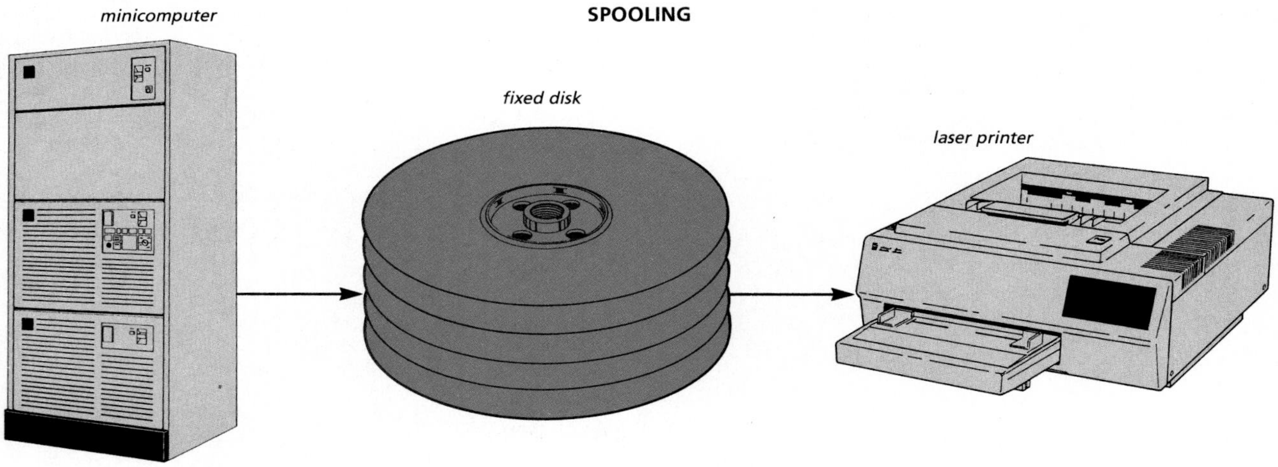

## Monitoring System Activities

Another function of the operating system is monitoring the system activity. This includes monitoring system performance and system security.

**System Performance** System performance can be measured in a number of ways but is usually gauged by the user in terms of response time. **Response time** is the amount of time from the moment a user enters data until the computer responds. Response time can vary based on what the user has entered. If the user is simply entering data into a file, the response time is usually within a second or two. However, if the user has just completed a request for a display of sorted data from several files, the response time could be minutes.

A more precise way of measuring performance is to run a program that is designed to record and report system activity. Among other information, these programs usually report **CPU utilization**, the amount of time that the CPU is working and not idle, waiting for data to process. Figure 10-9 shows a CPU performance measurement report.

Another measure of performance is to compare the CPU utilization with the disk input and output rate, referred to as disk I/O. We previously discussed how a virtual memory management operating system swaps pages or segments from disk to memory as they are needed. Systems with heavy workloads and insufficient memory or CPU power can get into a situation called **thrashing**, where the system is spending more time moving pages to and from the disk than processing the data. System performance reporting can indicate this problem.

CONNECT SEC : CPU SEC

| HOUR | CONNECT | CPU SEC |
|---|---|---|
| 12-1A | 1925. | 1742. |
| 1-2 | 802. | 2057. |
| 2-3 | 5788. | 5164. |
| 3-4 | 7200. | 4368. |
| 4-5 | 14692. | 3791. |
| 5-6 | 73585. | 3172. |
| 6-7 | 154932. | 2490. |
| 7-8 | 343274. | 3909. |
| 8-9 | 778287. | 4828. |
| 9-10 | 896538. | 4405. |
| 10-11 | 970041. | 4736. |
| 11-12 | 950215. | 4620. |
| 12-1P | 769632. | 3297. |
| 1-2 | 868651. | 4875. |
| 2-3 | 890501. | 4321. |
| 3-4 | 799440. | 4264. |
| 4-5 | 651196. | 3135. |
| 5-6 | 221613. | 3053. |

TO CONTINUE SCROLL PRESS RETURN

**FIGURE 10-9**
**System performance measurement programs report the amount of time the CPU is actually working and not waiting to process data.**

**System Security** Most multiuser operating systems provide for a logon code, a user ID, and a password that must all be entered correctly before a user is allowed to use an application program (Figure 10-10). Each is a word or series of characters. A **logon code** usually identifies the application that will be used, such as accounting, sales or manufacturing. A **user ID** identifies the user, such as Jeffrey Ryan or Mary Gonzales. The **password** is usually confidential; often it is known only to the user and the data processing manager. The logon code, user ID, and password must match entries in an authorization file. If they don't match, the user is denied access to the system. Both successful and unsuccessful logon attempts are often recorded in a file so that managers can review who is using or attempting to use the system. These logs can also be used to allocate data processing expenses based on the percentage of system use by an organization's various departments.

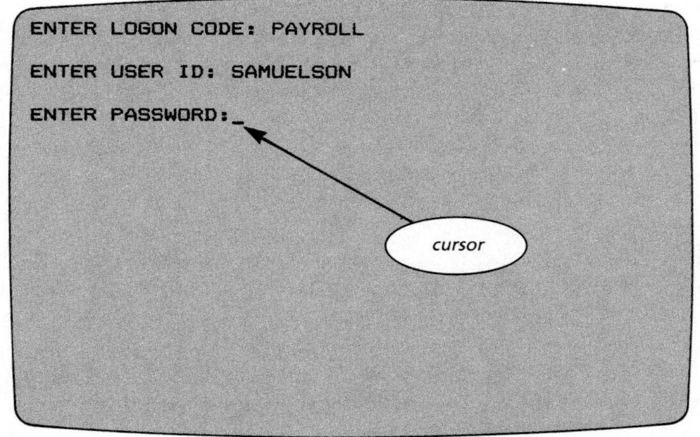


**FIGURE 10-10**
**The logon code, user ID, and password must all be entered correctly before the user is allowed to use the computer. Because the password is confidential, it is usually not displayed on the screen when the user types it in.**

## Utilities

In addition to allocating system resources and monitoring system activities, most operating systems contain programs called **utilities** that can perform functions such as file management, sorting, and editing. Some of the functions that the file management utility programs can perform include formatting disks and diskettes, deleting files from a disk, copying files from one auxiliary storage device to another, and renaming stored files. Sort utilities are used to place the data stored in files into ascending or descending order based on a value stored in the key field of each record in a file. For example, a sort utility program could be used to sort the records in a personnel file in alphabetical order by the employees' last names. **Editors** allow users to make direct changes to programs and data. An editor would be used by a programmer to change a program instruction that was incorrect or had to be modified.

## POPULAR OPERATING SYSTEMS

The first operating systems were developed by manufacturers for the computers in their product line. When the manufacturers came out with another computer or model, they often produced an "improved" and different operating system. Since programs are designed to be used with a particular operating system, this meant that users who wanted to switch computers, either from one vendor to another or to a different model from the same vendor, would have to convert their existing programs to run under the new operating system. Today, however, the trend is away from operating systems limited to a specific model and toward operating systems that will run on any model by a particular manufacturer. For example, part of Digital Equipment Corporation's success in recent years has been attributed to the fact that their VMS operating system is used on all their computer systems. Going even further, many computer users are supporting the move away from **proprietary operating systems** (meaning privately owned) and toward **portable operating systems** that will run on many manufacturers' computers. The advantage of portable operating systems is that the user is not tied to a particular manufacturer. Using a portable operating system, a user could change computer systems, yet retain existing software and data files, which usually represents a sizable investment in time and money. One of the most popular portable operating systems is UNIX, which we will discuss along with the popular personal computer operating system, MS-DOS, and IBM's latest personal computer operating system, O/S 2.

### UNIX

The **UNIX** operating system was developed in the early 1970s by scientists at Bell Laboratories. It was specifically designed to provide a way to manage a variety of scientific and specialized computer applications. Because of federal regulations, Bell Labs (a subsidiary of AT&T) was prohibited from actively promoting UNIX in the commercial marketplace. Instead, for a low fee Bell Labs licensed UNIX to numerous colleges and universities where it obtained a wide following. With the deregulation of the telephone companies in the 1980s, AT&T was allowed to enter the computer system marketplace. With AT&T's increased promotion and the trend toward portable operating systems, UNIX has aroused tremendous interest. One of the advantages of UNIX is its extensive library of over 400 instruction modules that can be linked together to perform almost any programming task. Today, most major computer manufacturers offer a multiuser version of the UNIX operating system to run on their computers.

With all its strengths, however, UNIX has not yet obtained success in the commercial business systems marketplace. Some people attribute this to the fact that UNIX has never been considered "user friendly." For example, most of the UNIX program modules are identified by obscure names such as MAUS, SHMOP, and BRK. Other critics contend that UNIX lacks the file management capabilities to support the online interactive databases that more and more businesses are implementing. With the support of most major computer manufacturers, however, these problems are being worked on and UNIX has a good chance of becoming one of the major operating systems of the coming years.

### MS-DOS

The Microsoft Disk Operating System or **MS-DOS** was released by Microsoft Corporation in 1981. MS-DOS was originally developed for IBM for their first personal computer system.

IBM calls their equivalent version of the operating system **PC-DOS**. Because so many personal computer manufacturers followed IBM's lead and chose MS-DOS for their computers, MS-DOS quickly became an industry standard. Other personal computer operating systems exist, but by far the majority of personal computer software is written for MS-DOS. This single-user operating system is so widely used that it is often referred to simply as DOS.

## OS/2

In 1988, IBM released the **OS/2** operating system for its new family of PS/2 personal computers (Figure 10-11). Microsoft Corporation, which developed OS/2 for IBM, also released their equivalent version, called MS-OS/2. OS/2 is designed to take advantage of the increased computing power of the 80286 and 80386 microprocessors and will only run on systems that use these chips. OS/2 also requires a lot more computing power to operate. For example, OS/2 requires 5MB of hard disk and a minimum of 2MB of main memory just to run the operating system. Additional features offered by OS/2 include the ability to run larger and more complex programs and the ability to do multiprogramming (OS/2 can have up to 12 programs running at the same time).

There are two versions and two editions of OS/2. One of the versions includes the *Presentation Manager*, a graphic windowing environment similar to that available on the Apple Macintosh. The difference between the Standard Edition and the Extended Edition of OS/2 is that the Extended Edition includes database management and communications capabilities.

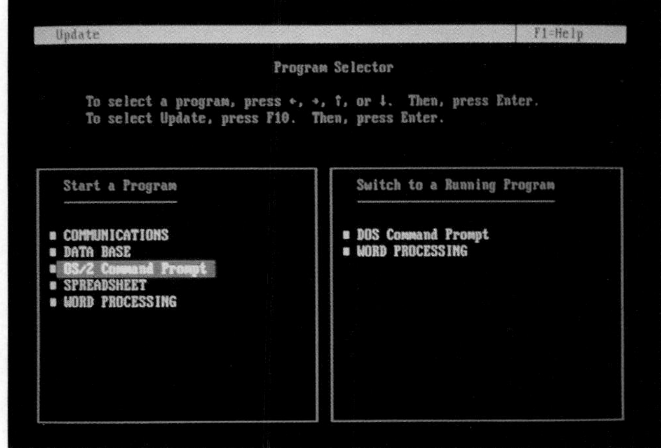


**FIGURE 10-11**
**IBM's OS/2 operating system takes advantage of the increased processing power of the latest personal computer systems.**

## Other Operating Systems

A number of other popular operating systems exist in addition to the ones just discussed. The Apple Macintosh multiprogramming operating system, currently available only on Apple systems, provides a unique graphic interface that uses icons (figures) and windows (Figure 10-12) that many people find easy to learn and use. The ProDos operating system is used on many of Apple's other computer systems. The PICK operating system is another portable operating system that runs on personal, mini, and mainframe computers. The PICK operating system incorporates a relational database manager and has had much success in the business data processing marketplace. Most mainframe operating systems are unique to a particular make of computer or are designed to be compatible with one of IBM's operating systems such as DOS/VS, MVS, or VM, IBM's virtual machine operating system.

**FIGURE 10-12**
**The Macintosh operating system offers a unique graphic interface and the ability to display information in separate "windows."**

## SUMMARY OF OPERATING SYSTEMS AND SYSTEM SOFTWARE

System software and the operating system are essential parts of any computer system and should be understood by users who want to obtain the maximum benefits from their computer. This is especially true for the latest personal computer operating systems that include features such as virtual memory management and multiprogramming. Understanding and being able to use these and other features will give users even more control over their computer resources.

## CHAPTER SUMMARY

1. **System software** consists of all the programs including the operating system that are related to managing the operations of the computer.
2. An **operating system** consists of one or more programs that manage the operations of a computer.
3. Operating systems function as an interface between the user, the application programs, and the computer equipment.
4. The essential and most frequently used instructions in an operating system are sometimes called the **supervisor** and must be stored in the main memory of a computer for the computer to operate.
5. **Booting** the system is the process of loading the operating system into the main memory of a computer.
6. **Single program** operating systems allow a single user to run a single program at one time.
7. **Multiprogramming** operating systems, also called **multitasking** operating systems, allow more than one program to be run at the same time.
8. A multiprogramming operating system that allows multiple users is called a **multiuser–multiprogramming** operating system.
9. A **multiprocessor** computer has more than one CPU. **Multiprocessor** operating systems coordinate the operations of these computers.
10. A **virtual machine (VM)** operating system allows a single computer to run two or more different operating systems.
11. The functions of an operating system include allocating system resources, monitoring system activities, and utilities.
12. The system resources that the operating system allocates include the CPU, main memory, and the input/output devices.
13. **Time slicing** is a common way for an operating system to allocate the CPU.
14. **Virtual memory management** expands the main memory by using portions of the disk space. With virtual memory management, the operating system transfers data between main memory and the disks by **segmentation** or **paging**.
15. The operating system is responsible for managing the input and output processes of the computer.
16. **Response time** is the amount of time from the moment a user enters data until the computer responds.
17. System performance can be measured by the response time and by comparing the **CPU utilization** with the disk I/O to determine if the system is **thrashing**.
18. System security is monitored by the operating system through the use of **passwords**.
19. Most operating systems contain programs called **utilities** that can perform functions such as file management and sorting.
20. Many computer users are supporting the move away from **proprietary operating systems** and toward **portable operating systems**.
21. Some of the popular operating systems being used today include UNIX, MS-DOS, and OS/2.

## KEY TERMS

Booting *10.3*
Buffers *10.7*
Control program *10.3*
CPU utilization *10.9*
Editors *10.9*
Executive *10.3*
Fault tolerance *10.5*
Frame *10.7*
Kernel *10.3*
Logon code *10.9*
Master program *10.3*
Monitor *10.3*
MS-DOS *10.11*
Multiprocessing *10.5*
Multiprocessors *10.5*
Multiprogramming *10.4*
Multitasking *10.4*
Multiuser-multiprogramming *10.5*
Operating system (OS) *10.3*
Operating system prompt *10.4*
OS/2 *10.11*
Page *10.7*
Paging *10.7*
Password *10.9*
Portable operating system *10.10*
Print spool *10.8*
Proprietary operating system *10.10*
PC-DOS *10.11*
Response time *10.8*
Segments *10.7*
Segmentation *10.7*
Single program *10.4*
Spooling *10.8*
Supervisor *10.3*
Swapping *10.8*
System software *10.2*
Time slice *10.6*
Thrashing *10.9*
UNIX *10.10*
User ID *10.9*
Utilities *10.9*
Virtual machine (VM) *10.5*
Virtual memory management *10.7*

## REVIEW QUESTIONS

1. Define system software. List some of the functions of system software.
2. Describe how to boot an operating system on a personal computer.
3. List the various types of operating systems and briefly describe their capabilities.
4. The functions of an operating system can be grouped into three areas. What are they?
5. How does an operating system use time slicing?
6. What is virtual memory management?
7. Describe how system performance can be measured.
8. What are three types of authorizations that an operating system uses to provide system security?
9. List several functions that the utilities of an operating system provide.
10. Explain the difference between proprietary and portable operating systems. Name and briefly describe three popular operating systems.

## CONTROVERSIAL ISSUE

1. Some users argue that portable operating systems should be avoided because they do not take full advantage of the unique capabilities of a computer. Other users feel that the advantages of using portable operating systems make them a better choice than proprietary operating systems. How do you feel? Be prepared to present your reasons in a class discussion.

## RESEARCH PROJECT

1. Visit a computer store and obtain information about the operating systems that are available for personal computers. Prepare a paper on the information you obtained.

# CHAPTER 11

# Commercial Application Software

## CHAPTER 11

# Commercial Application Software

### OBJECTIVES

- Define commercial application software.
- Describe the difference between general applications and functional applications.
- Describe the difference between horizontal and vertical applications.
- Discuss the factors to be considered in developing or buying application software.
- Discuss each of the five steps of acquiring commercial application software.
- Discuss the information that should be included on a request for proposal (RFP) for application software.
- Identify several sources for commercial application software.

---

The first computer users had few if any choices when it came to software. If users wanted the computer to perform a specific task, they usually had to develop and write their own computer programs to do the job. Today, however, users have several options when acquiring software. In addition to developing their own software, users may purchase prewritten software packages. Prewritten software is available for computers of all sizes. Most users know about the numerous application packages available for microcomputers. In addition, users should be aware that numerous packages are available for larger machines. This chapter discusses the type of prewritten application software that is available, how to determine your software requirements, and how to acquire the software you need. This information is important to know because it is very likely that some day you will either acquire application software for yourself or participate in software selection for your organization.

## WHAT IS COMMERCIAL APPLICATION SOFTWARE?

**Commercial application software** is software that has already been written and is available for purchase. It may be designed to perform either general or specific tasks. An example of software that performs a general task is word processing. Word processing is considered a "general" task because it can be performed by individuals throughout an organization to create documents. An example of a specific task is medical insurance claim processing. Software that performs this task would only be useful to a company that processes medical insurance claims. Software designed to perform general tasks is called general application software. Software designed to perform specific tasks is called functional application software. In the following sections, we discuss both of these categories in more detail.

# GENERAL APPLICATION SOFTWARE

**General application software** provides a way for tasks that are commonly performed in all types of businesses to be done on a computer. These applications are sometimes referred to as **productivity tools** because when they are used, they provide users with a more efficient way to do their work so that they become more productive. There are many popular types of general application software (Figure 11-1). The most common include word processing, spreadsheets, database, and graphics applications. In addition, three others that are commonly used include desktop publishing, electronic mail, and project management.

| TYPE | PURPOSE | POPULAR PACKAGES |
|---|---|---|
| Word processing | Creates documents | WordPerfect<br>Microsoft Word |
| Spreadsheet | Manipulates rows and columns of numbers | Lotus 1-2-3<br>Excel |
| Database | Stores, organizes, and retrieves data | dBASE III,<br>RBASE |
| Graphics | Pictorial representation of data | Chart-Master<br>Harvard Graphics |
| Electronic mail | Transmits electronic messages | Microsoft Mail<br>In Box |
| Desktop Publishing | Lay out and create documents containing text and graphics | Ventura<br>PageMaker |
| Project Management | Schedule and track a project's events and resources | Timeline<br>Super Project Expert |

**FIGURE 11-1**
A list of general application software packages. These packages can be used by most organizations and are not limited to a specific type of business.

## Review of the Four User Tools

The four user tools described in Chapter 2, word processing, electronic spreadsheets, database, and graphics software, are all examples of general applications software. To review, word processors are used to create documents; spreadsheets are used to manipulate rows and columns of numbers; databases allow data to be stored, organized, and retrieved efficiently; and graphics provide a way of representing data pictorially.

## Desktop Publishing

**Desktop publishing (DTP)** software allows users to design and produce professional-looking documents that contain both text and graphics (Figure 11-2). In business, this software is used to produce documents, such as newsletters, marketing literature, technical manuals, and annual reports, that were previously created by more traditional publishing methods. By using desktop publishing both the cost and time of producing quality documents is significantly decreased.

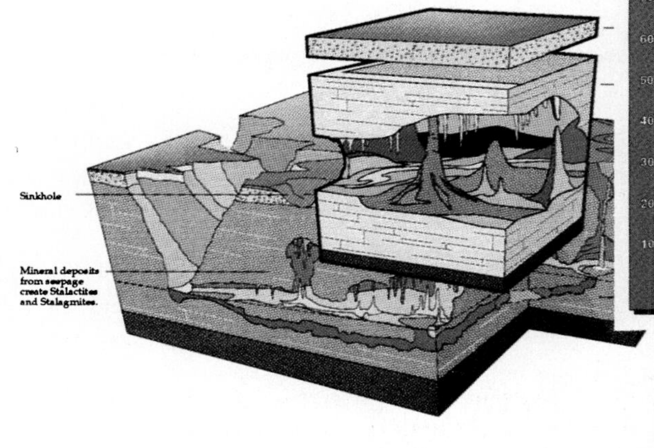

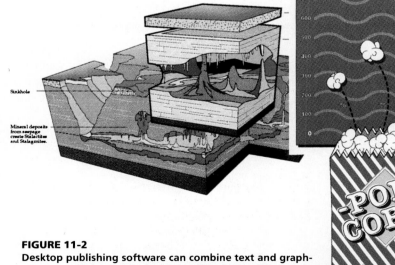

**FIGURE 11-2**
Desktop publishing software can combine text and graphics to produce documents that previously would have required the work of professional artists and printers. These two illustrations were producted using the Adobe Illustrator™ software programs.

An important feature of desktop publishing is page composition. This means that a user is able to design on the screen an exact image of what a printed page will look like. This capability is called **WYSIWYG**—an acronym for "What You See Is What You Get." Some of the page composition or layout features that are available include the use of columns for text, the choice of different font (type) styles, and the placement and size of art on the page.

The art used in the documents created with desktop publishing usually comes from one of three sources:

1. It can be created on the computer with software that has graphics capabilities, such as software packages that are specifically designed to create graphics, or software such as spreadsheet packages that can create pie, line, and bar charts.
2. A scanner can be used to digitize pictures, photographs, and drawings and store them as files on auxiliary storage for use with desktop publishing software.
3. Art can be selected from "clip art" collections. These are collections of art that are stored on disks and are designed to integrate with popular desktop publishing packages (Figure 11-3).

**FIGURE 11-3**
**Clip art consists of previously created figures, shapes, and symbols that can be added to documents. Users specify the numbers of the piece they want to use.**

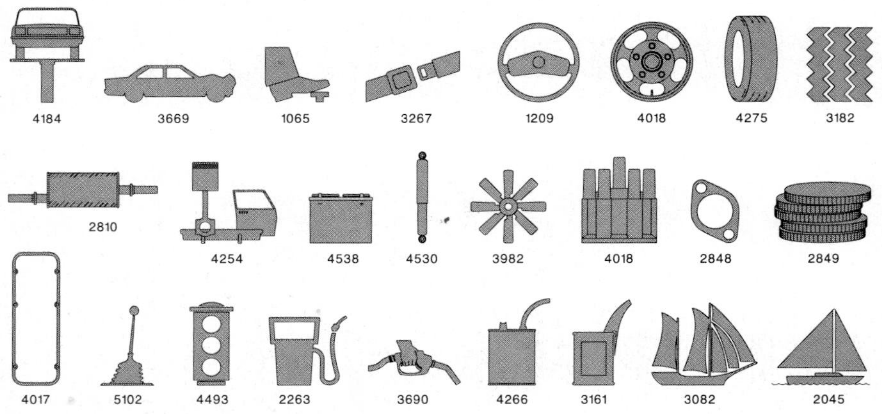


While the text for a document can be created with desktop publishing software, the word processing features of many desktop publishing packages are not as complete as those offered by word processing packages. Therefore, text is usually created with a word processor and then transferred into the desktop publishing package. As new versions of word processing and desktop publishing software are introduced, the capabilities of both applications will increase and the differences between the two applications will decrease. A number of word processing packages now offer desktop publishing features and the word processing features of desktop publishing packages continue to improve (Figure 11-4).

Desktop publishing software is usually executed on a microcomputer with graphics capabilities. Remember from the chapter on Output that graphics capability means that the computer can individually turn on or off the thousands of phosphor dots that make up the display screen. This ability is necessary in DTP to create different sizes and styles of letters and to produce other special DTP effects. Dot matrix and laser printers are used to print the letters and special graphic effects.

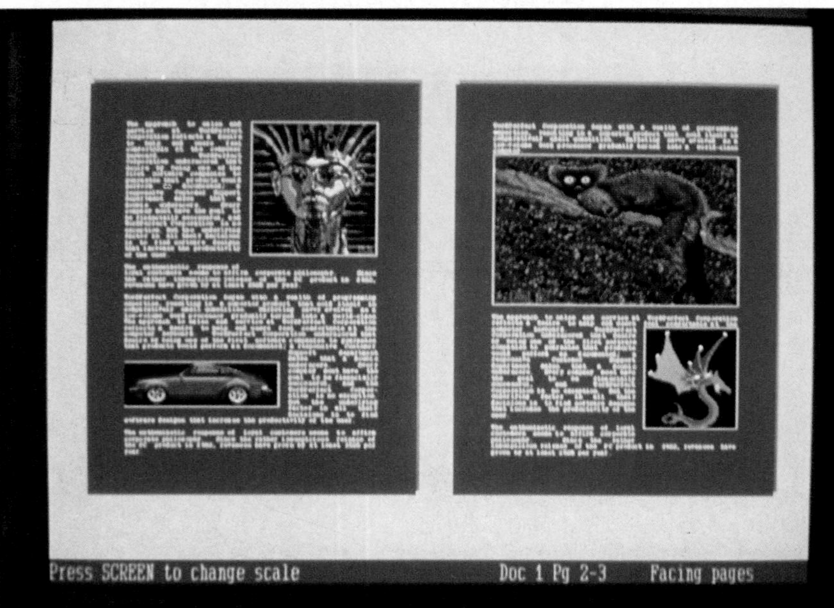


**FIGURE 11-4**
**This document was created using WordPerfect 5.0, which allows graphics to be imported into text.**

## Electronic Mail

Another type of general application software is electronic mail. **Electronic mail** software provides the ability for users to communicate directly with other users by sending text messages electronically over communication channels (Figure 11-5). For example, if the sales manager, Florence Bolduc, wants to send a message congratulating Terry Willis and Sue Rodriguez for closing a recent sale, she would use the electronic mail software to (1) enter the message on her computer, (2) specify that Terry and Sue are to receive the message, and (3) enter a command to send the message. The software places the message in a file referred to as an electronic mailbox. When Terry and Sue use their computers to check for electronic mail, the message from Florence is displayed on their screens. This method of communication is much more efficient than the traditional method of creating and physically delivering a printed document. Correspondence that once took days to reach an individual can now be electronically transmitted from one user to another in seconds.

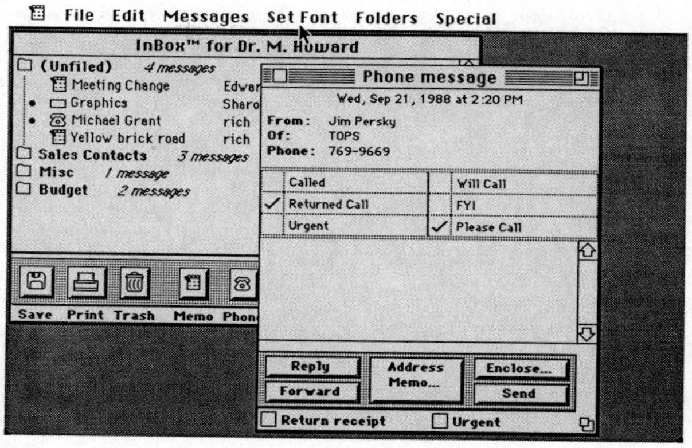

**FIGURE 11-5**
**Electronic mail software allows a user to transmit and receive messages without paperwork. Messages can be saved for future reference or sent back to the sender with a reply.**

## Project Management

**Project management software** allows users to plan, schedule, track, and analyze the events, resources, and costs of a project (Figure 11-6). For example, a construction company might use this type of software to manage the building of an apartment complex or a campaign manager might use it to coordinate the many activities of a politician running for office. The value of project management software is that it provides a method for managers to control and manage the variables of a project to help ensure that the project will be completed on time and within budget.

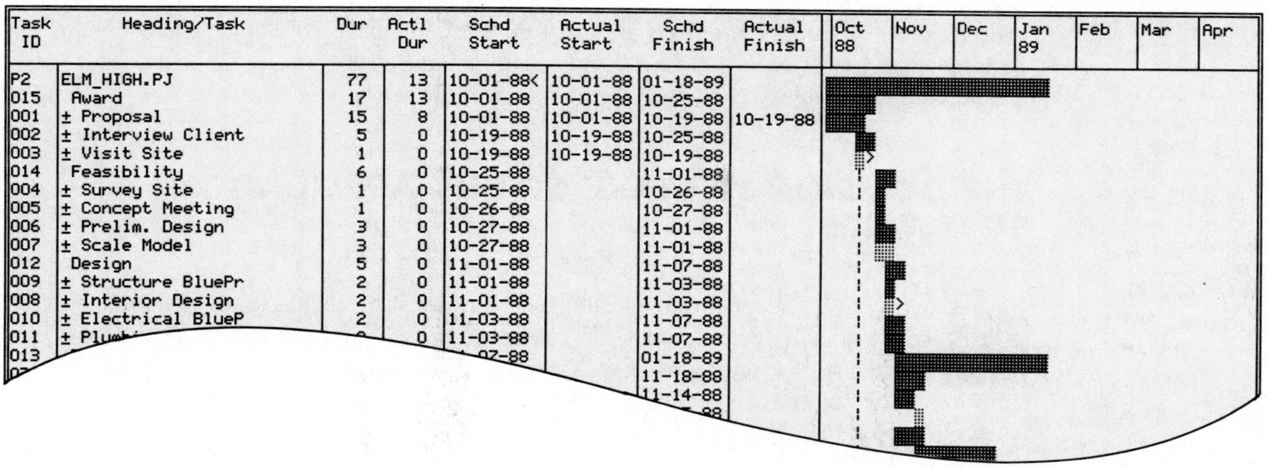

| Task ID | Heading/Task | Dur | Actl Dur | Schd Start | Actual Start | Schd Finish | Actual Finish | Oct 88 | Nov | Dec | Jan 89 | Feb | Mar | Apr |
|---|---|---|---|---|---|---|---|---|---|---|---|---|---|---|
| P2 | ELM_HIGH.PJ | 77 | 13 | 10-01-88< | 10-01-88 | 01-18-89 | | | | | | | | |
| 015 | Award | 17 | 13 | 10-01-88 | 10-01-88 | 10-25-88 | | | | | | | | |
| 001 | ± Proposal | 15 | 8 | 10-01-88 | 10-01-88 | 10-19-88 | 10-19-88 | | | | | | | |
| 002 | ± Interview Client | 5 | 0 | 10-19-88 | 10-19-88 | 10-25-88 | | | | | | | | |
| 003 | ± Visit Site | 1 | 0 | 10-19-88 | 10-19-88 | 10-19-88 | | | | | | | | |
| 014 | Feasibility | 6 | 0 | 10-25-88 | | 11-01-88 | | | | | | | | |
| 004 | ± Survey Site | 1 | 0 | 10-25-88 | | 10-26-88 | | | | | | | | |
| 005 | ± Concept Meeting | 1 | 0 | 10-26-88 | | 10-27-88 | | | | | | | | |
| 006 | ± Prelim. Design | 3 | 0 | 10-27-88 | | 11-01-88 | | | | | | | | |
| 007 | ± Scale Model | 3 | 0 | 10-27-88 | | 11-01-88 | | | | | | | | |
| 012 | Design | 5 | 0 | 11-01-88 | | 11-07-88 | | | | | | | | |
| 009 | ± Structure BluePr | 2 | 0 | 11-01-88 | | 11-03-88 | | | | | | | | |
| 008 | ± Interior Design | 2 | 0 | 11-01-88 | | 11-03-88 | | | | | | | | |
| 010 | ± Electrical BlueP | 2 | 0 | 11-03-88 | | 11-07-88 | | | | | | | | |
| 011 | ± Plumb | | 0 | 11-03-88 | | 11-07-88 | | | | | | | | |
| 013 | | | | 07-88 | | 01-18-89 | | | | | | | | |
| | | | | | | 11-18-88 | | | | | | | | |
| | | | | | | 11-14-88 | | | | | | | | |

**FIGURE 11-6**
**This output was prepared using project management software. It shows the individual tasks that make up the project and the elapsed time that each task is scheduled to take.**

# FUNCTIONAL APPLICATION SOFTWARE

Now that we've covered general applications, we'll discuss **functional application software**, software developed to perform a specific task or function.

With the increasing use of computers, a list of all functional applications might be as long as this book. It's probably safe to say that at least some part of every type of business, government branch, or recreational pastime has been computerized. Figure 11-7 is a category listing from an applications software catalog. Within each category, there are numerous programs available to perform different types of tasks. This catalog contains listings for over 20,000 individual software packages. Notice that this list is divided into two parts: non-industry specific and industry specific. More commonly used terms are horizontal and vertical applications.

**Horizontal application software** is software that can be used by many different types of organizations. Accounting packages are a good example of horizontal applications because they apply to most organizations. If, however, an organization has a unique way of doing business, then it requires a package that has been developed specifically for that job. Software developed for a unique way of doing business, usually within a specific industry, is called **vertical application software**. Examples of specific industries that utilize vertical software include food service, construction, and real estate. Each of these industries has unique information processing requirements.

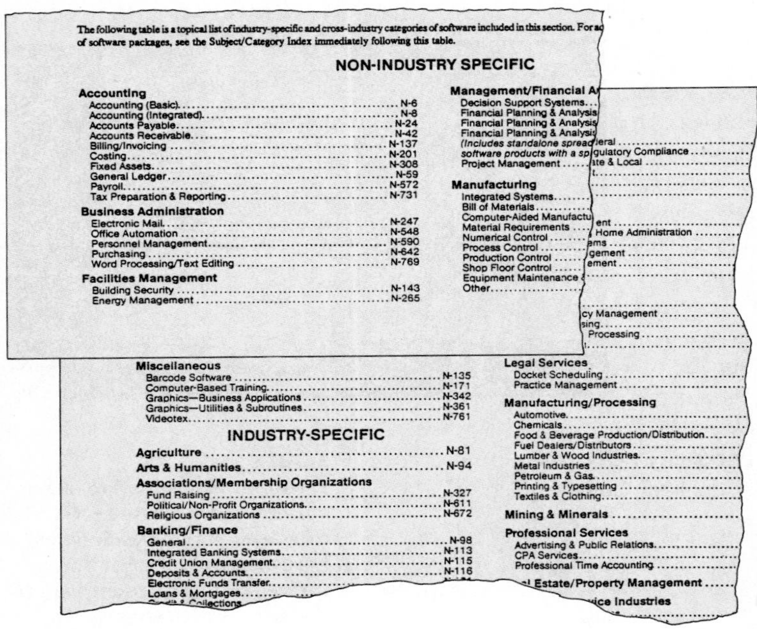
The following table is a topical list of industry-specific and cross-industry categories of software included in this section. For a... of software packages, see the Subject/Category Index immediately following this table.

NON-INDUSTRY SPECIFIC

**Accounting**
Accounting (Basic) ........ N-6
Accounting (Integrated) ........ N-8
Accounts Payable ........ N-24
Accounts Receivable ........ N-42
Billing/Invoicing ........ N-137
Costing ........ N-201
Fixed Assets ........ N-308
General Ledger ........ N-59
Payroll ........ N-572
Tax Preparation & Reporting ........ N-731

**Business Administration**
Electronic Mail ........ N-247
Office Automation ........ N-548
Personnel Management ........ N-590
Purchasing ........ N-642
Word Processing/Text Editing ........ N-769

**Facilities Management**
Building Security ........ N-143
Energy Management ........ N-265

**Management/Financial A...**
Decision Support Systems...
Financial Planning & Analysis
Financial Planning & Analysis
Financial Planning & Analysis
*(Includes standalone spread...*
*software products with a sp...*
Project Management ........

**Manufacturing**
Integrated Systems ........
Bill of Materials ........
Computer-Aided Manufactu...
Material Requirements ........
Numerical Control ........
Process Control ........
Production Control ........
Shop Floor Control ........
Equipment Maintenance ...
Other ........

**Miscellaneous**
Barcode Software ........ N-135
Computer-Based Training ........ N-171
Graphics—Business Applications ........ N-342
Graphics—Utilities & Subroutines ........ N-361
Videotex ........ N-761

INDUSTRY-SPECIFIC

**Agriculture** ........ N-81
**Arts & Humanities** ........ N-94
**Associations/Membership Organizations**
Fund Raising ........ N-327
Political/Non-Profit Organizations ........ N-611
Religious Organizations ........ N-672

**Banking/Finance**
General ........ N-98
Integrated Banking Systems ........ N-113
Credit Union Management ........ N-115
Deposits & Accounts ........ N-116
Electronic Funds Transfer ........
Loans & Mortgages ........

**Legal Services**
Docket Scheduling ........
Practice Management ........

**Manufacturing/Processing**
Automotive ........
Chemicals ........
Food & Beverage Production/Distribution ........
Fuel Dealers/Distributors ........
Lumber & Wood Industries ........
Metal Industries ........
Petroleum & Gas ........
Printing & Typesetting ........
Textiles & Clothing ........

**Mining & Minerals** ........

**Professional Services**
Advertising & Public Relations ........
CPA Services ........
Professional Time Accounting ........

**...Estate/Property Management** ........

**FIGURE 11-7**
**This is a category listing from an application software catalog that contains information on over 20,000 individual software packages.**

The difference between horizontal and vertical application software is important to understand. If you become involved in selecting software, one of the first things you will have to decide is how unique is the task for which you are trying to obtain software. If the task is not unique to your business, you will probably be able to use a horizontal application package. Horizontal application packages tend to be more widely available (because they can be used by a greater number of organizations) and less expensive. If your task is unique to your type of organization, you will probably have to look for a vertical software solution. Often an organization's total software requirements are made up of a combination of unique and common requirements. But before we discuss how to acquire application software, let's discuss if you should consider developing it yourself.

## THE DECISION TO MAKE OR BUY APPLICATION SOFTWARE

Each year, the number of application software packages increases. With all that software available, why would an organization choose to develop its own applications? There could be several reasons. The most common reason is that the organization's software requirements are so unique that it is unable to find a package that will meet its needs. In such a case, the organization would choose to develop the software itself or have it developed specifically for them. Application software that is developed by the user or at the user's request is called **custom software**. An example of a requirement for custom software might be a government agency that is implementing a new medical assistance service. If the service has new forms and procedures and is different from previous services, it is unlikely that any appropriate software exists. Another reason to develop rather than buy software is that the new software must work with existing custom software. This is an important point to keep in mind; once an organization chooses to use custom software, it will usually choose custom software for future applications as well. This is because it is often difficult to make custom software work with purchased software. The following example illustrates this point.

Let's say a company that has previously developed a custom inventory control software system now wants to computerize their order entry function. Order entry software packages allow the user to sell merchandise from stock and therefore must work closely with the inventory files. In fact, many order entry systems are sold together with inventory control systems. If the company wants to retain its existing inventory control application, it would probably have a hard time finding a commercial order entry package that would be able to work with its custom inventory files. This is because the software and the file structures used in the commercial package will not be the same as the existing software. For this reason, the company would probably decide to develop a custom order entry application.

Both custom and commercial software have their advantages and disadvantages. The advantage of custom software is that if it is correctly done, it will match an organization's exact requirements. The disadvantages of custom software are that it is "one of a kind," difficult to change, often poorly documented, and usually more expensive than commercial software. In addition, custom software projects are often difficult to manage and complete on time.

The advantage of commercial software is that it's ready to install immediately. After sufficient training, usually provided by the vendor who developed or sold the software, people can begin using the software for productive work. The disadvantage of commercial software is that an organization will probably have to change some of its methods and procedures to adapt to the way the commercial software functions.

A good guideline for evaluating your need for custom or commercial software is to look for a package with an 80% or better "fit" with your requirements. If there is less than an 80% fit, an organization should either consider custom software or reevaluate its requirements. Figure 11-8 shows the most likely software solutions for different application requirements.

| APPLICATION CHARACTERISTICS | APPLICATION EXAMPLE | MOST LIKELY SOFTWARE SOLUTION |
|---|---|---|
| Applicable to many different types or organizations | Accounts receivable | Horizontal application package |
| Specific to a particular type of business or organization | Hotel room reservations | Vertical application package |
| Unique to a specific organization or business | Space shuttle launch program | Custom software |

**FIGURE 11-8**
**A guide to the types of functional software applications.**

## HOW TO ACQUIRE COMMERCIAL APPLICATION SOFTWARE

The first companies to develop commercial application software were the computer manufacturers. Having software to solve specific problems made it easier for them to sell computers. Today, most mini and mainframe computer manufacturers still sell application software, but numerous other sources are available as well. The process of acquiring software involves five steps: (1) evaluating the application requirements, (2) identifying potential software vendors, (3) evaluating software alternatives, (4) making the purchase, and (5) installing the software.

## Evaluating the Application Requirements

Evaluating the application requirements is the first and probably the most important step in acquiring commercial application software. Decisions made during this step can determine the eventual success or failure of the software package implementation. The actual evaluation process can and should vary depending on the type of application, how many people will be using it, and how critical it is to the organization. For example, an application to keep track of office supplies is not as critical to an organization as one for processing the payroll. All evaluations should include at least the following steps:

1. **Identify the key features of the application.** If the application is an important one, you should prepare a key features list with features that are considered essential to the application. For example, if an organization is a wholesale distributor that makes (or loses) sales based on whether or not it has an item in stock, it would want current inventory status to be part of any order entry program it acquires. Software that only updates the inventory once a day probably would not be acceptable. Therefore, current inventory status should be listed as a key feature.

2. **Determine your current transaction volumes and estimate their growth over the next one to three years.** Figure 11-9 shows a transaction volume summary for an organization's accounts payable application. The figure shows that projected growth over the next year is moderate but increases significantly during the second and third years. This information needs to be considered for both the application software and the equipment that the software will run on. The user would want to be assured that the software and equipment could handle the increased volume of transactions and the corresponding increase in file storage requirements.

**FIGURE 11-9**
**A transaction volume summary should be prepared to avoid acquiring software that won't handle the projected growth.**

| MONTHLY VOLUME | | | |
|---|---|---|---|
| | CURRENT | 1 YEAR | 3 YEARS |
| # of Vendors | 50 | 60 | 200 |
| # of Invoices | 100 | 120 | 400 |
| # of Debit Memos | 20 | 25 | 80 |
| # of Checks | 75 | 100 | 300 |

3. **Decide if the software for the new application needs to work with any existing software or equipment.** It may be important that the new application transfer data to or receive data from an existing application. An example would be an accounts payable package that passes data to the general ledger, where all accounting transactions are summarized. In addition, if you already have a particular type of computer, you'll probably want to find software for that system first. On the other hand, if you don't have any equipment, make the decision about the software *first*. It's the software that is the most important element in any system. Choosing the software first is especially important with mini and mainframe systems. Application software for these systems is usually written for a specific manufacturer's computer.

One way organizations summarize their software requirements is in a request for proposal. A **request for proposal** or **RFP** is a written list of an organization's software requirements that is given to prospective software vendors to help the vendors determine if they have a product that is a possible software solution. Just as the depth of application evaluations varies, so too do RFPs. RFPs for simple applications may be only a single page consisting of the key features and a transaction volume summary. Other RFPs for large systems may consist of over a hundred pages that identify both key and secondary desired features. An example of a page from an RFP is shown in Figure 11-10.

**FIGURE 11-10**
**A request for proposal (RFP) documents the key features that a user wants in a software package.**

REQUEST FOR PROPOSAL

ACCOUNTS PAYABLE

| Features | Standard Feature | Comments |
|---|---|---|
| 1. Interface to general ledger | ✓ | |
| 2. Matching to receiving documents | ✓ | |
| 3. Matching to purchasing documents | ✓ | |
| 4. Automatic check printing | ✓ | |
| 5. Recurring payments | | PLANNING FOR NEXT RELEASE |
| 6. Flexible payment selection | ✓ | |
| 7. Checking statement reconciliation | | WILL DO ON CUSTOM BASIS |
| 8. Consolidated check preparation | ✓ | |
| 9. Duplicate invoice check | | NO PLANS FOR THIS FEATURE |
| 10. Manual check processing | ✓ | |
| **Reports** | | |
| 1. Vendor listing | ✓ | BY NAME, BUYER |
| 2. Invoice register | ✓ | |
| 3. Check register | ✓ | |
| 4. Cash requirements | ✓ | WEEKLY & MONTHLY |
| 5. Detail aging | ✓ | 30, 60, 90, 120 + DAYS |
| 6. Form 1099 reports | | PLANNED FOR NEXT RELEASE |
| 7. Account distribution | ✓ | |
| 8. Bank statement reconciliation | | WILL DO ON CUSTOM BASIS |

## Identifying Potential Software Vendors

After you have an idea of the software features you want, the next step is to locate potential vendors that sell the type of software you are interested in buying. If the software will be implemented on a personal computer, a good place to start looking for software is a local computer store. Most computer stores have a wide selection of application software and can suggest several alternatives to consider. If you have prepared an RFP, even a simple one, it will help the store representative to narrow the choices. If software is required for a mini or mainframe computer, however, you won't find it at the local personal computer store. For this type of software, which can cost tens to hundreds of thousands of dollars, the best place to start is the computer manufacturer. In addition to having some software themselves, most manufacturers have a list of software companies that they work with—companies that specialize in developing software for the manufacturer's equipment. **Software houses** are businesses that specialize in developing software for sale. **System houses** not only sell software but sell the equipment as well. System houses usually take full responsibility for equipment, software, installation, and training. Sometimes they even provide equipment maintenance, although this is usually left to the equipment manufacturer. The advantage of dealing with a system house is that the user only has to deal with a single company for the entire system.

Another place to find software suppliers, especially for vertical applications, is to look in trade publications, magazines written for specific businesses or industries. Companies and individuals who have written software for these industries often advertise in the trade publications. Some industry trade groups also maintain lists of companies that provide specific software solutions.

For horizontal applications, most computer magazines publish regular reviews of individual packages and often have annual reviews of several packages of the same type. Figure 11-11 shows a software review of an accounting package.

Another way to identify software suppliers is to hire a knowledgeable consultant. Although the fees paid to a consultant will increase the overall software investment, it may be worth it, considering the real cost of making a bad decision. Many consultants specialize in assisting organizations of all sizes identify and implement software packages. A good place to start looking for a consultant would be to contact professional organizations in your industry. Your accountant may also be able to recommend a possible software solution or a consultant.

INFO WORLD THE PC NEWS WEEKLY

REPORT CARD

ACCOUNTING SOFTWARE

**PEACHTREE COMPLETE II**

VERSION 4.21

| Criterion | (Weighting) | Score |
|---|---|---|
| Performance | (400) | Good |
| Documentation | (80) | Excellent |
| Ease of learning | (40) | Very Good |
| Ease of use | (120) | Very Good |
| Error handling | (80) | Very Good |
| Support | | |
| Policies | (40) | Satisfactory |
| Technical Support | (40) | Satisfactory |
| Value | (200) | Excellent |
| Final score | | 7.5 |

PRODUCT SUMMARY

**Company:** Peachtree Software, 4355 Shackleford Road, Norcross, GA 30093; (800) 247-3224 or (404) 564-5800.
**List Price:** $199.
**Requires:** IBM PC or compatible, PS/2 or compatible; 384K of RAM; hard disk; DOS 2.0 or later.
**Support:** No cost-free support from vendor. Charge: $1 per minute, $20 minimum, with toll-free number; useability warranty; 30-day money-back guarantee (minus $20 charge) if purchased direct from Peachtree.
**Pros:** Superb value; great manuals; easy to use.
**Cons:** Reporting capabilities rather inflexible; broad range of modules but shallow in depth; no cost-free support.
**Summary:** An entry-level accounting package with functions for general ledger, accounts receivable, accounts payable, inventory, job costing, fixed assets, and payroll.

**FIGURE 11-11**
Many publications regularly evaluate application software. This review also included a narrative discussion of this accounting package.

## Evaluating Software Alternatives

After you've identified several possible software solutions, you have to sort them out and choose one. First, match each choice against your original requirements list. Be as objective as possible—try not to be influenced by the salesperson or representative demonstrating the software or the appeal of the marketing literature. Match each package against your list or RFP and give each package a score. If some key features are more important than others, take that into consideration. Try to complete this rating either during or immediately after a demonstration of the package while the features are still fresh in your mind (Figure 11-12).

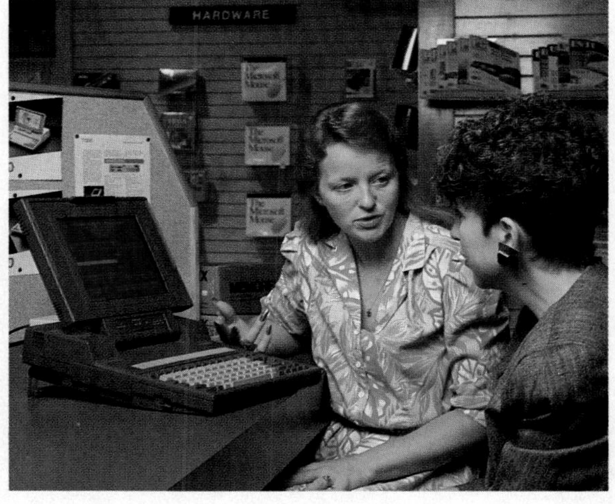


**FIGURE 11-12**
You should ask to see a demonstration of any program you are considering purchasing. During or after the demonstration, you should rate how well the package meets your requirements.

The next step is to talk to existing users of the software. For mini and mainframe software packages, software vendors routinely provide user references. For personal computer packages, if the computer store can't provide references, call the software manufacturer directly. User references are important because if a software package does (or doesn't) work for some organization like yours, it probably will (or won't) work for you.

Finally, try the software yourself. For a small application, this may be as simple as entering a few simple transactions using a demonstration copy of the software at the computer store. For large applications, it may require one or more days of testing at the vendor's office or on your existing computer to be sure that the software meets your needs.

If you are concerned about the ability of the software to handle a certain transaction volume efficiently, you may want to perform a benchmark test. A **benchmark test** involves measuring the time it takes to process a set number of transactions. For example, a benchmark might consist of measuring the time it takes a particular software package to produce a sales summary report using 1,000 sales transactions. Comparing the time it takes different packages to perform the same task using the same data and the same equipment is one way of measuring the packages' relative performance.

**FIGURE 11-13**
**A software license grants the purchaser the right to use the software but does not include ownership rights.**

## Making the Purchase

When you purchase software you usually don't own it. What you are actually purchasing is a **software license** (Figure 11-13), the right to use the software under certain terms and conditions. One of the usual terms and conditions is that you can use the software on a single computer only. In fact, some software is licensed to a specific computer and the serial number of the system is recorded in the license agreement. Other license restrictions include prohibitions against making the software available to others (for example, renting it or leasing it) and modifying or translating the software into another language. These restrictions are designed to protect the rights of the software developer who doesn't want someone else to benefit unfairly from the developer's work. For personal computer users, software license terms and conditions usually cannot be modified. But for mini and mainframe users, terms of the license agreements can be modified and therefore should be carefully reviewed and considered a part of the overall software selection process. Modifications to the software license are generally easier to obtain before the sale is made than after.

**FIGURE 11-14**
**Most application software comes with detailed installation instructions. Some packages include toll-free telephone numbers in case the user needs to call for assistance. The software seller will also usually offer support.**

## Installing the Software

After you've acquired the software, the next step is to install it. On small applications this could be a ten-minute task. On large systems, installation of a complete business system could be scheduled over a period of a year or more. Installation includes loading the software on the computer system, training the users, and testing to make sure the software is functioning correctly. Personal computer software can usually be installed by following the instructions in the user manual (Figure 11-14). Mini and mainframe computer software, however, usually requires a written installation plan tailored to the individual organization.

# SUMMARY OF COMMERCIAL APPLICATIONS SOFTWARE

This chapter discussed various aspects of commercial applications software including the types of software applications that are available, how to determine your software needs, and how to acquire applications software packages. Whether you need software for personal use or are involved in selecting software for your organization, a knowledge of commercial applications software and how to acquire it is useful.

# CHAPTER SUMMARY

1. **Commercial application software** is software that has already been written and is available for purchase.
2. Two categories of commercial application software are general application software and functional application software.
3. **General application software** provides a way for tasks that are commonly performed in all types of businesses to be done on a computer.
4. Software that allows a user to create professional-looking documents that include both text and graphics is called **desktop publishing** software.
5. Page composition, or the ability to design on the screen an exact image of what a printed page will look like, is an important feature of desktop publishing. This capability is called **WYSIWYG**, an acronym for "What You See Is What You Get."
6. **Electronic mail** software provides the ability for users to directly communicate with other users by sending text messages electronically over communication channels.
7. **Project management software** allows users to plan, schedule, track, and analyze the events, resources, and costs of a project.
8. **Functional application software**, developed to perform a specific task or function, can be classified as either horizontal or vertical applications.
9. Software packages that can be used by many different types of organizations, such as accounting packages, are called **horizontal applications**.
10. Software developed for a unique way of doing business, usually within a specific industry, is called **vertical application software**.
11. Application software that is developed by a user, or at the user's request, is called **custom software**.
12. The process of acquiring software involves five steps: evaluating the application requirements, identifying potential software vendors, evaluating software alternatives, making the purchase, and installing the software.
13. Evaluating the application requirements includes: identifying the key features of the application; determining your current transaction volumes and estimating their growth over the next three years; and deciding if the software for the new application needs to work with any existing software or equipment.
14. A **request for proposal** is a written list of an organization's software requirements that is given to prospective software vendors.
15. Identifying potential software vendors for personal computers can usually be done at a local computer store. For larger applications sources include computer manufacturers, **software houses**, **system houses**, trade publications, computer periodicals, and consultants.
16. To evaluate software alternatives, match the features of each possible solution against the original requirements list or RFP.
17. A **benchmark test** involves measuring the time it takes to process a set number of transactions.
18. A **software license** is the right to use software under certain terms and conditions.
19. Installation of the software includes loading the software on the computer system, training the users, and testing to make sure the software is functioning correctly.

## KEY TERMS

Benchmark test *11.10*
Commercial application software *11.2*
Custom software *11.6*
Desktop publishing (DTP) *11.3*
Electronic mail *11.5*
Functional application software *11.5*
General application software *11.3*
Horizontal application software *11.6*
Productivity tools *11.3*
Project management software *11.5*
Request for proposal (RFP) *11.8*
Software houses *11.9*
Software license *11.10*
System houses *11.9*
Vertical application software *11.6*
WYSIWYG *11.4*

## REVIEW QUESTIONS

1. What is commercial application software? Describe the difference between software that performs a general task and software that performs a specific task.
2. List several types of general applications software. Why are these applications called productivity tools?
3. What does the page composition feature of desktop publishing allow a user to do? What is WYSIWYG?
4. Explain the difference between horizontal and vertical applications.
5. What is custom software and why is it appropriate for some applications?
6. List the five steps in acquiring commercial applications software.
7. Describe the information that an RFP should contain and how the RFP is used.
8. List several ways to find sources for commercial applications software.
9. Describe several things that a user can do to evaluate a software package before purchasing it. What is a benchmark test?
10. What is a software license? Describe some of the terms and conditions that are included in a software license.

## CONTROVERSIAL ISSUES

1. Some personal computer users who have purchased application software off the shelf in a computer store have found that learning to use the software has been difficult and time consuming. Many of these users claim that the store that sold the software should provide training on how to use it. While some computer stores do provide limited training, other stores say that training is not their responsibility and explain that they cannot afford to provide training services for customers on all the various software packages that they sell. Do you think that software stores should provide training to customers?
2. Some organizations claim that consultants have saved them considerable sums of money when acquiring application software? Others say that they would have been better off not using a consultant. What role, if any, do you feel a consultant should play in helping an organization to select application software?

## RESEARCH PROJECTS

1. Compare the license agreements for three different microcomputer software packages. Prepare a report that discusses the terms and conditions of each license.
2. Visit a store that sells microcomputer software. Select three accounting packages and prepare a report that discusses the features of each package. In the conclusion of your report, state which package you would buy and give the reasons for your selection.

CHAPTER 12

# The Information System Development Life Cycle

CHAPTER 12

# The Information System Development Life Cycle

## OBJECTIVES

- Describe the six elements of an information system: equipment, software, data, personnel, users, and procedures.
- Define the term information system and describe the different types of information systems.
- Explain the five phases of the information system development life cycle: analysis, design, development, implementation, and maintenance.
- Explain the importance of documentation and project management in the information system development life cycle.
- Describe how various analysis and design tools, such as data flow diagrams, are used.
- Explain how program development is part of the information system development life cycle.
- Explain several methods that can be used for a conversion to a new system.
- Discuss the maintenance of an information system.

---

Every day, factors such as competition and government regulations cause people to face new challenges in obtaining the information they need to perform their jobs. A new product, a new sales commission plan, or a change in tax rates are just three examples of events that require a change in the way an organization processes information. Sometimes these challenges can be met by existing methods but other times, meeting the challenge requires an entirely new way of processing data. In these cases, a new or modified information system is needed. As a computer user, either as an individual or within your organization, it is very likely that someday you will participate in the development or modification of such a system. This chapter discusses information systems and how they are developed. To better explain the chapter material, we illustrate each phase of the system development cycle with a case study about the wholesale auto parts division of the Sutherland Company.

## WHAT IS AN INFORMATION SYSTEM?

An **information system** is a collection of elements that provide accurate, timely, and useful information. As discussed in Chapter 1, an information system is comprised of six elements: equipment, software, data, personnel, users, and procedures. Each element is important in order to obtain quality information from an information system.

The term information system is frequently used to describe the entire computer operation of an organization, as in a computer information system or the information system(s) department. The term is also used to mean an individual application or "system" that is processed on the computer. For example, an accounting system or an inventory control system can each be thought of as an information system.

Regardless of the scope implied by the use of the term information system, all information systems that are implemented on a computer are comprised of the six elements previously listed. Each element—equipment, software, data, personnel, users, and procedures—contributes to a successful information system and conversely, a weakness in any of these elements can cause an information system to fail. To help ensure success, all six elements should be considered by the people responsible for creating or changing any type of information system.

## TYPES OF INFORMATION SYSTEMS

The types of information systems that use a computer fall into four broad categories: (1) operational systems; (2) management information systems; (3) decision support systems; and (4) expert systems.

### Operational Systems

An **operational system** is designed to process data generated by the day-to-day business transactions of a company. Examples of operational systems are accounting systems, billing systems, inventory control systems, and order entry systems (Figure 12-1).

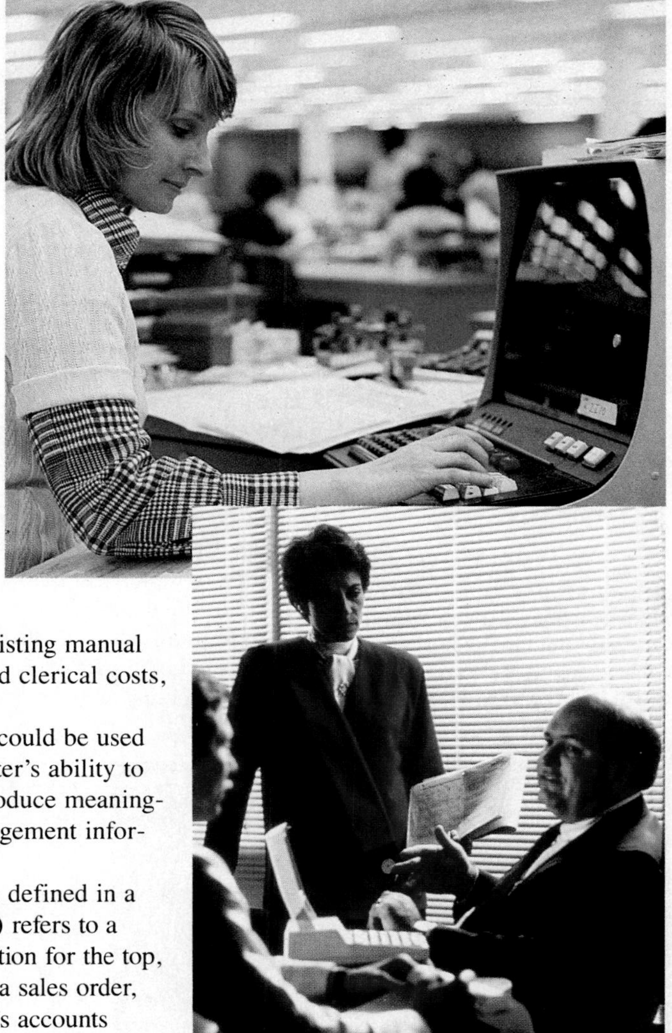

**FIGURE 12-1**
**Operational systems process the day-to-day transactions of an organization, such as the tax forms that are shown being entered into an IRS computer.**

### Management Information Systems

When computers were first used for processing business applications, the information systems developed were primarily operational systems. Usually, the purpose was to "computerize" an existing manual system. This approach often resulted in faster processing, reduced clerical costs, and improved customer service.

Managers soon realized, however, that computer processing could be used for more than just day-to-day transaction processing. The computer's ability to perform rapid calculations and compare data could be used to produce meaningful information for management. This led to the concept of management information systems.

Although the term management information system has been defined in a number of ways, today a **management information system (MIS)** refers to a computer-based system that generates timely and accurate information for the top, middle, and lower levels of management. For example, to process a sales order, the operational system would record the sale, update the customer's accounts receivable balance, and make a deduction from the inventory. In the related management information system, reports would be produced that show slow or fast moving items, customers with past due accounts receivable balances, and inventory items that need reordering. In the management information system, the focus is on the information that management needs to do its job (Figure 12-2).

**FIGURE 12-2**
**Management information systems focus on the summary information and exceptions that managers use to perform their jobs.**

## Decision Support Systems

Frequently management needs information that is not routinely provided by operational and management information systems. For example, a vice president of finance may want to know the effect on company profits if sales increase by 10% and costs increase by 5%. This type of information is not usually provided by operational or management information systems. To provide this information, decision support systems have been developed.

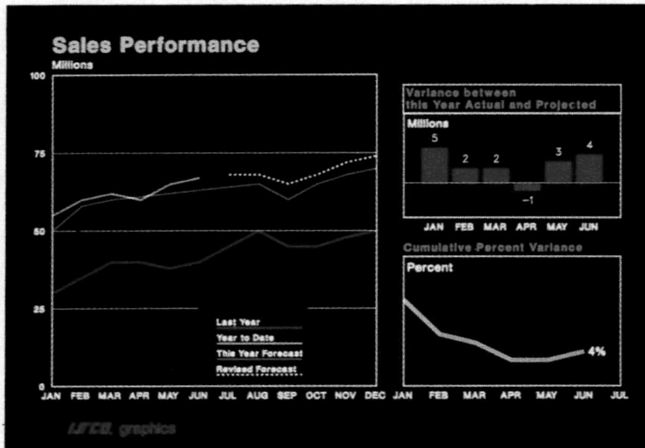


**FIGURE 12-3**
**Decision support systems often use graphics to help the user evaluate decision data.**

A **decision support system** is a system designed to help someone reach a decision by summarizing or comparing data from either or both internal and external sources. Internal sources include data from an organization's database such as sales, manufacturing, or financial data. Data from external sources could include information on interest rates, population trends, or new housing construction. Decision support systems often include query languages, statistical analysis capabilities, spreadsheets, and graphics to help the user evaluate the decision data (Figure 12-3). More advanced decision support systems also include capabilities that allow users to create a model of the factors affecting a decision. A simple model for determining the best product price would include factors for the expected sales volume at each price level. With a model, users can ask "what if" questions by changing one or more of the factors and seeing what the projected results would be. Many people use electronic spreadsheets for simple modeling tasks.

## Expert Systems

**Expert systems** combine the knowledge on a given subject of one or more human experts into a computerized system that simulates the human experts' reasoning and decision making processes (Figure 12-4). Thus, the computer also becomes an "expert" on the subject. Expert systems are made up of the combined subject knowledge of the human experts, called the **knowledge base** and the **inference rules** that determine how the knowledge is used to reach decisions. Although they may appear to "think," the current expert systems actually operate within narrow preprogrammed limits and cannot make decisions based on "common sense" or on information outside of their knowledge base. Expert systems have been successfully applied to problems as diverse as diagnosing illnesses, searching for oil, and making soup. These systems are part of an exciting branch of computer science called **artificial intelligence**, the application of human intelligence to computer systems.

**FIGURE 12-4**
**NEXpert Object is a powerful software tool that allows relatively unsophisticated users to create their own expert system.**

## The Integration of Information Systems

With today's sophisticated software, it can be difficult to classify a system as belonging uniquely to one of the four types of information systems. For example, much of today's application software provides both operational and management information system information and some of the more advanced software even includes some decision support capabilities. Although expert systems still operate primarily as separate systems, the trend is clear: to combine all of an organization's information needs into a single integrated information system.

To develop the information systems they need, many organizations use the information system development life cycle.

# WHAT IS THE INFORMATION SYSTEM DEVELOPMENT LIFE CYCLE?

The **information system development life cycle (SDLC)** is an organized approach to developing an information system.

Regardless of the type or complexity of an information system, the structured process of the information system development life cycle should be followed whenever an information system is developed. Although some experts group them differently, this chapter divides the activities of the information system development life cycle into five phases.

**FIGURE 12-5**
**The five phases of the information system development life cycle.**

phase 1 Analysis
phase 2 Design
phase 3 Development
phase 4 Implementation
phase 5 Maintenance

## The Five Phases of the Information System Development Life Cycle

Each of the five phases of the information system development life cycle includes important activities that relate to the development of an information system. The five phases are (Figure 12-5):

Phase 1 Analysis
Phase 2 Design
Phase 3 Development
Phase 4 Implementation
Phase 5 Maintenance

Before explaining each of the phases, we will discuss project management and documentation because these two activities are ongoing processes that are performed throughout the cycle. In addition, we will identify the information system specialists and users who participate in the various phases of the SDLC.

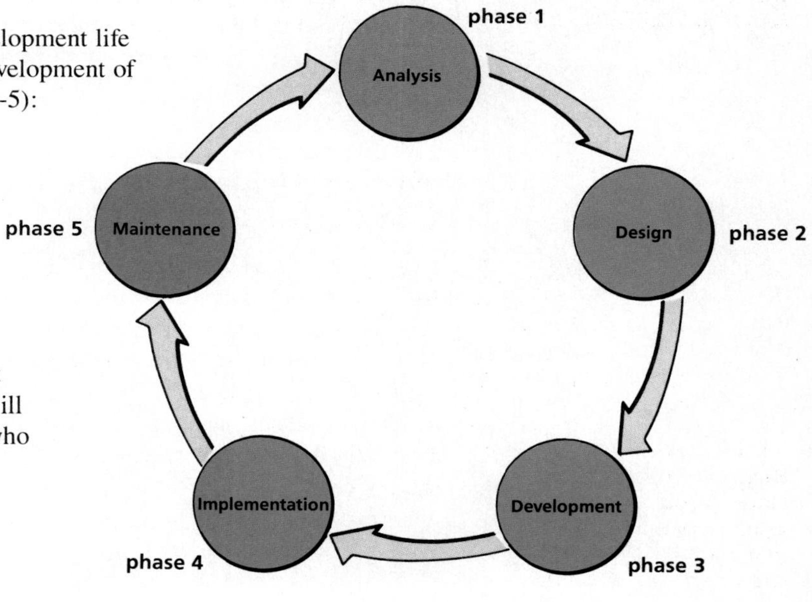

## Project Management

**Project management** involves planning, scheduling, reporting, and controlling the individual activities that make up the information system development life cycle. These activities are usually recorded in a **project plan** on a week-by-week basis that includes an estimate of the time to complete the activity and the start and finish dates. As you might expect, the start of many activities depends on the successful completion of other activities. For example, implementation (Phase 4) activities can't begin until you have completed at least some, if not all, of the development activities (Phase 3). An effective way of showing the relationship of project activities is with a Gantt chart (Figure 12-6).

**FIGURE 12-6**
**A Gantt chart is often used in project management to show the time relationships of the project activities.**

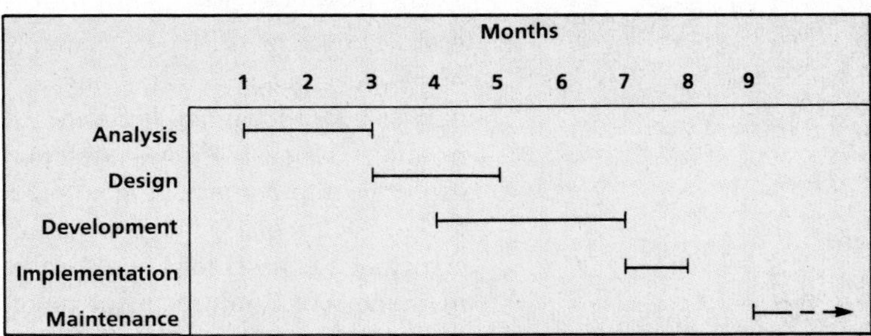

The importance of maintaining a realistic schedule for project management cannot be overstated. Without a realistic schedule, the success of a development project is in jeopardy from the start. If project members don't believe the schedule is realistic, they may not participate to the full extent of their abilities. Project management is a place for realistic and not wishful thinking.

Project management is a task that should be done *throughout* the development process. In most projects, activities need frequent rescheduling. Some activities will take less time than originally planned and others will take longer. To measure the impact of the actual results and revised estimates, they should be recorded regularly and a revised project plan issued. A number of project management software packages are available to assist in this task.

### Documentation

**Documentation** refers to written materials that are produced as part of the information system development life cycle, such as a report describing the overall purpose of the system or layout sheets that are used to design reports and screens. Documentation should be identified and agreed on prior to beginning the project. Well-written, thorough documentation makes it easier for users and others to understand why particular decisions are made. Too often, documentation is put off until the completion of a project and is never adequately finished. Documentation should be an ongoing part of the entire development process and should not be thought of as a separate phase.

### Who Participates in the Information System Development Life Cycle?

Every person who will be affected by the new system should have the opportunity to participate in its development. The participants fall into two categories: users and information system personnel such as systems analysts and computer programmers. As discussed in Chapter 1, the systems analyst works closely with both the users and the programmers. The systems analyst's job is challenging, requiring good communication, analytical, and diplomatic skills to keep the development process on track and on schedule. Good communication skills are especially important during analysis, the first phase of the information system development life cycle.

## PHASE 1—ANALYSIS

**Analysis** is the separation of a system into its parts to determine how the system works. In addition, the analysis phase of a development project also includes the identification of a proposed solution to the problems identified in the current system.

A system project can originate in several ways, but a common way is for the manager of a user department, such as accounting or personnel, to contact the information systems department with a request for assistance. The initial request may be oral, but it is eventually written on a standard form that becomes the first item of documentation (Figure 12-7). In most organizations, requests for new system projects exceed the capacity of the information systems department to implement them. Therefore, the manager of the systems department must review each request and make a preliminary determination as to the potential benefit for the company. Requests for large development projects, such as an entirely new system, are often reviewed by committees made up of both user and information systems personnel and representatives of top management. When the managers of both the user and information systems departments determine that a request warrants further review, one or more systems analysts will be assigned to begin a preliminary investigation, the first step in the analysis phase.

## The Preliminary Investigation

The purpose of the **preliminary investigation** is to determine if a request justifies further detailed investigation and analysis. The most important aspect of the preliminary investigation is **problem definition**, the identification of the true nature of the problem. Often the stated problem and the real problem are not the same. For example, the investigation of a request for a new accounts receivable report may reveal that the real problem is that customer payments are not being recorded in a timely manner. The existing accounts receivable reports may be fine if the payments are recorded when received instead of once a week. The purpose of the preliminary investigation is to determine the real source of the problem.

The preliminary investigation begins with an interview of the manager who submitted the request. Depending on the scope of the request, other users may be interviewed as well.

The duration of the preliminary investigation is usually quite short when compared to the remainder of the project. At the conclusion of the investigation, the analyst presents the findings to both user and information system management and recommends the next course of action. Sometimes the results of a preliminary investigation indicate an obvious solution that can be implemented at minimal cost. Other times, however, the only thing the preliminary investigation does is confirm that there is a problem that needs further study. In these cases, detailed system analysis is recommended.

REQUEST FOR SYSTEM SERVICES

ISD CONTROL #: 2143

I. To Be Completed By Person Requesting Services

SUBMITTED BY: MIKE CHARLES DEPT AUTO PARTS SALES DATE: 1-22-90

REQUEST TYPE: ☐ MODIFICATION ☑ NEW SYSTEM

NEED: ☐ ASAP ☑ IMMEDIATE ☐ LONG RANGE

BRIEF STATEMENT OF REQUEST (attach additional material, if necessary)

NEED AUTOMATED ORDER ENTRY AND INVOICING CAPABILITY. MANUAL PROCEDURES CAN NO LONGER KEEP UP WITH INCREASED SALES VOLUME.

☐ ADDITIONAL MATERIAL ATTACHED

II. To Be Completed By Information Systems Department

REQUEST INVESTIGATED BY: FRANK PEACOCK DATE: 2-4-90

COMMENTS: MANUAL INVOICING RUNNING 3 DAYS BEHIND SHIPMENTS. RECOMMEND DETAILED SYSTEM ANALYSIS FOR DEVELOPMENT OF COMPUTERIZED SYSTEM

III. Disposition

☑ REQUEST APPROVED FOR IMMEDIATE IMPLEMENTATION

☐ Analyst assigned: MARY RUIZ

☐ REQUEST APPROVED FOR IMPLEMENTATION AS SOON AS POSSIBLE

☐ REQUEST REJECTED

COMMENTS:

SIGNED: [signature] DATE: 2-15-90

**FIGURE 12-7**
**The system development project usually starts with a request from a user. The request should be documented on a form such as the one shown here to provide a record of the action taken.**

## Detailed System Analysis

**Detailed system analysis** involves both a thorough study of the current system and at least one proposed solution to any problems found.

The study of the current system is important for two reasons. First, it helps increase the analyst's understanding of the activities that the new system will perform. Second, and perhaps most important, studying the current system builds a relationship with the user. The analyst will have much more credibility with users if the analyst understands how the users currently do their job. This may seem an obvious point, but surprisingly, many systems are created or modified without studying the current system or without adequately involving the users.

The basic fact-gathering techniques used during the detailed system analysis are: (1) interviews; (2) questionnaires; (3) reviewing current system documentation; (4) observing current procedures. During this phase of the system study, the analyst must develop a critical, questioning approach to each procedure within the current system to determine what is actually taking place. Often it is found that operations are being performed not because they are efficient or effective, but because "they have always been done this way."

Information gathered during this phase includes: (1) the output of the current system; (2) the procedures used to produce the output; (3) the input to the current system.

An increasingly popular method for documenting this information is called structured analysis. **Structured analysis** is the use of analysis and design tools such as data flow diagrams, data dictionaries, structured English, and decision tables and trees to document the specifications of an information system.

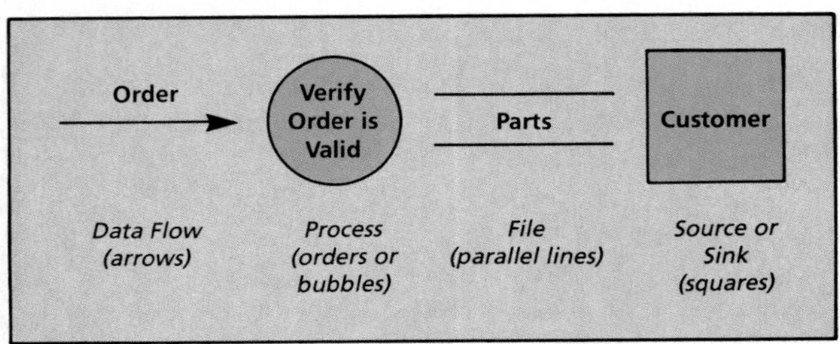


**FIGURE 12-8**
**The symbols used to create data flow diagrams.**

**Data Flow Diagrams** One of the difficulties with the analysis of any system is documenting the results in a way that others can understand. Structured analysis addresses this problem by using graphics to represent the flow of data between processes and files. These graphics are represented by data flow diagrams.

**Data flow diagrams (DFD)** graphically show the flow of data through a system. The key elements of a DFD (Figure 12-8) are arrows or vectors called data flows, representing data; circles (also called "bubbles") representing processes, such as verifying an order or creating an invoice; parallel lines representing data files; and squares, called sources or sinks, that represent either or both an originator or a receiver of data, such as a customer. Because they are visual, DFDs are particularly useful for reviewing the existing or proposed system with the user. (See Figure 12-9).

**FIGURE 12-9**
**Data flow diagrams (DFD) are used to graphically illustrate the flow of information through a system. The customer (box) both originates and receives data (arrows). The circles indicate where actions take place on the data. Files are shown as parallel lines.**

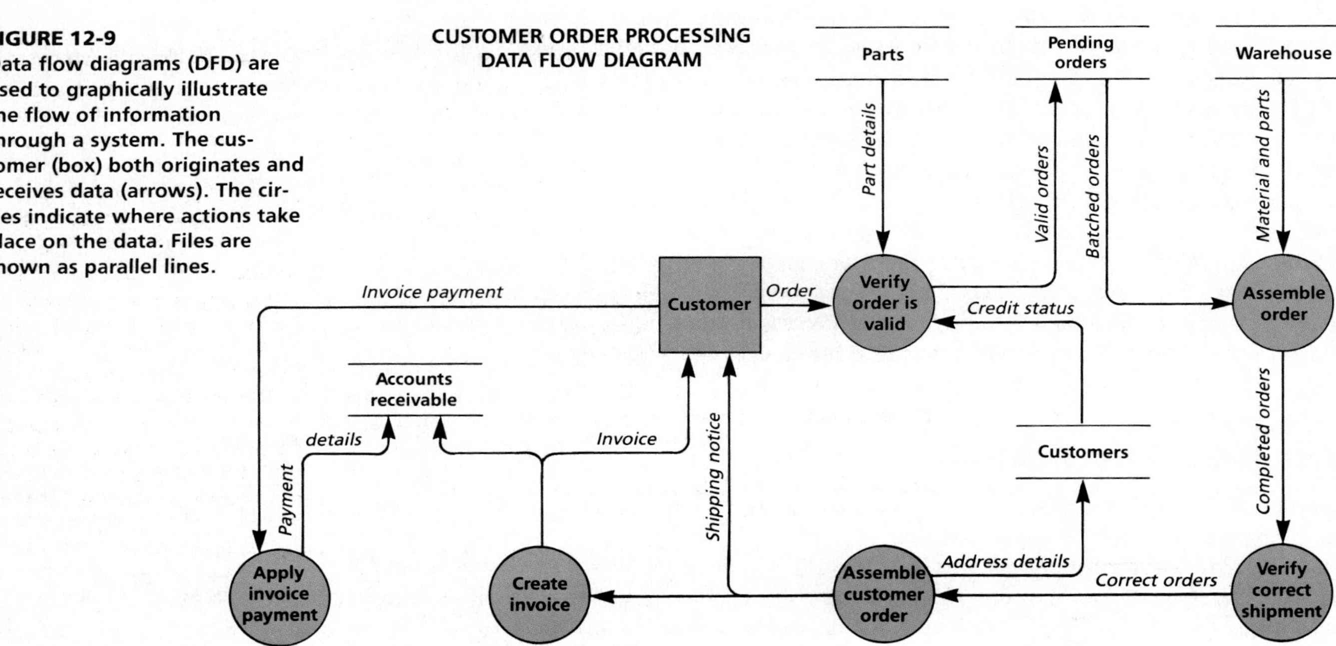


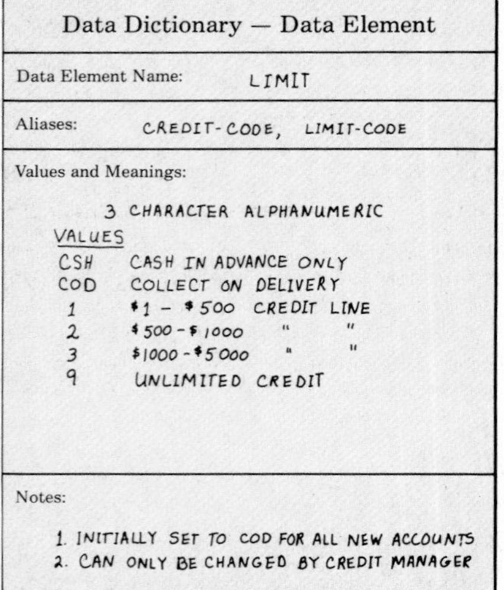
Data Dictionary — Data Element

Data Element Name: LIMIT

Aliases: CREDIT-CODE, LIMIT-CODE

Values and Meanings:

3 CHARACTER ALPHANUMERIC
VALUES
CSH CASH IN ADVANCE ONLY
COD COLLECT ON DELIVERY
1 $1 - $500 CREDIT LINE
2 $500 - $1000 " "
3 $1000 - $5000 " "
9 UNLIMITED CREDIT

Notes:

1. INITIALLY SET TO COD FOR ALL NEW ACCOUNTS
2. CAN ONLY BE CHANGED BY CREDIT MANAGER

**Data Dictionaries** The **data dictionary** describes the elements that make up the data flow. Elements can be thought of as equivalent to fields in a record. The data dictionary (Figure 12-10) includes information about the attributes of an element, such as length; where the element is used (what files and data flows include the element); and any values or ranges the element might have, such as a value of 2 for a credit limit code to indicate a purchase limit of $1,000.00. The data dictionary is created in the analysis phase and is used in all subsequent phases.

**FIGURE 12-10**
**The data dictionary is used to document the elements that are included in the data flows. This illustration shows the information on length, type of data, and possible values that is recorded for each data element in the dictionary.**

**Structured English** **Process specifications** document what action is taken on the data flows. Referring to the DFD in Figure 12-9, process specifications will describe what goes on in each of the circles. One way of writing process specifications is to use **structured English**, a style of writing and presentation that highlights the alternatives and actions that are part of the process. Figure 12-11 shows an example of a structured English process specification describing a policy for order processing.

```
If the order amount exceeds $1,000,
    If customer has any unpaid invoices over 90 days old,
        Do not issue order confirmation,
        Write message on order reject report.
    Otherwise (account is in good standing),
        Issue order confirmation.
Otherwise (order is $1,000 or less),
    If customer has any unpaid invoices over 90 days old,
        Issue order confirmation,
        Write message on credit follow-up report.
    Otherwise (account is in good standing),
        Issue order confirmation.
```

**FIGURE 12-11▲** Structured English is an organized way of describing what actions are taken on data. This structured English example describes an order processing policy.

**Decision Tables and Decision Trees** Another way of documenting the system during the analysis phase is with a decision table or decision tree. A **decision table** or **decision tree** identifies the actions that should be taken under different conditions. Figures 12-12 and 12-13 show a decision table and decision tree for the order processing policy described with structured English in Figure 12-11. Decision tables and trees are an excellent way of showing the desired action when the action depends on multiple conditions.

| | Rules | | | |
|---|---|---|---|---|
| | 1 | 2 | 3 | 4 |
| **Conditions** | | | | |
| 1. Order > $1,000 | Y | Y | N | N |
| 2. Unpaid invoices over 90 days old | Y | N | Y | N |
| **Actions** | | | | |
| 1. Issue confirmation | N | Y | Y | Y |
| 2. Reject order | Y | N | N | N |
| 3. Credit follow-up | N | N | Y | N |

**◄FIGURE 12-12** Decision tables help a user quickly determine the course of action based on two or more conditions. This decision table is based on the order processing policy described in Figure 12-11. For example, if an order is $1,000 or less and the customer has an unpaid invoice over 90 days old, the policy is to issue an order confirmation but to perform a credit follow-up on the past due invoice.

## Making the Decision on How To Proceed

Just as at the completion of the preliminary investigation, at the completion of the analysis phase, the user, systems analyst, and management face another decision on how to proceed. At this point the analyst should have completed a study of the current system and, using the same tools and methods, developed one or more proposed solutions to the current system's identified problems. Sometimes the systems analyst is asked to prepare a feasibility study and a cost/benefit analysis. These two reports are often used together. The **feasibility study** discusses whether the proposed solution is practical and capable of being accomplished. The **cost/benefit analysis** identifies the estimated costs of the proposed solution and the benefits (including potential cost savings) that are expected. If there are strong indications at the beginning of the project that some type of new system will be developed, the feasibility study and cost/benefit analysis are sometimes performed as part of the preliminary investigation.

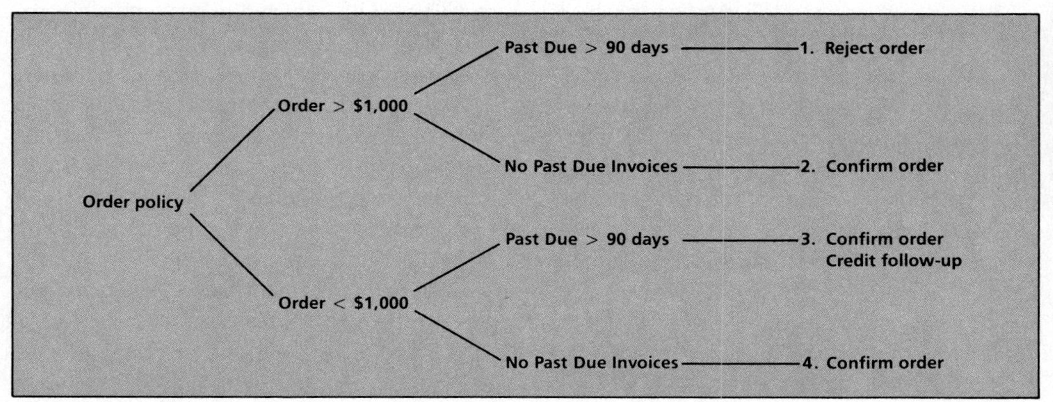


**◄FIGURE 12-13** Like a decision table, a decision tree illustrates the action to be taken based on the given conditions, but presents it graphically. This decision tree is based on the order processing policy described in Figure 12-11.

DATE: April 1
TO: Management Review Committee
FROM: George Lacey, Corporate Systems Manager
SUBJECT: Detailed Investigation and Analysis of Order Entry System

Introduction

A detailed system investigation and analysis of the order entry system was conducted as a result of approval given by the Management Review Committee on March 1. The findings of the investigation are presented below.

Objectives of Detailed Investigation and Analysis

The study was conducted to investigate two major complaints of the wholesale auto parts order entry system. Complaints have been received that orders were not being shipped promptly, and customers were not notified of out-of-stock conditions for many days after sending in orders. In addition, billing invoices are running several days behind shipments. The objective of this study was to determine where the problems existed and to develop alternative solutions.

Findings of the Detailed Investigation and Analysis

The following problems appear to exist within the order entry system:

2. Place the order entry and invoicing systems on the computer. Computer terminals would be installed in the sales department for order entry clerks. As orders are received, they would be entered into the computer. Orders could be immediately edited for proper customer and part numbers and a check could be made to determine if stock is available. Billing invoices could be mailed the same day as shipments. Estimated costs: (1) Systems analysis and design-$26,000; (2) Programming and implementation-$40,000; (3) Training, new forms, and maintenance-$7,000; (4) Equipment (four terminals)-$6,000.

Recommended Action

The systems department recommends the design of a computerized order entry and invoicing system utilizing alternative 2, which is believed to offer the most effective solution.

George Lacey

**FIGURE 12-14**
**Written reports summarizing the analyst's work are an important part of the development project. This report was prepared at the end of the analysis phase and recommends the development of a computerized order entry and invoicing system.**

The results of the analyst's work are presented in a written report (Figure 12-14) to both user and information systems management who consider the alternatives and the resources, such as time, people, and money, of the organization. The end of the analysis phase is usually where organizations decide either to acquire commercial software from an outside source, contract outside the organization for system development, or develop the system internally. If a decision is made to proceed, the project enters the design phase.

## PHASE 1—ANALYSIS AT SUTHERLAND

The Sutherland Company is a large corporation with separate divisions that sell tools, electric motors, and auto parts, respectively. Although the tool and electric motor divisions have been computerized for some time, the low sales volume of the auto parts division, started just two years ago, enabled it to rely on manual procedures. In the last six months, however, auto parts sales doubled and the manual order entry and invoicing systems were unable to keep up with the increased workload.

Because he believed the increased sales volume would continue, Mike Charles, the auto parts sales manager, turned in a request for system services to the information systems department that provided computer services for all three Sutherland divisions. Frank Peacock, a systems analyst, was assigned to investigate the request.

As part of the preliminary investigation, Frank interviewed Mike to try to determine the problem. During his interview with Mike and a subsequent tour of the auto parts sales department, Frank discovered that invoices were not being sent to customers until three days after their parts orders had shipped. In addition, Frank found that customers were complaining about shipments being late and about not being notified when parts they ordered were not available. As a result of his preliminary investigation, Frank recommended a detailed system analysis. George Lacey, the corporate systems manager, agreed with Frank's recommendation and assigned systems analyst Mary Ruiz.

Mary reviewed Frank's notes and began to perform a detailed analysis of the auto parts order entry and invoicing systems. As part of her study, Mary interviewed several people in the auto parts division and prepared several documents including a data flow diagram (Figure 12-9), a data dictionary definition for the different credit limits assigned to customers (Figure 12-10), and a structured English statement of the order processing policy (Figure 12-11).

After studying the manual procedures for a week, Mary discussed her findings with her supervisor, George Lacey. Based on Mary's work, George wrote a report to the management review committee recommending that the order entry and invoicing systems be computerized. The report contained two alternative solutions, one utilizing a separate minicomputer system and the other, considered the most effective solution, utilizing terminals connected to the company's central computer. The management review committee meets every month to review requests for additional computer equipment and software. The committee is made up of top management representatives from each division, the finance department, and the information systems department. Based on George's report, the management review committee authorized the corporate systems department to design a computerized order entry and invoicing system.

# PHASE 2—DESIGN

The proposed solution developed as part of the analysis phase usually consists of what is called a **logical design**, which means that the design was deliberately developed without regard to a specific computer or programming language and no attempt was made to identify which procedures should be automated and which procedures should be manual. This approach avoids early assumptions that may limit the possible solutions. During the **design** phase the logical design will be transformed into a **physical design** that will identify the procedures to be automated, choose the programming language, and specify the equipment needed for the system.

## Structured Design Methods

The system design usually follows one of two methods, top-down design or bottom-up design.

**Top-Down Design** **Top-down design**, also called **structured design**, focuses on the major functions of the system, such as recording a sale or generating an invoice, and keeps breaking those functions down into smaller and smaller activities, sometimes called modules, that can eventually be programmed. Top-down design is an increasingly popular method because it focuses on the "big picture" and helps users and systems analysts reach an early agreement on what the major functions of the new system are.

**Bottom-Up Design** **Bottom-up design** focuses on the data, particularly the output of the system. The approach used is to determine what output is needed and move "up" to the processes needed to produce the output.

In practice, most system analysts use a combination of the two methods. Some information requirements like payroll checks, for example, have data elements that lend themselves to bottom-up design. Other requirements, such as management-oriented exception reports, are better suited to a top-down design.

Regardless of the structured design method used, the system analyst will eventually need to complete the design activities.

## Design Activities

Design activities include a number of individual tasks that a system analyst performs to design an information system. These include designs for the output, input, database, processes, system controls, and testing.

**Output Design** The design of the output is critical to the successful implementation of the system because it is the output that provides the information to the users and that is the basis for the justification of most computerized systems. For example, most users don't know (or necessarily care) how the data will be processed, but they usually do have clear ideas on how they want the information output to look. Often requests for new or modified systems begin with a user-prepared draft of a report that the current system doesn't produce. During **output design**, the system analyst and the user document specific screen and report layouts that will be used for output to display or report information from the new system. The example in Figure 12-15 illustrates a report layout sheet.

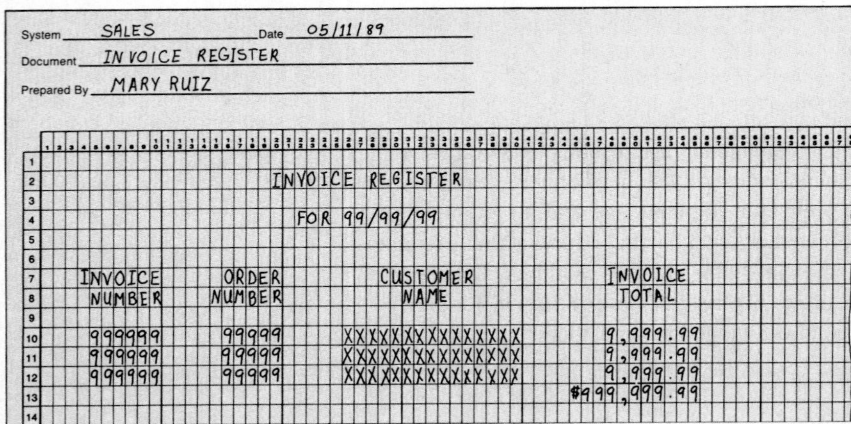

System SALES Date 05/11/89
Document INVOICE REGISTER
Prepared By MARY RUIZ

INVOICE REGISTER
FOR 99/99/99

| INVOICE NUMBER | ORDER NUMBER | CUSTOMER NAME | INVOICE TOTAL |
|---|---|---|---|
| 999999 | 99999 | XXXXXXXXXXXXXXXXXX | 9,999.99 |
| 999999 | 99999 | XXXXXXXXXXXXXXXXXX | 9,999.99 |
| 999999 | 99999 | XXXXXXXXXXXXXXXXXX | 9,999.99 |
| | | | $999,999.99 |

FIGURE 12-15
The report layout form is used to design printed output. Column titles, data width, and report totals are shown on the layout form.

**Input Design** During **input design** the analyst and user identify what information needs to be entered into the system to produce the desired output and where and how the data will be entered. With interactive systems, the systems analyst and user must determine the sequence of inputs and computer responses, called a **dialogue**, that the user will encounter when entering data. Figure 12-16 shows a display screen layout sheet commonly used to document the format of a screen display.

```
COLUMN
01 99/99    ** ENTER ORDERS **
02          -SCREEN 1-
03
04 CUSTOMER NUMBER: 9999999
05 ORDER NUMBER: 99999
06
07 BILL TO: XXXXXXXXXXXXXXXXXXXXX  SHIP TO: XXXXXXXXXXXXXXXXXXXXX
08          XXXXXXXXXXXXXXXXXXXXX           XXXXXXXXXXXXXXXXXXXXX
09          XXXXXXXXXXXXXXXXXXXXX           XXXXXXXXXXXXXXXXXXXXX
10
11 ORDER DATE: 99/99
12 TERMS: XXXXXXXXXX
13 SALESPERSON: XXXX
14 DISCOUNT %:   9999
ROW
```

FIGURE 12-16
The display screen layout sheet is similar to the report layout form. Each row and column correspond to a row and column on the screen.

**Database Design** During **database design** the systems analyst uses the data dictionary information developed during the analysis phase and merges it into new or existing system files. During this phase of the design, the analyst works closely with the database administrator to identify existing database elements that can be used to satisfy design requirements.

Efficient file design can be a challenging task, especially with relational database systems that stress minimum data redundancy (duplicate data). The volume of database activity must also be considered at this point. For example, large files that will be frequently accessed may need a separate index file (discussed in Chapter 8) to allow inquiries to be processed in an amount of time acceptable to the user.

**Process Design** During **process design** the system analyst specifies exactly what actions will be taken on the input data to create output information. Decisions on the timing of actions are added to the logical processes identified in the analysis phase. For example, the analysis phase might have found that an exception report should be produced if inventory balances fall below a certain level. During the process design phase, the frequency of the report would be determined.

One way to document the relationship of different processes is with a **system flowchart** (Figure 12-17). The system flowchart shows the major processes (each of which may require one or more programs), reports (including their distribution), data files, and the types of input devices such as terminals or tape drives, that will provide data to the system. The special symbols used in a system flowchart are shown in Figure 12-18.

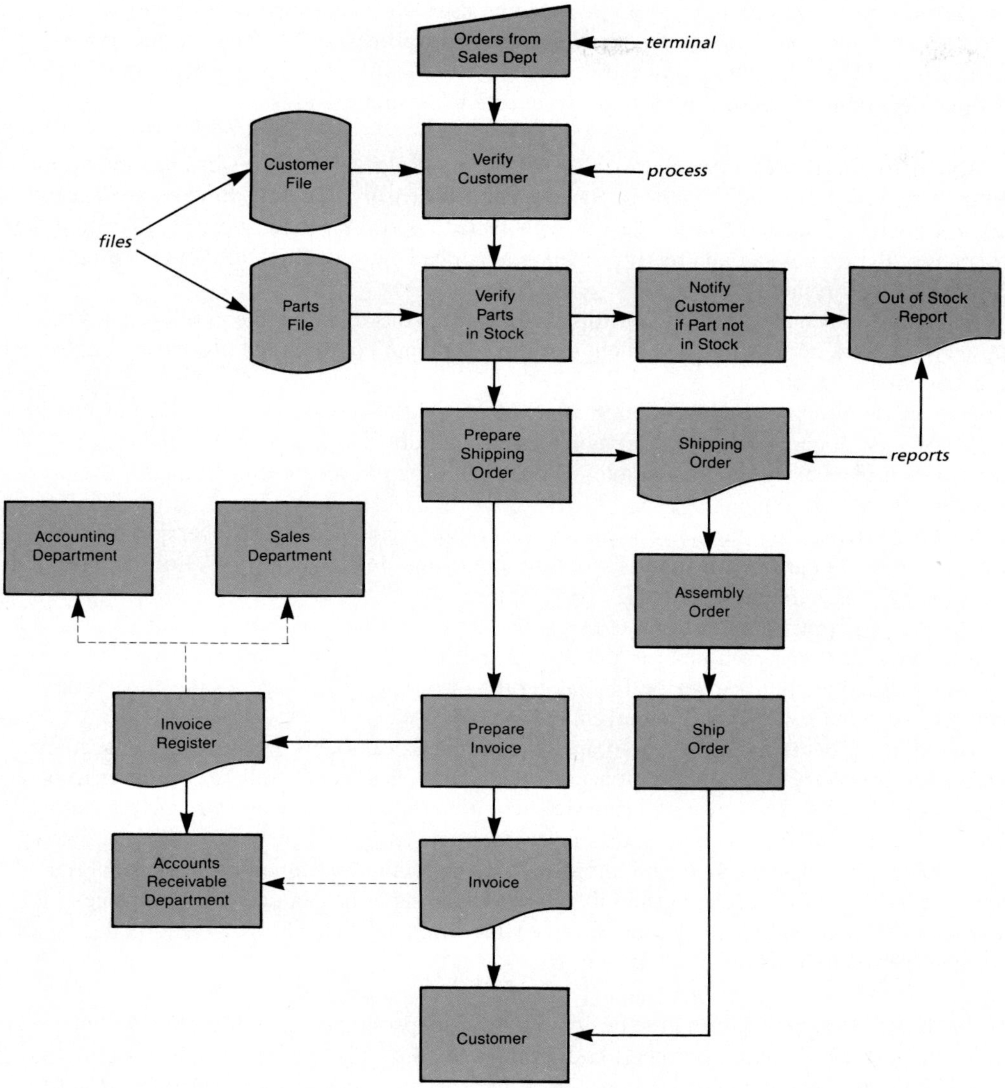

**FIGURE 12-17**
The system flowchart documents the equipment used to enter data, such as the terminals for the salespeople and the order department, the processes that will take place, such as ''Verify Customer,'' the files that will be used, such as the Parts and Customer files, and the reports that will be produced, such as the shipping order. Dotted lines indicate additional copies of reports, such as the copy of the invoice that is sent to the accounts receivable department.

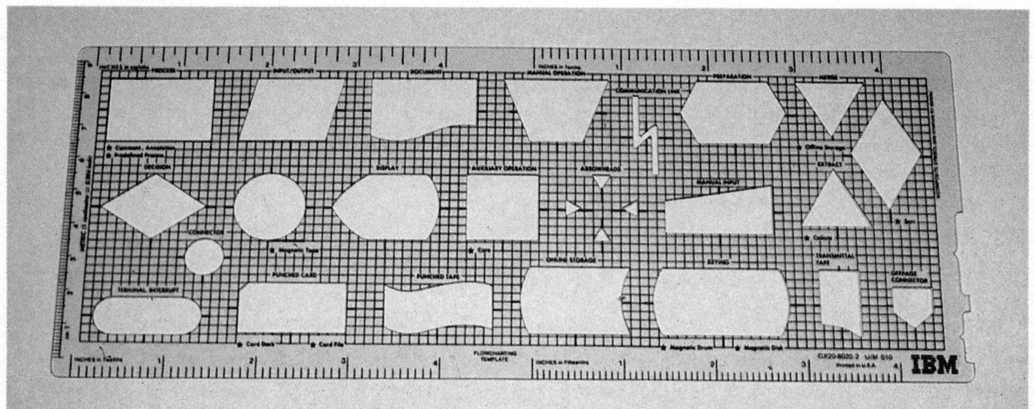


**FIGURE 12-18**
Symbols used for preparing a system flowchart.

During process design the system analyst, the user, and other members of the development project sometimes meet to conduct a **structured walkthrough**, a step-by-step review of the process design. The purpose of these sessions is to identify any design logic errors and to continue the communication between the systems analyst and the user.

**System Controls** An important aspect of the design phase is the establishment of a comprehensive set of system controls. **System controls** ensure that only valid data is accepted and processed. Adequate controls must be established for two basic reasons: (1) to ensure the accuracy of the processing and the information generated from the system; (2) to prevent computer-related fraud.

There are four basic types of controls that must be considered by the systems analyst. These controls are: (1) source document controls; (2) input controls; (3) processing controls; (4) accounting controls.

**Source document controls** include serial numbering of input documents such as invoices and paychecks, document registers in which each input document is recorded and time-stamped as it is received, and batch totaling and balancing to predetermined totals to assure the accuracy of processing.

**Input controls** are established to assure the complete and accurate conversion of data from the source documents or other sources to a machine-processable form. Editing data as it enters the system is the most important form of input controls.

**Processing controls** refer to procedures that are established to determine the accuracy of information after it has been input to the system. For example, the accuracy of the total accounts receivable could be verified by taking the prior day's total, adding the current day's sales invoices, and subtracting the current day's payments.

**Accounting controls** provide assurance that the dollar amounts recorded in the accounting records are correct. An important accounting control is an audit trail. An **audit trail** is one or more reports that provide a history of how transactions have been summarized before they are recorded in the general ledger. For example, an audit trail for sales would include a daily sales register that shows each individual sale transaction, a monthly sales journal that shows the total sales for each day, and the general ledger that has an entry for total sales for the month. With an audit trail, a user can trace any summary entry in the general ledger back to the individual transactions that make it up.

**Testing Design** During the design phase, test specifications are developed. The exact tests to be performed should be specified by someone other than the user or the systems analyst, although both should be consulted. Users and systems analysts have a tendency to test only what has been designed. An impartial third party, who has not been actively involved in the design, is more likely to design a test for, and therefore discover, a procedure or type of data that may have been overlooked in the design. Sometimes organizations avoid test design and test their systems with actual transactions. While such "live" testing is valuable, it might not test all conditions that the system is designed to process. This is especially true of error or exception conditions that do not occur regularly. For example, payroll systems are usually designed to reject input for hours worked over some limit, say 60 hours in a week. If only actual data are used to test the system, this limit may not be tested. Thus it is important to design testing specifications that will test each system control that is part of the system.

## Design Review

At the end of the design phase, management performs a **design review** and evaluates the work completed so far to determine whether or not to proceed (Figure 12-19). This is a critical point in any development project and all parties must take equal responsibility for the decision.

Usually the design review will result only in requests for clarification of a few items. But sometimes an entire project may be terminated. Although canceling or restarting a project from the beginning is a difficult decision, in the long run it is less costly than implementing the wrong or an inadequate solution. If the decision is made to proceed, the project enters the development phase. Before discussing the development phase, we describe prototyping, a development method that can be used in several phases of a system development project.

**FIGURE 12-19**
**The design review is a critical point in the development process. Representatives from the user and information systems departments and top management meet to determine if the system should be developed as designed or if additional design work is necessary.**

## Prototyping

**Prototyping** is building a working model of the new system. The advantage of prototyping is that it lets the user actually experience the system before it is completed. Some organizations use prototyping during the analysis phase, others use it during the design phase. Still other companies use prototyping to go directly from preliminary investigation to an implemented system. These companies just keep refining the prototype until the user says that it is acceptable. The disadvantage of such an accelerated approach is that key features of a new system, especially exception conditions, may be overlooked. Another disadvantage is that documentation, an important part of any system development effort, is usually not as well or as thoroughly prepared. When used as a tool to show the user how the system will operate, however, prototyping can be an important system development tool.

# PHASE 2—DESIGN AT SUTHERLAND

Upon approval by the management review committee, Mary Ruiz began designing the order entry and invoicing system. After studying existing manually prepared documents and talking to users, Mary designed printed reports and screen displays. According to Mike Charles, one of the most important reports is the daily invoice register. Using a report layout form (Figure 12-15), Mary showed Mike what the report would look like after it was programmed. Using a similar form for screen displays (Figure 12-16), Mary also showed Mike what the order clerks would see when they enter auto parts orders. To graphically show how the overall system would work, Mary prepared a system flowchart (Figure 12-17). The system flowchart showed that auto parts orders would be entered on terminals in the sales department and would use data in the Parts and Customer files to verify that the orders were valid. Shipping orders and invoices were two of the reports produced. An important part of Mary's design time involved specifying the system controls used during processing. These controls included verifying the customer number before processing the order and checking to see if the ordered part is in stock. If the ordered part is not in stock, the customer is notified immediately.

After completing her design work, Mary met with representatives from the user and information systems departments and top management to review her design. After Mary explained the design, the committee agreed to develop the system.

# PHASE 3—DEVELOPMENT

Once the system design phase has been completed, the project enters the system development phase. There are two parts to **development**: program development and equipment acquisition.

## Program Development

The process of developing the software, or programs, required for a system is called **program development** and includes the following steps: (1) reviewing the program specifications; (2) designing the program; (3) coding the program; (4) testing the program; and (5) finalizing the program documentation. The primary responsibility for completing these tasks is assumed by computer programmers who work closely with the system analyst who designed the system. Chapter 13 explains program development in depth. The important concepts to understand now are that this process is a part of the development phase of the information system life cycle and that its purpose is to develop the software required by the system.

## Equipment Acquisition

During the development phase, final decisions will be made on what additional equipment, if any, will be required for the new system. A preliminary review of the equipment requirements would have been done during the analysis phase and included in the written report prepared by the systems analyst. Making the equipment acquisition prior to the development phase would be premature because any equipment selected should be based on the requirements of the approved design from Phase 2. Equipment selection is affected by factors such as the number of users who will require terminals and the disk storage that will be required for new files and data elements. In some cases, even a new or upgraded CPU is required.

# PHASE 3—DEVELOPMENT AT SUTHERLAND

During the development phase, Mary worked closely with the two programmers who were assigned to the project. She regularly met with the programmers to answer questions about the design and to check on the progress of their work. Prior to starting the programming, Mary arranged for the programmers to meet with the auto parts sales employees so that the programmers would have a better understanding of the purpose of the new system.

When the programming was close to completion, Mary arranged for the terminals to be installed in the sales department.

# PHASE 4—IMPLEMENTATION

**Implementation** is the phase of the system development process when people actually begin using the new system. This is a critical phase of the project that usually requires careful timing and the coordination of all project participants. Important parts of this phase that will contribute to the success of the new system are training and education, conversion, and postimplementation evaluation.

## Training and Education

Someone once said, "If you think education is expensive, you should consider the cost without it." The point is that untrained users can prevent the estimated benefits of a new system from ever being obtained or worse, contribute to less efficiency and more costs than when the old system was operational. Training consists of showing people exactly how they will use the new system (Figure 12-20). This may include classroom-style lectures but should definitely include hands-on sessions with the equipment they will be using, such as terminals, and realistic sample data. Education consists of learning new principles or theories that help people to understand and use the system. For example, before implementing a modern manufacturing system, many companies now require their manufacturing personnel to attend classes on material requirements planning (MRP), shop floor control, and other essential manufacturing topics.

**FIGURE 12-20**
**All users should be trained on the system before they have to use it to process actual transactions. Training could include both classroom and hands-on sessions.**

## Conversion

**Conversion** refers to the process of changing from the old system to the new system. A number of different methods of conversion may be used including direct, parallel, phased, and pilot.

With **direct conversion**, the user stops using the old system one day and begins using the new system the next. The advantage of this approach is that it is fast and efficient. The disadvantage is that it is risky and can seriously disrupt operations if the new system does not work correctly the first time.

**Parallel conversion** consists of continuing to process data on the old system while some or all of the data is also processed on the new system. Results from both systems are compared, and if they agree, all data is switched to the new system (Figure 12-21).

**Phased conversion** is used with larger systems that can be broken down into individual modules that can be implemented separately at different times. An example would be a complete business system that could have the accounts receivable, inventory, and accounts payable modules implemented separately in phases. Phased conversions can be direct, parallel, or a combination of both.

**Pilot conversion** means that the new system will be used first by only a portion of the organization, often at a separate location such as a plant or office.

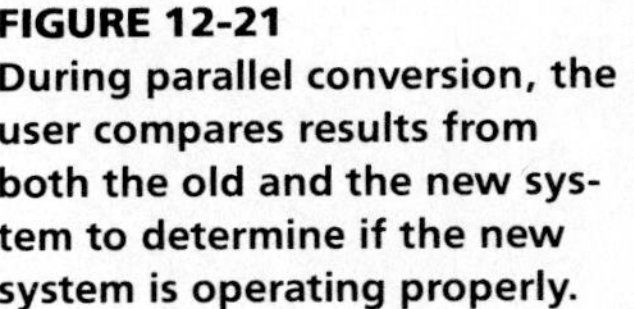

**FIGURE 12-21**
**During parallel conversion, the user compares results from both the old and the new system to determine if the new system is operating properly.**

## Postimplementation Evaluation

After a system is implemented, it is important to conduct a **postimplementation evaluation** to determine if the system is performing as designed, if operating costs are as anticipated, and if any modifications are necessary to make the system operate more effectively.

# PHASE 4—IMPLEMENTATION AT SUTHERLAND

Before they began using the new system to enter real transactions, the users participated in several training sessions about the equipment and the software. Because this was the first application in the auto parts division to be computerized, Mary began the training sessions with an overview of how the central computer system processes data. She conducted a basic data entry class to teach the employees how to use the terminals (Figure 12-20).

Before the system could be used, the Parts and Customer files had to be created from existing manual records. Temporary employees trained in data entry skills were hired for this task. Their work was carefully reviewed each day by Mike Charles and other permanent department employees.

Although he knew it would mean extra work, Mike decided that a parallel conversion would be the safest way to implement the new system. Using this method, Mike could verify the results of the new system with those of the existing manual system. Actual use of the system began on the first business day of the month so that transaction totals could be balanced to accounting reports.

Because they were thoroughly trained, the order clerks felt comfortable when they began entering real orders. A few minor problems were encountered, such as orders for special parts that were not on the Parts file. These errors became less frequent and at the end of the month, after comparing manual and computerized report totals, Mike decided to discontinue the use of the manual system.

During the postimplementation review, Mike and Mary discovered that nine out of ten customer orders were now shipped the same day as the order was received. Before the new system was implemented, less than half the orders were shipped within two days of receipt. Invoices, which once lagged three days behind shipments, were now mailed on the same day. Perhaps the most positive benefit of the new system was that customer complaints about order processing were practically eliminated.

## PHASE 5—MAINTENANCE

**Maintenance** is the process of supporting the system after it is implemented. Maintenance consists of three activities: performance monitoring, change management, and error correction.

### Performance Monitoring

**Performance monitoring** is the ongoing process of comparing response times, file sizes, and other system performance measures against the estimates that were prepared during the analysis, design, and implementation phases. Variances from these estimates may indicate that the system requires additional equipment resources, such as more memory or faster disk drives.

### Change Management

Change is an inevitable part of any system and should be provided for with methods and procedures that are made known to all users of the system. Sometimes changes are required because existing requirements were overlooked. Other times, new information requirements caused by external sources such as government regulations will force change. A key part of change management is documentation. The same documentation standards that were followed during the analysis and design phases should also be used to record changes. In fact, in many organizations, the same document that is used to request new systems (Figure 12-7) is used to request changes to an existing system (Figure 12-22). Thus the information system development cycle continues as Phase 1 (analysis) begins on the change request.

## Error Correction

Error correction deals with problems that are caused by programming and design errors that are discovered after the system is implemented. Often these errors are minor problems, such as the zip code not appearing on a name and address report, that can be quickly fixed by a programmer. Other times, however, the error requires some level of investigation by the systems analyst before a correction can be determined.

# PHASE 5—MAINTENANCE AT SUTHERLAND

During the months following the system implementation, a number of minor programming errors were discovered. Most of these errors were quickly corrected by the programming staff but in one case involving special credit terms for a large customer, Mary Ruiz had to become involved and had to prepare specifications for the necessary program changes.

Approximately one year after Mike Charles submitted his original request for a computerized order entry and invoicing system, he submitted another request (Figure 12-22) for a change to the system to provide for a new county sales tax. This type of request does not require a preliminary investigation and will be assigned to Mary Ruiz as soon as she is available. Mike submitted his request five months before the tax was scheduled to go into effect, which should allow ample time for the necessary program changes to be implemented.

REQUEST FOR SYSTEM SERVICES

ISD CONTROL #: 4703

I. To Be Completed By Person Requesting Services

SUBMITTED BY: MIKE CHARLES DEPT AUTO PARTS SALES DATE: 2-1-91

REQUEST TYPE: ☑ MODIFICATION ☐ NEW SYSTEM

NEED: ☑ ASAP ☐ IMMEDIATE ☐ LONG RANGE

BRIEF STATEMENT OF REQUEST (attach additional material, if necessary)

SALES INVOICE PROGRAM NEEDS TO PROVIDE FOR 1% COUNTY TAX THAT WILL GO INTO EFFECT JULY 1, 1991.

☑ ADDITIONAL MATERIAL ATTACHED COUNTY TAX RATE SCHEDULE

II. To Be Completed By Information Systems Department

REQUEST INVESTIGATED BY: ____ DATE: ____

COMMENTS: ____

III. Disposition

☐ REQUEST APPROVED FOR IMMEDIATE IMPLEMENTATION

☐ Analyst assigned: ____

☐ REQUEST APPROVED FOR IMPLEMENTATION AS SOON AS POSSIBLE

☐ REQUEST REJECTED

COMMENTS: ____

SIGNED: ____ DATE: ____

**FIGURE 12-22**
**The same form that was used to request a new system (see Figure 12-7) is also used to request a modification to an existing system.**

# SUMMARY OF THE INFORMATION SYSTEM DEVELOPMENT LIFE CYCLE

Although the information system development process may appear to be a straightforward series of steps, in practice it is a challenging activity that calls for the skills and cooperation of all involved. New development tools have made the process more efficient but the success of any project always depends on the commitment of the project participants. The understanding you have gained from this chapter will help you participate in information system development projects and give you an appreciation for the importance of each phase.

# CHAPTER SUMMARY

1. An **information system** is a collection of six elements, equipment, software, data, personnel, users, and procedures, that provide accurate, timely and useful information.
2. There are four types of information systems: (1) **operational systems**; (2) **management information systems**; (3) **decision support systems**; and (4) **expert systems**.
3. The trend is to combine all of an organization's information needs into a single integrated information system.
4. The **information system development life cycle** is an organized approach to developing an information system and consists of five phases: analysis, design, development, implementation, and maintenance.
5. Planning, scheduling, reporting, and controlling the individual activities that make up the information system development life cycle is called **project management**. These activities are usually recorded in a **project plan**.
6. **Documentation** refers to written materials that are produced throughout the information system development life cycle.
7. All users and information system personnel who will be affected by the new system should have the opportunity to participate in its development.
8. The systems analyst's job is a challenging one requiring good communication, analytical, and diplomatic skills to keep the development process on track and on schedule.
9. The **analysis** phase is the separation of a system into its parts in order to determine how the system works. This phase consists of the preliminary investigation, detailed system analysis, and making the decision to proceed.
10. The purpose of the **preliminary investigation** is to determine if a request warrants further detailed investigation. The most important aspect of this investigation is **problem definition**.
11. **Detailed system analysis** involves both a thorough study of the current system and as least one proposed solution to any problems found.
12. **Data flow diagrams** are a **structured analysis** tool that graphically show the flow of data through a system.
13. Other tools that are used in the analysis phase include **data dictionaries**, **process specifications**, **structured English**, **decision tables**, and **decision trees**.
14. A **feasibility study** and **cost/benefit analysis** are often prepared to show whether the proposed solution is practical and to show the estimated costs and benefits that are expected.
15. During the **design** phase the **logical design** that was created in the analysis phase is transformed into a **physical design**.
16. There are two major structured design methods: **top-down design** (or **structured design**) and **bottom-up design**.
17. **Output design**, **input design**, and **database design** all occur during the design phase.
18. When designing interactive systems, the systems analyst and user determine the sequence of inputs and computer responses, called a **dialogue**.
19. During the **process design** the systems analyst specifies exactly what actions will be taken on the input data to create output information.
20. One method of documenting the relationship of different processes is with a **system flowchart**.
21. A **structured walkthrough**, or a step-by-step review, is sometimes performed on the process design.
22. **System controls** ensure that only valid data is accepted and processed. Types of system controls include **source document controls**, **input controls**, **processing controls**, and **accounting controls**, including an **audit trail**.
23. At the end of the design phase, a **design review** is performed to evaluate the work completed so far.
24. **Prototyping** is building a working model of the new system.
25. The **development** phase consists of program development and equipment acquisition.
26. **Program development** includes: (1) reviewing the program specifications; (2) designing the program; (3) coding the program; (4) testing the program; and (5) finalizing the program documentation.
27. The **implementation** phase is when people actually begin using the new system. This phase includes training and education, conversion, and the **postimplementation evaluation**.
28. The process of changing from the old system to the new system is called a **conversion**. The conversion methods that may be used are **direct**, **parallel**, **phased**, and **pilot**.
29. The **maintenance** phase is the process of supporting the information system after it is implemented. It consists of three activities: **performance monitoring**, change management, and error correction.

## KEY TERMS

Accounting controls *12.14*
Analysis *12.6*
Artificial intelligence *12.4*
Audit trail *12.14*
Bottom-up design *12.11*
Conversion *12.17*
Cost/benefit analysis *12.9*
Database design *12.12*
Data dictionary *12.8*
Data flow diagram (DFD) *12.8*
Decision support systems *12.4*
Decision table *12.9*
Decision tree *12.9*
Design *12.11*
Design review *12.14*
Detailed system analysis *12.7*
Development *12.16*
Dialogue *12.12*
Direct conversion *12.17*
Documentation *12.6*
Expert systems *12.4*
Feasibility study *12.9*
Implementation *12.16*
Inference rules *12.4*
Information system *12.2*
Information system development life cycle (SDLC) *12.5*
Input controls *12.14*
Input design *12.12*
Knowledge base *12.4*
Logical design *12.11*
Maintenance *12.18*
Management information system (MIS) *12.3*
Operational system *12.3*
Output design *12.11*
Parallel conversion *12.17*
Performance monitoring *12.18*
Phased conversion *12.17*
Physical design *12.11*
Pilot conversion *12.17*
Postimplementation evaluation *12.17*
Preliminary investigation *12.7*
Problem definition *12.7*
Process design *12.12*
Processing controls *12.14*
Process specifications *12.9*
Program development *12.16*
Project management *12.5*
Project plan *12.5*
Prototyping *12.15*
Source document controls *12.14*
Structured analysis *12.8*
Structured design *12.11*
Structured English *12.9*
Structured walkthrough *12.14*
System controls *12.14*
System flowchart *12.12*
Top-down design *12.11*

## REVIEW QUESTIONS

1. List the six elements of an information system.
2. What are the four types of information systems? What is meant by integrated information systems?
3. List the five phases of the information system development life cycle.
4. Describe project management and when it should be performed.
5. What is the preliminary investigation? What is the most important aspect of the preliminary investigation?
6. Briefly describe detailed system analysis. What are the fact-finding techniques used during detailed system analysis?
7. What are the symbols used in data flow diagrams? Why are data flow diagram useful?
8. Explain the difference between the logical and physical design of an information system.
9. What are the two methods of structured design? Briefly describe each method.
10. List and describe four basic types of system controls.
11. What is prototyping?
12. What are the steps in program development?
13. Write a description of the four types of conversion methods.
14. Describe the three major activities of system maintenance.

## CONTROVERSIAL ISSUES

1. Large systems may take several years to design and implement. Some experts argue that undertaking such a task is ridiculous because the needs of the users and the technology will change so much during the time it takes to implement the system that it will be obsolete before it is implemented. Others point out that there are really no alternatives. What do you think?
2. "The difficulty in developing and implementing an information processing system is the user," proclaimed a systems analyst. "Users never know what they want. When they are shown what the system will do, they give their approval, but when the system is implemented they are never happy. They always want changes. It's impossible to satisfy them." How do you feel about these comments? Are the systems analyst's comments about users correct?

## RESEARCH PROJECTS

1. Today there are many software packages available for personal computers to help systems analysts with the tasks they perform during the information system development life cycle. Write a report on one of these packages and be prepared to discuss it in class.
2. Prepare a data flow diagram of how you registered for class. Document your work by obtaining copies of any forms that were used during the registration process.

CHAPTER 13

# Program Development

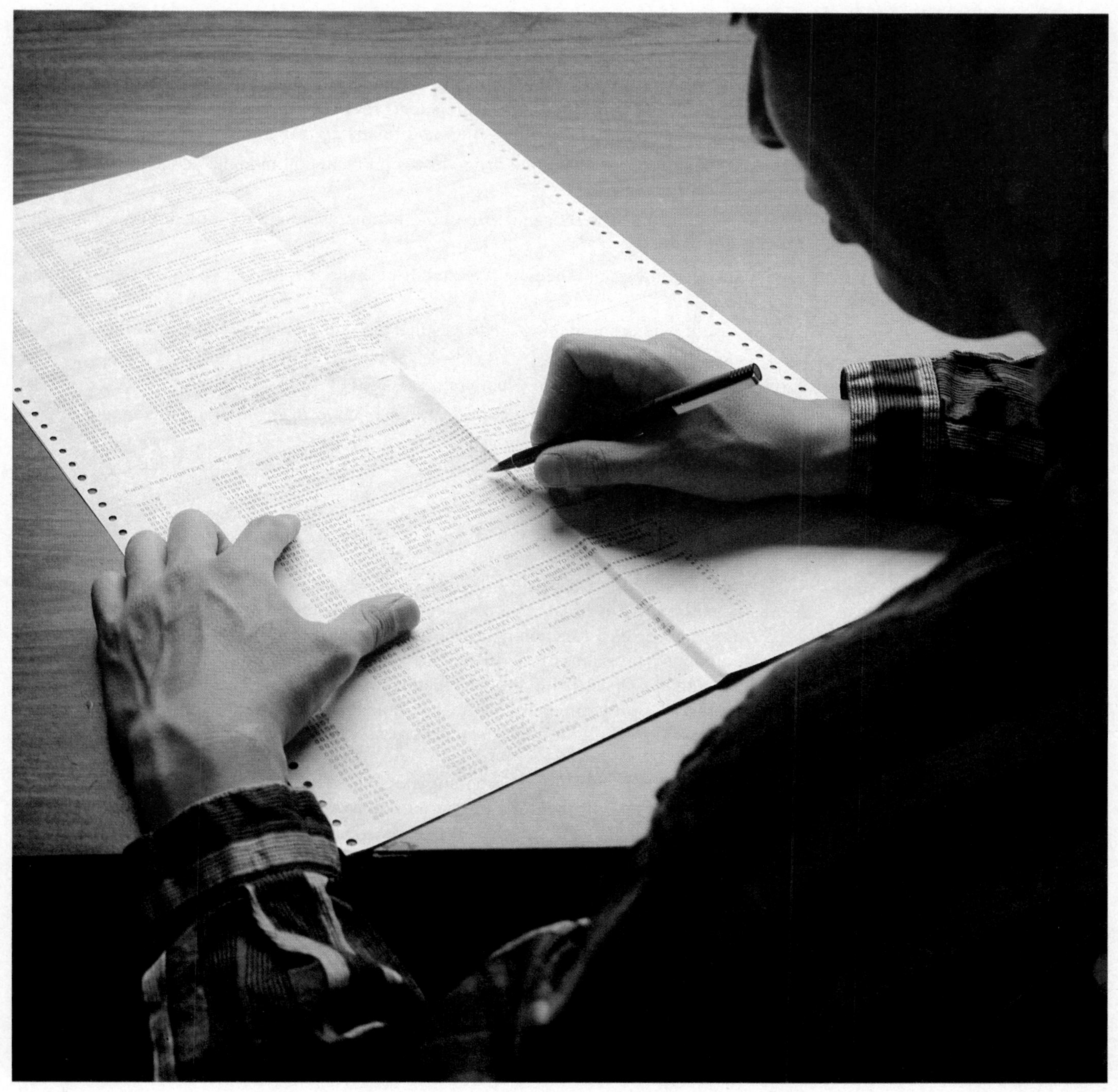

CHAPTER 13

# Program Development

## OBJECTIVES

- Define the term computer program.
- Describe the five steps in program development: review of program specifications, program design, program coding, program testing, and finalizing program documentation.
- Explain the concepts of structured program design including modules, control structures, and single entry/single exit.
- Explain and illustrate the sequence, selection, and iteration control structures used in structured programming.
- Define the term programming language and discuss the various categories of programming languages.
- Briefly discuss the programming languages that are commonly used today, including BASIC, COBOL, C, FORTRAN, Pascal, Ada, and RPG.
- Explain and discuss application generators.
- Explain the factors that should be considered when choosing a programming language.

---

As we discussed in Chapter 12, the information system development life cycle covers the entire process of taking a plan for processing information through various phases until it becomes a functioning information system. During the development phase of this cycle, computer programs are written. The purpose of these programs is to process data and produce output as specified in the information system design. This chapter focuses on the steps taken to write a program and the available tools that make the program development process more efficient. In addition, this chapter discusses the different languages used to write programs.

Although you may never write a program yourself, it is likely that you will someday request information that will require a program to be written or modified. Therefore it is important for you to understand the process that takes place when a computer program is developed.

## WHAT IS A COMPUTER PROGRAM?

A **computer program** is a detailed set of instructions that directs a computer to perform the tasks necessary to process data into information. These instructions, usually written by a computer programmer, can be coded (written) in a variety of programming languages that will be discussed later in this chapter. To create programs that are correct (produce accurate information) and maintainable (easy to modify), programmers follow a process called program development.

## WHAT IS PROGRAM DEVELOPMENT?

In the early days of computing, programming was considered an "art" and the programming process was left to the "interpretation" of the programmer. While there is still room for creativity, **program development**, the process of producing one or more programs to perform one or more specific tasks on a computer, has evolved into a series of five steps that most experts agree should take place when any program is developed. These five steps (Figure 13-1) are:

1. Review of program specifications. The programmer reviews the specifications created by the system analyst during the system design phase.
2. Program design. The programmer determines the specific actions the program will take to accomplish the desired tasks.
3. Coding. The programmer writes the actual program instructions.
4. Testing. The written programs are tested to make sure they perform as intended.
5. Finalizing documentation. The documentation produced during the program development process is brought together and organized.

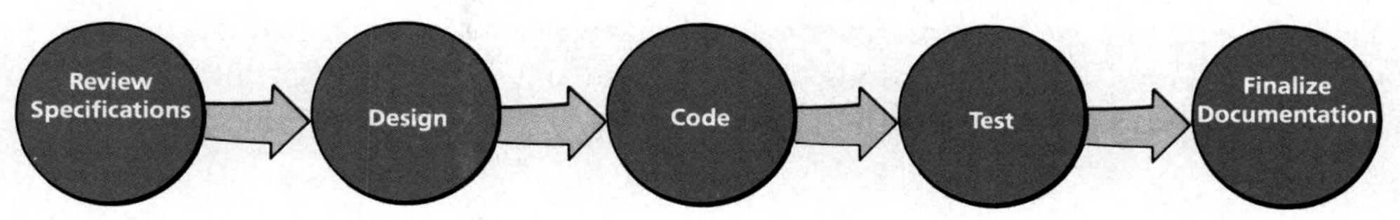


**FIGURE 13-1**
**The five steps of program development.**

## STEP 1—REVIEW OF PROGRAM SPECIFICATIONS

The first step in the program development cycle is a review of the program specifications. **Program specifications** can consists of data flow diagrams, system flowcharts, process specifications that indicate the action to be taken on the data, a data dictionary identifying the data elements that will be used, screen formats, and report layouts. These documents help the programmer understand the work that needs to be done by the program. Because it is important that the programmer understands the purpose of the program from the user's point of view, one or more meetings are usually held between the programmer, the user, and the systems analyst who designed the system.

If the programmer believes some aspect of the design should be changed, such as a screen layout, it is discussed with the analyst and the user. If the change is agreed on, the design specification is changed. However, the programmer should not change the specified system without the agreement of the analyst and user. If a change is authorized, it should be recorded in the system design. The analyst and user, through the system design, have specified *what* is to be done. It is the programmer's job to determine *how* to do it.

Large programming jobs are usually assigned to more than one programmer. In these situations, a good system design is essential so that each programmer can be given a logical portion of the system to be programmed.

# STEP 2—PROGRAM DESIGN

After the program specifications have been carefully reviewed, program design begins. During **program design** a logical solution to the programming task is developed and documented. The logical solution or **logic** for a program is a step-by-step solution to a programming problem. Determining the logic for a computer program can be an extremely complex task. To aid in program design and development, a method called structured program design is commonly used.

## Structured Program Design

**Structured program design** is a methodology that emphasizes three main program design concepts: modules, control structures, and single entry/single exit. Use of these concepts helps to create programs that are easy to write, read, understand, check for errors, and modify.

**Modules** With structured design, programming problems are "decomposed" (separated) into smaller parts called modules. Each **module**, sometimes referred to as a **subroutine** in programming, performs a given task within the program. The major benefit of this technique is that it simplifies program development because each module of a program can be developed individually. When the modules are combined, they form a complete program that accomplishes the desired result.

**Structure charts**, also called **hierarchy charts**, are often used to decompose and represent the modules of a program. When the program decomposition is completed, the entire structure of a program is illustrated by the hierarchy chart and the relationship of the modules within the program is shown (Figure 13-2).

**FIGURE 13-2**
**A structure chart graphically illustrates the relationship of individual program modules.**

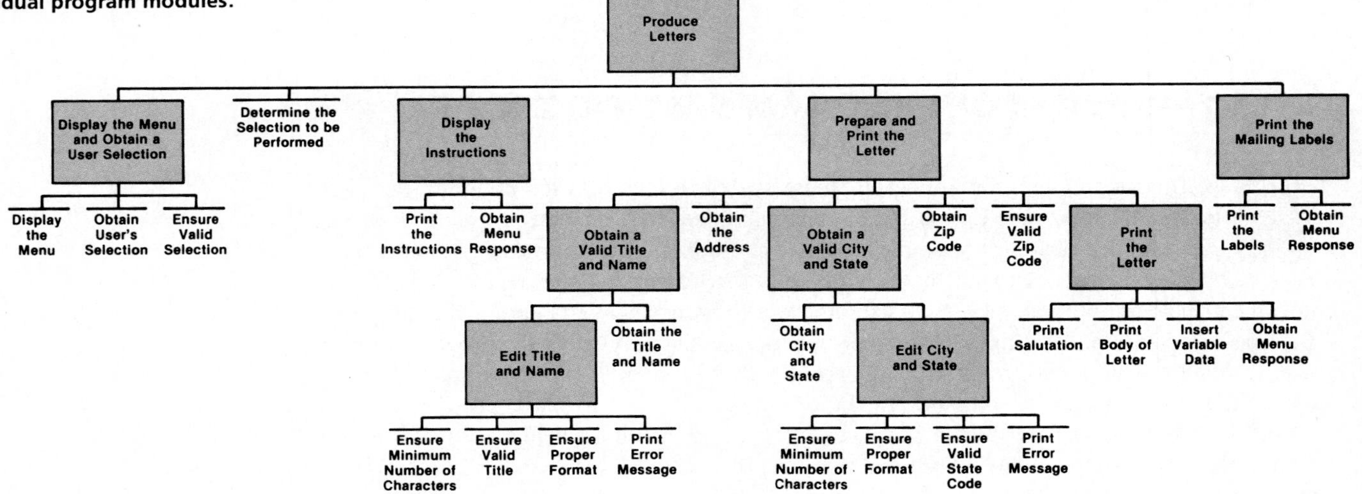


**Control Structures** In structured program design three basic **control structures** are used to form the logic of a program. All logic problems can be solved by a combination of these structures. The three basic control structures are: sequence, selection, and iteration.

In the **sequence structure**, one process occurs immediately after another. In Figure 13-3, each rectangular box represents a particular process that is to take place. For example, a process could be a computer instruction to move data from one location in main memory to another location. Each process takes place in the exact sequence specified, one process followed by the next.

The second control structure, called the **selection** or **if-then-else structure**, gives programmers a way to represent conditional program logic (Figure 13-4). Conditional program logic can be expressed in the following way: *If* the condition is true, *then* perform the true condition processing, *else* perform the false condition processing. When the if-then-else control structure is used, the "if" portion of the structure tests a given condition. The true portion of the statement is executed if the condition tested is true and the false portion of the statement is executed if the condition is false. For example, in a payroll program the number of hours worked might be tested to determine if an employee worked overtime. If the person did work overtime, the true portion of the statement would be executed and overtime would be calculated. If the employee did not work overtime, then the false portion of the statement would be executed and overtime would not be calculated. The selection or if-then-else structure is used by programmers to represent conditional logic problems.

The third control structure, called **iteration** or **looping**, means that one or more processes continue to occur so long as a given condition remains true. There are two forms of this control structure: the **do-while structure** and the **do-until structure** (Figure 13-5). In the do-while structure a condition is tested. If the condition is true, the process is performed. The program then "loops" back and tests the condition again. If the condition is still true, the process is performed again. This looping continues until the condition being tested is false. At that time, the program exits the loop and performs some other processing. An example of this type of testing would be a check to see if all records have been processed. The do-until control structure is similar to the do-while except that the conditional test is at the end instead of the beginning of the loop. Processing continues "until" the condition is met.

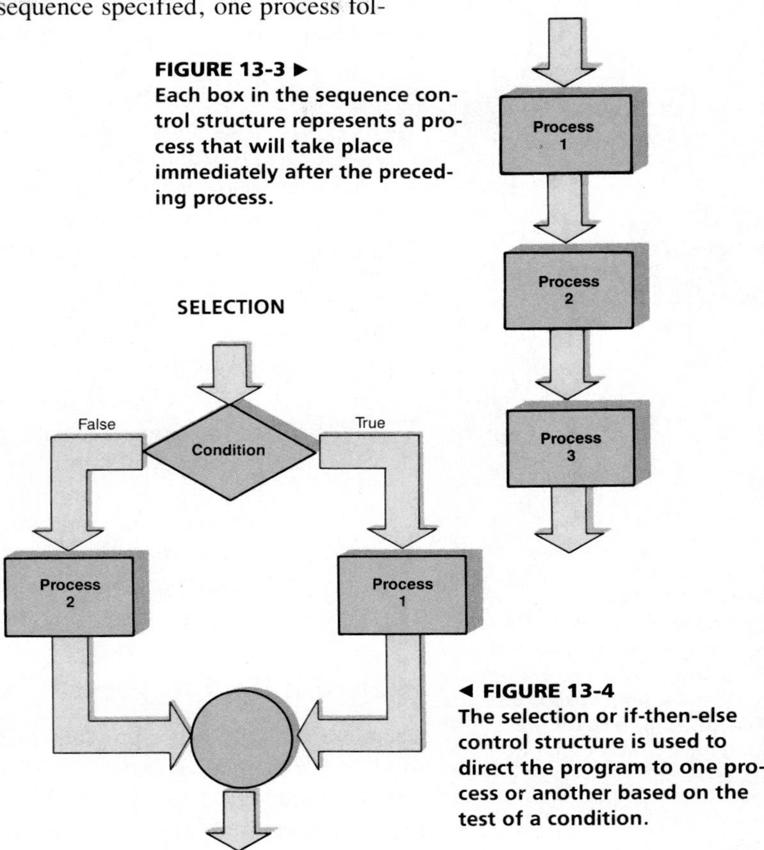


**FIGURE 13-3 ▶**
**Each box in the sequence control structure represents a process that will take place immediately after the preceding process.**

**◀ FIGURE 13-4**
**The selection or if-then-else control structure is used to direct the program to one process or another based on the test of a condition.**

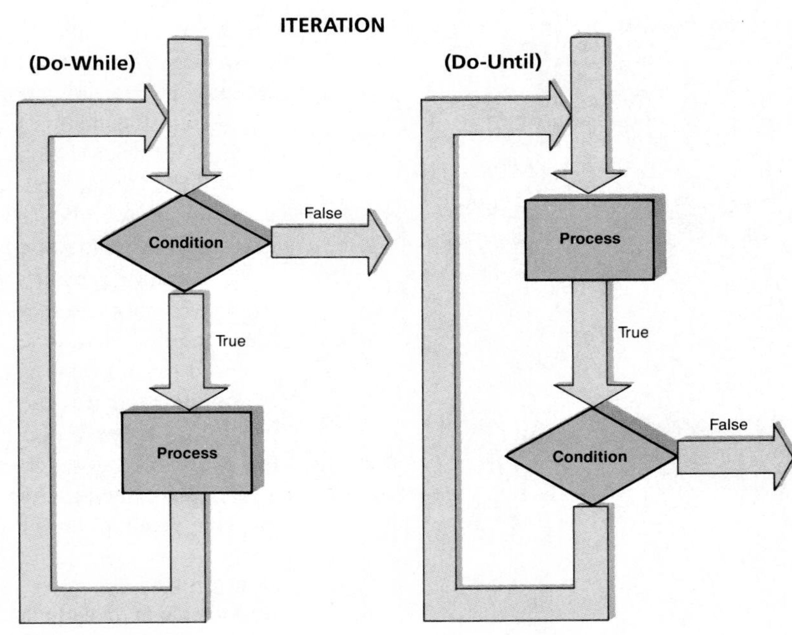


**FIGURE 13-5 ▶**
**The iteration control structure has two forms, do-while and do-until. In the do-while structure, the condition is tested before the process. In the do-until structure, the condition is tested after the process.**

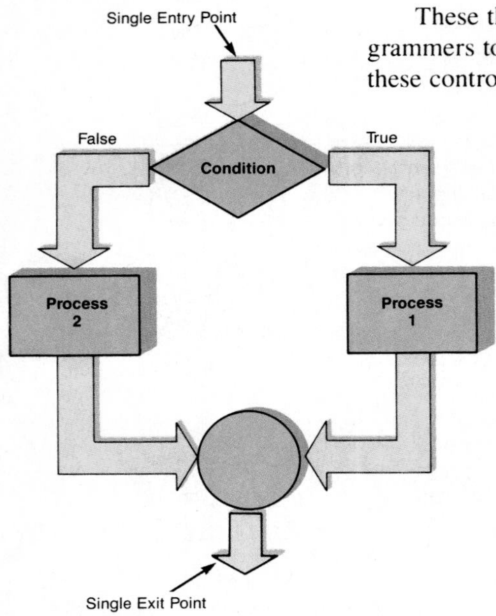


**FIGURE 13-6 ▲**
**Structured programming concepts require that all control structures have a single entry point and a single exit point. This contributes to programming logic that is easier to understand.**

These three control structures, sequence, selection, and iteration, are combined by programmers to create program logic solutions. A structured program design rule that applies to these control structures and how they are combined is the single entry/single exit rule.

**Single Entry/Single Exit** An important concept in structured programming is **single entry/single exit**, meaning that there is only one entry point and one exit point for each of the three control structures. An **entry point** is the point where a control structure is entered. An **exit point** is the point where the control structure is exited. For example, in Figure 13-6, when the if-then-else structure is used, the control structure is entered at the point where the condition is tested. When the condition is tested, one set of instructions will be executed if the condition is true and another set will be executed if the condition is false. Regardless of the result of the test, however, the structure is exited at the single exit point.

This feature substantially improves the understanding of a program because, when reading the program, the programmer can be assured that whatever happens within the if-then-else structure, the control structure will always be exited at a common point. Prior to the use of structured programming, many programmers would transfer control to other parts of a program without following the single entry/single exit rule. This practice led to poorly designed programs that were extremely difficult to read, check for errors, and modify.

## Program Design Tools

There are several popular program design tools through which structured program design concepts can be applied. These design tools are used by computer programmers to develop and document the logical solutions to the problems they are programming. Three of these design tools are program flowcharts, pseudocode, and Warnier-Orr.

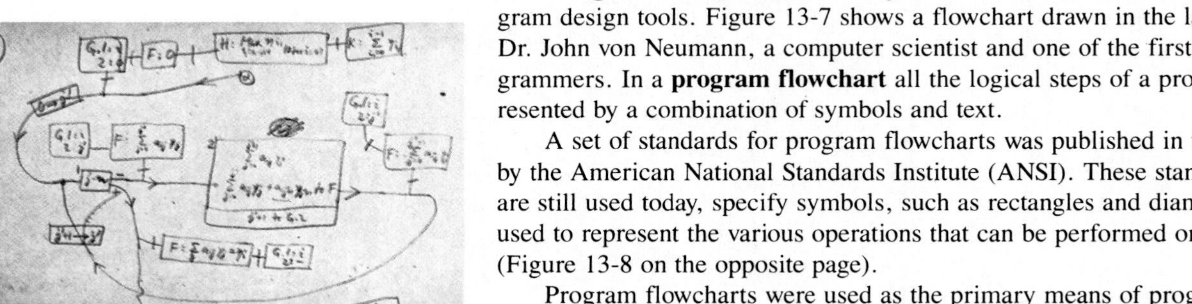

**Program Flowcharts** Program flowcharts were one of the first program design tools. Figure 13-7 shows a flowchart drawn in the late 1940s by Dr. John von Neumann, a computer scientist and one of the first computer programmers. In a **program flowchart** all the logical steps of a program are represented by a combination of symbols and text.

A set of standards for program flowcharts was published in the early 1960s by the American National Standards Institute (ANSI). These standards, which are still used today, specify symbols, such as rectangles and diamonds, that are used to represent the various operations that can be performed on a computer (Figure 13-8 on the opposite page).

Program flowcharts were used as the primary means of program design for many years prior to the introduction of structured program design. During these years, programmers designed programs by focusing on the detailed steps required for a program and creating logical solutions for each new combination of conditions as it was encountered. Developing programs in this manner led to programs that were poorly designed. Today, programmers are taught to apply the structured design concepts when preparing program flowcharts (Figure 13-9). When the basic control structures are utilized, program flowcharts are a valuable program design tool.

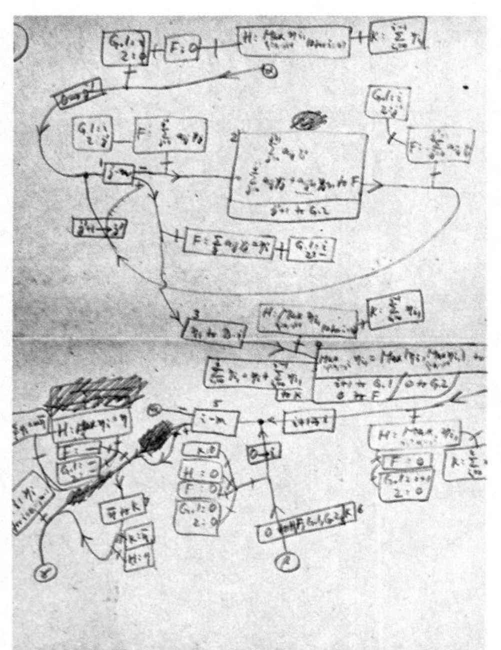

**◀ FIGURE 13-7**
**An example of an early flowchart developed by computer scientist Dr. John von Neumann in the 1940s to solve a problem involving game theory.**

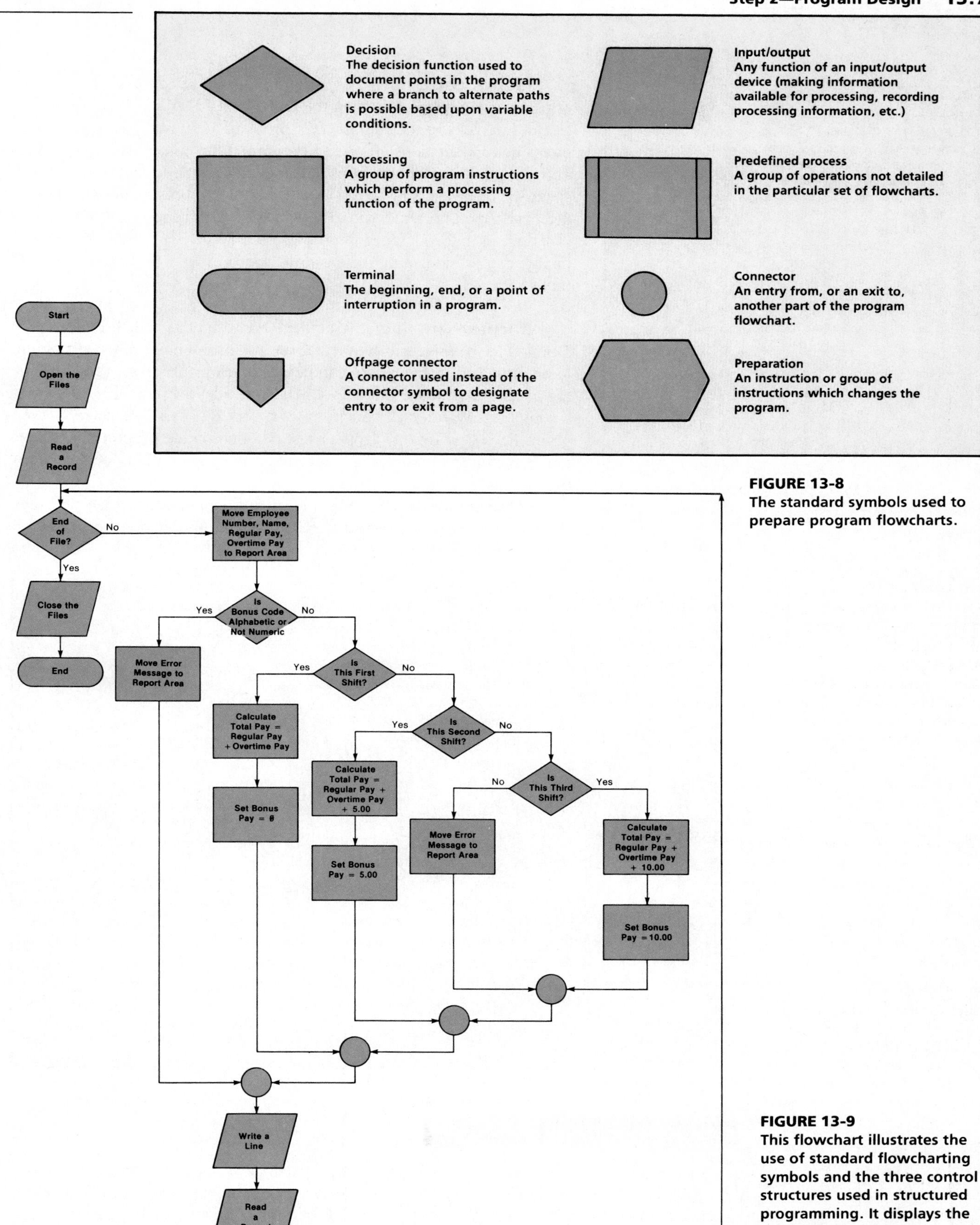


**FIGURE 13-8**
The standard symbols used to prepare program flowcharts.

**FIGURE 13-9**
This flowchart illustrates the use of standard flowcharting symbols and the three control structures used in structured programming. It displays the logic required to solve a payroll calculation task.

```
Open the files
Read a record
PERFORM UNTIL end of file
    Move employee number, name, regular pay, and
        overtime pay to the report area
    IF bonus code is alphabetic or not numeric
        Move error message to report area
    ELSE
        IF first shift
            Calculate total pay = regular pay +
                overtime pay
            Set bonus pay to zero
        ELSE
            IF second shift
                Calculate total pay = regular pay +
                    overtime pay + 5.00
                Set bonus pay to 5.00
            ELSE
                IF third shift
                    Calculate total pay = regular pay +
                        overtime pay + 10.00
                    Set bonus pay to 10.00
                ELSE
                    Move error message to report area
                ENDIF
            ENDIF
        ENDIF
    ENDIF
    Write a line
    Read a record
ENDPERFORM
Close the files
End the program
```

**FIGURE 13-10**
**This pseudocode is another way of documenting the logic shown in the flowchart in Figure 13-9.**

**Pseudocode** Some experts in program design advocate the use of pseudocode when designing the logic for a program. In **pseudocode** the logical steps in the solution of a problem are written as English statements and indentations are used to represent the control structures (Figure 13-10). An advantage of pseudocode is that it eliminates the time spent with flowcharting to draw and arrange symbols while attempting to determine the program logic. The major disadvantage is that unlike flowcharting, pseudocode does not provide a graphic representation, which many people find useful and easier to interpret when examining programming logic.

**Warnier-Orr** In the **Warnier-Orr** technique (named after Jean-Dominique Warnier and Kenneth Orr), the programmer analyzes output to be produced from an application and develops processing modules that are needed to produce the output. The example in Figure 13-11 illustrates a completed Warnier-Orr diagram for a checkbook-balancing report program. Each bracket ( { ) represents a module in the program. The statements within the brackets identify the processing that is to occur within the modules.

Regardless of the design tool used, it is important that the program design is efficient and correct. To help ensure this, many organizations use structured walkthroughs.

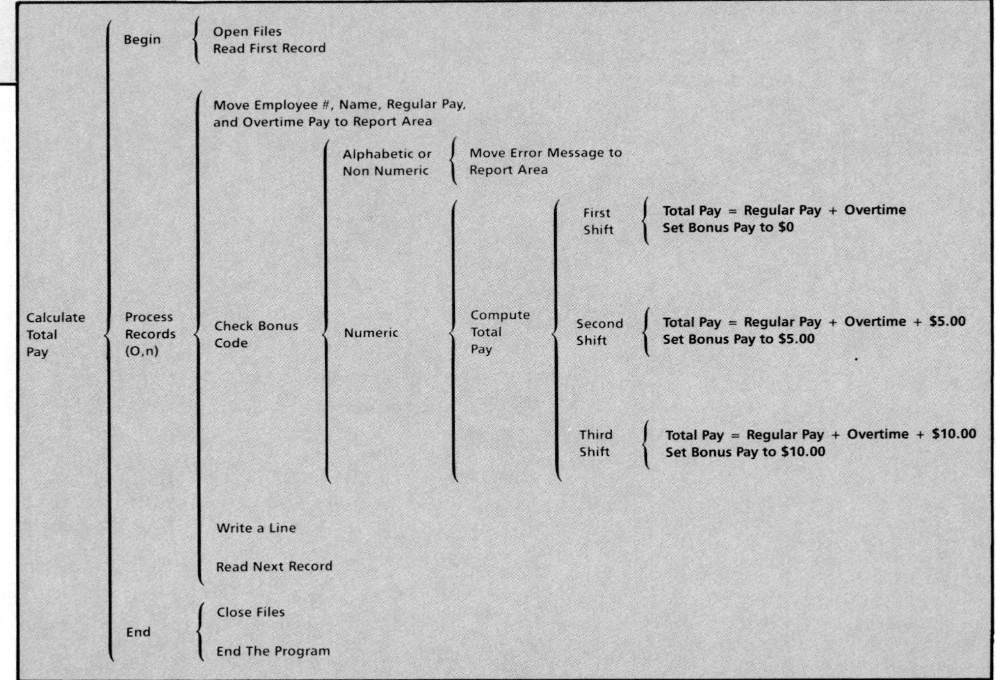


**FIGURE 13-11**
**This Warnier-Orr diagram illustrates the logic for the payroll calculation problem also used for Figures 13-9 and 13-10.**

## Structured Walkthroughs

After a program has been designed, the programmer schedules a structured walkthrough of the program. The programmer, other programmers in the department, and the systems analyst attend. During the walkthrough, the programmer who designs the program explains the program logic. The purpose of the design walkthrough is to review the logic of the program for errors, and if possible, improve program design. It is much better to find errors and make needed changes to the program during the design step than to make them later in the program development process.

Once the program design is complete, the coding of the program begins.

## STEP 3—PROGRAM CODING

**Coding** the program refers to the process of writing the program instructions that will process the data and produce the output specified in the program design. As previously mentioned, programs are written in different languages that each have particular rules on how to instruct the computer to perform specific tasks, such as read a record or multiply two numbers. The differences in these languages will be discussed later in this chapter.

If a thorough program design has been produced, the coding process is greatly simplified and can sometimes be a one-for-one translation of a design step into a program step. Today, program code, or instructions, are usually entered directly into the computer via a terminal and stored on a disk drive. Using this approach, the programmer can partially enter a program at one time and finish entering it at a later time. Program instructions are added, deleted, and changed until the programmer believes the program design has been fully translated into program instructions and the program is ready for testing.

## STEP 4—PROGRAM TESTING

Before a program is used to process "real" data and produce information that people rely on, it should be thoroughly tested to make sure it is functioning correctly. Several different types of tests can be performed.

**Desk checking** is the process of reading the program and mentally reviewing its logic. This is a simple process that can be performed by the programmer who wrote the program or by another programmer. This process can be compared with proofreading a letter before you put it in the mail. The disadvantage of this method is that it is difficult to detect other than obvious errors.

Another type of testing identifies program **syntax errors**, violations of the grammar rules of the language in which the program was written. An example of a syntax error would be the program command READ being misspelled REED. Syntax errors missed by the programmer are discovered by the computer when it decodes the program instructions.

Logic testing is what most programmers think of when the term testing is used. During **logic testing**, the sequence of program instructions is tested to make sure they provide the correct result. Logic errors may be the result of a programming oversight, such as using the wrong data to perform a calculation, or a design error, such as forgetting to specify that some customers do not have to pay sales tax when they purchase merchandise.

Logic testing is performed with **test data**, data that simulates the type of input that the program will process when it is implemented. In order to obtain an independent and unbiased test of the program, test data and the review of test results should be the responsibility of someone other than the programmer who wrote the program. The test data should be developed by referring to the system design but should also try to "break" the program by including data outside the range of data that will be input during normal operations. For example, even though a payroll program should never have more than 60 hours per week input, the program should be designed, coded, and tested to properly process transactions in excess of 60 hours by displaying an error message or in some other way indicating that an invalid number

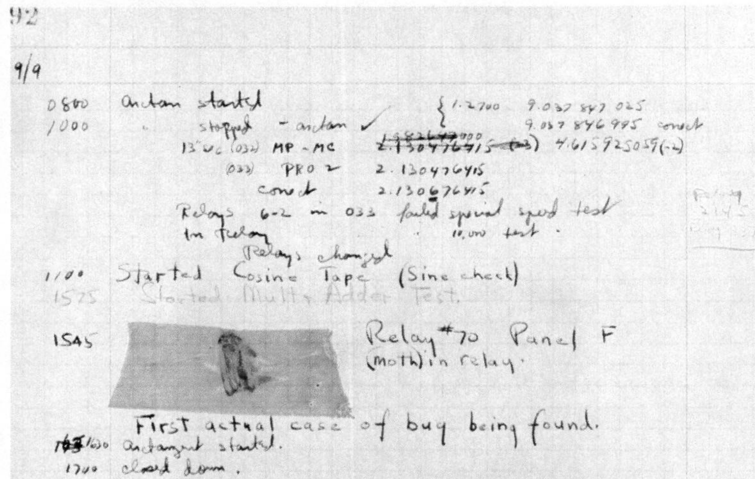


**FIGURE 13-12**
**In 1945, the cause of the temporary failure of the world's first electromechanical computer, the Mark I, was traced to a dead moth caught in the electrical components. The term "bug," meaning a computer error, has been part of computer jargon ever since.**

of hours has been entered. Other similar tests should include alphabetic data when only numeric data is expected, and negative numbers when only positive numbers are normally input.

One of the more colorful terms of the computer industry is **debugging**, which refers to the process of locating and correcting program errors or **bugs** found during testing. The term was coined when the failure of one of the first computers was traced to a moth that had become lodged in the electronic components (Figure 13-12).

## STEP 5—FINALIZING PROGRAM DOCUMENTATION

Documentation is an essential but sometimes neglected part of the programming process. As reflected in the title of this section, documentation should be an ongoing part of developing a program and should only be finalized, meaning organized and brought together, after the program is successfully tested and ready for implementation. The difficulty in sometimes obtaining adequate documentation is that many programmers can and do develop programs without it; when the program is completed, they have little incentive to go back and complete the documentation "after the fact." In addition to helping programmers develop programs, documentation is valuable because it helps the next programmer who, six months or one year later, is asked to make a change to the program. Proper documentation can substantially reduce the amount of time the new programmer will have to spend learning enough about the program to know how best to make the change.

Documentation developed during the programming process should include a narrative description of the program, program flowcharts, pseudocode, program listings, and test results. Comments in the program itself are also an important part of program documentation (Figure 13-13).

**FIGURE 13-13**
**Most programming languages allow explanatory comments to be placed directly in the program. This is an effective way of documenting the program.**

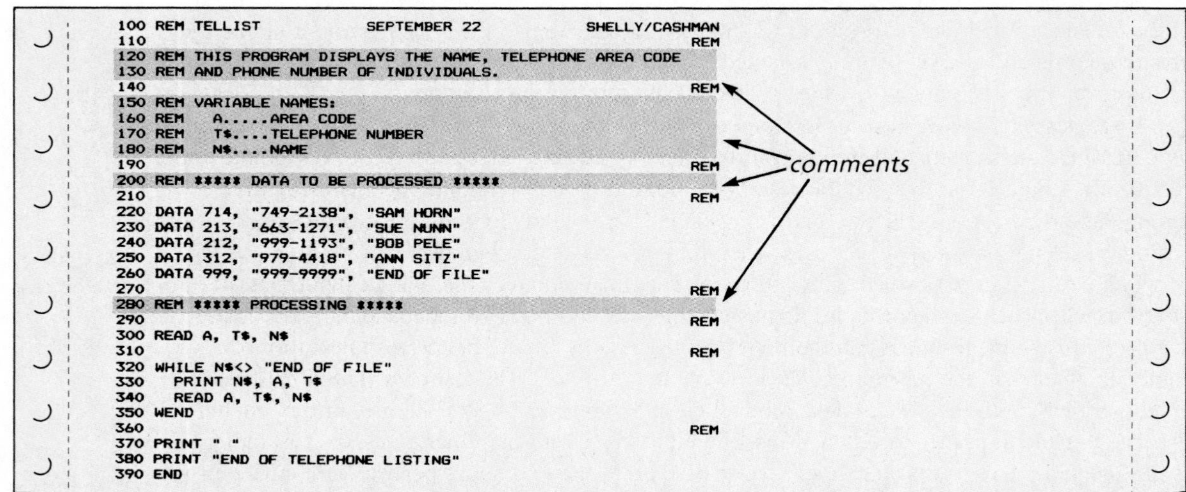

```
100 REM TELLIST           SEPTEMBER 22          SHELLY/CASHMAN
110                                                        REM
120 REM THIS PROGRAM DISPLAYS THE NAME, TELEPHONE AREA CODE
130 REM AND PHONE NUMBER OF INDIVIDUALS.
140                                                        REM
150 REM VARIABLE NAMES:
160 REM    A.....AREA CODE
170 REM    T$....TELEPHONE NUMBER
180 REM    N$....NAME
190                                                        REM
200 REM ***** DATA TO BE PROCESSED *****
210                                                        REM
220 DATA 714, "749-2138", "SAM HORN"
230 DATA 213, "663-1271", "SUE NUNN"
240 DATA 212, "999-1193", "BOB PELE"
250 DATA 312, "979-4418", "ANN SITZ"
260 DATA 999, "999-9999", "END OF FILE"
270                                                        REM
280 REM ***** PROCESSING *****
290                                                        REM
300 READ A, T$, N$
310                                                        REM
320 WHILE N$<> "END OF FILE"
330   PRINT N$, A, T$
340   READ A, T$, N$
350 WEND
360                                                        REM
370 PRINT " "
380 PRINT "END OF TELEPHONE LISTING"
390 END
```

## PROGRAM MAINTENANCE

**Program maintenance** includes all changes to a program once it is implemented and processing real transactions. Sometimes maintenance is required to correct errors that were not found during the testing step. Other times, maintenance is required to make changes that are the result of the user's new information requirements. It may surprise you to learn that the majority of all business programming today consists of maintaining existing programs, not writing new programs.

Because so much time is spent on maintenance programming, it should be subject to the same policies and procedures, such as design, testing, and documentation, that are required for new programs. Unfortunately, this is not always the case. Because maintenance tasks are usually shorter than new programming efforts, they often aren't held to the same standards. The result is that over time, programs can become unrecognizable when compared with their original documentation. Maintaining high standards for program maintenance can not only lower overall programming costs, but also lengthen the useful life of a program.

## SUMMARY OF PROGRAM DEVELOPMENT

The key to developing quality programs for an information system is to follow the steps of the program development process. Program specifications must be carefully reviewed and understood. Structured concepts should be used to design programs that are modular, use the three control structures, and follow the single entry/single exit rule. The program should be carefully coded and tested. Documentation should be finalized. If each of these steps is followed, quality programs will be developed that are correct and that can be easily read, understood, and maintained.

## WHAT IS A PROGRAMMING LANGUAGE?

As mentioned at the beginning of this chapter, computer programs can be written in a variety of programming languages. People communicate with one another through language, established patterns of words and sounds. A similar definition can also be applied to a **programming language**, which is a set of written words and symbols that allow the programmer or user to communicate with the computer. Just like English, Spanish, Chinese, or other spoken languages, programming languages have rules, called syntax, that govern their use.

## CATEGORIES OF PROGRAMMING LANGUAGES

There are hundreds of programming languages, each with its own syntax. Some languages were developed for specific computers and others, because of their success, have been standardized and adapted to a wide range of computers. Programming languages can be classified into one of four categories: machine language, assembly language, high-level languages, and fourth-generation languages.

## Machine Language

A **machine language** is the fundamental language of the computer's processor. Programs written in all other categories of languages are eventually converted into machine language before they are executed. Individual machine language instructions exist for each of the commands in the computer's instruction set, the operations such as add, move, or read that are specific to each computer. Because the instruction set is unique for a particular processor, machine languages are different for computers that have different processors. The advantage of writing a program in machine language is that the programmer can control the computer directly and accomplish exactly what needs to be done. Therefore, well-written machine language programs are very efficient. The disadvantages of machine language programs are that they take a long time to write and they are difficult to review if the programmer is trying to find an error. In addition, because they are written using the instruction set of a particular processor, the programs will only run on computers with the same type of processor. Because they are written for specific processors, machine languages are also called **low-level languages**. Figure 13-14a shows an example of machine language instructions.

**FIGURE 13-14**
**This chart shows program instructions for: (a) machine language (printed in a hexadecimal form); (b) assembly language; and (c) a high-level language called C. The machine language and assembly language instructions shown in this example correspond to the high-level instructions and were generated when the high-level language statements were translated into machine language.**

| (a) Machine Language | (b) Assembly Language | (c) High-level Language |
|---|---|---|
| 9b df 46 0c<br>9b d9 c0<br>9b db 7e f2<br>9b d9 46 04<br>9b d8 c9<br>9b d9 5e fc | fild WORD PTR [bp+12];qty<br>fld ST(0)<br>fstp TBYTE PTR [bp-14]<br>fld DWORD PTR [bp+4];price<br>fmul ST(0),ST(1)<br>fstp DWORD PTR [bp-4];gross | gross = qty * price; |
| 9b d9 c0<br>9b dc 16 ac 00<br>9b dd d8<br>9b dd 7e f0<br>90 9b<br>8a 66 f1<br>9e<br>9b dd c0<br>76 19 | fld ST(0)<br>fcom QWORD PTR $T20002<br>fstp ST(0)<br>fstsw WORD PTR [bp-16]<br>fwait<br>mov ah,BYTE PTR [bp-15]<br>sahf<br>ffreeST(0)<br>jbe $I193 | if (qty > ceiling) |
| 9b d9 46 fc<br>9b d9 46 fc<br>9b dc 0e b4 00<br>9b de e9<br>9b d9 5e 08<br>90 9b<br><br>eb 0d<br>90 | fld DWORD PTR [bp-4];gross<br>fld DWORD PTR [bp-4];gross<br>fmul QWORD PTR $T20003<br>fsub<br>fstp DWORD PTR [bp+8];net<br>fwait<br><br>jmp SHORT $I194<br>nop<br>$I193: | net = gross - (gross * discount_rate);<br><br><br><br><br><br><br>else |
| 8b 46 fc<br>8b 56 fe<br>89 46 08<br>89 56 0a | mov ax,WORD PTR [bp-4];gross<br>mov dx,WORD PTR [bp-2]<br>mov WORD PTR [bp+8],ax ;net<br>mov WORD PTR [bp+10],dx<br>$I194: | net = gross; |

## Assembly Language

To make it easier for programmers to remember the specific machine instruction codes, assembly languages were developed. An **assembly language** is similar to a machine language, but uses abbreviations called **mnemonics** or **symbolic operation code** to represent the machine operation code. Another difference is that assembly languages usually allow **symbolic addressing**, which means that a specific computer memory location can be referenced by a name or symbol, such as TOTAL, instead of by its actual address as it would have to be referenced in machine language. Assembly language programs can also include **macroinstructions** that generate more than one machine language instruction. Assembly language programs are converted into machine language instructions by a special program called an **assembler**. Even though assembly languages are easier to use than machine languages, they are still considered a low-level language because they are so closely related to the specific design of the computer. Figure 13-14b shows an example of assembly language instructions.

## High-Level Languages

The evolution of computer languages continued with the development of high-level languages in the late 1950s and 1960s. **High-level languages** more closely resemble what most people would think of as a language in that they contain nouns, verbs, and mathematical, relational, and logical operators that can be grouped together to form what appear to be sentences (Figure 13-14c). These sentences are called **program statements**. Because of these characteristics, high-level languages can be "read" by programmers and are thus easier to learn and use than machine or assembly languages. Another important advantage over low-level languages is that high-level languages are usually machine independent, which means they can run on different types of computers.

As mentioned previously, all languages must be translated into machine language before they can instruct the computer to perform processing. High-level languages are translated in one of two ways: with a compiler or an interpreter.

A **compiler** converts an entire program into machine language that is usually stored on a disk for later execution. The program to be converted is called the **source program** and the machine language produced is called the **object program** or **object code**. Compilers check the program syntax, perform limited logic checking, and make sure that data that is going to be used in comparisons or calculations, such as a discount rate, is properly defined somewhere in the program. An important feature of compilers is that they produce an error listing of all program statements that do not meet the program language rules. This listing helps the programmer make the necessary changes to correct the program. Figure 13-15 illustrates the process of compiling a program.

**FIGURE 13-15**
**When a compiler is used, a source language program is compiled into a machine language object program. Usually, both the source and object programs are stored on disk. When the user wants to run the program, the object program is loaded into the main memory of the CPU and the program instructions begin executing. Errors in the source program identified during compilation are shown on an error listing that can be used to make the necessary corrections.**

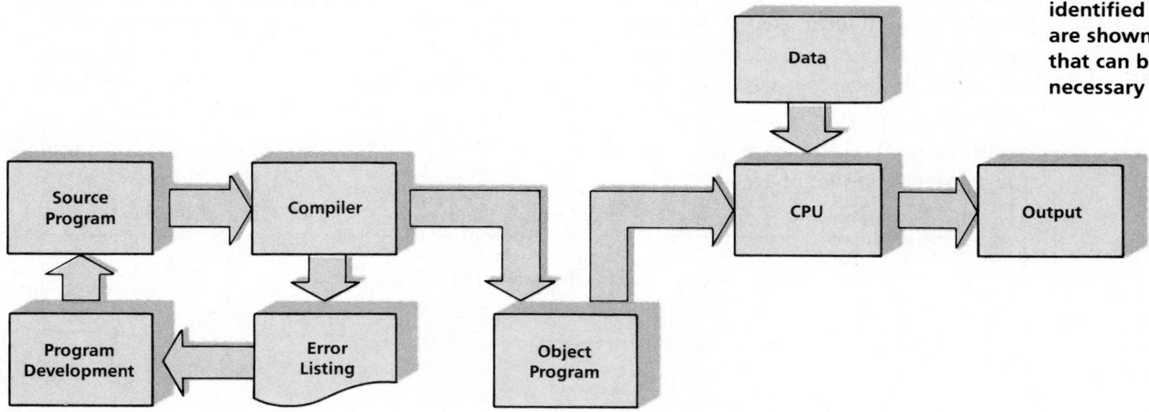


Because machine language is unique to each processor, different computers require different compilers for the same language. For example, a mainframe, minicomputer, and personal computer would each have different compilers that would translate the same source language program into the specific machine language for each computer.

While a compiler translates an entire program, an **interpreter** translates one program statement at a time and then executes the resulting machine language before translating the next program statement. When using an interpreter, each time the program is run, the source program is interpreted into machine language and executed. No object program is produced. Figure 13-16 illustrates this process.

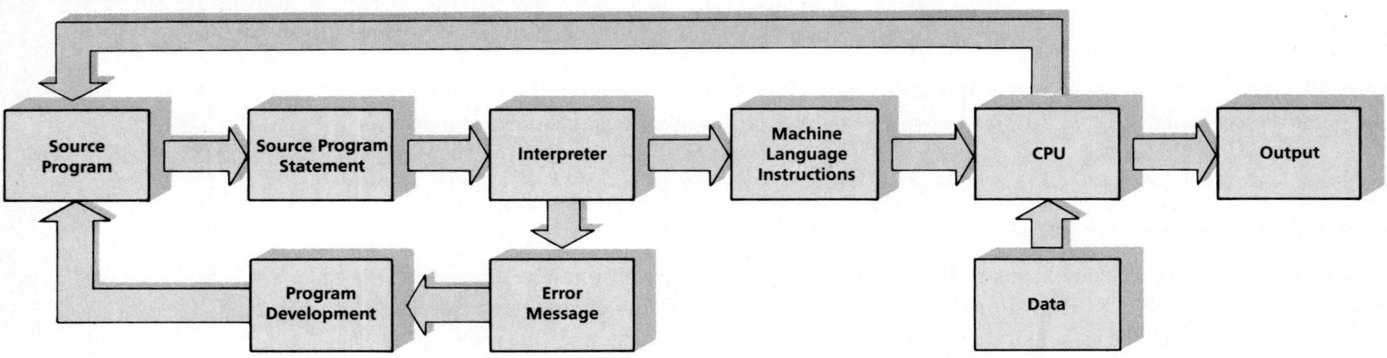


**FIGURE 13-16**
**When an interpreter is used, one source language statement at a time is interpreted into machine language instructions that are executed immediately. Error messages indicating an invalid source language statement are produced as each source program statement is interpreted.**

Interpreters are often used with personal computers that do not have the memory or computing power required by compilers. The advantage of interpreters is that the compiling process is not necessary before program changes can be tested. The disadvantage of interpreters is that interpreted programs do not run as fast as compiled programs because the translation to machine language occurs each time the program is run. Compilers for most high-level languages are now available for the newer and more powerful personal computers.

## Fourth-Generation Languages

The evolution of computer languages is sometimes described in terms of "generations" with machine, assembly, and high-level languages considered the first, second, and third generations, respectively. Each generation offered significant improvements in ease of use and programming flexibility over the previous generation. Although a clear definition doesn't yet exist, **fourth-generation languages (4GLs)**, sometimes called **very high-level languages**, continue the programming language evolution by being even easier to use than high-level languages for both the programmer and the nonprogramming user.

A common term used to describe fourth-generation languages is **nonprocedural**, which means that the programmer does not specify the procedures to be used to accomplish a task as is done with lower "procedural" language generations. Instead of telling the computer *how* to do the task, the programmer tells the computer *what* is to be done, usually by describing the desired output. A database query language (Figure 13-17) is an example of a nonprocedural fourth-generation language.

**FIGURE 13-17**
**This database query is considered an example of a fourth-generation language because it tells the computer what the user wants, not how to perform the processing.**

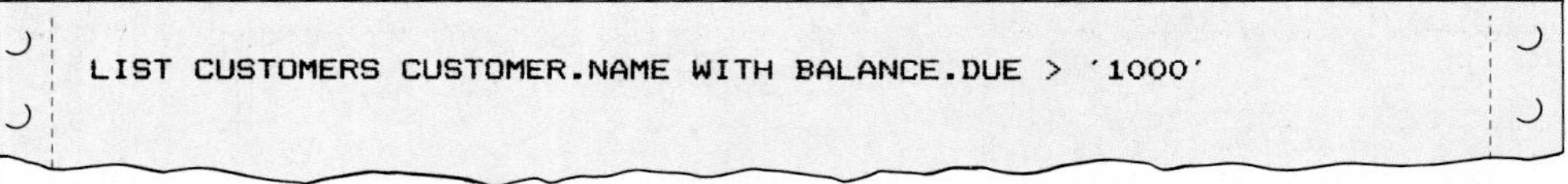

LIST CUSTOMERS CUSTOMER.NAME WITH BALANCE.DUE > '1000'


The advantage of fourth-generation languages is that they are "results" oriented ("what" is to be done, not "how") and they can be used by nonprogramming personnel such as users. The disadvantage of fourth-generation languages is that they do not provide as many processing options to the programmer nor are they as efficient as other language generations. Most experts, however, believe that their ease of use far outweighs these disadvantages and predict that fourth-generation languages will continue to be more widely used.

An extension of fourth-generation languages, sometimes called the fifth generation, is a natural language. A **natural language** is a type of query language that allows the user to enter a question as if the user were speaking to another person. For example, a fourth-generation query might be stated as LIST SALESPERSON TOTAL-SALES BY REGION. A natural language version of that same query might be TELL ME THE NAME OF EACH SALESPERSON AND THE TOTAL SALES FOR EACH REGION. The natural language allows the user more flexibility in the structure of the query and can even ask the user a question if it does not understand what is meant by the initial query statement.

## PROGRAMMING LANGUAGES USED TODAY

Although there are hundreds of programming languages, only a few are used extensively enough to be recognized as industry standards. Most of these are high-level programming languages that can be used on a variety of computers. This section discusses the popular programming languages that are commonly used, their origins, and their primary purpose.

To help you understand the differences, we show program code for each of the most popular languages. The code is from programs that solve the same problem, the computation of the net sale price using a discount if the gross sale is over $100.00.

### BASIC

**BASIC**, which stands for **B**eginner's **A**ll-purpose **S**ymbolic **I**nstruction **C**ode, was developed by John Kemeny and Thomas Kurtz in 1964 at Dartmouth College (Figure 13-18). Originally designed to be a simple, interactive programming language for college students to learn and use, BASIC has become one of the most commonly used programming languages on microcomputers and minicomputers.

**FIGURE 13-18**
**An excerpt from a BASIC program.**

```
5010 REM *****************P R O C E S S   A N D   D I S P L A Y*********
5040 GROSS = QTY * SLSPR
5050 IF QTY > CEILING THEN NET = GROSS - (GROSS * DISC) ELSE NET = GROSS
5070 PRINT "THE NET SALES IS $";
5080 PRINT USING "$$#,###.##"; NET
5090 RETURN
```

### COBOL

**COBOL** (**CO**mmon **B**usiness **O**riented **L**anguage) was introduced in 1960. Backed by the Department of Defense, COBOL was developed by a committee of representatives from both government and industry. Rear Admiral Grace M. Hopper was a key person on the committee and is recognized as one of the prime developers of the COBOL language. COBOL is one of the most widely used programming languages for business applications (Figure 13-19). Using an English-like format, COBOL instructions are arranged in "sentences" and grouped into "paragraphs." The English format makes COBOL easy to write and read, but also makes it a wordy language that produces lengthy program code. COBOL is very good for processing large files and performing relatively simple business computations. Other languages are stronger at performing complex mathematical formulas and functions.

```
016200 C010-PROCESS-AND-DISPLAY.
016400*****************************************************************
016600* FUNCTION:                          CALCULATE NET SALES AMOUNT     *
016700*                                    AND DISPLAY RESULTS            *
016800* ENTRY/EXIT:                        B000-LOOP-CONTROL              *
016900* CALLS:                             NONE                           *
017100*****************************************************************
017300     COMPUTE GROSS-SALES-WRK = QUANTITY-SOLD-WRK * SALES-PRICE-WRK.
017500     IF QUANTITY-SOLD-WRK IS GREATER THAN CEILING
017600         COMPUTE NET-SALES-WRK = GROSS-SALES-WRK -
017700              (GROSS-SALES-WRK * DISCOUNT-RATE)
017800     ELSE
017900         MOVE GROSS-SALES-WRK TO NET-SALES-WRK.
018100     MOVE NET-SALES-WRK TO NET-SALES-OUTPUT.
018300      DISPLAY CLEAR-SCREEN.
018500     WRITE PRINT-LINE FROM DETAIL-LINE
018600          AFTER ADVANCING 2.
```

**FIGURE 13-19**
**An excerpt from a COBOL program.**

## C

The **C** programming language was developed at Bell Laboratories in 1972 by Dennis Ritchie (Figure 13-20). Originally designed as a programming language for writing systems software, it is now considered a general-purpose programming language. C is a powerful programming language that requires professional programming skills to be used effectively. The use of C to develop various types of software on microcomputers and minicomputers is increasing.

**FIGURE 13-20**
**An excerpt from a C program.**

```
float gross;
gross = qty * price;
if (qty > ceiling)
    net = gross - (gross * discount_rate);
else
    net = gross;
return(net);
```

## FORTRAN

**FORTRAN** (**FOR**mula **TRAN**slator), developed by IBM and released in 1957, was designed as a programming language to be used by scientists, engineers, and mathematicians (Figure 13-21). The language is noted for its ability to easily express and efficiently calculate mathematical equations.

**FIGURE 13-21**
**An excerpt from a FORTRAN program.**

```
BEGIN                                  (* Begin procedure *)
    GROSS := SALES * QTY;
    IF QTY > CEILING
        THEN NET := GROSS - (GROSS * DISCOUNT_RATE)
        ELSE NET := GROSS;
    WRITELN('THE NET SALES IS $',NET:6:2);
END;                                   (* End of procedure *)
```

## Pascal

The **Pascal** language was developed by Niklaus Wirth, a computer scientist at the Institut fur Informatik in Zurich, Switzerland, in 1968. The name Pascal is not an abbreviation or acronym, but rather the name of a mathematician, Blaise Pascal (1623–1662), who developed one of the earliest calculating machines. Pascal, available for use on both personal and large computers, was one of the first programming languages that provided statements to encourage the use of structured program design (Figure 13-22).

**FIGURE 13-22**
**An excerpt from a Pascal program.**

```
      SUBROUTINE CALC(QTY,SALES,DISC,MAX,GROSS,NET)
      REAL SALES, DISC, MAX, GROSS, NET
      INTEGER QTY
      GROSS = QTY * SALES
      IF(QTY .GT. MAX) THEN
1        NET = GROSS - (GROSS * DISC)
1     ELSE
1        NET = GROSS
1     ENDIF
      PRINT *, "   "
      RETURN
```

## Ada

The programming language **Ada** is named for Augusta Ada Byron, Countess of Lovelace, a mathematician in the 1800s, who is thought to have written the first program. Introduced in 1980, the development of Ada was supported by the Department of Defense. Ada was designed to facilitate the writing and maintenance of large programs that would be used over a long period of time. The language encourages coding of readable programs that are also portable, allowing them to be transferred from computer to computer (Figure 13-23).

```
GROSS_SALES_PRICE := FLOAT(QUANTITY * SALES_PRICE);
if GROSS_SALES_PRICE > 100.0 then
   GROSS_SALES_PRICE := GROSS_SALES_PRICE - (GROSS_SALES_PRICE * 0.05);
end if;
```

**FIGURE 13-23**
**An excerpt from an Ada program.**

## RPG

**RPG**, which stands for **R**eport **P**rogram **G**enerator, was developed by IBM and introduced in 1964. As the name indicates, this language was primarily designed to allow reports to be generated quickly and easily. Instead of writing a set of instructions as in other languages, in RPG special forms are filled out that describe the desired report (Figure 13-24). With a minimum of training, a user can be taught to fill out the forms, enter the information into the computer, and produce the desired reports without having to design and develop a computer program.

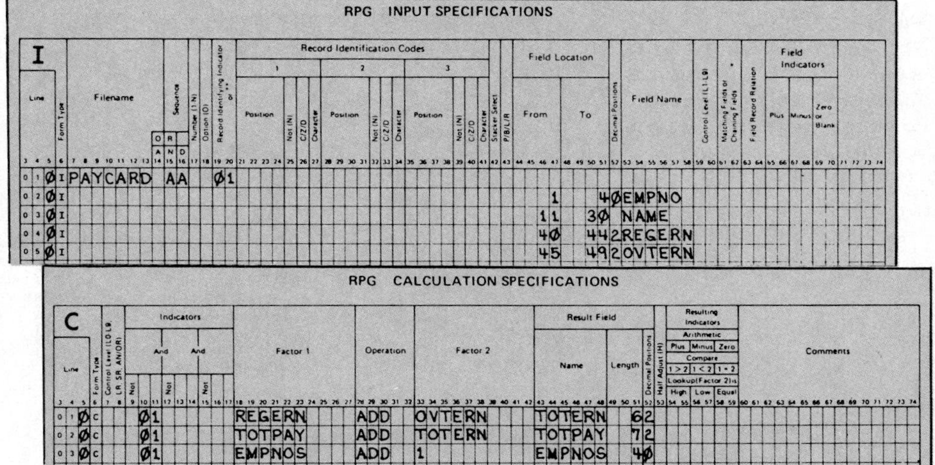

RPG INPUT SPECIFICATIONS

| Line | Form Type | Filename | Sequence | Record Identifying Indicator | Field Location From | To | Decimal Positions | Field Name |
|---|---|---|---|---|---|---|---|---|
| 01 | I | PAYCARD | AA | Ø1 | | | | |
| 02 | I | | | | 1 | 4Ø | | EMPNO |
| 03 | I | | | | 11 | 3Ø | | NAME |
| 04 | I | | | | 4Ø | 44 | 2 | REGERN |
| 05 | I | | | | 45 | 49 | 2 | OVTERN |

RPG CALCULATION SPECIFICATIONS

| Line | Form Type | Indicators | Factor 1 | Operation | Factor 2 | Result Field Name | Length | Decimal Positions |
|---|---|---|---|---|---|---|---|---|
| 01 | C | Ø1 | REGERN | ADD | OVTERN | TOTERN | 6 | 2 |
| 02 | C | Ø1 | TOTPAY | ADD | TOTERN | TOTPAY | 7 | 2 |
| 03 | C | Ø1 | EMPNOS | ADD | 1 | EMPNOS | 4 | Ø |

**FIGURE 13-24**
**Special forms help the RPG programmer to quickly specify the input, calculation, and output requirements of a program. The input and calculation forms are shown in this illustration.**

## Other Popular Programming Languages

In addition to the commonly used programming languages just discussed, there are several other popular languages. Figure 13-25 lists some of these languages and their primary uses.

| Language | Description |
|---|---|
| ALGOL | ALGOrithmetic Language. Structured programming language used for scientific and mathematical applications. |
| APL | A Programming Language. A powerful, easy to learn language that is good for processing data stored in a table (matrix) format. |
| FORTH | Similar to C. Creates fast and efficient program code. Originally developed to control astronomical telescopes. |
| LISP | LISt Processing. Popular artificial intelligence language. |
| LOGO | Primarily known as an educational tool to teach problem-solving skills. |
| MODULA-2 | Similar to Pascal. Used primarily for developing systems software. |
| PILOT | Programmed Inquiry Learning Or Teaching. Used by educators to write computer-aided instruction programs. |
| PL/1 | Programming Language/One. Business and scientific language that combines many of the features of FORTRAN and COBOL. |
| PROLOG | PROgramming in LOGic. Used for artificial intelligence. |

**FIGURE 13-25**
**Other popular computer languages.**

## APPLICATION GENERATORS

**A**pplication generators, also called **program generators**, are programs that produce source language programs, such as BASIC or COBOL, based on input, output, and processing specifications entered by the user. Application generators can greatly reduce the amount of time required to develop a program. They are based on the fact that most programs are comprised of standard processing modules, such as routines to read, write, or compare records, that can be combined together to create unique programs. These standard processing modules are stored in a library and are selected and grouped together based on user specifications. Application generators often use menu and screen generators to assist in developing an application.

A **menu generator** lets the user specify a menu (list) of processing options that can be selected. The resulting menu is automatically formatted with heading, footing, and prompt line text (Figure 13-26).

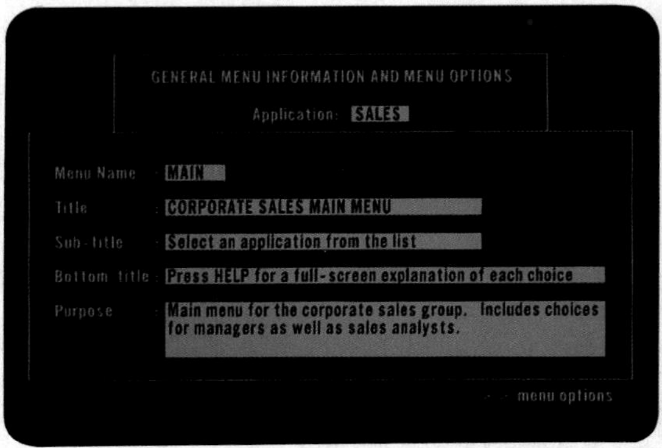


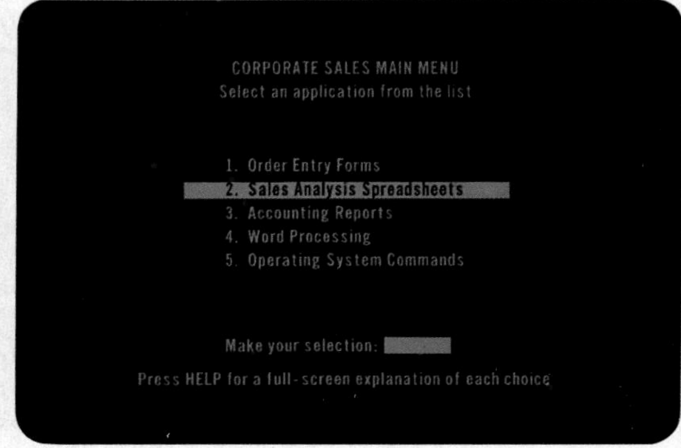


**FIGURE 13-26**
**The screen on the left is part of a menu generator from Oracle Corporation that can be used to quickly create professional-looking menus, as shown in the screen on the right.**

A **screen generator**, sometimes called a **screen painter**, allows the user to design an input or output screen by entering the names and descriptions of the input and output data directly on the screen. The advantage is that the user enters the data exactly as it will appear after the program is created. As each data name, such as Order No., is entered, the screen generator asks the user to specify the length and type of data that will be entered and what processing, if any, should take place before or after the data is entered. The order entry screen shown in Figure 13-27 was created in just one hour using SQL*FORMS, a screen generator product from ORACLE Corporation.

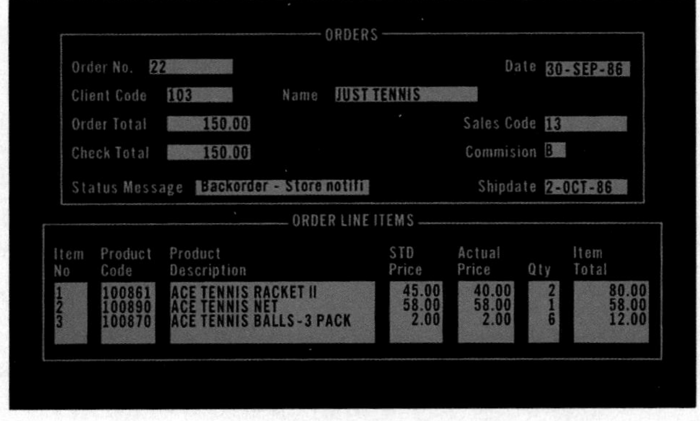


**FIGURE 13-27**
**This order entry screen and the program to process the data were created in just one hour using a screen generator from Oracle Corporation. Using the traditional programming technique of writing individual program instructions would have taken considerably longer.**

## HOW TO CHOOSE A PROGRAMMING LANGUAGE

Although each programming language has its own unique characteristics, selecting a language for a programming task can be a difficult decision. Following are some of the factors that should be considered in making a choice:

- The programming standards of the organization. Many organizations have programming standards that specify that a particular language is used for all applications.
- The need to interface with other programs. If a program is going to work with other existing or future programs, ideally it should be programmed in the same language as the other programs.
- The suitability of a language to the application to be programmed. As we discussed, most languages are best suited to a particular type of application. For example, FORTRAN works well with applications requiring many calculations.
- The expertise of the available programmers. Unless another language is far superior, the language used by the existing programmers probably should be chosen.
- The availability of the language. Not all languages are available on all machines.
- The need for the application to be portable. If the application will have to run on different machines, a common language should be chosen so the program only has to be written once.
- The anticipated maintenance requirements. If the user anticipates that the application will have to be modified frequently, a language that can be maintained easily and that supports structured programming concepts should be considered.

## SUMMARY OF PROGRAMMING LANGUAGES

Although procedural languages such as COBOL and BASIC will continue to be used for many years, there is a clear trend toward the creation of programs using nonprocedural tools, such as fourth-generation and natural languages, that allow users to specify what they want accomplished. Your knowledge of programming languages will help you to better understand the process that takes place when the computer converts data into information and to obtain better results if you directly participate in the programming process.

## CHAPTER SUMMARY

1. A **computer program** is a detailed set of instructions that directs a computer to perform the tasks necessary to process data into information.
2. **Program development** is a series of five steps that take place when a computer program is developed.
3. The five steps in program development are: (1) review of the program specifications; (2) program design; (3) program coding; (4) program testing; and (5) finalizing the documentation.
4. **Program specifications** can include many documents such as data flow diagrams, system flowcharts, process specifications, a data dictionary, screen formats, and report layouts.
5. During **program design** a logical solution or **logic** for a program is developed and documented.
6. **Structured program design** is methodology that emphasizes three main program design concepts: modules, control structures, and single entry/single exit.
7. **Modules** or **subroutines**, which perform a given task within a program, can be developed individually and then combined to form a complete program.
8. **Structure charts** or **hierarchy charts** are used to decompose the modules of a program.
9. The three **control structures** are: **sequence** where one process occurs immediately after another; **selection** or **if-then-else**, which is used for conditional program logic; and **iteration** which is used for **looping**.
10. The two forms of iteration are the **do-while structure** and the **do-until structure**.
11. **Single entry/single exit** means that there is only one **entry point** and one **exit point** from each of the control structures.
12. Three commonly used program design tools are **program flowcharts**, **pseudocode**, and **Warnier-Orr**.
13. Structured walkthroughs are used to review the design and logic of a program.
14. **Coding** is the process of writing the program instructions.
15. Before a program is used to process "real" data it should be thoroughly tested to make sure it is functioning correctly. A simple type of testing is **desk checking**.
16. Programs can be tested for **syntax errors** (grammar). **Logic testing** checks for incorrect results using **test data**.
17. **Debugging** refers to the process of locating and correcting program errors or **bugs** found during testing.
18. **Program maintenance** includes all changes to a program once it is implemented and processing real transactions.
19. A **programming language** is a set of written words and symbols that allow a programmer or user to communicate with the computer.
20. Programming languages fit into one of four categories: machine language; assembly language; high-level languages; and fourth-generation languages.
21. Before they can be executed, all programs are converted into **machine language**, the fundamental language of computers, also called **low-level language**.
22. **Assembly language** is a low-level language that is closely related to machine language. It uses **mnemonics** or **symbolic operation code**.
23. Assembly languages use **symbolic addressing** and include **macroinstructions**. Assembly language programs are converted into machine language instructions by an **assembler**.
24. **High-level languages** are easier to learn and use than low-level languages. They use sentences called **program statements**.
25. **Compilers** and **interpreters** are used to translate high-level **source programs** into machine language **object code** or **object programs**.
26. **Fourth-generation languages**, also called **very high-level languages**, are **nonprocedural**, which means that the user tells the computer "what" is to be done, not "how" to do it.
27. A **natural language** allows the user to enter a question as if the user were speaking to another person.
28. Commonly used programming languages include **BASIC**, **COBOL**, **C**, **FORTRAN**, **Pascal**, **Ada**, and **RPG**.
29. **BASIC** is one of the most commonly used programming languages on microcomputers and minicomputers.
30. **COBOL** is the most widely used programming language for business applications.
31. **C** is an increasingly popular programming language that requires professional programming skills to be used effectively.
32. **FORTRAN** is noted for its ability to easily express and efficiently calculate mathematical equations.

33. **Pascal** contains programming statements that encourage the use of structured program design.
34. **Ada**, developed and supported by the Department of Defense, was designed to facilitate the writing and maintenance of large programs that would be used over a long period of time.
35. **RPG** was primarily designed to generate reports quickly and easily.
36. **Application generators** or **program generators** produce source language programs based on input, output, and processing specifications entered by the user.
37. A **menu generator** lets the user specify a menu of options.
38. A **screen generator** or **screen printer** allows the user to design an input or output screen.
39. Some of the factors that should be considered when choosing a programming language are: the programming standards of the organization; the need to interface with other programs; the suitability of a language to the application to be programmed; the expertise of the available programmers; the availability of the language; the need for the application to be portable; and the anticipated maintenance requirements.

## KEY TERMS

Ada *13.17*
Application generators *13.18*
Assembler *13.12*
Assembly language *13.12*
BASIC *13.15*
Bugs *13.10*
C *13.16*
COBOL *13.15*
Coding *13.9*
Compiler *13.13*
Computer program *13.2*
Control structures *13.4*
Debugging *13.10*
Desk checking *13.9*
Do-until structure *13.5*
Do-while structure *13.5*
Entry point *13.6*
Exit point *13.6*
FORTRAN *13.16*
Fourth-generation language (4GL) *13.14*
Hierarchy charts *13.4*
High-level languages *13.13*
If-then-else structure *13.5*
Interpreter *13.13*
Iteration *13.5*
Logic *13.4*
Logic testing *13.9*
Looping *13.5*
Low-level language *13.12*
Machine language *13.12*
Macroinstruction *13.12*
Menu generator *13.18*
Mnemonics *13.12*
Module *13.4*
Natural language *13.14*
Nonprocedural *13.14*
Object code *13.13*
Object program *13.13*
Pascal *13.16*
Program design *13.4*
Program development *13.3*
Program flowchart *13.6*
Program generators *13.18*
Program maintenance *13.11*
Programming language *13.11*
Program specifications *13.3*
Program statements *13.13*
Pseudocode *13.8*
RPG (Report Program Generator) *13.17*
Screen generator *13.18*
Screen painter *13.18*
Selection structure *13.5*
Sequence structure *13.4*
Single entry/single exit *13.6*
Source program *13.13*
Structure charts *13.4*
Structured program design *13.4*
Subroutine *13.4*
Symbolic addressing *13.12*
Symbolic operation code *13.12*
Syntax errors *13.9*
Test data *13.9*
Very high-level languages *13.14*
Warnier-Orr *13.8*

## REVIEW QUESTIONS

1. What is a computer program?
2. List the five steps in program development and give a brief description of each step.
3. What is the purpose of reviewing the program specifications? List at least four types of documents that may be included in the program specifications.
4. Draw the three control structures used in structured program design.

5. Briefly describe three types of program design tools that are used by programmers.
6. What is the difference between a syntax error and a logic error?
7. Describe the four categories of programming languages.
8. Explain how a compiler and an interpreter work. What is a source program? What is an object program?
9. Why are high-level languages referred to as machine-independent languages?
10. List five commonly used programming languages and explain their primary uses.
11. How do application generators reduce the amount of time required to program?
12. List seven factors that should be considered when choosing a programming language.

## CONTROVERSIAL ISSUE

1. Computer literacy is defined in different ways. Some people believe that to be computer literate a person should learn a programming language and have experience programming a computer. Other people believe that programming knowledge is inappropriate for the general user and should be reserved for those who plan to become computer professionals. What do you think?

## RESEARCH PROJECT

1. Review the employment advertisements in your local newspaper for computer programming positions. Prepare a report discussing which programming languages are in demand.

CHAPTER 14

# Career Opportunities in the Age of Information Processing

CHAPTER 14

# Career Opportunities in the Age of Information Processing

## OBJECTIVES

- Discuss the three areas that provide the majority of computer related jobs.
- Describe the career positions available in an information systems department.
- Describe information processing career opportunities in sales, service and repair, consulting, and education and training.
- Discuss the compensation and growth trends for information processing careers.
- Discuss the three fields in the information processing industry.
- Discuss career development, including professional organizations, certification, and professional growth and continuing education.

---

In discussing career opportunities and computers, it's difficult to decide what to exclude. As society becomes more information oriented, computers are becoming an integral part of most jobs. For this reason, the knowledge you have gained from this text will apply in some way to any career you choose. Some of you, however, may want to consider a career in the information processing industry itself. The purpose of this chapter is to show you the opportunities that exist in the industry, present computer industry career trends, and discuss how to prepare for a career in information systems. Even if you don't choose a computer industry career, it is important to have an understanding of them, as it is likely that any job you choose will at some time provide contact with one or more computer industry representatives.

## THE INFORMATION PROCESSING INDUSTRY

The information processing industry is one of the largest industries in the world with annual sales of well over $100 billion. Job opportunities in the industry come primarily from three areas: the companies that provide the computer equipment; the companies that develop computer software; and the companies that hire information processing professionals to work with these products. As in any major industry, there is also a large group of service companies that support each of these three areas. An example would be a company that sells computer supplies such as printer paper and disks.

## The Computer Equipment Industry

The computer equipment or hardware industry includes all manufacturers and distributors of computers and computer-related equipment such as disk and tape drives, terminals, printers, and communication equipment (Figure 14-1). The five largest mini and mainframe computer manufacturers in the United States, IBM, Digital Equipment Corporation, UNISYS, Hewlett-Packard, and NCR, are huge organizations with tens of thousands of employees worldwide. Major microcomputer manufacturers include IBM, Apple, Compaq, and Tandy. The largest company, IBM, has had annual sales of over $54 billion. In addition to the major companies, the computer equipment industry is also known for the many new "start-up" companies that appear each year. These new companies take advantage of rapid changes in equipment technology, such as laser printers, video disks, and fiber optics, to create new products and new job opportunities. Besides the companies that make end user equipment, thousands of companies make components that most users never see. These companies manufacture chips (processor, memory, etc.), power supplies, wiring, and the hundreds of other parts that go into computer equipment.

**FIGURE 14-1**
**This photo shows newly manufactured computer keyboards being tested before shipping.**

## The Computer Software Industry

The computer software industry includes all developers and distributors of application and system software. In the early days, computer software was almost exclusively produced by the computer manufacturers. However, during the 1960s, numerous companies began producing software to compete with that offered by manufacturers. Today, thousands of companies provide a wide range of software from operating systems to complete business systems. The personal computer boom in the early 1980s provided numerous opportunities in the software industry. Thousands of individuals went into business for themselves by creating useful programs for the new microcomputers. Many of these people started by working out of their homes, developing their first software products on their own time while holding other jobs.

Today, software alone is a huge industry whose leaders include companies such as MSA, ASK, Microsoft, Lotus, and Ashton-Tate, with annual sales in the hundreds of millions of dollars. Most of these companies specialize in one particular type of software product such as business application software or productivity tools like word processing or spreadsheets.

**FIGURE 14-2**
**Computer professionals must be able to understand the end user's point of view and often meet with the user to review information processing requirements.**

## Information Processing Professionals

Information processing professionals are the people that put the equipment and software to work to produce information for the end user (Figure 14-2). This includes people such as programmers and systems analysts who are hired by companies to work in an information systems department. These and other positions available in the information processing industry will be discussed in the next section.

# WHAT ARE THE CAREER OPPORTUNITIES IN INFORMATION PROCESSING?

The use of computers in so many aspects of life has created thousands of new jobs. Some of these occupations, such as personal computer software sales representative, didn't even exist ten years ago. The following section describes some of the career opportunities that currently exist.

## Working in an Information Systems Department

In Chapter 1 we discussed the various types of career positions that exist within an information systems department. These positions include: data entry personnel, computer operators, computer programmers, systems analysts, database administrator, manager of information systems, and vice president of information systems.

The people in these positions work together as a team to meet the information demands of their organizations. Throughout this book, the responsibilities associated with many of these positions were discussed, including the role of the systems analysts in the information system development life cycle (Chapter 12) and the steps programmers perform in program development (Chapter 13). Another way to visualize the positions and their relationships is to look at an organization chart such as the one shown in Figure 14-3. In addition to management, the jobs in an information systems department can be classified into five categories:

1. Operations
2. Data administration
3. Systems analysis and design
4. Programming
5. Information center

Operations personnel are responsible for carrying out tasks such as operating the computer equipment that is located in the computer center. The primary responsibility of data administration is the maintenance and control of an organization's database. In systems analysis and design the various information systems needed by an organization are created and maintained. Programming develops the programs needed for the information systems, and the information center provides teaching and consulting services within an organization to help users meet their departmental and individual information processing needs. As you can see, an information systems department provides career opportunities for people with a variety of skills and talents.

**FIGURE 14-3**
**This organization chart shows some of the positions available in an information systems department.**

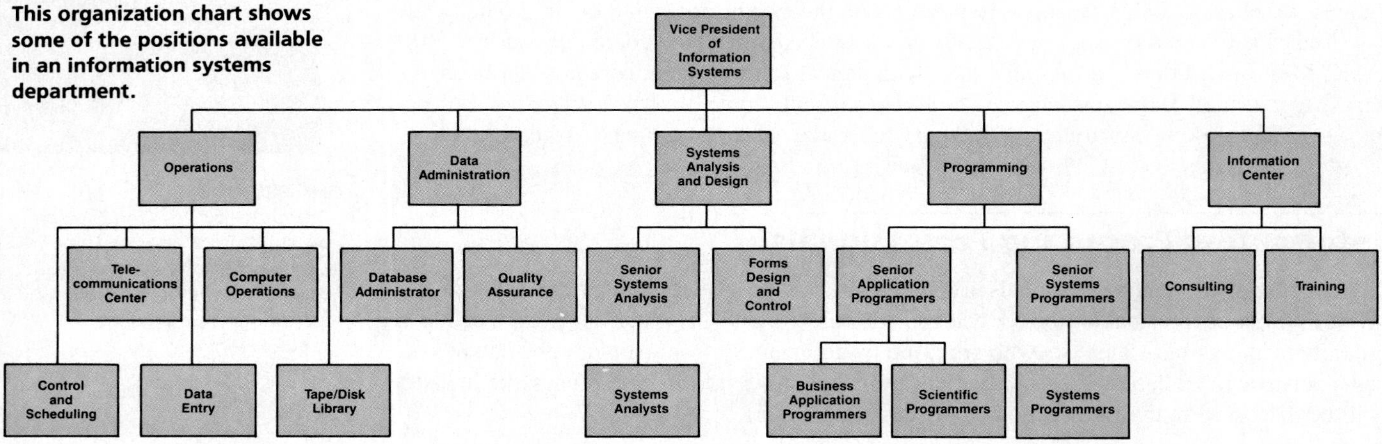

## Sales

**Sales representatives** must have a general knowledge of computers and a specific understanding of the product they are selling. Strong interpersonal or "people" skills are important, including the ability to listen and the ability to communicate effectively both verbally and in writing. Sales representatives are usually paid based on the amount of product they sell, and top sales representatives are often the most highly compensated employees in a computer company.

**FIGURE 14-4**
**Computer retailers, such as Computerland, need salespeople who understand personal computers and have good "people" skills.**

Some sales representatives work directly for equipment and software manufacturers and others work for resellers. Most personal computer products are sold through dealers such as Computerland or Businessland (Figure 14-4). Some dealers, such as Egghead Discount Software, specialize in selling the most popular software products.

## Service and Repair

Being a **service and repair technician** is a challenging job for persons who like to troubleshoot and solve problems and who have a strong background in electronics (Figure 14-5). In the early days of computers, repairs were often made at the site of the computer equipment. Today, however, malfunctioning components, such as circuit boards, are usually replaced and taken back to the service technician's office or sent to a special facility for repair. Many equipment manufacturers are now including special diagnostic software with their computer equipment that helps the service technician identify the problem. Using a modem, some advanced computer systems can automatically telephone a computer at the service technician's office and leave a message that a malfunction has been detected.

**FIGURE 14-5**
**Computer service and repair is one of the fastest growing computer-related professions. A knowledge of electronics is essential for this occupation.**

## Consulting

After building experience in one or more areas, some individuals become **consultants**, people who draw upon their experience to give advice to others. Consultants must not only have strong technical skills in their area of expertise, but must also have the people skills to convince their clients to follow their advice. Qualified consultants are in high demand for such tasks as computer system selection, system design, and communication network design and installation.

## Education and Training

The increased sophistication and complexity of today's computer products has opened wide opportunities in computer education and training (Figure 14-6). Qualified instructors are needed in schools, colleges, and universities and in private industry as well. In fact, the high demand for teachers has created a shortage at the university level, where many instructors have been lured into private industry because of higher pay. This shortage probably will not be filled in the near future; the supply of Ph.D.s, usually required at the university level, is not keeping up with the demand.

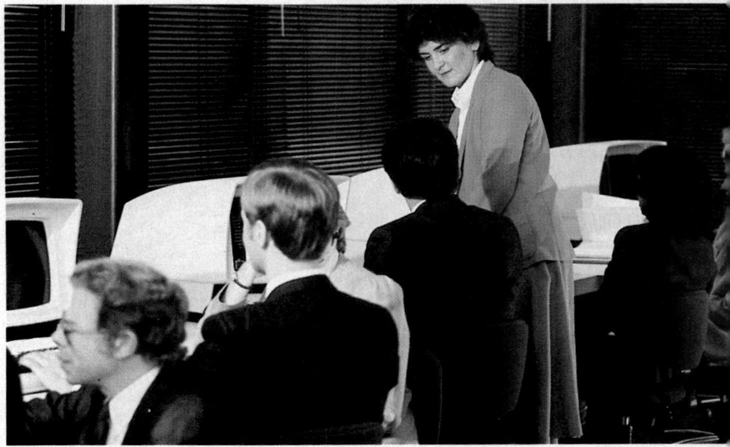

**FIGURE 14-6**
**There is a high demand in schools and industry for qualified instructors who can teach information processing subjects.**

# COMPENSATION AND GROWTH TRENDS FOR INFORMATION PROCESSING CAREERS

Compensation is a function of experience and demand for a particular skill. Demand is influenced by geographic location, with metropolitan areas usually having higher pay than rural areas where, presumably, the cost of living is lower. Figure 14-7 shows the result of a salary survey of over 70,000 computer professionals across the United States and Canada. These amounts represent an average increase of approximately 7% over the prior year. As shown in Figure 14-8, some industries pay higher than others for the same job position. According to the survey, the communications, utility, and aerospace industries paid the highest salaries. These industries have many challenging applications and are willing to pay the highest rate to obtain the best qualified employees. According to the U.S. Bureau of Labor Statistics, the fastest growing computer career positions between 1982 and 1995 will be systems analyst, applications programmer, machine operator, and computer repair technician (Figure 14-9).

**FIGURE 14-7**
**This table shows salary levels for various computer industry positions based on the number of years of experience. (Source: Source Edp, The Going Rate: 1988 Salaries.)**

| PROGRAMMING: | YRS. EXP. | 20% | MEDIAN | 80% |
|---|---|---|---|---|
| Commercial | <2 | 19.9 | 24.3 | 28.7 |
| | 2–3 | 23.5 | 28.0 | 32.5 |
| | 4–6 | 25.8 | 30.4 | 35.0 |
| | >6 | 30.6 | 36.0 | 42.5 |
| Engineering/Scientific | <2 | 23.4 | 30.0 | 34.2 |
| | 2–3 | 24.5 | 30.6 | 35.5 |
| | 4–6 | 29.6 | 34.8 | 40.7 |
| | <6 | 32.8 | 40.0 | 48.4 |
| Microcomputer | <2 | 18.0 | 22.0 | 27.1 |
| | 2–3 | 20.0 | 25.0 | 29.8 |
| | 4–6 | 26.1 | 33.0 | 38.9 |
| | >6 | 34.8 | 43.0 | 51.6 |
| Minicomputer | <2 | 19.3 | 23.2 | 28.8 |
| | 2–3 | 22.4 | 27.0 | 32.9 |
| | 4–6 | 25.4 | 31.0 | 37.2 |
| | >6 | 30.3 | 37.0 | 45.9 |
| Software Engineer | <2 | 23.2 | 28.6 | 31.7 |
| | 2–3 | 24.9 | 29.0 | 33.6 |
| | 4–6 | 29.1 | 35.0 | 40.6 |
| | >6 | 33.6 | 41.5 | 50.2 |
| Systems Software | <2 | 23.7 | 27.6 | 31.5 |
| | 2–3 | 23.5 | 28.0 | 31.9 |
| | 4–6 | 26.9 | 32.0 | 37.8 |
| | >6 | 36.1 | 42.0 | 50.0 |
| **MANAGEMENT:** | | | | |
| Data Center Operations | | 33.2 | 40.0 | 52.0 |
| Programming Development | | 39.8 | 48.0 | 58.1 |
| Software Development | | 44.0 | 53.0 | 64.1 |
| Systems Development | | 44.8 | 54.0 | 65.3 |
| Technical Services | | 42.5 | 50.0 | 61.5 |
| MIS Director | | 49.2 | 60.0 | 76.8 |
| **BUSINESS SYSTEMS:** | | | | |
| Consultant | <4 | 25.4 | 31.0 | 37.2 |
| | 4–6 | 30.1 | 35.0 | 41.3 |
| | >6 | 38.7 | 45.0 | 53.6 |
| Project Leader | <4 | 25.8 | 31.5 | 37.8 |
| | 4–6 | 30.1 | 35.0 | 41.3 |
| | >6 | 36.1 | 42.0 | 50.0 |

| BUSINESS SYSTEMS (Cont.): | YRS. EXP. | 20% | MEDIAN | 80% |
|---|---|---|---|---|
| System Analyst | <4 | 24.0 | 29.3 | 35.2 |
| | 4–6 | 28.4 | 33.0 | 38.9 |
| | >6 | 32.7 | 38.0 | 45.2 |
| **SPECIALISTS:** | | | | |
| Communications Analyst | <4 | 27.6 | 32.5 | 37.4 |
| | 4–6 | 27.3 | 35.0 | 44.5 |
| | >6 | 32.0 | 41.0 | 48.8 |
| Database/Management Analyst | <4 | 20.7 | 28.0 | 33.6 |
| | 4–6 | 28.5 | 33.5 | 40.5 |
| | >6 | 34.9 | 41.5 | 49.4 |
| Information Center Analyst | <4 | 20.0 | 26.0 | 29.1 |
| | 4–6 | 23.4 | 30.0 | 36.0 |
| | >6 | 30.2 | 38.2 | 45.8 |
| Office Automation Analyst | <4 | 20.0 | 26.0 | 29.1 |
| | 4–6 | 25.7 | 33.0 | 39.6 |
| | >6 | 30.5 | 38.6 | 46.3 |
| **SALES:** | | | | |
| Hardware | | 30.4 | 44.0 | 63.4 |
| Software | | 26.7 | 43.8 | 62.6 |
| Services | | 28.9 | 43.1 | 62.9 |
| Technical Support | <2 | 18.6 | 23.2 | 27.1 |
| | 2–3 | 23.9 | 29.5 | 35.1 |
| | 4–6 | 26.6 | 32.4 | 39.9 |
| | >6 | 36.0 | 45.0 | 54.0 |
| Management | | 45.5 | 61.5 | 85.5 |
| **OTHER:** | | | | |
| Computer Operator | <2 | 15.2 | 19.5 | 21.6 |
| | 2–3 | 16.0 | 20.0 | 22.8 |
| | 4–6 | 23.3 | 28.8 | 34.3 |
| | >6 | 26.3 | 33.7 | 41.5 |
| Edp Auditor | <4 | 30.8 | 35.0 | 42.0 |
| | 4–6 | 32.5 | 38.2 | 48.9 |
| | >6 | 34.0 | 40.0 | 48.4 |
| Technical Writer or Editor | <4 | 17.2 | 21.0 | 24.8 |
| | 4–6 | 27.3 | 32.5 | 40.0 |
| | >6 | 31.2 | 39.5 | 47.8 |

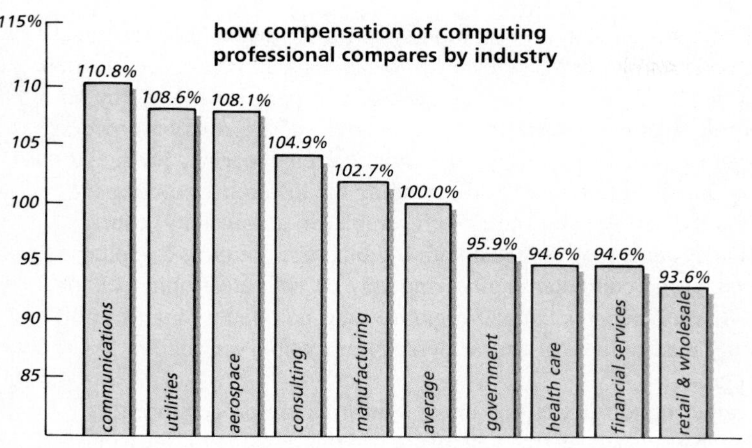


**FIGURE 14-8**
**This chart shows that some industries pay more for the same job position.**

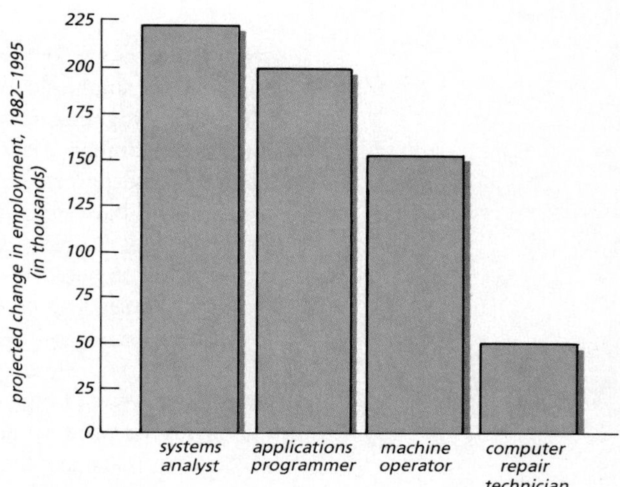


**FIGURE 14-9**
**This chart shows computer careers with the highest projected growth, as compiled by the U.S. Bureau of Labor Statistics.**

# PREPARING FOR A CAREER IN INFORMATION PROCESSING

To prepare for a career in the information processing industry, individuals must decide what computer field they are interested in and obtain education in the chosen field. This section discusses the three major computer fields and some of the opportunities for obtaining education in those fields.

## What Are the Fields in the Information Processing Industry?

While this book has primarily focused on the use of computers in business, there are actually three broad fields in the information processing industry (Figure 14-10): computer information systems; computer science; and computer engineering. **Computer information systems (CIS)** refers to the use of computers in areas relating to business. The field of **computer science** includes the technical aspects of computers such as hardware operation and systems software. **Computer engineering** deals with the design and manufacturing of electronic computer components and computer hardware. Each field provides unique career opportunities and has specialized study requirements. Several avenues of study are available to persons interested in obtaining formal education in information processing.

**FIGURE 14-10**
**There are three broad fields of study in the information processing industry. Each field has specialized study requirements.**

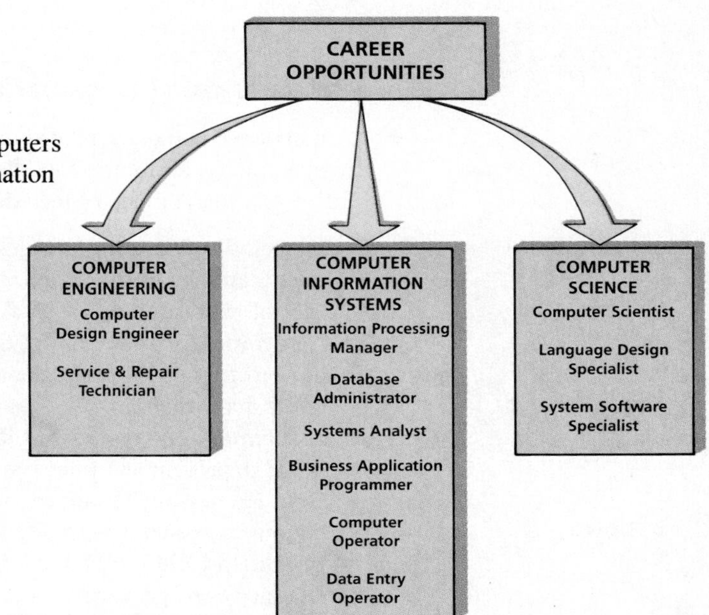

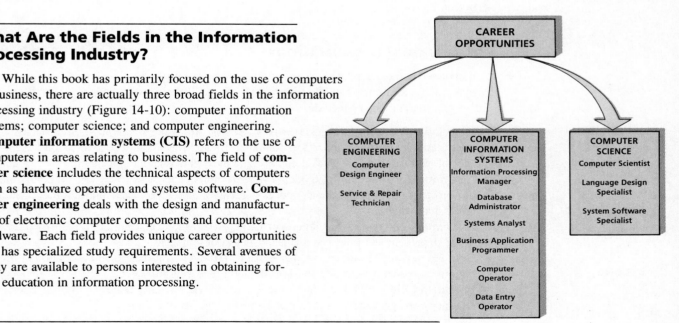

## Obtaining Education for Information Processing Careers

The expanded use of computers in today's world has increased the demand for properly trained computer professionals. Educational institutions have responded to this demand by providing a variety of options for students to study information systems. Trade schools, technical schools, community colleges, colleges and universities offer formal education and certification or degree programs in computer-related fields. If you are evaluating a program offered by one of these institutions, it is important that you remember the three areas of information processing: computer information systems, computer science, and computer engineering. Frequently schools will have separate programs for each area. Understanding the differences among the three fields will help you to find the courses you want. For example, in a university, courses relating to computer information systems may be listed with the business courses, computer science courses may be with math, and computer engineering may be with electronic technology or electrical engineering. Because schools list and organize their computer courses in different ways, you should carefully read individual course descriptions whenever you are selecting computer education classes.

With the wide variety of career opportunities that exist in information processing, it is difficult to make anything other than broad general statements when it comes to discussing degree requirements for employment in the industry. As in most other industries, the more advanced degree an individual has in a chosen field, the better that individual's chances are for success. While not having a degree may limit a person's opportunities for securing a top position, it will not prevent entry nor preclude success in information processing.

## CAREER DEVELOPMENT IN THE INFORMATION PROCESSING INDUSTRY

There are several ways for persons employed in the information processing industry to develop their skills and increase their recognition among their peers. These include professional organizations, certification, and professional growth and continuing education activities.

### Professional Organizations

A number of computer-related organizations have been formed by people who have common interests and a desire to share their knowledge. Some of the organizations that have been influential in the industry include:

- **Association for Computing Machinery (ACM)**. An association composed of persons interested in computer science and computer science education. The association has many special interest groups such as computer graphics, database, and business.
- **Association of Information Systems Professionals**. This association was originally aimed at word processing professionals, but now includes a much broader interest area, including office automation.
- **Association of Systems Management (ASM)**. A group composed of individuals interested in the improvement of the systems analysis and design field.
- **Data Processing Management Association (DPMA)**. A professional association of programmers, systems analysts, and information processing managers.
- **Institute of Electrical and Electronic Engineers (IEEE)** and **IEEE Computer Society**. Organizations primarily composed of computer scientists and engineers.

Each of the above organizations has chapters throughout the United States (several throughout the world), offers monthly meetings, and sponsors periodic workshops, seminars, and conventions. Some organizations have student chapters or offer reduced membership fees for students. Attending professional meetings provide an excellent opportunity for students to learn about the information processing industry and to meet and talk with professionals in the field. In addition to these and other professional organizations, user groups exist for most makes of computers. Most metropolitan areas have one or more local computer societies that meet monthly to discuss topics of common interest about personal computers. For anyone employed or just interested in the computer industry, these groups can be an effective and rewarding way to learn and continue career development.

## Certification

Many professions offer certification programs as a way of encouraging and recognizing the efforts of their members to attain a level of knowledge about their profession. The best known certification program in the information processing industry is the **Certificate in Data Processing (CDP)**, originated by DPMA but now administered by the **Institute for the Certification of Computer Professionals (ICCP)**. The CDP (Figure 14-11) is awarded to persons who pass an examination that has five parts: (1) computer equipment; (2) computer programming and software; (3) principles of management; (4) accounting and quantitative methods; and (5) systems analysis and design. To be eligible to take the examination, a person must have a minimum of five years of experience in the information processing industry. People who pass the examination are authorized to place the initials CDP after their name.

Data Processing Management Association

DPMA

Be it known that George W. Abbott has successfully completed all prescribed requirements and is hereby awarded by the Directors of the Association, the professional

Certificate in Data Processing

In Witness whereof, we have subscribed our signatures under the seal of the Association this 4th day of September 1962

DATA PROCESSING MANAGEMENT ASSOCIATION DPMA 1951

EXECUTIVE DIRECTOR

INTERNATIONAL PRESIDENT

**FIGURE 14-11**
**The Certificate in Data Processing (CDP) recognizes a high level of knowledge that the recipient has demonstrated by passing a five-part examination. This is a copy of the first CDP ever awarded.**

## Professional Growth and Continuing Education

Because of rapid changes in technology, staying aware of new products and services in the information processing industry can be a challenging task. One way of keeping up is by participating in professional growth and continuing education activities. This broad category includes events such as conferences, workshops, conventions, and trade shows that provide both general and specific information on equipment, software, services, and issues affecting the industry, such as computer security. Workshops and seminars usually last a day or two while conferences, conventions, and trade shows often last a week. Some of the larger trade shows, such as **COMDEX (COMputer Dealer EXposition)**, bring together over a thousand vendors to display their latest products and services (Figure 14-12).

**FIGURE 14-12**
**COMDEX is one of the largest computer product trade shows in the world. Thousands of vendors come together to demonstrate their new equipment, software, and services to prospective customers.**

## SUMMARY OF COMPUTER CAREER OPPORTUNITIES

With the increased use of computers, the prospects for computer-related career opportunities are excellent. Not only are the numbers of traditional information processing jobs, such as programmer and systems analyst, expected to increase, but the application of the computer to existing occupations will create additional job opportunities. Regardless of an individual's career choice, a basic understanding of computers should be an essential part of any employee's job skills.

## CHAPTER SUMMARY

1. As society becomes more information oriented, computers are becoming an integral part of most jobs.
2. Job opportunities in the information processing industry come from three areas: computer equipment companies, computer software companies, and companies that hire information processing professionals.
3. The computer equipment industry includes all manufacturers and distributors of computers and computer-related equipment.
4. The computer software industry includes all developers and distributors of application and system software.
5. Information processing professionals are the people that put the equipment and software to work to produce information for the end user.
6. Career opportunities in information processing include: working in an information systems department; sales; service and repair; consulting; education and training.
7. The jobs in an information systems department can be classified into five categories: (1) operations; (2) data administration; (3) systems analysis and design; (4) programming; and (5) information center.
8. **Sales representatives** are often the most highly compensated employees in a computer company.
9. Being a **service and repair technician** is a challenging job for persons who like to solve problems and who have a strong background in electronics.
10. **Consultants**, people who draw upon their experience to give advice to others, are in high demand for such tasks as computer system selection, system design, and communication network design and installation.
11. According to the U.S. Bureau of Labor and Statistics, the fastest growing computer career positions between 1982 and 1995 will be systems analyst, applications programmer, machine operator, and computer repair technician.
12. The three fields in information processing are computer information systems; computer science; and computer engineering.
13. **Computer information systems** refers to the use of computers in areas relating to business.
14. **Computer science** includes the technical aspects of computers such as hardware operation and systems software.
15. **Computer engineering** deals with the design and manufacturing of electronic computer components and computer hardware.
16. Trade schools, technical schools, community colleges, colleges, and universities offer formal education and certification or degree programs in computer related fields.
17. Computer professionals may continue to develop their skills and increase their recognition among their peers through professional organizations, certification, and professional growth and continuing education activities.
18. Professional organizations, such as the **Data Processing Management Association (DPMA)**, have been formed by people who have common interests and a desire to share their knowledge.
19. The **Certificate in Data Processing (CDP)** is the best known certification program in the information processing industry.
20. Computer professionals stay current by participating in professional growth and continuing education activities such as conferences, workshops, conventions, and trade shows.

## KEY TERMS

Association for Computing Machinery (ACM) *14.8*
Association of Information Systems Professionals *14.8*
Association of Systems Management (ASM) *14.8*
Certificate in Data Processing (CDP) *14.9*
COMDEX *14.9*
Computer engineering *14.7*
Computer information systems (CIS) *14.7*
Computer science *14.7*
Consultants *14.5*
Data Processing Management Association (DPMA) *14.8*
Institute for the Certification of Computer Professionals (ICCP) *14.9*
Institute of Electrical and Electronic Engineers (IEEE) *14.8*
Sales representatives *14.5*
Service and repair technician *14.5*

## REVIEW QUESTIONS

1. Briefly discuss the computer hardware and software industries.
2. The positions in an information systems department can be classified into what five categories?
3. List and discuss four information career opportunities other than working in an information systems department.
4. What are the four fastest growing computer career positions?
5. Describe the three fields in information processing.
6. List five computer-related professional organizations.
7. What are the five parts of the CDP exam?

## CONTROVERSIAL ISSUE

1. Some people believe that computer professions such as programming should be subject to mandatory certification or licensing, like certified public accountants. Others believe that because the industry is changing so rapidly, certification programs should be encouraged but remain voluntary. Discuss the advantages and disadvantages of mandatory programs.

## RESEARCH PROJECT

1. Contact one of the professional computer organizations listed in the chapter. Either attend a local meeting or write for membership information and prepare a report for your class.

## CHAPTER 15

# Trends and Issues in the Information Age

CHAPTER 15

# Trends and Issues in the Information Age

## OBJECTIVES

- Discuss the electronic devices and applications that are part of the automated office.
- Describe the technologies that are developing for the automated factory, including CAD, CAE, CAM, and CIM.
- Discuss the use of personal computers in the home.
- Explain guidelines for purchasing personal computers.
- Discuss social issues related to computers, such as computer crime and privacy.

After reading the preceding chapters, you know what a computer is, what a computer does, how it does it, and why a computer is so powerful. You have learned about computer equipment and software, and how the system development process is used to combine these elements with data, personnel, users, and procedures to create a working information system. The purpose of this chapter is to talk about current and future trends, including changes taking place in information systems in the workplace. We also discuss the use of personal computers in the home and some of the social issues related to computers, such as security and computer crime, privacy, ethics, and health.

## INFORMATION SYSTEMS IN BUSINESS

The largest single user of computers is business. Millions of systems ranging from mainframes to microcomputers are installed and used for applications such as inventory control, billing, and accounting. This section discusses how these traditional applications will be affected by changes in technology and methods. It also discusses two other areas of business applications, the automated office and the automated factory. Although the term automated can be applied to any process or machine that can operate without human intervention, the term is commonly used to describe computer-controlled functions.

### How Will Existing Information Systems Change?

Existing business information systems will continue to undergo profound changes as new technology, software, and methods are applied to the huge installed base of traditional business system users. Important overall trends include more online, interactive systems and less batch processing. In addition, the increased use of relational database systems means that users have a wider variety of data and information available for decision making, and more flexibility, presenting information on reports and displays (Figure 15-1).

**FIGURE 15-1**
Trends that will affect information systems of tomorrow.

**SOFTWARE**

- Fourth-generation and natural languages that will enable the user to communicate with the computer in a more conversational manner.
- Computer-aided software engineering (CASE) that will shorten the system development time frame.
- Increased use of decision support and artificial intelligence systems to help users make decisions.
- Increased implementation of graphic interfaces using icons and symbols to represent information and processes.

**EQUIPMENT**

- Increased use of personal computers networked to other personal computers and to central mini or mainframe computers.
- Increased storage capacity of disks using improved and new technologies such as laser disks.
- Terminals that can display 132 or more characters per line, as well as graphics and images.
- Faster, better quality printers.
- Reduced instruction set computers (RISC) and parallel processing that will greatly increase the number of instructions that can be processed at one time.

**DATA**

- Automatic input of data at the source where it is created.
- Storage and use of non-text data such as voice and image.

Profit and Loss Statement

| (in millions) | 1983 | 1984 | 1985 | 1986 | 1987 |
|---|---|---|---|---|---|
| | Actual | | | Projected | |
| Revenues | 3.551 | 5.300 | 6.170 | 6.787 | 7.465 |
| Expenses | | | | | |
| Labor | 0.300 | 0.370 | 0.550 | 0.616 | 0.727 |
| Energy | 0.165 | 0.284 | 0.350 | 0.392 | 0.462 |
| Materials | 1.108 | 1.626 | 2.513 | 2.814 | 3.321 |
| Administration | 0.317 | 0.365 | 0.388 | 0.435 | 0.513 |
| Other | 0.447 | 0.491 | 0.523 | 0.586 | 0.691 |
| Total Expenses | 2.337 | 3.136 | 4.323 | 4.842 | 5.714 |
| Profit (Loss) | 1.215 | 2.163 | 1.846 | 1.944 | 1.751 |

**INFORMATION SYSTEMS PERSONNEL**

- Increased interface with users.
- Emphasis will shift from how to capture and process data to how to use the available data more effectively.

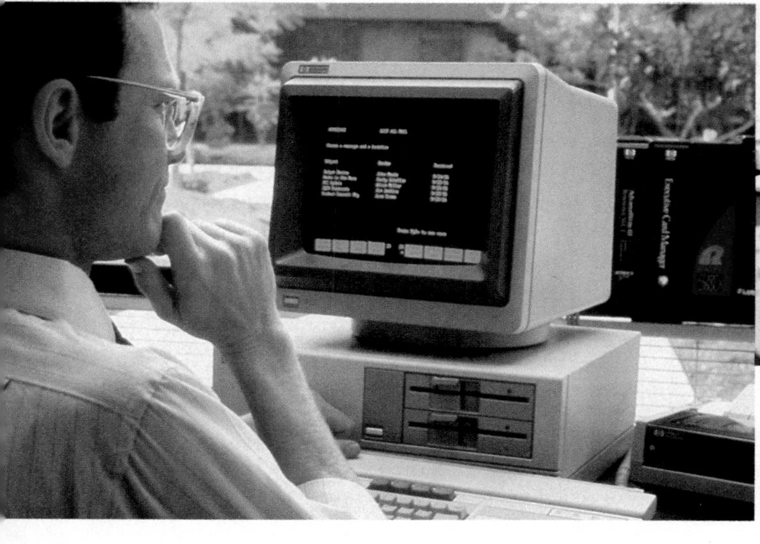

**USERS**

- Most people will be computer literate, with a basic understanding of how computers work and how they can use them in their jobs.

## The Automated Office

The **automated office**, sometimes referred to as the **electronic office**, is the term that describes the use of electronic devices such as computers, facsimile machines, and computerized telephone systems to make office work more productive. As was the case with traditional business applications such as accounting, automated office applications such as word processing, electronic mail, voice mail, desktop publishing, facsimile, image processing, and teleconferencing started out as separate, stand-alone applications. In recent years, however, the trend has been to integrate these applications into a network of devices and services that can share information. A brief review of each of these capabilities follows.

**Word Processing** Word processing is the ability to electronically create, store, revise, and print written documents. For many organizations, word processing was the first office application to be automated and among all organizations, word processing still ranks as the most widely used office automation technology. Today, most word processing systems are integrated with other applications. This allows the word processing applications to extract data such as names and addresses or financial data from other application files.

**Electronic Mail** Electronic mail is the ability to use computers to transmit messages to and receive messages from other computer users. The other users may be on the same computer network or on a separate computer system reached through the use of a modem or some other communications device. Electronic mail eliminates the need to hand deliver messages or use a delivery service, such as the post office or Federal Express. Electronic mail usage will grow as previously separate personal computers are attached to local area networks.

**Voice Mail** **Voice mail** can be considered verbal electronic mail. Made possible by the latest computerized telephone systems, voice mail reduces the problem of "telephone tag," where two people trying to reach each other wind up leaving a series of messages to "please call back." With voice mail, the caller can leave a message, similar to leaving a message on an answering machine. The difference is that with a voice mail system, the caller's message is digitized (converted into binary ones and zeros) so that it can be stored on a disk like other computer data. This allows the party who was called to hear the message later (by reconverting it to an audio form) and also, if desired, add a reply or additional comments and forward the message to someone else who has access to the system.

**Desktop Publishing** Desktop publishing involves the use of computers to produce printed documents that can combine different sizes and styles of text and graphics. Desktop publishing allows the user to control the process of creating high quality newsletters, brochures, and other documents that previously would have to have been developed by professional artists. The availability of desktop publishing systems for different computers and levels of user sophistication will increase their use in small as well as large organizations.

**Facsimile** **Facsimile** or **Fax** machines are used to transmit a reproduced image of a document over standard phone lines (Figure 15-2). The document can be printed, hand written, or a photograph. Fax machines optically scan the document and convert the image into digitized data that can be transmitted, using a modem, over the phone. A compatible Fax machine at the receiving end converts the digitized data back into its original image. Besides the separate Fax machines, plug-in circuit boards are also available for personal computers. Using a modem, these boards can directly transmit computer-prepared documents or documents that have been digitized with the use of a scanner. Fax machines are having an increasing impact on the way businesses transmit documents. Many documents that were previously sent through the mail are now sent by Fax. With the speed and convenience of a phone call, a document sent by Fax can be transmitted anywhere in the world.

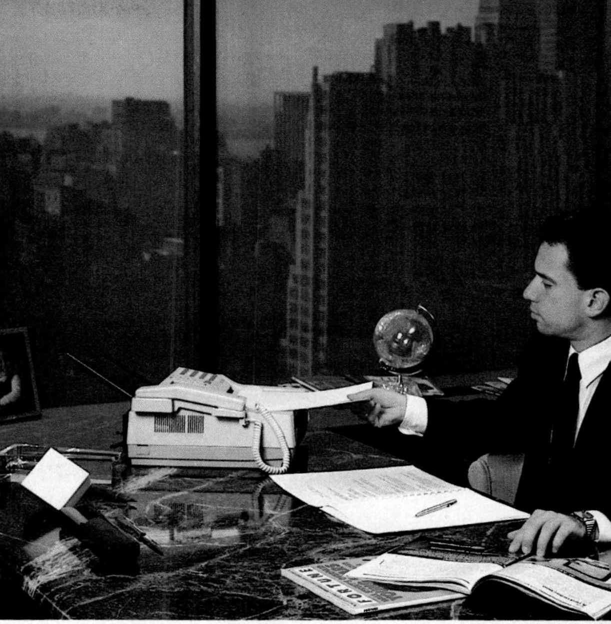

FIGURE 15-2
This facsimile (Fax) machine can send and receive copies of documents to and from any location where there is phone service and a compatible Fax machine.

**Image Processing** Image processing is the ability to store and retrieve a reproduced image of a document. Image processing is often used when an original document, such as an insurance claim, must be seen to verify data. Image processing and traditional applications will continue to be combined in many areas. For example, in 1988 American Express began sending cardholders copies of the individual charge slips that were related to the charges on their statement. These charge slips were recorded by an image processing system and then merged with the customer statement program.

**Teleconferencing** Teleconferencing once meant three or more people sharing a phone conversation. Today, however, **teleconferencing** usually means **video conferencing**, the use of computers and television cameras to transmit video images and the sound of the conference participants to other participants with similar equipment at a remote location (Figure 15-3). Special software and equipment is used to digitize the video image so that it can be transmitted along with the audio over standard communication channels. Although the video image is not as clear for moving objects as is commercial television, it does contribute to the conference discussion and is adequate for nonmoving objects such as charts and graphs.

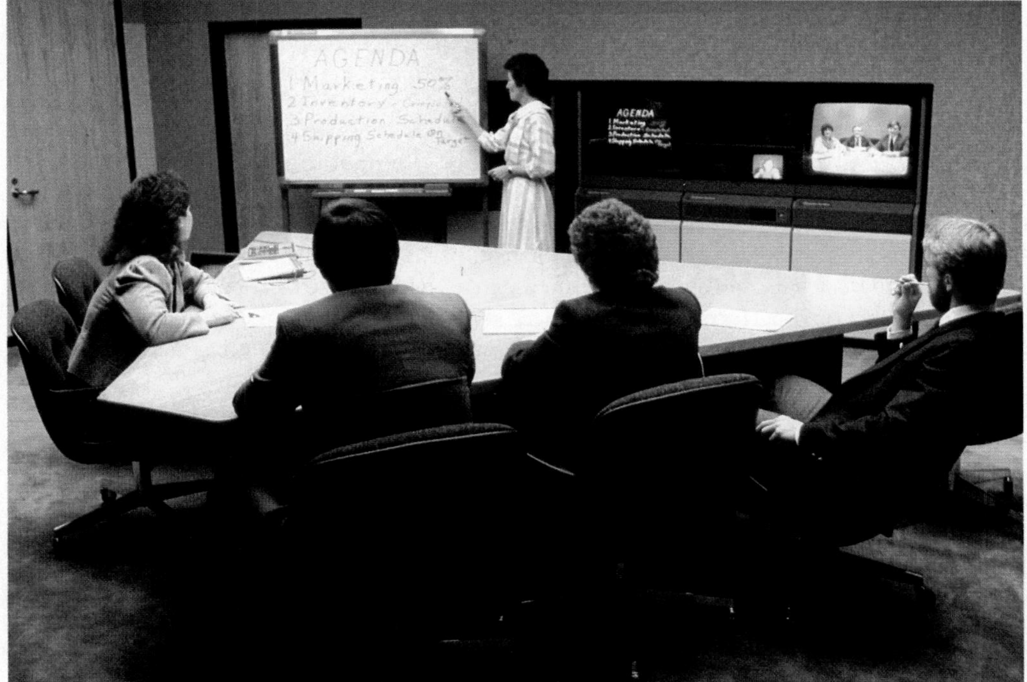


FIGURE 15-3
Video conferencing is used to transmit and receive video and audio signals over standard communication channels.

**Summary of the Automated Office** The trend toward integrated automated office capabilities will continue. Incompatible devices will be standardized or will be provided with software that will enable them to communicate and transfer data with other devices. The increased productivity provided by automated office devices will encourage more and more organizations to adopt them to help control costs and remain competitive.

FIGURE 15-4
Computer-aided design (CAD) is an efficient way to develop plans for new products.

## The Automated Factory

As in the automated office, the goal of the **automated factory** is to increase productivity through the use of automated, and often computer-controlled, equipment. Technologies used in the automated factory include computer-aided design, computer-aided engineering, computer-aided manufacturing, and computer-integrated manufacturing.

### Computer-Aided Design (CAD)

**Computer-aided design (CAD)** uses a computer and special graphics software to aid in product design (Figure 15-4). The CAD software eliminates the laborious drafting that used to be required and allows the designer to dynamically change the size of some or all of the product and view the design from different angles. The ability to store the design electronically offers several advantages over traditional manual methods. For one thing, the designs can be changed more easily than before. For another, the design database can be reviewed more easily by other design engineers. This increases the likelihood that an existing part will be used in a product rather than a new part designed. For example, if a support bracket was required for a new product, the design engineer could review the design database to see if any existing products used a support bracket that would be appropriate for the new product. This not only decreases the overall design time but increases the reliability of the new product by using proven parts.

### Computer-Aided Engineering (CAE)

**Computer-aided engineering (CAE)** is the use of computers to test product designs. Using CAE, engineers can test the design of an airplane or a bridge before they are built (Figure 15-5). Sophisticated programs are available to simulate the effects of wind, temperature, weight, and stress on product shapes and materials. Before the use of CAE, prototypes of products had to be built and subjected to testing that often destroyed the prototype.

### Computer-Aided Manufacturing (CAM)

**Computer-aided manufacturing (CAM)** is the use of computers to control production equipment. CAM production equipment includes software-controlled drilling, lathe, and milling machines as well as robots (Figure 15-6). The use of robots has aroused much interest, partially because of preconceived ideas of robots as intelligent, humanlike machines. In practice, most industrial robots rarely look like a human and can only perform preprogrammed tasks. Robots are often used for repetitive tasks in hazardous or disagreeable environments, such as welding or painting areas.

FIGURE 15-5 Computer-aided engineering (CAE) allows the user to test product designs before they are built and without damaging the product.

FIGURE 15-6 Computer-aided manufacturing (CAM) is used to control production equipment such as these welding robots on an automobile assembly line.

**Computer-Integrated Manufacturing (CIM)** **Computer-integrated manufacturing (CIM)** is the total integration of the manufacturing process using computers (Figure 15-7). Using CIM concepts, individual production processes are linked so that the production flow is balanced and optimized, and products flow smoothly through the factory. In a CIM factory, automated design processes are linked to automated machining processes that are linked to automated assembly processes that are linked to automated testing and packaging. Under ideal CIM conditions, a product will move through the entire production process under computer control. Because of its complexity, many companies may never fully implement CIM. But CIM's related concepts of minimum inventory and efficient demand-driven production are valid and will be incorporated into many manufacturers' business plans.

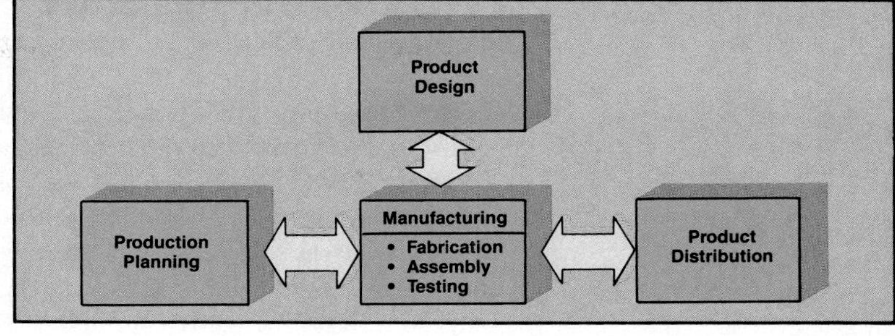


**FIGURE 15-7**
**The concept of computer-integrated manufacturing (CIM) is to use computers to integrate all phases of the manufacturing process from planning and design to manufacturing and distribution.**

## BRINGING THE INFORMATION AGE HOME

Since personal computers became available in the mid-1970s, millions of personal computers have been purchased for home use. It is expected that the use of personal computers in the home will continue to increase. Just as the use of computers in the workplace will change how we work, the use of computers in our homes will change various aspects of our personal lives. The next two sections discuss how personal computers are used in the home, including some possible new applications, and things you should consider when purchasing a personal computer system.

### The Use of Personal Computers in the Home

Personal computers can be used in many different ways in the home. Five general areas of use include: (1) personal services; (2) control of home systems; (3) telecommuting; (4) education; and (5) entertainment.

**Personal Services** In many ways running a home is similar to running a small business. The productivity tools that are used in the office, such as word processing, spreadsheet, and database, can also be used in the home to aid with creating documents, financial planning and analysis, and filing and organizing data. Personal computer software is also available to assist with home accounting applications such as balancing checkbooks, making household budgets, and preparing tax returns. In addition, using a personal computer to transmit and receive data over telephone lines allows home users to access a wealth of information and services. For example, teleshopping and electronic banking are two services that are becoming more popular, and information such as stock prices and airline schedules is available to home users who subscribe to database services such as CompuServe and The Source. The personal services provided by home computer use allows people to perform personal and business-related tasks quickly and conveniently in the comfort of their own homes. Without a personal computer, completing similar activities would take considerably more time because it would frequently require travel to other locations to conduct business and acquire information.

**Control of Home Systems** Another use of computers in the home is to control home systems such as security, environment control, lighting, and landscape sprinkler systems. Personal computers used in this manner are usually linked to special devices such as alarms for security; thermostats for environmental control; and timing devices for lighting and sprinkler systems. When the personal computer system has communication capabilities, a homeowner who is away can use a telephone or another computer to call home and change the operation of one of the control systems. For example, suppose a homeowner is on vacation in Texas and learns that heavy rains have been falling at home in Pennsylvania. It is possible for the homeowner to call home and use the keys of a touch-tone telephone to instruct the computer to turn off the garden sprinkler system. Near Orlando, Florida, an example of the ways that computers may be used in homes of the future is demonstrated in a showcase model called the Xanadu House. In this home computers are used in many ways including controlling home systems.

**Telecommuting** **Telecommuting** refers to the ability of individuals to work at home and communicate with their offices by using personal computers and communication lines. With a personal computer, an employee can access the main computer at the office. Electronic mail can be read and answered. Databases can be accessed and completed projects can be transmitted. It has been predicted that by the end of the 1990s 10 percent of the workforce will be telecommuters. Most of these people will probably arrange their business schedules so that they can telecommute two or three days a week. Telecommuting provides flexibility, allowing companies and employees to work out arrangements that can increase productivity and at the same time meet the needs of individual employees. Some of the advantages possible with telecommuting include reducing the time needed to commute to the office each week; eliminating the need to travel during poor weather conditions; providing a convenient and comfortable work environment for disabled employees or workers recovering from injuries or illnesses; and allowing employees to combine work with personal responsibilities such as child care.

**Education** The use of personal computers for education, called **computer-aided instruction (CAI)**, is another rapidly growing area. While CAI is frequently used to describe software that is developed and used in schools, much of the same software is available for home users. CAI software can be classified into three main types: drill and practice; tutorials; and simulations.

**Drill and practice software** uses a "flashcard" approach to teaching by allowing users to practice skills in subjects such as math and language. A problem or word is displayed on the computer screen and the user enters the answer. The computer accepts the answer and responds by telling the student whether or not the answer was correct. Sometimes the user gets second and third chances to select the correct answer before the computer software will display the correct answer. With **tutorial software**, the computer software displays text and graphics and sometimes uses sound to teach a user concepts about subjects such as chemistry, music theory, or computer literacy. Following the instruction, tutorial software may quiz the user with true/false or multiple choice questions to help ensure that the concepts being taught are understood. The increased use of optical disk storage that provides high quality graphics and direct access capability promises to greatly enhance this type of CAI.

The third type of CAI, **simulation software**, is designed to teach a user by creating a model. For example, many simulation packages are available to teach business concepts. One program designed for children simulates running a lemonade stand and another program for adults simulates the stock market. In the lemonade simulation, the user makes decisions about "How many quarts of lemonade to make" and "What price to charge customers for a glass of lemonade." The computer software accepts the user's decisions, performs computations using the software model, and then responds to the user with the amount of profit or loss for the day. Good CAI software is designed to be user friendly and motivate the user to succeed (Figure 15-8).

**FIGURE 15-8**
**Computer-aided instruction (CAI) software provides a structured yet motivating way to learn. This software package helps the user to develop deductive reasoning, reference, and research skills while learning geography, history, economics, government, and culture.**

In addition to CAI software, some trade schools, colleges and universities are now allowing students with personal computers to take electronic correspondence courses from their homes. Lessons and assignments for classes are transmitted between the student and the school over communication lines.

Education in the home through CAI or electronic correspondence courses allow home users to learn at their own pace, in the convenience of their home, and at a time that fits into their personal schedule. Well-written educational software can be so entertaining that it is sometimes difficult to distinguish between it and entertainment software.

**Entertainment** Entertainment software, or game playing, on home computers has always had a large following among the younger members of the family. However, many adults are surprised to find that entertainment software can also provide them with hours of enjoyment. Popular types of entertainment software include arcade games, board games, simulations, and interactive graphics programs. Most people are familiar with the arcade-type games (similar to video games such as Pac-Man) that are available for computers. A popular board game is computer chess. Simulations include games such as baseball and football and a variety of flight simulators that allow users to pretend they are controlling and navigating different types of aircraft (Figure 15-9). Also available are a wide variety of interactive graphic adventure games that range from rescuing a princess from a castle's dungeon to solving a murder mystery. Many of these games can be played either individually or in small groups. The software usually allows players to adjust the level of play to their skill level, that is, beginner through advanced. With entertainment software, the computer becomes a fun, skillful, and challenging game partner.

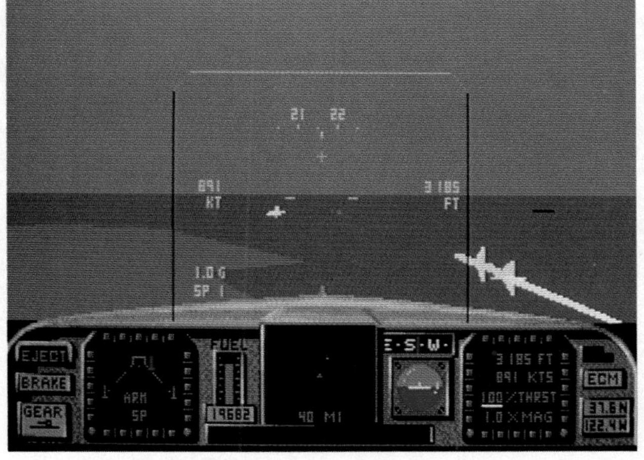


**FIGURE 15-9**
**Flight simulators can be part fun and part educational. Some simulators offer realistic instrument consoles and flight patterns that help teach the user about flying.**

A different type of entertainment available to users who have personal computers with communication capabilities is the access and use of electronic **bulletin board systems**, called **BBSs**, that allow users to communicate with one another and share information (Figure 15-10). While some bulletin boards provide specific services such as buying and selling used computer equipment, many bulletin boards function as electronic clubs for special interest groups and are used to share information about hobbies as diverse as stamp collecting, music, genealogy, and astronomy. Some BBSs are strictly social; users meet new friends and conduct conversations by entering messages through their keyboards.

**FIGURE 15-10**
**This is a list of just some of the bulletin boards available in the San Diego, California area. Bulletin board systems are an excellent source for answers to questions about personal computer equipment and software.**

**300/1200 BPS**

| | | |
|---|---|---|
| A&B Express | 447-1009 | * Z |
| Adventure Board | 224-2636 | |
| The After World | 679-7159 | |
| Back County PCBBS | 789-6377 | |
| The BBS | 447-8143 | |
| The C-64 Exchange | 292-9351 | |
| The Candy Shoppe | 474-5966 | |
| Clue Line | 566-2562 | |
| CMS—Bell Junior High | 267-2807 | |
| CMS—Kearny Mesa | 565-1321 | |
| CMS—Patrick Henry | 287-2644 | |
| CMUG | 433-3162 | |
| The Commodore Shop | 423-7910 | * |
| Cougar Country | 480-3056 | Z |
| Cuyamaca College | 465-3792 | |
| Digex—SDCS DIGSIG | 454-8078 | |
| Disk-Connection | 562-1989 | |
| Educational Technologies | 265-3428 | |
| Eight-Bit Tandy | 571-6366 | |
| Empty V | 425-5808 | Z |
| The Evergreen Forest | 426-2057 | * |
| F&L BBS | 670-7462 | |
| The Fifth Dimension | 670-3969 | * Z |
| Frog's Bible Board | 275-0506 | |
| The Fun House | 282-9124 | |
| Guardian's Cavern | 563-9004 | |
| Heath SIG MS/PC-DOS Support | 461-2417 | |
| His Majesty's Secret Service | 480-8403 | Z |
| JSR Service Net | 258-9078 | |
| Kit's Hideout | 741-0692 | |
| The Knight's Realm | 746-2029 | |
| The Lemonade Stand | 941-6158 | |
| The Looney Bin | 390-9470 | |
| Maui's CoCo Hotspot | 486-4249 | |
| Micro-80 of Oceanside | 439-9169 | |
| Money Works | 579-1403 | |
| The Monsoon | 259-1507 | |
| My Board | 743-7194 | |
| My House | 447-1422 | |
| Ocean Beach BBS | 224-4878 | |
| Outer Limits | 941-2424 | |
| Paulette's Playhouse | 743-3138 | |
| The Post Office | 479-8558 | |
| P.O.C. | 437-1911 | |
| Private Resort | 484-6437 | |
| Ramona Country BBS | 789-6235 | |
| Real-Net BBS | 464-4540 | |
| Sanyo Users Group BBS | 454-8876 | |
| SCCG-TIBBS | 278-8155 | |
| ST—SDACE | 284-3821 | |
| ST SIG Atari ST & Others | 726-4419 | |
| SunSplash | 297-3230 | |
| The 64 & More Store | 258-0951 | |
| Smart Users Group | 480-9686 | |
| also | 726-4419 | |
| Software, Etc. | 291-5790 | Z |
| Special Integrated Designs | 464-0048 | |
| The Surf Shack | 967-6017 | |
| The Torture Chamber | 452-2893 | |
| Zeke | 755-5675 | |

**300/1200/2400 BPS**

| | | |
|---|---|---|
| Adventures In Palancia | 222-1785 | |
| The Amiga Exchange | 223-2734 | Z |
| Apokolips | 488-4714 | |
| Bear Country | 541-7048 | |
| Brian Smith's BBS | 582-0875 | |
| Camelot 3000 | 462-0542 | |
| Classified Connection | 566-1745 | |
| CMS—El Cajon | 444-5442 | |
| COM2: Remote BBS | 471-8730 | |
| Computer Boulevard | 589-0565 | |
| ComputorEdge On-Line | 573-1675 | |
| Computer Outlet | 282-6815 | Z |
| Computer Outlet, North County | 740-0113 | * Z |
| The Computer Room | 287-6006 | |
| CORE BBS | 295-2912 | |
| Cornucopia | 283-0498 | |
| Coronado Wildcat! | 435-8070 | |
| Dollars and Bytes | 483-5477 | Z |
| The Dream Clinic | 670-9522 | |
| The Enchanted World | 692-9518 | |
| Enigma—The Next Generation | 453-1819 | |
| The Fish Express | 792-1653 | |
| Faultline BBS | 481-7340 | |
| FSMAO-2 | 725-6322 | |
| The Flare Path | 561-2999 | |
| The Fun House | 282-9124 | |
| The Information Center | 696-2568 | |
| Imperial Beach BBS | 575-1562 | |
| The Key Of David | 479-2104 | |
| Kingdom Age BBS | 586-7973 | |
| The Knowledge Works BBS | 528-1058 | * |
| Lakeside PC Board | 390-7328 | |
| MacBonsall | 726-1591 | |
| The MacConnection | 259-8735 | |
| Mainstreet Data | 439-6624 | |
| Mac INFONET | 944-3646 | |
| Milliway's | 268-9614 | |
| Morning Star | 575-3310 | |
| Mouse Trap BBS | 462-3975 | * |
| Multitech PC | 578-9221 | |
| Nassau Xpress | 433-9777 | |
| NEXUS Z-Node #63 | 486-0735 | |
| North San Diego Apple Club | 571-9010 | |
| Nova | 489-6975 | |
| PD-SIG | 749-2741 | |
| also | 749-2589 | |
| also | 566-6329 | |
| also | 466-3118 | |
| also | 727-0202 | |
| P-Net (pnet01) | 444-7006 | |
| P-Net (pnet03) | 569-9195 | |
| P-Net (pnet08) | 450-0052 | |
| Prides Crossing | 464-6271 | |
| ProLine [avalon] | 271-0131 | |
| ProLine [beagle] | 452-5565 | |
| ProLine [mercury] | 697-0261 | |
| The Rasta Connection | 282-1211 | |
| The RPC Library | 283-6365 | |
| Sabaline | 692-1961 | |
| San Diego Computer Society | 549-3788 | |
| San Diego Live | 584-1715 | $ |
| also | 584-4172 | $ |
| Scanline | 298-2023 | |
| Seastalker BBS | 581-9379 | |
| Sharky's MAChine | 747-8719 | |
| SomeWares Between Heaven & Hell | 436-9861 | |
| ST MIDI Connection | 452-7535 | |
| Star Base 23 | 560-2996 | |
| Surfer's Paradise | 724-9520 | * |
| Sysport MIDI BBS | 698-7155 | |
| TeleMac | 576-1820 | $ |
| Turnkey Technology | 563-6688 | |
| Z Node #9 | 270-3148 | |

**300/1200/2400/9600 HST STANDARD**

| | | |
|---|---|---|
| Another System | 792-0634 | |
| Bootcamp I | 941-0996 | |
| Bytes 'R Us | 428-9773 | |
| Casino West | 470-0771 | |
| Dead Zone | 755-3350 | |
| DOOGER'S PLACE | 588-8931 | |
| Dworkin's Castle | 438-5256 | |
| MediaLine BBS | 454-1629 | |
| The Final Experience | 670-4445 | |
| Sawyer College of Business BBS | 286-8614 | Z |
| Mushin BBS | 535-9580 | |
| Night Owl, Ham Radio | 279-3921 | |
| Nuggo's Place | 222-3097 | |
| ProLine [simasd] | 239-1397 | |
| ProLine [sol] | 670-5379 | * |
| PD-SIG | 749-6222 | |
| also | 749-3432 | |
| SCANIS | 565-0785 | |
| Serenity | 259-7757 | |
| South Bay BBS | 421-3189 | |
| Starhelm Graystaff | 479-3006 | |

**300/1200/2400/9600 BPS Trailblazer**

| | | |
|---|---|---|
| People-Net (pnet12) | 259-3704 | * |

**300/1200/2400/9600 BPS Racial Vadic**

| | | |
|---|---|---|
| PD-SIG | 749-6384 | * |

**LEGEND**

- * New or updated information.
- Z After hours or weekends.
- $ Requires a one-time donation for access.

*ComputorEdge* acknowledges this is not a complete listing of all BBSs in San Diego area. We reserve the right to reject or cancel any submission for publication.

**62** October 14, 1988 COMPUTOREDGE

In addition to sharing hobby information with other computer users on a BBS, some personal computer users use their home computer as a tool for personal hobbies. Computers are used by hobbyists to design quilt and stained glass patterns, run model trains, organize stamp, doll, and photography collections, and write, transpose, play, and print musical scores.

**Summary of the Use of Personal Computers in the Home** As you can see, personal computers are used in homes in a variety of ways. Whether or not you now use a personal computer in your home, it is very probable that you will at some time in the near future. In fact, it is very possible that within the next decade you will have multiple computers in your home. Because computers can be used in so many different ways and also because computer technology is changing so rapidly, it is important that you carefully choose any computer system that you may purchase. Some general guidelines for purchasing personal computers are discussed in the next section.

## Guidelines for Buying a Personal Computer

When purchasing a personal computer, make every effort to select a computer system that matches your individual needs as closely as possible. Six general steps recommended for purchasing a personal computer system include:

**Step 1. Become computer literate.** This is truly the first step and an important step in making a wise purchase. You might be surprised that many people go straight out and buy computer equipment without understanding the capability of a personal computer or the tasks it can and cannot perform. Many times these people buy a computer like the one their neighbor or friend purchased, and expect it to meet their needs. Sometimes it does, but frequently they are disappointed. Hopefully this will not happen to you. You already have an advantage because by reading this book, you now know a great deal about computers and have developed a foundation of knowledge on which you can base your software and equipment decisions. In short, you already are computer literate. Because computer technology is changing rapidly, to stay computer literate you will need to stay current with the changes in the field. You can do this by reading periodicals or attending seminars on "state of the art" computer technology.

**Step 2. Define and prioritize the type of tasks you want to perform on your computer.** This step will help you to see more clearly exactly what you want to do with your computer and will help you to select software and equipment that will match these needs. Define your needs in writing. Create a numbered list with the most important application at the top and the least important application at the bottom. General applications like word processing, spreadsheets, database, and communications are easy to include on the list. You may, however, have a special application in mind, such as controlling a household security system. Being computer literate will help you to know if a special application is feasible. It will also help you to discuss any special needs you may have with computer professionals who can help you. Once your list is completed you can begin to evaluate the available software.

**Step 3. Select the software packages that best meet your needs.** Periodicals, computer stores, and user groups are all good resources when it comes to evaluating the available software. For more on evaluating software, review the section in Chapter 2, "Guidelines for Purchasing Microcomputer Applications Software."

In addition to purchasing commercial software, another possibility is to consider selecting shareware and public domain software. **Shareware** is software that users may try out on their own systems before paying a fee. If a user decides to keep and use the software a registration fee is sent to the software publisher (Figure 15-11). **Public domain software** is free software that is not copyrighted and can therefore be distributed among users. While the quality of shareware and public domain software varies greatly, some of the software is quite good. This type of software can be obtained from BBSs and also from public domain software libraries.

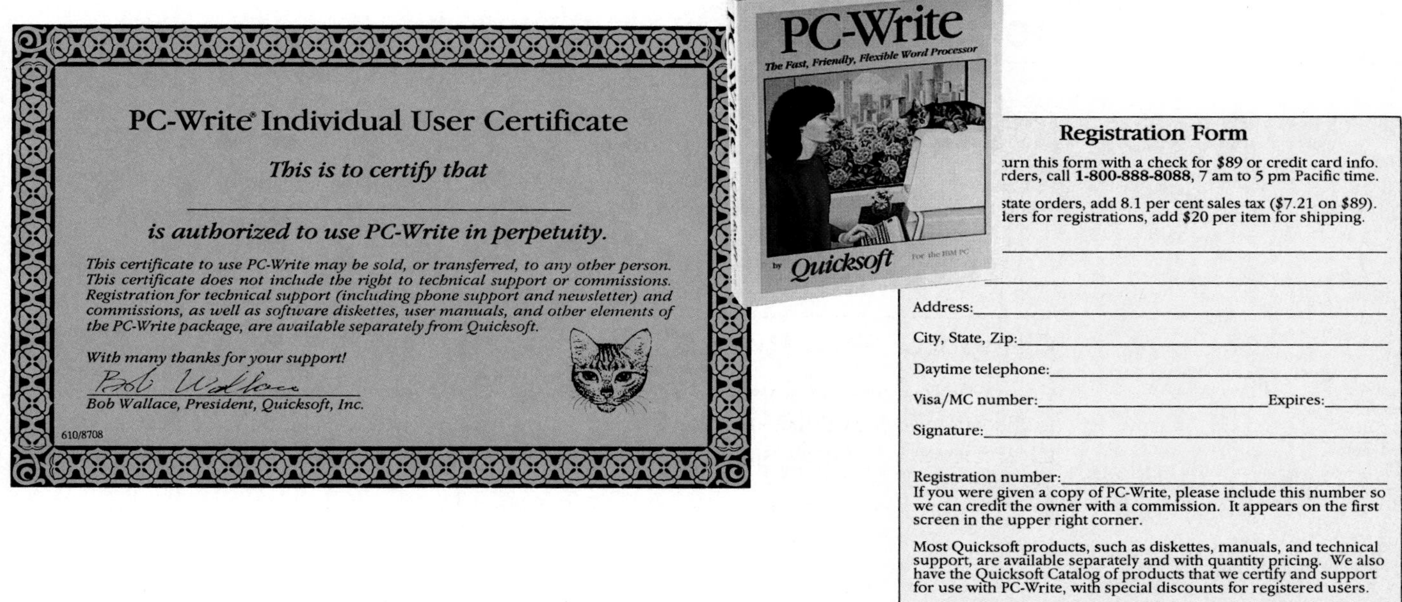

PC-Write® Individual User Certificate

*This is to certify that*

____________________

***is authorized to use PC-Write in perpetuity.***

*This certificate to use PC-Write may be sold, or transferred, to any other person. This certificate does not include the right to technical support or commissions. Registration for technical support (including phone support and newsletter) and commissions, as well as software diskettes, user manuals, and other elements of the PC-Write package, are available separately from Quicksoft.*

*With many thanks for your support!*

*Bob Wallace, President, Quicksoft, Inc.*

610/8708

PC-Write
The Fast, Friendly, Flexible Word Processor
by Quicksoft
For the IBM PC



**Registration Form**

urn this form with a check for $89 or credit card info.
rders, call **1-800-888-8088**, 7 am to 5 pm Pacific time.

state orders, add 8.1 per cent sales tax ($7.21 on $89).
lers for registrations, add $20 per item for shipping.

Address:__________

City, State, Zip:__________

Daytime telephone:__________

Visa/MC number:__________Expires:______

Signature:__________

Registration number:__________
If you were given a copy of PC-Write, please include this number so we can credit the owner with a commission. It appears on the first screen in the upper right corner.

Most Quicksoft products, such as diskettes, manuals, and technical support, are available separately and with quantity pricing. We also have the Quicksoft Catalog of products that we certify and support for use with PC-Write, with special discounts for registered users.

Quicksoft, 219 First Ave N #224, Seattle, WA 98109. 206/282-0452.

**FIGURE 15-11**
**After trying the PC-Write software, users fill out a registration form and mail it with a fee to Quicksoft, the publisher of PC-Write. A user certificate is then sent to the user.**

**Step 4. Select equipment that will run the software you have selected.** The capabilities of the different types of personal computers vary greatly. For example, some personal computers can perform extensive graphics while others cannot. Selecting the software that meets your needs before selecting your equipment guides you in selecting appropriate equipment. Some software only runs on certain types of personal computers. Also, knowing the software you want to run prevents overbuying (purchasing a machine that is more powerful than you need) or underbuying (purchasing a machine that is not powerful enough). Other things to consider when evaluating equipment include: processing speed of the microprocessor, memory size, system expandability, compatibility of the system with other personal computers, monochrome or color display, amount and type of auxiliary storage, printer type and speed, and communications capabilities.

**Step 5. Select the suppliers for the software and equipment.** Options include used equipment and software, mail order, and computer stores. Price, warranties, training, service, and repair are all things to consider when selecting a supplier. Obtaining the best overall value may not mean paying the lowest price. A store that is willing to provide you with assistance in assembling your system or providing some training may be well worth a slightly higher price.

**Step 6. Purchase the software and equipment.** If you have followed these guidelines you will probably feel both excited and confident with the decisions you have made. Your efforts to define your computing needs and to select software, equipment, and a supplier that will meet those needs should have helped you to select a personal computer system that is appropriate for you and with which you will be satisfied.

### Summary of Bringing the Information Age Home

Personal computers are used in homes to aid in a variety of tasks such as personal services, control of home systems, telecommuting, education, and entertainment. When purchasing a personal computer system for the home, users should first become computer literate and evaluate their computer processing needs, and then purchase software and equipment that meets those needs. The trend is clear. Personal computers will continue to bring the information age into our homes.

The changes that accompany the information age raise several issues that are related to society as a whole. Some of these issues will be discussed in the following section.

## SOCIAL ISSUES

Significant inventions such as the automobile and television have always challenged existing values and caused society to think about the right and wrong ways to use the new invention. So too has the computer. This section discusses some of the social issues related to computers, including security and computer crime and privacy.

### Computer Security and Crime

Computer security and computer crime are closely related topics. **Computer security** refers to the safeguards established to prevent and detect unauthorized use and deliberate or accidental damage to computer systems and data. **Computer crime** is the use of a computer to commit an illegal act. This section discusses the types of crimes that can be committed and the security measures that can be taken to prevent and detect them.

**Software Theft** Software theft, often called **software piracy**, became a major problem with the increased use of personal computers. Some people have a hard time understanding why they should pay hundreds, perhaps thousands of dollars for what appears to be an inexpensive diskette or tape, and instead of paying for an authorized copy of the software they make an illegal copy. This leads software manufacturers to install elaborate copy protection schemes designed to prevent anyone from copying the software. However, the copy protection also prevents authorized users who have paid the license fee from making backup copies of the software for security purposes. Today, software piracy is still an issue. It is estimated that for every authorized copy of a commercial program, there is at least one illegal copy. Although many companies have abandoned copy protection, they still take illegal copying seriously and vigorously prosecute offenders when caught. For large users, the financial incentives for stealing software have been lowered by site licensing and multiple copy discounts. Site licensing allows organizations to pay a single fee for multiple copies of a program used at a single location. Multiple copy discounts reduce the fee of each additional copy of a program license.

**Unauthorized Access and Use** **Unauthorized access** can be defined as computer trespassing, in other words, being logged on a system without permission. Many so-called computer hackers boast of the number of systems that they have been able to access by using a modem. These hackers usually don't do any damage and merely "wander around" the accessed system before logging off.

**Unauthorized use** is the use of a computer system or computer data for unapproved and possibly illegal activities. Unauthorized use may range from an employee using the company computer for keeping his child's soccer league scores to someone gaining access to a bank funds system and creating an unauthorized transfer. Unauthorized use could also include the theft of computerized information such as customer lists or product plans.

The key to preventing both unauthorized access and unauthorized use is an appropriate level of authorization. Authorization techniques range from simple passwords to advanced biometric devices that can identify individuals by their fingerprint, voice, or eye pattern. The level of authorization should match the degree of risk and should be regularly reviewed to determine if the level is still appropriate.

**Malicious Damage** Malicious or deliberate damage to the data in a computer system is often difficult to detect because the damaged data may not be used or carefully reviewed on a regular basis. A disgruntled employee or an outsider may gain access to the system and delete or alter individual records or an entire file. One of the most potentially dangerous types of malicious damage is done by a **virus**, a computer program designed to copy itself into other software and spread through multiple computer systems. Figure 15-12 on the following page shows how a virus can spread from one system to another. Although they have been known for a long time, it is only in recent years that viruses have become a serious problem. Besides developing specific programs called "vaccines" to locate and remove viruses, organizations are becoming more aggressive in prosecuting persons suspected of planting viruses. In what was described as the first computer virus trial, in 1988 a former programmer was convicted in Texas of planting a program in his employer's computer system that deleted 168,000 sales commission records.

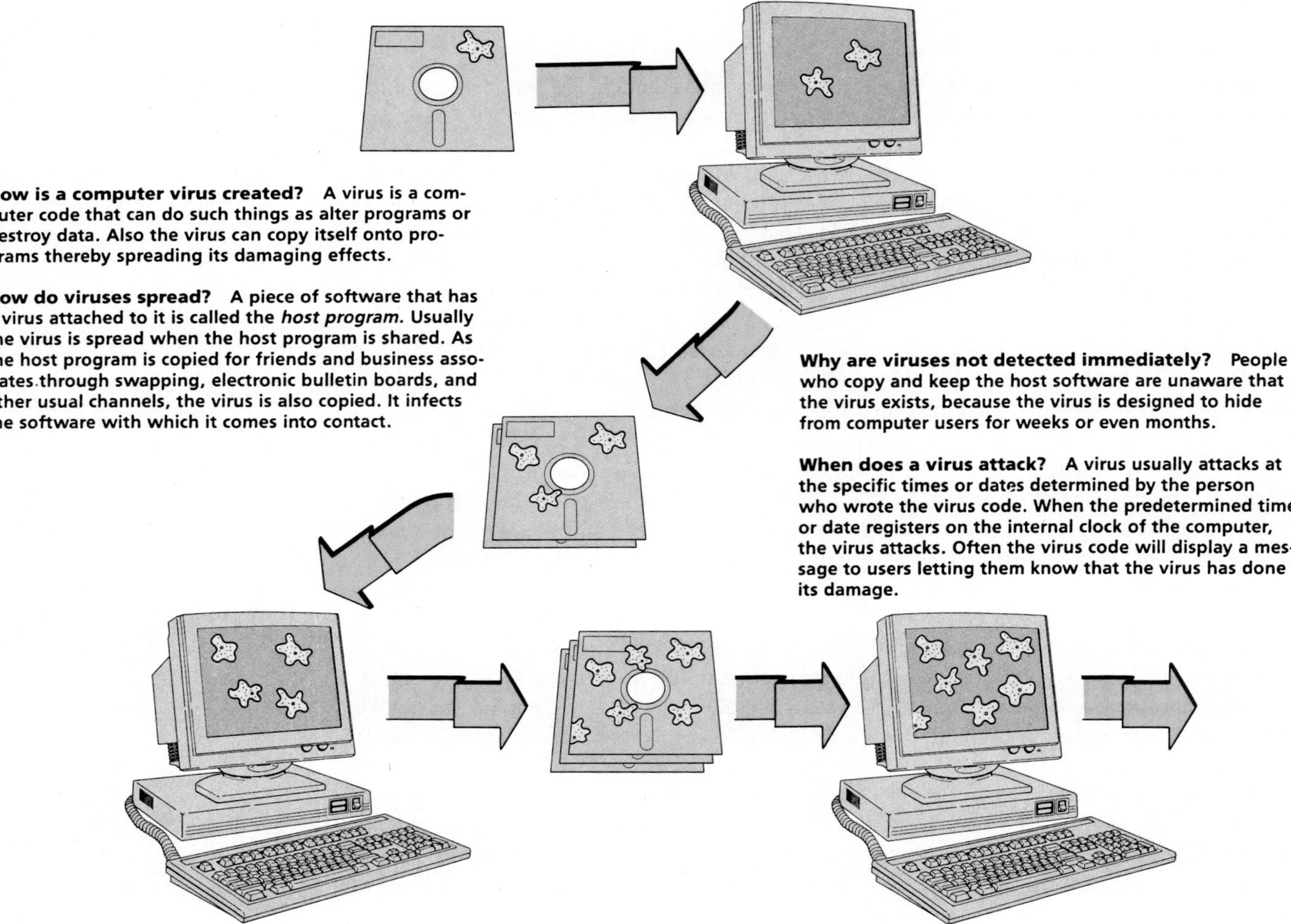

A COMPUTER VIRUS: WHAT IT IS AND HOW IT SPREADS

**How is a computer virus created?** A virus is a computer code that can do such things as alter programs or destroy data. Also the virus can copy itself onto programs thereby spreading its damaging effects.

**How do viruses spread?** A piece of software that has a virus attached to it is called the *host program*. Usually the virus is spread when the host program is shared. As the host program is copied for friends and business associates through swapping, electronic bulletin boards, and other usual channels, the virus is also copied. It infects the software with which it comes into contact.

**Why are viruses not detected immediately?** People who copy and keep the host software are unaware that the virus exists, because the virus is designed to hide from computer users for weeks or even months.

**When does a virus attack?** A virus usually attacks at the specific times or dates determined by the person who wrote the virus code. When the predetermined time or date registers on the internal clock of the computer, the virus attacks. Often the virus code will display a message to users letting them know that the virus has done its damage.


**FIGURE 15-12**
**This illustration shows how a virus program can be transmitted from one computer system to another.**

Single acts of malicious damage, especially when performed by employees with authorized access to the computer system, are very difficult to prevent. The best protection against this type of act remains adequate backup files that enable damaged data to be restored.

## Privacy

In the past, one way to maintain privacy was to keep information in separate locations—individual stores had their own credit files, government agencies had separate records, doctors had separate files, and so on. However, it is now technically and economically feasible to store large amounts of related data about individuals in one database. Some people believe that the easier access to the data increases the possibility for misuse. Others worry that the increased storage capacity of computers may encourage the storage of unnecessary personal data.

The concern about information privacy has led to federal and state laws regarding the storage and disclosure of personal data. Common points in these laws include: (1) Information collected and stored about individuals should be limited to what is necessary to carry out the function of the business or governmental agency collecting the data. (2) Once collected, provisions should be made to restrict access to the data to those employees within the organization who need access to it to perform their job duties. (3) Personal information should be released outside the organization collecting the data only when the person has agreed to its disclosure. (4) When information is collected about an individual, the individual should know that data is being collected and have the opportunity to determine the accuracy of the data.

## SUMMARY OF TRENDS AND ISSUES IN THE INFORMATION AGE

Based on current and planned developments, the impact of computers and the information age will be even greater in the future than it has been to date. However, as a society and as individuals, we have an obligation to use the computer responsibly and not abuse the power it provides. This presents constant challenges that sometimes weigh the rights of the individual against increased efficiency and productivity. The computer must be thought of as a tool whose effectiveness is determined by the skill and experience of the user. As a computer literate member of society, you will be better able to participate in decisions on how to best use computerized information systems.

## CHAPTER SUMMARY

1. Existing business information systems will continue to undergo profound changes as new technology, software, and methods become available.
2. Trends will include more online, interactive systems; less batch processing; and increased use of relational database systems.
3. The **automated office**, sometimes referred to as the **electronic office**, is the term that describes the use of electronic devices such as computers, facsimile machines, and computerized telephone systems to make office work more productive.
4. Word processing is the ability to electronically create, store, revise, and print written documents.
5. Electronic mail is the ability to transmit messages to and receive messages from other computer users.
6. **Voice mail** can be considered verbal electronic mail.
7. Desktop publishing involves the use of computers to produce printed documents that can combine different sizes and styles of text and graphics.
8. **Facsimile** or **Fax** machines are used to transmit a reproduced image of a document over standard phone lines.
9. Image processing is the ability to store and retrieve a reproduced image of a document.
10. **Teleconferencing** usually means **video conferencing**, the use of computers and television cameras to transmit video images and the sound of the conference participants to other participants with similar equipment at a remote location.
11. The goal of the **automated factory** is to increase productivity through the use of automated, and often computer-controlled, equipment.
12. **Computer-aided design (CAD)** uses a computer and special graphics software to aid in product design.
13. **Computer-aided engineering (CAE)** is the use of computers to test product designs.
14. **Computer-aided manufacturing (CAM)** is the use of computers to control production equipment.
15. **Computer-integrated manufacturing (CIM)** is the total integration of the manufacturing process using computers.
16. Personal computers are used in the home in many different ways, including: (1) personal services; (2) control of home systems; (3) telecommuting; (4) education; and (5) entertainment.
17. The personal services provided by home computer use allow people to perform personal and business-related tasks quickly and conveniently in the comfort of their own homes.
18. Another use of computers in the home is to control home systems such as security, environment control, lighting, and landscape sprinkler systems.
19. **Telecommuting** refers to the ability of individuals to work at home and communicate with their offices by using personal computers and communication lines.
20. The use of personal computers for education, called **computer-aided instruction (CAI)**, is a rapidly growing area.
21. CAI software can be classified into three main types: **drill and practice software**; **tutorial software**; and **simulation software**.
22. Popular types of entertainment software include arcade games, board games, simulations, and interactive graphics programs.

23. Electronic **bulletin board systems**, called **BBSs**, allow users to communicate with one another and share information.
24. The guidelines for purchasing a personal computer recommend that you: (1) become computer literate; (2) define and prioritize the type of tasks you want to perform on your computer; (3) select the software packages that best meet your needs; (4) select equipment that will run the software you have selected; (5) select the suppliers for the software and equipment; (6) purchase the software and equipment.
25. **Shareware** is software that users may try out on their own systems before paying a fee.
26. **Public domain software** is not copyrighted and can therefore be distributed among users.
27. **Computer security** refers to the safeguards established to prevent and detect unauthorized use and deliberate or accidental damage to computer systems and data.
28. **Computer crime** is the use of a computer to commit an illegal act.
29. Today, **software piracy** is still an issue and it is estimated that for every authorized copy of a commercial program, there is at least one illegal copy.
30. **Unauthorized access** can be defined as computer trespassing, in other words, being logged on a system without permission.
31. **Unauthorized use** is the use of a computer system or computer data for unapproved and possibly illegal activities.
32. The key to preventing both unauthorized access and unauthorized use is an appropriate level of authorization.
33. One of the most potentially dangerous types of malicious damage is done by a **virus**, a computer program designed to copy itself into other software and spread through multiple computer systems.
34. The concern about information privacy has led to federal and state laws regarding the storage and disclosure of personal data.

## KEY TERMS

Automated factory *15.6*
Automated office *15.4*
Bulletin board systems (BBSs) *15.10*
Computer-aided design (CAD) *15.6*
Computer-aided engineering (CAE) *15.6*
Computer-aided instruction (CAI) *15.8*
Computer-aided manufacturing (CAM) *15.6*
Computer crime *15.13*
Computer-integrated manufacturing (CIM) *15.7*
Computer security *15.13*
Drill and practice software *15.8*
Electronic office *15.4*
Facsimile (Fax) *15.4*
Public domain software *15.11*
Shareware *15.11*
Simulation software *15.9*
Software piracy *15.13*
Telecommuting *15.8*
Teleconferencing *15.5*
Tutorial software *15.8*
Unauthorized access *15.13*
Unauthorized use *15.13*
Video conferencing *15.5*
Virus *15.13*
Voice mail *15.4*

## REVIEW QUESTIONS

1. List three electronic devices that are used in an automated office. What is voice mail? How is a Fax machine used?
2. What is the goal of the automated factory? Briefly explain the four technologies that are used.
3. What are some of the personal services available to home computer users?
4. Describe the three general categories of educational software.
5. List the six guidelines for buying a personal computer. Why is it recommended that you select your software before your equipment?
6. What is software piracy?
7. What is unauthorized access and unauthorized use? How can they be prevented?
8. Explain why computer viruses are malicious. What is a "vaccine" program?
9. Discuss the four common points covered in the state and federal information privacy laws.

# Introduction to DOS

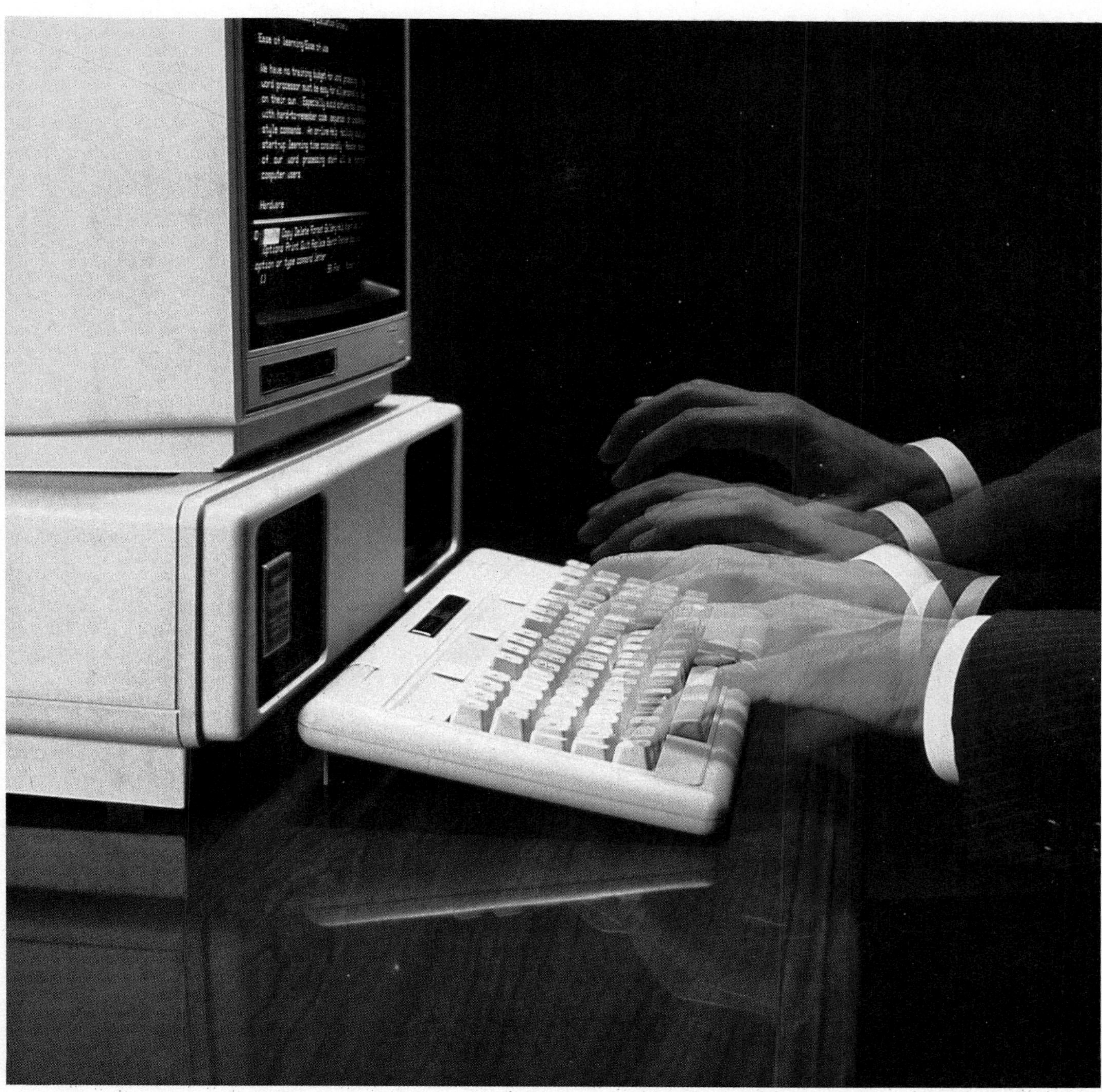

# Introduction to DOS

## OBJECTIVES

You will have mastered the basics of using DOS when you can:

- "Boot" your microcomputer
- Enter the time and date, if required
- Establish the system default disk drive
- List a disk directory
- Cancel commands
- Format diskettes, using /S and /V
- Use file specifications to address files on various disks
- Copy files on the same disk and from one disk to another
- Rename and erase files
- Organize and manage file subdirectories on a hard disk
- Start application programs

## INTRODUCTION

An **operating system** is one or more programs that control and manage the operation of the computer. These programs provide an interface among the user, the computer equipment, and the application programs. For instance, to use a computer to print a memo, you'd first use the operating system to start the computer. Next, you would enter a keyboard command that the operating system processes to activate the word processing program. When the word processing program instructs the computer to print the memo, the operating system finds the proper file on the disk, retrieves the data from the disk, and routes the output to the printer. The operating system is not part of the application program itself, but it provides essential services that the application program uses to perform its functions.

### Operating Systems for IBM PCs

Microsoft Corporation joined forces with IBM to develop the program known as **DOS**, an acronym for **Disk Operating System**, used since 1981 in IBM PC and IBM-compatible computers. **PC-DOS** is the name for versions of DOS distributed by IBM for its Personal Computer and Personal System/2 lines. All IBM-compatible computers use versions of this operating system distributed by Microsoft as **MS-DOS**. This book uses the term DOS to refer to any of the various editions of PC- or MS-DOS and covers information applicable to all versions of DOS, unless otherwise noted.

## DOS Versions

The numbers following the abbreviation DOS indicate the specific version and release of the product (Figure 1). The **version** number is the whole number and signifies a major improvement of the product. The **release** number is the decimal number and identifies minor corrections or changes to a version of the product. For example, DOS 1.1 corrected some minor problems with DOS 1.0.

Software developers try to maintain **upward compatibility**, that is, that all the features of an earlier version remain supported by a later one. However, "downward" compatibility is not common. Programs or equipment that require the features of DOS 3.3, for example, will not function with DOS 3.2 or earlier versions.

| DOS VERSION RELEASE | MAJOR FEATURE SUPPORTED | YEAR |
|---|---|---|
| 3.3 | Introduction of PS/2 | 1987 |
| 3.2 | Token-Ring Networks, 3.5" Diskette | |
| 3.1 | Addition of Networking, 1.2 mb 5.25 Diskette | |
| 3.0 | Introduction of PC/AT | 1985 |
| 2.1 | Enhancements to 2.0 | |
| 2.0 | Introduction of PC/XT | 1983 |
| 1.1 | Enhancements to 1.0 | |
| 1.0 | Introduction of IBM/PC | 1981 |

FIGURE 1

# USING THE DISK OPERATING SYSTEM (DOS)

## Starting the Computer

DOS programs are normally stored on a diskette or on a hard disk. To begin using the operating system, it must be read into main memory, a process known as **booting**. If you are using a system with two diskette drives, insert the diskette containing DOS into drive A of the computer and turn on the computer (Figure 2). If you are using a system with a hard disk, DOS is already available on the hard disk. Turn on the computer (Figure 3) and be certain you do not insert a diskette before the system has completed its startup process. If the computer is already on and your DOS diskette is in drive A (or DOS is on the hard disk and drive A is empty), you can restart the system by pressing the CTRL, ALT, and DEL keys simultaneously (Figure 4).

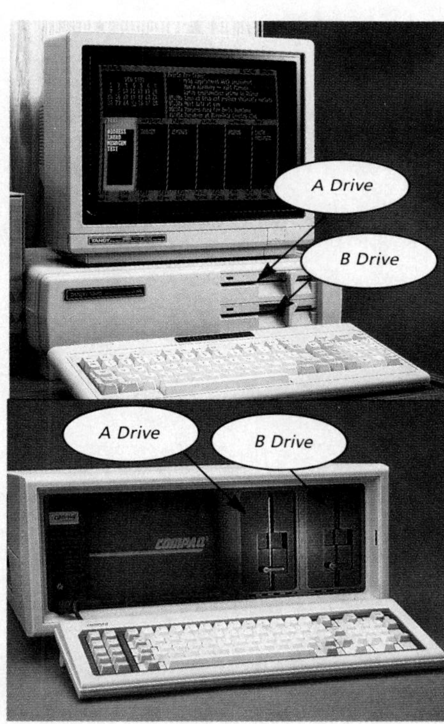


FIGURE 2

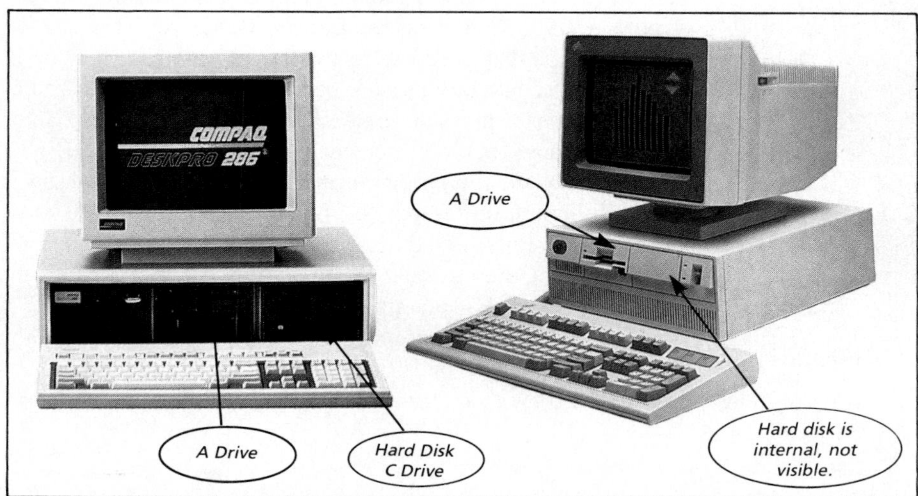


FIGURE 3

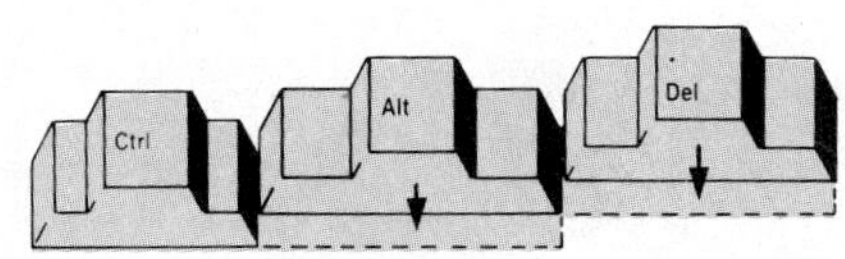


FIGURE 4

**The Cold Start.** Starting the computer by turning on the power switch is known as a **cold start** or **cold boot**. The computer will first run some tests to diagnose its own circuitry (known on some computers as a **power-on self-test**, or **POST** process). After running this test, the computer will begin to read the DOS diskette.

**The Warm Start or Reset.** Restarting the operating system by pressing the CTRL, ALT, and DEL keys simutaneously is called a **warm start**, or **warm boot**, because the computer has already been turned on. This procedure does not repeat the POST process, but it does erase all programs and data from main memory and reloads DOS. Do not worry about losing data from diskettes during this process, however, because data properly stored on diskettes will remain there.

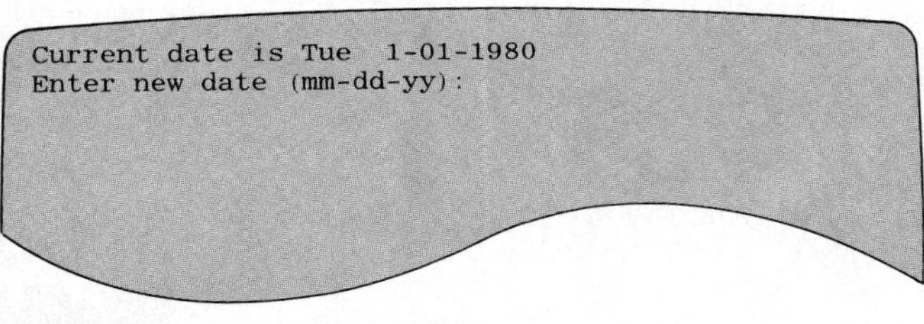

Current date is Tue 1-01-1980
Enter new date (mm-dd-yy):


FIGURE 5

**Loading DOS.** While the system is being booted, the status light on the disk drive flashes on and off, and the disk drive whirls for a few seconds. During this time, the program from the operating system is being loaded into main memory. When DOS has been loaded into main memory, an image similar to Figure 5 appears on the screen. When DOS has been loaded into main memory, the system will perform various activities depending upon how the startup procedure has been tailored for the specific computer.

## Setting the Date and Time

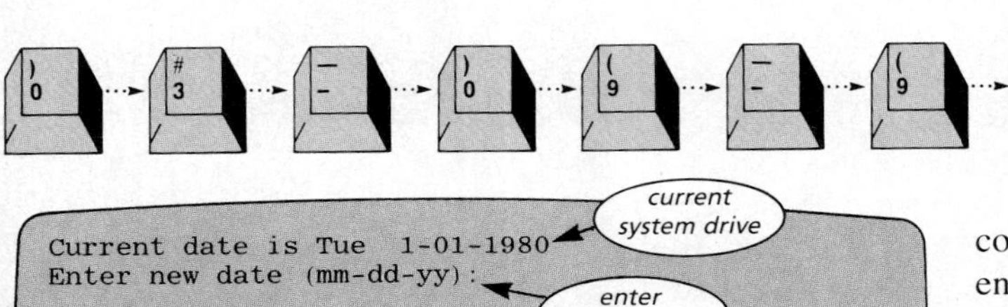


FIGURE 6

Although not required, it is a good practice to enter the date and time so that files you create are accurately documented. Enter the current date when the computer screen displays the message shown in Figure 6. To enter the date, always enter the month, day, and year separated by hyphens (-), slashes (/), or, in DOS 3.30 and later versions, periods (.). For example, assume that today is March 9, 1990. Type 03-09-90. Then press the Enter key (Figure 7).

If the date displayed is already correct—which it may be if your computer has an internal clock—you do not need to enter the date. Instead, press the Enter key when the message "Enter new date:" appears on the screen.

You enter the time in the format hh:mm:ss.xx, where hh stands for hours, mm stands for minutes, ss stands for seconds, and xx stands for hundredths of a second. As with the date, you are not required to enter the time, although it is a good practice to do so. For practice, type the time as 11:50 and press the Enter key (Figure 8). (If you do not include seconds and hundredths of seconds, the operating system assumes a value of zero for them.)

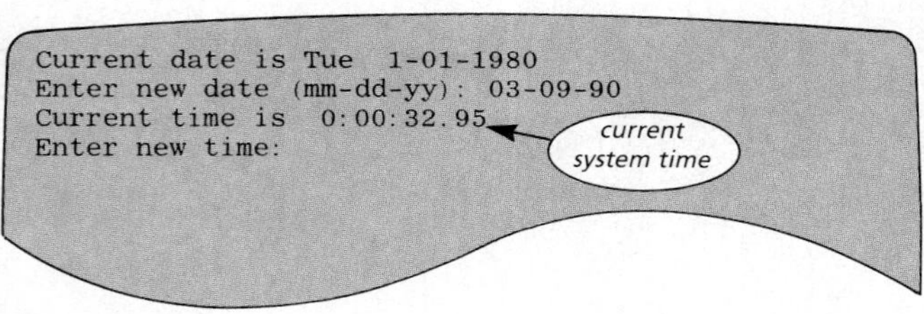


FIGURE 7

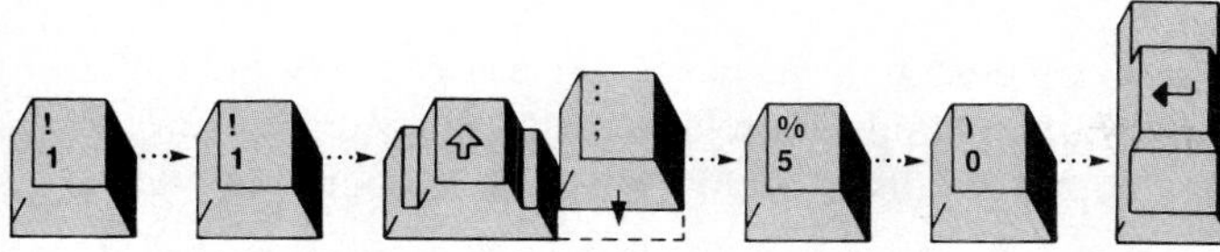


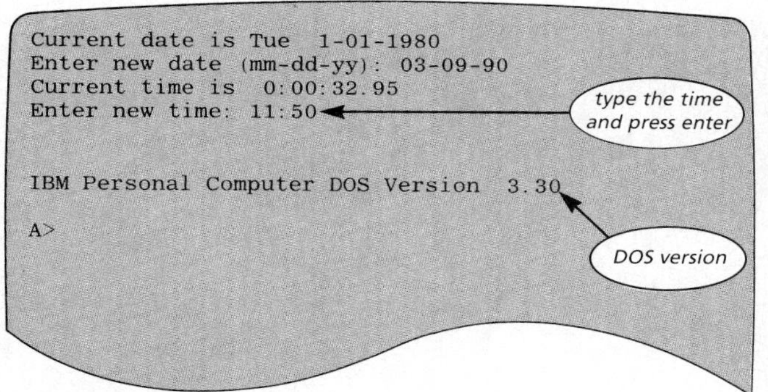

Current date is Tue 1-01-1980
Enter new date (mm-dd-yy): 03-09-90
Current time is 0:00:32.95
Enter new time: 11:50
type the time and press enter
IBM Personal Computer DOS Version 3.30
A>
DOS version


FIGURE 8

## The DOS Prompt

After the messages are displayed, the **system prompt**, also called the **DOS prompt**, indicates that the operating system is ready to receive your commands (Figures 9 and 10). The letter displayed within the prompt > indicates which drive has been assigned as the default disk drive. The **default drive** is the disk drive in which the operating system assumes the disk or diskette containing the operating system and other programs is located. Another term used for the default drive is **current drive**, because it is the drive that is assumed to be in current use.

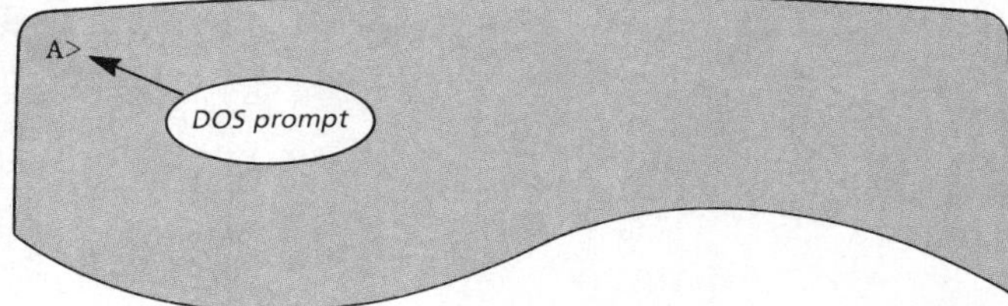


FIGURE 9

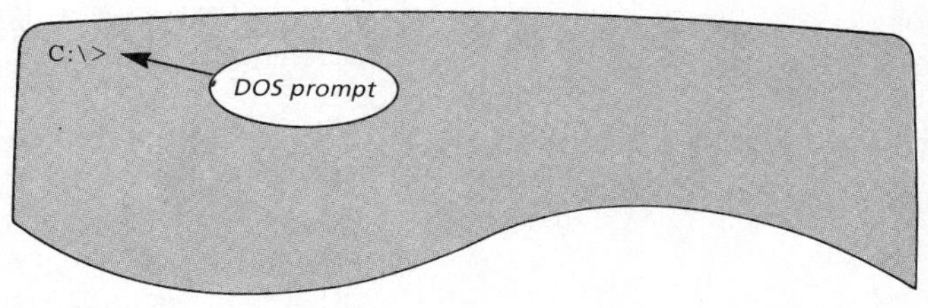


FIGURE 10

## The Default Drive

The default drive assignment will vary depending upon the specific hardware you are using. A two-diskette system typically assigns drive A as the default drive (Figure 9). If your computer has a hard disk, the default drive will initially be drive C, and the prompt will appear as it is shown in Figure 10.

At times you will need to change the default drive assignment. Before you do so, be certain that the new drive is ready. A hard disk is always installed, but in a two-diskette system the disk drive must have a diskette inserted before it can be assigned as the default drive. If the drive does not have a diskette in it, the computer will give you an error message.

To change the drive assignment, type the letter of the new drive to be used, followed by a colon, and then press the Enter key. For example, to change the default to drive B, type the letter B, followed by a colon (:), and then press the Enter key (Figure 11, step 1). The prompt will display drive B as the default drive. Now, change the default drive back to drive A by typing A:↵ (Figure 11, step 2).

FIGURE 11

Step 1: Change the default drive from A to B. Step 2: Change the default drive from B to A.

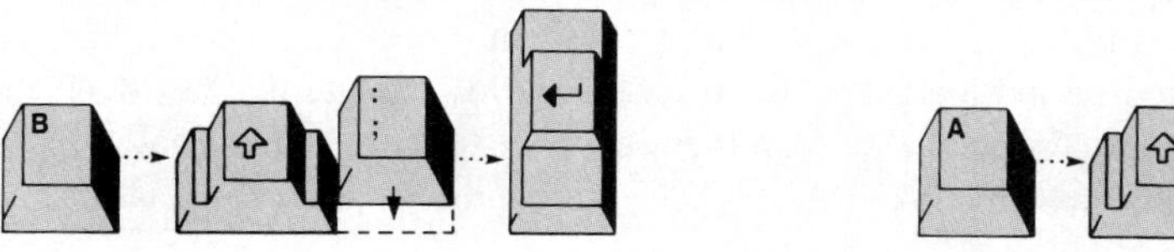

In most of the examples in this text, the default drive will be drive A. You will be told when the procedures for a hard disk are different than those for a diskette system. Figure 12 shows how to change the default drive for a hard disk system from drive C to drive A (step 1) and back to drive C (step 2).

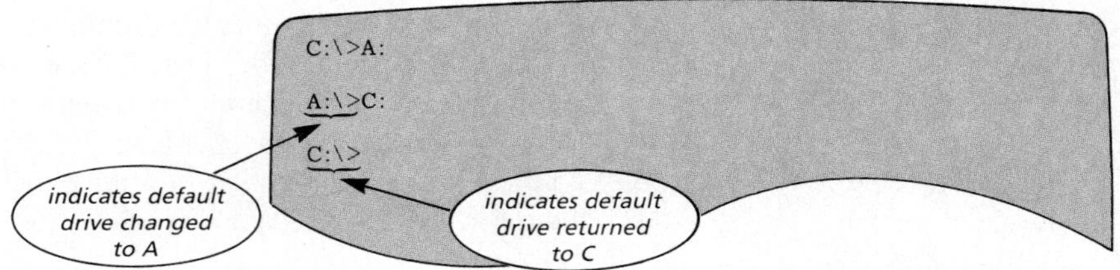


Step 1: Change the default drive from C to A.

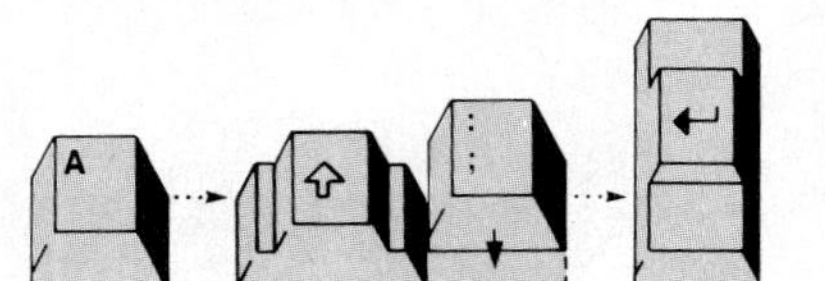

Step 2: Change the default drive from A to C.

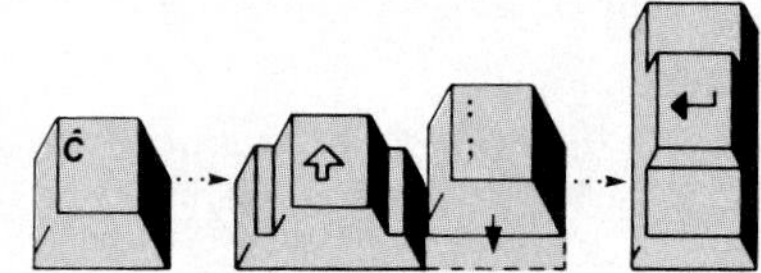

FIGURE 12

# ENTERING DISK OPERATING SYSTEM (DOS) COMMANDS

Now that you have booted the DOS system, you are able to enter commands to instruct the computer. DOS includes a variety of commands to assist you in using the computer. Some of the commands might be called "status" or "informative" commands because they instruct DOS to give you information about the system's operation. The directory command, DIR, is one such informative command. It lists the names of files stored on a disk. Other commands support DOS functions, helping you use the computer. FORMAT, for instance, prepares a new disk for use in storing files.

The DOS commands you have entered so far have been typed in capital letters. You can type capital letters either by pressing the Caps Lock key or by holding down one of the two shift keys. However, you do not have to enter all DOS commands in capital letters. Commands, drive specifiers, and other entries to the operating system can be entered in any combination of uppercase and lowercase letters.

## Internal and External Commands

An **internal command** is part of the operating system program. Once you have loaded DOS into main memory, an internal command is always started there. You can enter an internal command at any time. It does not matter whether the DOS system diskette is in the default drive. DIR, COPY, CLS, ERASE, RENAME, and DEL are examples of internal commands.

**External commands**, on the other hand, are stored on the DOS system disk as program files. They must be read from the disk into main memory before they can be executed. This means that the DOS system disk must be in the default drive or the specified drive so that the program can be found on the disk and loaded into main memory for execution. FORMAT and CHKDSK are examples of external commands. Another easy way to identify external commands is to look for the extensions .BAT, .COM, or .EXE following the filename, such as FORMAT.EXE.

# DIRECTORY COMMAND (DIR)

One of the functions of the operating system is to store files containing both programs and data on diskettes. To facilitate that storage, the operating system maintains a directory of all the files stored on a diskette. To display the directory of the diskette you have placed in drive A of your computer, use the **DIR command**. At the A> prompt, type DIR and press the Enter key (Figure 13).

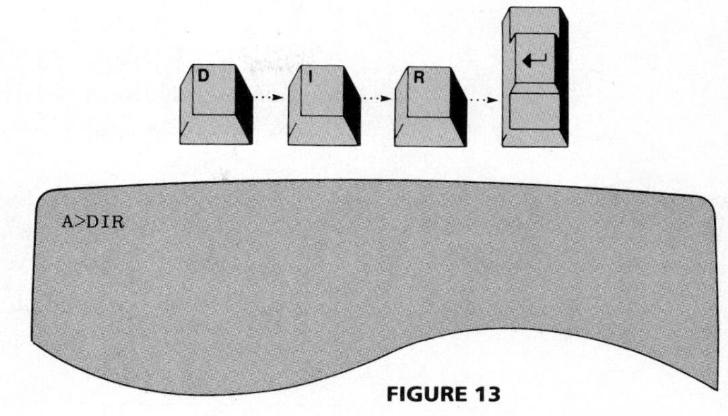


FIGURE 13

The directory of the diskette in the default drive will then be displayed as in Figure 14. Because the default drive is drive A (as specified by the system's A> prompt), the directory of the diskette in drive A is displayed. If you are using a hard disk and your default disk is drive C, the DIR command will display the directory of your hard disk.

The directory itself consists of the names of the files on the diskette, the number of bytes required to store the file on the diskette, the date of the last change of the file, and for some files, the time of the last change of the file. The message at the end of the directory listing indicates the number of files on the diskette (in Figure 14 there are 15 files on the diskette) and the remaining space available on the diskette (181248 unused bytes remain on the diskette in Figure 14). At the end of the directory display, the system prompt reappears on the screen, indicating that the system is ready for your next command.

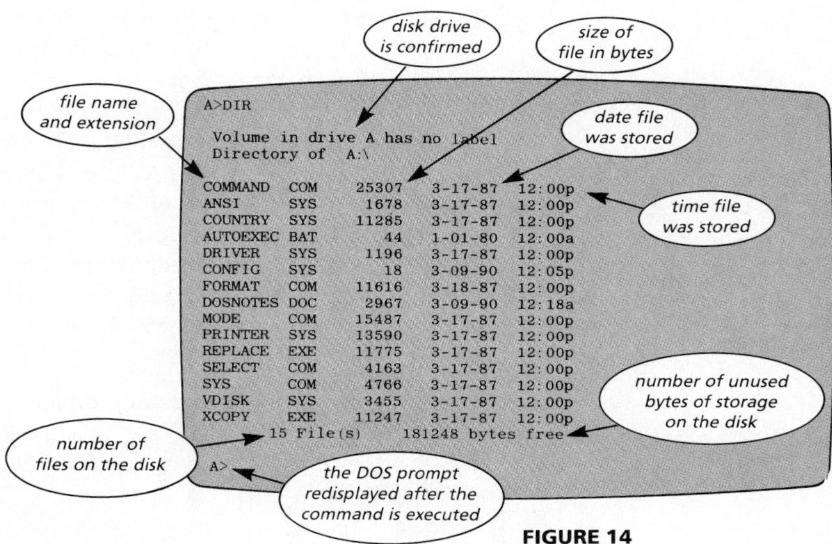


FIGURE 14

## Displaying Directories of Other Disks

The directories of files on diskettes in other disk drives of the computer can be displayed as well. For practice, remove your system diskette from drive A and move it to drive B. To display the directory, type the command DIR B: and press the Enter key, as in Figure 15. You have directed the operating system to display the directory of the diskette located in drive B. The entry B: specifies that drive B is to be used.

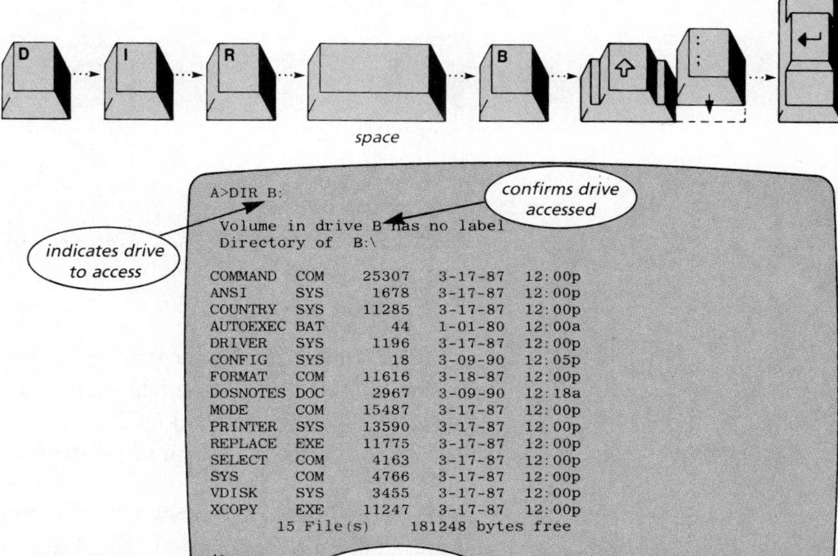


FIGURE 15

If your computer has a hard disk and you have been using drive C as the default drive, you can insert a diskette into drive A and then list the directory of that diskette drive by typing DIR A: and pressing the Enter key (Figure 16).

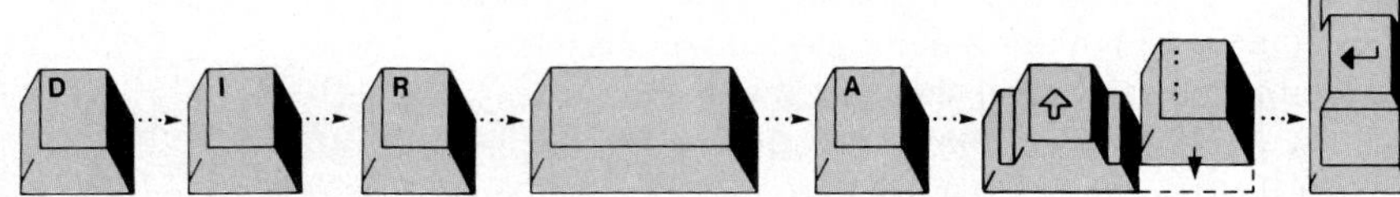


FIGURE 16

Note the use of the **colon**, **:**, with the disk drive letter. Whenever you refer to a specific disk drive, type the letter designating the drive followed by the colon, such as A:, B:, or C:.

## Pausing Directory Listings

The directory of your diskette will often contain more files than can be displayed on the screen at one time. DOS has two methods of handling this situation: the pause screen option and the DIR command options.

**Pause Screen (Control S).** To use a **pause screen** function, first make certain that your DOS diskette is in drive A. Type DIR and press the Enter key (Figure 17, step 1). When approximately one screenful of information is displayed, press Control-S. The directory display immediately halts (Figure 17, step 2). You can then examine the screen for any information you require. To continue the display, press any character key on the keyboard. The directory display will continue to scroll as if it had never halted. This pause screen operation can be used with many DOS commands.

**Step 1: Display a directory of the default drive.**

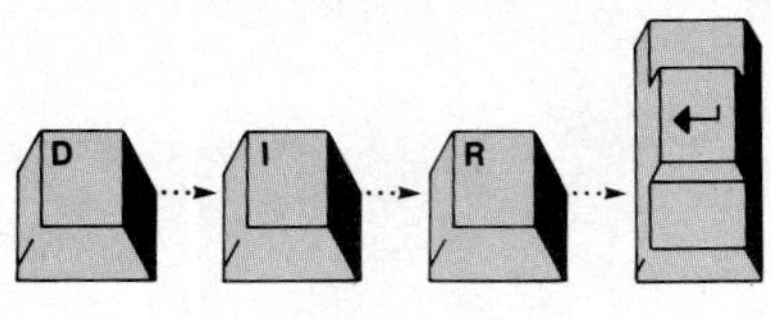


**Step 2: Halt the directory listing.**

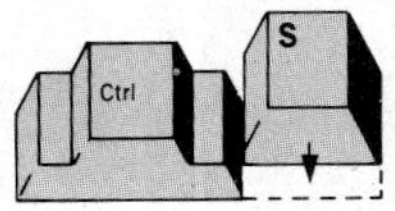


**Step 3: Continue the display by pressing any character key.**

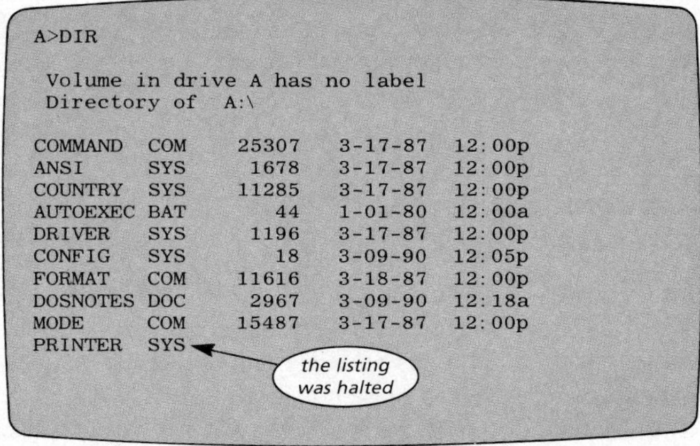


FIGURE 17

**DIR Command Options.** It is not always easy to pause the directory listing where you want it. Therefore, you might want to use two other options with the DIR command. One option, /P, causes the screen to pause. The second option, /W, displays more data on the screen by increasing the **width** of the display area.

**/P—the Pause Option.** To demonstrate the pause option, type DIR followed by /P and press the Enter key (Figure 18). When the screen is full, the listing stops and the message "Strike a key when ready . . ." appears at the bottom of the screen. When you are ready to continue the listing, press any character key.

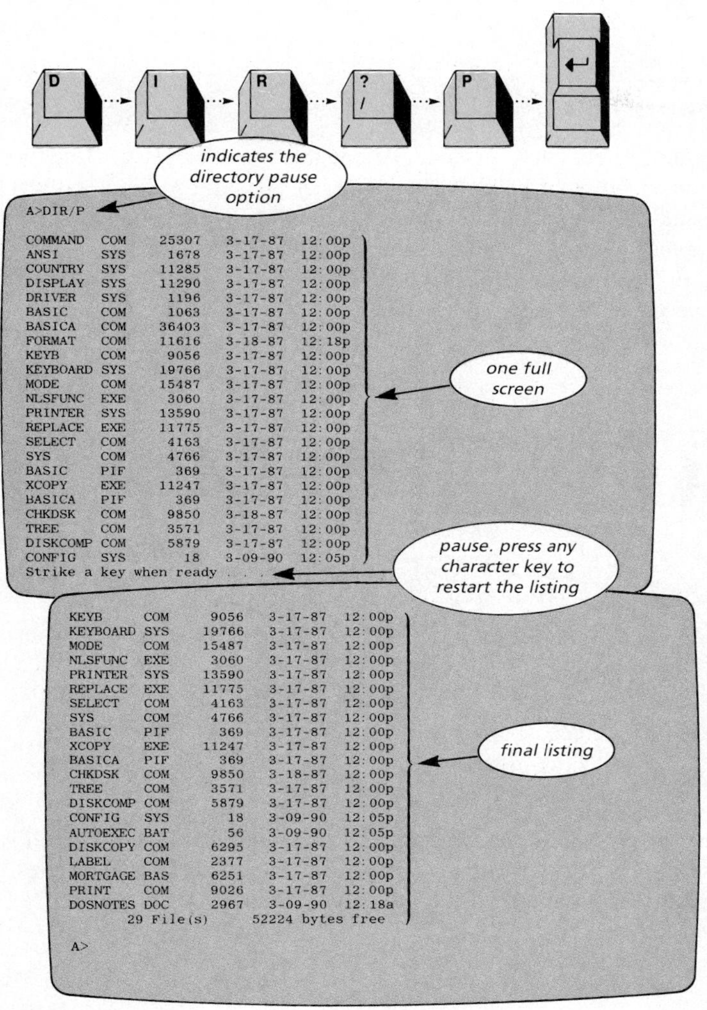


**FIGURE 18**

# FORMATTING A DISKETTE

You cannot use a brand new diskette to store files. The diskette must first be formatted using the DOS FORMAT program. The **formatting** process establishes sectors on the diskette and performs other functions that allow the diskette to store files. Be careful when selecting disks to be used with the FORMAT command. Formatting a diskette destroys all files previously stored on the diskette. Therefore, you must be extremely careful to place the correct diskette in the drive and to make the correct drive letter designation. With a hard disk, extra precaution is necessary to avoid losing files by formatting the hard disk accidentally. DOS versions 3.0 and later provide some protection against accidental formatting of a hard disk, but your own precautions are still the best insurance.

**/W—the Wide Display Option.** The second option for displaying a long list of files is the **/W option**, which displays the information in a wide format. To use the /W option, type DIR /W, then press the Enter key (Figure 19). Note that only the file and directory names are listed, not the size, time, or date of the files.

## Canceling a Command (Break)

In some cases, you only need to see a portion of the directory and so you might want to cancel the DIR command after you have seen that portion. To cancel a command you use the Break key. Locate this key on your keyboard; on many keyboards it is on the side of a key, often on the Scroll Lock key or the Pause key. When you press Ctrl-Break the characters ^C appear on the screen and the system prompt reappears. You will often hear this keystroke combination referred to as **Control-Break** or the **Break key**. The characters **^C** indicate that you canceled the command by using the Break key. In general, you can cancel any DOS command that has been initiated by pressing Control-Break. An alternate method of canceling DOS commands is pressing Control-C (Figure 20).

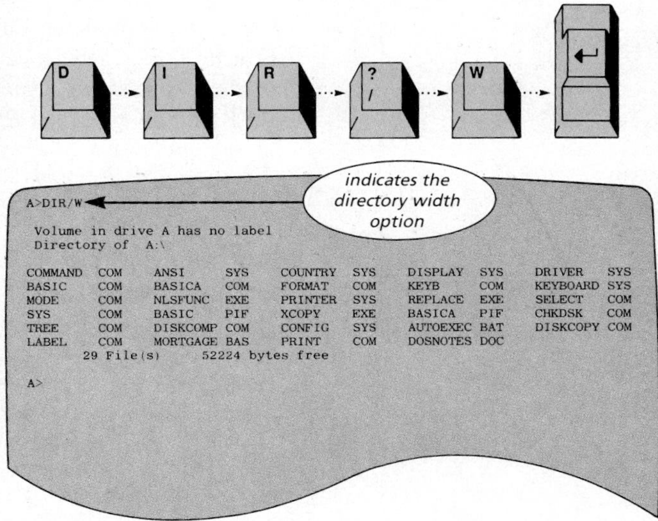


**FIGURE 19**

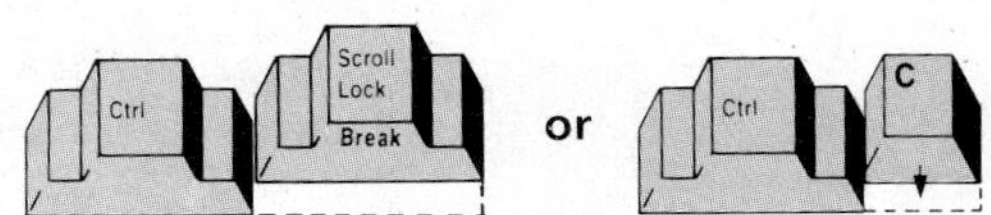


**FIGURE 20**

## The FORMAT Command

To initiate the FORMAT program, select a new diskette, or one that may be erased. (Use the DIR command to check the contents of your diskette if you are not certain it may be erased.) Because FORMAT is an external DOS command, the FORMAT.COM program file must be on the system disk in the computer when you use this command.

To format a diskette on a two-diskette system, place the DOS diskette in drive A. Type the command FORMAT B: and press the Enter key (Figure 21).

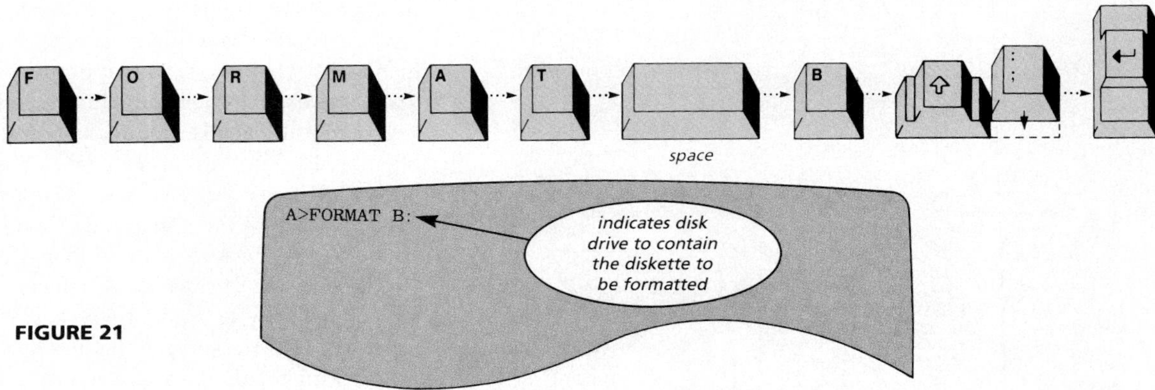


FIGURE 21

When you press the Enter key, the FORMAT program is loaded into main memory and is executed. A message appears on the screen instructing you to "Insert new diskette for drive B: and strike ENTER when ready" (Figure 22). If the disk you want to format is already in drive B, simply press the Enter key.

**Step 1: View the message and insert diskette.**

**Step 2: Press Enter.**

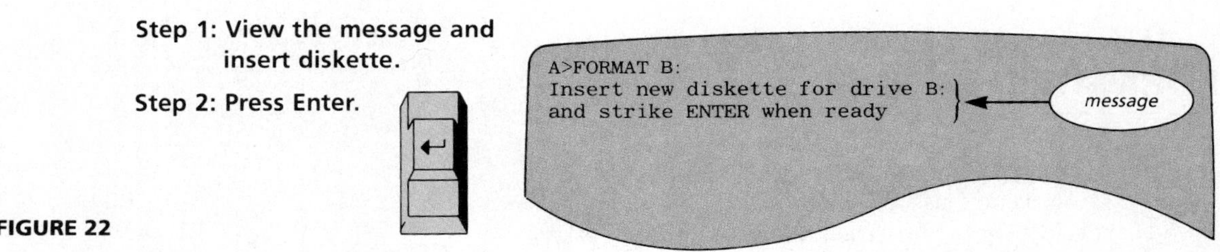


FIGURE 22

The FORMAT procedure on a hard-disk system is essentially the same as for a two-diskette system, except that the FORMAT program is stored on drive C, the hard disk. Be careful NOT to format drive C accidentally. To format a diskette in drive A at the C> prompt, type FORMAT A: and press the Enter key (Figure 23). The program will instruct you when to place the diskette to be formatted into drive A (Figure 24).

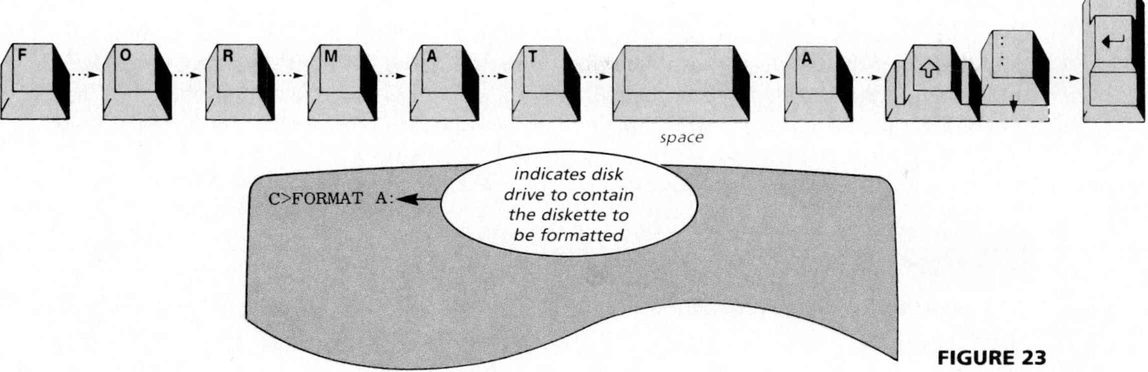
F
O
R
M
A
T
space
A
:
C>FORMAT A:
indicates disk drive to contain the diskette to be formatted

FIGURE 23

To complete the format process, place the diskette to be formatted into the appropriate drive (drive B for a two-diskette system; drive A for a computer with a hard-disk) and press the Enter key. While formatting occurs, a message appears indicating that the process is underway. Figure 25 shows the message from a two diskette system and Figure 26 illustrates the message on a computer with a hard-disk. Messages may differ slightly depending upon the version of DOS you are using. When the formatting process is complete, the messages shown in Figure 27 or 28 appear.

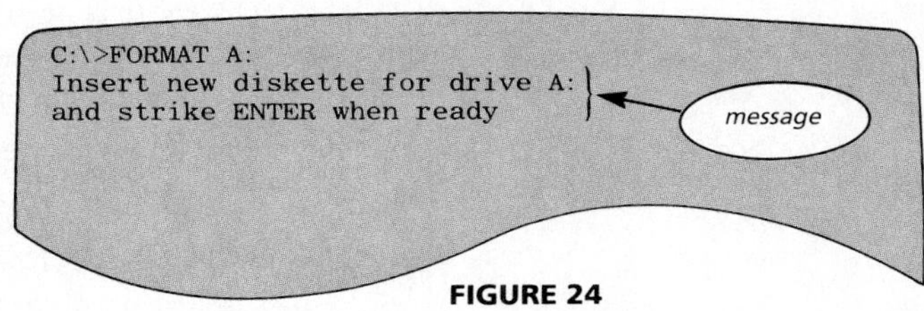
C:\>FORMAT A:
Insert new diskette for drive A:
and strike ENTER when ready
message

FIGURE 24

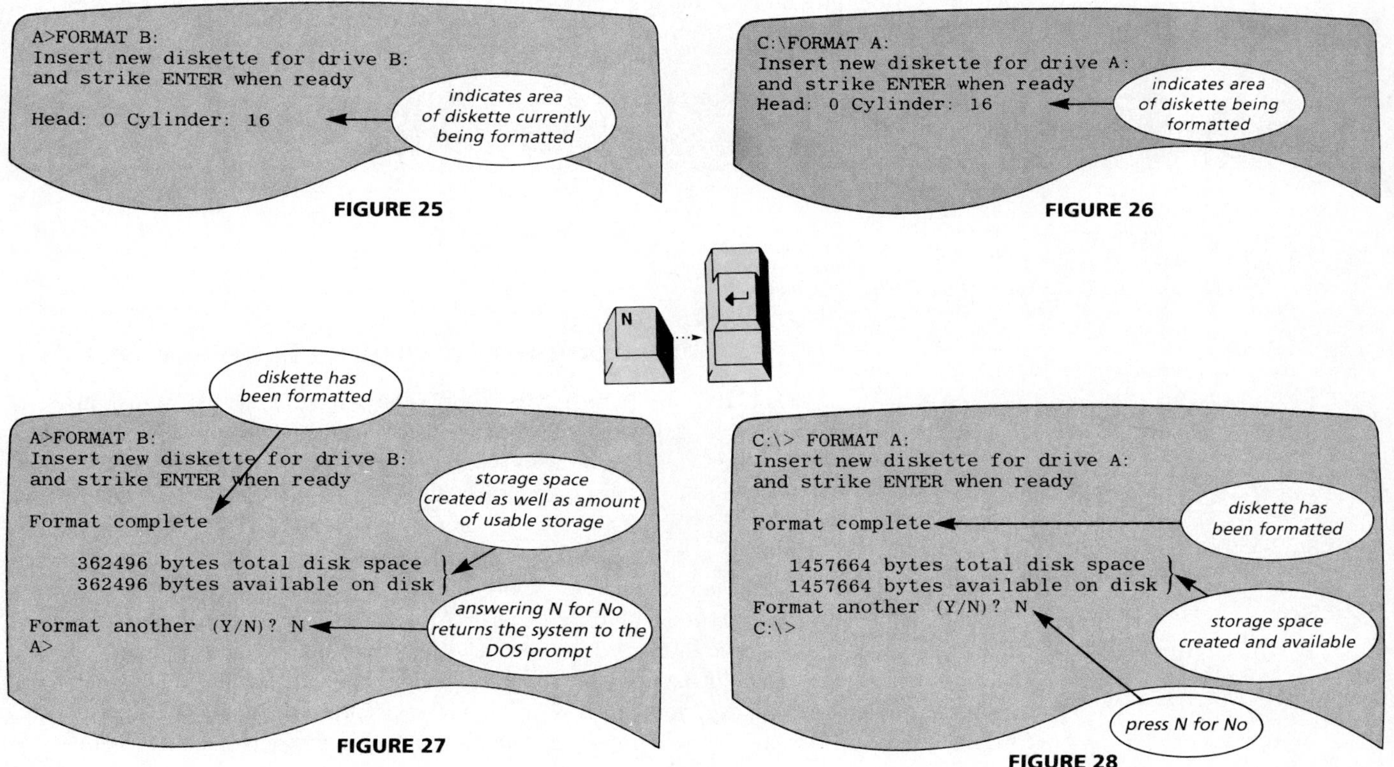
A>FORMAT B:
Insert new diskette for drive B:
and strike ENTER when ready
Head: 0 Cylinder: 16
indicates area of diskette currently being formatted
C:\FORMAT A:
Insert new diskette for drive A:
and strike ENTER when ready
Head: 0 Cylinder: 16
indicates area of diskette being formatted
N
diskette has been formatted
A>FORMAT B:
Insert new diskette for drive B:
and strike ENTER when ready
Format complete
362496 bytes total disk space
362496 bytes available on disk
Format another (Y/N)? N
A>
storage space created as well as amount of usable storage
answering N for No returns the system to the DOS prompt
C:\> FORMAT A:
Insert new diskette for drive A:
and strike ENTER when ready
Format complete
1457664 bytes total disk space
1457664 bytes available on disk
Format another (Y/N)? N
C:\>
diskette has been formatted
storage space created and available
press N for No

FIGURE 25

FIGURE 26

FIGURE 27

FIGURE 28

The FORMAT program specifies that the diskette is formatted for a total number of bytes and that all of these bytes are available for storage. Finally, the FORMAT program asks if there are other diskettes to be formatted. If there are, press the letter Y and then the Enter key to continue the formatting process. If there are no more diskettes to be formatted, press the letter N and then the Enter key to end the FORMAT program.

## Formatting a System Disk (/S Option)

The FORMAT command shown in Figures 26 and 27 will format a diskette so that it can be used for both data files and program files. However, the diskette cannot be used to boot the system because it does not contain the special system programs that are required for booting. To format a diskette so that it contains these special programs, thus creating what is called a **system disk**, you must use the **/S option**.

Use the same diskette you used in the last exercise. If you are using a two-diskette system, use the following commands. If you are using a hard-disk system, use drive C as the default drive and place the diskette to be formatted in drive A. Be very certain NOT to format drive C accidentally.

To create a system disk on a two-diskette system, type FORMAT B:/S and press the Enter key (Figure 29). On a hard-disk system, type FORMAT A:/S. You will be prompted to insert a new diskette in drive B (or A); if the diskette you formatted earlier is still in the disk drive, simply press the Enter key. After the diskette is formatted, the "System transferred" message appears. In general, if you are formatting a diskette to be used only for storing data files, do not place system programs on the diskette so that more space is available for the data files.

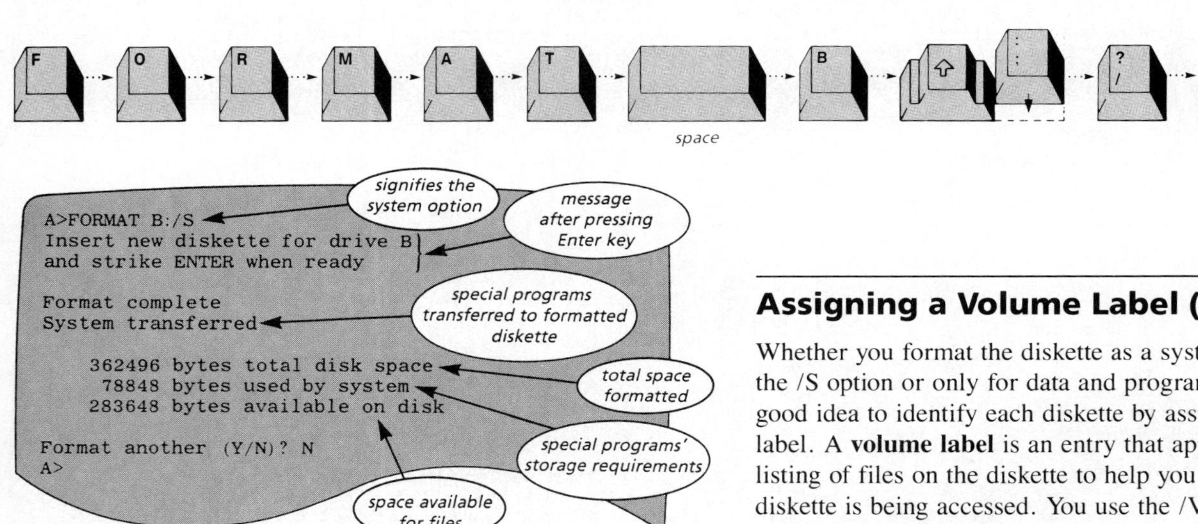


FIGURE 29

## Assigning a Volume Label (/V Option)

Whether you format the diskette as a system disk using the /S option or only for data and program files, it is a good idea to identify each diskette by assigning a volume label. A **volume label** is an entry that appears before the listing of files on the diskette to help you verify which diskette is being accessed. You use the /V command to assign a volume label.

To assign a volume label, you would type FORMAT B:/V and press the Enter key (Figure 30). You will again be instructed to insert a diskette into drive B. Insert a new diskette, or press the Enter key if the diskette from the previous exercise is still in drive B. When the format process is complete, you will receive the message "Volume label (11 characters, ENTER for none)?" as a prompt to enter your label. You may use 11 characters—letters, numbers, or spaces—but not punctuation or special characters. After you enter a label and press the Enter key, a message appears asking if you want to format another diskette. You would press N and the Enter key to return to the DOS prompt.

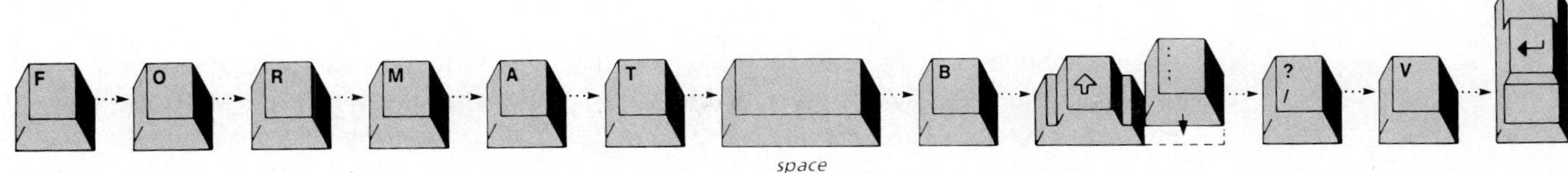


FIGURE 30

## CLS COMMAND

Quite often, as you issue several commands or perform lengthy processes, the display screen will become crowded and difficult to read and interpret (Figure 31). To clear the screen and place the system prompt on the first line of the screen, you can use the CLS (Clear Screen) command. Type the letters CLS, then press the Enter key to execute the Clear Screen command.

## MANAGING DATA AND PROGRAM FILES ON DISKS

A **data file** is a collection of data created by application or system programs and used by the programs. The data can be the figures used for a spreadsheet showing sales revenues, names and addresses in a database file, or a word processing document announcing the arrival of a new employee. A **program file** contains machine-readable instructions that the computer follows to perform its tasks. The program might be an operating system program or one of the application programs such as word processing that uses data files. Both data files and program files require your attention to be stored on a disk correctly.

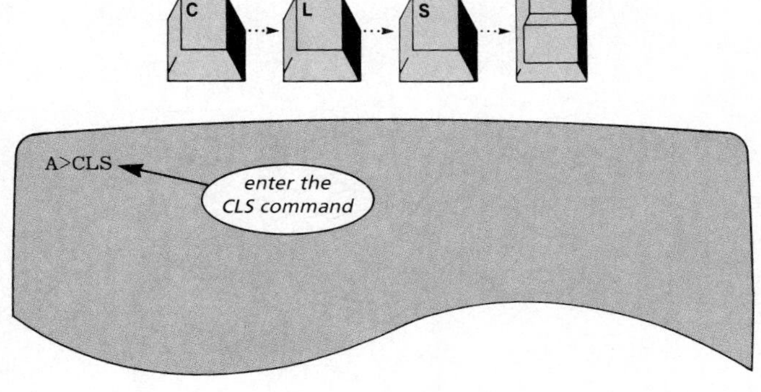


FIGURE 31

### Assigning File Specifications

DOS identifies the files on a disk by a combination of several specifications (Figure 32). A **file specification** lets DOS know exactly where to search for a file and gives its exact name. There are four parts to a DOS file specification: (1) the drive specifier, which you already know as drive A: or B: or C:, if there is a hard disk; (2) a directory specification (explained later); (3) the filename; (4) the filename extension.

FIGURE 32

| LEGEND | DEFINITION |
|---|---|
| d: | The disk drive letter specifies the drive containing the file you are requesting. For example, A: specifies disk drive A. If you omit the drive letter, DOS assumes the file is located on the default drive. A disk drive letter is always followed by a colon (:). |
| \path | A path is an optional reference to a subdirectory of files on the specified disk. It is preceded, and sometimes followed, by a backslash (\). |
| filename | The filename consists of from one to eight characters. |
| .ext | A filename may contain an optional extension of a period followed by from one to three characters. The extension is used to add further identity to files. |

**Filenames.** Regardless of the type of data in the file, you must assign a filename to every data file, as well as to every program file. A **filename** consists of one to eight characters and is used by DOS to identify a specific file. You may use any combination of characters except: period (.), quotation mark ("), slash (/), backslash (\), brackets ([ ]), colon (:), less than (<), greater than (>), plus (+), equals (=), semicolon (;), and comma (,).

In general, your filename should reflect the data stored in it. For example, if your file contains employee records, it is more meaningful to use the filename EMPLOYEE than to use the filename FILE1, even though DOS will accept either filename.

**Filename Extensions.** A filename can be made more specific by an optional extension. A **filename extension** consists of a period followed by one to three characters. The same characters that are permitted for a filename are permitted for a filename extension. The filename extension can identify a file more specifically or describe its purpose (Figure 33). For example, if you wish to create a copy of the EMPLOYEE file, you could use the filename extension .CPY to identify the file as a copied file. The entire file specification for the file would be EMPLOYEE.CPY.

FIGURE 33

| .COM Files | | .EXE Files | | .BAT Files | |
|---|---|---|---|---|---|
| COMMAND | COM | APPEND | EXE | AUTOEXEC | BAT |
| ASSIGN | COM | ATTRIB | EXE | WP | BAT |
| BACKUP | COM | FASTOPEN | EXE | INSTALL | BAT |
| BASIC | COM | FIND | EXE | | |
| BASICA | COM | JOIN | EXE | | |
| CHKDSK | COM | NLSFUNC | EXE | | |
| COMP | COM | REPLACE | EXE | | |
| DEBUG | COM | | | | |
| DISKCOMP | COM | | | | |
| DISKCOPY | COM | | | | |
| FORMAT | COM | | | | |
| LABEL | COM | | | | |

Certain programs associated with the Disk Operating System use special filename extensions. All files with the filename extensions .COM or .EXE are executable programs. Files with the extension .BAT are **DOS batch files** and contain a series of DOS commands to be executed in sequence. Any DOS command with one of these filename extensions is an external command. You can execute any external command simply by typing the filename (the extension is not required) and pressing the Enter key.

## COPY COMMAND

Once you have formatted a diskette and are ready to use it to store data or program files, you will need a method of placing these files on the diskette. Use the **COPY command** to copy one file or a series of files to the same or a different diskette. As a DOS internal command, COPY may be used at any time, with or without the system disk.

### Using the COPY Command

The COPY command is often used to make working copies of program and data diskettes. Copying original files from one diskette creates a second diskette that can be used for everyday work to protect the original disk from damage. A similar use for COPY is to make a **backup copy** of a diskette to guard against accidental loss of data. One frequently used technique is to make a backup copy of a file whenever you work on revisions to an existing file. In fact, some application programs will make a backup file automatically, using the filename extension .BAK or .BAC to indicate that it is a backup file.

## Copying Files from One Diskette to Another

In the following examples of the COPY command, you will copy files from drive A to drive B. Check to see that you have the Data Diskette provided to instructors in drive A and your formatted diskette in drive B. If you are using a hard disk system, use drive C as the default drive, copying the files to drive A.

For practice, copy the file DOSNOTES.DOC from drive A to drive B. Your instructor will make the DOSNOTES.DOC file available to you or will give you the name of another file to copy. Type COPY DOSNOTES.DOC B: and press the Enter key. Note that after the word COPY you leave one or more spaces, then state the file specification of the file to be copied. In DOS terminology, this file is called the **source file**. In Figure 34, the filename DOSNOTES.DOC is specified as the source file. Since no drive specification is included, the operating system assumes the file is located on the default drive, drive A.

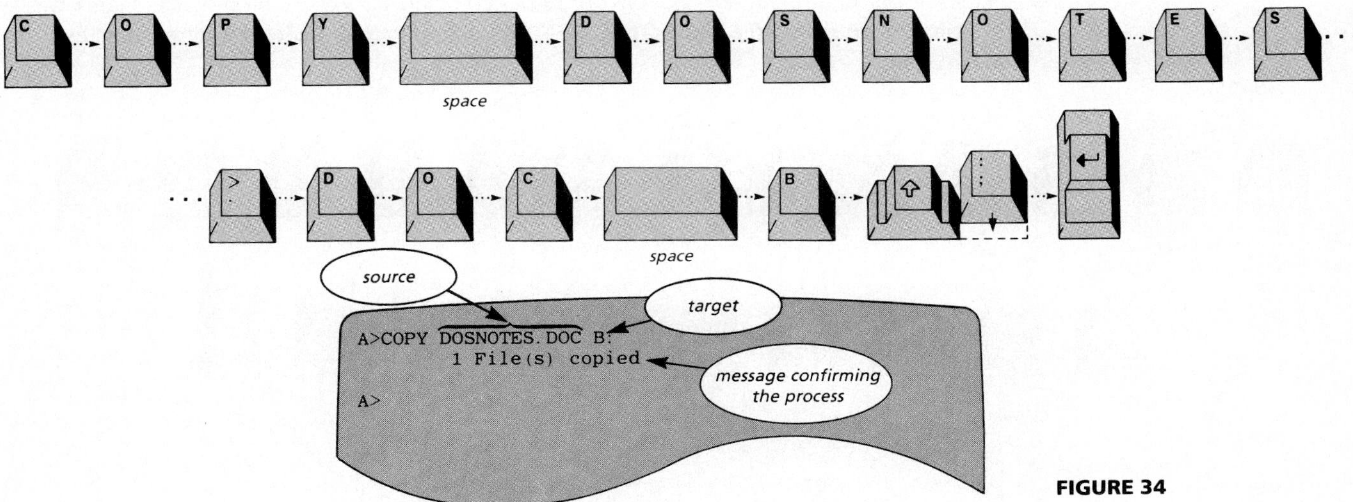


**FIGURE 34**

Following the source file is one or more blank spaces. Then, the **file specification**, which can include the drive specification, and the name of the **target file**, that is, the filename and filename extension of the source file after it is copied, is specified. In Figure 34, the drive specification B: states that the file is to be copied to a diskette in drive B. Because no filename is specified for the target file on drive B, DOS defaults to the same name as the source file, and so the name of the file on drive B will be DOSNOTES.DOC. The message "1 File(s) copied" signals that the command is completed.

When you copy a file from a diskette in one drive to a diskette in another drive, you can assign a new name to the target file. To copy the file DOSNOTES.DOC from the diskette in drive A to the diskette in drive B, giving the new file the name NOTECOPY on drive B, type COPY DOSNOTES.DOC B:NOTECOPY and press the Enter key (Figure 35). Again, the message "1 File(s) copied" appears when the task is completed, as in Figure 34.

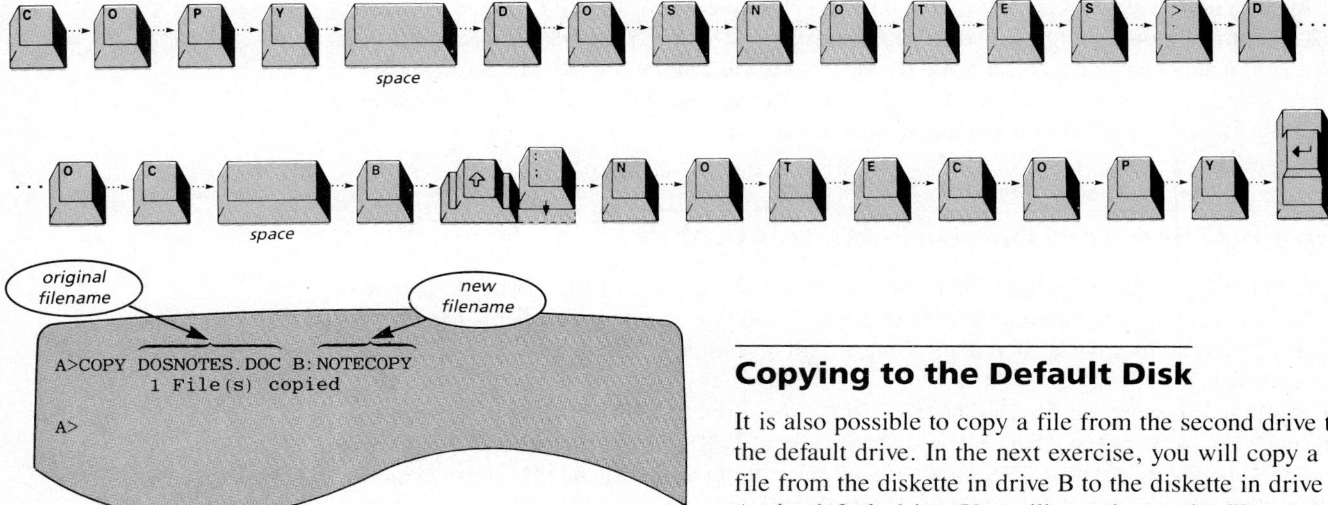


FIGURE 35

## Copying to the Default Disk

It is also possible to copy a file from the second drive to the default drive. In the next exercise, you will copy a file from the diskette in drive B to the diskette in drive A, the default drive. You will not change the filename. To accomplish this procedure, type COPY B:NOTECOPY A: and press the Enter key. This command copies the file named NOTECOPY from the diskette in drive B to the diskette in drive A. When the message "1 File(s) copied" appears, as in Figure 36, the copying process is completed. Because no target filename was given in the command, the file NOTECOPY will be on drive A under the same name as it is on drive B.

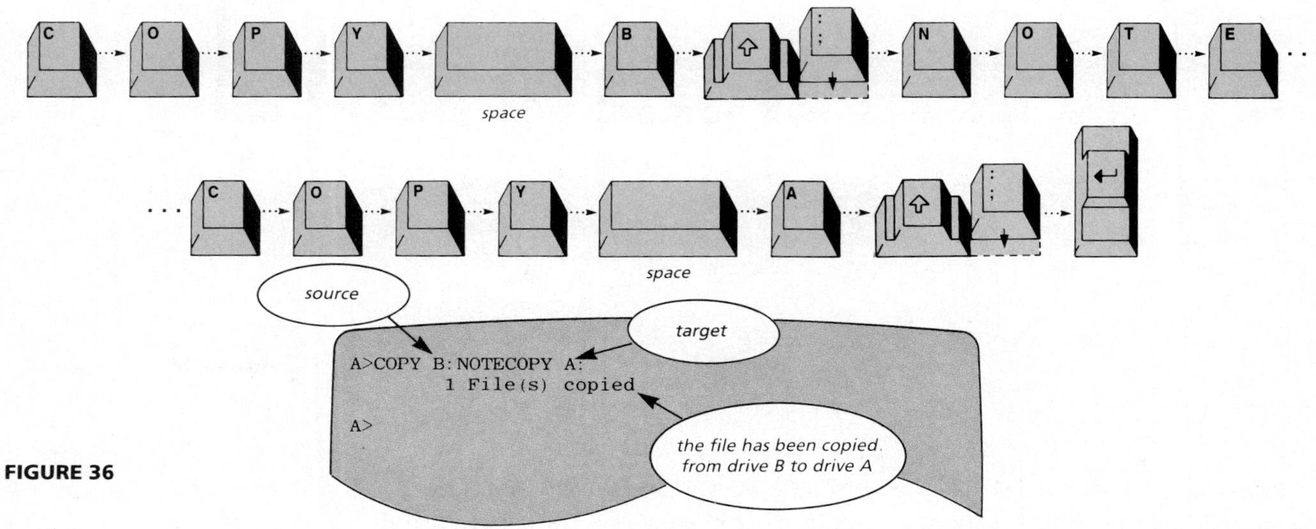


FIGURE 36

## Copying a File to the Same Diskette

It is possible to copy a file to the same diskette, but you must use a different filename. For practice, copy the file named DOSNOTES.DOC stored on drive A onto the same diskette. Give the filename DOSNOTES.BAK to the target file. Type the command COPY DOSNOTES.DOC DOSNOTES.BAK and press the Enter key.

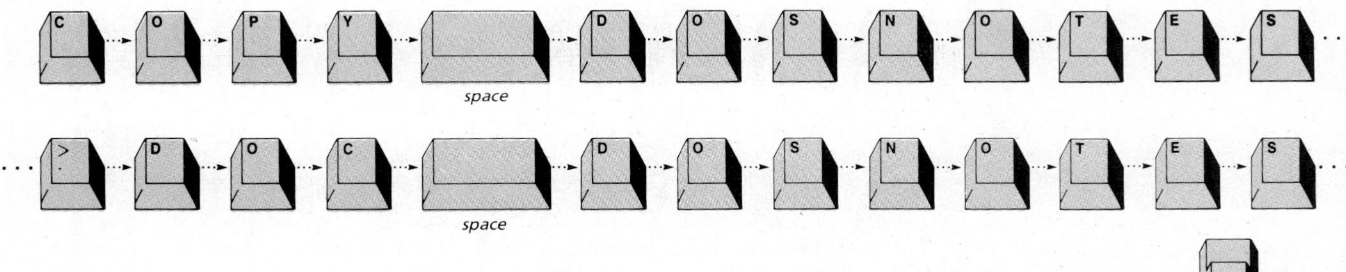


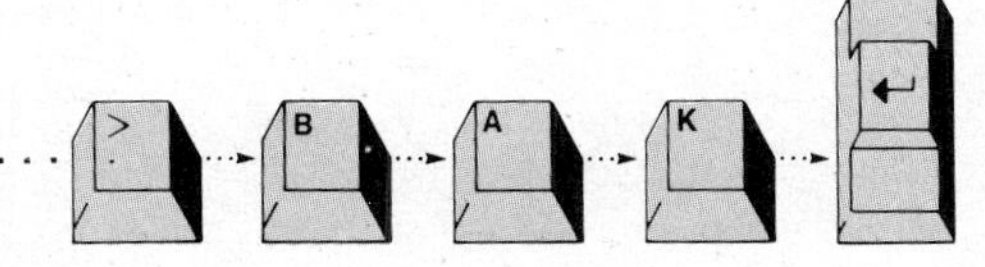


When your COPY command is executed, the file DOSNOTES.DOC in drive A is copied to the same diskette on drive A as DOSNOTES.BAK (Figure 37). The file extension .BAK is used to distinguish the files. If you had used the same filename to designate both the target and source files on the same diskette, an error message would be displayed, stating that a file cannot be copied onto itself. You would then have to reenter the COPY command using a different name for the target file.

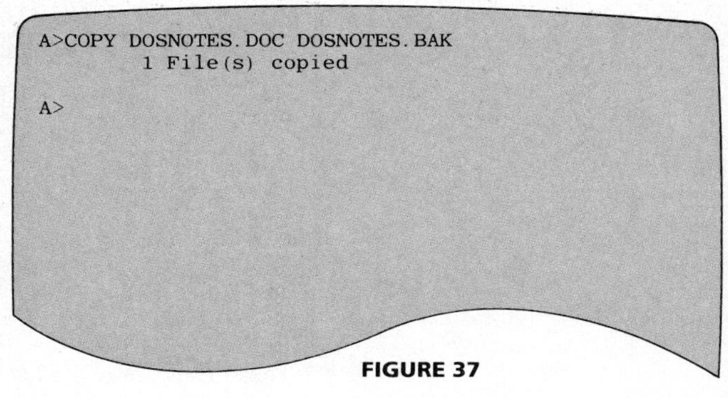

```
A>COPY DOSNOTES.DOC DOSNOTES.BAK
        1 File(s) copied

A>
```

FIGURE 37

## Global Filename Characters (''Wildcards'')

You can copy more than one file at a time using a single COPY command. To copy more than one file, you use **global characters**, or **wildcards**. These are special characters indicating that any character may occupy that specific location in the filename. The two global characters are the * (asterisk) and the ? (question mark).

To use wildcards, you need to know the files stored on the diskette. Figure 38 shows the directory of the diskette in drive A. (Your directory may look different.) Notice that the files DOSNOTES.BAK and NOTECOPY appear, a result of the COPY commands you used earlier. Notice also that several files have the same filename extensions. It is not uncommon, on any disk with many files, to find several files with similarities in filenames or extensions. These similarities can be exploited by using wildcard characters.

```
Volume in drive A has no label
Directory of  A:\

COMMAND  COM    25307   3-17-87  12:00p
ANSI     SYS     1678   3-17-87  12:00p
COUNTRY  SYS    11285   3-17-87  12:00p
AUTOEXEC BAT       44   1-01-80  12:00a
DRIVER   SYS     1196   3-17-87  12:00p
CONFIG   SYS       18   3-09-90  12:05p
NOTECOPY         2967   3-09-90  12:18a
FORMAT   COM    11616   3-18-87  12:00p
COPYNOTE         2967   3-09-90  12:18a
DOSNOTES DOC     2967   3-09-90  12:18a
MODE     COM    15487   3-17-87  12:00p
DOSNOTES BAK     2967   3-09-90  12:18a
PRINTER  SYS    13590   3-17-87  12:00p
REPLACE  EXE    11775   3-17-87  12:00p
SELECT   COM     4163   3-17-87  12:00p
SYS      COM     4766   3-17-87  12:00p
VDISK    SYS     3455   3-17-87  12:00p
XCOPY    EXE    11247   3-17-87  12:00p
        18 File(s)    172032 bytes free

A>
```

FIGURE 38

**The * Character.** You can use the global character * (asterisk) to indicate a portion of the filename or extension. When the * global character appears, any character can occupy that position and all the remaining positions in the filename or the filename extension.

For example, let us use the wildcard asterisk (*) to copy files with the filename extension .COM from the diskette in drive A to the diskette in drive B. Type COPY *.COM B: and press the Enter key. In Figure 39, the source files are specified by the entry *.COM. The asterisk (*) in the filename portion of the specification means that any filename can be used. The file extension .COM states that the file specification must include the file extension .COM. In Figure 38, five filenames satisfy this criterion: COMMAND.COM, FORMAT-.COM, MODE.COM, SELECT.COM, and SYS.COM.

FIGURE 39

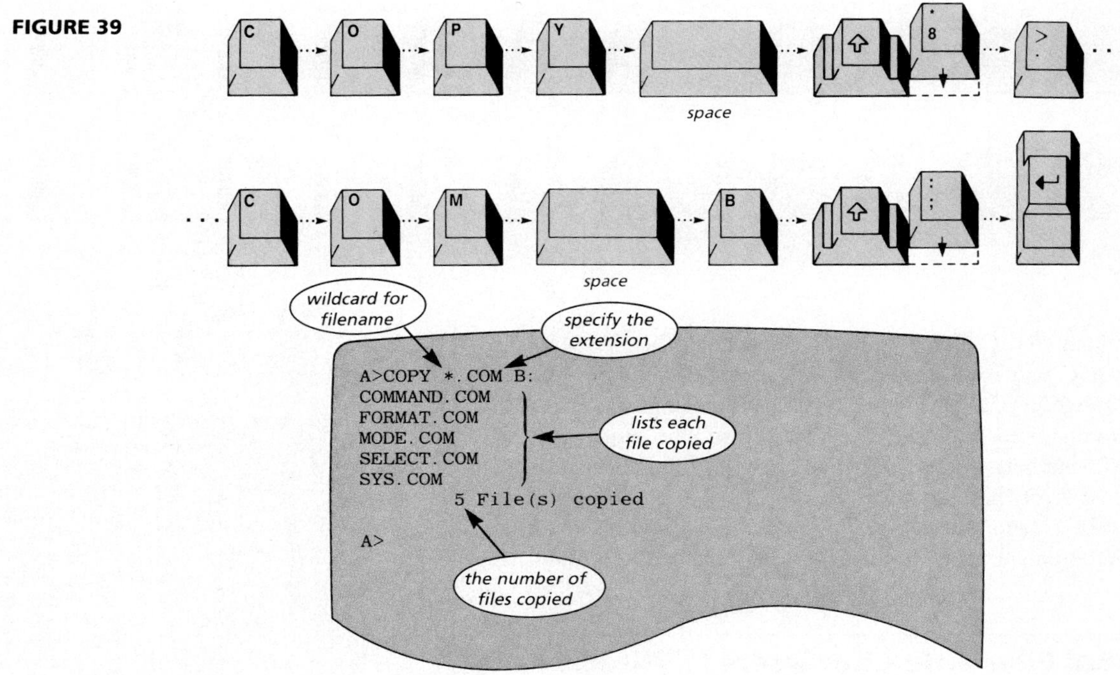


These files are copied to the diskette in disk drive B. The filenames for the copied files on the diskette in drive B remain the same as the source filenames on the diskette in drive A because you specified no new names in the copy command. When you copy files with a COPY command using the * global character, all files copied are listed by the COPY command. Figure 39 lists the five copied files.

You can also specify the global character * as the filename extension to copy a specific filename with any extension. For example, the diskette contains two files with the name DOSNOTES, DOSNOTES.BAK and DOSNOTES.DOC. Type the command COPY DOSNOTES.* B: as in Figure 40 and press the Enter key to copy both the files with the filename DOSNOTES to drive B.

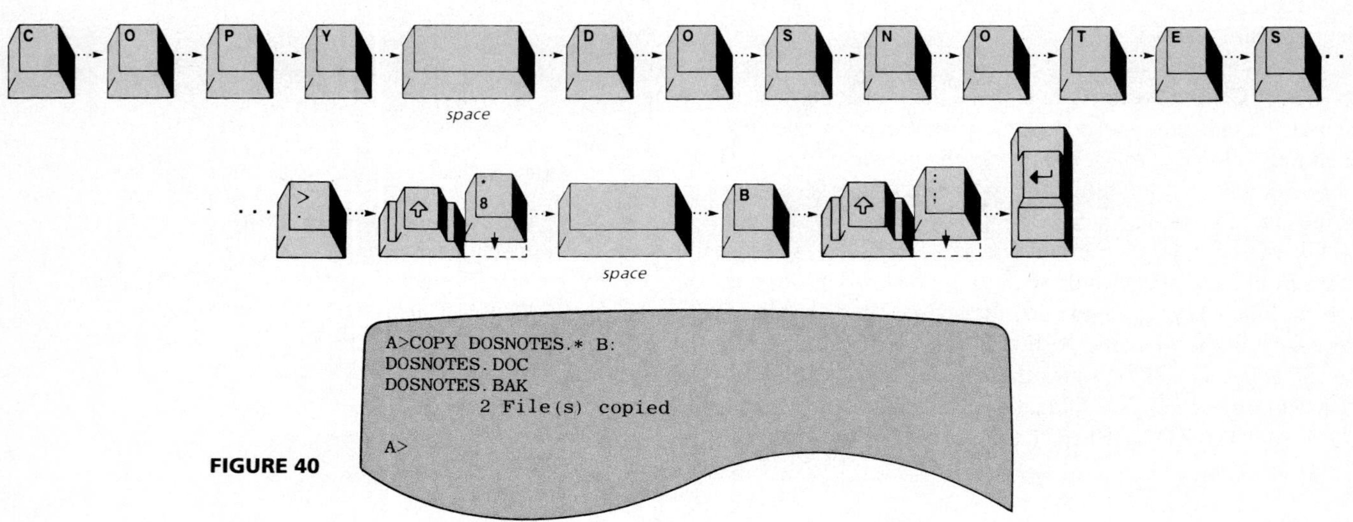


FIGURE 40

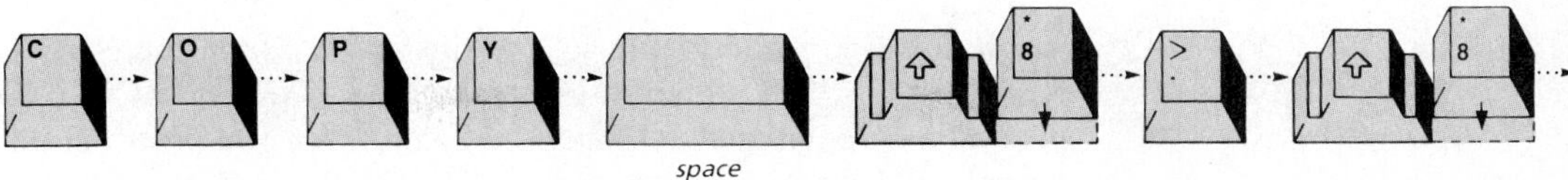


**Copying All Files from One Diskette to Another.** You can also use the COPY command to copy all of the files on one diskette to another diskette by using the * global character. This technique is useful in making backup or working copies of entire diskettes. You use the * wildcard in both the filename and extension positions to signify "all filenames.all extensions" in the command. Practice by typing COPY *.* B: and pressing the Enter key to copy all files on drive A to drive B (Figure 41).

**The ? Character.** The **?** (question mark) global character can also be used to represent any character occupying the position in which the wildcard character appears. However, the ? represents only a single character replacement, whereas the * can represent one or more characters. You can use a single ? or several in a command to identify files. Practice this option by typing COPY DOSNOTES.BA? B: and pressing the Enter key to copy DOSNOTES.BAK to drive B (Figure 42).

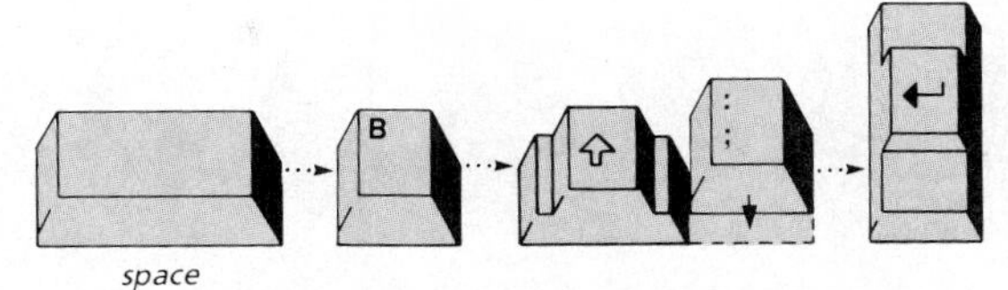


```
A>COPY *.* B:
COMMAND.COM
ANSI.SYS
COUNTRY.SYS
AUTOEXEC.BAT
DRIVER.SYS
CONFIG.SYS
NOTECOPY
FORMAT.COM
COPYNOTE
DOSNOTES.DOC
MODE.COM
DOSNOTES.BAK
PRINTER.SYS
REPLACE.EXE
SELECT.COM
SYS.COM
VDISK.SYS
XCOPY.EXE
        18 File(s) copied

A>
```

**FIGURE 41**

## Using Wildcards with DOS Commands

You have learned to use the wildcard characters with the COPY command. Many DOS commands support the use of global replacement characters. For example, you can use the wildcards with the DIR command to look for files of a common type. To look at all DOS batch files on a diskette, you would type the command DIR *.BAT and press the Enter key to display all files with the filename extension .BAT.

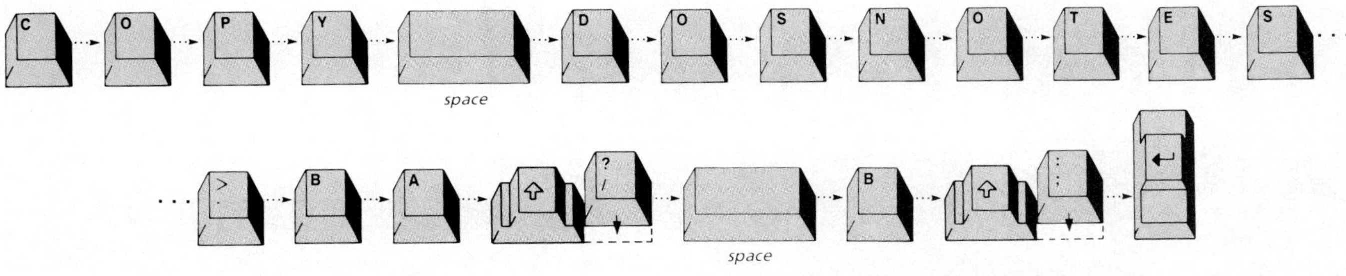


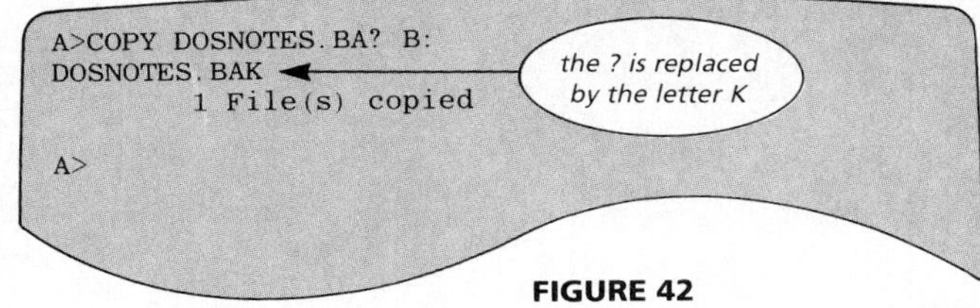

```
A>COPY DOSNOTES.BA? B:
DOSNOTES.BAK
        1 File(s) copied

A>
```


**FIGURE 42**

# RENAME COMMAND

Use the **RENAME command** when you want to rename a file on a diskette. If you assign a filename already used by a file currently on the diskette, DOS creates the new file on the diskette and destroys the previously existing file with that name. You will not receive any warning that this has happened. Thus, you should periodically check the filenames on a diskette to avoid accidental replacement of files. If you discover a filename you might reuse, you can use the RENAME command to change the name of the file.

In the example in Figure 43, the file with the filename NOTECOPY on drive A is to be renamed DOSFILE. Type the command RENAME NOTECOPY DOSFILE immediately after the system prompt and press the Enter key. When you press the Enter key, the filename on the diskette in drive A is changed from NOTECOPY to DOSFILE.

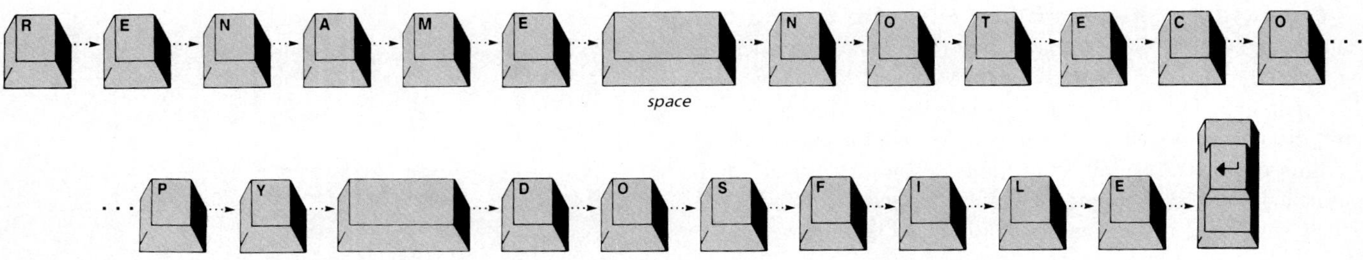


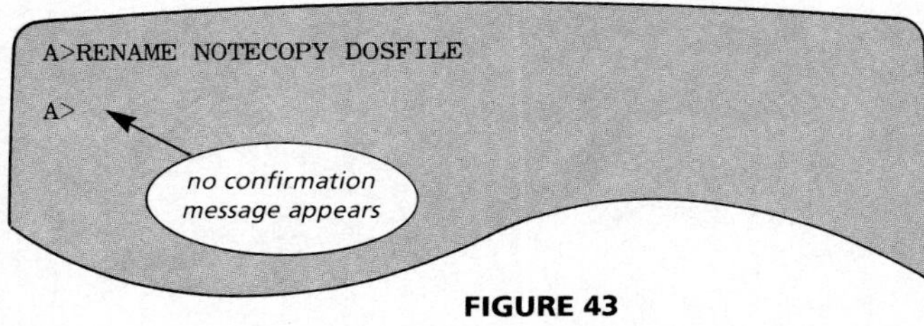


**FIGURE 43**

You can use the global characters * and ? with the RENAME command. In Figure 44, all files with the file extension .BAK are renamed with a file extension .BAC. Type the wildcard character * with the command RENAME *.BAK *.BAC and press the Enter key. All characters represented by the * will remain the same in the new filename. Thus, in Figure 44, all the filenames in the renamed files will remain the same, but the file extensions will change from .BAK to .BAC. RENAME does not confirm the operation on the screen, so you should use the DIR command before and after you use the RENAME command to assure the command was executed (Figure 45).

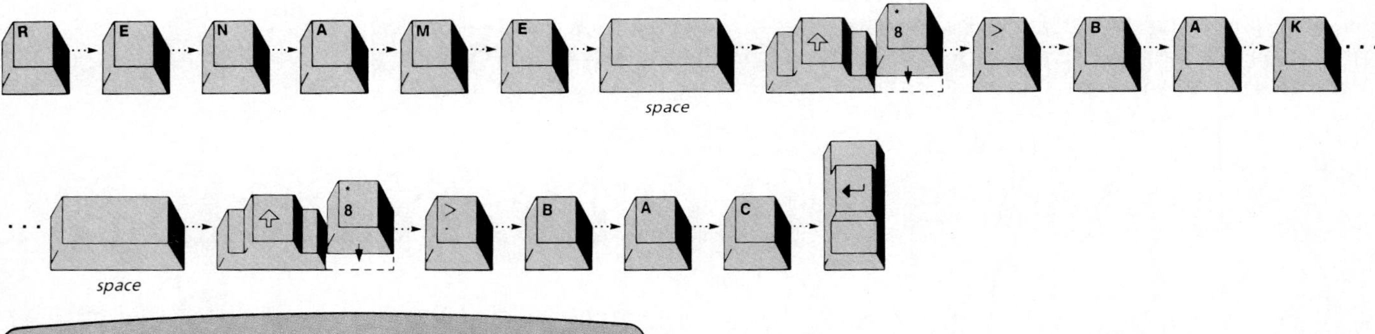


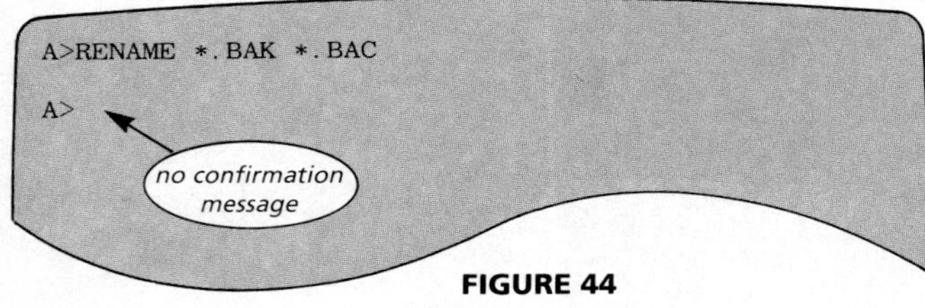


**FIGURE 44**

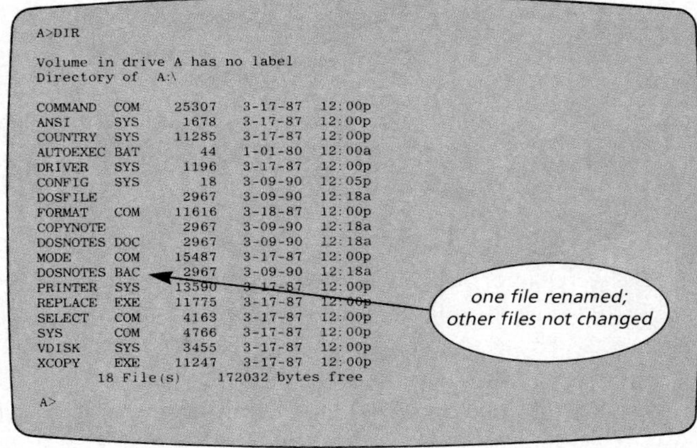


**FIGURE 45**

# ERASE AND DEL COMMANDS

As a part of diskette file management, you should periodically remove unneeded files from your diskette. The **ERASE command** will erase, or remove, a file from a diskette. An alternative command that functions like the erase command is the **DEL** (delete) command. Take care when using the ERASE or DEL commands, because once a file has been erased from the directory, it cannot be easily recovered. Such inadvertent erasing of a file is another reason for keeping backup files.

## Removing Files

We will begin by removing a single file, DOSFILE, from drive A. Type ERASE DOSFILE and press the Enter key, as shown in Figure 46. (You could use the DEL command instead, typing DEL DOSFILE and pressing the Enter key.) Use the DIR command to assure that the file has been removed from the diskette.

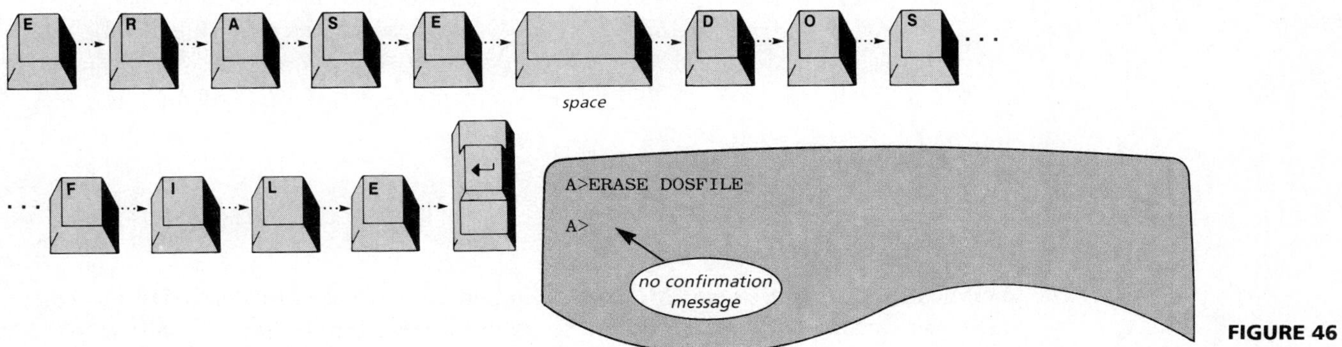


FIGURE 46

# USING DIRECTORIES AND SUBDIRECTORIES

## Directory Entries and Subdirectories

When you need to view the files on any disk, the computer does not actually read the entire disk looking for the file. Instead, a **file directory** or listing of each of the filenames on the disk is searched. This directory, created when the diskette is formatted, is called the **root directory**. Entries for subdirectories are made in the root directory. The root directory is the highest level directory of a disk (Figure 47).

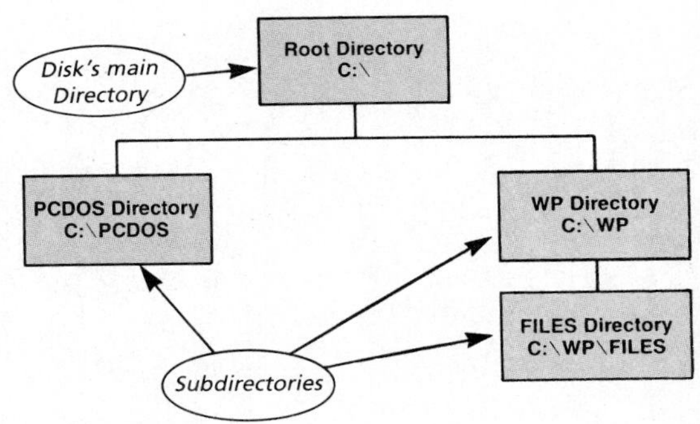


FIGURE 47

You can make three types of entries into a disk directory: (1) the filename and extension, (2) the volume label, (3) a subdirectory entry. We have previously discussed (1) and (2).

You can create a **subdirectory** to group all files of a similar type together (Figure 47). For example, you can create a subdirectory containing all the files related to DOS.

There are at least two good reasons to use subdirectories. First, the operating system provides a limited number of entries in the file directory. A diskette has room for only 112 entries; a hard disk allows up to 512 entries. This capacity may be sufficient on a diskette, but a hard disk with many millions of bytes of storage may have more files than the directory permits.

It is also easier to find files that are organized by related groups than to search randomly through all the files on a disk.

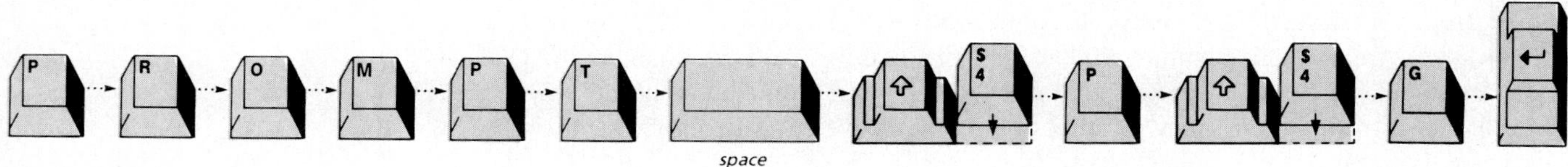


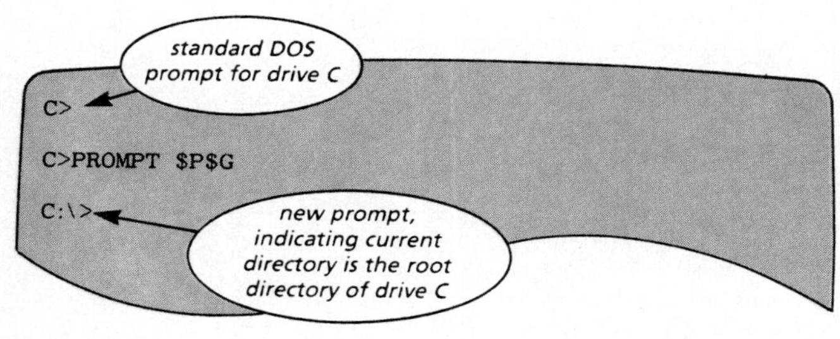


FIGURE 48

## The PROMPT Command

The standard DOS prompt, A>, B>, or C>, does not tell you what subdirectories you are using. DOS provides a way for you to monitor which directory is in use through the **PROMPT command**. To have DOS include the subdirectory information as a part of the DOS prompt, type PROMPT $P$G and press the Enter key (Figure 48). Whenever you change disk drive addresses, you will see the subdirectory information as a part of the prompt.

## Making Subdirectories

To create a subdirectory, use the **MKDIR command**, usually abbreviated as **MD**. If you have a hard disk, and *if your instructor approves*, create a subdirectory on drive C. Otherwise, practice the command on a diskette in drive A. To create a subdirectory called "PCDOS" on your diskette or disk drive, type MD A:\PCDOS and press the Enter key (Figure 49).

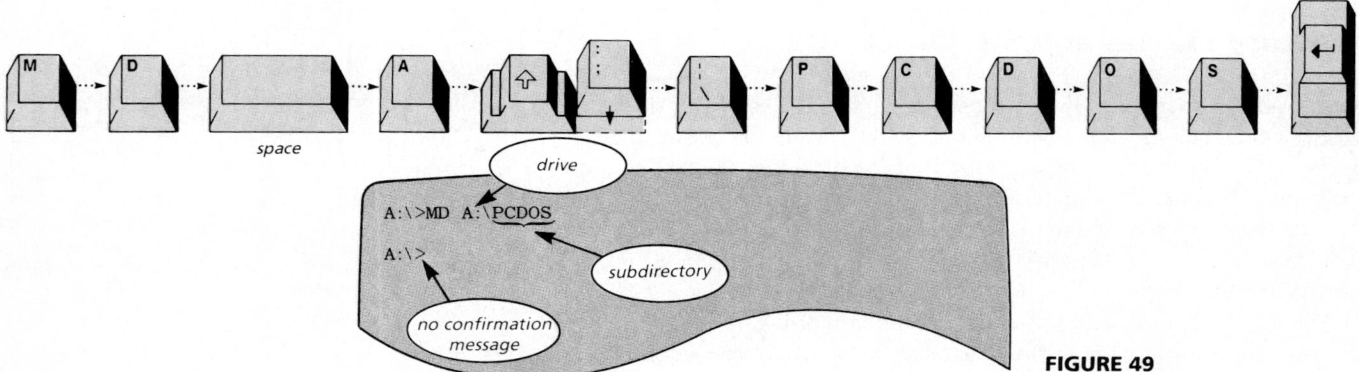


FIGURE 49

There are specific steps to the MD command. (1) Start a subdirectory entry with the drive designation. If the directory is to be on drive C, enter C: immediately after the MD command. Use the command MD A:\PCDOS to use drive A on a diskette. You can omit the drive specification if you are creating the directory on the default drive.

(2) Begin a subdirectory entry with the **backslash** character, \. The root directory for your hard disk is designated by a backslash alone. For example, C:\ designates the root

directory of drive C. The subdirectory made for the DOS files is C:\PCDOS. Notice that because you have issued the PROMPT command, the DOS prompt now includes the root or subdirectory name, C:\> or C:\PCDOS>.

(3) The subdirectory name, like any filename, can contain one to eight characters, followed optionally by a period and one to three characters in an extension. (Generally, subdirectory names do not include extensions.)

(4) You can assign a subdirectory entry to an existing subdirectory. For instance, you can create a subdirectory for a word processing program and a subordinate subdirectory for the data files created by the program. To create the word processing subdirectories shown in Figures 50 and 51, make the word processing subdirectory by typing MD A:\WP and press the Enter key. To make the subordinate subdirectory, type MD A:\WP\FILES and press the Enter key. The program subdirectory is A:\WP, and the word processing files can be stored in a second subdirectory, A:\WP\FILES. These two operations result in a series of related directories. Refer back to Figure 47 to see the relationships among the directories and subdirectories we have created.

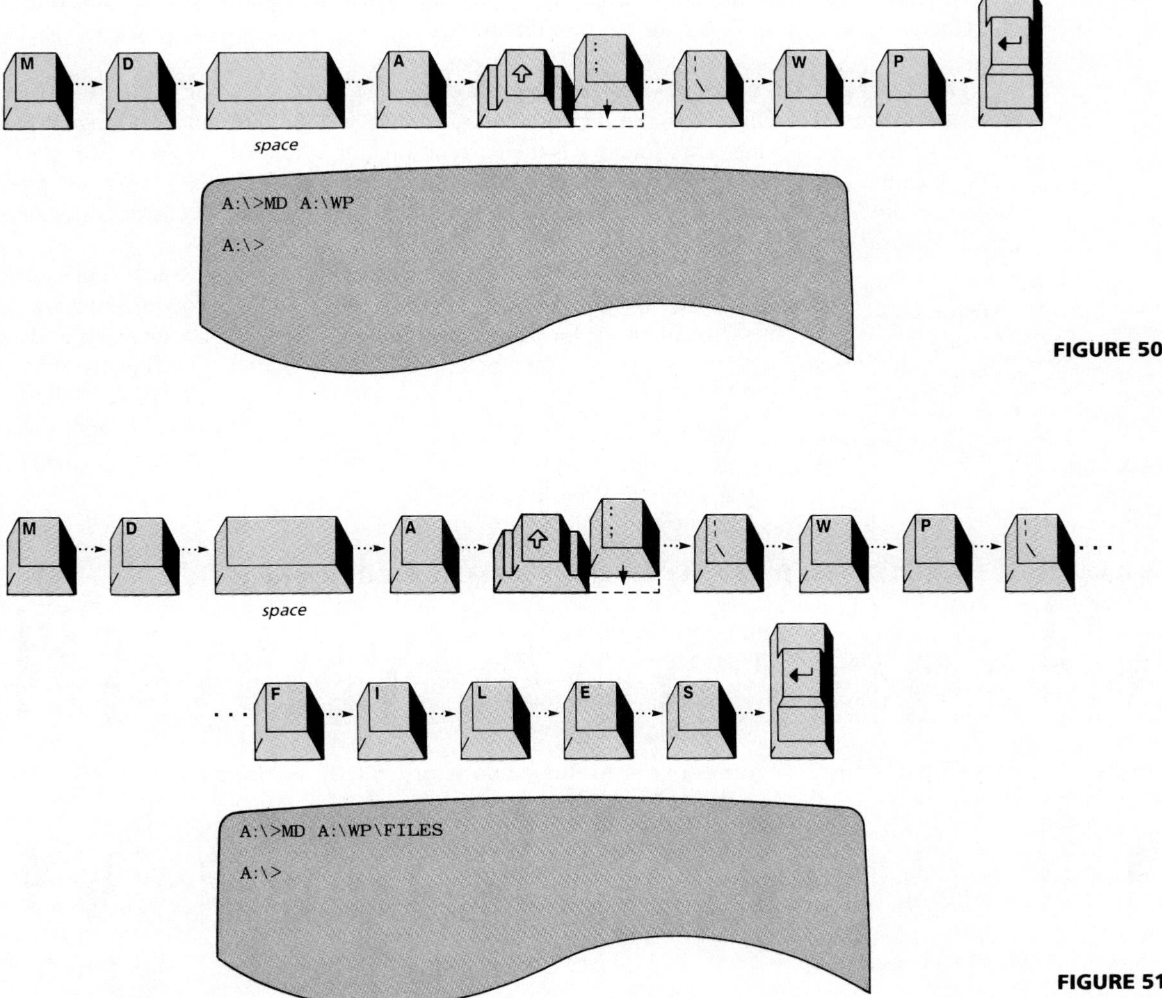


**FIGURE 50**



**FIGURE 51**

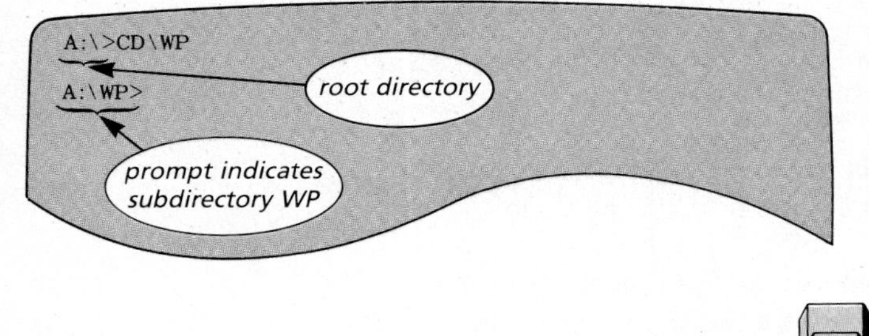


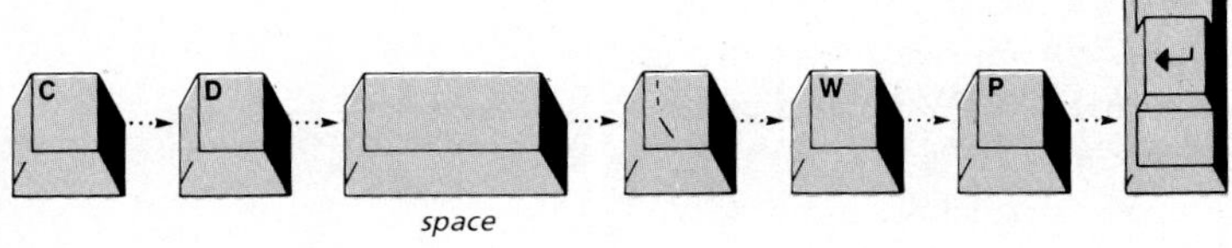


FIGURE 52

## Changing Directories

Use the **CHDIR command** to move from one directory to another. Enter the letters CD immediately following the DOS prompt. Then type the backslash character and the subdirectory name and press the Enter key. To change from the root directory to the WP directory, for instance, type the entry CD \WP and press the Enter key. The result shown in Figure 52 should appear on your screen. To move to a lower subdirectory, such as the FILES subdirectory, type CD \WP\FILES and press the Enter key.

If you are moving to a directory that is subordinate to the current subdirectory, you can simply type CD and the subdirectory name. For instance, if your current directory is WP, you can move to the FILES subdirectory by entering CD FILES. Note that the entry omits both the reference to WP (the current directory) and the backslash character.

To return to the root directory simply type CD\ and press the Enter key. The backslash character entered by itself signifies the root directory.

**The Current Directory.** Just as there is a default or current disk drive, there is a current directory. The **current directory** is the one in which you are currently working. When you first access a disk, the root directory is the current directory. You can, however, direct DOS to a subdirectory, which then becomes the current directory for that disk. If you temporarily set another drive as the default drive, the named directory remains the current directory for the first disk.

FIGURE 53

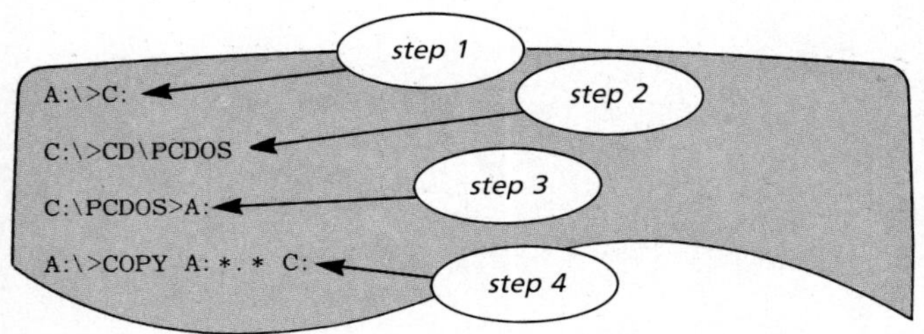


For practice, set your default drive to drive C by entering C: (Figure 53, step 1). Then set PCDOS as the current subdirectory for drive C by entering CD \PCDOS (step 2). Switch to drive A as the default drive (step 3) and copy files from drive A to drive C: type the copy command COPY A:*.* C: (step 4). Files are copied from the A drive to the PCDOS subdirectory on drive C even though the subdirectory is not specified in the copy command.

**Step 1: Change default to drive C.**

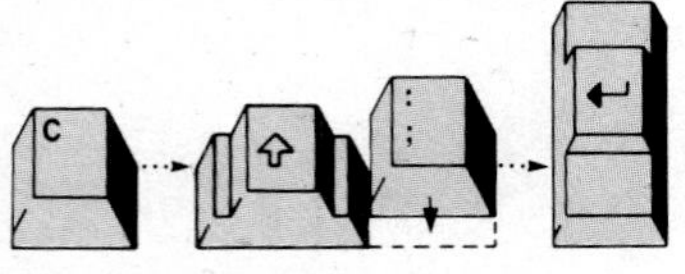


**Step 2: Change from root directory of drive C to PCDOS directory.**

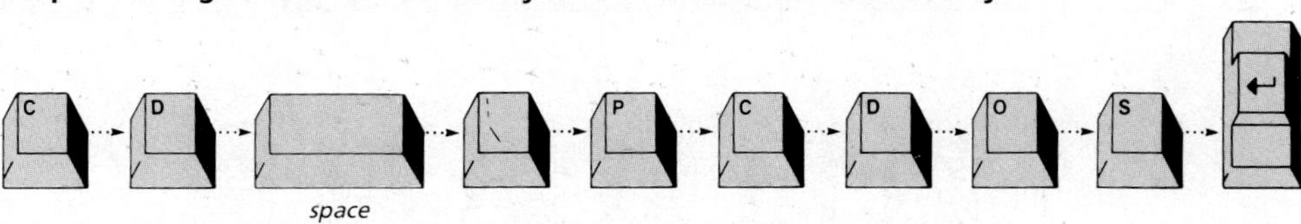


**Step 3: Return to A drive.** **Step 4: Copy files from drive A to the subdirectory PCDOS on drive C.**

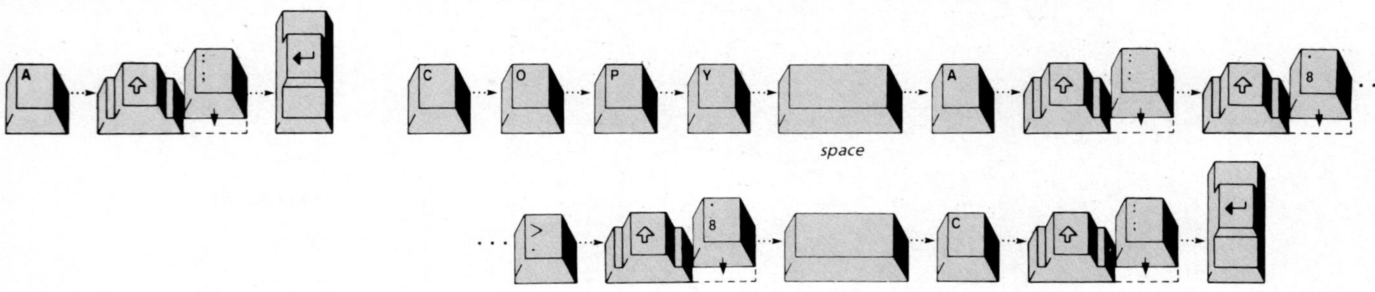

## Specifying a Path to Subdirectories and Files

You will find it very convenient to group files in subdirectories. To use the technique you must learn to specify the path to a file. The **path** includes three components: (1) the drive, (2) the name of the subdirectories, (3) the name of the file. The path specifies the route DOS is to take from the root directory through subdirectories leading to a file. Specify the path whenever you wish to access a file for DIR, COPY, or similar commands. Unless you specify a path, DOS may not find the file you desire because it would search only the current directory of the default drive.

**Specifying Paths in Commands.** One way to specify the path is to include it in the command you are using. For example, you can make a backup copy on a diskette of a file named DOSNOTES.DOC stored in the FILES subdirectory under the WP subdirectory, by typing the command COPY C:\WP\FILES\DOSNOTES.DOC A:. The COPY command includes the source drive (C:), both directories specified together (\WP\FILES), and the filename preceded by a backslash (\DOSNOTES.DOC). On drive A, the file is stored simply as DOSNOTES.DOC under the root directory, because no subdirectory has been made or referenced on that disk.

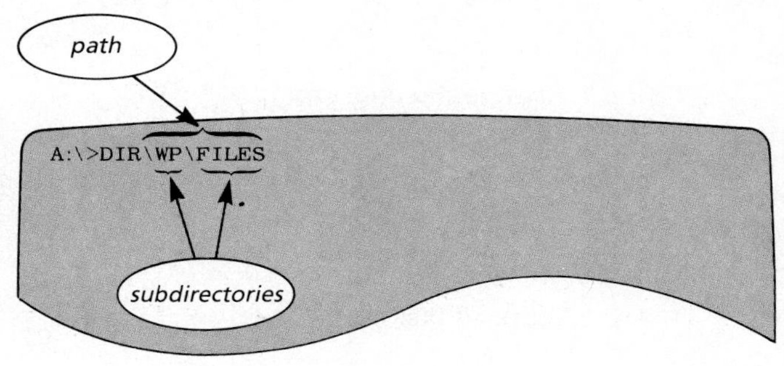


FIGURE 54

You can use this style with other DOS commands and when specifying files in many programs. For example, to display the file contents of the FILES subdirectory, enter DIR \WP\FILES and press the Enter key (Figure 54). Enter DIR \WP to list the program files for the word processing software stored under the WP subdirectory.

## Managing Files Within Subdirectories

To copy files or data to subdirectories, you can use the COPY command or any file storage techniques offered by your application program. Some programs may not recognize the subdirectory structure on your diskette, so you may need to set the current directory before you use the program. The RENAME, DIR, ERASE, and other DOS commands work in subdirectories in nearly the same way as they do in the main directory.

## Removing Subdirectories

When you no longer need a subdirectory, you can remove it. Use the **RMDIR command**, abbreviated to **RD**, to remove a specified directory from a disk.

**Erasing Subdirectory Files.** To remove a subdirectory, you must first remove all files stored within it. You can do so by using the global character * with the ERASE command. You can issue this command from the subdirectory to be removed or from another directory if you give the full path specification. If you issue the command from another directory, make certain to use the correct subdirectory and path information or you might inadvertently erase files from another part of the disk.

For practice, delete the FILES subdirectory (Figure 55, step 1). First, enter the FILES subdirectory by typing the command CD\WP\FILES and pressing the Enter key. Next, empty the subdirectory of files by typing ERASE *.* and pressing the Enter key (step 2). You will receive the message "Are you sure (Y/N)?", to which you must press Y and then the Enter key (step 3).

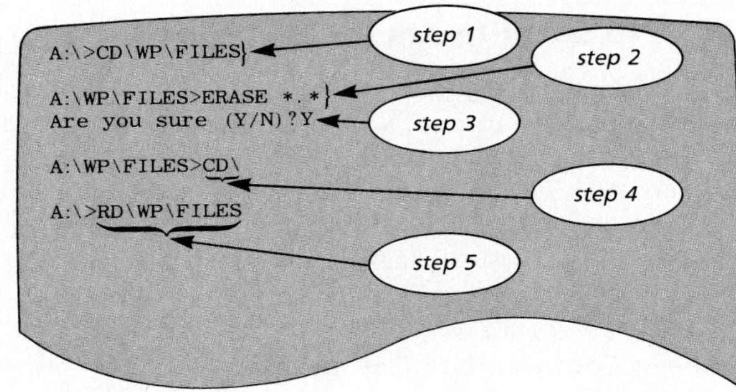


**Step 1: Change the directory to WP\FILES.**

**Step 2: Erase all files.**

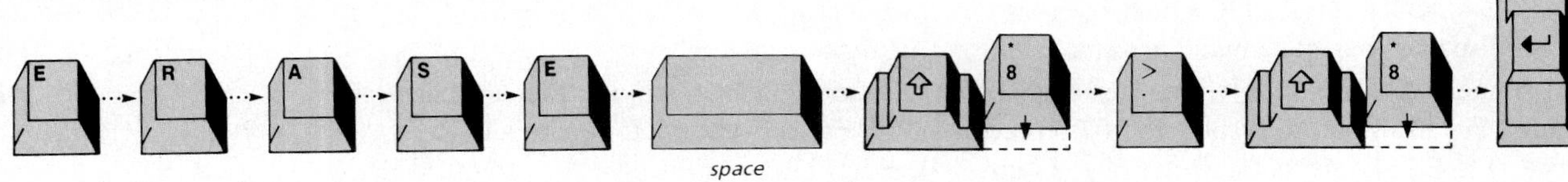


**Step 3: Respond "Yes" to the prompt.** **Step 4: Change to the root directory.**

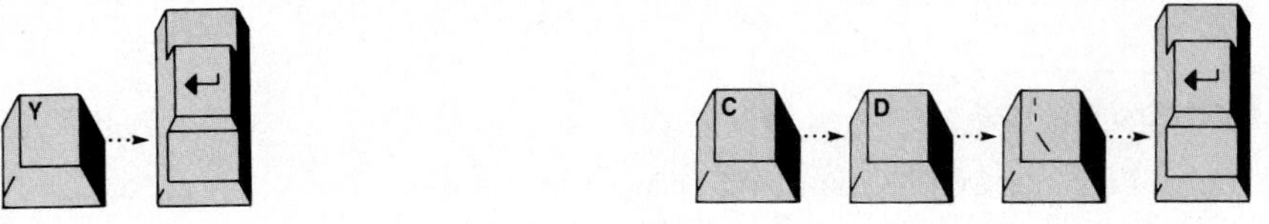

**Step 5: Remove the FILES subdirectory.**

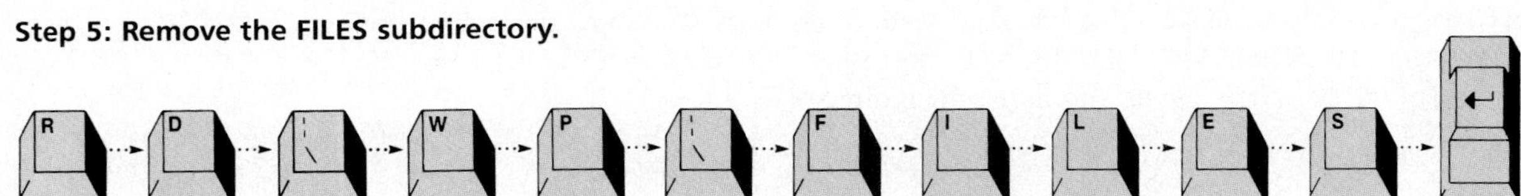

**FIGURE 55**

**Removing a Subdirectory.** After you have emptied the subdirectory files, you can remove the subdirectory. Enter the root directory by typing the command CD\ and pressing the Enter key (step 4). To remove the FILES subdirectory, enter RD \WP\FILES and press the Enter key (step 5). Note that you must specify the full path, even though the WP directory is to remain. You must specify the full path so that DOS follows the path from the root directory, where the WP directory entry is stored, through the WP directory to find and remove the FILES entry.

## LOADING A PROGRAM

A **program** is a series of instructions that specifies the steps your computer must perform to accomplish a specific purpose. To execute a program, you must first load the program into main memory from diskette or disk storage. The program must be stored either on a diskette, which you have inserted into one of the disk drives, or on the internal hard disk. If you are using a two-diskette system, place the diskette containing the program to be executed in the default drive, usually drive A. Then type the program name (or name abbreviation) and press the Enter key. (Notice that loading and executing an application program is essentially the same as issuing an external DOS command.)

## SUMMARY

1. An **operating system** is one or more programs that control and manage the operation of a computer.
2. The operating system for an IBM Personal Computer is **PC-DOS**. Other compatible computers use a similar program called **MS-DOS**.
3. The **version** number of a program is the whole number and signifies a major improvement of the product. The **release** number is the decimal number and identifies minor corrections or changes to a version of the product.
4. "**Booting**" the computer refers to loading the operating system from a disk into main memory.
5. The computer can be "booted" by turning it on with the operating system located on a disk in the computer. This is called a "cold start."
6. To reload the operating system when the computer is already switched on, hold down the **Control** and **Alternate** keys and press the **Delete** key. This process is called a "warm start" or "reset."
7. The operating system will **prompt** you for its commands. DOS has two general types of commands: (1) **internal commands** that are executed from the program stored in the main memory; (2) **external commands** that are programs loaded from a disk as the command is executed.
8. After the operating system has been loaded into main memory, you may be prompted to enter the date or time. Some systems have an internal clock that provides this information for you.
9. The **DOS prompt** includes the letter address of the **default disk drive**, the disk that is currently in use for data or program access.
10. The default drive of a two-diskette computer is usually drive A. A computer with a hard disk drive will generally use drive C as its default drive.
11. You can change the default drive by entering a valid drive letter, followed by a colon, and pressing the Enter key.
12. To examine files on a disk, issue the **DIR** (directory) command. Use the **/P** option to pause a long directory listing when the screen is full. Use the **/W** option to list files across the width of the screen.
13. Give the **pause-screen** command by holding down the Control key and pressing the S key.
14. Many commands can be canceled by holding down the **Control** key and pressing the **Break** key or by pressing Control-C.
15. Use the **FORMAT** command to prepare diskettes for storing data or program files. Several options are available for various types of diskettes. Use **/S** to format the diskette as a **system disk**. The **/V** option prompts a **volume label**.
16. Filenames must be created by following specific rules. A **filename** may consist of up to eight letters, numbers, or certain symbols. The filename **extension** is an optional one- to three-character addition, separated from the filename by a period.
17. Files with the extensions **.BAT**, **.COM**, or **.EXE** are external, executable command files.
18. Use the COPY command to transfer a file to another diskette or to create a backup file on the same diskette.
19. **Wildcards**, the ***** and **?** characters, can be used in conjunction with many DOS commands to replace specific characters.
20. A file to be copied is the **source** file. The resulting copy is called the **target** file.
21. You can change a file's name by specifying the target file used during the COPY command or by using the **RENAME** command.
22. To remove a file from a disk, execute the **ERASE** or the **DELETE** command.
23. Disks can be better organized through the use of **subdirectories**. A disk's primary directory is the **root** directory, signified by a **backslash** following the drive letter, such as C:\.
24. Use the **MKDIR** or the **MD** command to create a subdirectory. The entry includes the drive, backslash, and directory name, such as C:\WP.
25. To switch from one directory to another, use the **CHDIR** or **CD** command, for example, CD\WP.
26. A directory can be removed by first erasing all the files in the directory, then using the REMOVE DIRECTORY command, **RD**.
27. To **load a program** for execution, type the name of the program file at the DOS prompt.

# STUDENT ASSIGNMENTS

## True/False Questions

**Instructions:** Which of the following statements are true and which are false?

1. PC-DOS and MS-DOS are essentially the same operation system.
2. When DOS is updated for a new version, programs operating in prior versions may not work under the newer edition.
3. The programs comprising an operating system such as PC-DOS can be stored on a diskette.
4. "Booting" the computer refers to the procedure of starting the operating system.
5. DOS commands are divided into two types: internal and external commands.
6. As a part of the system startup procedures, you are requested to enter the computer's serial number.
7. After the operating system has been loaded, you can type the command DIR and press the Enter key to display a directory of the diskette in the default drive.
8. The computer may have a built-in clock that the operating system automatically accesses to input the date and time.
9. The symbol A>, which appears on the computer screen, is called the DOS prompt.
10. A defective disk drive is one that improperly stores data.
11. To change the disk drive assignment to drive C, type C:↵.
12. All DOS commands must be entered in uppercase characters.
13. You can list the directory of the default disk drive by typing DIR and pressing the Enter key.
14. The option /P used with the DIR command will cause the listing to pause when the screen is full.
15. Holding down the Control key and then pressing the Break key will cancel a command function.
16. To format a diskette, put the diskette to be formatted in disk drive A and enter the command FORMAT B:.
17. The command Copy A: can be used to copy all files from one disk drive to another.
18. The ERASE command can be used to remove a file from the file directory.
19. To include the operating system on a formatted disk, use the command FORMAT B:/S.
20. When you use the FORMAT option /V, the system will prompt you to enter a volume label.
21. To cancel a command, hold down the ALT key and press the END key.
22. A DOS filename may contain from 1 to 11 characters plus an optional extension of 1 to 3 characters.
23. The disk containing the file to be copied is known as the source disk.
24. Global replacement characters include *, ?, and \.
25. Hard disk drives are generally addressed as drive C.
26. Subdirectories on disks are used to group filename entries for convenient storage and retrieval.
27. A disk's main file directory is called the root directory.
28. The current directory is the one in which you are currently working.
29. To move from one current directory to another, use the MD command.
30. A file address contains the disk drive letter, the subdirectory path, and the filename.
31. A program cannot be loaded from a disk unless the program disk is in the current drive.

## Multiple-Choice Questions

1. "Booting" the computer refers to
   a. loading the operating system
   b. placing covers over the disk drives
   c. using application programs to access disk drives
   d. the system interface
2. "DOS" stands for
   a. Digital Organizing Software
   b. Data Output Stream
   c. Disk Operating System
   d. Dielectric Orthanographic Startup
3. PC-DOS is used on IBM Personal Computers and Personal System/2 systems. IBM-compatible computers generally use
   a. PC-OMD
   b. MS-DOS
   c. XD-DOS
   d. CP/DUZ
4. A term describing your ability to use newer editions of software while retaining features and data used in earlier ones is
   a. software generation
   b. compatibility curve
   c. upward compatibility
   d. version control
5. When you start up the computer, you load the operating system
   a. from a diskette in drive A
   b. from the computer's internal memory
   c. from the fixed disk if the computer is so equipped
   d. both a and c
6. The term for restarting the operating system in a computer already powered on is
   a. warm start
   b. cold start
   c. warm boot
   d. both a and c
7. The symbol A>
   a. is called a DOS prompt
   b. indicates the name of a program
   c. indicates the default disk drive
   d. both a and c
8. Listing the files on a disk is accomplished by
   a. typing DIR and pressing the Enter key
   b. typing LIST and pressing the Enter key
   c. typing CHKDSK and pressing the Enter key
   d. typing RUN FILES and pressing the Enter key

9. To pause a listing on the screen, press
   a. Control and Break
   b. Alternate, Control, and Delete
   c. Control and S
   d. either b or c
10. To cancel a command, press
    a. Control and Break
    b. Alternate, Control, and Delete
    c. Control and S
    d. either c or d
11. The ________ command establishes sectors on a diskette and performs other functions that allow the diskette to store files.
    a. CHKDSK
    b. DIR
    c. REUSE
    d. FORMAT
12. A valid DOS filename specification consists of
    a. 10 alphanumeric characters
    b. a 9-character filename
    c. an 11-character name, separated by a period at any position within the name
    d. an 8-character filename plus an optional extension of a period followed by 3 characters
13. A common use of the COPY command is to make working copies of program and data disks, producing
    a. file disks
    b. backup copies
    c. extension disks
    d. authorized disks
14. To copy the file PROGRAM.EXE from drive A to drive B, type the command
    a. COPY PROGRAM.EXE TO DRIVE B
    b. COPY A:PROGRAM.EXE TO B:PROGRAM.EXE
    c. COPY A:PROGRAM.EXE B:
    d. either b or c
15. To copy all files on drive A to drive C, type the command
    a. COPY DRIVE A TO DRIVE C
    b. COPY ALL FILES TO C
    c. COPY A:*.* C:*.*
    d. COPY A: C:
16. To change the name of a file from FILEX.DOC to FILEA.DOC, enter
    a. ALTER FILEX.DOC TO FILEA.DOC
    b. CHANGE FILEX.DOC TO FILEA.DOC
    c. ASSIGN FILEX.DOC AS FILEA.DOC
    d. RENAME FILEX.DOC FILEA.DOC
17. To remove a file from a disk, type
    a. REMOVE FILE
    b. DELETE FILEX.DOC
    c. ERASE FILEX.DOC
    d. either b or c
18. Filenames are grouped on disks into
    a. index lists
    b. directories and subdirectories
    c. subject and filename entries
    d. internally labeled entries

19. The MKDIR, or MD, command will
    a. manage directory files
    b. make a directory on a disk
    c. create a file copy
    d. either a or b
20. To shift from the root directory to a directory of files under a word processing directory, type the command
    a. CH /FILES
    b. GOTO WP FILES
    c. CD \WP\FILES
    d. C:\WP\FILES*.*

## Projects

1. Start your computer without a DOS disk in drive A. What is the display on the screen? Why did this display appear? Insert a DOS disk in drive A and restart the computer by pressing the Ctrl Alt Del keys simultaneously.
2. Start your computer with the DOS disk in the default disk drive. If permitted in your computer lab, prepare a new diskette as a system disk using the proper FORMAT command options for the task at hand and for the specific diskette your computer uses.
3. Prepare a diskette to be a file disk using the FORMAT command. Give the diskette a volume label using your own name. Determine the proper type of diskette to use on the computer and, after formatting, determine the amount of free space remaining on the diskette.
4. If permitted in your computer lab, create a working copy of your application program diskettes.
    a. First, format a new diskette. Will there be enough room on the diskette to contain both the operating system and the program? How can you know?
    b. Using one command, copy all files from the master copy of the disk to your newly prepared diskette.
5. Create a subdirectory named SUB1 on your diskette.
6. Make subdirectory SUB1 the current directory. Copy all .DOC files into SUB1 and display the directory.
7. Remove the subdirectory created in Project 6.

# DOS Index



**Photo Credits:** **Opening Page and Figure 2a**, Radio Shack, a division of Tandy Corp.; **Figures 2b and 3a**, Compaq Computer Corp.; **Figure 3b**, International Business Machines Corp.

# Word Processing Using WordPerfect

# PROJECT 1

## Typing, Saving, and Printing a Simple Letter

### Objectives

You will have mastered the material in this project when you can:

- Load WordPerfect into main memory
- Explain the function of the WordPerfect template
- Move the cursor in all directions
- View the reveal codes
- Type, save, and print a short letter
- Exit WordPerfect and return to the A> prompt

**WordPerfect**, developed by **WordPerfect Corporation**, Orem, Utah is a best-selling word processing program. WordPerfect is available for use on most microcomputers on the market. In this unit, you will learn how to use WordPerfect on an IBM personal computer (PC, XT, AT, PS/2, and compatibles) operating under MS-DOS, or PC-DOS. Like all word processing programs, WordPerfect is used to produce printed documents and is especially useful when documents require precise formatting and presentation. These documents can be prepared for many different applications, from business memos to student term papers.

In the following projects all the features of WordPerfect will not be explained. For an explanation of those features not covered, refer to the WordPerfect Reference Manual supplied with the software package by WordPerfect Corporation.

For the following Projects using WordPerfect we assume you are using a keyboard with the function keys at the *left* of the keyboard.

### Using the Training Version of WordPerfect

Boyd & Fraser Publishing Company, the publisher of this textbook, has contracted with WordPerfect Corporation to obtain the **Training Version of WordPerfect**, Release 4.2. This training version contains most of the features of the WordPerfect package available in the retail market. It was developed to help students *learn* the features of WordPerfect, not to be a fully usable tool for professional documents. The limitations of the training version are as follows:

- You may work with as large a document as you like in memory; however, you may save to disk a document no larger than about 4K (4,000 characters).
- A data file created with the training version can be used with the commercial version of WordPerfect, and a file created in the commercial version of WordPerfect can be used with the training version.
- Data files of any size may be printed through parallel printer port 1 without defining a printer.
- The training version supports one font but not the extended ASCII characters.
- The letters *WPC will appear randomly throughout your printed document. This is your indication that the document was prepared using the training version of WordPerfect.
- Using training examples, you will be able to learn all the functions of WordPerfect 4.2's speller and thesaurus. However, you may not use the speller and thesaurus with any of your own documents.
- The Help file of the training version allows you to view the function-key template on the screen, but as with the speller and the thesaurus, space does not allow the complete Help files to be included on the training disk.

Boyd & Fraser Publishing Company and the authors are grateful to WordPerfect Corporation for allowing students to have access to this word processing program.

# THE KEYBOARD

In Project 1 you will become familiar with the keyboard and the template used with WordPerfect. To learn the position and feel of the keys, you will practice pressing certain keys before turning the computer on. Then, after turning the computer on and loading WordPerfect, you will type, save, and print the short letter in Figure 1-1. You will then practice moving the cursor on a blank screen, after which you will exit the WordPerfect program.

December 1, 1990

Mr. Joseph Wright
236 Santo Domingo Cir.
Fountain Valley, Ca 92708

Dear Mr. Wright:

I received your letter today and wish to thank you for it.

Sincerely,

Mary Martinez
Director

**FIGURE 1-1**
**Letter for Project 1.**

The **keyboard** is used as an **input** device to input data into the computer. Look over the entire keyboard in Figure 1-2. In addition to the familiar typewriter keyboard keys, you will see some other keys. To the left of the typewriter section (or on top of the keyboard, depending on which keyboard you are using), you will notice keys F1 through F10. These are called **function keys** (some computers also have function keys 11 and 12). To the right of the keyboard is a **numeric keypad**, which looks similar to a 10-key adding machine. In addition to numbers, most keys on this numeric keypad have arrows pointing in different directions, or words such as Home and End.

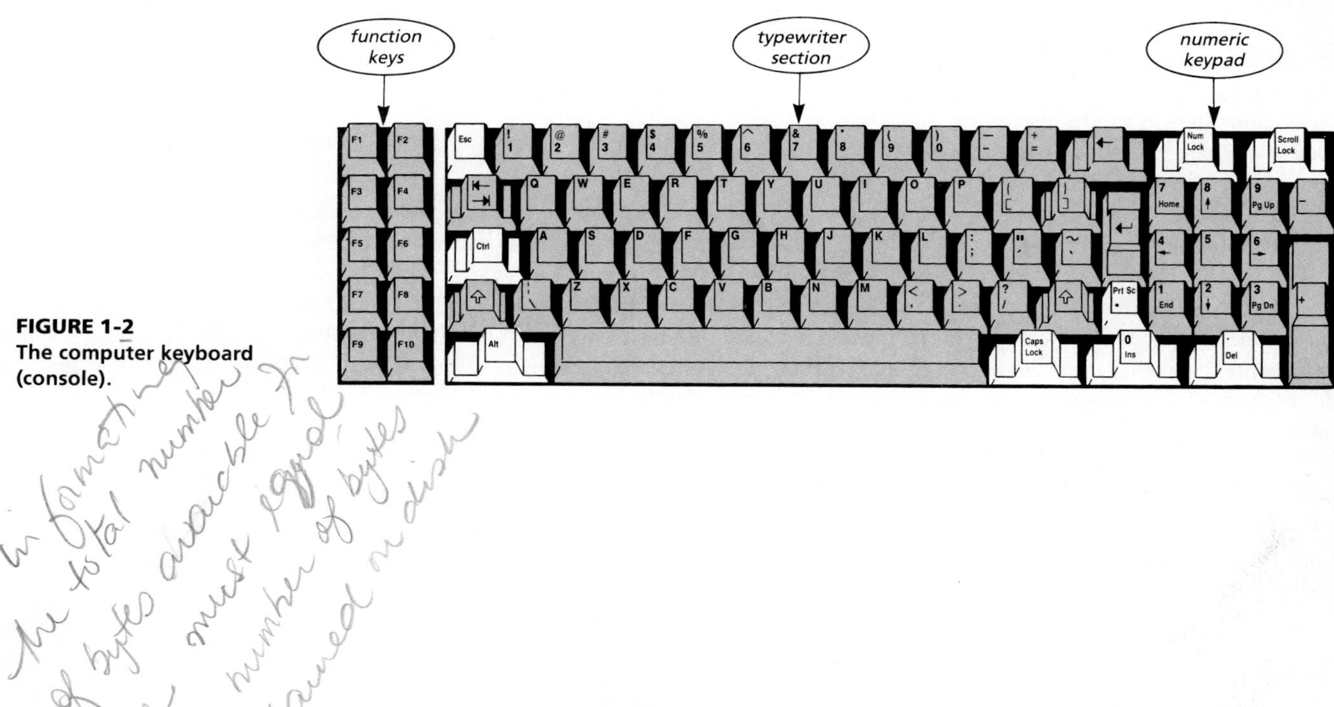


**FIGURE 1-2**
**The computer keyboard (console).**

## The Typewriter Section

In the typewriter section of the keyboard, the **Shift** keys may look familiar, but the **Ctrl** (Control) and **Alt** (Alternate) keys may be new to you.

As you may know, the Shift key is used to make lowercase letters into CAPITAL LETTERS, or to type the symbols above the number (#, $, %, &, *, etc.) on the keyboard. The Ctrl and Alt keys, as well as the Shift keys (Figure 1-3), are used along with the function keys to achieve specific word processing goals.

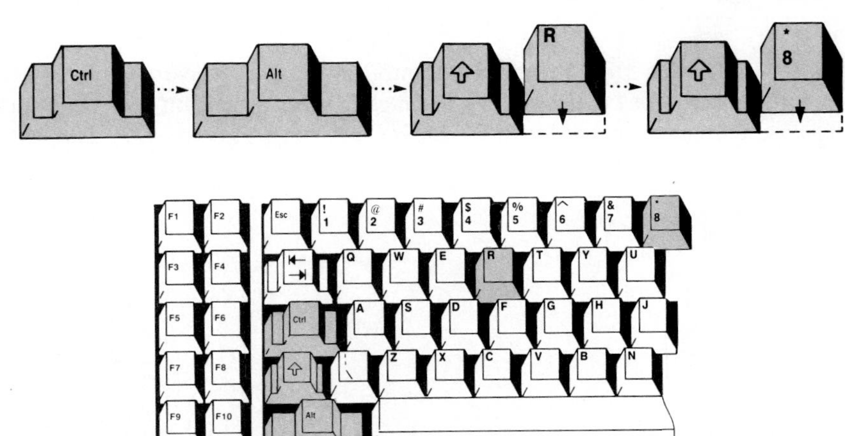


**FIGURE 1-3** **The Ctrl, Alt, and Shift keys.**

To become familiar with these keys *before* you turn on the computer, press the Ctrl key down, then let it up. Now press the Alt key, then let it up. Press the Right Shift key down and while holding it press the R key, then let them both up. Now hold the Left Shift key down and press the 8 key. Had the machine been on and WordPerfect loaded, the R key would have typed a capital R and the 8 key would have typed the asterisk, *.

The **Tab** key (Figure 1-4) is used for indenting to the next tab setting to the right, just as on a typewriter. Press the Tab key, and notice that there is one arrow that faces forward → and one arrow that faces backward ←. That is because this key, when pressed with the Shift key, also allows you to release the left margin. Hold the Shift key down firmly and press the Tab key. Had the machine been on and WordPerfect loaded, the margin would have been released to the next tab setting to the *left* of the cursor.

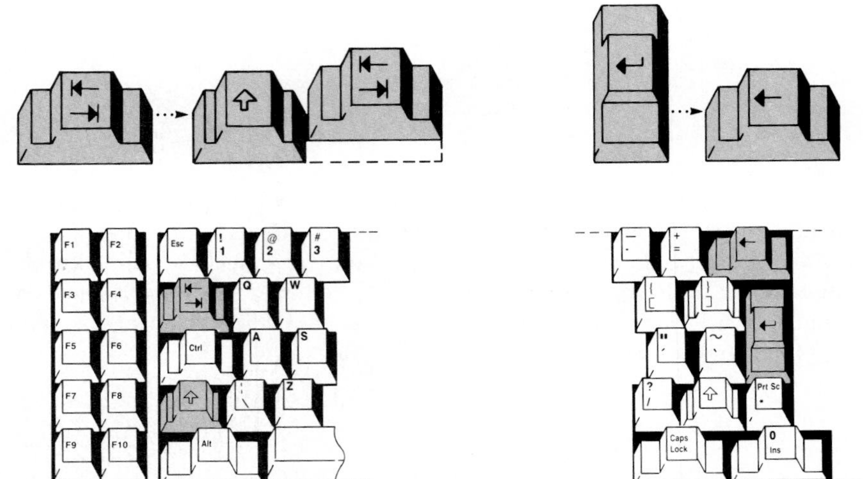


**FIGURE 1-4** **The Tab key**

**FIGURE 1-5** **The Return or Enter and Backspace keys**

The **Return** key (Figure 1-5), is used to do the same thing that the Return key is used for on a typewriter—to begin a new line. On most keyboards, however, the word **Enter** is on the key along with an arrow that looks like this ↵. That is because this key is also used to enter information into the computer.

Often while using a word processing package, such as WordPerfect, you will type a command and the letters or numbers you typed will stay on the screen; you may wonder what to do next. A good rule of thumb is that *if you have given a command and nothing happens, press Enter* ↵. In other words, the command you typed is only on the screen. It will not be entered into the memory of the computer until you press the Enter key. The few exceptions to this will be discussed individually. Now, for practice, press the Enter key.

Although Enter and Return are the same key, remember that sometimes the key will be referred to as Enter and sometimes as Return. When you were loading DOS into the computer, you had to type the date. After the date, you pressed the Enter key, because you wanted the date entered into the computer memory. When you press this key at the end of a paragraph or a short line, or when you want to add a blank line in your text, you refer to the key as the Return key, as you normally would if you were typing on a typewriter. Since the Enter (Return) key has an arrow like this ↵, many times throughout these projects you will see this arrow instead of the word Enter or Return. When you see the arrow, press the Enter key.

The **Backspace** key (Figure 1-5) is used to move the cursor backward on the screen, much like the Backspace key on a typewriter. However, in WordPerfect, as you backspace, the character or space directly to the left of the cursor (_) is deleted. Try pressing the Backspace key.

## The Numeric Keypad

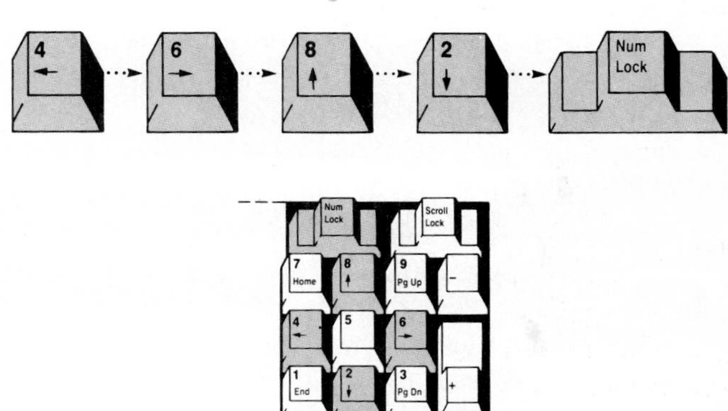


**FIGURE 1-6 The Numeric Keypad.**

Figure 1-6 shows the numeric keypad. The keys on the numeric keypad can be used to type numbers, but for most purposes it's better to use the number keys in the typewriter section of the keyboard to type numbers. It's more important to use the keys on the numeric keypad to move the cursor through the text on the screen. The arrow pointing to the left will move the cursor one character to the left. Press the **Left Arrow** key ← several times. The arrow pointing right will move the cursor one character to the right. Press the **Right Arrow** key → several times. The arrow pointing up will move the cursor up one line. Press the **Up Arrow** key ↑ several times. The arrow pointing down will move the cursor down one line. Press the **Down Arrow** key ↓ several times.

If you wish to use the numeric keypad to type numbers instead of using it to move the cursor, you will have to "lock" the numbers to the "on" position by pressing the Num Lock key. For practice, press the Num Lock key several times.

## The Function Keys

Find the function keys on the far left side of the keyboard (or at the top). They are numbered 1 to 10, with an F in front of each number. These function keys are special keys programmed to execute commonly used commands. Functions can be margin changes, tab setting changes, boldfacing, correcting the spelling of a document, and so on.

To understand how the function keys work, first look at the keyboard. If you have any typing experience, you know that if you were to type the G key, you would see a lowercase g on the screen. If you hold down the Shift key and type the *same* G key, the Shift key changes the function of that key and makes it a capital G. You type the same key, but you get a different value, depending on whether you press the key alone or hold down the Shift key and press the G key.

The Function keys are very similar. If you press a function key alone, you will be able to perform a certain function, such as saving a document. But if you hold the Shift key down and press the same function key, you will be able to perform an entirely different function, such as centering.

Further, you can hold down the Alt key or the Ctrl key and press the same Function key to perform additional functions such as moving parts of your text. *Each* function key can have *four* different values, depending on whether you press it alone or with the Ctrl, Alt, or Shift keys.

## THE WORDPERFECT TEMPLATE

Figure 1-7 is a picture of the WordPerfect **Template**, showing how it fits over the function keys. Most word processors show command messages on the screen that take up valuable space. The template takes command messages off the screen and puts them next to the function keys to which they correspond. This not only makes it easier to learn the keystrokes, it also unclutters the screen, making it easier to read.

The template is color coded, starting at the bottom with black, then blue, green, and red on the top. The colors signify the following:

**Black** means you press the key alone.

**Blue** means you hold down the **Alt** key firmly while pressing the desired F key.

**Green** means you hold down the **Shift** key firmly while pressing the desired F key.

**Red** means you hold down the **Ctrl** key firmly while pressing the desired F key.

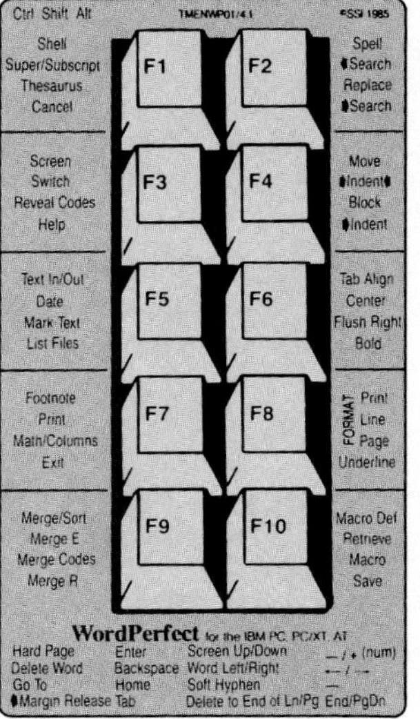


**FIGURE 1-7**
**Template around Function keys.**

To understand how to use this template and its color coding, look to the right of the F6 key on the template. Notice that the bottom item, in black, says Bold. Therefore, if you desire to have your typing boldfaced you would press the F6 key alone. For practice, press the F6 key. If the computer had been turned on and WordPerfect was loaded, after you pressed the F6 key, any typing you did would have been boldfaced, until you "turned off" the boldface by pressing the F6 key again.

Let's try another example. Look at the template next to the F2 key. You will see the word Spell in red. Because red signifies the Ctrl key on the template, hold down the Ctrl key firmly and while holding it, lightly press the F2 key to perform the Spell function. For practice, hold down the Ctrl key and press the F2 key. If the machine had been turned on and WordPerfect was loaded, it would have been ready to check the spelling of your text.

In summary, whenever you see Ctrl, Alt, or Shift followed by a hyphen and a function key—such as Ctrl-F8 or Alt-F3—remember to hold down the first key and, while holding it down, lightly press the function key.

Common mistakes made by users of WordPerfect are that they try to press the Ctrl, Alt, or Shift key *simultaneously* with the function key, or they press the Ctrl, Alt, or Shift key, release that key, and then press the function key. If you make either of those mistakes, the computer will react as if you had pressed the function key *only*.

If you press the function keys in error and get a message on the lower left corner of the screen that you wish to remove, press the F1 (Cancel) key. That will usually undo that error and remove the message.

Practice on the keyboard for a few minutes to feel more comfortable with it. After you have practiced with the Ctrl, Alt, and Shift keys, you will have just the right touch.

## DEFAULTS

One word that you will see throughout this text is **default**. This word simply means that *unless instructed otherwise* this is the action to be taken. For example, you will often be asked to give a yes or no answer, as in the message in Figure 1-8. The Y (for yes) will automatically appear on the screen, which means that Y is the default. Notice that after the (Y/N), WordPerfect displays an option outside the parentheses, and the cursor will be under that option. You may type Y or N, whichever is your choice. However, the choice above the cursor is WordPerfect's default choice. If you want the default choice, you may either type the letter or press the Enter key, which automatically accepts the default.

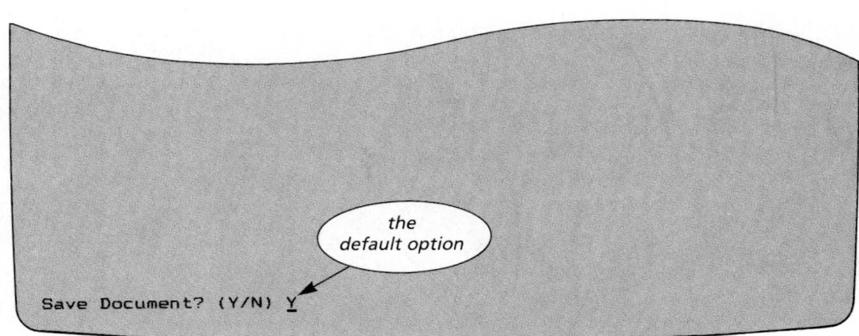


**FIGURE 1-8**

## LOADING WORDPERFECT

To place the WordPerfect training program into the memory of the computer, first load DOS into memory so that the A> prompt is displayed. Look at step 1 in Figure 1-9. Type b: and press the Enter key. This changes the default from drive A to drive B and enables your files to be saved to the disk in drive B. In step 2, at the B> prompt, type a:wp and press the Enter key. This instructs the computer to find the WordPerfect program in drive A.

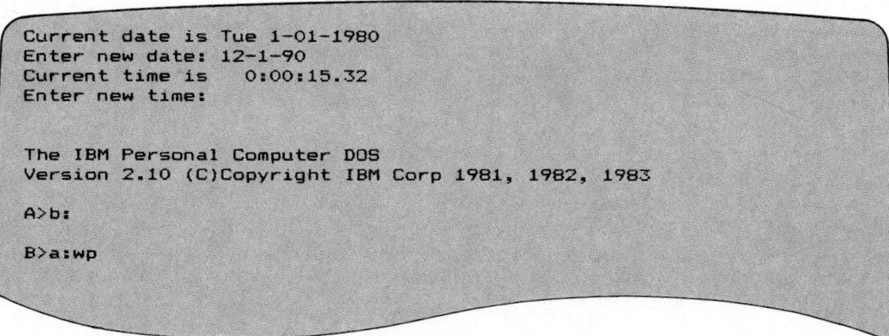

```
Current date is Tue 1-01-1980
Enter new date: 12-1-90
Current time is   0:00:15.32
Enter new time:

The IBM Personal Computer DOS
Version 2.10 (C)Copyright IBM Corp 1981, 1982, 1983

A>b:

B>a:wp
```

FIGURE 1-9

**Step 1: Change default to drive B** **Step 2: Load WordPerfect into main memory**

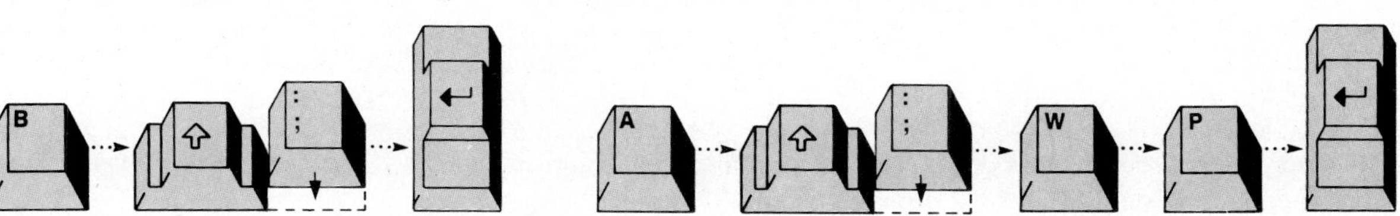


You hear the drives working, loading the WordPerfect program into the memory of the computer. Then you see the opening screen, informing you that you are using the training version of WordPerfect and explaining the licensing restrictions and the limitations of the training version (Figure 1-10). Press any key to continue. (If the last person to use the training version exited WordPerfect improperly, you may be stopped before this screen and asked, "Are other copies of WordPerfect currently running (Y/N)?" If you get this message, type N and WordPerfect will continue.)

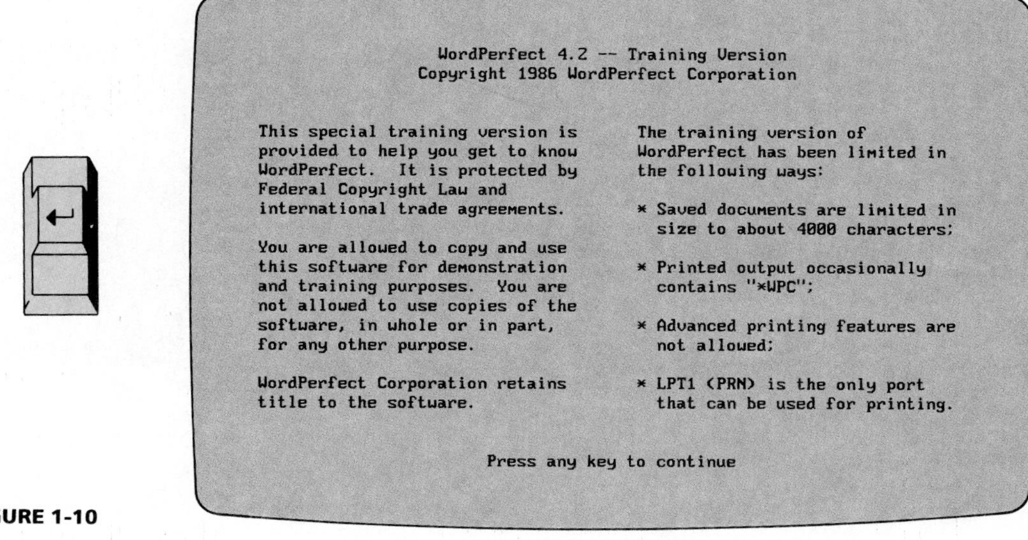

```
                WordPerfect 4.2 -- Training Version
              Copyright 1986 WordPerfect Corporation

This special training version is     The training version of
provided to help you get to know     WordPerfect has been limited in
WordPerfect.  It is protected by     the following ways:
Federal Copyright Law and
international trade agreements.      * Saved documents are limited in
                                       size to about 4000 characters;
You are allowed to copy and use
this software for demonstration      * Printed output occasionally
and training purposes.  You are        contains "*WPC";
not allowed to use copies of the
software, in whole or in part,       * Advanced printing features are
for any other purpose.                 not allowed;

WordPerfect Corporation retains      * LPT1 <PRN> is the only port
title to the software.                 that can be used for printing.

                       Press any key to continue
```

FIGURE 1-10

Some copies of the training version show a second screen welcoming you to WordPerfect, explaining how to use the function keys with the template and the Help function, and giving a few additional tips on how to use this software (Figure 1-11). If you see this screen, press any key to continue. If not, you are already into WordPerfect.

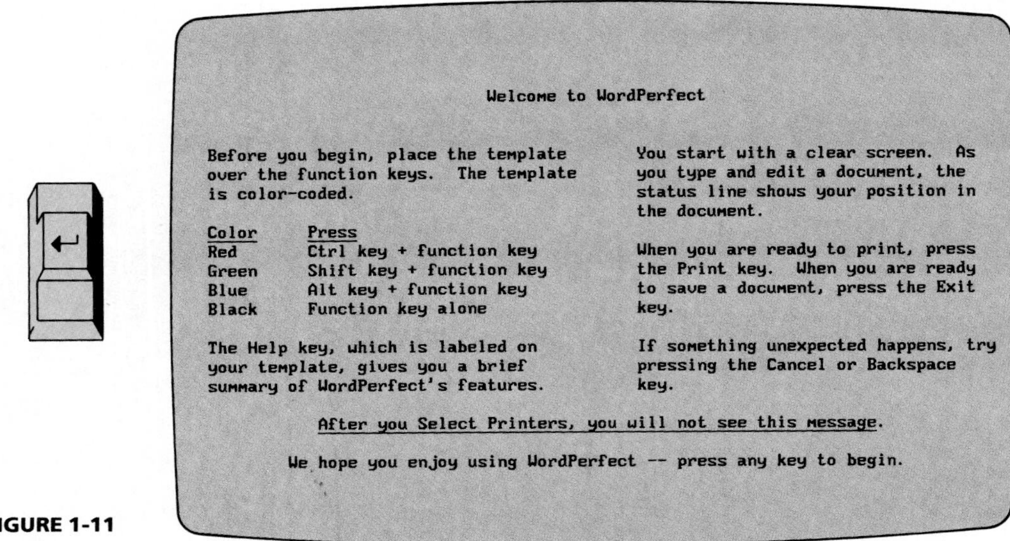

Welcome to WordPerfect
Before you begin, place the template over the function keys. The template is color-coded.
Color Press
Red Ctrl key + function key
Green Shift key + function key
Blue Alt key + function key
Black Function key alone
The Help key, which is labeled on your template, gives you a brief summary of WordPerfect's features.
You start with a clear screen. As you type and edit a document, the status line shows your position in the document.
When you are ready to print, press the Print key. When you are ready to save a document, press the Exit key.
If something unexpected happens, try pressing the Cancel or Backspace key.
After you Select Printers, you will not see this message.
We hope you enjoy using WordPerfect -- press any key to begin.


**FIGURE 1-11**

After you see the second opening screen, an almost blank screen appears, as shown in Figure 1-12. The only things on this screen are the status line and a blinking cursor. This blank screen is your work space, just as if you had put a blank piece of paper in your typewriter. The **cursor** is a visual reminder of where you are in the document. The **status line** informs you at all times about the exact document, page, line, and position of your cursor. For example, in Figure 1-12 the status line tells you that the cursor is in Document 1, on page 1, line 1, position 10.

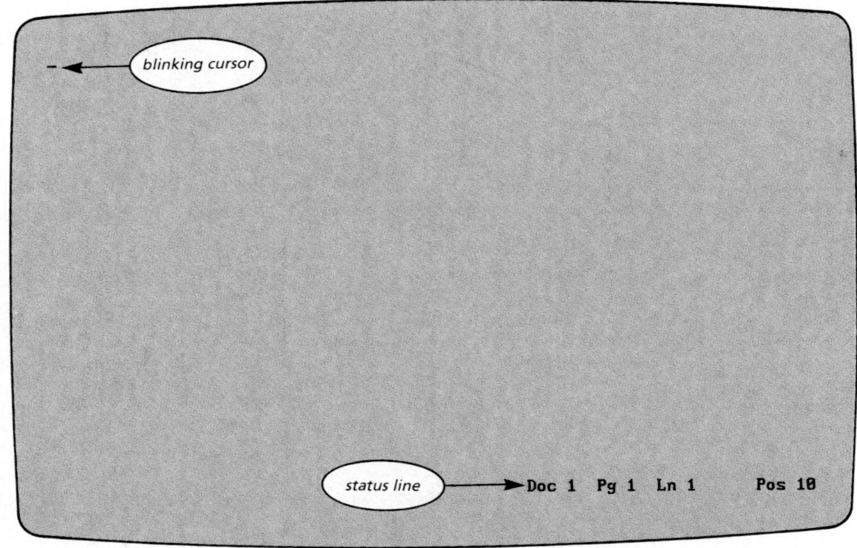


**FIGURE 1-12**

If you were typing on a typewriter, you would put one sheet of paper in at a time. Figure 1-13 illustrates how in WordPerfect all the pages seem to be attached together, with a so-called perforation between the pages. WordPerfect is programmed to advise you where the bottom of the page is and when you have started typing on the next page. When you have moved onto the next page, a line that looks much like a perforation will appear across the screen. After this line appears, the status line indicates that you are on the next page.

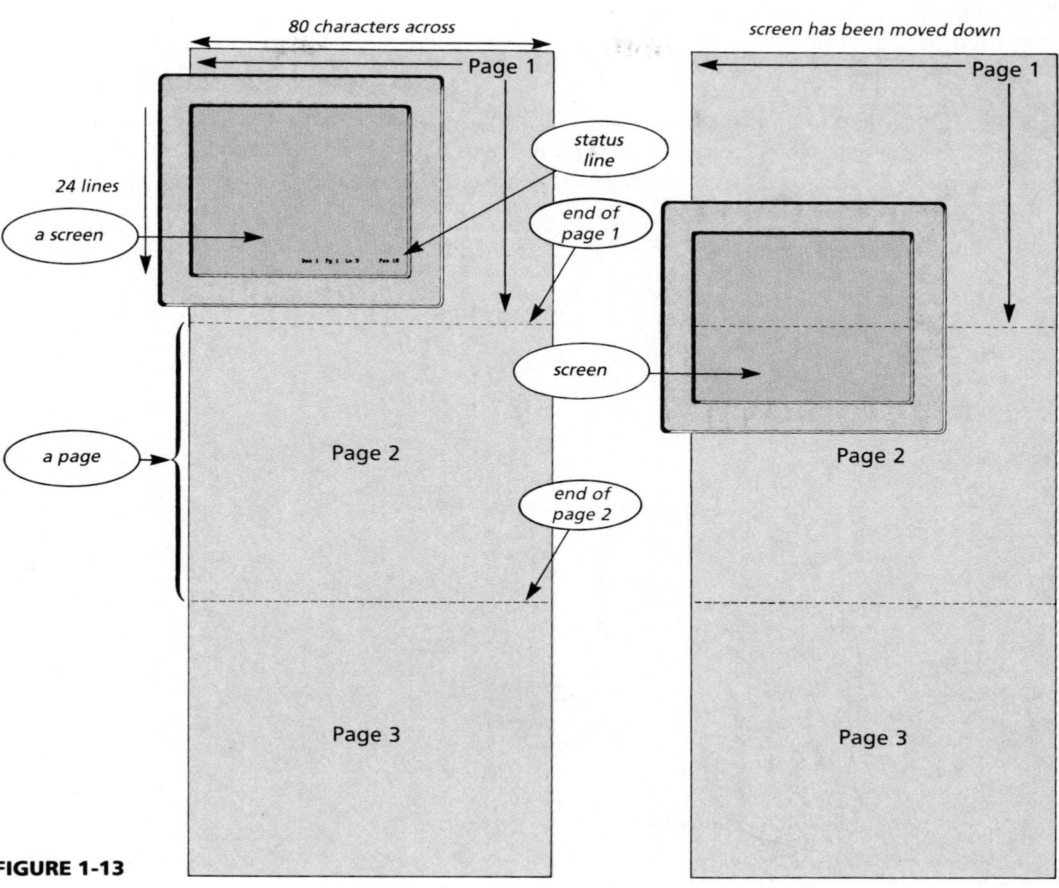


**FIGURE 1-13**

## THE SCREEN (OR WINDOW)

A **screen** or "window" is what appears on the computer monitor. Although you may have a four-page document, you can only view 24 lines down or 80 characters across at any one time on a screen. Imagine yourself looking out a window. You can only see a portion of the landscape outside. This does not mean that the rest of the world is not there, just that *your* view of the world is limited. If you went to another window, you would have a different view. This is the same as your "window" on your document. As Figure 1-13 shows, you can only see one screenful at a time. This does not mean that the rest of the document does not exist. Your view of your document depends on where your screen or "window" is situated.

## THE HELP FUNCTION

If you need help, you could use the **Help Function**. This is a collection of screens that you can access any time you are working on a document. These screens contain quick reminders on how to use WordPerfect.

Because the amount of memory available for the training version of WordPerfect is limited, the full version of the help screens are not included on the training version WordPerfect diskette. To view the help screen that is included on the training version, look at the template next to the F3 key. In black you will see the word **Help**. Press the F3 key. This displays the help screen. To exit the help screen press the space bar.

## CREATING A DOCUMENT

Now we are ready to create the letter to Mr. Wright (recall Figure 1-1). As you type, remember that if you type a mistake, all you need to do is press the Backspace key. As you do, your typing to the left of the Backspace key will be deleted. You can then retype correctly. If something unexpected happens, pressing the Backspace key may help. If you press a function key in error and you see a message at the bottom left corner of the screen, try pressing the **F1 (Cancel)** key.

Begin typing the first line of Figure 1-14, which is the date. As you type, notice that the position indicator (Pos) on the status line changes position with each letter or space you add.

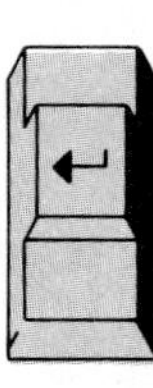

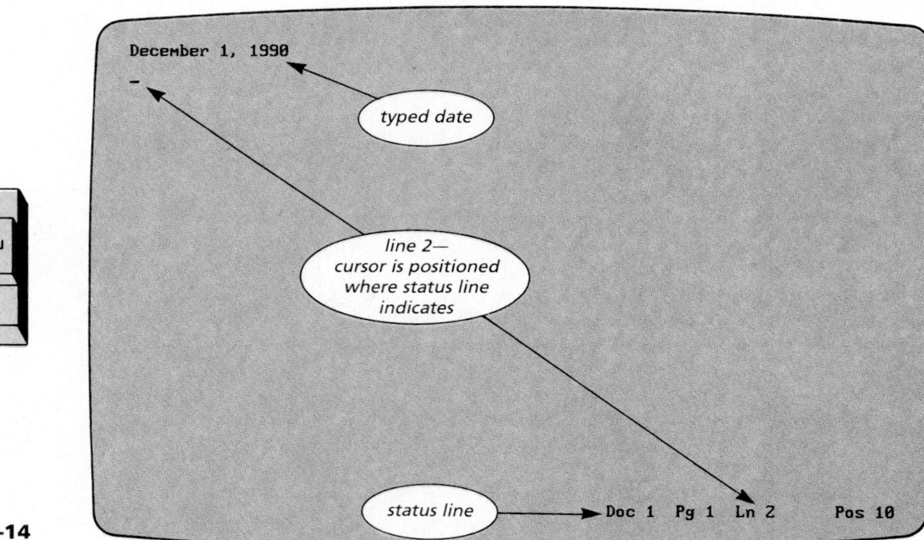


FIGURE 1-14

After typing the date, press the Return key. Pressing the Return key to start a new line is called a **hard return**. The cursor is now on line 2. Look at the status line for verification of the line where the cursor is. In order to insert four blank lines between the date and the addressee's name, press the Return key four more times. The status line now shows that the cursor is on line 6. Type the words Mr. Joseph Wright and then press the Return key, which takes the cursor to line 7. Type 236 Santo Domingo Cir. and press the Return key. The status line now indicates that the cursor is on line 8. Type the words Fountain Valley, CA 92708 and press the Return key. Figure 1-15 shows what your screen looks like with the date, name, and address.

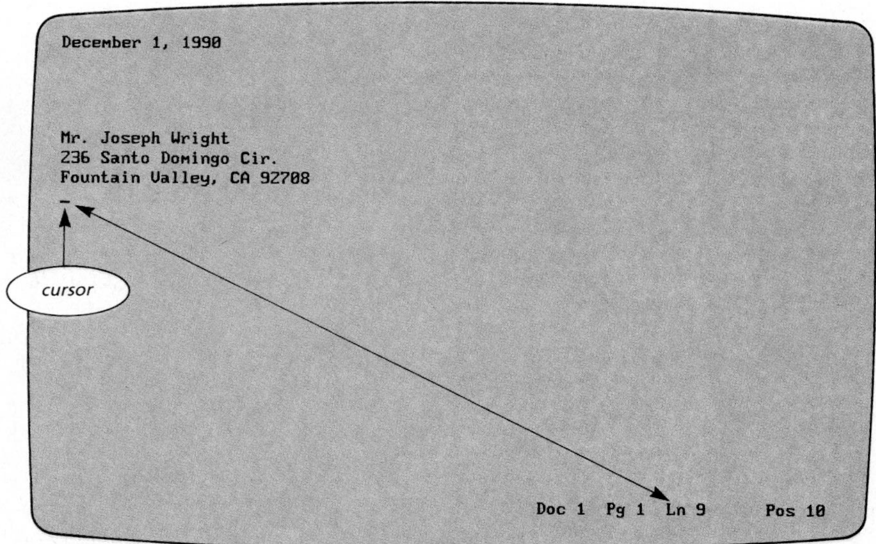

FIGURE 1-15

Now that you have typed the name and address, you want a blank line between the last address line and the greeting to Mr. Wright. Simply press the Return key. That will insert a blank line. Your status line now indicates that the cursor is on line 10, position 10. Type the words Dear Mr. Wright: and press the Return key. Press the Return key again to insert another blank line. On line 12, type: I received your letter today and wish to thank you for it. Press the Return key. Press it again to insert a blank line. On line 14, type the word Sincerely, and press the Return key, which will move the cursor to line 15, position 10 (Figure 1-16).

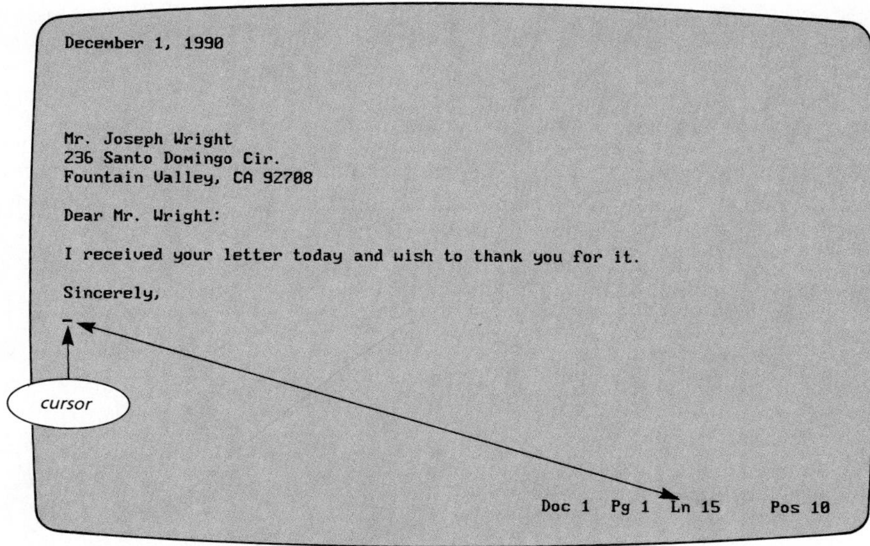
December 1, 1990
Mr. Joseph Wright
236 Santo Domingo Cir.
Fountain Valley, CA 92708
Dear Mr. Wright:
I received your letter today and wish to thank you for it.
Sincerely,
cursor
Doc 1 Pg 1 Ln 15 Pos 10

**FIGURE 1-16**

To add three more blank lines, press the Return key three more times. On line 18 type the words Mary Martinez followed by a Return. Type the word Director. The status line shows line 19, position 18. Press the Return key one more time, taking the cursor to line 20, position 10.

Figure 1-17 shows how the finished document should look on your screen.

If you neglected to insert a blank line somewhere, move the cursor to the beginning of that line and press Enter. If you omitted a word, move the cursor to the point where you wish to insert the word and type. All other text will move to accommodate the new text.

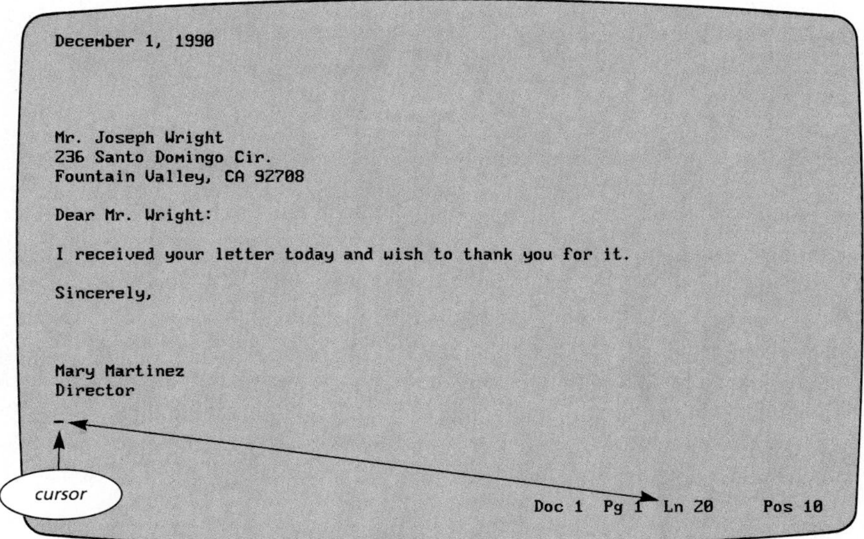
December 1, 1990
Mr. Joseph Wright
236 Santo Domingo Cir.
Fountain Valley, CA 92708
Dear Mr. Wright:
I received your letter today and wish to thank you for it.
Sincerely,
Mary Martinez
Director
cursor
Doc 1 Pg 1 Ln 20 Pos 10

**FIGURE 1-17**

# REVEAL CODES

The WordPerfect software "remembers" each keystroke you make, whether a letter, number, or space. In addition, when you change margins or when you press the Return key, the Tab key, or other keys, the WordPerfect software embeds **codes** into the text, thereby recording each key you have pressed. To keep the screen clean and free of codes, WordPerfect stores these embedded codes in a hidden screen. You can view the codes at any time, however, by using the Alt and F3 keys. To learn about these codes first press the Up Arrow key until the cursor is at the top of the document.

## Learning How to Read the Reveal Codes

For each function you perform in WordPerfect, a unique code is embedded into the text. When you type a line and then perform a hard return, for example, that hard return is registered by the WordPerfect software and the code **[HRt]** is entered into the text at that point.

As you look at the screen you cannot see any of the codes, because they are on a hidden screen. Hold down the Alt key firmly and press the F3 key. Your screen will look like the one in Figure 1-18.

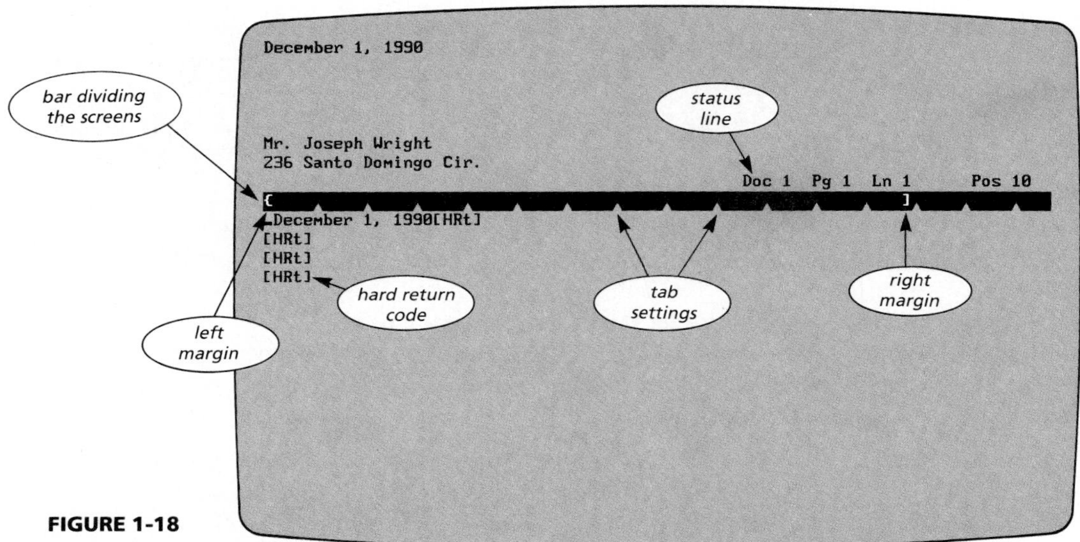


**FIGURE 1-18**

Look at your screen carefully. It appears that you have two different screens separated by a bar. First, look at the upper portion of the screen, at the numbers and letters above the bar. This is the screen you are used to viewing. You cannot see any codes, and your status line can still be viewed.

In the middle of the screen there appears to be a bar. On the left side you will notice a brace {. This indicates where your left margin is located. On the right side you will notice a bracket (]). This indicates where your right margin is located. The triangles (▲) you see between these symbols indicate where the tabs are currently set. Default is every five spaces.

On the bottom portion of the screen, notice that the text of the letter is the same as that on the top of the screen, with some differences. This lower screen is where your **reveal codes** are displayed. All the codes are in boldface. This is so that the codes will be easily recognized. The cursor in the reveal codes screen is also bolder than the cursor in the regular screen.

Figure 1-18 also shows, on the lower screen, that at the end of the first line you typed, you inserted a hard return. At the end of that line the code **[HRt]** is inserted, indicating that you pressed the Return key to start a new line.

Move your cursor one character to the right by pressing the Right Arrow → (step 1 in Figure 1-19). Notice that the cursor on the upper screen moves *underneath* each character, while the cursor on the lower screen moves *between* each character. Now move your cursor down one line by pressing the Down Arrow key ↓ (step 2 in Figure 1-19). Notice how both cursors move at the same time. They are, in fact, the same cursor, and move in relationship to each other.

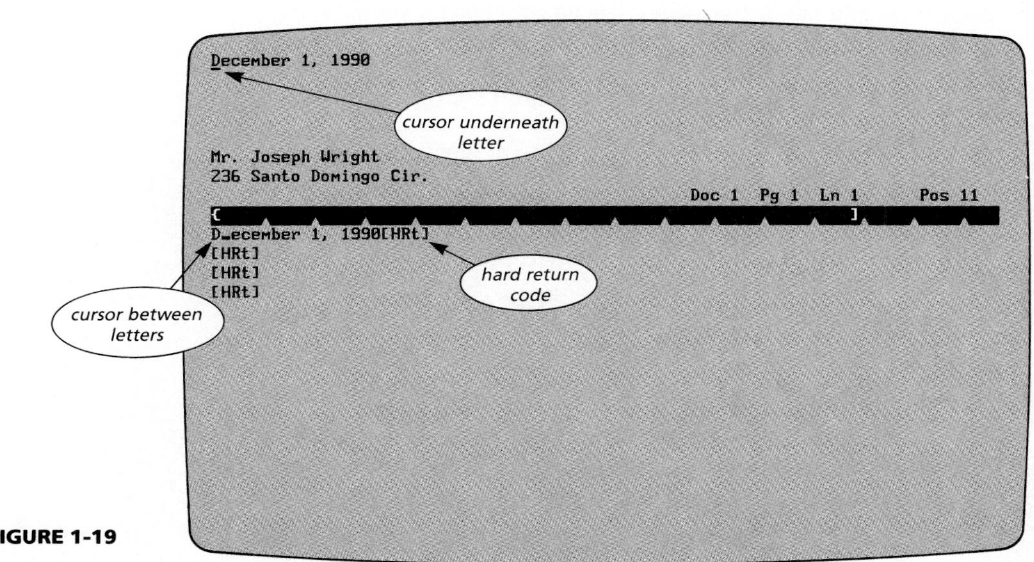


**FIGURE 1-19**

**Step 1: Move cursor one space to the right**

**Step 2: Move cursor down one line at a time**

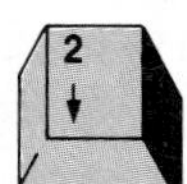


**Step 3: Exit reveal codes**

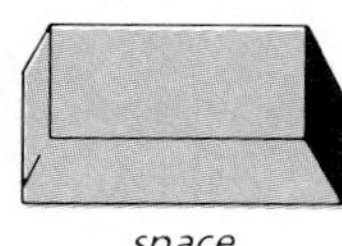

*space*

Continue pressing the Down Arrow key ↓ until the status line indicates the cursor is on line 9. As you do this, notice how each time you pressed the Return key in the letter, the reveal codes indicate that a hard return code was embedded into the document. The reveal codes function is a valuable feature of WordPerfect. As you become more familiar with this feature, you will notice how much control you have over your word processing.

To exit from the reveal codes press the spacebar (step 3 in Figure 1-19). (The Enter or Cancel keys will also let you exit from the reveal codes).

Because you will be instructed many times in this text to display the reveal codes, practice this a few times. Hold down the Alt key, then press the F3 key. See how quickly the reveal codes are displayed. Press your spacebar to exit the reveal codes.

## SAVING A DOCUMENT

The letter to Mr. Wright is now completed. Whenever a document is completed, it should be **saved** on a disk so that it can be retrieved for printing or modification at a later time. Look at the template next to the F10 key (Figure 1-20). Notice that the word Save is in black, indicating that the key is to be pressed alone. Now press the F10 key. At the lower left corner of your screen you will see the message "Document to be Saved:" (Figure 1-21).

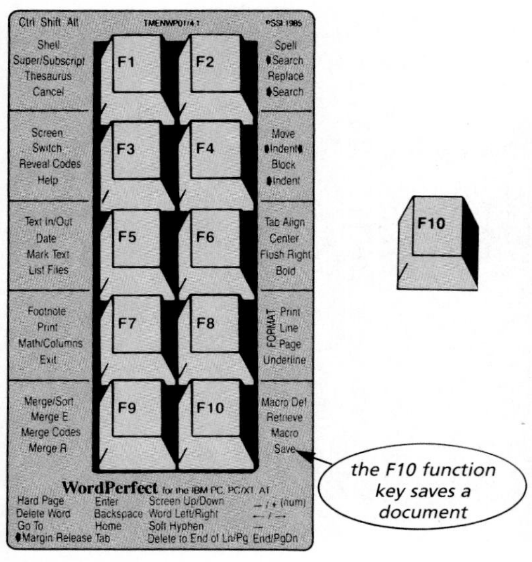


FIGURE 1-20

F10

Mr. Joseph Wright
236 Santo Domingo Cir.
Fountain Valley, CA 92708

Dear Mr. Wright:

I received your letter today and wish to thank you for it.

Sincerely,

Mary Martinez
Director

appears when you press F10

Document to be Saved:

FIGURE 1-21

Type the name Wright (in uppercase, lowercase, or a combination). After you have typed Wright you will notice that nothing else happens. Remember: When nothing happens, press Enter (Figure 1-22).

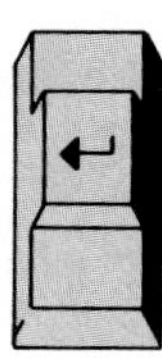

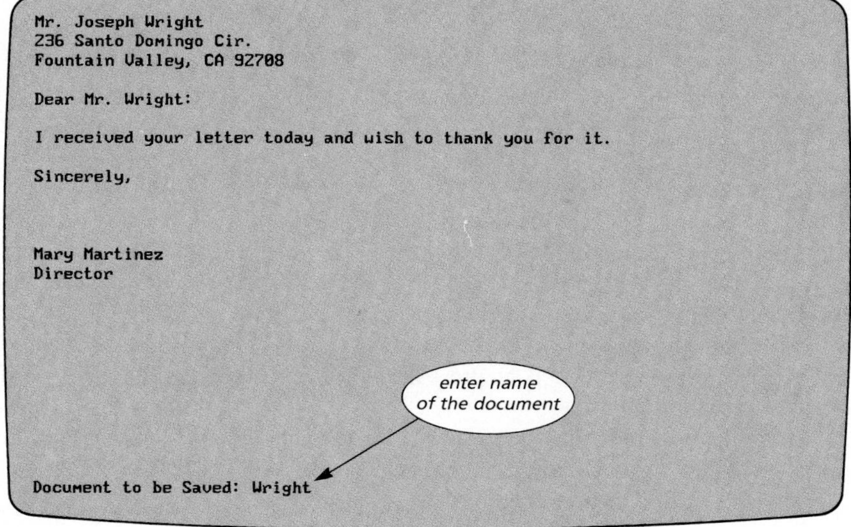


FIGURE 1-22

After you have pressed the Enter key you will notice that the light on drive B goes on, indicating that the document is being saved to drive B. That is because at the beginning of this project, before we loaded WordPerfect into the computer, we changed the default drive to B.

Your document is now named and saved. The name of your document appears in the lower left corner of your screen. As shown in Figure 1-23, the disk drive and directory that the document was saved to (B:\) are also displayed along with the document name.

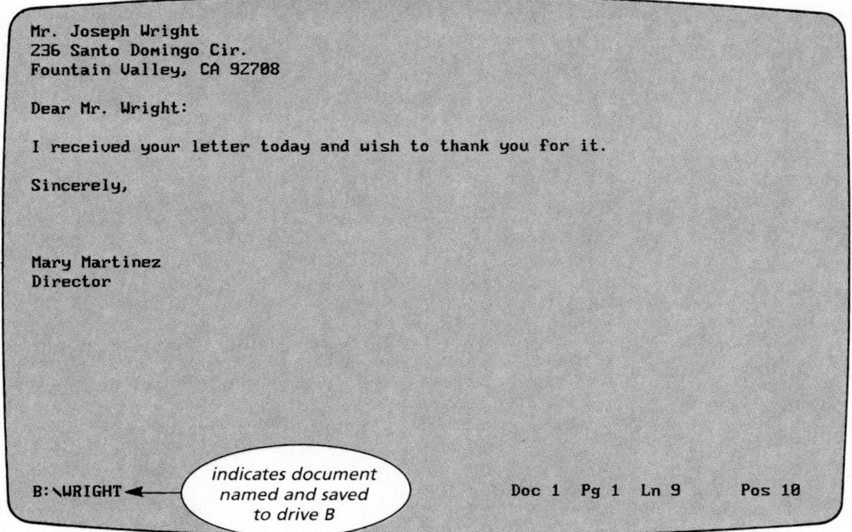


**FIGURE 1-23**

## PRINTING A DOCUMENT

After the document is typed and stored on the disk, you usually want to **print** it on paper. Before continuing, be sure that your printer has continuous feed paper inserted and that the printer is turned on and ready to print.

To print your document look at the template next to the **F7** key. Notice the word Print in green (Figure 1-24).

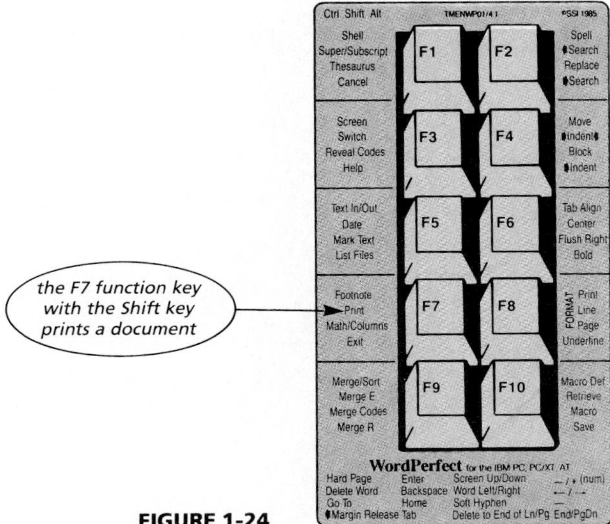


**FIGURE 1-24**

Hold down the Shift key and press the F7 key (step 1 in Figure 1-25). You will see the Print menu shown in Figure 1-25 at the bottom of your screen.

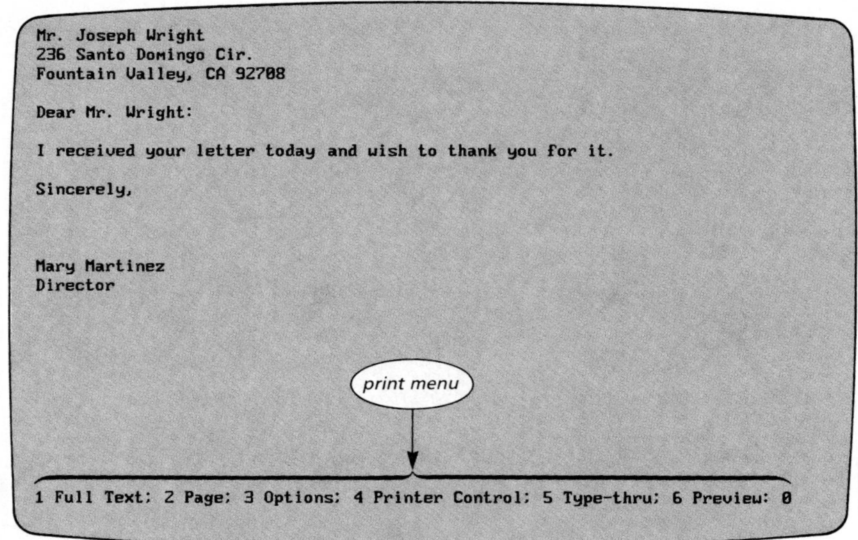


FIGURE 1-25

Step 1: Retrieve the Print menu

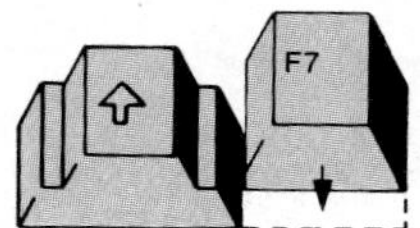


Step 2: Print the full text

Since we want to print the full text of this document, press the number 1 for full text (step 2 in Figure 1-25). At this point the printer will begin printing your document.

In Figure 1-26, notice that the document generated by the training version of WordPerfect contains the notation *WPC at random places throughout. This is your reminder that it is the training version and that it is copyrighted by WordPerfect Corporation.

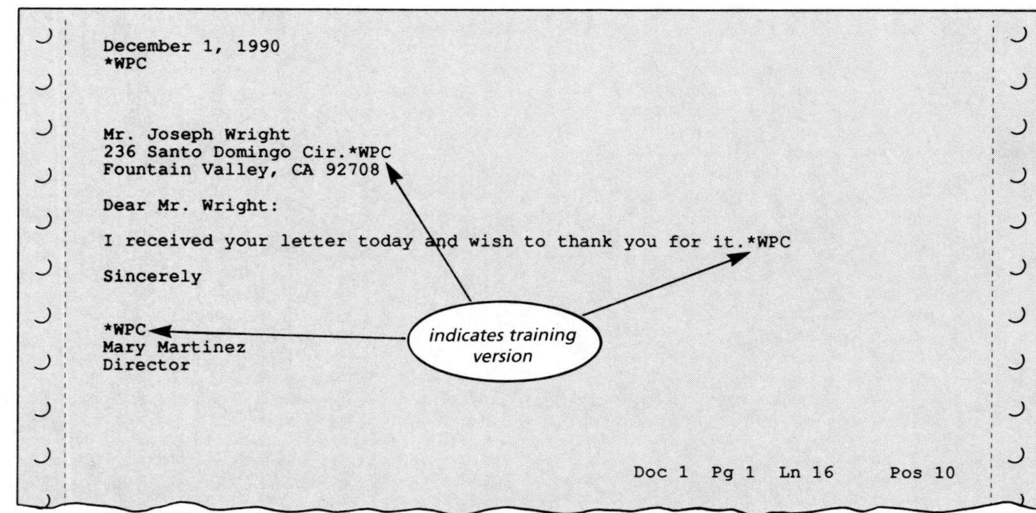

December 1, 1990
*WPC
Mr. Joseph Wright
236 Santo Domingo Cir.*WPC
Fountain Valley, CA 92708
Dear Mr. Wright:
I received your letter today and wish to thank you for it.*WPC
Sincerely
*WPC
Mary Martinez
Director
indicates training version
Doc 1 Pg 1 Ln 16 Pos 10


FIGURE 1-26

# MOVING THE CURSOR ON A BLANK SCREEN

Now that the letter to Mr. Wright has been typed, saved, and printed, we will use a blank screen to practice the Return, Tab, and spacebar functions. These are helpful keys for moving the cursor, shown in Figure 1-27. To be sure you are at the end of this document, press the **Home** key *two times*, then press the Down Arrow key ↓ one time (step 1 in Figure 1-28). This places the cursor at the end of your document. Press the Return key to insert a hard return (step 2 in Figure 1-28). This moves the cursor to a new line.

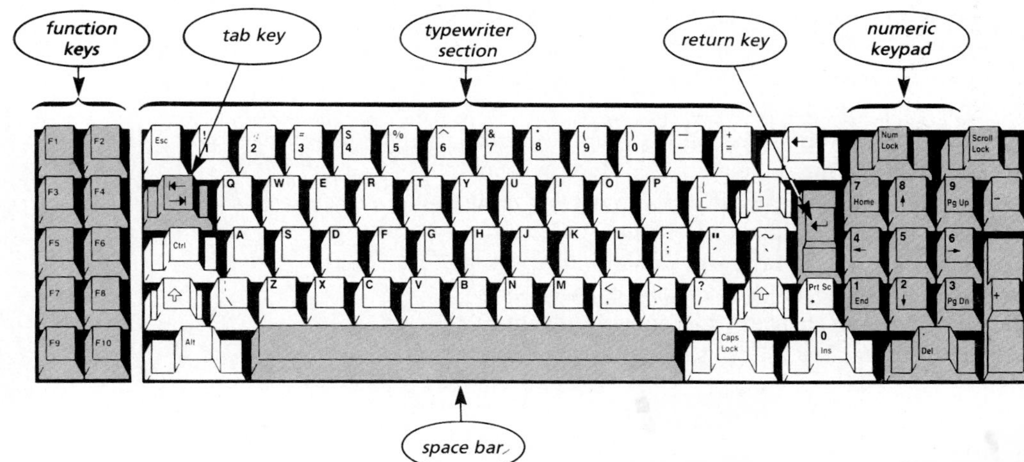


**FIGURE 1-27**

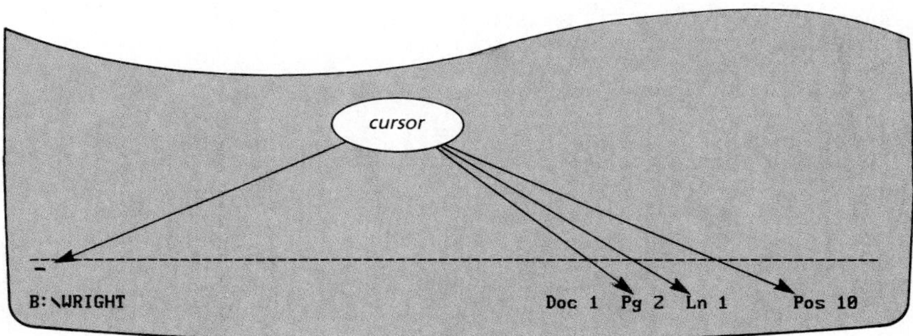


**FIGURE 1-28**

**Step 1: Move cursor to the end of the document**

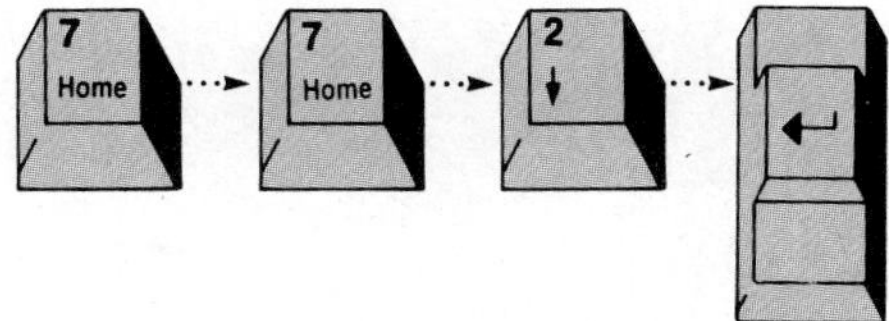


**Step 2: Move cursor to a new line**

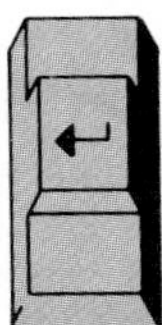

**Step 3: Move to page 2, line 1**

Recall that when you press the Return key, the cursor moves down one line at a time. The status line also indicates when the cursor has moved down a line. Press the Return key until the status line indicates that the cursor is on page 1, line 54. If you then press the Return key one more time (step 3 in Figure 1-28), a dotted line appears on the screen. This dotted line marks the end of page 1. The status line indicates that the cursor is now on page 2, line 1 as shown in Figure 1-28.

Press the Tab key once and you will see the cursor move to the right five spaces at a time. The status line also indicates with the position number that the cursor has moved five spaces at a time.

Press the spacebar and you will see the cursor move to the right one space at a time. The status line will also indicate with the position number that the cursor has moved one space at a time.

Now that you understand the meanings of Pg (page), Ln (line), and Pos (position) on the status line, you may wonder about Doc (document) 1. WordPerfect allows you to work on two different documents at the same time. For example, suppose you were working on a 30-page document and you needed to stop and quickly type a letter and print it out. You could switch to Doc (document) 2. In fact, you could switch back and forth between the two documents, making changes, printing, saving, and so on. The changes or printing of document 1 would not affect document 2 at all. This is like having two computers.

Look at the template next to the F3 key and notice the word Switch in green (Figure 1-29). To see document 2, hold down the Shift key firmly and press the F3 key (step 1 in Figure 1-30). You could type, save, and print a letter in document 2 without disturbing your letter to Mr. Wright in document 1. When finished with the letter in document 2, you could switch back to document 1. Your cursor will revert to where it was in document 1, allowing you to continue.

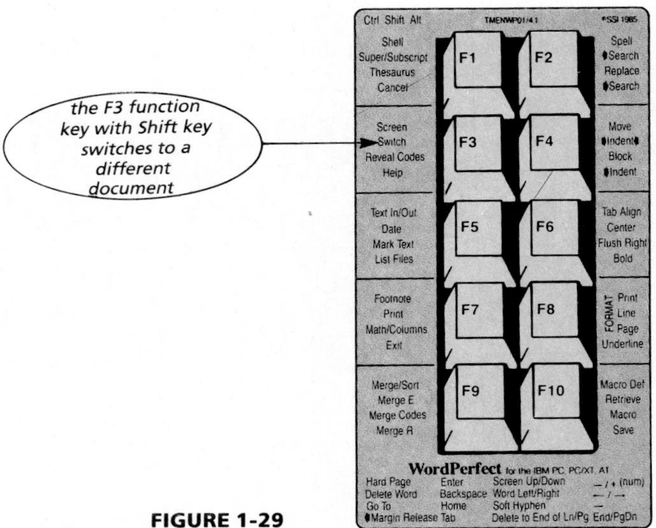


FIGURE 1-29

To return to document 1, hold the Shift key down and press the F3 key (step 2 in Figure 1-30). You are now back in document 1.

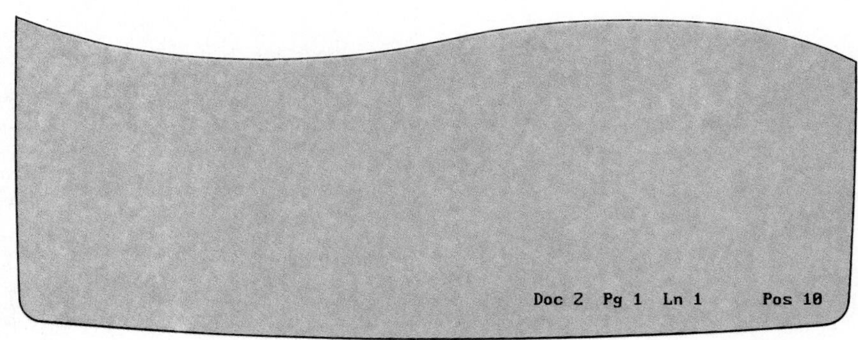


FIGURE 1-30

**Step 1: Switch to Doc 2**

**Step 2: Return to Doc 1**

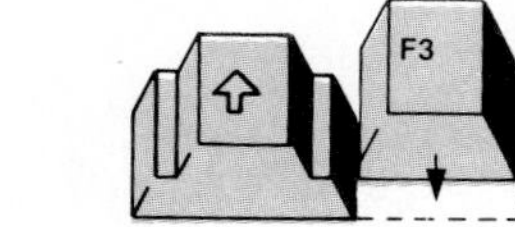

Since you have pressed the Return key, the spacebar, and the Tab key, you have changed your document. This altered document, with more spaces, tabs, and hard returns, has not been saved permanently to the disk, and we do not wish to do so. Remember that the *typed* portion of the document was saved. That saved portion was not changed on the disk. Since we want to exit from this document without saving again we will not use F10. To prepare to exit WordPerfect, move the cursor to the top of the document by pressing the Home key twice, then press the Up Arrow key ↑ (Figure 1-31). It is not necessary to move to the top of a document when exiting. We do so here to show that the letter to Mr. Wright is still in memory.

## EXITING WORDPERFECT

To exit this document, as well as WordPerfect, first look at the template next to the F7 key. The word Exit is in black, indicating that you press only the F7 key (Figure 1-32).

Press the F7 key (step 1 in Figure 1-33). The message "Save Document? (Y/N) Y" is shown in the lower left corner of the screen.

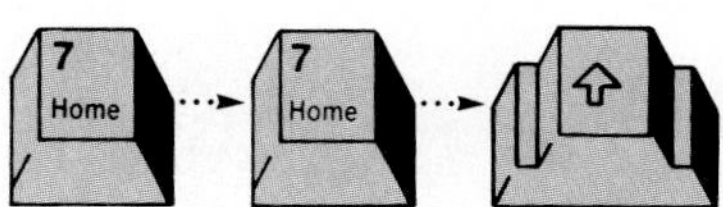


**FIGURE 1-31**

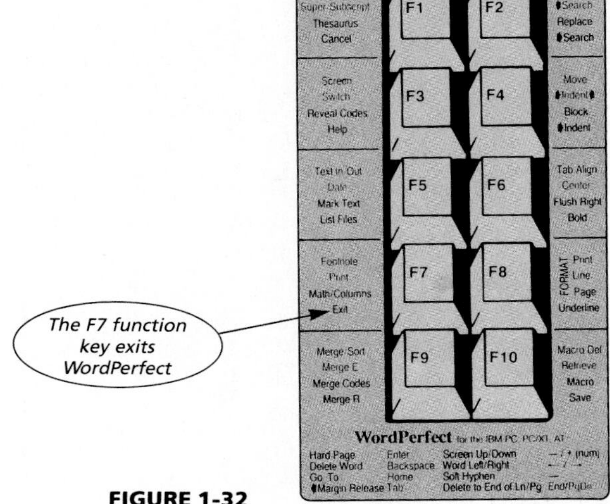


**FIGURE 1-32**

```
December 1, 1990



Mr. Joseph Wright
236 Santo Domingo Cir.
Fountain Valley, CA 92708

Dear Mr. Wright:

I received your letter today and wish to thank you for it.

Sincerely,



Mary Martinez
Director



Save Document? (Y/N) Y
```

choice for yes or no

default

**FIGURE 1-33**

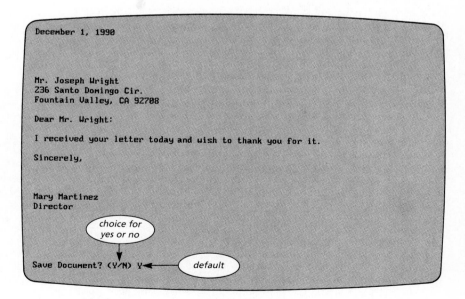

**Step 1: Initiate exit**

F7

**Step 2: Choose not to save document**

N

The (Y/N) means that if you press the Y (for yes) you want to save the document. If you press the N (for no) you do not want to save the document. The Y outside the parentheses means that the WordPerfect software has defaulted the answer to yes, so if you press either the Enter key or the spacebar the computer will accept yes as the default. However, type N for no (step 2 in Figure 1-33). You will then see "Exit WP? (Y/N) N" on your screen (Figure 1-34). Since we do want to exit the program, type Y. (If you failed to complete the printing of the document you may see the message "Cancel all print jobs (Y/N)?N". If this appears, type Y for yes.)

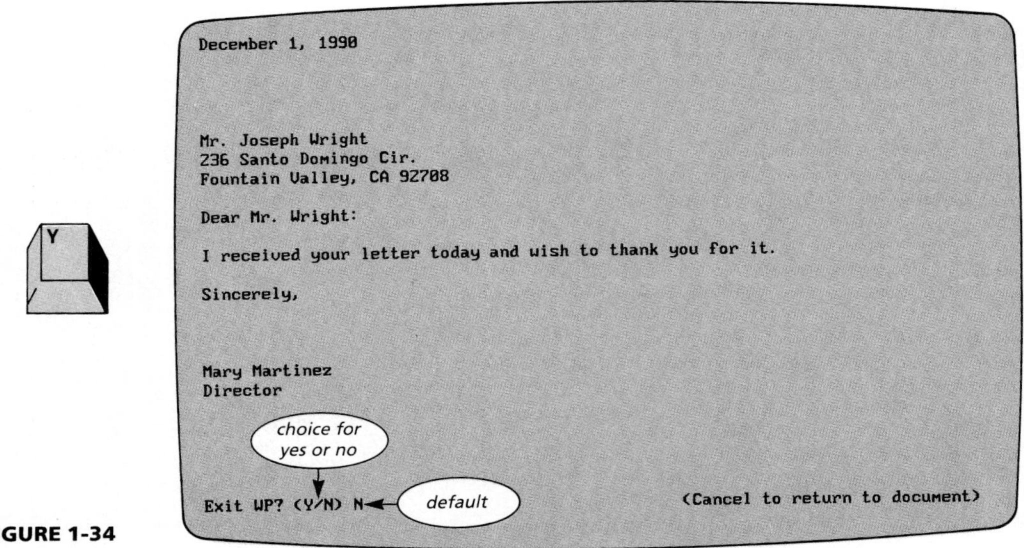
Y
December 1, 1990
Mr. Joseph Wright
236 Santo Domingo Cir.
Fountain Valley, CA 92708
Dear Mr. Wright:
I received your letter today and wish to thank you for it.
Sincerely,
Mary Martinez
Director
choice for yes or no
Exit WP? (Y/N) N
default
(Cancel to return to document)

**FIGURE 1-34**

To exit properly we must return to the DOS prompt. After you have typed Y, the message "Insert COMMAND.COM disk in drive A and strike any key when ready" appears on the screen (Figure 1-35). On some copies of the training version or if you have a hard disk system the DOS prompt will appear immediately and you will not see the message.

If you see the message "Insert COMMAND.COM disk in drive A and strike any key when ready" take your WordPerfect training version out of drive A and insert your DOS disk. Press any key. You will then see the DOS prompt indicating that WordPerfect is no longer in the computer's memory (Figure 1-35).

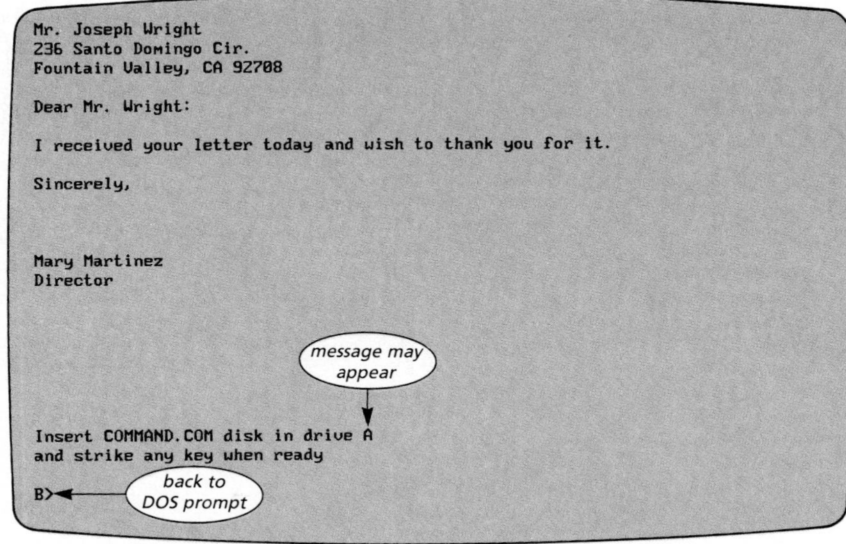
Mr. Joseph Wright
236 Santo Domingo Cir.
Fountain Valley, CA 92708
Dear Mr. Wright:
I received your letter today and wish to thank you for it.
Sincerely,
Mary Martinez
Director
message may appear
Insert COMMAND.COM disk in drive A
and strike any key when ready
B>
back to DOS prompt

**FIGURE 1-35**

# PROJECT SUMMARY

This project demonstrated how to use the function keys with the WordPerfect template. You learned how to enter the WordPerfect program and type a document using the hard return at the end of short sentences. You also learned the importance of reveal codes to a document, and that the hidden codes can be found by holding down the Alt key and pressing the F3 key. You learned how to save and print the document and how to move the cursor on a blank screen. Finally, you exited WordPerfect.

The following is a summary of the keystroke sequence we used in Project 1:

**SUMMARY OF KEYSTROKES—Project 1**

| STEPS | KEY(S) PRESSED | STEPS | KEY(S) PRESSED |
|---|---|---|---|
| 1 | b: [at the A> prompt] | 25 | ↵ |
| 2 | ↵ | 26 | Sincerely, |
| 3 | a:wp [at the B> prompt] | 27 | ↵ |
| 4 | ↵ | 28 | ↵ |
| 5 | ↵ [at first introductory screen] | 29 | ↵ |
| 6 | ↵ [only if you see a second introductory screen] | 30 | ↵ |
| 7 | December 1, 1990 | 31 | Mary Martinez |
| 8 | ↵ | 32 | ↵ |
| 9 | ↵ | 33 | Director |
| 10 | ↵ | 34 | ↵ |
| 11 | ↵ | 35 | Alt-F3 |
| 12 | ↵ | 36 | spacebar |
| 13 | Mr. Joseph Wright | 37 | F10 |
| 14 | ↵ | 38 | Wright |
| 15 | 236 Santo Domingo Cir. | 39 | ↵ |
| 16 | ↵ | 40 | Shift-F7 |
| 17 | Fountain Valley, CA 92708 | 41 | 1 |
| 18 | ↵ | 42 | F7 |
| 19 | ↵ | 43 | N |
| 20 | Dear Mr. Wright: | 44 | Y |
| 21 | ↵ | 45 | [remove disk from drive A if you see prompt "Insert COMMAND.COM disk in drive A and strike any key when ready"] |
| 22 | ↵ | 46 | [put DOS disk into drive A] |
| 23 | I received your letter today and wish to thank you for it. | 47 | [press any key] |
| 24 | ↵ | 48 | [remove disks from both drives] |

### Project Summary (continued)

The following list summarizes the material covered in Project 1.

1. The **keyboard** is used as an input device to input data into the computer.
2. **Function keys** numbered F1 through F10 are located to the left or at the top of the keyboard. Each function key has been assigned four specific functions to execute commonly used commands.
3. The keys on the **numeric keypad**, to the right of the keyboard, are used to move the cursor. When the Num Lock key is pressed, these keys can also be used to type numbers.
4. The **Shift key** is used to make lowercase letters into capital letters and to type the symbols above the numbers. It is also used with the function keys to accomplish specific word processing goals.
5. The **Ctrl** key, used in tandem with function keys, performs special functions.
6. The **Alt** key, used in tandem with function keys, also performs special functions.
7. The **Tab** key moves the cursor to the next tab setting, and when used with the Shift key releases the left margin.
8. The **Enter** or **Return** key is used to enter data in the computer, or as a **hard return** at the end of a line or paragraph.
9. The **Backspace** key moves the cursor backward on the screen, deleting the character to the left of the cursor.
10. The **Left Arrow** key moves the cursor one character to the left.
11. The **Right Arrow** key moves the cursor one character to the right.
12. The **Up Arrow** key moves the cursor up one line.
13. The **Down Arrow** key moves the cursor down one line.
14. A color-coded **template** is placed over the function keys to identify the keys to be used for specific functions.
15. The **Help function** is a collection of screens that gives reminders on how to use WordPerfect.
16. A **default** option is a preassigned choice. Unless instructed otherwise, the default option will be chosen.
17. The **cursor** is the blinking underscore on the screen that designates the current position in a document.
18. The **status line**, at the bottom right of the screen, identifies the exact location of the cursor.
19. The **screen** (window) is the monitor of the computer. It shows what has been entered into the computer.
20. Press the **Cancel (F1)** key when an undesired message appears at the bottom left of the screen.
21. **Reveal codes** are the commands embedded in the document by the WordPerfect software. They control how the input document appears on the screen, as well as how it is printed on a printer.
22. The **hard return [HRt]** code indicates the end of a short line or paragraph, or where a blank line is to be inserted into the document.
23. Press the Alt and F3 keys to view the screen that reveals the embedded codes that control the format of the document.
24. After a document has been entered into the computer, it must be **saved** to a disk for later retrieval or reference.
25. **Printing** a document that has been typed and stored produces a copy of the document on paper.

## STUDENT ASSIGNMENTS

### STUDENT ASSIGNMENT 1: True/False

**Instructions:** Circle T if the statement is true and F if the statement is false.

T F 1. It is not necessary to use the Ctrl, Alt, or Shift keys with any other key.
T F 2. A good rule of thumb is, if nothing happens on the screen, press Enter.
T F 3. The WordPerfect template fits above or around the function keys.
T F 4. When saving a document the file name must be typed in all capital letters.
T F 5. To exit WordPerfect, use the F7 key.
T F 6. To save a file, use the F10 key.
T F 7. The numeric keypad is usually on the left side of the keyboard.
T F 8. To print a document, use the Ctrl-F8 keys.
T F 9. On most monitors, you can only view 24 lines of typing at a time.
T F 10. To add a blank line, press the spacebar.

## STUDENT ASSIGNMENT 2: Multiple Choice

**Instructions:** Circle the correct response.

1. The WordPerfect template is used in conjunction with the
   a. numeric keypad
   b. alphabet keys
   c. function keys
   d. 1 through 10 keys
2. On the template, functions typed in red are used with the
   a. Ctrl key
   b. Shift key
   c. Alt and Ctrl key
   d. none of the above
3. The numeric keypad can be used to
   a. type numbers
   b. move the cursor
   c. neither a nor b
   d. both a and b
4. When some function keys are pressed a message may appear at the
   a. upper left corner of the screen
   b. lower left corner of the screen
   c. upper right corner of the screen
   d. lower right corner of the screen
5. After you press some function keys and a message appears on the screen, you can cancel the message by pressing the
   a. F2 key
   b. F7 key
   c. Shift-F10 keys
   d. F1 key
6. The Right Arrow key moves the cursor
   a. one character or space to the right
   b. one word to the right
   c. to the right end of the line
   d. one line down
7. To exit from reveal codes you can
   a. press the Right Arrow key
   b. press the spacebar
   c. press the Down Arrow key
   d. press the Home key twice, then the Up Arrow key
8. The Return key is used to
   a. end a paragraph
   b. put a [HRt] code in the document
   c. insert a blank line
   d. all of the above

## STUDENT ASSIGNMENT 3: Matching

**Instructions:** Put the appropriate number next to the words in the second column.

| | | |
|---|---|---|
| 1. Red | _____ | Alt plus a function key |
| 2. Blue | _____ | Alt-F3 |
| 3. Black | _____ | Shift-F7 |
| 4. Cancel | _____ | Ctrl plus a function key |
| 5. Save | _____ | Shift |
| 6. Print | _____ | F7 |
| 7. Bottom of document | _____ | F1 |
| 8. Green | _____ | Function key alone |
| 9. Exit | _____ | Home, Home, Up Arrow |
| 10. Reveal codes | _____ | Home, Home, Down Arrow |
| 11. Top of document | _____ | F10 |

## STUDENT ASSIGNMENT 4: Fill in the Blanks

1. To enter the WordPerfect program at the B> prompt, type _________ and then press _________ .
2. When WordPerfect has been brought into the memory of the computer, a screen appears that is blank except for a _________ line at the lower right corner of the screen.
3. The status line contains the default settings of Doc _________ Pg _________ Ln _________ Pos _________ .
4. The screen or window can show _________ lines of the document at any one time.
5. If something unexpected happens on the screen—for example, an extra space or a hard return—pressing the _________ key may help.
6. When you press the Return key at the end of a line, the code that is embedded into the document is _________ .
7. When the screen is split to reveal codes, the codes can be viewed in the _________ screen.
8. The Down Arrow moves the cursor down _________ lines.
9. "Document to be Saved:" appears on the screen when you press the _________ key.
10. If an unwanted message appears on the screen, you can usually press the _________ key to cancel the message.

## STUDENT ASSIGNMENT 5: Fill in the Blanks

1. When pressing Ctrl, Alt, or Shift with a function key, it is incorrect to press the keys simultaneously. The correct way is _________________________________________________ .
2. The ↵ key can be called either the _________ or the _________ key.
3. After pressing Shift-F7 to print, if you wish to print the full text, you must press the number _________ .
4. If you accept the tab default settings, the cursor will move _________ spaces when you press the Tab key.
5. After you press the Shift-F3 keys, the cursor will move to document _________ .
6. When you wish to exit, press the _________ key.
7. After you have pressed the Exit key, instead of exiting immediately, WordPerfect prompts: _________ Document? (Y/N) Y.
8. If you press N in answer to the message in question 7, the next prompt is: _________ WP? (Y/N) N.
9. If you press Y in answer to the message in question 8 you will then _________ from the WordPerfect program.

## STUDENT ASSIGNMENT 6

**Instructions:** On the keyboard shown here, label the keys with the names given below.

Ctrl
Shift (both keys)
Alt
Backspace
Tab
Enter (Return)
Spacebar

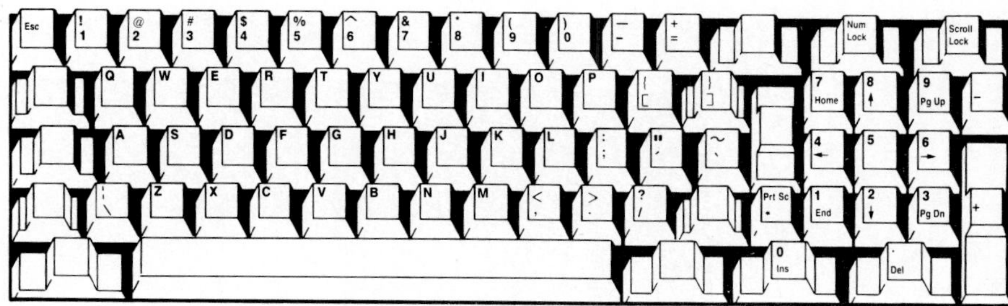


On the numeric keypad, fill in the correct direction of the cursor arrows.

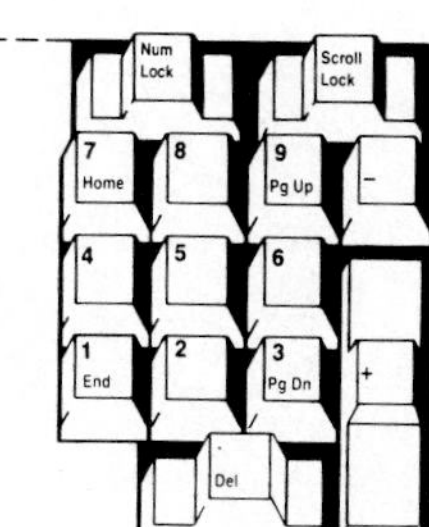


Label function keys 1 through 10 (write F1, F2, etc.).

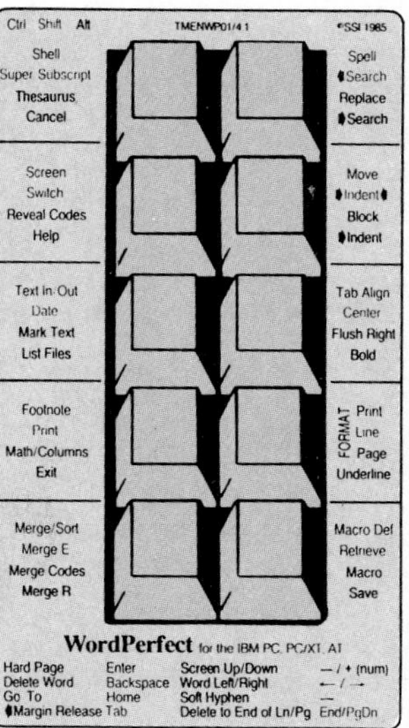


## STUDENT ASSIGNMENT 7: Correcting Errors

**Instructions:** The document illustrates the first part of a memo that is being prepared using WordPerfect. An error was made when typing the memo. The last word was typed todya. The word should be today. Explain in detail the steps necessary to correct the error.

Method of correction: ____________________

____________________

____________________

____________________

____________________

____________________

____________________

____________________

____________________

```
December 1, 1990



Mr. Joseph Wright
236 Santo Domingo Cir.
Fountain Valley, CA 92708

Dear Mr. Wright:

I received your letter todya_
```

## STUDENT ASSIGNMENT 8: Correcting Errors

**Instructions:** The screen illustrates a letter that has been prepared using WordPerfect. There are no hard returns between the body of letter and the word Sincerely, and there is no space between the words thankyou. Explain in detail the steps required to add a blank line above the word Sincerely, and to put a space between the words thankyou.

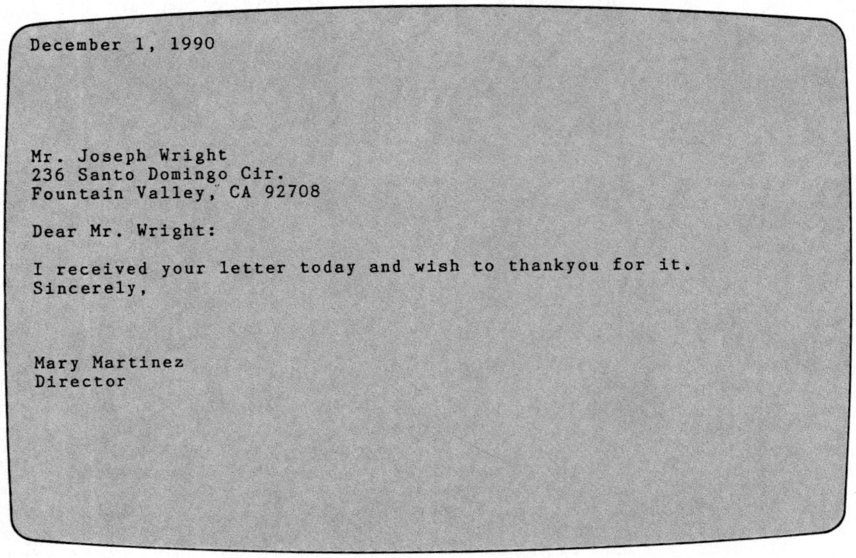

```
December 1, 1990



Mr. Joseph Wright
236 Santo Domingo Cir.
Fountain Valley, CA 92708

Dear Mr. Wright:

I received your letter today and wish to thankyou for it.
Sincerely,



Mary Martinez
Director
```

Method of correction: ______________________________________________

________________________________________________________________

________________________________________________________________

________________________________________________________________

## STUDENT ASSIGNMENT 9: Viewing Reveal Codes

Problem 1: Prepare the memo illustrated. Follow the step-by-step instructions you learned in this project.

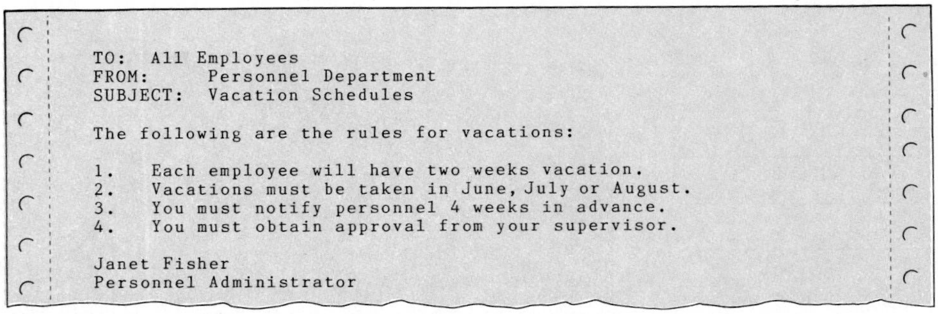

```
TO:  All Employees
FROM:      Personnel Department
SUBJECT:  Vacation Schedules

The following are the rules for vacations:

1.    Each employee will have two weeks vacation.
2.    Vacations must be taken in June, July or August.
3.    You must notify personnel 4 weeks in advance.
4.    You must obtain approval from your supervisor.

Janet Fisher
Personnel Administrator
```

Problem 2: After you have typed the letter, press the Alt-F3 keys to reveal the codes. To send what is on your screen to the printer press the PrtSc (Print Screen) key (on some computers there is a Print Screen key, and on others you must press Shift-PrtSc). After you have a hard copy of what is on the screen, circle all [HRt] codes on the page.

Problem 3: Save on disk as schedule.1.

## STUDENT ASSIGNMENT 10: Creating and Printing a Document

**Instructions:** Perform the following tasks.

1. Load the disk operating system into main memory.
2. Load the WordPerfect program into main memory by inserting the WordPerfect diskette into drive A and putting a data disk into drive B. Type b: and press Enter. At the B> prompt, type a:wp and press the Enter key.

Problem 1: Prepare the letter illustrated below.

```
March 15, 1990

Ms. Roberta Weitzman
President, SpaceTek Inc.
44538 Scroll Avenue
Monnett, NJ 08773

Dear Ms. Weitzman:

This letter confirms our purchase of 13 Pin Brackets.

James R. McMillan, AirFrame Inc.
```

Problem 2: Save the document on disk. Use the file name Weitzman.1.

Problem 3: After the document has been saved on disk, produce a printed copy of the letter.

## STUDENT ASSIGNMENT 11: Creating and Printing a Document

**Instructions:** Perform the following tasks.

1. Load the disk operating system into main memory.
2. Load the WordPerfect program into main memory by inserting the WordPerfect diskette into drive A and putting a data disk into drive B. Type b: and press enter. At the B> prompt, type a:wp and press the Enter key.

Problem 1: Prepare the letter illustrated below.

```
March 15, 1990


Dear Employees:

You must notify the Personnel department of your vacation plans.

Janet Fisher
Personnel Administrator
```

Problem 2: Save the document on disk. Use the file name Vacation.

Problem 3: After the document has been saved on disk, produce a printed copy of the letter.

# PROJECT 2

## Creating a Document with Word Wrap

### Objectives

You will have mastered the material in this project when you can:

- Type documents using word wrap
- Move the cursor using more efficient keystrokes
- Delete and restore text

```
December 1, 1990


TO:   All Sales Managers
RE:   New Bonus Plan

The new bonus plan approved by the Board of Directors will become
effective January 1.  If you have questions, contact Hanna Butler
prior to January 1, 1991.  All sales people are affected by the
new plan.

Rita Moeller

cc:   Board of Directors
```

**FIGURE 2-1**

### Loading the WordPerfect Program

At the A> prompt, type b: and press Enter; at the B> prompt type a:wp and press Enter. WordPerfect loads into main memory. First you see the screen informing you that you are using the educational version of WordPerfect. Press any key to continue. Next, you may see the screen explaining the WordPerfect template colors; if you see this second screen, press any key to continue. The next screen is your clean work space. As you saw in Project 1, the only thing you see is the status line in the lower right corner, indicating that the cursor is in document 1 on page 1, line 1, position 10.

## LEARNING ABOUT WORD WRAP

When you type on a typewriter, the first thing you do after putting the paper in is set the margins. In WordPerfect, the default margins are position 10 at the left and position 74 at the right. *Default* means that the margins have been preset at these positions. Unless you instruct the software otherwise, these are the margins it will follow.

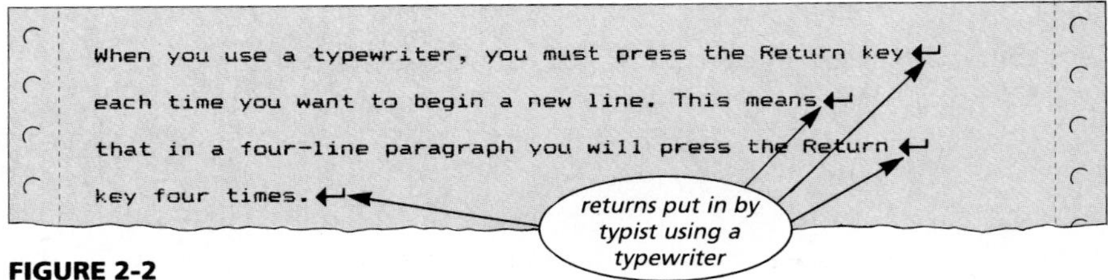


**FIGURE 2-2**

When you type on a typewriter with the margins set, every time you approach the end of a line, you hear a "ding" from the typewriter. This indicates that the margin is approaching and you should finish typing the current word and press the Return ↵ key to return the carriage to the next line, as illustrated in Figure 2-2.

Most word processing software, unlike a typewriter, allows you to type continuously. The software automatically "wraps" the typing to the next line when it reaches the right margin, as illustrated in Figure 2-3. The term for this is **word wrap**. The only time you need to press the Return ↵ key is when you reach the end of a paragraph, when you want to insert a blank line, or when you want to terminate the line before word wrap can take effect. Such is the case in the first three lines of the memo you will be typing (see Figure 2-1). Word wrap allows you to enter data much faster than if you had to press Return after each line. The word wrap feature is a major advantage of most word processing programs, including WordPerfect.

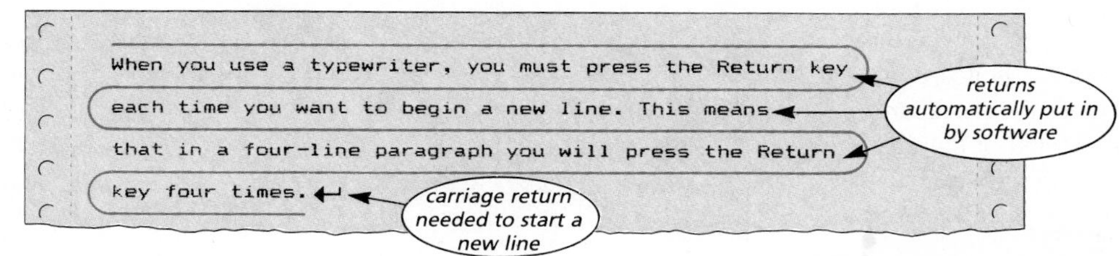


**FIGURE 2-3**

## Typing a Letter

Begin typing the memo in Figure 2-1. As you learned in Project 1, each time you press a key on the keyboard to enter a character, the cursor moves one position to the right, and the position number on the status line changes to indicate the cursor's position. The date line is not long enough to wrap. Therefore, after typing the date, press the Return ↵ key. The status line shows the cursor on line 2, position 10. Press the Return ↵ key four more times to move the cursor to line 6, position 10. Type TO: and press the Tab key, moving the cursor to position 15; then type the words All Sales Managers and press the Return ↵ key, putting the cursor on line 7, position 10. Type RE: and press the Tab key; then type the words New Bonus Plan. Press the Return key two times (↵ ↵), taking the cursor to line 9, position 10 (Figure 2-4).

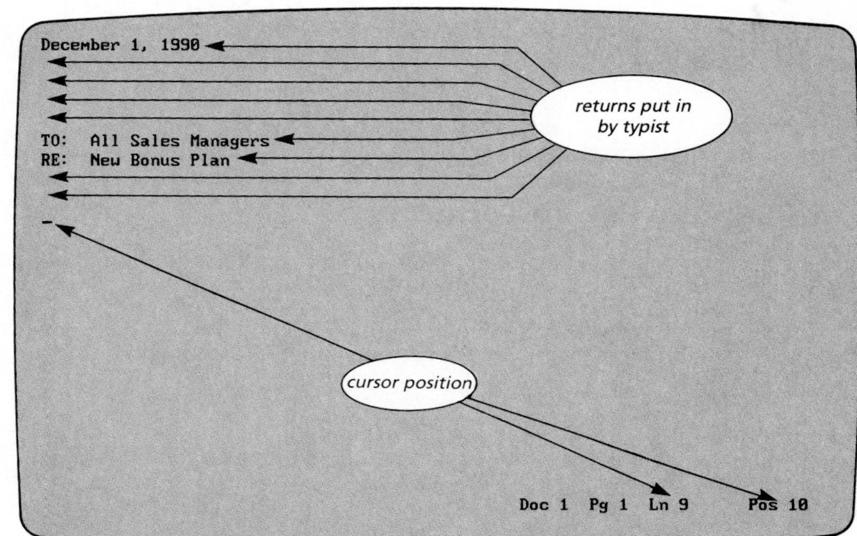


**FIGURE 2-4**

Now type the paragraph of the memo. As you type remember to press the spacebar twice after each period at the end of each sentence. Also, remember *not* to press the Return key at the end of each line. As you approach the end of the first line, watch the screen. When you begin to type the word "effective", notice that the word is too long to fit on the line. But before the word is completely typed it wraps down to the next line.

Type the entire paragraph. After you have typed the last word, Plan, followed by a period, the cursor is on line 12, position 19. Press the Return ↵ key because this last line of the paragraph is too short to wrap. Press the Return key again, moving the cursor to line 14, position 10. Type the name Rita Moeller and press the Return ↵ key two times. The cursor is now on line 16, position 10. Type the abbreviation cc:, then press the Tab key. Type the words Board of Directors.

The cursor should be on line 16, position 33. Press Return ↵, thereby putting the cursor on line 17, position 10 (Figure 2-5).

In Figure 2-5, all the text in the body of the memo has been typed. It consists of three full lines of text and a partial fourth line. Word wrap occurred for the three full lines of text. When you typed the fourth line of the paragraph, you reached the end of the text before word wrap took effect, so you pressed the Return to cause a hard return. When word wrap causes text to be moved to the next line, a **soft return** is said to have occurred.

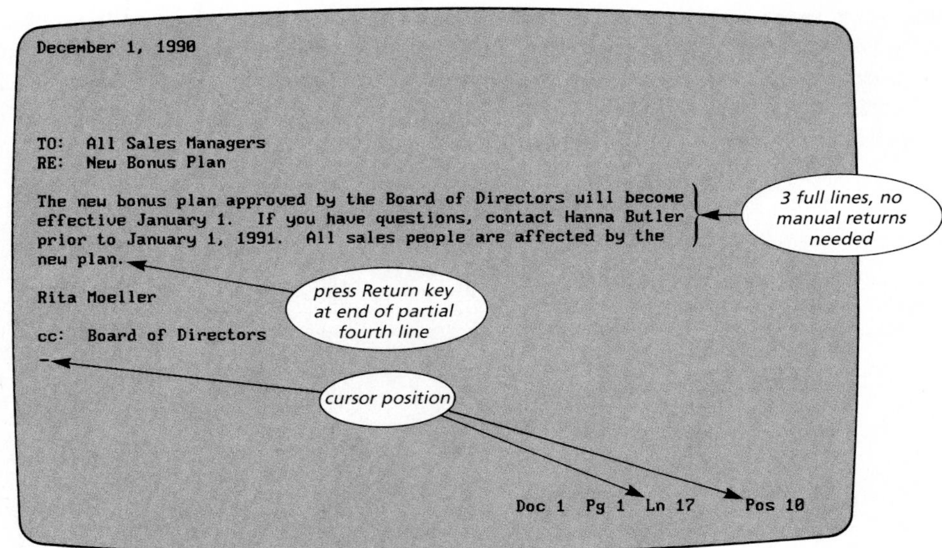

December 1, 1990
TO: All Sales Managers
RE: New Bonus Plan
The new bonus plan approved by the Board of Directors will become
effective January 1. If you have questions, contact Hanna Butler
prior to January 1, 1991. All sales people are affected by the
new plan.
Rita Moeller
cc: Board of Directors
3 full lines, no manual returns needed
press Return key at end of partial fourth line
cursor position
Doc 1 Pg 1 Ln 17 Pos 10

FIGURE 2-5

## Checking the Reveal Codes

It is always necessary to be conscious of the codes being embedded into your document. The entire format of your document is determined by the codes, and the printer is governed by codes. If something does not print the way you anticipated, it is wise to check the codes. As you learned in Project 1, the codes are embedded into the document automatically by the software and saved when the document is saved. Before you look at the codes, return to the top of the document. Press the Home, Home, Up Arrow ↑ keys (Figure 2-6). This takes the cursor immediately to the top of the document, line 1, position 10.

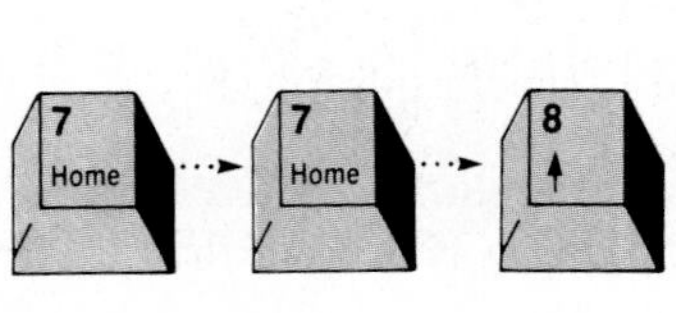

7 Home
7 Home
8 ↑

December 1, 1990

cursor position

TO: All Sales Managers
RE: New Bonus Plan

The new bonus plan approved by the Board of Directors will become
effective January 1. If you have questions, contact Hanna Butler
prior to January 1, 1991. All sales people are affected by the
new plan.

Rita Moeller

cc: Board of Directors

Doc 1 Pg 1 Ln 1 Pos 10

FIGURE 2-6

Look at the template next to the F3 key. Notice the words Reveal Codes in blue. Hold down the Alt key firmly and press the F3 key. When you do, the screen shown in Figure 2-7 appears.

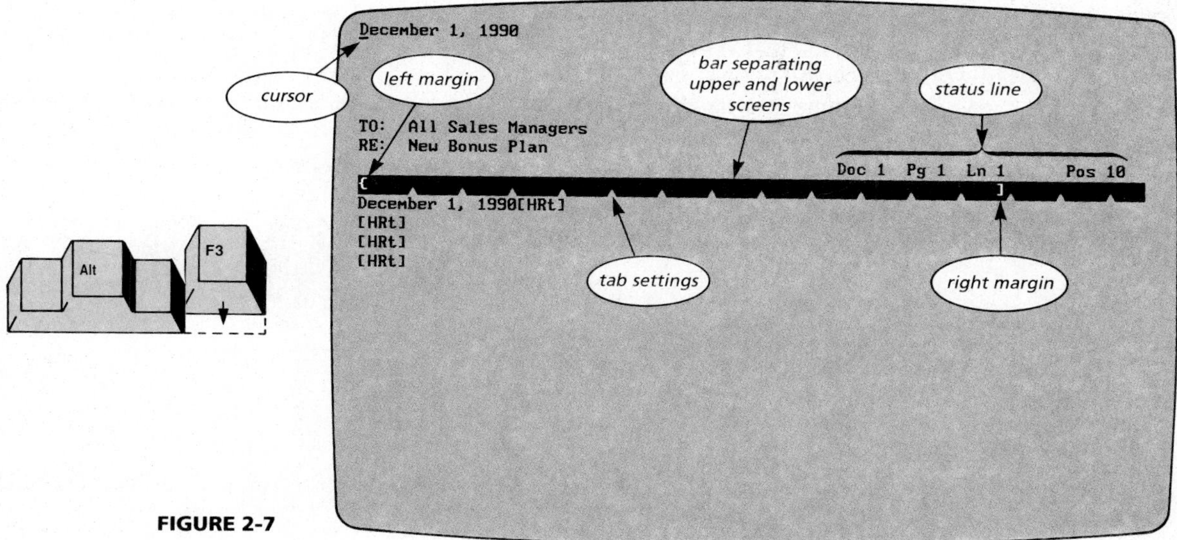


**FIGURE 2-7**

Look at your screen carefully. The bar indicating the left and right margins and tab settings separates the upper and lower screens. Above the bar is the screen you are familiar with. You cannot see any codes, and your status line can still be viewed.

Below the bar is the reveal codes screen. Notice that the typing is the same as on the upper screen, except the codes also appear. All the codes are in boldface so that they are easily recognizable (if you have a color monitor, boldface may appear as a particular color; in that case the codes will be that boldface color). The cursor in the lower screen is also bolder than the cursor in the regular screen.

In Figure 2-8, notice the [HRt] code at the end of line 1 where you typed the date. Move the cursor down to line 6 with the Down Arrow ↓ key. Notice that both cursors move at the same time. They are, in fact, the same cursor and move in relationship to each other.

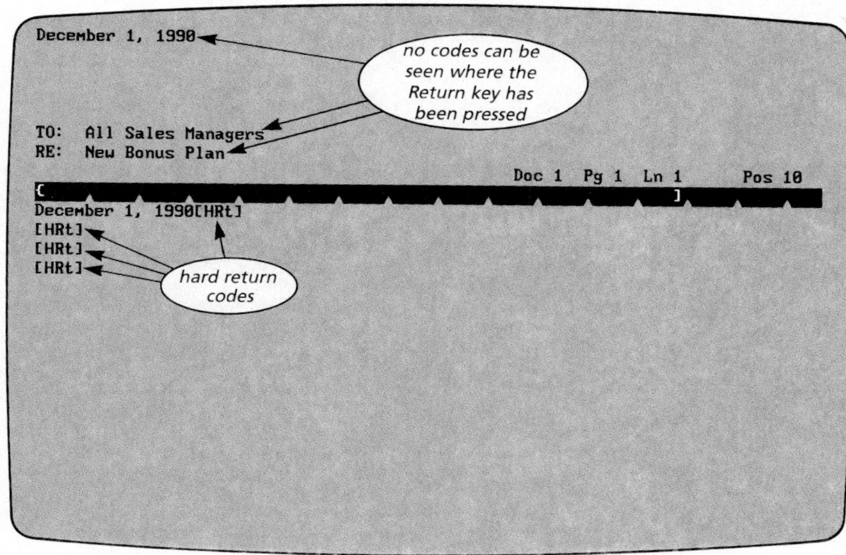


**FIGURE 2-8**

As you move the cursor, notice that wherever you inserted a hard return there is the [HRt] code. In Figure 2-9, on line 6 after TO: and on line 7 after RE: where you pressed the Tab key, notice the code **[TAB]**. Each of those lines is followed by a hard return.

Looking only at the lower screen, continue moving the cursor down with the Down Arrow ↓ key. When you get to the paragraph you typed, notice that instead of [HRt] codes at each line end, there are **[SRt]** codes (Figure 2-10). These are the lines where you allowed word wrap to occur, so there is a soft return [SRt] code at the end of each line.

With the Down Arrow ↓ key continue moving the cursor down to the end of the document, shown in Figure 2-11. The last code in the document is [HRt].

To exit from the reveal codes screen, press the spacebar or another key such as Enter.

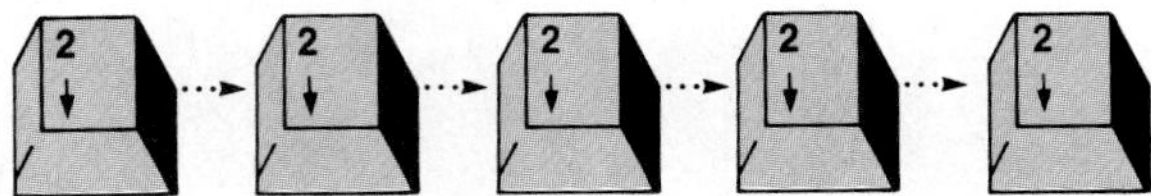
2
2
2
2
2

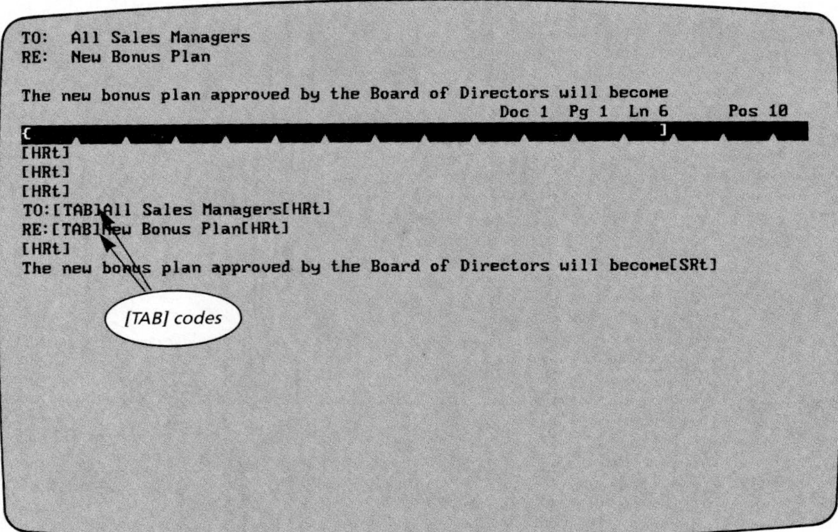
TO:  All Sales Managers
RE:  New Bonus Plan
The new bonus plan approved by the Board of Directors will become
Doc 1  Pg 1  Ln 6  Pos 10
[HRt]
[HRt]
[HRt]
TO:[TAB]All Sales Managers[HRt]
RE:[TAB]New Bonus Plan[HRt]
[HRt]
The new bonus plan approved by the Board of Directors will become[SRt]
[TAB] codes

**FIGURE 2-9**

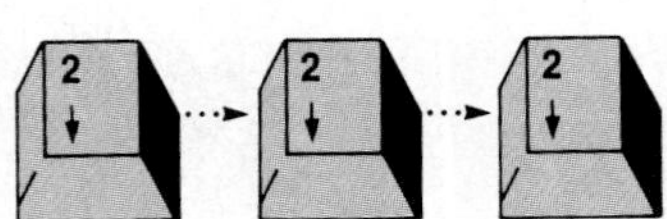
2
2
2

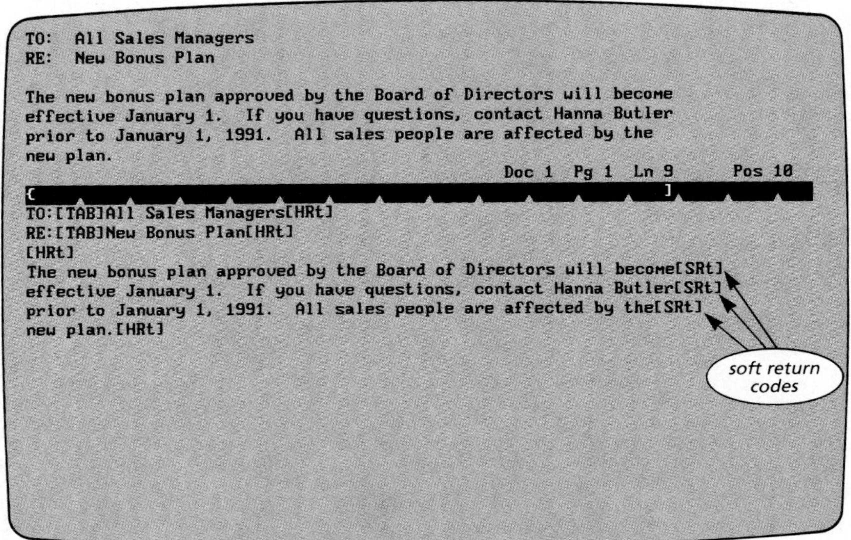
TO:  All Sales Managers
RE:  New Bonus Plan
The new bonus plan approved by the Board of Directors will become
effective January 1.  If you have questions, contact Hanna Butler
prior to January 1, 1991.  All sales people are affected by the
new plan.
Doc 1  Pg 1  Ln 9  Pos 10
TO:[TAB]All Sales Managers[HRt]
RE:[TAB]New Bonus Plan[HRt]
[HRt]
The new bonus plan approved by the Board of Directors will become[SRt]
effective January 1.  If you have questions, contact Hanna Butler[SRt]
prior to January 1, 1991.  All sales people are affected by the[SRt]
new plan.[HRt]
soft return codes

**FIGURE 2-10**

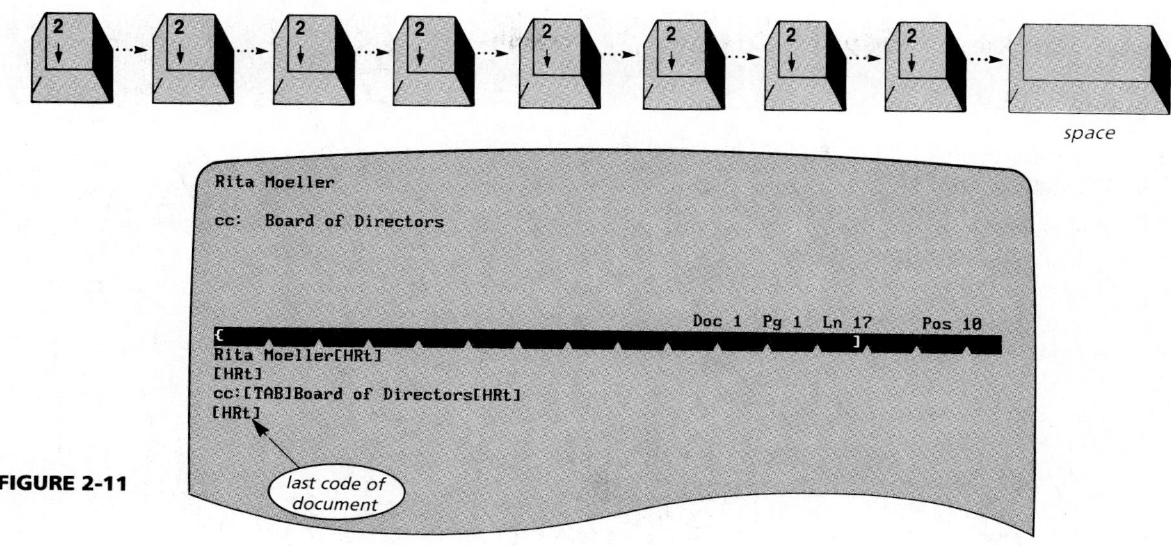
2
2
2
2
2
2
2
2
space
Rita Moeller
cc: Board of Directors
Doc 1 Pg 1 Ln 17 Pos 10
Rita Moeller[HRt]
[HRt]
cc:[TAB]Board of Directors[HRt]
[HRt]
last code of document

**FIGURE 2-11**

## Saving a Document

The memo to the sales managers shown in Figure 2-1 is completed. Whenever a document is completed, it should be saved onto the disk so that it can be retrieved for printing or modification at a later time. Look at the template next to the F10 key. Notice the word Save in black. Press the F10 key (step 1 in Figure 2-12). At the lower left corner of your screen you see the message "Document to Be Saved:". To name the document type the word MEMO as shown in step 2 of Figure 2-12 (you can type it in uppercase, lowercase, or a combination). After you have typed MEMO, notice that nothing else happens. Press the Enter key ↵.

After you press the Enter key, notice that the light on drive B goes on, indicating that the document is being saved to the diskette in drive B, the default disk drive.

Your document is now named and saved. The name of the document appears in the lower left corner of your screen. Although you did not enter B:\ before you typed the name, because WordPerfect defaults to drive B, B:\ appears to remind you that the document is saved to the diskette in drive B.

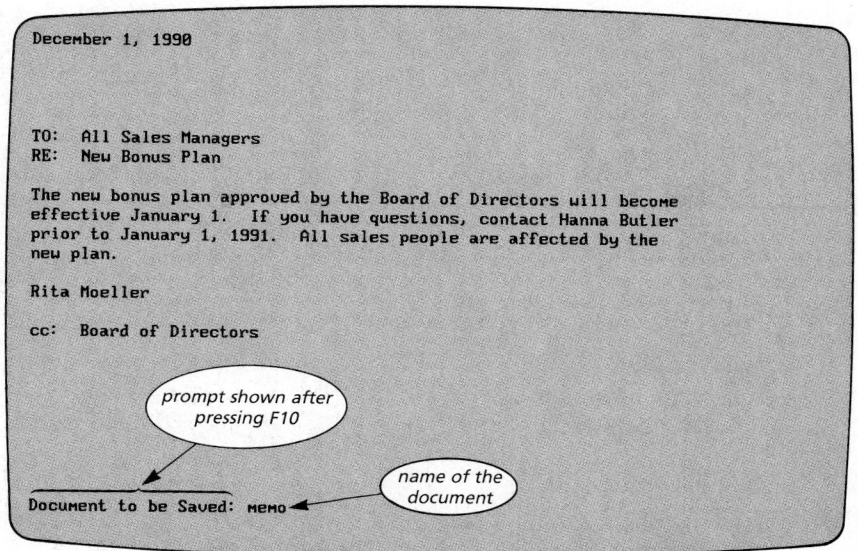
December 1, 1990
TO: All Sales Managers
RE: New Bonus Plan
The new bonus plan approved by the Board of Directors will become effective January 1. If you have questions, contact Hanna Butler prior to January 1, 1991. All sales people are affected by the new plan.
Rita Moeller
cc: Board of Directors
prompt shown after pressing F10
name of the document
Document to be Saved: MEMO

**Step 1: Save the document** **Step 2: Name the document**

F10

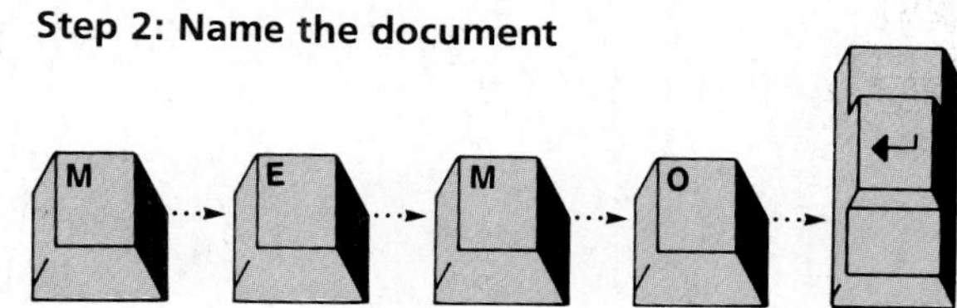
M
E
M
O

**FIGURE 2-12**

Figure 2-13 shows that that designation is now part of the name of this document.

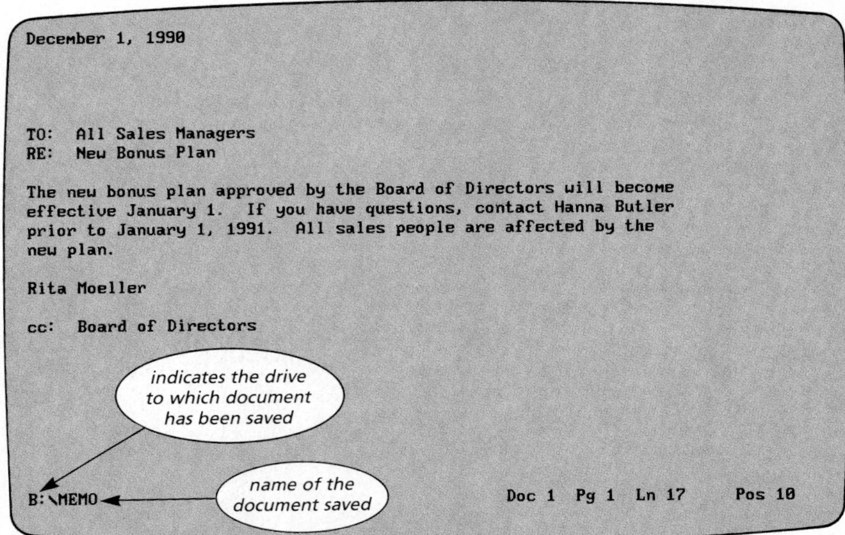
December 1, 1990
TO: All Sales Managers
RE: New Bonus Plan
The new bonus plan approved by the Board of Directors will become effective January 1. If you have questions, contact Hanna Butler prior to January 1, 1991. All sales people are affected by the new plan.
Rita Moeller
cc: Board of Directors
indicates the drive to which document has been saved
B:\MEMO
name of the document saved
Doc 1 Pg 1 Ln 17 Pos 10

**FIGURE 2-13**

## Printing a Document

After the file is entered and stored on the disk, the next task is normally to print the document. Be sure your printer has paper inserted correctly and that the printer is turned on and is ready to print.

From Project 1, remember that to print your document you must invoke the Print function. While holding down the Shift key, press the F7 key. Figure 2-14 shows that when you press those keys the print menu appears at the bottom of the screen.

Since you wish to print the full text of this document, press the number 1 for full text. At this point the printer begins printing your document. The printed document is illustrated in Figure 2-15.

The document generated by the training version of WordPerfect contains random *WPC notations throughout. The notations are your reminder that you are using the WordPerfect training version copyrighted by WordPerfect Corporation.

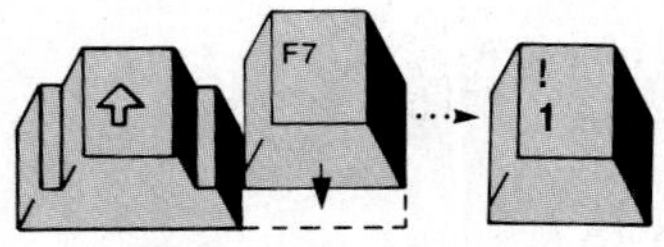
F7
!
1

December 1, 1990

TO: All Sales Managers
RE: New Bonus Plan

The new bonus plan approved by the Board of Directors will become effective January 1. If you have questions, contact Hanna Butler prior to January 1, 1991. All sales people are affected by the new plan.

Rita Moeller

cc: Board of Directors

option to print the complete text

the print menu

1 Full Text; 2 Page; 3 Options; 4 Printer Control; 5 Type-thru; 6 Preview: 0

**FIGURE 2-14**

December 1, 1990
*WPC

TO: All Sales Managers
RE: New Bonus Plan*WPC

The new bonus plan approved by the Board of Directors will become effective January 1. If you have questions, contact Hanna Butler prior to January 1, 1991. All sales people are affected by the new plan.*WPC

Rita Moeller

cc: Board of Directors
*WPC

indicates training version of WordPerfect

**FIGURE 2-15**

# MOVING THE CURSOR

## Arrow Keys

As you have learned, the arrow keys are used to move the cursor on the screen. However, to save time by moving more efficiently through your document, WordPerfect allows many combinations of cursor movements. Table 2-1 presents a complete list of cursor movements. Refer to the table during the following discussion about cursor movements.

**TABLE 2-1 Summary of Cursor Keystrokes**

| KEYSTROKES | RESULTS |
|---|---|
| ← | Moves cursor one character or space to the left. |
| → | Moves cursor one character or space to the right. |
| ↑ | Moves cursor up one line. |
| ↓ | Moves cursor down one line. |
| Ctrl → | Moves cursor to the first letter of the next word. |
| Ctrl ← | Moves cursor to the first letter of the previous word. |
| Home → | Moves cursor to the right edge of the current screen. If you continue to press Home, Right Arrow the cursor moves to the right edge of the next screen to the right. |
| Home ← | Moves cursor to the left edge of the current screen. If there are more screens to the left and you continue to press Home, Left Arrow, the cursor moves to the left edge of the next screen. |
| Home ↑ | Moves cursor to the top of the current screen, then to the top of the previous screen. |
| Home ↓ | Moves cursor to the bottom of the current screen, then to the bottom of the next screen. |
| − (on numeric keypad) | Moves cursor to the top of the current screen, then to the top of the previous screen (same as Home, Up Arrow). |
| + (on numeric keypad) | Moves cursor to the bottom of the current screen, then to the bottom of the next screen (same as Home, Down Arrow). |
| Home Home ↑ | Moves cursor to the top of the entire document. |
| Home Home ↓ | Moves cursor to the bottom of the entire document. |
| Home Home → | Moves cursor to the right end of the current line. |
| Home Home ← | Moves cursor to the beginning of the current line. |
| Home Home Home ← | Moves cursor in front of all codes and characters at the beginning of the current line. |
| End | Moves cursor to the right end of the current line. |
| PgDn | Moves cursor to line 1 of the next page. |
| PgUp | Moves cursor to line 1 of the previous page. |
| Ctrl-Home, page number, ↵ | "Go to" command. When "Go to" appears on the screen, type the page number desired and press Enter. Moves cursor to line 1 of page indicated. |
| Ctrl-Home ↑ | Moves cursor to line 1 of current page. |
| Ctrl-Home ↓ | Moves cursor to last line of current page. |
| Ctrl-Home Alt-F4 | Moves cursor to the beginning of a block. |
| Esc | Repeats the keystroke command the number of times indicated. The default number is 8. To change the number, type in the desired number when n = 8 appears on the screen. Refer to WordPerfect manual to change the default number permanently. |
| Esc ↓ | Moves cursor down the number of lines indicated, i.e., if n = 8, the cursor would move down 8 lines. |
| Esc ↑ | Moves cursor up the number of lines indicated. |
| Esc → | Moves cursor right the number of characters indicated. |
| Esc ← | Moves cursor left the number of characters indicated. |
| Esc PgDn | Moves cursor down the number of pages indicated. Cursor will be placed on line 1 of the new page. |
| Esc PgUp | Moves cursor up the number of pages indicated. Cursor will be placed on line 1 of the new page. |
| Tab | Moves the cursor right to the next tab setting, on the current line only when the Insert key has been pressed and the word Typeover appears on the screen. (Caution: if Typeover is not on, a [TAB] code will be inserted.) |

## Home Key Used with Arrow Keys

Move to the top of the document by pressing Home, Home, and then the Up Arrow key (Figure 2-16). To move to the end of the document, press Home, Home, and the Down Arrow key (step 1 in Figure 2-17). The cursor will go to the bottom of the document.

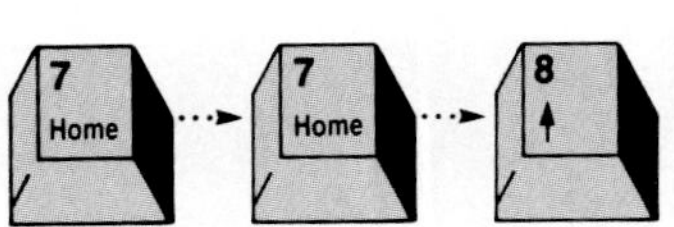
7
Home
7
Home
8

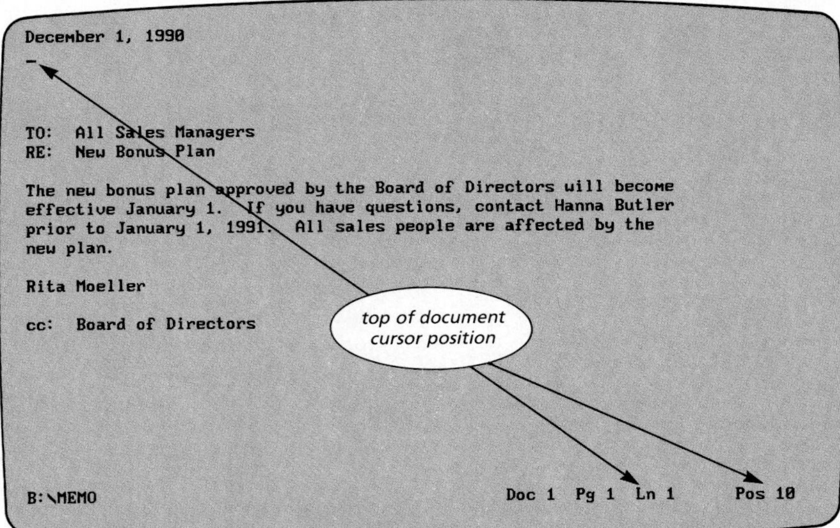
December 1, 1990
TO: All Sales Managers
RE: New Bonus Plan
The new bonus plan approved by the Board of Directors will become effective January 1. If you have questions, contact Hanna Butler prior to January 1, 1991. All sales people are affected by the new plan.
Rita Moeller
cc: Board of Directors
top of document
cursor position
B:\MEMO
Doc 1 Pg 1 Ln 1 Pos 10

FIGURE 2-16

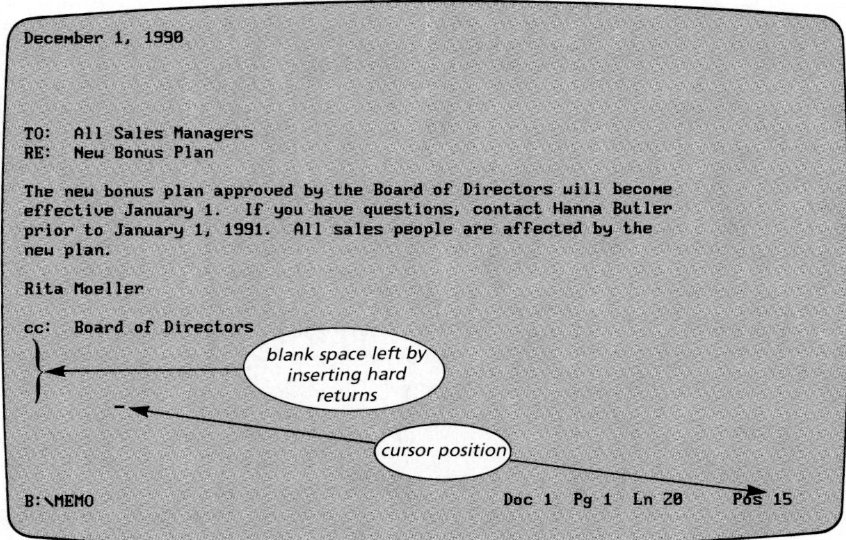
December 1, 1990
TO: All Sales Managers
RE: New Bonus Plan
The new bonus plan approved by the Board of Directors will become effective January 1. If you have questions, contact Hanna Butler prior to January 1, 1991. All sales people are affected by the new plan.
Rita Moeller
cc: Board of Directors
blank space left by inserting hard returns
cursor position
B:\MEMO
Doc 1 Pg 1 Ln 20 Pos 15

FIGURE 2-17

**Step 1: Move cursor to the end of the document**

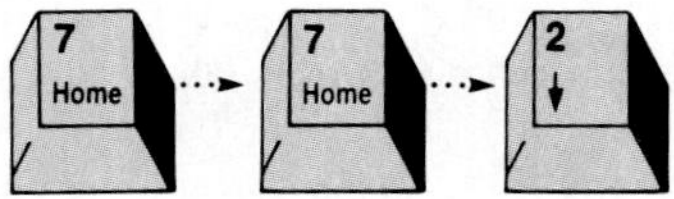
7
Home
7
Home
2

**Step 2: Insert 3 lines**

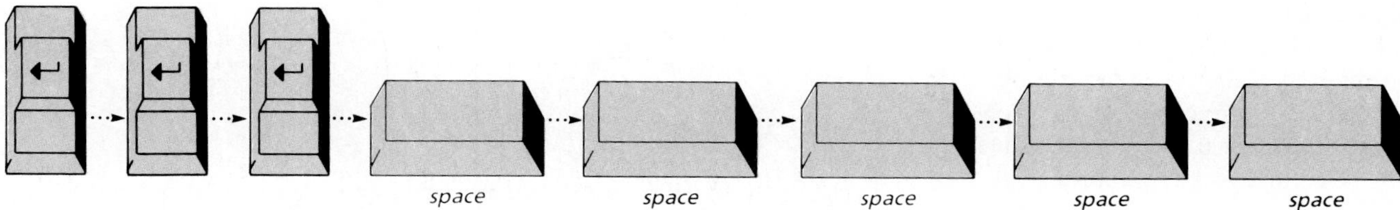


**Step 3: Move cursor to the top and bottom of the document**

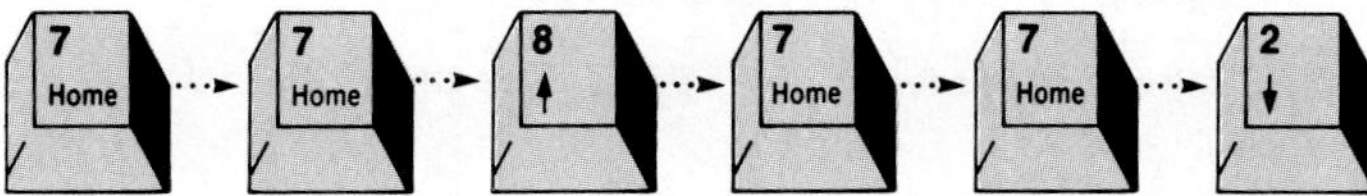


**FIGURE 2-17** (Steps 2 and 3)

The cursor cannot move past the bottom of the document, that is, it cannot move where there is no typing or codes. Press the Return key three times to put the cursor on line 20. Note the status line. Press the spacebar five times (step 2 in Figure 2-17), placing the cursor on line 20, position 15. Press Home, Home, and the Up Arrow key. The cursor returns to line 1, position 10. Then press Home, Home, and the Down Arrow key (step 3 in Figure 2-17). The cursor returns to line 20, position 15.

Many cursor movements can only be demonstrated over several pages of text. Since you have not yet typed several pages, do the following exercise first so you can practice additional cursor movements.

First, press a hard return ↵, which moves the cursor to line 21, position 10. Type the letter o followed by a hard return ↵. Continue to type the letter o followed by a hard return ↵ until the cursor is on line 54 of page 1 (this may seem awkward right now, but you will see its usefulness when we begin to move the cursor). Next type one more o followed by a hard return ↵ and as you do, watch for a dotted line to appear across the screen. This dotted line indicates that there has been a *page break*, which means that the document has moved from page 1 to page 2. Figure 2-18 shows that the status line also indicates that the cursor is now on page 2, line 1.

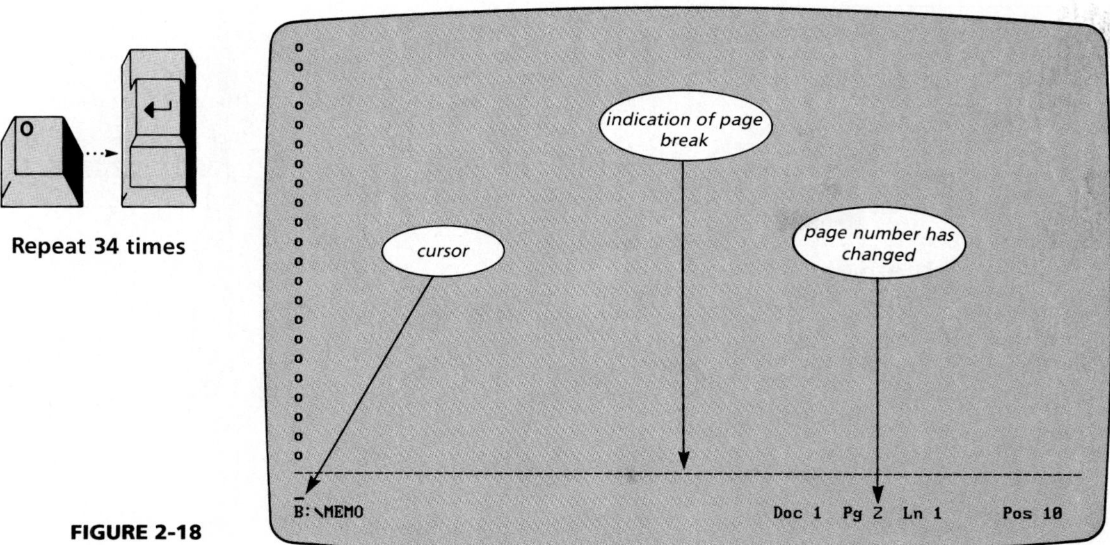


**FIGURE 2-18**

On page 2, line 1 type the letter a, then press the Enter key ↵. Continue to do this until another page break appears and the status line indicates that the cursor is on page 3, line 1, as shown in step 1 of Figure 2-19. To complete this exercise, type the letter u and press the Enter key ↵. Continue to do so until the cursor is on line 14, position 10 of page 3 (step 2 of Figure 2-19). If you could now see your entire document, it would look like Figure 2-20.

The cursor is at the bottom of your document. That is, the *last* position of the cursor is the end of the document. Now press Home, Home, Up Arrow to move to the beginning of your document, page 1, line 1, position 10 (step 1 of Figure 2-21). Press the Down Arrow until you are on line 9 of page 1, the paragraph portion of your letter (step 2 of Figure 2-21).

To move the cursor to the right, press the Right Arrow → (step 3 of Figure 2-21). This moves the cursor to the right one character at a time. To move the cursor to the left, press the Left Arrow ← (step 4 of Figure 2-21). This moves the cursor to the left one character at a time.

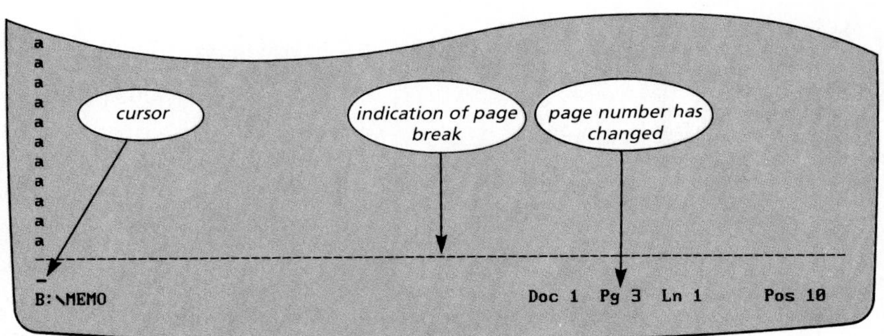


**Step 1: Repeat 54 times**

**Step 2: Repeat 13 times**

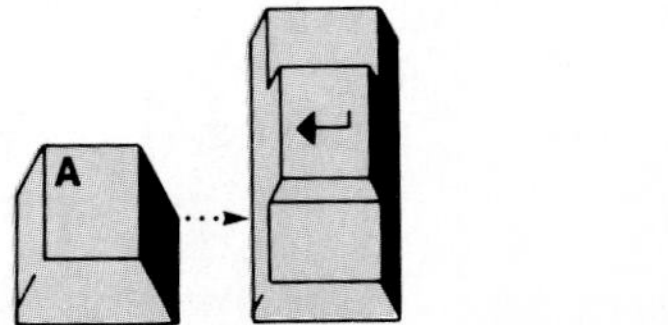


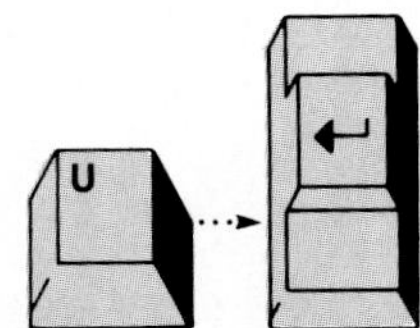


**FIGURE 2-19**

## Control Key Used with Arrow Keys

Move the cursor to position 41 of line 9 so that it is under the letter t in the word the (step 1 in Figure 2-22). To move one word at a time, hold the Ctrl key down firmly and while holding, press the Right Arrow key → (step 2 in Figure 2-22). If you continue to press the Right Arrow key, the cursor moves one word at a time. Hold down the Right Arrow key firmly while holding the Ctrl key; notice how fast the cursor moves through the document.

Hold down the Ctrl key and press the Left Arrow key ←. The cursor moves to the left one word at a time (step 3 in Figure 2-22).

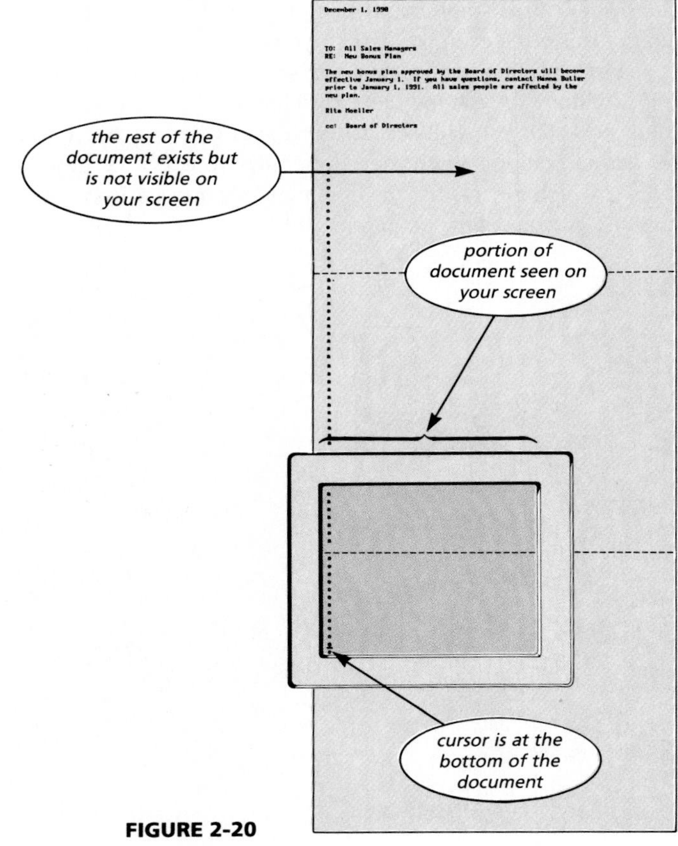
December 1, 1990

TO: All Sales Managers
RE: New Bonus Plan

The new bonus plan approved by the Board of Directors will become effective January 1. If you have questions, contact Hanna Butler prior to January 1, 1991. All sales people are affected by the new plan.

Rita Moeller

cc: Board of Directors



**FIGURE 2-20**

**Step 1:** **Move the cursor to top of the document**

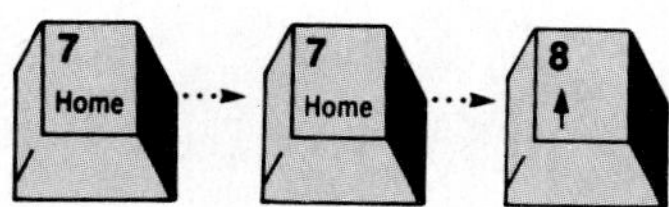

7
Home
7
Home
8

**Step 2:** **Move the cursor to line 9**

2

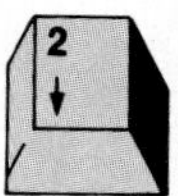

**Step 3:** **Practice using the Right Arrow key**

6

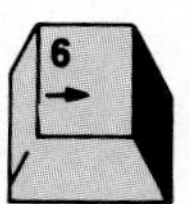

**Step 4:** **Practice using the Left Arrow key**

4

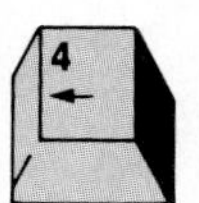

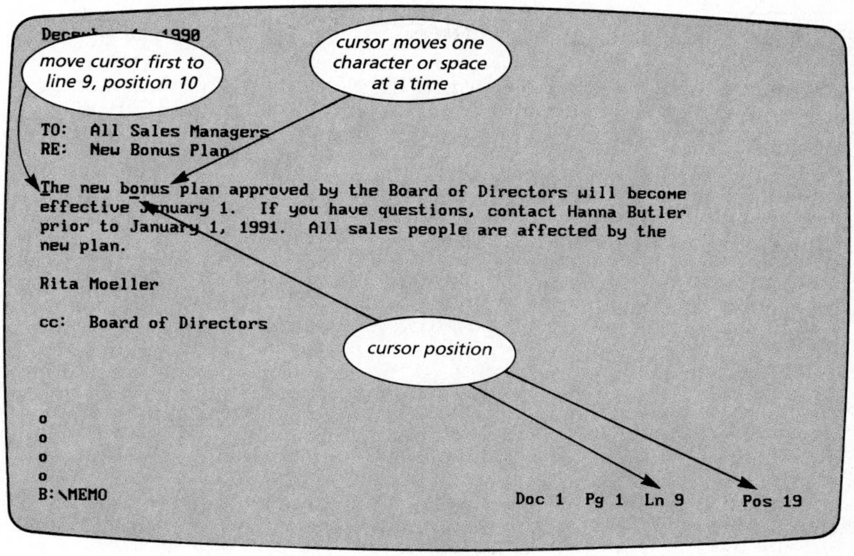

move cursor first to line 9, position 10
cursor moves one character or space at a time
TO: All Sales Managers
RE: New Bonus Plan
The new bonus plan approved by the Board of Directors will become effective January 1. If you have questions, contact Hanna Butler prior to January 1, 1991. All sales people are affected by the new plan.
Rita Moeller
cc: Board of Directors
cursor position
B:\MEMO
Doc 1 Pg 1 Ln 9 Pos 19

**FIGURE 2-21**

**Step 1:** **Move the cursor to line 9, position 41**

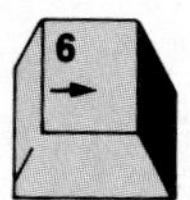

6

**Step 2:** **Move the cursor to the beginning of the next word**

Ctrl
6

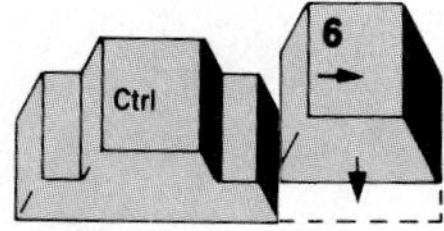

**Step 3:** **Move the cursor to the beginning of previous words**

Ctrl
4

December 1, 1990
cursor moves to the first letter of the next or previous word
TO: All Sales Managers
RE: New Bonus Plan
The new bonus plan approved by the Board of Directors will become effective January 1. If you have questions, contact Hanna Butler prior to January 1, 1991. All sales people are affected by the new plan.
Rita Moeller
cc: Board of Directors
cursor position
B:\MEMO
Doc 1 Pg 1 Ln 9 Pos 45

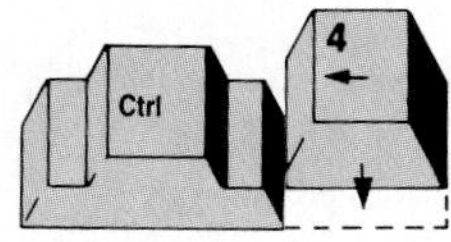

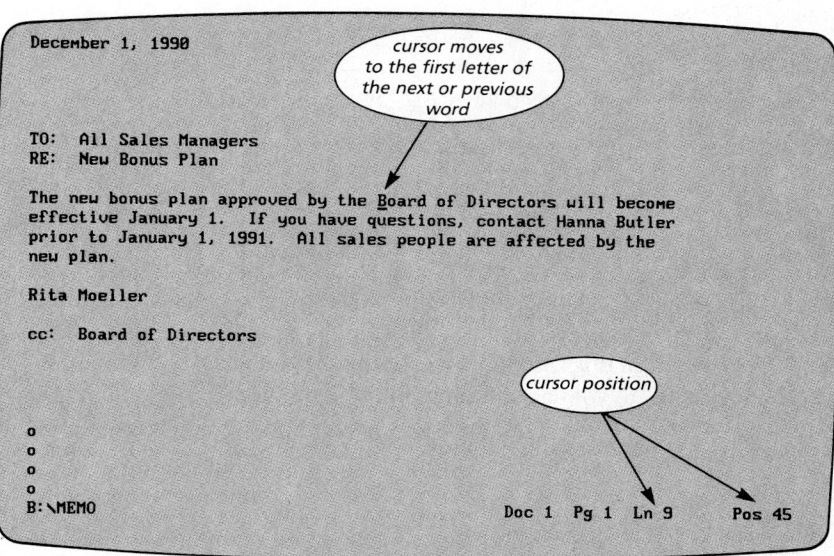

**FIGURE 2-22**

## End Key

Move the cursor again to line 9, position 10. Note that you are at the left edge of the line. Press the End key. Figure 2-23 shows how the End key moves the cursor to the end of the line.

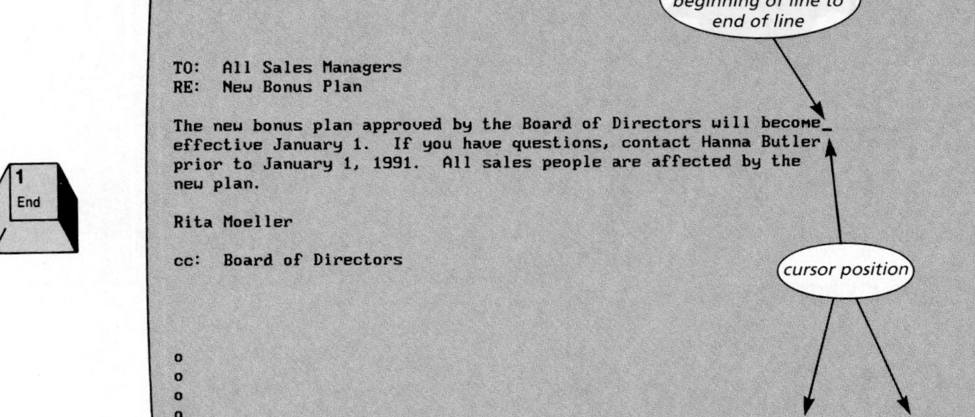
1
End
December 1, 1990
moves directly from beginning of line to end of line
TO: All Sales Managers
RE: New Bonus Plan
The new bonus plan approved by the Board of Directors will become
effective January 1. If you have questions, contact Hanna Butler
prior to January 1, 1991. All sales people are affected by the
new plan.
Rita Moeller
cc: Board of Directors
cursor position
o
o
o
o
B:\MEMO
Doc 1 Pg 1 Ln 9 Pos 75

**FIGURE 2-23**

## More Home Key, Arrow Key Sequences

Move to the top of the document again by pressing Home, Home, Up Arrow. The cursor is now on page 1, line 1, position 10.

As you learned in Project 1, you may have a large document, but the monitor can only show you one screenful at a time. If you wish to move the cursor to the top, the bottom, the left, or the right edges of your present screen, press the Home key *once*, then the Up, Down, Left, or Right arrow keys. Try pressing the Home key, then the Down Arrow key ↓. That moves the cursor to line 24 (step 1 in Figure 2-24). Press the Home key, then the Up Arrow key ↑. That moves the cursor to line 1 (step 2 in Figure 2-24). Press Down Arrow ↓ to move the cursor down to line 9. Now press Home, then Right Arrow →. The cursor moves to the right end of the line (step 3 in Figure 2-24). Press Home, then Left Arrow ←. The cursor moves to the left edge of the screen, in this case the left end of the line (step 4 in Figure 2-24). Thus, pressing the Home key once in combination with an arrow key moves the cursor to the edges of the screen.

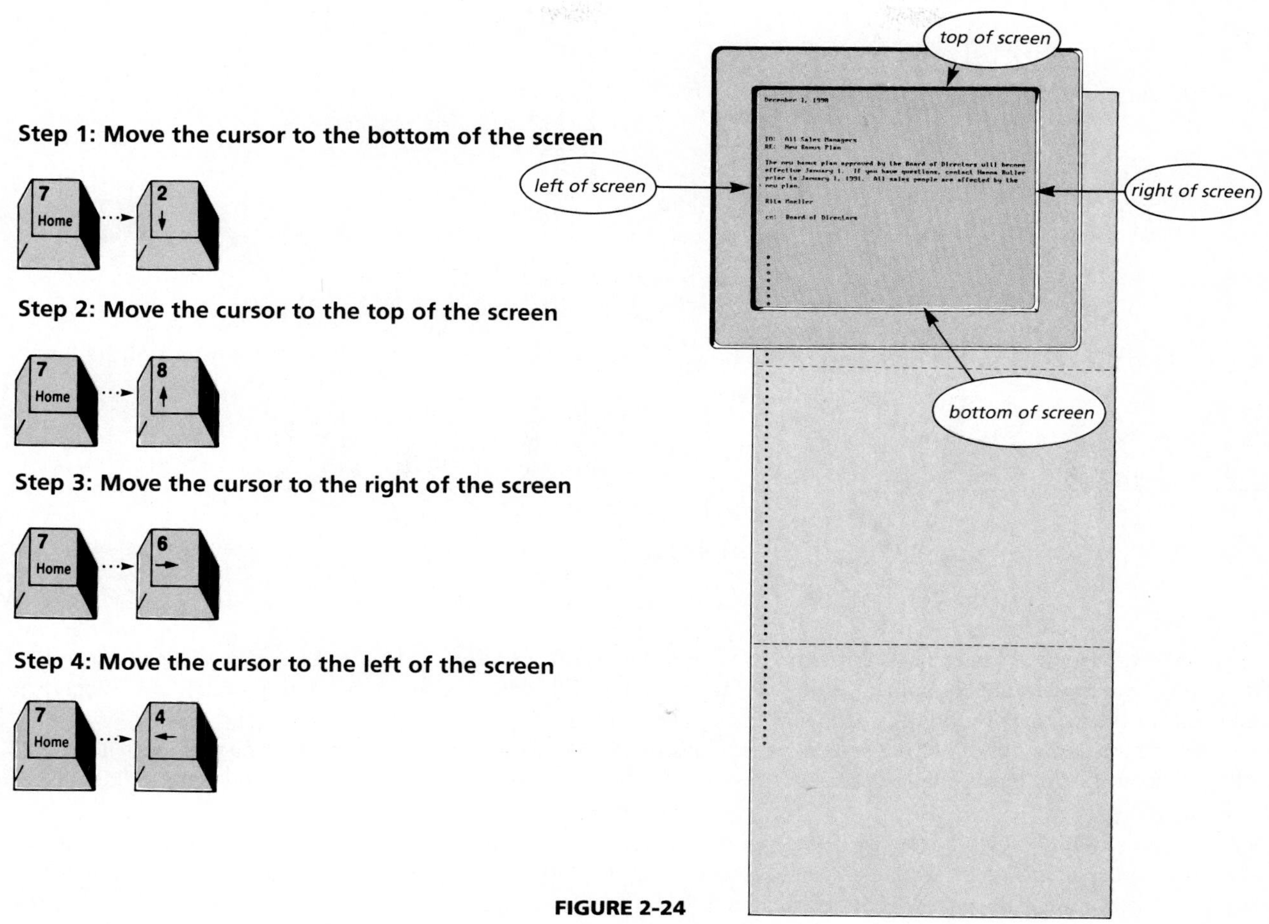
Step 1: Move the cursor to the bottom of the screen
7
Home
2
Step 2: Move the cursor to the top of the screen
7
Home
8
Step 3: Move the cursor to the right of the screen
7
Home
6
Step 4: Move the cursor to the left of the screen
7
Home
4
top of screen
left of screen
right of screen
bottom of screen

**FIGURE 2-24**

The margins of your document can be very wide, extending beyond the left or right edges of your screen, and you may wish to be able to move quickly to the left or right ends of a line in your document. With the cursor still on page 1, line 9, press Home, Home, Right Arrow (step 1 of Figure 2-25 on the following page). Notice that the cursor moves to the right end of the line, to position 75. Press Home, Home, Left Arrow, and the cursor moves back to position 10 at the left end of the line (step 2 in Figure 2-25). The cursor movements caused by Home, Right or Left Arrow, and Home, Home, Right or Left Arrow appear to be the same. But if you had lines longer than could be shown on one screen, you would notice that Home, Left or Right Arrow moves the cursor only to the edges of the screen you are viewing. Figure 2-25 illustrates that Home, Home, Right or Left Arrow causes the cursor to move immediately to the right or left ends of the line, even if the ends of the line cannot be seen on the current screen.

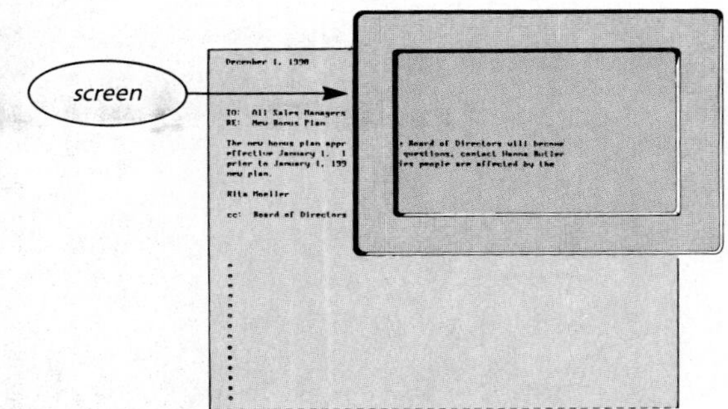


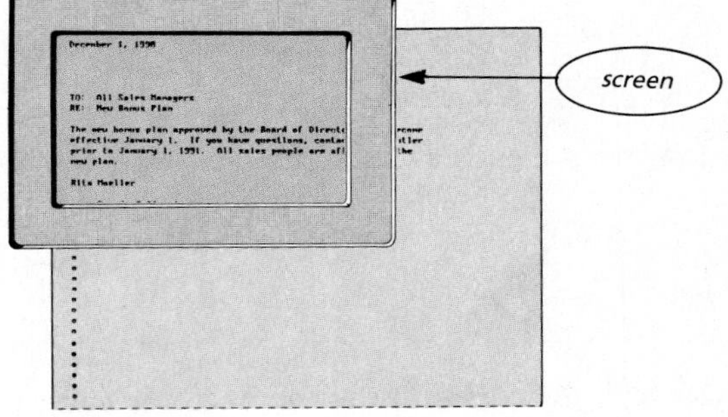


Step 1: Move the cursor to the right end of the line

Step 2: Move the cursor to the left end of the line

FIGURE 2-25

In addition to the Home, Home, Left Arrow function, you can use Home, Home, Home, Left Arrow. This keystroke sequence moves the cursor to the beginning of the line, even if codes are embedded at the beginning of the line. When text is moved, the codes have to be moved too.

Move your cursor to the bottom of the screen by pressing Home, Down Arrow ↓. The cursor is now on page 1, line 24, position 10. To go to the bottom of the *next* screen, press Home, Down Arrow ↓. The cursor is now on page 1, line 48, position 10.

When you press Home, Down Arrow or Home, Up Arrow, you will not miss viewing any lines of typing. The cursor moves down one screen at a time or up one screen at a time, without skipping any portions of the document. Figure 2-26 shows how the screen moves. Because WordPerfect automatically breaks a page at line 54, the next screen down shows the remainder of the lines on page 1, then the dotted line showing the break between the pages. The cursor is on line 17 of page 2. Press Home, Down Arrow again and again until the cursor is at the bottom of the document (page 3, line 14). Since that is as far as the cursor has been before, it cannot be moved any farther. To move the cursor up one screen at a time, press Home, Up Arrow ↑. The cursor moves to the top of the screen. Continue pressing Home, Up Arrow and watch how the cursor moves a screen at a time (watch the status line as well as the screen). Continue pressing Home, Up Arrow until the cursor is on page 1, line 1.

## Plus and Minus Keys on the Numeric Keypad

The **Plus** and **Minus** keys on the numeric keypad, when the Num Lock key is "off", perform the same functions as the Home, Up Arrow and Home, Down Arrow keys (Figure 2-27).

Look on the numeric keypad at the Plus ( + ) and the Minus (–) keys. Press the Plus key. Notice that the cursor moves to line 24, as shown in Figure 2-28.

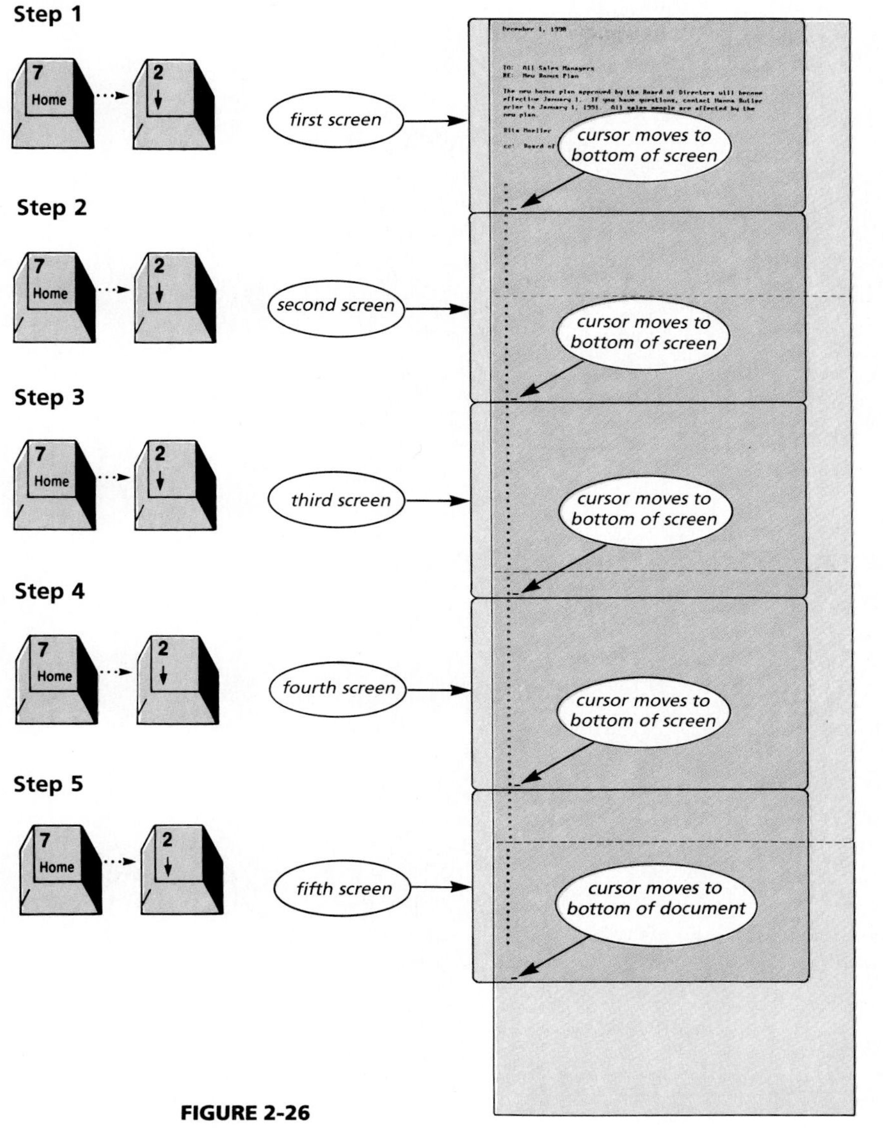


FIGURE 2-26

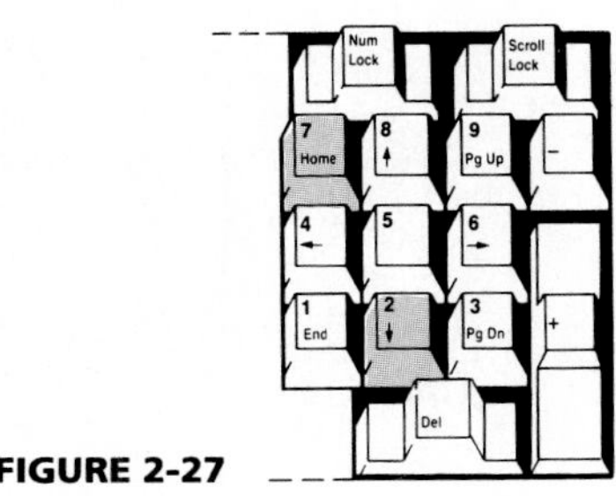


FIGURE 2-27

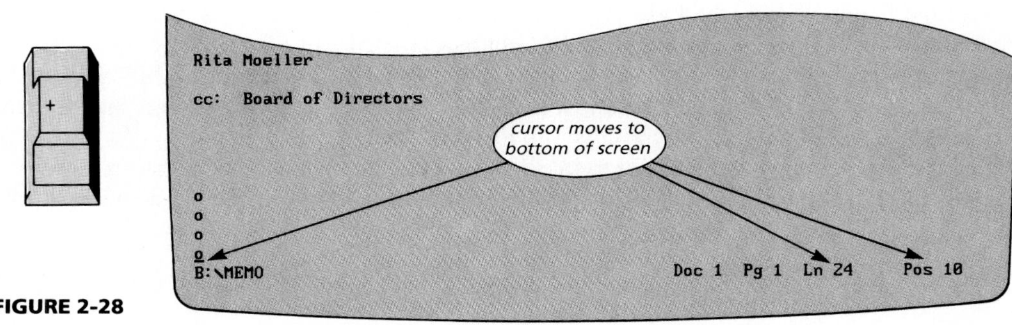


FIGURE 2-28

Press the Plus key again and the cursor moves to line 48 (Figure 2-29). This is the same result you would get from pressing the Home, Down Arrow keys. Press the Minus key and the cursor moves to the top of the screen, line 25 (Figure 2-30), just as if you had pressed the Home, Up Arrow keys. Press the Minus key again and the cursor moves to line 1 of page 1.

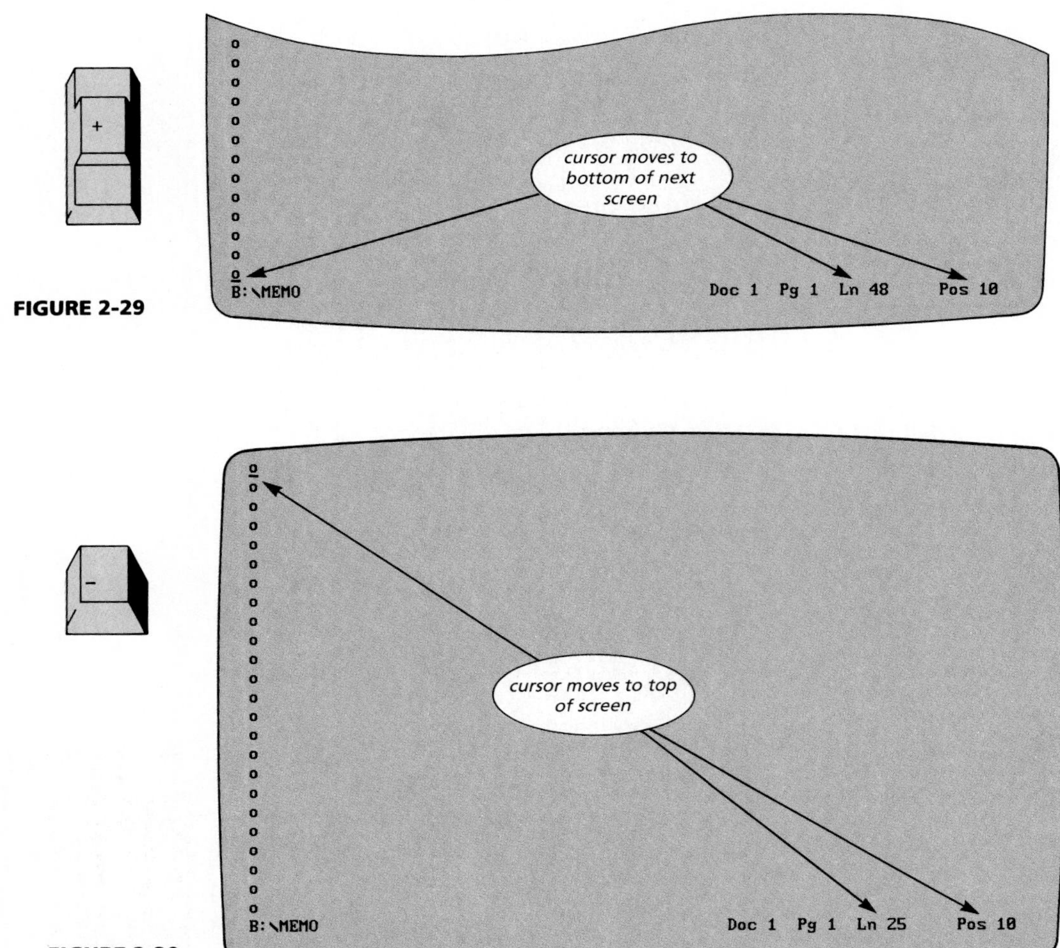


**FIGURE 2-29**

**FIGURE 2-30**

## Page Down and Page Up Keys

The **PgDn** (Page Down) key moves the cursor to line 1 of the *next* page. The **PgUp** (Page Up) key moves the cursor to line 1 of the *previous* page.

With the cursor on page 1, line 1, press the PgDn key (step 1 of Figure 2-31). Notice that the cursor moves to line 1 of page 2. Press the PgDn key again and the cursor moves to line 1 of page 3 (step 2 of Figure 2-31).

Now move the cursor up only one line by pressing the Up Arrow ↑ key (step 1 of Figure 2-32). The cursor moves to line 54 of page 2. Press the PgDn key (step 2 of Figure 2-32). Note that the cursor moves only one line, but the status line indicates the cursor is on page 3 because PgDn moved the cursor to line 1 of page 3.

Press the Up Arrow ↑ one time, moving the cursor to line 54 of page 2. Because the status line states page 2, you know that the previous page is page 1. Therefore the PgUp key will take the cursor almost two full pages to line 1, page 1. Press the PgUp key.

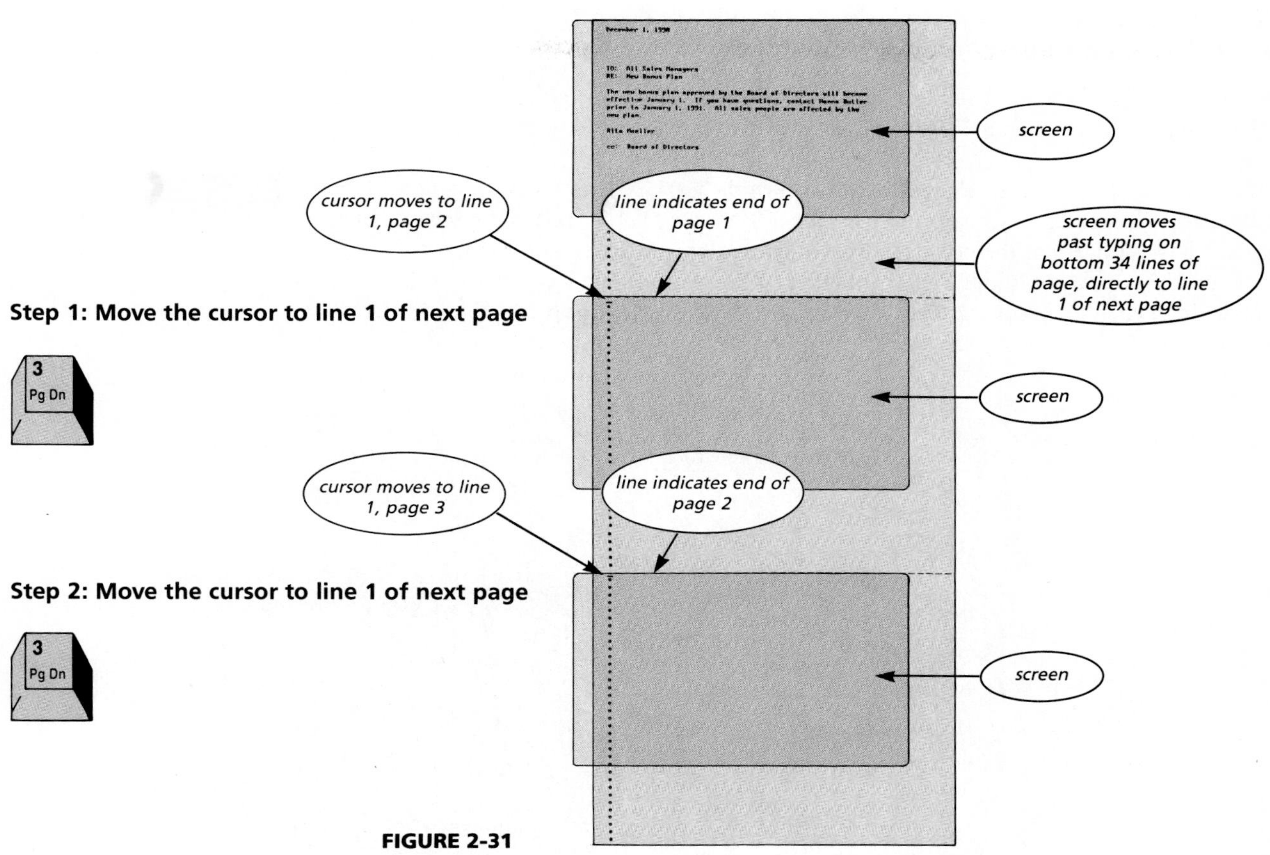


**FIGURE 2-31**

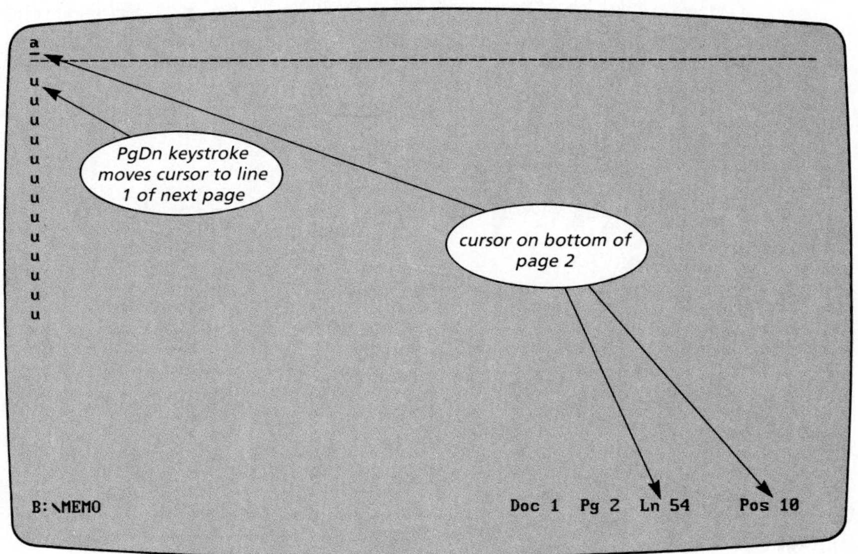


**FIGURE 2-32**

**Step 1: Move cursor up one line to line 54 of page 2**

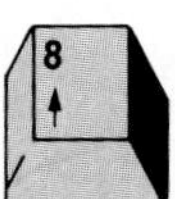


**Step 2: Move cursor to line 1 of page 3**

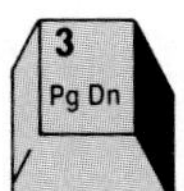

## "Go to" Cursor Function

There may be times when you want to go directly to a specific page, but repeatedly pressing the PgDn key would take too long. For example, if you had a 30-page document and you wished to go to page 15, pressing PgDn 15 times would be too time consuming.

To move directly to a particular page, hold down the Ctrl key and while holding it, press the Home key (step 1 of Figure 2-33). You see the message "Go to" in the lower left corner of the screen. Type the number 3 and then press Enter ↵ (step 2 of Figure 2-33). Notice that the cursor moves to page 3, line 1. To "Go to" a particular page, you can also go backward. While on page 3, line 1, hold the Ctrl key down and press the Home key (step 1 of Figure 2-34). The "Go to" message appears again. Type the number 2 and then press the Enter ↵ key (step 2 of Figure 2-34). The cursor is now on page 2, line 1. The cursor will always go to line 1 of the page number that you type.

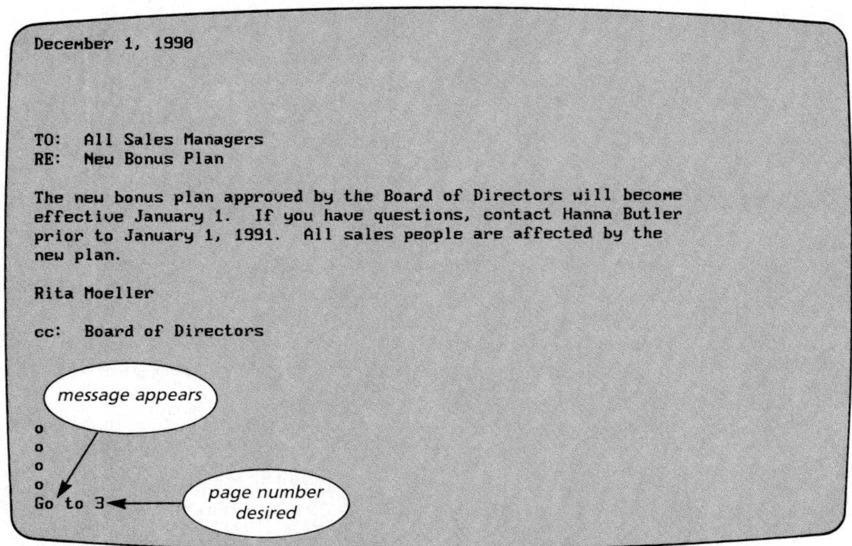

December 1, 1990
TO: All Sales Managers
RE: New Bonus Plan
The new bonus plan approved by the Board of Directors will become effective January 1. If you have questions, contact Hanna Butler prior to January 1, 1991. All sales people are affected by the new plan.
Rita Moeller
cc: Board of Directors
message appears
Go to 3
page number desired


**FIGURE 2-33**

**Step 1: Invoke the "Go to" message**  **Step 2: Go to page 3**

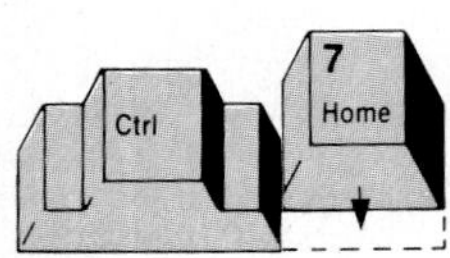


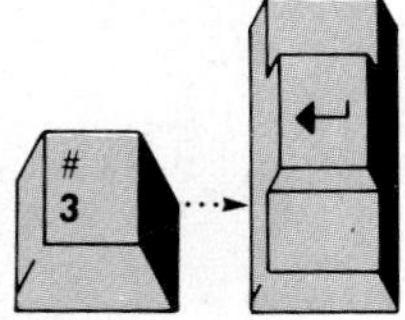

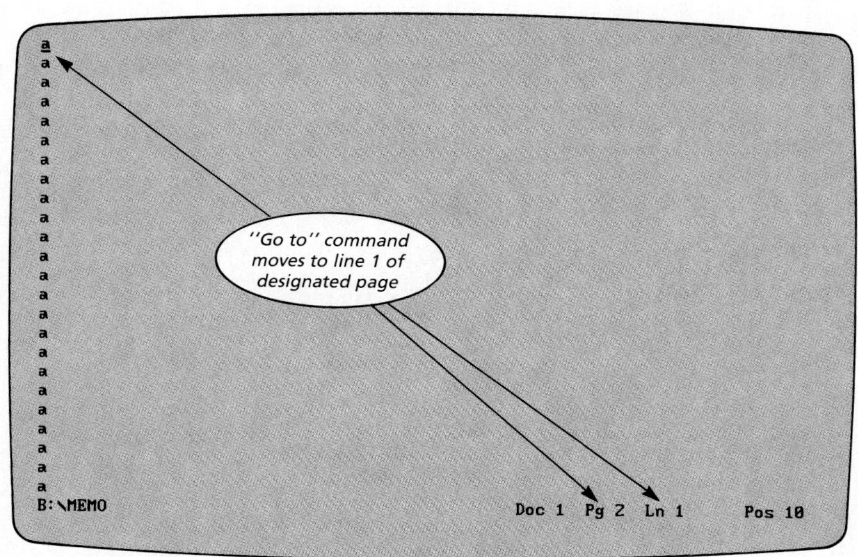


FIGURE 2-34

**Step 1: Invoke the "Go to" message**

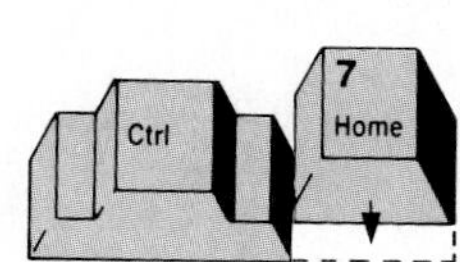


**Step 2: Go to page 2**

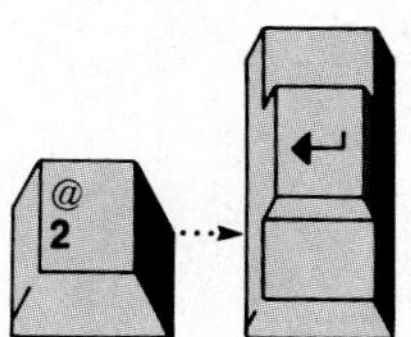


Another "Go to" command will take you either to the last line or the first line of the page you are currently on. The cursor should be on page 2, line 1. Hold down the Ctrl key and press the Home key. The "Go to" message appears. Press the Down Arrow key ↓ (see Figure 2-35). Look at the status line and notice that the cursor stayed on page 2, but went to the last line of that page, line 54.

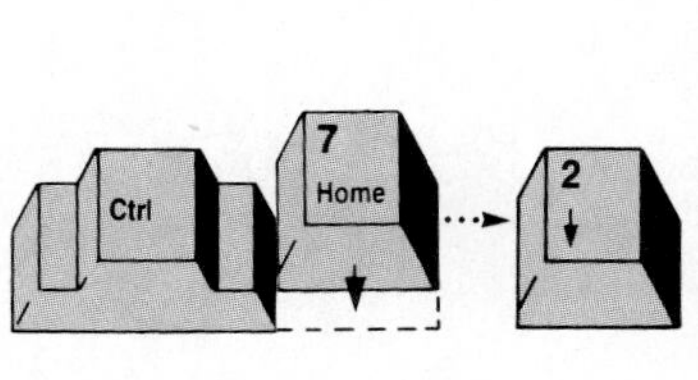


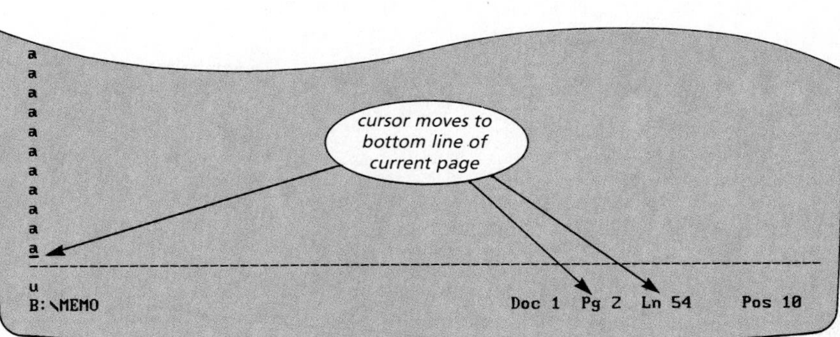


FIGURE 2-35

To move the cursor to the first line of page 2, hold the Ctrl key down and press the Home key. The "Go to" message appears. Press the Up Arrow ↑ key (see Figure 2-36). The cursor moves to page 2, line 1.

To move the cursor to the top of your document, press Home, Home, Up Arrow. The cursor is on page 1, line 1.

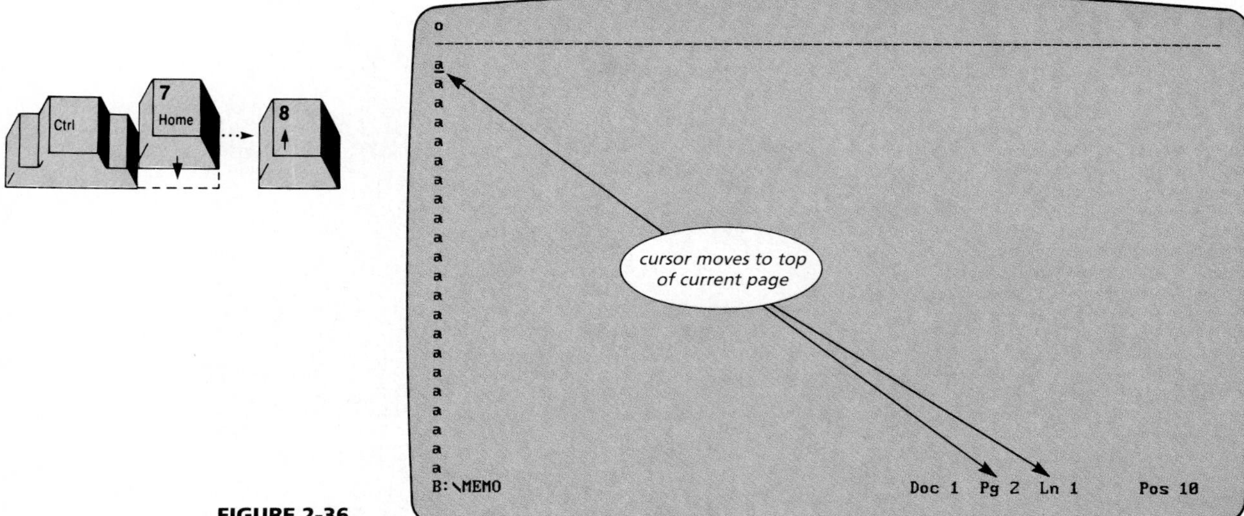
Ctrl
7
Home
8
cursor moves to top of current page
B:\MEMO
Doc 1 Pg 2 Ln 1 Pos 10

FIGURE 2-36

## Esc Key

Another key used to move the cursor is the **Esc** key. This is called a repeating key because it will repeat almost any stroke, whether a character or a cursor movement. For our purposes now, we will use it only to move the cursor.

Press the Esc key. Figure 2-37 shows the message "n = 8" at the bottom left corner of the screen. The message means that the default number is 8. Whatever keystroke you choose will be repeated eight times. After pressing Esc, press the Down Arrow ↓ key (step 1 of Figure 2-38). Instead of moving down one line, the cursor moves down eight lines, from line 1 to line 9. Press the Esc key again. The message "n = 8" appears again. Now press the Right Arrow key → (step 2 of Figure 2-38). The cursor moves to position 18 on line 9, moving eight characters to the right instead of just one.

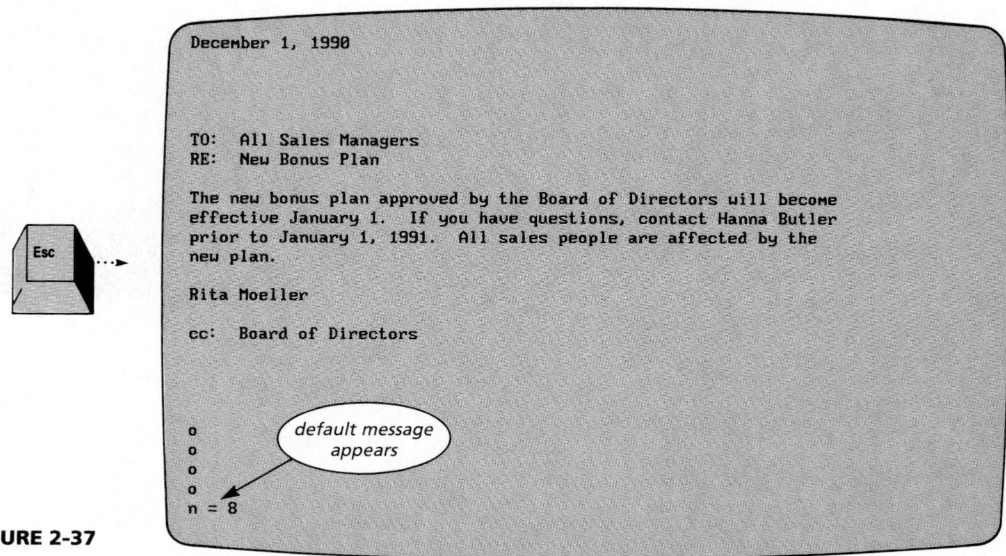
Esc
December 1, 1990
TO: All Sales Managers
RE: New Bonus Plan
The new bonus plan approved by the Board of Directors will become
effective January 1. If you have questions, contact Hanna Butler
prior to January 1, 1991. All sales people are affected by the
new plan.
Rita Moeller
cc: Board of Directors
default message appears
n = 8

FIGURE 2-37

You can also change the number of lines or characters that the cursor will move. Press the Esc key. The message "n = 8" appears on the screen. Instead of accepting the default, type the number 15. The 8 is replaced by the number 15 in the message. Next, press the Down Arrow key. The cursor moves down 15 lines to line 24, as shown in Figure 2-39.

You can see how important it is to memorize the keystroke sequences that move the cursor. You will save a lot of time by learning to use WordPerfect efficiently.

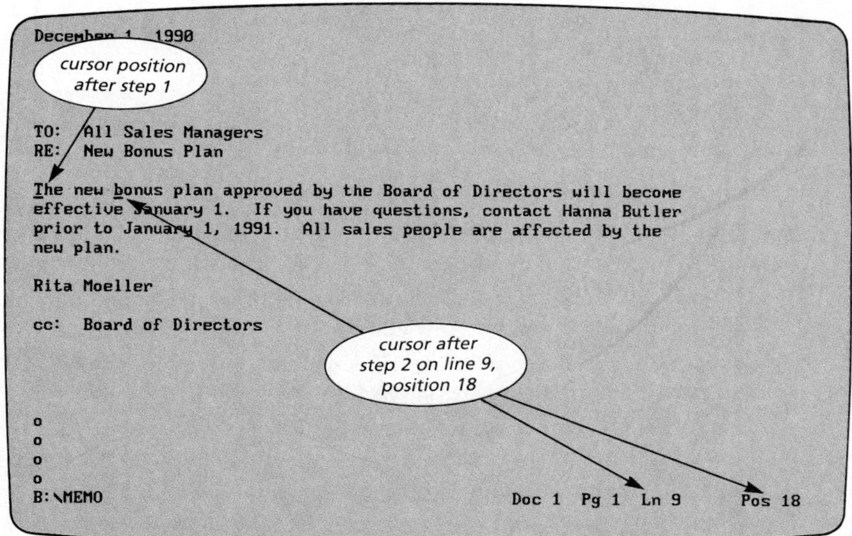
December 1, 1990
cursor position after step 1
TO: All Sales Managers
RE: New Bonus Plan
The new bonus plan approved by the Board of Directors will become effective January 1. If you have questions, contact Hanna Butler prior to January 1, 1991. All sales people are affected by the new plan.
Rita Moeller
cc: Board of Directors
cursor after step 2 on line 9, position 18
B:\MEMO
Doc 1 Pg 1 Ln 9 Pos 18

FIGURE 2-38

**Step 1: Move cursor down 8 lines**

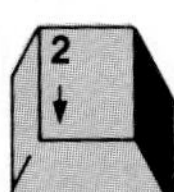

**Step 2: Move cursor 8 characters to the right**

Esc
6

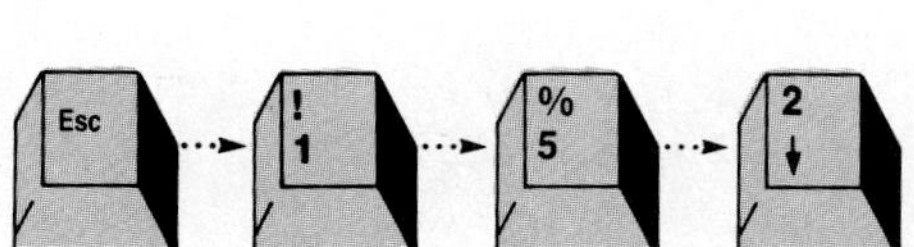
Esc
!
1
%
5
2

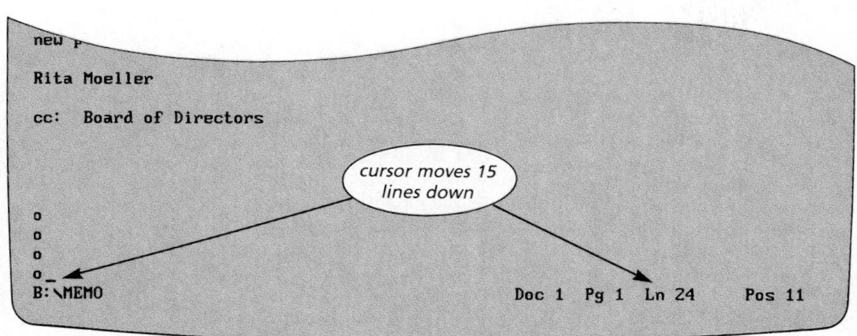
Rita Moeller
cc: Board of Directors
cursor moves 15 lines down
B:\MEMO
Doc 1 Pg 1 Ln 24 Pos 11

FIGURE 2-39

# DELETING TEXT

Learning how to use the deletion keys is as important as learning the cursor movements. Table 2-2 presents a comprehensive list of deletion keystrokes. Refer to the table during the following discussion about using the deletion keys.

Before we start, move the cursor to the bottom of the document by pressing Home, Home, Down Arrow. The cursor should be on page 3, line 14.

**TABLE 2-2 Summary of Deletion Keystrokes**

| KEYSTROKES | RESULTS |
|---|---|
| F1 1 | Restores deleted text. F1 highlights deleted text, then 1 restores that text. |
| Backspace | Deletes the character or code to the left of the cursor. |
| Delete | Deletes the character or code above the cursor moving to the right (as text is deleted, the typing to the right of the cursor moves left to the cursor). |
| Home Backspace | Deletes the word to the left of the cursor. |
| Ctrl-Backspace | Deletes the word above the cursor (as words are deleted, the typing to the right of the cursor moves left to the cursor). |
| Ctrl-End | Deletes from the cursor to the end of the current line. |
| Ctrl-PgDn | The prompt "Delete Remainder of Page? (Y/N) N" appears. Type the letter Y to delete from the cursor to the end of the current page. |
| Alt-F4 Delete | To delete a block place the cursor at the beginning of a block. Hold down the Alt key and press F4. Move the cursor to identify and highlight a block of text. Press the Delete key. At the prompt "Delete Block? (Y/N) N" type the letter Y. |

## Using the Backspace Key and Restoring Deleted Text

Type these words: This is how to use the Backspace key (see Figure 2-40). The cursor is now at position 46 in a blank space just to the right of the y in the word key. Think of the **Backspace** key as deleting *backward*. Press the Backspace key and notice that the character to the *left* of the cursor is deleted. Continue to press the Backspace key until you've deleted the words Backspace and key (Figure 2-40).

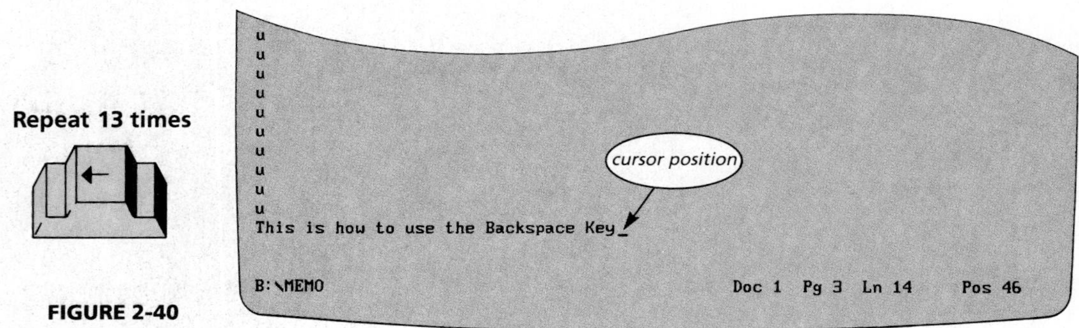


FIGURE 2-40

If you deleted text in error, and you have not moved the cursor to another position in the document, you can restore your text. Look at the template next to the F1 key. Notice the word Cancel in black. Press the F1 key. The text that was deleted reappears and is highlighted on the screen. The menu on the bottom of the screen shows that pressing the numeric key 1 will "undelete" or restore the highlighted text. Press 1 to see the text restored, putting the cursor back to position 46 to the right of the y (Figure 2-41).

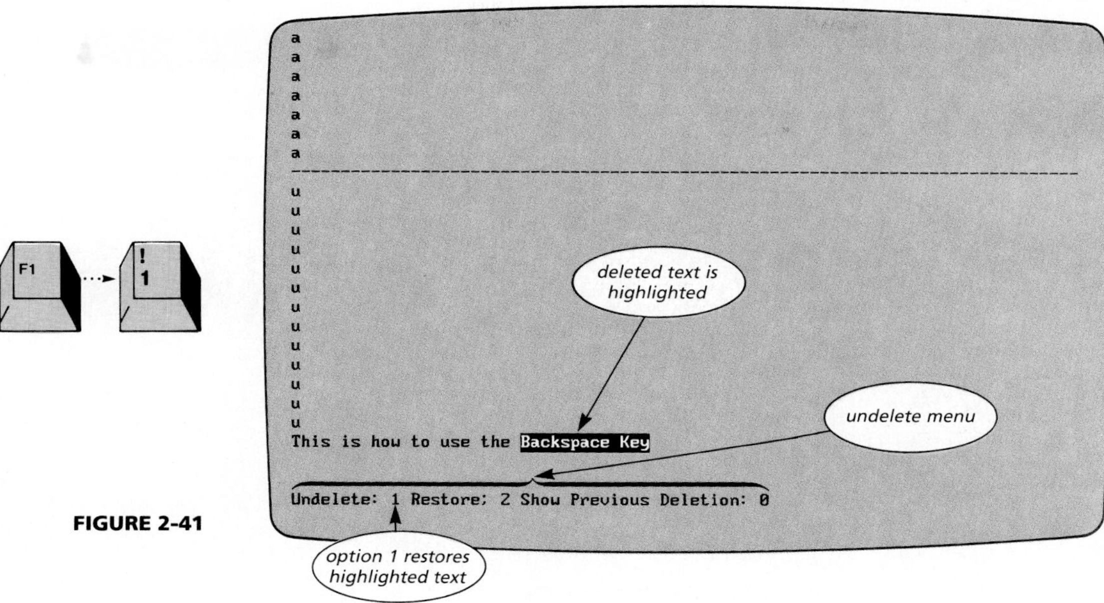


FIGURE 2-41

## Using the Delete Key and Restoring Deleted Text

The other key used to delete text is the Delete key. The **Delete** key deletes the space or character directly *above* the cursor. Think of the Delete key as deleting text going *forward*.

Press the Return key to move the cursor to page 3, line 15. Type these words: This is how to use the Delete key (see Figure 2-42). Press Home, Left Arrow to move the cursor to the beginning of the line, putting the cursor under the T in This. Press the Delete key and notice that the T that was directly above the cursor is deleted. Delete these words: This is how.

As before, to restore this deleted text press the F1 key. The "undelete" menu appears at the bottom of the screen. Press 1 to restore the highlighted text. The text is restored with the cursor on position 21.

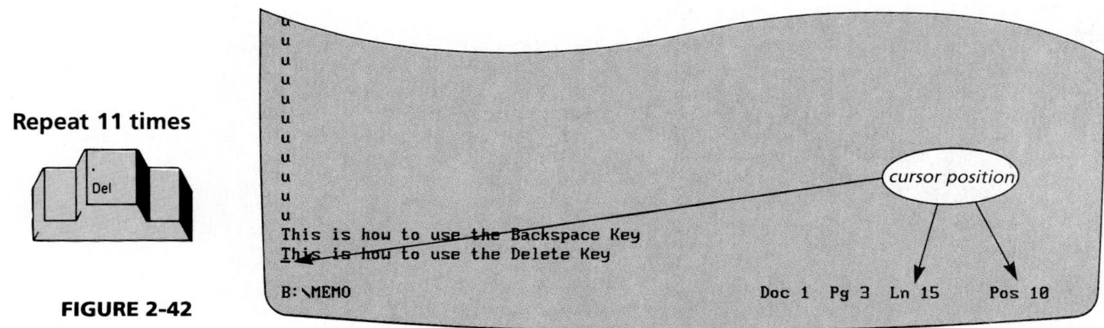


FIGURE 2-42

## Deleting One Line at a Time

To delete a line from where the cursor is to the end of the line, hold the Ctrl key down and press the End key. Figure 2-43 shows that the text from position 21 to the end of the line is deleted. To restore the deleted text, press the F1 key, then number 1.

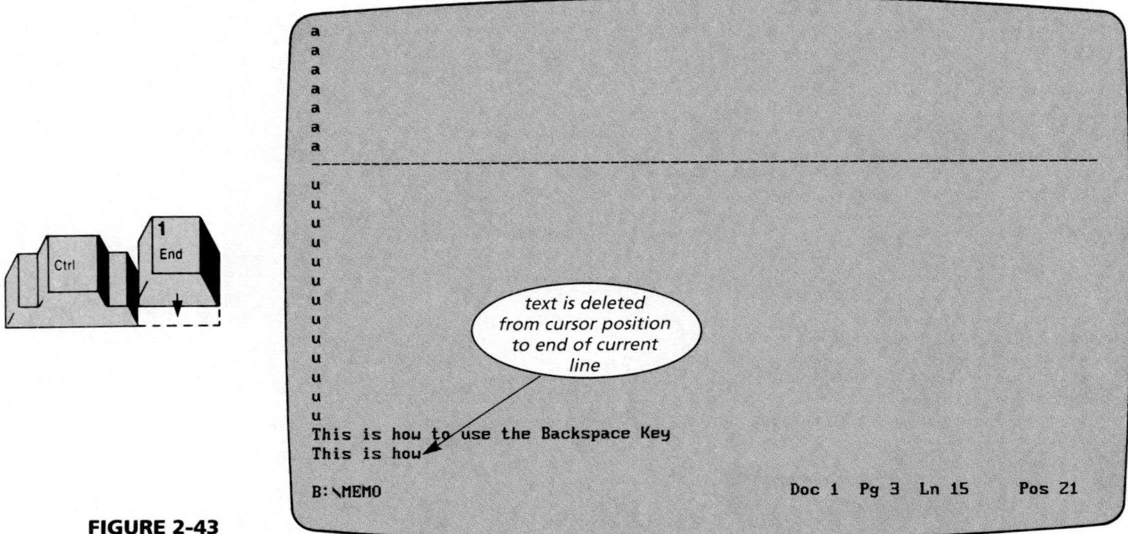


**FIGURE 2-43**

## Deleting One Page at a Time

The Ctrl-PgDn keys are used if you wish to delete from where the cursor is to the bottom of the page. Press Home, Home, Up Arrow to move the cursor to page 1, line 1. Since the cursor is on line 1, Ctrl-PgDn will delete from there to line 54, which is the bottom of this page. If your cursor were on line 9, Ctrl-PgDn would delete from there down to line 54. Hold down the Ctrl key and press the PgDn key (Figure 2-44). Since an entire page can contain a lot of work, WordPerfect has a built-in precaution. The message "Delete Remainder of Page? (Y/N) N" appears at the bottom left corner of the screen. The N at the end of the message means that the default is no. Therefore, if you press any key (besides Y), the answer no is accepted and nothing is deleted. Type the letter Y. Figure 2-45 shows that typing the letter Y deletes the entire text of page 1, bringing the text that was below page 1 up to line 1 of page 1.

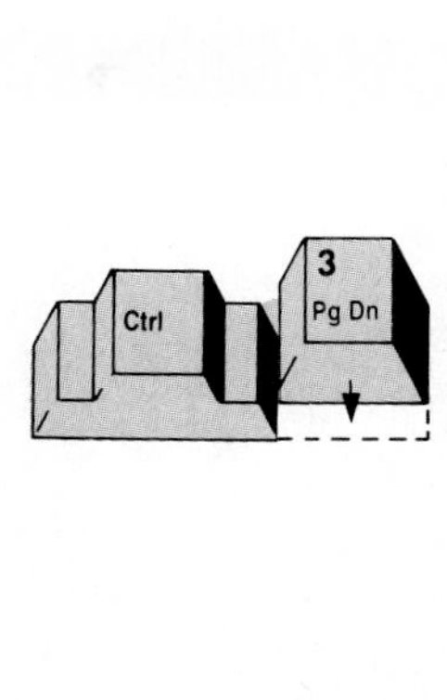
Ctrl
3
Pg Dn

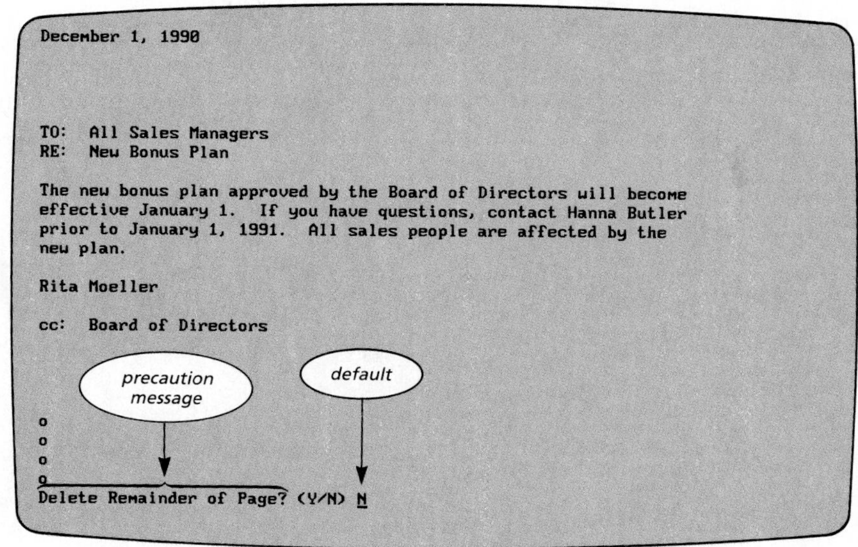
December 1, 1990
TO: All Sales Managers
RE: New Bonus Plan
The new bonus plan approved by the Board of Directors will become effective January 1. If you have questions, contact Hanna Butler prior to January 1, 1991. All sales people are affected by the new plan.
Rita Moeller
cc: Board of Directors
precaution message
default
Delete Remainder of Page? (Y/N) N

**FIGURE 2-44**

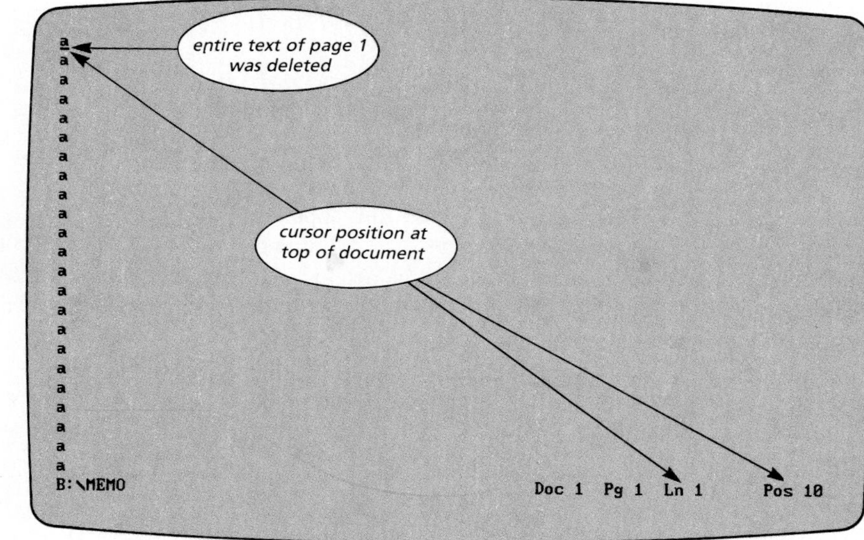
entire text of page 1 was deleted
cursor position at top of document
B:\MEMO
Doc 1 Pg 1 Ln 1 Pos 10

**FIGURE 2-45**

To restore the entire deleted text, press F1 to undelete and highlight the deleted text, then press the number 1 to restore the entire deleted text, bringing the cursor to line 54 on page 1. Press Home, Home, Up Arrow, moving the cursor to page 1, line 1. The entire text is restored.

## Deleting One Word at a Time

There will be times when you want to delete three or four words on a line. Move the cursor under the T in The, hold down the Ctrl key, and press the backspace key. Figure 2-46 shows that instead of just one character, the entire word The plus the space after it is deleted, bringing the first character of the next word to the cursor. Ctrl-Backspace deletes one word at a time going *forward* through the text. Continuing to hold down the Ctrl key and pressing the Backspace key, delete these words: new bonus plan. Then, to restore the deleted text, press the F1 key. Notice the highlight on the words The new bonus plan. Press the number 1 to restore those words to the text.

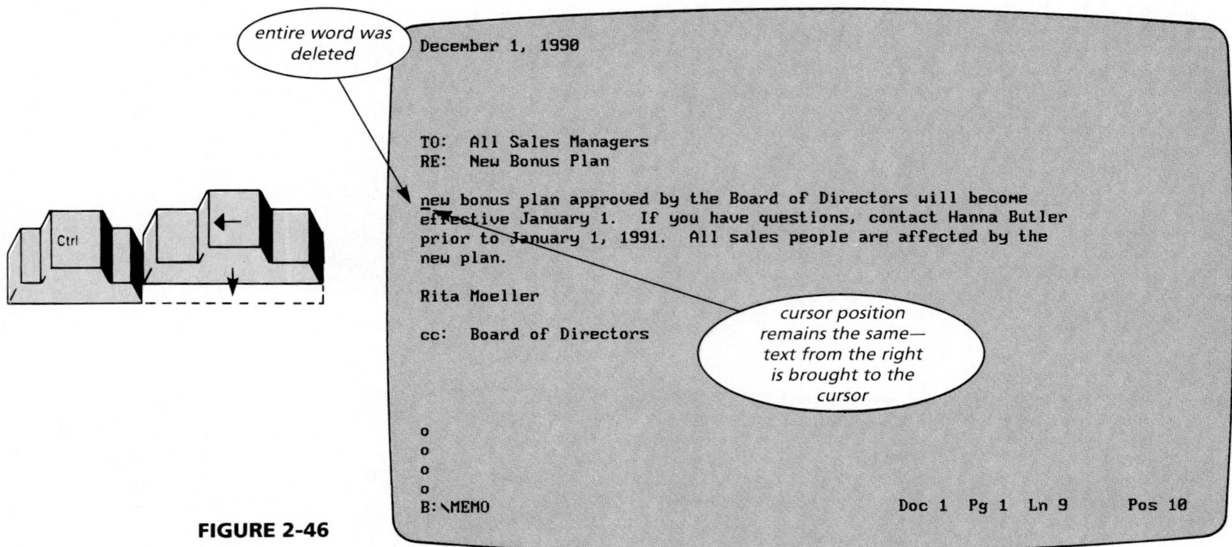
entire word was deleted
Ctrl
December 1, 1990
TO: All Sales Managers
RE: New Bonus Plan
new bonus plan approved by the Board of Directors will become
effective January 1. If you have questions, contact Hanna Butler
prior to January 1, 1991. All sales people are affected by the
new plan.
Rita Moeller
cc: Board of Directors
cursor position remains the same—text from the right is brought to the cursor
B:\MEMO
Doc 1 Pg 1 Ln 9 Pos 10

**FIGURE 2-46**

The cursor is at position 29 under the letter a in the word approved. To delete one word at a time going *backward* in your text, press the Home key once, then press the Backspace key. Notice that the word "plan" to the left of the cursor is deleted. Again press Home, then Backspace. The word "bonus" is deleted. Press Home, Backspace two more times, deleting first the word "new" and then the word "The" (see Figure 2-47). To restore these four words, press the F1 key and then the number 1. The text is restored to its original form.

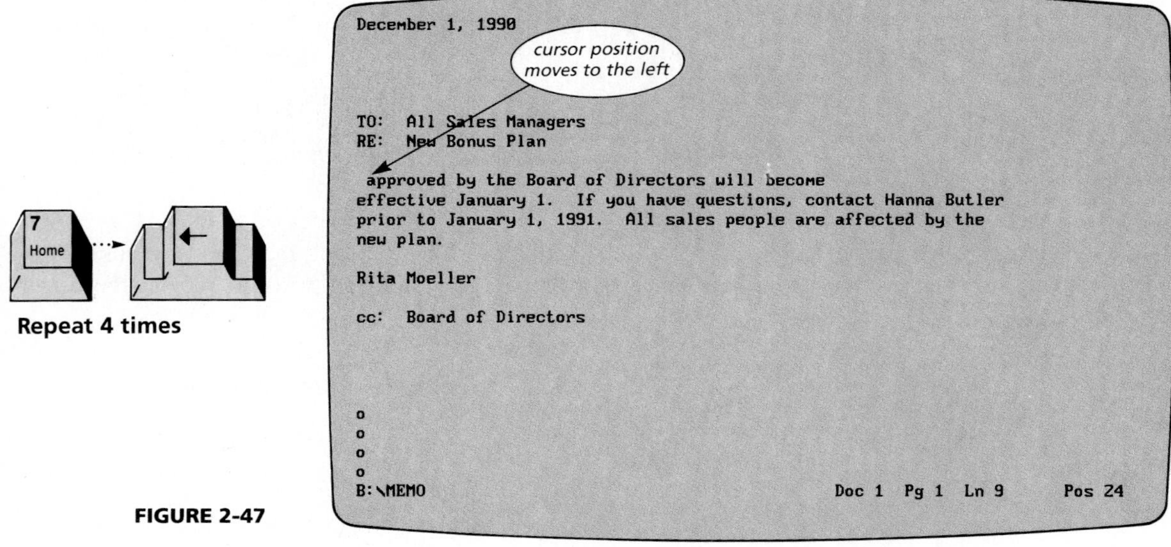
December 1, 1990
cursor position moves to the left
TO: All Sales Managers
RE: New Bonus Plan
approved by the Board of Directors will become
effective January 1. If you have questions, contact Hanna Butler
prior to January 1, 1991. All sales people are affected by the
new plan.
Rita Moeller
cc: Board of Directors
B:\MEMO
Doc 1 Pg 1 Ln 9 Pos 24
7
Home
Repeat 4 times

**FIGURE 2-47**

## Deleting One Block at a Time

Sometimes you may wish to delete an entire block of text. The **Block** feature highlights an area or "block" of text, thereby isolating that text from the rest of the document. Once the desired text is highlighted you can invoke the desired function.

Press Home, Home, Up Arrow to move the cursor to the top of your document (page 1, line 1). Press the Esc key, then the Down Arrow ↓ key, moving the cursor to page 1, line 9.

Look at the template next to the F4 key. You see the word Block in blue. Hold down the Alt key and press the F4 key (step 1 in Figure 2-48). The "Block on" message blinks in the lower left corner of your screen. To highlight text you must move the cursor in any of the ways you have learned in this project (step 2 in Figure 2-48). For example, press the Right Arrow → key and as you continue to press it, you see the word "The" highlighted. To highlight one *word* at a time, hold down the Ctrl key and while holding it, press the Right Arrow → key two or three times. Notice that words are highlighted one at a time. Press Down Arrow ↓ and notice that you can highlight one line at a time. Move the cursor to line 12, position 19, thereby highlighting the entire paragraph. Figure 2-49 shows how the entire paragraph should be highlighted.

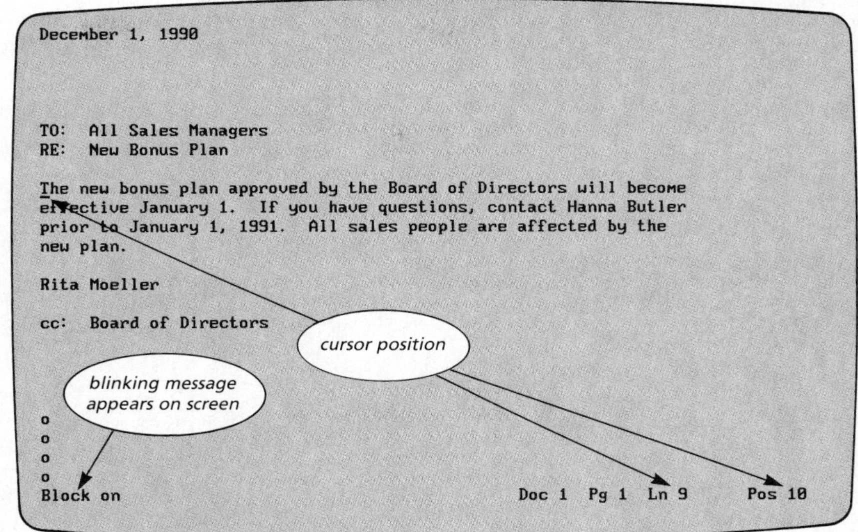
December 1, 1990
TO: All Sales Managers
RE: New Bonus Plan
The new bonus plan approved by the Board of Directors will become effective January 1. If you have questions, contact Hanna Butler prior to January 1, 1991. All sales people are affected by the new plan.
Rita Moeller
cc: Board of Directors
cursor position
blinking message appears on screen
Block on
Doc 1 Pg 1 Ln 9 Pos 10

**Step 1: Invoke Block on** **Step 2: Use cursor movements to highlight paragraph**

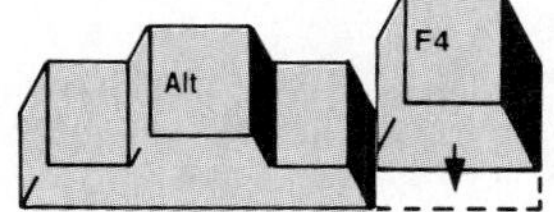
Alt
F4

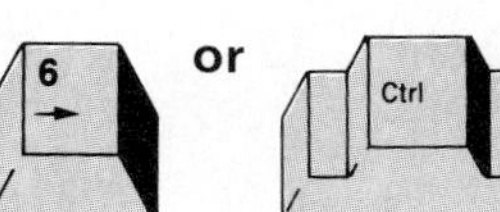
6
or

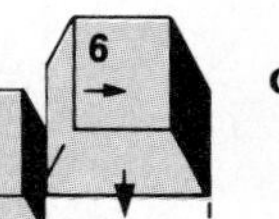
Ctrl
6

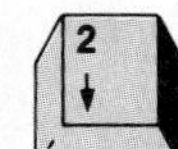
or
2

**FIGURE 2-48**

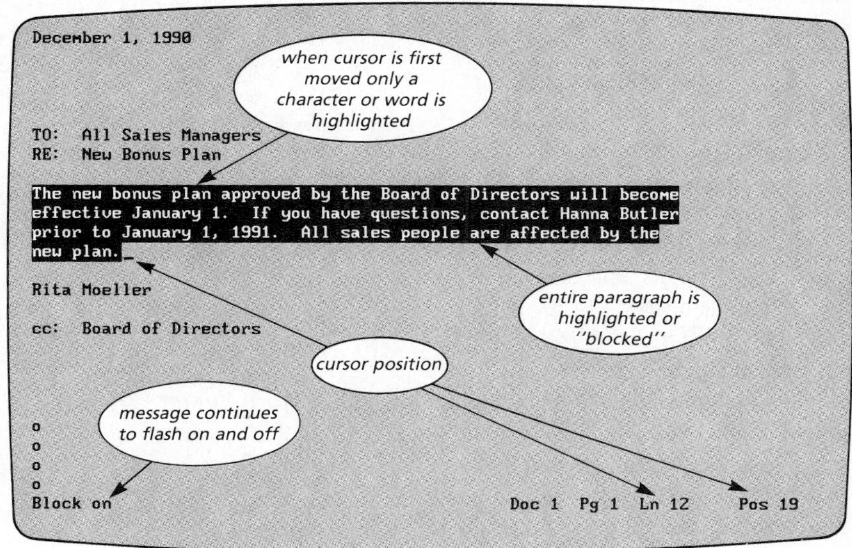
December 1, 1990
when cursor is first moved only a character or word is highlighted
TO: All Sales Managers
RE: New Bonus Plan
The new bonus plan approved by the Board of Directors will become effective January 1. If you have questions, contact Hanna Butler prior to January 1, 1991. All sales people are affected by the new plan.
Rita Moeller
cc: Board of Directors
entire paragraph is highlighted or "blocked"
cursor position
message continues to flash on and off
Block on
Doc 1 Pg 1 Ln 12 Pos 19

**FIGURE 2-49**

Now that the desired text is highlighted, press the Del key. Figure 2-50 shows that when you do, the message "Delete Block (Y/N)? N" appears at the bottom left corner of the screen. Delete the block of text you have highlighted by typing the letter Y. Restore the deleted text by pressing the F1 key. The deleted text is highlighted again. Press the number 1 and the text is restored.

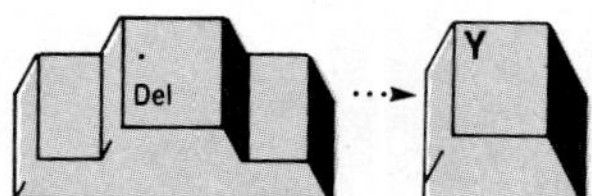
Del
Y

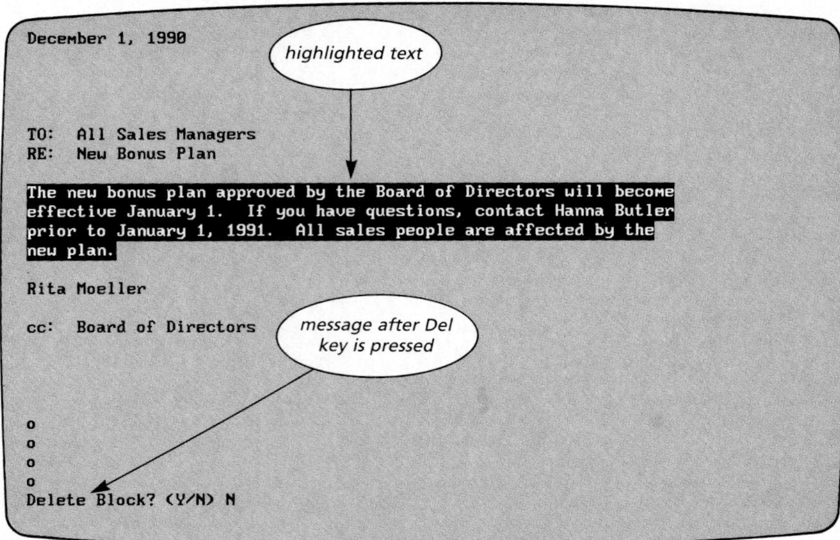
December 1, 1990
highlighted text
TO: All Sales Managers
RE: New Bonus Plan
The new bonus plan approved by the Board of Directors will become effective January 1. If you have questions, contact Hanna Butler prior to January 1, 1991. All sales people are affected by the new plan.
Rita Moeller
cc: Board of Directors
message after Del key is pressed
Delete Block? (Y/N) N

FIGURE 2-50

## EXITING PROJECT 2

Move the cursor to the top of the document by pressing Home, Home, Up Arrow. Look at the template next to the F7 key. Notice the word Exit in black. Press the F7 key (step 1 in Figure 2-51). The message "Save Document? (Y/N) Y" is shown in the lower left corner of the screen.

The (Y/N) indicates that if you press Y for yes, you would like to save the document. If you press N for no, you do not wish to save the document. The Y outside the brackets indicates that the default response to this question is yes, which means that if you press either the Enter key or the spacebar the software will process yes as your answer. In this project you altered the document since you last saved it to the disk. To save this latest version you should replace the old document with the newly revised version. To save the new version and replace the old version, press Y for yes (step 2 in Figure 2-51).

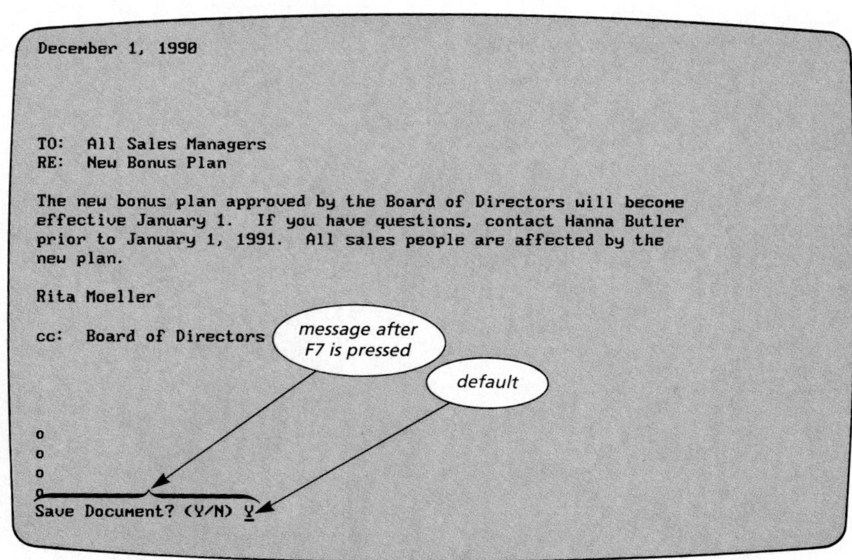
December 1, 1990
TO: All Sales Managers
RE: New Bonus Plan
The new bonus plan approved by the Board of Directors will become effective January 1. If you have questions, contact Hanna Butler prior to January 1, 1991. All sales people are affected by the new plan.
Rita Moeller
cc: Board of Directors
message after F7 is pressed
default
Save Document? (Y/N) Y

Step 1: Invoke Exit

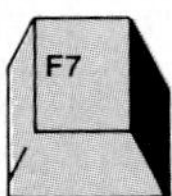
F7

Step 2: Save the document

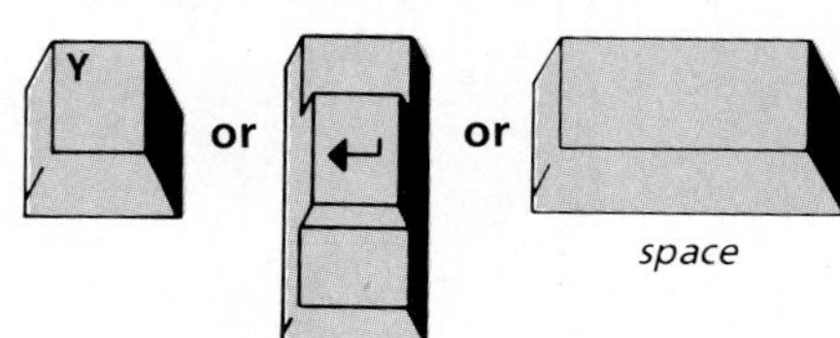
Y
or
or
space

FIGURE 2-51

Figure 2-52 shows that the message "Document to be Saved: B:\MEMO" appears at the bottom of the screen. It is not necessary to type MEMO again. Just press the Enter ↵ key. WordPerfect then presents the message "Replace B:\MEMO? (Y/N) N" (Figure 2-53). Type the letter Y. The light on drive B turns on, indicating that the document is being saved in its new form to the disk. Next, a message "Exit WP? (Y/N) N" appears (Figure 2-54). Type the letter Y. (If you failed to complete the printing of the document you may see the message "Cancel all print jobs (Y/N)? N" If this appears, type the letter Y for yes.)

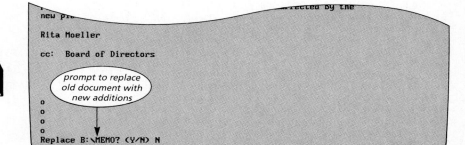

As you learned in Project 1, to exit properly we must return to the DOS prompt. After you have typed the letter Y, the message "Insert COMMAND.COM disk in drive A and strike any key when ready" appears on the screen. On some copies of the training version or if you have a hard disk system, the DOS prompt will appear immediately and you will not see the message. If you see the message, take your WordPerfect training version out of drive A and insert your DOS disk. Press any key. You then see the DOS prompt indicating that WordPerfect is no longer in main memory.

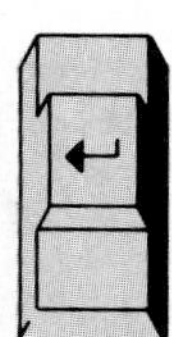

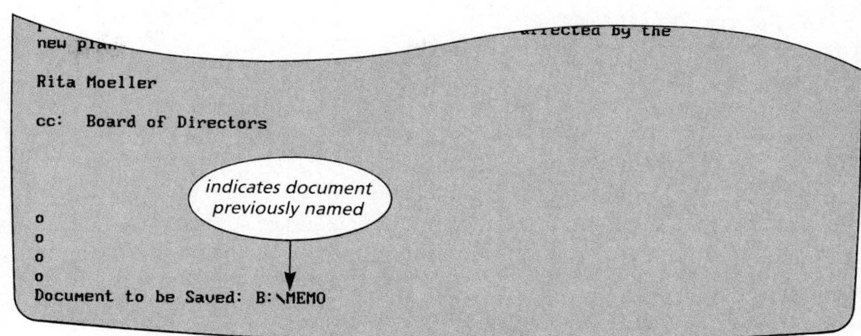
Rita Moeller
cc: Board of Directors
indicates document previously named
Document to be Saved: B:\MEMO

FIGURE 2-52

Rita Moeller
cc: Board of Directors
prompt to replace old document with new additions
Replace B:\MEMO? (Y/N) N

FIGURE 2-53

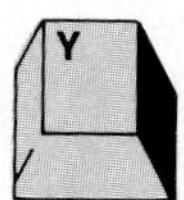

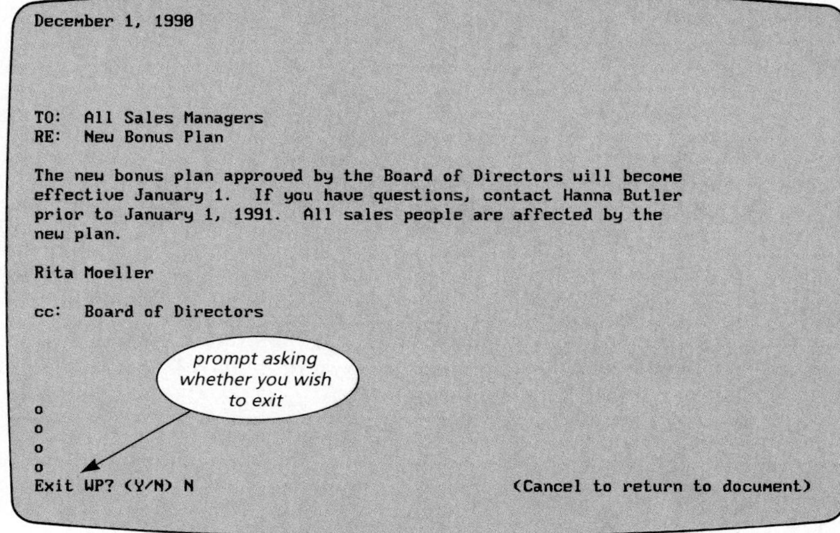
December 1, 1990
TO: All Sales Managers
RE: New Bonus Plan
The new bonus plan approved by the Board of Directors will become effective January 1. If you have questions, contact Hanna Butler prior to January 1, 1991. All sales people are affected by the new plan.
Rita Moeller
cc: Board of Directors
prompt asking whether you wish to exit
Exit WP? (Y/N) N
(Cancel to return to document)

FIGURE 2-54

## PROJECT SUMMARY

In Project 2, you learned how to type a document using the word wrap feature. After the document was typed, you learned more about the reveal codes, including how to read the [TAB] code, the hard return [HRt] code, and the soft return [SRt] code.

After saving the document, you printed it. To understand how the cursor moves through several pages of text, you added typing to page 3. Then you practiced several keystrokes that help to move the cursor quickly through a document. You learned that the screen can only show certain portions of the document at a time. You also learned how to edit the text by using several deletion keystrokes or functions.

The following is a list of the keystroke sequence we used in Project 2:

**SUMMARY OF KEYSTROKES—Project 2**

| STEPS | KEY(S) PRESSED | STEPS | KEY(S) PRESSED |
|---|---|---|---|
| 1 | b: [at the A> prompt] | 27 | ↵ |
| 2 | ↵ | 28 | ↵ |
| 3 | a:wp [at the B> prompt] | 29 | Rita Moeller |
| 4 | ↵ | 30 | ↵ |
| 5 | ↵ [at first introductory screen] | 31 | ↵ |
| 6 | ↵ [only if you see a second introductory screen] | 32 | cc: |
| 7 | December 1, 1990 | 33 | TAB |
| 8 | ↵ | 34 | Board of Directors |
| 9 | ↵ | 35 | ↵ |
| 10 | ↵ | 36 | F10 |
| 11 | ↵ | 37 | memo |
| 12 | ↵ | 38 | ↵ |
| 13 | Caps Lock | 39 | Shift-F7 |
| 14 | TO: | 40 | 1 |
| 15 | Caps Lock | 41 | [practice in text cursor movements and deleting text] |
| 16 | TAB | 42 | F7 |
| 17 | All Sales Managers | 43 | Y |
| 18 | ↵ | 44 | ↵ |
| 19 | Caps Lock | 45 | Y |
| 20 | RE: | 46 | Y |
| 21 | Caps Lock | 47 | [remove disk from drive A if you see prompt "Insert COMMAND.COM disk in drive A and strike any key when ready"] |
| 22 | TAB | | |
| 23 | New Bonus Plan | | |
| 24 | ↵ | | |
| 25 | ↵ | 48 | [put DOS disk into drive A] |
| 26 | The new bonus plan approved by the Board of Directors will become effective January 1. If you have questions, contact Hanna Butler prior to January 1, 1991. All sales people are affected by the new plan. | 49 | [press any key] |
| | | 50 | [remove disks from both drives] |

The following list summarizes the material covered in Project 2:

1. The **word wrap** function eliminates the need to press the Return (Enter) key until you come to the end of a paragraph, short line, or command, or if you want to insert a blank line.
2. A **soft return** has occurred when word wrap automatically moves text to the next line.
3. The **[SRt]** code is embedded in the document when a soft return occurs.
4. Pressing the Tab key embeds the **[TAB]** code into the document.
5. Cursor movement keys are the single keys or combinations of keys that move the cursor efficiently throughout the document (see Table 2-1).
6. The **Plus** and **Minus** keys on the numeric keypad perform the same functions as the Home, Up Arrow and Home, Down Arrow keys.
7. To move the cursor to line 1 of the next page, press the **PgDn** key. To move the cursor to line 1 of the previous page, press the **PgUp** key.
8. To move directly to a particular page, press Ctrl-Home, then enter the desired page number in response to the "**Go to**" message on the screen, and press Enter.
9. The **Esc** key lets you repeat a character or a cursor movement.
10. Deletion keys are the single keys or combinations of keys that delete a character, a word, a page, or blocks of text (see Table 2-2).
11. The **Backspace** key deletes the character or code to the left of the cursor.
12. The **Delete** key deletes the space or character directly above the cursor, moving to the right.
13. The **Block** function highlights a block of text in the document so that a specific function can be performed, such as deleting the text.

# STUDENT ASSIGNMENTS

## STUDENT ASSIGNMENT 1: True/False

**Instructions:** Circle T if the statement is true and F if the statement is false.

T F 1. When typing a paragraph at the computer, if you continue typing, the words will automatically wrap to the next line.

T F 2. When word wrap occurs, the code inserted in the document is [HRt].

T F 3. To view the reveal codes screen, press the Alt key, release it, and press F3.

T F 4. When a word is in black on the template, it signifies that the function key is to be pressed alone.

T F 5. To move the cursor to the bottom of the screen, press Home, Down Arrow.

T F 6. To move the cursor to the top of the current screen you press Home, Up Arrow.

T F 7. To move the cursor to the bottom of the document press the PgDn key.

T F 8. The Backspace key deletes the character or space above the cursor.

T F 9. To restore deleted text, press the F1 key, then 1.

## STUDENT ASSIGNMENT 2: Multiple Choice

**Instructions:** Circle the correct response.

1. To load WordPerfect into main memory, with the WordPerfect disk in drive A, type
   a. the characters WPC at the DOS A> prompt
   b. the word WORDPERFECT at the DOS A> prompt
   c. the characters a:wp at the DOS B> prompt
   d. the word WORDPERFECT at the DOS B> prompt
2. Which of the following is a valid file name?
   a. MEMO
   b. memo
   c. Memo
   d. all of the above
3. When typing a paragraph
   a. press the Enter key at the end of each sentence
   b. press the Enter key at the end of each line
   c. press the Enter key at the end of each paragraph
   d. press the Enter key at the end of the document
4. The command to move the cursor to line 1 of the next page is
   a. Home, Home, Down Arrow
   b. Home, Down Arrow
   c. End
   d. PgDn
5. The command to delete from the cursor to the end of the line is
   a. End
   b. Ctrl-End
   c. Delete
   d. Ctrl-Backspace
6. If the cursor is on line 54 of page 1, how many lines will the cursor move if you press the PgDn key?
   a. 1
   b. 54
   c. 53
   d. 2
7. To repeat a certain keystroke, you can press the Esc key before the keystroke. The default number of keystrokes is (Esc = ?)
   a. 10
   b. 9
   c. 8
   d. 6
8. The Cancel key can be used to restore a deletion. The Cancel key is
   a. Esc
   b. F1
   c. Shift-F1
   d. Alt-F1
9. The command Ctrl-PgDn can be used to delete
   a. the current page from the cursor down
   b. the entire current page, no matter where the cursor is
   c. 54 lines of type
   d. half a page

10. To invoke the Block function, press
    a. Ctrl-F4
    b. F4
    c. Shift-F4
    d. Alt-F4

## STUDENT ASSIGNMENT 3: Matching

**Instructions:** Put the appropriate number next to the words in the second column.

| | | |
|---|---|---|
| 1. PgDn | _____ | one word to the left |
| 2. Home, Home, Down Arrow | _____ | line 1 of previous page |
| 3. Right Arrow | _____ | line 1, page 3 |
| 4. Ctrl-Left Arrow | _____ | top of document |
| 5. Esc, Down Arrow | _____ | bottom of document |
| 6. PgUp | _____ | right end of line |
| 7. End | _____ | bottom line of current page |
| 8. Ctrl-Home, Down Arrow | _____ | line 1 of next page |
| 9. Ctrl-Home, 3, Enter | _____ | next right character |
| 10. Home, Home, Up Arrow | _____ | 8 lines down |

## STUDENT ASSIGNMENT 4: Fill in the Blanks

**Instructions:** Next to each keystroke or keystroke sequence, describe its effect.

| Keystroke(s) | Effect |
|---|---|
| 1. PgDn | ______________________ |
| 2. PgUp | ______________________ |
| 3. Right Arrow | ______________________ |
| 4. Left Arrow | ______________________ |
| 5. Down Arrow | ______________________ |
| 6. Up Arrow | ______________________ |
| 7. Home, Home, Up Arrow | ______________________ |
| 8. Home, Home, Down Arrow | ______________________ |
| 9. Ctrl-Left Arrow | ______________________ |
| 10. Ctrl-Right Arrow | ______________________ |
| 11. Home, Down Arrow | ______________________ |
| 12. Home, Up Arrow | ______________________ |
| 13. Home, Left Arrow | ______________________ |
| 14. Home, Right Arrow | ______________________ |

## STUDENT ASSIGNMENT 5: Fill in the Blanks

**Instructions:** Next to each delete function below, describe the effect of that deletion.

| Delete Function | Effect |
|---|---|
| 1. Backspace | ______________ |
| 2. Delete | ______________ |
| 3. Ctrl-Backspace | ______________ |
| 4. Ctrl-End | ______________ |
| 5. Ctrl-PgDn, Y | ______________ |
| 6. Alt-F4, Home, Home, Down arrow, Delete, Y | ______________ |
| 7. F1, 1 | ______________ |
| 8. Home, Backspace | ______________ |

## STUDENT ASSIGNMENT 6: Deleting Text

**Instructions:** The screen illustrates a memo that was prepared using WordPerfect. The words "approved by the Board of Directors" are to be deleted from the memo. Assume that the cursor is under the B in the word Board. Explain in detail the steps necessary to delete the words.

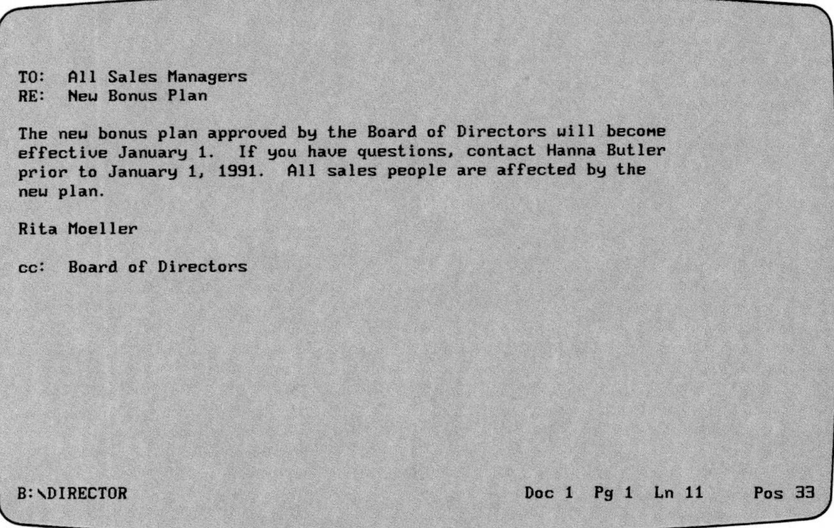
TO: All Sales Managers
RE: New Bonus Plan
The new bonus plan approved by the Board of Directors will become effective January 1. If you have questions, contact Hanna Butler prior to January 1, 1991. All sales people are affected by the new plan.
Rita Moeller
cc: Board of Directors
B:\DIRECTOR
Doc 1 Pg 1 Ln 11 Pos 33

Method of correction: ______________

______________

______________

______________

## STUDENT ASSIGNMENT 7: Reformatting the Text

**Instructions:** The screen illustrates a memo that was prepared using the word wrap feature in WordPerfect. Words were then deleted in the first line of the paragraph. Explain in detail the steps necessary to reformat the text so that all lines wrap at the margins.

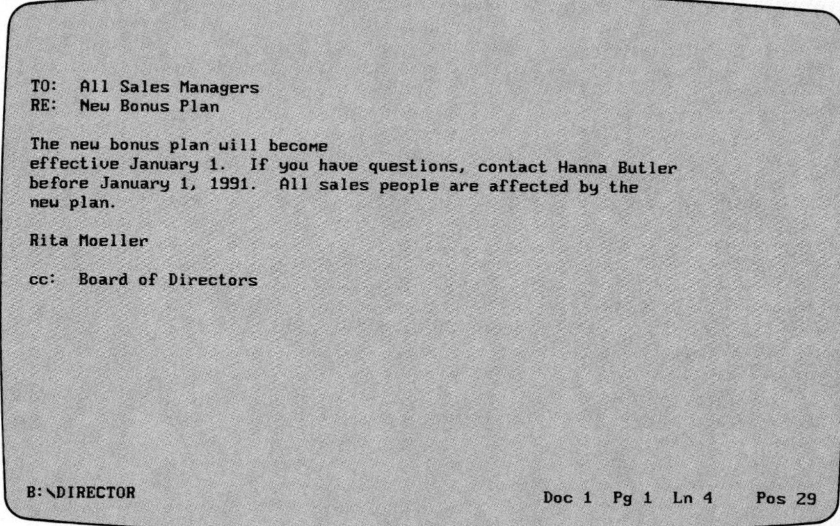

TO: All Sales Managers
RE: New Bonus Plan

The new bonus plan will become
effective January 1. If you have questions, contact Hanna Butler
before January 1, 1991. All sales people are affected by the
new plan.

Rita Moeller

cc: Board of Directors

B:\DIRECTOR Doc 1 Pg 1 Ln 4 Pos 29

Method of correction: ______________________________

______________________________

______________________________

______________________________

## STUDENT ASSIGNMENT 8: Modifying a WordPerfect Document

**Instructions:** Perform the following tasks.

1. Load DOS into main memory.
2. Load WordPerfect into main memory by inserting the WordPerfect diskette into drive A and putting a data disk into drive B. Type b:. At the B> prompt, type a:wp and press the Enter key.

Problem 1: Type the letter illustrated at right without corrections.

Problem 2: Make the corrections indicated and save the document. Name the document Director.

Problem 3: Print the document.

TO: All Sales Managers
RE: New Bonus Plan

The ~~bonus~~ new bonus plan ~~approved by the Board of Directors~~ will become
effective January 1. If you have questions, contact Hanna Butler
before ~~prior to~~ January 1, 1991. All sales people are affected by the
new plan.

Rita Moeller

cc: Board of Directors

## STUDENT ASSIGNMENT 9: Modifying a WordPerfect Document

**Instructions:** Perform the following tasks.

1. Load DOS into main memory.
2. Load WordPerfect into main memory by inserting the WordPerfect diskette into drive A, and putting a data disk into drive B. Type b:. At the B> prompt, type a:wp and press the Enter key.

Problem 1: Type the document illustrated below. Then make the following changes to the document. *NOTE:* In pencil, note the changes to the memo on this page before modifying the document using WordPerfect.

```
TO:  All Employees
FROM:  Personnel Department
SUBJECT:  Vacation Schedules

All employees that have been employed for more than one year are
eligible for two weeks vacation each year.  The vacations must be
taken during the months of June, July, or August.  You must
notify the Personnel Department at least 4 weeks in advance.  You
must also obtain approval from your immediate supervisor.

Janet Fisher
Personnel Administrator
```

1. Begin the memo on line 12 of the page.
2. Add the current date on the line above the word TO.
3. Delete the words "each year" from the second line of the body of the memo.
4. Insert the word May, a comma, and a space before the word June in the third line of the body of the memo.
5. Delete the sentence "You must notify the Personnel Department at least 4 weeks in advance."
6. Delete the word "also" from the last sentence.
7. Delete the period after the word "supervisor" in the last sentence and add these words to the last sentence: at least 4 weeks in advance.

Problem 2: Save the modified document. Name the document Schedule.2.

Problem 3: Print the modified document.

## STUDENT ASSIGNMENT 10: Modifying a WordPerfect Document

**Instructions:** Perform the following tasks.

1. Load DOS into main memory.
2. Load WordPerfect into main memory by inserting the WordPerfect diskette into drive A and putting a data disk into drive B. Type b:. At the B> prompt, type a:wp and press the Enter key.

```
DATE:     January 1, 1991
TO:  All Employees
FROM:  Personnel Department
SUBJECT:  Vacation Schedules

All employees that have been employed for more than one year are
eligible for two weeks vacation.  The vacations must be taken
during the months of May, June, July, or August.  You must obtain
approval from your immediate supervisor at least 4 weeks in
advance.

Janet Fisher
Personnel Administrator
```

Problem 1: Type the document illustrated below. Then make the following changes to the document. *NOTE:* In pencil, note the changes on the letter on this page before modifying the document using WordPerfect.

```
January 10, 1990



Ms. Roberta A. Morris
Editor, Computer Magazine
222 Edwin Drive
Arlington, VA 22289

Dear Ms. Morris:

Please enter my subscription to your magazine effective
immediately.  It is my understanding that you provide free
subscriptions to those employed in the computer industry.

Thank you for providing this valuable service to the computer
industry.

Sincerely,



Rodney C. Caine
Programmer/Analyst
Rockview International
111 Riverview Drive
Redlands, CA 92393
```

1. Begin the letter on line 8 of the page.
2. Change the name to Ms. Roberta A. Morrison.
3. Change the address to 222 Edwards Drive.
4. Delete the words "effective immediately" beginning on the first line of the text.
5. Add this sentence at the end of the first paragraph: I am currently employed as a programmer/analyst with Rockview International, Redlands, California.
6. Change the last sentence to: Thank you for providing this valuable service to those employed in the computer industry.

Problem 2: Save the modified document. Name it Morrison.

Problem 3: Print the modified document.

```
January 10, 1990



Ms. Roberta A. Morrison
Editor, Computer Magazine
222 Edwards Drive
Arlington, VA 22289

Dear Ms. Morris:

Please enter my subscription to your magazine.  It is my
understanding that you provide free subscriptions to those
employed in the computer industry.  I am currently employed as a
programmer/analyst with Rockview International, Redlands,
California.

Thank you for providing this valuable service to those employed
in the computer industry.

Sincerely,



Rodney C. Caine
Programmer/Analyst
Rockview International
111 Riverview Drive
Redlands, CA 92393
```

# PROJECT 3

## Learning Special Features

### Objectives

You will have mastered the material in this project when you can:

- Arrange text flush right and centered
- Underline and boldface text
- Insert text and typeover existing text
- Indent text using the indent key and the left/right indent function
- Save and replace a document

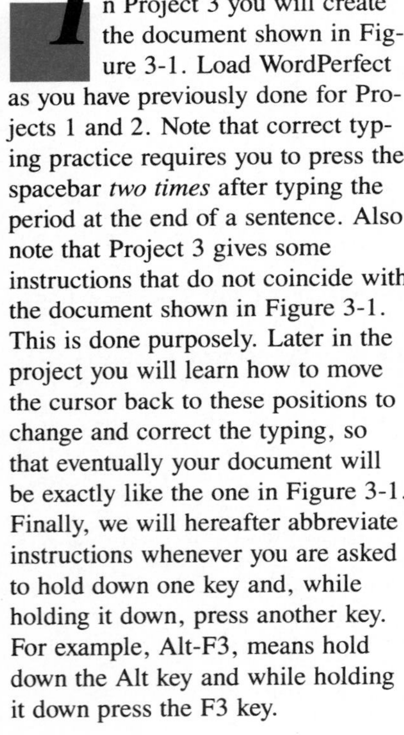

In Project 3 you will create the document shown in Figure 3-1. Load WordPerfect as you have previously done for Projects 1 and 2. Note that correct typing practice requires you to press the spacebar *two times* after typing the period at the end of a sentence. Also note that Project 3 gives some instructions that do not coincide with the document shown in Figure 3-1. This is done purposely. Later in the project you will learn how to move the cursor back to these positions to change and correct the typing, so that eventually your document will be exactly like the one in Figure 3-1. Finally, we will hereafter abbreviate instructions whenever you are asked to hold down one key and, while holding it down, press another key. For example, Alt-F3, means hold down the Alt key and while holding it down press the F3 key.

December 15, 1990

LICENSING AGREEMENT

You should **carefully** read the following terms and conditions. Your use of this program package indicates your acceptance of them. If you do not agree with them, you should not use this software package. Instead, you should return the package and your money will be returned to you.

PerSoft Inc. provides this program and licenses you to use it. You assume responsibility for the selection of this program to achieve your intended results. PerSoft Inc. assumes no responsibility for the results you obtain from the use of this software package.

**LICENSE**

You may perform the following functions:

a. Use the program on a single machine only. Use on more than one machine is considered "pirating" this software.

b. Copy the program into any machine readable or printed form for backup or modification purposes in support of your use of the program on a single machine. Certain programs from PerSoft Inc., however, may contain mechanisms to limit or inhibit copying. These programs are marked "copy protected."

c. Modify or merge the program into another PerSoft Inc. program for use on the single machine. Any portion of the program merged into another program will continue to be subject to the terms and conditions of this License.

You MAY NOT use, copy, modify, or transfer the program, in whole or in part, except as **expressly permitted** in this Licensing Agreement. PerSoft Inc. also reserves the right to do the following:

Withdraw your license if this software package is used for any illegal or immoral purpose which, in the sole judgment of PerSoft Inc., may damage the reputation of PerSoft Inc.

If you transfer possession of any copy, modification, or merged portion of the program to another person, **YOUR LICENSE IS AUTOMATICALLY TERMINATED.**

**FIGURE 3-1**

# MOVING TEXT FLUSH RIGHT

In Figure 3-1, notice that the date is against the right margin. The term to describe this placement of text is **flush right**. Look at the template next to the F6 key, as shown in Figure 3-2. You see the words Flush Right in blue. Press Alt-F6, (step 1 of Figure 3-3). The right margin defaults at position 74. Notice on the status line that the cursor is on position 75, just to the right of position 74. As you type, the text will move to the left of position 75. Type the date December 15, 1990. Figure 3-3 shows how the cursor is anchored at position 75 and how the letters move to the left as you type them. To end the Flush Right command press the Return key ↵ (step 2 of Figure 3-3). Next, insert two blank lines, by pressing Return twice ↵ ↵, placing the cursor on line 4, position 10.

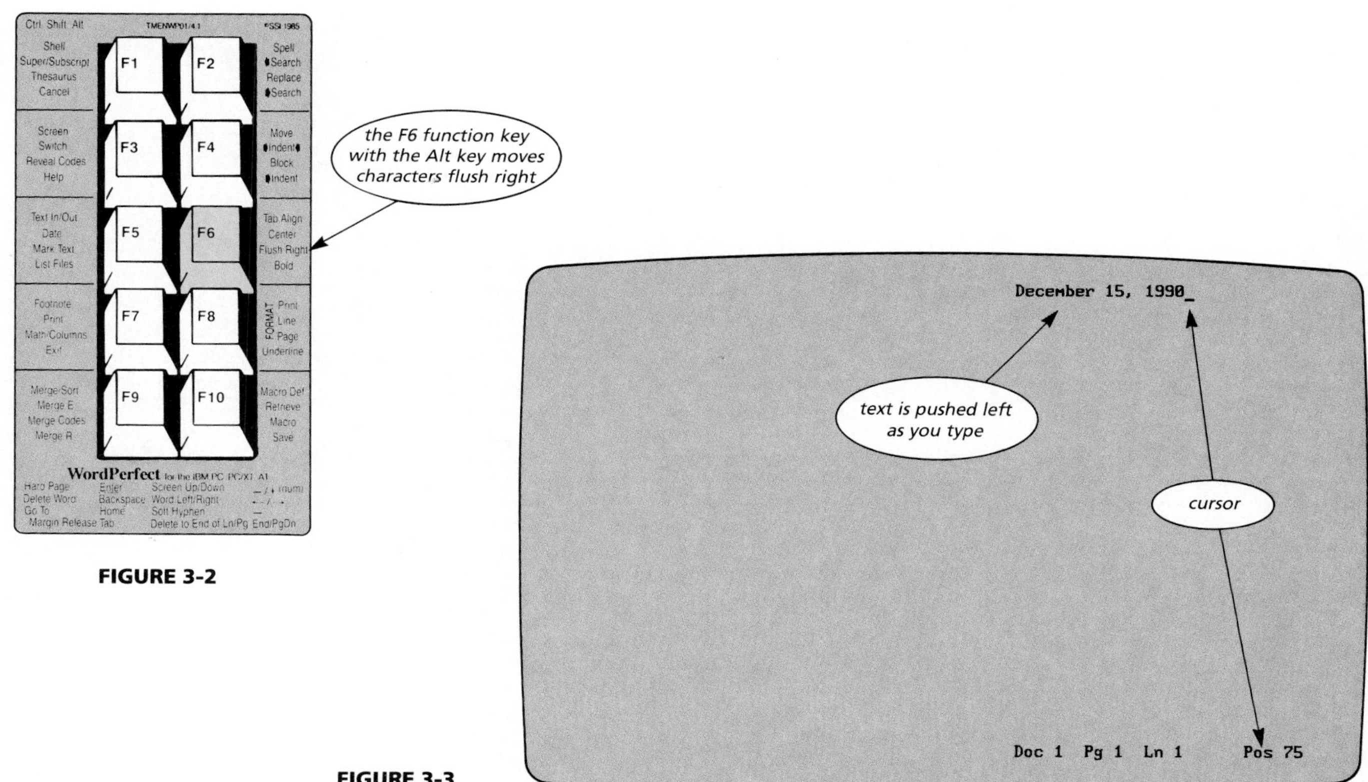


FIGURE 3-2

FIGURE 3-3

**Step 1: Align text flush right**

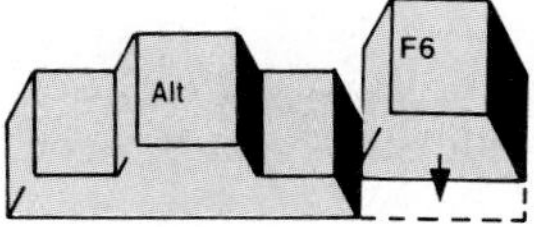


**Step 2: Stop aligning text flush right**

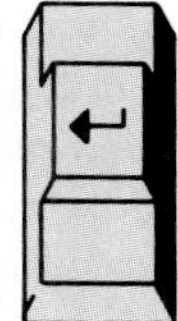

Now, view the code that is inserted when you align text flush right. Press Alt-F3 (step 1 of Figure 3-3). Figure 3-4 shows how the screen is divided. The lower screen reveals the codes that were embedded in your document. The first code you see is **[A]**, followed by the date. The capital [A] signifies the *beginning* of a Flush Right command. The A stands for text *aligned to the right*. After the date, notice a lowercase **[a]**, which signifies the end of a Flush Right command. After the [a] code is the [HRt] code, which indicates the hard return you pressed after typing the date. Then you see two more hard returns that inserted two blank lines. To exit the reveal codes screen and return to your typing screen, press the spacebar.

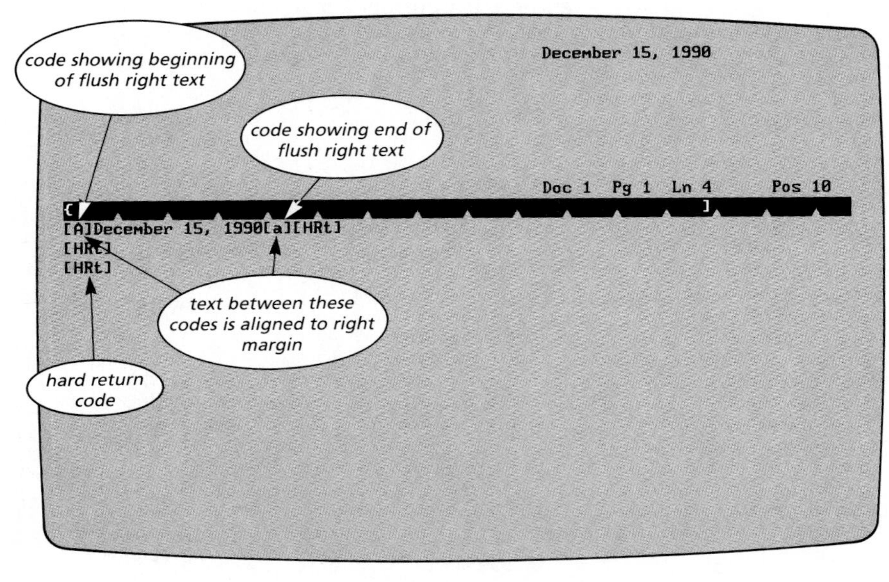


FIGURE 3-4

**Step 1: View reveal codes**

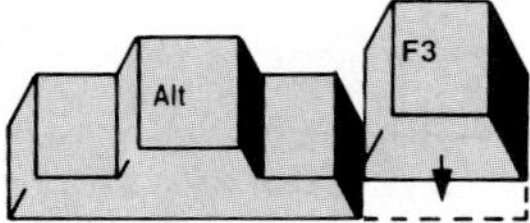


**Step 2: Exit reveal codes**

*space*

## CENTERING TEXT

**Center Text** is a useful command and one that is commonly used, such as when you wish to center a heading. In Projects 1 and 2, you learned that the margins in WordPerfect are preset at (or default to) position 10 at the left and position 74 at the right. Instead of figuring the middle of the text by hand, as you would with typewriting, when you invoke the center function in WordPerfect, the program does all the figuring automatically.

Look at the template next to the F6 key. You see the word Center in green. While holding down the Shift key, press the F6 key (step 1 of Figure 3-5). The status line indicates you are at position 42, which is the middle position between the margins of 10 and 74. Before you begin typing, note that the title in Figure 3-1 is in capital (uppercase) letters. To capitalize your title, press the Caps Lock key (step 2 of Figure 3-5). Look at the status line. Figure 3-5 shows that the letters Pos are now POS. This is your indication that anything you type now will be in uppercase letters. The Caps Lock key is a *toggle* key, which means you turn it off the same way you turn it on. In other words, you press it once to activate the capitalization function and press it again to turn it off. For practice you may want to press the Caps Lock key a few times.

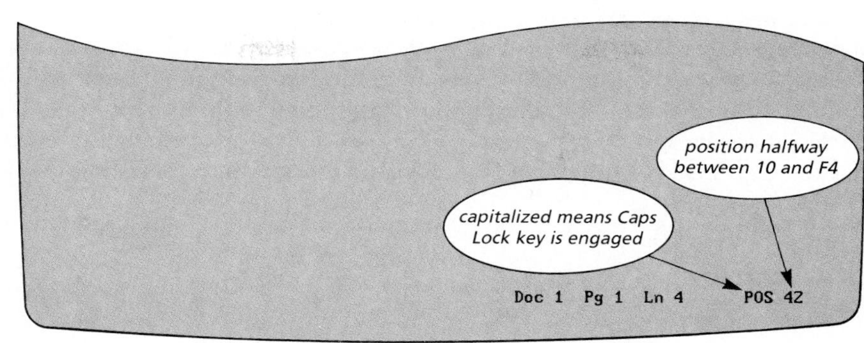


**FIGURE 3-5**

**Step 1: Center text** **Step 2: Capitalize text** **Step 3: Stop centering text**

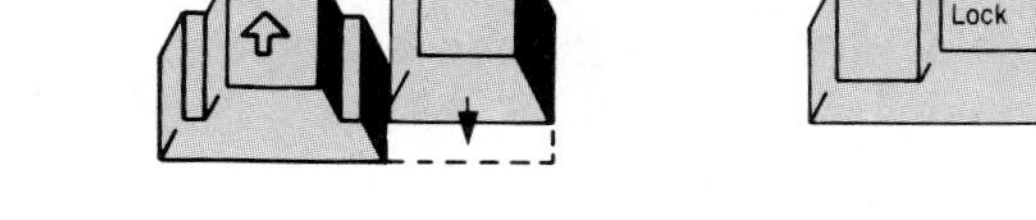


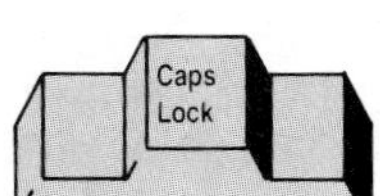


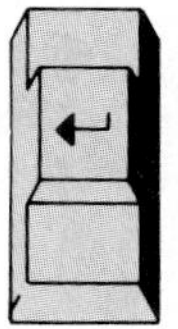

When you are ready to continue with the project, be sure you see POS on the status line, indicating that type will be in uppercase letters. Type the words LICENSING AGREEMENT and as you do, notice that the text is automatically centered. To end the centering of text, press the Return key ↵ (step 3 in Figure 3-5). To insert a blank line, press the Return key one more time ↵, placing the cursor on line 6, position 10.

Now, to see the codes that are embedded when you use the centering function, hold down the Alt key and press the F3 key (step 1 of Figure 3-6). Figure 3-6 shows the [HRt] code that you inserted before you centered the text.

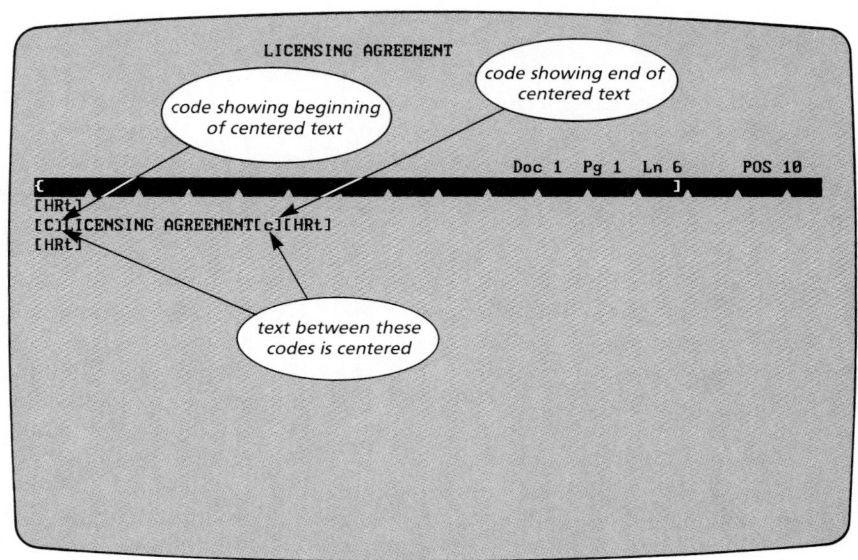


**FIGURE 3-6**

**Step 1: View reveal codes** **Step 2: Exit reveal codes** **Step 3: Stop capitalizing text**

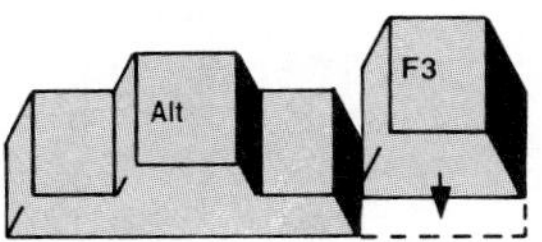


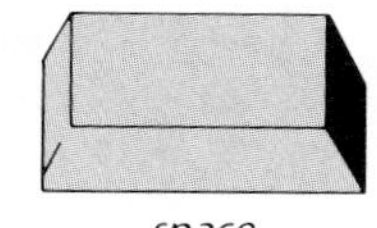

space

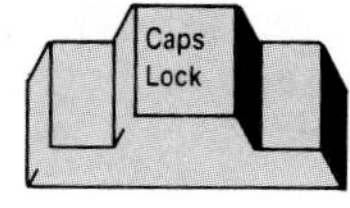

On the line where you centered text, you see the code **[C]**, indicating the beginning of centering. At the end of the text is the code **[c]** followed by another [HRt] code, indicating the end of centering. (Because centering is ended by pressing a hard return, which embeds the [c] code, if you were to look at the codes before you inserted the hard return, you would not see the [c] code.) In addition to the [HRt] after the [c] code you also see another [HRt] code, which inserted the blank line. To exit from the reveal codes, press the spacebar (step 2 in Figure 3-6). You are returned to your document. To turn off the capitalizing function, press the Caps Lock key (step 3 of Figure 3-6) and notice on the status line that POS is again Pos.

## BOLDFACING TEXT

Continue by typing the words You should, and then press the spacebar. The cursor is on line 6, position 21. Note that in Figure 3-1 the word "carefully" is in darker, bolder type. When letters are presented this way in a document, they are said to be **boldfaced** or in boldface type. Look at the template next to the F6 key. You see the word Bold in black. Press the F6 key (step 1 of Figure 3-7) and as you press it look at the position number. If you have a monochrome monitor, the number itself becomes bolder. If you have a color monitor, the number changes to a different color. For practice, press the F6 key several times while watching the position number on the status line.

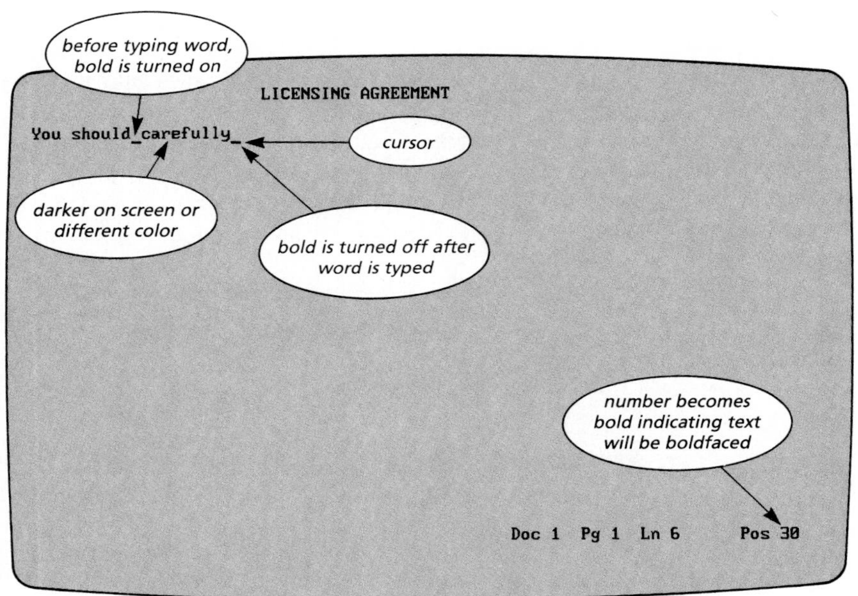


**FIGURE 3-7**

**Step 1: Boldface text**

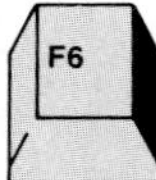


**Step 2: Stop boldfacing text**

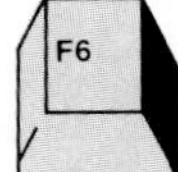

Be sure that the Bold command is on, and type the next word in Figure 3-1, which is the word carefully. As shown in Figure 3-7 the cursor is on line 6, position 30. Because you only want one word boldfaced, press F6 again to turn off the Bold command (step 2 of Figure 3-7). To view the codes that are inserted when typing in boldface mode, press Alt-F3 (step 1 of Figure 3-8). Figure 3-8 illustrates that preceding the word carefully is the code **[B]**, indicating the beginning of boldfacing. At the end of the word carefully is the code **[b]**, indicating the end of boldfacing. When the document is printed, the printer reads the codes, and only the typing between the boldface codes will be in boldface. To exit from the reveal codes press the spacebar (step 2 of Figure 3-8), and you are returned to your document.

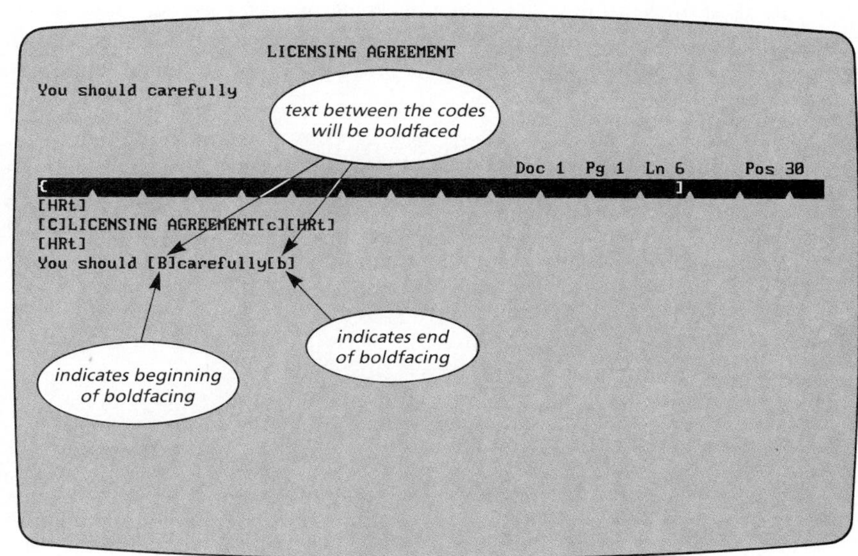


**FIGURE 3-8**

**Step 1: View reveal codes** **Step 2: Exit reveal codes**

Alt F3

*space*

To continue, press the spacebar one time and type these words:

read the following terms and conditions. Your use of this program package indicates your acceptance of them. If you do

Then press the spacebar. The cursor is now on line 8, position 27.

# UNDERLINING TEXT

At times, you may want your type to be underscored with a line. You would then want to use the **underline** function. Look at the template next to the F8 key. Note the word Underline in black. Press the F8 key (step 1 of Figure 3-9). The position number on the status line is underlined, indicating that any text you type now will be underlined. (If you have a color monitor, the color of the number will change.) For practice, press the F8 key several times, so that you can see how your monitor indicates that the words or letters you type will be underlined. Before you begin typing, be sure that the underline command is on. Type the word not. Then, before typing or even spacing, press the F8 key again and notice on the status line that the underline command is off (step 2 of Figure 3-9). The cursor is at position 30.

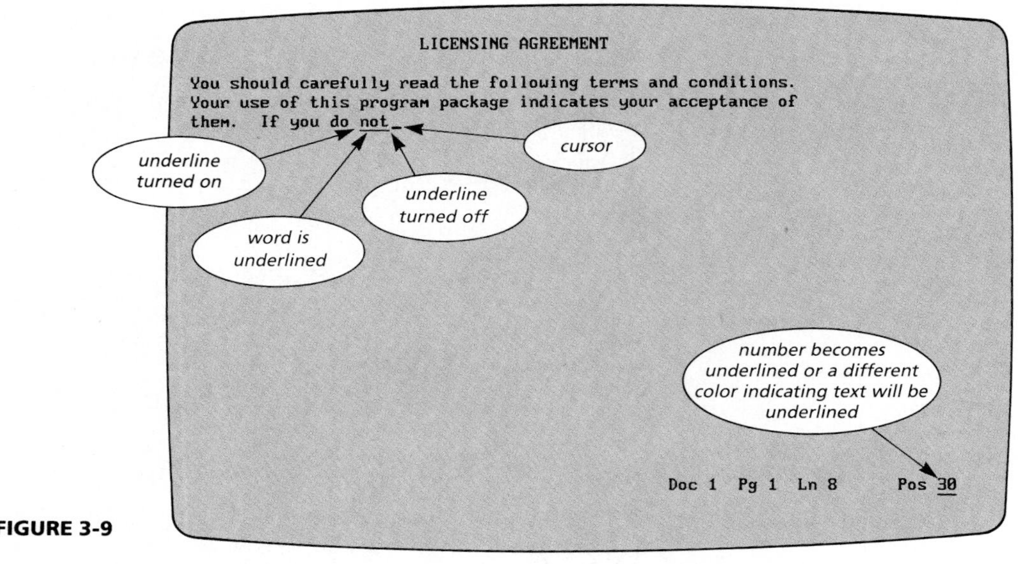


**FIGURE 3-9**

**Step 1: Underline text** **Step 2: Stop underlining text**

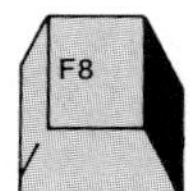


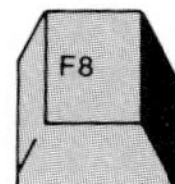


To view the codes used for underlining, press Alt-F3 (step 1 of Figure 3-10). Figure 3-10 shows in the lower screen that before the word not is the code **[U]**, indicating the beginning of underlining. After the word not is the code **[u]**, indicating the end of underlining. To exit from the reveal codes, press the spacebar, and you are back to your document.

To finish typing the paragraph, press the spacebar and, with the cursor at position 31, type these words:

agree with them, you should not use this software package. Instead, you should return the package and your money will be returned to you.

Next, press the return ↵ key twice, placing the cursor on line 12, position 10. Now type the second paragraph of Figure 3-1. Beginning on line 12, position 10, type these words:

PerSoft Inc. provides this program and licenses you to use it.

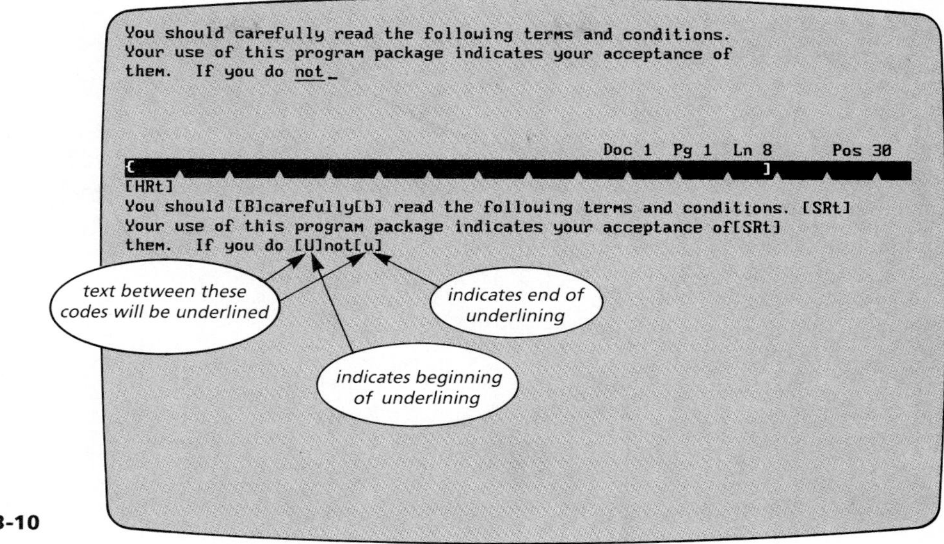
You should carefully read the following terms and conditions.
Your use of this program package indicates your acceptance of
them. If you do not_
Doc 1 Pg 1 Ln 8 Pos 30
[HRt]
You should [B]carefully[b] read the following terms and conditions. [SRt]
Your use of this program package indicates your acceptance of[SRt]
them. If you do [U]not[u]
text between these codes will be underlined
indicates end of underlining
indicates beginning of underlining

**FIGURE 3-10**

**Step 1: View reveal codes**

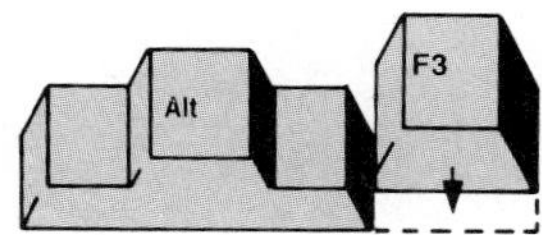
Alt
F3

**Step 2: Exit reveal codes**

space

After typing the period, press the spacebar twice, placing the cursor on line 12, position 74. Since the next word is to be underlined, press the F8 key (step 1 of Figure 3-11). Before you type, let's see how the codes appear. Press Alt-F3 (step 2 of Figure 3-11). The lower screen shows both the underline codes together, with only the cursor between them. Press the spacebar to exit from the reveal codes (step 3 of Figure 3-11), and type the word You.

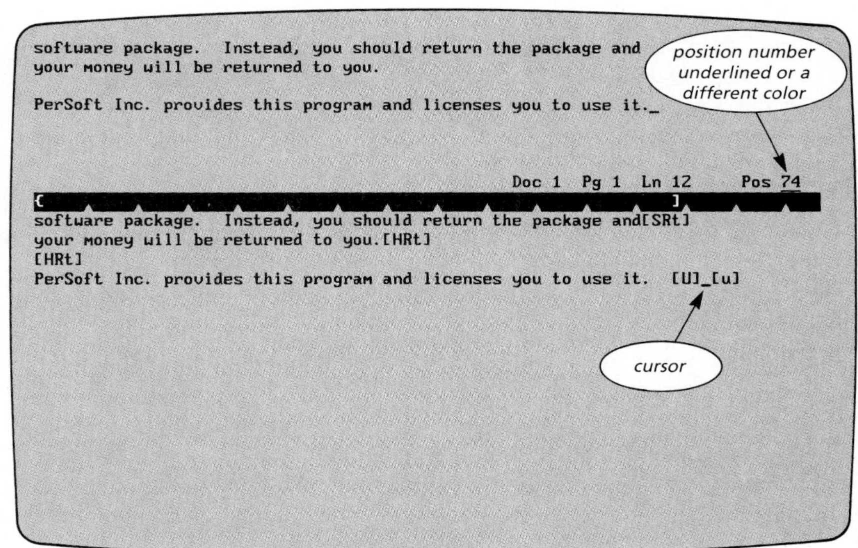
software package. Instead, you should return the package and
your money will be returned to you.
PerSoft Inc. provides this program and licenses you to use it._
position number underlined or a different color
Doc 1 Pg 1 Ln 12 Pos 74
software package. Instead, you should return the package and[SRt]
your money will be returned to you.[HRt]
[HRt]
PerSoft Inc. provides this program and licenses you to use it. [U]_[u]
cursor

**FIGURE 3-11**

**Step 1: Underline text**

F8

**Step 2: View reveal codes**

Alt F3

**Step 3: Exit reveal codes**

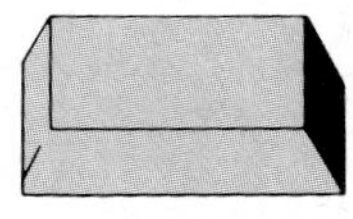
space

Before you turn off the underline command, look at the reveal codes again by pressing Alt-F3 (step 1 of Figure 3-12). Your screen will look like the one in Figure 3-12. Notice how the lowercase **[u]** code moved to the right and the word you typed appears between the codes. In addition, notice that because the Underline command is still turned on, the cursor is to the left of the [u] code. Press the spacebar to exit from the reveal codes (step 2 of Figure 3-12).

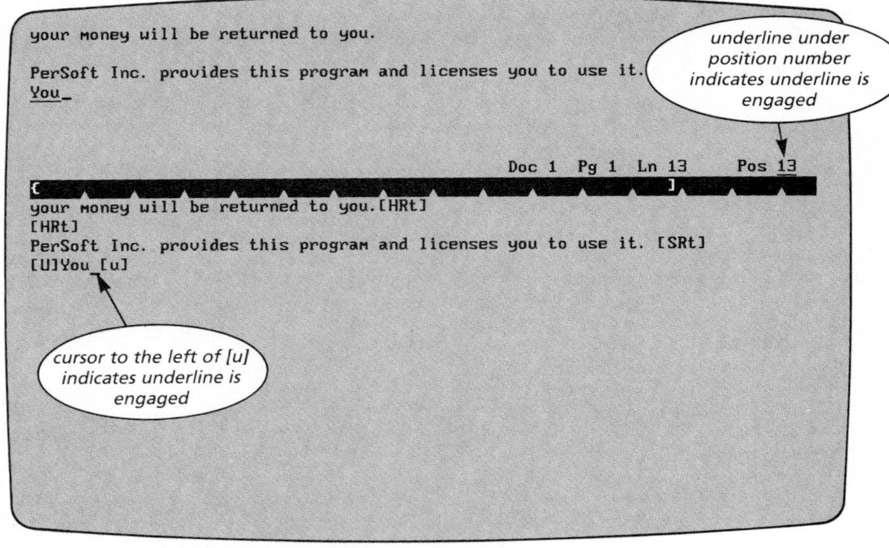
your money will be returned to you.
PerSoft Inc. provides this program and licenses you to use it.
You_
underline under position number indicates underline is engaged
Doc 1 Pg 1 Ln 13 Pos 13
your money will be returned to you.[HRt]
[HRt]
PerSoft Inc. provides this program and licenses you to use it. [SRt]
[U]You_[u]
cursor to the left of [u] indicates underline is engaged

**FIGURE 3-12**

**Step 1: View reveal codes**

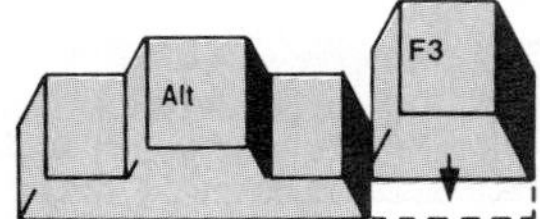
Alt
F3

**Step 2: Exit reveal codes**

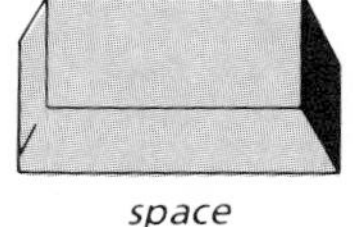
space

Press the F8 key to turn off the Underline command (step 1 of Figure 3-13). View the codes again by pressing Alt-F3 (step 2 of Figure 3-13). By turning off the Underline command, you have moved the cursor to the right of the [u] code. Press the spacebar to exit the reveal codes (step 3 of Figure 3-13).

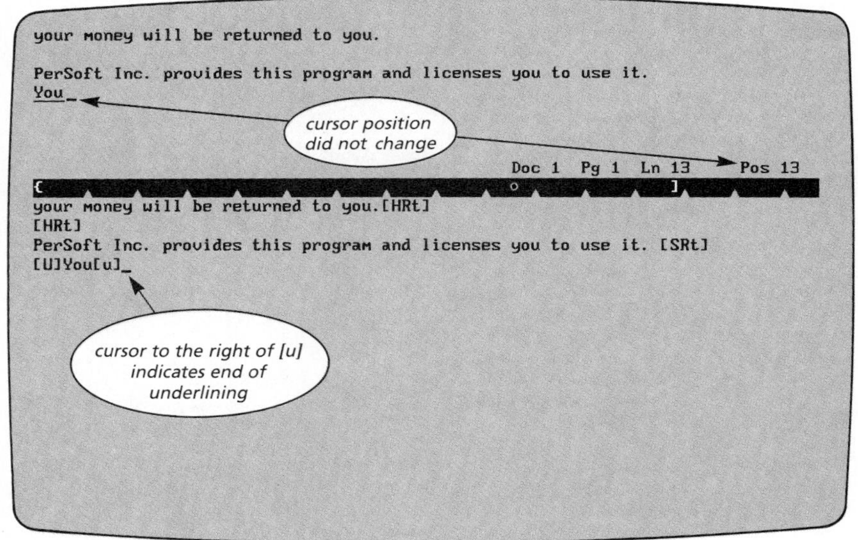
your money will be returned to you.
PerSoft Inc. provides this program and licenses you to use it.
You_
cursor position did not change
Doc 1 Pg 1 Ln 13 Pos 13
your money will be returned to you.[HRt]
[HRt]
PerSoft Inc. provides this program and licenses you to use it. [SRt]
[U]You[u]_
cursor to the right of [u] indicates end of underlining

**FIGURE 3-13**

**Step 1: Stop underlining text**

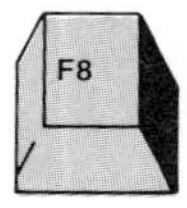
F8

**Step 2: View reveal codes**

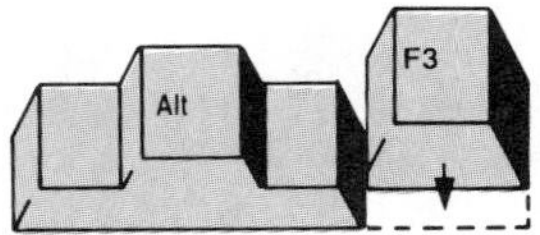
Alt
F3

**Step 3: Exit reveal codes**

space

# INSERTING TEXT

Sometimes you may wish to insert text between existing text. WordPerfect defaults to the **Insert Text** mode, which means that as you type, text will be inserted wherever the cursor is located.

Press the spacebar to put the cursor on line 13, position 14. Type these words:

assume responsibility for the selection of this program to achieve your intended results. PerSoft Inc. assumes no responsibility for the results you obtain from the use of this package.

When you finish, the cursor is on line 16, position 18. Compare what you typed to Figure 3-1. You see that you omitted the word software before the last word, package. Press the Left Arrow ← key to move the cursor to the left to position it under the p in the word package. Type the word software and as you do, notice that the word is inserted into the text and the word package is moved to the right (Figure 3-14). Finally, press the spacebar once to insert a space between the last two words of the paragraph.

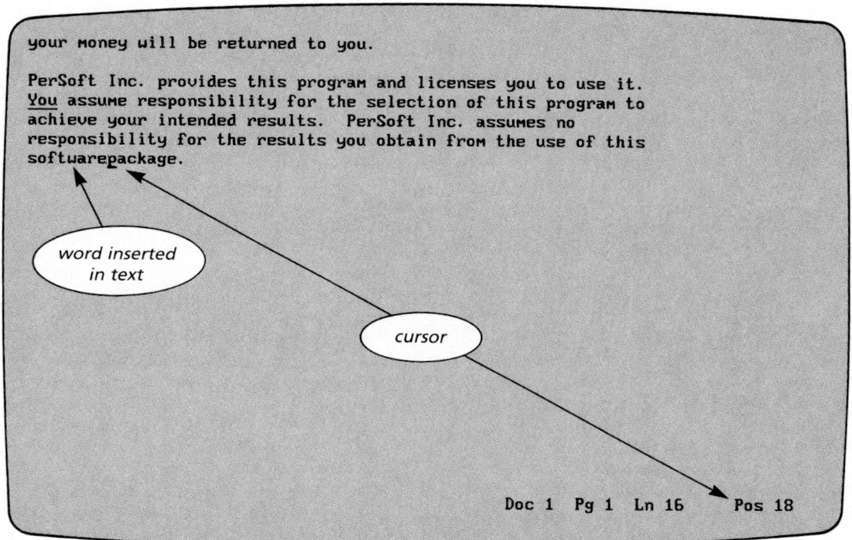


**FIGURE 3-14**

## USING THE BACKSPACE KEY TO CORRECT ERRORS

As you know, if you make a mistake in typing a word, you can press the Backspace key to delete the error. At other times you can use the Backspace key to correct other errors such as hard returns and spacing. For example, you may accidentally press the Return/Enter key ↵, thereby splitting lines of text on the screen. With the cursor still under the p in package, press the Return key ↵. Figure 3-15 shows how this splits the line. Press the Backspace key. Figure 3-16 shows how the word "package" returns to line 16.

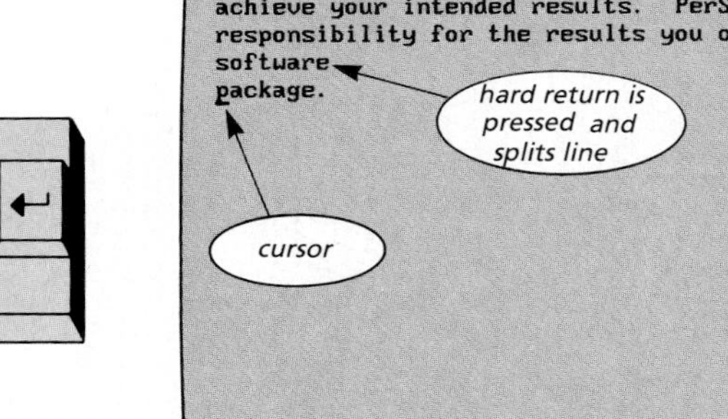

**FIGURE 3-15**

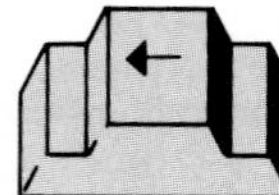

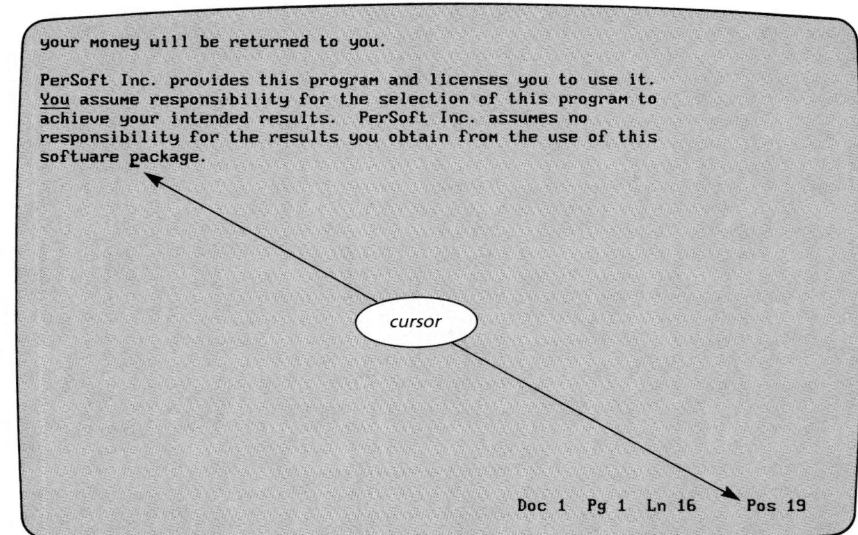


**FIGURE 3-16**

You can also use the Backspace key if you press the spacebar in error. Press the Spacebar two times (step 1 of Figure 3-17). To delete these extra spaces, press the Backspace key two times (step 2 of Figure 3-17) to return the word "package" to its original position.

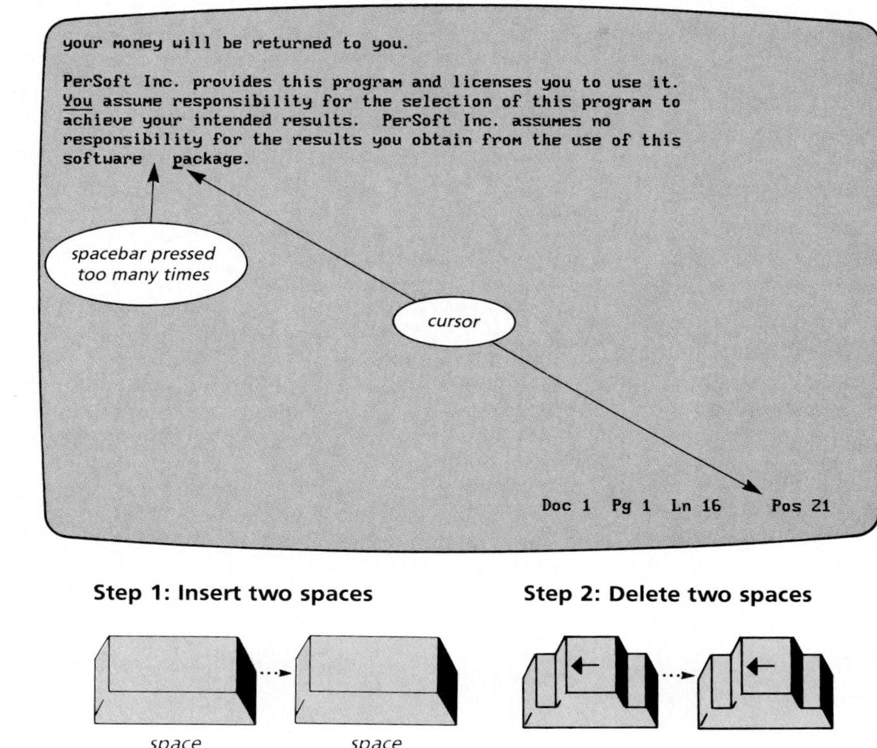


**FIGURE 3-17**

Because you wish to end the paragraph, press Home, then Right Arrow →, placing the cursor to the right of the period, on line 16, position 27. To end the paragraph, press Return ↵. To insert a blank line press Return ↵ again, placing the cursor on line 18, position 10.

## USING THE TYPEOVER COMMAND

As explained earlier, WordPerfect defaults to the Insert mode. However, if you wish to type over existing text instead of using the insert function, you must turn on the Typeover command. The Insert key is a toggle key, which means you turn it off the same way you turn it on.

Beginning at position 10 on line 18 type the word License. Comparing the word with the one in Figure 3-1 you note that it should have been typed in capital letters rather than upper and lowercase letters. One way to do this is to delete the word and then retype it completely. However, you can also use the **Typeover** mode to accomplish this.

Move the cursor to the left under the i in License as shown in Figure 3-18. Before you begin typing press the Caps Lock key, then press the Insert key (step 1 of Figure 3-18). At the bottom left corner of your screen you see the word "Typeover." It means that anything you type will type over existing text. Type the letters ICENSE and as you do notice how the lowercase letters become uppercase letters. When finished, press the Insert key to turn the Typeover command off. The word "Typeover" in the left corner of the screen disappears. Press the Caps Lock key to change from uppercase to lowercase typing (step 2 of Figure 3-18). Press the Return ↵ key to move the cursor to line 19, then press the Return ↵ key again to insert a blank line and move the cursor to line 20, position 10.

Type the words You may perform the following functions: followed by a hard return ↵. To insert a blank line press the hard return ↵ again, placing the cursor on line 22, position 10.

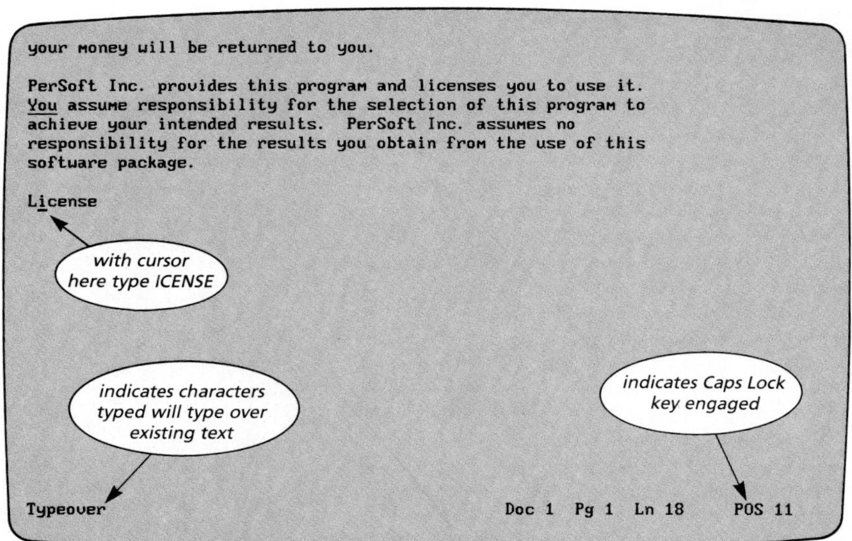


FIGURE 3-18

**Step 1: Type over text with capitalized letters**

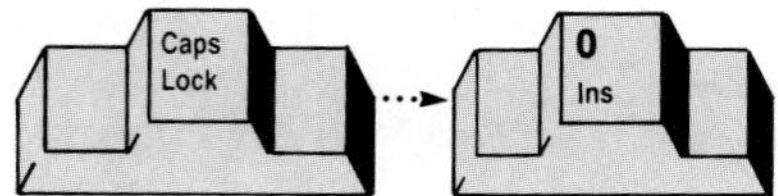


**Step 2: Return to Insert mode and stop capitalizing text**

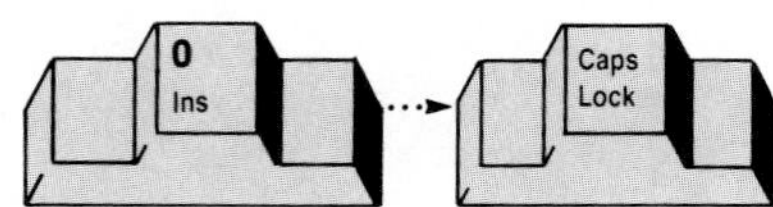


## USING THE INDENT KEY

Without actually changing the margin settings you may wish to change the left margin temporarily so that lines wrap to a specific position setting, making a wider margin, as shown in Figure 3-19. To accomplish this you must use the →**Indent** key, which is the F4 key. Look at the template next to the F4 key. You see the word →Indent in black. When you use the Indent key you will notice that the cursor always moves to where the Tabs are set. In WordPerfect the tabs setting defaults to every fifth position, or 0, 5, 10, 15, 20, and so on.

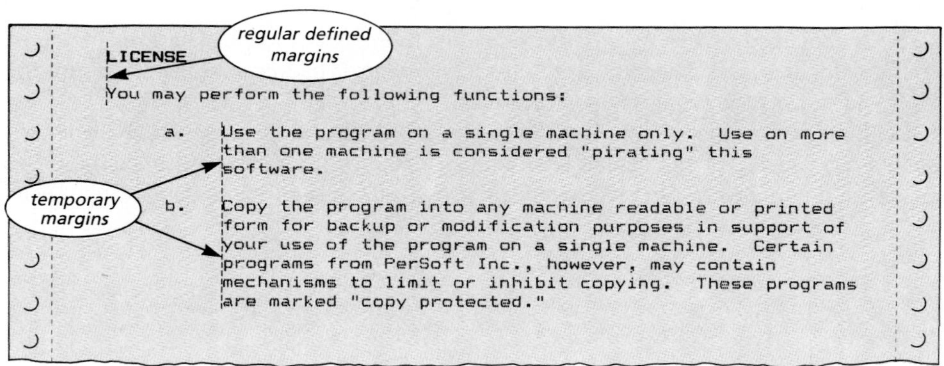


FIGURE 3-19

With the cursor at position 10, press the F4 key. The cursor moves to position 15, which is where the first tab is found to the right of the margin. At position 15 type a. then press the F4 key again. As shown in Figure 3-20, the cursor moves to position 20, which is now the new temporary left margin. All text typed will wrap around to position 20.

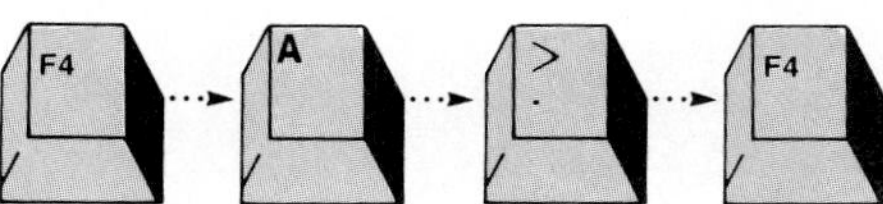


```
                                            December 15, 1990

                         LICENSING AGREEMENT

You should carefully read the following terms and conditions.
Your use of this program package indicates your acceptance of
them.  If you do not agree with them, you should not use this
software package.  Instead, you should return the package and
your money will be returned to you.

PerSoft Inc. provides this program and licenses you to use it.
You assume responsibility for the selection of this program to
achieve your intended results.  PerSoft Inc. assumes no
responsibility for the results you obtain from the use of this
software package.

LICENSE

You may perform the following functions:

     a.  _

                                            Doc 1  Pg 1  Ln 22      Pos 20
```

cursor

position of left temporary margin

**FIGURE 3-20**

To view the code that is embedded into the text when you press the Indent key, press Alt-F3. Figure 3-21 shows the reveal codes screen. You see the first [→Indent] code, then the letter a. Next you see the second [→Indent] code, which will change the left margin temporarily. Press the spacebar to exit from the reveal codes (step 2 of Figure 3-21).

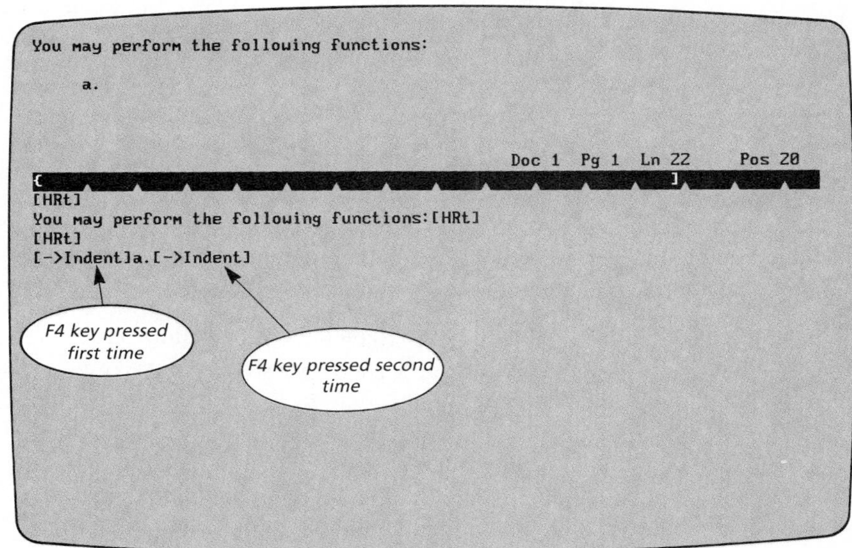


**FIGURE 3-21**

**Step 1: View reveal codes**

Alt F3

**Step 2: Exit reveal codes**

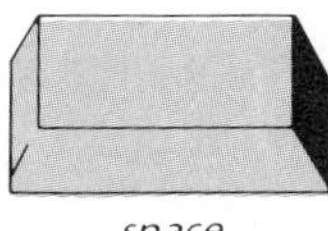

*space*

Beginning on line 22, position 20 type these lines:

Use the program on a single machine only. Use on more than one machine is considered "pirating" this software.

At the end of the first line when you begin typing the word than, notice that the word wraps to the next line, to position 20, which is the new temporary margin. After typing the word software, end indenting by pressing the Return key. The cursor moves to line 25, position 10, which is the default left margin.

To insert a blank line, press Return ↵ to move the cursor to line 26, position 10 (step 1 of Figure 3-22). Since you need to indent the next paragraph, press the F4 key and type b. then press the F4 key again (step 2 of Figure 3-22). With the cursor on position 20, type this paragraph:

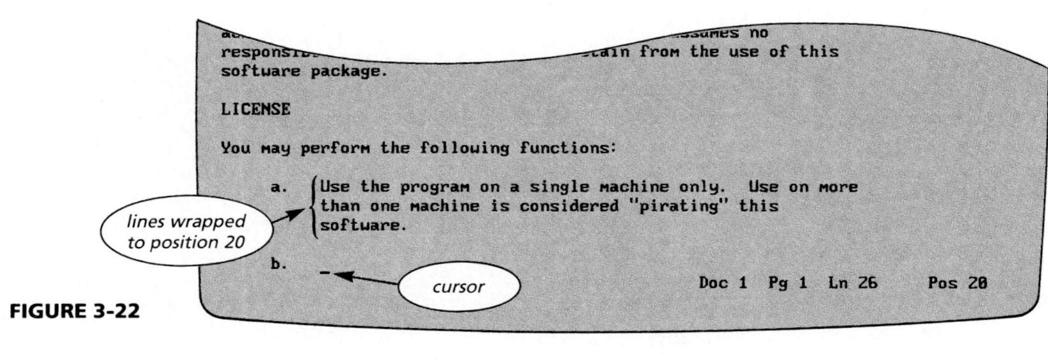


FIGURE 3-22

Step 1: Return to default margin

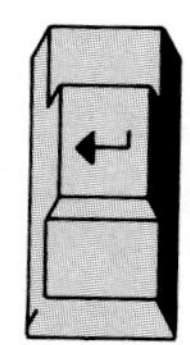

Step 2: Create temporary margin

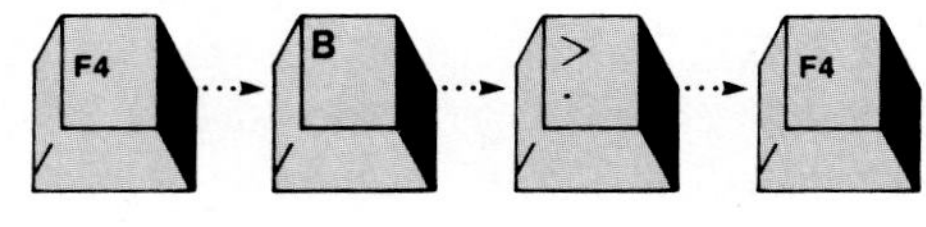


Copy the program into any machine readable or printed form for backup or modification purposes in support of your use of the program on a single machine. Certain programs from PerSoft Inc., however, may contain mechanisms to limit or inhibit copying. These programs are marked "copy protected."

When you have finished typing the paragraph the cursor will be on line 31, position 48. Press the Return key ↵ to end the indenting for this paragraph. Press the Return key ↵ again to insert a blank line, placing the cursor on line 33, position 10 (step 1 of Figure 3-23).

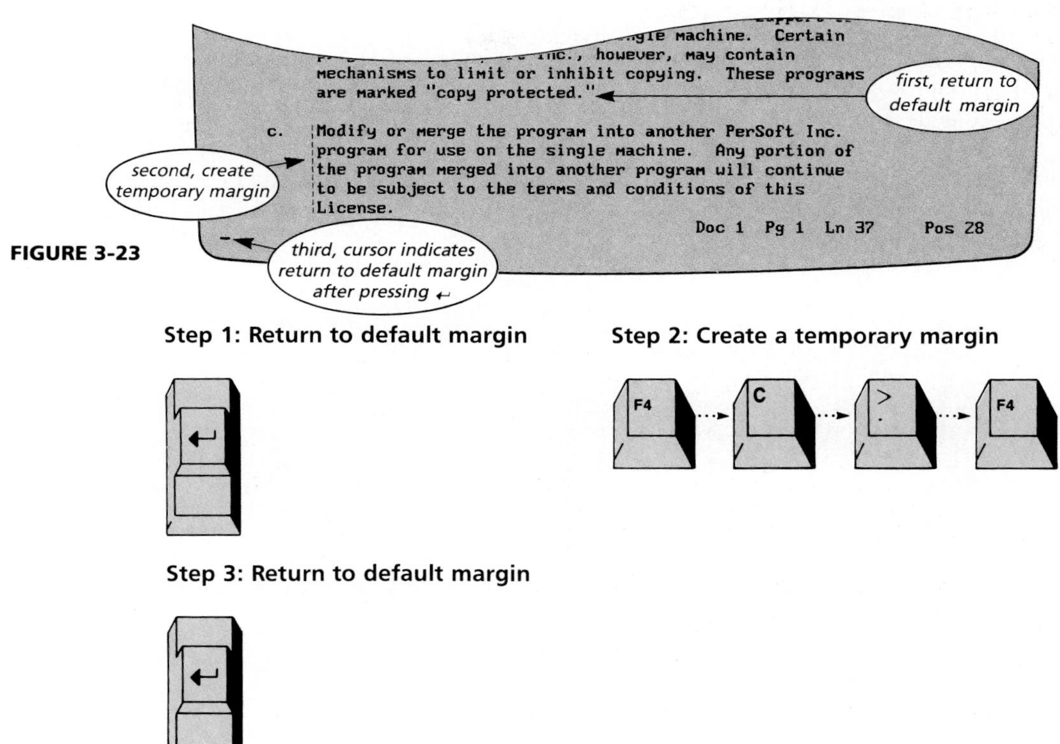


**FIGURE 3-23**

Before typing the last indented paragraph, press the F4 key and type c. then press the F4 key again (step 2 of Figure 3-23). Beginning on position 20, type this paragraph:

> Modify or merge the program into another PerSoft Inc. program for use on the single machine. Any portion of the program merged into another program will continue to be subject to the terms and conditions of this License.

Figure 3-23 shows that after you type the paragraph, the cursor is on line 37, position 28.

To end indenting the paragraph press the Return key ↵ (step 3 of Figure 3-23), then press the Return key ↵ again to insert a blank line.

With the cursor on Ln 39 Pos 10 type these words:

> You MAY NOT use, copy, modify, or transfer the program, in whole or in part, except as

Then press the spacebar, placing the cursor on line 40, position 32.

## BOLDFACING AND UNDERLINING AT THE SAME TIME

To emphasize important words in a document, you may wish to use boldface as well as underlining. Remember how to underline text: Press the F8 key. To boldface text, press the F6 key (step 1 of Figure 3-24). Type the words: expressly permitted. Figure 3-24 shows how your screen will look with the words both boldfaced and underlined (if you have a color screen, the words to be boldfaced and/or underlined appear in different colors). Before you resume typing you must turn off the Boldface and Underline commands. Press F8 to turn off the Underline, then press F6 to turn off the Boldface (step 2 of Figure 3-24).

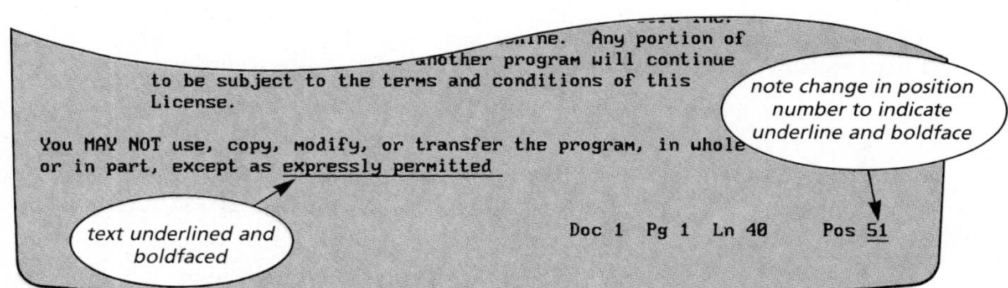


FIGURE 3-24

Step 1: Underline and Boldface text

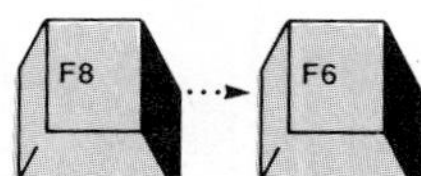

Step 2: Stop underlining and boldfacing

F8 F6

To view the codes in this document, press Alt-F3 (step 1 of Figure 3-25). Figure 3-25 shows both the underline [U][u] and boldface [B][b] codes at the beginning and end of the two words. Press the spacebar to exit from the reveal codes (step 2 of Figure 3-25).

Press the spacebar to insert a space after the word permitted and continue typing:

in this Licensing Agreement. PerSoft Inc. also reserves the right to do the following:

To end the paragraph press the Return key ↵ followed by another Return ↵ to insert a blank line. The cursor should now be on line 44, position 10.

## USING THE LEFT/RIGHT INDENT KEY

If you wish to define wider left and right margins temporarily, you can use the **Left/Right Indent** key. The Left/Right Indent key can be used for long quotes that will be indented from both the left and right margins. The left/right indent moves to where the tabs are currently set. When you use the left/right indent, the right margin will move in the same number of spaces as the left margin.

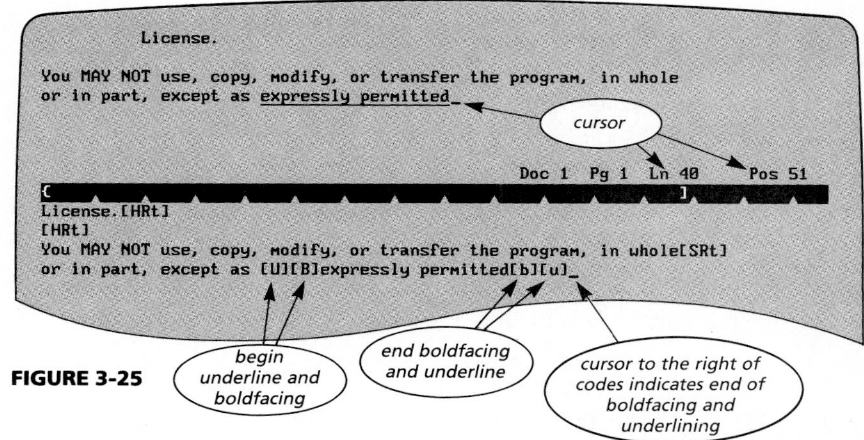
License.
You MAY NOT use, copy, modify, or transfer the program, in whole
or in part, except as expressly permitted_
cursor
Doc 1 Pg 1 Ln 40 Pos 51
License.[HRt]
[HRt]
You MAY NOT use, copy, modify, or transfer the program, in whole[SRt]
or in part, except as [U][B]expressly permitted[b][u]_
begin underline and boldfacing
end boldfacing and underline
cursor to the right of codes indicates end of boldfacing and underlining

FIGURE 3-25

Step 1: View reveal codes

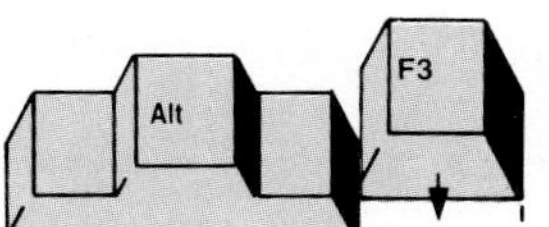
Alt
F3

Step 2: Exit reveal codes

space

Look at the template next to the F4 key. You see the word →**Indent**← in green. Press Shift-F4 (step 1 of Figure 3-26). To see the embedded code, press Alt-F3 (step 2 of Figure 3-26). In the lower screen shown in Figure 3-26 notice the code [→**Indent**←], indicating that any text that follows will be indented from both the left and right margins. To exit from the reveal codes, press the spacebar (step 3 of Figure 3-26).

Now type the left/right indented paragraph:

> Withdraw your license if this software package is used for any illegal or immoral purpose which, in the sole judgment of PerSoft Inc., may damage the reputation of PerSoft Inc.

When you finish typing this paragraph, the cursor is on line 47, position 27. To end the Left/Right Indent command, press the Return key ↵, then press the Return key ↵ again to insert a blank line, placing the cursor on line 49, position 10.

Beginning on line 49, position 10, type the last paragraph of the licensing agreement:

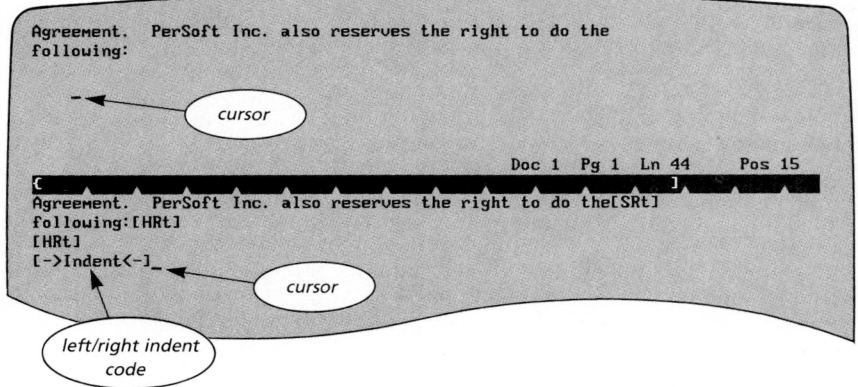
Agreement. PerSoft Inc. also reserves the right to do the
following:
cursor
Doc 1 Pg 1 Ln 44 Pos 15
Agreement. PerSoft Inc. also reserves the right to do the[SRt]
following:[HRt]
[HRt]
[->Indent<-]_
cursor
left/right indent code

FIGURE 3-26

Step 1: Indent text Step 2: View reveal codes

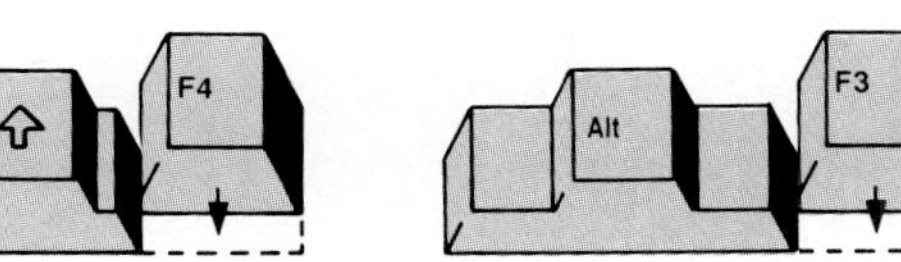
F4
Alt
F3

Step 3: Exit reveal codes

space

If you transfer possession of any copy, modification, or merged portion of the program to another person, YOUR LICENSE IS AUTOMATICALLY TERMINATED.

The entire document is now typed.

## SAVING A FILE TO THE DISK

It is necessary to save the document to disk so that it can be retrieved for printing or modification later. To save, follow the procedure you learned in Projects 1 and 2. Save this document under the name LICENSE.

## UNDERLINING AND BOLDFACING EXISTING TEXT

At the beginning of Project 3 you were told that you would be creating the document in Figure 3-1. If you compare the document in Figure 3-1 with your completed document as shown in Figure 3-27, you will notice the following differences:

1. In the title, the words LICENSING AGREEMENT are not underlined in Figure 3-27.
2. Farther down, the word LICENSE is not in boldface type.
3. The words MAY NOT are not underlined.
4. The last five words of the agreement are not in boldface type.

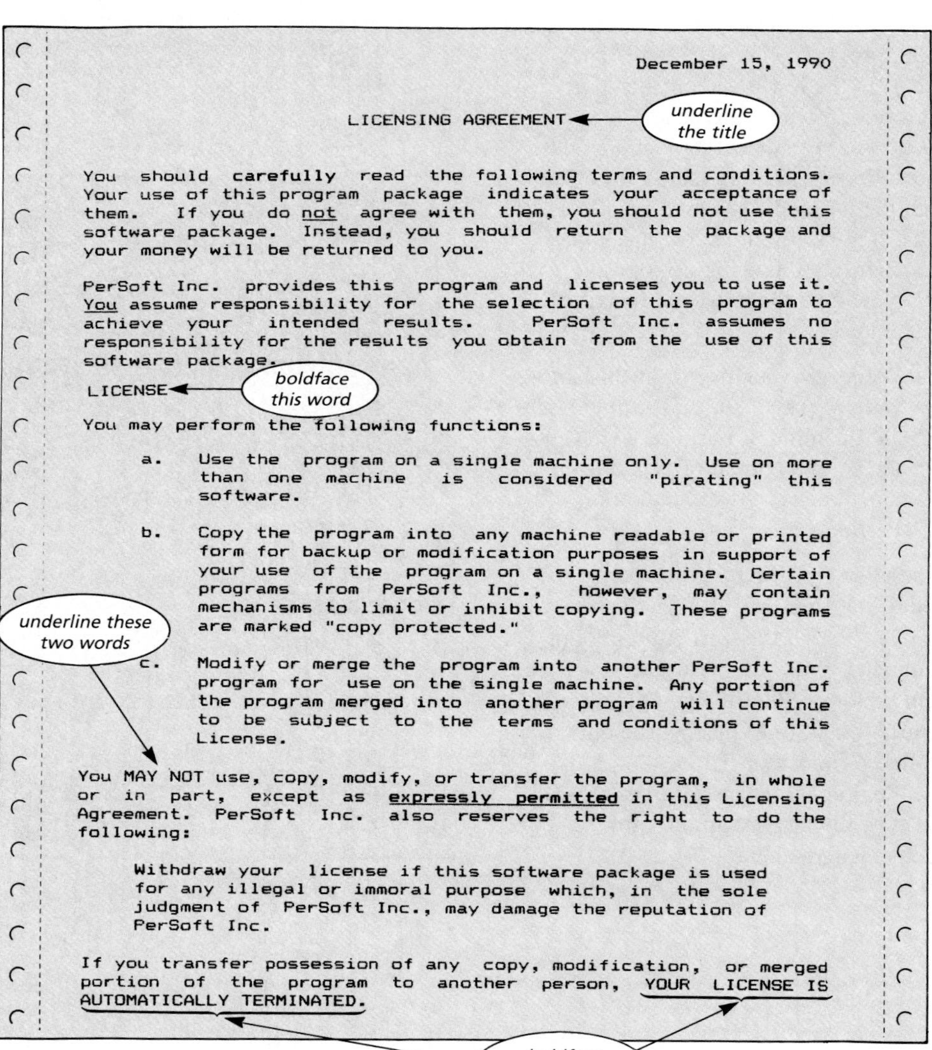

December 15, 1990

LICENSING AGREEMENT

You should **carefully** read the following terms and conditions. Your use of this program package indicates your acceptance of them. If you do <u>not</u> agree with them, you should not use this software package. Instead, you should return the package and your money will be returned to you.

PerSoft Inc. provides this program and licenses you to use it. <u>You</u> assume responsibility for the selection of this program to achieve your intended results. PerSoft Inc. assumes no responsibility for the results you obtain from the use of this software package.

LICENSE

You may perform the following functions:

a. Use the program on a single machine only. Use on more than one machine is considered "pirating" this software.

b. Copy the program into any machine readable or printed form for backup or modification purposes in support of your use of the program on a single machine. Certain programs from PerSoft Inc., however, may contain mechanisms to limit or inhibit copying. These programs are marked "copy protected."

c. Modify or merge the program into another PerSoft Inc. program for use on the single machine. Any portion of the program merged into another program will continue to be subject to the terms and conditions of this License.

You MAY NOT use, copy, modify, or transfer the program, in whole or in part, except as **<u>expressly permitted</u>** in this Licensing Agreement. PerSoft Inc. also reserves the right to do the following:

Withdraw your license if this software package is used for any illegal or immoral purpose which, in the sole judgment of PerSoft Inc., may damage the reputation of PerSoft Inc.

If you transfer possession of any copy, modification, or merged portion of the program to another person, YOUR LICENSE IS AUTOMATICALLY TERMINATED.



**FIGURE 3-27**

The comparison of the two figures shows that sometimes you need to boldface or underline *existing* text. It is not necessary to delete the text and retype it in boldface or underline mode. Move the cursor to the top of the document by pressing Home, Home, Up Arrow ↑. As the cursor moves to the top of the document, the word "Repositioning" appears in the lower left corner of the screen, advising you that the cursor is in the process of moving.

Move the cursor down so that it is under the L in LICENSING AGREEMENT. The cursor will be on line 4, position 33.

As we learned in Project 2, the block function highlights specified text, thereby isolating that text from the rest of the document. Once the desired text is highlighted you can perform the requested function. Here we use the **block** function to underline and then boldface a block of text.

Look at the template next to the F4 key. You see the word Block in blue. Press Alt-F4 (step 1 of Figure 3-28). The "Block on" message begins blinking in the lower left corner of the screen. To highlight or block the words LICENSING AGREEMENT, move the cursor to the right one character at a time with the Right Arrow → key, or move the cursor more quickly by pressing the Home key followed by the Right Arrow key → (step 2 of Figure 3-28). When the cursor is on position 52 just to the right of the letter T in AGREEMENT, the two words are blocked. You have now isolated these words from the rest of the document and can underline them. As noted on the template, the F8 key is used for underlining. Press the F8 key (step 3 of Figure 3-28). When you do, notice that the "Block on" message turns off on the screen and at the same time the block of text is underlined.

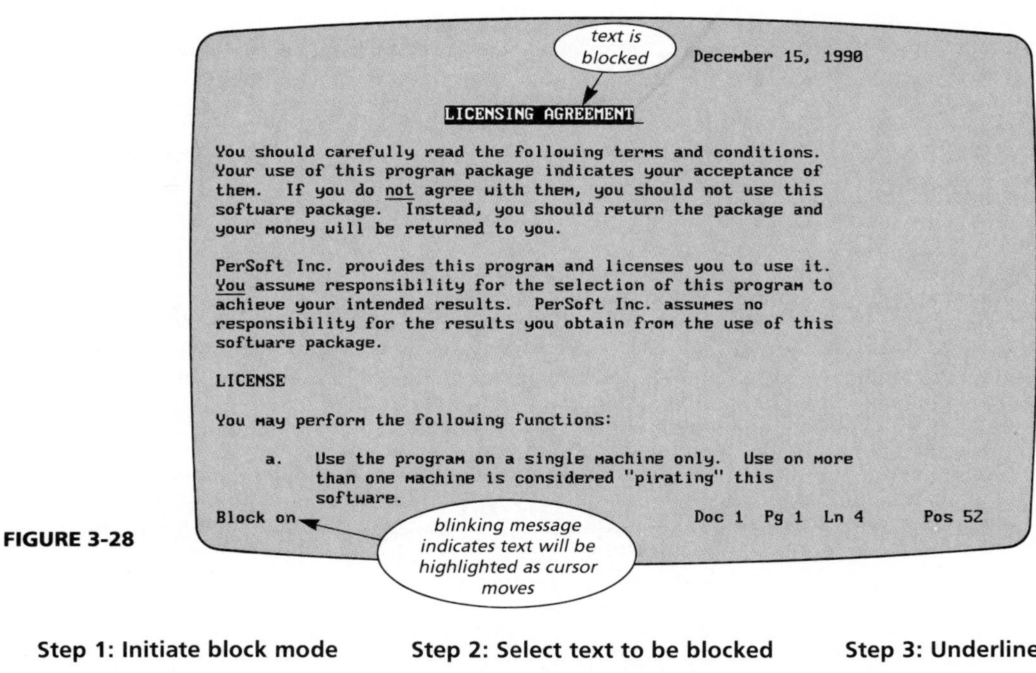


**FIGURE 3-28**

**Step 1: Initiate block mode** **Step 2: Select text to be blocked** **Step 3: Underline blocked text**

Alt F4 6 → or 7 Home 6 →

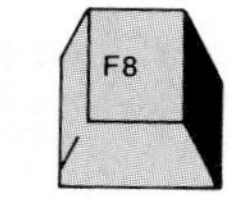

Move the cursor down to line 18, position 10 so that it is under the L in the word LICENSE. This is existing text you wish to boldface. The same method that was used to underline existing text is used to boldface existing text. Press Alt-F4 (step 1 of Figure 3-29). With the "Block on" message flashing in the lower left corner of your screen, move the cursor to the right to highlight the word LICENSE (step 2 of Figure 3-29). When the word is highlighted, note that the word Bold is in black next to the F6 key, and press the F6 key (step 3 of Figure 3-29). The blocked text is turned off and the word LICENSE is boldfaced.

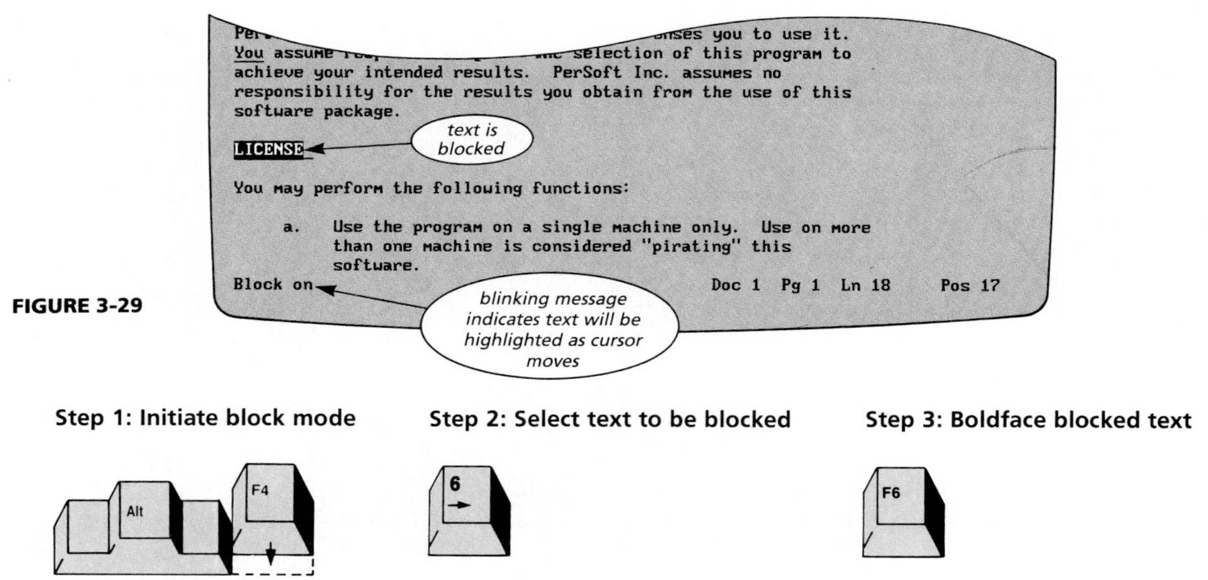


**FIGURE 3-29**

Move the cursor down to line 39 of your document, then to position 14. The cursor should be under the M in the word MAY. To block the words MAY NOT, press Alt-F4 (step 1 of Figure 3-30). With the message "Block on" flashing, move the cursor to the right to highlight the words MAY NOT (step 2 of Figure 3-30). When the words are highlighted, press the F8 key (step 3 of Figure 3-30). The block is turned off and the words are underlined.

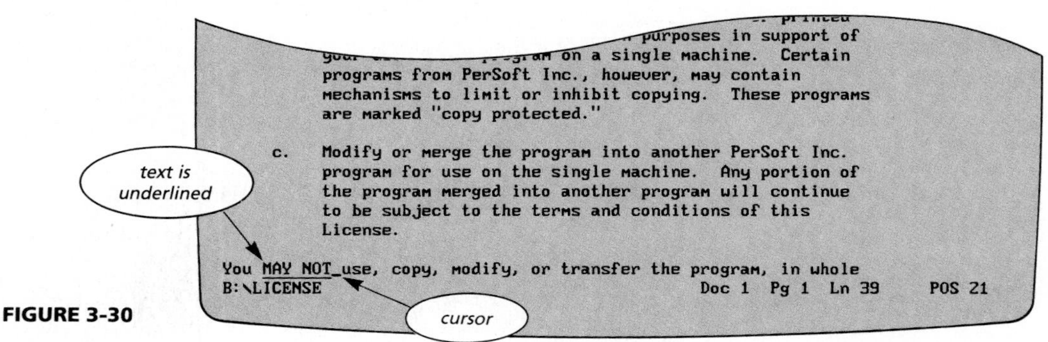


**FIGURE 3-30**

**Step 1: Initiate block mode** **Step 2: Select text to be blocked** **Step 3: Underline blocked text**

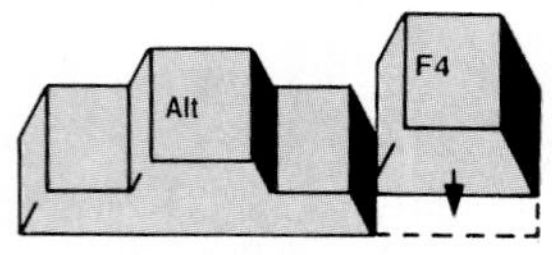


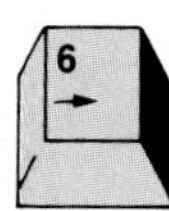

Move the cursor down to line 50. To move to the right, while holding down the Ctrl key, press the Right Arrow → until the cursor is under the letter Y in the word YOUR. The cursor should be at position 52. To highlight the last five words of the document, press Alt-F4 (step 1 of Figure 3-31). With the message "Block on" flashing, move the cursor to highlight the last five words of the document, YOUR LICENSE IS AUTOMATICALLY TERMINATED (step 2 of Figure 3-31). With the desired text highlighted, press the F6 key (step 3 of Figure 3-31). "Block on" is turned off and the text is placed in boldface mode.

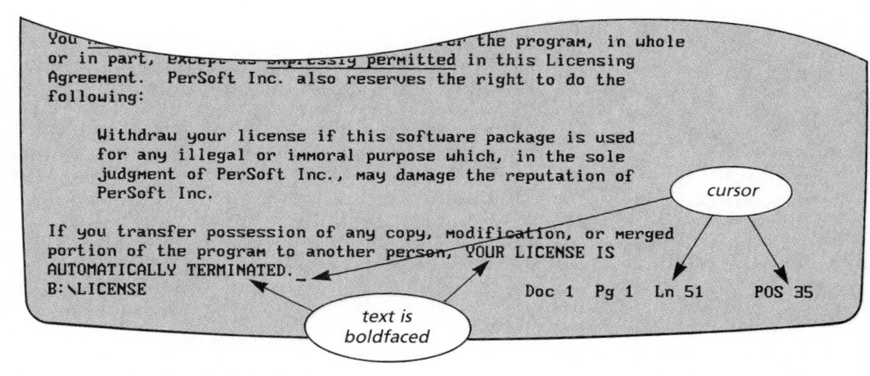


**FIGURE 3-31**

**Step 1: Initiate block mode**

Alt F4

**Step 2: Select text to be blocked**

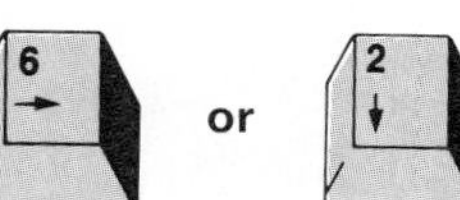


**Step 3: Boldface blocked text**

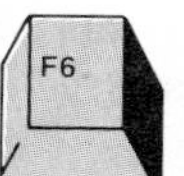


To view your last command in the reveal codes, press Alt-F3 (step 1 of Figure 3-32). In the lower screen the **[B]** code (beginning boldface) was placed before the Y and the **[b]** code (ending boldface) was placed after the period. When the document is printed, all type between those codes will be printed in boldface. To exit the reveal codes, press the spacebar (step 2 of Figure 3-32).

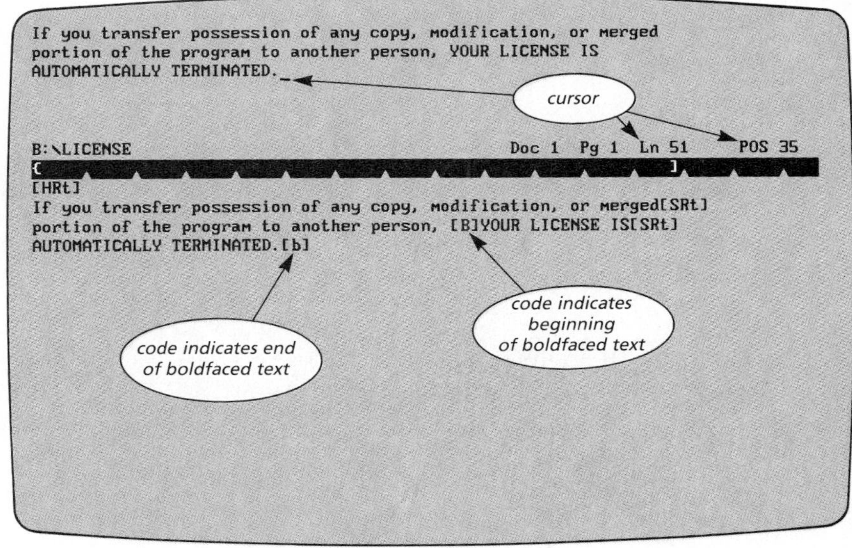


**FIGURE 3-32**

**Step 1: View reveal codes**

Alt F3

**Step 2: Exit reveal codes**

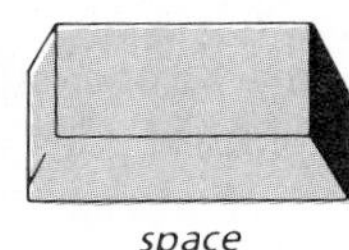

*space*

## SAVING AND REPLACING A DOCUMENT

When you finished typing this document, you saved it to your disk. But after saving it, you made several changes to the document on your screen. Those changes have not been saved to the disk. If there were a power failure or if you turned off the computer, the revised document in the main memory would be lost. Therefore, you must save the changes to the disk, replacing the old text with the new text. When you instruct the computer to replace the old document with the new one, the entire document will be saved, including any changes or additions.

To **save and replace** your document, press the F10 key (step 1 of Figure 3-33). Notice the message "Document to be Saved:" in the lower left corner of the screen, along with the name you previously gave your document. Once you have named a document, it is not necessary to type the name each time you wish to save and replace. Since that is the name you wish to keep, you only need to press the Enter ↵ key (step 2 of Figure 3-33). When you do, the message "Replace B:\LICENSE? (Y/N) N" appears on the screen (Figure 3-34). Since you want to replace the old document with the new one, type the letter Y for yes. You will hear drive B whirring and see the drive B light go on, indicating that the document is being saved to the diskette and that the new version is replacing the old version.

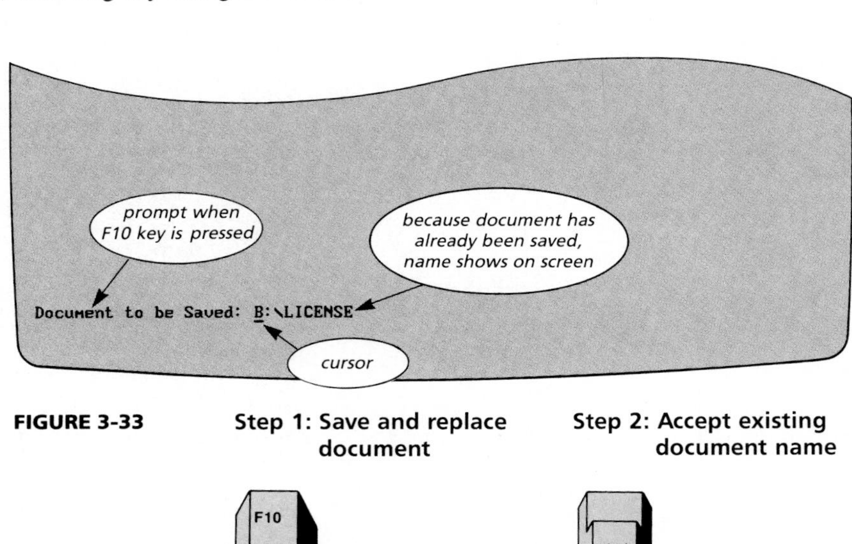


FIGURE 3-33

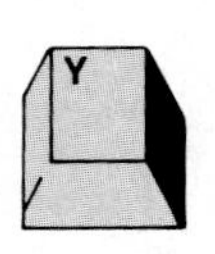


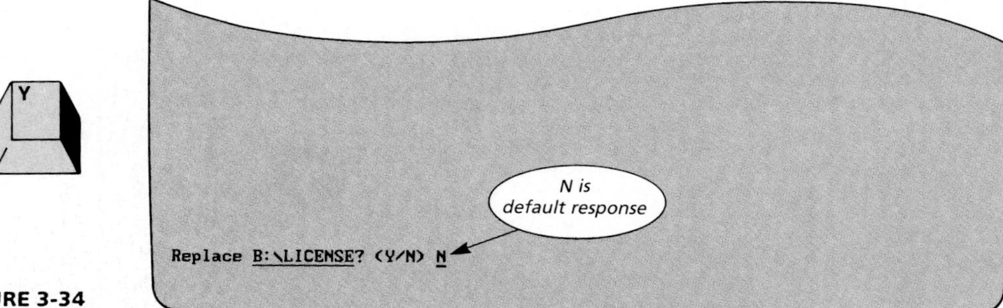


FIGURE 3-34

## PRINTING A DOCUMENT

Now you can print the document in its final form. Be sure the printer has paper in place and that the printer is turned on and ready to print.

From Project 1, remember that in order to print the document you must invoke the print function. Press Shift-F7. Figure 3-35 shows the print menu you see at the bottom of the screen.

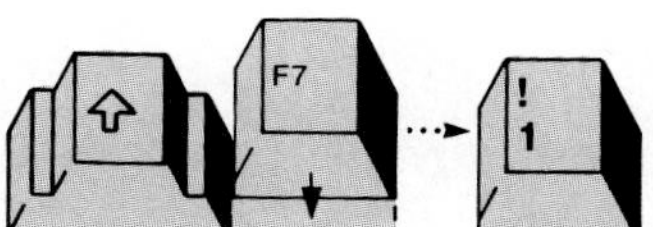


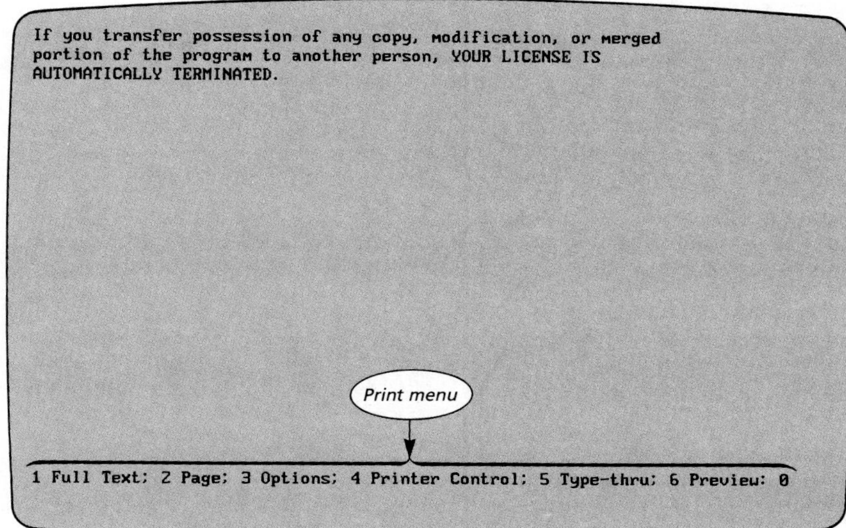


FIGURE 3-35

Because you wish to print the complete or full text of this document, press the number 1 for full text, and the printer will begin printing your document. The printed document is illustrated in Figure 3-36.

December 15, 1990

*WPC

LICENSING AGREEMENT

You should **carefully** read the following terms and conditions. Your use of this program package indicates your acceptance of them. If you do not agree with them, you should not use this software package. Instead, you should return the package and your money will be returned to you.*WPC

PerSoft Inc. provides this program and licenses you to use it. You assume responsibility for the selection of this program to achieve your intended results. PerSoft Inc. assumes no responsibility for the results you obtain from the use of this software package.*WPC

**LICENSE**

You may perform the following functions:
*WPC

a. Use the program on a single machine only. Use on more than one machine is considered "pirating" this software.

b. Copy the program into any machine readable or printed form for backup or modification purposes in support of your use of the program on a single machine. Certain programs from PerSoft Inc., however, may contain mechanisms to limit or inhibit copying. These programs are marked "copy protected." *WPC

c. Modify or merge the program into another PerSoft Inc. program for use on the single machine. Any portion of the program merged into another program will continue to be subject to the terms and conditions of this License. *WPC

You MAY NOT use, copy, modify, or transfer the program, in whole or in part, except as **expressly permitted** in this Licensing Agreement. PerSoft Inc. also reserves the right to do the following:*WPC

Withdraw your license if this software package is used for any illegal or immoral purpose which, in the sole judgment of PerSoft Inc., may damage the reputation of PerSoft Inc. *WPC

If you transfer possession of any copy, modification, or merged portion of the program to another person, **YOUR LICENSE IS AUTOMATICALLY TERMINATED.**

FIGURE 3-36

## EXITING PROJECT 3

In order to exit this document press the F7 key (step 1 of Figure 3-37). The message "Save Document? (Y/N) Y" appears in the lower left corner of the screen.

Remember that you have already saved this document in its new form to the disk, so it is not necessary to save it again. Look at the right corner of the screen in Figure 3-37. Notice the message "(Text was not modified)." That message is your assurance that everything in your document has been saved. If that message were completed it would say "Text was not modified since you last saved to disk." If you are ever exiting a document you wish to save and you do not see the "(Text was not modified)" message, be sure to save and replace as you exit.

Since you do see the message and are assured that your document has been saved in its entirety, you can answer the prompt by pressing the letter N for no (step 2 of Figure 3-37). The screen then displays the prompt "Exit WP? (Y/N) N" as shown in Figure 3-38. Since you do wish to exit the program, type the letter Y as you have done in Projects 1 and 2 to return to the DOS prompt.

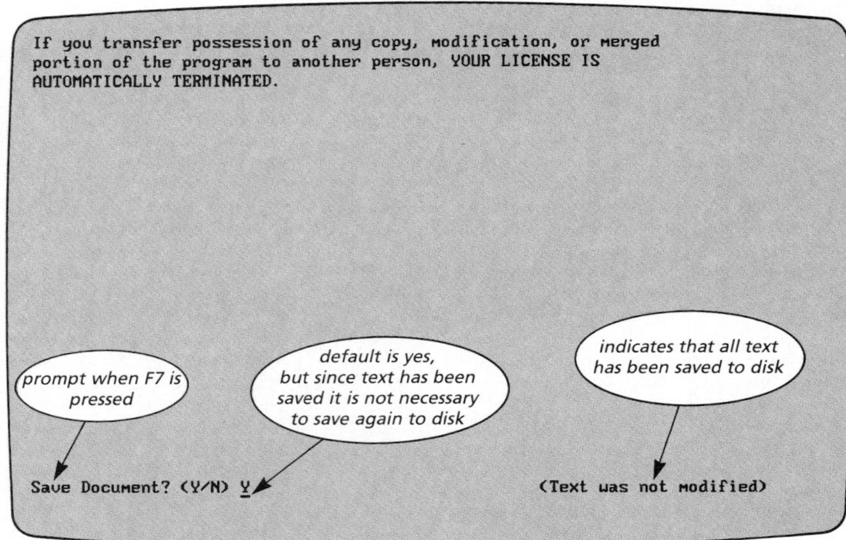


FIGURE 3-37

Step 1: Exit the document

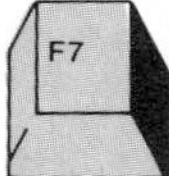


Step 2: Respond to prompt

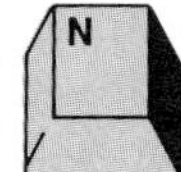


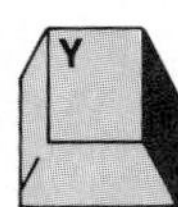


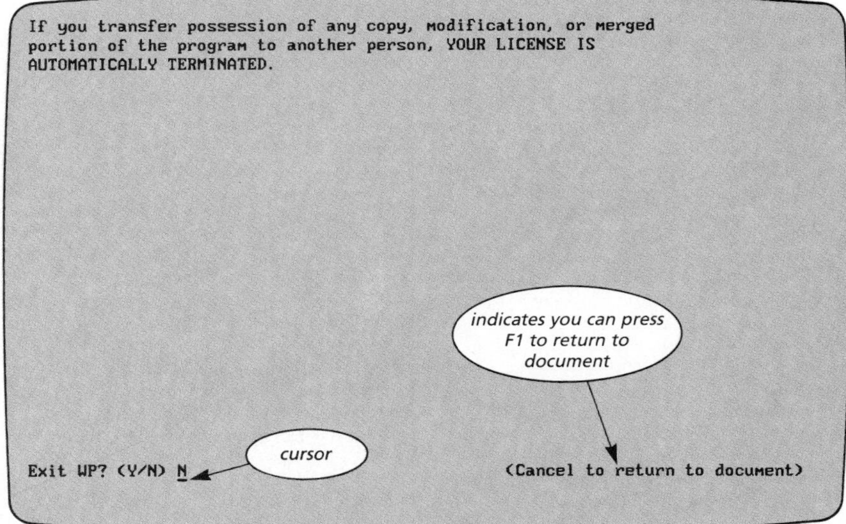


FIGURE 3-38

# PROJECT SUMMARY

In Project 3 you learned how to arrange text flush right and centered, how to boldface and underline text, and how to indent text. You saved the document to disk, then returned to existing text and boldfaced and underlined some key words. Then you saved the revised document to the disk, replacing the first version. You printed the document, making a hard copy of the text. Throughout the project, you practiced viewing the reveal codes screen to become familiar with the various codes that are embedded as you create a document.

The following is a list of the keystroke sequence we used in Project 3:

**SUMMARY OF KEYSTROKES—Project 3**

| STEPS | KEY(S) PRESSED |
|---|---|
| 1 | b: [at the A> prompt] |
| 2 | ↵ |
| 3 | a:wp [at the B> prompt] |
| 4 | ↵ |
| 5 | ↵ [at first introductory screen] |
| 6 | ↵ [only if you see a second introductory screen] |
| 7 | Alt-F6 |
| 8 | December 15, 1990 |
| 9 | ↵ |
| 10 | ↵ |
| 11 | ↵ |
| 12 | Shift-F6 |
| 13 | Caps Lock |
| 14 | LICENSING AGREEMENT |
| 15 | Caps Lock |
| 16 | ↵ |
| 17 | ↵ |
| 18 | You should |
| 19 | space |
| 20 | F6 |
| 21 | carefully |
| 22 | F6 |
| 23 | space |
| 24 | read the following terms and conditions. Your use of this program package indicates your acceptance of them. If you do |
| 25 | space |
| 26 | F8 |
| 27 | not |
| 28 | F8 |
| 29 | space |
| 30 | agree with them, you should not use this software package. Instead, you should return the package and your money will be returned to you. |
| 31 | ↵ |
| 32 | ↵ |
| 33 | PerSoft Inc. provides this program and licenses you to use it. |
| 34 | space |
| 35 | space |
| 36 | F8 |
| 37 | You |
| 38 | F8 |
| 39 | space |
| 40 | assume responsibility for the selection of this program to achieve your intended results. PerSoft Inc. assumes no responsibility for the results you obtain from the use of this software package. |
| 41 | ↵ |
| 42 | ↵ |
| 43 | Caps Lock |
| 44 | LICENSE |
| 45 | Caps Lock |
| 46 | ↵ |
| 47 | ↵ |
| 48 | You may perform the following functions: |
| 49 | ↵ |
| 50 | ↵ |
| 51 | F4 |
| 52 | a. |
| 53 | F4 |
| 54 | Use the program on a single machine only. Use on more than one machine is considered "pirating" this software. |
| 55 | ↵ |
| 56 | ↵ |
| 57 | F4 |
| 58 | b. |
| 59 | F4 |
| 60 | Copy the program into any machine readable or printed form for backup or modification purposes in support of your use of the program on a single machine. Certain programs from PerSoft Inc., however, may contain mechanisms to limit or inhibit copying. These programs are marked "copy protected." |
| 61 | ↵ |
| 62 | ↵ |
| 63 | F4 |

### SUMMARY OF KEYSTROKES—Project 3 (continued)

| STEPS | KEY(S) PRESSED |
|---|---|
| 64 | c. |
| 65 | F4 |
| 66 | Modify or merge the program into another PerSoft Inc. program for use on the single machine. Any portion of the program merged into another program will continue to be subject to the terms and conditions of this License. |
| 67 | ↵ |
| 68 | ↵ |
| 69 | You |
| 70 | space |
| 71 | Caps Lock |
| 72 | MAY NOT |
| 73 | Caps Lock |
| 74 | space |
| 75 | use, copy, modify, or transfer the program, in whole or in part, except as |
| 76 | space |
| 77 | F8 |
| 78 | F6 |
| 79 | expressly permitted |
| 80 | F8 |
| 81 | F6 |
| 82 | space |
| 83 | in this Licensing Agreement. PerSoft Inc. also reserves the right to do the following: |
| 84 | ↵ |
| 85 | ↵ |
| 86 | Shift-F4 |
| 87 | Withdraw your license if this software package is used for any illegal or immoral purpose which, in the sole judgment of PerSoft Inc., may damage the reputation of PerSoft Inc. |
| 88 | ↵ |
| 89 | ↵ |
| 90 | If you transfer possession of any copy, modification, or merged portion of the program to another person, |
| 91 | space |
| 92 | Caps Lock |
| 93 | YOUR LICENSE IS AUTOMATICALLY TERMINATED. |
| 94 | Caps Lock |
| 95 | F10 |
| 96 | license |
| 97 | ↵ [wait for document to be saved] |
| 98 | Home Home ↑ |
| 99 | [move cursor to line 4, position 33 under the L in LICENSING AGREEMENT] |
| 100 | Alt-F4 |
| 101 | [→ to highlight or block LICENSING AGREEMENT] |
| 102 | F8 |
| 103 | [move cursor down to line 18, position 10 under the L in LICENSE] |
| 104 | Alt-F4 |
| 105 | [→ to highlight or block LICENSE] |
| 106 | F6 |
| 107 | [move cursor to line 39, position 14 under the M in MAY NOT] |
| 108 | Alt-F4 |
| 109 | [→ to highlight or block MAY NOT] |
| 110 | F8 |
| 111 | [press cursor keys to move cursor to line 50, position 52 under the Y in YOUR] |
| 112 | Alt-F4 |
| 113 | [press cursor keys to highlight the words YOUR LICENSE IS AUTOMATICALLY TERMINATED.] |
| 114 | F6 |
| 115 | F10 |
| 116 | ↵ |
| 117 | Y [wait for document to be saved] |
| 118 | Shift-F7 |
| 119 | 1 |
| 120 | F7 |
| 121 | N |
| 122 | Y |
| 123 | [remove disk from drive A if you see prompt ''Insert COMMAND.COM disk in drive A and strike any key when ready''] |
| 124 | [put DOS disk into drive A] |
| 125 | [press any key] |
| 126 | [at B> remove disks from both drives] |

The following list summarizes the material covered in Project 3:

1. The term **flush right** describes text that is aligned to the right margin. The embedded codes are **[A]** and **[a]**.
2. The **Center Text** command centers text between the margins. The embedded codes are **[C]** and **[c]**.
3. **Boldfaced text** appears darker or bolder. The embedded codes are **[B]** and **[b]**.
4. The **underline** function is used to underline text. The embedded codes are **[U]** and **[u]**.
5. When you **insert** text, existing text is moved to the right.
6. Use the **Typeover** command to type over existing text by pressing the Insert key.

7. The **Indent** key sets a temporary left margin. The embedded code is **[→Indent]**. The temporary margin is removed with a hard return.
8. Use the **Left/Right Indent** key to set temporary left and right margins. The embedded code is **[→Indent←]**. Temporary margins are removed with a hard return.
9. Use the **block** function to highlight text, to isolate it from the rest of the document so that you can underline or boldface it.
10. If you have **saved** a document to disk and then made changes in it on the screen, you must **replace** the old document with the new version by saving it again to disk.

# STUDENT ASSIGNMENTS

## STUDENT ASSIGNMENT 1: True/False

**Instructions:** Circle T if the statement is true and F if the statement if false.

T F 1. To use the flush right function you would use the Shift-F6 keys.
T F 2. The paired codes to indicate boldfacing are [B] and [b].
T F 3. The Indent key moves the cursor to the next tab setting.
T F 4. To turn off the block function you could press the Exit (F7) key.
T F 5. With the Insert key turned on, the message "Typeover" appears on the screen.
T F 6. The command Alt-F6 can be used to cause boldface characters.
T F 7. Pressing the Indent key temporarily changes the left margin until a hard return is pressed.
T F 8. The Ctrl-F4 keys are used to turn on the block function.
T F 9. The left/right indent function is invoked with the Shift-F4 keys.
T F 10. To exit a document you can use the F1 (Cancel) key.

## STUDENT ASSIGNMENT 2: Multiple Choice

**Instructions:** Circle the correct response.

1. When the F6 key is pressed
   a. the position number changes appearance
   b. the codes [B] and [b] are embedded into the document
   c. boldface typing will occur until the F6 key is pressed again, turning boldfacing off
   d. all of the above
2. To underline a word in the body of the text
   a. the user must backspace and underline the characters just typed
   b. press the F8 key, type the text to be underlined, then press F8 again
   c. press the F6 key, type the text to be underlined, then press F6 again
   d. press the F8 key, type the text to be underlined, then press the F7 (Exit) key
3. The boldface function can be specified by pressing
   a. the F8 key
   b. the Shift-F8 keys
   c. the F6 key
   d. none of the above

### Student Assignment 2 (continued)

4. To center a heading on a page,
   a. the space bar must be used to cause spaces to appear to the left
   b. the Shift-F6 keys must be pressed
   c. a hard return must be pressed after the text has been typed
   d. both b and c are correct
5. The F4 or Indent key will do the following:
   a. temporarily change the left margin
   b. temporarily change the left and right margins
   c. move the cursor to the next tab stop setting
   d. both a and c are correct
6. The code(s) that are inserted when the Alt-F6 keys are pressed (followed by a hard return) are
   a. [Flsh Rt]
   b. [A] [a]
   c. [HRt]
   d. [SRt]
7. To invoke Boldfacing mode,
   a. press F6 at the beginning and end of the type to be boldfaced
   b. press F6 at the beginning and a hard return at the end of the type to be boldfaced
   c. press F8 at the beginning and end of the type to be boldfaced
   d. press Shift-F6 at the beginning of typing, and F7 at the end of the type to be boldfaced
8. To underline existing text,
   a. delete existing text, press F8, type text again, press F8
   b. put the cursor at the beginning of the text, press F8, then press the spacebar under the text
   c. block the existing text using the Alt-F4 keys, then press F8
   d. none of the above

## STUDENT ASSIGNMENT 3: Matching

**Instructions:** Put the appropriate number next to the words in the second column.

| | | |
|---|---|---|
| 1. Underline codes | _____ | [C] [c] |
| 2. Typeover | _____ | Alt-F4 |
| 3. Boldface codes | _____ | F6 |
| 4. Left/Right Indent | _____ | Insert key |
| 5. Center codes | _____ | Shift-F6 |
| 6. Indent key(s) | _____ | [B] [b] |
| 7. Boldface key(s) | _____ | [U] [u] |
| 8. Flush Right code | _____ | F4 |
| 9. Flush Right key(s) | _____ | Shift-F4 |
| 10. Center key(s) | _____ | [A] [a] |
| 11. Block function | _____ | Alt-F6 |

## STUDENT ASSIGNMENT 4: Writing WordPerfect Commands

**Instructions:** Next to each command, write its effect.

| Command | Effect |
|---|---|
| 1. Alt-F6 | ____________ |
| 2. F6 | ____________ |
| 3. Shift-F6 | ____________ |
| 4. F8 | ____________ |
| 5. Insert key | ____________ |
| 6. Caps Lock key | ____________ |
| 7. F4 | ____________ |
| 8. Shift-F4 | ____________ |
| 9. Alt-F4 (plus cursor keys) | ____________ |
| 10. F10 | ____________ |
| 11. Shift | ____________ |
| 12. F7 | ____________ |

## STUDENT ASSIGNMENT 5: WordPerfect Commands

**Instructions:** The heading shown below was typed in capital letters, centered and underlined. Describe in detail each of the keystrokes that were used to produce this heading.

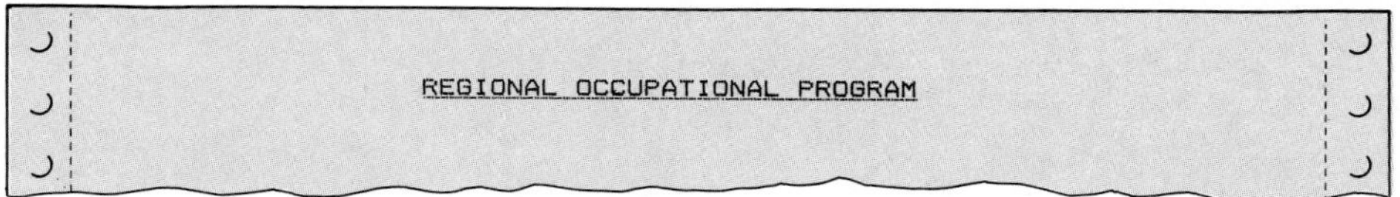


## STUDENT ASSIGNMENT 6: WordPerfect Commands

**Instructions:** The illustration below is the beginning of a document. After typing it, the user realized that the heading should have been underlined. Explain in detail how this existing text can be underlined without deleting the text.

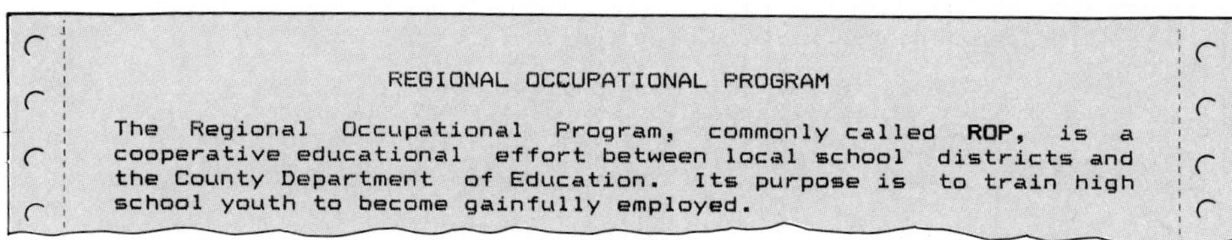

REGIONAL OCCUPATIONAL PROGRAM

The Regional Occupational Program, commonly called **ROP**, is a cooperative educational effort between local school districts and the County Department of Education. Its purpose is to train high school youth to become gainfully employed.

## STUDENT ASSIGNMENT 7: WordPerfect Commands

**Instructions:** The text in sample A below is typed incorrectly because the margins after each letter should be indented temporarily. The text in sample B is typed correctly. Identify the one function key that made the difference in appearance, and describe in detail where that key should have been used.

```
a.   Copy the program into any machine readable or printed form
for backup or modification purposes in support of your use of the
program on a single machine.  Certain programs from PerSoft Inc.,
however, may contain mechanisms to limit or inhibit copying.
These programs are marked "copy protected."

b.   Modify or merge the program into another PerSoft Inc.
program for use on the single machine.  Any portion of the
program merged into another program will continue to be subject
to the terms and conditions of this License.
```

Sample A

```
a.   Copy the program into any machine readable or printed form
     for backup or modification purposes in support of your use
     of the program on a single machine.  Certain programs from
     PerSoft Inc., however, may contain mechanisms to limit or
     inhibit copying.  These programs are marked "copy
     protected."

b.   Modify or merge the program into another PerSoft Inc.
     program for use on the single machine.  Any portion of the
     program merged into another program will continue to be
     subject to the terms and conditions of this License.
```

Sample B

## STUDENT ASSIGNMENT 8: WordPerfect Commands

**Instructions:** The text in sample A below is typed normally. The text in the first paragraph of sample B is indented five spaces from both the left and right margins. The text in the second paragraph of sample B is indented ten spaces from both the left and right margins. Describe in detail the keystrokes that were used to make the margins in both the first and second paragraphs of sample B.

```
Copy the program into any machine readable or printed form for
backup or modification purposes in support of your use of the
program on a single machine.  Certain programs from PerSoft Inc.,
however, may contain mechanisms to limit or inhibit copying.
These programs are marked "copy protected."

Modify or merge the program into another PerSoft Inc. program for
use on the single machine.  Any portion of the program merged
into another program will continue to be subject to the terms and
conditions of this License.
```

Sample A

```
Copy the program into any machine readable or printed
form for backup or modification purposes in support of
your use of the program on a single machine.  Certain
programs from PerSoft Inc., however, may contain
mechanisms to limit or inhibit copying.  These programs
are marked "copy protected."

     Modify or merge the program into another
     PerSoft Inc. program for use on the single
     machine.  Any portion of the program merged
     into another program will continue to be
     subject to the terms and conditions of this License.
```

**Sample B**

## STUDENT ASSIGNMENT 9: Creating a Document

**Instructions:** Create the document below and save it under the name Regional. Then print the document.

```
                    REGIONAL OCCUPATIONAL PROGRAM

The Regional Occupational Program, commonly called ROP, is a
cooperative educational effort between local school districts and
the County Department of Education. Its purpose is to train high
school youth to become gainfully employed.

ROP has served and trained over 95,000 students in some 42 trades
since 1988.

ROP plays an important role in the application of basic skills in
the world of work, endeavoring to assist the unskilled and
undertrained to become gainfully employed. ROP works in
cooperation with 1,054 local businesses in the community to provide
students on-the-job training. About 500 members of business and
industry are involved in an advisory committee role to assure
meaningful job skill training, a verified labor market demand, and
a high potential for student placement in every course offered
through ROP.

Important features of the Regional Occupational Program are:

     1.   Students from many schools meet at a centralized
          classroom. The teacher has a credential in the field
          being taught plus at least 5 years of directly related
          work experience.

     2.   Students are assigned to business training sites to
          receive realistic on-the-job skill development. An
          individualized training plan is developed for each
          student at each job training site.

     3.   Periodically students return to the classroom for
          additional training and to review progress from an
          employment point of view.


Courses are offered for three semesters during the year.
Enrollment time varies depending on the course topic or trade area.
Some programs permit entry on any day, others at the start of each
semester.
```

## STUDENT ASSIGNMENT 10: Correcting a Document

**Instructions:** The document that you created in Student Assignment 9 needs to be changed to look like the document below. Make the following corrections:

1. The characters ROP should appear in boldface type.
2. The heading should be underlined.
3. Add paragraph 4 after paragraph 3 as follows:

   4. There is no tuition charge for any ROP class.

4. Save the new document under the name Regional.2, then print the document.

REGIONAL OCCUPATIONAL PROGRAM

The Regional Occupational Program, commonly called **ROP**, is a cooperative educational effort between local school districts and the County Department of Education. Its purpose is to train high school youth to become gainfully employed.

**ROP** has served and trained over 95,000 students in some 42 trades since 1988.

**ROP** plays an important role in the application of basic skills in the world of work, endeavoring to assist the unskilled and undertrained to become gainfully employed. **ROP** works in cooperation with 1,054 local businesses in the community to provide students on-the-job training. About 500 members of business and industry are involved in an advisory committee role to assure meaningful job skill training, a verified labor market demand, and a high potential for student placement in every course offered through **ROP**.

Important features of the Regional Occupational Program are:

1. Students from many schools meet at a centralized classroom. The teacher has a credential in the field being taught plus at least 5 years of directly related work experience.

2. Students are assigned to business training sites to receive realistic on-the-job skill development. An individualized training plan is developed for each student at each job training site.

3. Periodically students return to the classroom for additional training and to review progress from an employment point of view.

4. There is no tuition charge for any **ROP** class.

Courses are offered for three semesters during the year. Enrollment time varies depending on the course topic or trade area. Some programs permit entry on any day, others at the start of each semester.

# PROJECT 4

## Modifying a WordPerfect Document

### Objectives

You will have mastered the material in this project when you can:

- Retrieve a document
- Format a document
- Adjust left and right margins and top and bottom margins
- Justify and unjustify text
- Center text on a page
- Set tabs

## RETRIEVING A DOCUMENT

In many word processing applications, a document must be modified after it has been created. In this project you will make some changes to the memo you created in Project 2. The old memo (Figure 4-1a) contains instructions for corrections to be made. The corrected memo is shown in Figure 4-1b. As you learned in the previous projects, first load WordPerfect into the computer.

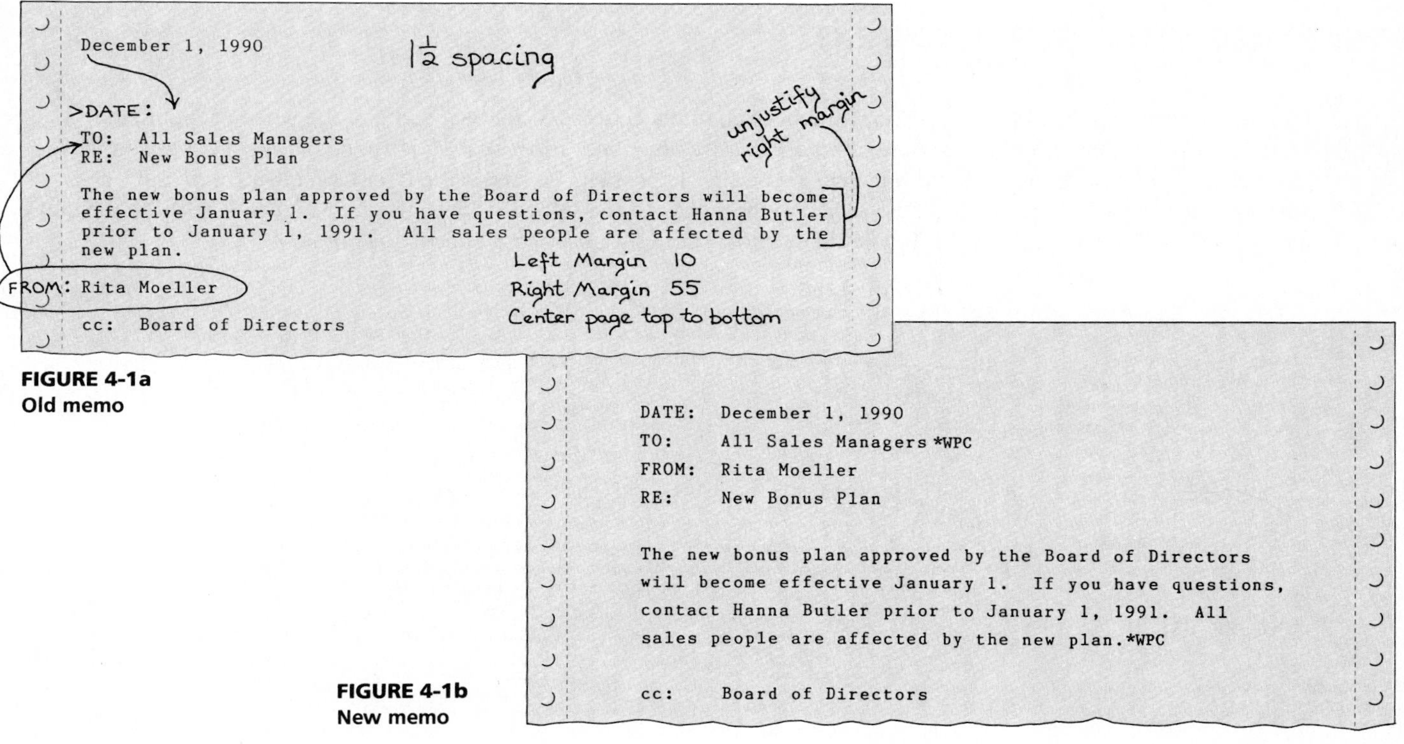

December 1, 1990
1½ spacing
>DATE:
TO: All Sales Managers
RE: New Bonus Plan
unjustify right margin
The new bonus plan approved by the Board of Directors will become effective January 1. If you have questions, contact Hanna Butler prior to January 1, 1991. All sales people are affected by the new plan.
Left Margin 10
Right Margin 55
Center page top to bottom
FROM: Rita Moeller
cc: Board of Directors
DATE: December 1, 1990
TO: All Sales Managers *WPC
FROM: Rita Moeller
RE: New Bonus Plan
The new bonus plan approved by the Board of Directors
will become effective January 1. If you have questions,
contact Hanna Butler prior to January 1, 1991. All
sales people are affected by the new plan.*WPC
cc: Board of Directors

**FIGURE 4-1a**
**Old memo**

**FIGURE 4-1b**
**New memo**

In Project 2 you created a document, named it Memo, and saved it. Now you'll retrieve that document and modify it. Look at the template next to the F10 key. The word Retrieve is in green. Press Shift-F10 (step 1 of Figure 4-2). The message "Document to be Retrieved:" appears. Type the name memo, then press Enter ↵ (step 2 of Figure 4-2). The light on drive B goes on, and the memo is retrieved from memory and displayed on the screen.

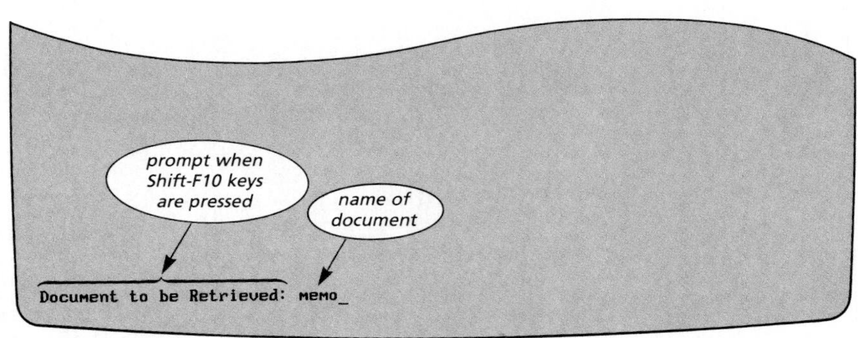
prompt when Shift-F10 keys are pressed
name of document
Document to be Retrieved: MEMO_

FIGURE 4-2

**Step 1: Retrieve a document**

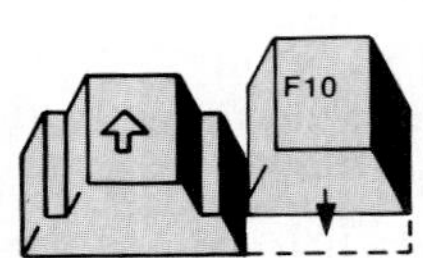
F10

**Step 2: Specify name of document to be retrieved**

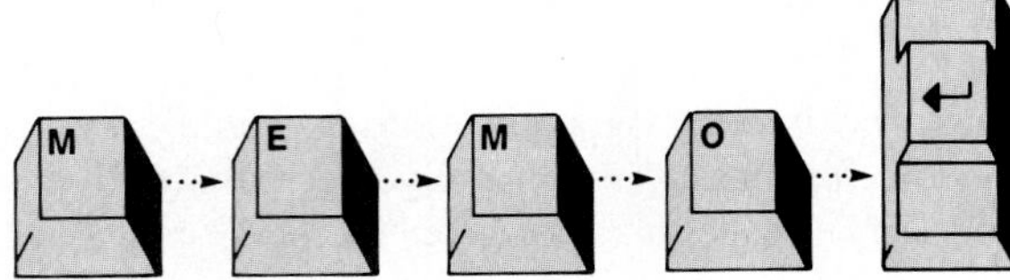
M
E
M
O

## INSERTING CHANGES INTO TEXT

In a memo's heading, the word DATE: is typed in front of the actual date and the name of the person sending the memo is placed at the top of the document after FROM:. Thus, the first task to modify the old memo is to add the word DATE: in front of the date. With the cursor on line 1, position 10, under the D in December, press the Caps Lock key and type the word DATE:. The date is pushed to the right and the word DATE is inserted (Figure 4-3). With the cursor still under the D in December, press the Tab key. The cursor moves to position 20 (step 1 of Figure 4-4).

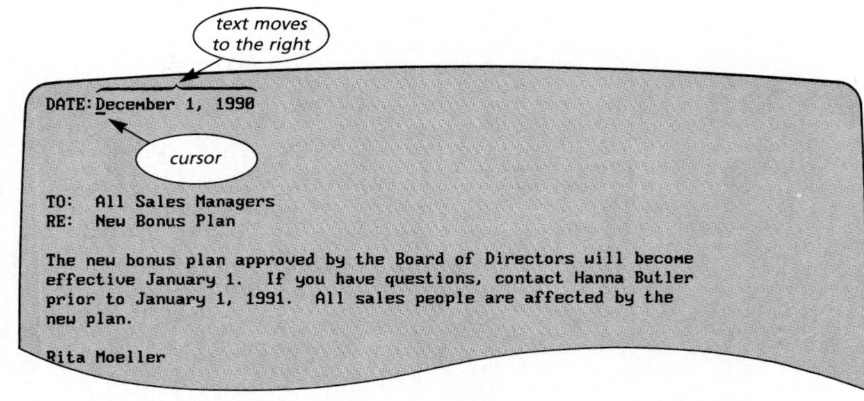
text moves to the right
DATE:December 1, 1990
cursor
TO: All Sales Managers
RE: New Bonus Plan
The new bonus plan approved by the Board of Directors will become
effective January 1. If you have questions, contact Hanna Butler
prior to January 1, 1991. All sales people are affected by the
new plan.
Rita Moeller

FIGURE 4-3

Now, remove the hard returns between the date and the line: TO: All Sales Managers. Press the Down Arrow ↓ to move the cursor to line 2, position 10, then press the Del key four times until the cursor is under the T in TO: on line 2, position 10 (step 2 of Figure 4-4). Press the Down Arrow ↓ to move the cursor under the R in RE: on line 3, position 10, then press Return ↵. You see a blank line inserted, as shown in Figure 4-5. Press the Up Arrow ↑ key to put the cursor on position 10 of line 3, the blank line. With Caps Lock still on, type the word FROM:. To turn off capitalizations, press the Caps Lock key.

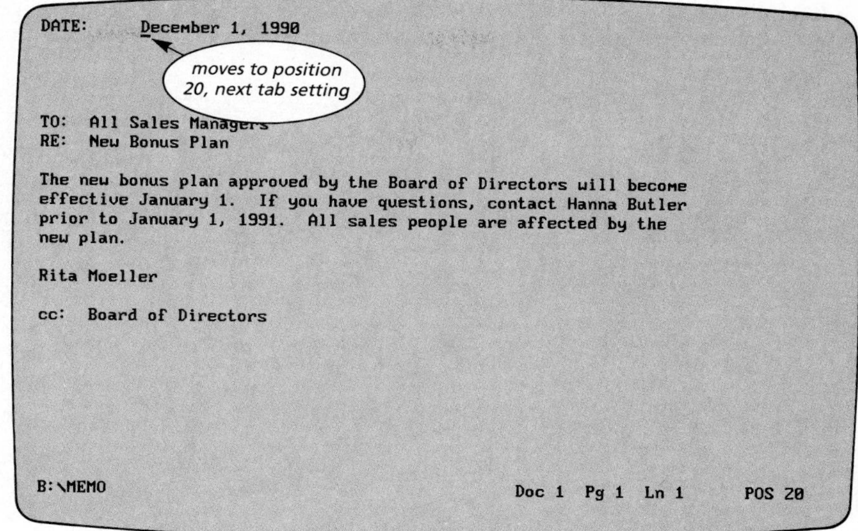
DATE: December 1, 1990
moves to position 20, next tab setting
TO: All Sales Managers
RE: New Bonus Plan
The new bonus plan approved by the Board of Directors will become effective January 1. If you have questions, contact Hanna Butler prior to January 1, 1991. All sales people are affected by the new plan.
Rita Moeller
cc: Board of Directors
B:\MEMO Doc 1 Pg 1 Ln 1 POS 20

**FIGURE 4-4**

**Step 1: Move cursor to the first tab setting**

**Step 2: Delete 4 lines**

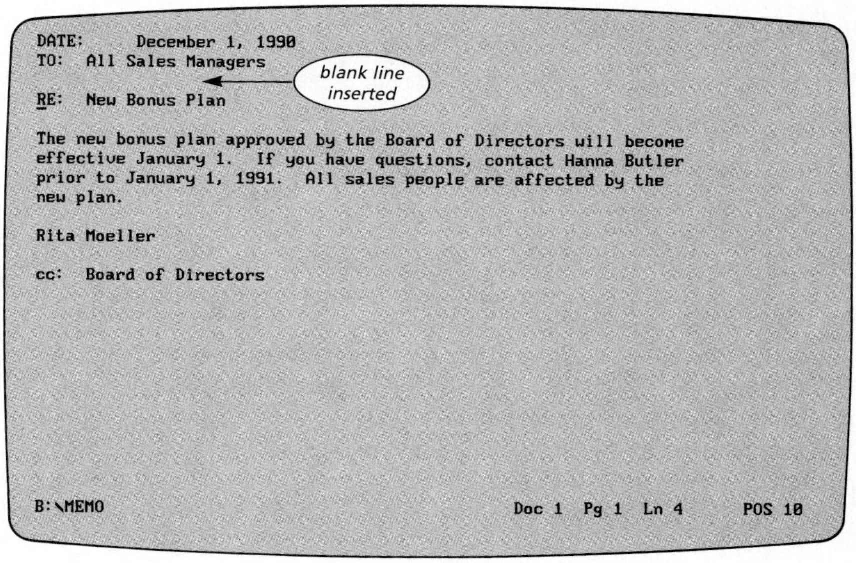

2
Del
Del
Del
Del

```
DATE:     December 1, 1990
TO:  All Sales Managers

RE:  New Bonus Plan

The new bonus plan approved by the Board of Directors will become
effective January 1.  If you have questions, contact Hanna Butler
prior to January 1, 1991.  All sales people are affected by the
new plan.

Rita Moeller

cc:  Board of Directors

B:\MEMO                                   Doc 1  Pg 1  Ln 4     POS 10
```

blank line inserted

**FIGURE 4-5**

Press the Tab key and type the name Rita Moeller (Figure 4-6). Notice that although you pressed the Tab key only once after each heading, the tabbed lines begin at different positions. Later in this project we will change the tab settings so that they line up.

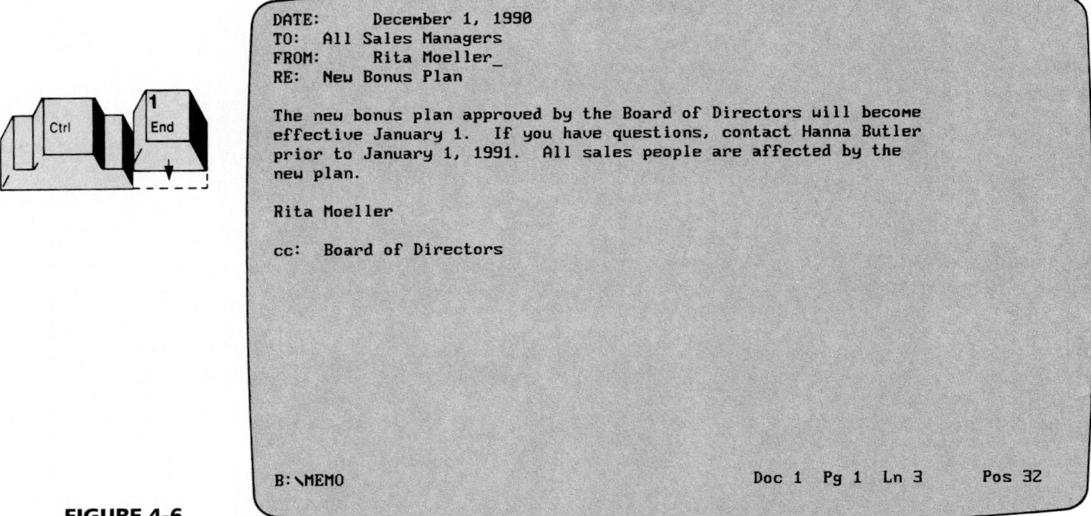
Ctrl
1
End
DATE:	December 1, 1990
TO:	All Sales Managers
FROM:	Rita Moeller_
RE:	New Bonus Plan
The new bonus plan approved by the Board of Directors will become effective January 1. If you have questions, contact Hanna Butler prior to January 1, 1991. All sales people are affected by the new plan.
Rita Moeller
cc:	Board of Directors
B:\MEMO
Doc 1 Pg 1 Ln 3 Pos 32

**FIGURE 4-6**

It is now necessary to remove the name that was typed at the bottom of the memo. Move the cursor to line 11, position 10. Press Ctl-End (Figure 4-6). The line is deleted. Press the Del key two times. You see the last line of typing move up to line 11.

## DEFAULT SETTINGS

The appearance of the documents in Projects 1 and 2 is governed by a number of default settings established by WordPerfect. In other words, if you do not change or add codes, your document will print with the parameters that have been set. You can, however, change the format of a document either before or after typing it.

## LEFT AND RIGHT MARGINS

A normal page of typing paper is 8 1/2" wide by 11" long. The WordPerfect default settings have the length of a line of type almost 6 1/2 inches wide, leaving approximately a 1-inch margin on both the left and right. The length of a line in characters can be easily figured.

Traditionally, typewriters used **pica** or **elite** type. Pica type fits 10 characters into 1 inch of space on a line, and elite type fits 12 characters into that same space. Therefore pica is the larger type and elite is the smaller. Some typewriters can type very small, placing 15 characters within 1 inch of space. When you use a word processor, some of the terminology is different. If you have used different type elements, you may have used the term "typing ball." The term used in word processing is **type font**. Instead of pica or elite, the term used is **10 pitch** (10 characters per inch) or **12 pitch** (12 characters per inch) (Figure 4-7). You could also use a *15 pitch font*. WordPerfect's default is a *10 pitch font*.

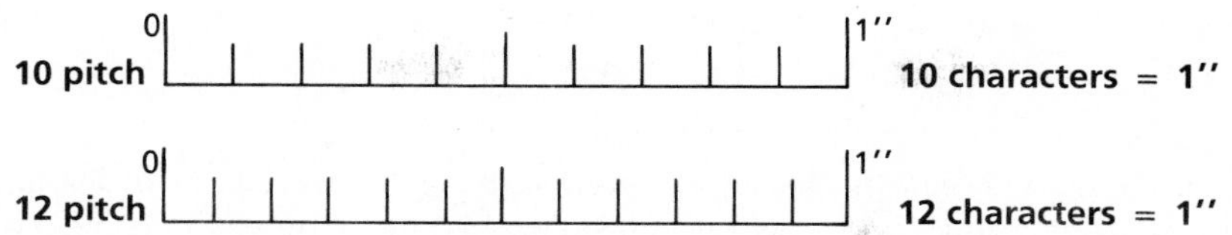


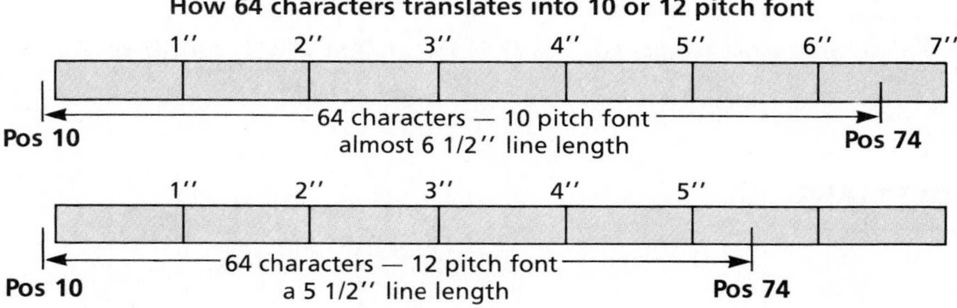


**FIGURE 4-7**

It is important to know which font you are using, because the margin is not set by inches but by characters. The margins default at position 10 on the left and position 74 on the right. If you subtract 10 from 74 you know WordPerfect's default uses 64 characters per line. With 64 characters per line and a default of a 10 pitch font, you can figure that each line of type will be almost 6 1/2 inches long (divide 64 by 10). If you were to leave the margins as they are and change the pitch to a 12 pitch font, divide 12 into 64 and you can see that the length of the line would be about 5 1/2 inches (Figure 4-7).

## TOP AND BOTTOM MARGINS

Figure 4-8 shows that a normal piece of paper is 11 inches long. Normal typewriting spacing allows for 6 lines per inch, making 66 lines from the top edge to the bottom edge of the paper. WordPerfect allows for 6 lines or a 1-inch top margin, and 6 lines or a 1-inch bottom margin. If you subtract the 6 lines on top and the 6 lines on the bottom (12 lines) from the total of 66, you know that there are 54 lines available for text. If you double space your typing, you will have 27 lines of type and 27 blank lines.

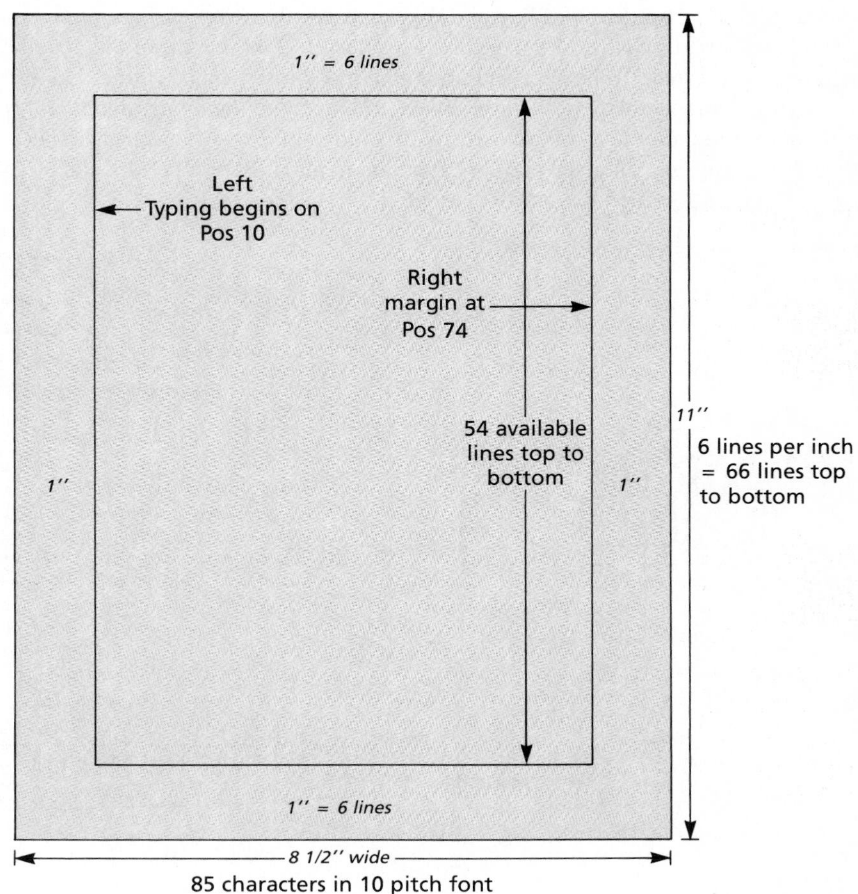


**FIGURE 4-8**
**WordPerfect Default Margins**

## FORMATTING

All the default settings we have discussed—pitch, font, lines per inch, line spacing, margin settings, tab settings, or anything that has to do with how the typing will appear on paper—are aspects of **formatting**. Any default setting can be changed by inserting a code, which will be embedded into the particular document on which you are working. You will learn many of the formatting functions in this project. To become familiar with the codes you will refer to the reveal codes screen many times. If you make an error in formatting, refer to the codes and analyze them to decide how they have affected the look of your document.

All the format settings are on the Format key, which is F8, either Ctrl-F8, Alt-F8, or Shift-F8. Next we will change default settings.

## LINE FORMATTING

To change anything having to do with the length of the line, the line spacing, or the tab settings on the line, we must use the **Line Format** key.

### Changing Margin Settings

Look at the memo to be corrected in Figure 4-1a. Notice that the margins are to be changed to 10 on the left and 55 on the right. With 45 characters per line and the default of the 10 pitch font, you can tell that you are going to have a 4 1/2" line.

If you want to change the margins, you must do it at the top of the document, because a code takes effect starting from where it is inserted. To be sure you are at the top, press Home, Home, Up Arrow.

Look at the template next to the F8 key. Notice that the word Line is in green. Press Shift-F8. The menu shown in Figure 4-9 appears at the bottom of the screen. Press the number 3 for margins. The screen changes to the one in Figure 4-10. The default margins are set at 10 and 74. Type the number 10 and press Enter ↵, then type the number 55 and press Enter ↵ again. You are returned to your document.

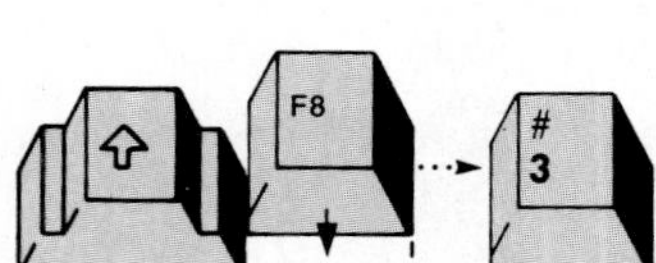
F8
#
3

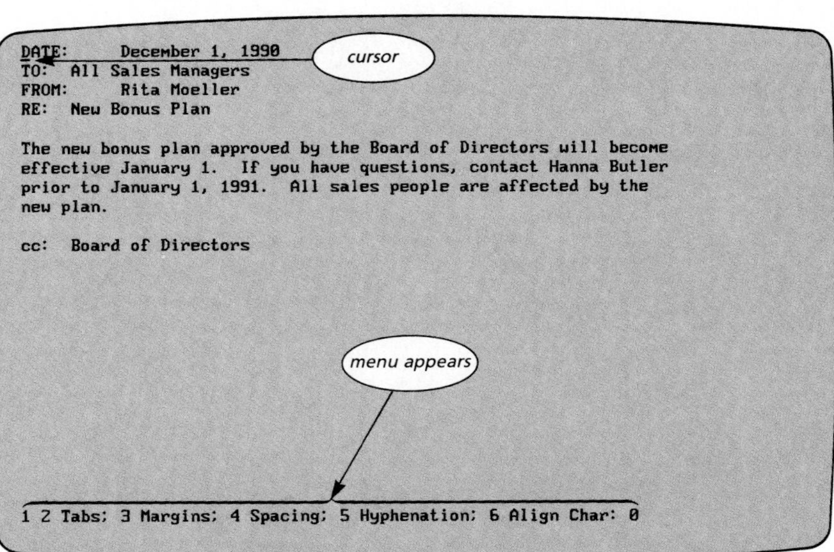
DATE: December 1, 1990
TO: All Sales Managers
FROM: Rita Moeller
RE: New Bonus Plan
The new bonus plan approved by the Board of Directors will become effective January 1. If you have questions, contact Hanna Butler prior to January 1, 1991. All sales people are affected by the new plan.
cc: Board of Directors
cursor
menu appears
1 2 Tabs; 3 Margins; 4 Spacing; 5 Hyphenation; 6 Align Char: 0

**FIGURE 4-9**

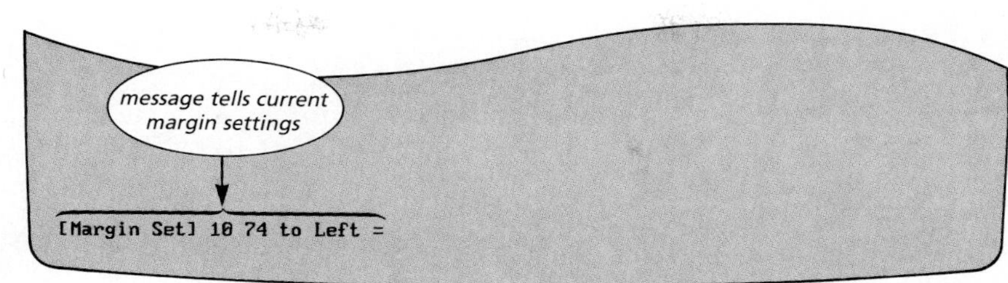


FIGURE 4-10

To see that a code for the new margin setting has been embedded into the document, look at the codes using Alt-F3 (Figure 4-11). Notice that the cursor is to the right of the code. Press the Left Arrow ← one time. Notice that an entire code is enclosed within brackets [ ] and that you cannot move the cursor inside the brackets. Also notice, on the bar that separates the two screens, that the right bracket has moved to show the new margin setting. Move the Left Arrow ← and Right Arrow → back and forth and notice how the right bracket moves. When you read a novel, you read from left to right, one line after another. You only understand what you have already read, not what might be coming. It is the same with how the codes work in WordPerfect. Think of the cursor reading left to right, line after line. When the cursor is to the left of the code, it follows the default setting of 10 and 74. When you move the cursor to the right of the code, the cursor in a sense "reads" or "interprets" that code, and the bracket on the bar moves according to what is read.

This code controls the margin until it is replaced by a different code. To see this, press Home, Home, Up Arrow to move the cursor to the top of the document. Press the spacebar to exit the reveal codes. You have decided that a 4 1/2-inch line is too short; you wish to change it to 5 1/2-inches. Because there are 10 characters per inch, you need to have 55 characters on the line. Press Shift-F8. Press the number 3 for margins. Type the number 10 and press Enter ↵. Type the number 65 and press Enter ↵.

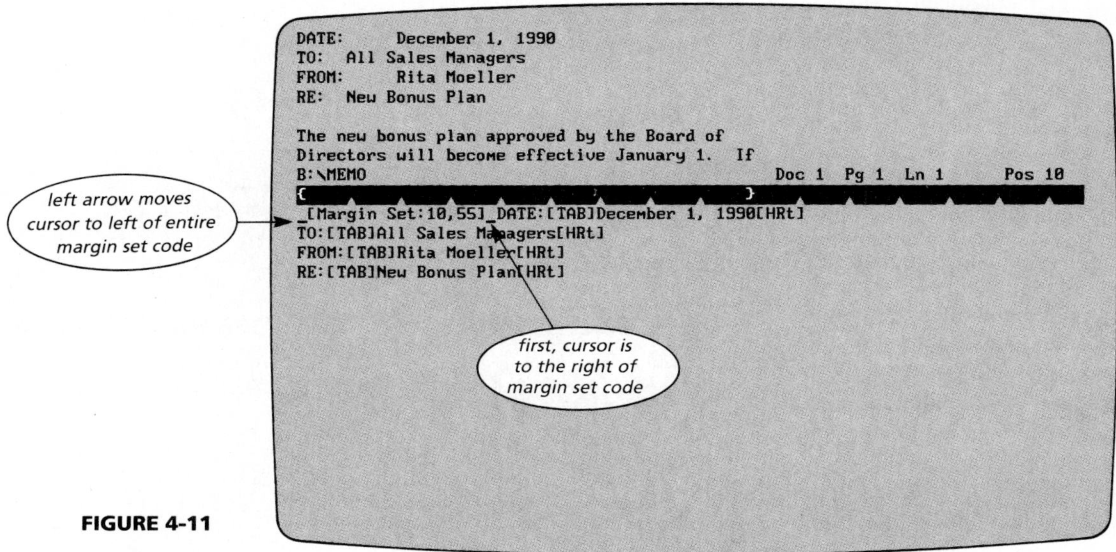


FIGURE 4-11

As you look at the screen you cannot see any changes to the length of the line. In Project 2 you learned that most problems with WordPerfect can be solved by analyzing the codes. Press Alt-F3. As you see in Figure 4-12 you have two margin setting codes, with the cursor between them. The first code is the new margin setting of 10,65. That code is in effect until it is overridden by a new code. As you see, it is immediately overridden by the old code of 10,55. Therefore, the typing will follow the command of the 10,55 code instead of the 10,65 code. Because you wish to delete the 10,55 code, you wish to delete going *forward*. Press the Delete key once. Be careful when you delete the code. Your tendency may be to press the Delete key many times. But because the margin setting is within brackets, it is only necessary to press the Delete key one time. Then press the spacebar to exit the reveal codes. Figure 4-13 shows how the new margin setting affects the typing.

To emphasize one more time the importance of where you insert a code, move the cursor down to line 8, position 10, under the c in contact. Press Shift-F8. Press the number 3 for margins. Type the number 10 and press Enter ↵. Type the number 30 and press Enter ↵ again. You see now that the code at the top of the memo remains in effect until it is overridden by a new code. Because the new code was inserted later in the document, the new code overrides the old code and will affect typing from where it is inserted *downward*. To view the new code, press Alt-F3 (Figure 4-14). You see the new code on the screen. The cursor is to the right of the code. Press the Backspace key *only one time* to delete the 10,30 code allowing the 10,65 code to take effect again.

After completing this exercise you can understand how important it is to have the cursor in the proper position before you invoke a code. You cannot be at the end of a document, then decide that you want to change the margins of the entire document, without pressing Home, Home, Up Arrow to place the code at the beginning of the document.

Press the spacebar to exit the reveal codes. Press Home, Home, Up Arrow to go to the top of the document.

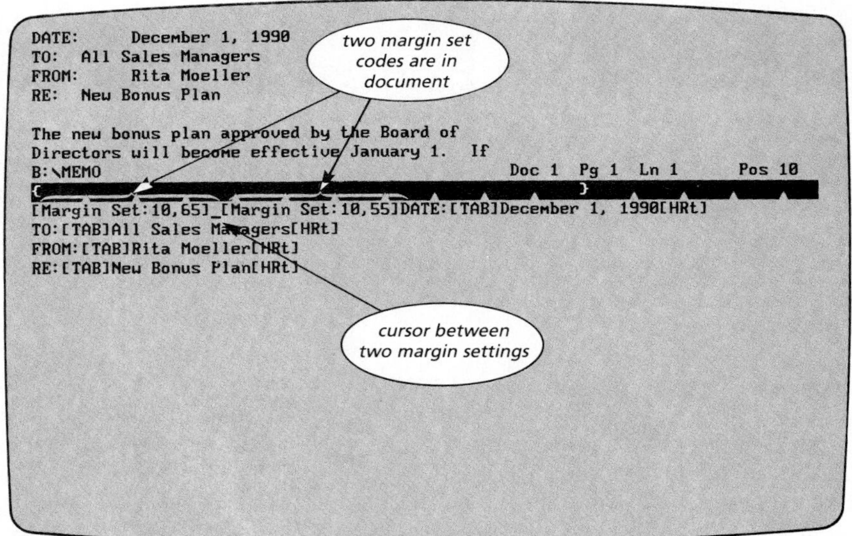
DATE: December 1, 1990
TO: All Sales Managers
FROM: Rita Moeller
RE: New Bonus Plan
The new bonus plan approved by the Board of
Directors will become effective January 1. If
B:\MEMO Doc 1 Pg 1 Ln 1 Pos 10
[Margin Set:10,65]_[Margin Set:10,55]DATE:[TAB]December 1, 1990[HRt]
TO:[TAB]All Sales Managers[HRt]
FROM:[TAB]Rita Moeller[HRt]
RE:[TAB]New Bonus Plan[HRt]
two margin set codes are in document
cursor between two margin settings

FIGURE 4-12

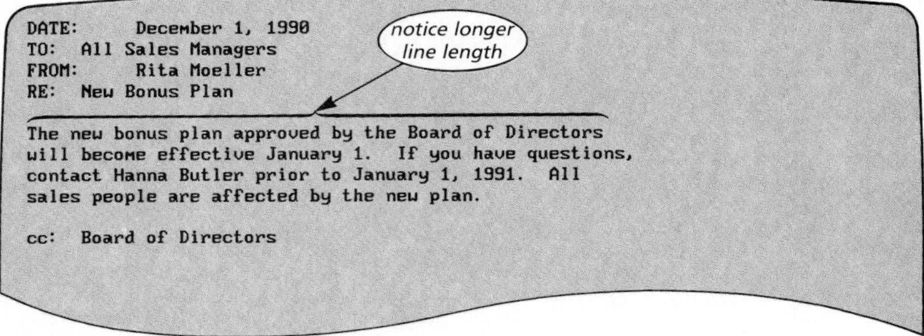
DATE: December 1, 1990
TO: All Sales Managers
FROM: Rita Moeller
RE: New Bonus Plan
The new bonus plan approved by the Board of Directors
will become effective January 1. If you have questions,
contact Hanna Butler prior to January 1, 1991. All
sales people are affected by the new plan.
cc: Board of Directors
notice longer line length

FIGURE 4-13

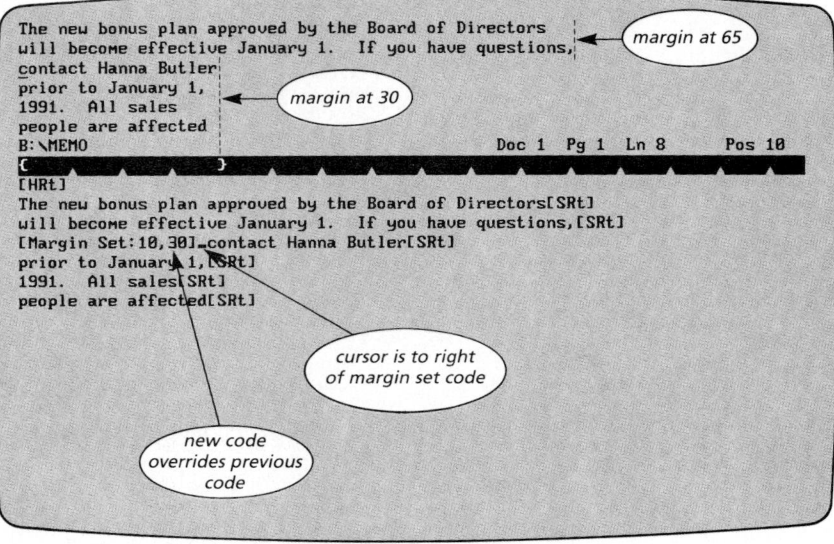
The new bonus plan approved by the Board of Directors
will become effective January 1. If you have questions,
contact Hanna Butler
prior to January 1,
1991. All sales
people are affected
B:\MEMO Doc 1 Pg 1 Ln 8 Pos 10
[HRt]
The new bonus plan approved by the Board of Directors[SRt]
will become effective January 1. If you have questions,[SRt]
[Margin Set:10,30]_contact Hanna Butler[SRt]
prior to January 1,[SRt]
1991. All sales[SRt]
people are affected[SRt]
margin at 65
margin at 30
cursor is to right of margin set code
new code overrides previous code

FIGURE 4-14

## Changing Tab Settings

So that the first four lines will line up at the tab, you need to add a tab setting at position 17 and delete the tab setting at position 15. Press Shift-F8. Either number 1 or number 2 will choose tabs. Press number 1. Figure 4-15 shows the tab settings on the lower portion of the screen. Type the number 17 and press Enter ↵ (step 1 of Figure 4-16). Notice that there is an L on position 17. To delete the tab setting on position 15, press the Left Arrow two times ← ← to move the cursor under the L on position 15. Press the Delete key one time (step 2 of Figure 4-16). The message on the screen instructs you to press Exit when done. This is how you exit the tab setting screen properly. If you press the Cancel key, you will exit but the changes will not be made. Therefore, press F7 to exit (step 3 of Figure 4-16). Now notice how the tabs have lined up properly, as in Figure 4-17 on the following page.

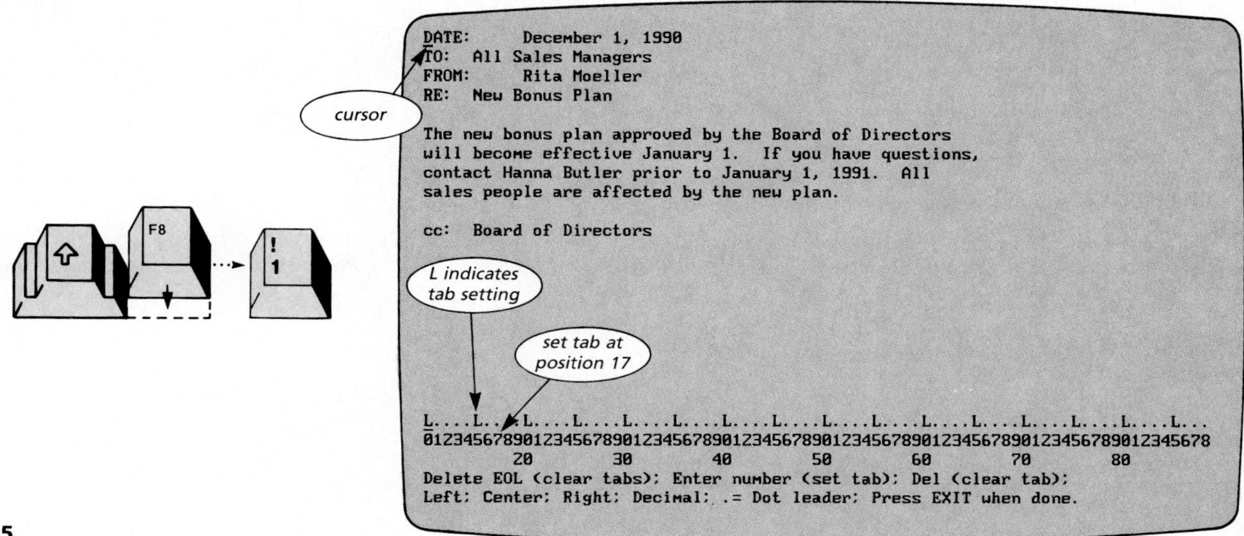


FIGURE 4-15

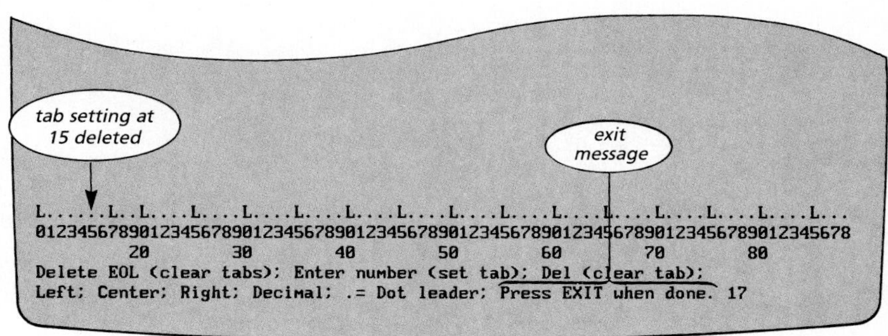


**Step 1: Set tab at 17** **Step 2: Delete tab at 15** **Step 3: Save tab changes and exit**

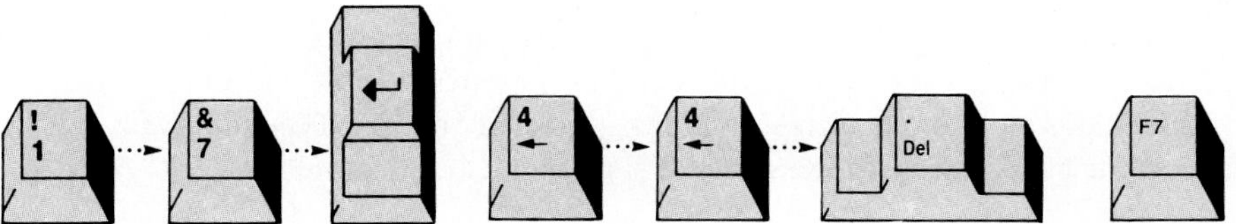


FIGURE 4-16

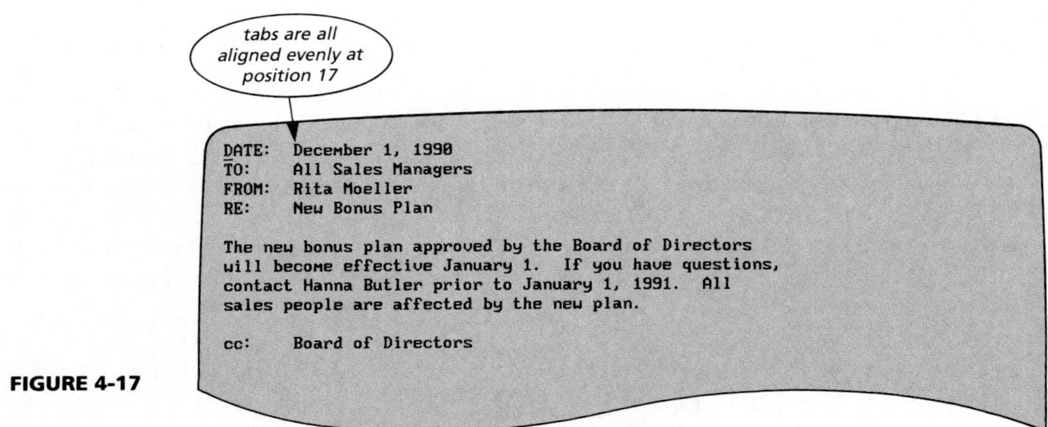
tabs are all aligned evenly at position 17
DATE: December 1, 1990
TO: All Sales Managers
FROM: Rita Moeller
RE: New Bonus Plan
The new bonus plan approved by the Board of Directors
will become effective January 1. If you have questions,
contact Hanna Butler prior to January 1, 1991. All
sales people are affected by the new plan.
cc: Board of Directors

FIGURE 4-17

To view the embedded codes, press Alt-F3 (Figure 4-18). All the tab settings that were present when you inserted the one at position 17 are listed. Remember that codes are within brackets [ ]. Therefore, this is only *one* code. If you were to press the Left Arrow ←, then the Right Arrow → back and forth, you would notice that the cursor cannot move inside the brackets. To exit the reveal codes press the spacebar.

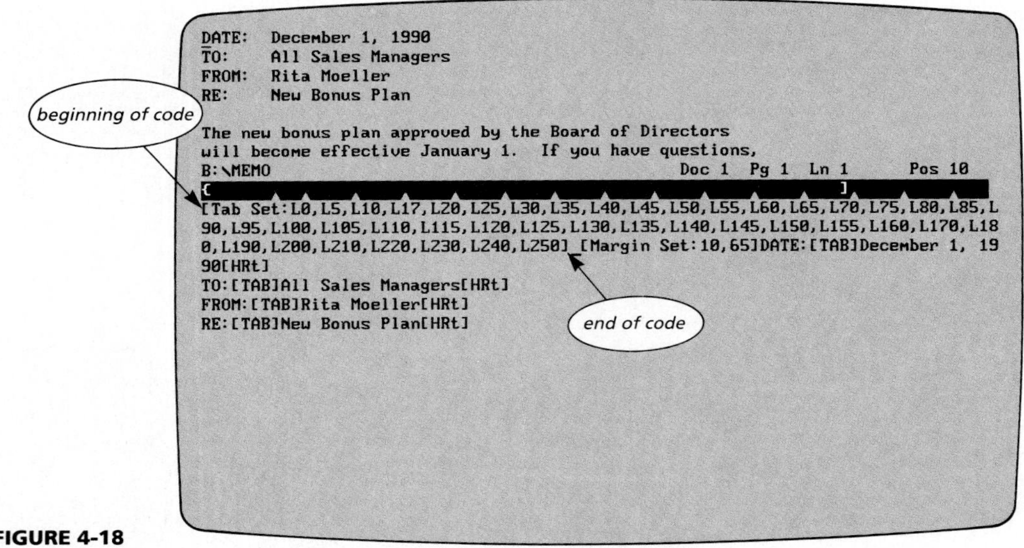
DATE: December 1, 1990
TO: All Sales Managers
FROM: Rita Moeller
RE: New Bonus Plan
beginning of code
The new bonus plan approved by the Board of Directors
will become effective January 1. If you have questions,
B:\MEMO Doc 1 Pg 1 Ln 1 Pos 10
[Tab Set:L0,L5,L10,L17,L20,L25,L30,L35,L40,L45,L50,L55,L60,L65,L70,L75,L80,L85,L
90,L95,L100,L105,L110,L115,L120,L125,L130,L135,L140,L145,L150,L155,L160,L170,L18
0,L190,L200,L210,L220,L230,L240,L250] [Margin Set:10,65]DATE:[TAB]December 1, 19
90[HRt]
TO:[TAB]All Sales Managers[HRt]
FROM:[TAB]Rita Moeller[HRt]
RE:[TAB]New Bonus Plan[HRt]
end of code

FIGURE 4-18

## Changing the Line Spacing

The next change to make in the memo is to change the line spacing from single space to 1 1/2 spacing. To change the line spacing, you must call up the line format menu. Press Shift-F8 (step 1 of Figure 4-19). At the Line Format menu, press the number 4 (step 2 of Figure 4-19). The prompt on the screen will be "[Spacing Set] 1". Type the number 1.5 and press Enter ↵ (Figure 4-20). To view the code that was inserted, press Alt-F3 (Figure 4-21).

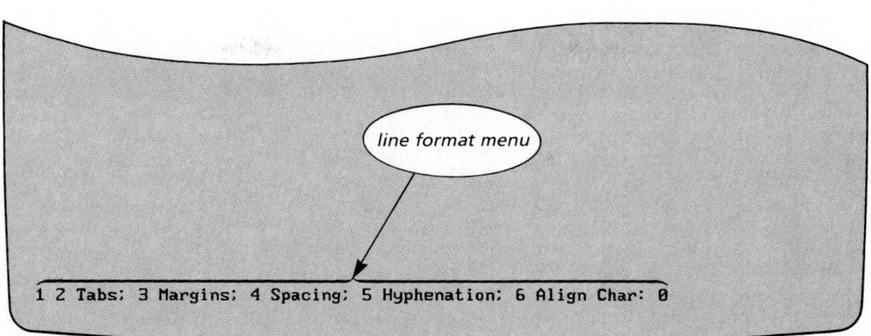


**Step 1: View Line Format menu**

**Step 2: View how spacing is set**

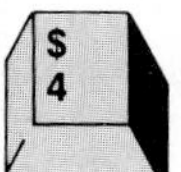


**FIGURE 4-19**

**FIGURE 4-20**

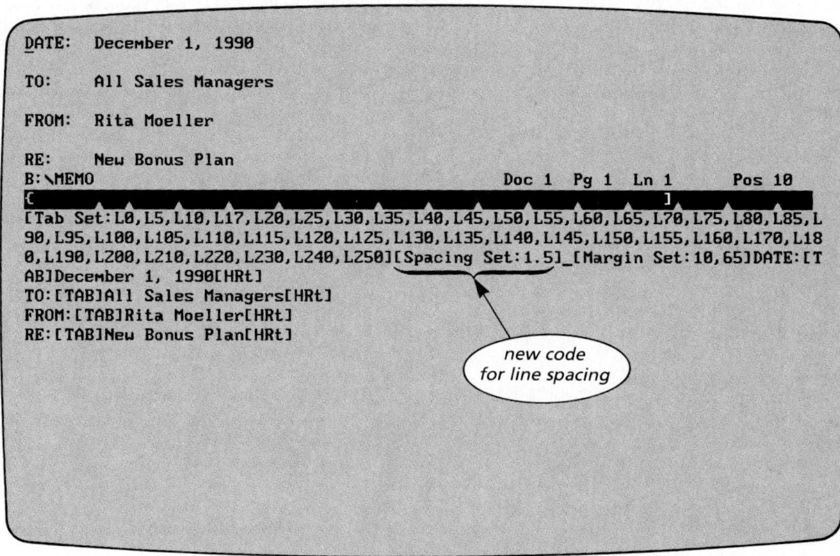


**FIGURE 4-21**

If you ever want to change back to single spacing, you can simply delete the code. WordPerfect would then return to the default, which is single spacing. If you wish to change to double spacing, you must be sure that the cursor *follows* any code you wish to override.

To exit the reveal codes, press the spacebar. The lines on the screen will appear to be double spaced. That is because the screen cannot show 1 1/2 spacing. However, the printer will read the code and print in 1 1/2 spacing. Watching the status line, press the Down Arrow ↓. Figure 4-22 shows how the code is interpreted: the next line is line 2.5. Continue pressing the Down Arrow ↓ and notice that the spacing is indeed 1 1/2 spacing. Press Home, Home, Up Arrow to move the cursor to the top of the document.

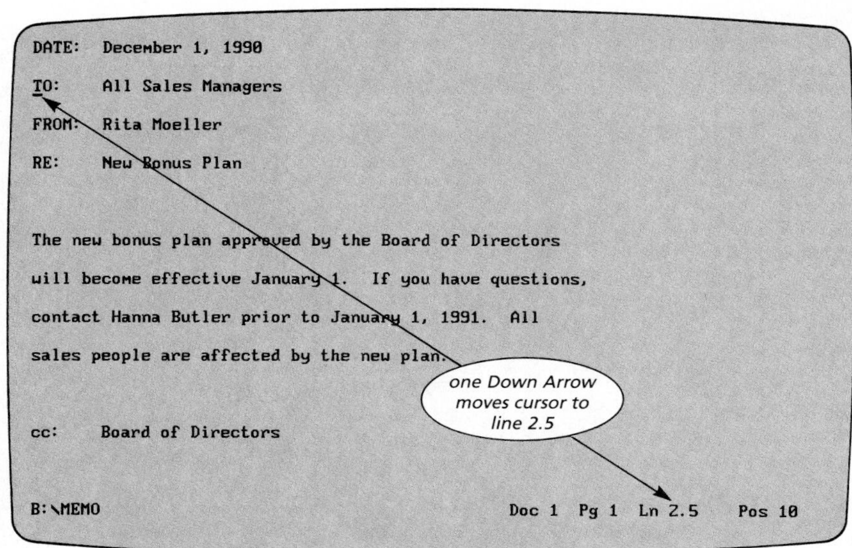
DATE: December 1, 1990
TO: All Sales Managers
FROM: Rita Moeller
RE: New Bonus Plan
The new bonus plan approved by the Board of Directors
will become effective January 1. If you have questions,
contact Hanna Butler prior to January 1, 1991. All
sales people are affected by the new plan.
one Down Arrow moves cursor to line 2.5
cc: Board of Directors
B:\MEMO
Doc 1 Pg 1 Ln 2.5 Pos 10

FIGURE 4-22

## PREVIEWING

You can **preview** your text exactly as it will be printed. Press Shift-F7 to reveal the Print menu, then press the number 6 for preview and press the number 1 to view the document (step 1 of Figure 4-23). As WordPerfect formats the document for previewing, the message "please wait" appears. Figure 4-23 shows the preview screen identified as Document 3 and shows the word "PREVIEW" in the lower left corner of the screen. This screen shows you exactly how your document will be printed. Notice the 1-inch heading at the top margin. The text has a justified right margin. The screen also shows where the *WPC markings will be printed. To exit the preview screen, press the F7 (Exit) key (step 2 of Figure 4-23).

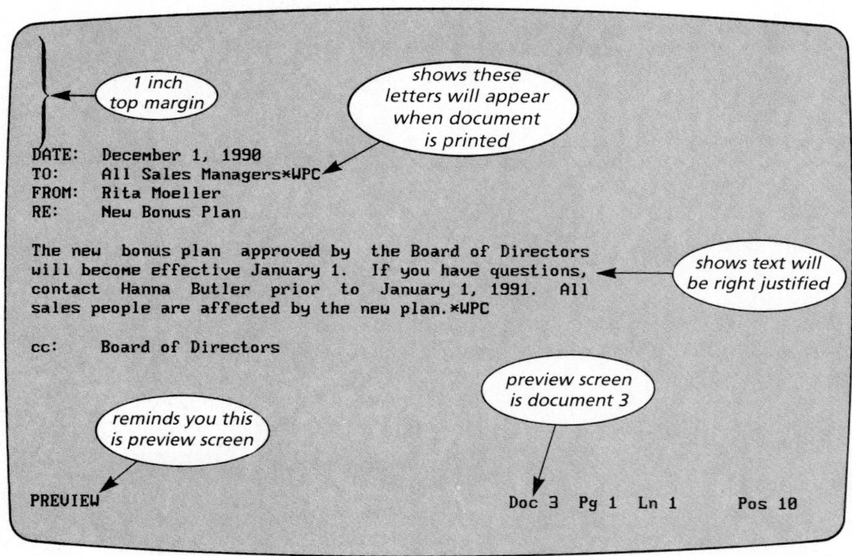
1 inch top margin
shows these letters will appear when document is printed
DATE: December 1, 1990
TO: All Sales Managers*WPC
FROM: Rita Moeller
RE: New Bonus Plan
The new bonus plan approved by the Board of Directors
will become effective January 1. If you have questions,
contact Hanna Butler prior to January 1, 1991. All
sales people are affected by the new plan.*WPC
shows text will be right justified
cc: Board of Directors
preview screen is document 3
reminds you this is preview screen
PREVIEW
Doc 3 Pg 1 Ln 1 Pos 10

Step 1: Preview the document

Step 2: Exit the preview screen

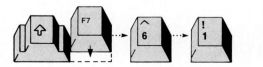

FIGURE 4-23

# PRINT FORMATTING

## Right Justified Text

Turning the justification on and off is part of the print formatting process for a document. Look at the template next to the F8 key. You see the words Print Format in red. Press Ctl-F8 (step 1 of Figure 4-24) to view how the document is formatted. Notice that the justification is turned on. Press the number 3 and notice that the justification is now turned off (step 2 of Figure 4-24). Press Enter to exit the print format screen (step 3 of Figure 4-24). To view the code that was inserted, press Alt-F3. Figure 4-25 shows the embedded code that turned the justification off. To exit the reveal codes, press the spacebar.

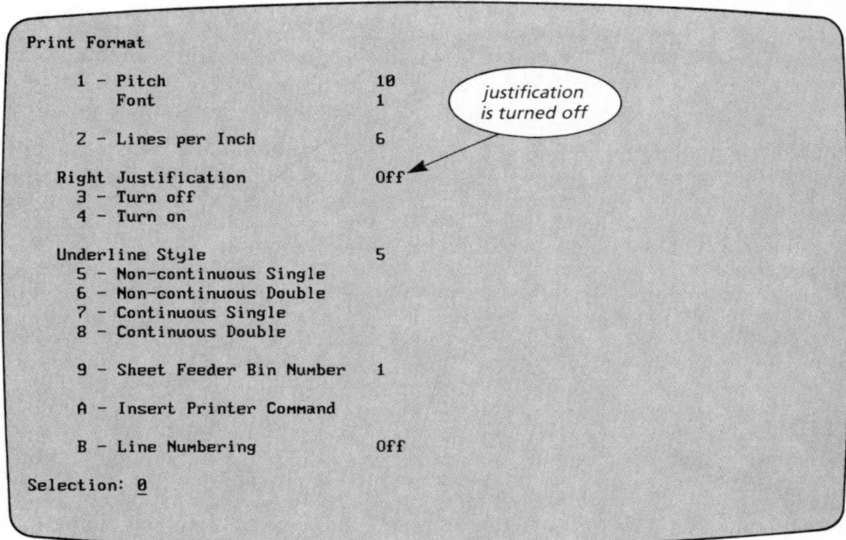


FIGURE 4-24

Step 1: View the print format screen

Step 2: Turn off right justification

Step 3: Exit the print format screen

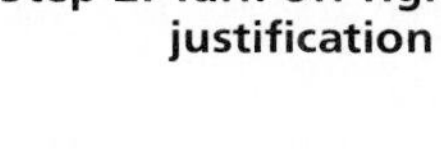

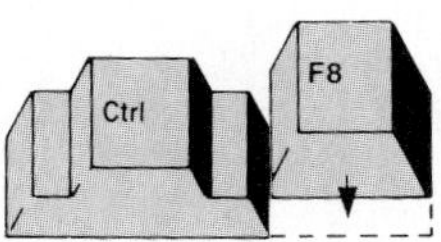


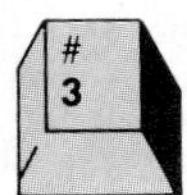


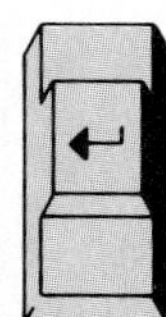

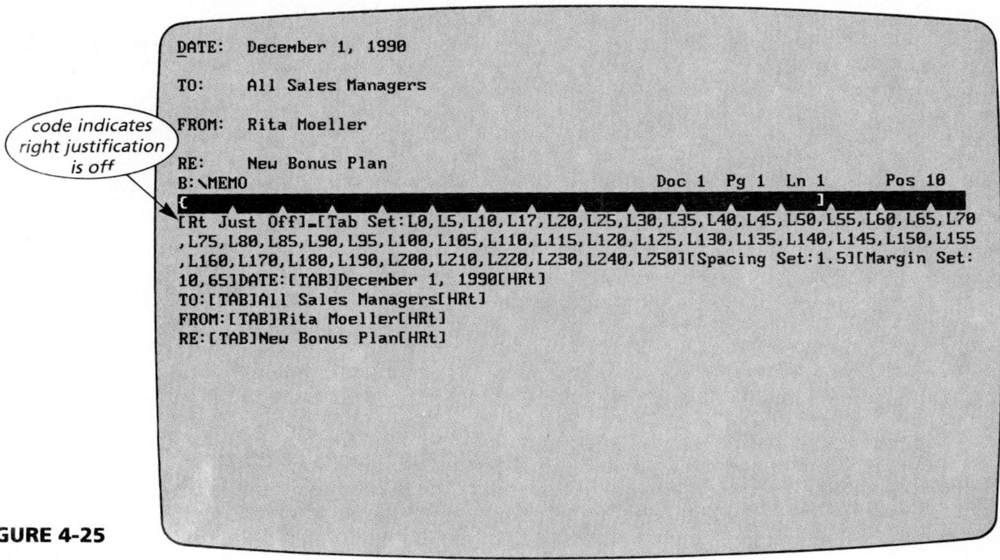


FIGURE 4-25

# PAGE FORMATTING

## Centering Page Top to Bottom

Because your memo is short, when it is printed it will only cover the top portion of the page as shown in Figure 4-1a. To print your document in the center of the paper, as shown in Figure 4-1b, with even margins on the top and the bottom of the page, you must choose the **Center Page Top to Bottom** option from the page format screen.

Press Alt-F8 (step 1 of Figure 4-26). Figure 4-26 shows the page format screen. Press the number 3 and then Enter ↵ to return to your document (steps 2 and 3 of Figure 4-26). To view the inserted code, press Alt-F3. Figure 4-27 shows the code that will tell the printer to center the page, giving it even top and bottom margins. To exit the reveal codes, press the spacebar.

Your document has all the desired changes, as shown in Figure 4-1a. Now you must save the document in its new form, then print the memo on paper.

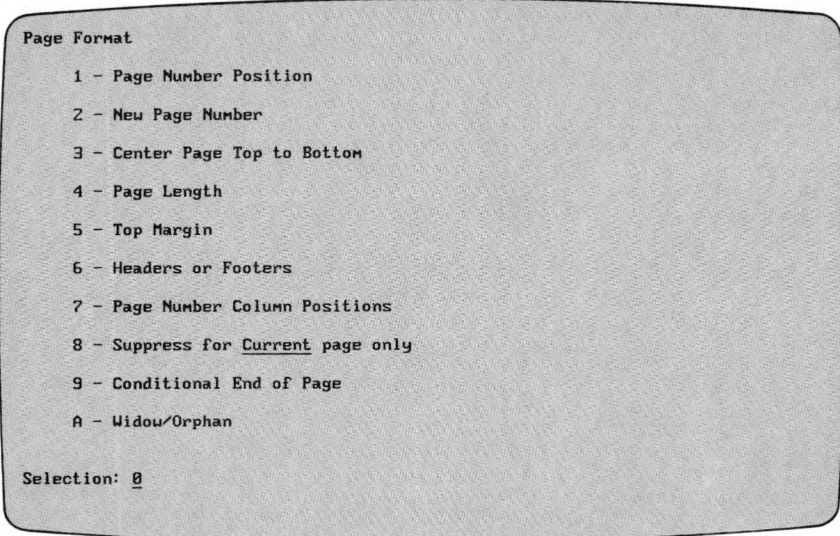

Page Format
1 - Page Number Position
2 - New Page Number
3 - Center Page Top to Bottom
4 - Page Length
5 - Top Margin
6 - Headers or Footers
7 - Page Number Column Positions
8 - Suppress for Current page only
9 - Conditional End of Page
A - Widow/Orphan
Selection: 0


FIGURE 4-26

**Step 1: View Page Format menu**

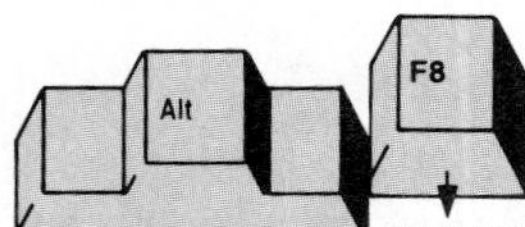


**Step 2: Select the Center Page Top to Bottom option**

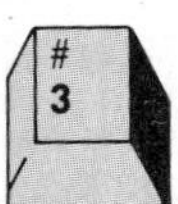


**Step 3: Return to the document**

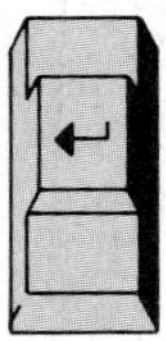

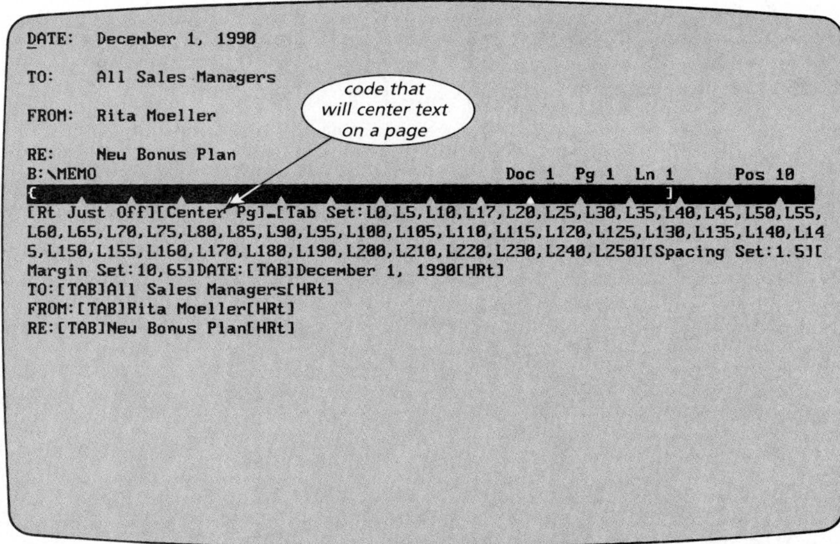


**FIGURE 4-27**

## SAVING, REPLACING, AND PRINTING THE DOCUMENT

When you finished typing this document in Project 2, you saved the document to your disk. Since that time, you have made several changes to the document on your screen. However, those changes have not been saved to the disk. As you learned in Project 3, it is necessary to save these changes to the disk, replacing the old text with the new text. Keep in mind that you are not just adding but also replacing text. Save and replace your document now as you did in Project 3 (F10, Enter, Y).

The document is now ready to be printed. Be sure that your printer has paper inserted and that the printer is turned on and ready to print. As you have done in previous projects, print the full text of this document. The printed document generated should look like Figure 4-1b.

## OTHER PRINT FORMAT FEATURES

Now that the document has been changed, saved, and printed, we can learn some other print format features. Let's return to the print format screen by pressing Ctrl-F8 (Figure 4-24).

## Pitch

If you wish to change the pitch from 10 to 12 or 15 (Figure 4-28), or the font number, you would press the number 1, then type the preferred pitch followed by the Enter key. Then you'd type the preferred font number followed by the Enter key.

```
This is  a 10 pitch font defined as font #1.  The margins are set
at 10 on the left and 74 on  the right.   There  are 6  lines per
inch.

This is  a 12 pitch font defined as font #1.  The margins are set
at 10 on the left and 74 on  the right.   There  are 6  lines per
inch.

This is  a 15 pitch font defined as font #1.  The margins are set
at 10 on the left and 74 on the right.  Because  the letters are
small, the  computer has  been programmed at 8 lines per inch, so
that there is not too much white space between the lines.
```

FIGURE 4-28

## Lines per Inch

If you were using a 15 pitch font where the type is very small, you may wish to have more lines per inch than the default of 6. In the print format screen, you would press number 2, then type the number 8 for 8 lines per inch. WordPerfect will not accept spacing other than 6 or 8, so if you were to type something else, the cursor would not move and when you press Enter, 6 will be inserted automatically.

## Underline Style

If you have some underlined text, you may wish to change the underline style, such as to a double continuous line. On the print format screen, select the desired number, such as number 8 for a continuous double line. Figure 4-29 shows examples of the underline styles available.

```
Non-continuous                  Single underlining

Non-continuous                  Double underlining

Continuous                      Single underlining

Continuous                      Double underlining
```

FIGURE 4-29

## ADVANCED TAB SETTINGS

**H**ere we will learn some of the more advanced tab setting features. You do not want to confuse this lesson with the memo on your screen. WordPerfect has the ability to have two documents in memory and to let you switch quickly back and forth between the two documents. As we learned in Project 1, we can switch to Document 2, while keeping Document 1 as it is. Refer to the template next to the F3 key. You'll see that Shift-F3 will shift documents. Press Shift-F3. Your typing disappears, and you have a blank screen. Notice that the status line indicates document 2. This is a new blank screen; anything you do in this screen will be totally separate from document 1. For practice, press Shift-F3 and notice that you are back in document 1. Press Shift-F3 again and you are in document 2.

Remember that tabs are set by pressing Shift-F8. Press Shift-F8 and then the number 1 for tabs (Figure 4-30). Remember that tab settings are indicated by the letter L.

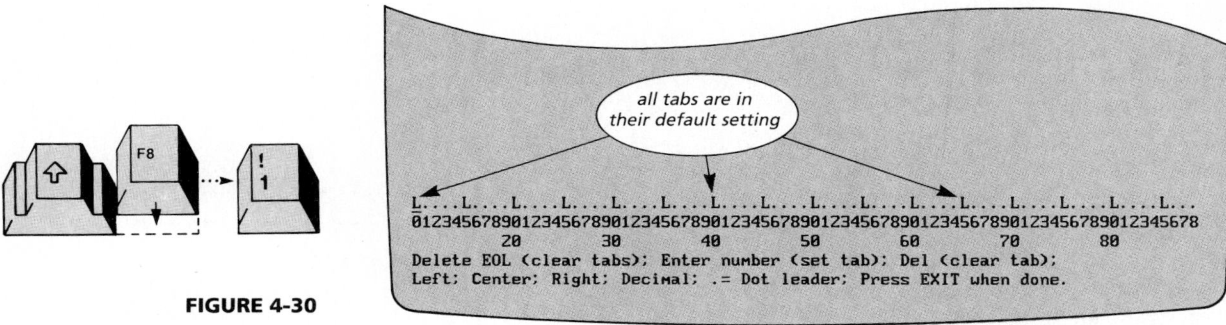


**FIGURE 4-30**

First we need to clear all tab settings. Press Home, Home, Left Arrow to move the cursor to position 0. As the bottom of the screen indicates, "Delete EOL" (Delete End of Line) will clear all tabs. Press Ctrl-End and all tab settings will clear (Figure 4-31).

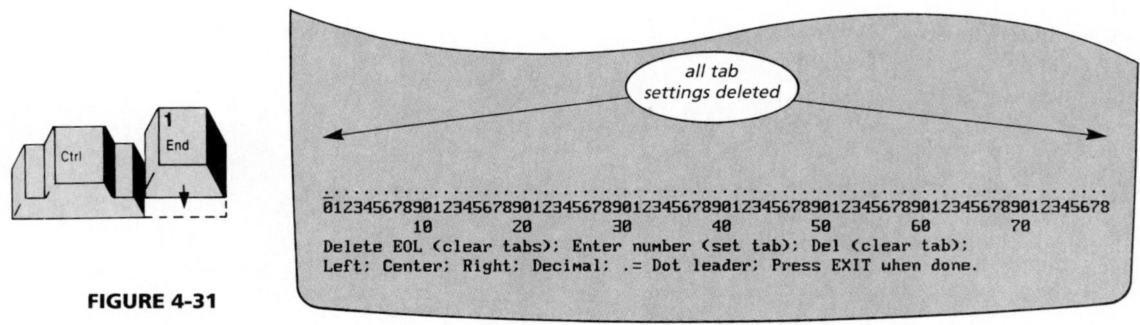


**FIGURE 4-31**

First, let's set the desired tab settings; then their functions will be explained. Type the number 15 and press Enter ↵. You see an L above position 15. Type the number 30 and press Enter ↵. You see an L above position 30. Press the letter c and notice how the L changes to a capital C. Type the number 48 and press Enter ↵. Press the letter r and notice how the L changes to a capital R. Type the number 60 and press Enter ↵. Press the letter d and notice once more how the L changes to a capital D. The screen should now look like the Figure 4-32.

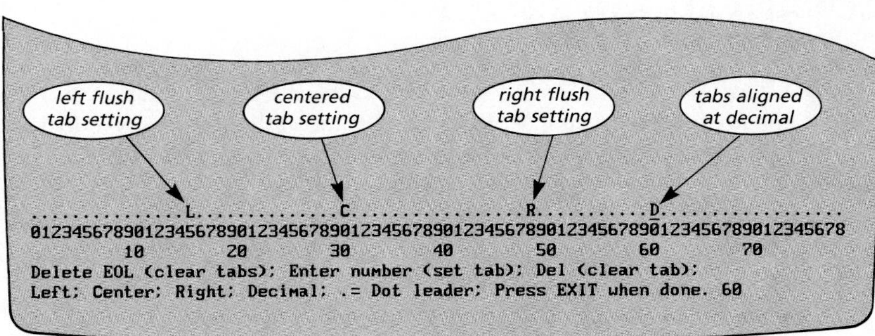


FIGURE 4-32

When you set each tab, the default of L appeared first at each setting. Imagine that the tab settings are like anchors. Wherever there is an L, the typing anchors to the *left* and the typing flows to the *right*. When you changed the L at position 30 to C, you were instructing WordPerfect to anchor in the *center*, so the typing will be centered over the tab setting as it does when you use the center function. When you changed the L at position 48 to R, you were instructing WordPerfect to anchor at the right, so the typing flows to the left as it does when you use the flush right function. When you changed the L at position 60 to D, you were instructing WordPerfect to anchor at a decimal point (a period). Figure 4-33 illustrates how each tab setting will be anchored and where the type will flow from the specific tab setting.

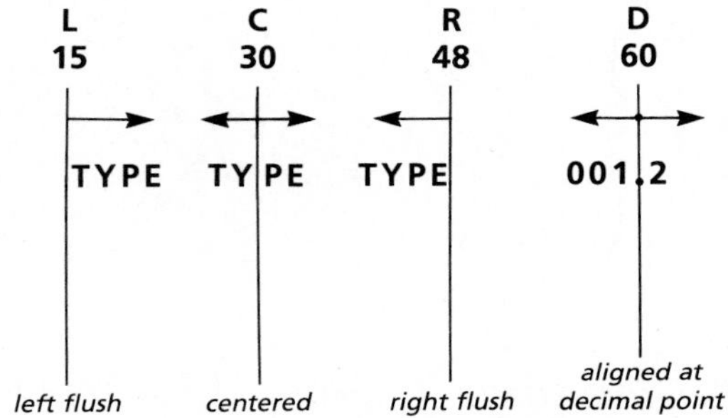


FIGURE 4-33

To exit from the tab setting screen, press F7. You are returned to the blank screen of document 2. To view the inserted codes, press Alt-F3. Figure 4-34 shows that each tab setting is identified with the proper letter. To exit the codes press the spacebar.

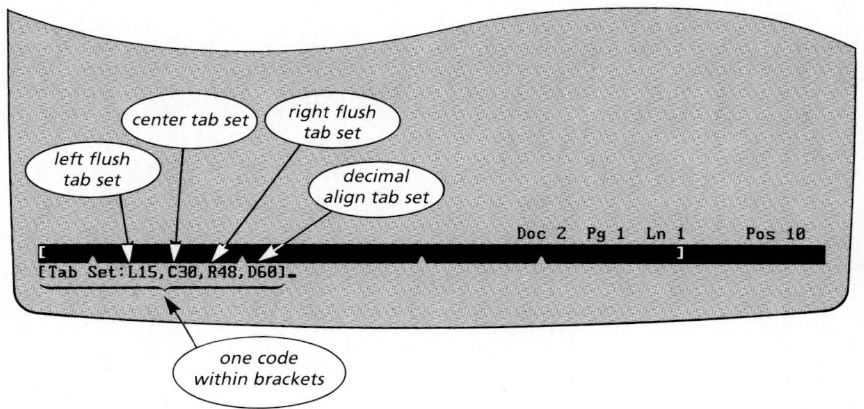


FIGURE 4-34

To use each tab setting, first press the Tab key. The cursor stops at the first tab setting, which is 15. The type will flow to the right of the tab setting. Type the two words Now is, and press the Tab key again. The cursor moves to position 30, the next tab setting. This is where the C for center was placed. Type the word Heading. As you do, try to watch the screen and notice how the word centers over position 30. Press the Tab key again and the cursor moves to position 48, the next tab setting. This is where an R was placed for right justified. Type the amount $1,000.00 and as you do notice how the typing anchors at the tab setting and flows to the left of the tab, making the number flush right. For the last setting, press the Tab key, moving the cursor to position 60 where the D was placed, for aligning at the decimal point. In the lower left corner of the screen you see the message "Align Char = ." As you type now, try to watch the screen so you can see how the type anchors at the decimal point and the last two zeros are placed to the right of the decimal. Type the amount $2,000.00. The screen should look like Figure 4-35.

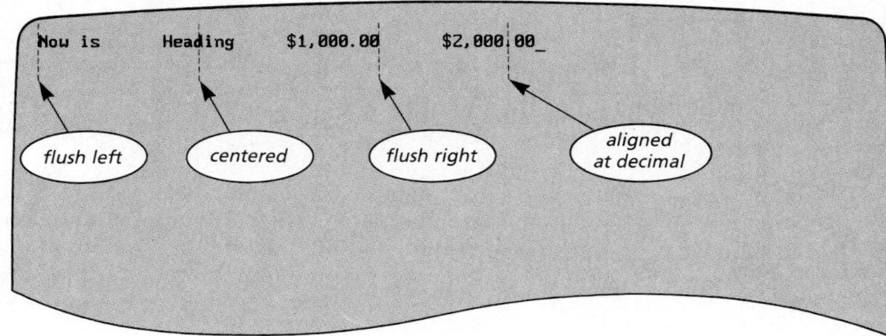


**FIGURE 4-35**

Press the hard return ↵ so you can use each tab setting one more time. The cursor should be on line 2, position 10. Press the Tab key and type these two words: the time. As you do so watch the typing anchor at the left. Press the Tab key again and type the word Head, and the typing centers at the tab setting. Press the Tab key again and type the number 60.00, and notice how the typing anchors at the right. Press the Tab key one more time. Type the number 120.34 and the typing will anchor at the decimal point, putting the 34 to the right of the decimal. Press the hard return two times ↵ ↵, placing the cursor on line 4, position 10.

There is one more tab setting that is also very useful. To use it we must change the present tab settings. As before, press Shift-F8 and the number 1 for tabs. To delete the present settings press Ctrl-End. Type the number 74 and press Enter. An L is placed above position 74. Press the letter r, changing the L to an R. Now type . (a period) and notice how the R is shown in reverse video (Figure 4-36). You know that the R setting will anchor at the right and the text will flow to the left, as in flush right. By placing the decimal over the R, you are indicating that you want *leader dots* to be inserted automatically from where the cursor is to the tab setting. While you are only placing a period over the R in this particular exercise, you can also place a period over the L (left flush) or D (decimal align) settings. You cannot place a period over the C (center) tab setting.

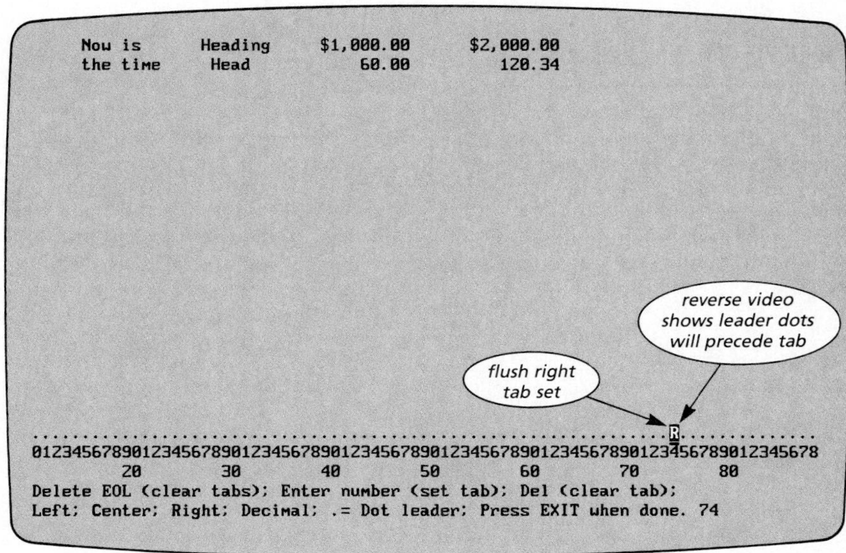


**FIGURE 4-36**

To exit from the tab setting screen, press F7 and you are returned to your document. To demonstrate how this tab setting works, we will type this as if it were part of a program you may be typing. With the cursor on line 4, position 10, type the words Piano Prelude, then press the Tab key. The cursor moves to position 74, which is the tab setting, and as it does, leader dots are inserted from the end of your typing to the tab setting. Now type the name Francis Holt and notice how the type moves to the left of the tab. As it does, it eliminates leader dots where the name is typed (Figure 4-37).

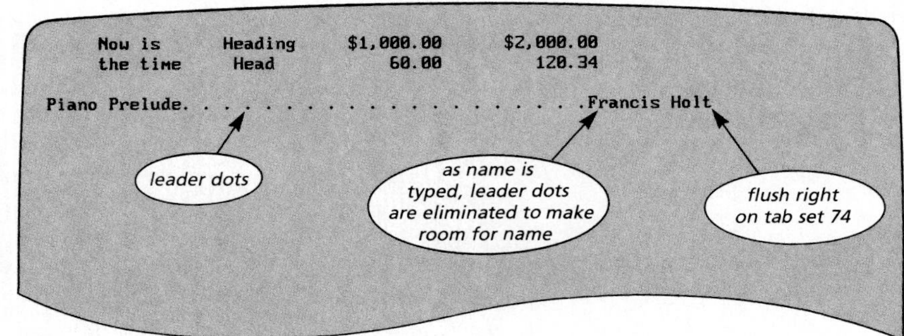


**FIGURE 4-37**

Leader dots can be used as above in programs, or, for example, in a table of contents. The dots lead the reader's eye to the right to follow the line of typing.

Save this document under the name Tabs. Press F10, type Tabs, then press Enter.

## EXITING PROJECT 4

You may remember that document 1 still remains in memory. You will not be able to exit WordPerfect without seeing a reminder that another document remains in memory. Press F7. Press N to the prompt "Save document?". The next prompt is "Exit Doc 2? (Y/N) N." It indicates that MEMO is still in memory in document 1. Type the letter Y to exit document 2 and return to document 1. If you had typed the letter N for no, you would have remained in document 2 and received a blank screen. Then you would have had to use the Shift-F3 function to return to document 1.

Because document 1 has already been saved, it is not necessary to save it again before you exit WordPerfect. Exit WordPerfect as you have in previous projects (F7, N, Y).

## PROJECT SUMMARY

In Project 4 you retrieved an existing document and made changes to it. You learned how to change the default margin settings, tab settings, and line spacing, how to justify text, and how to center a short document on the page. You learned about the print format functions of pitch, lines per inch, and underline style. Finally, you practiced advanced tab setting functions and moving back and forth between two documents in memory.

The following is a list of the keystroke sequence we used in Project 4:

## SUMMARY OF KEYSTROKES—Project 4

| STEPS | KEY(S) PRESSED | STEPS | KEY(S) PRESSED | STEPS | KEY(S) PRESSED |
|---|---|---|---|---|---|
| 1 | Shift-F10 | 45 | 30 | 90 | ↵ |
| 2 | memo | 46 | ↵ | 91 | d |
| 3 | ↵ | 47 | Alt-F3 | 92 | F7 |
| 4 | Caps Lock | 48 | Backspace | 93 | TAB |
| 5 | DATE: | 49 | Space | 94 | Now is |
| 6 | TAB | 50 | Home Home ↑ | 95 | TAB |
| 7 | ↓ | 51 | Shift-F8 | 96 | Heading |
| 8 | Del | 52 | 1 | 97 | TAB |
| 9 | Del | 53 | 17 | 98 | $1,000.00 |
| 10 | Del | 54 | ↵ | 99 | TAB |
| 11 | Del | 55 | ← | 100 | $2,000.00 |
| 12 | ↓ | 56 | ← | 101 | ↵ |
| 13 | ↵ | 57 | Del | 102 | TAB |
| 14 | ↑ | 58 | F7 | 103 | the time |
| 15 | FROM: | 59 | Shift-F8 | 104 | TAB |
| 16 | Caps Lock | 60 | 4 | 105 | Head |
| 17 | TAB | 61 | 1.5 | 106 | TAB |
| 18 | Rita Moeller | 62 | ↵ | 107 | 60.00 |
| 19 | [move cursor to line 11, position 10, under R in Rita] | 63 | Home Home ↑ | 108 | TAB |
|  |  | 64 | Ctrl-F8 | 109 | 120.34 |
| 20 | Ctrl-End | 65 | 3 | 110 | ↵ |
| 21 | Del | 66 | ↵ | 111 | ↵ |
| 22 | Del | 67 | Alt-F8 | 112 | Shift-F8 |
| 23 | Home Home ↑ | 68 | 3 | 113 | 1 |
| 24 | Shift-F8 | 69 | ↵ | 114 | Ctrl-End |
| 25 | 3 | 70 | F10 | 115 | 74 |
| 26 | 10 | 71 | ↵ | 116 | ↵ |
| 27 | ↵ | 72 | y | 117 | r |
| 28 | 55 | 73 | [be sure printer is on] | 118 | . |
| 29 | ↵ | 74 | Shift-F7 | 119 | F7 |
| 30 | Home Home ↑ | 75 | 1 | 120 | Piano Prelude |
| 31 | Shift-F8 | 76 | Shift-F3 | 121 | TAB |
| 32 | 3 | 77 | Shift-F8 | 122 | Francis Holt |
| 33 | 10 | 78 | 1 | 123 | F7 |
| 34 | ↵ | 79 | Home Home ← | 124 | y |
| 35 | 65 | 80 | Ctrl-End | 125 | tabs |
| 36 | ↵ | 81 | 15 | 126 | ↵ |
| 37 | Alt-F3 | 82 | ↵ | 127 | y |
| 38 | Del | 83 | 30 | 128 | F7 |
| 39 | Space | 84 | ↵ | 129 | n |
| 40 | [move cursor to line 8, position 10] | 85 | c | 130 | y |
|  |  | 86 | 48 | 131 | [if not at the DOS prompt, take WordPerfect disk out of drive A and insert DOS disk] |
| 41 | Shift-F8 | 87 | ↵ |  |  |
| 42 | 3 | 88 | r |  |  |
| 43 | 10 | 89 | 60 | 132 | [press any key] |
| 44 | ↵ |  |  |  |  |

The following list summarizes the material covered in Project 4:

1. The term **type font** refers to the typeface or print style of a document.
2. Traditionally, typewriters used the terms **pica** or **elite** to describe type size. Pica type fits 10 characters into 1 inch of space on a line; elite type fits 12 characters into 1 inch of space.

### Project Summary (continued)

3. Instead of pica or elite, the terms used in word processing are **10 pitch font** and **12 pitch font**.
4. **Formatting** is the process of defining how a document will look when printed.
5. The **Line Format** key is used to define tab settings, margins, and line spacing.
6. The **preview** function allows the user to see how a document will look when it is printed.
7. The **Center Page Top to Bottom** option from the page format screen centers the print on a page evenly between the top and bottom of the page.

## STUDENT ASSIGNMENTS

### STUDENT ASSIGNMENT 1: True/False

**Instructions:** Circle T if the statement is true and F if the statement is false.

T F 1. On the template, the word Retrieve is in red, meaning the user presses Ctrl-F10 to retrieve a document.
T F 2. WordPerfect default margin settings are at position 10 on the left and position 74 on the right.
T F 3. A piece of paper that is 11" long has 60 typing lines from the top edge of the paper to the bottom edge.
T F 4. To change any of the line format settings, press Shift-F8.
T F 5. The default letter setting for tabs is the letter L.
T F 6. When changing the line spacing to 1 1/2 spacing, press Shift-F8, then 4, then type 1.5 and press Enter.
T F 7. To change the type to be unjustified on the right margin, press the number 3 on the page format screen.
T F 8. When setting tab stops, if the user changes the L to R, the type will anchor at the right.
T F 9. When setting tab stops, changing the L to D will cause leader dots to be typed on the screen.
T F 10. When setting tab stops, changing the L to C will enable type to be centered over the tab stop.

### STUDENT ASSIGNMENT 2: Multiple Choice

**Instructions:** Circle the correct response.

1. Circle all answers that refer to formatting functions.
   a. Shift-F8
   b. F6
   c. Alt-F8
   d. Ctrl-F8
2. It is possible to invoke leader dots when setting a tab stop by pressing which key?
   a. D for decimal
   b. L for leaders
   c. . (period)
   d. none of the above
3. To change the line spacing to double space, press the following keys:
   a. Alt-F8, 3, 2, Enter
   b. Ctrl-F8, 4, 2, Enter
   c. Shift-F8, 4, 2, Enter
   d. Shift-F8, 3, 2, Enter

4. To turn off right justification, press the following keys:
   a. Ctrl-F8, 3
   b. Alt-F8, 3
   c. Alt-F8, 4
   d. Ctrl-F8, 4
5. The code embedded into the document to signify that right justification has been turned off is:
   a. [Rt Just Off]
   b. [Right Just Off]
   c. [R Justification Off]
   d. [Rt Justification Off]
6. When the tab setting has been changed to one tab stop at position 30, the code embedded into the document shows the following:
   a. [Tab Set]
   b. [Tab Set: 30]
   c. [Tab Set: Pos 30]
   d. [Tab Set: L30]
7. If the user were to change the margins to 15 on the left and 75 on the right, the code embedded into the document would read:
   a. [Margin Set]
   b. [Margin Set: 15,75]
   c. [Margin Set: 15 left, 75 right]
   d. none of the above

## STUDENT ASSIGNMENT 3: Matching

**Instructions:** Put the appropriate number next to the words in the second column.

| | | |
|---|---|---|
| 1. Margin set | _____ | Shift-F8 |
| 2. Top margin line default | _____ | Home, Home, Up arrow |
| 3. Default tab set letter | _____ | Shift-F8, 3 |
| 4. Justification off | _____ | Shift-F8, 1 or 2 |
| 5. Line format | _____ | Alt-F8, 3 |
| 6. Print format | _____ | 6 lines |
| 7. Tab set | _____ | L |
| 8. Top of document | _____ | Ctrl-F8, 3 |
| 9. Line spacing | _____ | Ctrl-F8 |
| 10. Center page, top to bottom | _____ | Shift-F8, 4 |

## STUDENT ASSIGNMENT 4: Understanding WordPerfect Commands

**Instructions:** Next to each command, describe its effect.

| Command | Effect |
|---|---|
| Shift-F8, 1 | ______________________________ |
| Shift-F8, 3 | ______________________________ |
| Shift-F8, 4 | ______________________________ |
| Ctrl-F8, 3 | ______________________________ |
| Alt-F8, 3 | ______________________________ |
| Shift-F7, 1 | ______________________________ |

## STUDENT ASSIGNMENT 5: Identifying Default Settings

**Instructions:** Describe what default means. Then identify the default settings for the following commands.

| Command | Default setting |
|---|---|
| Top margin | ______________ |
| Bottom margin | ______________ |
| Left margin | ______________ |
| Right margin | ______________ |
| Line spacing | ______________ |
| Lines per inch | ______________ |
| Pitch | ______________ |
| Font | ______________ |
| Right justification | ______________ |
| Tab settings | ______________ |
| Letter tab setting | ______________ |
| Lines from top edge of paper | ______________ |
| to bottom edge | ______________ |
| Number of single-spaced text lines | ______________ |

## STUDENT ASSIGNMENT 6: Modifying a WordPerfect Document

**Instructions:** The screen below illustrates a memo that was prepared using WordPerfect. The margins are to be changed to 15 on the left and 75 on the right. The letter is to be centered top to bottom, and the right justification is to be turned off. Explain in detail the steps necessary to perform those changes.

```
DATE:      December 15, 1990
TO:  All Sales Managers
FROM:      Rita Moeller
RE:  New Bonus Plan

The new  bonus plan will become effective January 1.  If you have
questions, contact Hanna Butler.  All  sales people  are affected
by the new plan.
```

## STUDENT ASSIGNMENT 7: Creating a WordPerfect Document

**Instructions:** Perform the following tasks.

1. Load DOS into main memory.
2. Load WordPerfect into main memory by inserting the WordPerfect diskette into drive A, putting a data disk into drive B, typing b: and pressing Enter. At the B> prompt, type a:wp and press Enter.

Problem 1:

1. Set the left margin to 12 and the right margin to 50.
2. Turn the right justification off.
3. Center the page top to bottom.
4. Type the letter on the following page.

```
March 15, 1990

Ms. Roberta Weitzman
President, SpaceTek Inc.
44538 Scroll Avenue
Monnett, NJ 08773

Dear Ms. Weitzman:

This letter confirms our purchase of
thirteen DF-132 Modular Pin Brackets
from your company, delivery by April 1.

James R. McMillan, AirFrame Inc.
```

Problem 2: Save the document, using the name Weitzman.
Problem 3: Print the document.

## STUDENT ASSIGNMENT 8: Modifying a WordPerfect Document

**Instructions:** Perform the following tasks.

1. Load DOS into main memory.
2. Load WordPerfect into main memory by inserting the WordPerfect diskette into drive A, putting a data disk into drive B, typing b: and pressing Enter. At the B> prompt, type a:wp and press Enter.

Problem 1:

1. Retrieve the document named Weitzman, created in Student Assignment 7.
2. Change the margins to 10 on the left and 60 on the right (Hint: Either delete the old margin codes or be sure the new margin code is to the right of the old one. The last code governs).
3. The correct address is 44358 Scroll Street.
4. Change the purchase to 35 Pin Brackets.
5. Remove the words "from your company" on line 2 and end the sentence following the word "Brackets."
6. Insert the words "We expect" in front of the word "delivery" on the second line.
7. The last name of the sender of the letter is MacMillan, not McMillan.

Problem 2: Save the document again, replacing the old version with the new version.
Problem 3: Print the modified document. It should look like the letter below.

```
March 15, 1990

Ms. Roberta Weitzman
President, SpaceTek Inc.
44358 Scroll Street
Monnett, NJ 08773

Dear Ms. Weitzman:

This letter confirms our purchase of 35 DF-132
Modular Pin Brackets.  We expect delivery by April
1.

James R. MacMillan, AirFrame Inc.
```

## STUDENT ASSIGNMENT 9: Advanced Tab Settings

**Instructions:** Perform the following tasks.

1. Load DOS into main memory.
2. Load WordPerfect into main memory by inserting the WordPerfect diskette into drive A, putting a data disk into drive B, typing b: and pressing Enter. At the B> prompt, type a:wp and press Enter.

```
                    GRADUATION PROGRAM

Opening Procession. . . . . . . . Graduating Class

Flag Ceremony . . . . . . . . . . . . . . . . ROTC

Greeting. . . . .Vice President of Student Affairs

Special number. . . . . . . . . . . String Quartet

Remarks . . . . . . . . . . . University President

Song. . . . . . . . . . . . . . . A Cappella Choir

Presentation of Diplomas. . . . . . .College Deans

School Song . . . . . . . . . . . Graduating Class

                      Recessional


                         *****


            Refreshments served in the foyer


                         *****
```

Problem 1:
1. Set margins to 15 on the left and 65 on the right.
2. Begin typing on line 7.
3. Center and capitalize heading, followed by three hard returns.
4. Change line spacing to 2 (double space).
5. Clear all tab settings. Place one tab stop at position 65. Change the L to R. Type a . (period) over the R. Exit out of tab setting.
6. Type remaining portion of program.

Problem 2: Save the document to disk as Program.
Problem 3: Print the document.

## STUDENT ASSIGNMENT 10: Advanced Tab Settings

**Instructions:** Perform the following tasks.

1. Load DOS into main memory.
2. Load WordPerfect into main memory by inserting the WordPerfect diskette into drive A, putting a data disk into drive B, typing b: and pressing Enter. At the B> prompt, type a:wp and press Enter.

```
                          PRICE LIST

       Products          Wholesale Price      Retail Price

     Ladies Skirts            34.00               59.95
      Mens Shirts             13.50               26.95
  Childrens T-Shirts           5.95                9.95
      Hair clips                .25                 .49
```

Problem 1:
1. Center and capitalize the heading, followed by three hard returns.
2. Enter the tab setting screen, clear all current tab stops.
3. Enter a C (Center) tab stop at positions 20, 42 and 62.
4. Type the first line of headings (Products, Wholesale Price, Retail Price).
5. After typing the column headings, press two Hard Returns. Enter the tab setting screen again and change the tab designations on positions 42 and 62 to a D.
6. Type the remainder of the price list.

Problem 2: Save the document to disk, using the name Price.
Problem 3: Print the document.

# PROJECT 5

## Formatting Functions, File Management, and Macros

### Objectives

You will have mastered the material in this project when you can:

- Invoke the List Files option
- Change page length and insert hard page breaks
- Add headers and footers
- Specify date format and employ the date function
- Create and invoke macros

## FILE MANAGEMENT

Load WordPerfect as you have in the previous projects. In this project you will revise a document to look like Figure 5-1. In Project 4 you retrieved a file using the Shift-F10 (retrieve) function. At the prompt you typed the name of the file to be retrieved. It is possible that you may not remember the name of the file, or perhaps you need to see how many bytes of memory a particular file uses. In these situations and to perform other file management functions, it is not necessary to exit WordPerfect, you can use the **List Files** function.

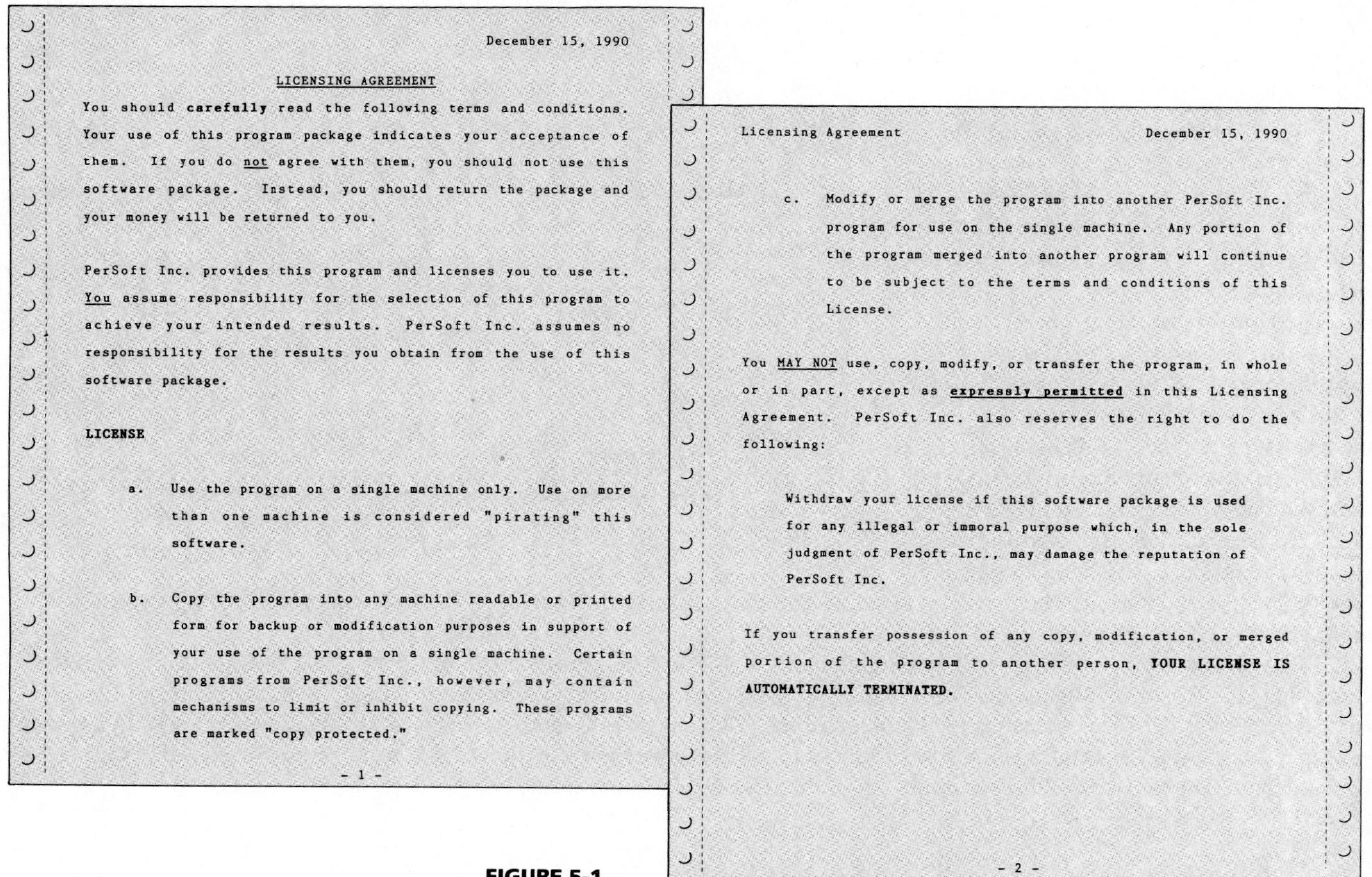

December 15, 1990

LICENSING AGREEMENT

You should **carefully** read the following terms and conditions. Your use of this program package indicates your acceptance of them. If you do not agree with them, you should not use this software package. Instead, you should return the package and your money will be returned to you.

PerSoft Inc. provides this program and licenses you to use it. You assume responsibility for the selection of this program to achieve your intended results. PerSoft Inc. assumes no responsibility for the results you obtain from the use of this software package.

**LICENSE**

a. Use the program on a single machine only. Use on more than one machine is considered "pirating" this software.

b. Copy the program into any machine readable or printed form for backup or modification purposes in support of your use of the program on a single machine. Certain programs from PerSoft Inc., however, may contain mechanisms to limit or inhibit copying. These programs are marked "copy protected."

- 1 -

Licensing Agreement December 15, 1990

c. Modify or merge the program into another PerSoft Inc. program for use on the single machine. Any portion of the program merged into another program will continue to be subject to the terms and conditions of this License.

You MAY NOT use, copy, modify, or transfer the program, in whole or in part, except as **expressly permitted** in this Licensing Agreement. PerSoft Inc. also reserves the right to do the following:

Withdraw your license if this software package is used for any illegal or immoral purpose which, in the sole judgment of PerSoft Inc., may damage the reputation of PerSoft Inc.

If you transfer possession of any copy, modification, or merged portion of the program to another person, **YOUR LICENSE IS AUTOMATICALLY TERMINATED.**

- 2 -

**FIGURE 5-1**

Look at the template next to the F5 key. You see the words List Files in black. Press the F5 key. Figure 5-2 shows that the message "Dir B:*.*" appears in the lower left corner of your screen. As you learned in the Introduction to DOS, the * is a global character. B:/*.*, therefore, stands for drive b and *all the files* (*) before the period and *all the files* (*) after the period. To accept this default and to see all the files on drive B, press the Enter key. Figure 5-3 shows a screen similar to what your screen will look like. (You may see some other files not shown in Figure 5-3).

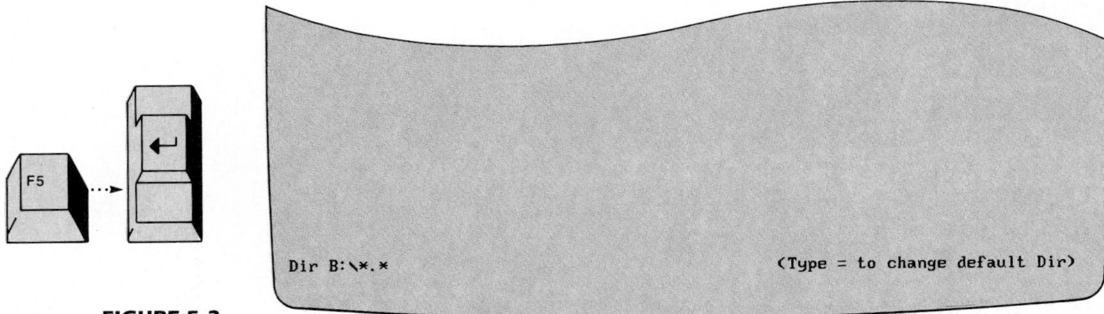


FIGURE 5-2

The top left corner shows the date and time you entered when you loaded WordPerfect into main memory. At the top middle is the directory you are currently in. At the top right you are shown the disk space that is still free. As each file is saved, bytes (each character or space is approximately equivalent to one byte) are subtracted from the free disk space. The Current Directory and Parent Directory are reserved if you are using a hard disk. Because you are using diskettes all files on drive B are listed in alphabetical order. After the name of the file, you see a dot or period and then the file extension name, if any. To the right of the file name are the number of bytes used by that particular file, then the date and time that particular file was saved. If you have since saved and then replaced a file, the last date and time of saving is shown. This is one reason why it is so important to enter the date when turning on the computer. Because all files are saved by date, you can often find a particular file you are looking for just by knowing when you last saved it. The Files menu at the bottom of the screen shows all the options that are available.

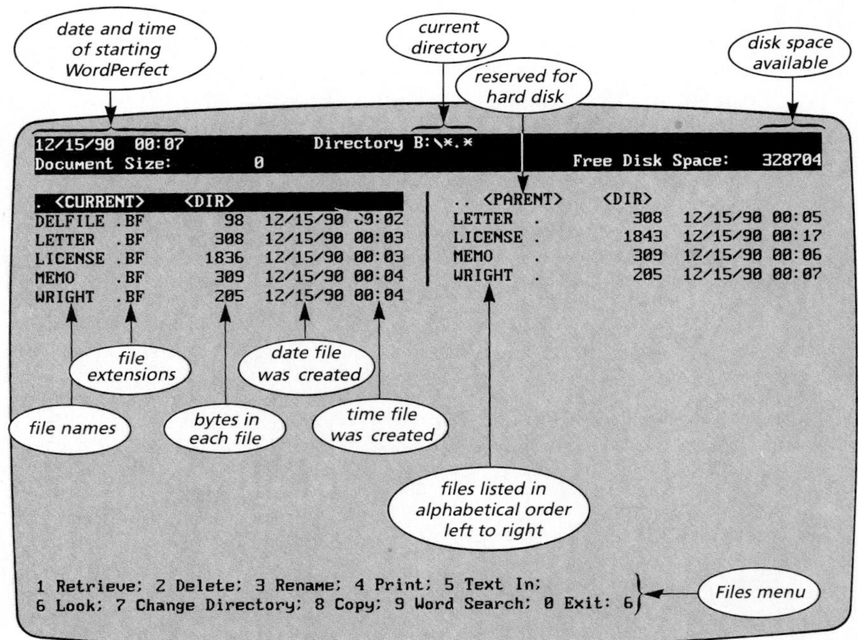


FIGURE 5-3

To invoke any of the options, you must highlight a file. To do this, press the Down Arrow ↓ and then the Right Arrow →. Notice how the cursor highlights one file at a time. If you have many files you may have more than one screenful of file names. To view other files you can press PgDn or Home, Down Arrow to move down a screen at a time. To move up a screen at a time, press PgUp or Home, Up Arrow. To move to the last document listed (even if it were several screens down), press Home, Home, Down Arrow. To move to the top of the files listing, press Home, Home, Up Arrow.

Notice that there is a file named MEMO. To go quickly to this file press the letter M (capital or lowercase). Figure 5-4 shows that the menu at the bottom of the screen is replaced by the letter M. When you press a letter, the first file beginning with that letter is highlighted. If you do not wish to type any more letters to view other files, press the spacebar to bring the menu back. (If you press the spacebar too long or press it twice, you will lose the files screen. If that happens, press F5 and then Enter to retrieve it.)

At the files screen, press Home, Home, Up Arrow to move the cursor to the top of the list of files. You now wish to highlight the document you saved as LICENSE. Since there is more than one file that begins with the letter L it will be necessary to type more than just L. Type L (lowercase or capital) (Step 1 in Figure 5-5). Notice how the file LETTER is highlighted and the letter L is shown at the bottom of the screen. Type the letter I and notice in Step 2 of Figure 5-5 how the highlighting moves to the first file that begins with LI. If you had many files, you could continue typing more letters of a file name, or you could move the cursor to the desired file name. Press any of the cursor keys or the spacebar, and the menu is restored (Step 2, Figure 5-5). To exit the List Files menu press the spacebar (Step 3 in Figure 5-5). You can now see that you have a blank screen or a clean work space.

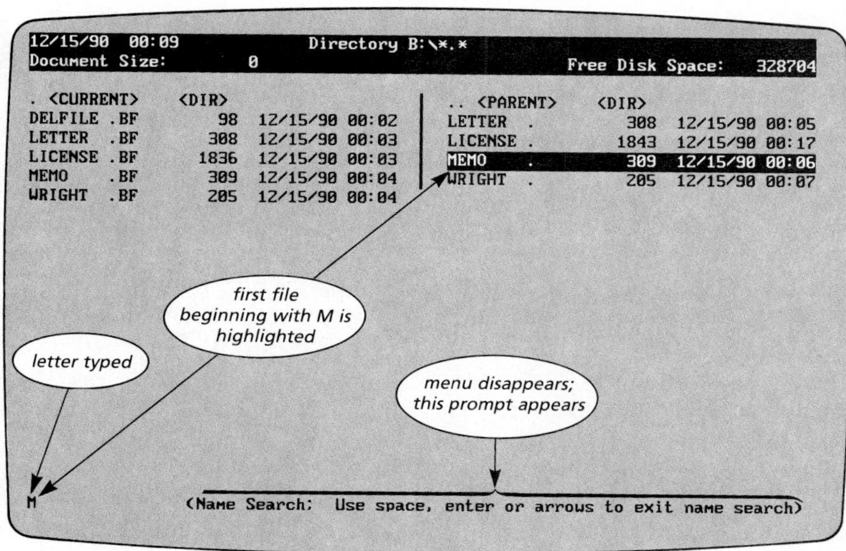


**FIGURE 5-4**

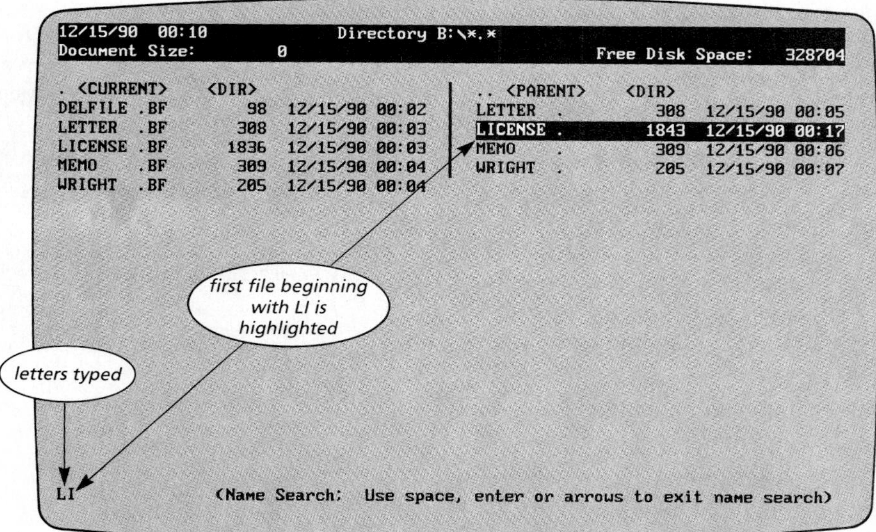


**FIGURE 5-5**

**Step 1: Type the first letter of the file name**

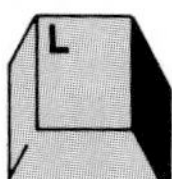


**Step 2: Type the second letter of the file name. To retrieve the menu press the spacebar**

I

*space*

**Step 3: Exit the List Files function**

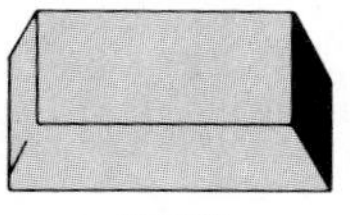

*space*

## Look Function

You will now retrieve a copy of a file from disk and place it into main memory. Note that you have a blank screen on which to retrieve that file. If you did not have a clean work space, and you retrieved a document on the screen, text that was on the screen would be pushed down below the incoming text. Since it might not be visible, you'd think it was gone, but you might find later that you saved two documents together. Remember to *clean the workspace* before you retrieve a new document into memory. The workspace can only be cleared using the Exit (F7) key.

To look at the entire listing of files on drive B, press F5, then Enter ↵. To work on the file named LICENSE, retrieve a copy of that file into the main memory of the computer. The term "copy" is used because the original file remains on the disk, and only a copy of that file is retrieved and placed in main memory. You will be changing that file, but all changes are made to the copy in main memory. To save all the changes you will have to use the Save key and then replace the old file on disk with the new changes that are in main memory.

Type LI and the document LICENSE that you created is highlighted. Press the spacebar to restore the menu. Since there are many files, you would waste time if you retrieved the wrong document into memory only to have to exit out again. WordPerfect includes an option to look at a document that is on the disk without actually retrieving a copy into main memory.

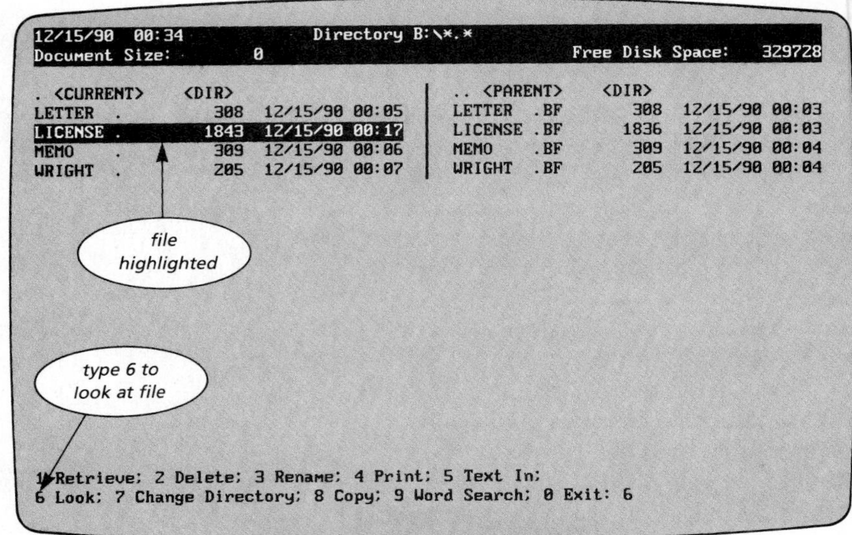


**FIGURE 5-6**

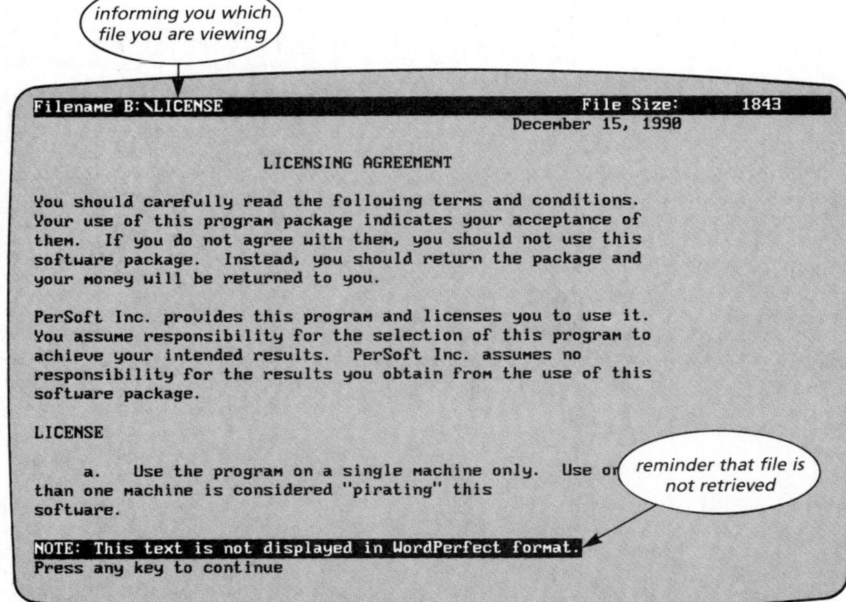


**FIGURE 5-7**

Look at the menu at the bottom of the screen as shown in Figure 5-6. Next to number 6 is the word Look. Press number 6 and the document LICENSE is displayed on your screen. Figure 5-7 shows, however, that you are just viewing the document. The bar at the top of the screen tells you which file you are looking at and how large the file is. At the bottom of the screen the highlighted message warns you that this is not displayed in WordPerfect format, that is, that the document has not been loaded into main memory. The document looks the same as you typed it. But in some documents (such as those that have columns or tabbed numbers) the typing may appear strange. Since the document has not been loaded into main memory you cannot do any editing. You can move the cursor down or even press the PgDn key to view more of the document, but you cannot press any other key or you will exit the look function.

To return to the Files menu press the spacebar. The file you were just viewing remains highlighted in the Files menu.

## Retrieving a Document

Because the highlighted file you just viewed is the file you wish to retrieve, look at the menu at the bottom of the screen. Next to the number 1, notice the word Retrieve. With the file name LICENSE still highlighted, press the number 1. The document named B:\LICENSE, which you typed in Project 3, is retrieved and placed in memory and displayed on your screen.

Press F5 and then Enter ↵. You now see the list files screen again. If you were to highlight a document and then retrieve it by pressing the number 1 you would be retrieving another document on top of the one already in main memory. Press the spacebar, and you are returned to your document still on the screen.

Now that you have the document named LICENSE retrieved and loaded into main memory, you will use this document to learn more formatting features. First, it is necessary to delete a line of type in the document. It may seem that the line is needed in the text, but deleting it rearranges the page breaks so that you can learn more formatting features in this project.

To delete the line of type, press the Down Arrow 19 times to move the cursor to line 20, position 10. Then press Ctrl-End. Press the Delete key two times to delete the blank lines. Press Home, Home, Up Arrow to move the cursor to the top of the document.

# MORE FORMATTING FEATURES

Now that you have deleted the one line, note that the body of the text should be in 1 1/2 spacing instead of single spacing. Since you do not want to change the spacing for the date and heading, press the Down Arrow ↓ five times to place the cursor on line 6, position 10 under the Y in You. To change the line spacing press Shift-F8. Press number 4 for spacing. Type 1.5 and press Enter ↵. Figure 5-8 shows that typing below the code is now in 1 1/2 line spacing.

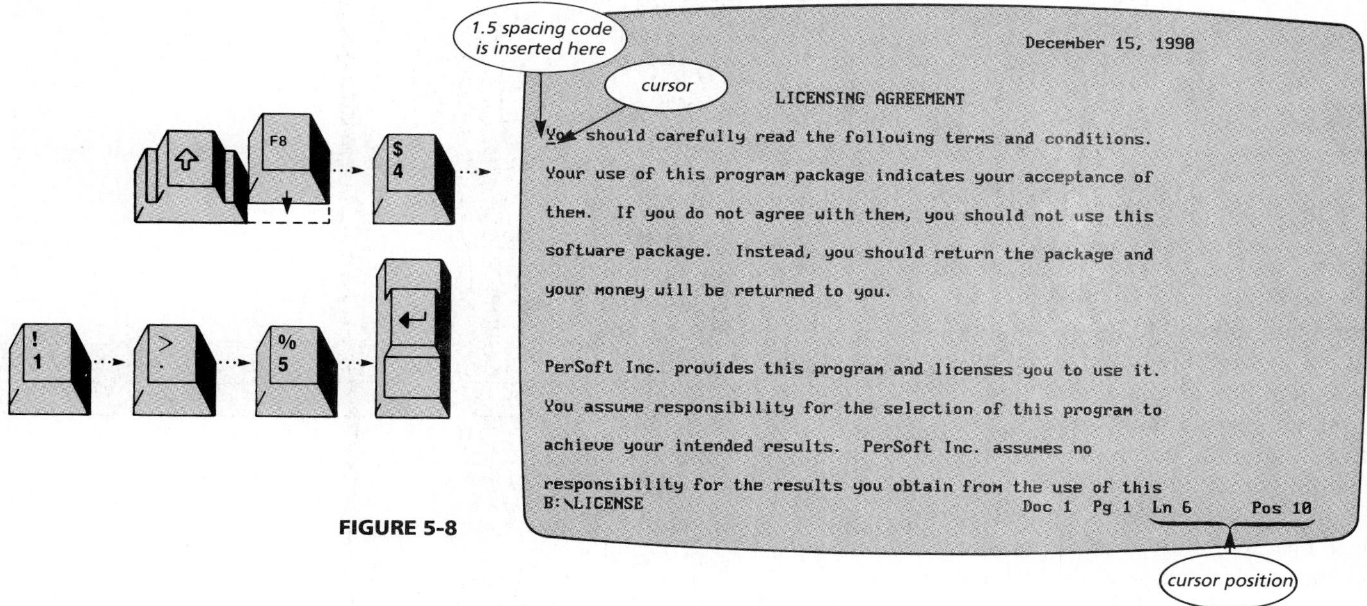


FIGURE 5-8

Before printing any document, it is important to view each screen to see if the format and the page breaks make reading easy. To do this, press the Plus (+) key on the numeric keypad to move to the bottom of the current screen. To move to the bottom of the next screen press the + key again. The cursor moves to line 37.5. To continue moving to the next screen, press the + key. Notice that the cursor crosses the page break and is on page 2, line 1. To view the code that is embedded when the page breaks, press Alt-F3. The code **[SPg]** is inserted because the page break was invoked by the computer, causing a **soft page break**. To exit the reveal codes, press the spacebar.

The page break comes in an awkward place; the four lines of the paragraph should be kept together. There are three ways in which the document can be formatted to keep these lines together. All three ways will now be demonstrated. When you type other documents in the future, you can decide which way will be most advantageous for each document.

## Changing the Page Length

As discussed in Project 4, WordPerfect defaults to a one-inch margin on the top and bottom of each page; that is why the page breaks at line 54. Knowing this, you can invoke a code that will make the page break at line 57, which is below the four-line paragraph. Remembering that a code is only good going downward from where it is invoked, you must move the cursor above the page break in order to lengthen page 1. Press the Up Arrow ↑ ↑ two times to move the cursor to line 52.5. Look at the template next to the F8 key. You see Page Format in blue. Press Alt-F8. The menu shown in Figure 5-9 appears on the screen.

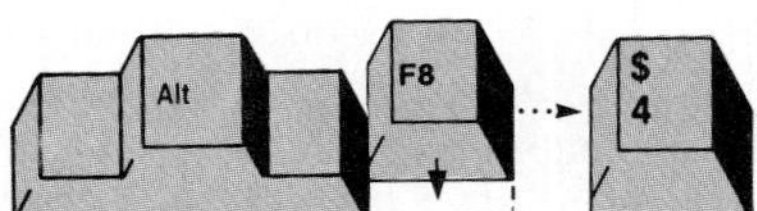
Alt
F8
$
4

```
Page Format

     1 - Page Number Position

     2 - New Page Number

     3 - Center Page Top to Bottom

     4 - Page Length

     5 - Top Margin

     6 - Headers or Footers

     7 - Page Number Column Positions

     8 - Suppress for Current page only

     9 - Conditional End of Page

     A - Widow/Orphan

Selection: 0
```

**FIGURE 5-9**

Because you wish to **change the page length**, press the number 4. Figure 5-10 shows that option 1 describes the default setting. Option 2 would be chosen if you had a page that would be printed on legal size paper. Since neither one of these options are what you wish to use, press the number 3 for "other." You will still be printing on 8 1/2 × 11-inch paper, which is 66 lines long from top to bottom, so it is not necessary to change the 66. Just press Enter ↵ to accept the 66. The cursor moves underneath the 54. Type the number 57 to change the number of typed lines on the page. Press Enter ↵ and you are returned to the page format screen.

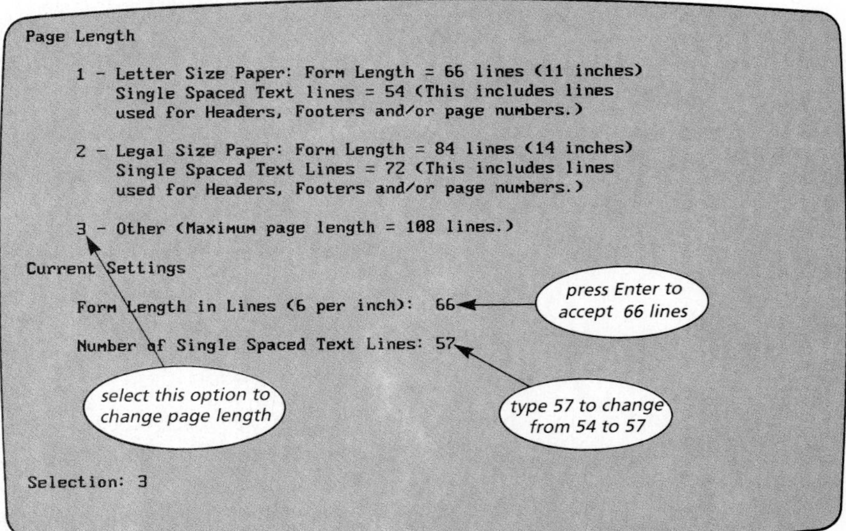
Page Length
1 - Letter Size Paper: Form Length = 66 lines (11 inches)
Single Spaced Text lines = 54 (This includes lines
used for Headers, Footers and/or page numbers.)
2 - Legal Size Paper: Form Length = 84 lines (14 inches)
Single Spaced Text Lines = 72 (This includes lines
used for Headers, Footers and/or page numbers.)
3 - Other (Maximum page length = 108 lines.)
Current Settings
Form Length in Lines (6 per inch): 66
Number of Single Spaced Text Lines: 57
Selection: 3
press Enter to accept 66 lines
select this option to change page length
type 57 to change from 54 to 57

**FIGURE 5-10**

Press Enter ↵ again and you are returned to your document. Note that the page break is still in the same place. This is because the code has not yet been interpreted by the WordPerfect software, and so the screen has not yet rewritten itself to reflect this code. To view the code that was embedded into the document, press Alt-F3. The embedded code shows that the page has 66 lines and that the typing will be 57 lines long (Figure 5-11). Notice that the [SPg] code still follows the word Licensing. To exit the reveal codes, press the spacebar. As you do, notice that the screen rewrites itself and that the four lines are now above the page break (Figure 5-12). Return to the reveal codes by pressing Alt-F3.

To try another way to keep the four lines together, it is necessary to delete the code that was just inserted into the document. The cursor should be to the right of the page length code. To delete backward, press the Backspace key one time, and the code is deleted. Press the spacebar to exit the reveal codes. As you do, notice that the four lines are split again by a dotted line, indicating the page break. The cursor should still be under the Y in You.

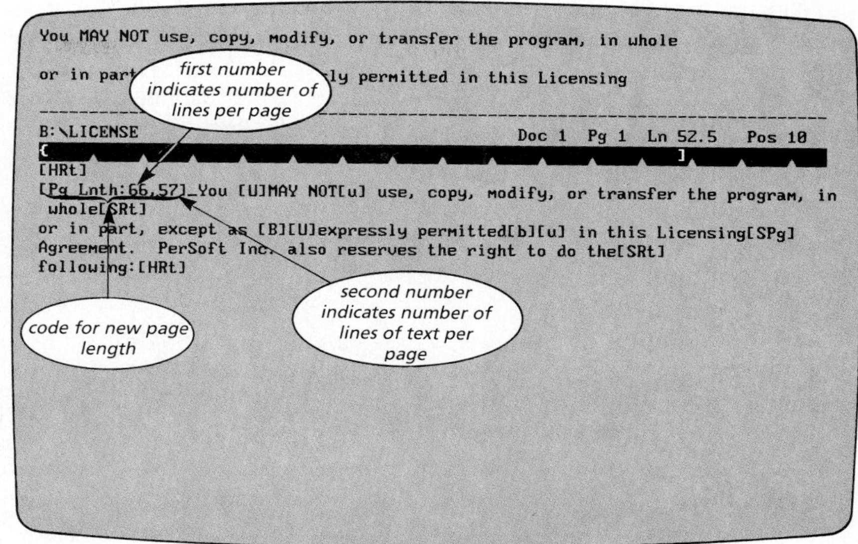


FIGURE 5-11

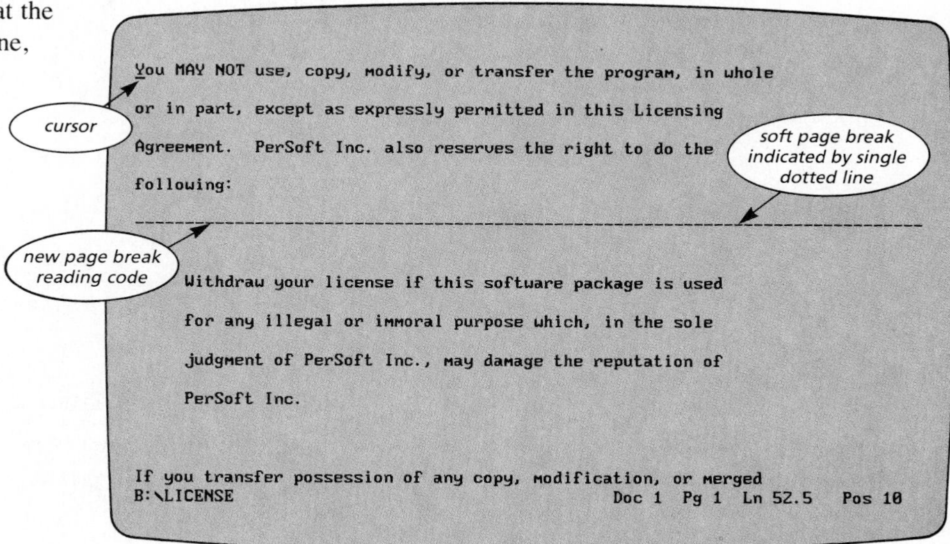


FIGURE 5-12

## Hard Page Break

When you see a dotted line across the page, you know that it is a page break invoked by the WordPerfect software as it interprets the page length codes, or the conditional end of page. You have viewed the [SPg] code that is embedded when the computer interprets Page Length commands. There could be times when you wish to invoke a page break code to ensure that no typing can be inserted below a certain point on a page. This is called a **hard page** break. Even if margins or page lengths are redefined, the hard page break will continue to be invoked by the software as long as the code exists.

With the cursor on line 52.5 under the Y in You, press Ctrl-Enter. You can see how the page break has occurred (Figure 5-13), and you can also see that instead of a single dotted line, WordPerfect uses a double dotted line when you invoke a hard page break.

To view the code, press Alt-F3. Notice that above the first line of the paragraph a **[HPg]** code is embedded (Figure 5-14). To delete the hard page break, press the Backspace key. Press the spacebar to exit the codes.

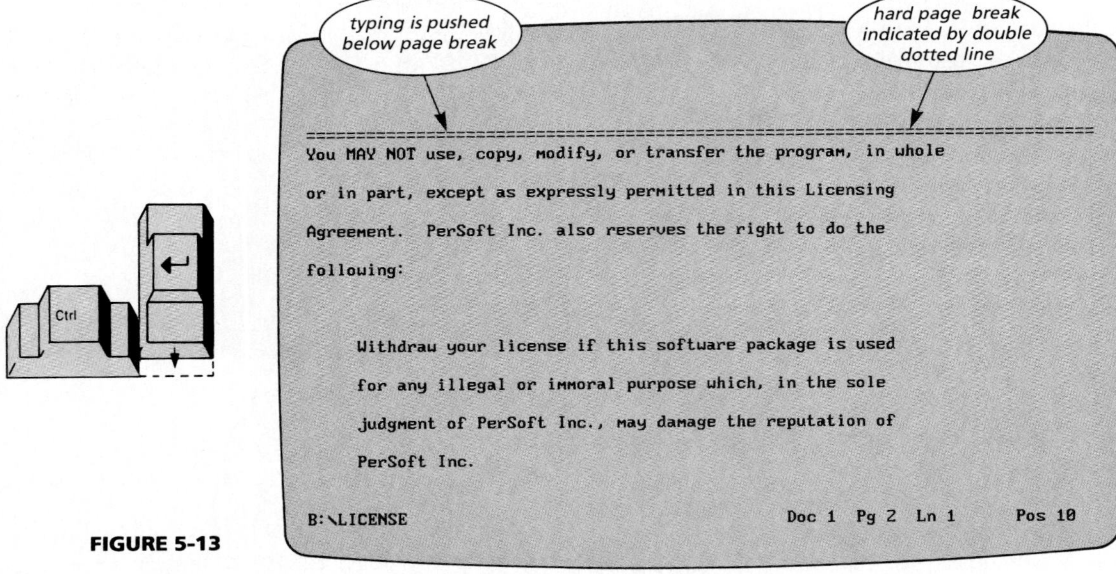


**FIGURE 5-13**

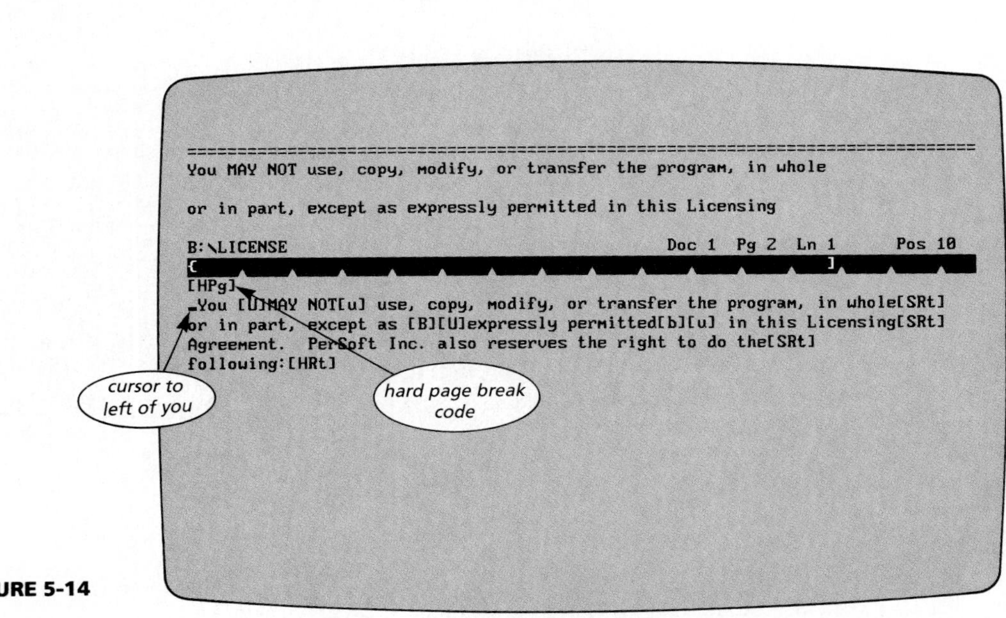


**FIGURE 5-14**

## Conditional End of Page

Another formatting feature, **conditional end of page**, is found on the Page Format key. This feature keeps a specified number of lines together on one page. If the current page is not long enough, it will move all lines specified to the next page. This is helpful if you have a table or graph that must be kept on one page.

The cursor must be *above* the lines to be kept together, so press the Up Arrow ↑ to move the cursor to line 51, which is the blank line before the paragraph. Press Alt-F8. The Page Format menu appears. Press number 9 for conditional end of page. The message "Number of lines to keep together = " appears on the screen. Type the number 4 (because there are four lines you wish to keep together), as shown in Figure 5-15. Press Enter ↵, then press Enter ↵ again to exit the Page Format menu. The lines will reformat after you have looked at the codes.

To view the code that was inserted, press Alt-F3. Figure 5-16 shows the conditional end of page code, **[CndlEOP]**, embedded in your document. Before you exit the codes, notice that the [SPg] code again follows the word Licensing. Press the spacebar to exit the codes. As you do, notice that all four lines have been kept together by being moved down to the next page below the dotted line (see Figure 5-17 on the following page).

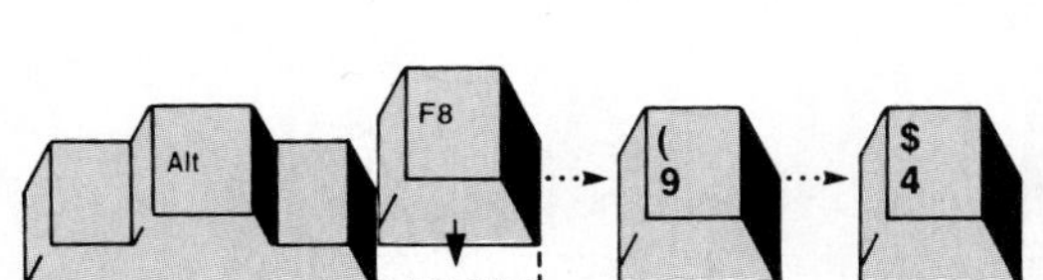


```
Page Format

     1 - Page Number Position

     2 - New Page Number

     3 - Center Page Top to Bottom

     4 - Page Length

     5 - Top Margin

     6 - Headers or Footers

     7 - Page Number Column Positions

     8 - Suppress for Current page only

     9 - Conditional End of Page

     A - Widow/Orphan

Number of lines to keep together = 4
```

this option keeps specified number of lines together

type 4 to keep 4 lines of paragraph together

**FIGURE 5-15**

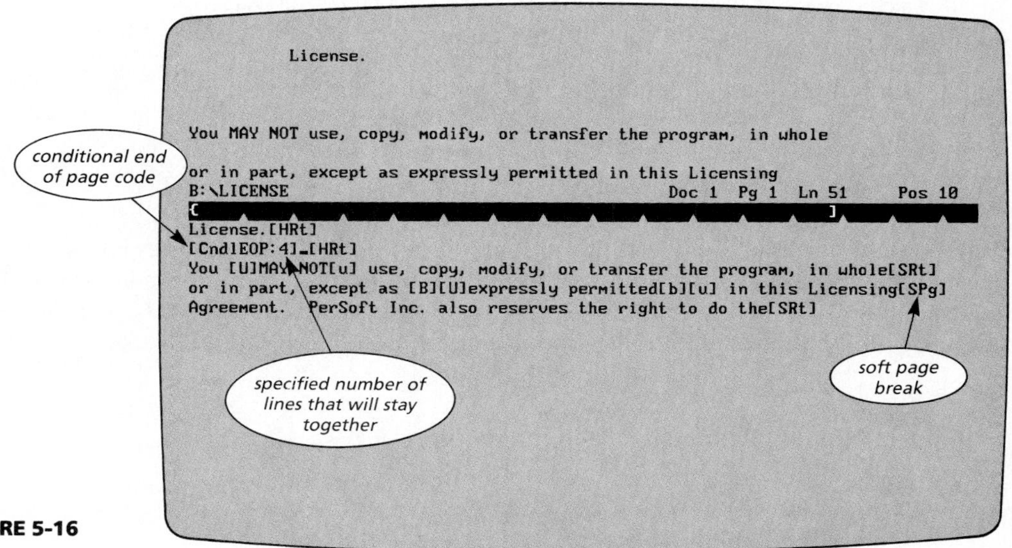


**FIGURE 5-16**

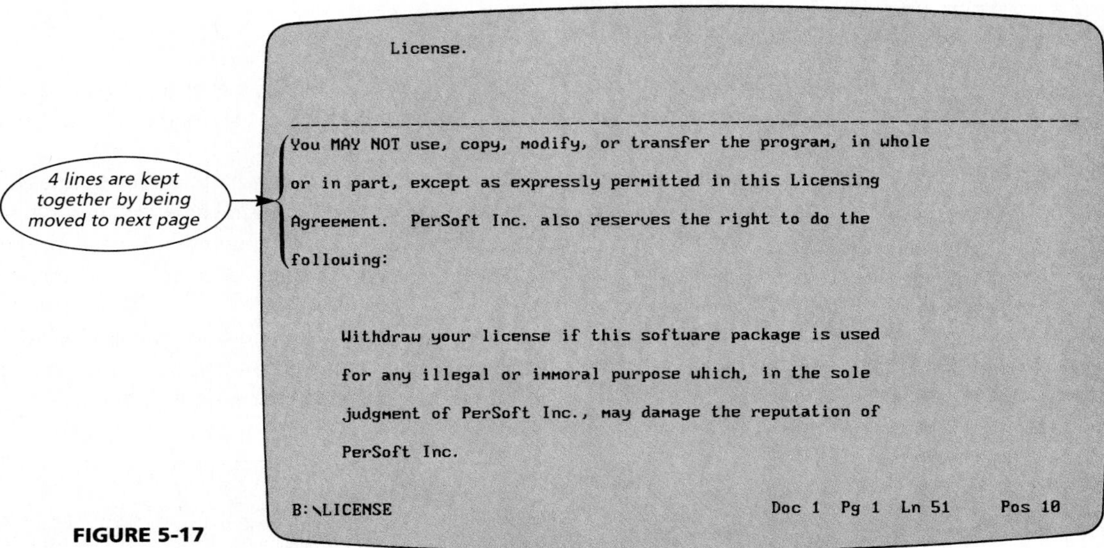

4 lines are kept together by being moved to next page
License.
You MAY NOT use, copy, modify, or transfer the program, in whole
or in part, except as expressly permitted in this Licensing
Agreement. PerSoft Inc. also reserves the right to do the
following:
Withdraw your license if this software package is used
for any illegal or immoral purpose which, in the sole
judgment of PerSoft Inc., may damage the reputation of
PerSoft Inc.
B:\LICENSE
Doc 1 Pg 1 Ln 51 Pos 10


FIGURE 5-17

## HEADERS AND FOOTERS

Whenever your document contains more than one page, you will most likely wish to number the pages. You may also wish to have a heading at the top or bottom of each page, or perhaps both. A heading and page number placed at the top of a page is called a **header**; placed at the bottom of a page, it is called a **footer**. You may have noticed headers and footers in your textbooks. It is not necessary to type headers and footers on each and every page when you compose a document. It can be done once for the entire document.

WordPerfect allows you to have as many as two headers and/or two footers per page, which is helpful if you are typing a document that will have facing pages. Facing pages are normally used in books or magazines. You have probably noticed that in books odd pages are normally on the right side and even pages on the left side, either at the top or bottom of the page. This type of numbering is called facing pages numbering. For our exercise, we will use only one position for the numbering.

After you type headers and footers, a code is embedded and they are held in screens separate from the normal typing screen. When the pages are printed, headers will be printed at the top of each page and footers at the bottom of each page. WordPerfect allows one blank line to be inserted between either the header or footer and the body of the text. The lines required for the headers and/or footers are typed within the 54 lines of typing, leaving the top and bottom margins intact. Headers and footers should always be typed at the beginning of a document. If you have invoked a margin set change, the headers and footers code should follow the margin set code.

### Headers

To move to the top of the document, press Home, Home, Up Arrow ↑. Headers and footers are found on the Page Format key. Press Alt-F8. The Page Format menu that was shown in Figure 5-15 appears on the screen. Press number 6 for headers or footers. Figure 5-18 shows the screen you will see. Look at the menu on the left. You have a choice of header A or B and/or footer A or B. The menu on the right shows the options you can choose for each header or footer.

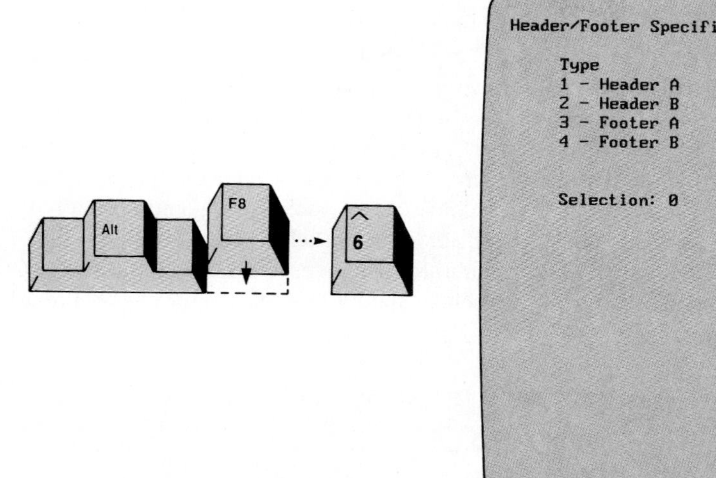


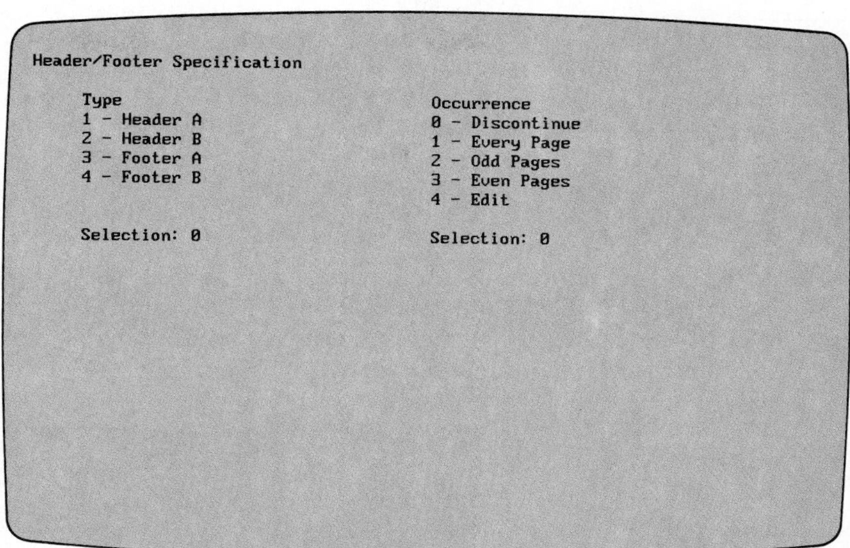


**FIGURE 5-18**

For this document, you will define one header and then one footer. Press the number 1 for header A. The 1 is accepted and the cursor moves to the next column. To place the header on every page type the number 1 again. A totally blank screen with a mini status line appears. This screen is reserved for header A. What you type is held in reserve and will be printed when the document is sent to the printer. Type the words Licensing Agreement. Because you also want the date to appear in the upper right corner, you must add the date flush right. Press Alt-F6. The cursor moves to position 75. Type the date December 15, 1990 (or the current date, if you wish). Because you want an extra blank line between the header and the text, press the hard return ↵ key. Your screen should look like Figure 5-19. As indicated on the screen, press F7 to exit. You are returned to the Page Format menu (Figure 5-15).

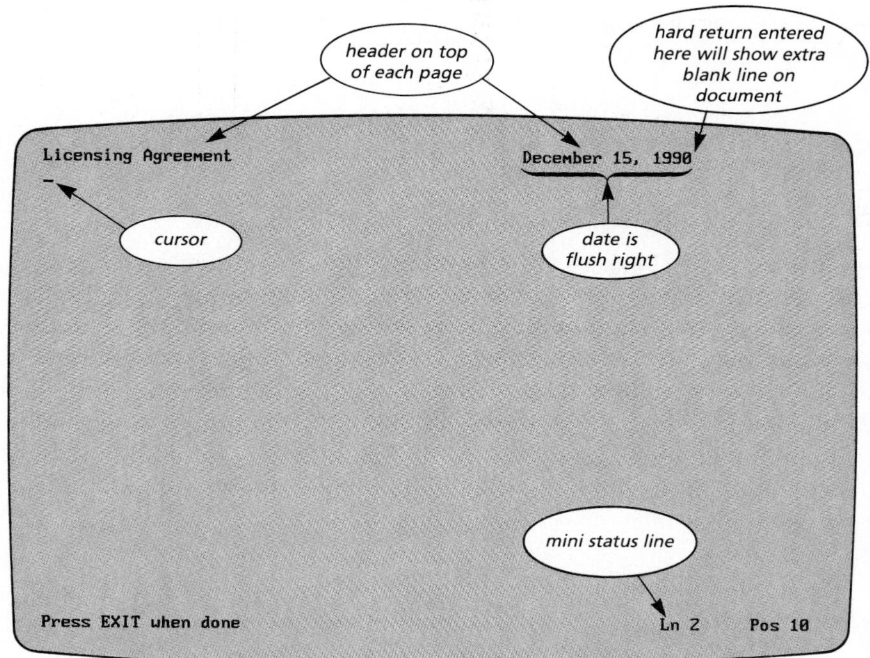


**FIGURE 5-19**

## Footers

Because you also wish to add a footer, press the number 6 for headers or footers. The screen you saw in Figure 5-18 appears again. This time press the number 3 for footer A. Next, press the number 1 for every page. Again you have a blank screen, which is reserved for footer A. The typing will be at the bottom of the page, and you want an extra blank line between the body of the text and the footer, so first press the hard return ↵ key. The cursor should be on line 2, position 10. Because you are going to put in page numbering, which you want centered at the bottom of each page, you must center the typing. Press Shift-F6. The cursor moves to position 42. Type a hyphen (–) followed by the spacebar. At this point you would normally type the number. You need to put in a code that will merge with the status line, so that, for instance, when page 2 is typed, the printer will read the status line and invoke that particular page number. To put in a numbering merge code, hold down the Ctrl key and type the letter B. Press the spacebar and then type another hyphen. The screen should look like Figure 5-20. Press F7 to exit. You are returned to the page format screen.

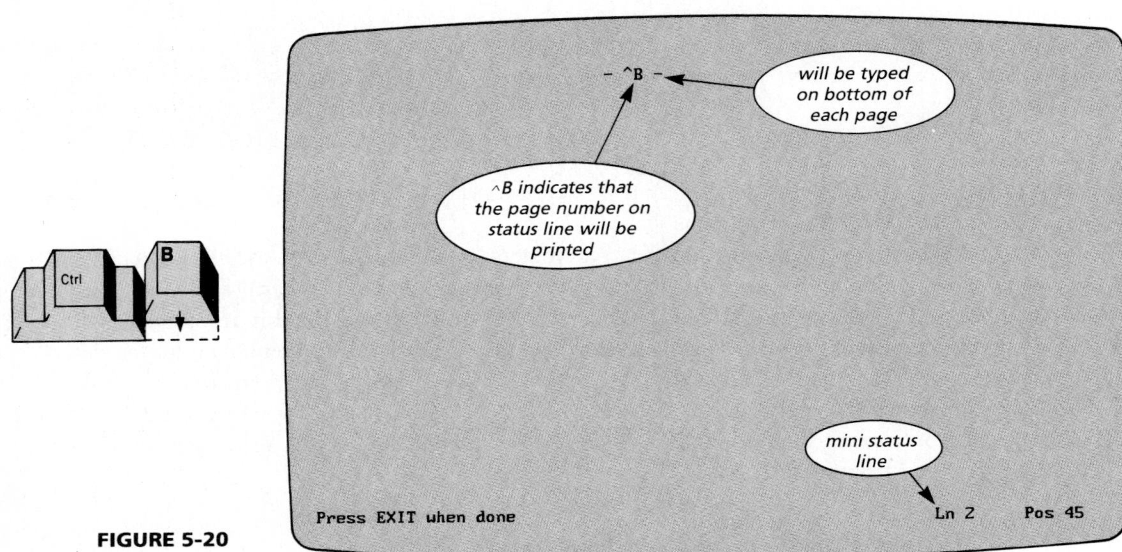


FIGURE 5-20

## Suppress for Current Page Only

The codes for headers and footers are being invoked at the top of your document, but you do not wish to have the header typed on the first page, since that page has its own heading. To suppress the header for page 1, which is the current page, press the number 8 for **suppress for current page only**. The menu in Figure 5-21 shows that you can suppress any number of options. You only wish to suppress the header, not the footer, so press the number 5 to turn off header A. Press Enter ↵, then press Enter ↵ again to return to your document.

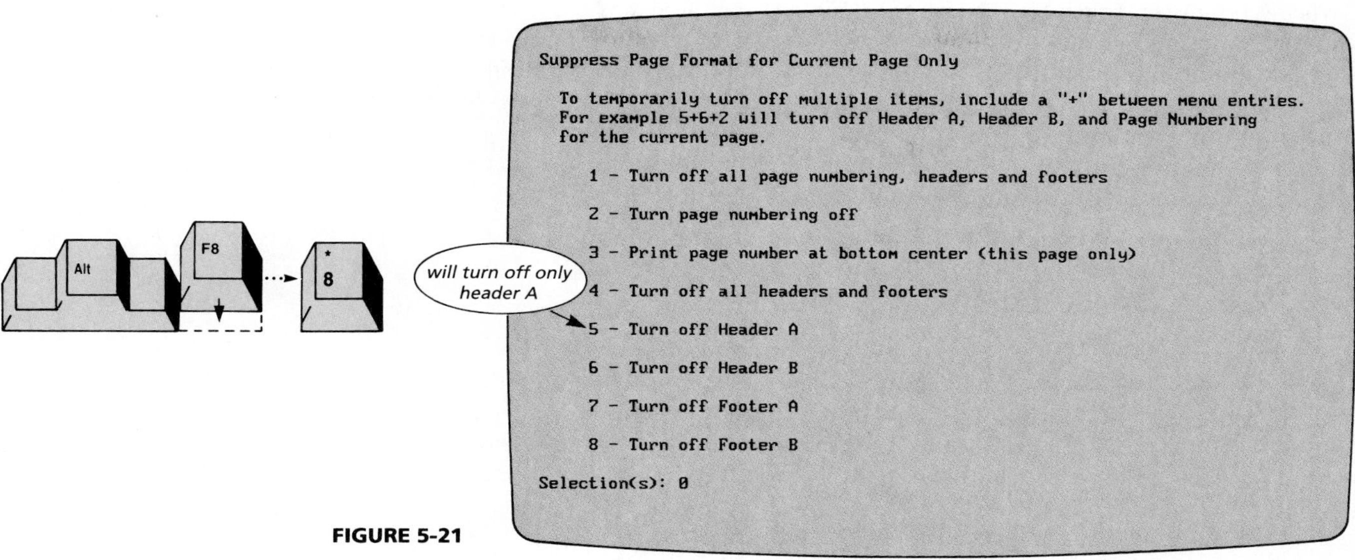


**FIGURE 5-21**

To view the three codes you just invoked, press Alt-F3. Figure 5-22 shows that first you have the header code, then the footer code, and then the suppress code. To exit the reveal codes, press the spacebar.

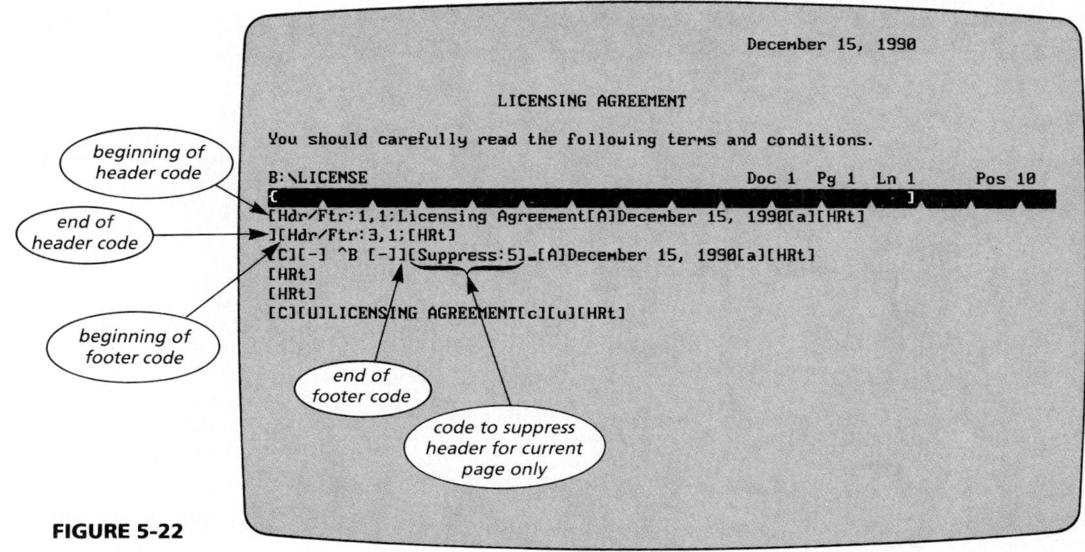


**FIGURE 5-22**

## SAVING AND REPLACING A DOCUMENT

Before you save your document, it is necessary to delete the 1.5 line spacing, since the training version of WordPerfect cannot send that command to the printer. It can, however, accept the command of double spacing. Press the Down Arrow five times to move the cursor to line 6 and then press Alt-F3. In reveal codes the cursor is to the right of the 1.5 spacing code. To delete the code press the backspace key. Press the spacebar to exit reveal codes. To make the document print in double spacing press Shift-F8. Press the number 4 for spacing. Type the number 2 for double spacing, then press Enter ↵.

When you finished typing this document in Project 3, you saved the document to your disk. However, you have now made several changes to the document on your screen, but those changes have not been saved to the disk. As you learned in Projects 3 and 4, it is possible to save these changes to the disk by replacing the old text with the new text. In this case, you want to save both the version made in Project 3 as well as the changes made here in Project 5. Therefore, when you save you will give this document a different name.

To save your document, press the F10 key. At the prompt "Document to be Saved: B:\LICENSE" type the new name license.2 and press Enter. The document is saved to the disk in drive B.

## PRINTING A DOCUMENT

You have saved and replaced your document, and it is now ready to be printed. At this point be sure that your printer has paper inserted, and that the printer is on and ready to print.

Press Shift-F7. You will see the Print menu at the bottom of the screen. Because you wish to print the full text of this document, press the number 1 for full text. At this point, the printer begins printing your document. The printed document generated is illustrated in Figure 5-23.

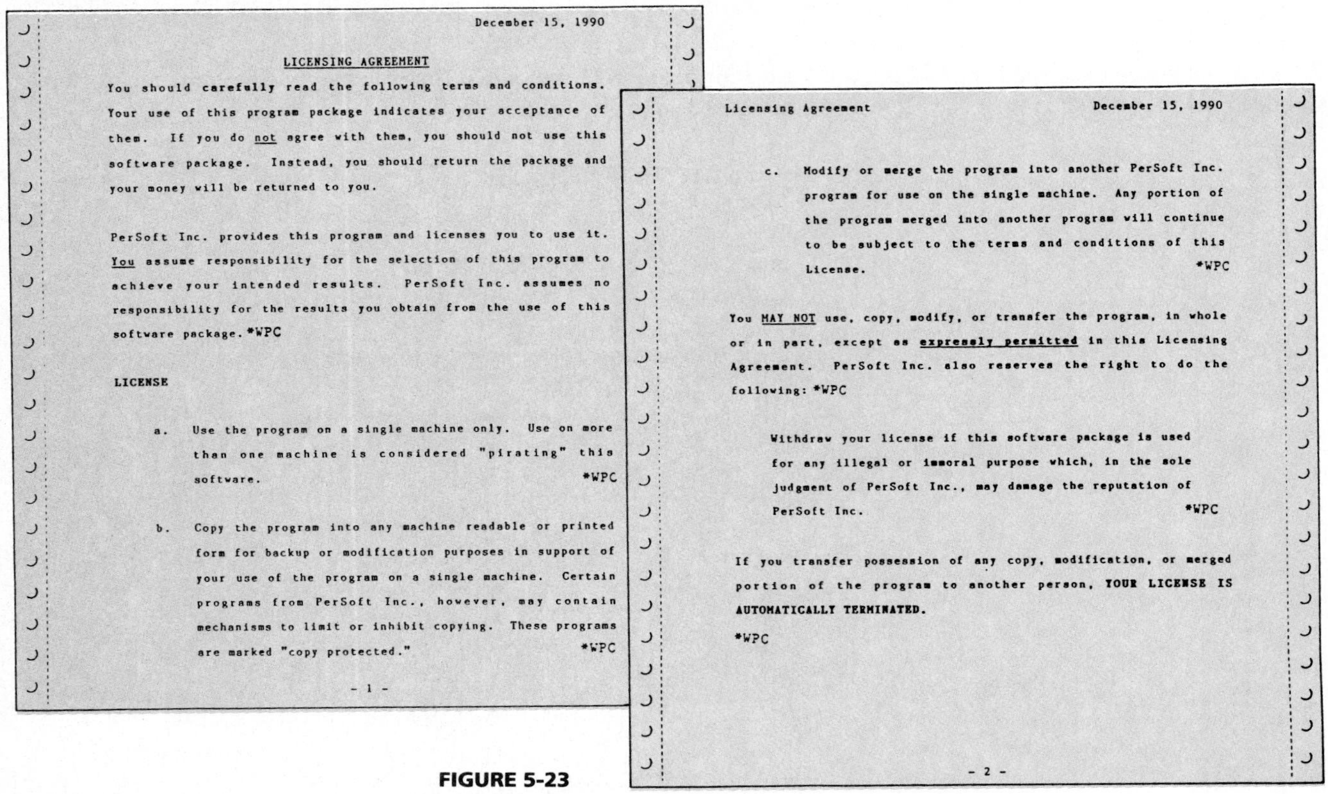

December 15, 1990

LICENSING AGREEMENT

You should **carefully** read the following terms and conditions. Your use of this program package indicates your acceptance of them. If you do not agree with them, you should not use this software package. Instead, you should return the package and your money will be returned to you.

PerSoft Inc. provides this program and licenses you to use it. You assume responsibility for the selection of this program to achieve your intended results. PerSoft Inc. assumes no responsibility for the results you obtain from the use of this software package. *WPC

LICENSE

a. Use the program on a single machine only. Use on more than one machine is considered "pirating" this software. *WPC

b. Copy the program into any machine readable or printed form for backup or modification purposes in support of your use of the program on a single machine. Certain programs from PerSoft Inc., however, may contain mechanisms to limit or inhibit copying. These programs are marked "copy protected." *WPC

- 1 -

Licensing Agreement December 15, 1990

c. Modify or merge the program into another PerSoft Inc. program for use on the single machine. Any portion of the program merged into another program will continue to be subject to the terms and conditions of this License. *WPC

You MAY NOT use, copy, modify, or transfer the program, in whole or in part, except as **expressly permitted** in this Licensing Agreement. PerSoft Inc. also reserves the right to do the following: *WPC

Withdraw your license if this software package is used for any illegal or immoral purpose which, in the sole judgment of PerSoft Inc., may damage the reputation of PerSoft Inc. *WPC

If you transfer possession of any copy, modification, or merged portion of the program to another person, **YOUR LICENSE IS AUTOMATICALLY TERMINATED.**
*WPC

- 2 -

**FIGURE 5-23**

## EXITING A DOCUMENT

Your document has been saved to disk and printed. It is now necessary to exit the document and clear the screen, but not exit the WordPerfect program.

Press the F7 key. At the prompt "Save Document? (Y/N) Y" type the letter N because the document has already been saved. At the prompt "Exit WP? (Y/N) N" type the letter N. The document exits and a clear screen appears.

## DATE FORMAT FUNCTION

When you first turned on your computer you were prompted to enter the date. It is always important to enter the date, because all files are saved by their date. Another good reason for inserting the date is that you can invoke the date with the F5 key. But when you use F5, the date you invoke will be the date you entered when first turning the machine on.

Look at the template next to the F5 key. Notice the word Date in green. Press Shift-F5. The menu shown in Figure 5-24 appears. Press the number 1 to enter today's date on your blank screen. Press a hard return ↵ to move the cursor to line 2.

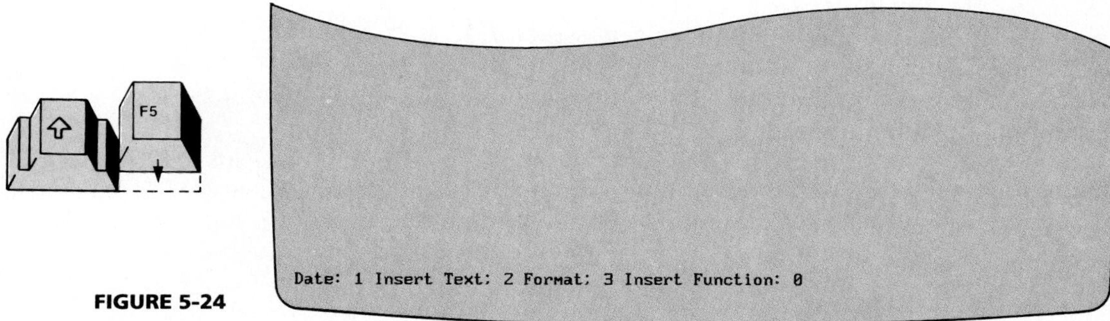


**FIGURE 5-24**

Whatever date you entered when you booted DOS will appear on the screen. For example, if you had entered 12-15-90 you would see December 15, 1990—the same date but in a different form. (If you did not enter a date you will see the system default date.) You can understand why the date appears in the form it does by viewing the **Date Format** menu.

To view the Date Format menu, press Shift-F5 and type the number 2. Figure 5-25 shows what your screen will look like. At the bottom in boldface typing you see "Date Format: 3 1, 4." The numbers are the default characters used. To understand the meaning of each number, look at the menu above. The 3 1, 4 stands for the following: 3 = month (word), 1 = day of the month (a comma is placed after the day because if you were typing it you would include a comma), 4 = year (all four digits). This explains how a date can be displayed or printed in one format when it was inserted in a different format. Press F7 to exit the Date Format menu.

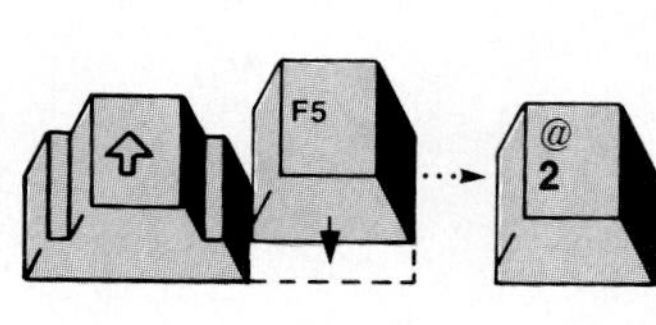


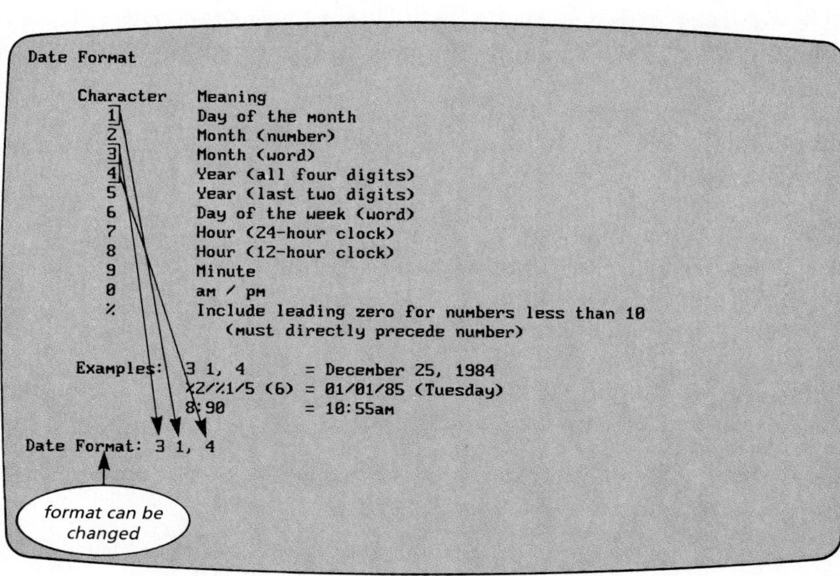


**FIGURE 5-25**

With the Date menu at the bottom of the screen, now press the number 3 for Insert Function. As you can see on the screen, the date is typed again.

To see the difference between 1 Insert Text and 3 Insert Function you need to view the codes. Press Alt-F3. The screen in Figure 5-26 shows that in the upper screen the date appears twice in exactly the same format. But the codes show that two different things happen. The first date is when you inserted text, exactly as if you had typed the date by hand. If you were to save this document and bring it up tomorrow, it would still have the same typing you see now. The second date is not a date at all in the codes. All you see is the code [3 1, 4]. The code inserts the current month, day, and year, which you entered when turning on the computer. If you were to bring this document up tomorrow, the date that would be invoked by the code would have tomorrow's date on the screen. This is especially useful if you type a letter today, but will be printing it out at some time in the future. Press the spacebar to exit the reveal codes.

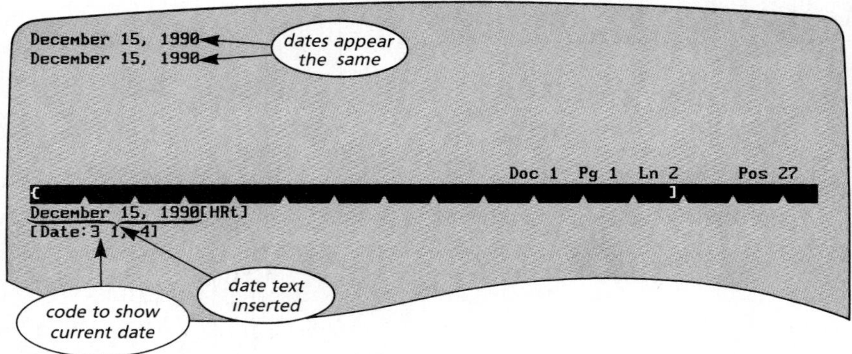


FIGURE 5-26

## MACROS

Probably the single most time-saving feature of WordPerfect is its capability of using macros. Simply stated, a **macro** stores frequently used keystrokes that make up phrases, paragraphs, or commands, so that instead of having to press a sequence of keystrokes each time, you only have to press a few keys. If any typing or string of commands is used frequently, you can make a macro of those keystrokes. You will learn how to create two macros, and then whenever keystrokes become repetitive, you can create and then invoke your own macros.

You have just learned how to invoke a date function. You will now learn how to put those keystrokes into main memory in a macro.

Press a hard return ↵ to move to a clean line. To define a macro look at the template next to the F10 key. You see the words Macro Def in red. Press Ctrl-F10. The prompt "Define Macro:" appears on your screen (step 1 of Figure 5-27). First, you must name the macro. You can use letters of the alphabet or a word or abbreviation to name a macro. To save time, you should make the name short and representative of what the macro does. In this case hold down the Alt key and press the letter D for date (step 2 of Figure 5-27). The prompt "Macro Def" begins flashing in the lower left corner of the screen (Figure 5-28). Any and all keys you press now will be stored in sequence until you turn the macro define

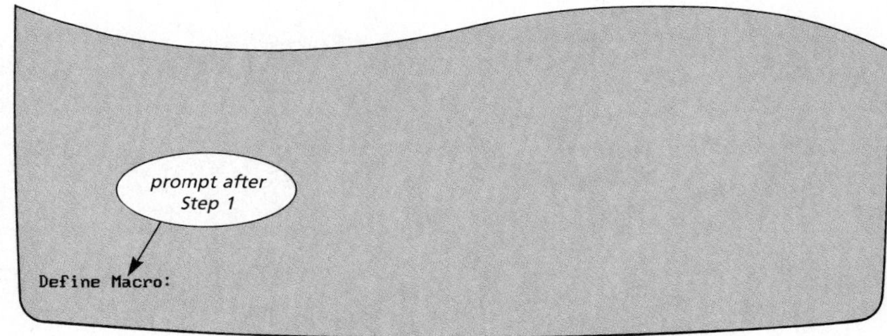


Step 1: Invoke macro function

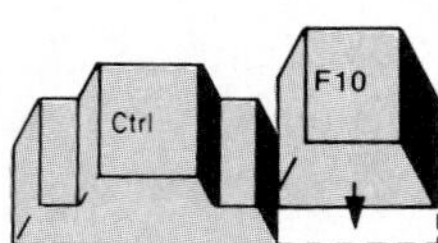


Step 2: Ready the software to receive the macro

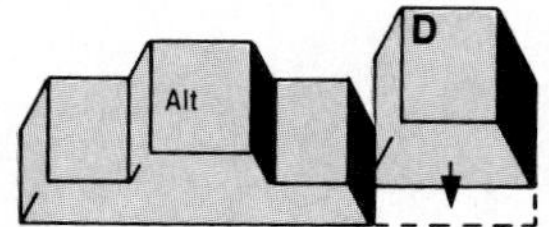


FIGURE 5-27

off. Recalling what we did before to retrieve the current date, press Shift-F5. When you receive the Date menu press the number 3 (step 1 of Figure 5-28). The current date appears on the screen.

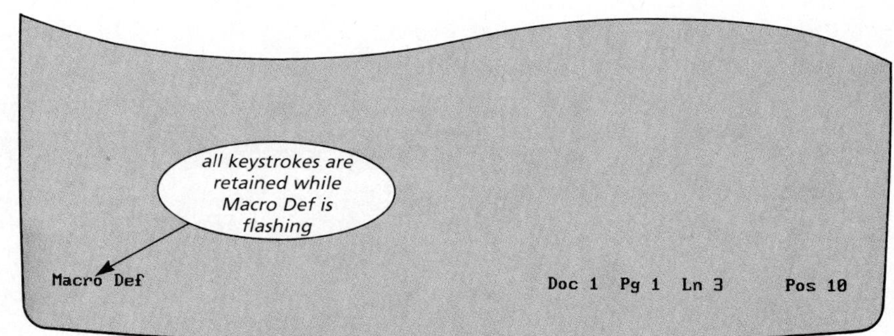


**FIGURE 5-28**

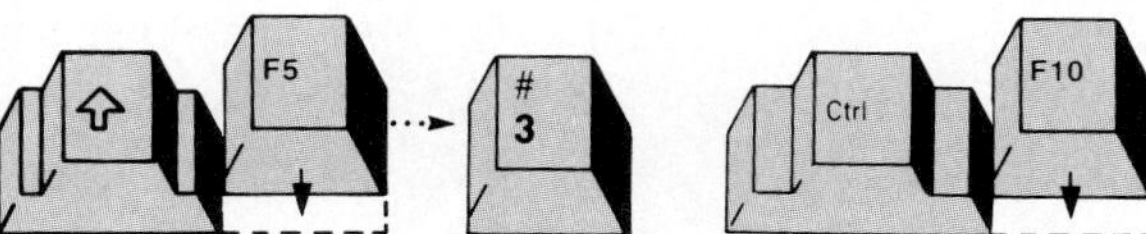


Turn off the macro define the same way you turned it on, by pressing Ctrl-F10 (step 2 of Figure 5-28). The light on drive B goes on, indicating that the macro is being saved to the disk. The prompt then stops flashing. Press a hard return ↵ to put the cursor on a clean line. To invoke the macro, press Alt-D. Immediately you see the date on the screen.

When you use this macro, the date will be inserted wherever the cursor is. To make the date flush right, press Alt-F6. When the cursor is flush right, press Alt-D. The date types out flush right. Press a hard return ↵ to move the cursor to a clean line. To center the date press Shift-F6. With the cursor centered, press Alt-D. Press a hard return. The date types out centered.

Because the macro has the code of 3 1, 4, no matter on which date you invoke the macro, the current date will appear on the screen in the form of month (word), day, and year (all four digits).

To learn the second way to invoke a macro it is best to clear the screen. Press F7 then the letter N to not save the document, then the letter N again to not exit WordPerfect.

The second macro you will learn is the ending of a letter. This is a sequence of keystrokes that is often repeated. To define a macro, press Ctrl-F10. Name the macro by typing the letters SY (for sincerely yours), and press Enter ↵. When "Macro Def" begins flashing, press the Tab key eight times, moving the cursor to position 50. (If you go too far or make a mistake, backspace and correct the error.) When the cursor is on position 50 type the phrase Sincerely yours, then press a hard return ↵. Press a hard return three more times ↵ ↵ ↵. Press the Tab key eight times to move to position 50. Type the name Francis Morris and press a hard return ↵. Press the Tab key eight times to move to position 50 again. Type the word Manager and press hard return. All your keystrokes are now defined. To turn off the macro define, press Ctrl-F10. The light on drive B goes on, indicating that the macro is being saved to the disk.

To invoke the macro this time, look at the template next to the F10 key. Notice the word Macro in blue. Press Alt-F10. The prompt "Macro:" appears. Type the letters SY and press Enter ↵. The macro is invoked and the typing appears on the screen.

To view how WordPerfect lists the macros, look at the List Files menu. Press F5 and then Enter ↵ (step 1 of Figure 5-29). Notice that the macro files have the extension of .MAC for macro (Figure 5-29). Do not try to retrieve the macro files from this screen. If you do try to retrieve a macro file from the List Files menu, you will receive the message "ERROR: Invalid file name". Press the spacebar to exit from this screen (step 2 of Figure 5-29).

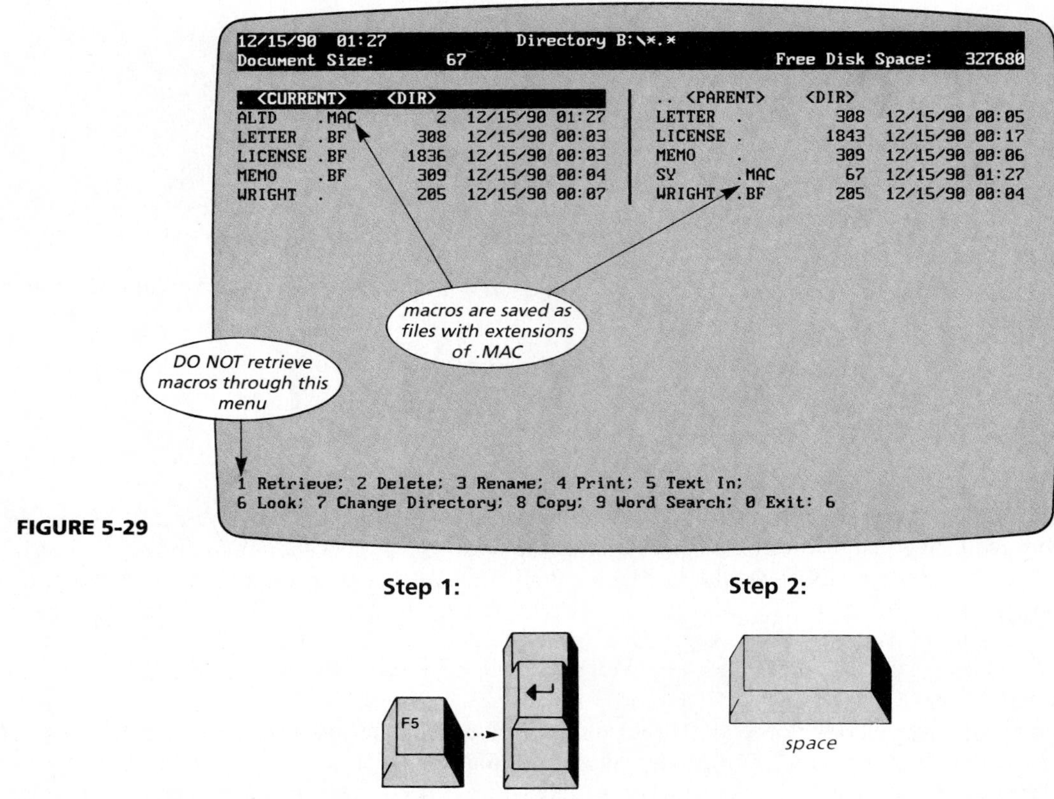


**FIGURE 5-29**

## EXITING WORDPERFECT

As you have done before, exit this document and WordPerfect. It is not necessary to save this document because the macros have already been saved to disk.

## PROJECT SUMMARY

In Project 5 you learned about file management with the List File options. You retrieved the document you typed in Project 3 and practiced more formatting features on that document. You changed the page length, put in a conditional end of page, and used a hard page break. You added a header and a footer to the document. After you saved, replaced, and exited the document, you learned about the date format and how to create macros.

The following is a list of the keystroke sequence we used in Project 5:

## SUMMARY OF KEYSTROKES—Project 5

| STEPS | KEY(S) PRESSED | STEPS | KEY(S) PRESSED | STEPS | KEY(S) PRESSED |
|---|---|---|---|---|---|
| 1 | F5 | 52 | 1 | 103 | ↵ |
| 2 | ↵ | 53 | 1 | 104 | Ctrl-F10 |
| 3 | LI | 54 | Licensing Agreement | 105 | Alt-D |
| 4 | Space | 55 | Alt-F6 | 106 | Shift-F5 |
| 5 | 1 | 56 | December 15, 1990 | 107 | 3 |
| 6 | [↓ 19 times to | 57 | ↵ | 108 | Ctrl-F10 |
| | line 20, position 10] | 58 | F7 | 109 | ↵ |
| 7 | Ctrl-End | 59 | 6 | 110 | Alt-D |
| 8 | Del | 60 | 3 | 111 | Alt-F6 |
| 9 | Del | 61 | 1 | 112 | Alt-D |
| 10 | Home Home ↑ | 62 | ↵ | 113 | ↵ |
| 11 | ↓ | 63 | Shift-F6 | 114 | Shift-F6 |
| 12 | ↓ | 64 | - | 115 | Alt-D |
| 13 | ↓ | 65 | Space | 116 | ↵ |
| 14 | ↓ | 66 | Ctrl-B | 117 | F7 |
| 15 | ↓ | 67 | Space | 118 | N |
| 16 | Shift-F8 | 68 | - | 119 | N |
| 17 | 4 | 69 | F7 | 120 | Ctrl-F10 |
| 18 | 1.5 | 70 | 8 | 121 | SY |
| 19 | ↵ | 71 | 5 | 122 | ↵ |
| 20 | + (on numeric keypad) | 72 | ↵ | 123 | Tab [8 times to move cursor to |
| 21 | + | 73 | ↵ | | position 50] |
| 22 | + | 74 | ↓ | 124 | Sincerely yours, |
| 23 | ↑ | 75 | ↓ | 125 | ↵ |
| 24 | ↑ (to line 52.5) | 76 | ↓ | 126 | ↵ |
| 25 | Alt-F8 | 77 | ↓ | 127 | ↵ |
| 26 | 4 | 78 | ↓ | 128 | ↵ |
| 27 | 3 | 79 | Alt-F3 | 129 | Tab [8 times to move cursor to |
| 28 | ↵ | 80 | Backspace [delete | | position 50] |
| 29 | 57 | | spacing code] | 130 | Francis Morris |
| 30 | ↵ | 81 | Space | 131 | ↵ |
| 31 | ↵ | 82 | Shift-F8 | 132 | Tab [8 times to move cursor to |
| 32 | Alt-F3 [view codes] | 83 | 4 | | position 50] |
| 33 | Space | 84 | 2 | 133 | Manager |
| 34 | Alt-F3 | 85 | ↵ | 134 | ↵ |
| 35 | Backspace [delete code] | 86 | F10 | 135 | Ctrl-F10 |
| 36 | Space | 87 | license.2 | 136 | ↵ |
| 37 | Ctrl-Enter | 88 | ↵ | 137 | ↵ |
| 38 | Alt-F3 | 89 | Shift-F7 | 138 | Alt-F10 |
| 39 | Backspace [delete code] | 90 | 1 | 139 | SY |
| 40 | Space | 91 | F7 | 140 | ↵ |
| 41 | ↑ (to Ln 51) | 92 | N | 141 | F5 |
| 42 | Alt-F8 | 93 | N | 142 | ↵ |
| 43 | 9 | 94 | Shift-F5 | 143 | Space |
| 44 | 4 | 95 | 1 | 144 | F7 |
| 45 | ↵ | 96 | ↵ | 145 | N |
| 46 | ↵ | 97 | Shift-F5 | 146 | Y |
| 47 | Alt-F3 [view codes] | 98 | 2 | 147 | [if not at a DOS prompt, take WP |
| 48 | Space | 99 | F7 | | disk out and put DOS disk in |
| 49 | Home Home ↑ | 100 | 3 | | drive A] |
| 50 | Alt-F8 | 101 | Alt-F3 | 148 | ↵ |
| 51 | 6 | 102 | Space | | |

### Project Summary (continued)

The following list summarizes the material covered in Project 5:

1. **File Management** is done through the **List Files** menu. After a file is highlighted, it can be retrieved, renamed, printed, looked at, or copied under another name or to another directory. A word search can also be done through the List Files menu.
2. A **soft page break** is one invoked by the software. The embedded code is **[SPg]**.
3. **Changing the page length** is a page format function that can be used to shorten or lengthen the number of lines on a page.
4. A **hard page break** is invoked by the user to prevent typing from being inserted past a certain point on the page. The embedded code is **[HPg]**.
5. The **conditional end of page** feature keeps a specified number of lines together on one page. The embedded code is **[CndlEOP]**.
6. A **header** is typing found at the top of every page. Headers only have to be typed one time, then they are held in reserve to be printed on top of every page. Headers can consist of several lines of type, or perhaps just a code so the printer will print the current page number.
7. A **footer** is typing found at the bottom of every page. Footers only have to be typed one time, then they are held in reserve to be printed on the bottom of every page. Footers can consist of several lines of type, or perhaps just a code so the printer will print the current page number.
8. The **suppress for current page only** function can instruct the printer *not* to print a combination of page numbering or headers and footers on specified pages.
9. The **date format** function allows you to place a code in a document, so that the current date (or the date entered when loading DOS into the computer) will always be present in a document. Any combination of date formats can be used, such as day of month first, month as a word, and year in all four digits.
10. A **macro** is defined and invoked by the user to replace a sequence of keystrokes that is used frequently. When a macro is defined, all keystrokes are stored under one short name and can be invoked quickly by pressing just a few keys.

# STUDENT ASSIGNMENTS

## STUDENT ASSIGNMENT 1: True/False

**Instructions:** Circle T if the statement is true and F if the statement is false.

T F 1. Headers and footers are found on the Shift-F8 keys.
T F 2. To delete a file from the List Files menu, highlight the file, press the number 2, and respond Y for yes.
T F 3. WordPerfect lets you define two headers and two footers.
T F 4. WordPerfect defaults at 50 single lines of type per page.
T F 5. To list the files on the default drive, press F5 and Enter.
T F 6. To suppress a header/footer for the current page only, choose option 8 in the Page Format menu.
T F 7. To access the Macro Define option, press Alt-F8.
T F 8. The date function is found by pressing Shift-F5.
T F 9. Each time a document is saved, the name must be retyped.
T F 10. To cause a hard page break, press the Scroll Lock/Break key.

## STUDENT ASSIGNMENT 2: Multiple Choice

**Instructions:** Circle the correct response.

1. It is possible to delete a file by
   a. highlighting the file in List Files and pressing the Cancel key.
   b. highlighting the file in List Files and pressing the 2 key, then Y.
   c. highlighting the file in List Files and pressing the Exit key.
   d. pressing Ctrl-F5.
2. When defining headers and footers, WordPerfect allows for
   a. one header and one footer.
   b. two headers and one footer.
   c. either two headers or two footers but not both.
   d. two headers and/or two footers.
3. The Date format and function can be found on the following key(s):
   a. F5
   b. Ctrl-F5
   c. Alt-F5
   d. Shift-F5
4. To invoke a macro,
   a. define the macro with Ctrl-F10
   b. while "Macro Def" is flashing, press all keys to be stored.
   c. call up the macro through either Alt-F10 or Alt-(letter).
   d. all of the above
5. When defining a conditional end of page,
   a. press Alt-F8, 9 and all lines will be kept together until you press a hard return.
   b. press Alt-F8, 9, and designate how many lines are to be kept together.
   c. press Ctrl-F8, 2, and designate how many lines to an inch.
   d. none of the above
6. By pressing Ctrl-Enter, a hard page break occurs. The code embedded in the document for a hard page break is:
   a. [HPg]
   b. [HPgBrk]
   c. [Hard Page]
   d. [Page Brk]
7. In the List Files function, feature 6 will
   a. retrieve the document into memory.
   b. allow the user to look at the entire document, without retrieving it into memory.
   c. not allow the user to do any editing in the document.
   d. both b and c
8. "Suppress for current page only" will
   a. allow the user to cancel all headers and/or footers.
   b. allow the user to cancel specific headers.
   c. allow the user to cancel specific footers.
   d. all of the above

## STUDENT ASSIGNMENT 3: Matching

**Instructions:** Put the appropriate number next to the words in the second column.

| | | |
|---|---|---|
| 1. Delete a file | _____ | Alt-F8, 4, 3 |
| 2. Conditional end of page | _____ | Ctrl-Enter |
| 3. Macro define | _____ | 2 on List Files menu |
| 4. Look option on List Files menu | _____ | Shift-F5, 3 |
| 5. Date format | _____ | 6 on List Files menu |
| 6. Hard page break | _____ | Alt-F8, 9 |
| 7. Retrieve a file | _____ | 1 on List Files menu |
| 8. Change page length | _____ | Ctrl-F10 |
| 9. Define a header | _____ | Shift-F5, 2 |
| 10. Insert date function | _____ | Alt-F8, 6, 1, 1 |

## STUDENT ASSIGNMENT 4: Understanding WordPerfect Commands

**Instructions:** Next to each command, describe its effect.

| Command | Effect |
|---|---|
| Alt-F8, 9 | ______________________ |
| Ctrl-F10 | ______________________ |
| Ctrl-Enter | ______________________ |
| Alt-F8, 4 | ______________________ |
| F5, Enter | ______________________ |
| 1 on List Files menu | ______________________ |
| 2 on List Files menu | ______________________ |
| 6 on List Files menu | ______________________ |
| Alt-F8, 8 | ______________________ |
| Alt-F8, 6 | ______________________ |

## STUDENT ASSIGNMENT 5: Describing a Footer

**Instructions:** At the bottom of the following document is a footer created on WordPerfect. Describe in detail how that footer was created.

The Regional Occupational Program, commonly called ROP, is a cooperative educational effort between local school districts and the County Department of Education. Its purpose is to train high school youth to become gainfully employed.

ROP has served and trained over 95,000 students in some 42 trades since 1988.

ROP plays an important role in the application of basic skills in the world of work, endeavoring to assist the unskilled and under-trained to become gainfully employed. ROP works in cooperation with 1,054 local businesses in the community to provide students on-the-job training. About 500 members of business and industry are involved in an advisory committee role to assure meaningful job skill training, a verified labor market demand, and a high potential for student placement in every course offered through ROP.

Important features of the Regional Occupational Program are:

1. Students from many schools meet at a centralized classroom. The teacher has a credential in the field being taught plus at least 5 years of directly related work experience.

2. Students are assigned to business training sites to receive realistic on-the-job skill development. An individualized training plan is developed for each student at each job training site.

3. Periodically students return to the classroom for additional training and to review progress from an employment point of view.

Courses are offered three semesters during the year. Enrollment time varies depending on the course topic or trade area. Some programs permit entry on any day, others at the start of each semester.

Regional Occupational Program Page number 1

## STUDENT ASSIGNMENT 6: Identifying the List Files Menu

**Instructions:** Look at this screen of a List Files menu. Circle the following areas and place the identifying number within the circle.

1. Amount of free disk space
2. Columns with names of files
3. Columns with names of extensions
4. Number of bytes used for files
5. Dates files were made
6. Directory of files

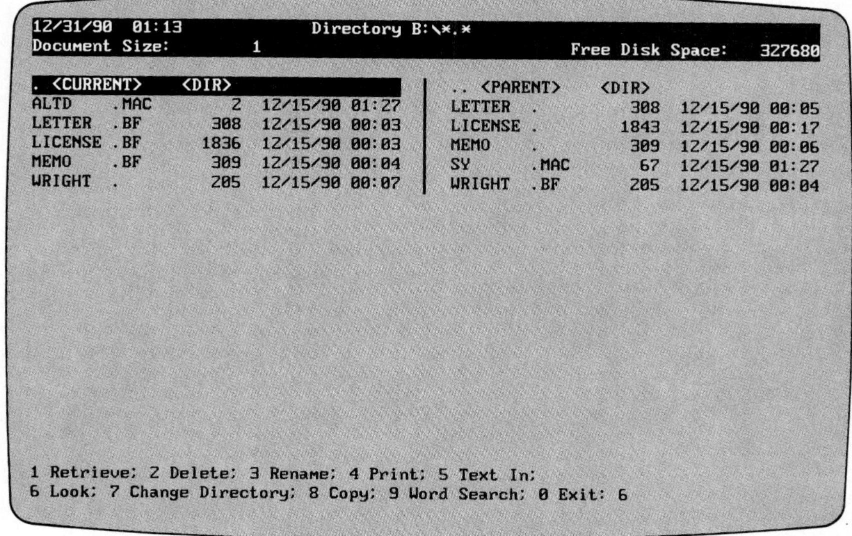

## STUDENT ASSIGNMENT 7: Identifying Codes

**Instructions:** This screen shows several codes. Circle the entire code and identify it with the appropriate number from the list below.

1. Margin setting
2. Header
3. Tab setting
4. Date function
5. Suppress for current page only
6. Hard page break
7. Page length
8. Conditional end of page

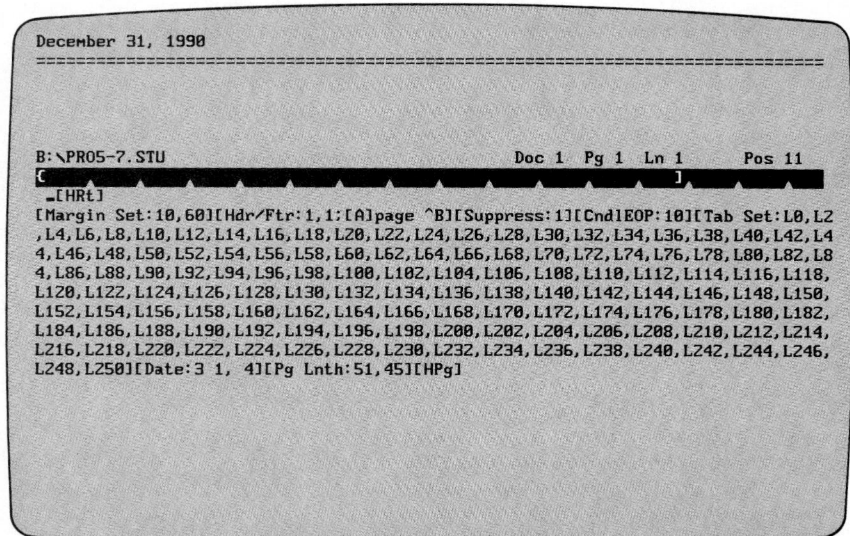


## STUDENT ASSIGNMENT 8: Making a Macro

**Instructions:** This heading will be used frequently.

Robert B. Jones
Attorney
Jones, Richards, and Smith
534 Harrison Blvd.
Salt Lake City, UT 84106

Problem 1: Define the heading as a macro. Define the name as HEAD.
Problem 2: Practice retrieving the heading with Alt-F10.
Problem 3: Print the page of typing.

## STUDENT ASSIGNMENT 9: Making a Macro

**Instructions:** Here is an ending that will be used frequently.

Problem 1: Define the ending as a macro. Define the name by using Alt-M.

Problem 2: Practice retrieving the ending with Alt-M.

Problem 3: Print the page of typing.

Sincerely yours,

Robert B. Jones
Attorney
Jones, Richards, and Smith

RBJ/rg

## STUDENT ASSIGNMENT 10: Modifying a Document

**Instructions:** Perform the following tasks.

1. Load DOS into main memory.
2. Load WordPerfect into main memory by inserting the WordPerfect diskette into drive A, putting a data disk into drive B, typing b: and pressing Enter. At the B> prompt, type a:wp and press Enter.

Problem 1:
1. Retrieve the file named Regional.
2. Change the margins to 15 on the left and 75 on the right.
3. Delete all existing tabs. Set tab stops at every third interval, beginning with position 0.
4. Change the line spacing to 2
5. Create a footer as follows:
   Regional Occupational Program (flush left)
   Page number (flush right)
6. Suppress the footer for the first page only.

Problem 2: Save the new document to disk under the new name of Regional.3.

Problem 3: Print the revised document; it should look like the document below.

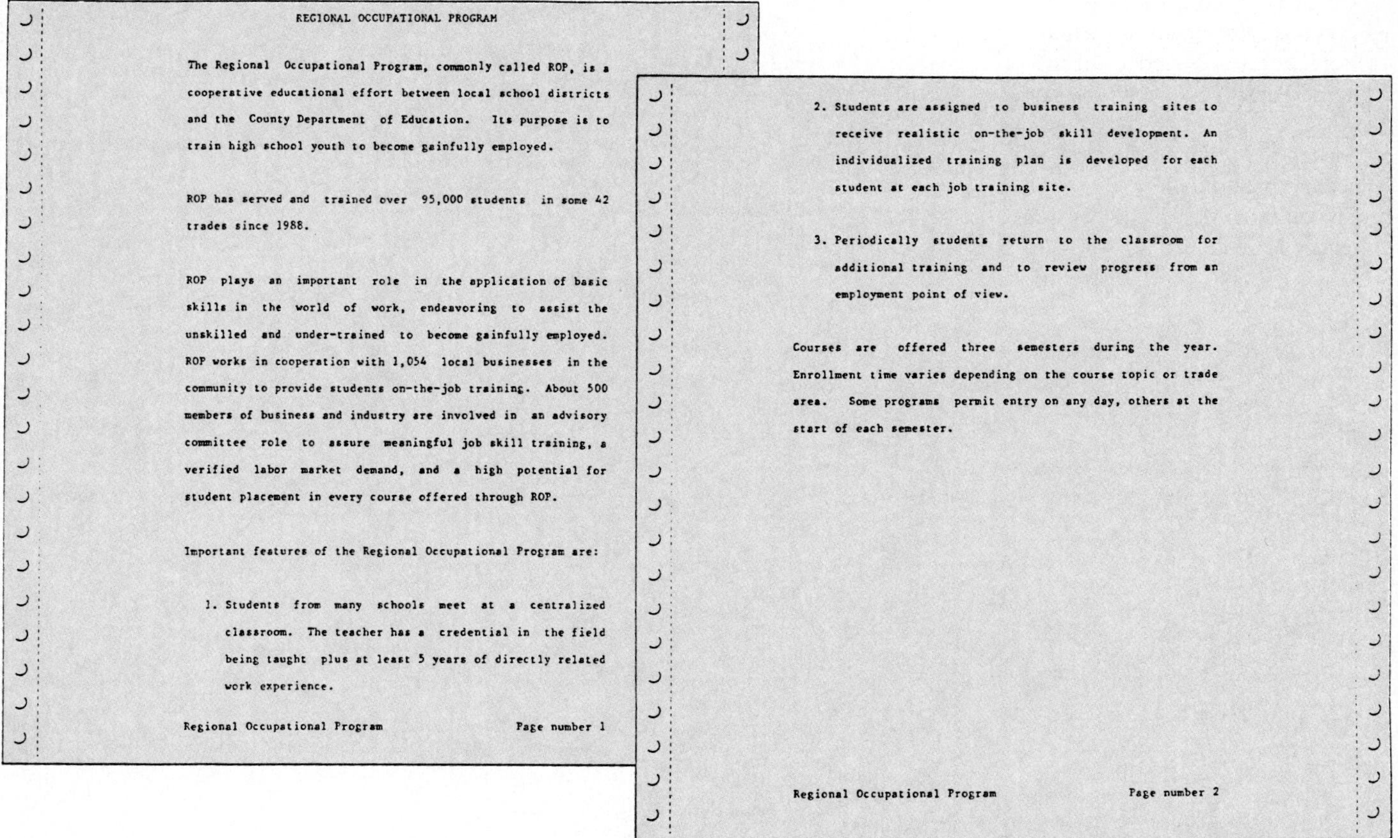

REGIONAL OCCUPATIONAL PROGRAM

The Regional Occupational Program, commonly called ROP, is a cooperative educational effort between local school districts and the County Department of Education. Its purpose is to train high school youth to become gainfully employed.

ROP has served and trained over 95,000 students in some 42 trades since 1988.

ROP plays an important role in the application of basic skills in the world of work, endeavoring to assist the unskilled and under-trained to become gainfully employed. ROP works in cooperation with 1,054 local businesses in the community to provide students on-the-job training. About 500 members of business and industry are involved in an advisory committee role to assure meaningful job skill training, a verified labor market demand, and a high potential for student placement in every course offered through ROP.

Important features of the Regional Occupational Program are:

1. Students from many schools meet at a centralized classroom. The teacher has a credential in the field being taught plus at least 5 years of directly related work experience.

Regional Occupational Program Page number 1

2. Students are assigned to business training sites to receive realistic on-the-job skill development. An individualized training plan is developed for each student at each job training site.

3. Periodically students return to the classroom for additional training and to review progress from an employment point of view.

Courses are offered three semesters during the year. Enrollment time varies depending on the course topic or trade area. Some programs permit entry on any day, others at the start of each semester.

Regional Occupational Program Page number 2

# PROJECT 6

## Advanced WordPerfect Features

### Objectives

You will have mastered the material in this project when you can:

- Search and reverse search the text of a document
- Employ the search and replace function
- Practice using the thesaurus and speller demonstration example

**B**oot up and load WordPerfect into main memory. Retrieve License.2, the document you saved in Project 5, by pressing Shift-F10. Type the name License.2 and press Enter ↵. The document appears on the screen.

Let's assume that we must modify this document because PerSoft Inc. has been acquired by a company called UMC Corp. The modified document to be prepared is shown in Figure 6-1. Six changes must be made to the existing licensing agreement so that it can be used for the new company's products:

1. Remove the double spacing.
2. Emphasize the fact that the company assumes no responsibility.
3. Change the word License to License Agreement in section c.
4. Replace all occurrences of the name PerSoft Inc. with the name UMC Corp.
5. Switch the order of the first and second paragraphs.
6. Switch the order of the two sentences in section a.

```
                                              December 15, 1990
*WPC

                         LICENSING AGREEMENT

UMC Corp.  provides this program and licenses you to use it.  You
assume  responsibility  for  the  selection  of  this  program to
achieve your  intended results.   UMC Corp. assumes absolutely no
responsibility for the results  you obtain  from the  use of this
software package.*WPC

You  should  carefully  read  the following terms and conditions.
Your use of this program  package  indicates  your  acceptance of
them.   If you  do not  agree with  them, you should not use this
software package.  Instead, you  should  return  the  package and
your money will be returned to you.*WPC

LICENSE

     a.   Use on  more than  one machine is considered "pirating"
          this software.  Use the  program  on  a  single machine
          only.                                              *WPC

     b.   Copy the  program into  any machine readable or printed
          form for backup or modification purposes  in support of
          your use  of the  program on a single machine.  Certain
          programs  from   UMC   Corp.,   however,   may  contain
          mechanisms to limit or inhibit copying.  These programs
          are marked "copy protected."                       *WPC

     c.   Modify or merge  the  program  into  another  UMC Corp.
          program for  use on the single machine.  Any portion of
          the program merged into  another program  will continue
          to  be  subject  to  the  terms  and conditions of this
          License Agreement.                                 *WPC

You MAY NOT use, copy, modify, or transfer the program,  in whole
or  in  part,  except  as  expressly  permitted in this Licensing
Agreement.    UMC  Corp.  also  reserves  the  right  to  do  the
following:*WPC

     Withdraw your  license if this software package is used
     for any illegal or immoral purpose  which, in  the sole
     judgment of UMC Corp., may damage the reputation of UMC
     Corp.                                              *WPC

If you transfer possession of any  copy, modification,  or merged
portion  of  the  program  to  another  person,  YOUR  LICENSE IS
AUTOMATICALLY TERMINATED.
*WPC

                               - 1 -
```

**FIGURE 6-1**

# SEARCH FUNCTIONS

## Searching for Codes

Before you begin manipulating text in the license, you decide that you do not want the document double spaced. Knowing that a code was inserted, you can **search** or look for that code among the reveal codes. But instead of manually searching for it, you can issue a command in WordPerfect to have the program search for you. A search can be conducted within or outside the reveal codes screen. In this case, let's search in reveal codes, so press Alt-F3. Look at the template next to the F2 key. Notice the word Search in black. Press the F2 key. The message "→Srch:" appears on your screen. Notice that the arrow is pointing forward, indicating a forward search. To search for a code, you must invoke it the way you invoked the original code. Recall that double spacing is invoked by pressing Shift-F8 and the number 4 for the spacing option. Thus, press Shift-F8 and 4. Figure 6-2 shows that your screen now displays the search command followed by the invoked code **[Spacing Set]**. To invoke the search press F2. Your tendency will be to press the Enter key. But if you do that a [HRt] code will be inserted, and you will need to backspace to delete the [HRt] code. As you press the F2 key, notice that the cursor moves to the right of the first code it finds (Figure 6-3 on the following page).

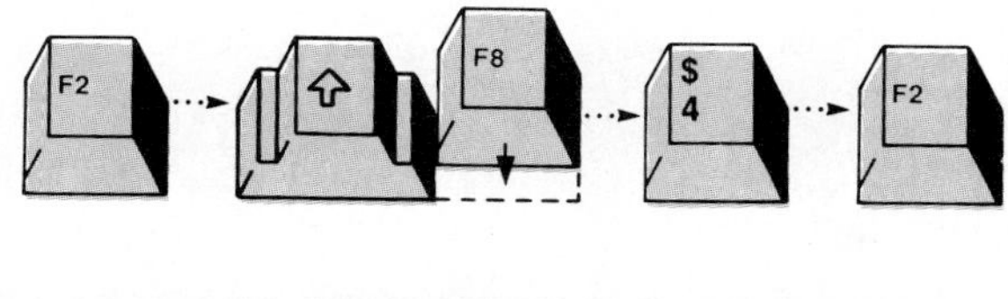


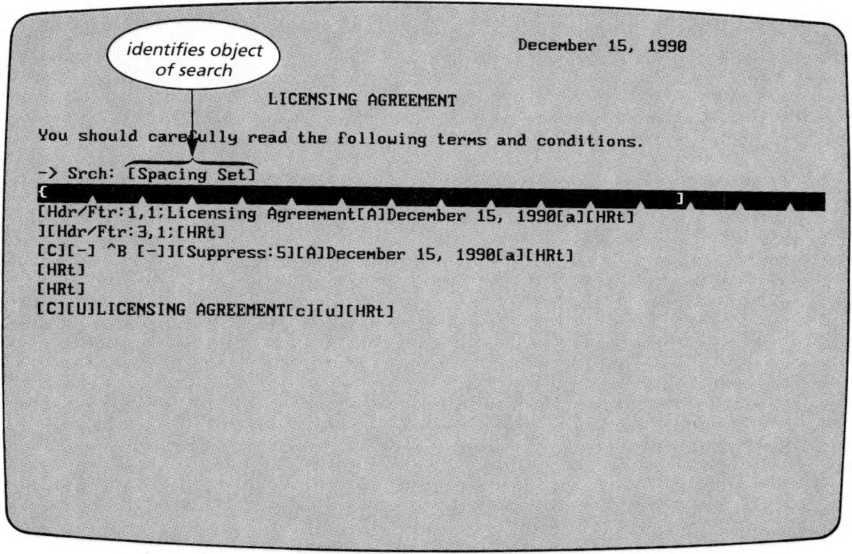


FIGURE 6-2

To delete the code press the Backspace key (step 1 of Figure 6-3). Because there may be more than one spacing code, you want to continue the search. Press the F2 key (step 2 of Figure 6-3), and notice that the words "Spacing Set" appear again to remind you that you are searching for spacing set codes. Press F2 again to continue the search. Because you have another spacing set code, the cursor will stop at that code. Press the Backspace key to delete the code.

To be sure there are no more spacing set codes, press the F2 key again. The words "Spacing Set" will appear again to remind you that you are searching for spacing set codes. Press the F2 key again to continue the search. When the prompt "* Not Found *" appears you are assured that all spacing codes have been deleted. Press the spacebar to exit the reveal codes screen.

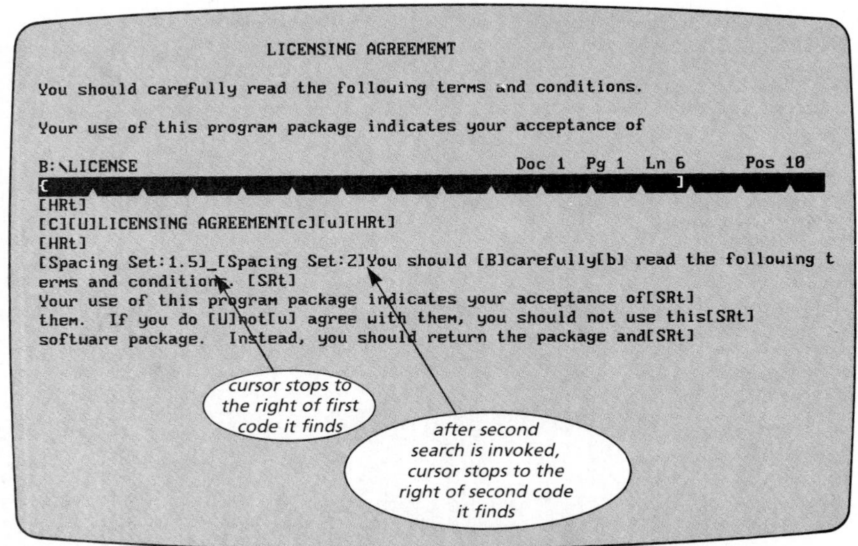


**FIGURE 6-3**

**Step 1: Delete the code**

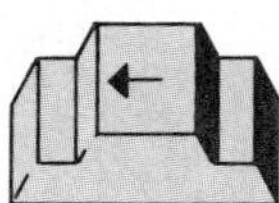

**Step 2: Continue to search for the code then backspace to delete**

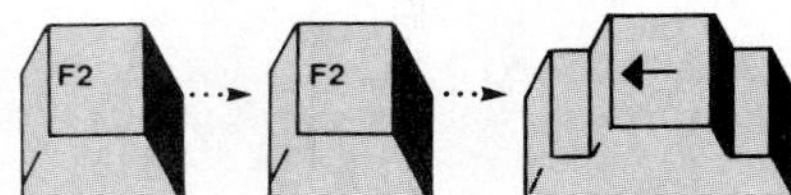

## Forward Search

Move the cursor to the top of the document by pressing Home, Home, Up Arrow.

In the second paragraph of the document you wish to emphasize the fact that the company assumes no responsibility. You can do this by searching for the word assumes and inserting the word absolutely, so the phrase will read: assumes absolutely no responsibility. To search forward for the word "assumes", press the F2 key. The last command to search for, spacing set codes, is still within brackets next to the search forward prompt. But you do not wish to use that command. Type the word assumes, because that is the object of your search (step 1 of Figure 6-4). The code "Spacing Set" is deleted and the word assumes appears next to the Srch: command. To begin the search, press the F2 key (step 2 of Figure 6-4). The cursor moves immediately to the right of the word. Press the spacebar and type the word absolutely.

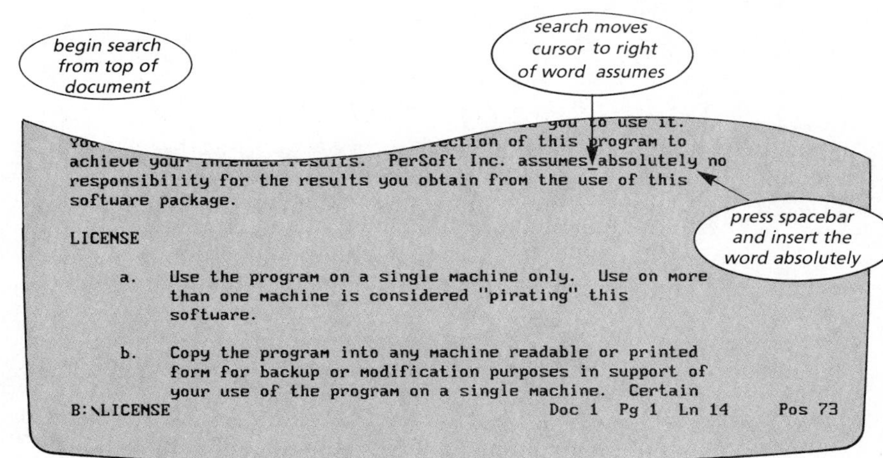


FIGURE 6-4

Step 1: Specify the object of the search

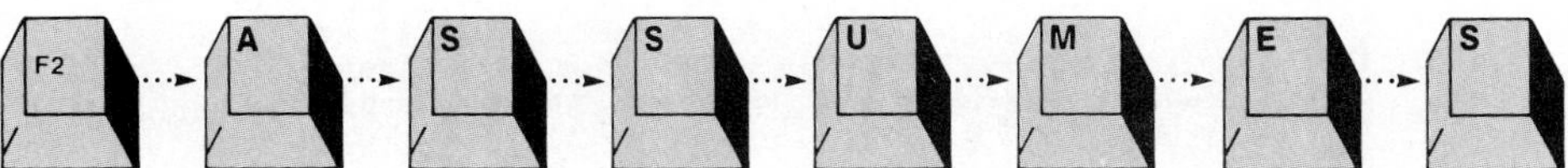


Step 2: Begin the search

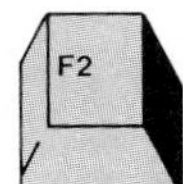

## Reverse Search

Move the cursor to the bottom of the document by pressing Home, Home, Down Arrow. At the end of section c is the word License, which you want to change to License Agreement. You may search backward with the Reverse Search key, which is Shift-F2. Press Shift-F2, and you will see the message "←Srch:" at the bottom left corner of the screen. Notice that the arrow points in the reverse direction, indicating that the search will be going backward from the cursor position. Type the word license in all lowercase letters. This causes WordPerfect to search for a word in lowercase, uppercase, or a combination of the two. If, however, you type in uppercase or upper and lowercase letters, WordPerfect will look only for those exact characters. Press the F2 key to begin the search. The cursor stops at the first license it finds, even though it is in uppercase letters. This is not the one you wish to change. To continue the search backward through the document, press Shift-F2, then press F2 again. The cursor stops again at the word license but it is still not the one you desire. To continue, press Shift-F2, then the F2 key. The cursor stops at the desired spot. Press the spacebar and type the word Agreement. The period moves to the right as the word is inserted into the text (Figure 6-5).

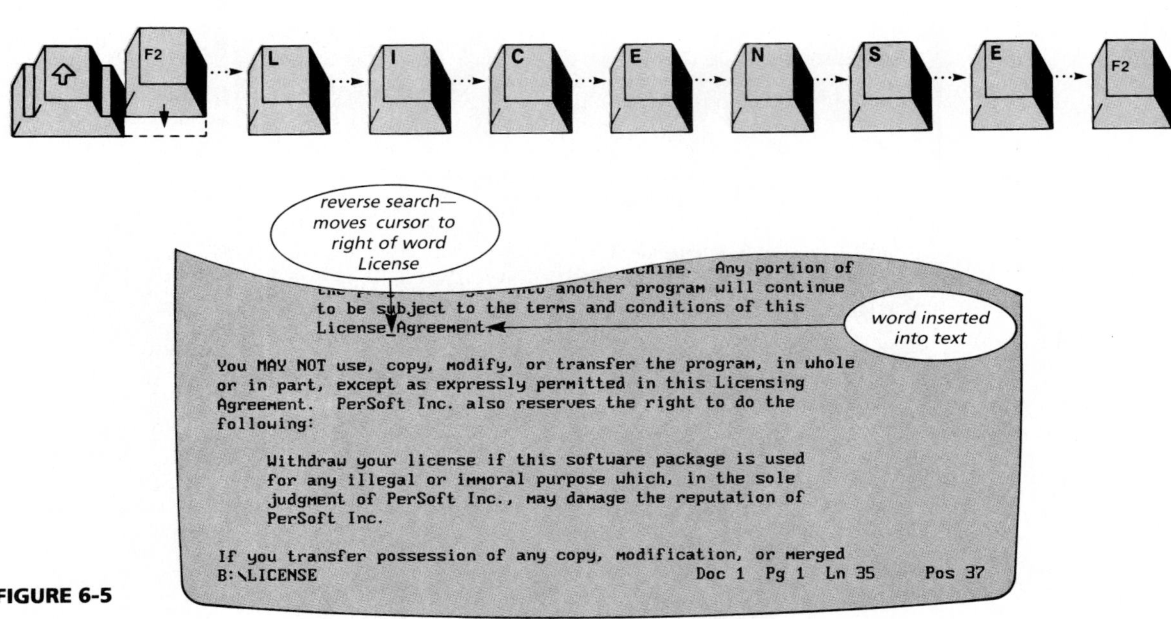


**FIGURE 6-5**

## Search and Replace

Move the cursor to the top of the document by pressing Home, Home, Up Arrow.

WordPerfect provides commands that allow you to search the document for specific characters and, after finding these characters, automatically replace them with other characters. This series of commands is called **Search and Replace**.

Recall that we are changing the document named License because the company for which the document was prepared, PerSoft Inc., has been acquired by a company called UMC Corp. Look at the template next to the F2 key. Notice the word Replace in blue. Press Alt-F2. A prompt message appears asking if you want to confirm each occurrence of the change. Type the letter Y for yes. You are prompted with "→Srch:". Type the name PerSoft Inc. (Figure 6-6). Press F2 to produce the prompt "Replace with:" (Figure 6-7). Type the name UMC Corp., then press the F2 key again. The cursor stops at the first occurrence of PerSoft Inc. and prompts "Confirm? (Y/N) N" (Figure 6-8); you may see the message "please wait" prior to seeing the prompt. Type the letter Y to change the name. The name will change and the cursor will move to the next occurrence of the name PerSoft Inc. and prompt again "Confirm? (Y/N) N". Type Y and the process will repeat itself. At each occurrence of the name, to confirm type Y until the prompt no longer appears at the lower left corner of the screen. That is your indication that there are no more occurrences of the name PerSoft Inc.

As you can see, you also could have typed N to not confirm each change. The WordPerfect software would have automatically made each change without stopping at each occurrence. You must be sure, however, that you do wish to change all occurrences of the searched-for word. For instance, you may have typed U.S. throughout a document and decided to change all occurrences of U.S. to United States. But you may have typed U.S. Grant for Ulysses S. Grant, in which case, had you not confirmed each change, his name would be changed to United States Grant. If you are *sure* all occurrences should be changed, there is no need to confirm.

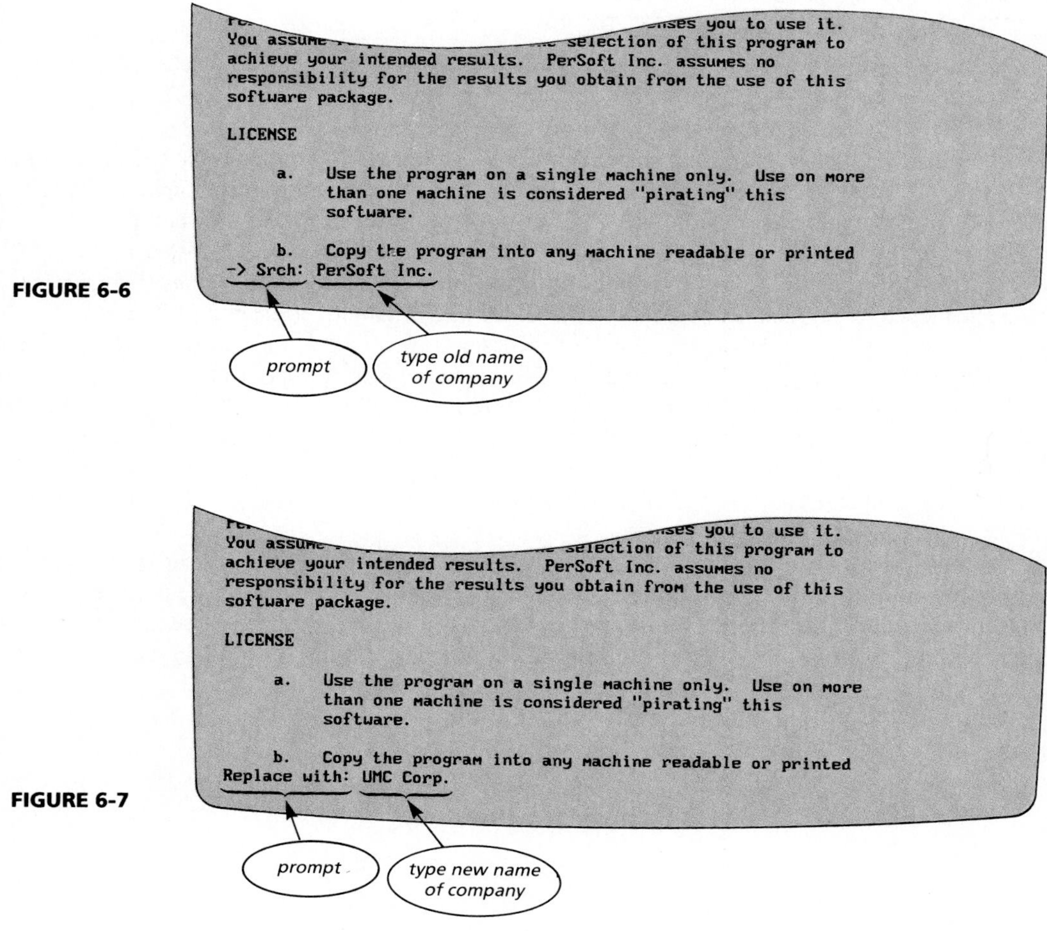


**FIGURE 6-6**

**FIGURE 6-7**

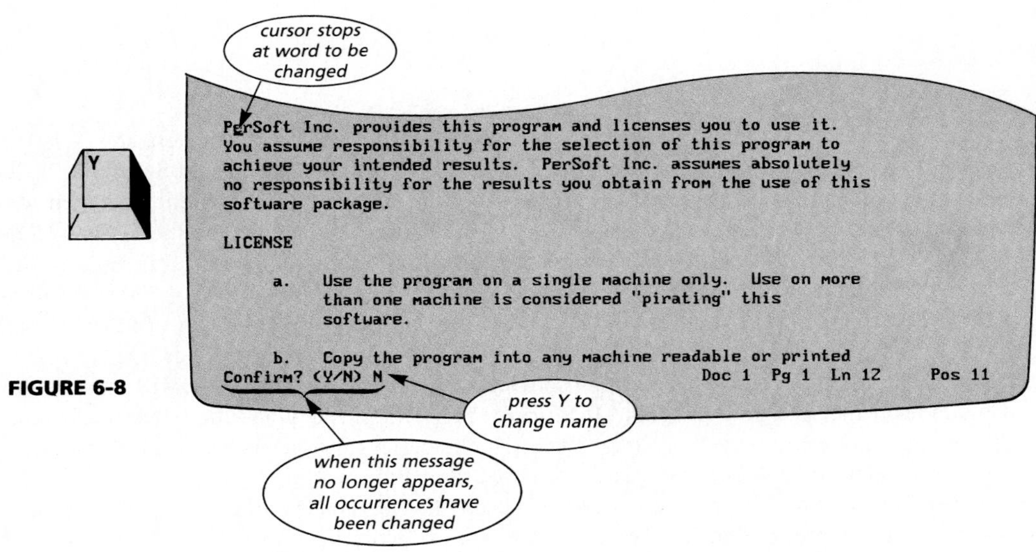


FIGURE 6-8

# MOVING TEXT WITHIN A DOCUMENT

## Cut and Paste a Paragraph

To move the cursor to the top of the document, press Home, Home, Up Arrow.

There are times when you wish to move text from one place in a document to another place. This is called **cut and paste**. Recall that you want to reverse paragraphs one and two. To **move** an entire paragraph, first you must move the cursor to the beginning of the paragraph. Press the Down Arrow to move to line 6, position 10 so that the cursor is under the Y in You in the first paragraph. Look at the template next to the F4 key. Notice the word Move in red. Press Ctrl-F4 (step 1 of Figure 6-9). The menu shown in Figure 6-9 gives you three options to move text, then three options to retrieve text. Notice the options to move a sentence, paragraph, or page. Type the number 2 for paragraph (step 2 of Figure 6-9). Figure 6-10 on the opposite page shows how the entire paragraph following the cursor is highlighted, indicating the text to be cut and pasted elsewhere. The figure also shows that at the bottom of the screen, you are given the options to cut, copy, or delete the highlighted text. Press the number 1 to cut the text for placement elsewhere (step 1 of Figure 6-10). The text of the highlighted first paragraph is cut and the second paragraph moves up to be in the first paragraph's position. Although the text of the first paragraph has been deleted from the screen, it has not been deleted from memory. Imagine that the text has been placed on a clipboard, and will be held there until the cursor has been moved to the desired new position, at which time you will retrieve the text from the clipboard.

Press the Down Arrow ↓ to move the cursor to line 12, position 10 so that it is under the L in License. When the text is retrieved, this text will be moved down to make room for the incoming paragraph. Now, to retrieve the text that was cut, press Ctrl-F4. The Move menu appears again. This time use the retrieve option on the menu to retrieve the text on the clipboard. Because number 5 indicates text, press the number 5 (step 2 of Figure 6-10). The cut text is inserted in place and text at the cursor is moved down.

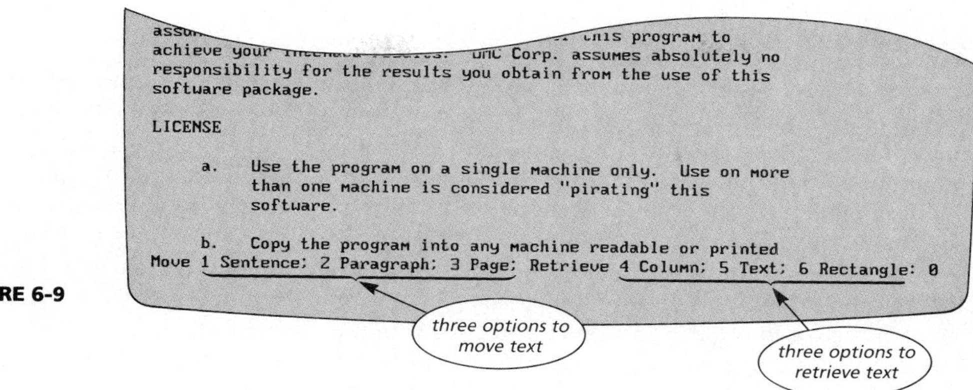


**FIGURE 6-9**

**Step 1: View the Move menu**

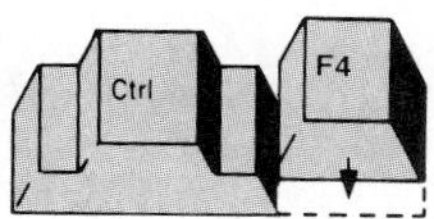


**Step 2: Identify text to be moved**

**Step 1: Cut highlighted text**

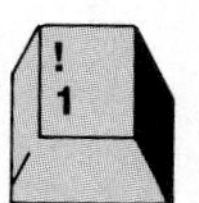


**Step 2: Move cursor to line 12, position 10 and retrieve the cut text**

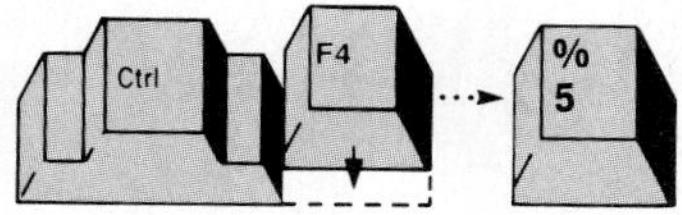


December 15, 1990

LICENSING AGREEMENT

You should carefully read the following terms and conditions. Your use of this program package indicates your acceptance of them. If you do not agree with them, you should not use this software package. Instead, you should return the package and your money will be returned to you.

UMC Corp. provides this program and licenses you to use it. You assume responsibility for the selection of this program to achieve your intended results. UMC Corp. assumes absolutely no responsibility for the results you obtain from the use of this software package.

LICENSE

a. Use the program on a single machine only. Use on more than one machine is considered "pirating" this software.

b. Copy the program into any machine readable or printed

1 Cut; 2 Copy; 3 Delete: 0

*cursor*

*paragraph is highlighted*

*copy leaves text on screen and holds it off screen as if it were on a clipboard*

*cut removes highlighted text and holds it off screen as if it were on a clipboard*

**FIGURE 6-10**

## Cut and Paste a Block

Sometimes you may wish to move a specific block of text rather than a whole sentence, paragraph, or page. To illustrate this, you will reverse the two sentences of section a. Move the cursor down to line 20, position 63 so that it is under the U in the word Use (if you only inserted one space between the sentences, the cursor would be on position 62).

As you have learned, to turn the block on press Alt-F4 and notice the message "Block on" flashing in the lower left corner of the screen. To highlight the sentence you can either move the cursor to the right one character at a time or press the Down Arrow key two times ↓ ↓ to highlight the entire sentence, as shown in Figure 6-11. Using the block function you can be exact about the text you wish to cut and paste. To move the highlighted or blocked text press Ctrl-F4. The prompt asks you to cut or copy the block (Figure 6-12). Press number 1 to cut the block (step 1 of Figure 6-12). The text is deleted and placed on the "clipboard." Move the cursor to line 20, position 20 under the U in Use. To retrieve the text from the "clipboard," press Ctrl-F4, then the number 5 (step 2 of Figure 6-12). Figure 6-13 shows no spaces between the first and second sentence. If you have spaces between the first and second sentence, it is not necessary to add any more. However, if you have no spaces, move the cursor down one line and to the right, under the U in Use. Press the spacebar two times to insert the two needed spaces. Press the Down Arrow key two times ↓ ↓ to reformat the text.

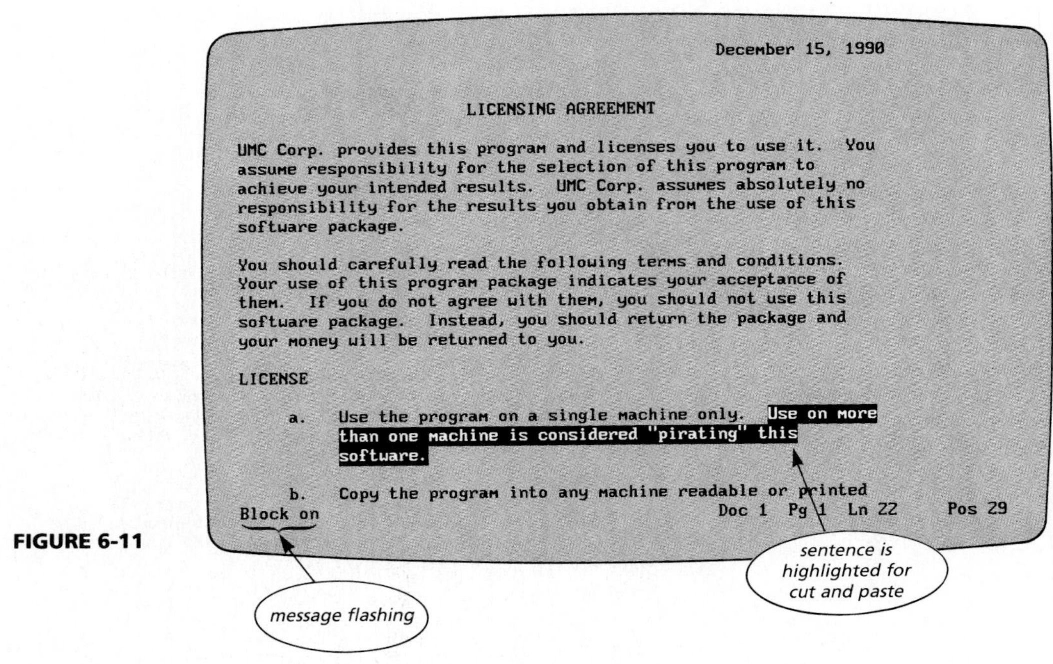


**FIGURE 6-11**

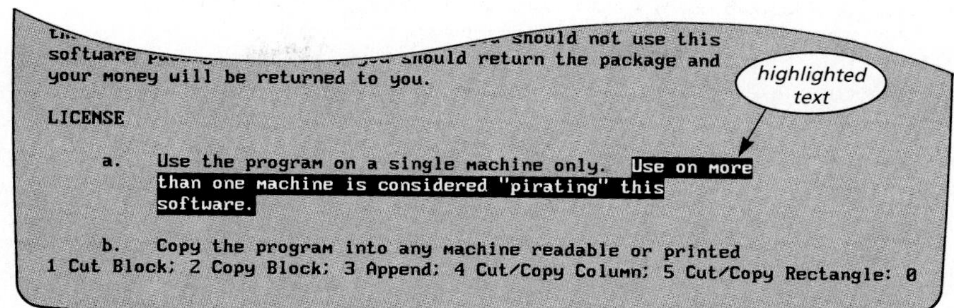


**FIGURE 6-12**

**Step 1: View the Move menu; cut the block and move it to the clipboard**

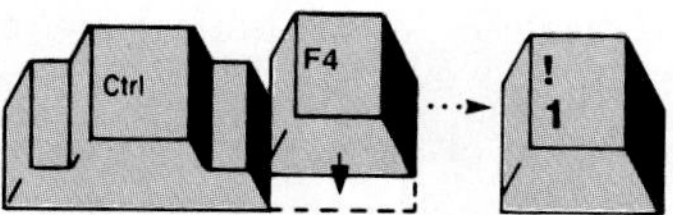


**Step 2: Move cursor to line 20, position 20; retrieve and insert cut text**

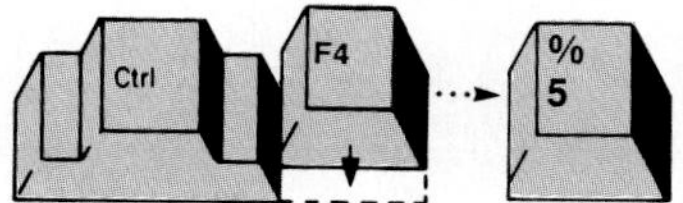


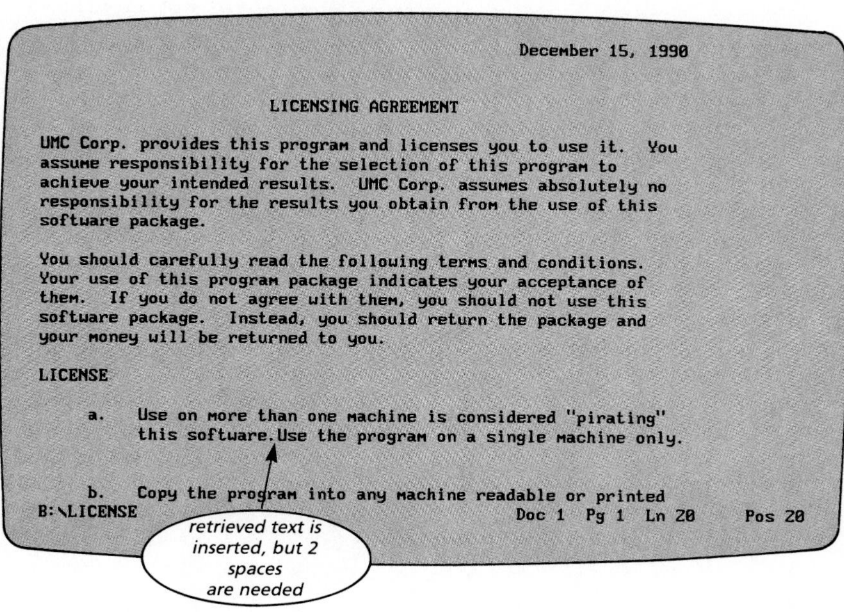


**FIGURE 6-13**

## SAVING THE DOCUMENT UNDER A NEW NAME

Now that the document has been changed, you decide that you wish to leave the document as it is on the disk, saved as it was in Project 5. You also wish to save this new version of the document. Therefore, as you save this document, you must give it another name. Look at the template by the F10 key. Notice the word Save in black. Press the F10 key. At the prompt "Document to be Saved:" type License.3 and press the Enter ↵ key. The document is saved under the new name.

## PRINTING A DOCUMENT

Now that you have saved your document, it is ready to be printed. At this point be sure that your printer has paper inserted and that the printer is on and ready to print.

Press Shift-F7. You will see the Print menu at the bottom of the screen. Press number 1 for full text. At this point the printer will begin printing your document. The printed document generated is illustrated in Figure 6-14.

December 15, 1990

LICENSING AGREEMENT

UMC Corp. provides this program and licenses you to use it. You assume responsibility for the selection of this program to achieve your intended results. UMC Corp. assumes absolutely no responsibility for the results you obtain from the use of this software package.

You should **carefully** read the following terms and conditions. Your use of this program package indicates your acceptance of them. If you do not agree with them, you should not use this software package. Instead, you should return the package and your money will be returned to you.

**LICENSE**

a. Use on more than one machine is considered "pirating" this software. Use the program on a single machine only.

b. Copy the program into any machine readable or printed form for backup or modification purposes in support of your use of the program on a single machine. Certain programs from UMC Corp., however, may contain mechanisms to limit or inhibit copying. These programs are marked "copy protected."

c. Modify or merge the program into another UMC Corp. program for use on the single machine. Any portion of the program merged into another program will continue to be subject to the terms and conditions of this License Agreement.

You MAY NOT use, copy, modify, or transfer the program, in whole or in part, except as **expressly permitted** in this Licensing Agreement. UMC Corp. also reserves the right to do the following:

Withdraw your license if this software package is used for any illegal or immoral purpose which, in the sole judgment of UMC Corp., may damage the reputation of UMC Corp.

If you transfer possession of any copy, modification, or merged portion of the program to another person, **YOUR LICENSE IS AUTOMATICALLY TERMINATED.**

- 1 -

**FIGURE 6-14**

## EXITING A DOCUMENT

Your document has been saved to disk and printed. It is now necessary to exit the document and clear the screen, but not exit the WordPerfect program.

Press the F7 key. At the prompt "Save Document? (Y/N) Y" type N because the document has already been saved. At the prompt "Exit WP? (Y/N) N" type N. The document is exited and a clear screen appears.

## THESAURUS/SPELLER USING THE README.WP FILE

Because of space restrictions on the disk containing the training version of WordPerfect, you are unable to use the thesaurus or speller on the documents you have created yourself. WordPerfect has, however, provided a sample sentence for the thesaurus and a sample paragraph for the speller. By practicing with these samples, you will learn the most valuable functions of the WordPerfect thesaurus and speller.

To use the sample thesaurus and speller it is necessary to retrieve the sample document WordPerfect has prepared. Press Shift-F10. At the prompt of "Document to be Retrieved:" type a:readme.wp and press Enter ↵. The screen shown in Figure 6-15 explains about the specially designed thesaurus and speller and gives you instructions on how to use them.

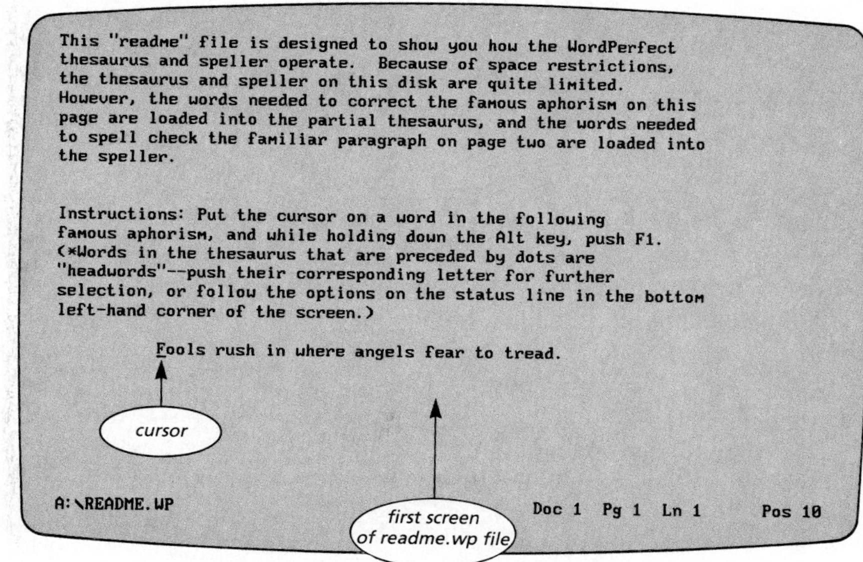

This "readme" file is designed to show you how the WordPerfect thesaurus and speller operate. Because of space restrictions, the thesaurus and speller on this disk are quite limited. However, the words needed to correct the famous aphorism on this page are loaded into the partial thesaurus, and the words needed to spell check the familiar paragraph on page two are loaded into the speller.
Instructions: Put the cursor on a word in the following famous aphorism, and while holding down the Alt key, push F1. (*Words in the thesaurus that are preceded by dots are "headwords"--push their corresponding letter for further selection, or follow the options on the status line in the bottom left-hand corner of the screen.)
Fools rush in where angels fear to tread.
cursor
A:\README.WP
first screen of readme.wp file
Doc 1 Pg 1 Ln 1 Pos 10


FIGURE 6-15

### Thesaurus

A thesaurus is a collection of words and their synonyms and antonyms. We'll use the WordPerfect **thesaurus** to choose different words for the famous saying shown. The words that you can use in this special version of the thesaurus are in boldface typing on your screen.

Move the cursor down to line 17, position 20 under the F in Fools. Look at the template next to the F1 key. Notice the word Thesaurus in blue. Press Alt-F1. Figure 6-16 shows the list of nouns (n), verbs (v), and antonyms (ant) that relate to the word Fools. A letter of the alphabet is next to each word in the first column, which will facilitate choosing a replacement for the word Fools. The words with dots are called **headwords**. If you wish to see other possible choices you can look up a word using one of the headwords. Press the number 3. The prompt "Word:" appears in the lower left corner of the screen. Type the word idiot and press Enter ↵.

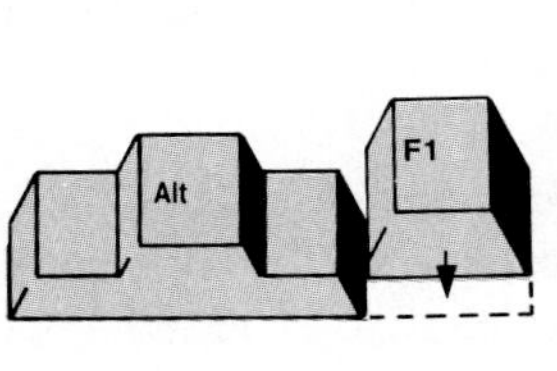


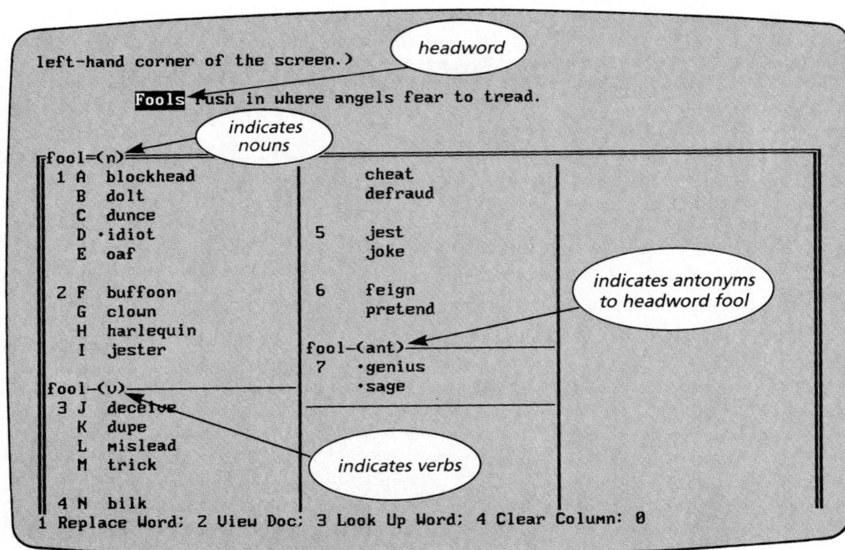


FIGURE 6-16

The screen will look like Figure 6-17. Notice that the second column shows the word idiot as the headword, giving synonyms and an antonym. The letter choices have moved from the first column to the second column. To look for more choices, press the number 3 again, then type the word simpleton and press Enter ↵.

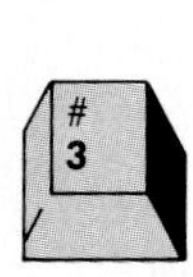


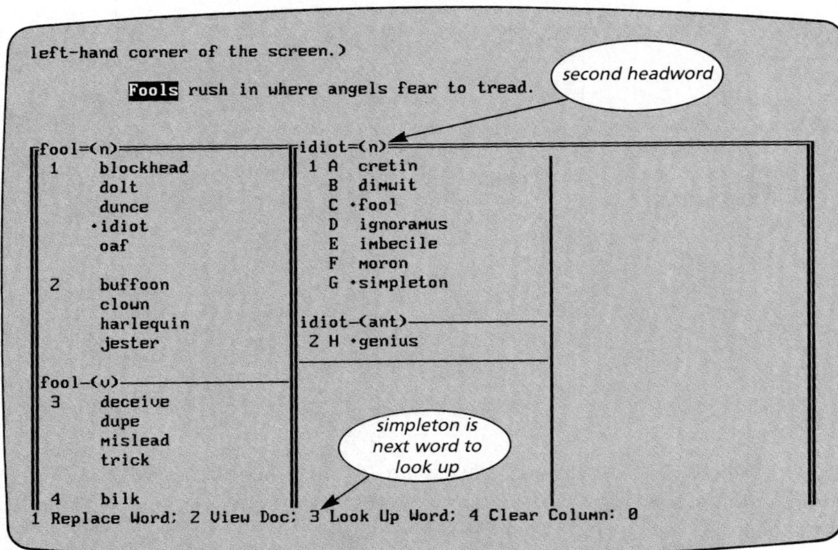


FIGURE 6-17

Figure 6-18 shows that the third column is now headed by the word simpleton and that the letters for choices have moved to the third column. Because you do not wish to use any of the words in columns two or three, press the Left Arrow ← to move the letter choices to the middle column. Instead of moving the cursor again to the left, notice that option number 4 is to clear a column. Type the number 4 and notice how the simpleton list is moved from column three to column two and that the letter choices are by the words in column two. Type the number 4 again and the letter choices are moved to column one (step 1 of Figure 6-18). Notice that the word clown is next to the letter G. To replace the word Fools with Clown press the number 1. The prompt "Press letter for word" appears on the screen. Press the letter G and notice that the word Fools is replaced by the word Clown. Type an s to make clown plural (step 2 of Figure 6-18). Because the word you are replacing, Fools, begins with a capital letter, the lowercase c in clown in the thesaurus will become uppercase when inserted into the document.

**Step 1: Clear columns**

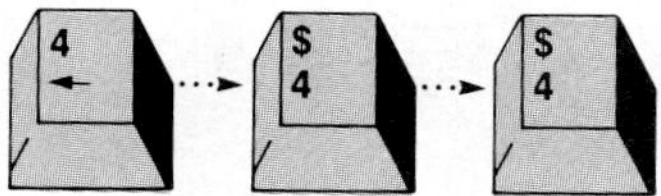


**Step 2: Replace the word Fools with the word Clowns and add the letter s**

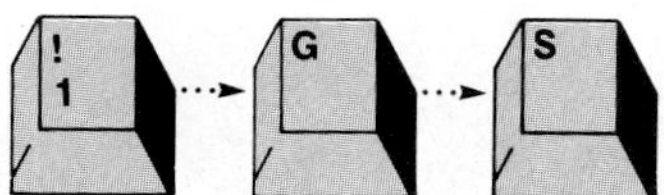


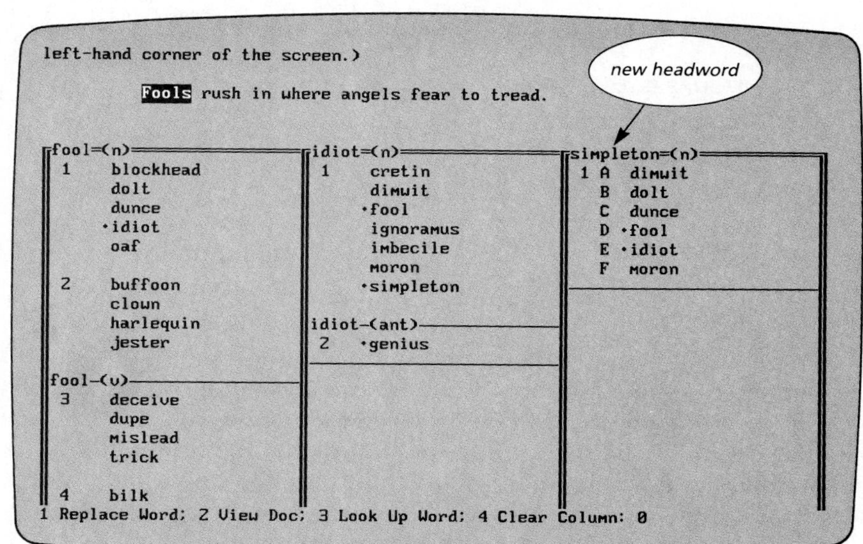


**FIGURE 6-18**

Continue practicing with the thesaurus. Press the Right Arrow → to move to the word angels. Press Alt-F1. Synonyms and an antonym appear on the screen (Figure 6-19).

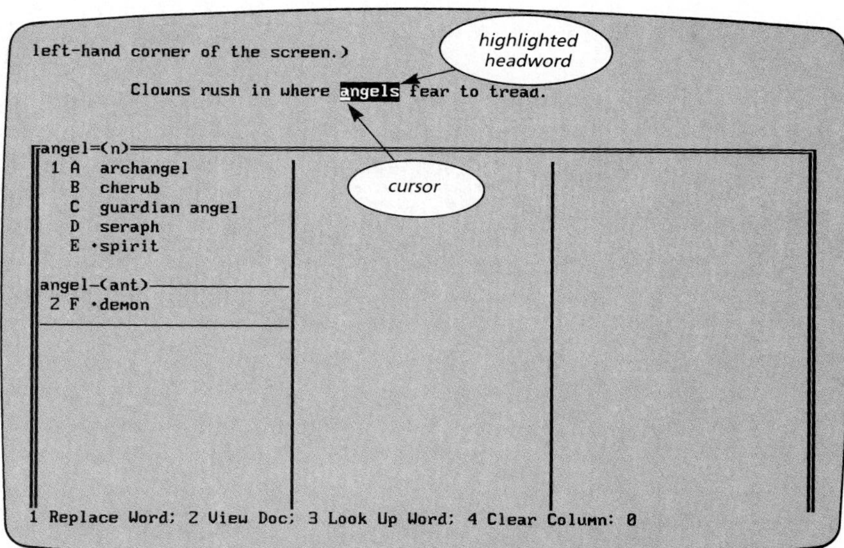


**FIGURE 6-19**

Press the number 1 to replace the word. Type the letter c and notice how angels changes to guardian angel. Type an s to make angel plural. Figure 6-20 shows how the corrected sentence appears.

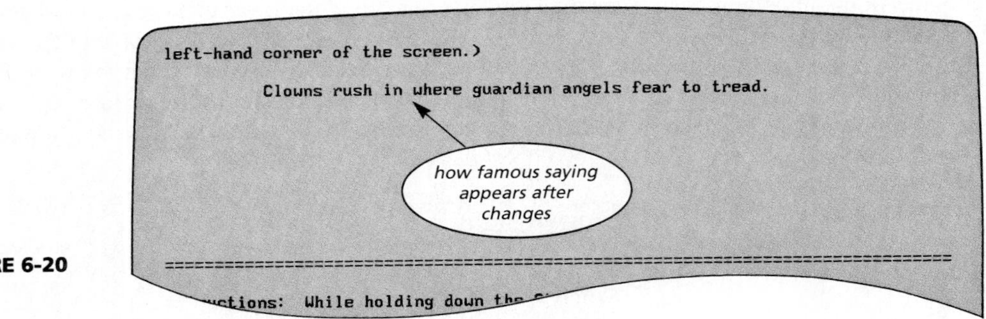
left-hand corner of the screen.)
Clowns rush in where guardian angels fear to tread.
how famous saying appears after changes
ctions: While holding down the

FIGURE 6-20

## Speller

Many word processing programs include a **speller**, a feature that checks the spelling of words you have typed. To demonstrate the WordPerfect speller press the PgDn key to move the cursor to page 2, line 1, position 10. Figure 6-21 shows the practice paragraph provided by the training version of WordPerfect. You can see that there are misspelled words in the paragraph.

Look at the template next to the F2 key. Notice the word Spell in red. Press Ctrl-F2. Figure 6-22 shows the menu at the bottom of the screen. Since you only want to use the speller on page 2, press the number 2 for Page.

Each word on the page will be matched against the words in the speller. If a word is not recognized it will be highlighted. Then a menu will appear from which you can make a choice of what you wish to do with that particular highlighted word.

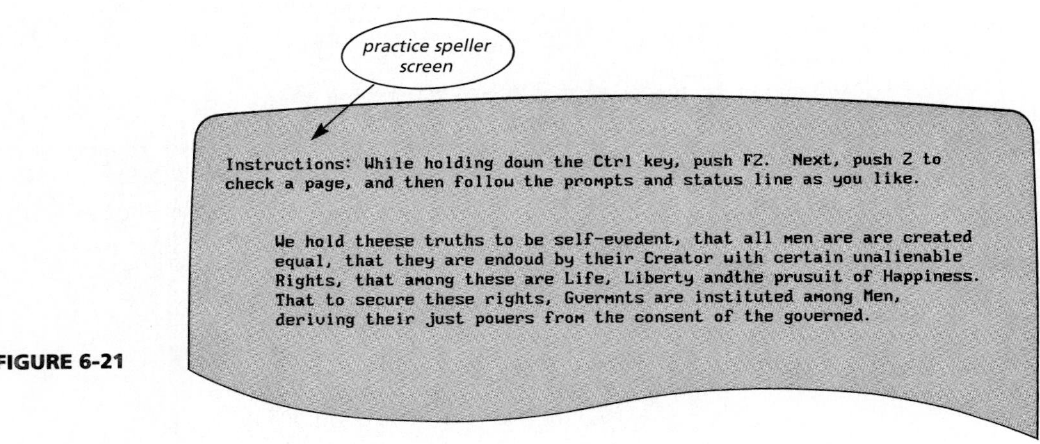
practice speller screen
Instructions: While holding down the Ctrl key, push F2. Next, push 2 to
check a page, and then follow the prompts and status line as you like.
We hold theese truths to be self-evedent, that all men are are created
equal, that they are endoud by their Creator with certain unalienable
Rights, that among these are Life, Liberty andthe prusuit of Happiness.
That to secure these rights, Guermnts are instituted among Men,
deriving their just powers from the consent of the governed.

FIGURE 6-21

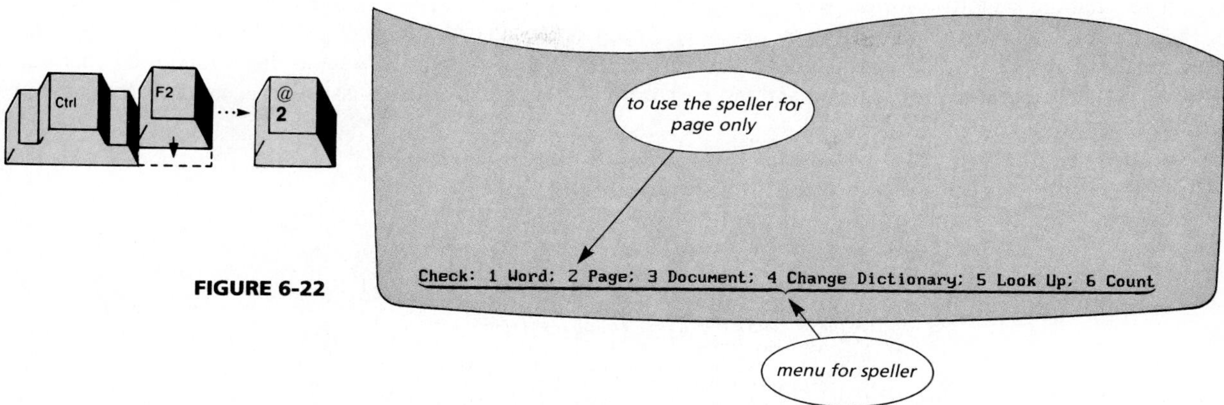


**FIGURE 6-22**

The first word to be highlighted is F2 (see Figure 6-23). Look at the menu. Words that mix letters and numbers are not recognized. If you were to press number 4, the cursor would move to the word F2 so that you could make a manual correction. Choosing number 3 on the menu allows you to ignore all words in your document that contain both numbers and letters. Because the word F2 is correct in this paragraph you simply wish to skip over it without changing it. Press number 1. The speller skips over F2 and highlights the next word it does not recognize.

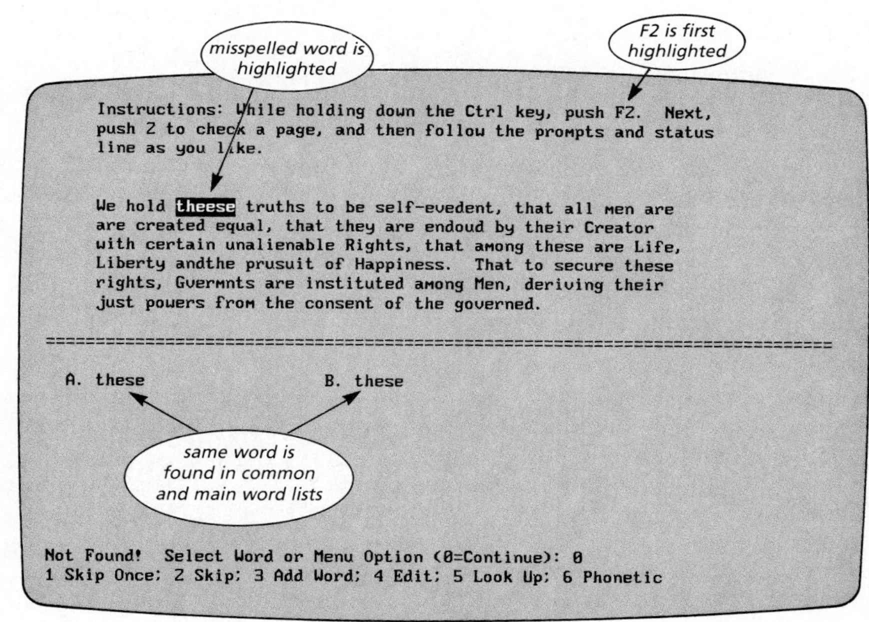


**FIGURE 6-23**

The next word to be highlighted is the misspelled word theese. When the WordPerfect speller does not recognize a word, it scans two lists: a *common* word list and a *main* word list. For speed's sake, WordPerfect first checks the common word list, then the main word list. Thus, it is possible that the correct spelling may be listed twice, as shown in Figure 6-23. In other words, you can choose either A or B and the misspelling will be corrected. Press the letter A, then notice on the screen how the misspelling is corrected and evedent, the next misspelled word, is highlighted. Two choices again appear. Press the letter A to correct the word.

Next you see that the same two words were typed together. The speller recognizes double words and gives you the menu shown in Figure 6-24. There are times when you purposely type two words together, such as in the sentence "I had had enough." In that case you would skip over the double words. In the case shown on the screen, the second are is not needed, so press the number 3. The second are is deleted and the next word to be highlighted as misspelled is endoud. Press the letter A to correct the word.

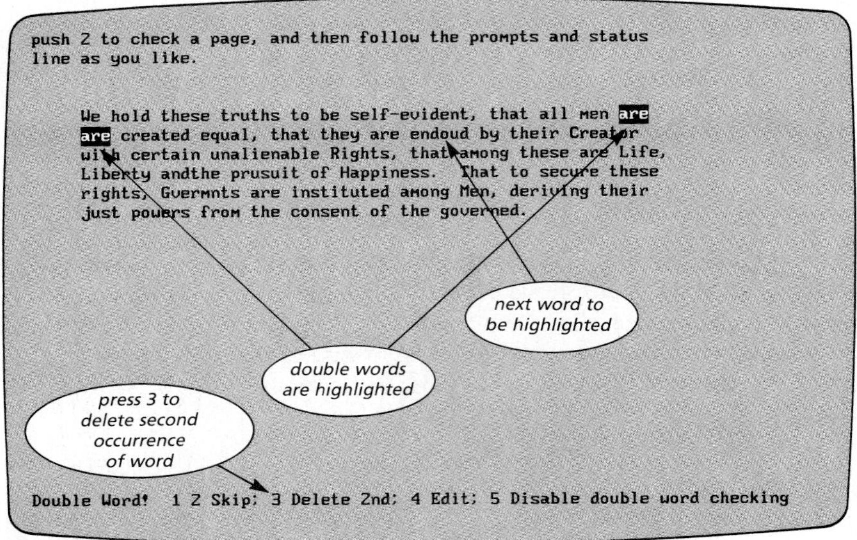
push 2 to check a page, and then follow the prompts and status line as you like.
We hold these truths to be self-evident, that all men are are created equal, that they are endoud by their Creator with certain unalienable Rights, that among these are Life, Liberty andthe prusuit of Happiness. That to secure these rights, Guermnts are instituted among Men, deriving their just powers from the consent of the governed.
next word to be highlighted
double words are highlighted
press 3 to delete second occurrence of word
Double Word! 1 2 Skip; 3 Delete 2nd; 4 Edit; 5 Disable double word checking

FIGURE 6-24

Next to be highlighted are the words andthe, which were typed with no space in between. The speller recognizes this as a misspelling but cannot find it in either the common or main word lists. Since you know what the problem is, you can correct the error. Press the number 4 and the cursor moves to the beginning of the misspelled word. Press the Right Arrow → three times to move the cursor under the t in the. Press the spacebar to insert a space between the words (Figure 6-25). As noted on the screen, press Enter ↵ when done. The speller recognizes the two words as correct and moves on to highlight the word prusuit. Press the letter A to correct the word.

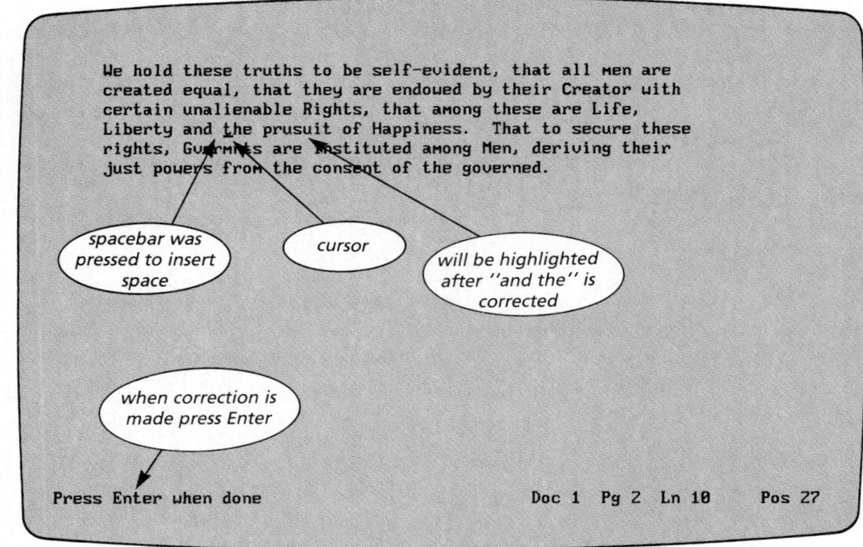
We hold these truths to be self-evident, that all men are created equal, that they are endowed by their Creator with certain unalienable Rights, that among these are Life, Liberty and the prusuit of Happiness. That to secure these rights, Guermnts are instituted among Men, deriving their just powers from the consent of the governed.
spacebar was pressed to insert space
cursor
will be highlighted after "and the" is corrected
when correction is made press Enter
Press Enter when done
Doc 1 Pg 2 Ln 10 Pos 27

FIGURE 6-25

The next word that the speller does not recognize is Gvermnts (see Figure 6-26). Although the word governments is in the speller, there are not enough vowels in the misspelling for the speller to recognize it and give you an option on the lower screen. If you were not sure how to spell this word and were typing on a typewriter, you would probably go to the dictionary and look up the word. In WordPerfect you can also *look up* a misspelled word. Look at the menu at the bottom of the screen. Press the number 5 for Look Up. The prompt "Word pattern:" appears on the screen. Type the word gov*ts. Because you know the word begins with gov and ends with ts, but you may not be sure what is in between, you place the asterisk (*) between the beginning and the end. As you learned in *Introduction to DOS*, the asterisk is a global command. Using it in the look-up function causes WordPerfect to look in its dictionary for all words that begin with gov and end with ts, no matter how many letters are in between. If you were to type g*s it would look for all words that begin with g and end with s. You can see there would probably be many more words given as an option if you were to type g*s. If you are not sure how a word ends, you could also type gov* and the speller would look for all the words that begin with gov no matter what the ending. Using the question mark can also help, but the question mark can only stand in the place of one character. For instance, the word pattern could be gover?ments and the speller would find the n where the question mark is. Since the asterisk stands for one or more characters, it is better to use the asterisk.

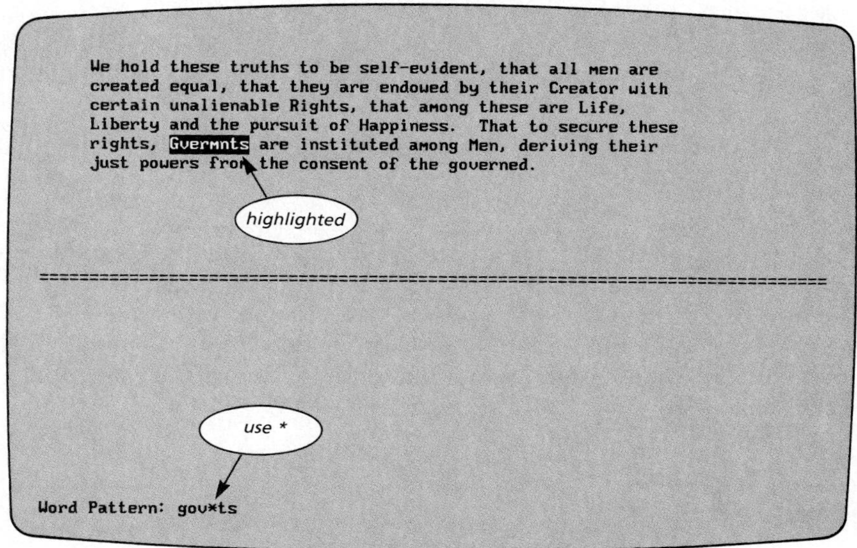
We hold these truths to be self-evident, that all men are
created equal, that they are endowed by their Creator with
certain unalienable Rights, that among these are Life,
Liberty and the pursuit of Happiness. That to secure these
rights, Gvermnts are instituted among Men, deriving their
just powers from the consent of the governed.
highlighted
use *
Word Pattern: gov*ts

**FIGURE 6-26**

With gov*ts on the screen as the word pattern, press the Enter ↵ key. The word governments is shown under the letter A. Press the letter A and the word is spelled correctly in the document. Because the word you are replacing begins with a capital letter, the lowercase g in government in the speller will become uppercase when inserted into the document.

Since there are no more misspelled words, the speller reviews the menu shown in Figure 6-27 on the following page. WordPerfect automatically counts the number of words on the page. If you had checked the spelling for the entire document, the number of words in the entire document would have been counted.

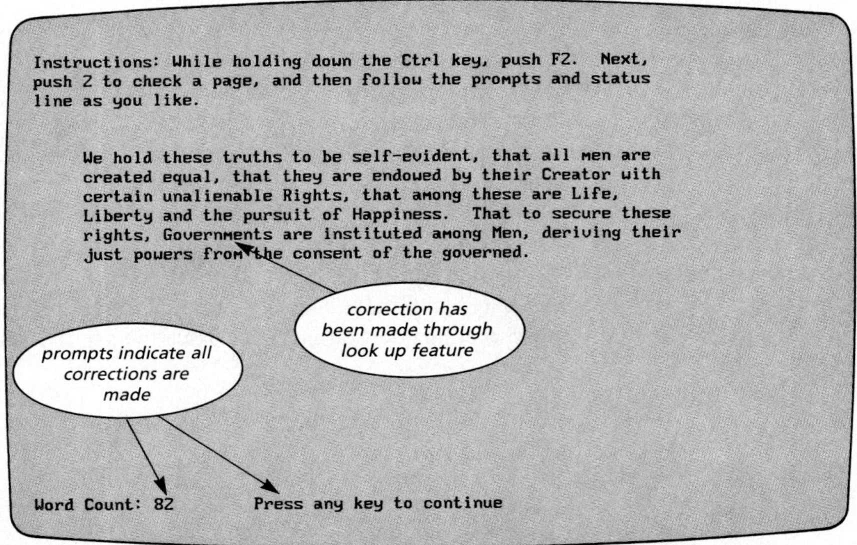
Instructions: While holding down the Ctrl key, push F2. Next,
push 2 to check a page, and then follow the prompts and status
line as you like.
We hold these truths to be self-evident, that all men are
created equal, that they are endowed by their Creator with
certain unalienable Rights, that among these are Life,
Liberty and the pursuit of Happiness. That to secure these
rights, Governments are instituted among Men, deriving their
just powers from the consent of the governed.
correction has been made through look up feature
prompts indicate all corrections are made
Word Count: 82
Press any key to continue

**FIGURE 6-27**

Press the spacebar to continue. The original menu appears again and shows that you have the option to look up a word directly from the speller without having it highlighted in a document. The option is number 5, the same option you use when checking the spelling of a word. To exit from the speller, press the spacebar. You are returned to your document.

It is important to remember that all corrections that you made to your document with the speller have been made only in the memory of the computer and have not been saved to disk. Immediately after checking the spelling of a document, save and replace the corrected version to the disk.

## Exiting the Thesaurus/Speller

If you wish to save the changes you made when using the thesaurus and the speller on your document you must exit by saving and replacing, as you have done in previous projects. If you wish to leave this thesaurus/speller document as it originally was so that you can practice again, you must exit without saving the changes to disk. To do this, press the F7 key. At the prompt "Save Document? (Y/N) Y" press the letter N for no. At the prompt "Exit WP? (Y/N) N" type Y for yes. You have exited the document without replacing the misspellings.

# PROJECT SUMMARY

In Project 6, you learned how to use the search function, the reverse search function, search and replace, and the move function. You used these functions to make changes to your document. In addition, you learned how to use the WordPerfect thesaurus and speller to change words in your document and to correct misspelled words.

The following is a list of keystroke sequences we used in Project 6:

**SUMMARY OF KEYSTROKES—Project 6**

| STEPS | KEY(S) PRESSED |
|---|---|
| 1 | [Be in WP at a blank screen] |
| 2 | Shift-F10 |
| 3 | License.2 |
| 4 | ↵ |
| 5 | Alt-F3 |
| 6 | F2 |
| 7 | Shift-F8 |
| 8 | 4 |
| 9 | F2 |
| 10 | Backspace |
| 11 | F2 |
| 12 | F2 |
| 13 | Backspace |
| 14 | F2 |
| 15 | F2 ["Not Found" should appear on screen] |
| 16 | Space |
| 17 | Home Home ↑ |
| 18 | F2 |
| 19 | assumes |
| 20 | F2 |
| 21 | Space |
| 22 | absolutely |
| 23 | Home Home ↓ |
| 24 | Shift-F2 |
| 25 | license |
| 26 | F2 |
| 27 | Shift-F2 |
| 28 | F2 |
| 29 | Shift-F2 |
| 30 | F2 |
| 31 | Space |
| 32 | Agreement |
| 33 | Home Home ↑ |
| 34 | Alt-F2 |
| 35 | Y |
| 36 | PerSoft Inc. |
| 37 | F2 |
| 38 | UMC Corp. |
| 39 | F2 |
| 40 | Y |
| 41 | Y |
| 42 | [continue to type "Y" to change each occurrence of PerSoft Inc. to UMC Corp] |
| 43 | Home Home ↑ |
| 44 | [↓ to line 6, position 10, under Y in You] |
| 45 | Ctrl-F4 |
| 46 | 2 |
| 47 | 1 |
| 48 | [↓ to line 12, position 10 under L in License] |
| 49 | Ctrl-F4 |
| 50 | 5 |
| 51 | [↓ then → to line 20, position 63 under U in Use] |
| 52 | Alt-F4 |
| 53 | ↓ |
| 54 | ↓ |
| 55 | Ctrl-F4 |
| 56 | 1 |
| 57 | [← to line 20, position 20 under U in Use] |
| 58 | Ctrl-F4 |
| 59 | 5 |
| 60 | [↓ then → to U in Use] |
| 61 | Space |
| 62 | Space |
| 63 | ↓ |
| 64 | ↓ |
| 65 | F10 |
| 66 | License.3 |
| 67 | ↵ |
| 68 | Shift-F7 |
| 69 | 1 |
| 70 | F7 |
| 71 | N |
| 72 | N |
| 73 | Shift-F10 |
| 74 | a:readme.wp |
| 75 | ↵ |
| 76 | [↓ then → to line 17, position 20 under F in Fools] |
| 77 | Alt-F1 |
| 78 | 3 |
| 79 | idiot |
| 80 | ↵ |
| 81 | 3 |
| 82 | simpleton |
| 83 | ↵ |
| 84 | ← |
| 85 | 4 |
| 86 | 4 |
| 87 | 1 |
| 88 | G |
| 89 | s |
| 90 | [→ to the word angels] |
| 91 | Alt-F1 |
| 92 | 1 |
| 93 | C |
| 94 | s |
| 95 | PgDn |
| 96 | Ctrl-F2 |
| 97 | 2 |
| 98 | 1 |
| 99 | A |
| 100 | A |
| 101 | 3 |
| 102 | A |
| 103 | 4 |
| 104 | → |
| 105 | → |
| 106 | → |
| 107 | Space |
| 108 | ↵ |
| 109 | A |
| 110 | 5 |
| 111 | gov*ts |
| 112 | ↵ |
| 113 | A |
| 114 | Space |
| 115 | Space |
| 116 | F7 |
| 117 | N |
| 118 | Y |
| 119 | [take WordPerfect disk out of Drive A and place DOS disk in Drive A] |
| 120 | ↵ |

The following list summarizes the material covered in Project 6:

1. The **search** function allows you to find a character, a code, or a string of text within a document.
2. **Search and replace**, also known as a global search and replace, allows you to look for every occurrence of a specified character, code, or string of text and either delete them or replace them with another specified code or text.
3. The **move** function allows you to highlight a specific block of text, then cut or copy the text, move it to another part of the document or to another document, and retrieve the cut or copied text.
4. The **thesaurus** allows you to point to a specific word, then invoke a search for possible replacement words. The thesaurus displays not only synonyms but also antonyms for the marked word. Use **headword** to look up other words in the thesaurus.
5. The **speller** provided in the full version of WordPerfect has a dictionary of more than 115,000 words with which it checks the spelling of the words in a document. You can add up to 20,000 words to the speller.

# STUDENT ASSIGNMENTS

## STUDENT ASSIGNMENT 1: True/False

**Instructions:** Circle T if the statement is true and F if the statement if false.

T F 1. When you invoke the search function, the cursor stops to the left of what you are searching for.
T F 2. A reverse search is invoked by pressing Shift-F2, typing what is to be searched for, then pressing F2.
T F 3. The search feature cannot search for codes embedded in the document.
T F 4. When moving text, either cut or copy a block of text.
T F 5. The move function is invoked through Ctrl-F4.
T F 6. Alt-F1 will access the thesaurus.
T F 7. The reveal codes function can be accessed through Alt-F4.
T F 8. The speller will only spell words that are typed on the screen; it cannot look up words.

## STUDENT ASSIGNMENT 2: Multiple Choice

**Instructions:** Circle the correct response.

1. The move function can
   a. move paragraphs
   b. move sentences
   c. move specific blocks of text
   d. all of the above
2. When invoking the search function and the desired code or words are defined, the user must
   a. press Enter
   b. press F2
   c. press Alt-F2
   d. press Shift-F2
3. When using the speller the user can
   a. look up a word by giving the word pattern
   b. skip over words whose spelling is not to be changed
   c. add words to the dictionary
   d. all of the above

## STUDENT ASSIGNMENT 3: Matching

**Instructions:** Put the appropriate number next to the words in the second column.

| | | | | | |
|---|---|---|---|---|---|
| 1. Ctrl-F2 | ____ | Reverse Search | 5. Alt-F3 | ____ | Speller |
| 2. Ctrl-F4 | ____ | Search | 6. F2 | ____ | Reveal codes |
| 3. Alt-F1 | ____ | Speller, Look Up | 7. Shift-F2 | ____ | Thesaurus |
| 4. Ctrl-F2, 5 | ____ | Move function | 8. Alt-F2 | ____ | Search and Replace |

## STUDENT ASSIGNMENT 4: Moving text

**Instructions:** In the paragraph below, it is necessary to move the second sentence in the paragraph to be the first sentence. Describe in detail the steps to accomplish this.

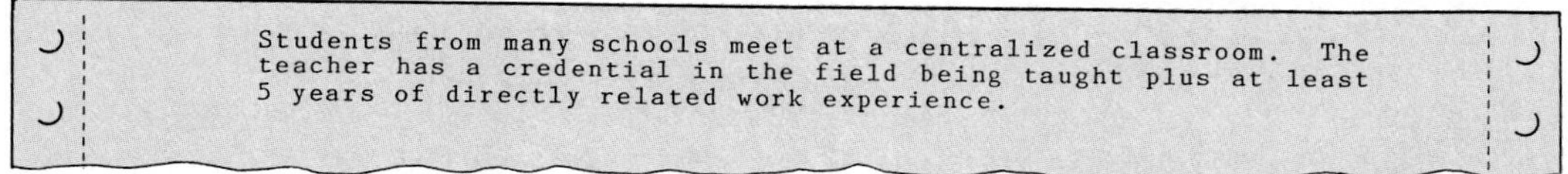

Students from many schools meet at a centralized classroom. The teacher has a credential in the field being taught plus at least 5 years of directly related work experience.

## STUDENT ASSIGNMENT 5: Using Search and Replace

**Instructions:** Perform the following tasks.

1. Load DOS into main memory.
2. Load WordPerfect into main memory by inserting the WordPerfect diskette into drive A, putting a data disk into drive B, typing b: and pressing Enter. At the B> prompt, type a:wp and press the Enter key.

Problem 1:

1. Create the resume as shown at the right. The titles in the left column should be in boldface type. (Hint: Don't forget the Indent [F4] key, or the hanging indent function [F4, Shift-Tab]).
2. Save the document under the name Cook.
3. Print the document.

```
                         JEREMY L. COOK
                     2311 No. Hickorey Street
                       Anaheim, CA 33245
                        (714) 555-6712

EDUCATION       CA State University, Fullerton
                Management Science Major, BS June 1984

                Anaheim, CA High School
                Major Area of Study - College Preparation

                University of CA, Los Angeles
                Graduate Business Courses

EMPLOYMENT      Farmers East, Inc., Garden Grove, CA
                August 1988 - present
                    Chief Accountant
                        Designed complete computer accounting
                            system
                        Responsible for 42 employees within the
                            accounting department
                        Corporation has gross revenues in excess
                            of $150 million per annum
                        Entire accounting operation reports to
                            me

                Peterson Manufacturing, Inc.
                Fountain Valley, CA
                June 1984 - August 1988
                    Senior Accountant
                        Responsible for all accounts payable for
                            $300 million company
                        Supervised 21 junior accountants
                        Received most valuable employee - 1987

OTHER SKILLS    Computer Programmer - COBOL, BASIC

PERSONAL DATA   Married, one child
                Age: 25
                Good health

REFERENCES      Available upon request
```

## Student Assignment 5 (continued)

Problem 2:

1. Beginning at the top of the document, search for all designations of CA and replace them with California. (Hint: Type Y to confirm).
2. Save the document as Cook.2.
3. Print the document.

```
                        JEREMY L. COOK
                   2311 No. Hickorey Street
                  Anaheim, California 33245
                        (714) 555-6712

EDUCATION        California State University, Fullerton
                 Management Science Major, BS June 1984

                 Anaheim, California High School
                 Major Area of Study - College Preparation

                 University of California, Los Angeles
                 Graduate Business Courses

EMPLOYMENT       Farmers East, Inc., Garden Grove, California
                 August 1988 - present
                     Chief Accountant
                         Designed complete computer accounting
                             system
                         Responsible for 42 employees within the
                             accounting department
                         Corporation has gross revenues in excess
                             of $150 million per annum
                         Entire accounting operation reports to
                             me

                 Peterson Manufacturing, Inc.
                 Fountain Valley, California
                 June 1984 - August 1988
                     Senior Accountant
                         Responsible for all accounts payable for
                             $300 million company
                         Supervised 21 junior accountants
                         Received most valuable employee - 1987

OTHER SKILLS     Computer Programmer - COBOL, BASIC

PERSONAL DATA    Married, one child
                 Age: 25
                 Good health

REFERENCES       Available upon request
```

## STUDENT ASSIGNMENT 6: Modifying a Document with the Move Function

**Instructions:** Perform the following tasks:

1. Load DOS into main memory.
2. Load WordPerfect into main memory by inserting the WordPerfect diskette into drive A, putting a data disk into drive B, typing b: and pressing Enter. At the B> prompt, type a:wp and press the Enter key.

Problem 1:

1. Retrieve the document named Cook.2 created in Student Assignment 5.
2. Using the block function, move the whole section of type under EDUCATION to be second after the heading EMPLOYMENT as shown below.

```
                         JEREMY L. COOK
                     2311 No. Hickorey Street
                     Anaheim, California 33245
                          (714) 555-6712

EMPLOYMENT     Farmers East, Inc., Garden Grove, California
               August 1988 - present
                    Chief Accountant
                         Designed complete computer accounting
                              system
                         Responsible for 42 employees within the
                              accounting department
                         Corporation has gross revenues in excess
                              of $150 million per annum
                         Entire accounting operation reports to
                              me

               Peterson Manufacturing, Inc.
               Fountain Valley, California
               June 1984 - August 1988
                    Senior Accountant
                         Responsible for all accounts payable for
                              $300 million company
                         Supervised 21 junior accountants
                         Received most valuable employee - 1987

EDUCATION      California State University, Fullerton
               Management Science Major, BS June 1984

               Anaheim, California High School
               Major Area of Study - College Preparation

               University of California, Los Angeles
               Graduate Business Courses

OTHER SKILLS   Computer Programmer - COBOL, BASIC

PERSONAL DATA  Married, one child
               Age: 25
               Good health

REFERENCES     Available upon request
```

Problem 2: Save the document to disk as Cook.3.

Problem 3: Print the revised document.

## STUDENT ASSIGNMENT 7: Using the Speller

**Instructions:** Perform the following tasks:

1. Load DOS into main memory.
2. Load WordPerfect into main memory by inserting the WordPerfect diskette into drive A, putting a data disk into drive B, typing b: and pressing Enter. At the B> prompt, type a:wp and press the Enter key.

Problem 1: Create the document exactly as written below, even the spelling errors.

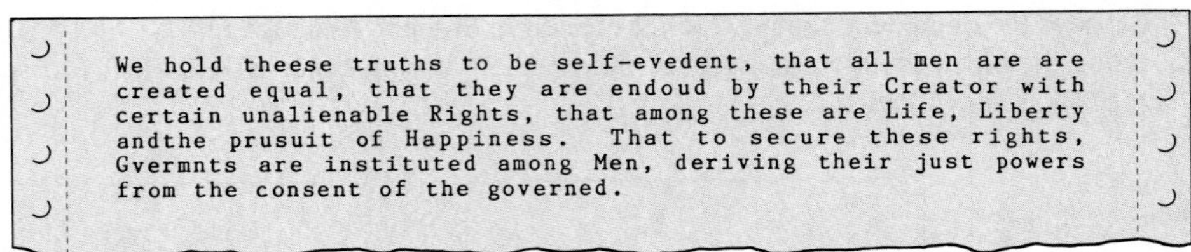
We hold theese truths to be self-evedent, that all men are are
created equal, that they are endoud by their Creator with
certain unalienable Rights, that among these are Life, Liberty
andthe prusuit of Happiness.  That to secure these rights,
Gvermnts are instituted among Men, deriving their just powers
from the consent of the governed.

Problem 2: Save the document to disk as Speller.

Problem 3: Print the document.

Problem 4: Invoke the speller and correct any misspellings.

Problem 5: Save the corrected document to disk as Speller.1.

Problem 6: Print the revised document.

## STUDENT ASSIGNMENT 8: Using the Thesaurus

**Instructions:** Perform the following tasks:

1. Load DOS into main memory.
2. Load WordPerfect into main memory by inserting the WordPerfect diskette into drive A, putting a data disk into drive B, typing b: and pressing Enter. At the B> prompt, type a:wp and press the Enter key.

Problem 1: Type the sentence: Fools that rush to step on me.

Problem 2: Position the cursor under the word Fools. Invoke the Thesaurus. Press the Print Screen option to print a hard copy of the screen as shown below.

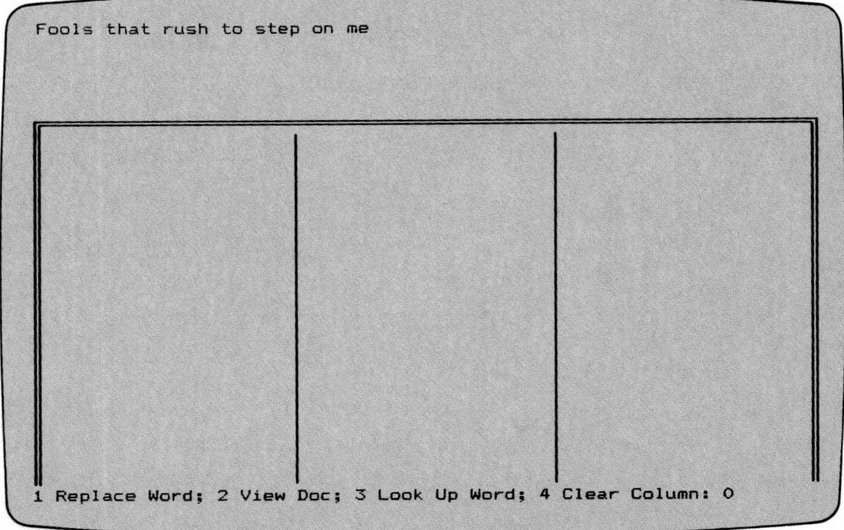


Problem 3: Repeat the process in problem 2 for the words rush and step, making a print screen hard copy.

# WordPerfect Index

# Spreadsheets Using Lotus 1-2-3

# PROJECT 1

## Building a Worksheet

## Objectives

You will have mastered the material in this Project when you can:

- Start 1-2-3
- Describe the worksheet
- Move the cell pointer around the worksheet
- Enter labels, numbers, and formulas into a worksheet
- Save a worksheet
- Print the screen image of the worksheet
- Correct errors in a worksheet
- Answer your questions regarding 1-2-3 using the online help facility
- Quit 1-2-3

In Project 1 we will develop the worksheet illustrated in Figure 1-1. It contains a company's first quarter sales report. To build this worksheet, we will enter the revenues and costs for January, February, and March. 1-2-3 calculates the profit for each month by subtracting the cost from the revenue.

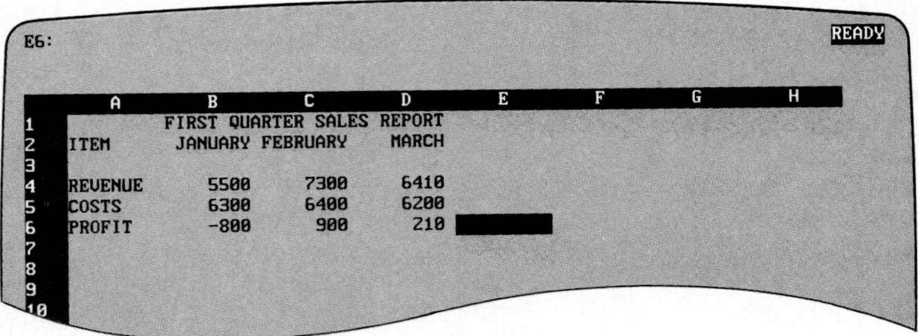


**FIGURE 1-1**
**The worksheet we will build in Project 1.**

## STARTING 1-2-3

Boot the computer following the procedures presented earlier in the Introduction to DOS. Next, follow the steps listed below if your computer has no fixed disk. If your computer has a fixed disk, follow the steps at the bottom of the next page. Several seconds will elapse while the 1-2-3 program is loaded from the disk into main computer memory. The red light on the disk drive turns on during this loading process. After 1-2-3 is loaded into main computer memory, it is automatically executed. The first screen displayed by 1-2-3 contains the copyright message shown in Figure 1-2. After a few seconds the copyright message disappears, leaving the worksheet illustrated in Figure 1-3.

### Computer with One or Two Floppy Disks and No Fixed Disk

To start 1-2-3 from a computer with one or two floppy disks and no fixed disk, do the following:

1. Replace the DOS disk in drive A with the 1-2-3 system disk. If you have two floppy disk drives, place your data disk in drive B.
2. At the A> prompt, type 123 and press the Enter key.
3. If you have only one floppy disk, replace the system disk in drive A with your data disk after the program is loaded.

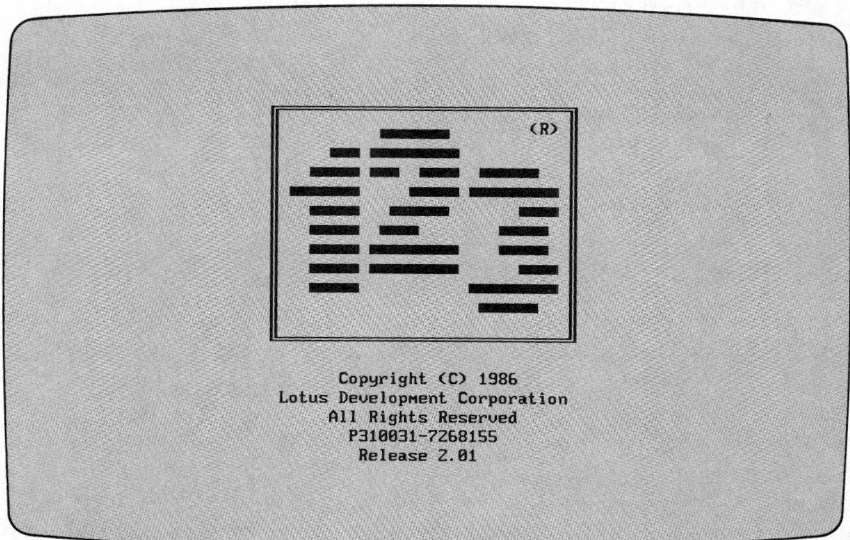


**FIGURE 1-2**
The copyright screen displays when you load 1-2-3.

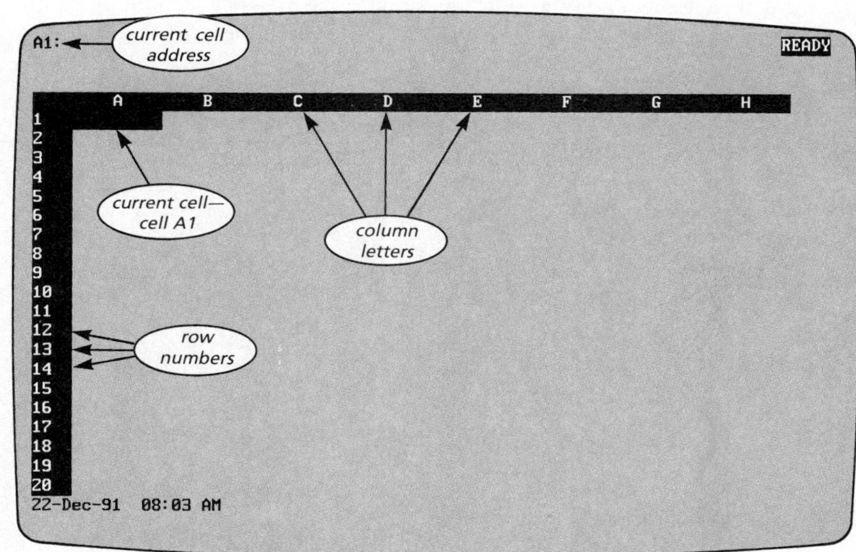


**FIGURE 1-3**
The worksheet.

## Computer with a Fixed Disk

To start 1-2-3 from a fixed disk, do the following:

1. Use the DOS command CD to change to the subdirectory containing the 1-2-3 program.
2. Place your data disk in drive A.
3. At the DOS prompt, type 123 and press the Enter key.

# THE WORKSHEET

The worksheet is organized into a rectangular grid containing columns (vertical) and rows (horizontal). In the border at the top, each **column** is identified by a column letter. In the border on the left side, each **row** is identified by a row number. As shown in Figure 1-3 on the previous page, eight columns (A to H) and twenty rows (1 to 20) of the worksheet appear on the screen.

## Cell, Cell Pointer, and Window

Within the borders is the worksheet. It has three parts: cell, cell pointer, and window. A **cell** is the intersection of a column and a row. It is referred to by its **cell address**, the coordinates of the intersection of a column and a row. When you specify a cell address, you must name the column first, followed by the row. For example, cell address D3 refers to the cell located at the intersection of column D and row 3.

One cell on the worksheet is designated the current cell. The **current cell** is the one in which you can enter data. The current cell in Figure 1-3 is A1. It is identified in two ways. First, a reverse video rectangle called the **cell pointer** displays over the current cell. Second, the **current cell address** displays on the first of three lines at the top of the screen. It is important to understand the layout of the worksheet and how to identify all cells, including the current cell.

1-2-3 has 256 columns and 8,192 rows for a total of 2,097,152 cells. Only a small portion of the rectangular worksheet displays on the screen at any one time. For this reason, the area between the borders on the screen is called a **window**. Think of your screen as a window through which you can see parts of the worksheet as illustrated in Figure 1-4.

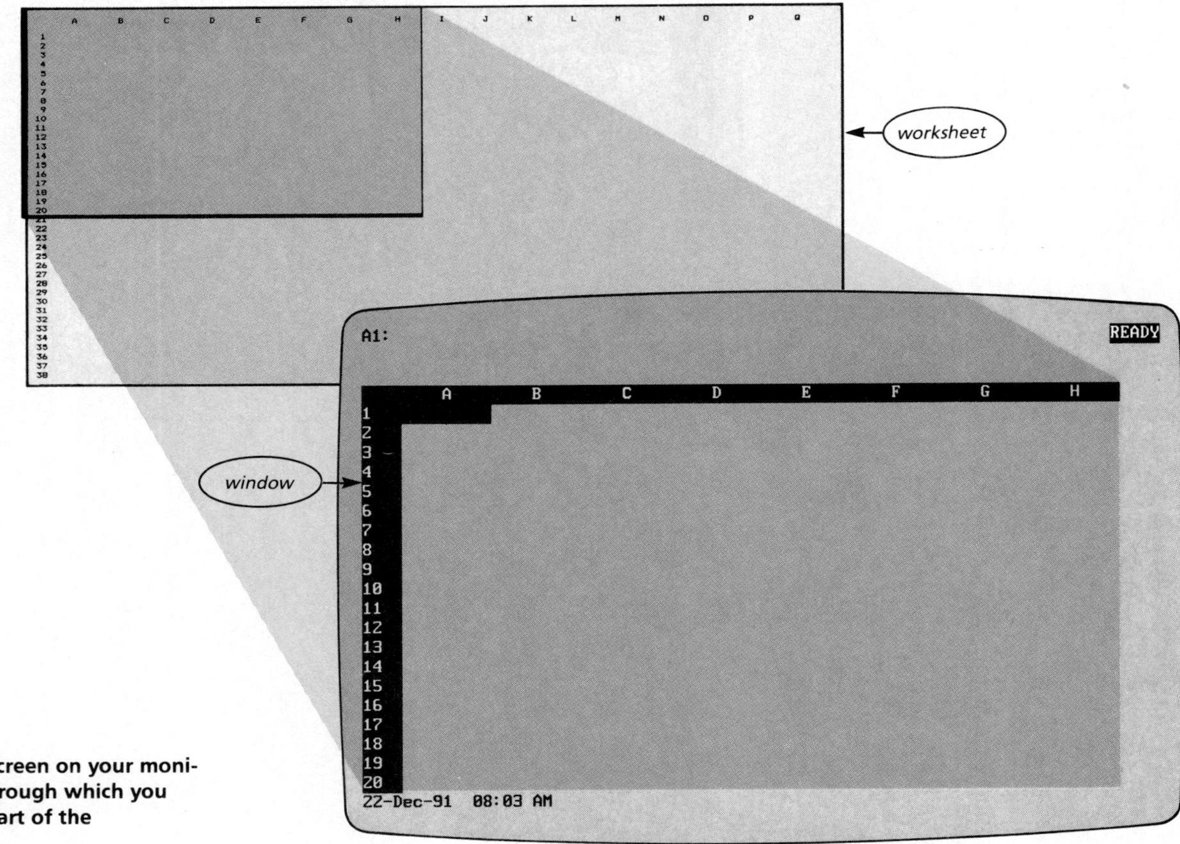


**FIGURE 1-4 The screen on your monitor is a window through which you can view a small part of the worksheet.**

## The Control Panel and the Indicator Line

The three lines above the window at the top of the screen display important information about the worksheet. The three lines—status line, input line, and menu line—are collectively called the **control panel**. Below the window, at the bottom of the screen, is the indicator line. These four lines are illustrated in Figure 1-5.

**Status Line** The first line in the control panel at the top of the screen is the **status line**. It identifies the current cell address and displays the mode of operation. If data is already in the current cell, the status line also shows the type of entry and its contents.

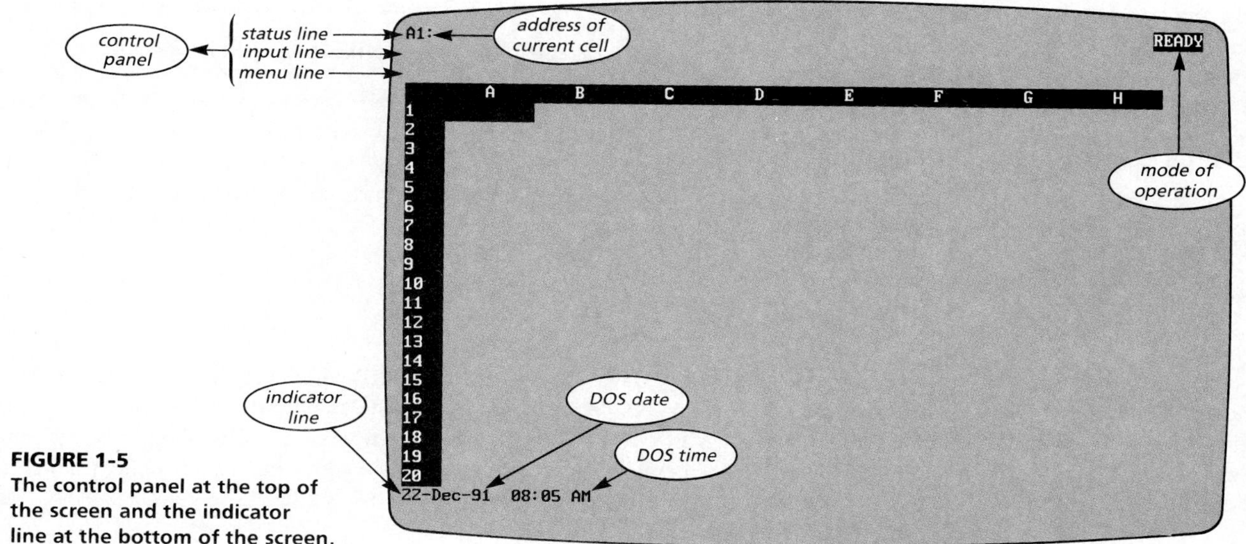


**FIGURE 1-5**
**The control panel at the top of the screen and the indicator line at the bottom of the screen.**

The mode of operation displays on the right side of the status line at the top of the screen. Mode indicators, like EDIT, ERROR, LABEL, MENU, POINT, READY, VALUE, and WAIT tell you the current mode of operation of 1-2-3. For now you should know that when the mode READY displays (see Figure 1-5), 1-2-3 is ready to accept your next command or data entry. When the mode indicator WAIT displays in place of READY, 1-2-3 is busy performing some operation that is not instantaneous, like saving a worksheet to disk.

**Input Line** Just below the status line is the input line. The **input line** displays one of three things: the characters you type as you enter data or edit cell contents; the command menu; or input prompts asking for additional command specifications.

**Menu Line** The **menu line**, the third line in the control panel, displays information about the menu item highlighted on the input line when 1-2-3 is in the MENU mode.

**Indicator Line** The line at the very bottom of the screen is the **indicator line**. It displays three items: the date, the time of day as maintained by DOS, and the status indicators of 1-2-3. Status indicators, like CALC, CAPS, CIRC, END, NUM, OVR, and SCROLL, tell you which keys are engaged and alert you to special worksheet conditions.

## MOVING THE CELL POINTER ONE CELL AT A TIME

Before you can build a worksheet, you must learn how to move the cell pointer to the cells in which you want to make entries. Several methods let you easily move to any cell in the worksheet. The most popular method is to use the four arrow keys located on the numeric keypad. Figure 1-6 illustrates a numeric keypad on a computer keyboard.

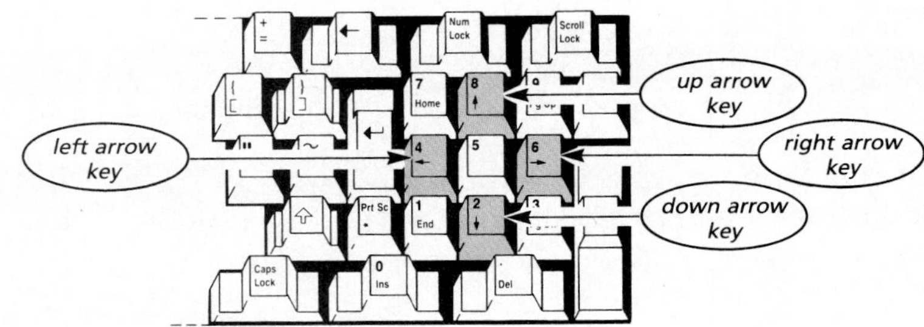


**FIGURE 1-6 The arrow keys on the keyboard.**

On some computers, you have a choice of two sets of arrow keys. One set, as shown in Figure 1-6, is part of the numeric keypad. The other set is located just to the left of the numeric keypad. If you have two sets of arrow keys, use the **Num Lock key** to activate one set or the other. When the Num Lock key is on, a red light on the key indicates that the arrow keys to the left are active. When the red light is off, the arrow keys on the numeric keypad are active.

For these projects we will use the arrow keys located on the numeric keypad. The arrow keys work as follows:

1. **Down Arrow key** (↓) moves the cell pointer directly down one cell.
2. **Left Arrow key** (←) moves the cell pointer one cell to the left.
3. **Right Arrow key** (→) moves the cell pointer one cell to the right.
4. **Up Arrow key** (↑) moves the cell pointer directly up one cell.

In the sample worksheet in Figure 1-1, the title FIRST QUARTER SALES REPORT begins in cell B1. Therefore, we must move the cell pointer from cell A1, where it is when 1-2-3 starts, to cell B1 so we can enter the title. Do this by pressing the Right Arrow key one time, as shown in Figure 1-7. Notice that the current cell address on the status line in the upper left corner of the screen changes from A1 to B1. Remember, the current cell address on the status line always identifies the current cell—the one where the cell pointer is.

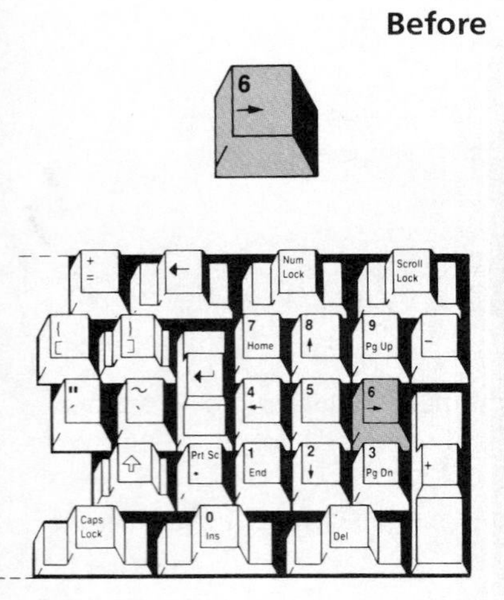

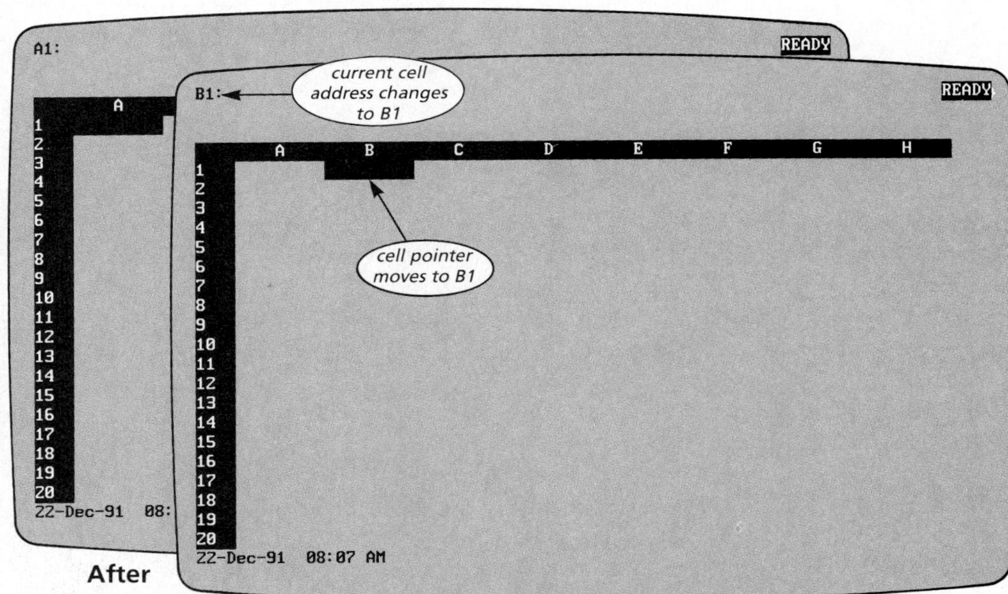


**FIGURE 1-7**
**Press the Right Arrow key to move the cell pointer from A1 to B1.**

# ENTERING LABELS

With the cell pointer on the proper cell (B1), we can enter the title of the worksheet. In the title FIRST QUARTER SALES REPORT, all the letters are capitals. While it is possible to enter capital letters by holding down one of the Shift keys on the keyboard each time we type a letter, a more practical method is to press the **Caps Lock key** one time (see Figure 1-8).

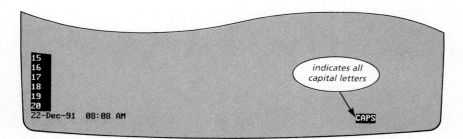

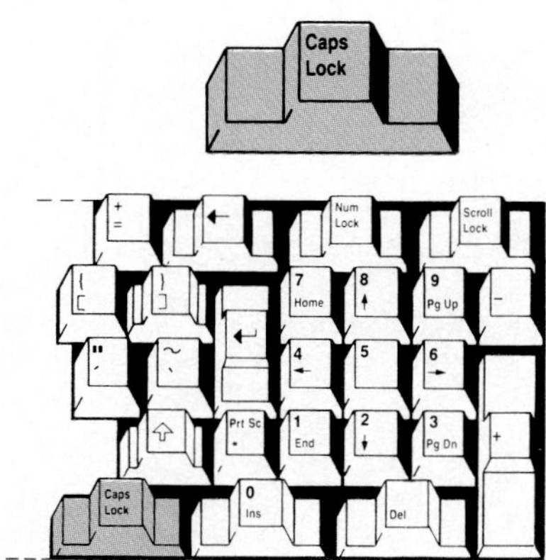

**FIGURE 1-8** **Press the Caps Lock key to type all capital letters.**

The word CAPS on the indicator line at the bottom of the screen in Figure 1-8 tells you that the Caps Lock key is engaged. Therefore, all subsequent letters you type will be accepted by 1-2-3 as capital letters. Note, however, that both uppercase and lowercase letters are valid in a worksheet, and that the letters appear in the same case as they are entered. The Caps Lock key affects only the keys representing letters. Digit and special-character keys continue to transmit the lower character on the key when you press them, unless you hold down a Shift key while pressing the key. To enter a lowercase letter when the Caps Lock key is engaged, hold down the Shift key while typing the letter.

## Labels That Begin with a Letter

Entering the title is simple. Just type the required letters on the computer keyboard. Type the words FIRST QUARTER SALES REPORT on the keyboard to get the display shown in Figure 1-9.

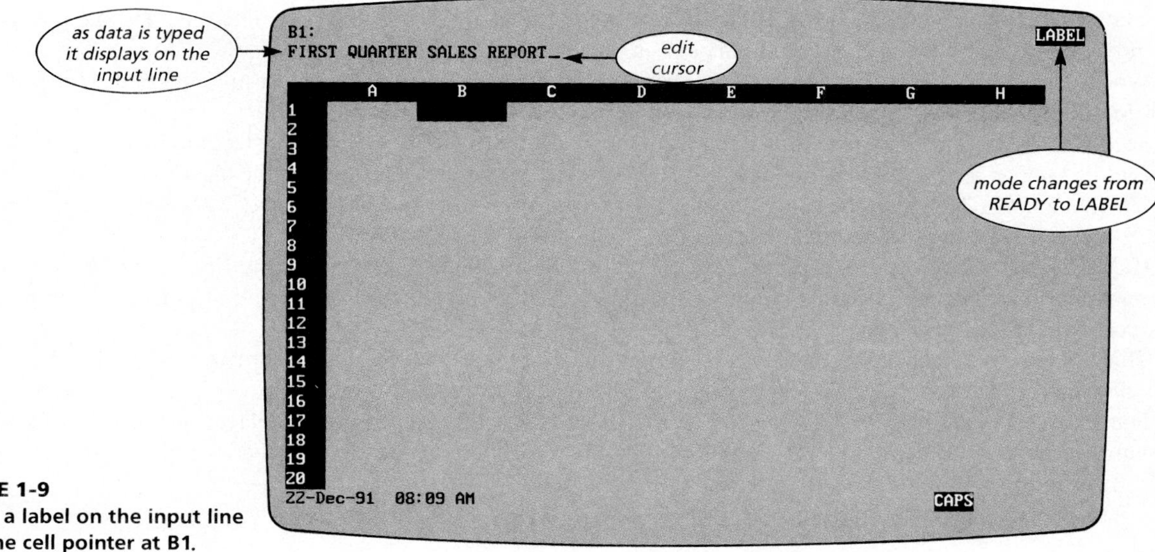


**FIGURE 1-9**
**Typing a label on the input line with the cell pointer at B1.**

Figure 1-9 shows two important features. First, as soon as we enter the first character of the report title, the mode on the status line changes from READY to LABEL. 1-2-3 determines that the entry is a **label** and not a number because the first character typed is a letter.

Second, as we type the report title, it displays on the input line followed immediately by the edit cursor. The **edit cursor** is a small, blinking underline symbol. It indicates where the next character typed will be placed on the input line.

Although the data appears at the top of the screen on the input line, it still is not in cell B1. To assign the title to cell B1, press the Enter key as shown in Figure 1-10. This causes the report title displayed on the input line to be placed in the worksheet beginning at cell B1, the cell identified by the cell pointer.

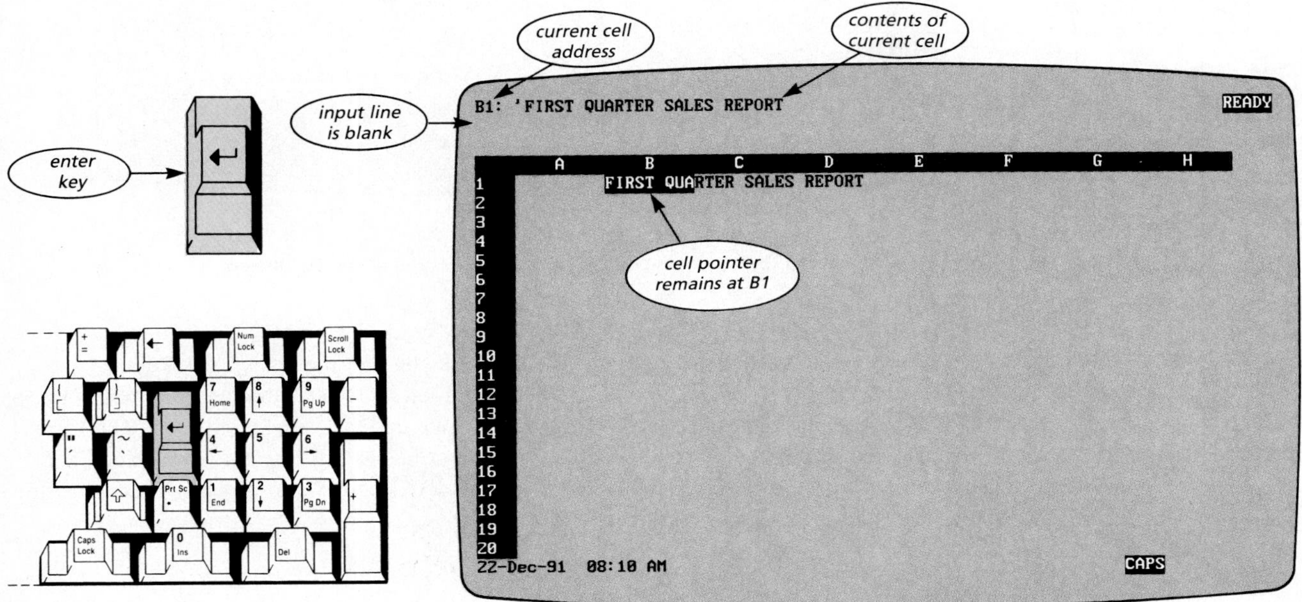


**FIGURE 1-10** Pressing the Enter key assigns the label on the input line to cell B1. The cell pointer remains at B1.

If you type the wrong letter and notice the error while it is on the input line at the top of the screen, use the **Backspace key** (above the Enter key on the keyboard) to erase all the characters back to and including the ones that are wrong. If you see an error in a cell, move the cell pointer to the cell in question and retype the entry.

When you enter a label, a series of events occurs. First, the label is positioned left-justified in the cell where it begins. Therefore, the F in the word FIRST begins in the leftmost position of cell B1.

Second, when a label has more characters than the width of the column, the characters are placed in adjacent columns to the right so long as these columns are blank. In Figure 1-10, the width of cell B1 is nine characters. The words we entered have 26 characters. Therefore, the extra letters display in cell C1 (nine characters) and cell D1 (eight characters), since both cell C1 and cell D1 were blank when we made the 26-character entry in cell B1.

If cell C1 had data in it, only the first nine characters of the 26-character entry in cell B1 would show on the worksheet. The remaining 17 characters would be hidden, but the entire label that belongs to the cell displays in the upper left corner of the screen on the status line whenever the cell pointer is moved to cell B1.

Third, when you enter data into a cell by pressing the Enter key, the cell pointer remains on the cell (B1) in which you make the entry.

Fourth, a label, in this case FIRST QUARTER SALES REPORT, appears in two places on the screen: in the cell and on the status line, next to the cell address. Note that 1-2-3 adds an apostrophe (') before the label on the status line (see Figure 1-10). This apostrophe identifies the data as a left-justified label.

With the title in cell B1, the next step is to enter the column titles in row 2 of the worksheet. Therefore, move the cell pointer from cell B1 to cell A2 by using the arrow keys (see Figure 1-11). Press the Down Arrow key and then the Left Arrow key. Pressing the Down Arrow key once causes the cell pointer to move to cell B2. Then pressing the Left Arrow key once causes the cell pointer to move to cell A2. Remember that pressing an arrow key one time moves the cell pointer one cell in the direction of the arrow. The current cell address changes on the status line from B1 to A2.

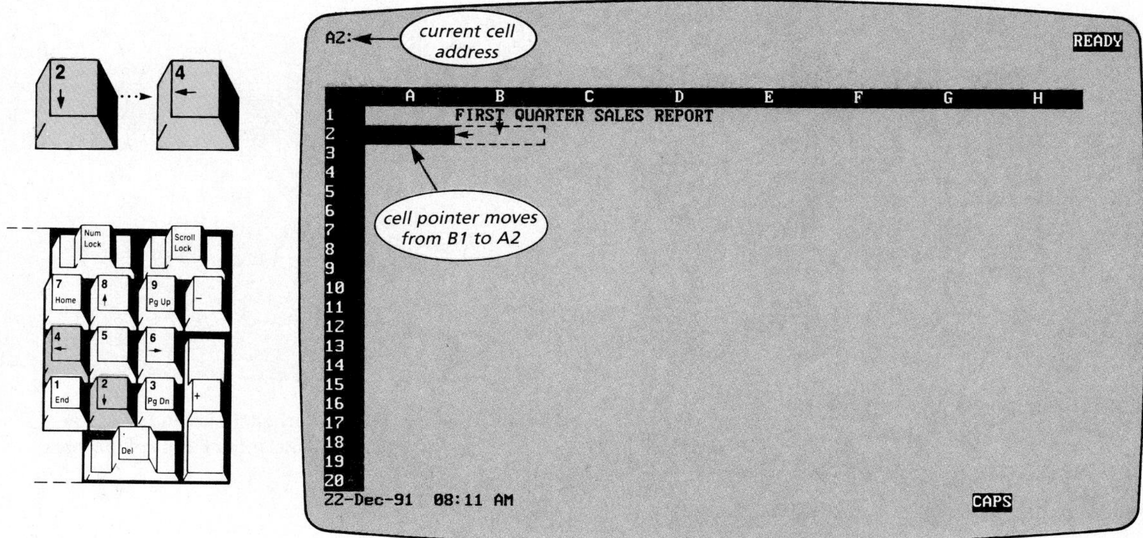


**FIGURE 1-11 Moving the cell pointer from B1 to A2 using the arrow keys.**

With the cell pointer on A2, enter the label ITEM as shown on the input line in Figure 1-12. Since the entry starts with a letter, 1-2-3 positions the label left-justified in the current cell. To enter the label in cell A2 we could press the Enter key as we did for the report title in cell B1. But another way is to press any one of the four arrow keys, as shown in Figure 1-13 on the next page. In this case, press the Right Arrow key. This is the better alternative because not only is the data entered into the current cell, but the cell pointer also moves one cell to the right. The cell pointer is at cell B2, the location of the next entry.

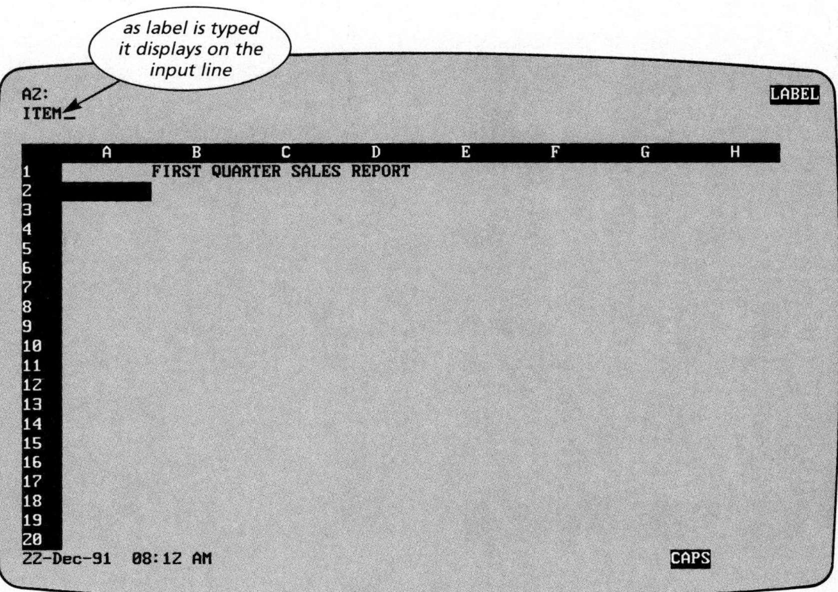


**FIGURE 1-12**
**Typing a label on the input line.**

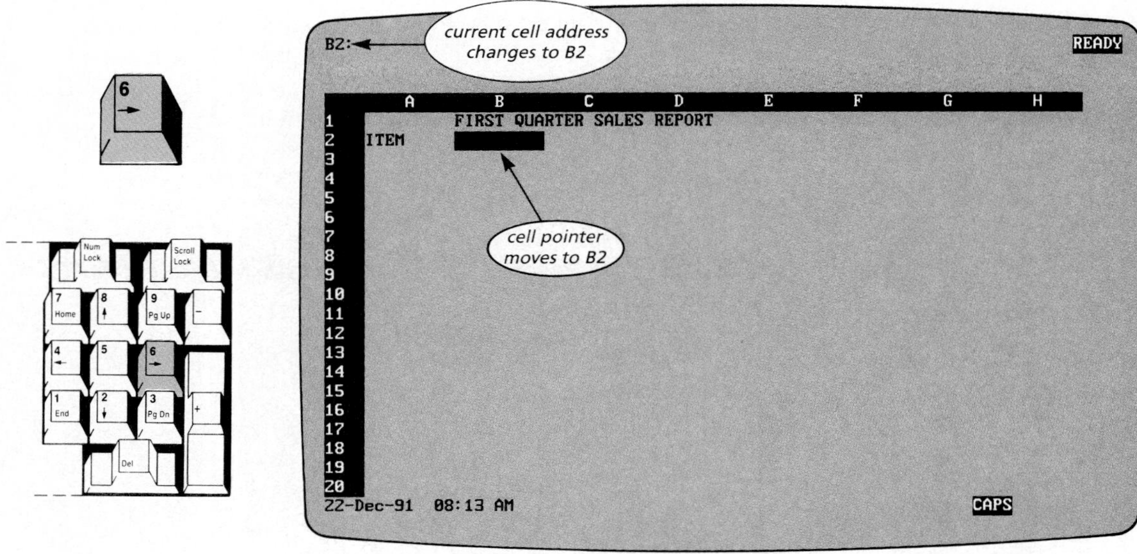


**FIGURE 1-13 Pressing the Right Arrow key rather than the Enter key assigns the label on the input line to cell A2 and moves the cell pointer one cell to the right to B2.**

## Labels Preceded by a Special Character

The worksheet in Figure 1-1 that we are in the process of building requires that the column headings JANUARY, FEBRUARY, and MARCH be positioned right-justified in the cell, rather than left-justified. There are three different ways to position labels in a cell: left-justified, right-justified, or centered. Remember that the first character of the entry instructs 1-2-3 how to place the label in the cell.

If a label begins with a letter or apostrophe ('), 1-2-3 positions the label left-justified in the current cell. If a label begins with a quotation mark ("), it is positioned right-justified. Finally, if a label begins with a circumflex (^), it is centered within the cell. When the first character is an apostrophe, quotation mark, or circumflex, 1-2-3 does not consider the special character to be part of the label and it will not appear in the cell. However, the special character will precede the label on the status line when the cell pointer is on the cell in question. Table 1-1 summarizes the positioning of labels in a cell.

**TABLE 1-1 Positioning Labels within a Cell**

| FIRST CHARACTER OF DATA | DATA ENTERED | POSITION IN CELL | REMARK |
|---|---|---|---|
| 1. Letter | ITEM | ITEM | Left-justified in cell. |
| 2. Apostrophe (') | '9946 | 9946 | Left-justified in cell. The label 9946 is a name, like the address on a house, and not a number. |
| 3. Quotation Mark (") | "MARCH | MARCH | Right-justified in cell. This always results in one blank character at the end of the label in the cell. |
| 4. Circumflex (^) | ^MARCH | MARCH | Centered in the cell. |

With the cell pointer located at cell B2, enter the column heading JANUARY preceded by a quotation mark (") as shown in Figure 1-14, and then press the Right Arrow key. The word JANUARY appears, right-justified, in cell B2 and the cell pointer moves to cell C2 in preparation for the next entry (see Figure 1-15).

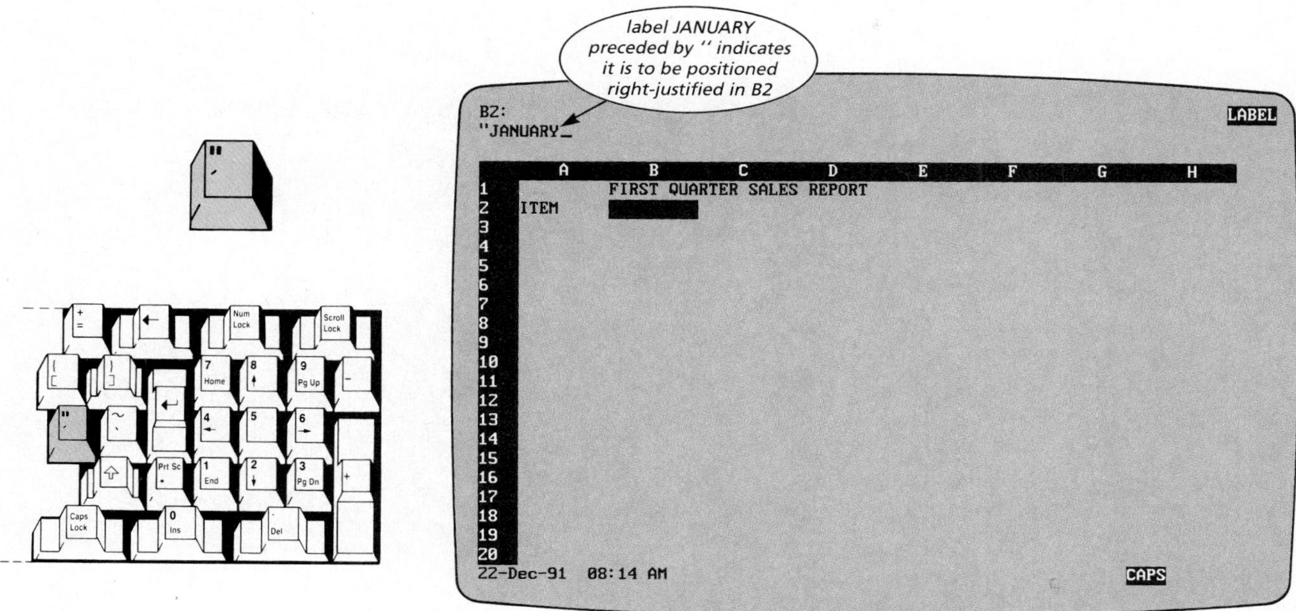


**FIGURE 1-14** Begin a label with a quotation mark (") to make it right-justified.

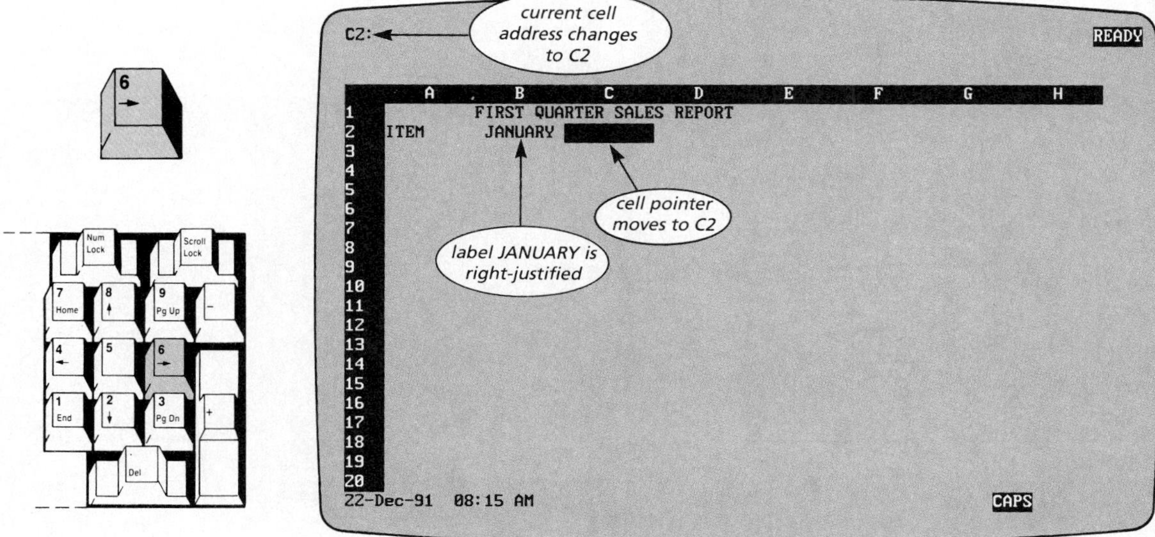


**FIGURE 1-15** Pressing the Right Arrow key assigns the label on the input line to cell B2 and moves the cell pointer one cell to the right to C2.

Next, enter the month name FEBRUARY in cell C2 and the month name MARCH in cell D2. Enter both labels right-justified. That is, precede each month name with the quotation mark ("). Press the Right Arrow key after typing each label. With these latest entries, the worksheet appears as illustrated in Figure 1-16.

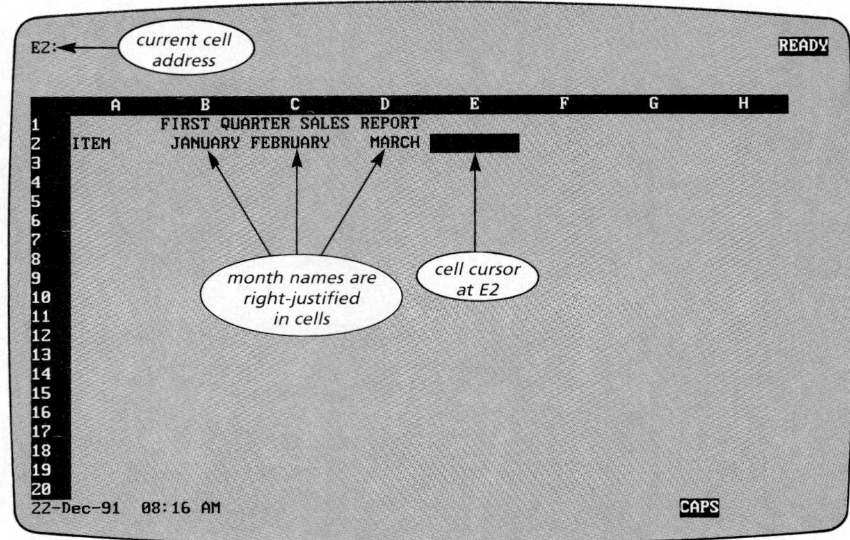


**FIGURE 1-16**
**The three month names entered right-justified.**

The cell pointer is now located at cell E2. According to Figure 1-1 no data is to be entered into cell E2. The next entry is the label REVENUE in cell A4. Therefore, move the cell pointer from cell E2 to cell A4. Press the Down Arrow key twice and the Left Arrow key four times, as shown in Figure 1-17.

With the cell pointer at A4, type the label REVENUE and press the Right Arrow key. The cell pointer moves to cell B4 as shown in Figure 1-18.

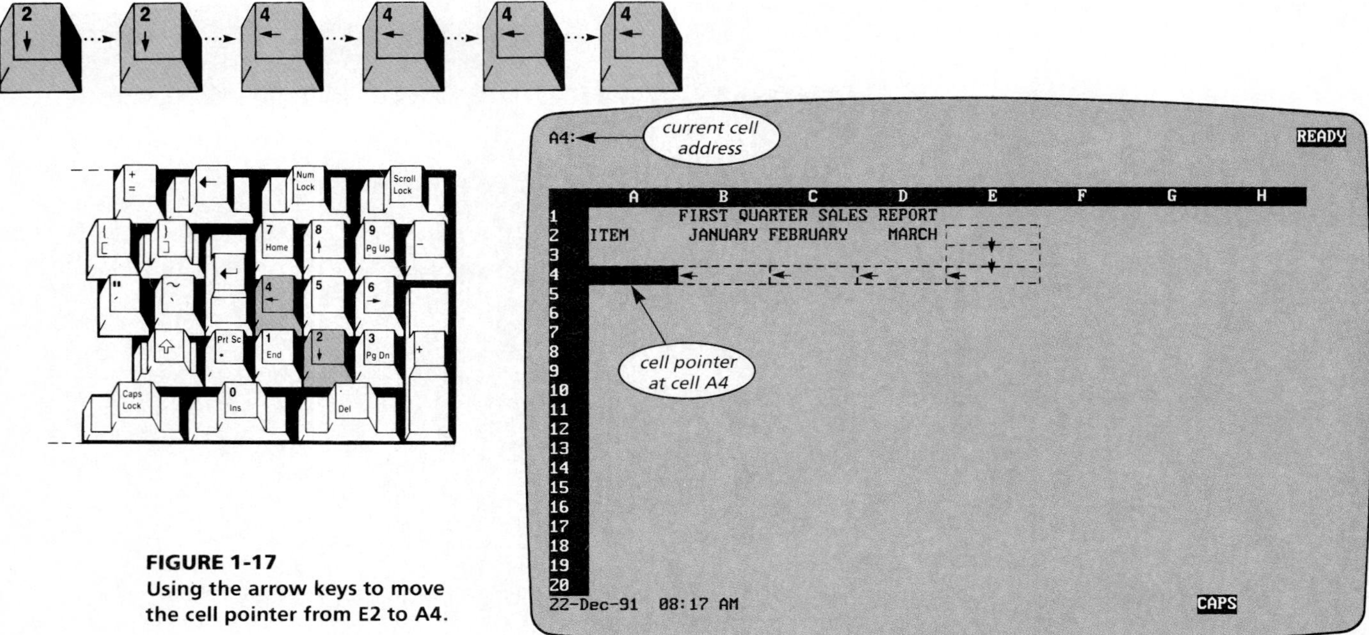


**FIGURE 1-17**
**Using the arrow keys to move the cell pointer from E2 to A4.**

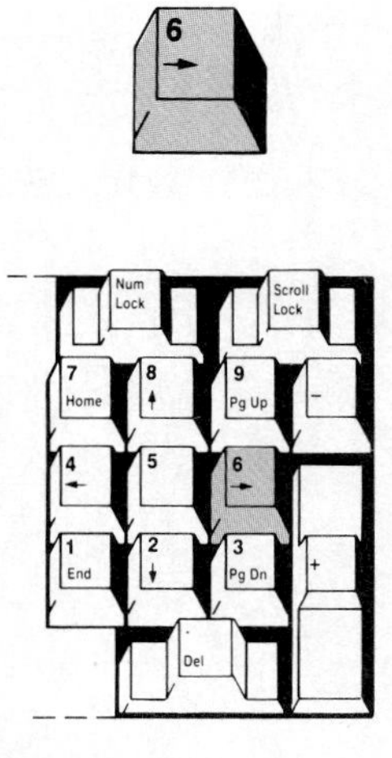


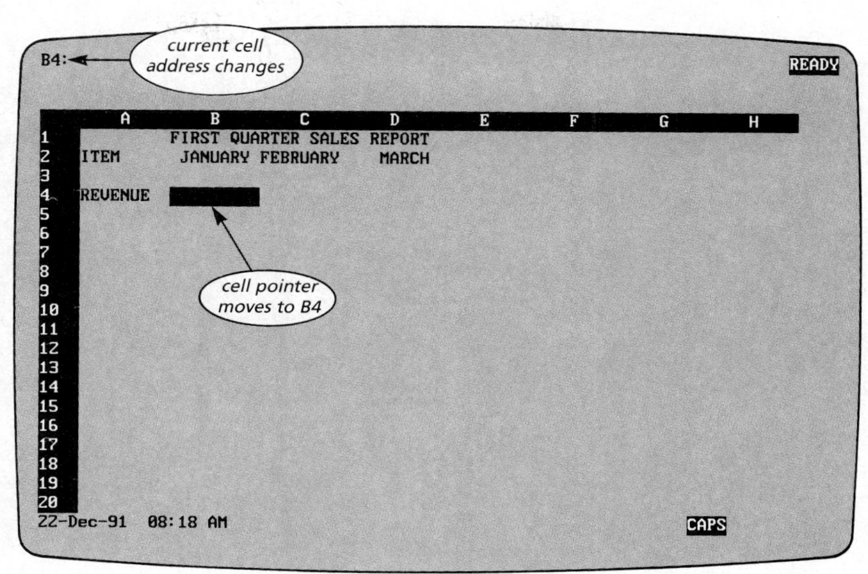


**FIGURE 1-18**
**Pressing the Right Arrow key assigns the label on the input line to cell A4 and moves the cell pointer to B4.**

## ENTERING NUMBERS

**Numbers** are entered into cells to represent amounts. Numbers are also called **values**. 1-2-3 assumes that an entry for a cell is a number or a formula if the first character you type is one of the following:

0 1 2 3 4 5 6 7 8 9 ( @ + – . # $

### Whole Numbers

With the cell pointer located at cell B4, enter the revenue amount for January. As shown in Figure 1-1, this amount is 5500. Type the amount 5500 on the keyboard without any special character preceding the number. The screen should now look like Figure 1-19 on the next page. Remember, the CAPS indicator affects only the keys that represent letters on the keyboard. Therefore, never hold down a Shift key to enter a number.

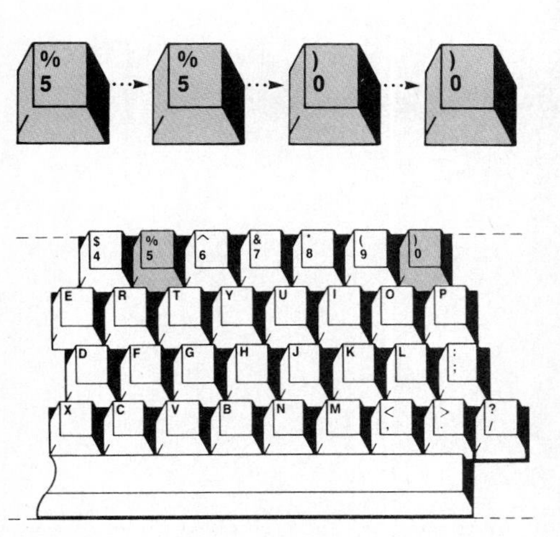

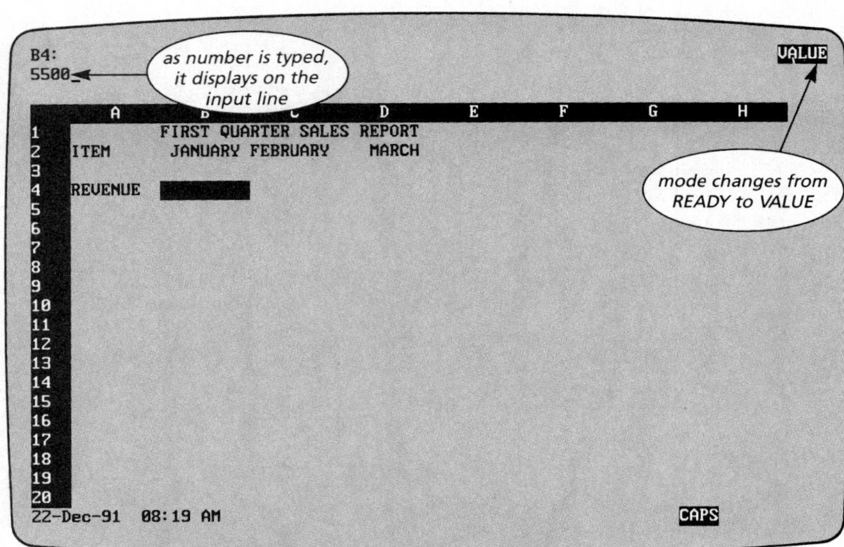


**FIGURE 1-19** Entering a number on the input line.

As soon as we enter the first digit, 5, the mode of operation on the status line changes from READY to VALUE. As we type the value 5500, it displays in the upper left corner of the screen on the input line followed immediately by the edit cursor.

Press the Right Arrow key to enter the number 5500 in cell B4 and move the cell pointer one cell to the right. The number 5500 displays right-justified in cell B4 as shown in Figure 1-20. Numbers always display right-justified in a cell. As with right-justified labels, a blank is added to the right side of a number when it is assigned to a cell.

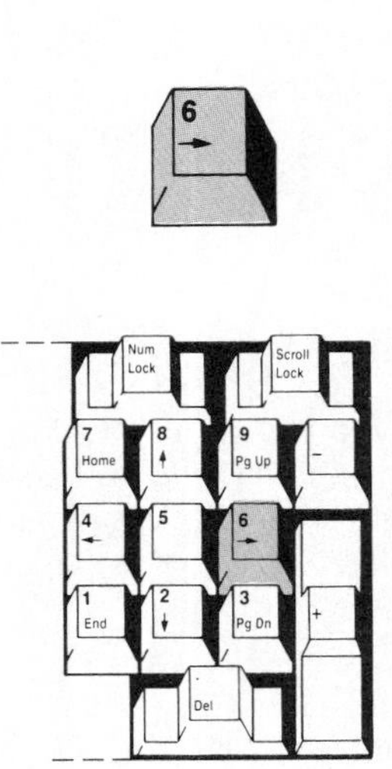

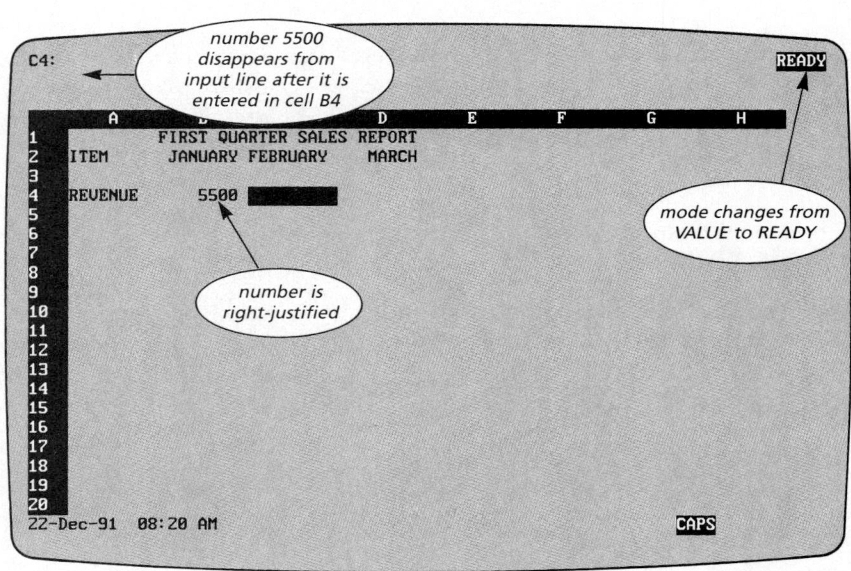


**FIGURE 1-20** Pressing the Right Arrow key assigns the number on the input line to cell B4 and moves the cell pointer to C4.

After we enter the data in cell B4, the cell pointer moves to cell C4. At this point, enter the revenue values for February (7300) and March (6410) in cells C4 and D4 in the same manner as we entered the number 5500 into cell B4. After we make the last two revenue entries, the cell pointer is located in cell E4 as shown in Figure 1-21.

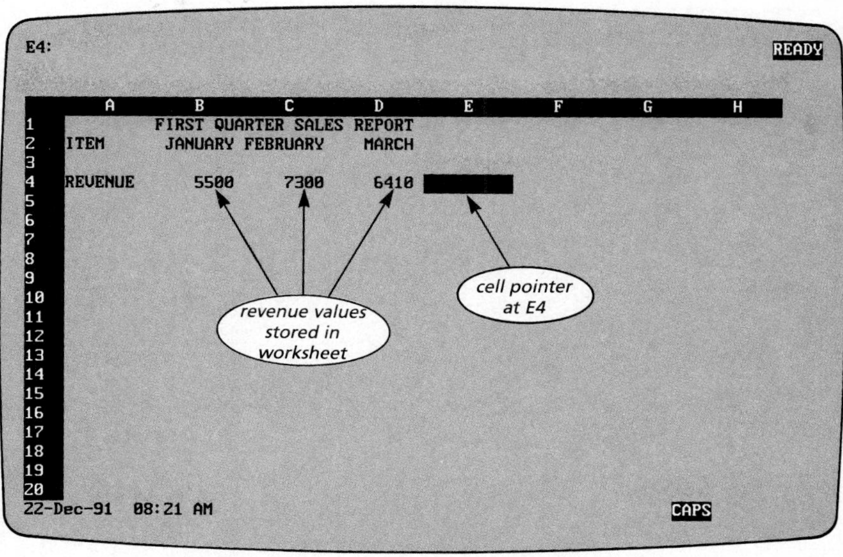


**FIGURE 1-21** The revenues for the three months entered into cells B4, C4, and D4.

## Decimal Numbers

Although the numeric entries in this project are all whole numbers, you can enter numbers with a decimal point, a dollar sign, and a percent sign. However, the dollar sign and percent sign will not appear in the cell. Other special characters, like the comma, are not allowed in a numeric entry. Table 1-2 gives several examples of numeric entries.

**TABLE 1-2** Valid Numeric Entries

| NUMERIC DATA ENTERED | CELL CONTENTS | REMARK |
|---|---|---|
| 1.23 | 1.23 | Decimal fraction numbers are allowed. |
| 32.20 | 32.2 | Insignificant zero dropped. |
| 320. | 320 | Decimal point at the far right is dropped. |
| $67.54 | 67.54 | Dollar sign dropped. |
| 47% | .47 | Percent converted to a decimal fraction. |

# MOVING THE CELL POINTER MORE THAN ONE CELL AT A TIME

After entering the revenue values for the three months, the cell pointer resides in cell E4. Since there are no more revenue values to enter, move the cell pointer to cell A5 so that we can enter the next line of data. While we can use the arrow keys on the right side of the keyboard to move the cell pointer from E4 to A5, there is another method that is faster and involves fewer keystrokes. This second method uses the GOTO command.

## The GOTO Command

The **GOTO command** moves the cell pointer directly to the cell you want. Issue the GOTO command by pressing function key F5. The function keys may be located at the far left side or at the top of the keyboard. In either case, the function keys work the same. For these projects, we assume that the function keys are located at the far left side of the keyboard (see Figure 1-22). When the function key F5 is pressed the message "Enter address to go to: E4" displays in the upper left corner of the screen on the input line and the mode changes from READY to POINT. This is illustrated in Step 1 of Figure 1-23. When the mode is POINT, 1-2-3 is requesting a cell address.

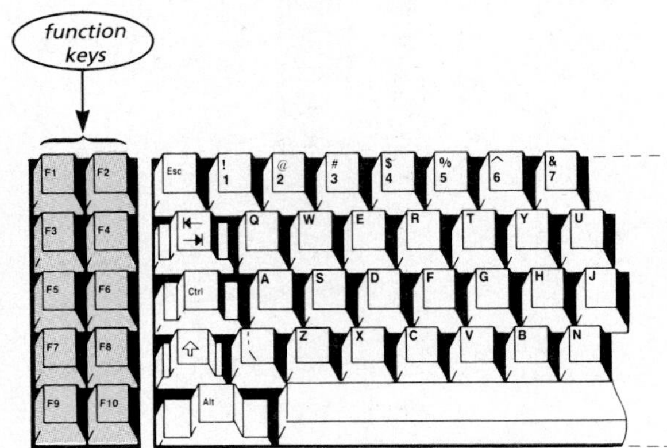


**FIGURE 1-22**
**The function keys on the keyboard.**

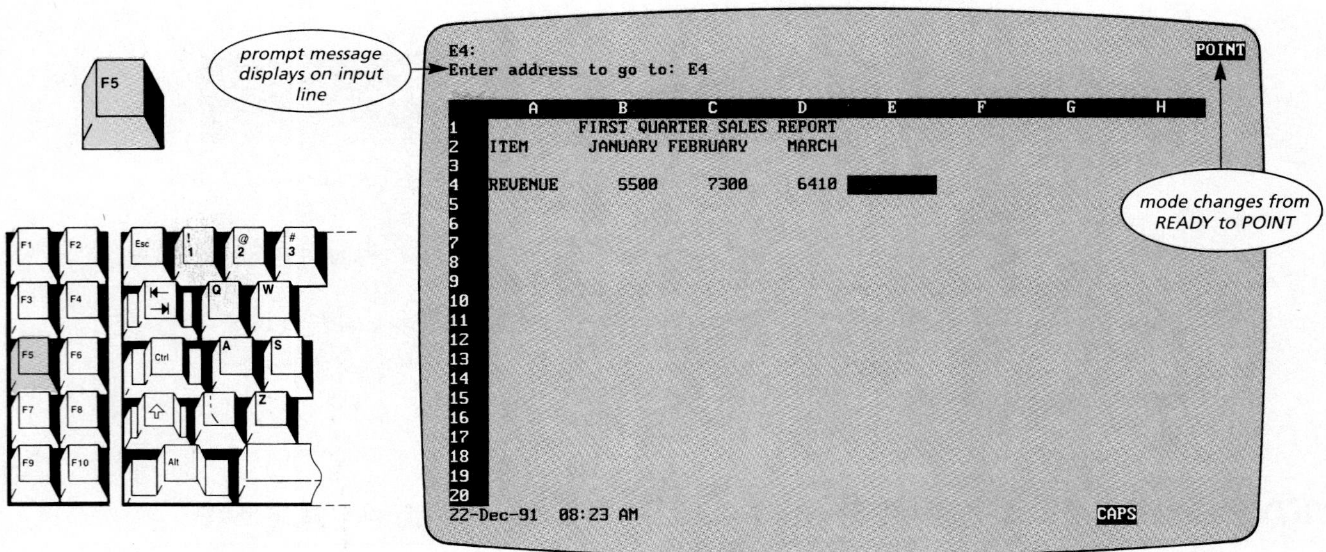


**FIGURE 1-23 (Step 1 of 3)** **Press function key F5 to issue the GOTO command to move the cell pointer from E4 to A5.**

Enter the cell address A5 as shown in Step 2 of Figure 1-23. Remember to enter the column letter first, followed by the row number. Now press the Enter key. The cell pointer immediately moves to cell A5 as shown in Step 3 of Figure 1-23. Note that not only does the cell pointer move, but also the current cell address on the status line in the upper left corner changes from E4 to A5.

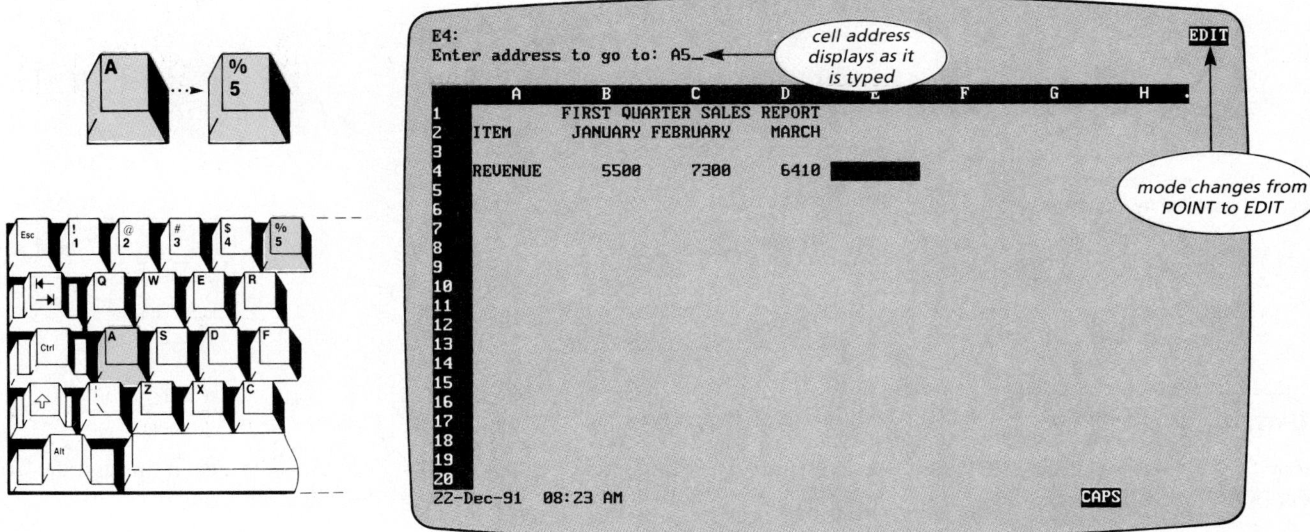


**FIGURE 1-23 (Step 2 of 3)** Enter the cell address A5.

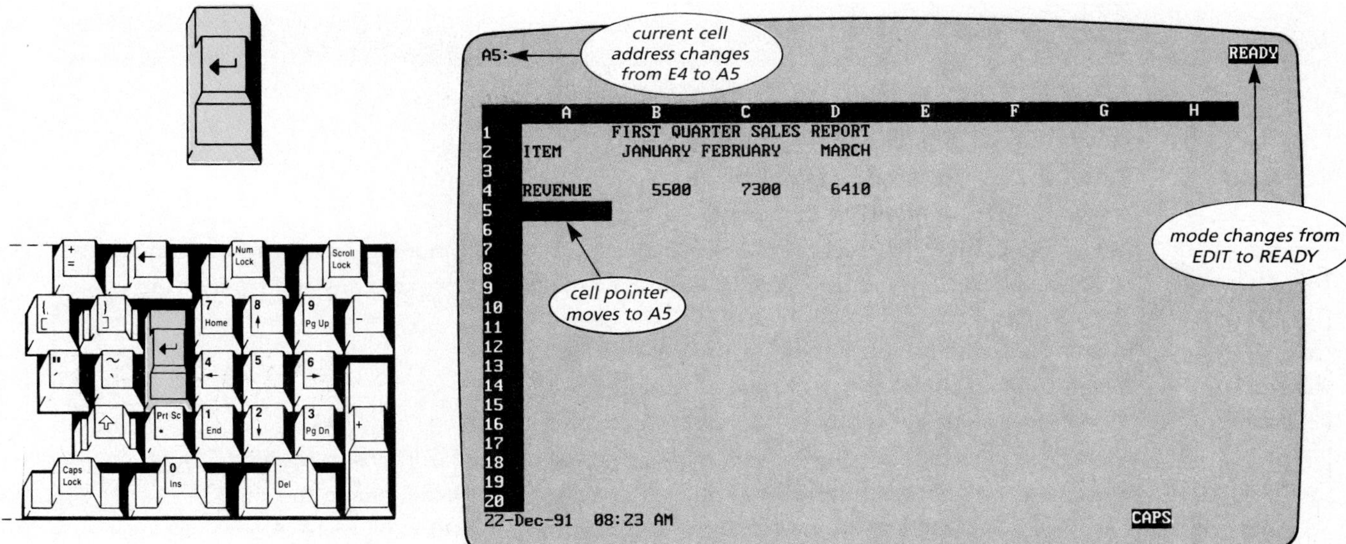


**FIGURE 1-23 (Step 3 of 3)** Press the Enter key and the cell pointer moves to A5.

With the cell pointer at cell A5, enter the label COSTS followed by the costs for January, February, and March in the same manner as for the revenues on the previous row. After entering the costs, enter the label PROFIT in cell A6. Figure 1-24 illustrates these entries.

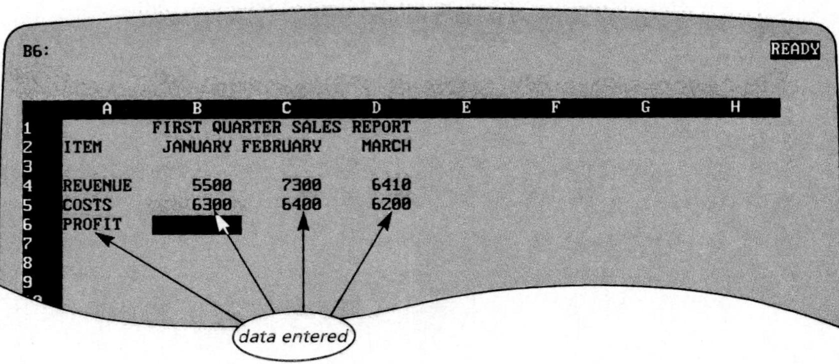


**FIGURE 1-24**
**Costs for the three months entered into cells B5, C5, and D5 and the label PROFIT entered into cell A6.**

## Summary of Ways to Move the Cell Pointer

Table 1-3 summarizes the various ways you can move the cell pointer around the worksheet. As we proceed through the projects in this book, this table will be a helpful reference. Practice using each of the keys described in Table 1-3.

**TABLE 1-3 Moving the Cell Pointer Around the Worksheet**

| KEY(S) | RESULT |
|---|---|
| ↓ | Moves the cell pointer directly down one cell. |
| ← | Moves the cell pointer one cell to the left. |
| → | Moves the cell pointer one cell to the right. |
| ↑ | Moves the cell pointer directly up one cell. |
| Home | Moves the cell pointer to cell A1 no matter where the cell pointer is located on the worksheet. |
| End | Used in conjunction with the arrow keys to move to the border columns and rows of the worksheet. |
| F5 | Moves the cell pointer to the designated cell address. |
| PgDn | Moves the worksheet under the cell pointer 20 rows down. |
| PgUp | Moves the worksheet under the cell pointer 20 rows up. |
| Tab | Moves the worksheet under the cell pointer one screenful of columns to the left. |
| Shift and Tab | Moves the worksheet under the cell pointer one screenful of columns to the right. |
| Scroll Lock | Causes the worksheet to move under the cell pointer when the cell pointer movement keys are used. |

## ENTERING FORMULAS

The profit for each month is calculated by subtracting the costs for the month from the revenue for the month. Thus, the profit for January is obtained by subtracting 6300 from 5500. The result, –800, belongs in cell B6. The negative sign preceding the number indicates that the company lost money and made no profit in January.

One of the reasons why 1-2-3 is such a valuable tool is because you can assign a formula to a cell and it will be calculated automatically. In this example, the formula subtracts the value in cell B5 from the value in cell B4 and assigns the result to cell B6.

### Assigning Formulas to Cells

In Figure 1-25, the cell pointer is located at cell B6. Type the formula +B4–B5 on the input line. This formula instructs 1-2-3 to subtract the value in cell B5 from the value in cell B4 and place the result in the cell to which the formula is assigned.

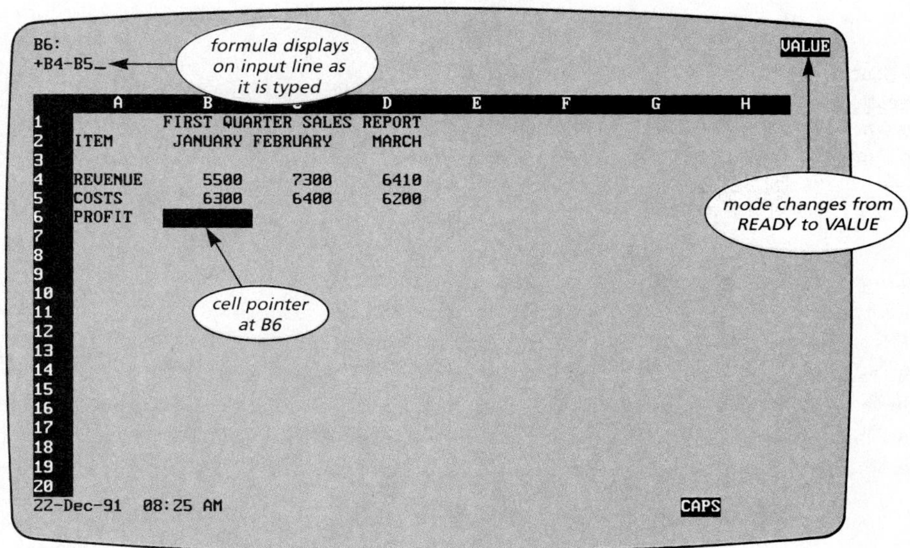


**FIGURE 1-25**
**Entering a formula on the input line.**

The plus sign (+) preceding B4 is an important part of the formula. It alerts 1-2-3 that you are entering a formula and not a label. The minus sign (–) following B4 is the **arithmetic operator**, which directs 1-2-3 to perform the subtraction operation. Other valid arithmetic operators include addition (+), multiplication (*), division (/) and exponentiation (^).

Pressing the Right Arrow key assigns the formula +B4–B5 to cell B6. Instead of displaying the formula in cell B6, however, 1-2-3 completes the arithmetic indicated by the formula and stores the result, –800, in cell B6. This is shown in Figure 1-26. Note that the negative number displays in cell B6 with the minus sign on the left side of the number. Positive numbers display without any sign.

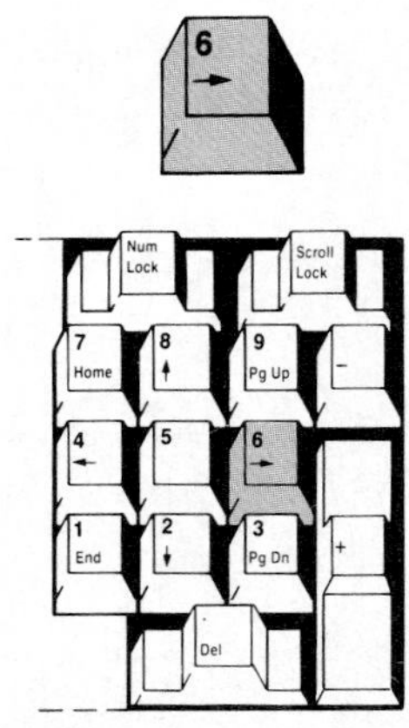


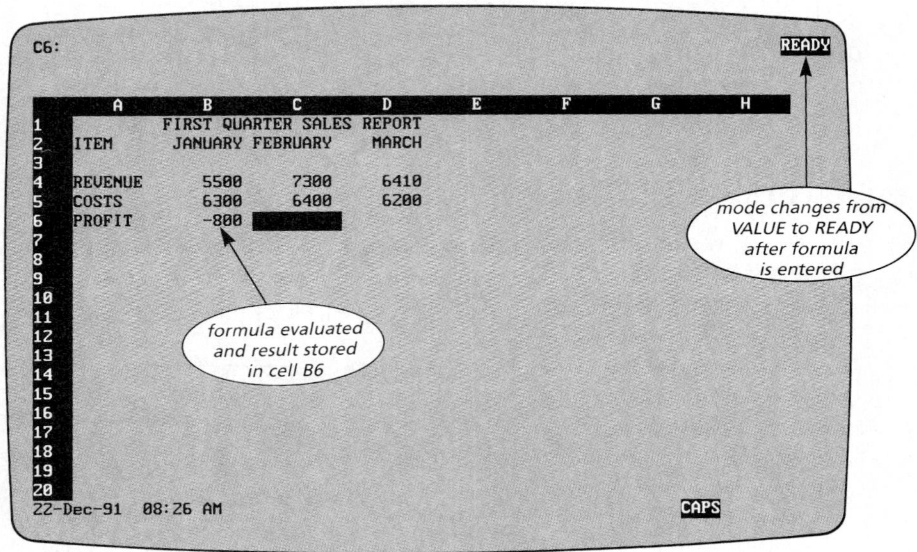


**FIGURE 1-26**
**Pressing the Right Arrow key assigns the formula to cell B6 and moves the cell pointer to C6.**

Formulas may be entered in uppercase or lowercase. That is, +b4–b5 is the same as +B4–B5. Like a number, a valid formula begins with one of the following characters: 0 1 2 3 4 5 6 7 8 9 ( @ + – . # $

Otherwise, the formula is accepted as a label. Therefore, an alternative to the formula +B4–B5 is (B4–B5). The entry B4–B5 is a label and not a formula, because it begins with the letter B.

To be sure that you understand the relationship of a formula, the associated cell, and the contents of the cell, move the cell pointer back to cell B6. This procedure is shown in Figure 1-27. In the upper left corner of the screen, the status line shows the assignment of the formula +B4–B5 to cell B6. However, in the cell itself, 1-2-3 displays the result of the formula (–800).

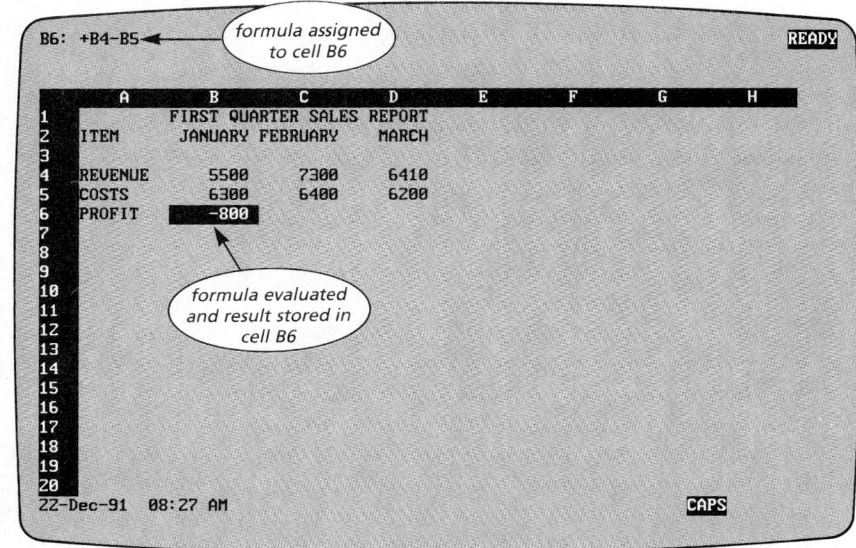


**FIGURE 1-27**
**When the cell pointer is moved to a cell assigned a formula, the formula displays on the status line.**

Next move the cell pointer to C6 and type the formula +C4–C5. As shown in Figure 1-28, the formula for determining the profit for February displays on the input line.

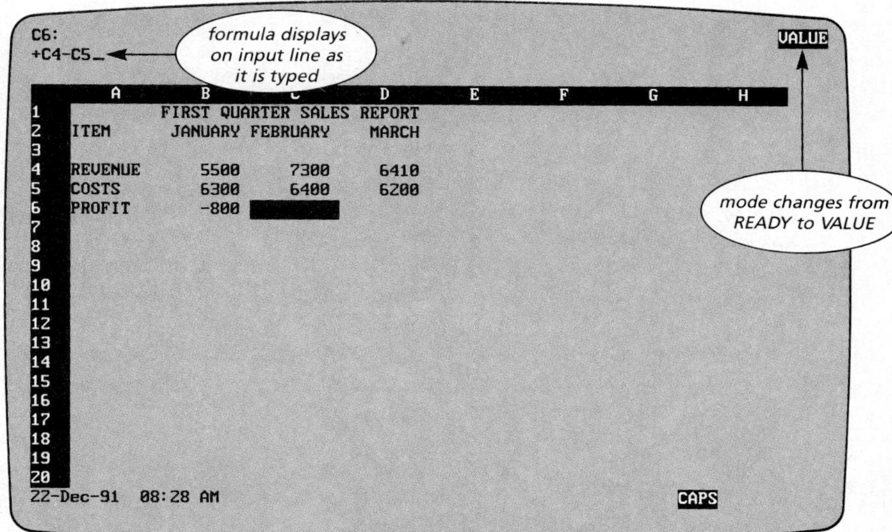


**FIGURE 1-28**
**Entering the profit formula for February on the input line.**

Press the Right Arrow key. The value in cell C5 (February costs) is subtracted from the value in cell C4 (February revenue) and the result of the computation displays in cell C6 (February profit). The cell pointer also moves to cell D6, as shown in Figure 1-29. As you can see, the process for entering a formula into a cell is much the same as for entering labels and numbers.

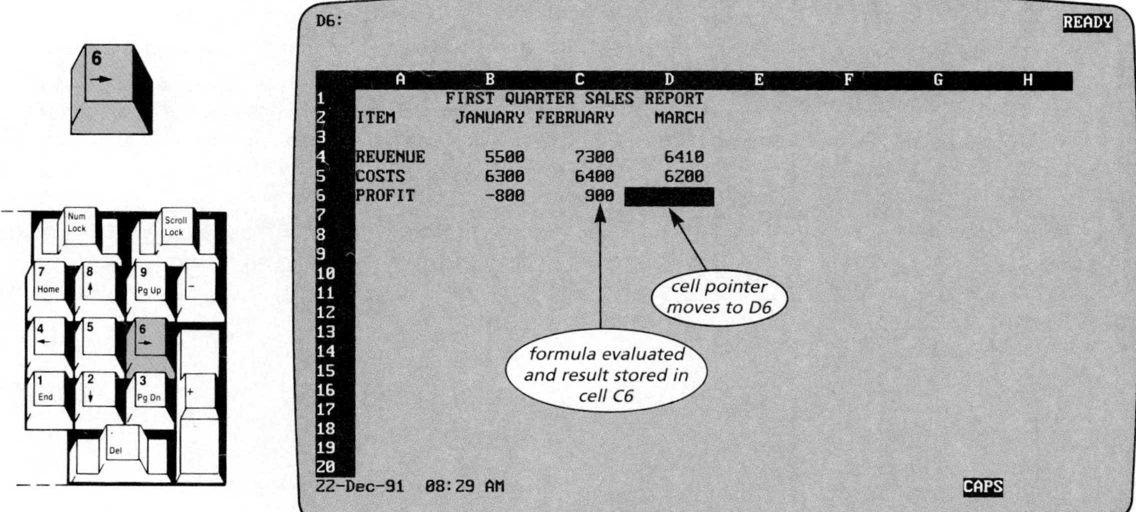


**FIGURE 1-29 Pressing the Right Arrow key assigns the formula on the input line to cell C6 and the cell pointer moves to D6.**

The same technique can be used to assign the formula +D4–D5 to cell D6. After pressing the Right Arrow key to conclude the entry in D6, the worksheet is complete, as illustrated in Figure 1-30.

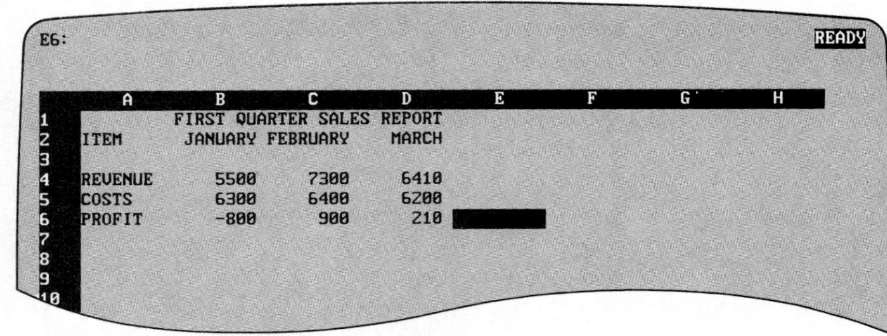


**FIGURE 1-30**
Worksheet for Project 1 is complete.

## Order of Operations

The formulas in this project involve only one arithmetic operator, subtraction. But when more than one operator is involved in a formula, the same order of operations is used as in algebra. Moving from left to right in a formula, the **order of operations** is as follows: first all exponentiations (^), then all multiplications (*) and divisions (/), and finally all additions (+) and subtractions (–). You can use parentheses to override the order of operations. Table 1-4 illustrates several examples of valid formulas.

**TABLE 1-4** Valid Formula Entries

| FORMULA | REMARK |
|---|---|
| +E3 or (E3) | Assigns the value in cell E3 to the current cell. |
| 7*F5 or +F5*7 or (7*F5) | Assigns 7 times the contents of cell F5 to the current cell. |
| –G44*G45 | Assigns the negative value of the product of the values contained in cells G44 and G45 to the current cell. |
| 2*(J12–F2) | Assigns the product of 2 and the difference between the values contained in cells J12 and F2 to the current cell. It is invalid to write this formula as 2(J12–F2). The multiplication sign (*) between the 2 and the left parenthesis is required. |
| +A1/A1–A3*A4+A5^A6 | From left to right: exponentiation (^) first, followed by multiplication (*) and division (/), and finally addition (+) and subtraction (–). |

# SAVING A WORKSHEET

You use 1-2-3 either to enter data into the worksheet, as we did in the last section, or to execute a command. In this section we discuss the first of a series of commands that allows you to instruct 1-2-3 to save, load, modify, and print worksheets.

When a worksheet is created, it is stored in main computer memory. If the computer is turned off or if you quit 1-2-3, the worksheet is lost. Hence, it is mandatory to save to disk any worksheet that will be used later.

## The Command Mode

To save a worksheet, place 1-2-3 in **command mode**. Do this by pressing the **Slash key** (/) as illustrated in Figure 1-31. First note in Figure 1-31 that the mode at the top right side of the screen is MENU. This means that 1-2-3 is now in the command mode. Next, notice the menus on the input line and menu line in the control panel. A **menu** is a list from which you can choose. The **command menu** appears on the input line. A second-level menu appears immediately below the input line on the menu line.

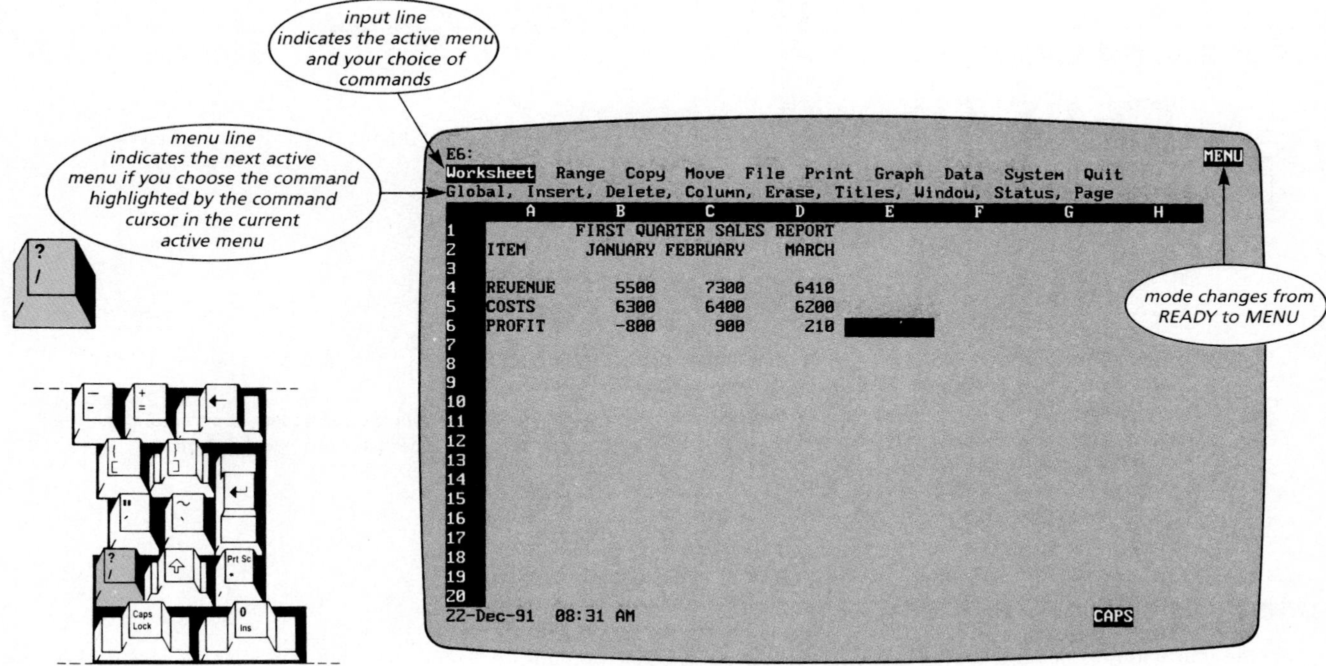


**FIGURE 1-31** To save a worksheet to disk, press the Slash key (/) to switch 1-2-3 to command mode.

The second-level menu lists the secondary commands that are available if you select the command highlighted by the command cursor in the command menu. The **command cursor** is a reverse video rectangle that can be moved from command to command in the active menu on the input line, using the Right Arrow and Left Arrow keys. Although there are two menus on the screen, only the one on the input line is active. The command menu is always the active one when you first press the Slash key. If you press the Right Arrow key four times, the command cursor rests on the File command. This procedure is shown in Figure 1-32. Now compare Figure 1-31 to Figure 1-32. Note that the second level of commands on the menu line has changed in Figure 1-32 to show the list of secondary commands that are available if you select the File command.

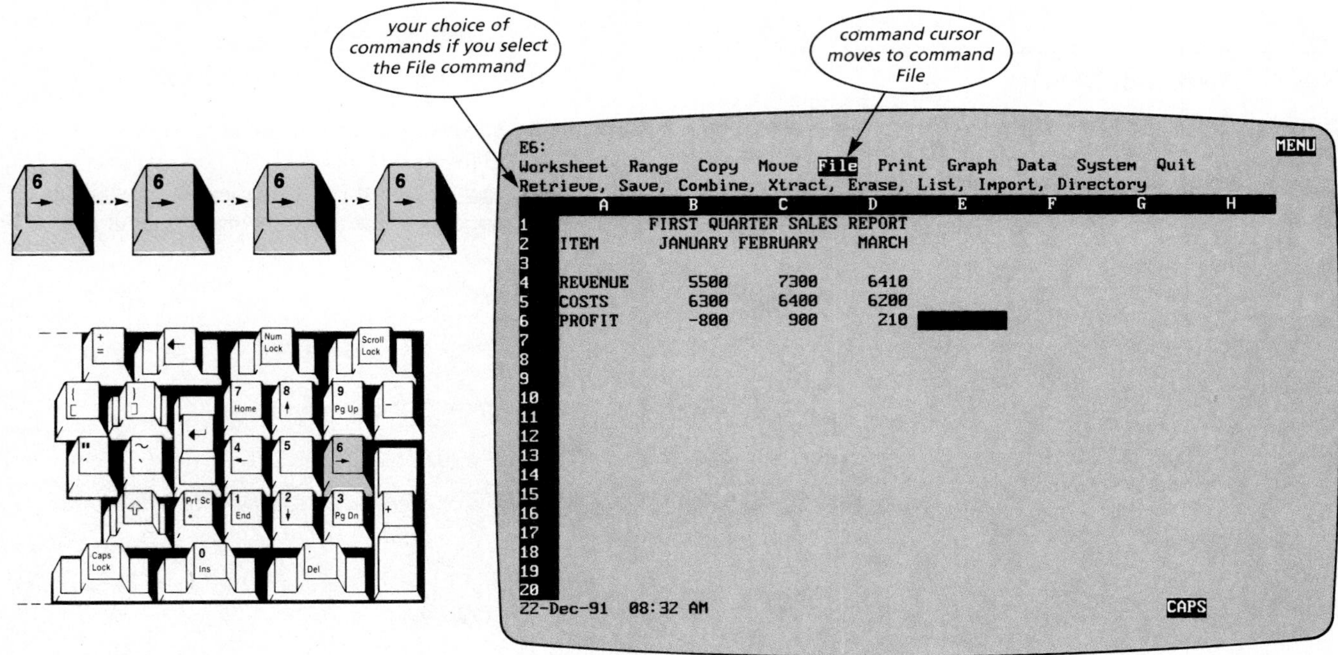


**FIGURE 1-32 As you move the command cursor to each command on the input line, the menu line indicates what the command can do.**

## Backing Out of the Command Mode

If you decide that you do not want to issue a command, press the **Esc key** until the mode of operation changes to READY. The Esc key, located on the top left side of the keyboard next to the digit 1 key, instructs 1-2-3 to exit MENU mode and return to READY mode.

Press the Esc key and the control panel changes from the one in Figure 1-32 to the one in Figure 1-30. Press the Slash key once and the Right Arrow key four times and the command menu in Figure 1-32 reappears in the control panel.

The Esc key allows you to *back out* of any command or entry on the input line. So if you become confused while making any kind of entry (command or data), use the Esc key to reset the current entry. When in doubt, press the Esc key.

## The File Save Command

To save a file, select the File command from the command menu. There are two ways to select the File command.

1. Press the F key for File. Each command in the command menu begins with a different letter. Therefore, the first letter uniquely identifies each command.
2. Use the Right Arrow key to move the command cursor to the word File (see Figure 1-32). With the command cursor on the word File, press the Enter key.

Use the first method and press the F key as shown in Figure 1-33. This causes the **File menu** to replace the command menu on the input line. The command cursor is now active in the File menu.

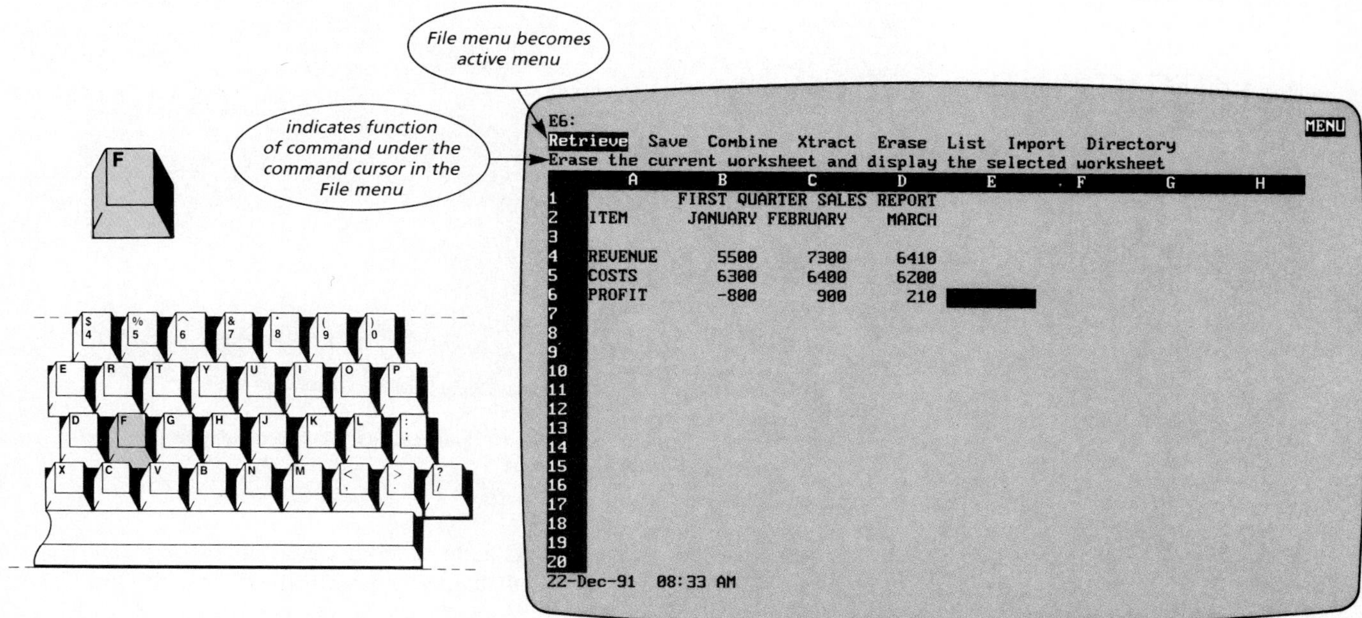


**FIGURE 1-33** Typing the letter F moves the File menu from the menu line to the input line.

Pressing the S key for Save causes the message "Enter save file name: A:\" followed by the blinking edit cursor to appear on the input line at the top of the screen. The mode also changes from MENU to EDIT. This procedure is shown in Figure 1-34.

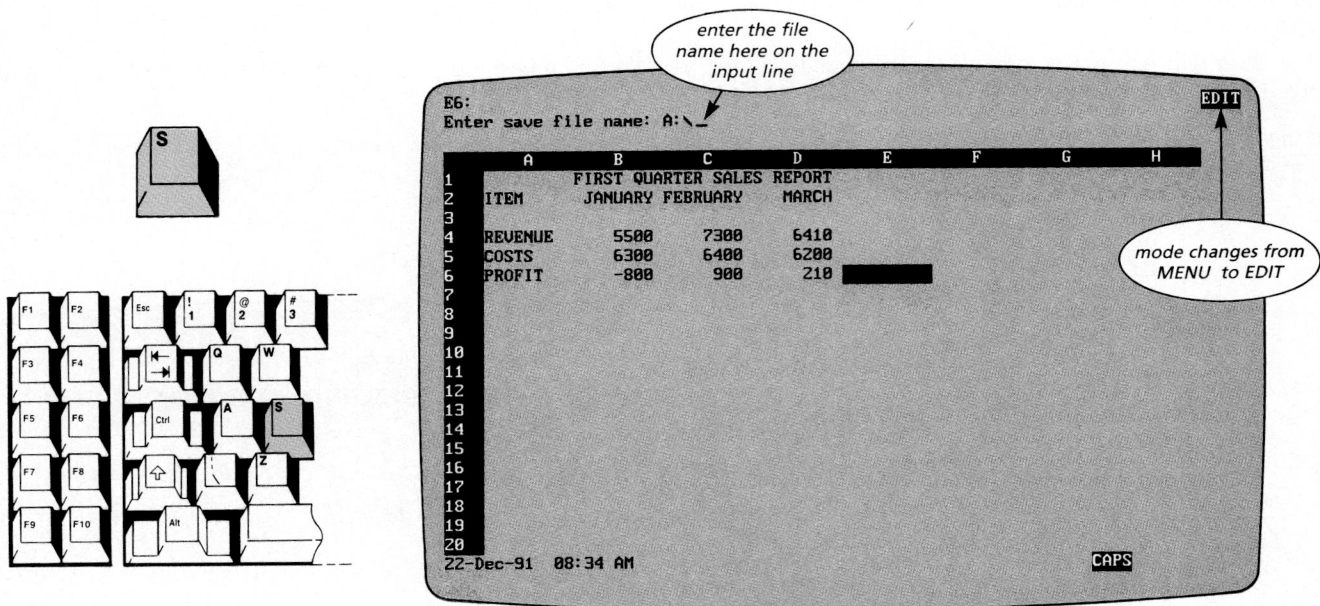


**FIGURE 1-34 Typing the letter S for Save causes 1-2-3 to display the prompt message on the input line.**

The next step is to select a file name. Any file name will do, so long as it is eight or fewer characters in length and includes only the characters A–Z (uppercase or lowercase), 0–9, and the special characters described earlier in the Introduction to DOS. 1-2-3 automatically adds the file extension .WK1 to the file name. The file extension .WK1 stands for worksheet.

In this example, let's choose the file name PROJS-1. Type the file name PROJS-1 as shown in Figure 1-35. Next, press the Enter key. The file is stored on the A drive with the file name PROJS-1.WK1. Remember, 1-2-3 does not distinguish between uppercase and lowercase letters. Therefore, you can type PROJS-1 or projs-1 or ProJS-1. All three file names will be treated the same.

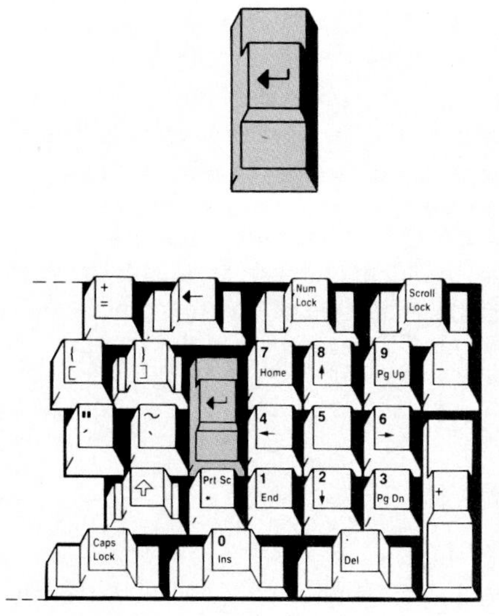


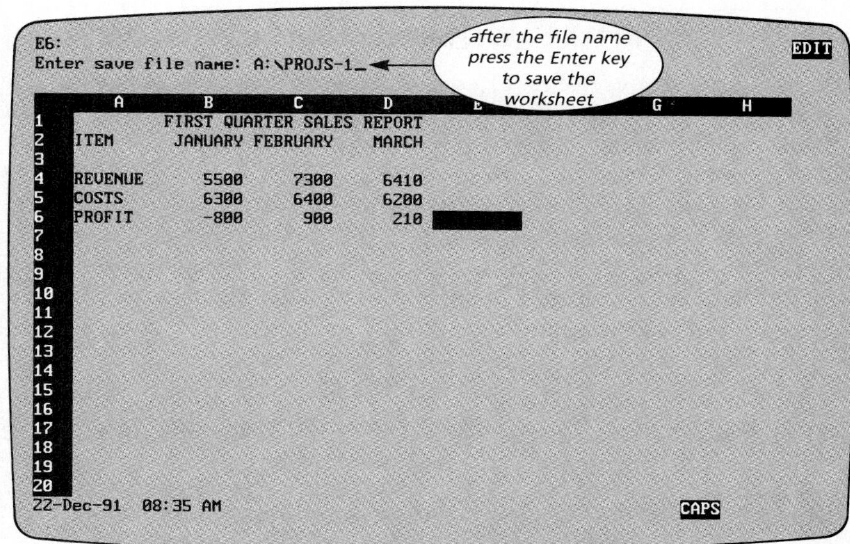


**FIGURE 1-35** After you enter the file name on the input line, press the Enter key to complete the /FS command.

While 1-2-3 writes the worksheet on the disk, the mode changes from EDIT to WAIT. The red light on the A drive also lights up to show it is in use. As soon as the writing is complete, the red light goes off and 1-2-3 returns to the READY mode. This is shown in Figure 1-36.

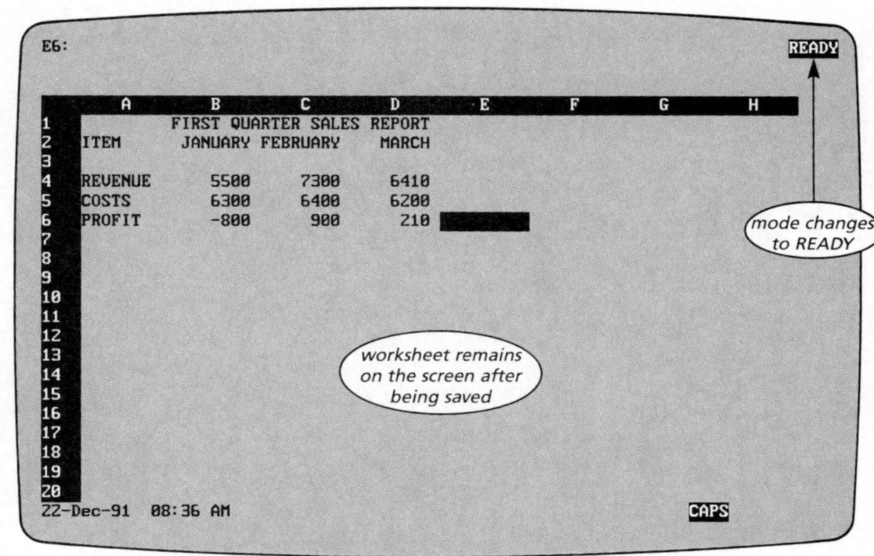


**FIGURE 1-36**
**When the computer is finished saving the worksheet to disk, 1-2-3 returns to READY mode.**

## Saving Worksheets to a Different Disk Drive

If you want to save the worksheet to a different drive, enter the command /**F**ile **S**ave (/FS). Next, press the Esc key twice to delete the "A:*.wk1" from the prompt message "Enter save file name: A:*.wk1". Enter the drive of your choice followed by the file name. For example, to save the worksheet on the disk in drive B, enter B:PROJS-1 in response to the prompt "Enter save file name:". Do not attempt to save a worksheet to the B drive if it is unavailable.

To change the default drive permanently from A to B, enter the command /**W**orksheet **G**lobal **D**efault **D**irectory (/WGDD). That is, press the Slash key, then type the letters WGDD. Press the Esc key to delete the current default drive and type B: for drive B. Press the Enter key. Next, enter the commands Update and Quit (UQ). The Update command permanently changes the default drive in the 1-2-3 program. The Quit command quits the Default menu. The examples in the remainder of this book use the B drive as the default drive.

# PRINTING A SCREEN IMAGE OF THE WORKSHEET

The **screen image** of the worksheet is exactly what you see on the screen, including the window borders and control panel. A printed version of the worksheet is called a **hard copy**.

Anytime you use the printer, you must be sure that it is ready. To make the printer ready, turn it off and use the platen knob to align the perforated edge of the paper with the top of the print head mechanism. Then turn the printer on.

With the printer in READY mode, hold down one of the Shift keys and press the PrtSc key. The screen image of the worksheet immediately prints on the printer. When the printer stops, eject the paper from the printer and carefully tear off the printed version of the worksheet (see Figure 1-37).

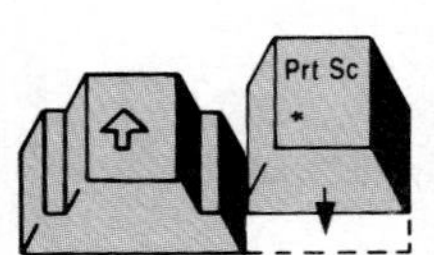


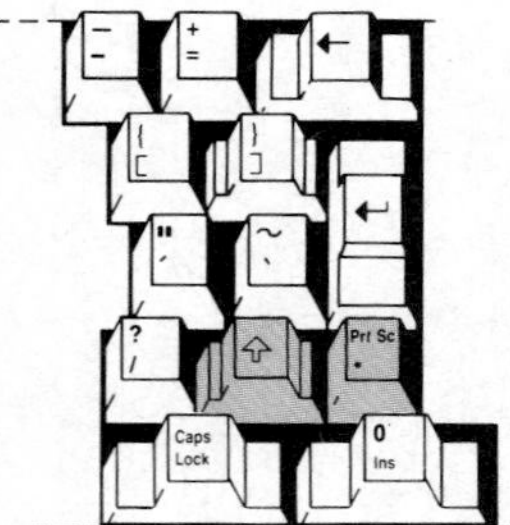


```
E6:                                                                  READY

       A          B         C         D         E         F         G         H
1              FIRST QUARTER SALES REPORT
2   ITEM        JANUARY FEBRUARY   MARCH
3
4   REVENUE        5500      7300      6410
5   COSTS          6300      6400      6200
6   PROFIT         -800       900       210
7
8
9
10
11
12
13
14
15
16
17
18
19
20
22-Dec-91  08:37 AM                                              CAPS
```

**FIGURE 1-37** Hold down the Shift key and press the PrtSc key to obtain a hard copy of the worksheet.

# CORRECTING ERRORS

There are five methods for correcting errors in a worksheet. The one you choose will depend on the severity of the error, and whether you notice it while typing the data on the input line or after the data is in the cell.

The error-correcting examples that follow are not part of the worksheet we are building in Project 1. However, you should carefully step through them since they are essential to building and maintaining worksheets.

## Correcting Errors While the Data Is on the Input Line

Move the cell pointer to cell A5 and type the label COTTS, rather than COSTS, on the input line. This error is shown in Figure 1-38.

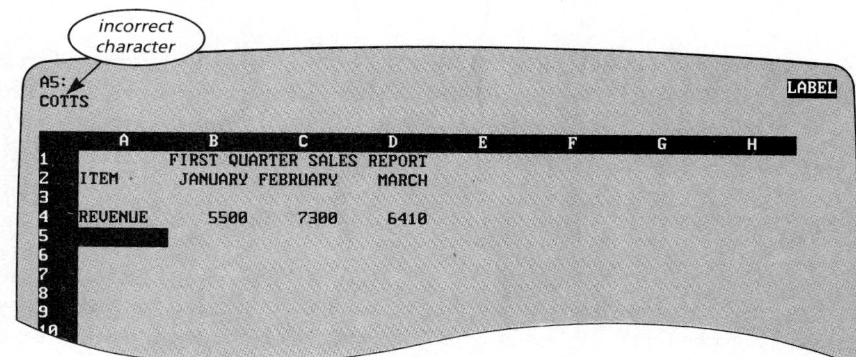


**FIGURE 1-38**
**Incorrect data spotted on the input line.**

To correct the error, move the edit cursor back to position 3 on the input line by pressing the Backspace key three times (see Figure 1-39). Each time you press the Backspace key, the character immediately to the left of the edit cursor is erased.

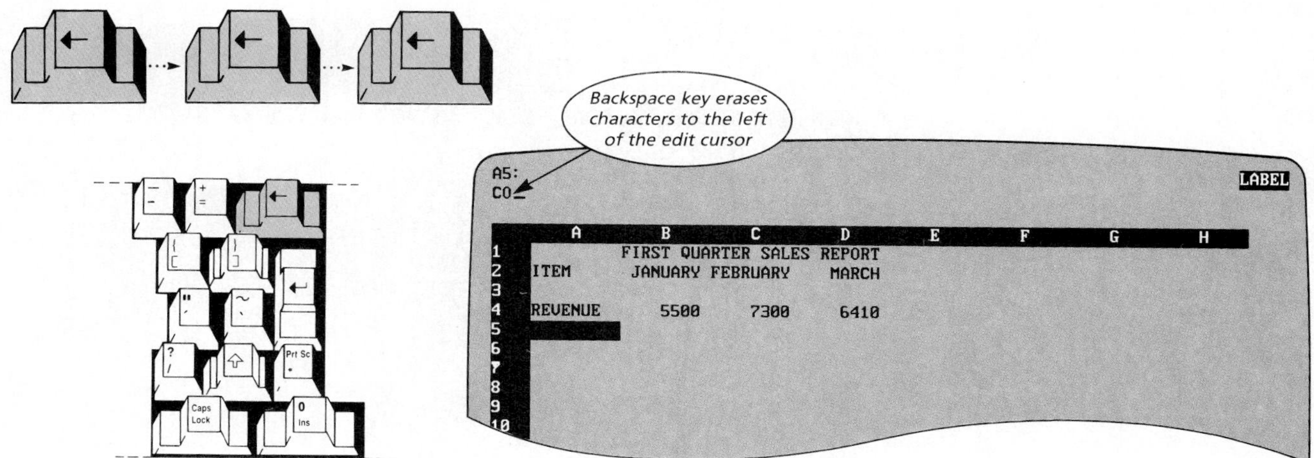


**FIGURE 1-39 Press the Backspace key three times to erase the characters up to and including the first T in COTTS.**

Then, as in Figure 1-40, type the correct letters STS. Now the entry is correct. Press the Right Arrow key to enter the label COSTS into cell A5.

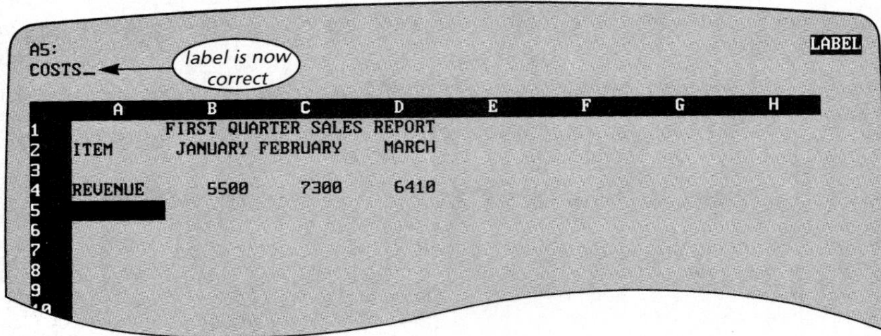


**FIGURE 1-40**
**Enter the correct characters and press the Enter key or one of the arrow keys.**

In summary, if you notice an error while the label, number, or formula is on the input line, you can do one of two things. You can use the Backspace key to erase the portion in error and then type the correct characters. Or, if the error is too severe, you can press the Esc key to erase the entire entry on the input line and reenter the data item from the beginning.

## Editing Data in a Cell

If you spot an error in the worksheet, move the cell pointer to the cell with the error. You then have two ways to correct the error. If the entry is short, simply type it and press the Enter key. The new entry will replace the old entry. Remember, the cell pointer must be on the cell with the error before you begin typing the correct entry.

If the entry in the cell is long and the errors are minor, using the EDIT mode may be a better choice, rather than retyping. Move the cell pointer to cell A4 and enter the label GROSS PAY incorrectly as GRSS PSY. Figure 1-41 shows the label GRSS PSY in cell A4. You will have to insert the letter O between the letters R and S in GRSS and change the letter S in PSY to the letter A.

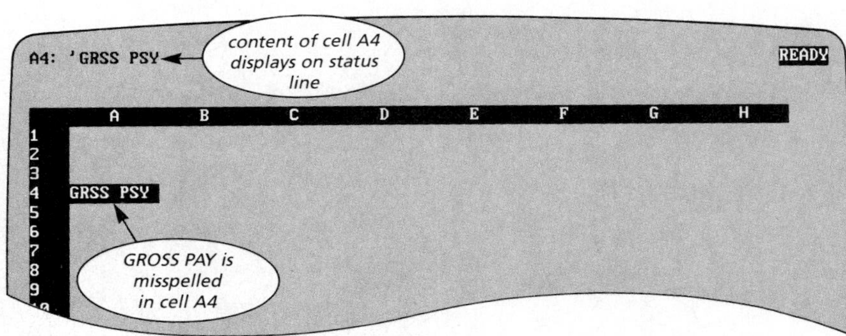


**FIGURE 1-41**
**Error spotted in cell.**

The six steps in Figure 1-42 illustrate how to use the EDIT mode to correct the entry in cell A4. As shown in Step 1, first press function key F2 to switch 1-2-3 to EDIT mode. The contents of cell A4 immediately display on the input line, followed by the edit cursor. The contents of the cell can now be corrected. Table 1-5 on page 33 lists the edit keys available in EDIT mode and their functions.

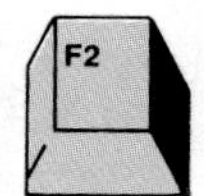


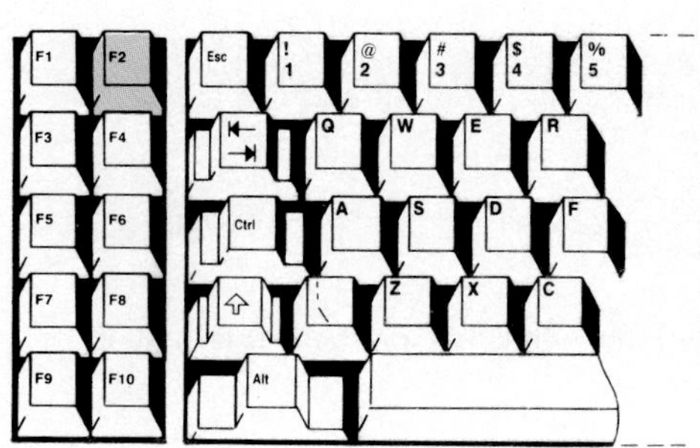

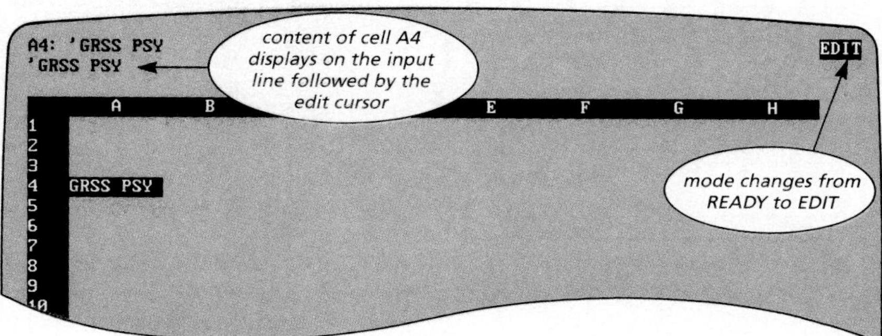


**FIGURE 1-42 (Step 1 of 6)** **Press function key F2 to switch 1-2-3 to EDIT mode.**

With 1-2-3 in EDIT mode, the next step in changing GRSS PSY to GROSS PAY is to move the edit cursor on the input line to the leftmost S in GRSS PSY. Press the Left Arrow key six times as shown in Step 2 of Figure 1-42.

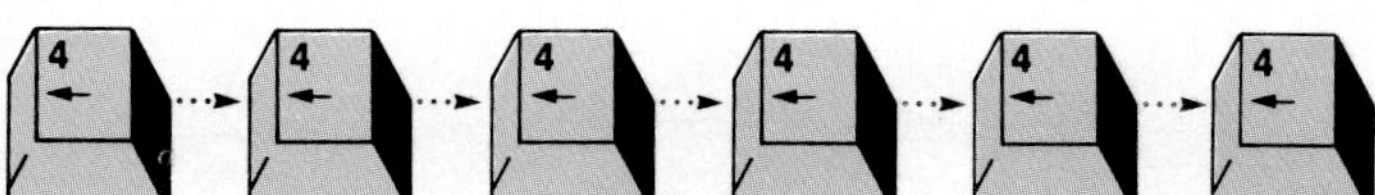

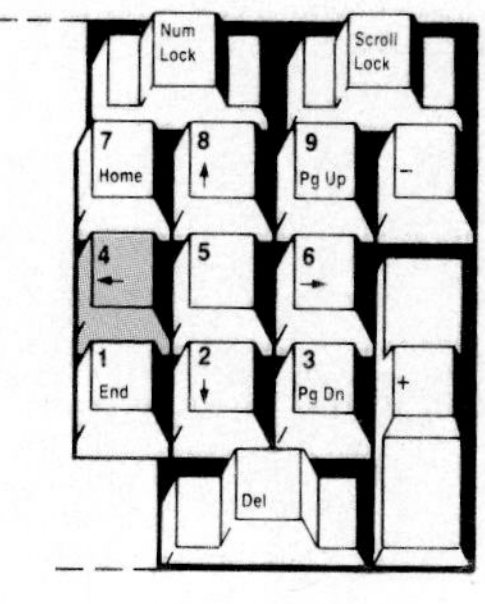

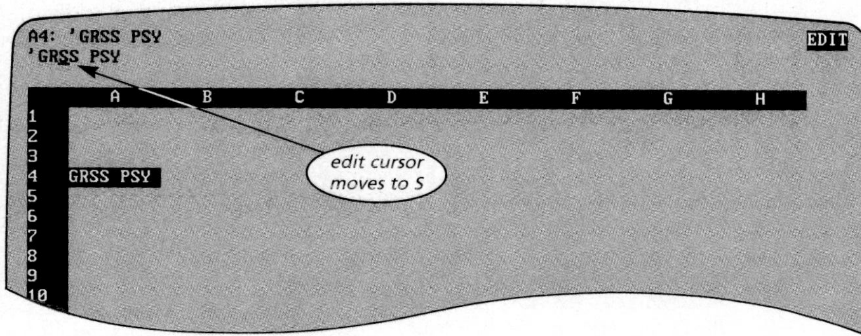


**FIGURE 1-42 (Step 2 of 6)** **Press the Left Arrow key six times to move the edit cursor on the input line to the first S in GRSS PSY.**

Next, type the letter O. Typing the letter O "pushes" the leftmost letter S and all the letters to the right of it to the right. The O is inserted as shown in Step 3 of Figure 1-42.

**FIGURE 1-42 (Step 3 of 6) With the edit cursor on the first letter S in GRSS PSY, type the letter O.**

The next step calls for moving the edit cursor to the S in PSY and changing it to the letter A. Use the Right Arrow key as shown in Step 4 of Figure 1-42. After moving the edit cursor, press the **Ins key** (Insert key) to switch from inserting characters to overtyping characters.

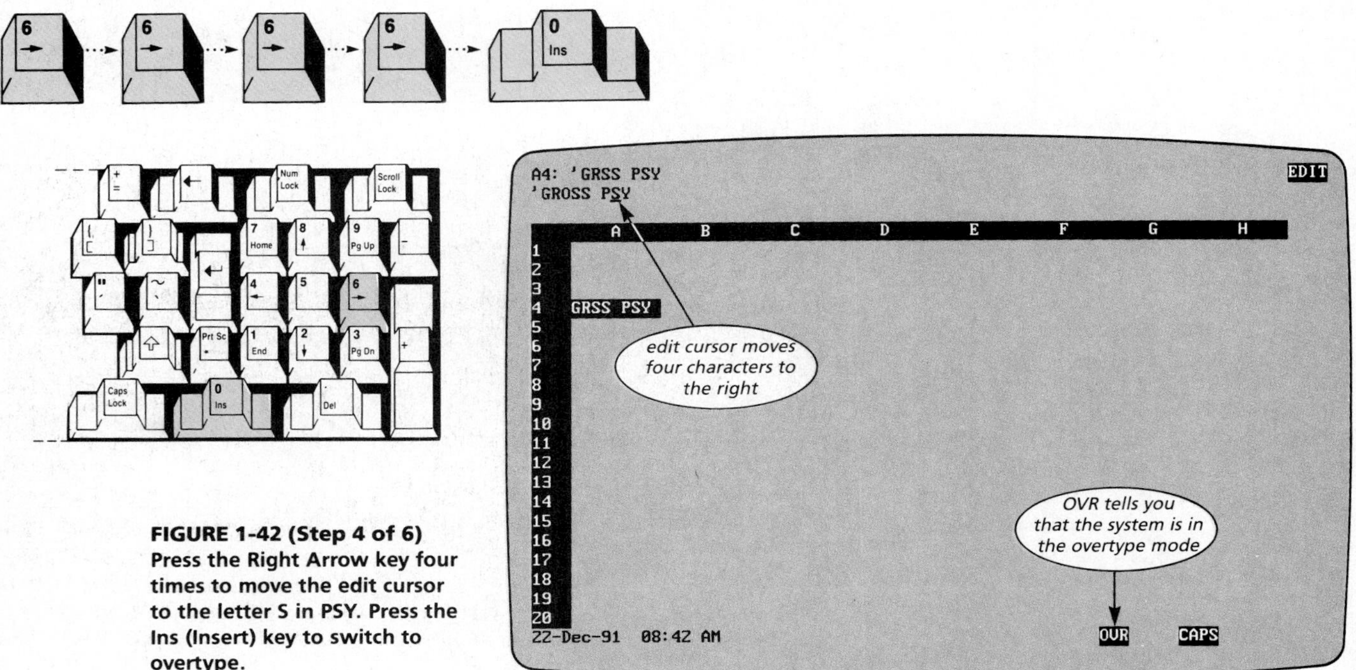


**FIGURE 1-42 (Step 4 of 6) Press the Right Arrow key four times to move the edit cursor to the letter S in PSY. Press the Ins (Insert) key to switch to overtype.**

Type the letter A. The correct label GROSS PAY now resides on the input line (see Step 5 of Figure 1-42). Press the Enter key to replace GRSS PSY in cell A4 with GROSS PAY. This is illustrated in Step 6 of Figure 1-42.

Pay careful attention to the six steps in Figure 1-42. It is easy to make keyboard and grammatical errors. Understanding how to use the EDIT mode will make it easier to correct mistakes.

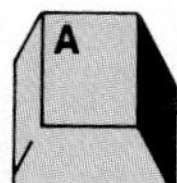


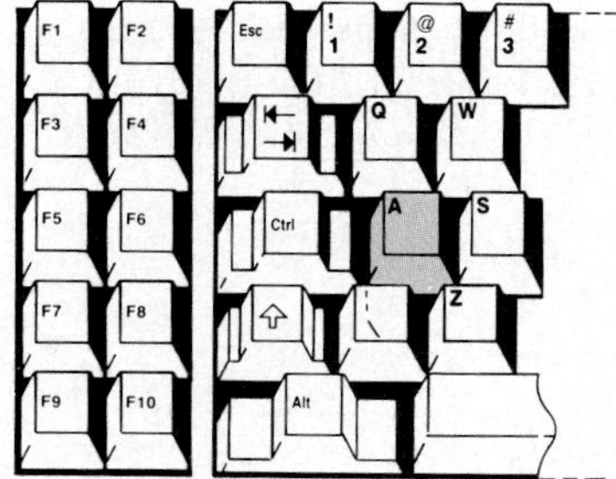


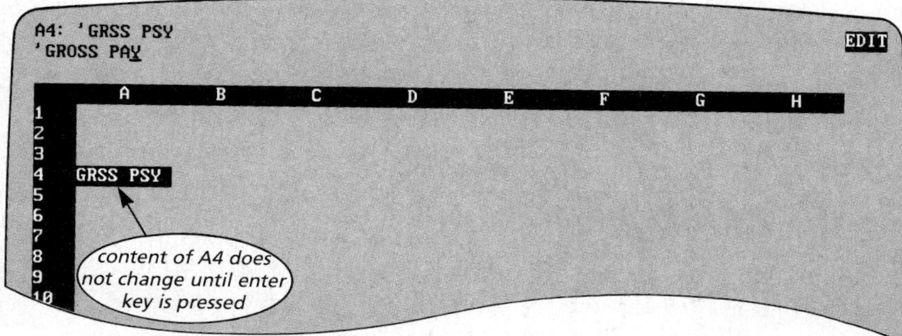


**FIGURE 1-42 (Step 5 of 6)** With the edit cursor on the letter S in PSY, type the letter A.

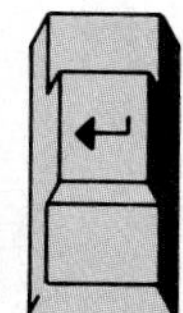

**FIGURE 1-42 (Step 6 of 6)** Press the Enter key to assign the edited value to cell A4.

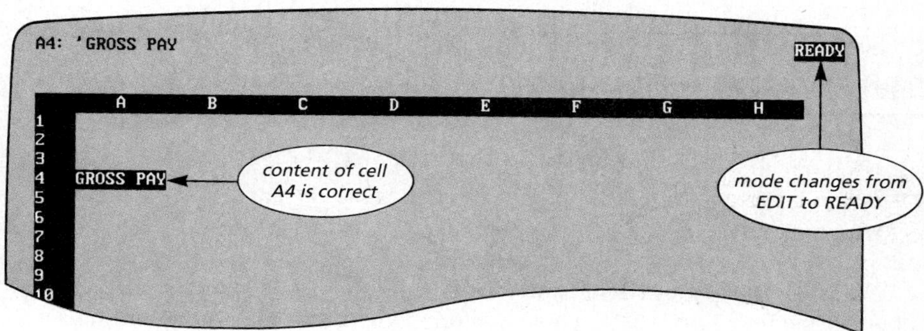


**TABLE 1-5** Keys for Editing Cell Entries

| KEY | FUNCTION |
|---|---|
| F2 | Switches 1-2-3 to EDIT mode. |
| Enter | Completes entry. Up Arrow key or Down Arrow Key also completes an entry. Either key also moves the cell pointer in the corresponding direction. |
| Backspace | Erases the character immediately to the left of the edit cursor. |
| Del | Deletes the character the edit cursor is on. |
| Ins | Used to switch between inserting characters and overtyping characters. In EDIT mode, characters are inserted when the status indicator OVR does not display at the bottom of the screen. Characters are overtyped when the status indicator OVR displays at the bottom of the screen. |
| Right Arrow | Moves the edit cursor one character to the right on the input line. |
| Left Arrow | Moves the edit cursor one character to the left on the input line. |
| End | Moves the edit cursor to the end of the entry on the input line. |
| Home | Moves the edit cursor to the first character in the entry on the input line. |

## Erasing the Contents of a Cell

It is not unusual to enter data into the wrong cell. In such a case, to correct the error, you may want to erase the contents of the cell. Let's erase the label GROSS PAY in cell A4. Make sure the cell pointer is on cell A4. Enter the command /**R**ange **E**rase (/RE). That is, press the Slash key to display the command menu. Then press the R key for Range and the E key for Erase. When the message "Enter range to erase: A4..A4" appears on the input line at the top of the screen, press the Enter key. 1-2-3 immediately erases the entry GROSS PAY in cell A4.

## Erasing the Entire Worksheet

Sometimes, everything goes wrong. If the worksheet is such a mess that you don't know where to begin to correct it, you may want to erase it entirely and start over. To do this, enter the command /**W**orksheet **E**rase **Y**es (/WEY). That is, first type the Slash key to display the command menu. Next, type the letters W for Worksheet, E for Erase and Y for Yes.

The /**W**orksheet **E**rase **Y**es (/WEY) command does not erase the worksheet PROJS-1 from disk. This command only affects the worksheet in main computer memory. Remember that the /**W**orksheet **E**rase **Y**es (/WEY) command can also be a method for clearing the worksheet on the screen of its contents after you have saved it. This is especially useful when you no longer want the current worksheet displayed because you want to begin a new one.

# ONLINE HELP FACILITY

At any time while you are using 1-2-3, you can press function key F1 to gain access to the online help facility. When you press F1, 1-2-3 temporarily suspends the current activity and displays valuable information about the current mode or command. If you have a one-disk or two-disk system and no fixed disk drive, make sure the 1-2-3 system disk is in drive A before pressing the F1 key.

With 1-2-3 in READY mode, press the F1 key. The help screen shown in Figure 1-43 displays. Directions are given at the bottom of the help screen for accessing information or any 1-2-3 program subject, including how to use the online help facility. To display an index of help screens, use the Arrow keys to highlight "Help Index" at the bottom of the screen (see Figure 1-43) and press the Enter key. With the index on the screen, use the Arrow key to select any one of the many 1-2-3 topics. To exit the help facility and return to the worksheet, press the Esc key.

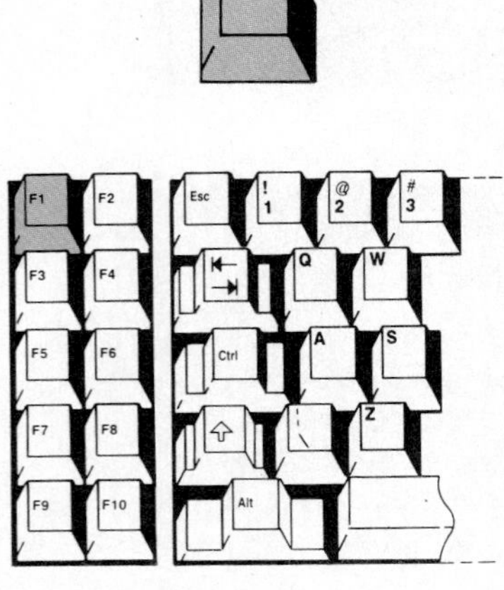


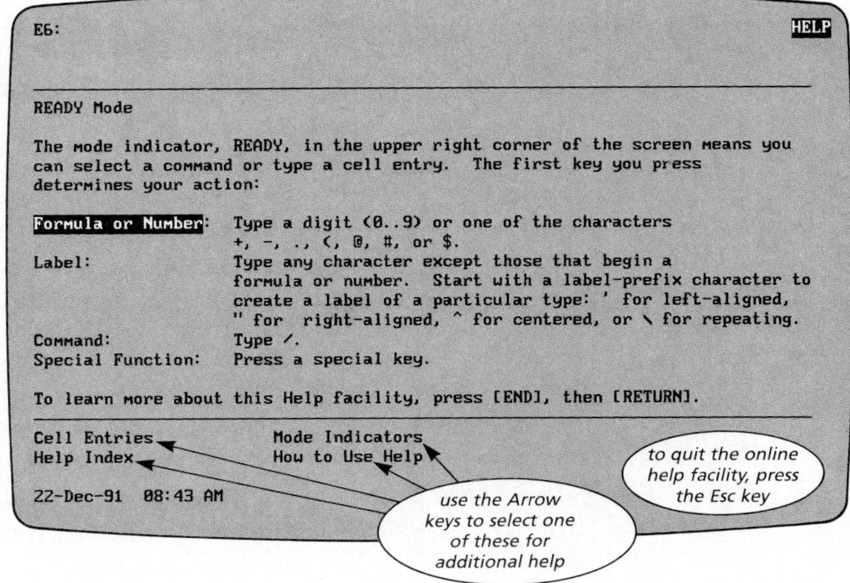

E6:
HELP
READY Mode
The mode indicator, READY, in the upper right corner of the screen means you can select a command or type a cell entry. The first key you press determines your action:
Formula or Number: Type a digit (0..9) or one of the characters +, -, ., (, @, #, or $.
Label: Type any character except those that begin a formula or number. Start with a label-prefix character to create a label of a particular type: ' for left-aligned, " for right-aligned, ^ for centered, or \ for repeating.
Command: Type /.
Special Function: Press a special key.
To learn more about this Help facility, press [END], then [RETURN].
Cell Entries
Mode Indicators
Help Index
How to Use Help
22-Dec-91 08:43 AM
to quit the online help facility, press the Esc key
use the Arrow keys to select one of these for additional help


**FIGURE 1-43**
**Press function key F1 to use the online help facility of 1-2-3.**

The best way to familiarize yourself with the online help facility is to use it. When you have a question about how a command works in 1-2-3, press F1. You may want to consider printing a hard copy of the information displayed on the screen. To print a hard copy, ready the printer, hold down one of the Shift keys, and press the PrtSc key.

## QUITTING 1-2-3

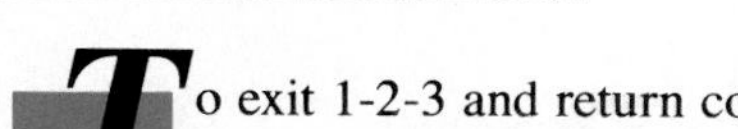

To exit 1-2-3 and return control to DOS, do the following:

1. Save the current worksheet if you made any changes to it since the last save.
2. If you loaded 1-2-3 from drive A, place the DOS disk in drive A.
3. Enter the **Q**uit command (/Q). First, press the Slash key to display the command menu. Next, type the letter Q for Quit.
4. When the message shown at the top of the screen in Figure 1-44 displays, type the letter Y to confirm your exit from 1-2-3.

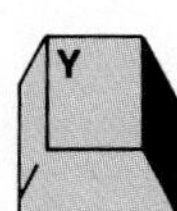


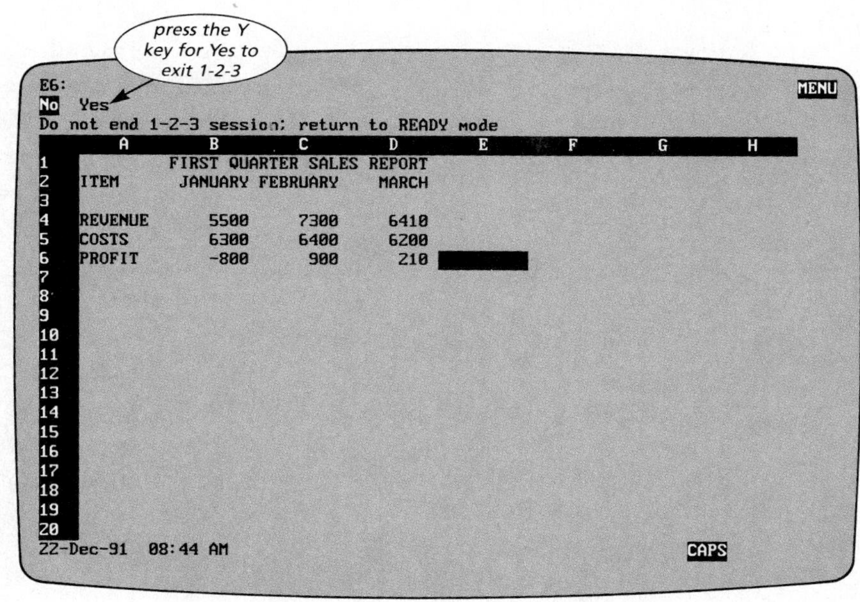

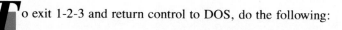

**FIGURE 1-44**
**To quit 1-2-3 and return control to DOS, enter the command /Q and type the letter Y.**

## PROJECT SUMMARY

In Project 1 you learned how to move the cell pointer around the worksheet, enter data into the worksheet, and save a worksheet. Each of the steps required to build the worksheet in this project is listed in the following table. Review the steps in detail to make sure you understand them.

**SUMMARY OF KEYSTROKES—Project 1**

| STEPS | KEY(S) PRESSED | RESULTS |
|---|---|---|
| 1 | Caps Lock | Set Caps Lock on |
| 2 | → | Move the cell pointer to B1 |
| 3 | FIRST QUARTER SALES REPORT ↵ | Enter report heading |
| 4 | ↓ ← | Move the cell pointer to A2 |
| 5 | ITEM → | Enter column heading |
| 6 | "JANUARY → | Enter column heading |
| 7 | "FEBRUARY → | Enter column heading |
| 8 | "MARCH → | Enter column heading |
| 9 | ↓ ↓ ← ← ← ← | Move the cell pointer to A4 |
| 10 | REVENUE → | Enter row identifier |
| 11 | 5500 → | Enter January revenue |
| 12 | 7300 → | Enter February revenue |
| 13 | 6410 → | Enter March revenue |
| 14 | F5 A5 ↵ | Move the cell pointer to A5 |
| 15 | COSTS → | Enter row identifier |
| 16 | 6300 → | Enter January costs |
| 17 | 6400 → | Enter February costs |
| 18 | 6200 → | Enter March costs |
| 19 | F5 A6 ↵ | Move the cell pointer to A6 |
| 20 | PROFIT → | Enter row identifier |
| 21 | + B4–B5 → | Enter January profit formula |
| 22 | + C4–C5 → | Enter February profit formula |
| 23 | + D4–D5 → | Enter March profit formula |
| 24 | /FS PROJS-1 ↵ | Save the worksheet as PROJS-1 |
| 25 | Shift - PrtSc | Print the screen image of the worksheet |

The following list summarizes the material covered in Project 1.

1. The worksheet is organized in two dimensions—columns (vertical) and rows (horizontal).
2. In the border at the top of the screen, each **column** is identified by a column letter. In the border on the left side, each **row** is identified by a row number.
3. A **cell** is the intersection of a row and a column. A cell is referred to by its **cell address**, the coordinates of the intersection of a column and row.
4. The **current cell** is the cell in which data (labels, numbers, and formulas) can be entered. The current cell is identified in two ways. A reverse video rectangle called the **cell pointer** is displayed over the current cell, and the current cell address displays on the status line at the top of the screen.
5. The area between the borders on the screen is called a **window**.
6. The three lines immediately above the window—status line, input line, and menu line—are collectively called the **control panel**.
7. The **status line** is the first line in the control panel. It indicates the current cell address and displays the mode of operation. If a value is already in the cell, the status line also shows the type of entry and its contents.
8. The second line in the control panel is the **input line**. Depending on the mode of operation, it shows the characters you type as you enter data or edit cell contents; the command menu; or input prompts asking for additional command specifications.
9. The third line in the control panel is the **menu line**. It displays information about the menu item highlighted on the input line when 1-2-3 is in the MENU mode.
10. The line at the bottom of the screen is the **indicator line**. It displays three items: the date and time of day as maintained by DOS and status indicators.
11. To move the cell pointer one cell at a time use the arrow keys found on the right side of the keyboard.
12. No matter where the cell pointer is on the worksheet, if you press the Home key, the cell pointer always moves to cell A1.
13. You may use the **GOTO command** (function key F5) to move the cell pointer to any cell in the worksheet.
14. Three types of entries may be made in a cell: labels, numbers, and formulas.
15. A cell entry is a **number** or a **formula** if the first character typed is one of the following: 0 1 2 3 4 5 6 7 8 9 ( @ + – . # $
16. A number or formula is also called a **value**.
17. A cell entry is a **label** if the first character is any character other than one that identifies it as a number or formula.
18. If a label begins with a letter or apostrophe, it is positioned in the cell left-justified. If a label begins with a quotation mark ("), it is positioned right-justified. If a label begins with a circumflex (^), it is centered in the cell.
19. One of the most powerful features of 1-2-3 is the ability to assign a formula to a cell and calculate it automatically. The result of the calculation is displayed in the cell.
20. 1-2-3 uses the same order of operations as in algebra. Moving from left to right in a formula, the order of operations is as follows: all exponentiations (^) are completed first, then all multiplications (*) and divisions (/), and finally all additions (+) and subtractions (–). Parentheses may be used to override the order of operations.
21. To put 1-2-3 in command mode, press the **Slash key (/)**. To leave command mode, press the Esc key.
22. There are two different cursors: edit cursor and command cursor. The **edit cursor** shows where the next character will be placed on the input line. The **command cursor** moves from command to command in the command menu.
23. If you get confused while making any kind of entry (command or data), press the **Esc key** to reset the current entry. When in doubt, press the Esc key.
24. In order to save a worksheet, enter the command /**F**ile **S**ave (/FS) and the file name that you plan to call the worksheet.
25. 1-2-3 automatically appends the file extension .WK1 (worksheet) to the file name.
26. To print the screen image of the worksheet, make sure the printer is in READY mode. Next, hold down one of the Shift keys and press the PrtSc key. After the worksheet has printed, eject the paper from the printer and carefully tear off the printed worksheet. A printed version of the worksheet is called a **hard copy**.
27. To edit the contents of a cell, press function key F2.
28. To erase the contents of a cell, move the cell pointer to the cell in question, enter the command /**R**ange **E**rase (/RE), and press the Enter key.
29. To erase the entire worksheet, enter the command /**W**orksheet **E**rase **Y**es (/WEY).
30. At any time while you are using 1-2-3, you may press function key F1 to gain access to the online help facility.
31. To exit 1-2-3 and return control to DOS, enter the command /**Q**uit (/Q). Press the Y key to confirm your exit. Before entering the Quit command, be sure that the DOS program COMMAND.COM is available to the system.

# STUDENT ASSIGNMENTS

## STUDENT ASSIGNMENT 1: True/False

**Instructions:** Circle T if the statement is true or F if the statement is false.

T F 1. The current cell address on the status line identifies the cell that the cell pointer is on in the worksheet.
T F 2. With 1-2-3, each column is identified by a number and each row by a letter of the alphabet.
T F 3. A cell is identified by specifying its cell address, the coordinates of the intersection of a column and a row.
T F 4. When 1-2-3 first begins execution, the column width is nine characters.
T F 5. One method of moving the worksheet cell pointer is by using the arrow keys on the right side of the keyboard.
T F 6. A cell entry that consists of just words or letters of the alphabet is called a label.
T F 7. When text data is entered that contains more characters than the width of the column, an error message displays.
T F 8. If a cell entry begins with a circumflex (^), the data is right-justified in the cell.
T F 9. To move the cell pointer from cell C1 to cell A2, press the Down Arrow key one time and the Left Arrow key one time.
T F 10. Numeric data entered into a worksheet is stored right-justified in a cell.
T F 11. The GOTO command moves the cell pointer directly to a designated cell.
T F 12. Typing GOTO A1 causes the worksheet cell pointer to be positioned in cell A1.
T F 13. A formula may begin with a letter.
T F 14. When you enter a formula in a cell, the formula is evaluated and the result is displayed in the same cell on the worksheet.
T F 15. The cell pointer is at C6. The formula +C4–C5 causes the value in cell C5 to be subtracted from the value in cell C4. The answer is displayed in cell C5.

## STUDENT ASSIGNMENT 2: Multiple Choice

**Instructions:** Circle the correct response.

1. In the border at the top of the screen, each column is identified by a ________ .
   a. number
   b. letter
   c. pointer
   d. none of the above
2. If the first character typed on the input line is the letter F, the mode on the status line changes from READY to ________ .
   a. VALUE
   b. LABEL
   c. MENU
   d. EDIT
3. A cell is identified by a cell ________ .
   a. pointer
   b. address
   c. entry
   d. none of the above
4. The command /File Save (/FS) is used to ________ .
   a. load a new worksheet
   b. save a worksheet on disk
   c. suspend work on the current worksheet and return to the operating system
   d. make corrections in the current entry

5. To exit from 1-2-3, ________ .
   a. type /Q for Quit and then Y
   b. type /E for Exit
   c. type /FS for Finally Stop
   d. both b and c are correct
6. Which one of the following should you press to put 1-2-3 in EDIT mode?
   a. function key F1
   b. function key F2
   c. function key F3
   d. function key F5
7. Which one of the following best describes the function of the Backspace key?
   a. deletes the value in the current cell
   b. deletes the character on the input line under which the edit cursor is located
   c. deletes the character to the right of the edit cursor on the input line
   d. deletes the character to the left of the edit cursor on the input line
8. Which one of the following should you press to activate the online help facility of 1-2-3?
   a. function key F1
   b. function key F2
   c. function key F3
   d. function key F4

## STUDENT ASSIGNMENT 3: Understanding the Worksheet

**Instructions:** Answer the following questions.

1. In Figure 1-45, a series of arrows points to the major components of a worksheet. Identify the various parts of the worksheet in the space provided in the figure.

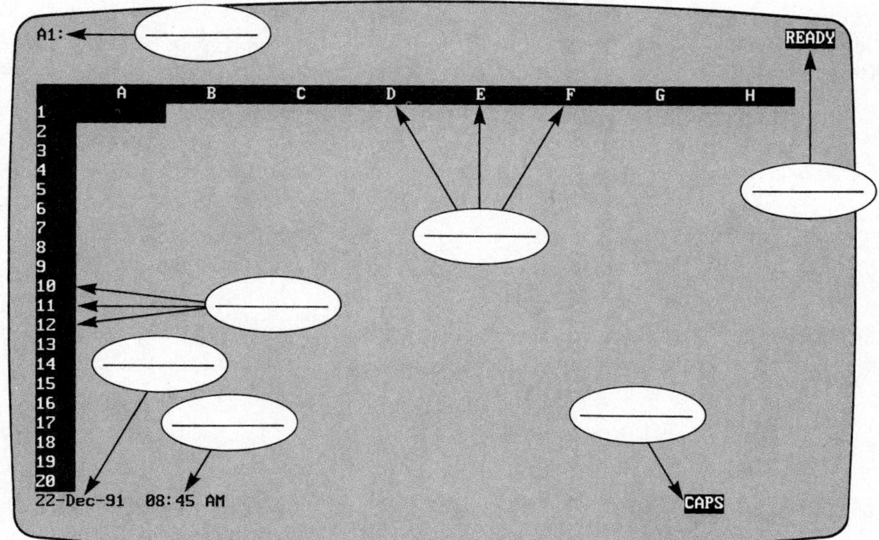


**FIGURE 1-45**
**Problem 1 of Student Assignment 3**

**Student Assignment 3 (continued)**

2. Explain the following entries that may be contained on the indicator line at the bottom of the screen.

   a. OVR ______________________________

   b. 13:15 ______________________________

   c. SCROLL ______________________________

   d. CAPS ______________________________

## STUDENT ASSIGNMENT 4: Understanding 1-2-3 Commands

**Instructions:** Answer the following questions.

1. Use Figure 1-46 to answer the following two questions. Where is the cell pointer located in the worksheet? Which keystroke causes the display on the input line?

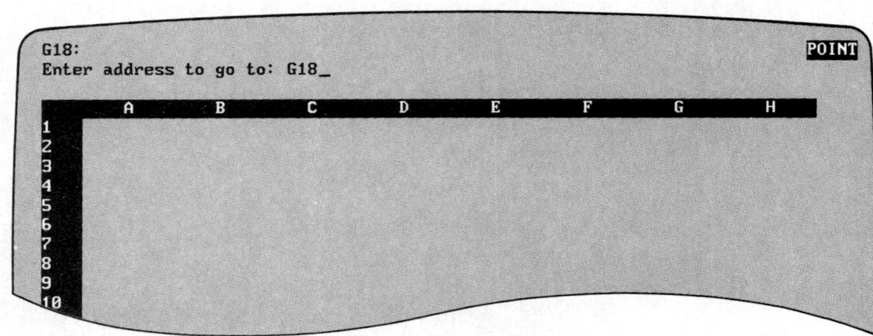


**FIGURE 1-46**
**Problem 1 of Student Assignment 4**

Cell pointer location: __________

Keystroke: ____________________

2. Indicate the sequence of keystrokes for saving a worksheet that causes the display shown on the input line in Figure 1-47. Assume that the first letter of each command is entered to issue the commands that cause the display.

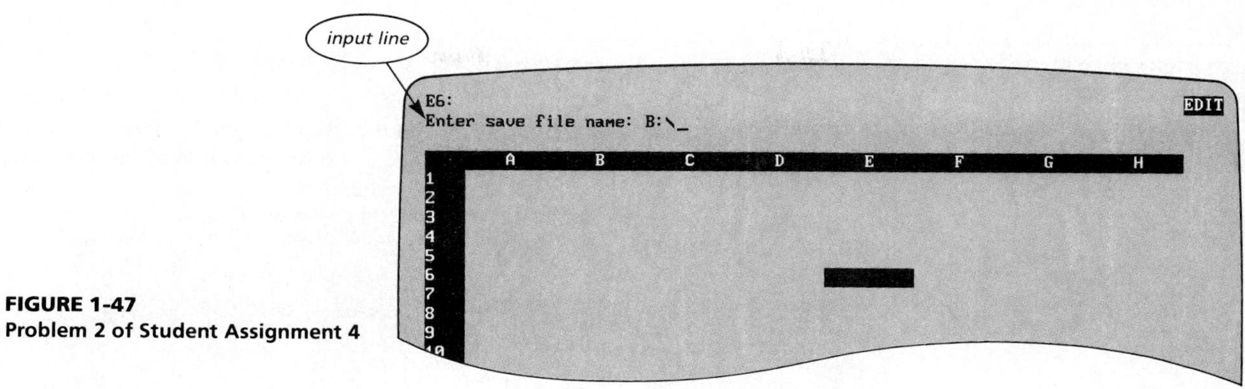


**FIGURE 1-47**
**Problem 2 of Student Assignment 4**

Keystroke sequence: ______________________________

3. Indicate the value assigned to the current cell caused by the entry on the input line in Figure 1-48. Assume that cell I23 contains the value 6 and cell I24 contains the value 7.

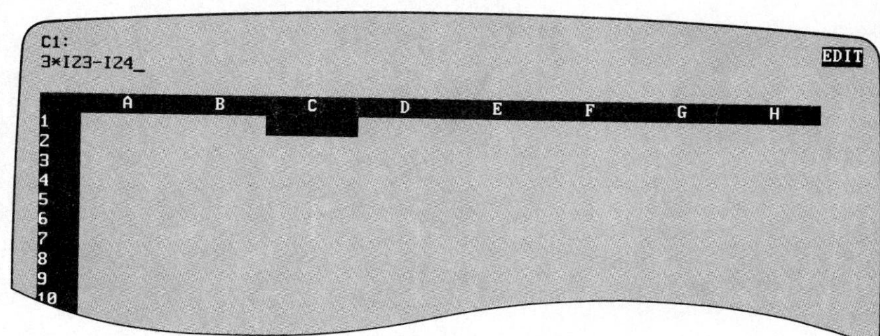


**FIGURE 1-48**
**Problem 3 of Student Assignment 4**

Value: ______________________

4. Which keystroke causes 1-2-3 to display the current mode shown in Figure 1-49?

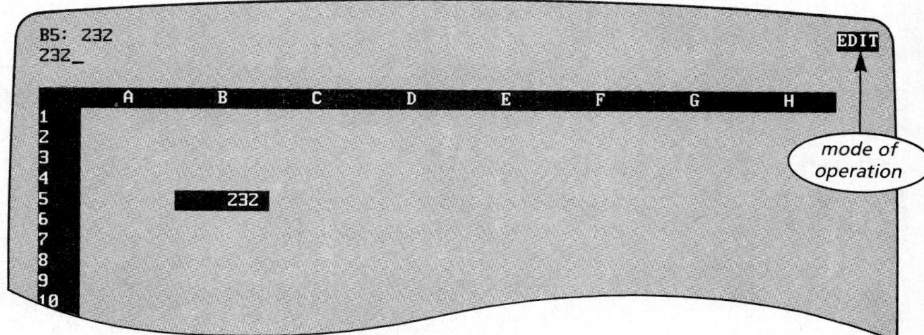


**FIGURE 1-49**
**Problem 4 of Student Assignment 4**

Keystroke: ________________

## STUDENT ASSIGNMENT 5: Correcting Formulas in a Worksheet

**Instructions:** The worksheet illustrated in Figure 1-50 contains an error in the PROFIT row for January. Analyze the entries displayed on the worksheet. Explain the cause of the error and the method of correction in the space provided below.

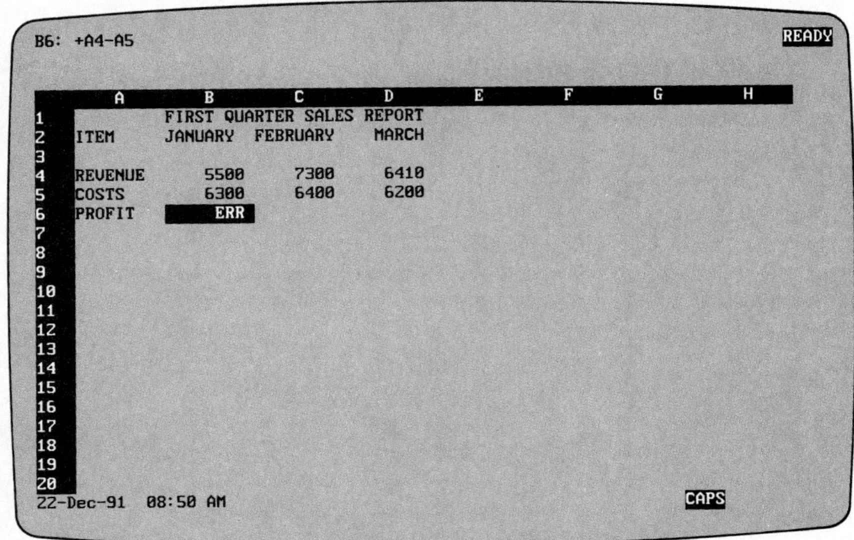


**FIGURE 1-50**
**Student Assignment 5**

Cause of error: ____________________

Method of correction: ____________________

## STUDENT ASSIGNMENT 6: Correcting Worksheet Entries

**Instructions:** The worksheet illustrated in Figure 1-51 contains errors in the PROFIT row for February (cell C6) and March (cell D6). Analyze the entries displayed on the worksheet. Explain the cause of the errors for the two months and the methods of correction in the space provided on page 43.

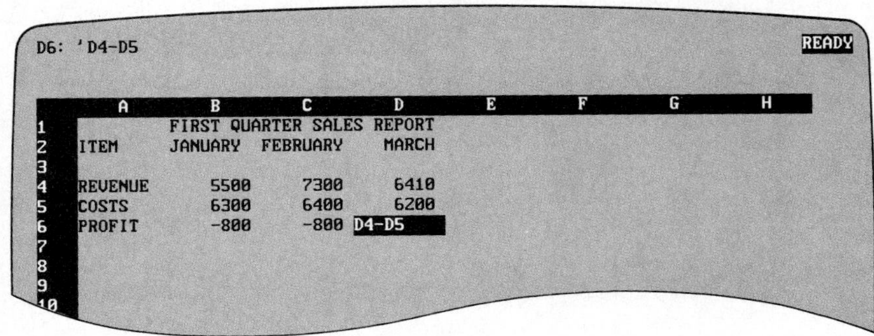


**FIGURE 1-51**
**Student Assignment 6**

Cause of error in C6: ______________________________

______________________________

Method of correction for C6: ______________________________

______________________________

Cause of error in D6: ______________________________

______________________________

Method of correction for D6: ______________________________

______________________________

## STUDENT ASSIGNMENT 7: Entering Formulas

**Instructions:** For each worksheet below, write the formula that accomplishes the specified task and manually compute the value assigned to the specified cell.

1. See Figure 1-52. Assign to cell A4 the product of cell A2 and cell A3.

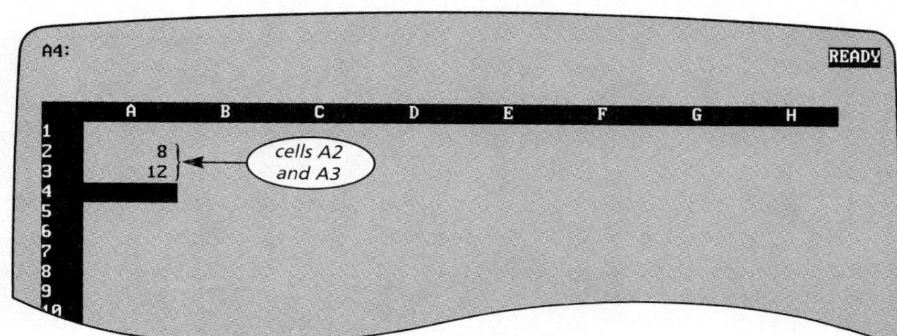


**FIGURE 1-52**
**Problem 1 of Student Assignment 7**

Formula: ______________________________

Result assigned to cell A4: ____________

2. See Figure 1-53. Assign to cell B5 the sum of cells B2, B3, and B4, minus cell A5.

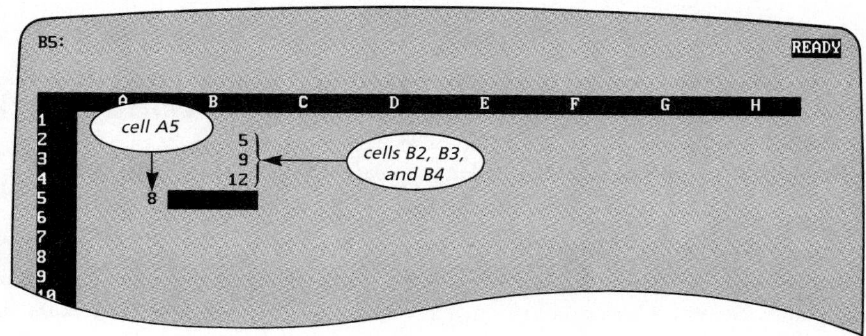


**FIGURE 1-53**
**Problem 2 of Student Assignment 7**

Formula: ______________________________

Result assigned to cell B5: ____________

### Student Assignment 7 (continued)

3. See Figure 1-54. Assign to cell C3 two times the quotient of cell D2 divided by cell C2.

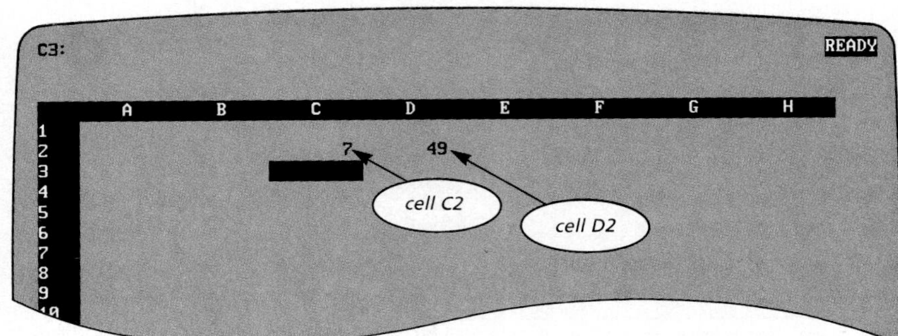


**FIGURE 1-54**
**Problem 3 of Student Assignment 7**

Formula: ______________________________

Result assigned to cell C3: ______________

4. See Figure 1-55. Assign to cell D5 the sum of cells D2 through D4 minus the sum of cells C3 and C4.

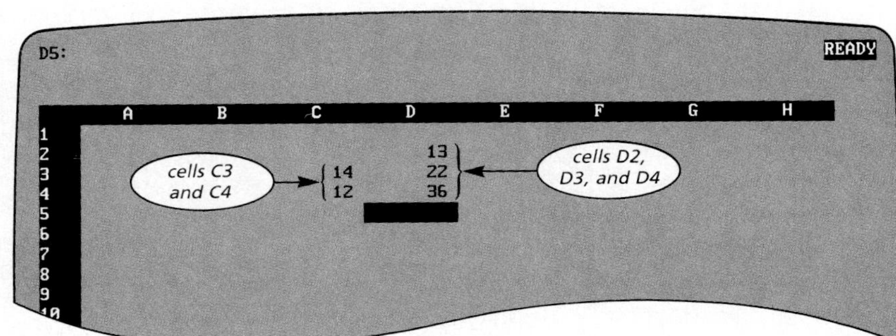


**FIGURE 1-55**
**Problem 4 of Student Assignment 7**

Formula: ______________________________

Result assigned to cell D5: ______________

## STUDENT ASSIGNMENT 8: Building an Inventory Listing Worksheet

**Instructions:** Perform the following tasks using a personal computer.

1. Boot the computer.
2. Load 1-2-3 into main computer memory.
3. Build the worksheet illustrated in Figure 1-56. The TOTAL line in row 7 contains the totals for Part A, Part B, and Part C for each of the plants (Seattle, Omaha, and Flint). For example, the total in cell B7 is the sum of the values in cells B4, B5, and B6.
4. Save the worksheet. Use the file name STUS1-8.
5. Print the screen image of the worksheet.

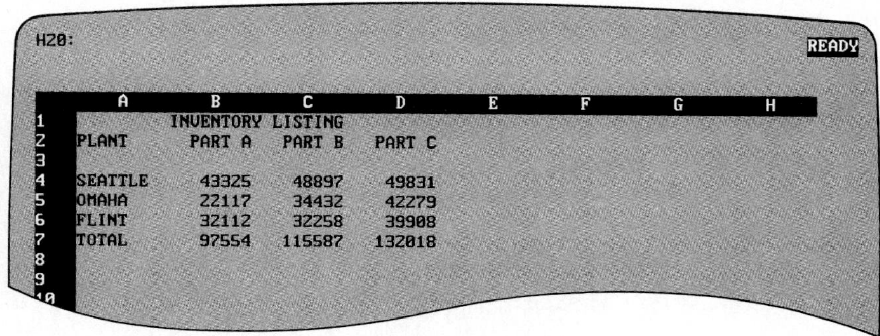


**FIGURE 1-56**
**Student Assignment 8**

## STUDENT ASSIGNMENT 9: Building a Yearly Personal Expenses Comparison Worksheet

**Instructions:** Load 1-2-3 and perform the following tasks.

1. Build the worksheet illustrated in Figure 1-57. Calculate the total expenses for THIS YEAR in column C and LAST YEAR in column D by adding the values in the cells representing the rent, food, utilities, auto, insurance, and entertainment expenses.
2. Save the worksheet. Use the file name STUS1-9.
3. Print the screen image of the worksheet.

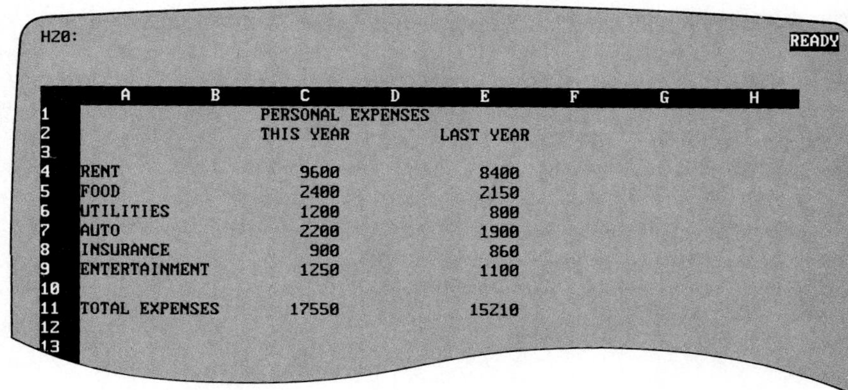


**FIGURE 1-57**
**Student Assignment 9**

## STUDENT ASSIGNMENT 10: Building a Quarterly Income and Expense Worksheet

**Instructions:** Load 1-2-3 and perform the following tasks.

1. Build the worksheet illustrated in Figure 1-58. Calculate the total income in row 10 by adding the income for gas and oil, labor, and parts. Calculate the total expenses in row 17 by adding salaries, rent, and cost of goods. Calculate the net profit in row 19 by subtracting the total expenses from the total income.
2. Save the worksheet. Use the file name STUS1-10.
3. Print the screen image of the worksheet.

### Student Assignment 10 (continued)

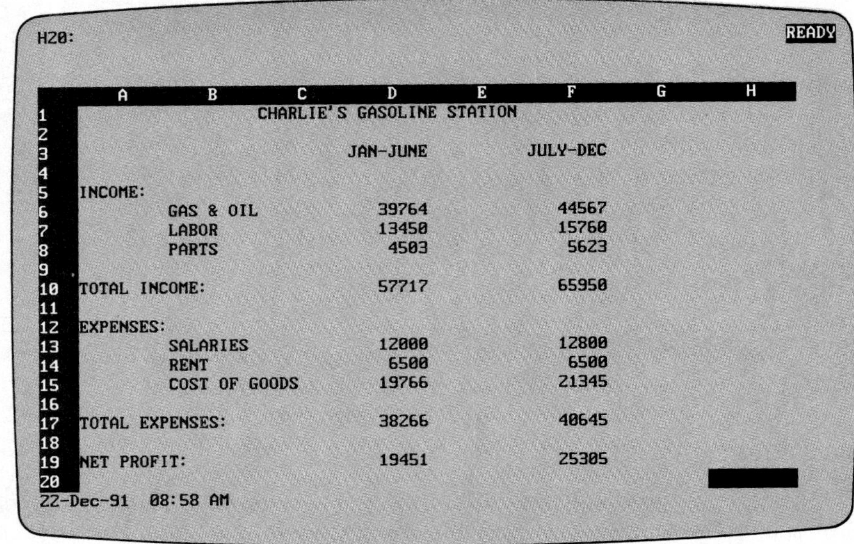

H20:
READY
A B C D E F G H
CHARLIE'S GASOLINE STATION
JAN-JUNE JULY-DEC
INCOME:
GAS & OIL 39764 44567
LABOR 13450 15760
PARTS 4503 5623
TOTAL INCOME: 57717 65950
EXPENSES:
SALARIES 12000 12800
RENT 6500 6500
COST OF GOODS 19766 21345
TOTAL EXPENSES: 38266 40645
NET PROFIT: 19451 25305
22-Dec-91 08:58 AM


**FIGURE 1-58**
Student Assignment 10

## STUDENT ASSIGNMENT 11: Using the Online Help Facility

**Instructions:** Load 1-2-3 and perform the following tasks.

1. With 1-2-3 in READY mode, press function key F1. Print the screen image.
2. Use the Down Arrow key to select the topic "Help Index" at the bottom of the screen. Press the Enter key. Read and print the image of the screen.
3. Select the following help screens: Using the Help Facility; Control Panel; Modes and Indicators; and Moving the Cell Pointer. Read and print the image of each screen.
4. Press the Esc key to quit the online help facility.

## STUDENT ASSIGNMENT 12: Changing Data in the Quarterly Income and Expense Worksheet

**Instructions:** If you did not do Student Assignment 10, do it before you begin this assignment. With the worksheet in Student Assignment 10 stored on the disk, load 1-2-3 and perform the following tasks.

1. Retrieve the worksheet STUS1-10 (see Figure 1-58) from disk. Use the command /**F**ile **R**etrieve (/FR). When the list of worksheet names displays on the menu line, use the arrow keys to move the command cursor to the worksheet name STUS1-10. Press the Enter key. The worksheet illustrated in Figure 1-58 will display on the screen.
2. Make the changes to the worksheet described in Table 1-6. Use the EDIT mode of 1-2-3. Recall that to use EDIT mode to change an entry in a cell, move the cell pointer to the cell and then press function key F2.

**TABLE 1-6 List of Corrections to the Quarterly Income and Expense Worksheet**

| CELL | CURRENT CELL CONTENTS | CHANGE THE CELL CONTENTS TO |
|---|---|---|
| C1 | CHARLIE'S GASOLINE STATION | CHUCK'S GAS STATION |
| D6 | 39764 | 39564 |
| F6 | 44567 | 40592 |
| D8 | 4503 | 45003 |
| F8 | 5623 | 45623 |
| D13 | 12000 | 22000 |
| F13 | 12800 | 19765 |

As you edit the values in the cells containing numeric data, keep an eye on the total income, total expenses, and net profit cells. The values in these cells are based on formulas that reference the cells you are editing. You will see that each time a new value is entered into a cell referenced by a formula, 1-2-3 automatically recalculates a new value for the formula. It then stores the new value in the cell assigned the formula. This automatic recalculation of formulas is one of the more powerful aspects of 1-2-3.

After you have successfully made the changes listed in Table 1-6, the net profit for Jan-June in cell D19 should equal 49751 and the net profit for July-Dec should equal 54365.

3. Save the worksheet. Use the file name STUS1-12.
4. Print the screen image of the worksheet on the printer.

# Project 2

## Formatting and Printing a Worksheet

### Objectives

You will have mastered the material in this project when you can:

- Retrieve a worksheet from disk
- Increase the width of the columns in a worksheet
- Define a range of cells
- Format a worksheet
- Enter repeating characters into a cell using the Backslash key
- Copy one range of cells to another range of cells
- Add the contents of a range using the SUM function
- Determine a percentage
- Print a partial or complete worksheet without window borders
- Print the cell-formulas version of a worksheet
- Display the formulas assigned to cells, rather than their numeric results

The Sales Report worksheet created in Project 1 contains the revenue, costs, and profit for each of the three months of the first quarter, but it is not presented in the most readable manner. For example, as you can see in Figure 2-1, the columns are too close together and the numbers are displayed as whole numbers, even though they are dollar figures.

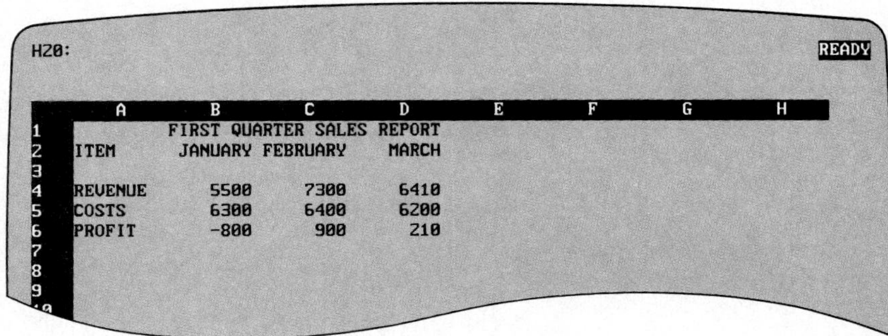


**FIGURE 2-1**
**The worksheet we completed in Project 1.**

In this project we will use the formatting capabilities of 1-2-3 to make the worksheet more presentable and easier to read. We will also add summary totals for the quarter, using formulas. As shown in Figure 2-2, the total revenue in cell B12 is the sum of the revenue values for January, February, and March. The total cost in cell B13 is the sum of the cost values for January, February, and March; and the total profit in cell B14 is the sum of the profit values for January, February, and March. The percent profit in cell B15 is determined by dividing the total profit by the total revenue. After the worksheet is complete, we will print it without the window borders.

E20: READY

| | A | B | C | D | E |
|---|---|---|---|---|---|
| 1 | | FIRST QUARTER SALES REPORT | | | |
| 2 | ITEM | JANUARY | FEBRUARY | MARCH | |
| 3 | | | | | |
| 4 | REVENUE | 5500.00 | 7300.00 | 6410.00 | |
| 5 | COSTS | 6300.00 | 6400.00 | 6200.00 | |
| 6 | PROFIT | -800.00 | 900.00 | 210.00 | |
| 7 | | | | | |
| 8 | ------------------------- | ------------- | ------------- | ------------- | |
| 9 | | | | | |
| 10 | QUARTER RESULTS | | | | |
| 11 | | | | | |
| 12 | TOTAL REVENUE | $19,210.00 | | | |
| 13 | TOTAL COSTS | $18,900.00 | | | |
| 14 | TOTAL PROFIT | $310.00 | | | |
| 15 | % PROFIT | 1.6% | | | |
| 16 | | | | | |

**FIGURE 2-2** The worksheet we will complete in Project 2.

## RETRIEVING A WORKSHEET FROM DISK

Recall that at the end of Project 1, we used the Save command to store the worksheet shown in Figure 2-1 on disk under the name PROJS-1.WK1. Since Project 2 involves making modifications to this stored worksheet, we can eliminate retyping the whole worksheet and save a lot of time by retrieving it from disk and placing it into main computer memory.

After booting the computer and loading the 1-2-3 program, retrieve the worksheet PROJS-1 from the data disk. To retrieve the worksheet, enter the command /**F**ile **R**etrieve (/FR). First, press the Slash key (/) as illustrated in Figure 2-3. This causes 1-2-3 to display the command menu on the input line at the top of the screen. Next, use the Right Arrow key to move the command cursor to the word File. The result of this activity is shown in Figure 2-4 on the next page. With the command cursor on the word File, the File menu displays on the menu line, immediately below the command menu. To select the File menu, press the Enter key or type the letter F.

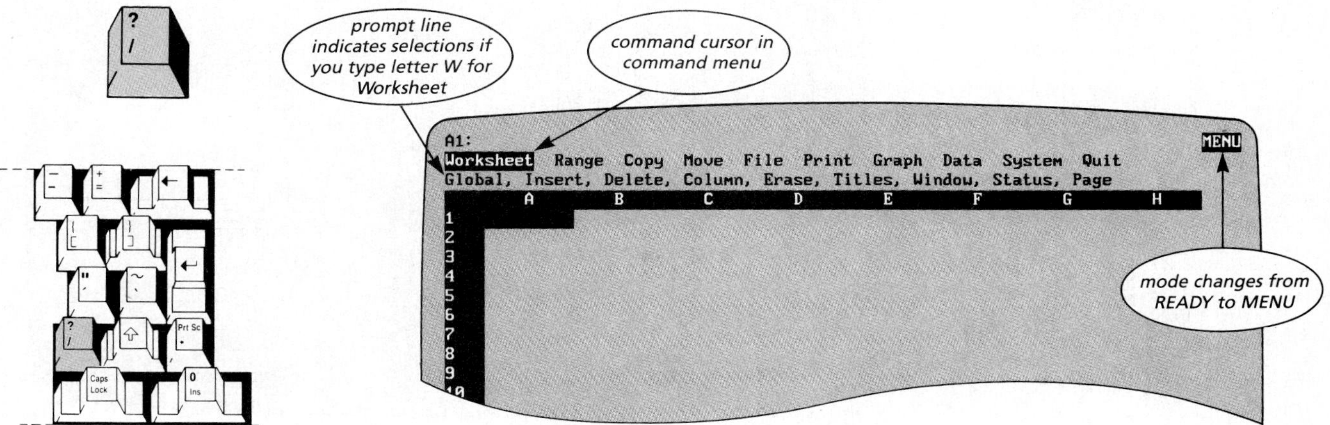


**FIGURE 2-3** Step 1 of retrieving a worksheet from disk—press the Slash key (/).

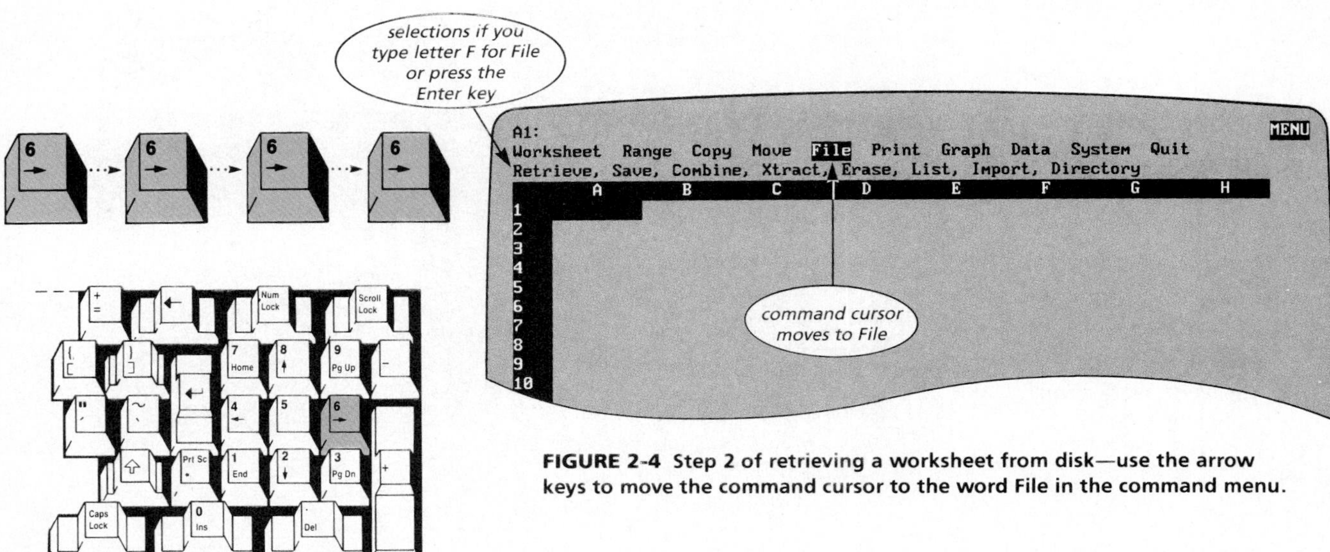


FIGURE 2-4 Step 2 of retrieving a worksheet from disk—use the arrow keys to move the command cursor to the word File in the command menu.

Press the Enter key. The command cursor is now active in the File menu as illustrated in Figure 2-5. The Retrieve command is the first command in the list. The message on the menu line indicates the function of this command. With the command cursor on the Retrieve command, type the letter R for Retrieve.

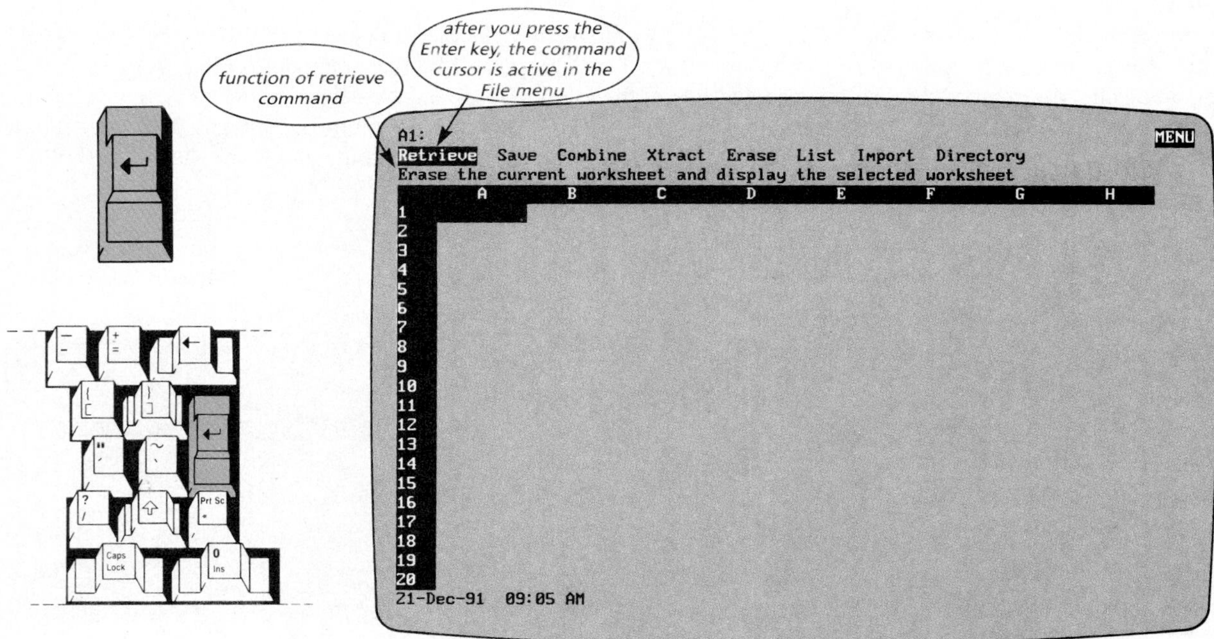


FIGURE 2-5 Step 3 of retrieving a worksheet from disk—press the Enter key to select the File command.

As illustrated in Figure 2-6, 1-2-3 displays on the menu line an alphabetized list of the file names on the default drive that have the extension .WK1. This helps you remember the names of the worksheets stored on the data disk. The list includes all the worksheets you were told to save in Project 1, including PROJS-1.WK1.

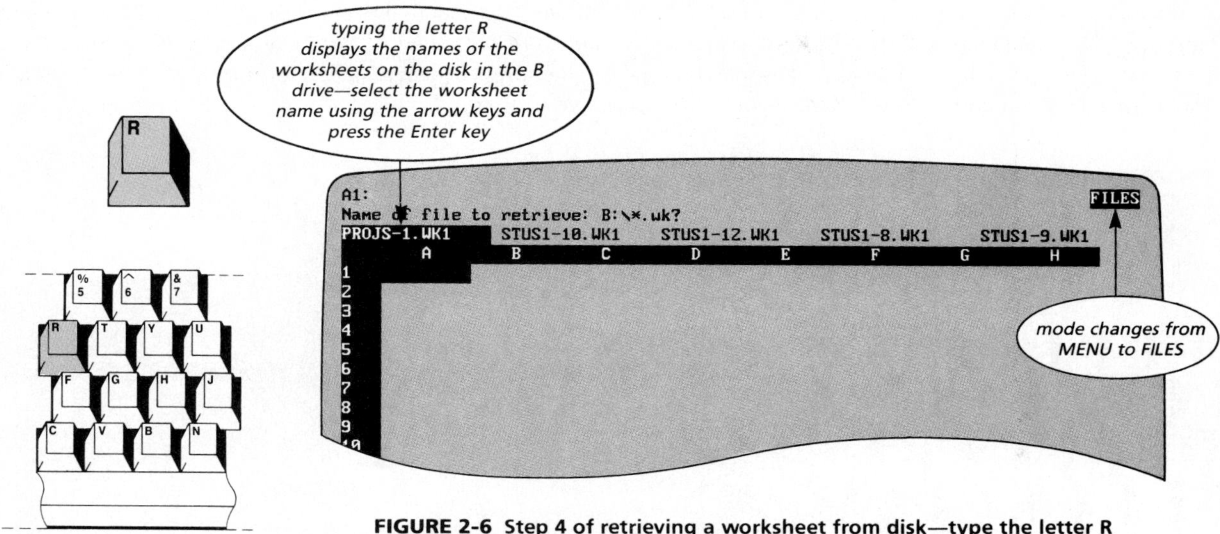


**FIGURE 2-6 Step 4 of retrieving a worksheet from disk—type the letter R for Retrieve, select the worksheet name and press the Enter key.**

One way to select the worksheet you want to retrieve is to type PROJS-1 on the input line and press the Enter key. Better yet, because the command cursor is on the file name PROJS-1.WK1 in the list in Figure 2-6, press the Enter key. This method saves keying time. While 1-2-3 is accessing the worksheet, the mode indicator in the upper right corner of the screen changes to WAIT and the red light flashes on the default drive. After the worksheet is retrieved, the screen appears as shown in Figure 2-1.

According to Figure 2-2, all the new labels are in capitals. Therefore, before modifying the worksheet, press the Caps Lock key.

The tasks in this project are to widen the columns, format the dollar amounts, and add the quarter results. The tasks may be completed in any sequence. Let's complete them in the following sequence:

1. Widen the columns from 9 characters to 13 characters to allow the quarter result titles and other numeric data to fit in the columns.
2. Change the numeric representations for the three months to dollars and cents—two digits to the right of the decimal place.
3. Determine the quarter results.
4. Change the percent profit to a number in percent.
5. Change the numeric representations of the quarter results to dollars and cents with a leading dollar sign.

## CHANGING THE WIDTH OF THE COLUMNS

When 1-2-3 first executes and the blank worksheet appears on the screen, all the columns have a default width of nine characters. But you might want to change the width of the columns to make the worksheet easier to read or to ensure that entries will display properly in the cells to which they are assigned.

There are two ways to change the width of the columns in a worksheet. First, make a global change, which uniformly increases or decreases the width of all the columns in the worksheet. **Global** means the entire worksheet. Second, make a change in the width of one column at a time.

## Changing the Width of All the Columns

To change the width of all the columns, enter the command /Worksheet Global Column-Width (/WGC). When you press the Slash key, the command menu displays at the top of the screen with the first command, Worksheet, highlighted as shown earlier in Figure 2-3. The **Worksheet menu** displays immediately below the command menu. Note that the first command in the Worksheet menu is Global. This command makes the changes to the entire worksheet. Therefore, type the letter W for Worksheet to move the command cursor to the Worksheet menu, as shown in Figure 2-7.

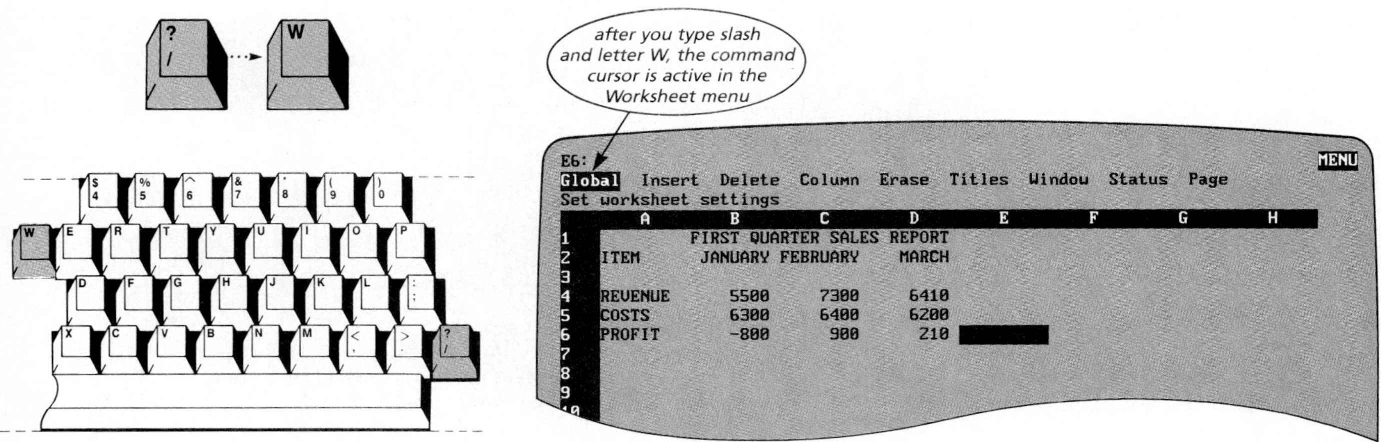


**FIGURE 2-7** Step 1 of increasing the width of the columns—press the Slash key (/) and type the letter W.

Type the letter G for Global. This causes the **Global menu** to display on the input line. Next, use the Right Arrow key to move the command cursor to Column-Width. Now the menu line explains the purpose of the Column-Width command. This procedure is illustrated in Figure 2-8.

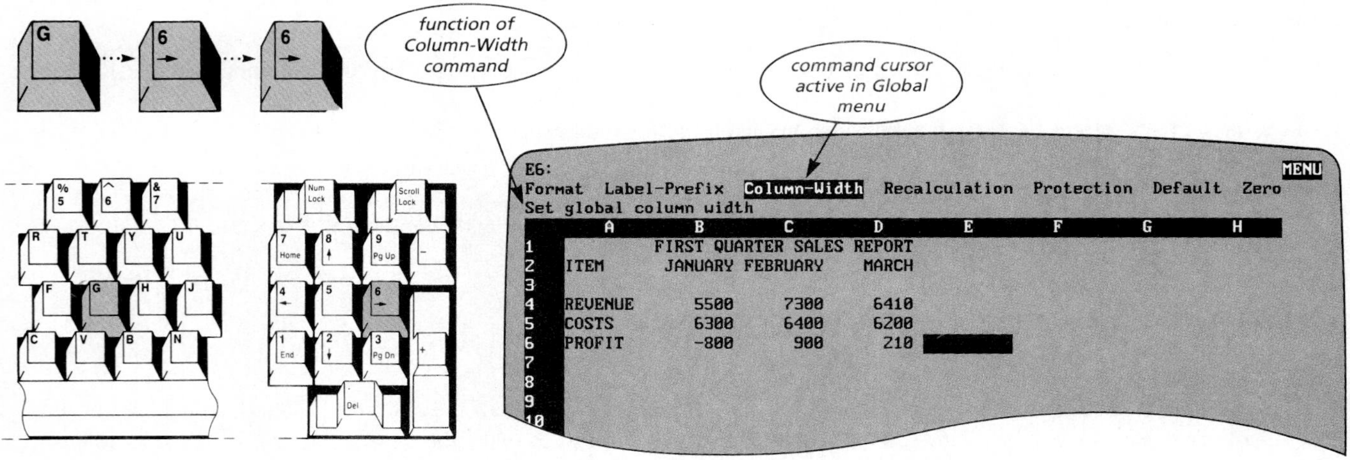


**FIGURE 2-8** Step 2 of increasing the width of the columns—type the letter G and use the Right Arrow key to move the command cursor to Column-Width in the Global menu.

Before typing the letter C for Column-Width, if you decided that you did not want to increase the width of the columns, how many times would you have to press the Esc key to *back out* of the command mode in Figure 2-8 and return to the READY mode? If your answer is three, you're right—once for the Global command, once for the Worksheet command, and once for the Slash key (/).

Now type the letter C for Column-Width. The prompt message "Enter global column width (1..240): 9" displays on the input line at the top of the screen. This message is illustrated on the screen in Figure 2-9. The numbers "1–240" define the range of valid entries. The number 9 following the colon indicates the current global (default) column width.

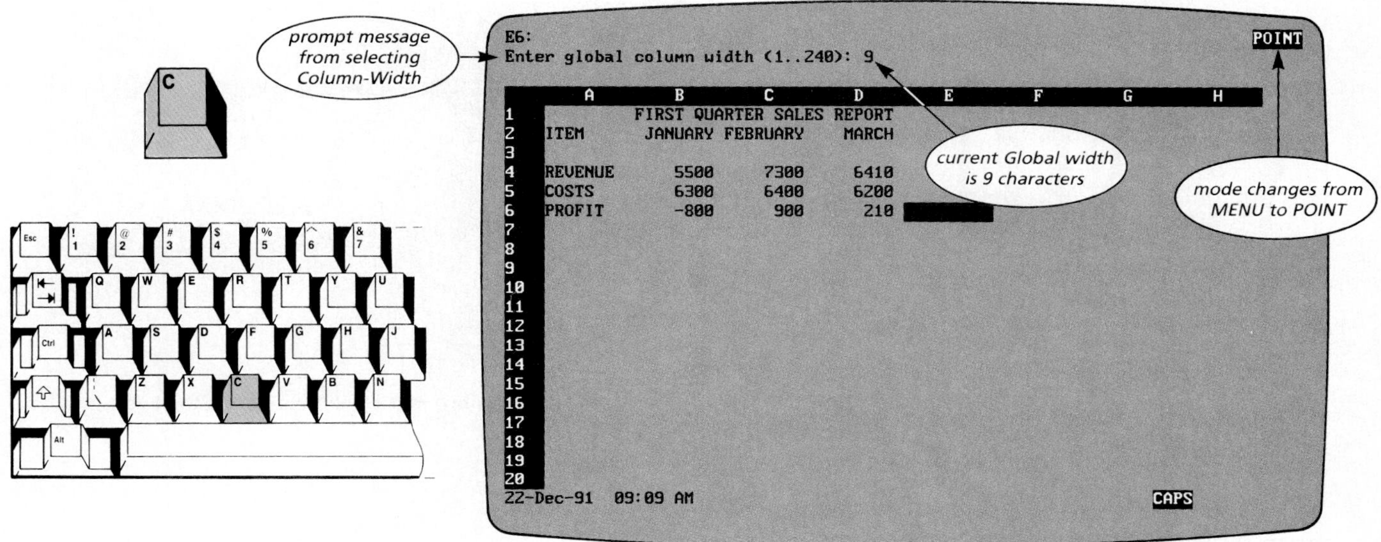


**FIGURE 2-9** **Step 3 of increasing the width of the columns—type the letter C for Column-Width.**

Type the number 13 as shown in Figure 2-10, then press the Enter key. An alternative to typing the number 13 is to use the Right and Left arrow keys to increase or decrease the number on the input line.

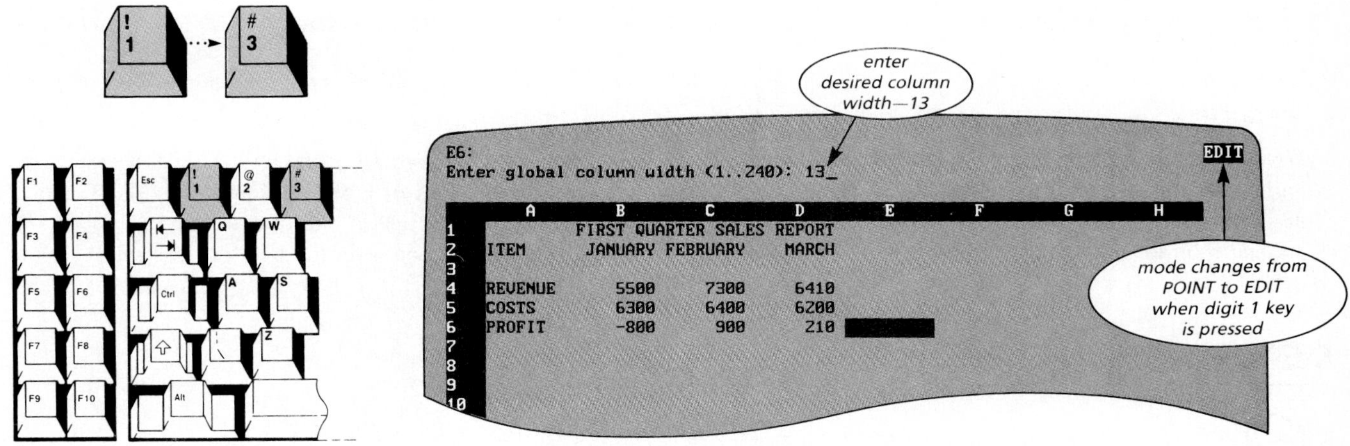


**FIGURE 2-10** **Step 4 of increasing the width of the columns—enter the number 13.**

Figure 2-11 illustrates the worksheet with the new column width of 13 characters. Compare Figure 2-11 to Figure 2-1. Because the columns in Figure 2-11 are wider, the worksheet is easier to read. But because the columns are wider, fewer show on the screen.

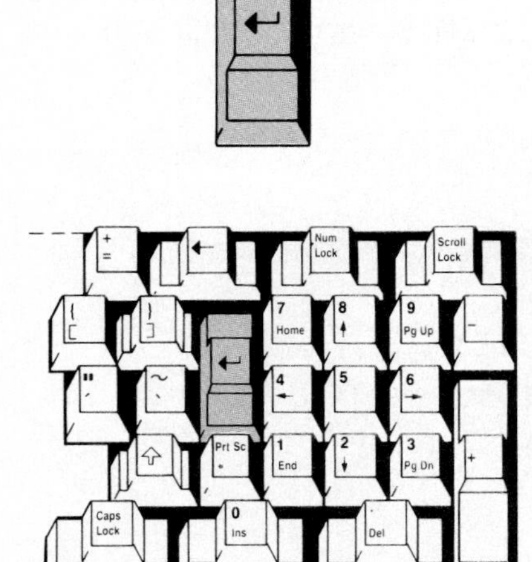

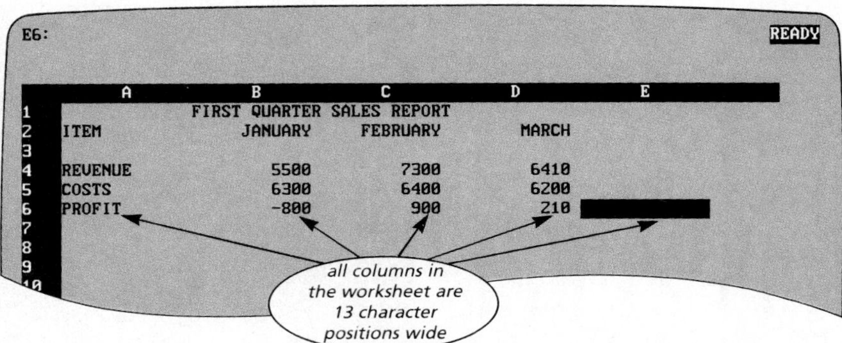


**FIGURE 2-11** Step 5 of increasing the width of the columns—press the Enter key.

## Changing the Width of One Column at a Time

You can change the width of one column at a time in the worksheet. Let's change the width of column A to 20 characters while leaving the width of the other columns at 13 characters. To change the width of column A to 20 characters, do the following:

1. Press the Home key to move the cell pointer into column A.
2. Type the command /**W**orksheet **C**olumn **S**et-Width (/WCS). The Slash key switches 1-2-3 to the command mode. The letter W selects the Worksheet command. The letter C selects the command Column and the letter S selects the command Set-Width.
3. In response to the prompt message "Enter column width (1..240): 13" on the input line, type the number 20 and press the Enter key.

Now column A is 20 characters wide while the other columns in the worksheet are 13 characters wide. Let's change column A back to the default width of 13 characters. With the cell pointer in column A, enter the command /**W**orksheet **C**olumn **R**eset-Width (/WCR). This command changes column A back to the default width—13 characters. Use the GOTO command to move the cell pointer back to cell E6, where it was before we set and then reset the width of column A.

# DEFINING A RANGE

Our next step is to format the monthly dollar amounts. The Format command requires you to specify the cells you want to format. For this reason, you need to understand the term *range* before using the Format command.

A **range** in 1-2-3 means one or more cells on which an operation can take place. A range may be a single cell, a series of adjacent cells in a row or column, or a rectangular group of adjacent cells. Hence, a range may consist of one cell or many cells. However, a range cannot be made up of cells that only run diagonally or are separated. Figure 2-12 illustrates several valid and invalid ranges of cells.

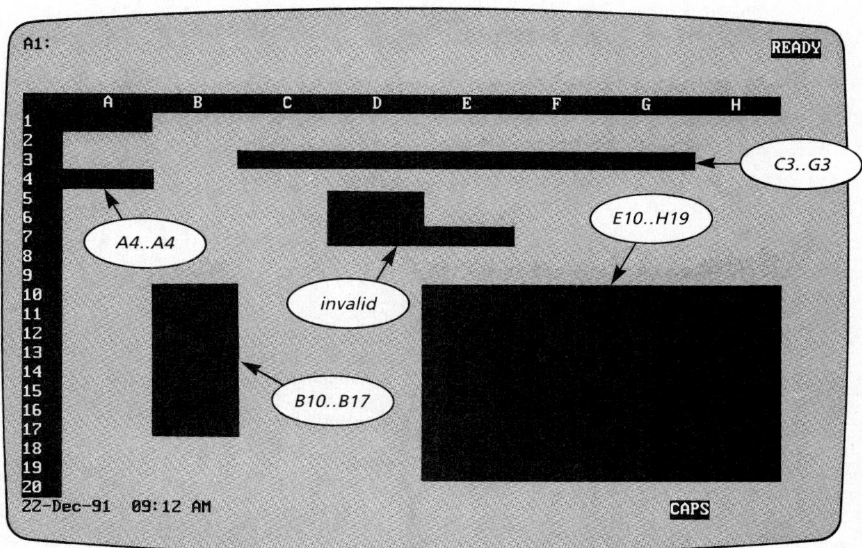


**FIGURE 2-12**
**Valid and invalid ranges.**

When you are asked by 1-2-3 to specify a range, you simply type the cell address for the first cell in the range, followed by a **period** (.), followed by the cell address for the last cell in the range. If a range defines a rectangular group of cells, any pair of diagonally opposite corner cells may be used to identify it. For example, the upper left cell and the lower right cell of the rectangular group of cells identify the range. Table 2-1 summarizes the ranges described in Figure 2-12.

**TABLE 2-1 A Summary of the Ranges Specified in Figure 2-12**

| RANGE | COMMENT |
|---|---|
| A4..A4 | The range is made up of one cell, A4. |
| C3..G3 | The range is made up of five adjacent cells in row 3. The five cells are C3, D3, E3, F3, and G3. |
| B10..B17 | The range is made up of eight adjacent cells in column B. The eight cells are B10, B11, B12, B13, B14, B15, B16, and B17. |
| E10..H19 | The range is made up of a rectangular group of cells. The upper left cell (E10) and the lower right cell (H19) define the rectangle. The ranges H19..E10, H10..E19, and E19..H10 define the same range as E10..H19. |

Now that you know how to define a range, we can move on to the next step in Project 2: formatting the numeric values in the worksheet.

## FORMATTING NUMERIC VALUES

The Format command is used to control the manner in which numeric values appear in the worksheet. As shown in Figure 2-2, we want to change the numeric values in the range B4 through D6 to display as dollars and cents with two digits to the right of the decimal point.

## Invoking the Format Command

There are two ways to invoke the Format command. First, you can use the series of commands /**W**orksheet **G**lobal **F**ormat (/WGF) to format all the cells in the worksheet the same way. Second, you can use the commands /**R**ange **F**ormat (/RF) to format just a particular range of cells. Since this project involves formatting a range rather than all the cells in the worksheet, type /RF to activate the command cursor in the Format menu as shown in Figure 2-13. The **Format menu** on the input line lists the different ways to format a range. As indicated on the third line of the control panel, the first format type in the menu, Fixed, formats cells to a fixed number of decimal places. This is the format we want to use to display the monthly amounts to two decimal places. Therefore, type the letter F for Fixed.

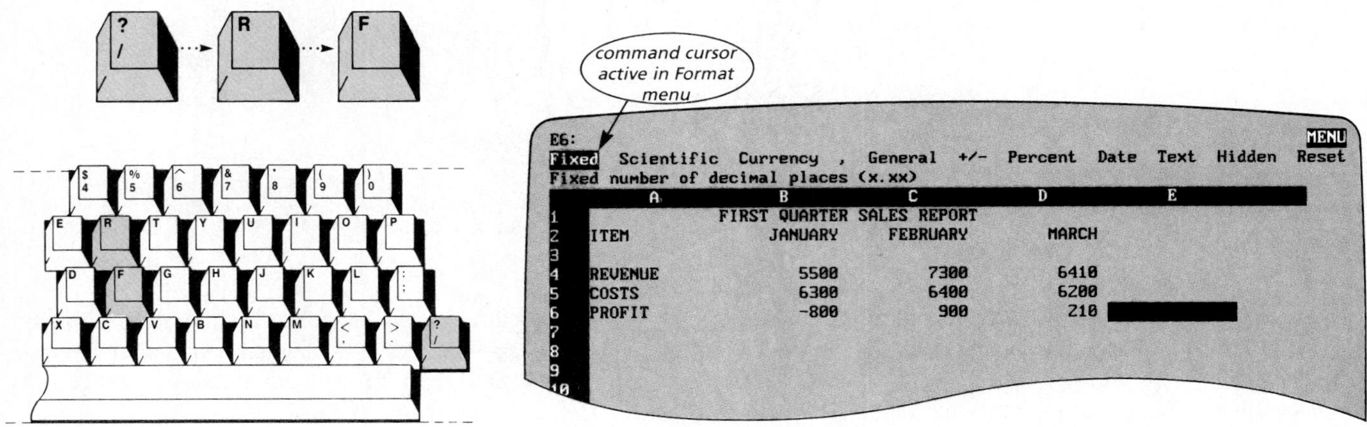


**FIGURE 2-13 Step 1 of formatting a range of cells—press the Slash key (/) and type the letters R for Range and F for Format.**

As shown in Figure 2-14, 1-2-3 displays the message "Enter number of decimal places (0..15): 2" on the input line at the top of the screen. Since most spreadsheet applications require two decimal positions, 1-2-3 displays 2 as the entry to save you time. Press the Enter key to enter two decimal positions. Next, 1-2-3 changes to POINT mode and displays the message "Enter range to format: E6..E6" (see Figure 2-15). The range E6..E6 displays at the end of the input line because the cell pointer is at cell E6. Enter the range by typing B4.D6, or use the arrow keys to select the range. (Don't be concerned that 1-2-3 displays two periods between the cell address when you press the Period key once. It is the program's way of displaying a range.) Using the arrow keys to select a range is called **pointing**. Let's use the pointing method, because it requires less effort.

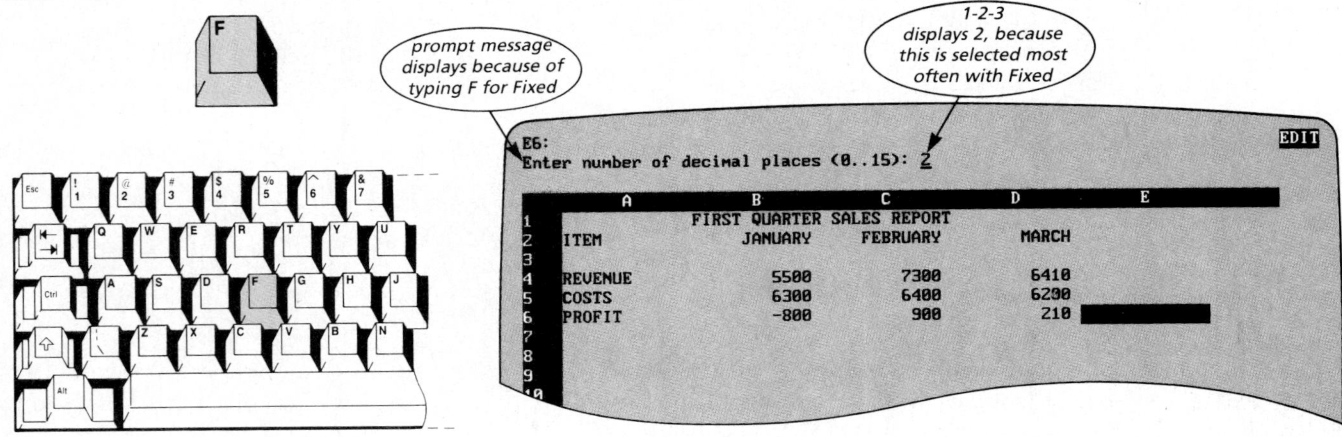


**FIGURE 2-14 Step 2 of formatting a range of cells—type the letter F for Fixed and 1-2-3 displays a prompt message on the input line.**

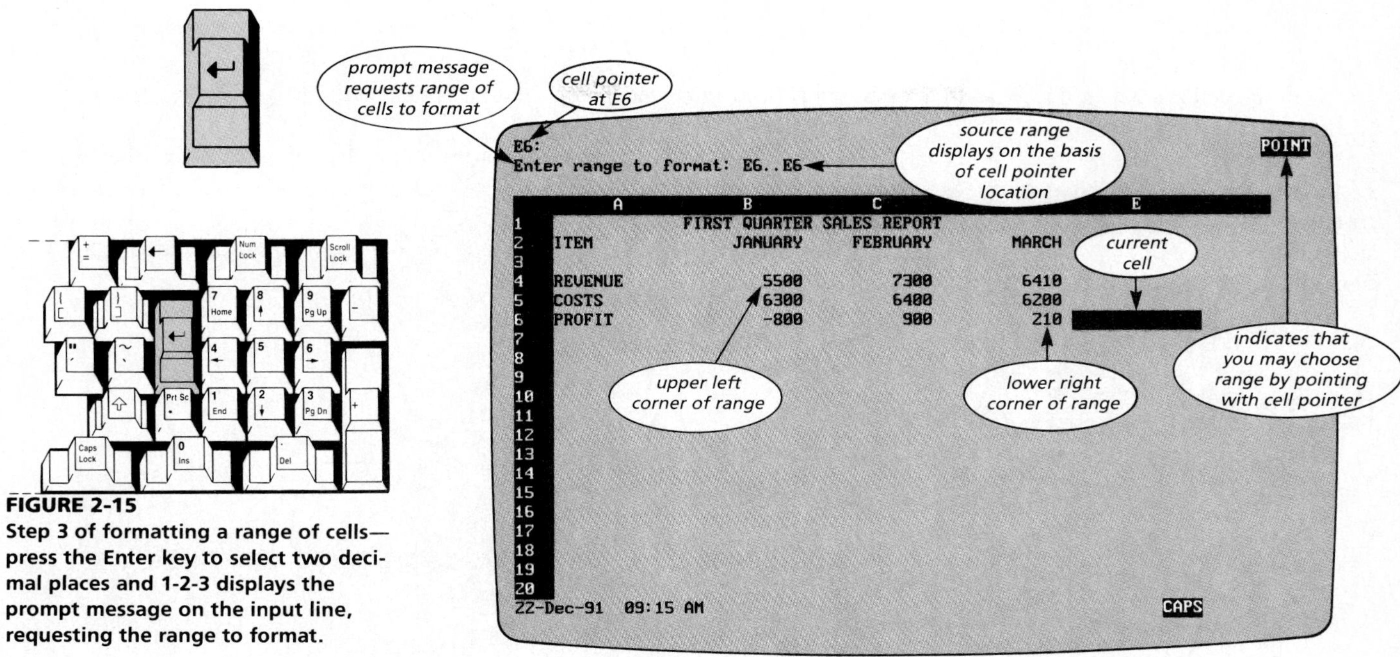


**FIGURE 2-15**
**Step 3 of formatting a range of cells—press the Enter key to select two decimal places and 1-2-3 displays the prompt message on the input line, requesting the range to format.**

## Selecting a Range by Pointing

To select a range by pointing, first press the Backspace key (or Esc key) to change the default entry on the input line in Figure 2-15 from E6..E6 to E6. Next, use the arrow keys to move the cell pointer to B4, the upper left corner cell of the desired range. This procedure is shown in Figure 2-16.

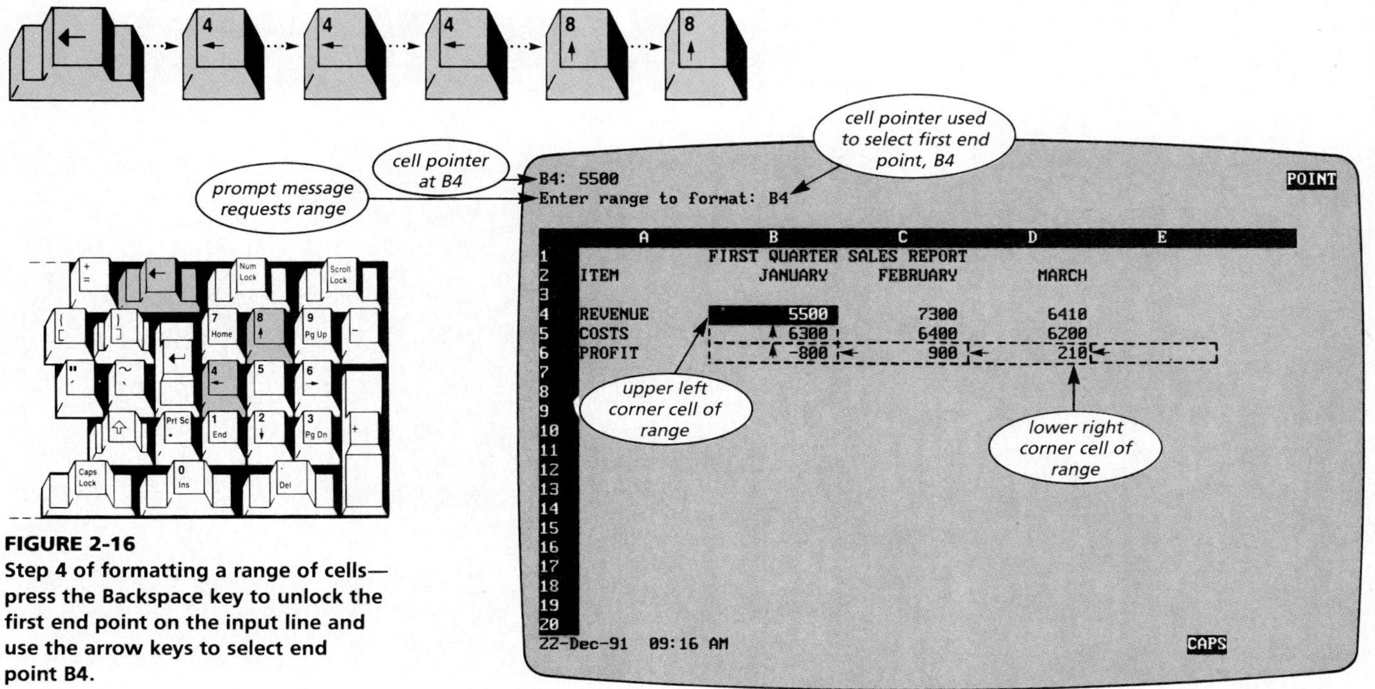


**FIGURE 2-16**
**Step 4 of formatting a range of cells—press the Backspace key to unlock the first end point on the input line and use the arrow keys to select end point B4.**

With the cell pointer at B4, press the Period key to *lock in* or *anchor* the first end point, B4. The B4 on the input line changes to B4..B4.

Now use the arrow keys to move the cell pointer to cell D6, the lower right corner of the desired range. Press the Down Arrow key twice and the Right Arrow key twice. As the cell pointer moves, a reverse video rectangle forms over the range covered. The range on the input line changes from B4..B4 to B4..D6 (see Figure 2-17). Press the Enter key. 1-2-3 immediately displays the monthly values in cells B4, C4, D4, B5, C5, D5, B6, C6, and D6 with two decimal places (dollars and cents). Everything else in the worksheet remains the same as shown in Figure 2-18.

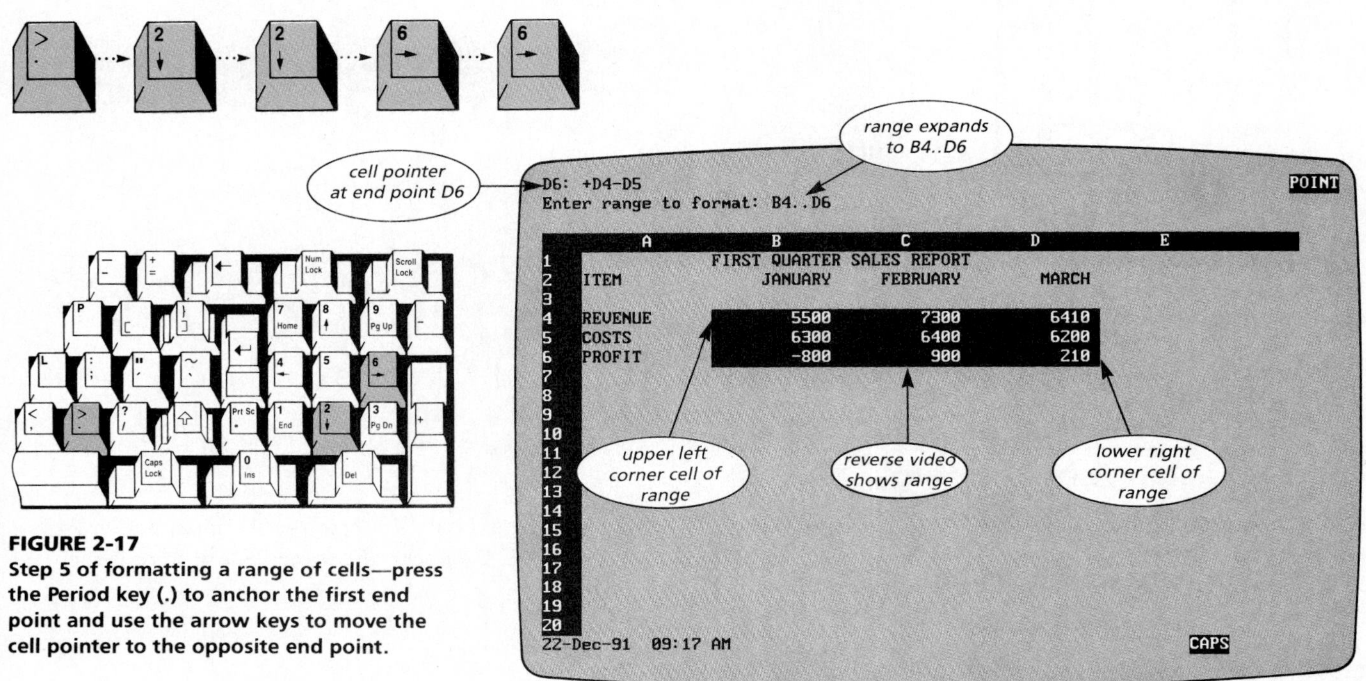


**FIGURE 2-17**
**Step 5 of formatting a range of cells—press the Period key (.) to anchor the first end point and use the arrow keys to move the cell pointer to the opposite end point.**

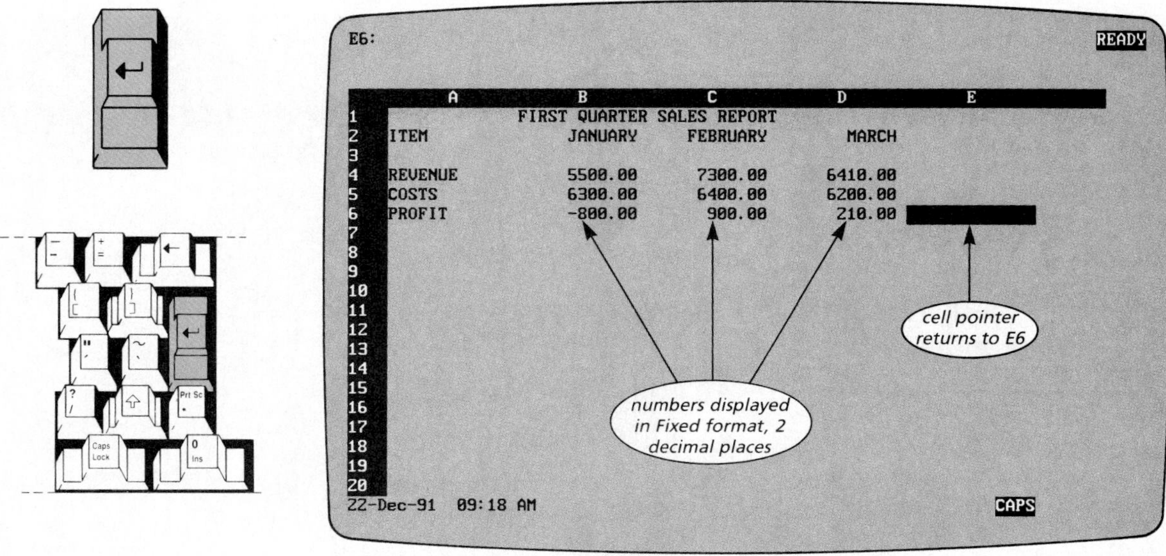


**FIGURE 2-18 Step 6 of formatting a range—press the Enter key and the numbers in the range B4..D6 display in Fixed format.**

We could have used three other ways to describe the rectangular group of cells B4..D6 to 1-2-3. B6..D4 and D4..B6 are two other ways. Can you identify the third way?

## Summary of Format Commands

You can format numbers in cells in a variety of ways using the /**W**orksheet **G**lobal **F**ormat (/WGF) or /**R**ange **F**ormat (/RF) commands. Table 2-2 summarizes the various format options. You will find Table 2-2 helpful when you begin formatting your own worksheets. Also, remember that 1-2-3 rounds a number to the rightmost position if any digits are lost because of the format or number of decimal positions chosen.

**TABLE 2-2 Format Types for Numeric Values in the Format Menu**

| MENU ITEM | DESCRIPTION |
|---|---|
| Fixed | Displays numbers to a specified number of decimal places. Negative values are displayed with a leading minus sign. Examples: 38; 0.912; –45.67. |
| Scientific | Displays numbers in a form called **scientific notation**. The letter E stands for "times 10 to the power." Examples: 3.7E+01; –2.357E–30. |
| Currency | Displays numbers preceded by a dollar sign next to the leftmost digit, with a specified number of decimal places (0–15), and uses commas to group the integer portion of the number by thousands. Negative numbers display in parentheses. Examples: $1,234.56; $0.98; $23,934,876.15; ($48.34). |
| , | The , (comma) is the same as the Currency format, except the dollar sign does not display. Examples: 2,123.00; 5,456,023.34; (22,000). |
| General | This is the default format in which a number is stored when it is entered into a cell. Trailing zeros are suppressed and leading integer zeros display. Negative numbers display with a leading minus sign. Examples: 23.981; 0.563; 23401; –500.45. |
| +/– | Displays a single horizontal bar graph composed of plus (+) or minus (–) signs that indicate the sign of the number and the magnitude of the number. One plus or minus sign displays for each unit value. Only the integer portion of the number is used. Examples: + + + + + + for 6; --- for –3.8. |
| Percent | Displays numbers in percent form. Examples: 34% for 0.34; .11% for 0.0011; –13.245% for –0.13245. |
| Date | Used to format cells that contain a date or time. |
| Text | Displays formulas rather than their values. Numbers appear in General format. Examples: +B4–B5; 2*(F5 – G3). |
| Hidden | Prevents the display of the cell contents on the screen and when printed. To see what's in a hidden cell, move the pointer to that cell. The contents will display on the status line. |
| Reset | Resets cells back to Global format. |

## Determining the Format Assigned to a Cell

You can determine the format assigned to a cell by the Range Format command by moving the cell pointer to that cell. The format displays on the status line in the upper left corner of the screen, next to the cell address. In Figure 2-19, the cell pointer is at cell D6. Format F2 displays on the status line in parentheses next to the cell address. F2 is an abbreviation for the format "Fixed, 2 decimal places." Recall that we assigned this format to cell D4 in Figures 2-13 through 2-18.

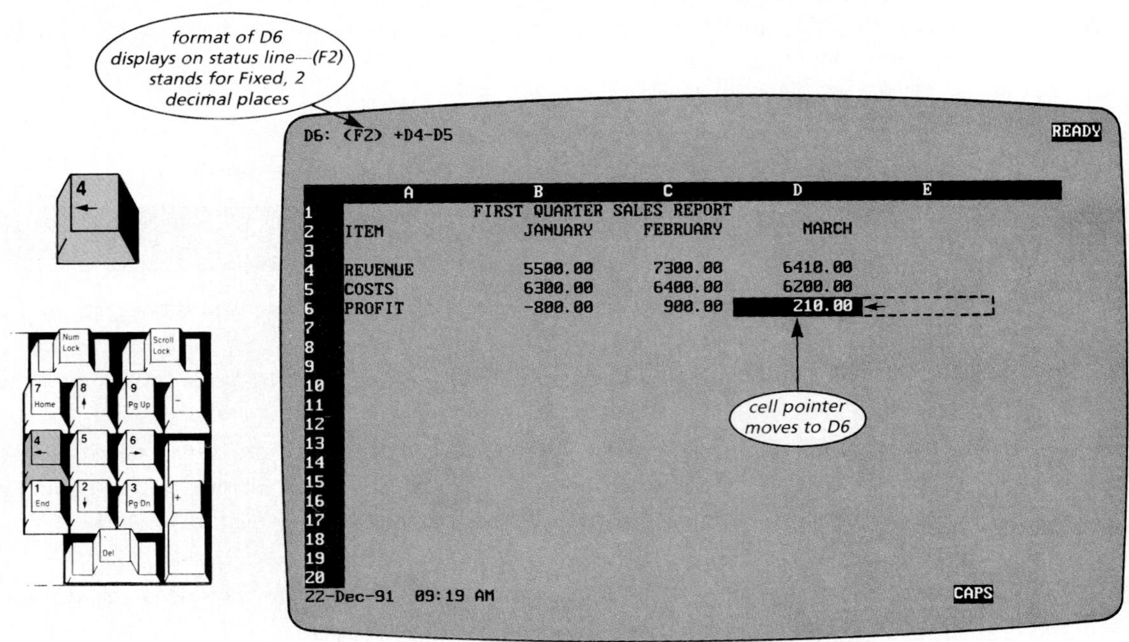


**FIGURE 2-19 The format assigned to a cell displays on the status line when the cell pointer is on the cell.**

# REPEATING CHARACTERS IN A CELL

In Figure 2-2, row 8 contains a dashed line. We will add the dashed line to the worksheet using **repeating characters**—characters that are repeated throughout a cell.

To enter the dashed line, move the cell pointer to cell A8 using the GOTO command. Recall that function key F5 invokes the GOTO command. Next, enter the cell address A8 and press the Enter key. The cell pointer immediately moves to cell A8 as shown in Figure 2-20.

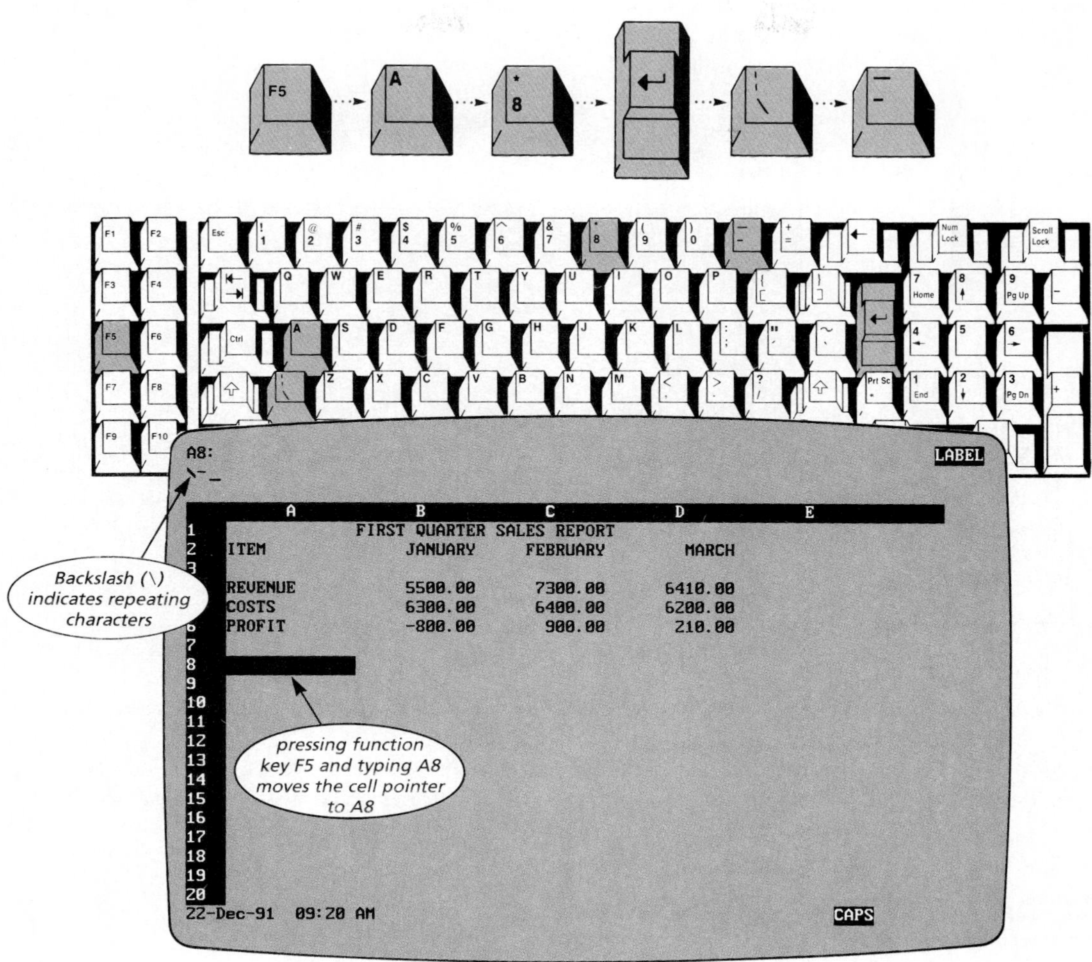


**FIGURE 2-20 Moving the cell pointer to A8 and entering a repeating dash on the input line.**

With the cell pointer at A8, press the Backslash key (\). The **Backslash key** signals 1-2-3 that the character or sequence of characters that follow it on the input line are to be repeated throughout the cell. Repeating the minus sign (-) creates the dashed line shown in Figure 2-2. Therefore, immediately after the Backslash key, press the Minus Sign key once as illustrated at the top of the screen in Figure 2-20.

To enter the repeating dash, press the Enter key. The dash repeats throughout cell A8 as shown in Figure 2-21. Note that the Backslash key is not included as part of the cell entry. Like the quotation mark ("), circumflex (^), and apostrophe ('), the backslash (\) is used as the first character that instructs 1-2-3 what to do with the characters that follow on the input line.

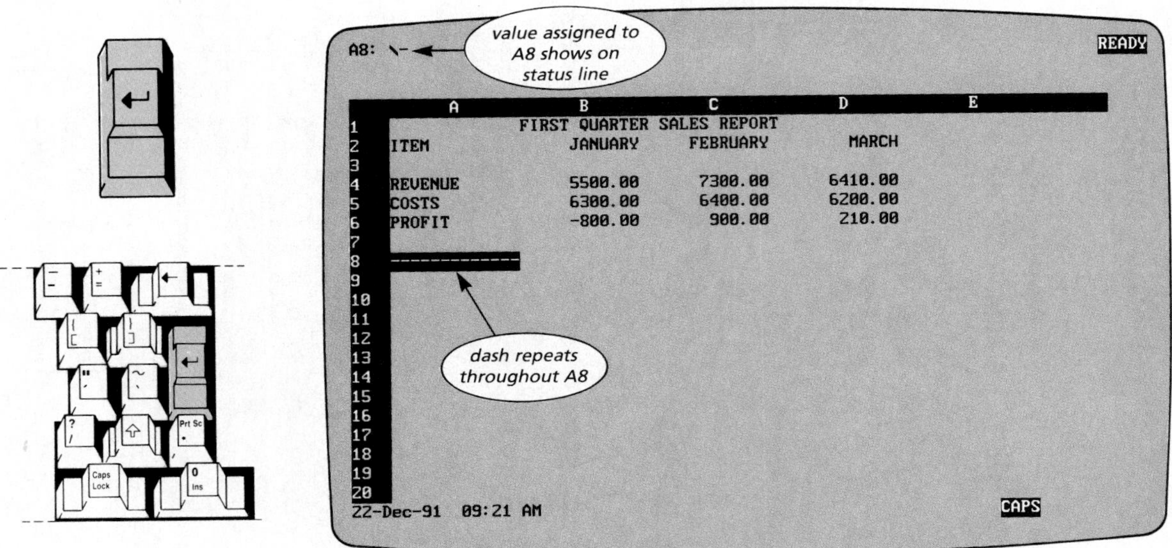


**FIGURE 2-21** **Press the Enter key to assign the repeating dash to cell A8.**

We still need to extend the dashed line through cells B8, C8, and D8. We can move the cell pointer to each individual cell and make the same entry we made in cell A8, or we can use the Copy command. Let's use the Copy command.

## REPLICATION—THE COPY COMMAND

The /Copy command (/C) is used to copy or replicate the contents of one group of cells to another group of cells. This command is one of the most useful because it can save you both time and keystrokes when you build a worksheet. We will use the Copy command to copy the dashes in cell A8 to cells B8 through D8. Type the Slash key (/) to place 1-2-3 in the command mode. In the command menu list, the Copy command is the third one. Type the letter C to invoke the Copy command.

### Source Range

When the Copy command is selected, the prompt message "Enter range to copy FROM: A8..A8" displays on the input line as shown in Figure 2-22. The **source range** is the range we want to copy. Since A8 is the cell that we want to copy to B8 through D8, press the Enter key (see Figure 2-23).

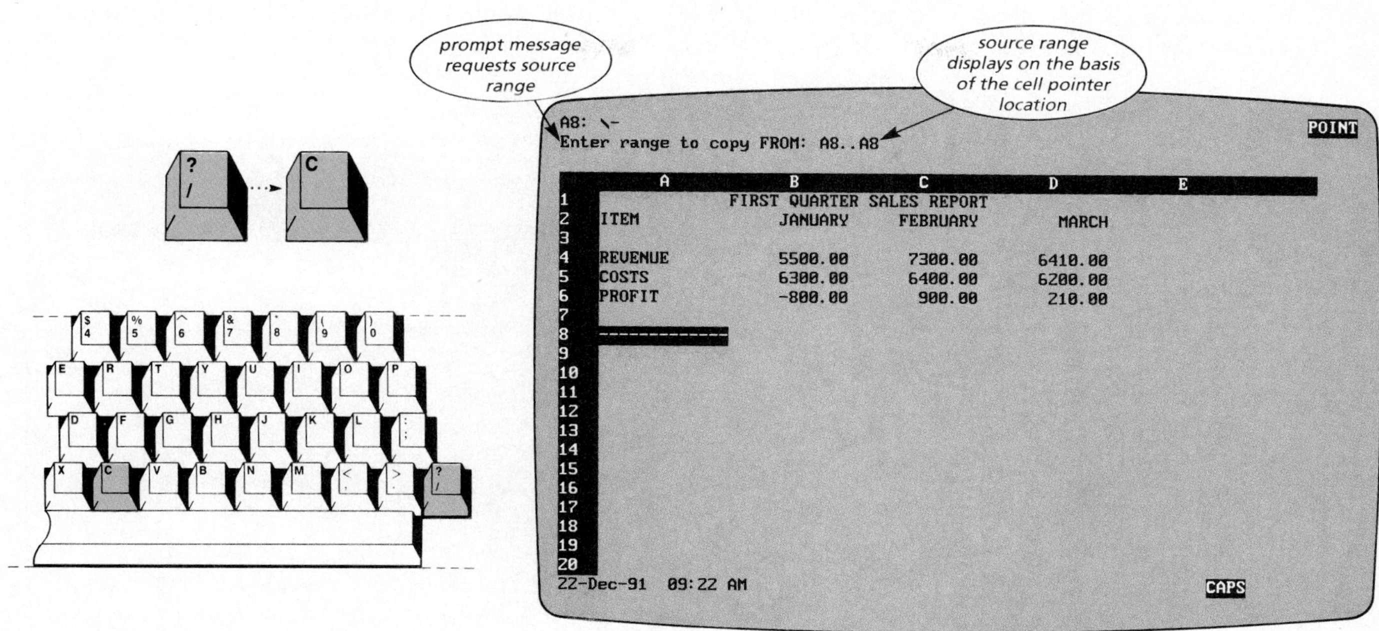


**FIGURE 2-22** Step 1 of copying a range of cells—press the Slash key (/) and type the letter C for Copy.

## Destination Range

After you press the Enter key, the prompt message "Enter range to copy TO: A8" displays on the input line as shown in Figure 2-23. The **destination range** is the range to which we want to copy the source range.

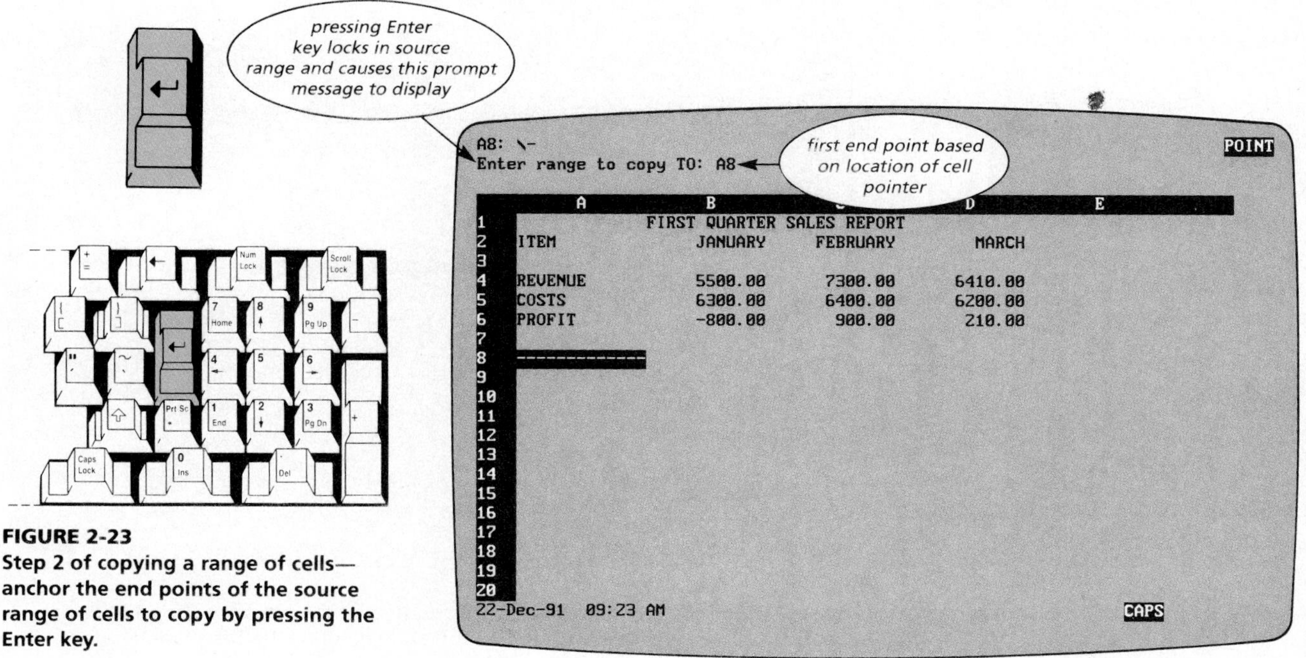


**FIGURE 2-23**
**Step 2 of copying a range of cells—anchor the end points of the source range of cells to copy by pressing the Enter key.**

Move the cell pointer to B8, the left end point of the range to copy to (see Figure 2-24). Note that following the prompt message on the input line, the cell address is now B8, the location of the cell pointer.

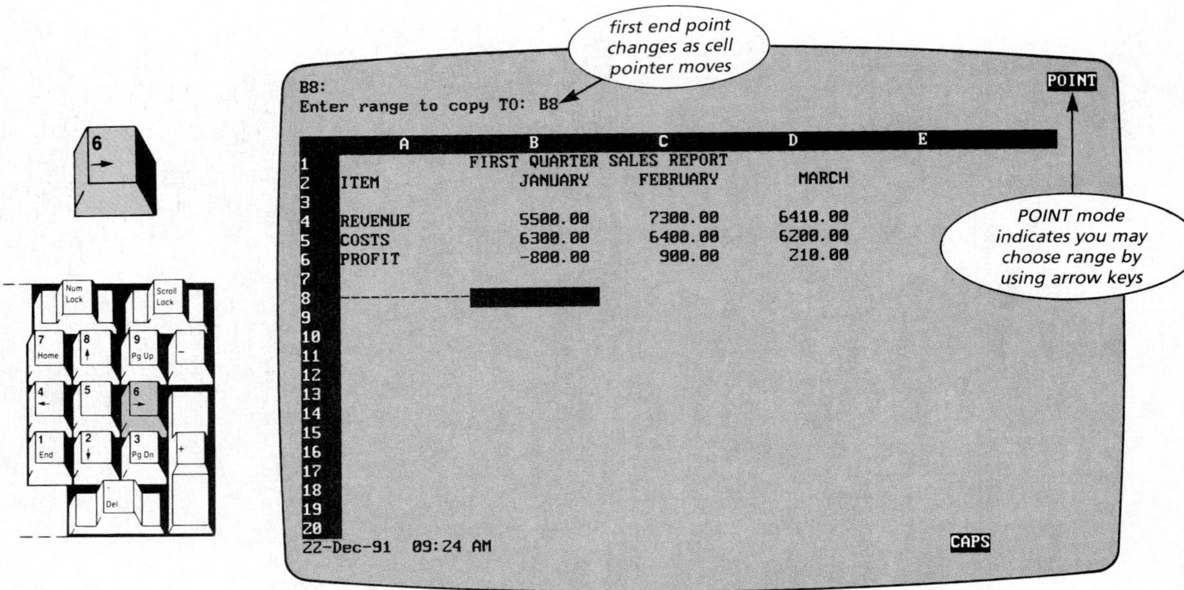


FIGURE 2-24 Step 3 of copying a range of cells—move the cell pointer to one of the end points of the destination range.

Press the Period key to anchor end point B8 and move the cell pointer to D8 as shown in Figure 2-25. Finally, press the Enter key to copy cell A8 to cells B8 through D8 (see Figure 2-26).

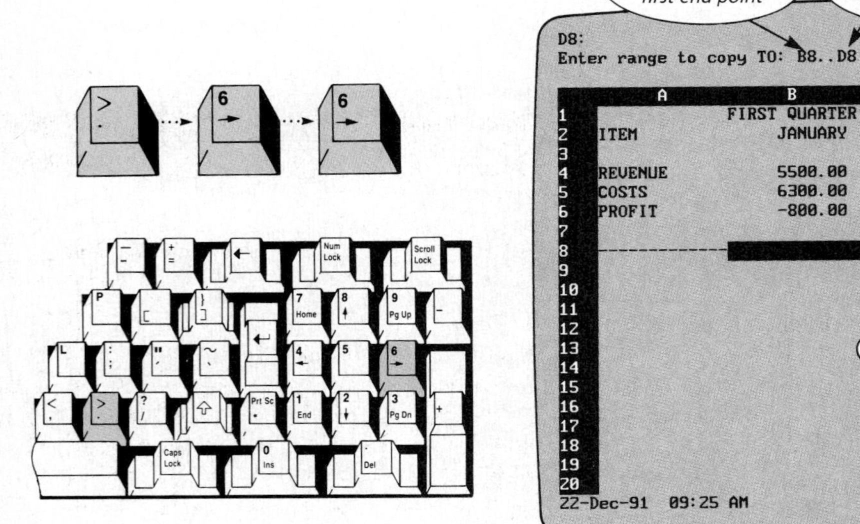

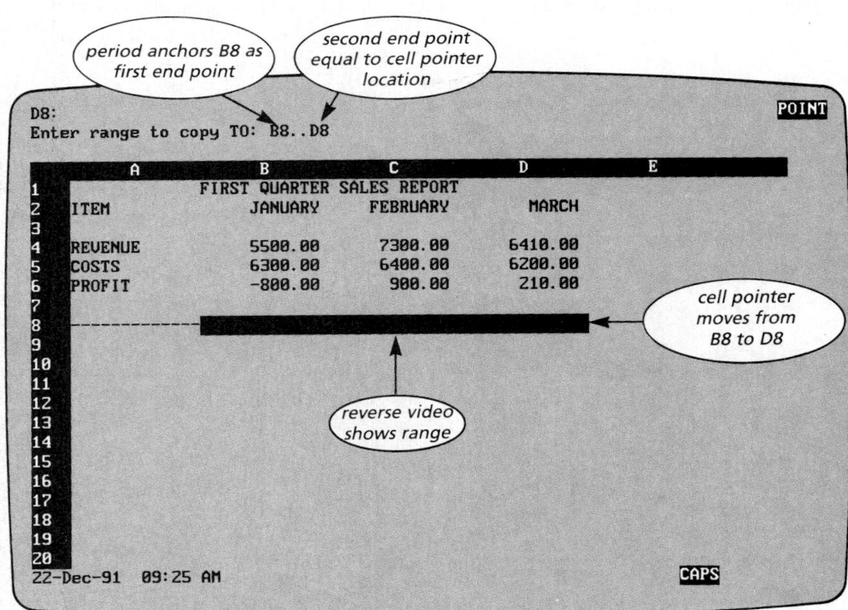


FIGURE 2-25 Step 4 of copying a range of cells—press the Period key and move the cell pointer to the opposite end point of the destination range.

As illustrated in Figure 2-26, the dashed line is complete and the cell pointer is back at cell A8, where it was before invoking the Copy command.

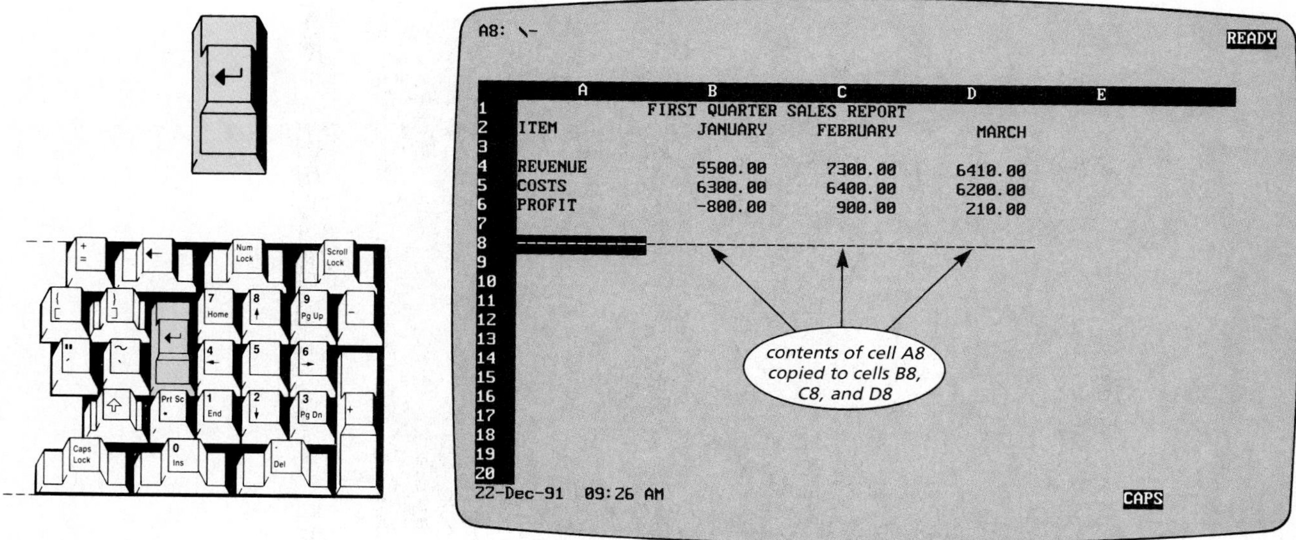


**FIGURE 2-26** **Step 5 of copying a range of cells—press the Enter key to anchor the end points of the destination range and complete the copy.**

With the dashed line complete, move the cell pointer to A10 and begin entering the labels that identify the quarter results. First enter the label QUARTER RESULTS and press the Down Arrow key twice as shown in Figure 2-27.

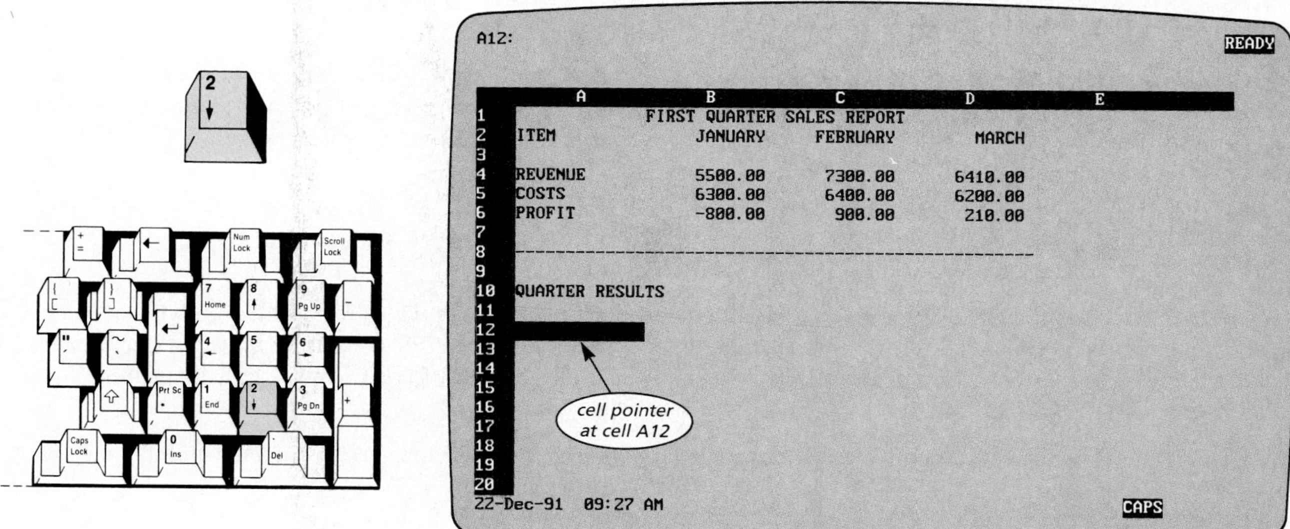


**FIGURE 2-27** **Step 1 of entering the total labels.**

Enter the remaining labels that identify the quarter results in cells A12 through A15. Use the Down Arrow key to enter each one. After the label entries are complete, the cell pointer ends up at cell A16 as illustrated in Figure 2-28. Use the GOTO command to move the cell pointer to cell B12, the location of the next entry.

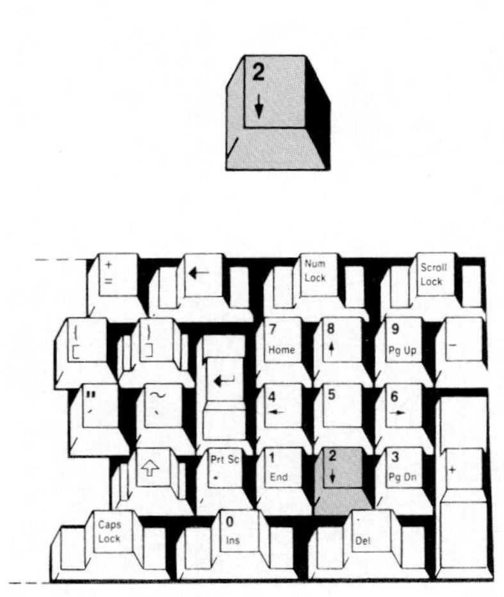

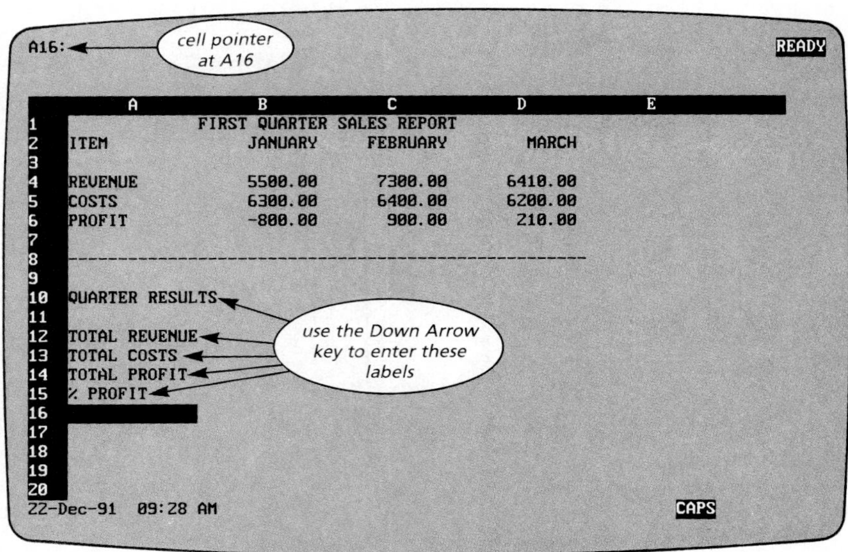


**FIGURE 2-28** Step 2 of entering the total labels.

## SAVING AN INTERMEDIATE COPY OF THE WORKSHEET

It's good practice to save intermediate copies of your worksheet. That way, if the computer loses power or you make a serious mistake, you can always retrieve the latest copy on disk. We recommend that you save an intermediate copy of the worksheet every 50 to 75 keystrokes. It makes sense to use the Save command often, because it saves keying time later if the unexpected happens.

Before we continue with Project 2, let's save the current worksheet as PROJS-2. Recall that to save the worksheet displayed on the screen you must do the following:

1. Enter the command /File Save (/FS).
2. In response to the prompt message on the input line, type the new file name, PROJS-2. As soon as you type the letter P in PROJS-2, the old file name, PROJS-1, disappears from the input line. File name PROJS-1 is on the input line because we retrieved it to begin this project and 1-2-3 assumes we want to save the revised worksheet under the same name.
3. Press the Enter key.

After 1-2-3 completes the save, the worksheet remains on the screen. You can immediately continue with the next entry.

## USING BUILT-IN FUNCTIONS

1-2-3 has many **built-in functions** that automatically handle calculations. These built-in functions save you a lot of time and effort because they eliminate the need to enter complex formulas. The first built-in function we will discuss is the SUM function, since it is one of the most widely used. For the remainder of the projects in this book, the term *function* will mean built-in function.

## The SUM Function

In the worksheet for Project 2, the total revenue is calculated by adding the values in cells B4, C4, and D4. While the calculation can be written in cell B12 as +B4+C4+D4, an easier and more general method to produce the same result is to use the SUM function. The **SUM function** adds the values in the specified range.

With the cell pointer at B12, enter @SUM(B4.D4) as illustrated on the input line at the top of the screen in Figure 2-29. Note that the SUM function begins with the **at sign** (@). Beginning an entry with the @ symbol indicates to 1-2-3 that the entry is a function.

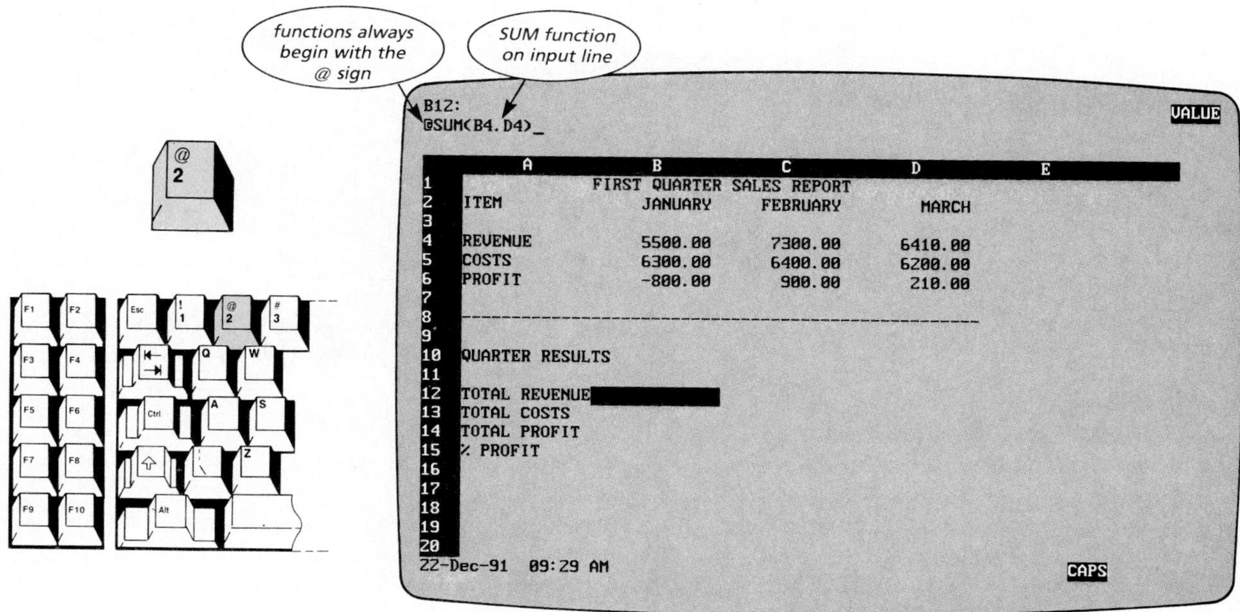


**FIGURE 2-29** Entering a function on the input line.

After the @ symbol, type the function name SUM (or sum) followed by a left parenthesis. Next, enter B4.D4, the range to be added. The range can be specified either by typing the beginning and ending cells or by using the pointing feature described earlier. In this case, type the two end points of the range separated by a period (.). Finally, type the right parenthesis.

Press the Enter key as shown in Figure 2-30 on the next page. As a result, 1-2-3 evaluates the sum of the entries in cells B4, C4, and D4 and displays the result in cell B12. Functions belong to the broader category called *formulas*. Therefore, 1-2-3 handles functions the same way it handles formulas—it evaluates the function and places a number in the cell. For example, in Figure 2-30, you can see on the status line that the formula @SUM(B4..D4) is assigned to cell B12. However, the value 19210 displays in cell B12 of the worksheet. The value 19210 is the sum of the numbers in cells B4, C4, and D4.

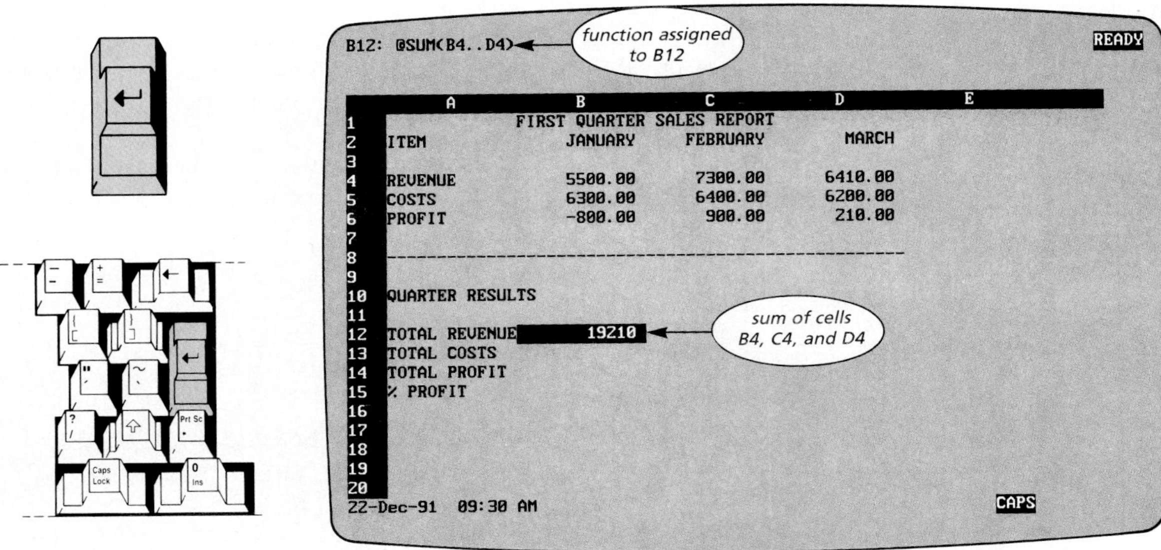


**FIGURE 2-30** **Press the Enter key to assign the function to B12. When a function is assigned to a cell, it is evaluated and the value displays in the cell.**

## Copying Functions

According to Figure 2-2, the two cells B13 and B14 require the identical function and similar ranges that we assigned to cell B12 in Figure 2-30. That is, cell B13 should contain the total costs for the quarter, or the sum of cells B5, C5, and D5. Cell B14 should contain the total profit for the quarter, or the sum of cells B6, C6, and D6. Table 2-3 illustrates the similarity between the entry in cell B12 and the entries required in cells B13 and B14.

**TABLE 2-3** **Three Function Entries for Cells B12, B13, and B14**

| CELL | FUNCTION ENTRIES |
|---|---|
| B12 | @SUM(B4..D4) |
| B13 | @SUM(B5..D5) |
| B14 | @SUM(B6..D6) |

There are two methods for entering the functions in cells B13 and B14. The first method involves moving the cell pointer to B13, entering the function @SUM(B5..D5), then moving the cell pointer to B14 and entering the function @SUM(B6..D6).

The second method, the one we are going to use, involves using the Copy command. That is, copy cell B12 to cells B13 and B14. Note in Table 2-3, however, that the ranges do not agree exactly. Each cell below B12 has a range that is one row below the previous one. Fortunately, when the Copy command copies cell addresses, it adjusts them for the new position. This cell-address adjustment used by the Copy command is called **relative addressing**. In other words, after cell B12 is copied to cells B13 and B14, the contents of B13 and B14 are identical to the entries shown in Table 2-3.

Let's complete the copy from cell B12 to cells B13 and B14. With the cell pointer at B12 as shown in Figure 2-30, enter the command /Copy (/C). The prompt message "Enter range to copy FROM: B12..B12" displays on the input line as shown in Figure 2-31. Since B12 is the cell that we want to copy to cells B13 and B14, press the Enter key.

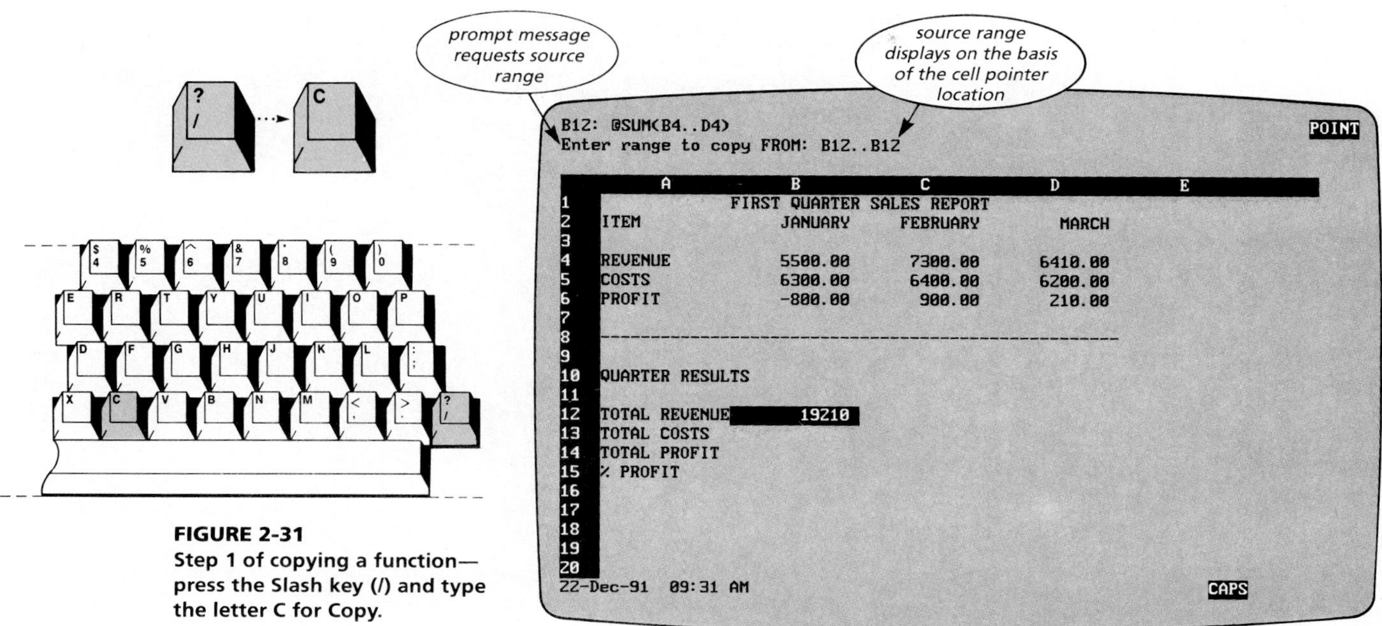


**FIGURE 2-31**
**Step 1 of copying a function—press the Slash key (/) and type the letter C for Copy.**

When we press the Enter key, the prompt message "Enter range to copy TO: B12" displays on the input line. This message is shown in Figure 2-32. Use the Down Arrow key to move the cell pointer to B13, the topmost end point of the destination range.

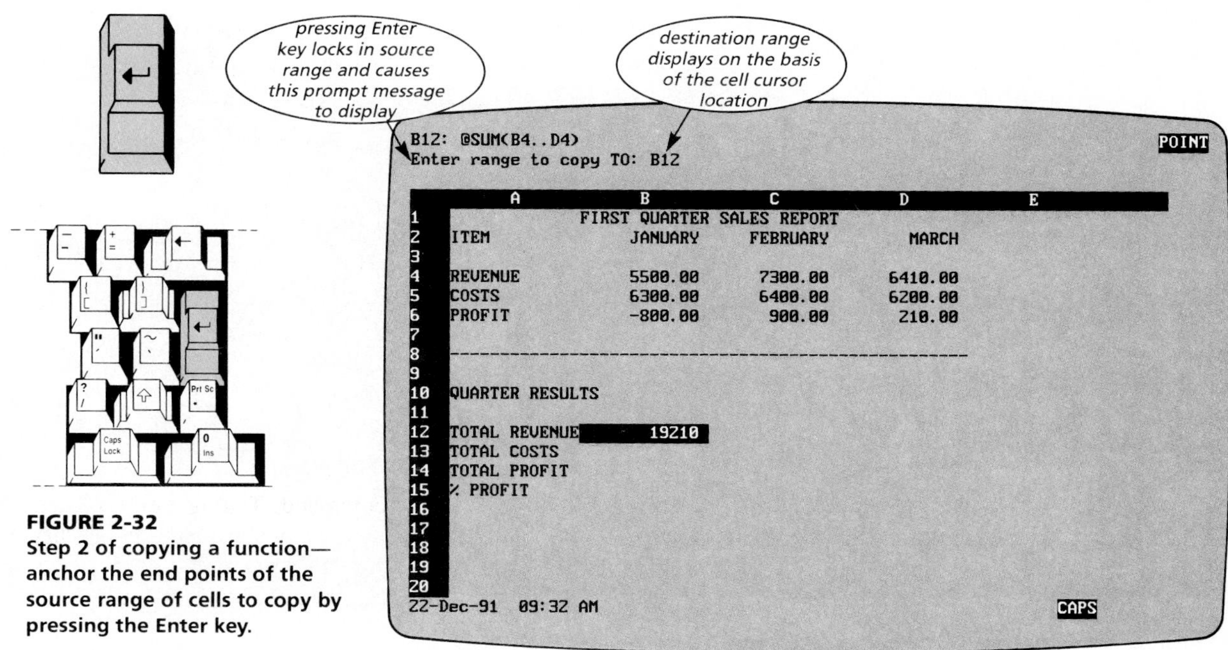


**FIGURE 2-32**
**Step 2 of copying a function—anchor the end points of the source range of cells to copy by pressing the Enter key.**

As shown in Figure 2-33, the cell address following the prompt message on the input line has changed from B12 to B13.

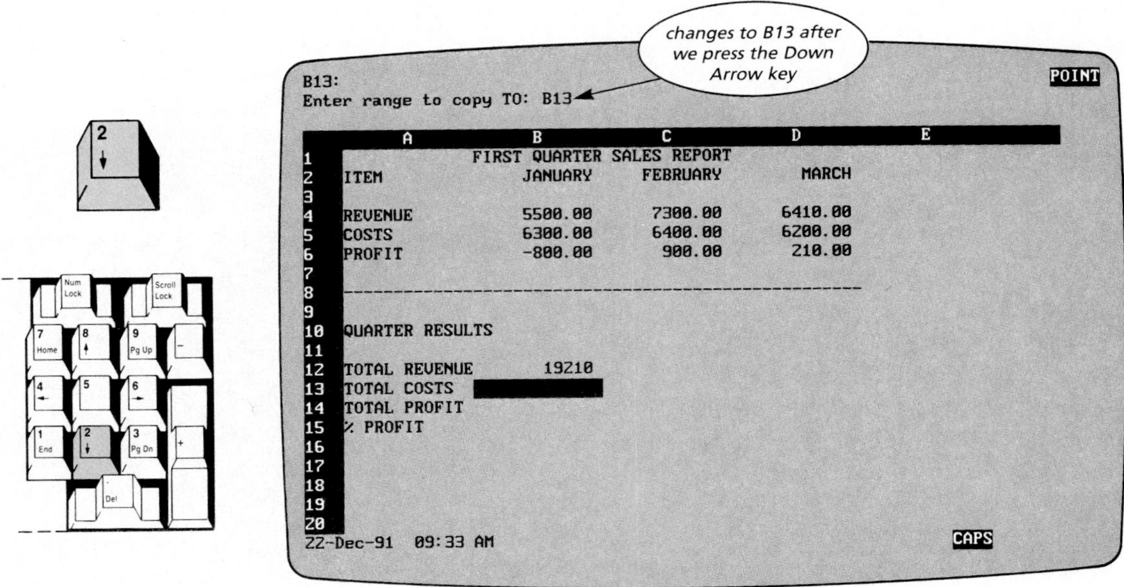


**FIGURE 2-33** Step 3 of copying a function—move the cell pointer to one of the end points of the destination range.

Press the Period key to anchor the topmost end point, B13. Next, move the cell pointer to B14 as shown in Figure 2-34. Finally, press the Enter key to copy the function in cell B12 to cells B13 and B14. As illustrated in Figure 2-35 on the next page, cell B13 contains the total costs for the quarter and cell B14 contains the total profit for the quarter. The cell pointer remains at cell B12, where it was before invoking the Copy command.

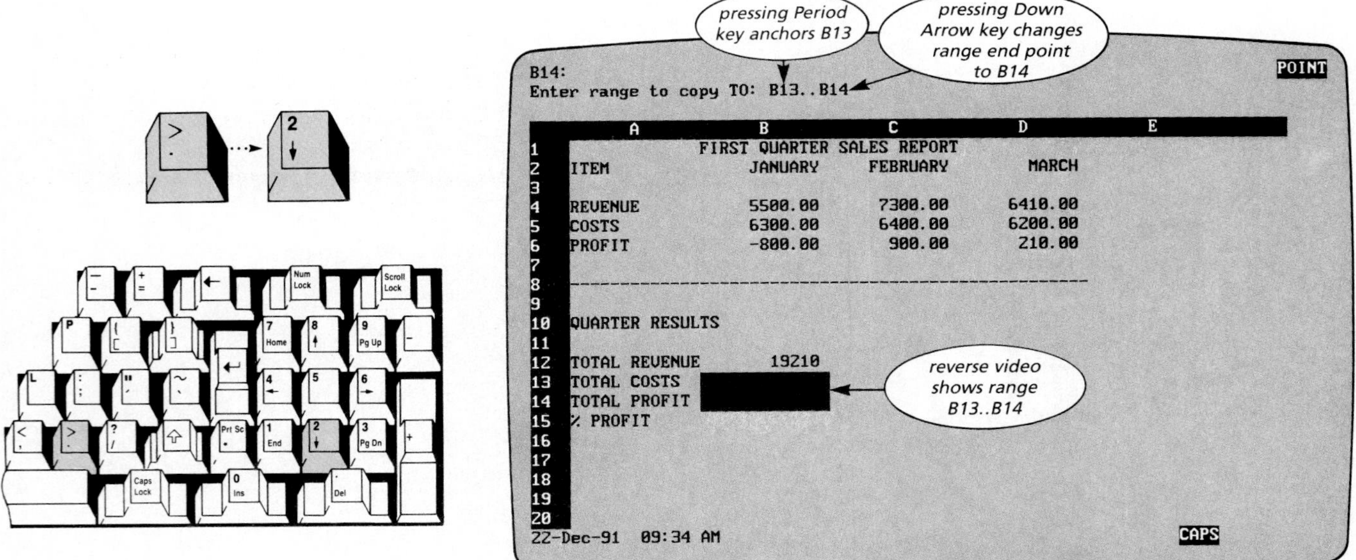


**FIGURE 2-34** Step 4 of copying a function—move the cell pointer to the opposite end point of the destination range.

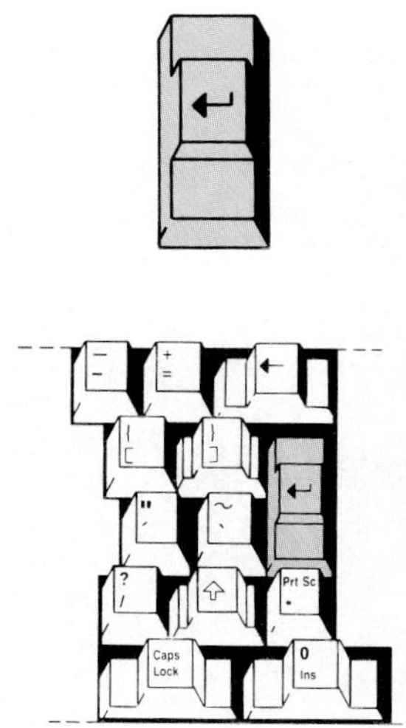

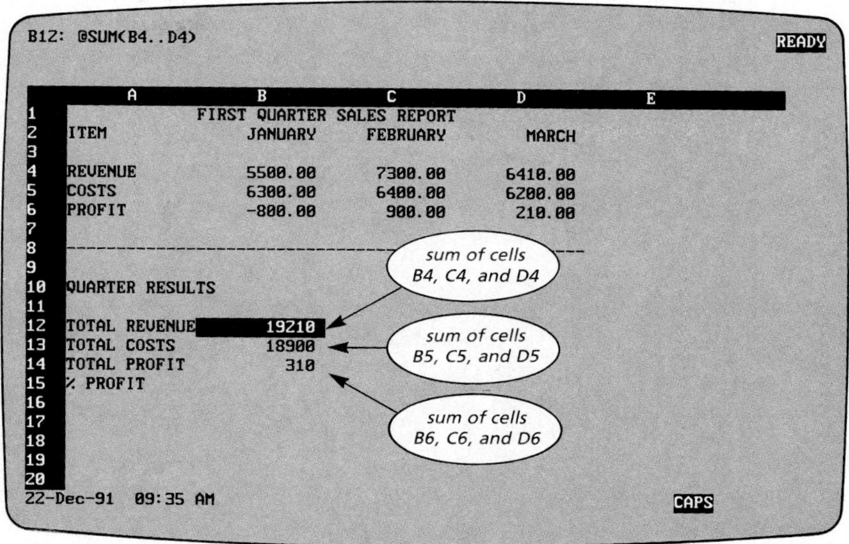


**FIGURE 2-35** Step 5 of copying a function—press the Enter key to anchor the end points of the destination range and complete the copy.

## DETERMINING A PERCENT VALUE

According to Figure 2-2, the percent profit appears in cell B15. The percent profit is determined by assigning a formula that divides the total profit (cell B14) by the total revenue (cell B12). Recall that the Slash key (/) represents the operation of division, provided it is not the first key typed in the READY mode and the entry is not a label.

Move the cell pointer to cell B15 and enter the formula +B14/B12 as shown on the input line in Step 1 of Figure 2-36 on the next page. Next, press the Enter key. 1-2-3 determines the quotient of +B14/B12 and stores the result, 0.0161374284, in cell B15. This is shown in Step 2 of Figure 2-36.

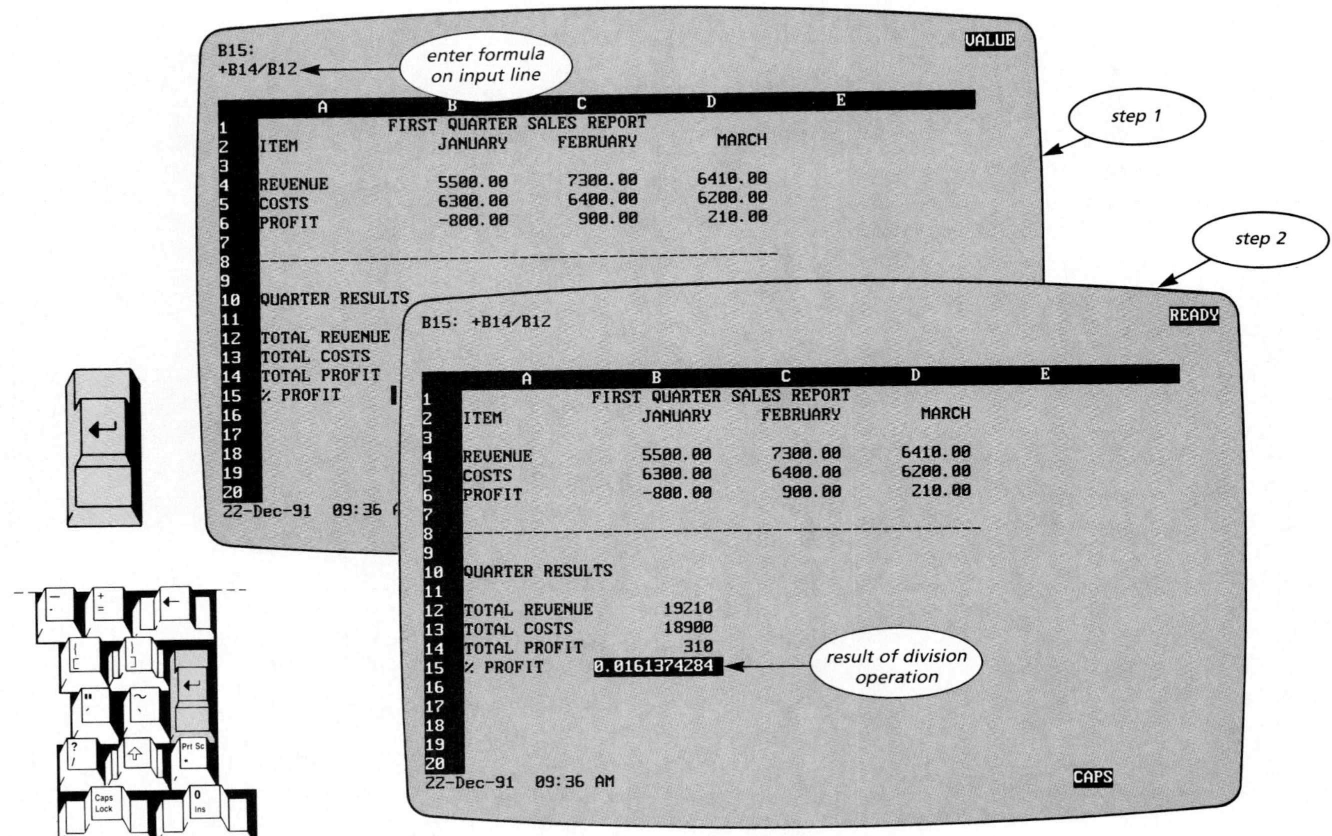


FIGURE 2-36 Entering a percentage. Step 1, enter the formula +B14/B12. Step 2, press the Enter key.

## FORMATTING TO PERCENT AND CURRENCY

Although the quarter totals displayed on the worksheet in Figure 2-36 are correct, they are not in an easy-to-read format. The dollar values are displayed as whole numbers and the percentage value is displayed as a decimal number carried out to 10 places. In Figure 2-2, the dollar figures in the quarter results are displayed as dollars and cents with a leading dollar sign. Furthermore, the quotient in cell B15 is displayed as a percent with one decimal place. Let's complete the formatting for this project.

### The Percentage Format

Since the cell pointer is at B15, first format the decimal value to a percentage value. With the pointer on cell B15, enter the command /**R**ange **F**ormat (/RF) as illustrated in Figure 2-37. With the command cursor active in the Format menu, type the letter P to select the Percent format. Remember, you can also select the command Percent by moving the command cursor to highlight the word Percent and pressing the Enter key.

When you type the letter P, 1-2-3 displays the prompt message "Enter number of decimal places (0..15): 2" on the input line. Type the digit 1 for one decimal position. This procedure is shown in Figure 2-38.

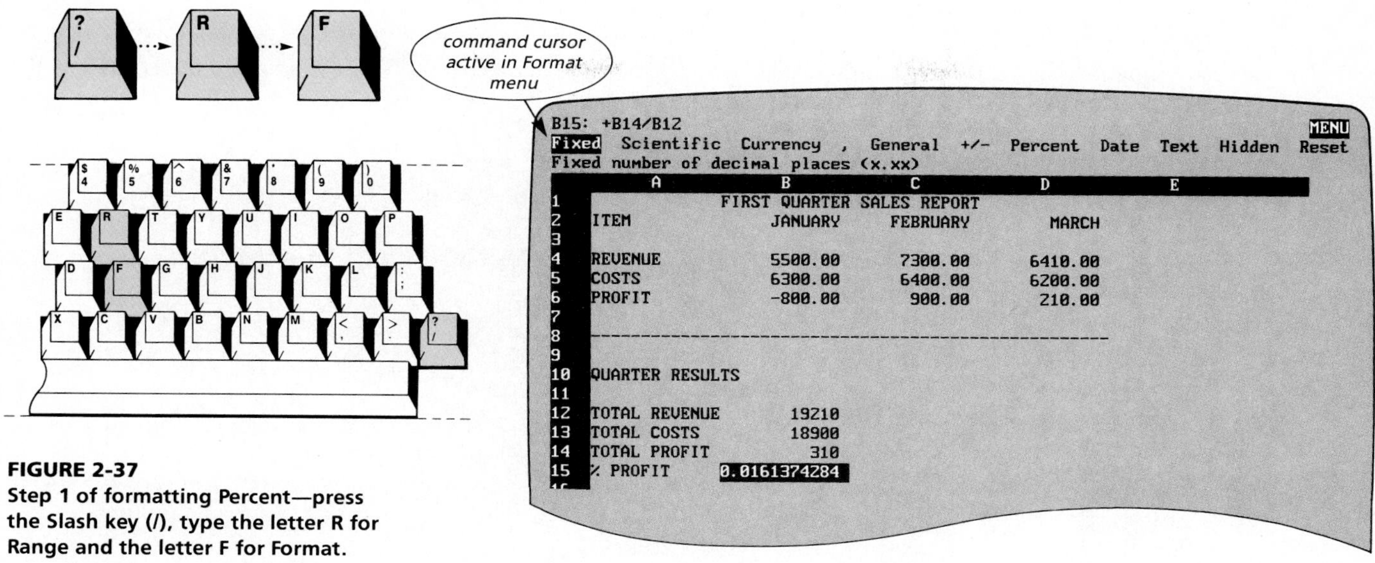


**FIGURE 2-37**
**Step 1 of formatting Percent—press the Slash key (/), type the letter R for Range and the letter F for Format.**

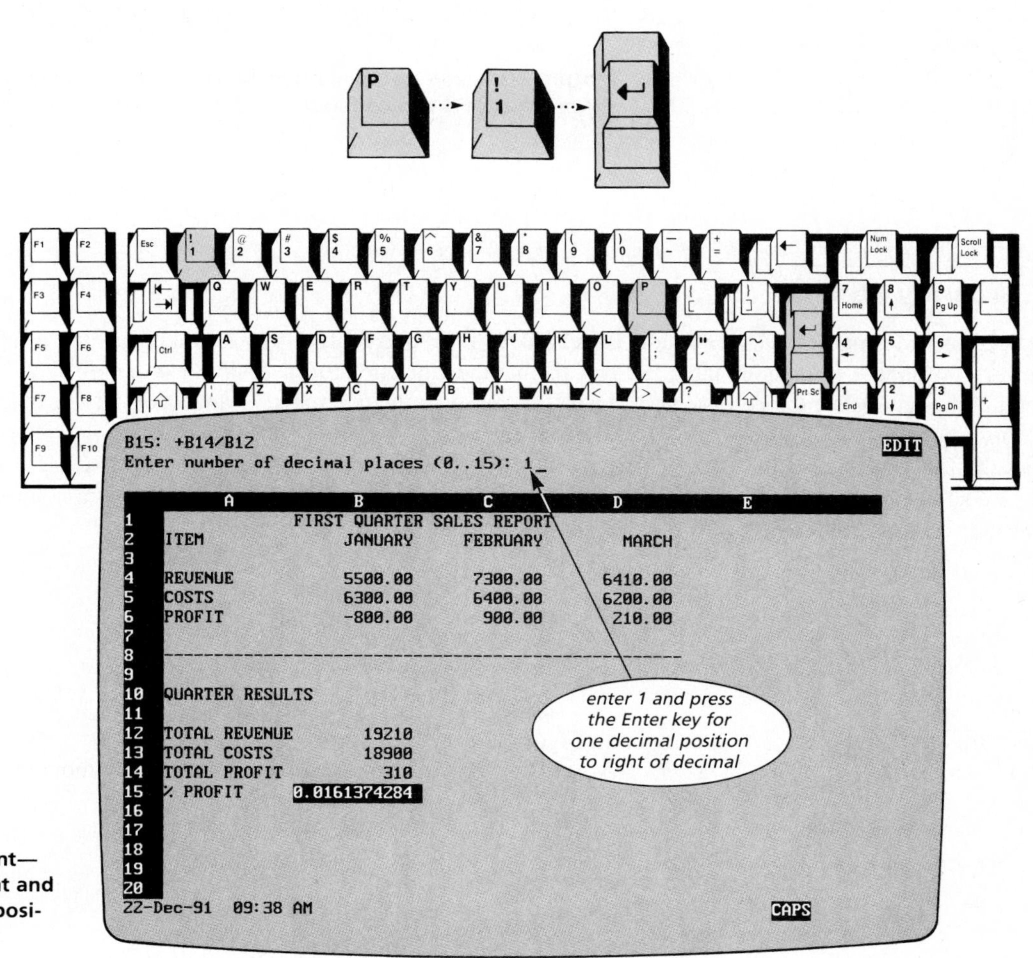


**FIGURE 2-38**
**Step 2 of formatting Percent—type the letter P for Percent and the number 1 for decimal positions desired.**

Next, press the Enter key. 1-2-3 displays the prompt message "Enter range to format: B15..B15" on the input line. Press the Enter key, since we want to assign this format only to cell B15. The decimal number 0.061374284, assigned to cell B15 by the formula +B14/B12, now displays as 1.6%. This result is shown in Figure 2-39.

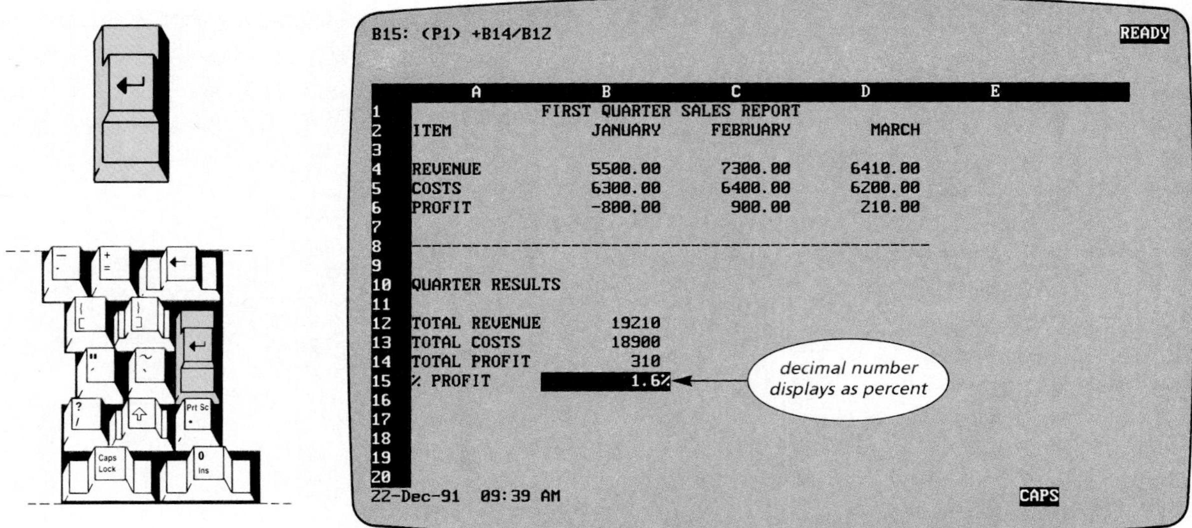


**FIGURE 2-39** Step 3 of formatting Percent—press the Enter key, because the range of cells to be affected is only the cell where the cell pointer is.

## The Currency Format

The next step is to format the quarter results in cells B12, B13, and B14 to dollars and cents with a leading dollar sign. Scanning the list of available formats in Table 2-2 reveals that the Currency format is the one that displays monetary amounts with a leading dollar sign. Move the cell pointer to cell B12 and type the command /**R**ange **F**ormat **C**urrency (/RFC). This activity is shown in Figure 2-40.

Press the Enter key in response to the prompt message "Enter number of decimal places (0..15): 2" because the desired number of decimal positions is 2. As shown on the input line in Figure 2-41, 1-2-3 wants to know the range to assign the Currency format. Use the pointing method to enter the range.

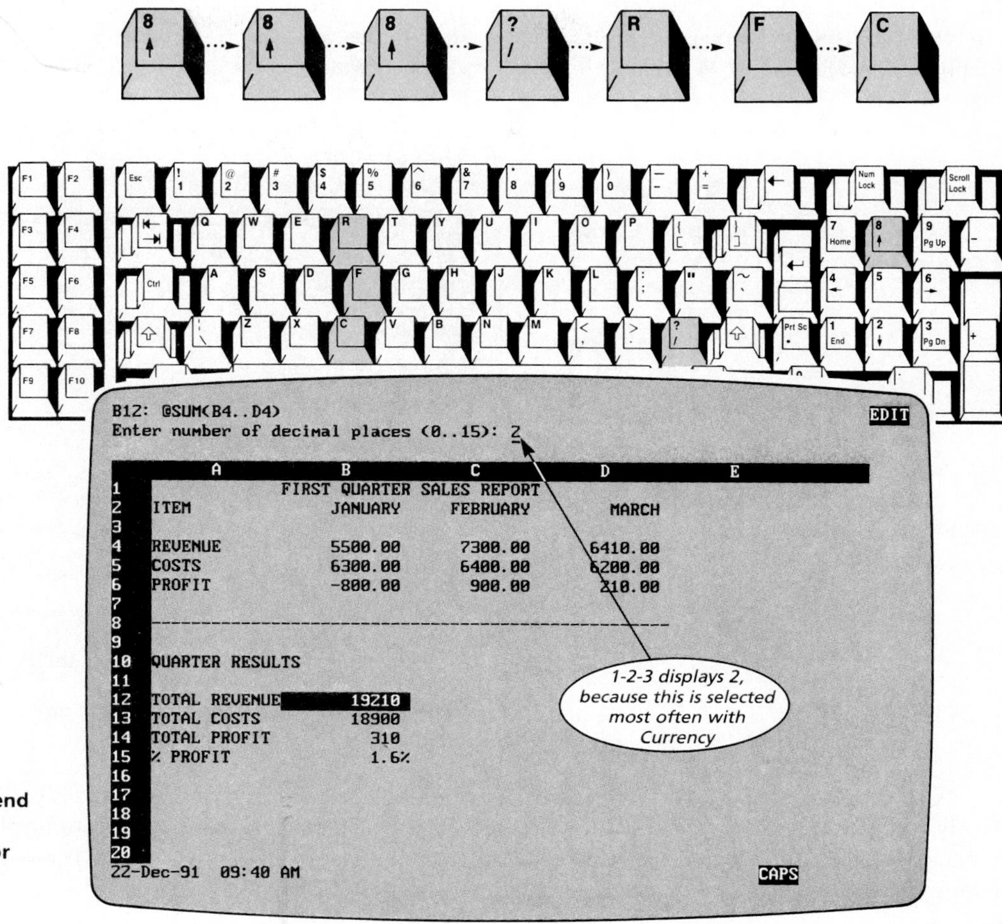


**FIGURE 2-40**
**Step 1 of formatting Currency—move the cell pointer to one of the end points of the range of cells to be affected, press the Slash key (/), R for Range, F for Format, and C for Currency.**

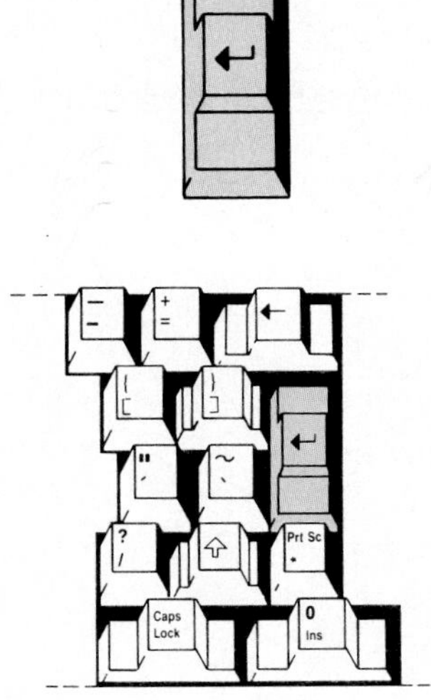

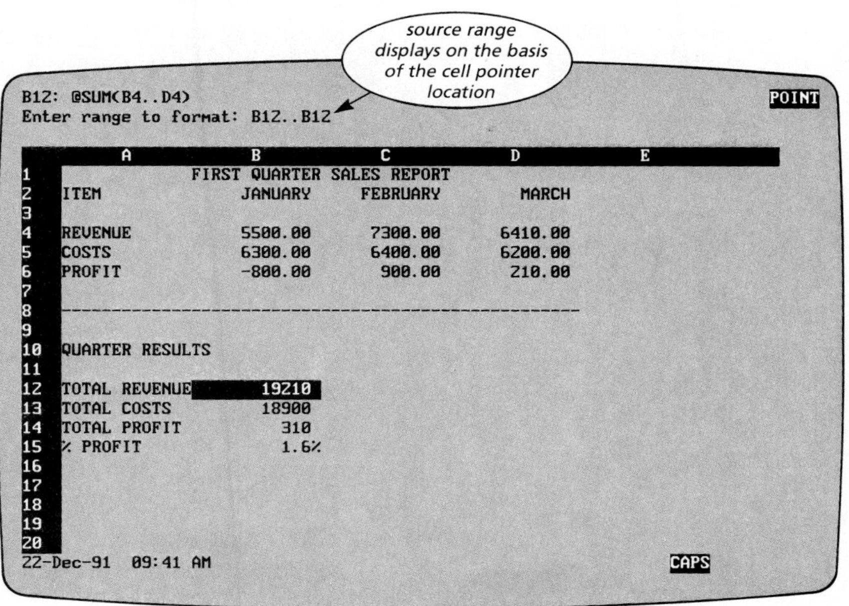


**FIGURE 2-41**
**Step 2 of formatting Currency—press the Enter key. This sets decimal places to 2 and displays the prompt message on the input line.**

The first cell address, B12, on the input line is correct. Therefore, move the cell pointer down to B14. As the cell pointer moves, 1-2-3 displays the range in reverse video. Also, the second cell address on the input line changes to agree with the location of the cell pointer. With the cell pointer on B14, the range we want to assign the Currency format is now correct (see Figure 2-42).

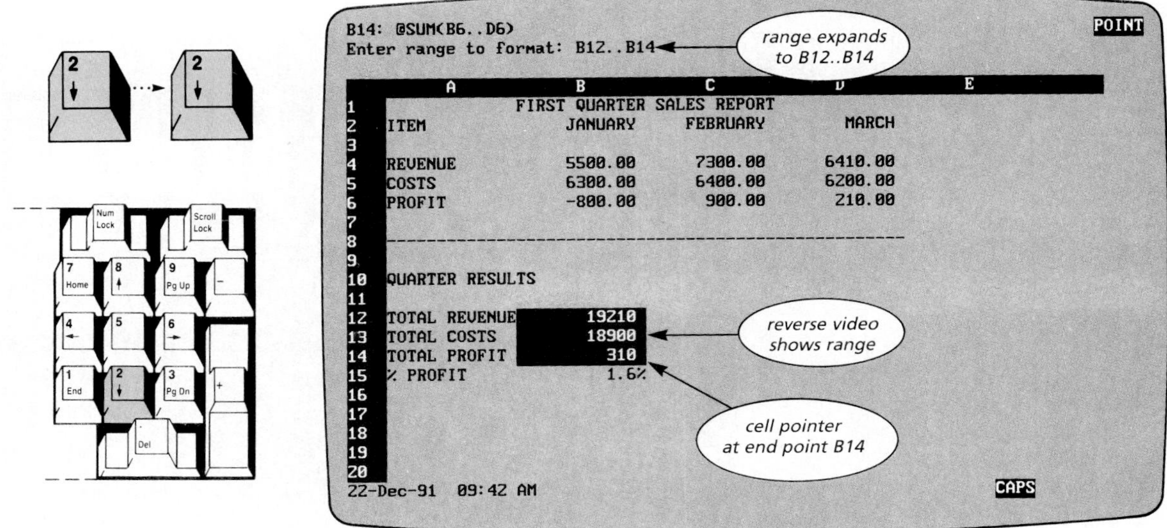


**FIGURE 2-42 Step 3 of formatting Currency—use the arrow keys to select the range of cells to be affected.**

Next, press the Enter key to assign the Currency format to the designated range in Figure 2-42, cells B12 through B14. Finally, press the Home key to move the cell pointer from cell B12 to cell A1 to prepare for the final step, printing the worksheet. Recall from Project 1 that no matter where the cell pointer is in the worksheet, it immediately moves to cell A1 when you press the Home key. The complete worksheet is shown in Figure 2-43.

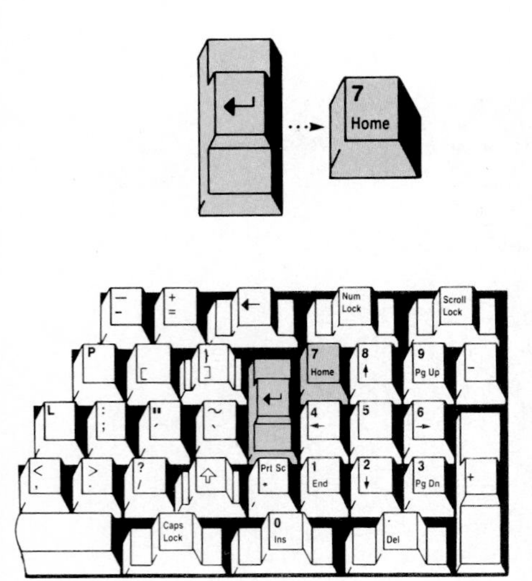

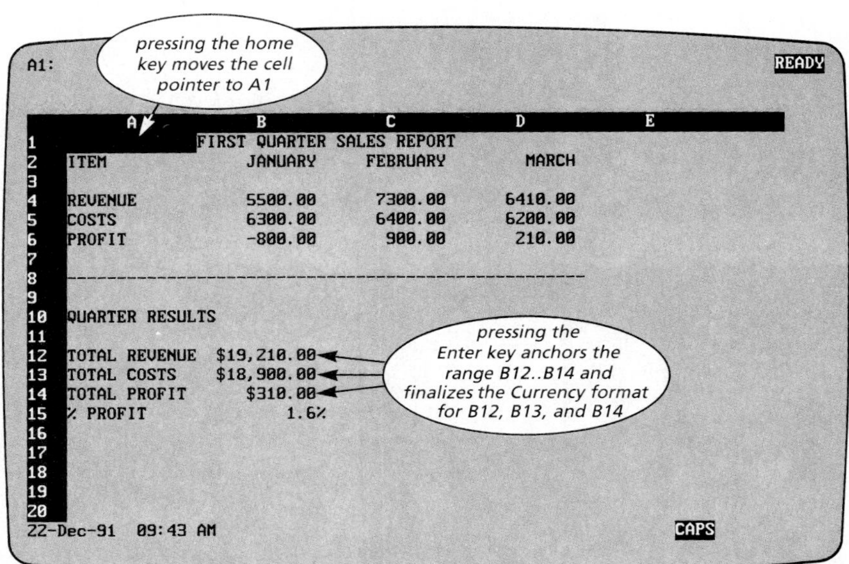


**FIGURE 2-43 Step 4 of formatting Currency—press the Enter key to lock in the range B12..B14. The worksheet is complete. Press the Home key to move the cell pointer to A1.**

## SAVING THE WORKSHEET A SECOND TIME

We already saved an intermediate version of the worksheet as PROJS-2. To save the worksheet again, do the following:

1. Enter the command /**F**ile **S**ave (/FS).
2. Since we saved this worksheet earlier in the session, 1-2-3 assumes we want to save it under the same file name. Therefore, it displays the name PROJS-2.WK1 on the input line at the top of the screen as shown in the first screen in Figure 2-44. This saves keying time. Press the Enter key.
3. The menu at the top of the lower screen in Figure 2-44 gives two choices—Cancel or Replace. Type the letter R for Replace. 1-2-3 replaces the worksheet we saved earlier on disk with the worksheet on the screen. If we had typed the letter C for Cancel rather than R for Replace, the Save command would have been terminated.

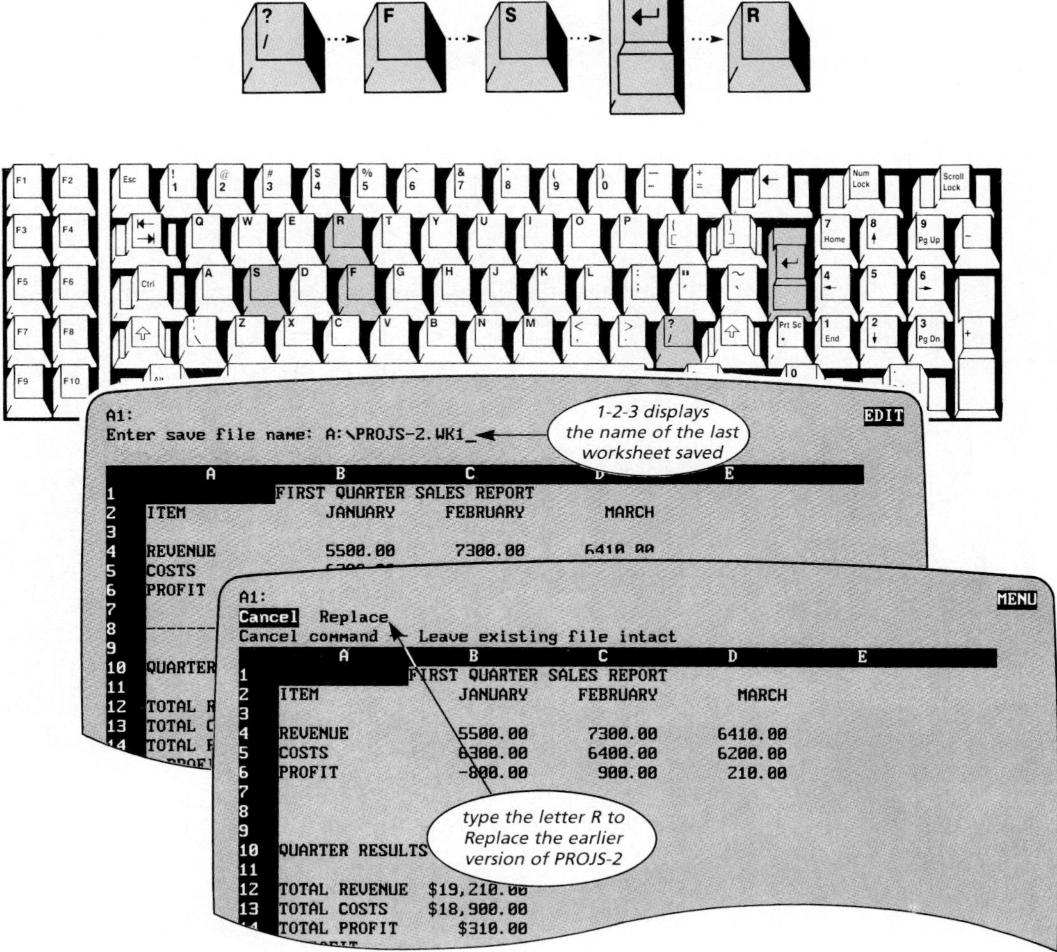


**FIGURE 2-44** When a worksheet is saved a second time under the same file name, type the letter R to replace the previous version on disk.

# PRINTING THE WORKSHEET

In Project 1, we printed the worksheet by holding down a Shift key and pressing the PrtSc key. The printed report included the window borders as well as the control panel and indicator line. However, window borders clutter the report and make it more difficult to read. In this section, we will discuss how to print the worksheet without the window borders, how to print sections of the worksheet, and how to print the actual entries assigned to the cells in a worksheet.

## The Print Printer Command

To print the worksheet without window borders, type the command /**P**rint **P**rinter (/PP). This activates the command cursor in the **Print menu** at the top of the screen as shown in Figure 2-45. Since this is the first time we will print this report using the Print command, we must enter the range to print. Therefore, type the letter R to select Range from the Print menu. The entire worksheet is in the range A1..D15. With the cell pointer at cell A1, press the Period key to anchor A1. Next, use the arrow keys to move the cell pointer to D15. As the cell pointer moves, the reverse video enlarges to encompass the entire range (see Figure 2-46). Press the Enter key to anchor end point D15. The Print menu reappears as shown in Figure 2-47.

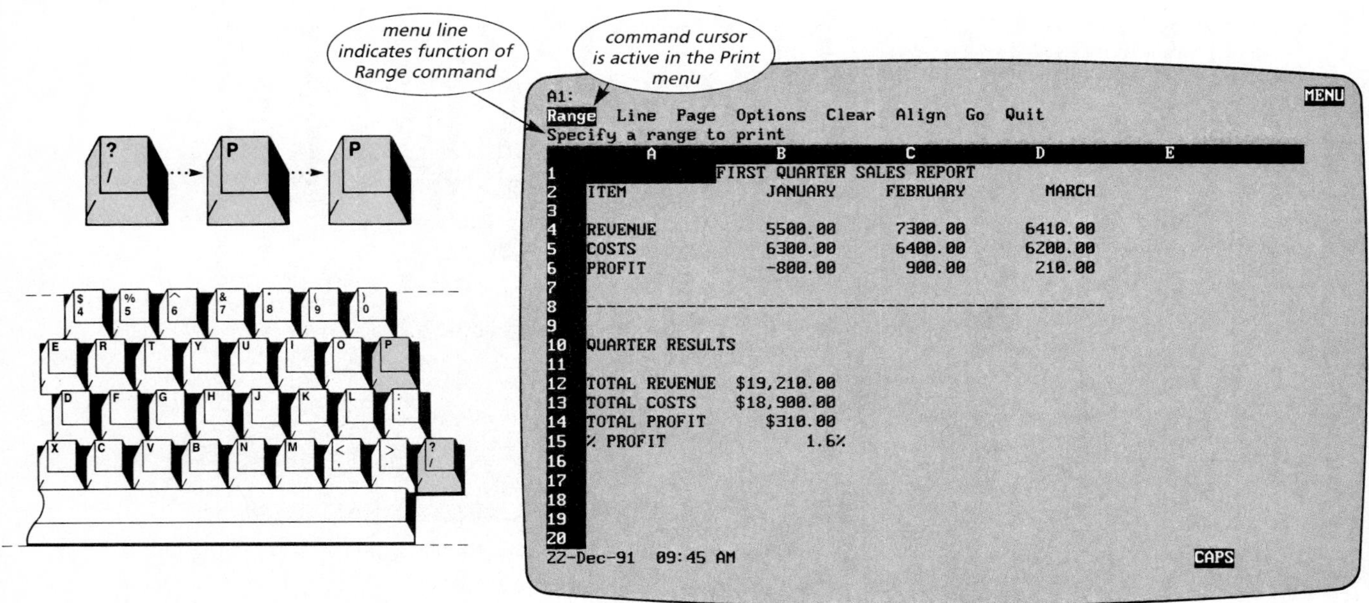


**FIGURE 2-45 Step 1 of printing a worksheet using the Print command—press the Slash key (/) and type the letter P twice, once for Print and once for Printer.**

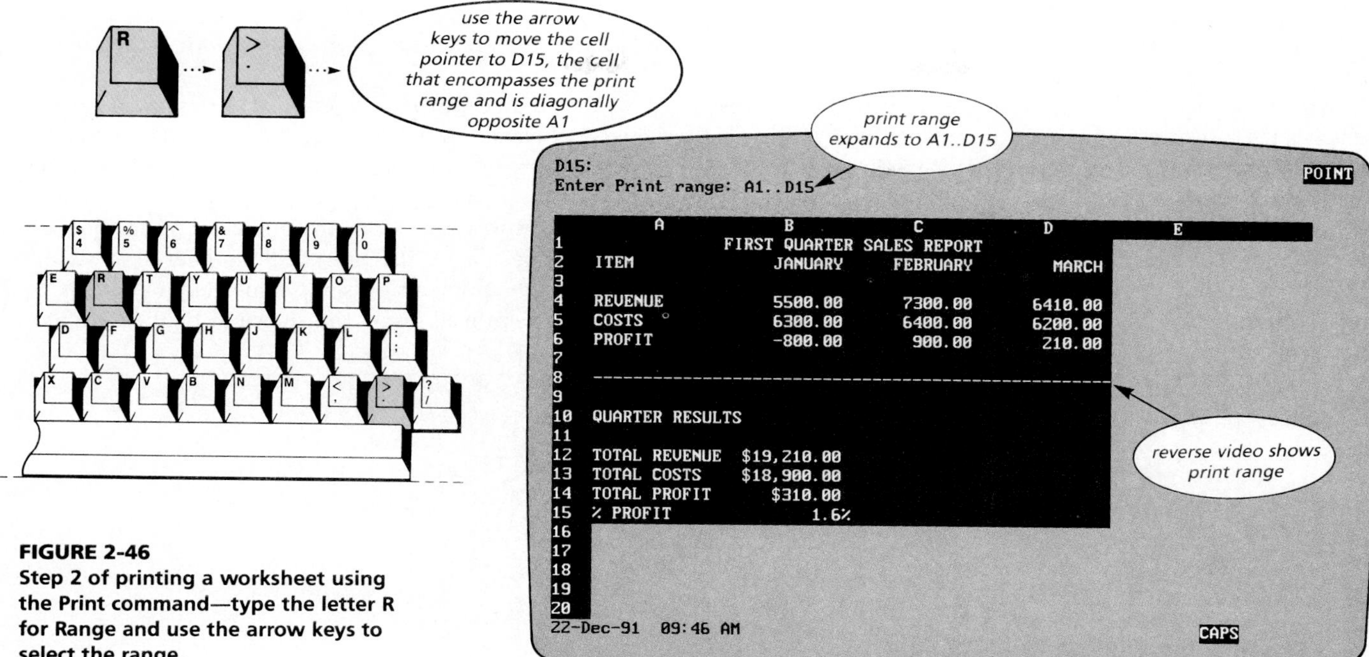


**FIGURE 2-46**
**Step 2 of printing a worksheet using the Print command—type the letter R for Range and use the arrow keys to select the range.**

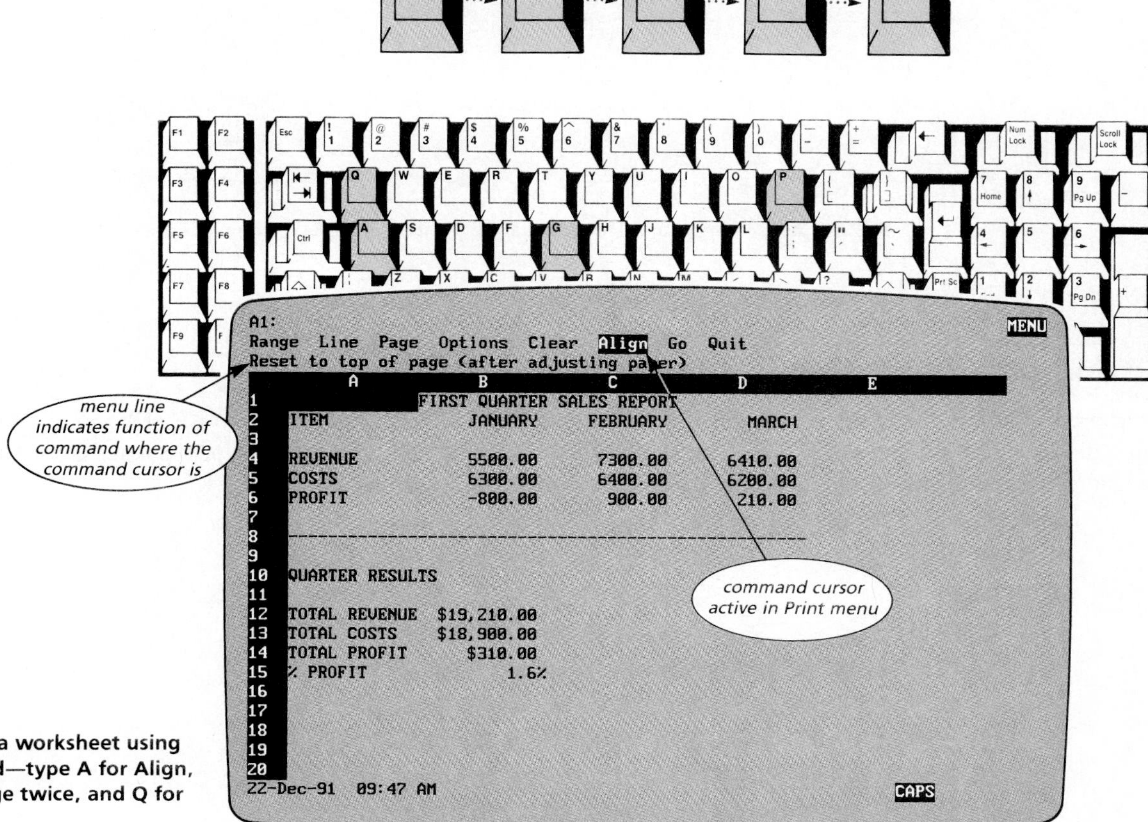


**FIGURE 2-47**
**Step 3 of printing a worksheet using the Print command—type A for Align, G for Go, P for Page twice, and Q for Quit.**

With the printer turned off, use the platen knob on the printer to align the perforated edge of the paper with the top of the print-head mechanism. Turn the printer on.

Type the letter A for Align. 1-2-3 has its own line counter. Invoking the Align command ensures that the program's line counter is the same as the printer's line counter, that is, that both counters are equal to zero after you turn the printer on and enter the Align command. If the two counters do not agree, the printed version of the worksheet may end up with a few inches of white space in the middle.

Next, type the letter G for Go. The printer immediately begins to print the worksheet. When the printer stops printing, type the letter P twice. Typing the letter P once invokes the Page command, which causes the paper in the printer to move to the top of the next page. Typing the letter P a second time moves the page with the printed worksheet completely out of the printer. Carefully tear the paper just below the report at the perforated edge. The printed results are shown in Figure 2-48(a).

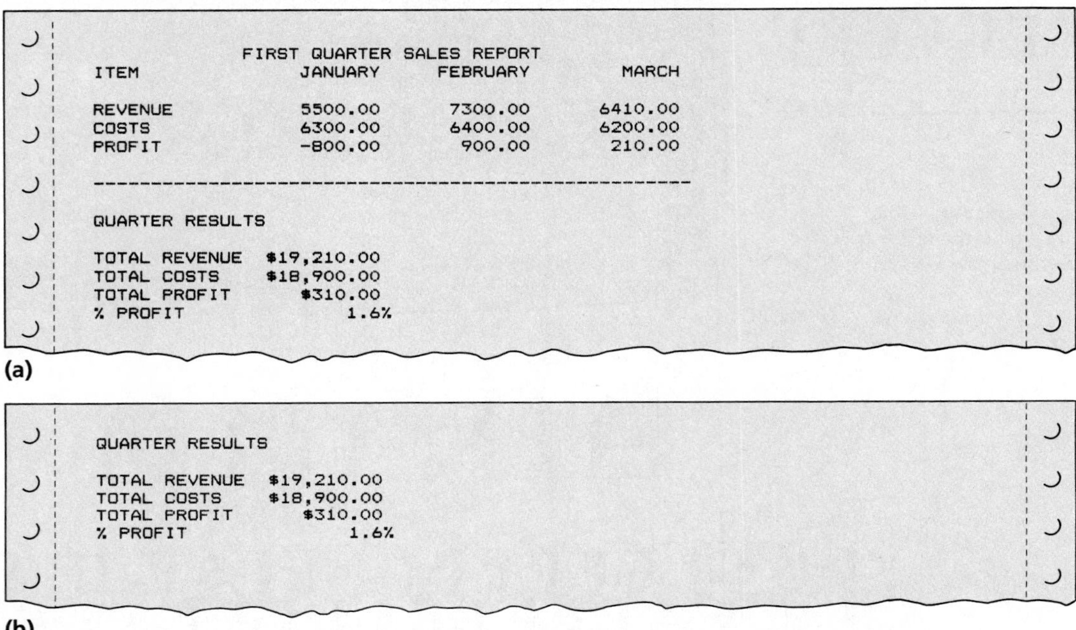

```
                 FIRST QUARTER SALES REPORT
ITEM                      JANUARY      FEBRUARY         MARCH

REVENUE                   5500.00       7300.00       6410.00
COSTS                     6300.00       6400.00       6200.00
PROFIT                    -800.00        900.00        210.00

-----------------------------------------------------------

QUARTER RESULTS

TOTAL REVENUE   $19,210.00
TOTAL COSTS     $18,900.00
TOTAL PROFIT       $310.00
% PROFIT              1.6%
```

(a)

```
QUARTER RESULTS

TOTAL REVENUE   $19,210.00
TOTAL COSTS     $18,900.00
TOTAL PROFIT       $310.00
% PROFIT              1.6%
```

(b)

**FIGURE 2-48** Complete (a) and partial (b) printed versions of the worksheet.

## Quitting the Print Command

The Print command is one of the few commands that does not immediately return 1-2-3 to READY mode when the command is finished executing. To return to READY mode after the Print command is complete, type the letter Q for Quit. This Quit command clears the menus from the control panel and returns 1-2-3 to READY mode.

## Printing a Section of the Worksheet

You may not always want to print the entire worksheet. Portions of the worksheet can be printed by entering the selected range in response to the Range command. Let's assume that you want to print only the quarter results as shown in Figure 2-48(b). From Figure 2-43, you can see that the quarter results are in the range A10..B15.

To print the quarter results, enter the command /**P**rint **P**rinter (/PP) as shown in Figure 2-45. Next, type the letter R for Range. The screen in Figure 2-46 displays because 1-2-3 always remembers the last range entered for the Print command. Recall that we entered the range A1..D15 when we printed the complete worksheet earlier.

To change the range, press the Backspace key to free the end points A1 and D15 on the input line. Use the arrow keys to move the cell pointer to A10. Press the Period key (.) to anchor the upper left end point of the range containing the quarter results. Move the cell pointer to B15. At this point, the screen appears as shown in Figure 2-49. Press the Enter key to anchor the lower right end point.

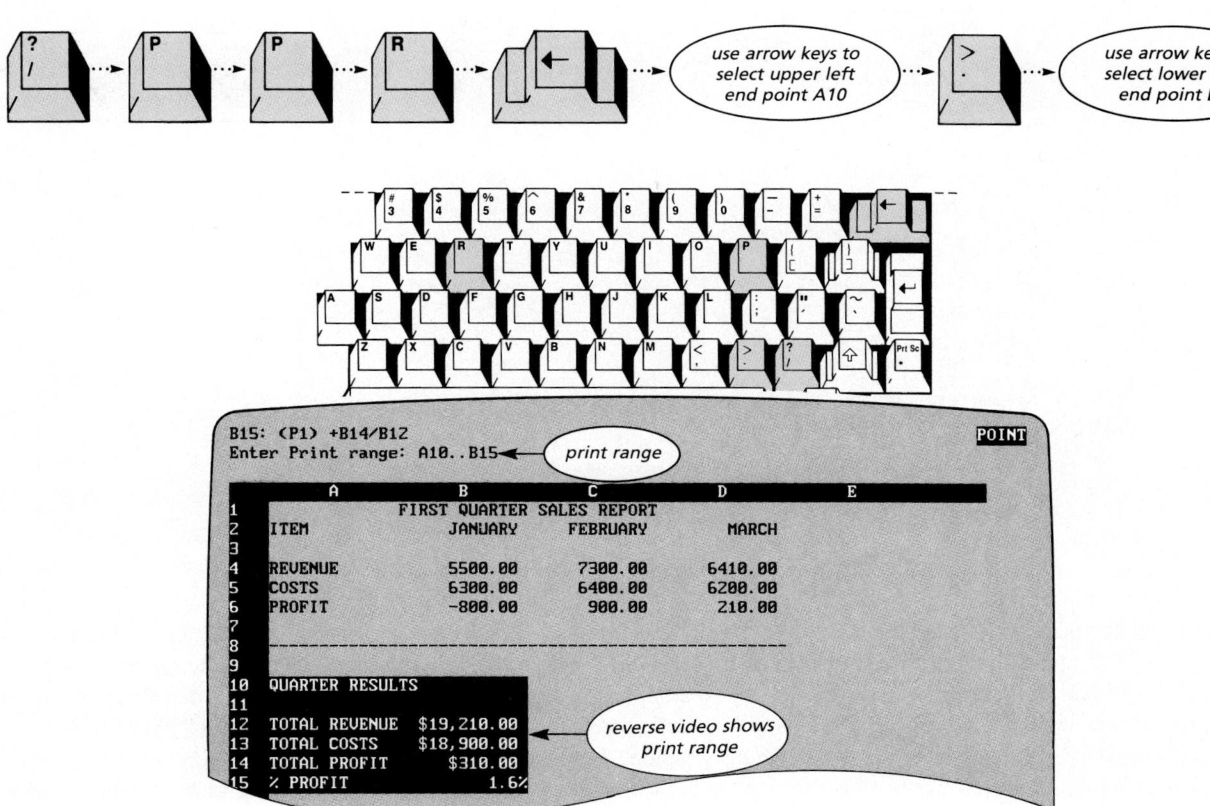


**FIGURE 2-49** Printing a portion of the worksheet.

Next, make sure the paper is aligned and the printer is ready. As described in Figure 2-47, type the letter A for Align and the letter G for Go to print the partial report. The partial report shown in Figure 2-48(b) prints on the printer. When the report is complete, type the letter P twice to eject the paper from the printer. Finally, type the letter Q for Quit to complete the Print command. The Print menu disappears from the control panel and 1-2-3 returns to the READY mode.

## Printing the Cell-Formulas Version of the Worksheet

Thus far, we have printed the worksheet exactly as it is on the screen. This is called the **as-displayed** version of the worksheet. Another variation that we print is called the cell-formulas version. The **cell-formulas** version prints what was assigned to the cells, rather than what's in the cells. It is useful for debugging a worksheet because the formulas and functions print out, rather than the numeric results.

Figure 2-50 illustrates the printed cell-formulas version of this worksheet. Each filled cell in the selected range is printed on a separate line. The cell address is printed in the left column, followed by any special formatting that was assigned to the cell, and the actual contents. The information displayed in the report is identical to the display on the status line for the current cell.

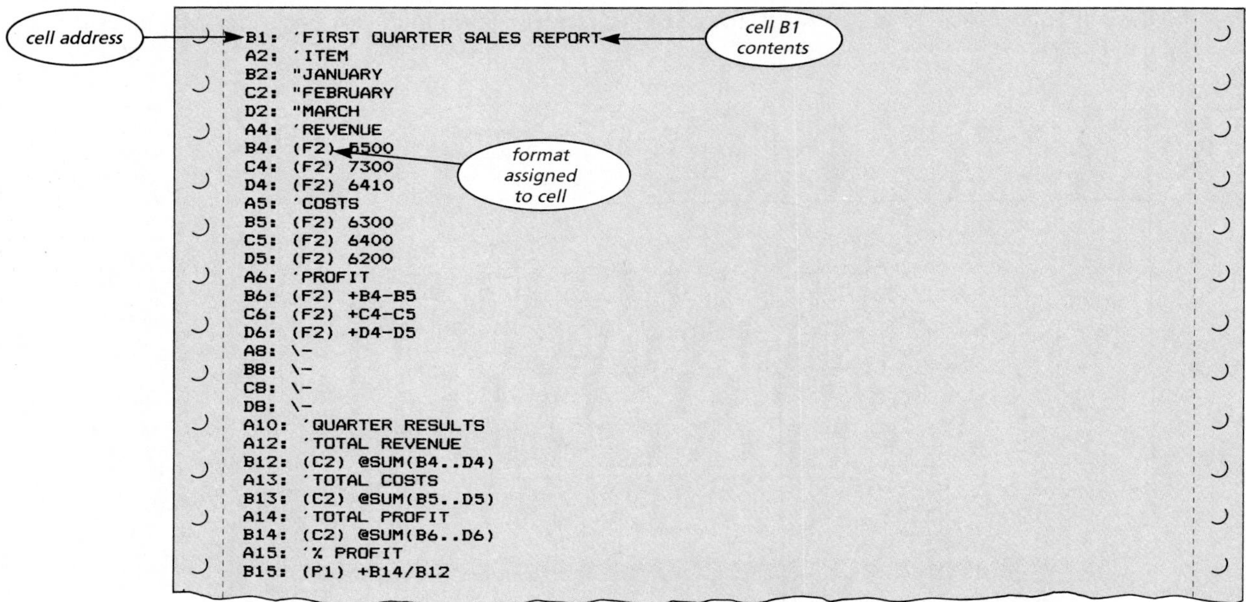

```
B1: 'FIRST QUARTER SALES REPORT
A2: 'ITEM
B2: "JANUARY
C2: "FEBRUARY
D2: "MARCH
A4: 'REVENUE
B4: (F2) 6500
C4: (F2) 7300
D4: (F2) 6410
A5: 'COSTS
B5: (F2) 6300
C5: (F2) 6400
D5: (F2) 6200
A6: 'PROFIT
B6: (F2) +B4-B5
C6: (F2) +C4-C5
D6: (F2) +D4-D5
A8: \-
B8: \-
C8: \-
D8: \-
A10: 'QUARTER RESULTS
A12: 'TOTAL REVENUE
B12: (C2) @SUM(B4..D4)
A13: 'TOTAL COSTS
B13: (C2) @SUM(B5..D5)
A14: 'TOTAL PROFIT
B14: (C2) @SUM(B6..D6)
A15: '% PROFIT
B15: (P1) +B14/B12
```



**FIGURE 2-50** Cell-formulas version of the worksheet.

To print the cell-formulas version of the worksheet, type the command /Print **P**rinter **R**ange (/PPR). Enter the range A1..D15 and press the Enter key. (If we had not printed a portion of the worksheet in the previous step, the range already would have been set to A1..D15. In this case we would have skipped the Range command.) With the command cursor still active in the Print menu, enter the command **O**ptions **O**ther **C**ell-formulas **Q**uit **A**lign **G**o **P**age **P**age (OOCQAGPP). With the printer in READY mode, 1-2-3 will print the cell-formulas version of Project 2 as shown in Figure 2-50.

Once the Print command option has been set to print the cell-formulas version, 1-2-3 will continue to print this variation each time you use the /**P**rint **P**rinter (/PP) command until you change the print option back to as-displayed. Therefore, after printing the cell-formulas version, but before quitting the Print command, enter the command **O**ptions **O**ther **A**s-displayed **Q**uit **Q**uit (OOAQQ). The last Quit in the chain of commands causes 1-2-3 to return to READY mode. The next time the Print command is used, 1-2-3 will print the as-displayed version.

### Printing a Worksheet to a File

You can instruct 1-2-3 to transmit the printed version of a worksheet to a file. This can be useful if your printer is not functioning or if you prefer to print the worksheet at a later time. Use the command /**P**rint **F**ile (/PF), rather than /**P**rint **P**rinter (/PP). When you enter the command /PF, 1-2-3 requests a file name. After you enter the file name, the Print menu in Figure 2-47 displays. From this point on, you can select commands from the Print menu as if you were printing the worksheet directly to the printer.

Later, after quitting 1-2-3, you can use the DOS command Type to display the worksheet on the screen or the DOS command Print to print the worksheet on the printer. The file extension .PRN, which stands for printer file, automatically appends to the file name you select.

### Summary of Commands in the Print Menu

Table 2-4 summarizes the commands available in the Print menu.

**TABLE 2-4 Commands Available in the Print Menu**

| COMMAND | FUNCTION |
|---|---|
| Range | Allows you to specify what part of the worksheet is printed. |
| Line | Moves the paper in the printer one line. |
| Page | Advances the paper in the printer to the top of the next page on the basis of the program's page-length setting. |
| Options | Sets header, footer, margins, page length, borders, and special printer commands. |
| Clear | Sets Print command settings to their default and clears the current print-range setting. |
| Align | Resets the line counter for the printer. |
| Go | Starts printing the worksheet on the printer. |
| Quit | Returns 1-2-3 to READY mode. |

## DEBUGGING THE FORMULAS IN A WORKSHEET USING THE TEXT FORMAT

Debugging is the process of finding and correcting errors in a worksheet. When formulas are assigned to the cells in a worksheet, the cell-formulas version is a handy tool for debugging it. Recall that the cell-formulas version shows the formulas associated with a worksheet (see Figure 2-50). An alternative to printing the cell-formulas version of the worksheet is to format the worksheet to the Text type. This format allows you to see the formulas in the cells on the screen, instead of their numeric result. When the worksheet is formatted to the Text type, it is called the **text version**.

To view the text version of the worksheet, do the following:

1. Save the worksheet to disk so that you don't lose the formats currently assigned to the cells in the worksheet.
2. Enter the command /**R**ange **F**ormat **T**ext (/RFT) and enter the range A1..D15.

As shown in Figure 2-51, the formulas display in the cells instead of their numeric results. One problem with this procedure is that if a formula is longer than the width of the cell, a portion of it is hidden.

When you are finished viewing or printing the worksheet formatted to the Text type, retrieve from disk the original version—the one that contains the properly formatted cells.

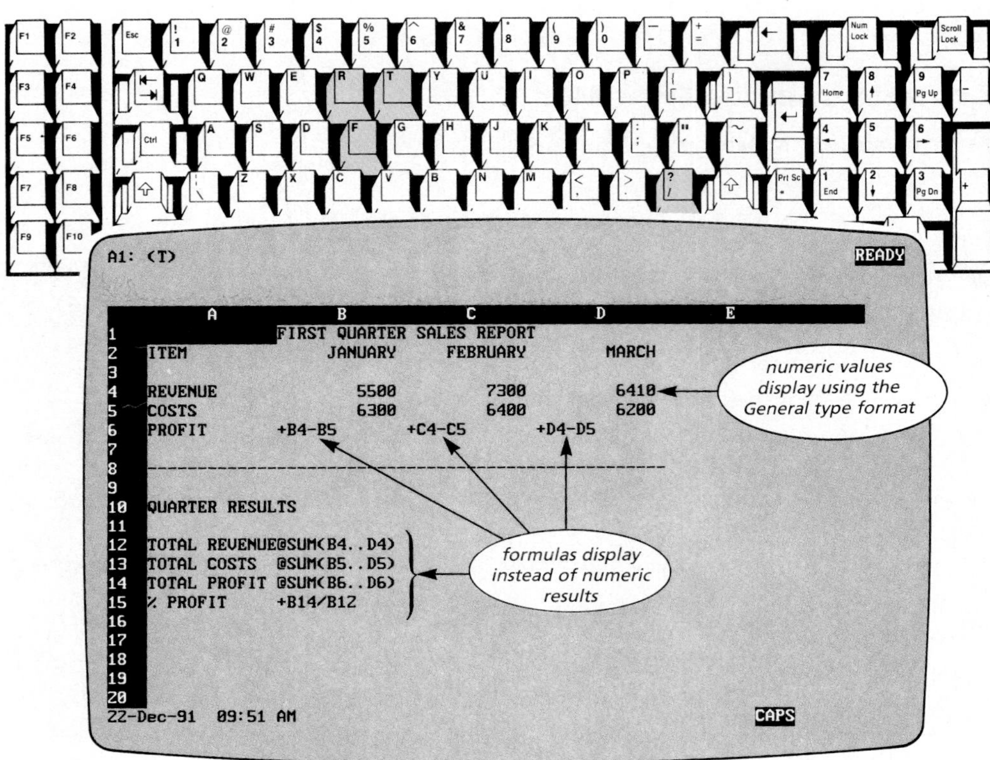


**FIGURE 2-51 Display of the formulas in the cells instead of the numeric results. Use the command /Range Format Text (/RFT) and enter the range A1..D15.**

# PROJECT SUMMARY

In Project 2 we formatted the numeric values entered in Project 1, added summaries, and formatted the summaries. Although this sequence of performing operations works well in many applications, it is not mandatory. For example, it may be more economical in terms of time and effort to enter portions of the data and then format it immediately, or it might be advisable to format the cells before entering the data into the worksheet. You will learn which sequence to choose as you gain experience with 1-2-3.

In Project 2 you learned how to load a worksheet, increase the size of columns, specify a range, copy cells, format a worksheet, and print a worksheet without window borders. The steps for Project 2 are summarized in the table on the next page. Review each step in the table in detail to make sure you fully understand the commands and concepts.

**SUMMARY OF KEYSTROKES—Project 2**

| STEPS | KEY(S) PRESSED | RESULTS |
|---|---|---|
| 1 | /FR↵ | Retrieve PROJS-1 from disk |
| 2 | Caps Lock | Set Caps Lock on |
| 3 | /WGC13↵ | Set column width to 13 |
| 4 | /RFF↵ Backspace ←←←↑↑.↓↓ →→↵ | Set monthly revenue, costs, and profit to a fixed format with two decimal places |
| 5 | F5 A8↵ | Move the cell pointer to A8 |
| 6 | \-↵ | Repeat dashes in cell A8 |
| 7 | /C↵→.→→↵ | Copy dashes in cell A8 to cells B8, C8, and D8 |
| 8 | ↓↓QUARTER RESULTS↓↓ | Enter title |
| 9 | TOTAL REVENUE↓ | Enter title |
| 10 | TOTAL COSTS↓ | Enter title |
| 11 | TOTAL PROFIT↓ | Enter title |
| 12 | % PROFIT↓ | Enter title |
| 13 | F5 B12↵ | Move the cell pointer to B12 |
| 14 | /FSPROJS-2↵ | Save worksheet as PROJS-2 |
| 15 | @SUM(B4.D4)↵ | Enter SUM function for total revenue |
| 16 | /C↵↓.↓↵ | Copy SUM function from cell B12 to B13 and B14 |
| 17 | ↓↓↓+B14/B12↵ | Enter % profit formula |
| 18 | /RFP1↵↵ | Format decimal number in cell B15 to percent |
| 19 | ↑↑↑/RFC↵↓↓↵ | Format the total revenue, costs, and profit to the Currency type |
| 20 | Home | Move the cell pointer to A1 |
| 21 | /FS↵R | Save worksheet as PROJS-2 |
| 22 | /PPRA1.D15↵AGPPQ | Print the as-displayed version of the worksheet |
| 23 | /PPRA10.B15↵AGPPQ | Print a portion of the worksheet |
| 24 | /PPRA1.D15↵OOCQAGPP | Print the cell-formulas version of the worksheet |
| 25 | OOAQQ | Change the print option to as-displayed |
| 26 | /RFTA1.D15↵ | Format the worksheet to the Text type |

The following list summarizes the material covered in Project 2.

1. To retrieve a worksheet from disk, enter the command /**F**ile **R**etrieve (/FR). Use the Left and Right Arrow keys to move the command cursor in the alphabetized list on the menu line to the worksheet name you wish to retrieve and then press the Enter key.
2. To change the width of all the columns in the worksheet, type the command /**W**orksheet **G**lobal **C**olumn-Width (/WGC). Enter the desired column width (1–240) on the input line and press the Enter key.
3. To change the width of a specific column in the worksheet, move the cell pointer to the column in question and type the command /**W**orksheet **C**olumn **S**et-Width (/WCS). Enter the new width and press the Enter key.
4. The column width may be entered in response to the /WGC or /WCS commands by pressing the Right Arrow or Left Arrow keys.
5. A **range** is one or more cells upon which you want to complete an operation. A range may be a single cell, a series of adjacent cells in a column or row, or a rectangular group of adjacent cells. A range cannot be made up of cells that only run diagonally or are separated.

## Project Summary (continued)

6. To enter a range, type the cell address at one end point of the range, followed by a period (.) to anchor the first end point, followed by the cell address at the opposite end point of the range. If it is necessary to change the first end point after it is *anchored*, press the Backspace key.
7. If a range defines a rectangular group of cells, the two end points must be diagonally opposite corner cells of the rectangle.
8. To format a range, type the command /**R**ange **F**ormat (/RF). Select the type of format you wish to use from the menu. Enter the number of decimal places if required. Enter the range to be affected and press the Enter key.
9. To format the entire worksheet, type the command /**W**orksheet **G**lobal **F**ormat (/WGF). Follow the same steps described for formatting a range.
10. You can also enter a range by **pointing**. Pointing involves using the arrow keys to move the cell pointer to select the end points.
11. When you use pointing to select the range, use the Backspace key to *unlock* the end points of the range on the input line.
12. 1-2-3 displays the range with the end points separated by two periods (..), even though you enter only a single period (.) to anchor the first end point.
13. There are several ways to format numeric values. See Table 2-2.
14. Move the cell pointer to a cell to determine the format assigned to it. The format displays in parentheses next to the cell address on the status line at the top of the screen.
15. To repeat a series of characters throughout a cell, begin the entry by typing the Backslash key (\).
16. To copy a range to another range, type the command /**C**opy (/C). Enter the source range and then the destination range.
17. It is good practice to save a worksheet to disk after every 50 to 75 keystrokes.
18. A **built-in function** automatically handles calculations.
19. All built-in functions begin with the @ symbol.
20. The SUM function adds the contents of the range specified in parentheses.
21. When you copy a function, the Copy command adjusts the range for the new position.
22. If the Slash key (/) is the first key pressed, 1-2-3 switches to command mode. If the Slash key follows any character in a nonlabel entry on the input line, it represents division.
23. When you save a worksheet the second time using the same file name, 1-2-3 requires that you type the letter R for Replace.
24. To print the **as-displayed** version of the worksheet without borders, type the command /**P**rint **P**rinter (/PP). If the range has not yet been established from a previous printout of the worksheet, you must enter the range to print. With the printer off, use the platen knob to align the perforated edge of the paper with the top of the print head mechanism. Turn the printer on. Type the letter A for Align and the letter G for Go. After the worksheet is printed, type the letter P (for Page) twice. Carefully remove the printed version of the worksheet from the printer. Finally, type the letter Q for Quit.
25. To print a section of the worksheet, enter the command /**P**rint **P**rinter **R**ange (/PPR). Use the Backspace key to *unlock* the range. Enter the desired range and continue with the steps just outlined.
26. To print the **cell-formulas** version of the worksheet, type the command /**P**rint **P**rinter **O**ptions **O**ther **C**ell-formulas **Q**uit **A**lign **G**o **P**age **P**age (/PPOOCQAGPP). It is important to change the print option back to as-displayed, so that future printouts will print the as-displayed version rather than the cell-formulas version.
27. To print the worksheet to a file, use the command /**P**rint **F**ile (/PF). Later, after you have quit 1-2-3, you may use the DOS command TYPE to display the worksheet on the screen or the DOS command PRINT to print the worksheet on the printer.
28. To display formulas assigned to cells rather than their numeric result, assign the Text type format to the cells in the worksheet.

# STUDENT ASSIGNMENTS

## STUDENT ASSIGNMENT 1: True/False

**Instructions:** Circle T if the statement is true or F if the statement is false.

T F 1. With the /**F**ile **R**etrieve (/FR) command, you are required to type the name of the worksheet you want loaded into main computer memory on the input line.

T F 2. The command /**W**orksheet **G**lobal **C**olumn-Width (/WGC) is used to set the width of all the columns in the worksheet.

T F 3. If you want to *back out* of the command /FR, press the Esc key three times.

T F 4. When using the command /**R**ange **F**ormat (/RF), entire columns can be formatted; however, entire rows cannot be formatted.

T F 5. For a rectangular group of cells, you must enter the cell addresses of two opposite corners to define the range.

T F 6. A range can be made up of one cell.

T F 7. If you decide to use the pointing method when 1-2-3 requests a range, press the Tab key to *unlock* the first end point, if necessary.

T F 8. A range can be referenced by an entry such as B4..D6.

T F 9. With the format Fixed, negative numbers display in parentheses.

T F 10. When in POINT mode, anchor the first cell end point by moving the cell pointer to it and pressing the Period key.

T F 11. The type of format assigned to a cell displays on the indicator line at the bottom of the screen when the cell pointer is on the cell.

T F 12. If the Backslash key (\) is the first character typed on the input line, the characters that follow will repeat throughout the cell when you press the Enter key or one of the arrow keys.

T F 13. The command /**C**opy (/C) is used to copy the contents of a range to another range of cells.

T F 14. If the function @SUM(B4..D4) is assigned to cell A20, A20 will be equal to the sum of the contents of cells B4, C4, and D4.

T F 15. It is not possible to copy a single cell to a group of cells.

T F 16. If the function @SUM(B4..B8) assigns a value of 10 to cell B9, and B9 is copied to C9, C9 will be equal to 10.

T F 17. If you save a worksheet a second time, you cannot use the same file name originally assigned to the worksheet.

T F 18. The Align command on the Print menu is used to align the cells on the screen.

## STUDENT ASSIGNMENT 2: Multiple Choice

**Instructions:** Circle the correct response.

1. Which of the following is the correct command for retrieving the worksheet PROJS-1.WK1 stored on the disk in the default drive?
   a. /FRPROJS-1 ↵
   b. /WRPROJS-1 ↵
   c. /CPROJS-1 ↵
   d. none of these
2. When the command /**W**orksheet **G**lobal (/WG) is used, it means that ________ .
   a. only a single cell will be affected
   b. only a single column will be affected
   c. only a single row will be affected
   d. the entire worksheet will be affected
3. Which one of the following is a valid range of cells?
   a. B2,D2
   b. B2:D2
   c. B2.D2
   d. both b and c are correct
4. The format Currency with two decimal places causes 5000 to display as:
   a. $5,000.00
   b. 5000.00
   c. 5,000.00
   d. $5000.00

5. Which one of the following causes the data in cells B4, C4, and D4 to be added together?
   a. @SUM(B4.D4)
   b. @ADD(B4.D4)
   c. @SUM(B4:D4)
   d. @SUM(B4 C4 D4)
6. Which one of the following correctly identifies the range of the rectangular group of cells with corner cells at A10, A18, D10, and D18?
   a. A10.D18
   b. A18.D10
   c. D18.A10
   d. all of these
7. Which one of the following instructs 1-2-3 to repeat characters in the current cell?
   a. circumflex (^)
   b. quotation mark (")
   c. apostrophe (')
   d. backslash (\)
8. A listing on the printer of what was entered into each cell of a worksheet is called the _________ version of the worksheet.
   a. cell-formulas
   b. as-displayed
   c. formatted
   d. content

## STUDENT ASSIGNMENT 3: Understanding Ranges

**Instructions:** List all the possible ranges for each of the designated areas in Figure 2-52. For example, one range that identifies the first group of cells is A1..B3. There are three other ways to identify this first group of cells.

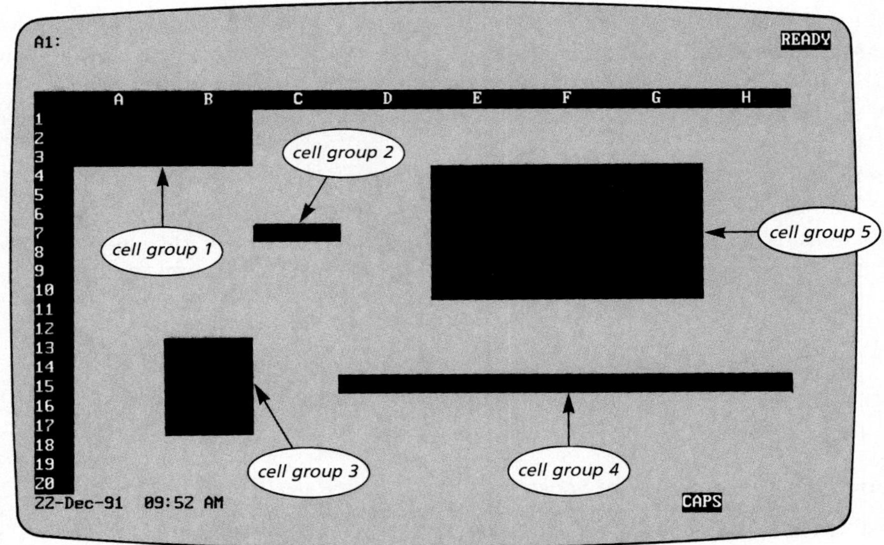


**FIGURE 2-52**
**Student Assignment 3**

Cell group 1: _________ _________ _________ _________

Cell group 2: _________

Cell group 3: _________ _________

Cell group 4: _________ _________

Cell group 5: _________ _________ _________ _________

## STUDENT ASSIGNMENT 4: Understanding Formats

**Instructions::** Using Table 2-1, fill in the *Results In* column of Table 2-5 below. Assume that the column width of each cell is 10 characters. Use the character b to indicate positions containing the blank character. As examples, the first two problems in Table 2-5 are complete.

**TABLE 2-5 Determining the Value of a Number Based on a Given Format**

| PROBLEM | CELL CONTENTS | FORMAT TO | DECIMAL PLACES | RESULTS IN |
|---|---|---|---|---|
| 1 | 25 | Fixed | 1 | bbbbb25.0b |
| 2 | 1.26 | Currency | 2 | bbbb$1.26b |
| 3 | 5000 | ,(comma) | 2 | ________ |
| 4 | 3.87 | Fixed | 0 | ________ |
| 5 | .137 | Percent | 2 | ________ |
| 6 | 5 | +/– | Not reqd. | ________ |
| 7 | –45.87 | , (comma) | 3 | ________ |
| 8 | 9523.6 | General | Not reqd. | ________ |
| 9 | 25 | Percent | 2 | ________ |
| 10 | .16 | Fixed | 2 | ________ |
| 11 | 109234 | Currency | 0 | ________ |
| 12 | 2357.85 | Scientific | 1 | ________ |
| 13 | 1903.4 | Currency | 2 | ________ |
| 14 | 23.56 | Scientific | 0 | ________ |
| 15 | –34.95 | Currency | 2 | ________ |

## STUDENT ASSIGNMENT 5: Correcting the Range in a Worksheet

**Instructions:** The worksheet illustrated in Figure 2-53 contains errors in cells B12 through B15. Analyze the entries displayed in the worksheet. Explain the cause of the errors and the method of correction in the space provided below.

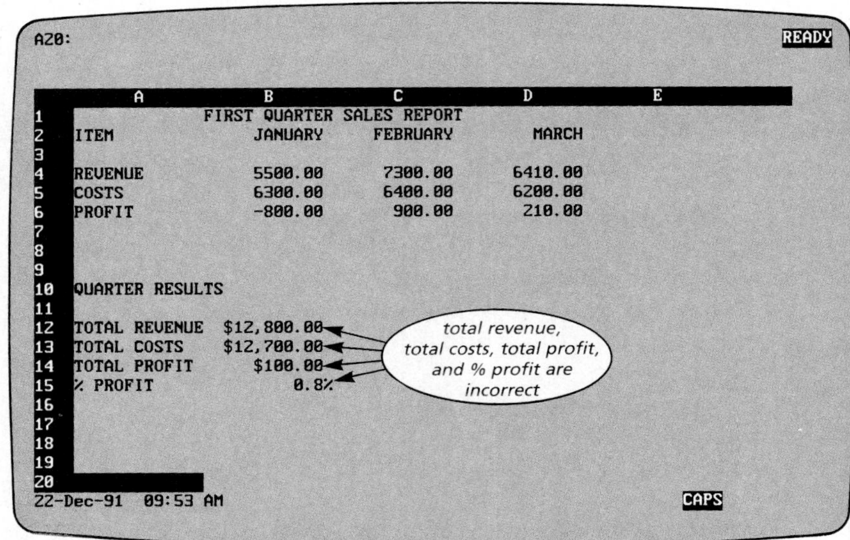


**FIGURE 2-53**
**Student Assignment 5**

Cause of error: ______________________________

______________________________

Method of correction for cell B12: ______________________________

______________________________

Method of correction for cells B13, B14, and B15: ______________________________

______________________________

______________________________

## STUDENT ASSIGNMENT 6: Correcting Functions in a Worksheet

**Instructions:** The worksheet illustrated in Figure 2-54 contains invalid function entries in cells B12, B13, and B14. The invalid entries in these cells cause the diagnostic message ERR to display in cell B15. Analyze the entries displayed in the worksheet. Explain the cause of the errors and the method of correction in the space provided below.

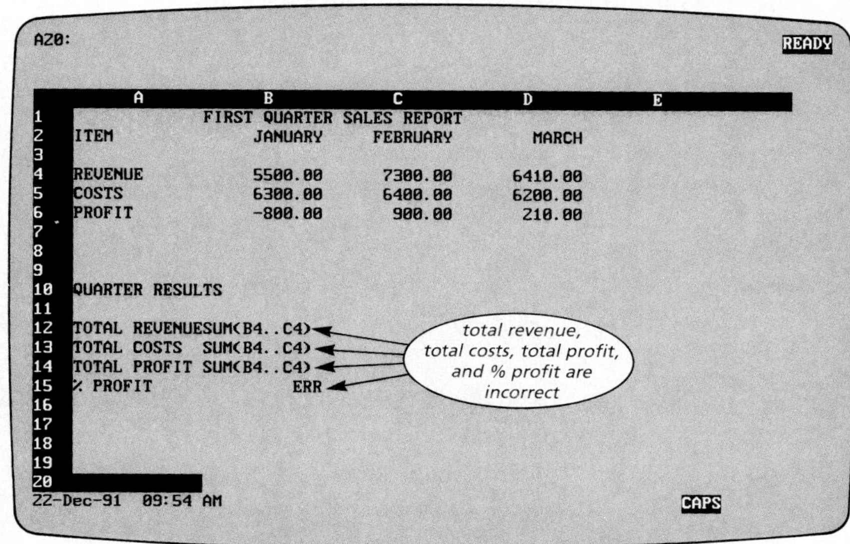


**FIGURE 2-54**
**Student Assignment 6**

Cause of error: ______________________________

______________________________

Method of correction for cell B12: ______________________________

______________________________

Method of correction for cells B13, B14, and B15: ______________________________

______________________________

______________________________

## STUDENT ASSIGNMENT 7: Modifying an Inventory Worksheet

**Instructions:** Load 1-2-3 and perform the following tasks.

1. Load the worksheet that was created in Project 1, Student Assignment 8. This worksheet is illustrated in Figure 2-55(a).
2. Perform the following modifications:
   a. Use the Comma (,) format with zero decimal places for the numbers in rows 4, 5, 6, and 7.
   b. Include the inventory total in the worksheet, as illustrated in Figure 2-55(b). The inventory total consists of a total for each plant (B13..B16). For example, the total for Seattle is the sum of cells B4 through D4. Separate the inventory total from the other values by a double line in row 9 (use the equal sign).
   c. Use the Comma (,) format with zero decimal places for the inventory totals.
3. Save the modified worksheet. Use the file name STUS2-7.
4. Print the entire worksheet on the printer using the /**P**rint **P**rinter (/PP) command.
5. Print only the inventory totals in the range A11..B16.
6. Print the worksheet after formatting all the cells to the Text type.

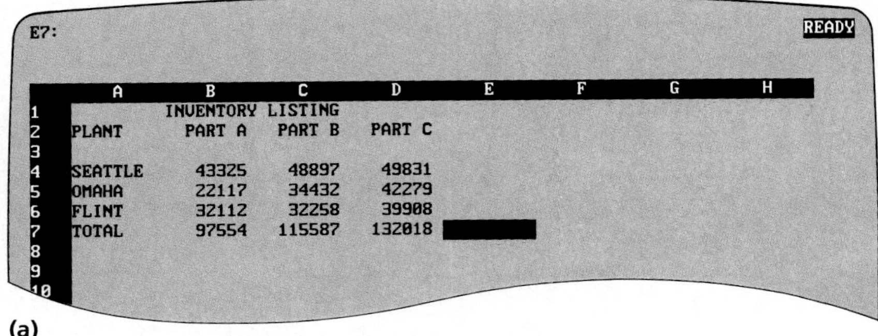


(a)

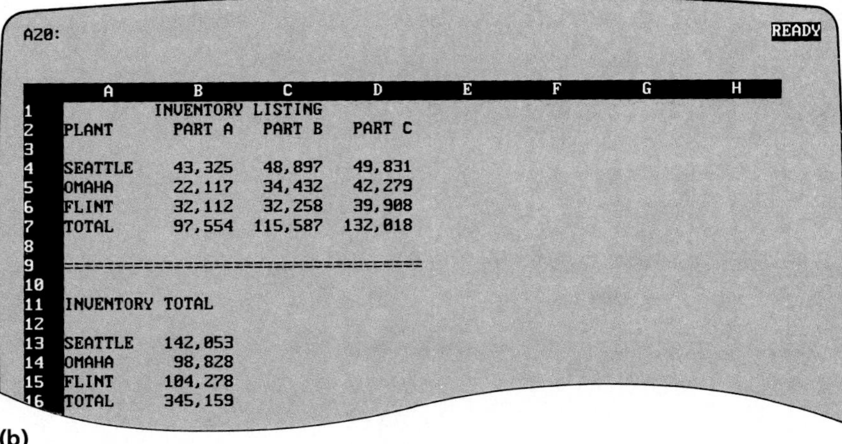


(b)

**FIGURE 2-55(a) & (b) Student Assignment 7. Worksheet before (a) and after (b) modification**

## STUDENT ASSIGNMENT 8: Building an Employee Payroll Comparison Worksheet

**Instructions:** Load 1-2-3 and perform the following tasks.

1. Build the worksheet illustrated in Figure 2-56. Change the width of all the columns to 14 characters. The totals displayed in row 9 of the worksheet are the sum of the salaried personnel in column B and the hourly personnel in column C. The store totals (B15..B18) are the sum of the salaried personnel and the hourly personnel for each store. The total in B20 is the sum of the store totals.
2. Save the worksheet. Use the file name STUS2-8.
3. Print the as-displayed and cell-formulas versions of this worksheet.
4. Print the portion of the worksheet in the range A1..C9.

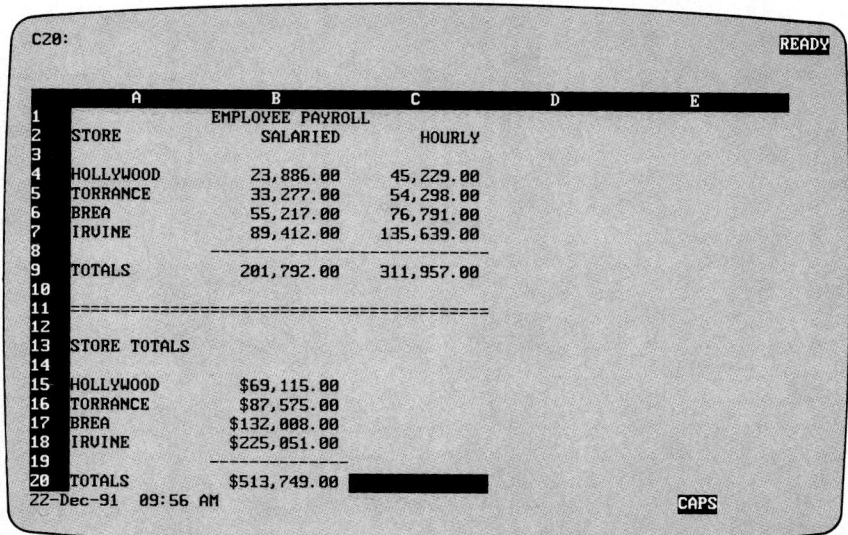


**FIGURE 2-56**
**Student Assignment 8**

## STUDENT ASSIGNMENT 9: Building a Monthly Expense Worksheet

**Instructions:** Load 1-2-3 and perform the following tasks.

1. Build the worksheet illustrated in Figure 2-57. Change the width of all the columns to 15 character positions. The variances in column D of the worksheet are obtained by subtracting the actual expenses from the budgeted expenses. In the summary portion of the worksheet, the percentage of budget used (C17) is obtained by dividing the total actual amount (C15) by the total budgeted amount (C14).
2. Save the worksheet. Use the file name STUS2-9.
3. Print the as-displayed and cell-formulas versions of this worksheet.
4. Print the portion of the worksheet in the range A3..B8.
5. Print the worksheet after formatting all the cells to the Text type.

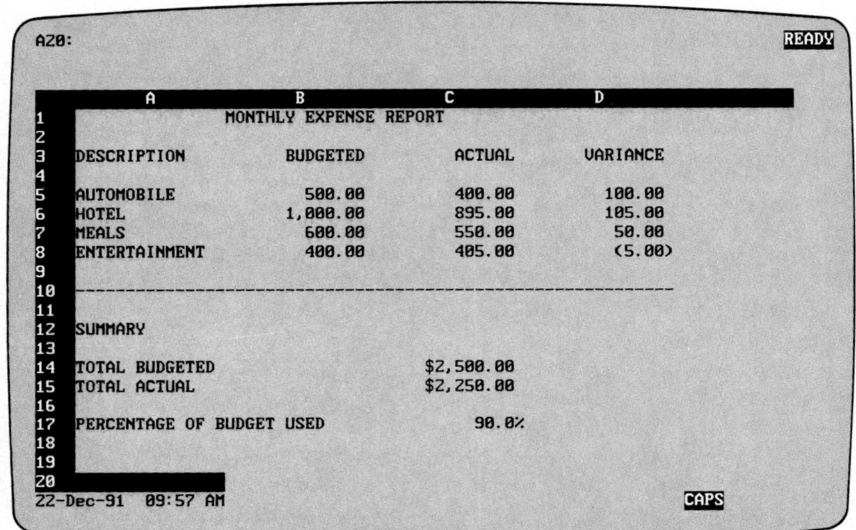


**FIGURE 2-57**
**Student Assignment 9**

## STUDENT ASSIGNMENT 10: Building a Monthly Sales Analysis Worksheet

**Instructions:** Load 1-2-3 and perform the following tasks.

1. Build the worksheet illustrated in Figure 2-58. Change the width of all the columns to 12 characters. Then change the width of column A to 14 positions. Center all the column headings using the circumflex (^). The net sales in column D of the worksheet is determined by subtracting the sales returns in column C from the sales amount in column B. The above/below quota amount in column F is obtained by subtracting the sales quota in column E from the net sales in column D. In the summary section of the worksheet, the totals for each group are obtained by adding the values for each salesperson. The percent of quota sold in cell C20 is obtained by dividing the total net sales amount in Cell 17 by the total sales quota amount in C18.
2. Save the worksheet. Use the file name STUS2-10.
3. Print the as-displayed and cell-formulas versions of this worksheet.
4. Print the portion of the worksheet in the range A1..F9.
5. Print the worksheet after formatting all the cells to the Text type.

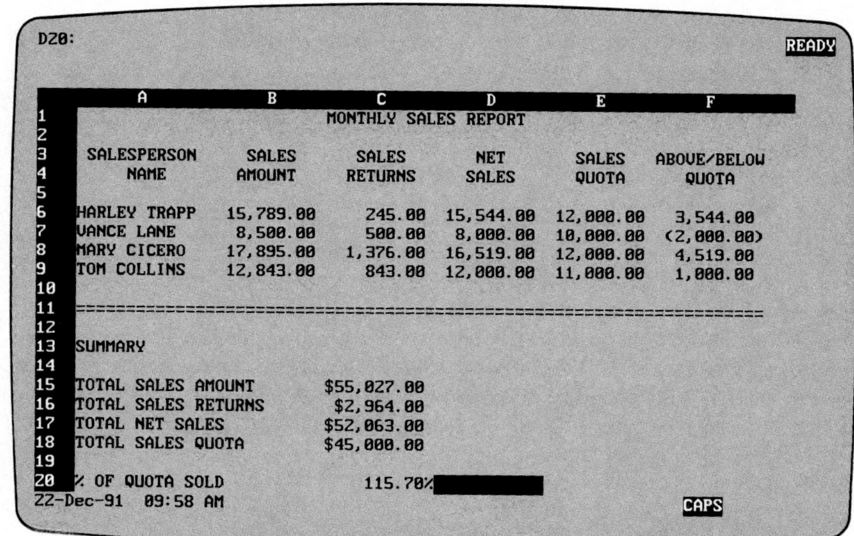


**FIGURE 2-58**
**Student Assignment 10**

## STUDENT ASSIGNMENT 11: Changing Data in the Monthly Expense Worksheet

**Instructions:** Load 1-2-3 and perform the following tasks.

1. Retrieve the worksheet STUS2-9 from disk. The worksheet is illustrated in Figure 2-57.
2. Decrement each of the four values in the ACTUAL column by $30.00 until the percentage of budget used in C17 is as close as possible to 80%. All four values in column C must be decremented the same number of times. You should end up with a percentage of budget used in C17 equal to 80.4%.
3. After successfully modifying the worksheet, print it on the printer.
4. Save the modified worksheet. Use the file name STUS2-11.

## STUDENT ASSIGNMENT 12: Changing Data in the Monthly Sales Analysis Worksheet

**Instructions:** Load 1-2-3 and perform the following tasks.

1. Retrieve the worksheet STUS2-10 from disk. The worksheet is illustrated in Figure 2-58.
2. Increment each of the four values in the sales quota column by $1000.00 until the percent of quota sold in cell C20 is below, yet as close as possible to 100%. All four values in column E must be incremented the same number of times. The percent of quota sold in C20 should be equal to 98.23%.
3. Decrement each of the four values in the sales returns column by $100.00 until the percent of quota sold in cell C20 is below, yet as close as possible to 100%. All four values in column C must be decremented the same number of times. Your worksheet is correct when the percent of quota sold in C20 is equal to 99.74%.
4. After successfully modifying the worksheet, print it on the printer.
5. Save the modified worksheet. Use the file name STUS2-12.

# PROJECT 3

## Enhancing Your Worksheet

## Objectives

You will have mastered the material in this project when you can:

- Display today's date and time in a worksheet using the NOW function.
- Move a group of rows or columns to another area of the worksheet.
- Insert and delete rows and columns.
- Freeze the horizontal and vertical titles.
- Enter percentage values using the percent sign (%).
- Copy absolute cell addresses.
- Employ the pointing method to enter a range to be summed.
- Print a worksheet in condensed mode.
- Print selected nonadjacent columns.
- Answer what-if questions.
- Switch between manual and automatic recalculation of a worksheet.
- Change the default settings.
- Temporarily exit 1-2-3 and return control to DOS.

In the first two projects you learned to build, save, retrieve, format, copy, and print worksheets. In this project we continue to emphasize these topics and discuss some new ones. We especially want to examine the Copy command in greater detail. The ability to copy one range to another range is one of the most powerful features of 1-2-3.

The new topics in this project teach you to insert and delete rows and columns in a worksheet and move the contents of a range to another range. In general, they make the job of creating, saving, and printing a worksheet easier.

Finally, this project illustrates using 1-2-3 to answer **what-if questions**, like "What if the marketing expenses decrease 3%—how would the decrease affect net income for the first quarter of the year?" This capability of quickly analyzing the effect of changing values in a worksheet is important in making business decisions. To illustrate answering what-if questions, we will prepare the quarterly budget report shown in Figure 3-1.

| | A | B | C | D | E |
|---|---|---|---|---|---|
| 1 | Quarterly Report - January through March | | | | 12/22/91 |
| 2 | Prepared by SAS | | | | 10:01 AM |
| 3 | | | | | |
| 4 | | | | | |
| 5 | ITEM | JANUARY | FEBRUARY | MARCH | QUARTER TOTAL |
| 6 | ==================== | ============ | ============ | ============ | ============== |
| 7 | | | | | |
| 8 | REVENUE | | | | |
| 9 | Sales Revenue | 232,897.95 | 432,989.76 | 765,998.61 | 1,431,886.32 |
| 10 | Other Revenue | 1,232.93 | 3,265.81 | 2,145.99 | 6,644.73 |
| 11 | | | | | |
| 12 | Total Revenue | 234,130.88 | 436,255.57 | 768,144.60 | 1,438,531.05 |
| 13 | | | | | |
| 14 | EXPENSES | | | | |
| 15 | Manufacturing | 88,969.73 | 165,777.12 | 291,894.95 | 546,641.80 |
| 16 | Research | 25,754.40 | 47,988.11 | 84,495.91 | 158,238.42 |
| 17 | Marketing | 37,460.94 | 69,800.89 | 122,903.14 | 230,164.97 |
| 18 | Administrative | 39,802.25 | 74,163.45 | 130,584.58 | 244,550.28 |
| 19 | Fulfillment | 18,730.47 | 34,900.45 | 61,451.57 | 115,082.48 |
| 20 | | | | | |
| 21 | Total Expenses | 210,717.79 | 392,630.01 | 691,330.14 | 1,294,677.95 |
| 22 | | | | | |
| 23 | NET INCOME | 23,413.09 | 43,625.56 | 76,814.46 | 143,853.10 |
| 24 | | | | | |
| 25 | Budget % Values | | | | |
| 26 | | | | | |
| 27 | Manufacturing | 38% | | | |
| 28 | Research | 11% | | | |
| 29 | Marketing | 16% | | | |
| 30 | Administrative | 17% | | | |
| 31 | Fulfillment | 8% | | | |

**FIGURE 3-1** The worksheet we will build in Project 3.

The worksheet in Figure 3-1 contains a company's budgeted revenue and expenses for the quarterly period of January through March. In addition, this worksheet includes the quarter total for all revenues and budgeted expenses. The total revenues for each month and the quarter total in row 12 are determined by adding the corresponding sales revenue and other revenue.

Each of the budgeted expenses—manufacturing, research, marketing, administrative, and fulfillment—is determined by taking a percentage of the total revenue. The budget percent values located in rows 27–31 are as follows:

1. The manufacturing expense is 38% of the total revenue.
2. The research expense is 11% of the total revenue.
3. The marketing expense is 16% of the total revenue.
4. The administrative expense is 17% of the total revenue.
5. The fulfillment expense is 8% of the total revenue.

The total expenses for each month in row 21 of Figure 3-1 are determined by adding all the corresponding budgeted expenses together. The net income for each month in row 23 is determined by subtracting the corresponding total expenses from the total revenue. Finally, the quarter totals in the far right column are determined by summing the monthly values in each row.

Begin this project by booting the computer and loading 1-2-3. A few seconds after the copyright message displays, an empty worksheet appears on the screen. All the columns in the empty worksheet are nine characters wide. This default width is not enough to hold some of the larger numbers in the worksheet we plan to build. Therefore, let's change the width of the columns.

## VARYING THE WIDTH OF THE COLUMNS

In the worksheet shown in Figure 3-1, column A is 17 characters wide, columns B through D are 13 characters wide, and column E is 16 characters wide. You select a column width setting on the basis of the longest column entry and the general appearance of the worksheet. Change the widths of the columns in the following manner:

1. Enter the command /**W**orksheet **G**lobal **C**olumn-Width (/WGC) to change the width of all the columns to 13 characters. Change the number on the input line from 9 to 13 by pressing the Right Arrow key four times followed by the Enter key as shown in Figure 3-2. We can also enter the number 13 in response to the prompt message on the input line and press the Enter key. The Global command is used to change the width of all the cells in the worksheet to 13 characters because that is the desired width of most of the columns for this project.

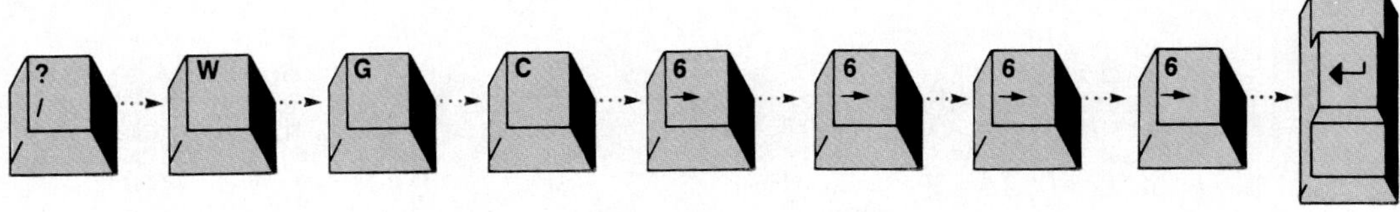


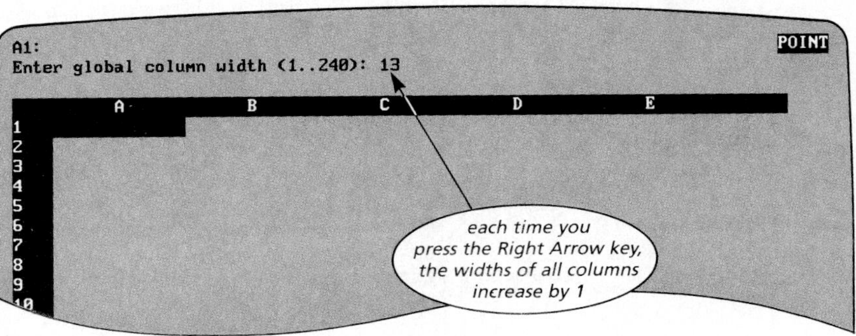


**FIGURE 3-2**
**Using the command /WGC and the Right Arrow key to increase the width of all the columns in the worksheet to 13 characters.**

2. With the cell pointer at A1, enter the command /**W**orksheet **C**olumn **S**et-Width (/WCS) to change the width of column A to 17 characters. Again, press the Right Arrow key four times to change the number 13 to 17 on the input line. To complete the command, press the Enter key as shown in Figure 3-3.

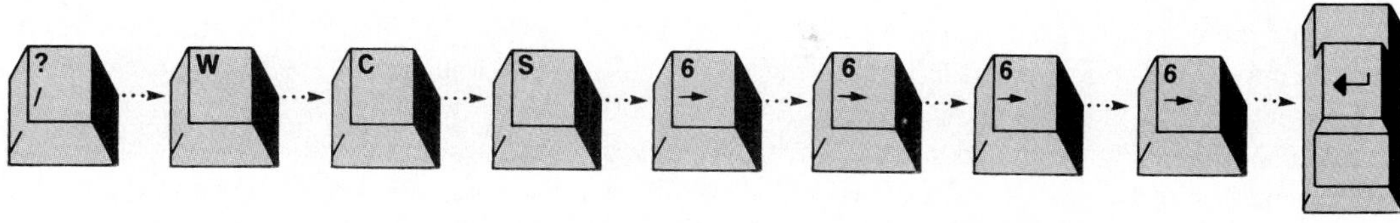

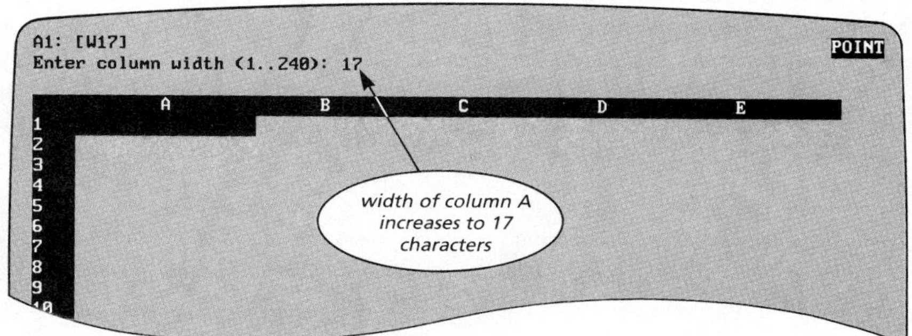


**FIGURE 3-3**
**Using the command /WCS and the Right Arrow key to increase the width of column A to 17 characters.**

3. Move the cell pointer to E1 and enter the command /**W**orksheet **C**olumn **S**et-Width (/WCS) to change the width of column E to 16 characters. This is shown in Figure 3-4.

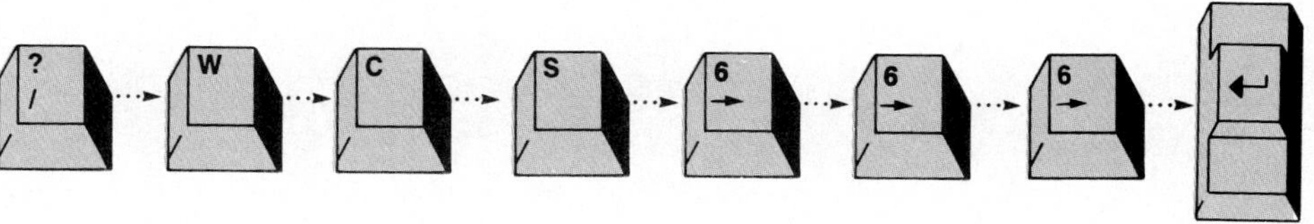

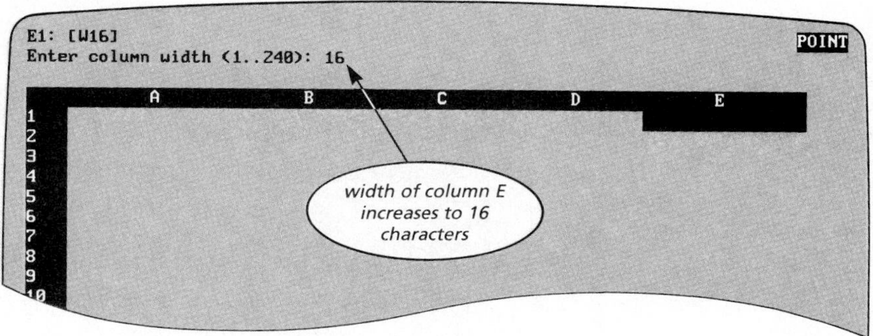


**FIGURE 3-4**
**Using the command /WCS and the Right Arrow key to increase the width of column E to 16 characters.**

With the columns set to their designated widths, we can move on to the next step, formatting the worksheet globally.

## FORMATTING THE WORKSHEET GLOBALLY

In Project 2, we formatted the numbers after we entered the data. In some cases, especially when developing a large worksheet, you should consider issuing a global format before entering any data. This formats the numbers as you enter them, which makes them easier to read. The way to do this is to choose the format that is common to most of the cells. In choosing the format, don't count the empty cells or the ones with labels, because a numeric format does not affect them.

You can see from Figure 3-1 that, except for the budget percent values and the date and time, all the numbers appear as decimal numbers with two places of accuracy. These numbers also use the comma to group the integer portion by thousands. If you refer to Table 2-2 in Project 2, you will see that the required format corresponds to the Comma (,) type. Therefore, use this format for all the cells in the worksheet.

To invoke the global format command, enter the command /Worksheet Global Format (/WGF). This is shown in Figure 3-5. With the command cursor active in the Format menu, press the Comma key (,). The prompt message "Enter number of decimal places (0..15): 2" displays on the input line (see Figure 3-6). Since we are working with dollars and cents, we want two decimal places to display. Therefore, press the Enter key.

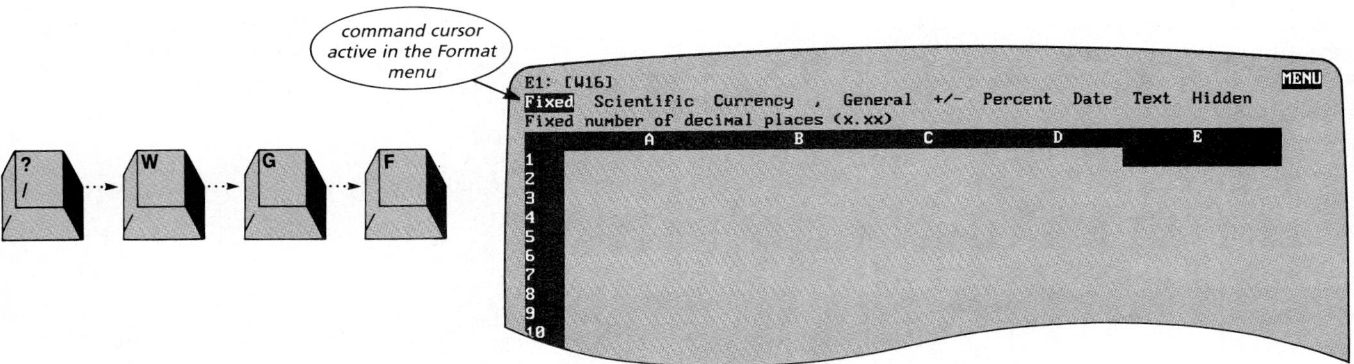


**FIGURE 3-5 Step 1 of using the /WGF command to format all the cells in the worksheet to the Comma (,) type—press the Slash key (/) and type the letters W for Worksheet, G for Global, and F for Format.**

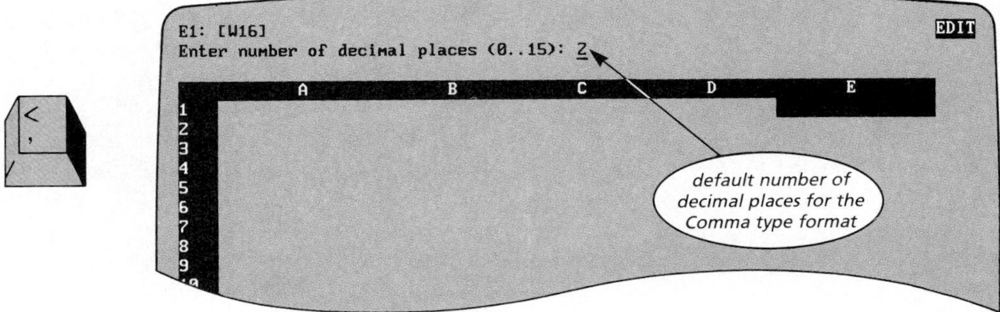


**FIGURE 3-6 Step 2 of using the /WGF command to format all the cells in the worksheet to the Comma (,) type—press the Comma key (,).**

The empty worksheet shown in Figure 3-7 displays. You can see that the columns are wider than nine characters. However, there is no indication of the Comma format we assigned to all the cells. The format will appear as we enter data, because 1-2-3 will automatically use the Comma format for any number entered into a cell.

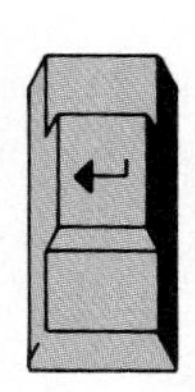

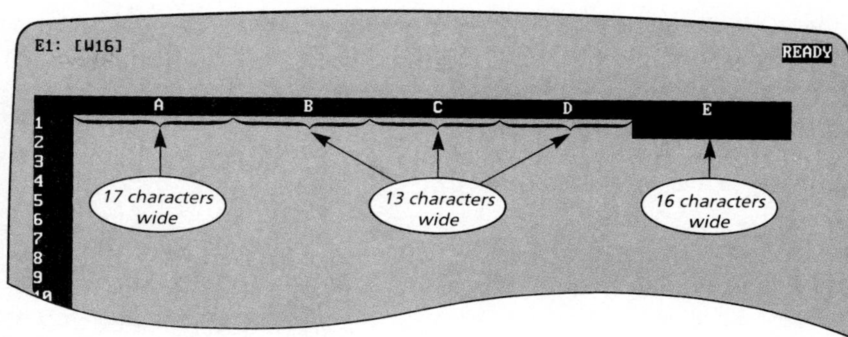


**FIGURE 3-7**
**Step 3 of using the /WGF command to format all the cells in the worksheet to the Comma (,) type—press the Enter key.**

# DISPLAYING THE DATE AND TIME

With the column widths and the global format set, the next step is to enter the data into the worksheet. Enter the titles in cells A1 and A2 as you learned in Project 1 (see Figure 3-8). Cells E1 and E2 require today's date and time. Both values can be displayed by assigning each cell the NOW function.

## The NOW Function

The NOW function uses the current DOS date and time to determine the number of days since December 31, 1899. It displays the value in the assigned cell as a decimal number. For this project assume that the DOS date is December 22, 1991 and the time is approximately 10:08 AM. For the NOW function to display the correct value, it is important that you check the accuracy of the system date and system time. Recall that in the Introduction to DOS, you learned how to set the system time and system date.

To complete the time and date entries in the worksheet, move the cell pointer to E1 and enter the NOW function on the input line as illustrated in Figure 3-8.

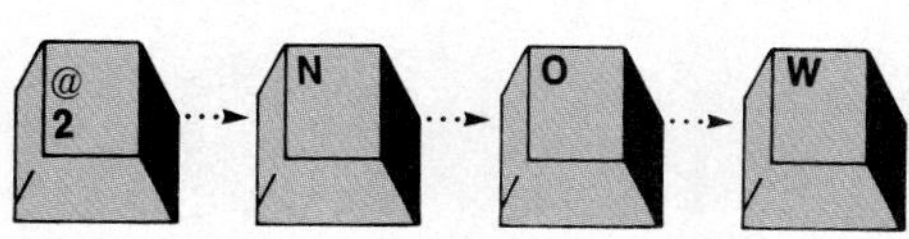


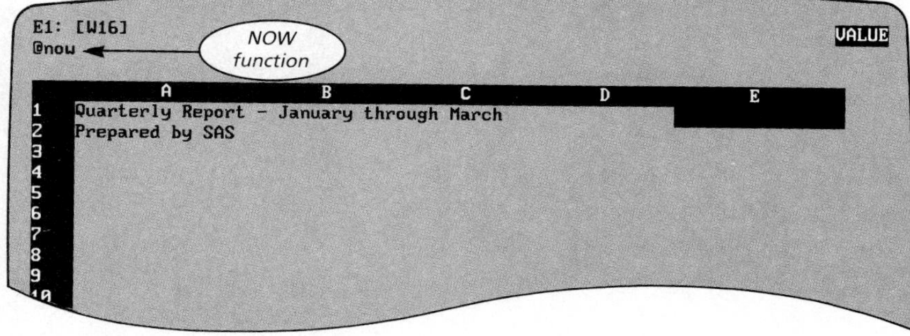


**FIGURE 3-8**
**Entering the NOW function on the input line with the cell pointer at E1.**

Next, press the Down Arrow key and enter the same function in E2. Use the Up Arrow key to enter the function in E2. This places the cell pointer in E1 as shown in Figure 3-9. The value 33,594.42 in cells E1 and E2 represents the number of days since December 31, 1899. The integer portion of the number (33,594) represents the number of complete days, and the decimal portion (.42) represents the first 10 hours of December 22, 1991. Note that the two entries are displayed in the Comma (,) format, the one we assigned earlier to the entire worksheet. The next step is to format the date and time so that they display in a more meaningful way.

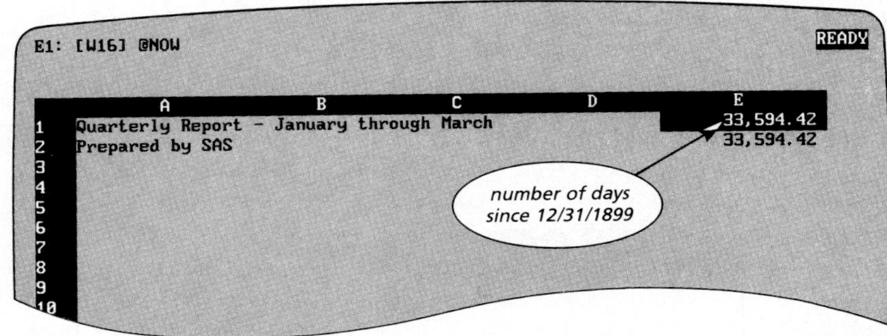


**FIGURE 3-9**
**The NOW function assigned to cells E1 and E2.**

## Formatting the Date

In Figure 3-9, the cell pointer is at E1. To format the date, enter the command /**R**ange **F**ormat **D**ate (/RFD) as shown in Figure 3-10. With the command cursor active in the **Date menu**, select the fourth date format Long Intn'l (MM/DD/YY). To select the desired format, move the command cursor to the fourth one in the menu and press the Enter key. 1-2-3 responds by displaying the prompt message "Enter range to format: E1..E1" on the input line. E1 is the only cell we want to format, so press the Enter key. The date immediately changes in cell E1 to 12/22/91 as shown in Figure 3-11.

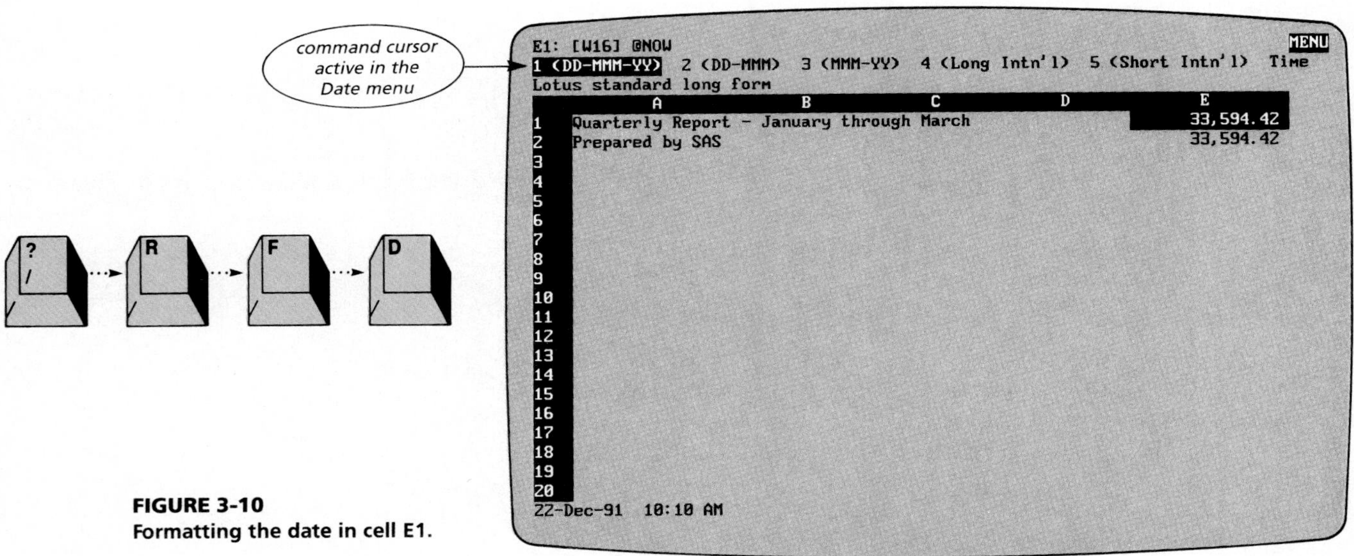


**FIGURE 3-10**
**Formatting the date in cell E1.**

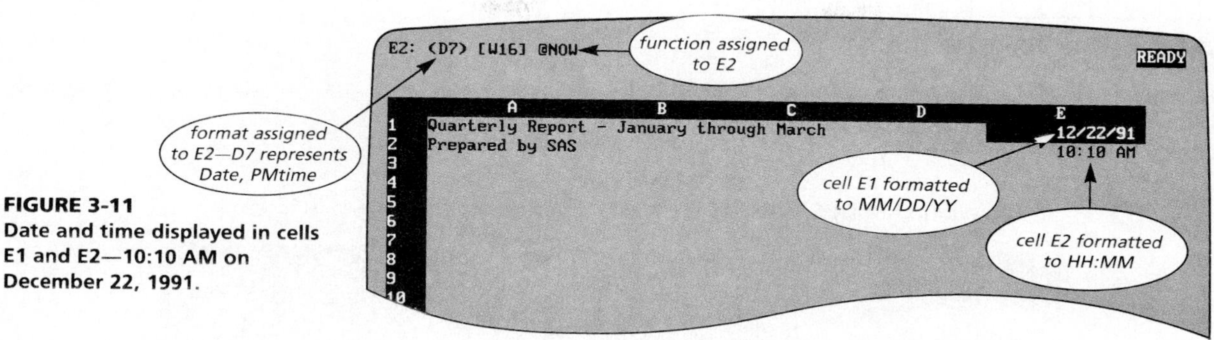


**FIGURE 3-11**
**Date and time displayed in cells E1 and E2—10:10 AM on December 22, 1991.**

## Formatting the Time

Move the cell pointer to E2. To format the time, enter the same command as for the date—/**R**ange **F**ormat **D**ate (/RFD). This is shown in Figure 3-10. With the command cursor active in the Date menu, type the letter T for Time. The **Time menu** replaces the Date menu at the top of the screen. Select the second Time format (HH:MM AM/PM) by pressing the 2 key. Next, press the Enter key and the time in E2 displays as 10:10 AM (see Figure 3-11).

## Updating the Time—Recalculation

The time displayed on the indicator line at the bottom of the screen updates every minute. However, the time displayed in a cell, as in E2, only updates when you enter a value into a cell in the worksheet. Any entry causes 1-2-3 to recalculate all the formulas and functions in the worksheet automatically.

If you are not entering any numeric values and want to instruct 1-2-3 to recalculate all formulas and functions, press function key F9. Pressing F9 updates the time as illustrated in Figure 3-12.

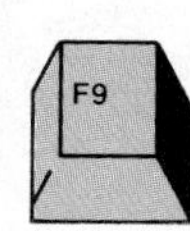


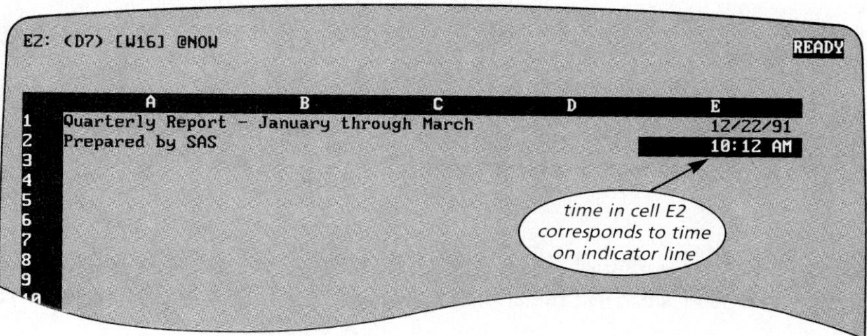


**FIGURE 3-12**
**Press function key F9 to manually update the time in cell E2.**

## Date and Time Formats

Table 3-1 summarizes the date and time formats available in 1-2-3. Use this table to select formats when you want to display the date and time in a worksheet.

**TABLE 3-1 Date and Time Formats**
**(Assume the DOS date is December 22, 1991 and the time is 3:12 PM.)**

| FORMAT NUMBER | FORMAT TYPE | FORMAT CODE ON STATUS LINE | DATE OR TIME DISPLAYED |
|---|---|---|---|
| 1 | DD-MMM-YY | D1 | 22-Dec-91 |
| 2 | DD-MMM | D2 | 22-Dec |
| 3 | MMM-YY | D3 | Dec-91 |
| 4 | Long Intn'l (MM/DD/YY) | D4 | 12/22/91 |
| 5 | Short Intn'l (MM/DD) | D5 | 12/22 |
| 1 | HH:MM:SS AM/PM | D6 | 3:12:00 PM |
| 2 | HH:MM AM/PM | D7 | 3:12 PM |
| 3 | Long Intn'l | D8 | 15:12:00 |
| 4 | Short Intn'l | D9 | 15:12 |

# ENTERING THE QUARTERLY BUDGET LABELS

With the date and time formatted, we can enter the column headings, group titles, and row titles. Move the cell pointer to A5. Since the column headings consist of capital letters, press the Caps Lock key before entering them. Left-justify the first column heading and right-justify the rest. Recall that to right-justify a label, you begin the label with a quotation mark ("). The worksheet with the column headings is shown in Figure 3-13.

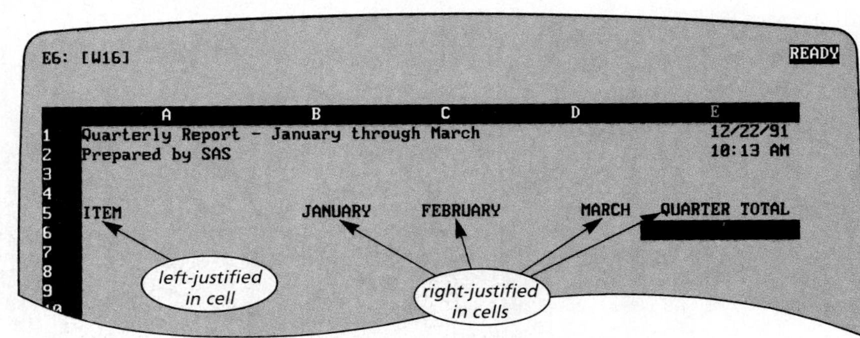


**FIGURE 3-13**
**Column headings entered into row 5.**

After completing the column headings, move the cell pointer to A6. Use the Backslash key (\) to repeat the equal sign (=) throughout cell A6. Next, use the command /Copy (/C) to copy the contents of cell A6 to cells B6 through E6. The result is a double-dashed line in row 6 as illustrated in Figure 3-14.

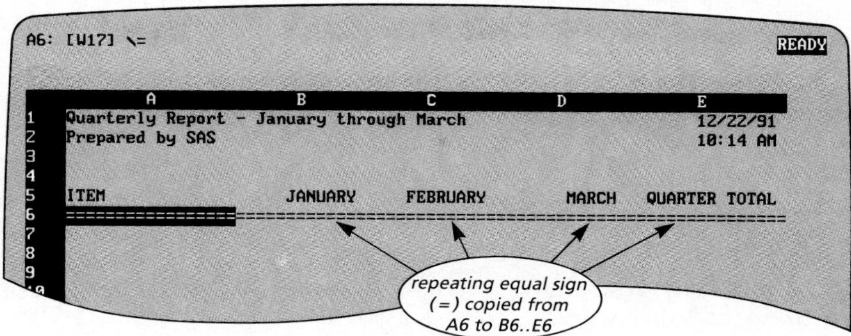


**FIGURE 3-14**
**Column headings underlined.**

Once the column headings are complete, begin entering the group titles and row titles that are shown on the left side of Figure 3-1. All the labels are left-justified. The group subtitles are indented by two spaces to make the worksheet easier to read. Since most of the remaining labels are in lower-case letters, press the Caps Lock key to toggle off capital letters after entering the group title REVENUE in cell A8.

Do not enter the two subtitles Marketing and Administrative under the group title EXPENSES. We will add these subtitles shortly.

Figure 3-15 shows the group titles and row identifiers up to row 24. Note in Figure 3-15 that with the cell pointer at A24 the window has moved down four rows, displaying rows 5 through 24 rather than rows 1 through 20. Once the cell pointer moves past row 20, the window begins to move down. The same applies when the cell pointer moves beyond the last column on the screen.

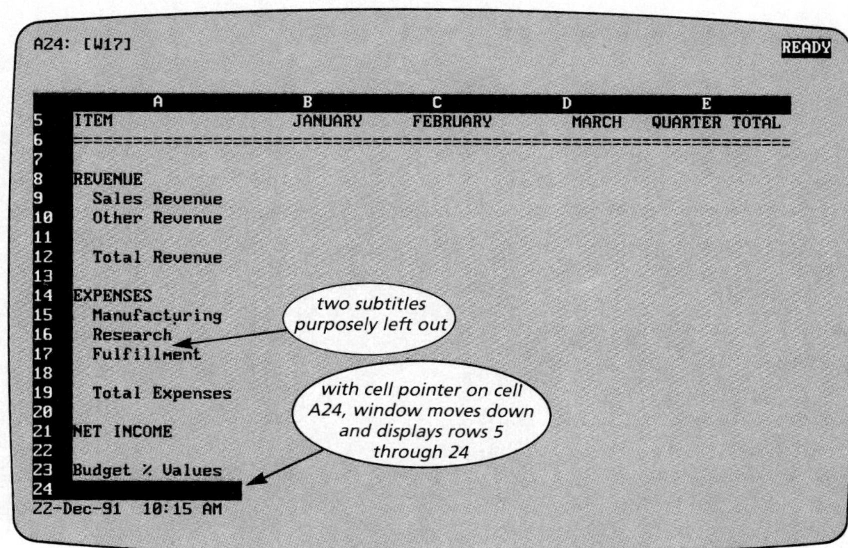


**FIGURE 3-15**
**Group titles and subtitles entered.**

# INSERTING AND DELETING ROWS AND COLUMNS

It is not unusual to forget to include rows or columns of data when building a worksheet, or to include too many rows or columns. 1-2-3 is forgiving. It has commands to insert or delete as many rows or columns as required. Furthermore, you can do this at any time, even after a worksheet is well under way.

## The Insert Command

The command /**W**orksheet **I**nsert (/WI) is used to insert empty rows or columns anywhere in the worksheet. To make room for the new rows, 1-2-3 simply opens up the worksheet by *pushing down* the rows below the insertion point. If you are inserting columns, those to the right of the insertion point are *pushed* to the right. More importantly, if the *pushed* rows or columns include any formulas, 1-2-3 adjusts the cell references to the new locations.

Remember that we purposely left out the two subtitles Marketing and Administrative from the group title EXPENSES (compare Figure 3-15 to Figure 3-1). Let's insert—open up—two blank rows in the worksheet so that we can add the two subtitles. According to Figure 3-1, the two subtitles belong immediately before Fulfillment in cell A17. Therefore, move the cell pointer to A17. To complete a row insert, always position the cell pointer on the first row you want *pushed* down. This is shown in Figure 3-16. For a row insert, the column location of the cell pointer is not important.

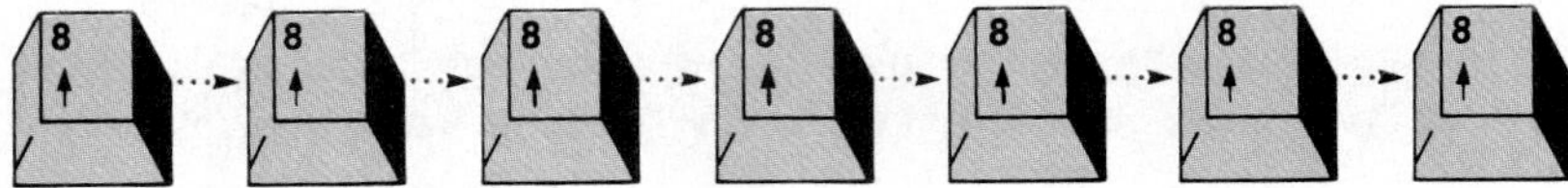


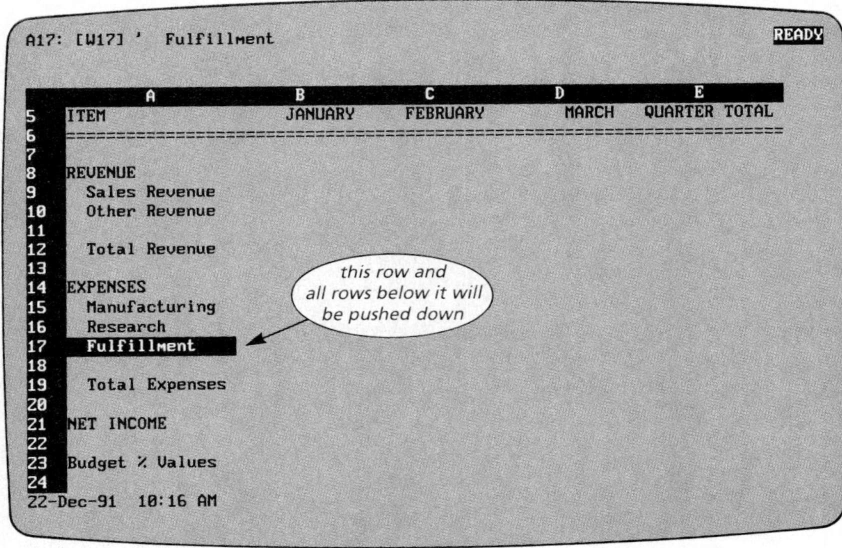


**FIGURE 3-16**
**Step 1 of using the /WI command to insert rows—move the cell pointer to A17, the first row we want *pushed* down.**

Enter the command /**W**orksheet **I**nsert (/WI) as shown in Figure 3-17. With the command cursor active in the **Insert menu**, type the letter R for Row. 1-2-3 immediately responds on the input line at the top of the screen with the prompt message, "Enter row insert range: A17..A17". We want to add two new rows, A17 and A18. Therefore, use the Down Arrow key to increase the range on the input line from A17..A17 to A17..A18. This is illustrated in Figure 3-18.

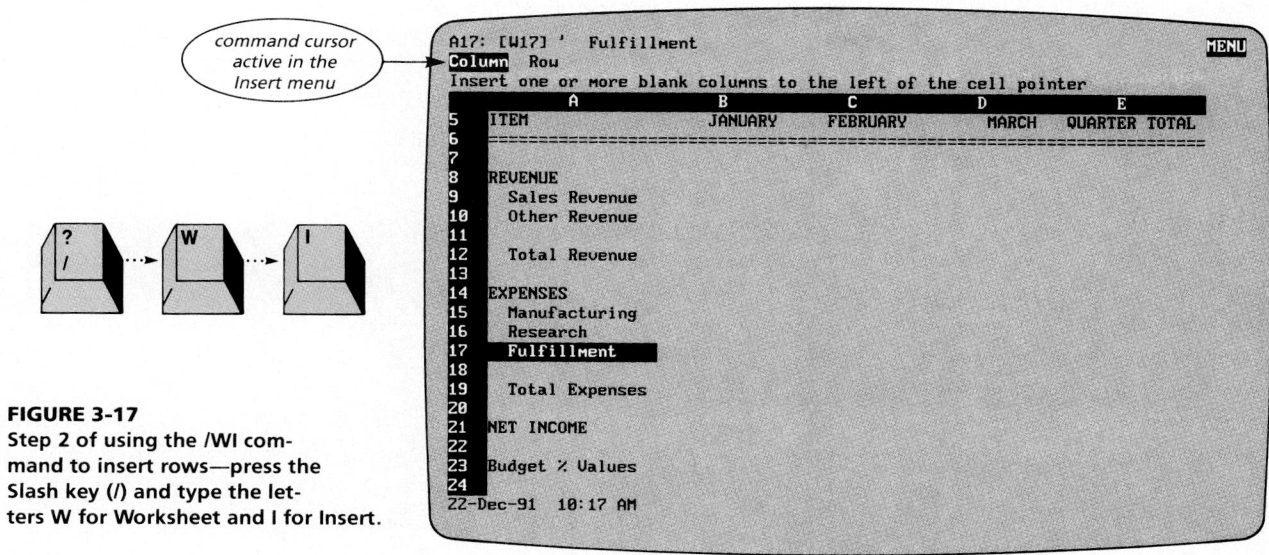


**FIGURE 3-17**
Step 2 of using the /WI command to insert rows—press the Slash key (/) and type the letters W for Worksheet and I for Insert.

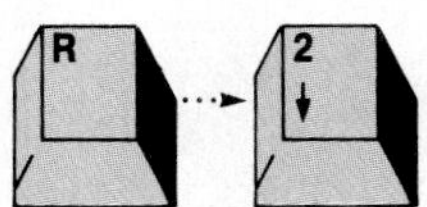


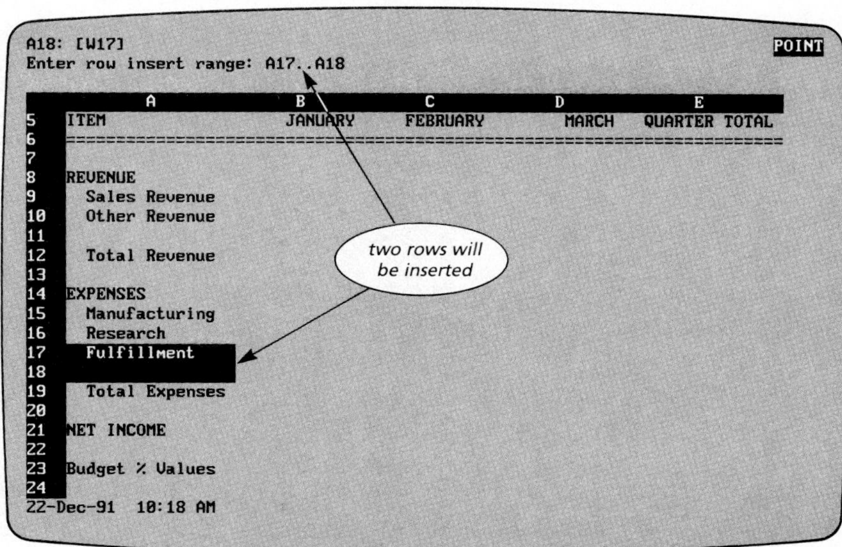


**FIGURE 3-18**
Step 3 of using the /WI command to insert rows—type the letter R for Row and use the Down Arrow key to select the number of rows you want to insert.

Press the Enter key and the worksheet *pushes down* all the rows beginning with row 17—the first row in the range A17..A18. This leaves rows 17 and 18 empty as shown in Figure 3-19. Enter the subtitle Marketing in cell A17 and the subtitle Administrative in cell A18 (see Figure 3-20).

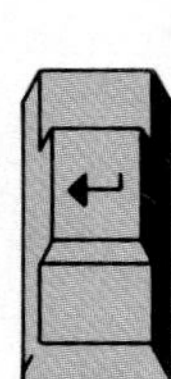

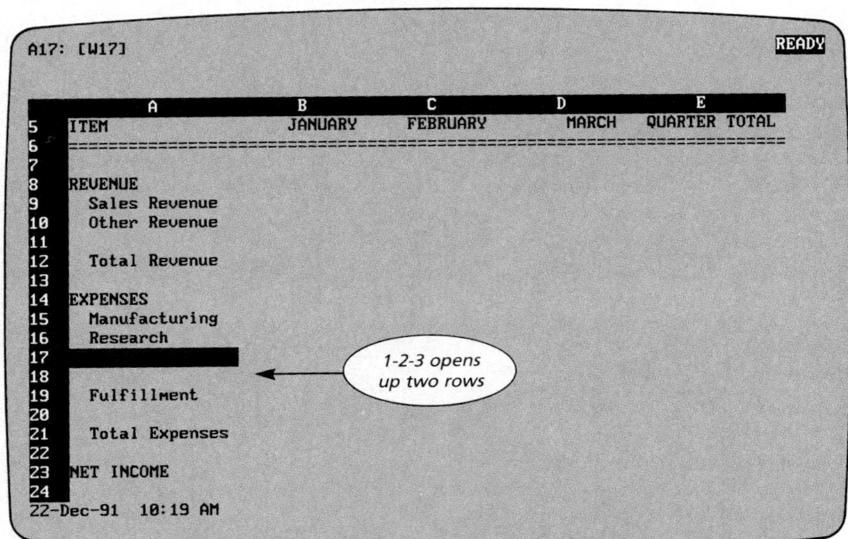


**FIGURE 3-19**
**Step 4 of using the /WI command to insert rows—press the Enter key.**

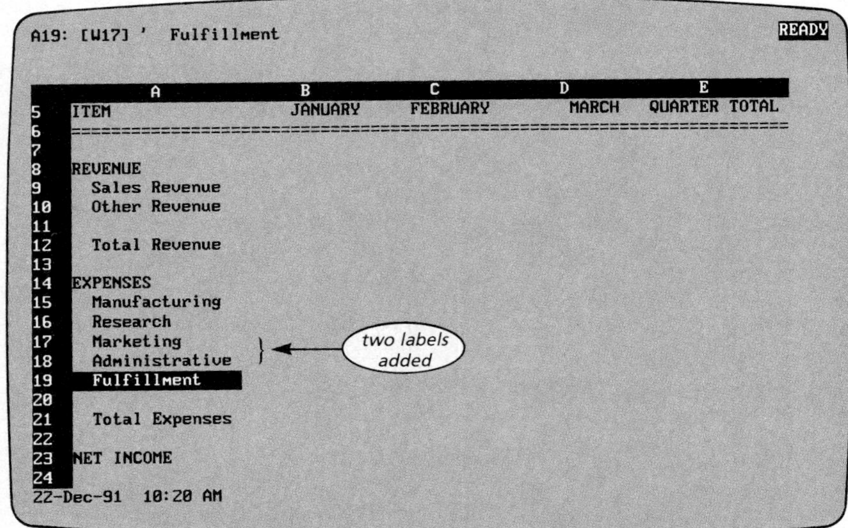


**FIGURE 3-20**
**The two subtitles inserted into the worksheet.**

## The Delete Command

You can delete unwanted rows or columns from a worksheet by using the command /**W**orksheet **D**elete (/WD). Let's delete rows 17 and 18 in Figure 3-20. After deleting these two rows, we will reinsert them using the command /**W**orksheet **I**nsert (/WI).

With the cell pointer at cell A17, enter the command /**W**orksheet **D**elete (/WD). Next, type the letter R to instruct 1-2-3 to delete rows rather than columns. To delete columns you would type the letter C. When 1-2-3 requests the range to delete, press the Down Arrow key to change the range from A17..A17 to A17..A18. Press the Enter key. 1-2-3 immediately *closes up* the worksheet—rows 17 and 18 disappear. The worksheet appears as it did earlier in Figure 3-16.

Be careful when you use the /Worksheet Delete command. You do not want to delete rows or columns that are part of a range used in a formula or function elsewhere in the worksheet without carefully weighing the consequences. If any formula references a cell in a deleted row or column, 1-2-3 displays the diagnostic message ERR in the cell assigned the formula. ERR means that it was impossible for 1-2-3 to complete the computation.

Before moving on, reinsert the two rows above row 17 and enter the row titles (Marketing and Administrative). Follow the keystroke sequence just described and shown in Figures 3-16 through 3-20.

## COPYING CELLS WITH EQUAL SOURCE AND DESTINATION RANGES

We are not yet finished with the labels. We need to enter the subtitles in cells A27 through A31 (see Figure 3-1). These subtitles are the same as the ones entered earlier in cells A15 through A19. Therefore, we can use the Copy command to copy the contents of cells A15 through A19 to A27 through A31.

As shown in Figure 3-20, the cell pointer is at cell A19, one of the end points of the source range. Enter the command /**C**opy (/C). On the input line, the first end point of the source cell range (A19) is already anchored. Use the Up Arrow key to select the range A19..A15. Press the Enter key. Next, select the destination range by moving the cell pointer to A27 as shown in Figure 3-21. Press the Enter key to conclude the Copy command (see Figure 3-22 on the following page).

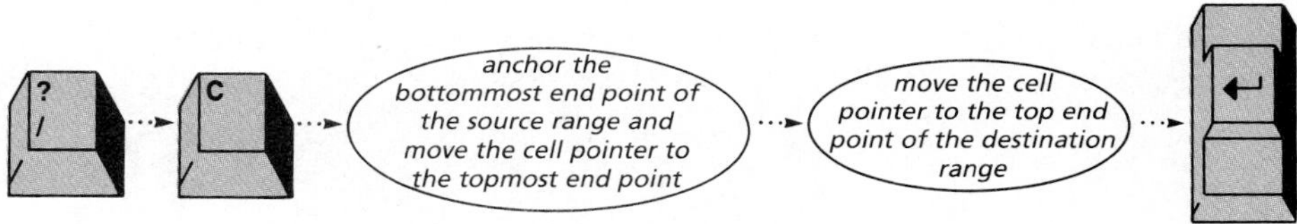


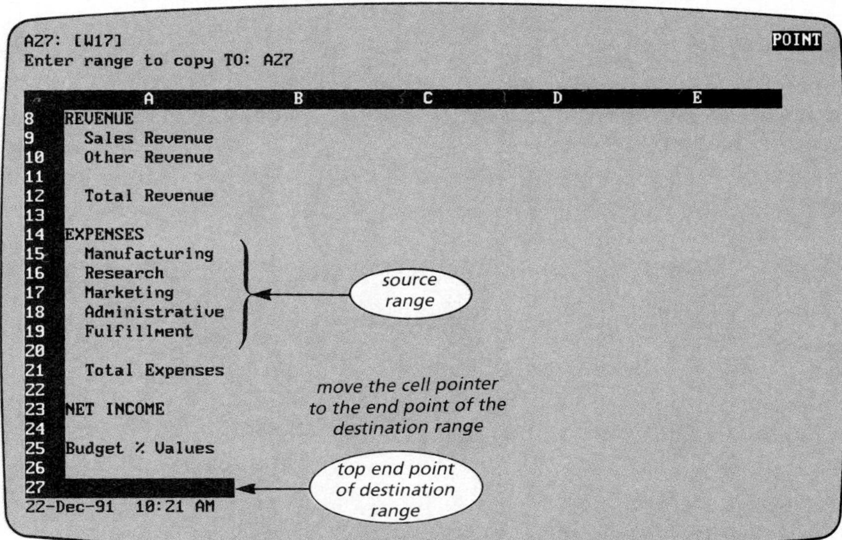


**FIGURE 3-21**
**Step 1 of using the /C command to copy—press the Slash key (/), type the letter C for Copy, select the source range, press the Enter key, and move the cell pointer to A27.**

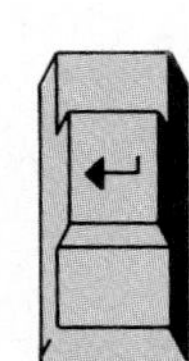

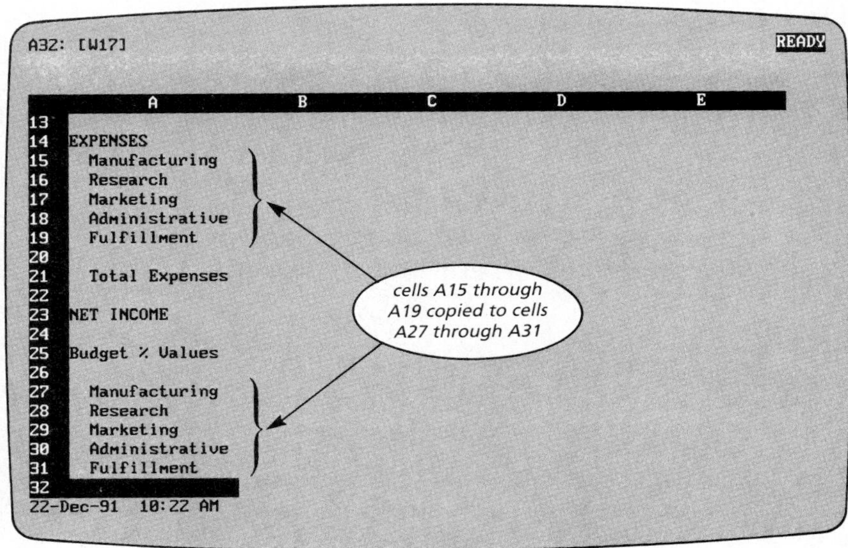


**FIGURE 3-22**
**Step 2 of using the /C command to copy—press the Enter key. The source range (A15..A19) is copied to the destination range (A27..A31).**

As shown in Figure 3-22, the source range (A15..A19) and the destination range (A27..A31) are identical. Two important points to note about copying the range A15..A19:

1. We selected the source range by entering A19..A15. Remember that the range A19..A15 is the same as A15..A19.
2. When both the source and destination ranges are the same size, it is not necessary to anchor the second end point of the destination range. 1-2-3 only needs to know the upper left end point, in this case A27. 1-2-3 copies the five cells in the source range beginning at cell A27. It always copies below the upper left end point of the destination range.

## ENTERING NUMBERS WITH A PERCENT SIGN

Next we will enter the five budget percent values that begin in cell B27 and extend through cell B31. Use the arrow keys to move the cell pointer from its present location to B27. Rather than entering the percent value as a decimal number (.38), as we did in Project 2, enter it as a whole number followed immediately by a percent sign (%). 1-2-3 accepts the number (38%) as a percent and displays it in the cell using the global format assigned earlier to the worksheet. After entering the five budget percent values, the worksheet appears as shown in Figure 3-23.

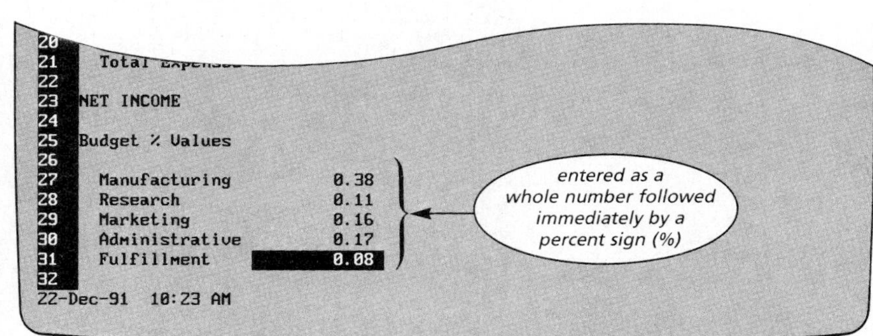


**FIGURE 3-23**
**The five budget percent values in cells B27 through B31.**

To format the five budget percent values to the Percent format, enter the command /**R**ange **F**ormat **P**ercent (/RFP). When 1-2-3 displays the prompt message "Enter number of decimal places (0..15): 2" on the input line, type the digit zero and press the Enter key. The prompt message "Enter range to format: B31..B31" displays on the input line. Enter the range B31..B27. The first end point (B31) is anchored. Use the Up Arrow key to move the cell pointer to B27. The range on the input line now reads B31..B27. Press the Enter key. The five budget percent values display in percent form as shown in Figure 3-24.

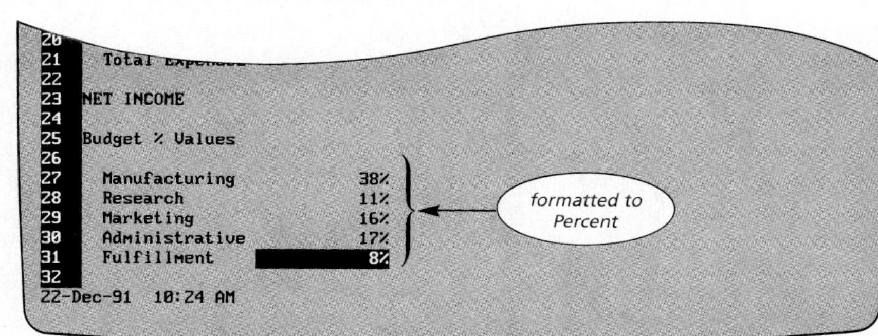


**FIGURE 3-24**
**The five budget percent values in cells B27 through B31 formatted to the Percent type.**

## FREEZING THE TITLES

The worksheet for this project extends beyond the size of the window. When you move the cell pointer down or to the right, the column and row titles disappear off the screen. This makes it difficult to remember where to enter the data. To alleviate this problem, 1-2-3 allows you to "freeze the titles" so that they remain on the screen no matter where you move the cell pointer. The title and column headings in rows 1 through 6 are called the **horizontal titles** and the row titles in column A are called the **vertical titles**.

### The Titles Command

To freeze the titles in this worksheet, press the Home key so that most of the titles are visible on the screen. Next, use the GOTO command to move the cell pointer to B7. The horizontal titles are just above cell B7 and the vertical titles are just to the left of cell B7. Enter the command /**W**orksheet **T**itles (/WT) as shown in Figure 3-25.

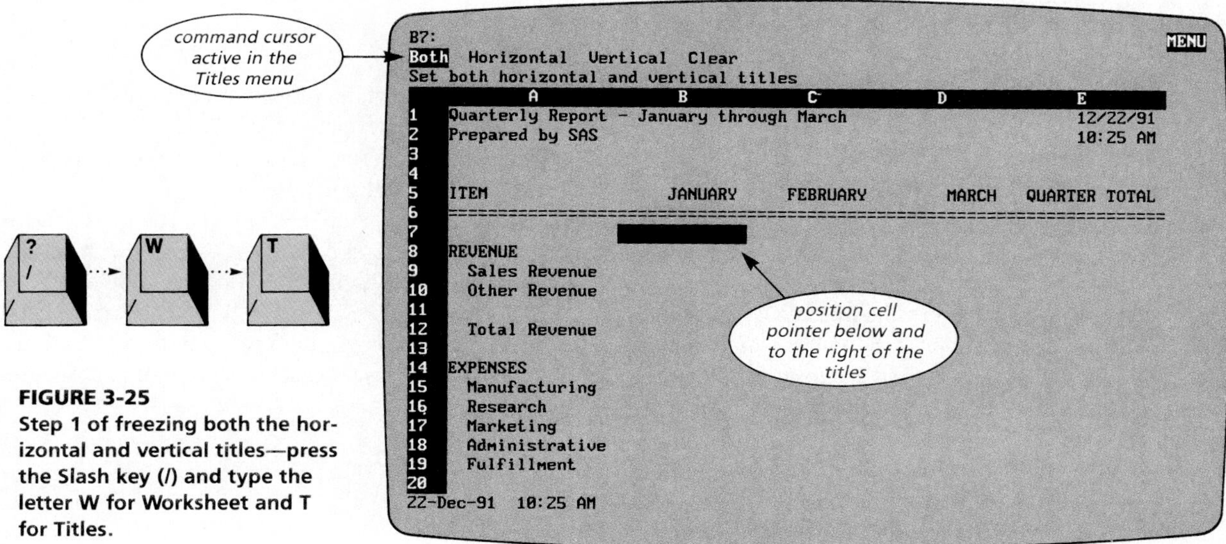


**FIGURE 3-25**
**Step 1 of freezing both the horizontal and vertical titles—press the Slash key (/) and type the letter W for Worksheet and T for Titles.**

With the command cursor active in the **Titles menu**, type the letter B for Both. This keeps the titles visible regardless of where you move the cell pointer, as shown in Figure 3-26.

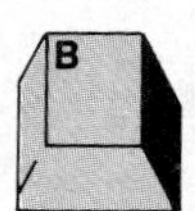


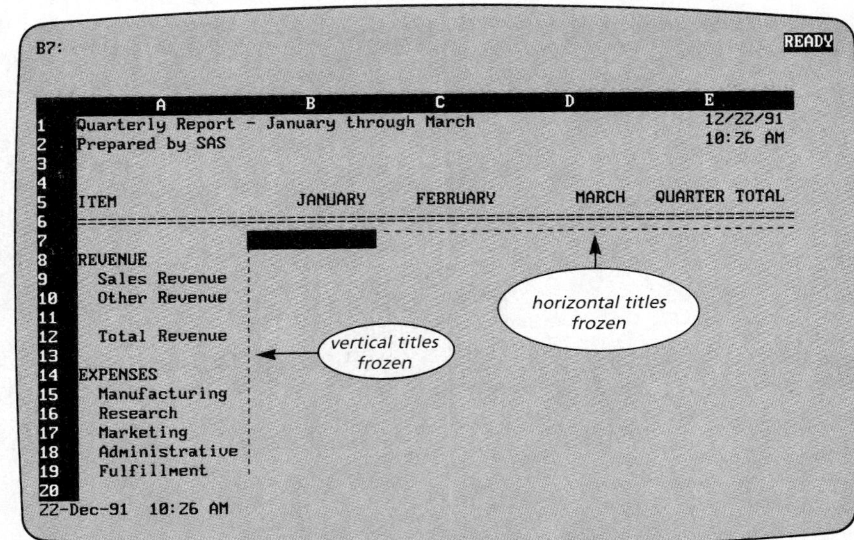


**FIGURE 3-26**
**Step 2 of freezing both the horizontal and vertical titles—type the letter B to freeze both.**

## Unfreezing the Titles

Once you specify a title area, you cannot move the cell pointer into this area of the worksheet using the keys on the numeric keypad. If you want to make a change to the titles after freezing them, you must "unfreeze" them. To unfreeze the titles, enter the command /**W**orksheet **T**itles **C**lear (/WTC). Once the titles are unfrozen, you can move the cell pointer anywhere on the worksheet, including the title area, to make your desired changes. To refreeze the titles, move the cell pointer to the cell (B7) just below the horizontal titles and just to the right of the vertical titles. Next, enter the command /**W**orksheet **T**itles **B**oth (/WTB).

# MOVING THE CONTENTS OF CELLS

The command /**M**ove (/M) moves the contents of a cell or range of cells to a different location in the worksheet. To illustrate the use of this command, let's make a mistake by entering the sales revenue (232897.95, 432989.76, and 765998.61) that belongs in cells B9 through E9 into cells B7 through E7—two rows above its location according to Figure 3-1. This type of error is common, especially when you're not careful about cell pointer placement.

The sales revenues for January, February, and March are 232,897.95, 432,989.76, and 765,998.61. The quarter total in column E is the sum of the sales revenue for the three months. Enter the three numbers in cells B7, C7, and D7. Use the Right Arrow key after typing each number on the input line. With the cell pointer at E7, enter the function @SUM(B7..D7). 1-2-3 evaluates the function and stores the number 1,431,886.32 in E7 (232,897.95 + 432,989.76 + 765,998.61). The values in cells C7, D7, and E7 are shown in Figure 3-27. Note that with the cell pointer at F7, the row identifiers in column A display along with columns C, D, E, and F. However, column B does not display because the titles in column A are frozen.

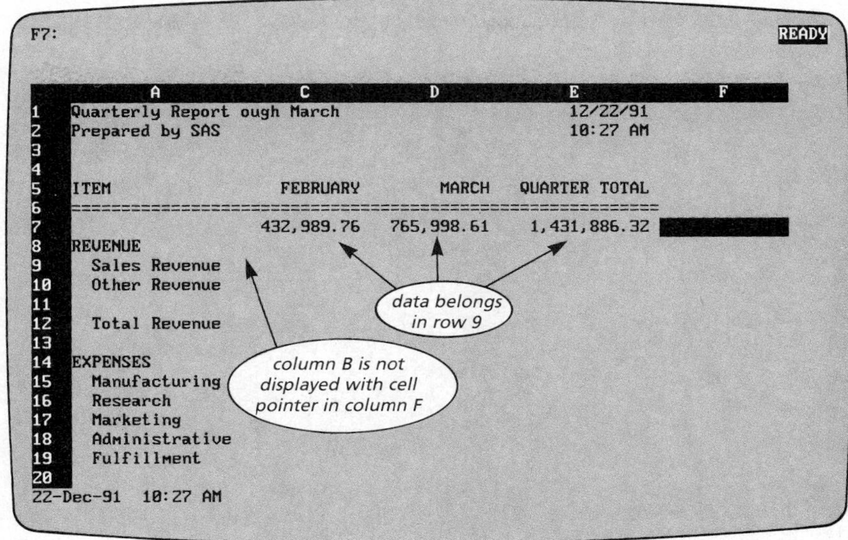


**FIGURE 3-27**
**The sales revenue data entered into the wrong row.**

As indicated earlier, the data we just entered in row 7 belongs in row 9. Let's correct the mistake and move the data from row 7 to row 9. With the cell pointer at F7, enter the command /**M**ove (/M). 1-2-3 displays the message "Enter range to move FROM: F7..F7" on the input line. Press the Backspace key to *unlock* the first end point. Move the cell pointer to E7 and press the Period key. Next, move the cell pointer to B7. The range to be moved is shown in Figure 3-28. Press the Enter key to lock in the range to be moved.

? / ... M ... ← ... use the arrow keys to select the range to move

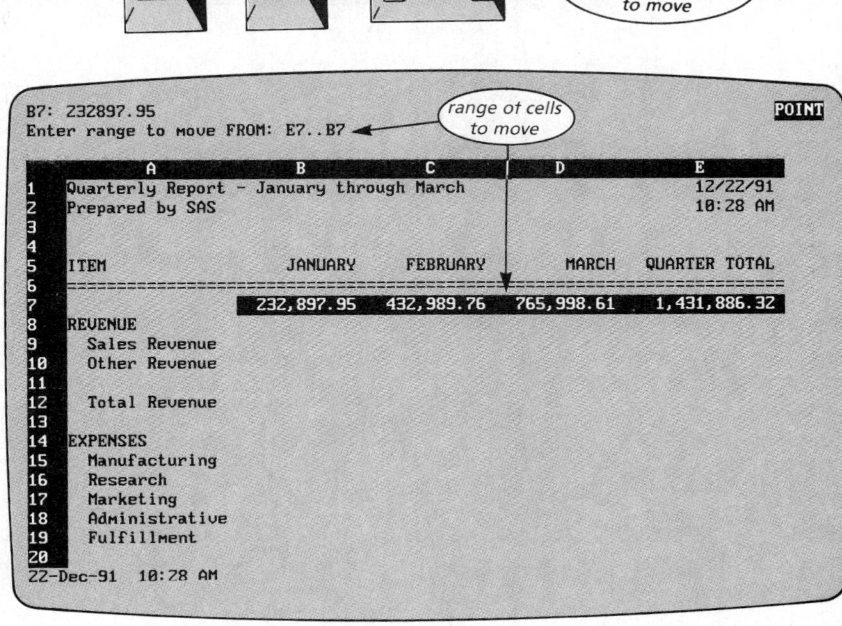


**FIGURE 3-28**
**Step 1 of using the /M command to move data from one range to another—press the Slash key (/), type the letter M, and select the range of cells to move.**

Next, 1-2-3 displays the message "Enter range to move TO: F7" on the input line. Move the cell pointer to E9. Press the Period key to anchor the first end point. Move the cell pointer to B9 as shown in Figure 3-29. To complete the command, press the Enter key and move the cell pointer to B10. Figure 3-30 illustrates the result of moving the contents of cells B7 through E7 to B9 through E9.

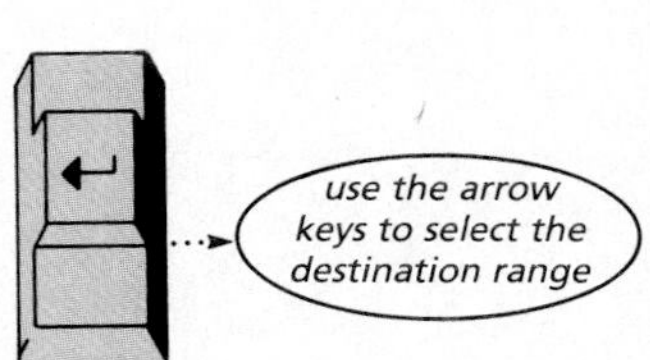


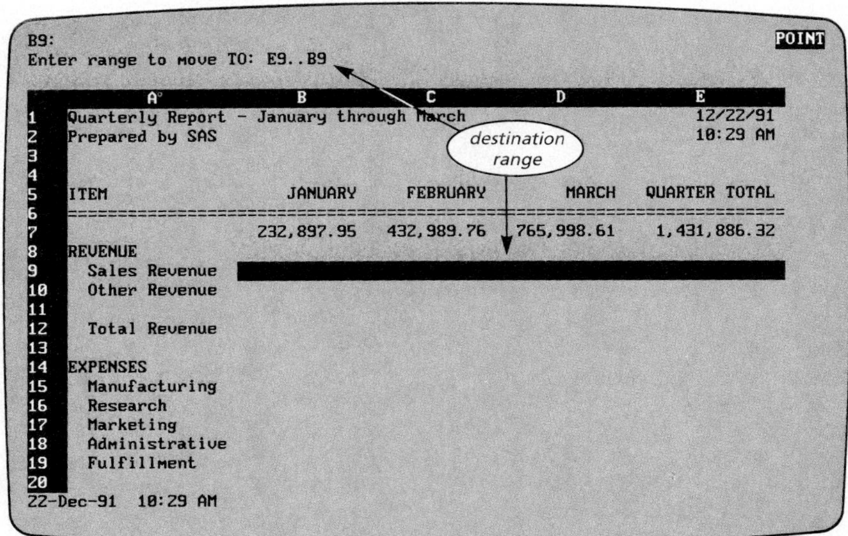


**FIGURE 3-29**
**Step 2 of using the /M command to move data from one range to another—press the Enter key to lock in the range to move and select the destination range.**

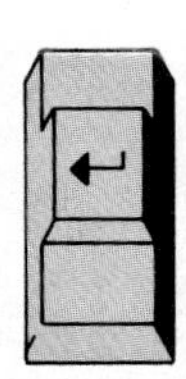

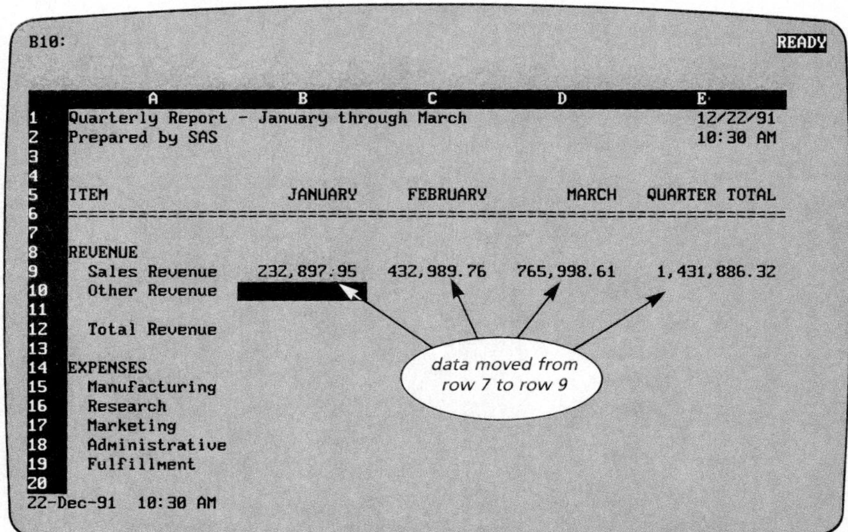


**FIGURE 3-30**
**Step 3 of using the /M command to move data from one range to another—press the Enter key.**

Here are some points regarding the Move command:

1. The Move and Copy commands are not the same. Where the Copy command copies one range to another, the Move command moves the contents of one range to another. Use the Move command to rearrange your worksheet. Use the Copy command to duplicate a range.
2. When you move a range containing a formula or function that references cell addresses, the referenced cell addresses are not changed relative to the new position, unless they refer to cells within the moved range. This was the case with the function in cell E7. Recall that we assigned the function @SUM(B7..D7) to cell E7. Following the Move command, the function assigned to cell E9 reads @SUM(B9..D9).

## DISPLAYING FORMULAS AND FUNCTIONS IN THE CELLS

The next step in this project is to enter the other revenue in cells B10 through D10. Enter the three values for January, February, and March as described in Figure 3-1. Leave the quarter total in column E alone for now.

The monthly total revenue in row 12 is equal to the sum of the corresponding monthly revenues in rows 9 and 10. Therefore, assign cell B12 the function @SUM(B9..B10). This is illustrated in Figure 3-31.

Use the /Copy (/C) command to copy the SUM function in cell B12 to cells C12 and C13. Remember, the Copy command adjusts the cell references in the function so that it adds the contents of the cells above the cell the SUM function is copied to. Once the Copy command has been entered, 1-2-3 requests the source cell range and the destination cell range. In this case the source cell range is B12 and the destination cell range is C12..D12 (see Figure 3-32).

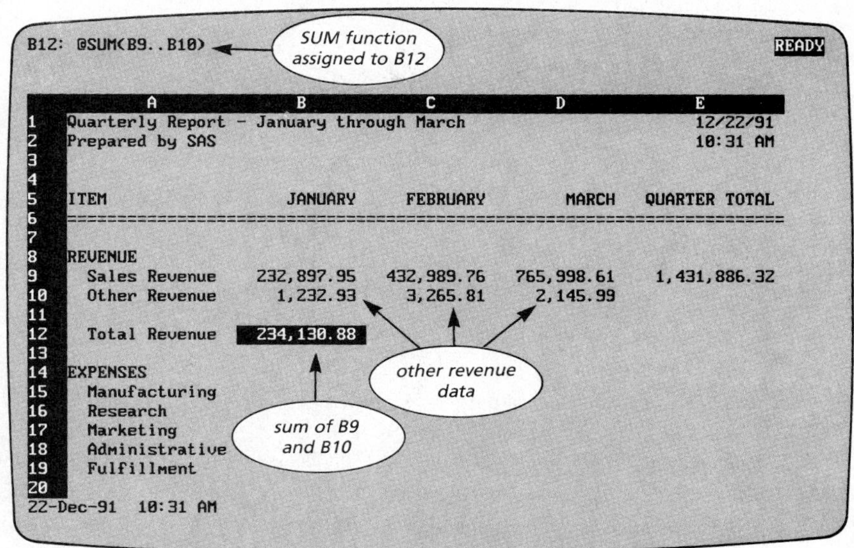


**FIGURE 3-31** Other revenue and formula for January total revenue entered into worksheet.

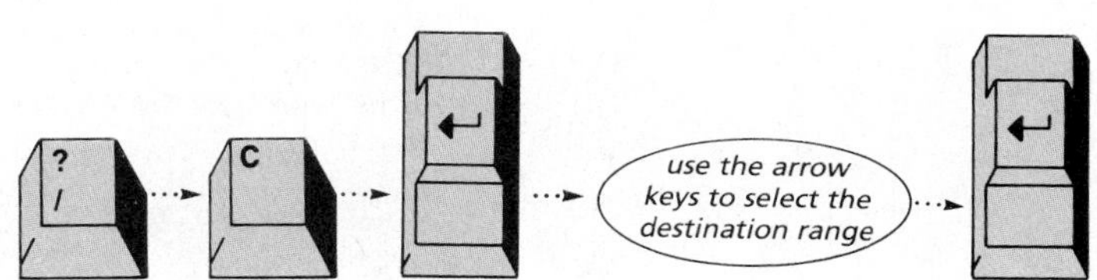


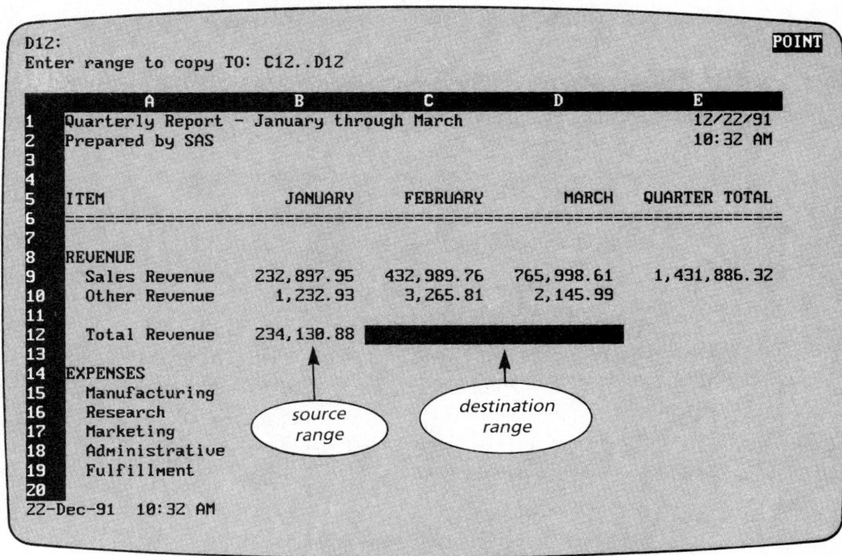


**FIGURE 3-32**
**Using the /C command to copy cell B12 to C12 and D12—press the Slash key (/), type the letter C, press the Enter key to select the source range, use the arrow keys to select the destination range, and press the Enter key.**

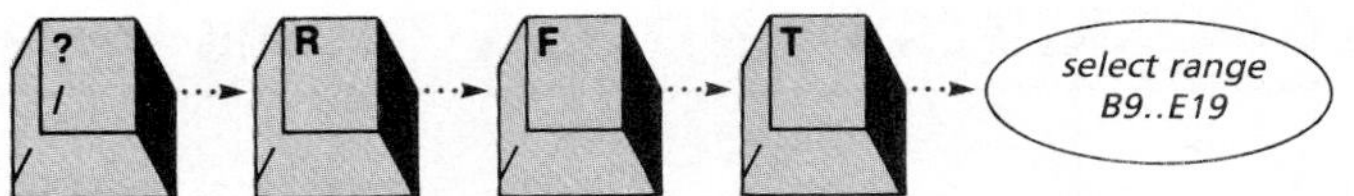


After entering each range, press the Enter key. The result of the copy is shown in cells C12 and D12 in Figure 3-33.

When entering or copying formulas, it is often useful to view them in the cells, instead of their numeric result. Therefore, to illustrate what is actually copied, let's change the format from Comma (,) to Text for the range B9..E19 in the worksheet. Remember from Project 2 that the Text format instructs 1-2-3 to display the formula assigned to a cell, rather than the numeric result.

Enter the command /**R**ange **F**ormat **T**ext (/RFT). 1-2-3 responds with the prompt message "Enter range to format: B12..B12" on the input line. Enter the range B9..E19 as shown in Figure 3-33 and press the Enter key. The functions in the worksheet (cells E9, B12, C12, and D12) now display in their respective cells and the numeric entries display using the General type format. This is shown in Figure 3-34. Later, we will reassign the Comma (,) format to the range B9..E19.

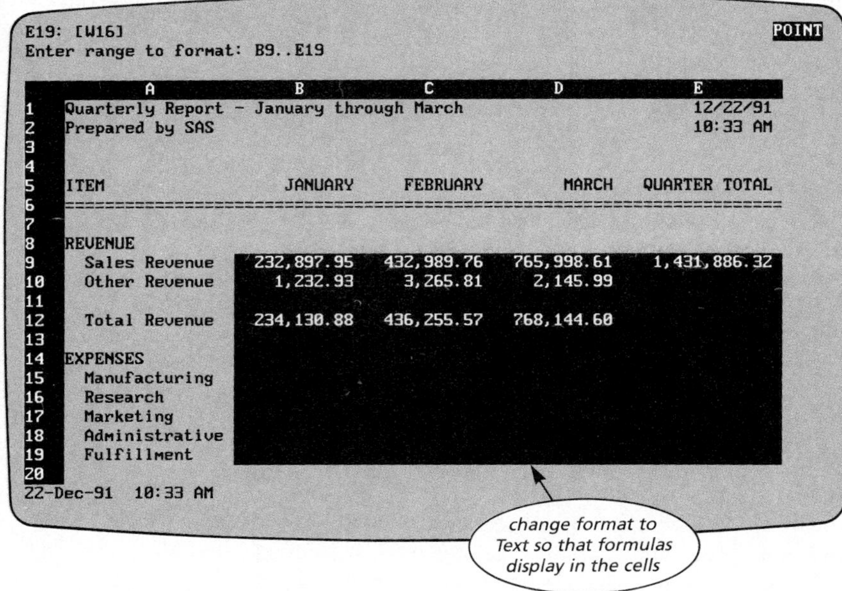


**FIGURE 3-33** Step 1 of using the /RFT command to format cells B9..E19 to the Text type—press the Slash key (/), type the letters R for Range, F for Format and T for Text, and select the range B9..E19.

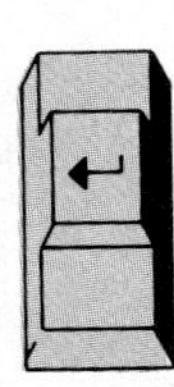

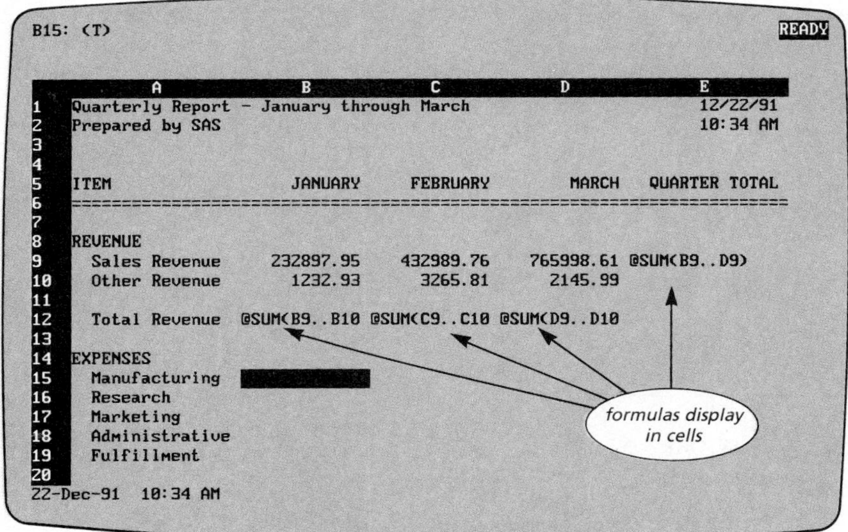


**FIGURE 3-34**
**Step 2 of using the /RFT command to format cells B9..E19 to the Text type—press the Enter key.**

# ABSOLUTE VERSUS RELATIVE ADDRESSING

The next step is to determine the five monthly budgeted expenses in the rectangular group of cells B15 through D19. Each of these budgeted expenses is equal to the corresponding budgeted percent (cells B27 through B31) times the monthly total revenue (cells B12 through D12). The formulas for each of the cells in this range are similar. They differ in that the total revenue varies by the month (column) and the budgeted percent value varies by the type of expense (row).

## Relative Addressing

It would be great if we could enter the formula +B27*B12 once in cell B15 (January budgeted manufacturing expense) and then copy this formula to the remaining cells in the rectangular group B15 through D19. However, we know that when a formula with relative addresses, like B27 and B12, is copied across a row or down a column, 1-2-3 automatically adjusts the cell references in the formula as it copies to reflect its new location.

Specifying cells in a formula using relative addressing has worked well in the previous examples of copying formulas, but it won't work here because the five budgeted percent values are all located in one column and the monthly total revenues are all located in one row. For example, if we copy +B27*B12 in cell B15 to cell C15, then cell C15 equals +C27*C12. This adjustment by the Copy command is because B27 and B12 are relative addresses. The C12 is okay, because it represents the total revenue for February, but cell C27 is blank. What we need here is for 1-2-3 to maintain cell B27 as it copies across the first row.

## Absolute and Mixed Cell Addressing

1-2-3 has the ability to keep a cell, a column, or a row constant when it copies a formula or function by using a technique called **absolute addressing**. To specify an absolute address in a formula, add a dollar sign ($) to the beginning of the column name, row name, or both.

For example, $B$27 is an absolute address and B27 is a relative address. Both reference the same cell. The difference shows when they are copied. A formula using $B$27 instructs 1-2-3 to use the same cell (B27) as it copies the formula to a new location. A formula using B27 instructs 1-2-3 to adjust the cell reference as it copies. Table 3-2 gives some additional examples of absolute addressing. A cell address with one dollar sign before either the column or the row is called a **mixed cell address**—one is relative, the other is absolute.

**TABLE 3-2 Absolute Addressing**

| CELL ADDRESS | MEANING |
|---|---|
| $A$22 | Both column and row reference remains the same when this cell address is copied. |
| A$22 | The column reference changes when you copy this cell address to another column. The row reference does not change—it is absolute. |
| $A22 | The row reference changes when you copy this cell address to another row. The column reference does not change—it is absolute. |
| A22 | Both column and row references are relative. When copied to another row and column, both the row and column in the cell address are adjusted to reflect the new location. |

## Copying Formulas with Mixed Cell Addresses

With the cell pointer at B15, enter the formula $B27*B$12 as shown in Figure 3-35. Because B15 was in the range we formatted to Text earlier, the formula displays in the cell, rather than the value. Note that it is not necessary to enter the formula $B27*B$12 with a leading plus sign because, in this case, the $ indicates that the entry is a formula or a number. The cell reference $B27 (budgeted manufacturing % value) means that the row reference (27) changes when you copy it to a new row, but the column reference (B) remains constant through all columns in the destination range. The cell reference B$12 (January expenses) in the formula means that the column reference (B) changes when you copy it to a new column, but the row reference (12) remains constant through all rows in the destination range. Let's copy the formula $B27*B$12 in cell B15 to the rectangular group of cells B15 through D19.

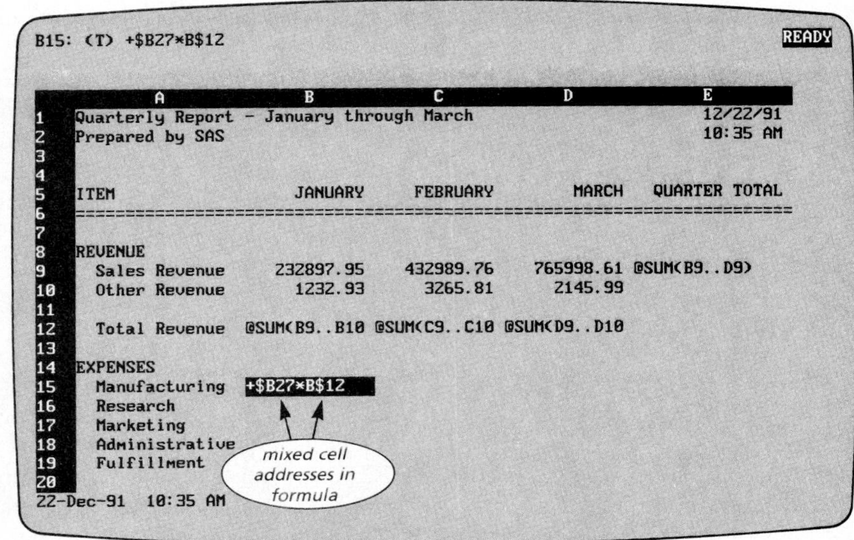


**FIGURE 3-35**
**Formula with mixed cell addresses entered into cell B15.**

The cell pointer is at B15 as shown in Figure 3-35. Enter the command /Copy (/C). When the prompt message "Enter range to copy FROM: B15..B15" displays on the input line, press the Enter key. When the message "Enter range to copy TO: B15" displays on the input line, use the arrow keys to select the range B15..D19. This is shown in Figure 3-36. Note that cell B15 is copied on top of itself, because B15 is one of the end points of the destination range.

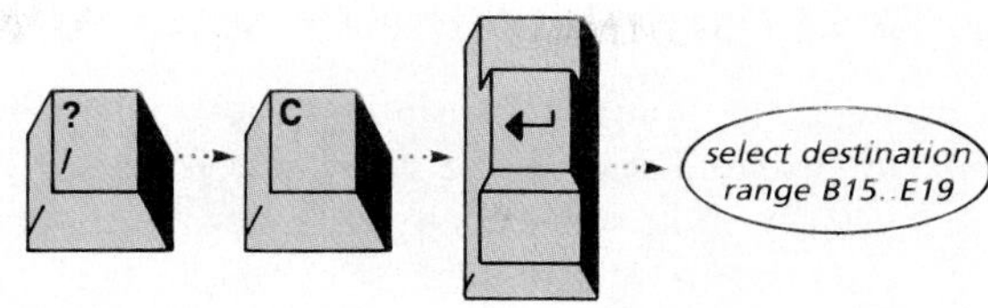


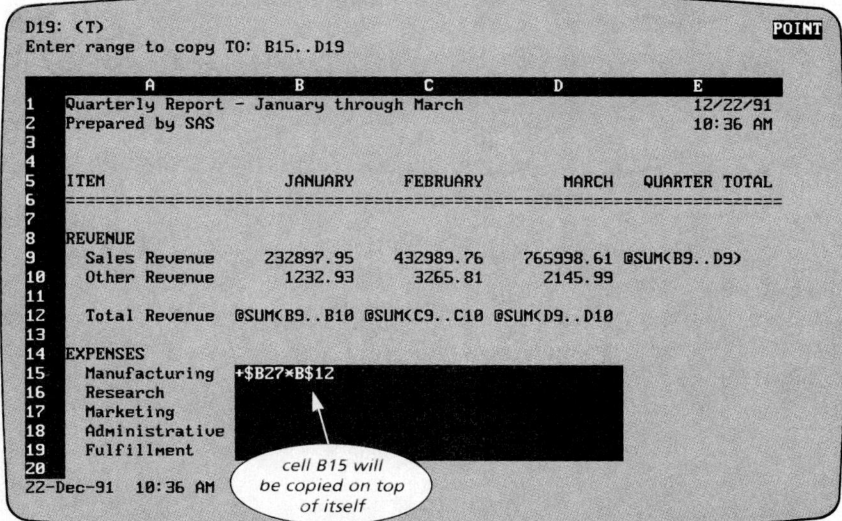


**FIGURE 3-36**
**Step 1 of using the /C command to copy cell B15 to the range B15..D19—press the Slash key (/), type the letter C for Copy, press the Enter key, and select the destination range.**

Press the Enter key. The Copy command copies the formula in cell B15 to the rectangular group of cells B15 through D19 as shown in Figure 3-37. Take a few minutes to study the formulas in Figure 3-37. You should begin to see the significance of mixed cell addressing. For example, every aspect of the five formulas in cells B15 through B19 is identical, except for the row in the first cell reference (budgeted % value). Also note, in columns C and D, that the column in the second cell reference (monthly total revenue) changes based on the column the formula is in.

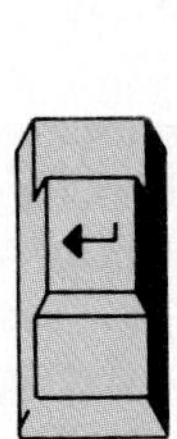

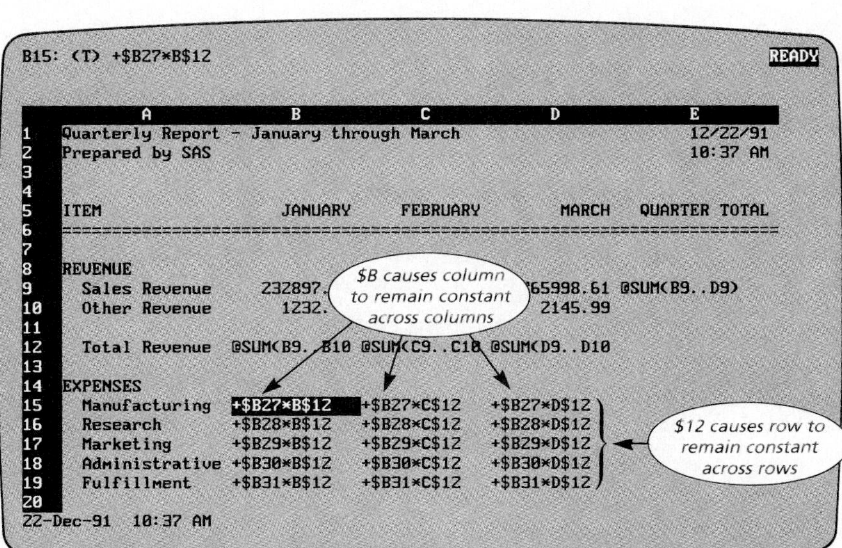


**FIGURE 3-37**
**Step 2 of using the /C command to copy cell B15 to the range B15..D19—press the Enter key.**

## Switching from Text Format to the Comma Format

Let's change cells B9 through E19 from the Text format back to the Comma format. Recall that we switched the format of these cells from Comma to Text so that we could view the formulas in the cells. To change the format, move the cell pointer to the lower left end point (B19) of the range B19..E9. Enter the command /**R**ange **F**ormat **,** (/RF,).

Press the Enter key when the prompt message "Enter number of decimal places (0..15): 2" displays on the input line. Finally, when 1-2-3 requests the range, use the arrow keys to select the rectangular group of cells B19..E9. Press the Enter key. The results of the formulas, rather than the formulas themselves, display in the cells (see Figure 3-38).

```
B19: (,2) +$B31*B$12                                                          READY

      A                    B              C              D              E
1  Quarterly Report - January through March                           12/22/91
2  Prepared by SAS                                                    10:38 AM
3
4
5  ITEM                    JANUARY        FEBRUARY       MARCH     QUARTER TOTAL
6  ============================================================================
7
8  REVENUE
9    Sales Revenue       232,897.95     432,989.76     765,998.61    1,431,886.32
10   Other Revenue         1,232.93       3,265.81       2,145.99
11
12   Total Revenue       234,130.88     436,255.57     768,144.60
13
14 EXPENSES
15   Manufacturing        88,969.73     165,777.12     291,894.95
16   Research             25,754.40      47,988.11      84,495.91
17   Marketing            37,460.94      69,800.89     122,903.14
18   Administrative       39,802.25      74,163.45     130,584.58
19   Fulfillment          18,730.47      34,900.45      61,451.57
20
22-Dec-91  10:38 AM
```

**FIGURE 3-38**
**Range B9..E19 reformatted to the Comma (,) type.**

# POINTING TO A RANGE OF CELLS TO SUM

The total expenses for January (cell B21) are determined by adding the five monthly budgeted expenses in cells B15 through B19. The total expenses for February (C21) and March (D21) are found in the same way.

To sum the five monthly budgeted expenses for January, move the cell pointer to B21 and begin entering the SUM function. For this entry, let's apply the pointing method to enter the range to sum. Enter @sum( on the input line. Remember that function names can be entered in lowercase. After typing the open parenthesis, use the Up Arrow key to move the cell pointer to B15, the topmost end point of the range to sum.

As the cell pointer moves upward, 1-2-3 changes the cell address following the open parenthesis on the input line. When the cell pointer reaches B15 (see Figure 3-39), press the Period key (.) to lock in the first end point of the range to sum. Next, use the Down Arrow key to move the cell pointer to B19 (see Figure 3-40). To complete the entry, press the Close Parenthesis key and the Enter key.

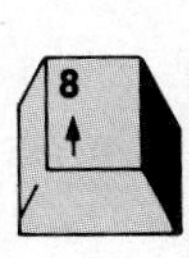

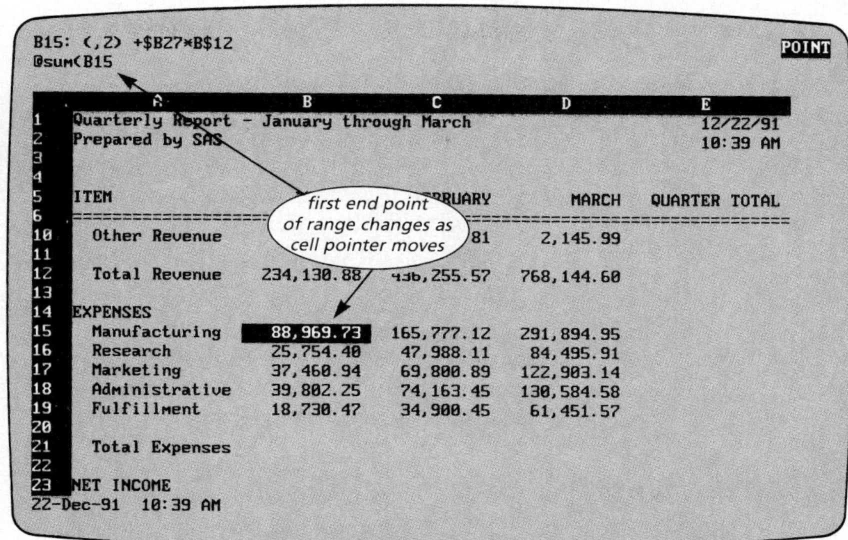


**FIGURE 3-39**
**Step 1 of entering the SUM function using the pointing method—after the open parenthesis, use the arrow keys to select the first end point of the range.**

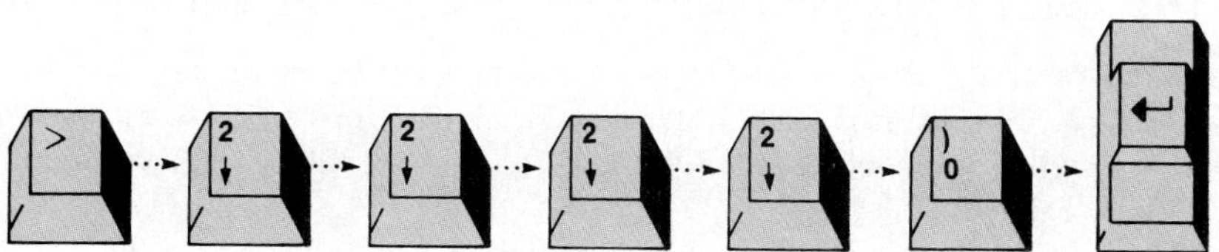

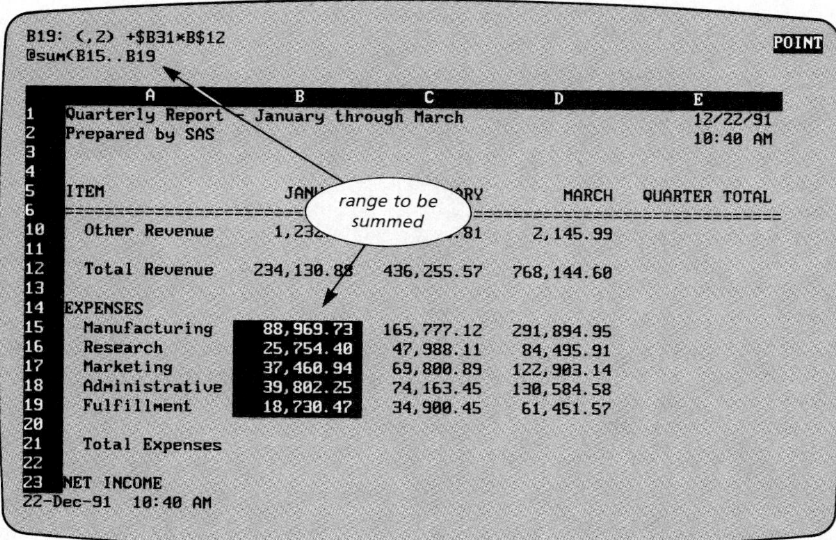


**FIGURE 3-40**
**Step 2 of entering the SUM function using the pointing method—press the Period key (.), use the arrow keys to select the second end point of the range, type the Close Parenthesis key, and press the Enter key.**

As shown in cell B21 of Figure 3-41, 1-2-3 displays the sum (210,717.79) of the five January budgeted expenses stored in cells B15 through B19.

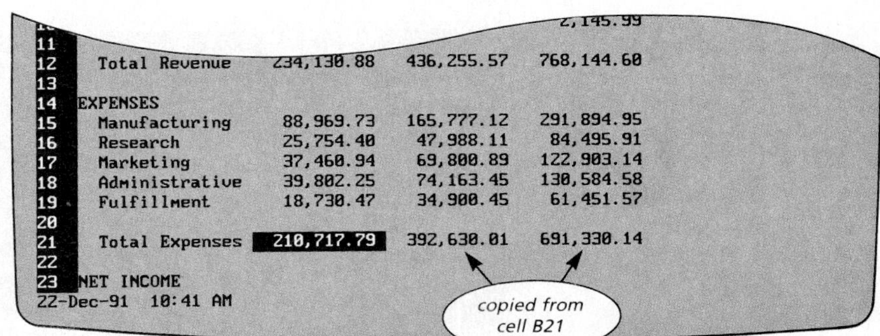

| | A | B | C | D |
|---|---|---|---|---|
| 11 | | | | |
| 12 | Total Revenue | 234,130.88 | 436,255.57 | 768,144.60 |
| 13 | | | | |
| 14 | EXPENSES | | | |
| 15 | Manufacturing | 88,969.73 | 165,777.12 | 291,894.95 |
| 16 | Research | 25,754.40 | 47,988.11 | 84,495.91 |
| 17 | Marketing | 37,460.94 | 69,800.89 | 122,903.14 |
| 18 | Administrative | 39,802.25 | 74,163.45 | 130,584.58 |
| 19 | Fulfillment | 18,730.47 | 34,900.45 | 61,451.57 |
| 20 | | | | |
| 21 | Total Expenses | 210,717.79 | 392,630.01 | 691,330.14 |
| 22 | | | | |
| 23 | NET INCOME | | | |

22-Dec-91 10:41 AM



**FIGURE 3-41**
**SUM function in cell B21 copied to cells C21 and D21.**

## Pointing versus Entering a Range of Cells

The pointing method used to enter the range for the SUM function in cell B21 saves keying time. Anytime you need to enter a range, you may use the arrow keys to point to it. Alternatively, you may type the cell addresses. Once you begin typing a cell address, 1-2-3 is no longer in POINT mode.

## Copying the Total Expenses and Net Income for Each Month

The next step in this project is to determine the total expenses for February and March. To accomplish this task, copy the function in cell B21 to cells C21 and D21. Enter the command /Copy (/C). After entering the source range (B21), press the Enter key. Next, select the destination range (C21..D21) and press the Enter key. Figure 3-41 shows the result of copying cell B21 to cells C21 and D21.

We can now determine the net income for each month in row 23 by subtracting the total expenses for each month in row 21 from the total revenue for each month in row 12. Move the cell pointer to B23 and enter the formula +B12–B21. Copy this formula to cells C23 and D23. The result of entering the formula in cell B23 and copying it to C23 and D23 is shown in Figure 3-42.

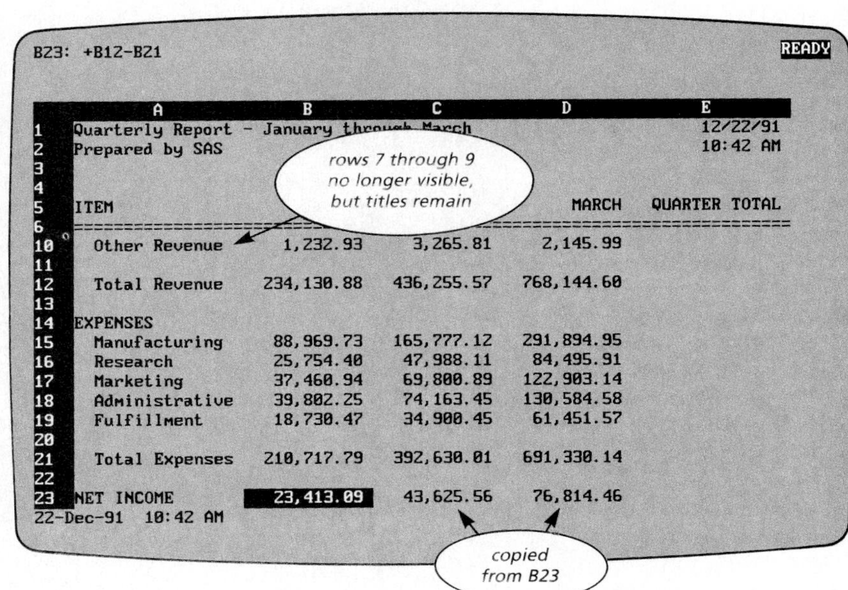

B23: +B12-B21 READY

| | A | B | C | D | E |
|---|---|---|---|---|---|
| 1 | Quarterly Report - January through March | | | | 12/22/91 |
| 2 | Prepared by SAS | | | | 10:42 AM |
| 3 | | | | | |
| 4 | | | | | |
| 5 | ITEM | | | MARCH | QUARTER TOTAL |
| 6 | ======================= | | | | |
| 10 | Other Revenue | 1,232.93 | 3,265.81 | 2,145.99 | |
| 11 | | | | | |
| 12 | Total Revenue | 234,130.88 | 436,255.57 | 768,144.60 | |
| 13 | | | | | |
| 14 | EXPENSES | | | | |
| 15 | Manufacturing | 88,969.73 | 165,777.12 | 291,894.95 | |
| 16 | Research | 25,754.40 | 47,988.11 | 84,495.91 | |
| 17 | Marketing | 37,460.94 | 69,800.89 | 122,903.14 | |
| 18 | Administrative | 39,802.25 | 74,163.45 | 130,584.58 | |
| 19 | Fulfillment | 18,730.47 | 34,900.45 | 61,451.57 | |
| 20 | | | | | |
| 21 | Total Expenses | 210,717.79 | 392,630.01 | 691,330.14 | |
| 22 | | | | | |
| 23 | NET INCOME | 23,413.09 | 43,625.56 | 76,814.46 | |

22-Dec-91 10:42 AM



**FIGURE 3-42**
**Formula in cell B23 copied to cells C23 and D23.**

## Summing Empty Cells and Labels

One more step and the worksheet is complete. We need to determine the quarter totals in column E. Use the GOTO command to move the cell pointer to the quarter total in cell E9. Since cell E9 is not on the screen (see Figure 3-42), the GOTO command causes the window to move so that cell E9 is positioned in the upper left corner, just below and to the right of the titles.

Recall that we determined the quarter total for the sales revenue after we entered the monthly sales revenue (see Figure 3-30). The functions required for all the row entries (E10, E12, E15 through E19, E21, and E23) are identical to the function in cell E9. Therefore, let's copy the function in cell E9 to these cells.

Unfortunately, the cells in the destination range are not contiguous, that is, connected. For example, in the range E10 through E23, the function is not needed in E11, E13, E14, E20, and E22. We have three choices here: (1) use the copy command several times and copy the function in E9 to E10, E12, E15 through E19, E21, and E23; (2) enter the function manually in each required cell; or (3) copy the function to the range E10 through E23. If we select the third method, we have to use the command /**R**ange **E**rase (/RE) to erase the function from E11, E13, E14, E20, and E22, the cells in which the function is not required. Let's use the third method.

With the cell pointer at E9, enter the command /**C**opy (/C). When 1-2-3 displays the prompt message "Enter range to copy FROM: E9..E9", press the Enter key. For the destination range, leave E9 anchored as the first end point and use the Down Arrow key to move the cell pointer to E23. This is shown in Figure 3-43.

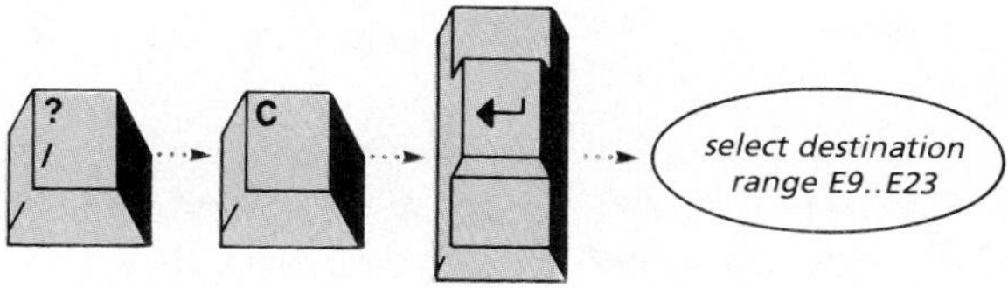


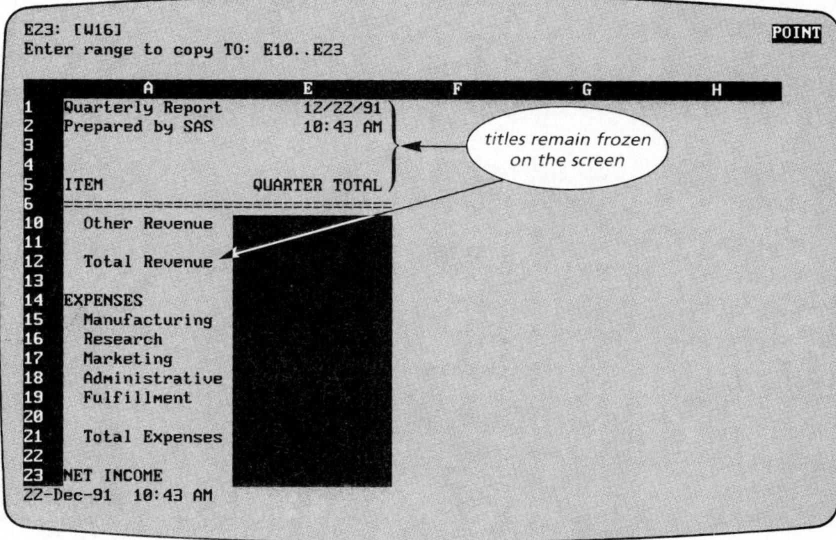


**FIGURE 3-43**
**Step 1 of using the /C command to copy cell E9 to the range E9..E23—press the Slash key (/), type the letter C for Copy, press the Enter key, and select the destination range.**

Press the Enter key and the function in cell E9 is copied to the cells in the range E9..E23 (see Figure 3-44).

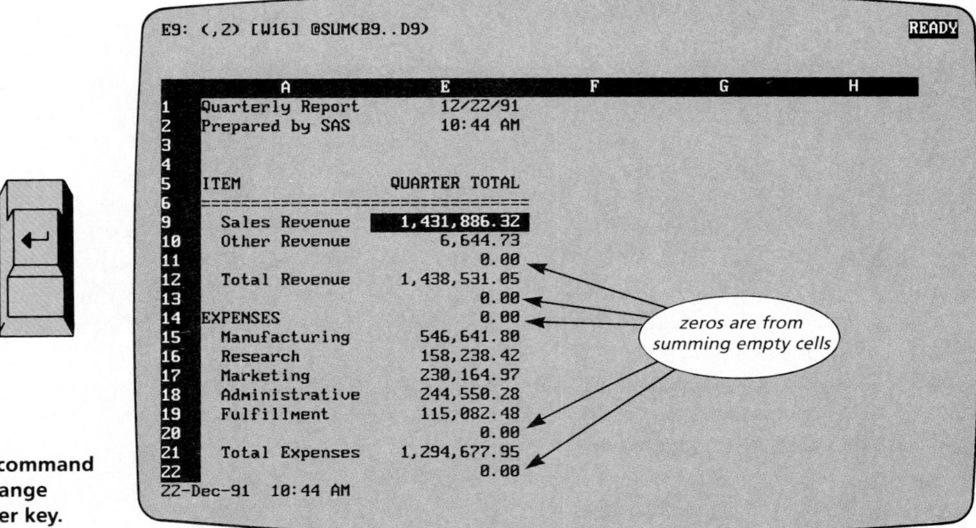


**FIGURE 3-44**
**Step 2 of using the /C command to copy cell E9 to the range E9..E23—press the Enter key.**

Notice the zeros in cells E11, E13, E14, E20, and E22. The formula in cell E11 reads @SUM(B11..D11). 1-2-3 considers empty cells and cells with labels to be equal to zero when they are referenced in a formula or function. Since cells B11, C11, and D11 are empty, the SUM function assigned to E11 produces the zero display. We need to erase the functions in the cells displaying zero. Recall from Project 1 that the command /**R**ange **E**rase (/RE) erases the contents of a cell. Use this command to erase the zeros in cells E11, E13, E14, E20, and E22.

After the zeros in column E are erased, use the command /**W**orksheet **T**itles **C**lear (/WTC) to unfreeze the titles. Finally, press the Home key to move the cell pointer to A1. The worksheet is complete as shown in Figure 3-45.

A1: [W17] 'Quarterly Report - January through March READY

| | A | B | C | D | E |
|---|---|---|---|---|---|
| 1 | Quarterly Report - January through March | | | | 12/22/91 |
| 2 | Prepared by SAS | | | | 10:45 AM |
| 3 | | | | | |
| 4 | | | | | |
| 5 | ITEM | JANUARY | FEBRUARY | MARCH | QUARTER TOTAL |
| 6 | ========== | ========== | ========== | ========== | ========== |
| 7 | | | | | |
| 8 | REVENUE | | | | |
| 9 | Sales Revenue | 232,897.95 | 432,989.76 | 765,998.61 | 1,431,886.32 |
| 10 | Other Revenue | 1,232.93 | 3,265.81 | 2,145.99 | 6,644.73 |
| 11 | | | | | |
| 12 | Total Revenue | 234,130.88 | 436,255.57 | 768,144.60 | 1,438,531.05 |
| 13 | | | | | |
| 14 | EXPENSES | | | | |
| 15 | Manufacturing | 88,969.73 | 165,777.12 | 291,894.95 | 546,641.80 |
| 16 | Research | 25,754.40 | 47,988.11 | 84,495.91 | 158,238.42 |
| 17 | Marketing | 37,460.94 | 69,800.89 | 122,903.14 | 230,164.97 |
| 18 | Administrative | 39,802.25 | 74,163.45 | 130,584.58 | 244,550.28 |
| 19 | Fulfillment | 18,730.47 | 34,900.45 | 61,451.57 | 115,082.48 |
| 20 | | | | | |

22-Dec-91 10:45 AM

zeros removed with the /Range Erase command

**FIGURE 3-45**
**The completed worksheet.**

## SAVING AND PRINTING THE WORKSHEET

Save the worksheet on disk for later use. Use the command /File Save (/FS) and the file name PROJS-3. As we discussed in Project 2, when you create a large worksheet such as this one, it is prudent to save the worksheet periodically—every 50 to 75 keystrokes. Then, if there should be an inadvertent loss of power to the computer or other unforeseen mishap, you will not lose the whole worksheet.

### Printing the Worksheet

After saving the worksheet as PROJS-3, obtain a hard copy by printing the worksheet on the printer. Recall from Project 2, that to print the worksheet you use the command /**P**rint **P**rinter (/PP). This command activates the command cursor in the Printer menu (see Figure 3-46). Type the letter R for Range. The cell pointer is at one end point of the range we wish to print, A1. Use the arrow keys to move the cell pointer to E31. Press the Enter key to anchor the second end point.

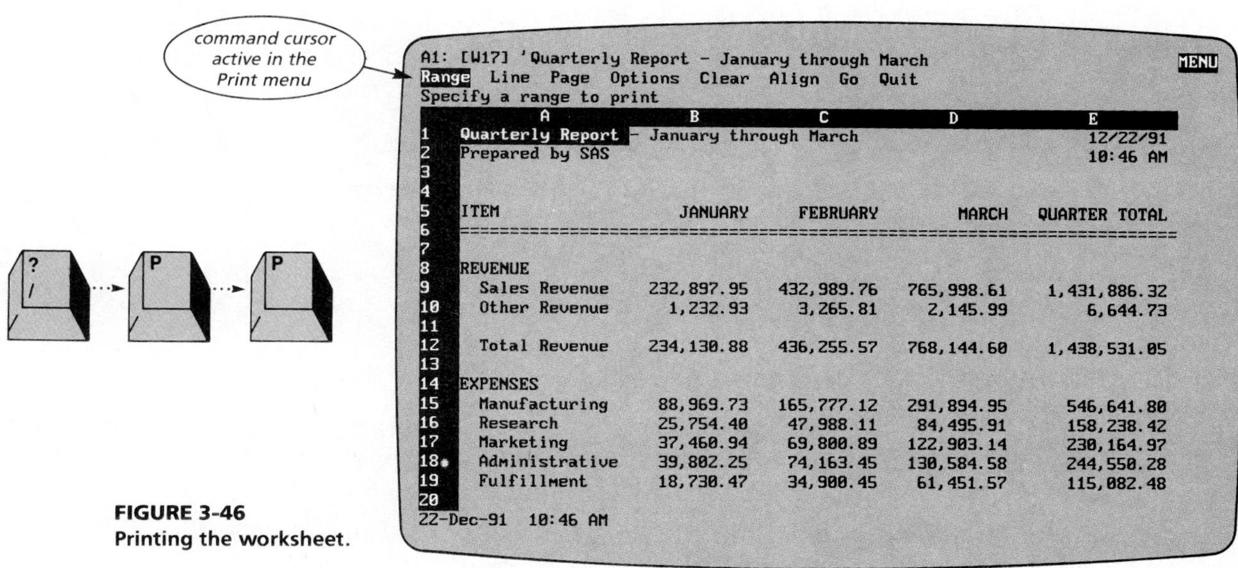


**FIGURE 3-46**
**Printing the worksheet.**

Next, check the printer to be sure it is in READY mode. Type the letter A for Align and the letter G for Go. The worksheet prints on the printer as shown in Figure 3-47. Finally, type the letter P for Page twice to move the paper through the printer so that you can tear the paper at the perforated edge below the printed version of the worksheet.

Quarterly Report - January through March 12/22/91
Prepared by SAS 10:47 AM

| ITEM | JANUARY | FEBRUARY | MARCH | QUARTER TOTAL |
|---|---|---|---|---|
| REVENUE | | | | |
| Sales Revenue | 232,897.95 | 432,989.76 | 765,998.61 | 1,431,886.32 |
| Other Revenue | 1,232.93 | 3,265.81 | 2,145.99 | 6,644.73 |
| Total Revenue | 234,130.88 | 436,255.57 | 768,144.60 | 1,438,531.05 |
| EXPENSES | | | | |
| Manufacturing | 88,969.73 | 165,777.12 | 291,894.95 | 546,641.80 |
| Research | 25,754.40 | 47,988.11 | 84,495.91 | 158,238.42 |
| Marketing | 37,460.94 | 69,800.89 | 122,903.14 | 230,164.97 |
| Administrative | 39,802.25 | 74,163.45 | 130,584.58 | 244,550.28 |
| Fulfillment | 18,730.47 | 34,900.45 | 61,451.57 | 115,082.48 |
| Total Expenses | 210,717.79 | 392,630.01 | 691,330.14 | 1,294,677.95 |
| NET INCOME | 23,413.09 | 43,625.56 | 76,814.46 | 143,853.10 |
| Budget % Values | | | | |
| Manufacturing | 38% | | | |
| Research | 11% | | | |
| Marketing | 16% | | | |
| Administrative | 17% | | | |
| Fulfillment | 8% | | | |

**FIGURE 3-47** The printed version of the worksheet in Project 3.

## Printing the Worksheet in Condensed Mode

If you have a graphics printer, you can print more than 80 characters per line by printing the worksheet in condensed mode. This mode can be helpful if the worksheet is wider than the screen. The **condensed mode** allows nearly twice as many characters to fit across the page. To print a worksheet in the condensed mode, do the following:

1. Enter the command /**P**rint **P**rinter **O**ptions **S**etup (/PPOS). Enter the code \015 and press the Enter key.
2. With the Printer Options menu at the top of the screen, enter the command **M**argins **R**ight. Type in a right margin of 132. Press the Enter key and type the letter Q to quit the Printer Options menu.
3. Select the range to print and follow the usual steps for printing the worksheet. The condensed printed version of the worksheet prints on the printer as shown in Figure 3-48.

```
Quarterly Report - January through March                       12/22/91
Prepared by SAS                                                10:48 AM

ITEM                   JANUARY     FEBRUARY        MARCH  QUARTER TOTAL
=======================================================================

REVENUE
  Sales Revenue     232,897.95   432,989.76   765,998.61   1,431,886.32
  Other Revenue       1,232.93     3,265.81     2,145.99       6,644.73

  Total Revenue     234,130.88   436,255.57   768,144.60   1,438,531.05

EXPENSES
  Manufacturing      88,969.73   165,777.12   291,894.95     546,641.80
  Research           25,754.40    47,988.11    84,495.91     158,238.42
  Marketing          37,460.94    69,800.89   122,903.14     230,164.97
  Administrative     39,802.25    74,163.45   130,584.58     244,550.28
  Fulfillment        18,730.47    34,900.45    61,451.57     115,082.48

  Total Expenses    210,717.79   392,630.01   691,330.14   1,294,677.95

NET INCOME           23,413.09    43,625.56    76,814.46     143,853.10

Budget % Values

  Manufacturing            38%
  Research                 11%
  Marketing                16%
  Administrative           17%
  Fulfillment               8%
```

**FIGURE 3-48 A printout of the worksheet in the condensed mode.**

If the printer does not print in condensed mode, check the printer manual to be sure the current dip switch settings on the printer allow for it. You may have to change these settings. If you continue to experience problems, check the printer manual to be sure that code \015 instructs the printer to print in condensed mode. This code works for most printers.

To change 1-2-3 back to the normal print mode, do the following:

1. Enter the command /**P**rint **P**rinter **O**ptions **S**etup (/PPOS). Enter the code \018 and press the Enter key.
2. With the Printer Options menu at the top of the screen, enter the command Margins Right. Type in a right margin of 76. Press the Enter key and type the letter Q to quit the Printer Options menu.
3. With the command cursor in the Print menu, follow the steps outlined earlier for printing the worksheet in the normal mode.

## Using Borders to Print Nonadjacent Columns

Up to this point, we have only printed columns that are side by side in the worksheet. Consider Figure 3-49. This partial printout is called a summary report, since only the row titles in column A and the corresponding totals in column E are printed.

We can print such a report through the use of the Borders command in the Printer Options menu. The Borders command prints specified columns to the left of the selected range or it prints specified rows above the selected range. To print the summary report in Figure 3-49, do the following:

1. Move the cell pointer to column A and enter the command /**P**rint **P**rinter **O**ptions **B**orders (/PPOB). Type C for Column and press the Enter key to select column A as the border. Type Q to quit the Printer Options menu.
2. With the Print menu at the top of the screen, select E1..E23 as the range to print.
3. Press A for Align and G for Go.

In Figure 3-49, column A prints as the border and column E prints because it was selected as the range to print.

To clear column A as the border, select the Clear command in the Print menu. When the Clear menu displays at the top of the screen, type B for Borders.

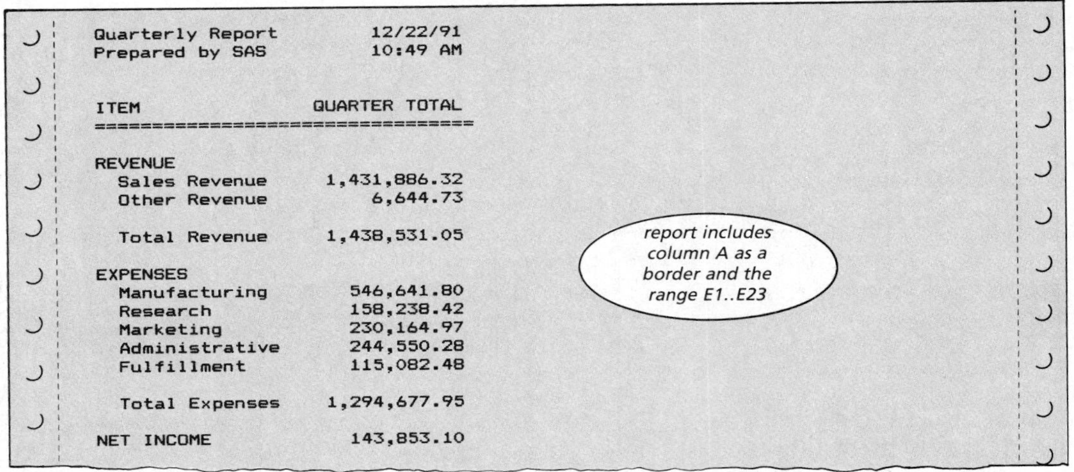

Quarterly Report 12/22/91
Prepared by SAS 10:49 AM
ITEM QUARTER TOTAL
REVENUE
Sales Revenue 1,431,886.32
Other Revenue 6,644.73
Total Revenue 1,438,531.05
EXPENSES
Manufacturing 546,641.80
Research 158,238.42
Marketing 230,164.97
Administrative 244,550.28
Fulfillment 115,082.48
Total Expenses 1,294,677.95
NET INCOME 143,853.10
report includes column A as a border and the range E1..E23


**FIGURE 3-49** A summary report made up of nonadjacent columns.

## Other Printer Options

There are other printer options that can enhance your worksheet. Table 3-3 summarizes the commands found in the **P**rinter **O**ptions menu.

**TABLE 3-3** Printer Options

| OPTION | DEFAULT SETTING | PURPOSE |
|---|---|---|
| HEADER | none | Print a line of text at the top of every page of the worksheet. |
| FOOTER | none | Print a line of text at the bottom of every page of the worksheet. |
| MARGINS | Left 4<br>Right 76<br>Top 2<br>Bottom 2 | Set the margins. |
| BORDERS | none | Print specified columns or rows on every page. |
| SETUP | none | Send commands to the printer, for example, to print the worksheet in condensed mode. |
| PAGE-LENGTH | 66 | Set printed lines per page. |
| OTHER | | Select the As-Displayed or Cell-Formulas version to print. |
| QUIT | | Return to the Print menu. |

Many of the options you set with the /Print Printer Options (/PPO) command are saved with the worksheet and stay in effect when you retrieve it. So remember, if you change any of the printer options and you want the changes to stay with the worksheet, be sure to save the worksheet after you finish printing it. That way you won't have to change the options the next time you retrieve the worksheet.

If you use the command /Worksheet Erase (/WE) to clear the worksheet on the screen or restart 1-2-3, the printer options revert back to the default settings shown in Table 3.3.

## WHAT-IF QUESTIONS

A powerful feature of 1-2-3 is the ability to answer what-if questions. Quick responses to these questions are invaluable when making business decisions. Using 1-2-3 to answer what-if questions is called performing **what-if analyses** or **sensitivity analyses**.

A what-if question for the worksheet in Project 3 might be, "What if the manufacturing budgeted percentage is decreased from 38% to 35%—how would this affect the total expenses and net income?" To answer questions like this, you need only change a single value in the worksheet. The recalculation feature of 1-2-3 answers the question immediately by displaying new values in any cells with formulas or functions that reference the changed cell.

Let's change the manufacturing budgeted percentage from 38% to 35% (see Figure 3-50). In the "before change" screen in Figure 3-50, the manufacturing budgeted percentage is 38%. After the change is made, the manufacturing budgeted percentage is 35%. When we make the change, all the formulas are immediately recalculated. This process generally requires less than one second, depending on how many calculations must be performed.

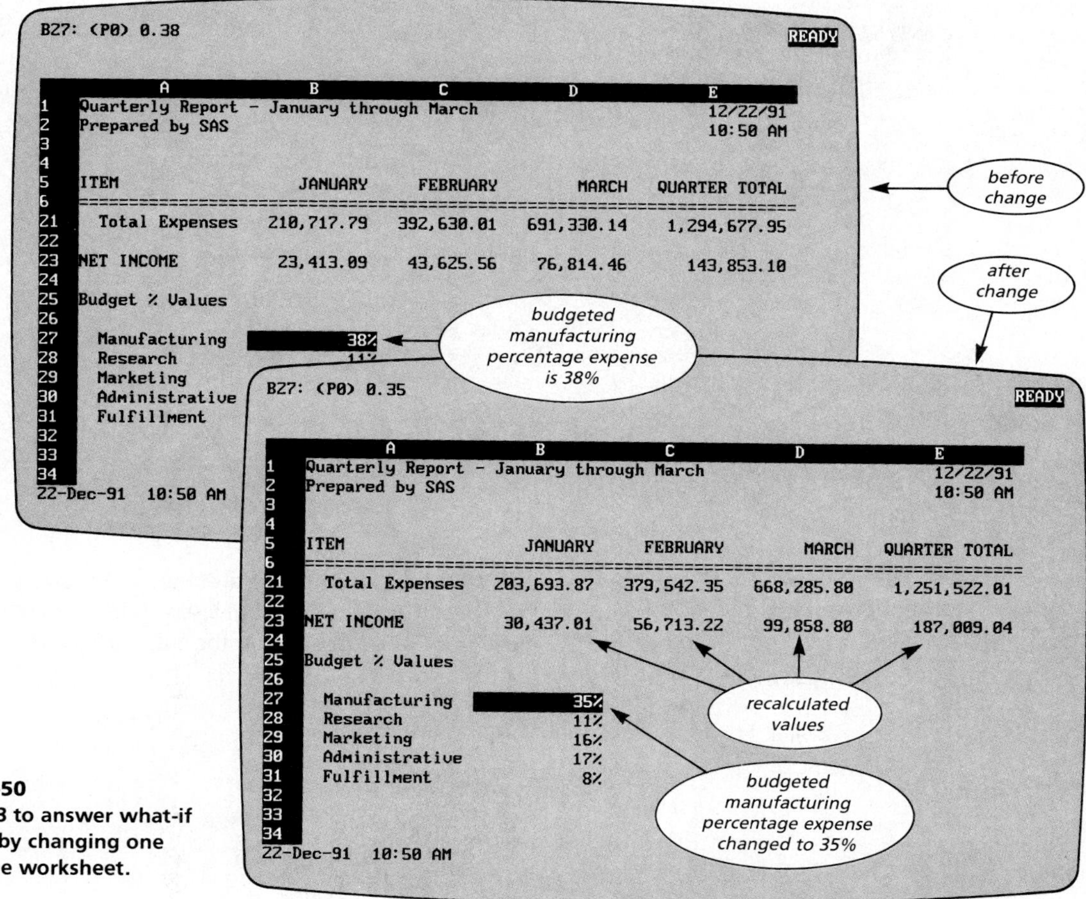


**FIGURE 3-50**
Using 1-2-3 to answer what-if questions by changing one value in the worksheet.

As soon as the 35% replaces the 38% in cell B27, the new expenses and new net income values can be examined (see the "after change" screen in Figure 3-50). By changing the value in B27 from 38% to 35%, the total January expenses decrease from 210,717.79 to 203,693.87, and the January net income increases from 23,413.09 to 30,437.01. The February and March figures change the same way. The quarter total expenses decrease from 1,294,677.95 to 1,251,522.01, and the quarter net income increases from 143,853.11 to 187,009.04. Thus, if the budgeted manufacturing expenses are reduced, it is clear that net income increases.

As shown in the "after change" screen in Figure 3-51, you can change more than one percentage. Let's change all the percentages. The new calculations display immediately.

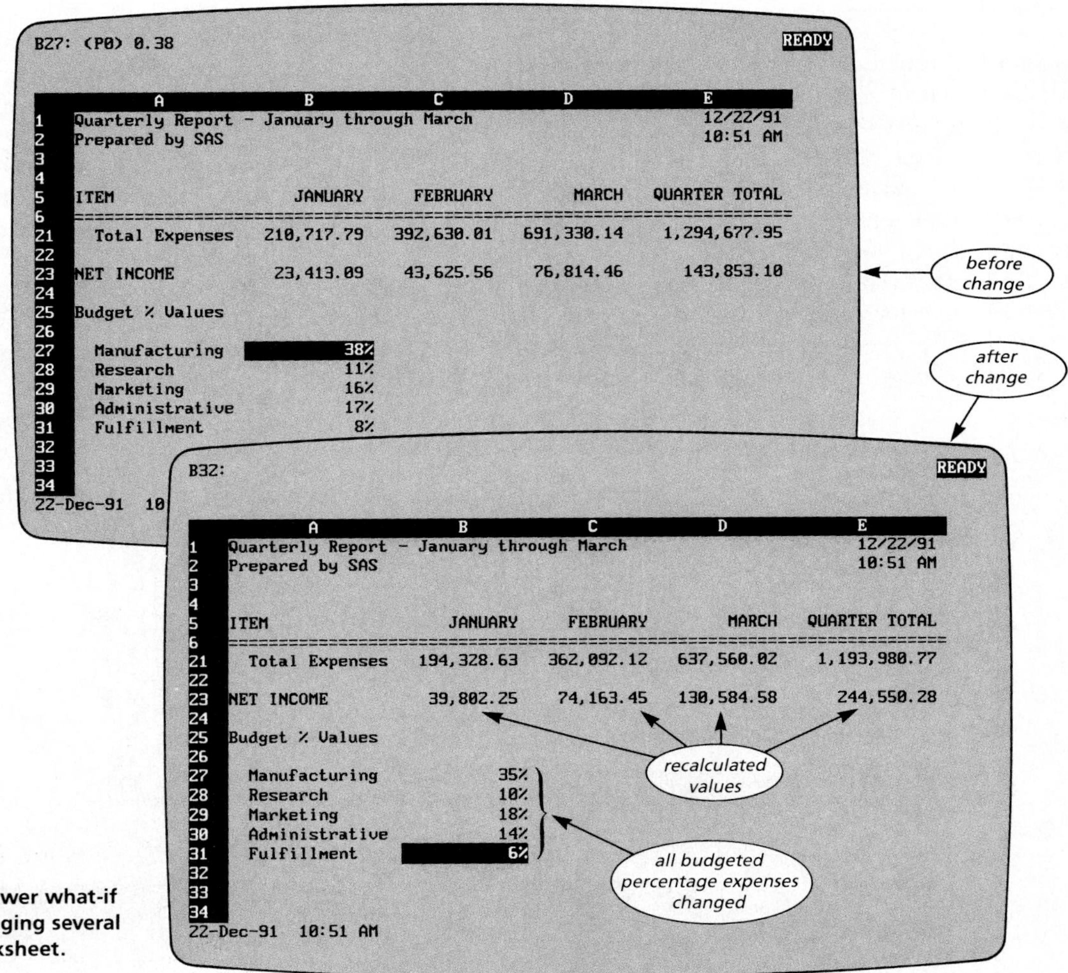


**FIGURE 3-51**
**Using 1-2-3 to answer what-if questions by changing several values in the worksheet.**

In Figure 3-51, we ask the question, "What if we change all the budgeted percent values to the following: Manufacturing (35%); Research (10%); Marketing (18%); Administrative (14%); Fulfillment (6%)—how would these changes affect the total expenses and the net income?" By merely changing the five values on the worksheet, all formulas are automatically recalculated to provide the answer to this question.

## Manual versus Automatic Recalculation

Each time you enter a value in the worksheet, 1-2-3 automatically recalculates all formulas and functions in the worksheet. This feature is called **automatic recalculation**.

An alternative to automatic recalculation is manual recalculation. With **manual recalculation**, 1-2-3 only recalculates after you tell it to do so. To change recalculation from automatic to manual, enter the command /**W**orksheet **G**lobal **R**ecalculate (/WGR). With the command cursor active in the **Recalculate menu**, type the letter M for Manual. Then recalculation of formulas takes place *only* after you press function key F9. To change back to automatic recalculation, use the same command but type the letter A for Automatic rather than M for Manual.

When you save a worksheet, the current recalculation mode is saved along with it. For an explanation of the other types of recalculation available with 1-2-3, enter the command /WGR and press function key F1. When you are finished with the online help facility, press the Esc key to return to your worksheet.

# CHANGING THE WORKSHEET DEFAULT SETTINGS

1-2-3 comes with default settings. We have already discussed some of the more obvious ones—column width is nine characters, format is General, and recalculation of formulas is Automatic. Some of the default settings, like the format, can be changed for a range or for the entire worksheet. When you make a change to the entire worksheet using the command /**W**orksheet **G**lobal (/WG), the change is saved with the worksheet when you issue the /**F**ile **S**ave (/FS) command.

There is another group of default settings that affect all worksheets created or retrieved during the current session, until you quit 1-2-3. To view or change these settings, type the command /**W**orksheet **G**lobal **D**efault (/WGD). This command displays the **Global Default menu** at the top of the screen as shown in Figure 3-52. Then use the arrow keys or first letters to select features to change.

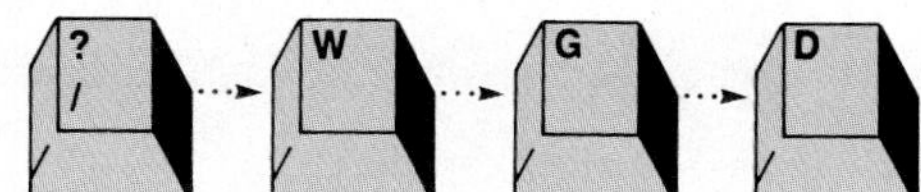


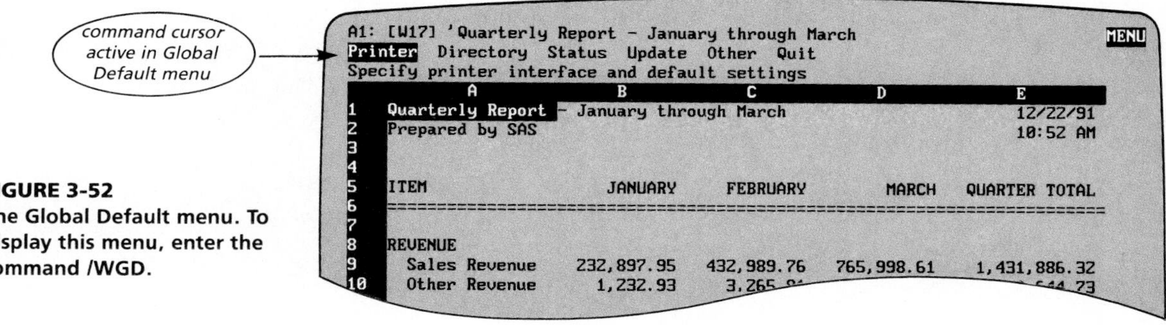


**FIGURE 3-52**
**The Global Default menu. To display this menu, enter the command /WGD.**

Once you pick the desired settings, you have the choice of saving the changes for the current session or saving them permanently. To save the changes for the current session, type the letter Q to quit the Global Default menu. To save the changes permanently, type the letters U for Update and then Q for Quit. If you typed the letter U for update, the new settings become the defaults for the current and future 1-2-3 sessions. Table 3-4 describes the features you can change by typing the command /WGD.

**TABLE 3-4 Global Defaults**

| FEATURE | DESCRIPTION |
|---|---|
| PRINTER | Specify printer interface and default settings. |
| DIRECTORY | Changes the default directory. |
| STATUS | Display default settings. |
| UPDATE | Permanently changes default settings in configuration file. |
| OTHER | Change international, help, and clock settings. |
| QUIT | Quit Global Default menu. |

## INTERACTING WITH DOS

Up to this point, we have used the File command to save and retrieve worksheets from disk. This command may also be used to carry out several other file management functions normally done at the DOS level. Table 3-5 summarizes the major file management commands available in 1-2-3.

**TABLE 3-5 File Management Commands**

| COMMAND | FUNCTION | DUPLICATE DOS COMMAND |
|---|---|---|
| /FE | Erases a file from disk. | ERASE or DEL |
| /FL | Displays the names of the files of a particular type. | DIR |
| /FD | Changes the current directory to a new one. | CHDIR or CD |

Other DOS commands and programs can be executed by placing 1-2-3 and your worksheet in a wait state. A **wait state** means that 1-2-3 has given up control to another program, like DOS, but still resides in main computer memory. To leave 1-2-3 temporarily, enter the command /System (/S). (If you do not have a fixed disk, place the DOS disk in the A drive before entering the /S command.)

You can use the System command to leave 1-2-3 to format a disk. Once the disk is formatted, you can return to 1-2-3 and the worksheet by typing the command Exit in response to the DOS prompt. One word of advice—save your worksheet before using the System command, especially if you plan to execute an external DOS command.

## PROJECT SUMMARY

In this project you learned a variety of ways to enhance a worksheet and simplify the steps of building, formatting, and printing large worksheets. You were introduced to the capabilities of 1-2-3 to answer what-if questions. Finally, you learned how to change the default settings and interact with DOS through 1-2-3.

Each of the steps required to build the worksheet in Project 3 is listed in the following table.

**SUMMARY OF KEYSTROKES—Project 3**

| STEPS | KEY(S) PRESSED | STEPS | KEY(S) PRESSED |
|---|---|---|---|
| 1 | /WGC→ → → → ↵ | 30 | /RFP0↵↑↑↑↑↵ |
| 2 | /WCS17↵ | 31 | [Home] [F5] B7↵ |
| 3 | → → → → /WCS16↵ | 32 | /WTB |
| 4 | /WGF,↵ | 33 | 232897.95→432989.76→765998.61→ |
| 5 | ← ← ← ← Quarterly Report – January through March↓ | 34 | @SUM(B7.D7)→ |
| 6 | Prepared by SAS↵ | 35 | /M [Backspace] ←.← ← ← ↵↓↓←.← ← ← ↵ |
| 7 | [F5] E1↵@now↓ | 36 | ↓↓↓← ← ← ← |
| 8 | @now↑ | 37 | 1232.93→3265.81→2145.99↓↓← ← |
| 9 | /RFD→ → → ↵↵ | 38 | @SUM(B9.B10)↵ |
| 10 | ↓/RFDT→ ↵↵ | 39 | /C↵ →.→ ↵ |
| 11 | [F5] A5↵ [Caps Lock] | 40 | /RFTB9.E19↵ |
| 12 | ITEM→"JANUARY→ | 41 | ↓↓↓$B27*B$12↵ |
| 13 | "FEBRUARY→"MARCH→ | 42 | /C↵.↓↓↓↓→ → ↵ |
| 14 | "QUARTER TOTAL↵ | 43 | [F5] B19↵/RF,↵B19.E9↵ |
| 15 | [F5] A6↵\=↵ | 44 | ↓↓@SUM(↑↑↑↑↑↑.↓↓↓↓)↵ |
| 16 | /C↵ →.→ → → ↵ | 45 | /C↵ →.→ ↵ |
| 17 | ↓↓REVENUE↓ [Caps Lock] | 46 | ↓↓+B12–B21↵ |
| 18 | ' Sales Revenue↓' Other Revenue↓↓ | 47 | /C↵ →.→ ↵ |
| 19 | ' Total Revenue↓↓ | 48 | [F5] E9↵ |
| 20 | EXPENSES↓' Manufacturing↓ | 49 | /C↵E9.E23↵ |
| 21 | ' Research↓' Fulfillment↓↓ | 50 | ↓↓/RE↵ |
| 22 | ' Total Expenses↓↓NET INCOME↓↓ | 51 | ↓↓/RE↓↵ |
| 23 | Budget % Values↓ | 52 | ↓↓↓↓↓↓↓/RE↵ |
| 24 | [F5] A17↵ | 53 | ↓↓/RE↵ |
| 25 | /WIR↓↵ | 54 | /WTC [Home] |
| 26 | ' Marketing↓' Administrative↓ | 55 | /FSPROJS-3↵ |
| 27 | /CA15.A19↵A27↵ | 56 | /PPRA1.E31↵ |
| 28 | [F5] B27↵ | 57 | AGPPQ |
| 29 | 38%↓11%↓16%↓17%↓8%↵ | | |

The following list summarizes the material covered in Project 3.

1. After setting the column width for the entire worksheet, use the command /**W**orksheet **C**olumn **S**et-Width (/WCS) to set the width of individual columns requiring a different width.
2. Use the command /**W**orksheet **G**lobal **F**ormat (/WGF) to format all the cells in the worksheet to the same type.
3. To display the date and time as a decimal number, use the NOW function. The whole number portion is the number of complete days since December 31, 1899. The decimal portion represents today's time.
4. Use the command /**R**ange **F**ormat **D**ate (/RFD) to format today's date and time. See Table 3-1 for a summary of the date and time formats.
5. The time stored in a cell is updated only after you make an entry into the worksheet or after you press function key F9.

## Project Summary (continued)

6. To insert rows or columns into a worksheet, move the cell pointer to the point of insertion and enter the command /**W**orksheet **I**nsert (/WI). Type the letter R to insert rows or the letter C to insert columns. Use the arrow keys to select how many rows or columns you want to insert.
7. To delete rows or columns from a worksheet, move the cell pointer to one of the end points of the range you plan to delete. Enter the command /**W**orksheet **D**elete (/WD). Type the letter R to delete rows or the letter C to delete columns. Use the arrow keys to select how many rows or columns you want to delete.
8. Enter a percentage value in percent form by appending a percent sign (%) to the right of the number.
9. To freeze the titles so that they remain on the screen as you move the cell pointer around the worksheet, use the command /**W**orksheet **T**itles (/WT). You then have the choice of freezing vertical (row) titles, horizontal (column) titles, or both. Use the same command to unfreeze the titles.
10. To move a range to another range, use the command /**M**ove (/M).
11. With respect to the Copy command, a cell address with no dollar sign ($) is a **relative address**. A cell address with a dollar sign appended to the front of both the column name and row number is an **absolute address**. A cell address with a dollar sign added to the front of the column name or to the front of the row number is a **mixed cell address**.
12. When entering a formula or function, you may use the arrow keys to point to the range.
13. It is valid to copy a cell to itself. This is necessary when you copy the end point of the destination range.
14. An empty cell or a cell with a label has a numeric value of zero.
15. Use the command /**P**rint **P**rinter **O**ption (/PPO) to change the printer default settings.
16. The ability to answer what-if questions is a powerful and important feature of 1-2-3.
17. Once a worksheet is complete, you can enter new values into cells. Formulas and functions that reference the modified cells are immediately recalculated, thus giving new results.
18. Use the command /**W**orksheet **G**lobal **R**ecalculation (/WGR) to change from automatic to manual recalculation.
19. To change the default settings for the worksheet, use the command /**W**orksheet **G**lobal **D**efault (/WGD).
20. Default settings changed with the command /WGD remain in force for the entire session, until you quit 1-2-3.
21. To permanently change the default settings, type the letter U for Update before quitting the Global Default menu.
22. The File command may be used to list the names of the files on disk, delete files, and change the current directory.
23. The System command allows you to temporarily place 1-2-3 in a wait state and return control to DOS. Once control returns to DOS, you may execute DOS commands. To return to 1-2-3, enter the command Exit.

# STUDENT ASSIGNMENTS

## STUDENT ASSIGNMENT 1: True/False

**Instructions:** Circle T if the statement is true or F if the statement is false.

T F 1. The /**W**orksheet **G**lobal **F**ormat (/WGF) command requires that you enter a range in the worksheet to be affected.
T F 2. Use the NOW function to display the date and time as a decimal number.
T F 3. The time displayed in a cell is automatically updated every minute.
T F 4. You can format the cell assigned the NOW function to display today's name (i.e., Sunday, Monday, etc.).
T F 5. When you insert rows in a worksheet, 1-2-3 *pushes up* the rows above the point of insertion to open up the worksheet.
T F 6. A percentage value, like 5.3%, can be entered exactly as 5.3% on the input line.
T F 7. The range B10..B15 is the same as B15..B10.
T F 8. When using the /**W**orksheet **T**itles (/WT) command, the title and column headings are called vertical titles.
T F 9. Use the command /**W**orksheet **T**itles **R**eset (/WTR) to unfreeze the titles.
T F 10. Use the /**M**ove (/M) command to move the contents of a cell or range of cells to a different location in the worksheet.
T F 11. When numbers are displayed using the Text format, they display left-justified in the cells.
T F 12. D23 is a relative address and $D$23 is an absolute address.

T F 13. You cannot use the arrow keys to select the range for the SUM function.
T F 14. If a cell within the range summed by the SUM function contains a label, 1-2-3 displays an error message.
T F 15. A worksheet printed in the condensed mode includes only the title lines and summary lines.
T F 16. Even a worksheet with no formulas or functions can be used to answer what-if questions.
T F 17. Manual recalculation means that you must tell 1-2-3 when to recalculate formulas by pressing function key F9.
T F 18. The System command is identical to the Quit command, except that the Quit command reminds you to save your worksheet.
T F 19. To permanently change the default settings of 1-2-3, type the letter U for Update before quitting the Global Default menu.
T F 20. The command /**F**ile (/F) can be used to erase and list the names of worksheets on disk.

## STUDENT ASSIGNMENT 2: Multiple Choice

**Instructions:** Circle the correct response.

1. Which one of the following functions is used to display the time?
   a. TODAY b. TIME c. NOW d. CLOCK
2. Which one of the following commands is used to delete rows or columns from a worksheet?
   a. /**W**orksheet **D**elete (/WD) c. /**W**orksheet **L**abel (/WL)
   b. /**W**orksheet **E**rase (/WE) d. /**W**orksheet **U**nprotect (/WU)
3. Which one of the following is an absolute address?
   a. G45 b. !G!45 c. $B$45 d. #G#45
4. If cell B14 is assigned the label TEN, then the function @SUM(B10.B14) in cell C25 considers B14 to be equal to ________ .
   a. 10 b. 0 c. an undefined value d. 3
5. The command /**P**rint **P**rinter **O**ptions (/PPO) may be used to change ________ .
   a. the margins c. from normal mode to condensed mode
   b. the page-length d. all of these
6. The /**F**ile (/F) command can be used to ________ .
   a. format disks c. erase worksheets from disk
   b. change the current directory d. both b and c
7. The command /**W**orksheet **G**lobal **D**efault (/WGD) can be used to ________ .
   a. delete files c. return control to DOS
   b. select a format for the worksheet d. display default settings
8. The command /**M**ove (/M) results in the same change to the worksheet as ________ .
   a. /**W**orksheet **E**rase (/WE) c. /**W**orksheet **I**nsert (/WI)
   b. /**C**opy (/C) d. none of these

## STUDENT ASSIGNMENT 3: Understanding Absolute, Mixed, and Relative Addressing

**Instructions:** Fill in the correct answers.

1. Write cell B1 as a relative address, absolute address, mixed address with the row varying, and mixed address with the column varying.

Relative address: __________ Mixed, row varying: __________

Absolute address: __________ Mixed, column varying: __________

2. In Figure 3-53, write the formula for cell B8 that multiplies cell B1 times the sum of cells B4, B5, and B6. Write the formula so that when it is copied to cells C8 and D8, cell B1 remains absolute. Verify your formula by checking it with the values found in cells B8, C8, and D8 in Figure 3-53.

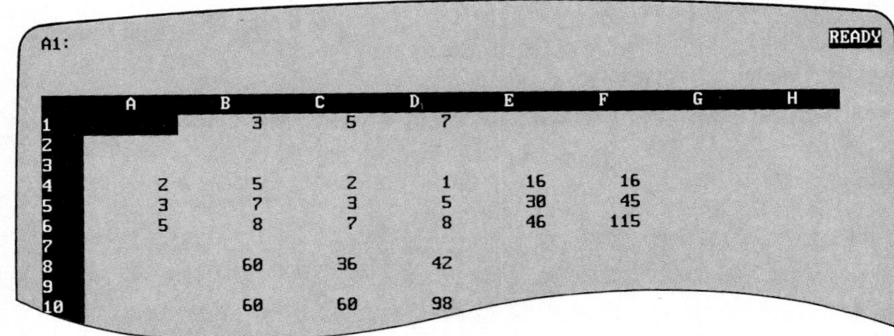


**FIGURE 3-53**
**Student Assignment 3**

Formula for cell B8: ______________________________

3. In Figure 3-53, write the formula for cell E4 that multiplies cell A4 times the sum of cells B4, C4, and D4. Write the formula so that when it is copied to cells E5 and E6, cell A4 remains absolute. Verify your formula by checking it with the values found in cells E4, E5, and E6 in Figure 3-53.

Formula for cell E4: ______________________________

4. In Figure 3-53, write the formula for cell B10 that multiplies cell B1 times the sum of cells B4, B5, and B6. Write the formula so that when it is copied to cells C10 and D10, 1-2-3 adjusts all the cell addresses according to the new location. Verify your formula by checking it with the values found in cells B10, C10, and D10 in Figure 3-53.

Formula for cell B10: ______________________________

5. In Figure 3-53, write the formula for cell F4 that multiplies cell A4 times the sum of cells B4, C4, and D4. Write the formula so that when it is copied to cells F5 and F6, 1-2-3 adjusts all the cell addresses according to the new location. Verify your formula by checking it with the values found in cells F4, F5, and F6 in Figure 3-53.

Formula for cell F4: ______________________________

## STUDENT ASSIGNMENT 4: Writing 1-2-3 Commands

**Instructions:** Write the 1-2-3 command to accomplish the task in each of the problems below. Write the command up to the point where you enter the range or type the letter Q to quit the command.

1. Delete columns A, B, and C. Assume the cell pointer is at A1.

   Command: ______________________________

2. Insert three rows between rows 5 and 6. Assume the cell pointer is at A6.

   Command: ______________________________

3. Move the range of cells A12..C15 to F14..H17. Assume the cell pointer is at A12.

   Command: ______________________________

4. Freeze the vertical and horizontal titles. Assume that the cell pointer is immediately below and to the right of the titles.

   Command: ______________________________

5. Return control to DOS temporarily.

   Command: ______________________________

6. List the worksheet names on the default drive.

   Command: ______________________________

7. Set columns A and B as borders. Assume the cell pointer is at B1.

   Command: ______________________________

8. Change the left print margin to 1 and the right print margin to 79 for the current worksheet only.

   Command: ______________________________

9. Change to print in condensed mode with a right margin of 132.

   Command: ______________________________

10. Change 1-2-3 from automatic to manual recalculation.

    Command: ______________________________

## STUDENT ASSIGNMENT 5: Correcting the Range in a Worksheet

**Instructions:** The worksheet illustrated in Figure 3-54 contains errors in cells E9 through E21. Analyze the entries displayed on the worksheet, especially the formula assigned to E9 and displayed at the top of the screen. Explain the cause of the errors and the method of correction in the space provided below.

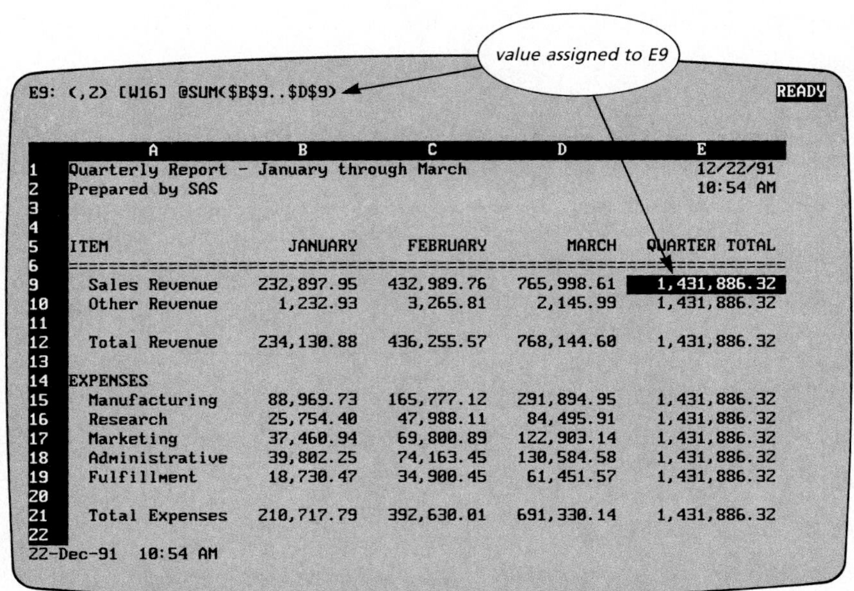


| | A | B | C | D | E |
|---|---|---|---|---|---|
| 1 | Quarterly Report - January through March | | | | 12/22/91 |
| 2 | Prepared by SAS | | | | 10:54 AM |
| 3 | | | | | |
| 4 | | | | | |
| 5 | ITEM | JANUARY | FEBRUARY | MARCH | QUARTER TOTAL |
| 6 | ============ | ============ | ============ | ============ | ============ |
| 9 | Sales Revenue | 232,897.95 | 432,989.76 | 765,998.61 | 1,431,886.32 |
| 10 | Other Revenue | 1,232.93 | 3,265.81 | 2,145.99 | 1,431,886.32 |
| 11 | | | | | |
| 12 | Total Revenue | 234,130.88 | 436,255.57 | 768,144.60 | 1,431,886.32 |
| 13 | | | | | |
| 14 | EXPENSES | | | | |
| 15 | Manufacturing | 88,969.73 | 165,777.12 | 291,894.95 | 1,431,886.32 |
| 16 | Research | 25,754.40 | 47,988.11 | 84,495.91 | 1,431,886.32 |
| 17 | Marketing | 37,460.94 | 69,800.89 | 122,903.14 | 1,431,886.32 |
| 18 | Administrative | 39,802.25 | 74,163.45 | 130,584.58 | 1,431,886.32 |
| 19 | Fulfillment | 18,730.47 | 34,900.45 | 61,451.57 | 1,431,886.32 |
| 20 | | | | | |
| 21 | Total Expenses | 210,717.79 | 392,630.01 | 691,330.14 | 1,431,886.32 |
| 22 | | | | | |

22-Dec-91 10:54 AM

**FIGURE 3-54**
**Student Assignment 5**

Cause of errors: ______________________________

______________________________

Method of correction for cell E9: ______________________________

______________________________

Method of correction for cells E10 through E21: ______________________________

______________________________

______________________________

## STUDENT ASSIGNMENT 6: Correcting Errors in a Worksheet

**Instructions:** The worksheet illustrated in Figure 3-55 contains errors in the range B15..E23. This worksheet contains the same formulas as the worksheet in Project 3. Analyze the entries displayed on the worksheet. Explain the cause of the errors and the method of correction in the space provided below. (Hint: Check the cells that are referenced in the range B15..E23.)

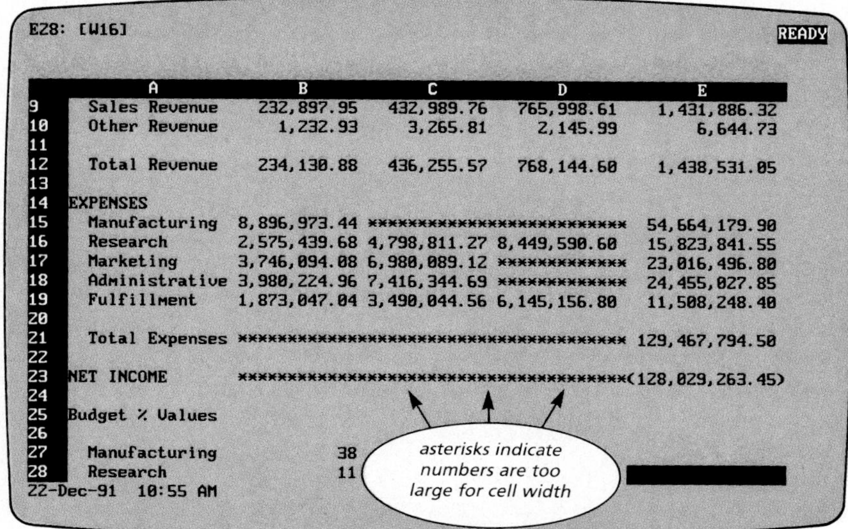

E28: [W16] READY

| | A | B | C | D | E |
|---|---|---|---|---|---|
| 9 | Sales Revenue | 232,897.95 | 432,989.76 | 765,998.61 | 1,431,886.32 |
| 10 | Other Revenue | 1,232.93 | 3,265.81 | 2,145.99 | 6,644.73 |
| 11 | | | | | |
| 12 | Total Revenue | 234,130.88 | 436,255.57 | 768,144.60 | 1,438,531.05 |
| 13 | | | | | |
| 14 | EXPENSES | | | | |
| 15 | Manufacturing | 8,896,973.44 | ************* | ************* | 54,664,179.90 |
| 16 | Research | 2,575,439.68 | 4,798,811.27 | 8,449,590.60 | 15,823,841.55 |
| 17 | Marketing | 3,746,094.08 | 6,980,089.12 | ************* | 23,016,496.80 |
| 18 | Administrative | 3,980,224.96 | 7,416,344.69 | ************* | 24,455,027.85 |
| 19 | Fulfillment | 1,873,047.04 | 3,490,044.56 | 6,145,156.80 | 11,508,248.40 |
| 20 | | | | | |
| 21 | Total Expenses | ************* | ************* | ************* | 129,467,794.50 |
| 22 | | | | | |
| 23 | NET INCOME | ************* | ************* | ************* | (128,029,263.45) |
| 24 | | | | | |
| 25 | Budget % Values | | | | |
| 26 | | | | | |
| 27 | Manufacturing | 38 | | | |
| 28 | Research | 11 | | | |

22-Dec-91 10:55 AM



**FIGURE 3-55**
**Student Assignment 6**

Cause of errors: ______________________________________________

______________________________________________

Method of correction: ______________________________________________

______________________________________________

## STUDENT ASSIGNMENT 7: Building a Projected Price Increase Worksheet

**Instructions:** Load 1-2-3 and perform the following tasks.

1. Build the worksheet illustrated in Figure 3-56. Increase the width of columns B through E to 13 characters. Enter the title, column headings, model numbers in column A, and corresponding current prices in column B. The entries in the columns labeled 10% INCREASE, 15% INCREASE, and 20% INCREASE are determined from formulas. Multiply one plus the percent specified in the column heading by the current price. For example, assign C8 the formula 1.10*B8. To determine the total current price in cell B18, enter a formula that adds the products of the on-hand column and the corresponding current price. Copy this total formula in cell B18 to cells C18 through E18 to determine the totals in the remaining columns.

A20: READY

| | A | B | C | D | E | F |
|---|---|---|---|---|---|---|
| 1 | | | VIDEOLAND | | | 22-Dec |
| 2 | | PROJECTED PRICE INCREASES FOR NEXT QUARTER | | | | 10:56 AM |
| 3 | | | | | | |
| 4 | MODEL | CURRENT | 10% | 15% | 20% | |
| 5 | NUMBER | PRICE | INCREASE | INCREASE | INCREASE | ON HAND |
| 6 | ========== | ============= | ============= | ============= | ============= | ========== |
| 7 | | | | | | |
| 8 | VCR-101 | 250.00 | 275.00 | 287.50 | 300.00 | 12 |
| 9 | VCR-201 | 295.00 | 324.50 | 339.25 | 354.00 | 23 |
| 10 | VCR-325 | 350.00 | 385.00 | 402.50 | 420.00 | 8 |
| 11 | VCR-500 | 495.00 | 544.50 | 569.25 | 594.00 | 17 |
| 12 | VCR-750 | 600.00 | 660.00 | 690.00 | 720.00 | 16 |
| 13 | VCR-800 | 675.00 | 742.50 | 776.25 | 810.00 | 25 |
| 14 | VCR-825 | 700.00 | 770.00 | 805.00 | 840.00 | 41 |
| 15 | VCR-900 | 750.00 | 825.00 | 862.50 | 900.00 | 19 |
| 16 | VCR-990 | 800.00 | 880.00 | 920.00 | 960.00 | 7 |
| 17 | | | | | | |
| 18 | TOTAL | $96,025.00 | $105,627.50 | $110,428.75 | $115,230.00 | |
| 19 | | | | | | |
| 20 | | | | | | |

22-Dec-91 10:56 AM

**FIGURE 3-56**
**Student Assignment 7**

2. Save the worksheet as STUS3-7.
3. Print the worksheet in the condensed mode. Reset 1-2-3 back to the normal print mode.
4. Print the cell-formulas version of the worksheet.
5. Print only the first 18 rows of the model number and current price columns.
6. Print the worksheet after formatting all the cells to the Text type.

## STUDENT ASSIGNMENT 8: Building a Payroll Analysis Worksheet

**Instructions:** Load 1-2-3 and perform the following tasks.

1. Build the worksheet illustrated in Figure 3-57. Change the global width to 13 characters. Change the width of column A to 19 characters. Enter the title, column headings, row titles, employee names in column A, and corresponding current hourly pay rate in column B. Use the NOW function to display the date and time in cells E18 and E19. Finally, enter the proposed percent increase in cell B15 and hours per week in cell B16. Enter the following formulas once and copy them to complete the remainder of the worksheet:
   a. Cell C8—current weekly pay = hours per week × current hourly pay rate
   b. Cell D8—proposed hourly pay rate = current hourly pay rate × (1 + proposed percent increase in B15)
   c. Cell E8—proposed weekly pay = hours per week × proposed hourly pay rate

Format the numbers in rows 8 through 12 to the Fixed type with two decimal places. Format the totals in rows 18 through 20 to the Currency type with two decimal places.

E20: READY

| | A | B | C | D | E |
|---|---|---|---|---|---|
| 1 | | PAYROLL ANALYSIS REPORT | | | |
| 2 | | | | | |
| 3 | | CURRENT | CURRENT | PROPOSED | PROPOSED |
| 4 | | HOURLY | WEEKLY | HOURLY | WEEKLY |
| 5 | EMPLOYEE NAME | PAY RATE | PAY | PAY RATE | PAY |
| 6 | ==================== | ============= | ============= | ============= | ============= |
| 7 | | | | | |
| 8 | BAKER, MARY A. | 7.00 | 280.00 | 7.35 | 294.00 |
| 9 | DAVIS, STEPHEN D. | 9.00 | 360.00 | 9.45 | 378.00 |
| 10 | LONG, CLARENCE R. | 8.00 | 320.00 | 8.40 | 336.00 |
| 11 | MONROE, JAMES L. | 10.00 | 400.00 | 10.50 | 420.00 |
| 12 | CHANG, JUSTIN M. | 5.00 | 200.00 | 5.25 | 210.00 |
| 13 | -------------------- | ------------- | ------------- | ------------- | ------------- |
| 14 | | | | | |
| 15 | PROPSED % INCREASE | 5% | | | |
| 16 | HOURS PER WEEK | 40 | | | |
| 17 | | | | | |
| 18 | TOTAL PROPOSED PAY | $1,638.00 | | | 22-Dec-91 |
| 19 | TOTAL CURRENT PAY | $1,560.00 | | | 10:57:03 AM |
| 20 | AMOUNT OF INCREASE | $78.00 | | | |

22-Dec-91 10:57 AM

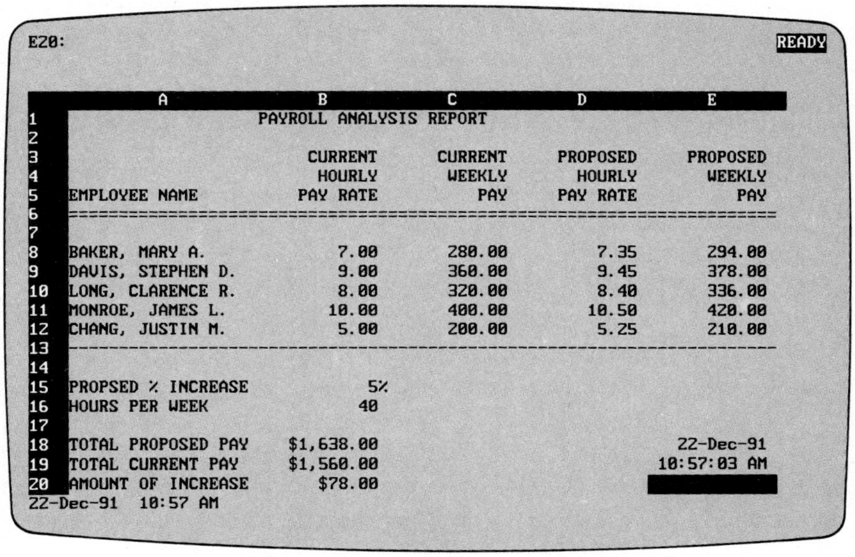

**FIGURE 3-57**
**Student Assignment 8**

2. Save the worksheet as STUS3-8.
3. Print the worksheet in condensed mode. Reset 1-2-3 back to the normal print mode.
4. Print only the range A1..C13.
5. Answer the following what-if questions. Print the worksheet for each question.
   a. What is the total proposed pay if the proposed percent increase is changed to 10%?
   b. What is the total proposed pay if the proposed percent increase is changed to 7.5%?

## STUDENT ASSIGNMENT 9: Building a Book Income Worksheet

**Instructions:** Load 1-2-3 and perform the following tasks.

1. Build the worksheet illustrated in Figure 3-58. Set column A to a width of 18 characters and columns B through E to a width of 13 characters. The calculations for each author are determined as follows:
   a. The royalty in column C is the net sales of the book multiplied by the author's royalty percentage in cell B30 or B31.
   b. The manufacturing costs in column D are the net sales of the book multiplied by the manufacturing budgeted percent in cell B35.
   c. The net income in column E for each book is determined by subtracting the royalty and manufacturing costs from the net sales.
   d. The report totals in rows 25 and 26 are the sum of the individual book titles for each author.

```
            A                  B              C             D             E
 1                                    BOOK INCOME REPORT
 2 -----------------------------------------------------------------------------
 3 AUTHOR:                HANSEN
 4
 5 BOOK TITLE                NET SALES        ROYALTY  MANU. COSTS    NET INCOME
 6
 7 Fury in the Sky          122,356.61      15,906.36    32,179.79     74,270.46
 8 Night Crawler            543,667.92      70,676.83   142,984.66    330,006.43
 9 White Feathers           885,443.91     115,107.71   232,871.75    537,464.45
10
11 -----------------------------------------------------------------------------
12 AUTHOR:                MERRRIT
13
14 BOOK TITLE                NET SALES        ROYALTY  MANU. COSTS    NET INCOME
15
16 The Sharp Beak           553,889.04      74,775.02   145,672.82    333,441.20
17 Webbed Intrique          657,443.25      88,754.84   172,907.57    395,780.84
18 Information Blight       956,441.89     129,119.66   251,544.22    575,778.02
19
20 -----------------------------------------------------------------------------
21 REPORT TOTALS
22
23 AUTHOR                    NET SALES        ROYALTY  MANU. COSTS    NET INCOME
24
25 Hansen                 1,551,468.44     201,690.90   408,036.20    941,741.34
26 Merrit                 2,167,774.18     292,649.51   570,124.61  1,305,000.06
27
28 =============================================================================
29 Royalty:
30 Hansen                        13.0%
31 Merrit                        13.5%
32
33
34 Manufacturing Cost                                                    Dec-91
35 All Books                     26.3%                                 10:58 AM
36
```

**FIGURE 3-58** Student Assignment 9

2. Save the worksheet. Use the file name STUS3-9.
3. Print the worksheet.
4. Print only the range A3..E9.
5. Print the worksheet after formatting all the cells to the Text type.

## STUDENT ASSIGNMENT 10: Building a Salary Budget Worksheet

**Instructions:** Load 1-2-3 and perform the following tasks.

1. Build the worksheet illustrated in Figure 3-59. Change the width of all the columns in the worksheet to 15 characters. Then change the width of column A to 20 characters. Enter the title, column headings, row titles, date, time, and current salary for full- and part-time employees. Determine the projected salaries in column C by using the salary increase in cell B27 and the current salaries in column B. Determine the salaries by department by multiplying the total salaries in row 12 by the corresponding sales allocation percent value in the range B21..B24. Use the SUM function to determine the annual totals in column D.

| | A | B | C | D |
|---|---|---|---|---|
| 1 | SALARY BUDGET - CURRENT AND PROJECTED SALARIES | | | 12/22/91 |
| 2 | PREPARED BY ACCOUNTING | | | 10:59 AM |
| 3 | | | | |
| 4 | | | | |
| 5 | | CURRENT | PROJECTED | |
| 6 | SALARY TYPE | JAN - JUNE | JULY - DEC | ANNUAL TOTAL |
| 7 | ==================== | =============== | =============== | =============== |
| 8 | | | | |
| 9 | FULL TIME | 1,250,500.00 | 1,313,025.00 | 2,563,525.00 |
| 10 | PART TIME | 750,500.00 | 788,025.00 | 1,538,525.00 |
| 11 | | | | |
| 12 | TOTAL SALARIES | 2,001,000.00 | 2,101,050.00 | 4,102,050.00 |
| 13 | | | | |
| 14 | SALARIES BY DEPARTMENT | | | |
| 15 | Accounting | 200,100.00 | 210,105.00 | 410,205.00 |
| 16 | Production | 600,300.00 | 630,315.00 | 1,230,615.00 |
| 17 | Sales | 500,250.00 | 525,262.50 | 1,025,512.50 |
| 18 | Distribution | 700,350.00 | 735,367.50 | 1,435,717.50 |
| 19 | | | | |
| 20 | SALES ALLOCATION % VALUES | | | |
| 21 | Accounting | 10% | | |
| 22 | Production | 30% | | |
| 23 | Sales | 25% | | |
| 24 | Distribution | 35% | | |
| 25 | | | | |
| 26 | | | | |
| 27 | SALARY INCREASE % | 5% | | |
| 28 | | | | |

**FIGURE 3-59** Student Assignment 10

2. Save the worksheet using the file name STUS3-10.
3. Print the worksheet.
4. Print the portion of the worksheet in the range A14..D18.

## STUDENT ASSIGNMENT 11: Changing Manufacturing Costs and Royalty Rates in the Book Income Worksheet

**Instructions:** Load 1-2-3 and perform the following tasks.

1. Retrieve the worksheet STUS3-9 from disk. The worksheet is illustrated in Figure 3-58.
2. Answer the following what-if questions. Print the worksheet for each question. Each question is independent of the others.
   a. If the manufacturing percentage cost in cell B35 is reduced from 26.3% to 24.7%, what is the net income from all of Hansen's books?
   b. If Merrit's royalty percentage in cell B31 is changed from 13.5% to 14.8%, what would be the royalty amount for the book *Webbed Intrigue*?
   c. If Hansen's royalty percentage in cell B30 is reduced from 13% to 12.5%, Merrit's royalty percentage is increased from 13.5% to 14.1%, and the manufacturing percentage costs are reduced from 26.3% to 25%, what would be the net incomes for Hansen and Merrit?

## STUDENT ASSIGNMENT 12: Changing Sales Allocation Percent Values and Salary Increase Percent in the Salary Budget Worksheet

**Instructions:** Load 1-2-3 and perform the following tasks.

1. Retrieve the worksheet STUS3-10 from disk. The worksheet is illustrated in Figure 3-59.
2. Answer the following what-if questions. Print the worksheet for each question. Each question is independent of the other.
   a. If the four sales allocation percent values in the range B21..B24 are each decreased by 1% and the salary increase in cell B27 is changed from 5% to 4%, what are the annual totals in the Salary Budget worksheet?
   b. If the salary increase percent is cut in half, what would be the total projected salaries?

# PROJECT 4

## Building Worksheets with Functions and Macros

### Objectives

You will have mastered the material in this project when you can:

- Assign a name to a range and refer to the range in a formula using the assigned name.
- Apply the elementary statistical functions AVG, COUNT, MAX, MIN, STD, and VAR.
- Determine the monthly payment of a loan using the financial function PMT.
- Enter a series of numbers into a range using the Data Fill command.
- Employ the IF function to enter one value or another in a cell on the basis of a condition.
- Determine the present value of an annuity using the financial function PV.
- Determine the future value of an investment using the financial function FV.
- Build a data table to perform what-if analyses.
- Store keystrokes as a macro and execute the macro.
- Write program-like macros to automate your worksheet.
- Divide the screen into multiple windows.
- Protect and unprotect cells.

In this project we will develop two worksheets, Project 4A and Project 4B. The worksheet for Project 4A, shown in Figure 4-1, is a grading report that displays a row of information for each student enrolled in DP 101. The student information includes a student identification number, three test scores, a test score total, and total percent correct. At the bottom of the worksheet is summary information for each test and all three tests grouped together. The summary includes the number of students that took the test, the highest and lowest test scores, the average test score, standard deviation, and variance. The **standard deviation** is a statistic used to measure the dispersion of test scores. The **variance** is used to make additional statistical inferences about the test scores.

| DP 101 | | Grading Report | | | 22-Dec-91 |
|---|---|---|---|---|---|
| Student | Test 1<br>139 | Test 2<br>142 | Test 3<br>150 | Total<br>431 | Percent<br>Correct |
| 1035 | 121 | 127 | 142 | 390 | 90.5 |
| 1074 | 114 | 113 | 132 | 359 | 83.3 |
| 1265 | 79 | 97 | 101 | 277 | 64.3 |
| 1345 | 85 | 106 | 95 | 286 | 66.4 |
| 1392 | 127 | 124 | 120 | 371 | 86.1 |
| 3167 | 101 | 120 | 109 | 330 | 76.6 |
| 3382 | 110 | 104 | 120 | 334 | 77.5 |
| 3597 | 92 | 104 | 100 | 296 | 68.7 |
| 4126 | 105 | 100 | 96 | 301 | 69.8 |
| 5619 | 125 | 135 | 143 | 403 | 93.5 |
| 7561 | 112 | 130 | 123 | 365 | 84.7 |
| Count | 11 | 11 | 11 | 11 | |
| Lowest Grade | 79 | 97 | 95 | 277 | |
| Highest Grade | 127 | 135 | 143 | 403 | |
| Average Grade | 106.5 | 114.5 | 116.5 | 337.5 | |
| Std Deviation | 15.2 | 12.6 | 16.8 | 41.4 | |
| Variation | 230.2 | 159.0 | 282.8 | 1711.2 | |

**FIGURE 4-1** The grading report we will build in Project 4A.

Project 4B has three parts. The first part is shown in Figure 4-2. This worksheet determines the monthly payment and an amortization table for a car loan. An **amortization table** shows the beginning and ending balances and the amount of payment that applies to the principal and interest for each period. This type of worksheet can be very useful if you are planning to take out a loan and want to see the effects of increasing the down payment, changing the interest rate, or changing the length of time it takes to pay off the loan.

```
A1: PR [W12]                                                                    READY

        A           B               C               D               E
1                            Crown Loan Company                         12/22/91
2
3  Item:         1988 Chevy Van                 Rate:                      11.5%
4
5  Price:            $18,500.00                 Years:                         5
6
7  Down Pymt:         $4,000.00                 Monthly Pymt:            $318.89
8  ==========================================================================
9                     Beginning          Ending        Paid On         Interest
10          Year        Balance         Balance      Principal             Paid
11 --------------------------------------------------------------------------
12             1      14,500.00       12,223.26       2,276.74         1,549.98
13             2      12,223.26        9,670.45       2,552.81         1,273.90
14             3       9,670.45        6,808.08       2,862.37           964.35
15             4       6,808.08        3,598.63       3,209.45           617.26
16             5       3,598.63            0.00       3,598.63           228.08
17 --------------------------------------------------------------------------
18                                     Subtotal      14,500.00         4,633.57
19                                    Down Pymt                        4,000.00
20                                   Total Cost                       23,133.57
22-Dec-91   11:02 AM
```

**FIGURE 4-2**
**The monthly payment and amortization table we will build for the Crown Loan Company in Part 1 of Project 4B.**

The second part of this worksheet is shown in Figure 4-3. Here we use a data table to analyze the effect of different interest rates on the monthly payment and total amount paid for the car loan. A **data table** is an area of the worksheet set up to contain answers to what-if questions. By using a data table you can automate your what-if questions and organize the answers returned by 1-2-3 into a table. For example, the data table in Figure 4-3 displays the monthly payments and total cost of the loan for interest rates that vary between 8.5% and 15% in increments of 0.5%.

```
I20: PR                                                                         READY

           F               G               H               I
1  Payments for Varying Interest Rates
2
3       Varying         Monthly           Total
4          Rate         Payment            Paid
5  ==========================================
6                        318.89       23,133.57
7          8.5%          297.49       21,849.38
8          9.0%          301.00       22,059.77
9          9.5%          304.53       22,271.62
10        10.0%          308.08       22,484.93
11        10.5%          311.66       22,699.69
12        11.0%          315.27       22,915.91
13        11.5%          318.89       23,133.57
14        12.0%          322.54       23,352.67
15        12.5%          326.22       23,573.21
16        13.0%          329.92       23,795.17
17        13.5%          333.64       24,018.57
18        14.0%          337.39       24,243.38
19        14.5%          341.16       24,469.60
20        15.0%          344.95       24,697.24
22-Dec-91   11:03 AM
```

**FIGURE 4-3**
**The data table we will build for the Crown Loan Company in Part 2 of Project 4B.**

The third part of Project 4B involves writing the four macros shown in Figure 4-4. A **macro** is a series of keystrokes or instructions that are stored in a cell or a range of cells associated with that particular worksheet. They are executed by pressing only two keys: the Alt key and the single letter macro name. Macros save you time and effort. For example, they allow you to store a complex sequence of commands in a cell. Later you can execute the macro (stored commands) as often as you want by simply typing its name.

```
        A                  B              C               D                  E
22                Crown Loan Company Worksheet Macros
23
24    Macro                           Macro Name     Function
25    ============                    ==========     ==============================
26    /FS~R                           \S             Saves worksheet
27
28    /PPAGPPQ                        \P             Prints worksheet
29
30    /PPOOCQAGOOAQPPQ                \C             Prints cell-formulas version
31
32
33    {HOME}                          \D             Accept loan information
34    {GOTO}B3~/RE~                                  --Clear cell B3
35    {DOWN}{DOWN}/RE~                               --Clear cell B5
36    {DOWN}{DOWN}/RE~                               --Clear cell B7
37    {GOTO}E3~/RE~                                  --Clear cell E3
38    {DOWN}{DOWN}/RE~                               --Clear cell E5
39    {HOME}                                         --Move to cell A1
40    /XLPurchase Item:~B3~                          --Accept item
41    /XNPurchase Price:~B5~                         --Accept price
42    /XNDown Payment:~B7~                           --Accept down payment
43    /XNInterest Rate in %:~E3~                     --Accept interest rate
44    /XNTime in Years:~E5~                          --Accept time in years
45    {HOME}                                         --Move to cell A1
46    /XQ                                            --End of macro
47
```

**FIGURE 4-4 The four macros we will build for the Crown Loan Company in Part 3 of Project 4B.**

When executed, the macro in cell A26 of Figure 4-4 saves the worksheet. The one in cell A28 prints the worksheet on the basis of the previously defined range. The macro in cell A30 prints the cell-formulas version of the worksheet on the basis of the previously defined range. The multicell macro in the range A33..A46 is a type of computer program. When it executes, it automatically clears the cells containing the loan information in Figure 4-2, requests new loan data on the input line, and displays the new loan information.

## PROJECT 4A—ANALYZING STUDENT TEST SCORES

Begin Project 4A with an empty worksheet and the cell pointer at A1, the home position. The first step is to change the widths of the columns in the worksheet. Set the width of column A to 13 characters, so that the row identifier "Std Deviation" fits in cell A22 (see Figure 4-1). Change the width of the rest of the columns in the worksheet from 9 to 11 characters so that all the student information fits across the screen. To change the columns to the desired widths, do the following:

1. Enter the command /**W**orksheet **G**lobal **C**olumn-Width (/WGC). Change the default width on the input line from 9 to 11 and press the Enter key.
2. With the cell pointer at A1, enter the command /**W**orksheet **C**olumn **S**et-Width (/WCS). Change the number 11 on the input line to 13 and press the Enter key.

If you reverse steps 1 and 2, the results will still be the same. That is, you can change the width of column A first and then change the width of the rest of the columns. The command /WGC affects only those columns that were not previously changed by the /WCS command.

The next step is to add the titles and student data to the worksheet. Enter the course number, worksheet title, date, column headings, maximum possible points for each test, student number, test scores, and summary identifiers as specified in Figure 4-1. Note that the numbers in column A identify the students in the class and are not used in any computations. Therefore, enter these numbers with a leading apostrophe ('). After entering the last row identifier in cell A23, press the Home key. The first 20 rows display as shown in Figure 4-5.

```
A1: [W13] 'DP 101                                                        READY

            A              B          C          D          E          F
1   DP 101                      Grading Report                    22-Dec-91
2
3                         Test 1     Test 2     Test 3      Total     Percent
4   Student                  139        142        150                Correct
5   ===========================================================================
6   1035                     121        127        142
7   1074                     114        113        132
8   1265                      79         97        101
9   1345                                106         95
10  1392                                124        120
11  3167                                120        109
12  3382                                104        120
13  3597                                104        100
14  4126                     105        100         96
15  5619                     125        135        143
16  7561                     112        130        123
17  ---------------------------------------------------------------------------
18  Count
19  Lowest Grade
20  Highest Grade
22-Dec-91  11:05 AM
```



**FIGURE 4-5**
**Labels and student data entered into the grading report.**

With the student data in the worksheet, we can determine the totals and summaries. Let's start with the maximum number of points for all three tests in cell E4. Use the GOTO command to move the cell pointer from cell A1 to cell E4 and enter the function @SUM(B4..D4). The range B4..D4 contains the maximum possible points for each test.

The SUM function in cell E4 is the same one required in the range E6..E16 to determine the total number of points received by each student. Hence, use the Copy command to copy cell E4 to the range E6..E16. With the cell pointer at E4, enter the command /Copy (/C), press the Enter key to lock in the source range, and use the Down Arrow key and Period key to select the destination range E6..E16. Press the Enter key. The total number of points received by each student displays in the range E6..E16 (see Figure 4-6).

```
E4: @SUM(B4..D4)                                                         READY

            A              B          C          D          E          F
1   DP 101                      Grading Report                    22-Dec-91
2
3                         Test 1     Test 2     Test 3      Total     Percent
4   Student                  139        142        150        431     Correct
5   ===========================================================================
6   1035                     121        127        142        390
7   1074                     114        113        132        359
8   1265                      79         97        101        277
9   1345                      85        106         95        286
10  1392                     127        124        120        371
11  3167                     101        120        109        330
12  3382                     110        104        120        334
13  3597                      92        104        100        296
14  4126                     105        100         96        301
15  5619                     125        135        143        403
16  7561                     112        130        123        365
17  ---------------------------------------------------------------------------
18  Count
19  Lowest Grade
20  Highest Grade
22-Dec-91  11:06 AM
```



**FIGURE 4-6**
**Student test totals entered into column E of the grading report.**

Once the total number of points received by each student is part of the worksheet, we can determine the total percent correct in column F. Move the cell pointer to F6 and enter the formula + E6/$E$4*100. The numerator in this formula, cell E6, is equal to the total number of points for the first student. The denominator, cell E4, is equal to the maximum number of points for the three tests. Multiplying the quotient + E6/$E$4 by 100 converts the ratio to a percent value. We use this procedure to display a percent value rather than formatting it in the Percent type because the column heading already indicates that the values in column E are in percent. Recall that the Percent type adds a percent sign (%) to the right side of the number.

Copy cell F6 to the range F7..F16. Note that we use the dollar sign ($) character in the denominator of the formula in cell E6 to make cell E4 an absolute cell address. Therefore, when we copy the formula in cell F6, the relative address E6 in the numerator changes based on the new location and the absolute address $E$4 in the denominator stays the same.

Format the percent correct in column F to the Fixed type with one decimal place. Enter the command /**R**ange **F**ormat **F**ixed (/RFF). Select one decimal position and press the Enter key. Enter the range F6..F16 and press the Enter key. The worksheet with each student's percent correct formatted to the Fixed type with one decimal place is illustrated in Figure 4-7.

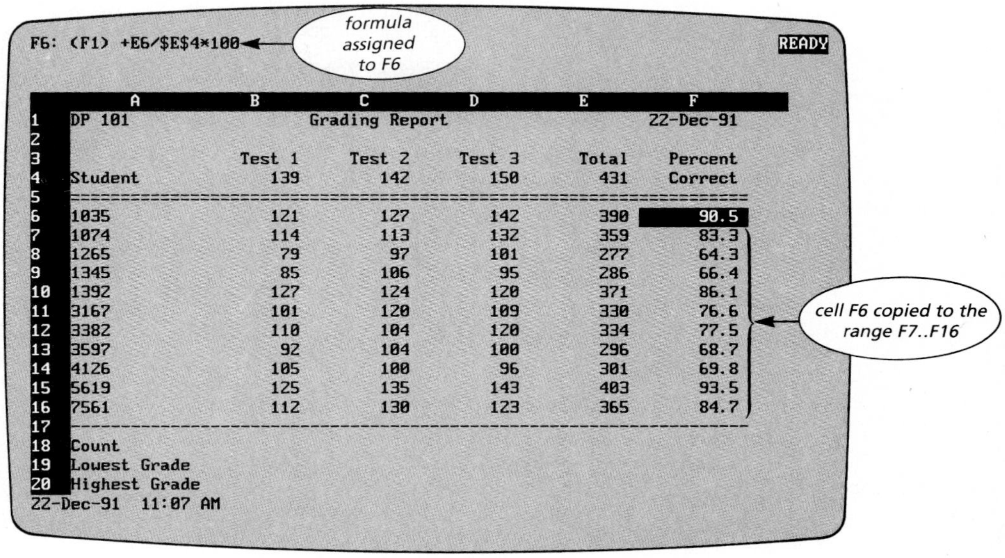

```
F6: (F1) +E6/$E$4*100                                              READY

       A              B          C          D          E          F
1   DP 101                    Grading Report                  22-Dec-91
2
3                   Test 1     Test 2     Test 3     Total     Percent
4   Student            139        142        150       431     Correct
5   ===================================================================
6   1035               121        127        142       390        90.5
7   1074               114        113        132       359        83.3
8   1265                79         97        101       277        64.3
9   1345                85        106         95       286        66.4
10  1392               127        124        120       371        86.1
11  3167               101        120        109       330        76.6
12  3382               110        104        120       334        77.5
13  3597                92        104        100       296        68.7
14  4126               105        100         96       301        69.8
15  5619               125        135        143       403        93.5
16  7561               112        130        123       365        84.7
17  -------------------------------------------------------------------
18  Count
19  Lowest Grade
20  Highest Grade
22-Dec-91  11:07 AM
```



**FIGURE 4-7**
**Total percent correct for each student formatted to the Fixed type with one decimal position.**

The next step is to determine the summaries in rows 18 through 23. To make the job of entering these summaries easier, we need to discuss range names.

## Assigning a Name to a Range of Cells

One of the problems with using a range is remembering the end points that define it. The problem becomes more difficult as worksheets grow in size and the same range is referred to repeatedly. This is the situation in the summary rows at the bottom of the grading report. For example, each summary item for Test 1 in cells B18 through B23 reference the same range, B6..B16. To make it easier to refer to the range, 1-2-3 allows you to assign a name to it. You may then use the name to reference the range, rather than the cell addresses of the end points. Let's assign the name TEST1 to the range B6..B16.

Move the cell pointer to B6, one of the end points of the range B6..B16. Enter the command /**R**ange **N**ame (/RN). With the command cursor active in the **Range Name** menu (see Figure 4-8), type the letter C for Create. 1-2-3 responds with the prompt message "Enter name:" on the input line (see Figure 4-9). Enter the name TEST1 and press the Enter key. The prompt message "Enter range: B6..B6" immediately displays on the input line. Use the arrow keys to select the range B6..B16 as shown in Figure 4-9. Press the Enter key. The range name TEST1 can now be used in place of B6..B16.

```
B6: 121                                                            MENU
Create  Delete  Labels  Reset  Table
Create or modify a range name
        A          B          C          D          E          F
1  DP 101                   Grading Report                    22-Dec-91
2
3                     Test 1     Test 2     Test 3     Total     Percent
4  Student               139        142        150       431     Correct
5  ===================================================================
6  1035                  121        127        142       390        90.5
7  1074                  114        113        132       359        83.3
8  1265                   79         97        101       277        64.3
9  1345                   85        106         95       286        66.4
10 1392                  127        124
                         101
```



**FIGURE 4-8** The display after entering the command /**R**ange **N**ame (/RN).

```
B16: 112                                                          POINT
Enter name: TEST1                     Enter range: B6..B16

        A          B          C          D          E          F
1  DP 101                   Grading Report
2
3                     Test 1     Test 2     Test 3     Total
4  Student               139        142        150       431
5  ===================================================================
6  1035                  121        127        142       390        90.5
7  1074                  114        113        132       359        83.3
8  1265                   79         97        101       277        64.3
9  1345                   85        106         95       286        66.4
10 1392                  127        124        120       371        86.1
11 3167                  101        120        109       330        76.6
12 3382                  110        104        120       334        77.5
13 3597                   92        104        100       296        68.7
14 4126                  105        100         96       301        69.8
15 5619                  125        135        143       403        93.5
16 7561                  112        130        123       365        84.7
17 -------------------------------------------------------------------
18 Count
19 Lowest Grade
20 Highest Grade
22-Dec-91  11:09 AM
```



**FIGURE 4-9**
**Range name TEST1 assigned to the range B6..B16.**

As shown in the Range Name menu in Figure 4-8, there are several Range Name commands. These commands are summarized in Table 4-1. When 1-2-3 is in the POINT mode, you can display a list of all the range names associated with the current worksheet by pressing function key F3.

**TABLE 4-1 Summary of the Range Name Commands**

| COMMAND | KEYSTROKES | FUNCTION |
|---|---|---|
| Create | /RNC | Assigns a name to a range. The name can be no longer than 14 characters. |
| Delete | /RND | Deletes the specified range name. |
| Labels | /RNL | Assigns the label in the current cell as a name to the cell above, below, to the right, or to the left of the current cell. |
| Reset | /RNR | Deletes range names associated with the worksheet. |
| Table | /RNT | Places an alphabetized list of range names in the worksheet beginning at the upper left corner cell of the specified range. |

## Statistical Functions—AVG, COUNT, MIN, MAX, STD, and VAR

1-2-3 has several statistical functions that return values that are handy for evaluating a group of numbers, like the test scores in the grading report. The statistical functions are summarized in Table 4-2.

**TABLE 4-2 Statistical Functions**

| FUNCTION | FUNCTION VALUE |
|---|---|
| AVG(R) | Returns the average of the numbers in range R by summing the nonempty cells and dividing by the number of nonempty cells. Labels are treated as zeros. |
| COUNT(R) | Returns the number of cells that are not empty in range R. |
| MAX(R) | Returns the largest number in range R. |
| MIN(R) | Returns the smallest number in range R. |
| STD(R) | Returns the standard deviation of the numbers in range R. |
| SUM(R) | Returns the sum of the numbers in range R. |
| VAR(R) | Returns the variance of the numbers in range R. |

In the grading report, cell B18 displays the number of students that received a grade for Test 1. This value can be obtained by using the COUNT function. With the cell pointer at B18, enter the function @COUNT(TEST1). 1-2-3 immediately displays the value 11—the number of students that received a grade for Test 1. This is shown in Figure 4-10. Remember, the range name TEST1 is equal to the range B6..B16.

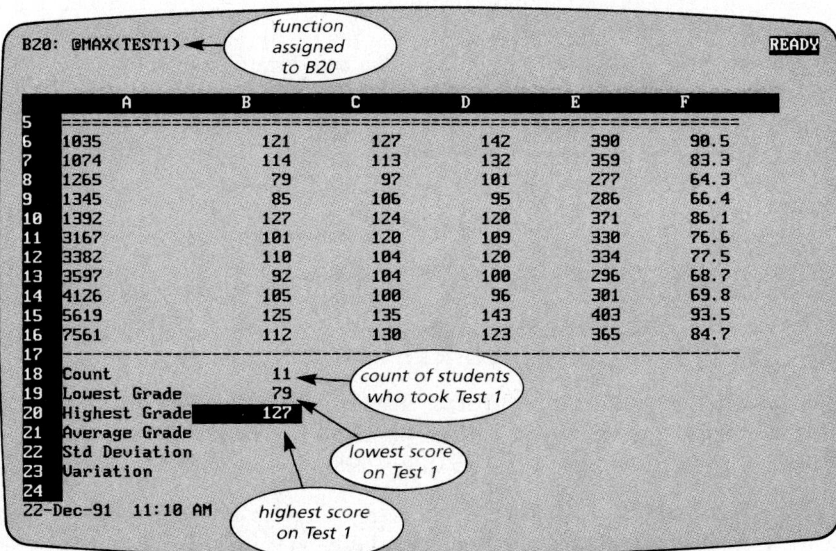


**FIGURE 4-10**
**COUNT, MIN, and MAX functions entered into the grading report for Test 1.**

In cells B19 and B20, the grading report contains the lowest score and the highest score received on Test 1. Student 1265 received the lowest score—79. Student 1392 received the highest score—127. To display the lowest score obtained on Test 1, enter the function @MIN(TEST1) in cell B19. To display the highest score, enter the function @MAX(TEST1) in cell B20. The results of entering these functions are shown in cells B19 and B20 in Figure 4-10.

The next step is to determine the average of the scores received on Test 1. Enter the function @AVG(TEST1) in cell B21. As illustrated in Figure 4-11, the average score for Test 1 in cell B21 is 106.454545. 1-2-3 arrives at this value by summing the scores for Test 1 and dividing by the number of non-empty cells in the range B6..B16.

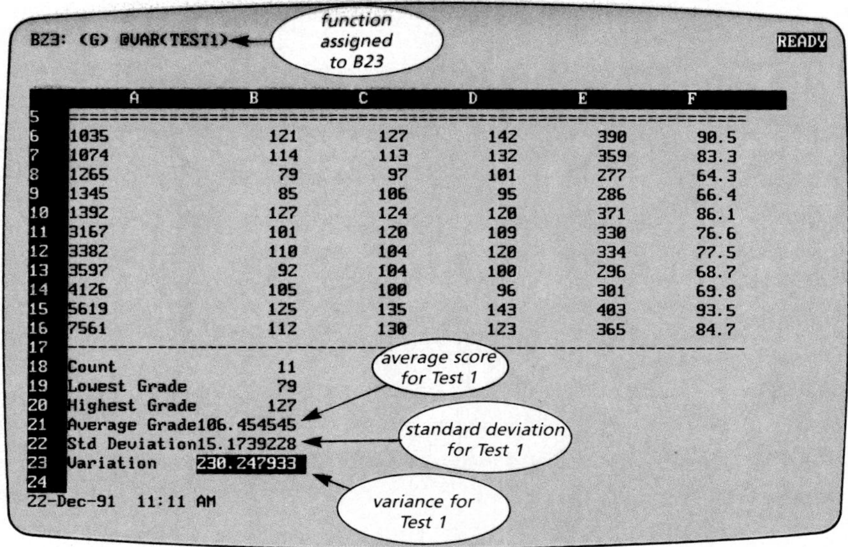


**FIGURE 4-11**
**AVG, STD, and VAR functions entered into the grading report for Test 1.**

The last two summary lines require we use the functions STD and VAR. As indicated in Table 4-2, the STD function returns the standard deviation and the VAR function returns the variance. To complete the summary lines for Test 1, enter the functions @STD(TEST1) in cell B22 and @VAR(TEST1) in cell B23. The results are shown in Figure 4-11.

The same six functions that are used to summarize the results for Test 1 are required for Test 2, Test 3, and the sum of the test scores for each student in column E. With the cell pointer at B23, enter the command /**C**opy (/C). Copy the source range B23..B18 to the destination range C23..E18.

As the functions in column B are copied to the new locations in columns C, D, and E, 1-2-3 adjusts the range TEST1 (B6..B16) to C6..C16 for Test 2, D6..D16 for Test 3, and E6..E16 for the sum of the test scores in column E.

To complete the worksheet, format the last three rows in the worksheet to the Fixed type with one decimal place. With the cell pointer at B23, enter the command /**R**ange **F**ormat **F**ixed (/RFF). In response to the prompt message "Enter number of decimal places (0..15):2" on the input line, type the digit 1 and press the Enter key. Next, 1-2-3 displays the prompt message "Enter range to format: B23..B23". Use the arrow keys to select the range B23..E21 and press the Enter key. The complete grading report is shown in Figure 4-1.

## Saving and Printing the Worksheet

To save the grading report worksheet to disk, enter the command /**F**ile **S**ave (/FS). In response to the prompt message on the input line, enter the file name PROJS-4A and press the Enter key.

To obtain a printed version of the worksheet, follow these steps:

1. Make sure the printer is in READY mode.
2. Press the Home key to move the cell pointer to A1.
3. Enter the command /**P**rint **P**rinter **R**ange (/PPR) and select the range A1..F23.
4. Type the letters A for Align and G for Go.
5. After the worksheet prints on the printer, type the letter P for Page twice. Recall that the Page command moves the paper through the printer to the top of the next page.
6. Type the letter Q to quit the /PP command and carefully remove the grading report from the printer.

## Erasing the Worksheet from Main Computer Memory

After saving and printing the grading report, we can erase it from main computer memory so that we can begin Project 4B. Recall from Project 1, that to erase the current worksheet, enter the command /**W**orksheet **E**rase (/WE). Finally, type the letter Y for Yes. 1-2-3 responds by clearing all the cells in the worksheet and changing all the settings to their default values.

## PROJECT 4B—DETERMINING THE MONTHLY PAYMENT FOR A CAR LOAN

With the grading report worksheet cleared from main computer memory, we can begin entering Project 4B. The car loan payment worksheet is shown in Figures 4-2, 4-3, and 4-4. It is by far the most complex worksheet undertaken thus far. For this reason, use the divide and conquer strategy to build it. This strategy involves completing a section of the worksheet and testing it before moving on to the next section. Let's divide the worksheet into five sections:

1. Determine the monthly payment on a five-year loan for a 1988 Chevy Van with a sticker price of $18,500.00, down payment of $4,000.00, at an interest rate of 11.5%—range A1..E7 in Figure 4-2.
2. Display the amortization schedule—range A8..E20 in Figure 4-2.
3. Generate the data table—range F1..H20 in Figure 4-3.
4. Create the simple macros—range A22..E30 in Figure 4-4.
5. Create the multicell macro—range A33..E46 in Figure 4-4.

The first step in determining the car loan payment is to change the column widths. Set the width of column A to 12 characters and set the global width of the columns in the worksheet to 15 characters. To change the widths of the columns, do the following:

1. With the cell pointer at A1, enter the command /**W**orksheet **C**olumn **S**et-Width (/WCS) to change the width of column A to 12 characters.
2. Enter the command /**W**orksheet **G**lobal **C**olumn-**W**idth (/WGC). Change the default value 9 on the input line to 15 and press the Enter key.

With the column widths set, enter the worksheet title, date, the six cell titles and the five data items in the range A1..E7 (see Figure 4-12). Assign cell E1 the NOW function.

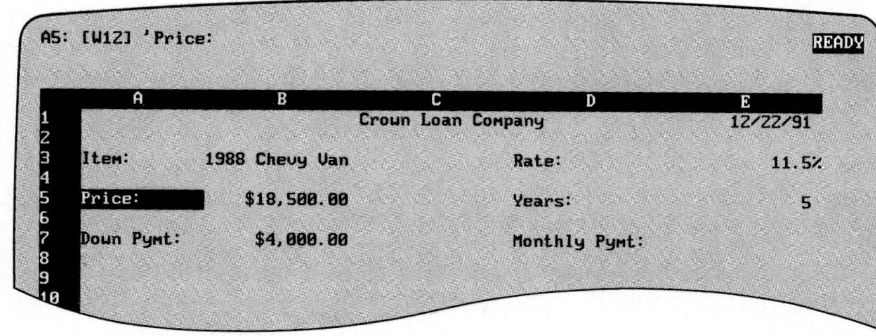


**FIGURE 4-12**
**Labels and data entered into the Crown Loan Company worksheet.**

Use the command /**R**ange **F**ormat (/RF) to change the format of the cells assigned numeric data in the range A1..E7 as follows:

1. Cell E1 to the Long Intn'l (MM/DD/YY) type.
2. Cells B5, B7, and E7 to the Currency type with two decimal positions.
3. Cell E3 to the Percent type with one decimal position.

The formatted worksheet with the cell pointer at A5 is shown in Figure 4-12.

## Assigning a Label Name to an Adjacent Cell

In Project 4A we used the command /**R**ange **N**ame **C**reate (/RNC) to assign the name TEST1 to the range B6..B16. Later, when we built the summary lines, we used the name TEST1 several times in functions to reference the range B6..B16, because the name TEST1 is easier to remember than the range B6..B16. Another advantage of using range names is that they make it easier to remember what the range represents in the worksheet. This is especially helpful when working with complex formulas or functions.

The function for determining the monthly payment in cell E7 uses the purchase price (B5), down payment (B7), rate (E3), and years (E5). Let's name each of these cells. In this case, we'll use a second technique for assigning names to the individual cells. Rather than typing in a new name for each cell, use the adjacent cell title—the label located immediately to the left of each cell we want to name. For example, use the label Price: in cell A5 to name cell B5.

With the cell pointer at A5, enter the command /**R**ange **N**ame **L**abel (/RNL). By entering the command Label, we instruct 1-2-3 to use a label in the worksheet as the name, rather than to create a new name. With the command cursor active in the **Range Name Label menu** (see Figure 4-13), type the letter R for Right. Note that this command allows us to assign any adjacent cell to the label name. Typing the letter R tells 1-2-3 that we want to assign the cell to the right of the label name.

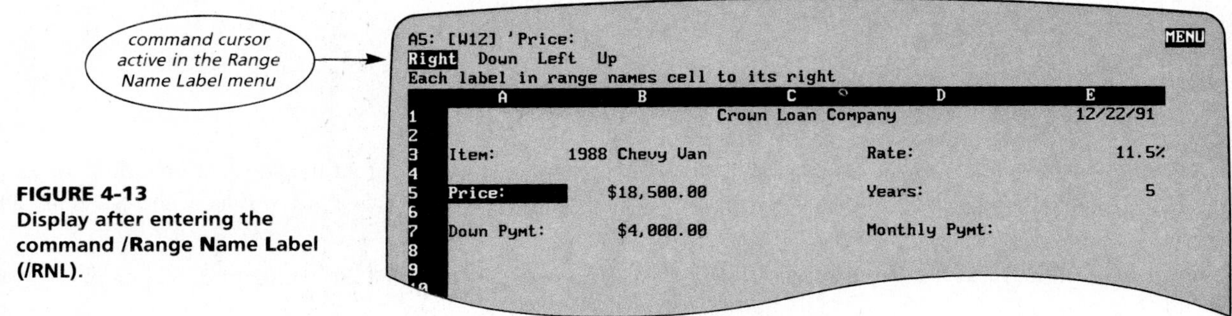


**FIGURE 4-13**
**Display after entering the command /Range Name Label (/RNL).**

Next, 1-2-3 requests that we enter the range containing the labels that we wish to assign to the cells to the right. Use the Down Arrow key to select the range A5..A7. Press the Enter key. We can now use the name Price: to refer to cell B5 and Down Pymt: to refer to cell B7.

Name cells E3, E5, and E7 in a similar fashion. Move the cell pointer to D3. Enter the command /**R**ange **N**ame **L**abel (/RNL). Type the letter R for Right, select the range D3..D7, and press the Enter key. We can now use Rate: to refer to cell E3, Years: to refer to cell E5, and Monthly Pymt: to refer to cell E7.

Three points to remember about the /RNL command: first, if a label in a cell is subsequently changed, the old label remains the name of the range; second, numbers cannot be used as range names; and third, only the first 14 characters of the label can be used as the name.

## Determining the Loan Payment—PMT

1-2-3 has several financial functions that save you from writing out long complicated formulas. One of the most important of these is the PMT function. This function determines the payment of a loan on the basis of the amount of the loan (principal), the interest rate (interest), and the length of time required to pay the loan back (term). If the term is in months, the PMT function returns the monthly payment. The PMT function is written in the following form:

@PMT(principal,interest,term)

To display the monthly payment of the car loan in cell E7, move the cell pointer to E7 and enter the following function:

@PMT($Price:-$Down Pymt:,$Rate:/12,$Years:*12)

The first argument ($Price:–$Down Pymt:) is the principal. The second argument ($Rate:/12) is the interest rate charged by the Crown Loan Company compounded monthly. The third argument ($Years:*12) is the number of months required to pay back the loan. As illustrated in cell E7 of Figure 4-14, it will cost $318.89 per month for 5 years to purchase the 1988 Chevy Van with a sticker price of $18,500.00, down payment of $4,000.00, at an annual interest rate of 11.5%.

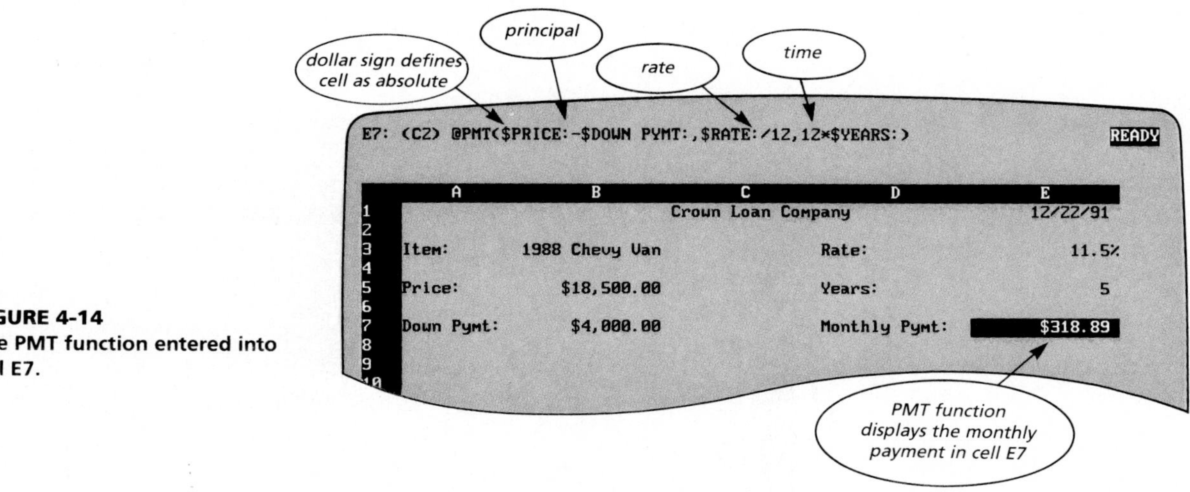


**FIGURE 4-14**
**The PMT function entered into cell E7.**

Note that we preceded all the names in the function arguments with a dollar sign ($). This is necessary because the function will be copied to another part of the worksheet later, and we want the cell references to remain the same.

Remember, 1-2-3 automatically recalculates all functions and formulas in a worksheet when an entry is made. If we change the purchase price, the amount of the down payment, the interest rate, the number of years, or any combination of these, 1-2-3 immediately adjusts the monthly payment displayed in cell E7.

## The Data Fill Feature

The next step is to add the amortization table in cells A8..E16 (see Figure 4-2). Enter the double underline in row 8, the column headings in rows 9 and 10, and the single underline in row 11 as shown in Figure 4.15.

In the range A12..A16, the series of numbers 1 though 5 represent the years. We can enter these numbers one at a time or we can use the Data Fill command. The Data Fill command allows you to quickly enter a series of numbers into a range using a specified increment or decrement. In this case, we want to enter a series of numbers in the range A12..A16 that begins with 1, increments by 1, and ends with 5.

With the cell pointer at A12, enter the command /**D**ata **F**ill (/DF). In response to the prompt message "Enter Fill range: A12" on the input line, press the Period key to anchor the first end point, A12. Use the Down Arrow key to move the cell pointer to the second end point (A16) and press the Enter key. Next, 1-2-3 requests that we enter the start, increment, and stop values. In response to the prompt messages on the input line, enter a start value of 1, an increment value of 1, and a stop value of 8191. The length of the range (five cells) will terminate the Data Fill command before it reaches the stop value 8191. The three entries are shown on the input line in Figure 4-15. Press the Enter key and the range A12..A16 is filled with the series of numbers 1 through 5 (see Figure 4-16).

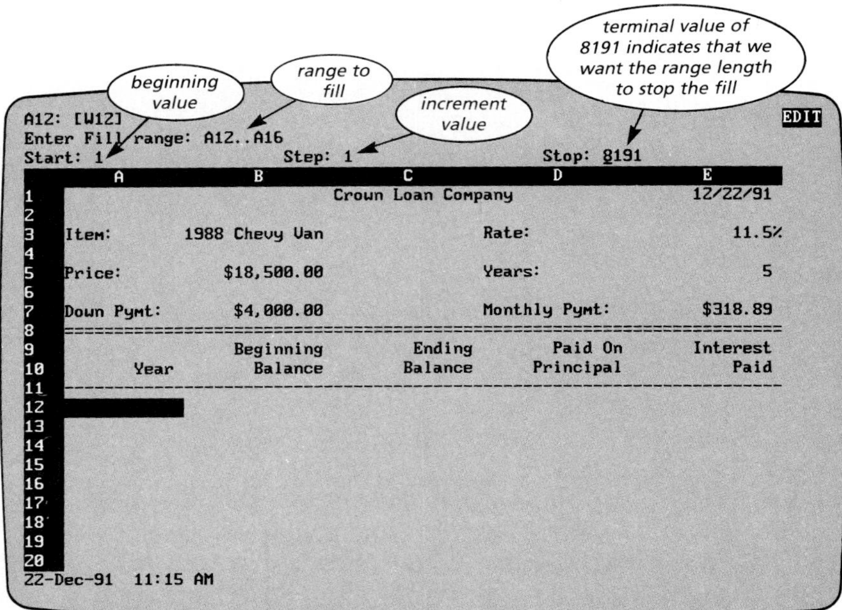


**FIGURE 4-15**
**The display due to entering the command /Data Fill (/DF).**

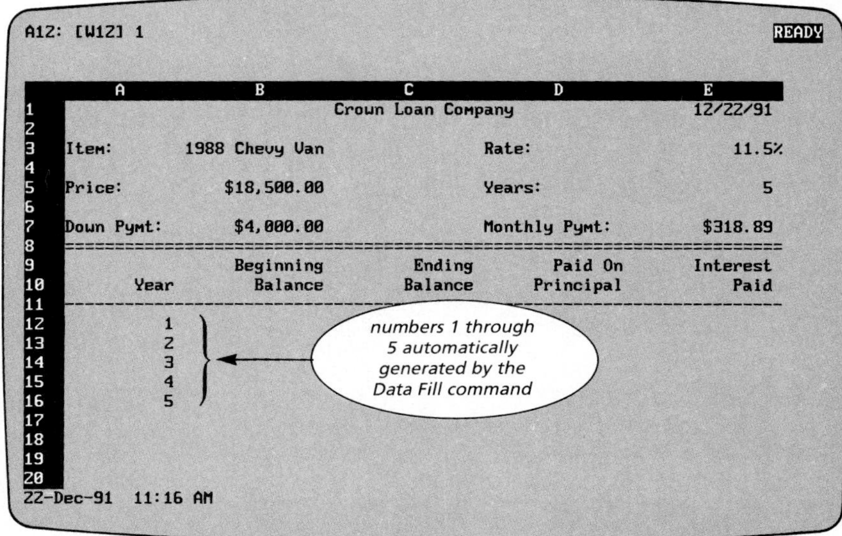


**FIGURE 4-16**
**The display after using the Data Fill command.**

Move the cell pointer to B12 and enter the beginning balance for year 1. This value is equal to the amount of the loan— + Price:-Down Pymt: or ( + B5–B7).

Before we enter any more values in the amortization table, format cells B12 through E20 to the Comma (,) type with two decimal positions. The Comma (,) type with two decimal positions displays the numbers in the form of dollar and cents. Although labels will be part of the range (B12..E20), recall that a numeric format is only used if a numeric value is stored in the cell. Enter the command /**R**ange **F**ormat , (/RF,). Press the Enter key to select two decimal positions. Enter the range B12..E20 and press the Enter key.

## Determining the Yearly Ending Balance—PV

Another important financial function is the PV function. This function returns the present value of an annuity. An **annuity** is a series of fixed payments made at the end of each of a fixed number of terms at a fixed interest rate. This function can be used to determine how much the borrower of the car loan still owes at the end of each year (C12..C16).

The general form of the PV function is:

@PV(payment,interest,term)

Use this function to determine the ending balance after the first year (C12) by using a term equal to the number of months the borrower must still make payments. For example, if the loan is for five years (60 months, therefore 60 payments), as it is in Figure 4-16, then the borrower still owes 48 payments after the first year. After the second year, the number of payments remaining is 36, and so on.

The entry for cell C12 that determines the ending balance reads as follows:

@PV($Monthly Pymt:, $Rate:/12, 12*($Years:-A12))

The first argument, $Monthly Pymt:, refers to cell E7, the monthly payment. The second argument, $Rate:/12, refers to the interest rate in cell E5. The third argument, 12*($Years:-A12), indicates the number of monthly payments that still must be made—48 after the first year. Note that each name in the three arguments of the PV function for cell C12 is preceded by a dollar sign ($). This tells 1-2-3 to treat these cell references as absolute. That is, when we copy the PV function in cell C12 to cells C13 through C16, the cell references in the arguments will not be adjusted.

## Making Decisions—The IF Function

If we assign the PV function just described to cell C12 and copy it to cells C13 through C16, the ending balances for each year of a five-year loan will display properly as illustrated in Figure 4-2. If the loan is for a period of time less than five years, the ending balances displayed for the years beyond the time the loan is due are invalid. For example, if a loan is taken out for three years, the ending balance for years four and five in the amortization table should be zero. However, the PV function will display negative values even though the loan has already been paid off.

What we need here is a way to assign the PV function to the range C12..C16 as long as the corresponding year in the range A12..A16 is less than or equal to the number of years in cell E5, which contains the number of years of the loan. If the corresponding year in column A is greater than the number of years in cell E5, we need to assign C12 through C16 the value zero. 1-2-3 has a function that can handle this type of decision making. It is called the IF function.

The IF function is useful when the value you want assigned to a cell is dependent on a condition. A **condition** is made up of two expressions and a relation. Each **expression** may be a cell, a number, a label, a function, or a formula.

The general form of the IF function is:

@IF(condition,true,false)

The argument **true** is the value you want to assign to the cell when the condition is true. The argument **false** is the value you want to assign to the cell when the condition is false. For example, assume @IF(A1 = A2,C3 + D4,C3–D4) is assigned to cell B12. If the value assigned to A1 is equal to the value assigned to A2, then the sum of the values in C3 and D4 is assigned to B12. If the value assigned to A1 does not equal the value assigned to A2, then B12 is assigned the difference between the values in C3 and D4.

Valid relations and examples of their use in IF functions are shown in Table 4-3.

**TABLE 4-3 Valid Relational Operators and Their Use in Conditions**

| RELATIONAL OPERATOR | MEANING | EXAMPLE |
|---|---|---|
| = | Equal to | @IF(A5 = B7,A22–A3,G5^E3) |
| < | Less than | @IF(E12/D5 < 6,A15,B13–5) |
| > | Greater than | @IF(@SUM(A1..A5) > 100,1,0) |
| < = | Less than or equal to | @IF(A12 < = $YEARS,A4*D5,1) |
| > = | Greater than or equal to | @IF(@NOW > = 30000,H15,J12) |
| < > | Not equal to | @IF(5 < > F6,"Valid","Invalid") |

Logical operators like NOT, AND, and OR may also be used to write a **compound condition**—two or more conditions in the same IF function. A summary of the logical operators is given in Table 4-4.

**TABLE 4-4 Valid Logical Operators and Their Use in Conditions**

| LOGICAL OPERATOR | MEANING | EXAMPLE |
|---|---|---|
| #NOT# | The compound condition is true if, and only if, the simple condition is false. | @IF(#NOT#($A$2 = A6),2,4) |
| #AND# | The compound condition is true if, and only if, both simple conditions are true. | @IF($J6 = R$4#AND#G5–S2 > D2, D4*D6,T3/D2) |
| #OR# | The compound condition is true if, and only if, either simple condition is true, or both simple conditions are true. | @IF(A1 > $PRINCIPAL#OR#B7 = E4, "Contact","OK") |

By using the IF function, we can assign the PV function or zero as the ending balance to cells C12 through C16. Enter the following IF function in cell C12:

@IF(A12< = $Years:,@PV($Monthly Pymt:,$Rate:/12,12*($Years:–A12)),0)

*condition* *true task* *false task*

If the condition A12< = $Years: is true, then C12 is assigned the PV function. If the condition is false, then C12 is assigned the value zero. Use the command /Copy (/C) to copy cell C12 to the range C13..C16. The results of this copy are shown in Figure 4-17.

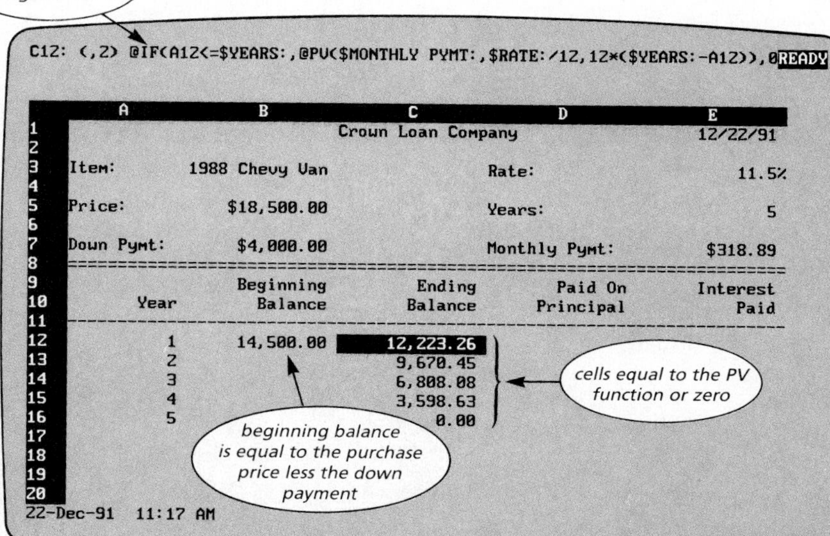


**FIGURE 4-17**
**The IF function entered into cell A12 and copied to the range C13..C16.**

Let's go back now and complete the entries in the beginning balance column, cells B13 through B16. The beginning balance in B13 is equal to the ending balance in cell C12. Therefore, enter +C12 in cell B13 and copy this cell to B14 through B16. The beginning balance for each year in cells B12 through B16 displays as shown in Figure 4-18.

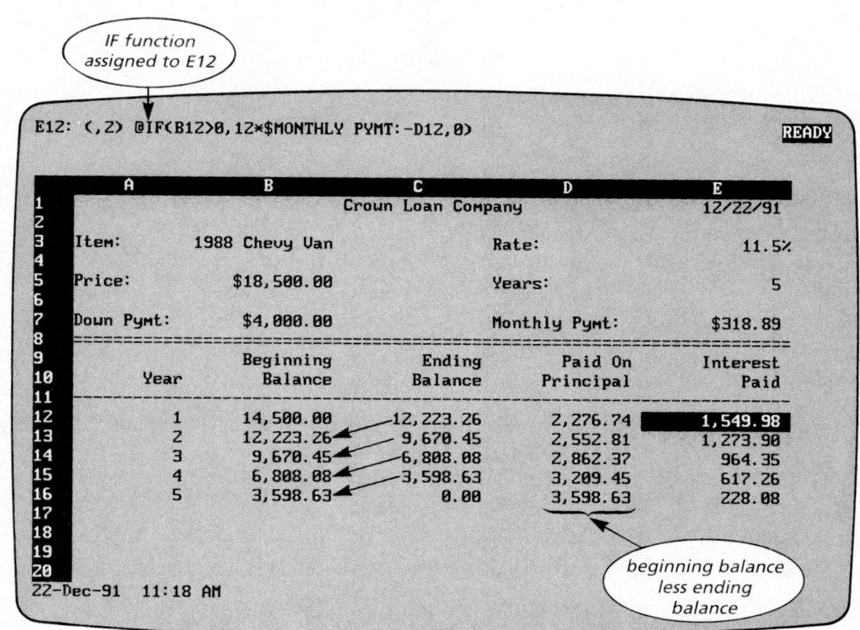


**FIGURE 4-18**
**The amortization table filled in.**

The total amount paid on the principal each year in column D is determined by subtracting the ending balance from the beginning balance. Enter the formula +B12–C12 in cell D12. Copy cell D12 to cells D13 through D16 (see Figure 4-18).

The total amount of interest paid each year by the lender to the borrower in column E is equal to 12 times the monthly payment in cell E7 less the amount paid on the principal. Here again, use the IF function because the loan may be for less than five years. Interest is paid in any year in which the beginning balance is greater than zero. Therefore, in cell E12, enter the IF function @IF(B12>0,12*$Monthly Pymt:–D12,0). Copy cell E12 to cells E13 through E16. The interest paid each year for a loan of $14,500.00 at 11.5% for 5 years is shown in column E of the worksheet in Figure 4-18.

To complete the amortization table, add the single underline in row 17 and the labels that identify the totals in cells C18 through C20. In cell D18, enter the SUM function @SUM(D12..D16). Note that this agrees with the original amount of the loan, $14,500.00. In cell E18, enter the SUM function @SUM(E12..E16). Cell E18 displays the total interest paid for the loan, $4,633.57. In cell E19, enter the name +Down Pymt:. Cell E19 displays $4,000.00, the amount in cell B7. Finally, in cell E20, enter the formula +D18+E18+E19. Cell E20 displays the total cost of the 1988 Chevy Van (see Figure 4-19).

E20: (,2) +D18+E18+E19 READY

| | A | B | C | D | E |
|---|---|---|---|---|---|
| 1 | | | Crown Loan Company | | 12/22/91 |
| 2 | | | | | |
| 3 | Item: | 1988 Chevy Van | | Rate: | 11.5% |
| 4 | | | | | |
| 5 | Price: | $18,500.00 | | Years: | 5 |
| 6 | | | | | |
| 7 | Down Pymt: | $4,000.00 | | Monthly Pymt: | $318.89 |
| 8 | ========== | ========== | ========== | ========== | ========== |
| 9 | | Beginning | Ending | Paid On | Interest |
| 10 | Year | Balance | Balance | Principal | Paid |
| 11 | ---------- | ---------- | ---------- | ---------- | ---------- |
| 12 | 1 | 14,500.00 | 12,223.26 | 2,276.74 | 1,549.98 |
| 13 | 2 | 12,223.26 | 9,670.45 | 2,552.81 | 1,273.90 |
| 14 | 3 | 9,670.45 | 6,808.08 | 2,862.37 | 964.35 |
| 15 | 4 | 6,808.08 | 3,598.63 | 3,209.45 | 617.26 |
| 16 | 5 | 3,598.63 | 0.00 | 3,598.63 | 228.08 |
| 17 | ---------- | ---------- | ---------- | ---------- | ---------- |
| 18 | | | Subtotal | 14,500.00 | 4,633.57 |
| 19 | | | Down Pymt | | 4,000.00 |
| 20 | | | Total Cost | | 23,133.57 |

22-Dec-91 11:19 AM

total cost of car

**FIGURE 4-19**
**Part 1 of Project 4B complete.**

With the amortization table complete, try various combinations of loan data to evaluate the what-if capabilities of 1-2-3. If we change the purchase price (B5), down payment (B7), interest rate (E3), time (E5) or any combination of these values, 1-2-3 will immediately change the monthly payment and the numbers in the amortization table.

## Saving the Worksheet

Before we continue with Project 4B, save the worksheet as PROJS-4B. Enter the command /**F**ile **S**ave (/FS). Enter the file name PROJS-4B and press the Enter key. The worksheet is saved on the default drive.

## Using a Data Table to Answer What-If Questions

The next step is to build the data table at the right side of the amortization table (see Figure 4-3). As described earlier, a data table has one purpose—it organizes the answers to what-if questions into a table. We have already seen that if a value is changed in a cell referenced elsewhere in a formula, 1-2-3 immediately recalculates and stores the new value in the cell assigned the formula. You may want to compare the results of the formula for several different values, but it would be unwieldy to write down or remember all the answers to the what-if questions. This is where a data table comes in handy.

Data tables are built in an unused area of the worksheet. You may vary one or two values and display the results of the specified formulas in table form. Figure 4-20 illustrates the makeup of a data table.

In Project 4B, the data table shows the impact of changing interest rates on the monthly payment and the total cost of the loan. The interest rates range from 8.5% to 15% in increments of 0.5%. Therefore, in this data table we are varying one value, the interest rate (E3). We are interested in its impact on two formulas: the monthly payment (E7) and the total cost (E20).

To construct the data table, enter the headings in the range F1..H5 as described in Figure 4-3. Next, move the cell pointer to F7 and use the command /**D**ata **F**ill (/DF) to enter the varying interest rates. Select the range F7..F20. Use a start value of 8.5%, an increment value of 0.5%, and a stop value of 8191. After we press the Enter key, the range F7..F20 contains the varying interest rates. Format the interest rates to the Percent type with one decimal position (see Figure 4-21).

| THIS CELL MUST BE EMPTY | FORMULA-1 FORMULA-2 . . . FORMULA-k |
|---|---|
| Value-1<br>Value-2<br>Value-3<br>Value-4<br><br>Value-n | 1-2-3 places results of formulas here on the basis of the values in the left-hand column. |

**(a) Data table with one value varying**

| ASSIGN FORMULA TO THIS CELL | VALUE-2a VALUE-2b . . . VALUE-2k |
|---|---|
| Value-1a<br>Value-1b<br>Value-1c<br>Value-1d<br><br>Value-1n | 1-2-3 places results of the formula in the upper left corner cell here on the basis of the two corresponding values. |

**(b) Data table with two values varying**

**FIGURE 4-20**
**General forms of a data table with one value varying (a) and two values varying (b).**

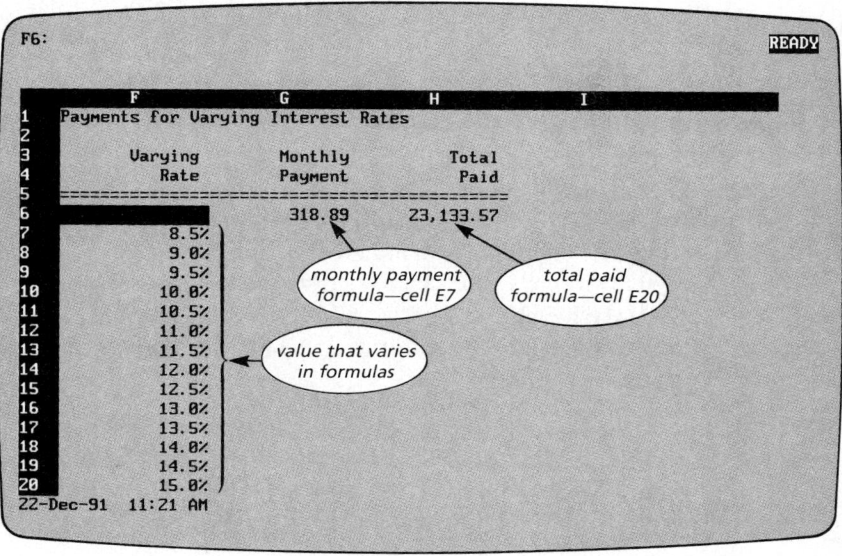


**FIGURE 4-21**
**Monthly payment formula, total paid formula, and varying interest rates entered into the worksheet in preparation for applying a data table in the range F6..H20.**

In cell G6 enter +E7, the cell with the monthly payment formula. In cell H6 enter +E20, the cell with the total cost of the loan formula. Format the range G6..H20 to the Comma (,) type with two decimal positions. Move the cell pointer to F6. The range F1..H20 of the worksheet is shown in Figure 4-21.

To define the data table, enter the command /**D**ata **T**able **1** (/DT1). 1-2-3 responds by displaying the prompt message "Enter Table range: F6" on the input line. Press the Period key to anchor F6 as one of the end points. Use the arrow keys to move the cell pointer to H20 and press the Enter key. (Note that the data table itself does not include the headings above F6.) 1-2-3 responds with the prompt message "Enter Input cell 1: F6" on the input line. The **input cell** is defined as the cell in the worksheet that contains the value we want to vary. For this data table, we want to vary the interest rate in cell E3 (also called Rate:). Therefore, enter the name Rate: in response to the prompt message on the input line and press the Enter key.

The data table, in the range F6..H20, immediately fills with monthly payments and total loan costs for the corresponding varying interest rates, as shown in Figure 4-22. Look over the table. Note how it allows you to compare the monthly payments and total loan costs for different interest rates. For example, at 10%, the monthly payment on the loan of $14,500.00 for 5 years is $308.08. At 10.5%, the monthly payment is $311.66 for the same loan. The two numbers at the top of the table, in cells G6 and H6, are the same as the monthly payment and total cost displayed in cells E7 and E20.

```
F6:                                                        READY

          F                 G                  H          I
 1  Payments for Varying Interest Rates
 2
 3       Varying          Monthly            Total
 4          Rate          Payment             Paid
 5  ==========================================
 6                        318.89         23,133.57
 7          8.5%          297.49         21,849.38
 8          9.0%          301.00         22,059.77
 9          9.5%          304.53         22,271.62
10         10.0%          308.08         22,484.93
11         10.5%          311.66         22,699.69
12         11.0%          315.27         22,915.91
13         11.5%          318.89         23,133.57
14         12.0%          322.54         23,352.67
15         12.5%          326.22         23,573.21
16         13.0%          329.92         23,795.17
17         13.5%          333.64         24,018.57
18         14.0%          337.39         24,243.38
19         14.5%          341.16         24,469.60
20         15.0%          344.95         24,697.24
22-Dec-91  11:22 AM
```

answers to what-if questions

**FIGURE 4-22**
**Data table in the range F6..H20 filled with answers to what-if questions regarding varying interest rates.**

Here are some important points to remember about data tables:

1. You can have only one active data table in a worksheet. If you want to move or establish a new data table, use the command /**D**ata **T**able **R**eset (/DTR) to deactivate the current data table.
2. For a data table with one varying value, the cell in the upper left corner of the table (F6) must be empty. With two values varying, assign the formula you want to analyze to the upper left corner cell of the table (see Figure 4-20b).
3. If you change any value in a cell referenced by the formula that is part of the data table but does not vary in the data table, you must press function key F8 to instruct 1-2-3 to recalculate the data table values.

# MACROS

A **macro** is a series of keystrokes entered into a cell or a range of cells. The macro is assigned a name using the command /**R**ange **N**ame **C**reate (/RNC). Later, when you enter the macro name, the keystrokes stored in the cell or range of cells execute one after another, as if you entered each keystroke manually at the keyboard. A macro can be as simple as the series of keystrokes required to save a worksheet or as complex as a sophisticated computer program.

Whether simple or complex, macros save time and help remove the drudgery associated with building and using a worksheet. You should consider using a macro when you find yourself typing the same keystrokes over and over again; when the series of keystrokes required is difficult to remember; or if you want to automate the use of the worksheet.

## Designing a Simple Macro

In Project 2, we suggested that you save your worksheet every 50 to 75 keystrokes. If you follow this suggestion, you will be entering the series of keystrokes shown in Table 4-5 often. This is an excellent example of how a macro can save you time and effort.

**TABLE 4-5 Series of Keystrokes for Saving a Worksheet Under the Same File Name**

| KEYSTROKE | PURPOSE |
|---|---|
| / | Switch 1-2-3 to command mode. |
| F | Select File command. |
| S | Select Save command. |
| ↵ | Save worksheet under the same file name. |
| R | Replace the worksheet on disk. |

One of the keystrokes in Table 4-5 is the Enter key(↵). In a macro, we use the **tilde character** (~) to represent the Enter key. Therefore, /FS~R represents the series of keystrokes in Table 4-5.

After determining the makeup of the macro, the next step is to move the cell pointer to a cell in an unused area of the worksheet. According to Figure 4-4, the macros for this project are to be placed below the amortization table. Hence, use the GOTO command and move the cell pointer to A22.

## Documenting Macros

We recommend that all macros be documented, even the simple ones. *Documenting* a macro means writing a comment off to the side of the cell or range containing the macro. The comment explains the purpose of the macro, and if it is complex, how it works. To document this macro, as well as the other macros in this worksheet, first enter the macro title and column headings in cells A22 through E25 (see Figure 4-23).

## Entering and Naming a Macro

Move the cell pointer to A26 and enter the macro '/FS~R. It is important that you begin the macro with an apostrophe or one of the other characters that defines the entry as a label (^, "). If you don't begin the macro with an apostrophe, 1-2-3 immediately switches to the command mode because the Slash key (/) is the first character entered.

With the macro assigned to A26, enter the command /**R**ange **N**ame **C**reate (/RNC) and assign the name \S to cell A26. A macro name must consist of two characters. The first character is the **backslash** (\). The second character is a letter. Choose the letter S for the name of the macro because it **S**aves the worksheet.

Complete the documentation in cells C26 and D26. Figure 4-23 illustrates the \S macro in cell A26 and the corresponding documentation.

## Invoking a Macro

After entering the macro '/FS˜R in cell A26 and naming it \S, execute it by holding down the Alt key and pressing the letter S. 1-2-3 automatically executes the series of keystrokes in cell A26 and saves the worksheet. Note that the \S macro is part of the worksheet that is saved. Hence, the macro will be available the next time we load the worksheet into main computer memory.

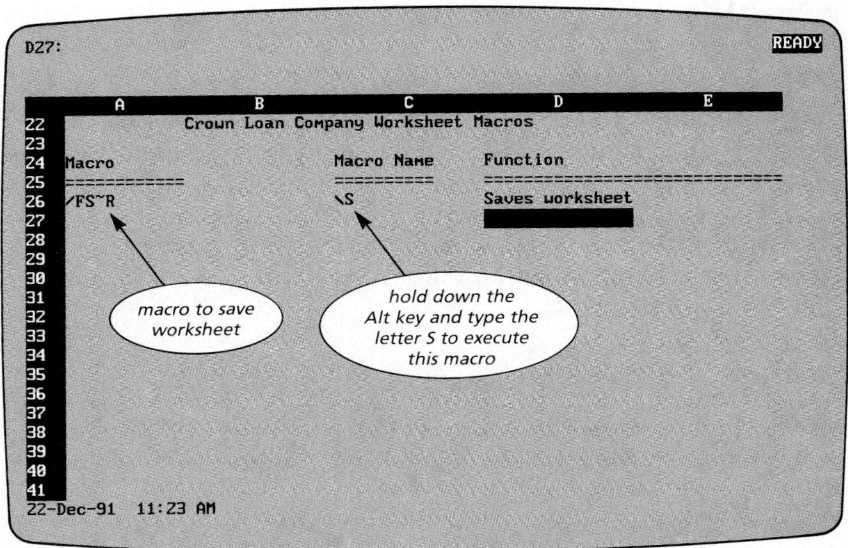


**FIGURE 4-23** The macro \S entered into cell A26 and documented in cells C26 and D26.

## Adding More Macros to the Worksheet

When 1-2-3 executes a macro, it starts at the specified cell. After executing the keystrokes in this cell, it inspects the adjacent cells. First it checks the cell below, then the cell to the right. If they are empty, the macro terminates. If they are not empty, 1-2-3 considers the non-empty cell to be part of the macro and executes its contents. Hence, 1-2-3 is finished executing a macro when the cells below and to the right are empty. It is for this reason that when you add additional macros to a worksheet, make sure that there is at least one empty cell between each macro.

With this rule in mind, enter the macro /PPAGPPQ in cell A28 and /PPOOCQAGOOAQPPQ in cell A30. Also enter the corresponding documentation in cells C28 through D30 (see Figure 4-24). Use the command /**R**ange **N**ame **C**reate (/RNC) and assign the names \P to cell A28 and \C to cell A30.

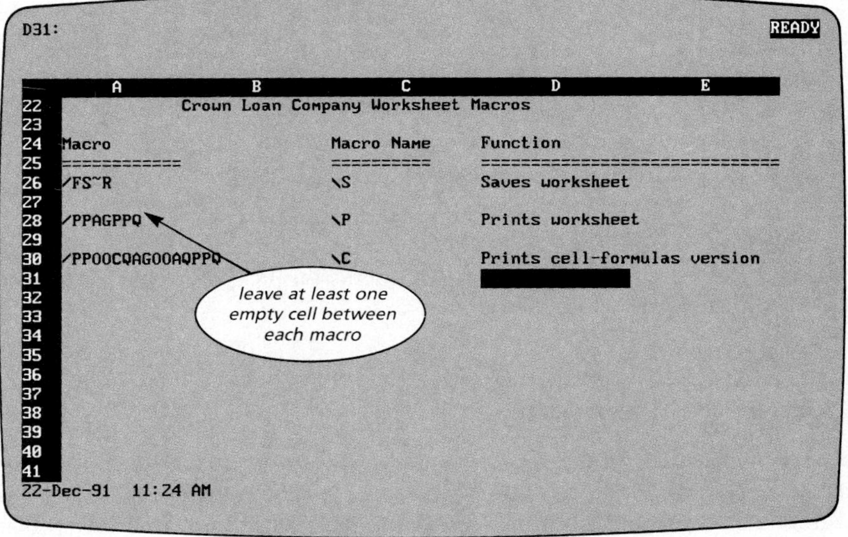


**FIGURE 4-24** The macros \P and \C entered into cells A28 and A30 and documented in the range C28..D30.

The \P macro in cell A28 prints the worksheet on the basis of the previous printer range setting. It also ejects the paper in the printer and quits the Print command. Build a print macro like this one when you expect to print the worksheet often. To prepare to execute the \P macro, use the /**P**rint **P**rinter **R**ange (/PPR) command to set the range to A1..E20. Invoke the \S macro again to save the print range permanently.

Now, imagine you are the loan officer for the Crown Loan Company. A customer comes in and requests information on the 1988 Chevy Van we discussed earlier. With the monthly payment and the amortization table on the screen, you can print a copy of the loan information and pass it to the customer. First, make sure the printer is ready. Next, hold down the Alt key and press the letter P. The monthly payment and amortization table shown in Figure 4-19 prints on the printer.

The \C macro in cell A30 prints the cell-formulas version of the worksheet according to the previously defined printer range. After printing the as-displayed version of the range A1..E20, hold down the Alt key and press the C key. This invokes the \C macro. Note that after the printer is done printing the cell-formulas version, the macro resets the print setting to the as-displayed version.

## Guarding Against Macro Catastrophes

Take care when applying macros to a worksheet. If you enter the wrong letter, forget the tilde (~) when required, place macros in adjacent cells, or transpose characters in a macro, serious damage in the form of lost data can occur. For this reason we recommend you save the worksheet before executing a macro for the first time.

You should also use the **STEP mode** of 1-2-3 to test the macro. The STEP mode allows you to watch 1-2-3 execute the macro keystroke by keystroke just as if you entered the keystrokes one at a time at the keyboard. Let's execute the \S macro again using the STEP mode. To place 1-2-3 in STEP mode, hold down the Alt key and press function key F2. The indicator STEP appears on the indicator line at the bottom of the screen. Next, invoke the \S macro by holding down the Alt key and pressing the S key. Now press any key on the keyboard to execute the next keystroke in the macro. When you press any key, a flashing SST indicator replaces the STEP indicator at the bottom of the screen on the indicator line. The flashing SST reminds you that you are executing a macro in the STEP mode.

If you encounter an error while in STEP mode, you could terminate the macro by holding down the Ctrl key and pressing the Break key. This combination of keys terminates the macro immediately. If the macro error displays an error message, press the Enter key or Esc key. In either case you may then edit the macro and execute it once again using STEP mode. Continue in this fashion until the macro is doing exactly what you intend it to do. To quit the STEP mode, hold down the Alt key and press function key F2. This process of finding and correcting errors in a macro is called **debugging**.

## /X Macro Commands and Macro Words

The final step in Project 4B is to enter the macro that extends from cell A33 through A46. Before entering this macro, we need to discuss macro commands and macro words. **Macro commands** are used to write programs that can guide you or another user of the worksheet through complex tasks, like accepting data into various cells. Some of the macro commands are listed in Table 4-6 on the following page. For a complete list of the macro commands, press function key F1 and go to the Help Index of the online help facility. Select the title Macros from the Help Index. After reading or printing the screens, press the Esc key to return to the worksheet.

**TABLE 4-6 Macro Commands**

| COMMAND | EXAMPLE | EXPLANATION |
|---|---|---|
| /XC | /XCBONUS~ | Executes the macro beginning at the cell named BONUS. Saves the return cell address—the one below the cell containing /XCBONUS~. The return cell address is used by the /XR command. |
| /XG | /XGB10~ | Executes the macro beginning at a specified cell. |
| /XI | /XIB10<=40~/XCREG~ | Executes the macro at the cell named REG if B10 contains a value less than or equal to 40; otherwise it executes the macro in the cell below. |
| /XL | /XLPurchase Item:~B3~ | Displays a prompt message on the input line, accepts a label, and assigns it to cell B3. |
| /XN | /XNPurchase Price:~B5~ | Displays a prompt message on the input line, accepts a number, and assigns it to cell B5. |
| /XQ | /XQ | Ends the execution of a macro. |
| /XR | /XR | Returns control to the cell below the corresponding /XC. |

**Macro words** are used to handle special circumstances in a macro, like moving the cell pointer from one cell to another. Except for the tilde (~), which represents the Enter key, all macro words are enclosed in curly braces { }. The important macro words are listed in Table 4-7. For a complete list of the macro words, load 1-2-3, press function key F1, and select Macros from the Help Index. After reading or printing the screens, press the Esc key to return to the worksheet.

**TABLE 4-7 Macro Words That Represent Special Keys on the Keyboard**

| CATEGORY | MACRO WORD |
|---|---|
| Cell pointer | {UP} {DOWN} {RIGHT} {LEFT} {PGUP} {PGDN} {HOME} {END} {BACKSPACE} {ESC} {DEL} |
| Function keys | {EDIT} {NAME} {ABS} {GOTO} {WINDOW} {QUERY} {TABLE} {CALC} {GRAPH} |
| Enter key | ~ |
| Interaction | {?} |

The cell pointer movement macro words in Table 4-7 move the pointer, as if you pressed the key named within the curly braces. The function key macro words operate the same as pressing one of the function keys. The macro word {?} makes the macro pause and wait for keyboard input from the user. For example, the macro /FR{?}~ may be used to retrieve a worksheet from disk. The macro word {?} following /FR tells the macro to pause and wait for the user to select a file name. When you press the Enter key after entering the file name, the macro resumes execution and accepts the name entered on the input line.

## Interactive Macros

The macro defined in cells A33 through A46 in Figure 4-4 automates the entry of the loan data in cells B3, B5, B7, E3, and E5. The instructions in cells A34 through A39 clear the cells that contain the loan data. The instructions in cells A40 through A44 prompts the user to enter the loan data. Each /XL and /XN command displays a prompt message and halts the execution of the macro until the user responds by entering a value on the input line. /XQ in cell A46 terminates the macro.

Enter the macro and documentation in the range A33..D46 as shown in Figure 4-4. Use the command /**R**ange **N**ame **C**reate (/RNC) and assign cell A33 the macro name \D. Note that it is not necessary to assign the range A33..A46 to the macro name \D, since a macro executes downward until it comes across an empty cell. Invoke the \D macro and reenter the loan data for the 1988 Chevy Van shown in Figure 4-19. In a step-by-step fashion, Table 4-8 explains how the \D macro works. Use Table 4-8 to step through the macro activity when you execute it.

**TABLE 4-8 Step-by-Step Explanation of the \D Macro in the Range A33..A46**

| STEP | CELL | ENTRY | FUNCTION |
|---|---|---|---|
| 1 | A33 | {HOME} | Move the cell pointer to A1. |
| 2 | A34 | {GOTO}B3~/RE~ | Move the cell pointer to B3 and erase the contents. |
| 3 | A35 | {DOWN}{DOWN}/RE~ | Move the cell pointer to B5 and erase the contents. |
| 4 | A36 | {DOWN}{DOWN}/RE~ | Move the cell pointer to B7 and erase the contents. |
| 5 | A37 | {GOTO}E3~/RE~ | Move the cell pointer to E3 and erase the contents. |
| 6 | A38 | {DOWN}{DOWN}/RE~ | Move the cell pointer to E5 and erase the contents. |
| 7 | A39 | {HOME} | Move the cell pointer to A1. |
| 8 | A40 | /XLPurchase Item:~B3~ | Accept the purchase item (1988 Chevy Van) and assign it to cell B3. |
| 9 | A41 | /XNPurchase Price:~B5~ | Accept the purchase price (18500) and assign it to cell B5. |
| 10 | A42 | /XNDown Payment :~B7~ | Accept the down payment (4000) and assign it to cell B7. |
| 11 | A43 | /XNInterest Rate in %: ~E3~ | Accept the interest rate (11.5) and assign it to cell E3. |
| 12 | A44 | /XNTime in Years:~E5~ | Accept the time (5) and assign it to cell E5. |
| 13 | A45 | {HOME} | Move the cell pointer to A1. |
| 14 | A46 | /XQ | Quit the macro. |

## WINDOWS

When you have a large worksheet like the one in Project 4B, it is helpful to view two parts of the worksheet at one time. 1-2-3 lets you divide the screen into two horizontal windows or two vertical windows. For example, by dividing the screen into two horizontal windows, you can view the \D macro in cells A33..A46 and the cells (A1..E7) that are affected by this macro at the same time.

To show two windows, press the Home key and use the arrow keys to move the cell pointer to A8. Enter the command /**W**orksheet **W**indow **H**orizontal (/WWH). The rows above row 8 display in the top window and rows 8 through 19 display in the lower window.

Immediately after a window split, the cell pointer is active in the window above or to the right of the split. You can move the cell pointer from window to window by pressing function key F6. Press function key F6 and use the PgDn and Down Arrow keys to move the cell pointer to A44. As shown in Figure 4-25, the top window shows the cells that are modified by the \D macro in the lower window.

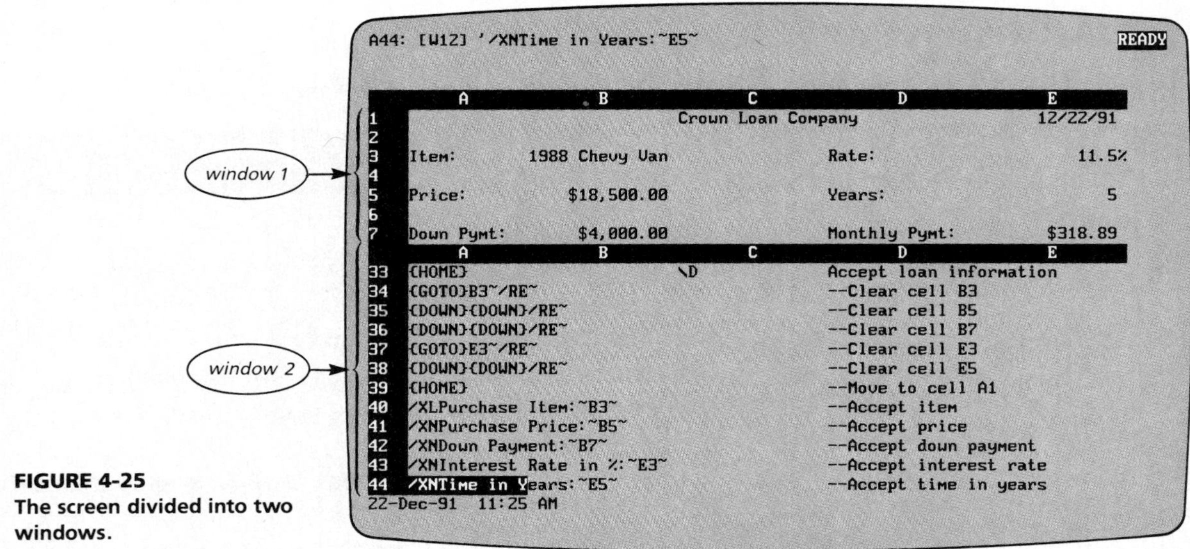


**FIGURE 4-25**
**The screen divided into two windows.**

Press function key F6 to move the cell pointer to the top window. Execute the \D macro a second time. Step through the macro in the lower window and watch the cells change in the top window.

It is important to understand that the entire worksheet is available through any window. If you make a change to a cell in one window, the change will show up in any other window. Table 4-9 summarizes the window commands available when you enter the command /**W**orksheet **W**indow (/WW).

**TABLE 4-9 Summary of the Worksheet Window Commands**

| COMMAND | KEYSTROKES | FUNCTION |
|---|---|---|
| Horizontal | /WWH | Splits the screen from side to side. |
| Vertical | /WWV | Splits the screen from top to bottom. |
| Sync | /WWS | Causes windows that are aligned horizontally or vertically to scroll together. |
| Unsync | /WWU | Causes each window to scroll independently. |
| Clear | /WWC | Returns the screen to a single window. |

## Synchronizing Windows

If you look closely at the two windows in Figure 4-25, you'll notice that they are **synchronized**, that is, the same column letters are aligned in both windows. The windows scroll together. They are **synchronized**. You can unsynchronize the windows so that they scroll independent of one another. To unsynchronize the windows, enter the command /**W**orksheet **W**indow **U**nsync (/WWU). To synchronize the windows after unsynchronizing them, enter the command /**W**orksheet **W**indow **S**ync (/WWS).

## Clearing the Windows

To return to the normal worksheet display with one window, enter the command /**W**orksheet **W**indow **C**lear (/WWC). This command switches the screen from two windows back to one window.

# CELL PROTECTION

Cells are either protected or unprotected. When you create a new worksheet, all cells are unprotected. **Unprotected cells** are cells whose values may be changed at any time, but **protected cells** cannot be changed. If a cell is protected and the user attempts to change its value, the computer beeps and 1-2-3 displays the error message "Protected cell" on the indicator line at the bottom of the screen.

Once the worksheet has been fully tested and displays the correct results, you should protect the cells that you don't want changed by mistake. You should protect cells that contain information that will not change or is unlikely to change, cells that contain macros, and cells whose values are determined by formulas. In the case of Project 4B, we want to protect all the cells in the worksheet except for B3, B5, B7, E3, E5, and the data table in the range F6..H20.

The first step in protecting cells is to protect all the cells in the worksheet. Once all the cells are protected, we can be selective and "unprotect" those that we want to change. To protect all the cells in the worksheet, enter the command /**W**orksheet **G**lobal **P**rotection **E**nable (/WGPE).

Next, move the cell pointer to B3. Enter the command /**R**ange **U**nprotect (/RU). Press the Enter key when 1-2-3 requests the range to unprotect. Do the same for cells B5, B7, E3, and E5. Finally, move the cell pointer to F6 and unprotect the range F6..H20, which contains the data table information.

You can check whether a cell is unprotected by moving the cell pointer to the cell in question. The letter U displays on the status line if the cell is unprotected. The letters PR display if the cell is protected. If you mistakenly unprotect the wrong cell, you may protect it by using the command /**R**ange **P**rotect (/RP). This command is meaningless unless global protection has been enabled (turned on).

If for some reason you need to modify the cells that are in a protected area, such as the macros, disable (turn off) global protection by using the command /**W**orksheet **G**lobal **P**rotection **D**isable (/WGPD). Once you are finished modifying the cells, enable (turn on) global protection. The worksheet will be protected exactly as it was before you disabled (turned off) global protection.

## Saving and Printing the Worksheet

To save the Crown Loan Company worksheet to disk with the cells protected, invoke the \S macro by holding down the Alt key and pressing the S key.

To obtain a printed version of the worksheet, do the following:

1. Enter the command /**P**rint **P**rinter **R**ange (/PPR) and select the range A1..H46.
2. Type the letter Q to quit the Print menu.
3. Invoke the \P macro by holding down the Alt key and pressing the P key.

1-2-3 prints the three parts of the worksheet on multiple pages. After the printer stops, carefully remove the Crown Loan Company worksheet from the printer. The complete worksheet is shown in Figures 4-2, 4-3, and 4-4.

## OBTAINING A SUMMARY OF ALL THE 1-2-3 FUNCTIONS

1-2-3 has over 100 useful functions. We have discussed the most widely used ones. You may find the others to be useful in certain situations. For a complete listing and description of the functions available, load 1-2-3, press function key F1, and go to the Help Index screen. Select the title @ Functions. Print the screen for each category of functions using the Shift and PrtSc keys. After you are finished, press the Esc key to return to the worksheet.

## PROJECT SUMMARY

In Project 4 we developed two worksheets. Project 4A introduced you to statistical functions and range names. Project 4B taught you how to use the IF, PMT, and PV functions, the data fill feature, data tables, and macros. You also learned how to protect cells in the worksheet and how to use multiple windows to see different parts of the worksheet at the same time.

Each of the steps required to build the worksheets in Projects 4A and 4B is listed in the following tables.

**SUMMARY OF KEYSTROKES—Project 4A**

| STEPS | KEY(S) PRESSED | STEPS | KEY(S) PRESSED |
|---|---|---|---|
| 1 | /WGC→ → ↵ | 18 | F5 A16↵'7561→112→130→123↵ |
| 2 | /WCS→ → ↵ | 19 | F5 A17↵\-↵/C↵.→ → → → → ↵ |
| 3 | DP 101→ →Grading Report→ → → | 20 | ↓Count↓Lowest Grade↓Highest Grade↓Average Score↓Std Deviation↓Variation↵ Home |
| 4 | @NOW↵/RFD1↵ | 21 | F5 E4↵@SUM(B4.D4)↵ |
| 5 | F5 B3↵"Test 1→"Test 2→"Test 3→ "Total→"Percent↵ | 22 | /C↵E6.E16↵ |
| 6 | F5 A4↵Student→139→142→150→ → "Correct↵ | 23 | F5 F6↵ +E6/$E$4*100↵ |
| 7 | F5 A5↵\=↵/C↵.→ → → → → ↵ | 24 | /C↵F6.F16↵ |
| 8 | ↓'1035→121→127→142↵ | 25 | /RFF1↵F6.F16↵ |
| 9 | F5 A7↵'1074→114→113→132↵ | 26 | F5 B6↵/RNCTEST1↵B6.B16↵ |
| 10 | F5 A8↵'1265→79→97→101↵ | 27 | F5 B18↵@COUNT(TEST1)↓@MIN(TEST1)↓ @MAX(TEST1)↓ |
| 11 | F5 A9↵'1345→85→106→95↵ | 28 | @AVG(TEST1)↓@STD(TEST1)↓@VAR(TEST1)↵ |
| 12 | F5 A10↵'1392→127→124→120↵ | 29 | /CB18.B23↵C18.E23↵ |
| 13 | F5 A11↵'3167→101→120→109↵ | 30 | /RFF1↵↑↑ → → → ↵ |
| 14 | F5 A12↵'3382→110→104→120↵ | 31 | /FSPROJS-4A↵ |
| 15 | F5 A13↵'3597→92→104→100↵ | 32 | Home /PPRA1.F23↵ |
| 16 | F5 A14↵'4126→105→100→96↵ | 33 | AGPPQ |
| 17 | F5 A15↵'5619→125→135→143↵ | 34 | /WEY |

## SUMMARY OF KEYSTROKES—Project 4B

| STEPS | KEY(S) PRESSED | STEPS | KEY(S) PRESSED |
|---|---|---|---|
| 1 | /WCS12↵ | 40 | [F5] A22↵ → Crown Loan Company Worksheet Macros↵ |
| 2 | /WGC15↵ | 41 | [F5] A24↵ Macro → → Macro Name → Function↓ |
| 3 | → → Crown Loan Company → → | 42 | \ = → \ = ← ← ========== ← ← \ = ↓ |
| 4 | @NOW↵ /RFD4↵ | 43 | '/FS˜R → → '\S → Saves worksheet under same name↵ |
| 5 | [F5] A3↵ Item:↓↓Price:↓↓Down Pymt:↵ | 44 | ← ← ← /RNC\S↵↵ |
| 6 | [F5] D3↵ Rate:↓↓Years:↓↓Monthly Pymt:↵ | 45 | [Alt]-S |
| 7 | [F5] B3↵ '1988 Chevy Van↓↓18500↓↓4000↵ /RFC↵ .↑↑↵ | 46 | ↓↓'/PPAGPPQ → → '\P → Prints worksheet↵ |
| 8 | [F5] E3↵ 11.5%↵ /RFP1↵↵↓↓5↓↓/RFC↵↵ | 47 | ← ← ← /RNC\P↵↵ |
| 9 | [F5] A5↵ /RNLR.↓↓↵ | 48 | ↓↓'/PPOOCQAGOOAQPPQ → → '\C → Prints cell-formulas version↵ |
| 10 | [F5] D3↵ /RNLR.↓↓↓↓↵ | 49 | ← ← ← /RNC\C↵↵ |
| 11 | [F5] E7↵ @PMT($PRICE:–$Down Pymt:, $Rate:/12,$Years:*12)↵ | 50 | /PPRA1.E20↵ Q |
| 12 | [F5] A8↵ \ = ↵ /C↵ . → → → → ↵ | 51 | [Alt]-P |
| 13 | [F5] B9↵ "Beginning → "Ending → "Paid On → "Interest↓ | 52 | [Alt]-C |
| 14 | "Paid ← "Principal ← "Balance ← "Balance ← "Year↓ | 53 | ↓↓↓{HOME} → → '\D → Accept loan information↵ |
| 15 | \-↵ /C↵ . → → → → ↵ | 54 | ← ← ← /RNC\D↵↵ |
| 16 | ↓/DF.↓↓↓↓↵ 1↵↵↵ | 55 | ↓{GOTO}B3˜/RE˜ → → → '--Clear cell B3↵ |
| 17 | → + Price:–Down Pymt:↵ | 56 | [F5] A35↵ {DOWN}{DOWN}/RE˜ → → → '--Clear cell B5↵ |
| 18 | /RF,↵ B12.E20↵ | 57 | [F5] A36↵ /CA35↵ A36↵ → → → '--Clear cell B7↵ |
| 19 | → @IF(A12< = $YEARS:,@PV($Monthly Pymt:,$Rate:/12,12*($Years:–A12)),0)↵ | 58 | [F5] A37↵ {GOTO}E3˜/RE˜ → → → '--Clear cell E3↵ |
| 20 | /C↵ .↓↓↓↓↵ | 59 | [F5] A38↵ {DOWN}{DOWN}/RE˜ → → → '--Clear cell E5↵ |
| 21 | ↓ ← + C12↵ /C↵ .↓↓↓↵ | 60 | [F5] A39↵ {HOME} → → → '--Move to cell A1↵ |
| 22 | [F5] D12↵ + B12–C12↵ /C↵ .↓↓↓↓↵ | 61 | [F5] A40↵ '/XLPurchase Item:˜B3˜ → → → '--Accept purchase item↵ |
| 23 | → @IF(B12>0,12*$Monthly Pymt:–D12,0) ↵ /C↵ .↓↓↓↓↵ | 62 | [F5] A41↵ '/XNPurchase Price:˜B5˜ → → → '--Accept purchase price↵ |
| 24 | [F5] A17↵ \-↵ /C↵ . → → → → ↵ | 63 | [F5] A42↵ '/XNDown Payment:˜B7˜ → → → '--Accept down payment↵ |
| 25 | [F5] C18↵ "Subtotal↓"Down Pymt↓ "Total Cost↵ | 64 | [F5] A43↵ '/XNInterest Rate in %:˜E3˜ → → → ' --Accept interest rate↵ |
| 26 | [F5] D18↵ @SUM(D12.D16) → | 65 | [F5] A44↵ '/XNTime in Years:˜E5˜ → → → '--Accept time in years↵ |
| 27 | @SUM(E12.E16)↓ | 66 | [F5] A45↵ {HOME} → → → '--Move to cell A1↵ |
| 28 | + Down Pymt:↓ | 67 | [F5] A46↵ '/XQ → → → '--End of macro↵ |
| 29 | + D18 + E18 + E19↵ | 68 | [Alt]-D1988 Chevy Van↵ 18500↵ 4000↵ 11.5%↵ 5↵ |
| 30 | /FSPROJS-4B↵ | 69 | /WGPE |
| 31 | [F5] F1↵ Payments for Varying Interest Rates↓↓ | 70 | → ↓↓/RU↵ |
| 32 | "Varying → "Monthly → "Total↓ | 71 | ↓↓/RU↵ |
| 33 | "Paid ← "Payment ← "Rate↓ | 72 | ↓↓/RU↵ |
| 34 | \ = → \ = → \ = ↓ | 73 | [F5] E3↵ /RU↵ |
| 35 | [F5] F7↵ /DFF7.F20↵ 8.5%↵ 0.5%↵↵ | 74 | ↓↓/RU↵ |
| 36 | /RFP1↵ F7.F20↵ | 75 | [F5] F6↵ /RUF6.H20↵ [Home] |
| 37 | ↑ → + E7 → + E20↵ | 76 | [Alt]-S |
| 38 | /RF,↵ G6.H20↵ | 77 | /PPRA1.H46↵ Q |
| 39 | /DT1H6.F20↵ Rate:↵ | 78 | [Alt]-P |

## Project Summary (continued)

The following list summarizes the material covered in Project 4:

1. If you plan to reference a range often, assign a name to it. To name a range, use the command /**R**ange **N**ame **C**reate (/RNC).
2. The Range Name command allows you to create range names, delete range names, assign labels as range names, clear all range names, and insert the list of range names in the worksheet. See Table 4-1.
3. 1-2-3 has several statistical functions, like AVG, COUNT, MAX, MIN, STD, and VAR. See Table 4-2.
4. The command /**R**ange **N**ame **L**abel (/RNL) allows you to assign a label in a cell as the name of the cell immediately above, below, to the right, or to the left.
5. The PMT function determines the payment of a loan on the basis of the amount of the loan (principal), the interest rate (interest), and the length of time required to pay the loan back (term). The general form of the PMT function is @PMT(principal,interest,term).
6. The command /**D**ata **F**ill (/DF) allows you to quickly enter a series of numbers into a range using a specified increment or decrement.
7. The PV function can be used to return the amount the borrower still owes at the end of a period at any time during the life of a loan. The general form of the PV function is @PV(payment,interest,term).
8. The general form of the IF function is @IF(condition,true,false). When the IF function is assigned to a cell, the value displayed will depend on the condition. If the condition is true, the cell is assigned the true value. If the condition is false, the cell is assigned the false value.
9. The true and false values in an IF function may be a number, label (in quotation marks), function, or formula.
10. A condition is made up of two expressions and a relation. Each expression may be a number, label (in quotation marks), function, or formula. See Table 4-3 for a list of the valid relations.
11. A compound condition is one that includes a logical operator like #AND#, #OR#, and #NOT#. See Table 4-4 for examples.
12. A data table is used to automate asking what-if questions and organize the values returned by 1-2-3.
13. A data table may have one value or two varying values. See Figure 4-20.
14. A **macro** is a series of keystrokes entered into a cell or range of cells. The macro is assigned a name using the command /**R**ange **N**ame **C**reate (/RNC).
15. A macro name begins with the backslash (\) character followed immediately by a letter.
16. If you have more than one macro associated with a worksheet, each macro should be separated by an empty cell.
17. The tilde character (~) is used to represent the Enter key in a macro.
18. All macros should be documented.
19. To invoke a macro, hold down the Alt key and type the single letter name of the macro.
20. A poorly designed macro can damage a worksheet. Before you execute a new macro, save the worksheet. To test a macro, place 1-2-3 in STEP mode, hold down the Alt key, and press function key F2. When you are finished testing the macro, hold down the Alt key and press function key F2 to toggle the STEP mode off.
21. If you encounter an error in a macro while in STEP mode, hold down the Ctrl key and press the Break key to stop the macro. If an error message displays, press the Esc or Enter key rather than the Ctrl and Break keys.
22. /X macro commands are used to write programs. See Table 4-6.
23. Macro words represent special keys, like the pointer movement and function keys. See Table 4-7.
24. 1-2-3 allows you to divide the screen into two windows for viewing different parts of the worksheet at the same time. Use the command /**W**orksheet **W**indow (/WW). See Table 4-9.
25. To protect cells in a worksheet that you do not want the user to change, enter the command /**W**orksheet **G**lobal **P**rotection **E**nable (/WGPE). Once all the cells in the worksheet are protected, use the command /**R**ange **U**nprotect (/RU) to unprotect the cells you want the user to be able to change. If you unprotect the wrong cell, use the command /**R**ange **P**rotect (/RP) to protect it.
26. To correct the values in protected cells, enter the command /**W**orksheet **G**lobal **P**rotection **D**isable (/WGPD). After the cells are corrected, enable (turn on) global protection. 1-2-3 remembers the cells you unprotected earlier.

# STUDENT ASSIGNMENTS

## STUDENT ASSIGNMENT 1: True/False

**Instructions:** Circle T if the statement is true or F if the statement is false.

T F 1. A data table allows you to automate what-if questions.
T F 2. The @COUNT(R) function returns the largest number in the range R.
T F 3. You may assign a single cell to a name using the /**R**ange **N**ame **C**reate (/RNC) command.
T F 4. If there are seven cells in range R and five of the cells have a value of 10 and two of the cells are empty, then the function @AVG(R) returns a value of 50.
T F 5. The command /**W**orksheet **E**rase (/WE) may be used to erase the contents of a single cell without affecting the remaining cells in the worksheet.
T F 6. The @NOW function returns a whole number equal to the number of days since December 31, 1899 on the basis of the system date.
T F 7. The command /**R**ange **N**ame **L**abel (/RNL) is used to name a cell that contains a label.
T F 8. The PMT function may be used to determine the monthly payment on a loan.
T F 9. To fill a range from top to bottom with the sequence of numbers 5, 4, 3, 2, and 1, use the /**D**ata **F**ill (/DF) command with a start value of 5, a step value of 1, and a stop value of 1.
T F 10. The IF function is used to assign one value or another to a cell on the basis of a condition that may be true, false, or both true and false.
T F 11. The logical operator #AND# requires both conditions to be true for the compound condition to be true.
T F 12. You may vary one or two values in a data table.
T F 13. 1-2-3 recalculates the values in a data table when you press function key F9.
T F 14. To invoke a macro, hold down the Ctrl key and type the letter that names the macro.
T F 15. To name a macro, use the /**R**ange **N**ame **C**reate (/RNC) command.
T F 16. The STEP mode is used to enter a macro into a cell.
T F 17. Each macro should be separated by at least one empty cell.
T F 18. To protect cells in the worksheet, global protection must be enabled (turned on).
T F 19. The /**W**orksheet **W**indow (/WW) command allows you to divide the screen into two to six windows.
T F 20. The /X macro commands allow you to write programs.

## STUDENT ASSIGNMENT 2: Multiple Choice

**Instructions:** Circle the correct response.

1. Which one of the following allows you to assign a name to one or more adjacent cells?
   a. /**R**ange **N**ame **C**reate (/RNC) c. /**R**ange **N**ame **L**abel (/RNL)
   b. /**W**orksheet **N**ame **C**reate (/WNC) d. /**R**ange **N**ame **T**able (/RNT)
2. Which one of the following functions returns the average of the numbers in a range?
   a. AVG b. COUNT c. MAX d. MIN
3. Which one of the following functions returns the payment on a loan?
   a. TERM b. PMT c. PV d. RATE
4. Which one of the following functions is used to assign one value or another value to a cell on the basis of a condition?
   a. CHOOSE b. FALSE c. IF d. TRUE
5. Which one of the following is used to instruct 1-2-3 to terminate the Data Fill command?
   a. The last cell in the selected range terminates the command.
   b. The STOP parameter terminates the command.
   c. Either a or b can terminate the command.
   d. None of the above.

**Student Assignment 2 (continued)**

6. Which one of the following relations is used to represent not equal to?
   a. < b. > c. <> d. none of these
7. In a Data table, you may vary up to __________ values.
   a. one b. two c. three d. four
8. Which one of the following characters represents the Enter key in a macro?
   a. backslash (\) b. curly braces ({ }) c. circumflex (^) d. tilde (~)

## STUDENT ASSIGNMENT 3: Understanding Functions

**Instructions:** Fill in the correct answers.

1. Write a function that will count the nonempty cells in the range B10..B50.

Function: ______________________________

2. Write a function that will find the average of the nonempty cells in the range A12..E12.

Function: ______________________________

3. Write a function that will display the largest value in the range D1..D13.

Function: ______________________________

4. Write a function that will determine the monthly payment on a loan of $85,000, over a period of 30 years, at an interest rate of 9.9% compounded monthly.

Function: ______________________________

5. The cell pointer is at F15. Write a function that assigns the value zero or 1 to cell F15. Assign zero to cell F15 if the value in cell A12 is less than the value in cell B15. Assign 1 to cell F15 if the value in A12 is not less than the value in cell B15.

Function: ______________________________

6. The cell pointer is at F15. Write a function that assigns the value Credit OK or Credit Not OK to cell F15. Assign the label Credit OK if the value in cell A1 is equal to the value in cell B1 or the value of cell C12 is greater than 500. If both conditions are false, assign the label Credit Not OK.

Function: ______________________________

7. When there are multiple logical operators in a compound condition, 1-2-3 determines the truth value of each simple condition. It then evaluates the logical operators, left to right, in the following order: #NOT#, #AND#, #OR#. Determine the truth value of the compound conditions below, given the following: E1 = 300 F1 = 500 G1 = 1 H1 = 50 I1 = 40

   a. E1<400#OR#G1=1 Truth value: __________
   b. F1<300#AND#I1<50#OR#G1=2 Truth value: __________
   c. #NOT#(F1>600)#OR#G1=0#AND#I1=40 Truth value: __________
   d. E1+F1=800#AND#H1*4/10=30 Truth value: __________

## STUDENT ASSIGNMENT 4: Understanding Macros

**Instructions:** Fill in the correct answers.

1. Describe the function of each of the following macros.
   a. /FS~R/QY

   Function of macro: ____________________

   b. /RE~

   Function of macro: ____________________

   c. /RFC2~{?}~

   Function of macro: ____________________

   d. /C~{?}~

   Function of macro: ____________________

   e. /PPOML2~MR78~Q

   Function of macro: ____________________

   f. /PPR{?}~AGPPQ

   Function of macro: ____________________

   g. {DOWN}{DOWN}/RE~

   Function of macro: ____________________

   h. /DF{?}~1~2~~

   Function of macro: ____________________

2. Describe the function of each of the following macro commands and macro words.

| | | | |
|---|---|---|---|
| a. tilde (~) | Function: ______ | f. {GOTO} | Function: ______ |
| b. curly braces ({}) | Function: ______ | g. {UP} | Function: ______ |
| c. /XN | Function: ______ | h. /XQ | Function: ______ |
| d. {?} | Function: ______ | i. /XI | Function: ______ |
| e. {HOME} | Function: ______ | j. {ESC} | Function: ______ |

## STUDENT ASSIGNMENT 5: Using the Data Fill Command

**Instructions:** Enter the worksheet illustrated in Figure 4-26. The worksheet is a multiplication table. Change the global width of the columns to 6 characters. Use the Data Fill command twice, once to enter the numbers 1 to 18 in column A, and once to enter the numbers 2 to 22 by 2 in row 1. Enter the formula $A3*B$1 in cell B3. Copy the formula to the range B3..L20. Save the worksheet as STUS4-5. Print the as-displayed version of the worksheet. Format all the cells in the worksheet to the Text type and print the worksheet.

A1: "x READY

| | A | B | C | D | E | F | G | H | I | J | K | L |
|---|---|---|---|---|---|---|---|---|---|---|---|---|
| 1 | x | 2 | 4 | 6 | 8 | 10 | 12 | 14 | 16 | 18 | 20 | 22 |
| 2 | ------ | ------ | ------ | ------ | ------ | ------ | ------ | ------ | ------ | ------ | ------ | ------ |
| 3 | 1 | 2 | 4 | 6 | 8 | 10 | 12 | 14 | 16 | 18 | 20 | 22 |
| 4 | 2 | 4 | 8 | 12 | 16 | 20 | 24 | 28 | 32 | 36 | 40 | 44 |
| 5 | 3 | 6 | 12 | 18 | 24 | 30 | 36 | 42 | 48 | 54 | 60 | 66 |
| 6 | 4 | 8 | 16 | 24 | 32 | 40 | 48 | 56 | 64 | 72 | 80 | 88 |
| 7 | 5 | 10 | 20 | 30 | 40 | 50 | 60 | 70 | 80 | 90 | 100 | 110 |
| 8 | 6 | 12 | 24 | 36 | 48 | 60 | 72 | 84 | 96 | 108 | 120 | 132 |
| 9 | 7 | 14 | 28 | 42 | 56 | 70 | 84 | 98 | 112 | 126 | 140 | 154 |
| 10 | 8 | 16 | 32 | 48 | 64 | 80 | 96 | 112 | 128 | 144 | 160 | 176 |
| 11 | 9 | 18 | 36 | 54 | 72 | 90 | 108 | 126 | 144 | 162 | 180 | 198 |
| 12 | 10 | 20 | 40 | 60 | 80 | 100 | 120 | 140 | 160 | 180 | 200 | 220 |
| 13 | 11 | 22 | 44 | 66 | 88 | 110 | 132 | 154 | 176 | 198 | 220 | 242 |
| 14 | 12 | 24 | 48 | 72 | 96 | 120 | 144 | 168 | 192 | 216 | 240 | 264 |
| 15 | 13 | 26 | 52 | 78 | 104 | 130 | 156 | 182 | 208 | 234 | 260 | 286 |
| 16 | 14 | 28 | 56 | 84 | 112 | 140 | 168 | 196 | 224 | 252 | 280 | 308 |
| 17 | 15 | 30 | 60 | 90 | 120 | 150 | 180 | 210 | 240 | 270 | 300 | 330 |
| 18 | 16 | 32 | 64 | 96 | 128 | 160 | 192 | 224 | 256 | 288 | 320 | 352 |
| 19 | 17 | 34 | 68 | 102 | 136 | 170 | 204 | 238 | 272 | 306 | 340 | 374 |
| 20 | 18 | 36 | 72 | 108 | 144 | 180 | 216 | 252 | 288 | 324 | 360 | 396 |

22-Dec-91 11:26 AM

## STUDENT ASSIGNMENT 6: Using the Data Table Command

**Instructions:** Create the following worksheets.

1. The worksheet illustrated in Figure 4-27 contains a data table with one value (time) varying. At the top of the worksheet, the PMT function is used to determine the monthly mortgage payment for a loan of $85,000.00 at 9.9% annual interest for 30 years. The data table indicates the monthly payment for the same loan for different terms (5 years, 10 years, 15 years, etc.).

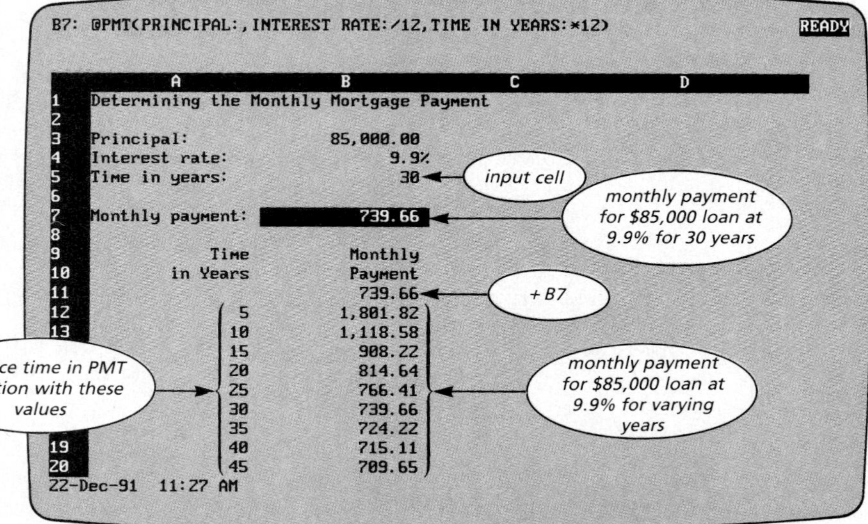


**FIGURE 4-27**
**Student Assignment 6A**

Do the following to create the worksheet in Figure 4-27:

a. Increase the global column width to 17.
b. Format the entire worksheet to the Comma (,) type with two decimal places.
c. Enter the labels and numeric values in the range A1 through B5 and in cell A7. Format cell B4 to the Percent type with one decimal position. Format cell B5 to the Fixed type with zero decimal positions.
d. Use the Range Name Label command to assign the labels in cells A3 through A7 to B3 through B7.
e. Assign the PMT function shown on the input line in Figure 4-27 to cell B7.

f. Enter the labels in the range A9..B10.
g. Use the Data Fill command to enter the multiples of five shown in the range A12..A20. Format A12..A20 to the Fixed type with zero decimal positions.
h. Assign cell B11 the formula +B7.
i. Use the command /**D**ata **F**ill 1 (/DF1) to create a data table in the range A11..B20. Use B5 (time in years) as the input cell.
j. After the data table displays, save the worksheet using the file name STUS4-6A.
k. Print the worksheet.
l. Select and enter several other sets of numbers into cells B3, B4, and B5. When necessary, use function key F8 to reset the data table.

2. The worksheet illustrated in Figure 4-28 contains a data table with two values varying. It also uses the FV function in cell B7 to determine the future value of a fund. The FV function tells you how much money you will have in a fund if you pay a fixed payment and earn a fixed interest rate over a period of time.

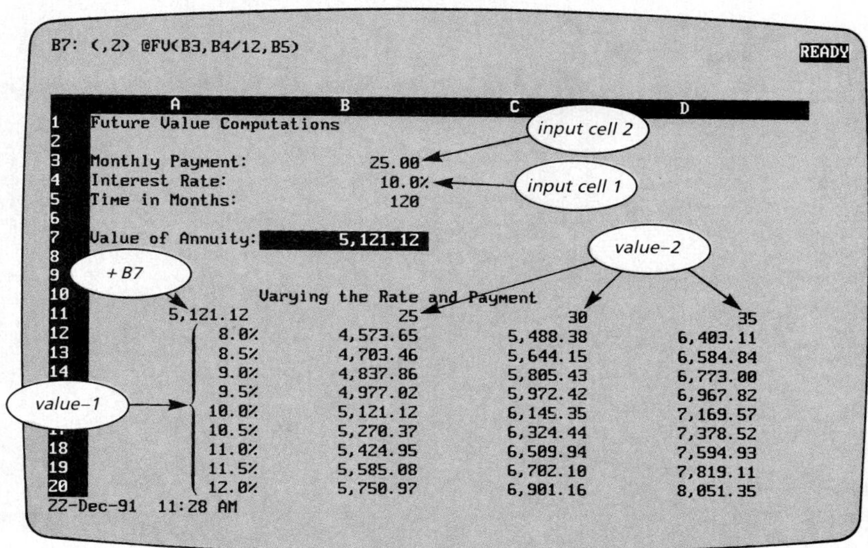


**FIGURE 4-28**
**Student Assignment 6B**

The data table describes the future values for varying interest rates and varying monthly payments. For example, if you invest $35.00 per month instead of $25.00 per month and if the interest rate is 11.5%, then you will have $7,819.11 rather than $5,585.08 at the end of 10 years.

Do the following to create the worksheet in Figure 4-28:

a. Increase the global column width to 17.
b. Enter the labels and numeric values in the range A1 through B5 and in cell A7.
c. Assign the FV function @FV(B3,B4/12,B5) to cell B7 to determine the future value of a fund in which you invest $25.00 per month at 10% interest, compounded monthly, for 10 years (120 months).
d. Use the Data Fill command to build the percent values in the range A12..A20. Assign +B7 to cell A11.
e. With the cell pointer at A11, enter the command /**D**ata **T**able **2** (/DT2). Enter the data table range A11..D20.
f. Enter an input cell-1 value of B4 and an input cell-2 value of B3. Press the Enter key. The data table should fill as shown in Figure 4-28.
g. Format the worksheet according to Figure 4-28.
h. Save the worksheet using the file name STUS4-6B.
i. Print the worksheet.
j. Try several different investment combinations in cells B3, B4, and B5. Use function key F8 to instruct 1-2-3 to recalculate the data table if you change the value in cell B5.

## STUDENT ASSIGNMENT 7: Building a Weekly Payroll Worksheet

**Instructions:** Load 1-2-3 and perform the following tasks.

1. Build the worksheet illustrated in Figure 4-29. For each employee, use the following formulas to determine the gross pay in column E, federal tax in column F, state tax in column G, and net pay in column H:
   a. If Hours ≤ 40, then Gross Pay = Rate ∗ Hours, otherwise Gross Pay = Rate ∗ Hours + 0.5 ∗ Rate ∗ (Hours – 40).
   b. If (Gross Pay – Dependents ∗ 38.46) > 0, then Federal Tax = 20% ∗ (Gross Pay – Dependents ∗ 38.46), otherwise Federal Tax = 0.
   c. State Tax = 3.2% ∗ Gross Pay.
   d. Net Pay = Gross Pay – (Federal Tax + State Tax).

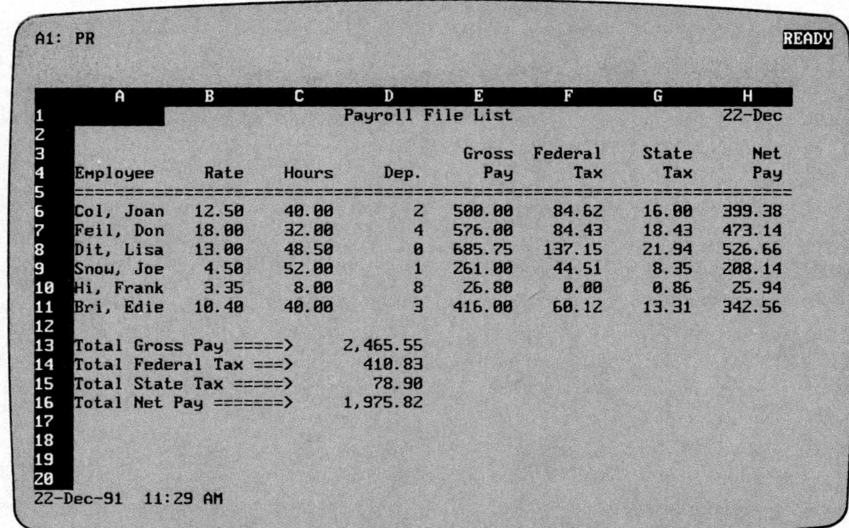

A1: PR READY

| Employee | Rate | Hours | Dep. | Gross Pay | Federal Tax | State Tax | Net Pay |
|---|---|---|---|---|---|---|---|
| | | | Payroll File List | | | | 22-Dec |
| Col, Joan | 12.50 | 40.00 | 2 | 500.00 | 84.62 | 16.00 | 399.38 |
| Feil, Don | 18.00 | 32.00 | 4 | 576.00 | 84.43 | 18.43 | 473.14 |
| Dit, Lisa | 13.00 | 48.50 | 0 | 685.75 | 137.15 | 21.94 | 526.66 |
| Snow, Joe | 4.50 | 52.00 | 1 | 261.00 | 44.51 | 8.35 | 208.14 |
| Hi, Frank | 3.35 | 8.00 | 8 | 26.80 | 0.00 | 0.86 | 25.94 |
| Bri, Edie | 10.40 | 40.00 | 3 | 416.00 | 60.12 | 13.31 | 342.56 |

Total Gross Pay =====> 2,465.55
Total Federal Tax ===> 410.83
Total State Tax =====> 78.90
Total Net Pay =======> 1,975.82

22-Dec-91 11:29 AM

**FIGURE 4-29**
**Student Assignment 7**

2. Use the Range Name Create command to name cells B6, C6, and D6 so that you can use the variable names described in step 1 when you enter the formulas in cells E6, F6, G6, and H6.
3. Protect all the cells in the worksheet except those in the range C6..C11. Try to enter values into the protected cells.
4. Save the worksheet as STUS4-7.
5. Print the worksheet.
6. Print the cell-formulas version of the worksheet.
7. Print the worksheet after formatting all the cells to the Text type.
8. Increase the number of hours worked for each employee by 7.5 hours. Print the worksheet with the new values.

## STUDENT ASSIGNMENT 8: Building a Future Value Worksheet

**Instructions:** Load 1-2-3 and perform the following tasks.

1. Build the worksheet illustrated in Figure 4-30. Set column A to a width of 16 characters and the rest of the columns to a width of 14 characters. Use the Range Name Label command to name B3, B5, E3, and E5. Use the label to the right of each cell in Figure 4-30 as the label name. Determine the future value in cell E5 from the function @FV($Monthly Pymt;, $Rate:/12,12*$Time:). The FV function tells you how much money you will have in a fund if you pay a fixed payment and earn a fixed interest rate over a period of time.

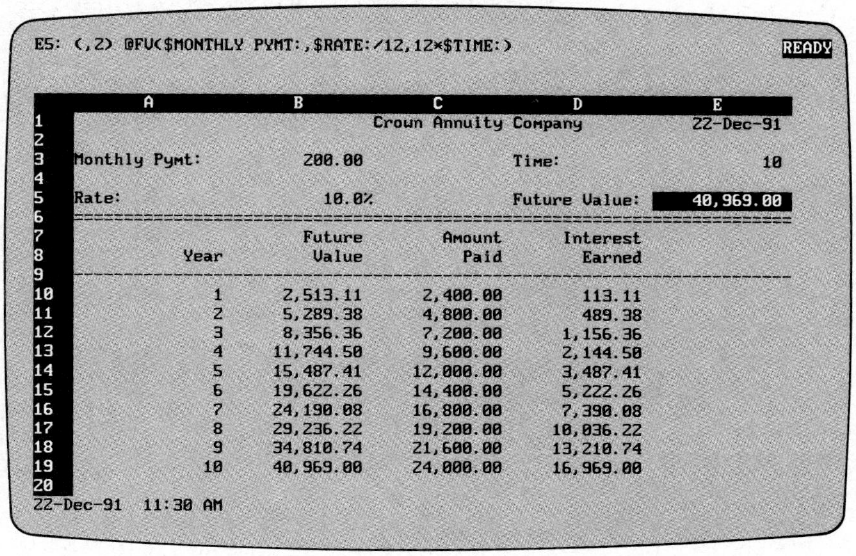

E5: (,2) @FV($MONTHLY PYMT:,$RATE:/12,12*$TIME:) READY

| | A | B | C | D | E |
|---|---|---|---|---|---|
| 1 | | | Crown Annuity Company | | 22-Dec-91 |
| 2 | | | | | |
| 3 | Monthly Pymt: | 200.00 | | Time: | 10 |
| 4 | | | | | |
| 5 | Rate: | 10.0% | | Future Value: | 40,969.00 |
| 6 | ============== | ============== | ============== | ============== | ============== |
| 7 | | Future | Amount | Interest | |
| 8 | Year | Value | Paid | Earned | |
| 9 | -------------- | -------------- | -------------- | -------------- | -------------- |
| 10 | 1 | 2,513.11 | 2,400.00 | 113.11 | |
| 11 | 2 | 5,289.38 | 4,800.00 | 489.38 | |
| 12 | 3 | 8,356.36 | 7,200.00 | 1,156.36 | |
| 13 | 4 | 11,744.50 | 9,600.00 | 2,144.50 | |
| 14 | 5 | 15,487.41 | 12,000.00 | 3,487.41 | |
| 15 | 6 | 19,622.26 | 14,400.00 | 5,222.26 | |
| 16 | 7 | 24,190.08 | 16,800.00 | 7,390.08 | |
| 17 | 8 | 29,236.22 | 19,200.00 | 10,036.22 | |
| 18 | 9 | 34,810.74 | 21,600.00 | 13,210.74 | |
| 19 | 10 | 40,969.00 | 24,000.00 | 16,969.00 | |
| 20 | | | | | |

22-Dec-91 11:30 AM

**FIGURE 4-30**
**Student Assignment 8**

Determine the values in the table in rows 10 through 19 as follows:

a. Use the Data Fill command to create the series of numbers in the range A10..A19.
b. Assign the function @IF(A10< = $Time:,@FV($Monthly Pymt:,$Rate:/12,12*A10),0) to B10 and copy B10 to B11..B19.
c. Assign the function @IF(A10< = $Time:,12*A10*$Monthly Pymt:,0) to C10 and copy C10 to C11..C19.
d. Assign the formula +B10–C10 to D10 and copy D10 to D11..D19.
e. Format the cells in the worksheet as shown in Figure 4-30.

2. Save the worksheet. Use the file name STUS4-8.
3. Determine the future value for the following: monthly payment, 500; rate of interest, 11.5%; time in years, 10.
4. Print the worksheet with the future value for the data described in step 3.
5. Print only the range A1..E5 with the future value for the data described in step 3.

## STUDENT ASSIGNMENT 9: Building a Data Table for the Future Value Worksheet

**Instructions:** Load 1-2-3 and perform the following tasks.

1. Load STUS4-8, the future value worksheet, which you created in Student Assignment 8. This worksheet is illustrated in Figure 4-30.
2. Add the data table shown in Figure 4-31. Do the following to complete the data table:

```
I20:                                                              READY

         F                  G                  H             I             J
1   Future Values for Varying Interest Rates
2
3
4        Varying            Future           Interest
5           Rate             Value             Earned
6   ==========================================================
7                       149,476.47          53,476.47
8           8.5%        136,821.45          40,821.45
9           9.0%        139,856.16          43,856.16
10          9.5%        142,975.19          46,975.19
11         10.0%        146,181.08          50,181.08
12         10.5%        149,476.47          53,476.47
13         11.0%        152,864.08          56,864.08
14         11.5%        156,346.73          60,346.73
15         12.0%        159,927.29          63,927.29
16         12.5%        163,608.76          67,608.76
17         13.0%        167,394.23          71,394.23
18         13.5%        171,286.85          75,286.85
19         14.0%        175,289.93          79,289.93
20         14.5%        179,406.83          83,406.83
22-Dec-91  11:31 AM
```

**FIGURE 4-31**
**Student Assignment 9**

a. Use the Data Fill command to enter the series of numbers 8.5% to 14.5% in increments of 0.5% in the range F8..F20.
b. Assign +E5 (future value) to cell G7.
c. Assign the formula +Future Value:-Time:*12*Monthly Pymt: to cell H7.
d. Use the command /**D**ata **T**able **1** (/DT1) to establish the range F7..H20 as a data table.
e. Enter an input cell value of B5, the interest rate.
f. Format the data table as shown in Figure 4-31.

3. Save the worksheet using the file name STUS4-9.
4. Print the data table (F1..H20).
5. Determine the future value for the following: monthly payment, 1000; rate of interest, 10.5%; time in years, 8.
6. Press function key F8 to recalculate the data table.
7. Print the complete worksheet (A1..H20) with the future value for the data described in step 5.

## STUDENT ASSIGNMENT 10: Building Macros for the Future Value Worksheet

**Instructions:** Load 1-2-3 and perform the following tasks.

1. Load STUS4-9, the future value worksheet, which was created in Student Assignments 8 and 9. This worksheet is illustrated in Figures 4-30 and 4-31.
2. Enter the three macros shown in Figure 4-32.

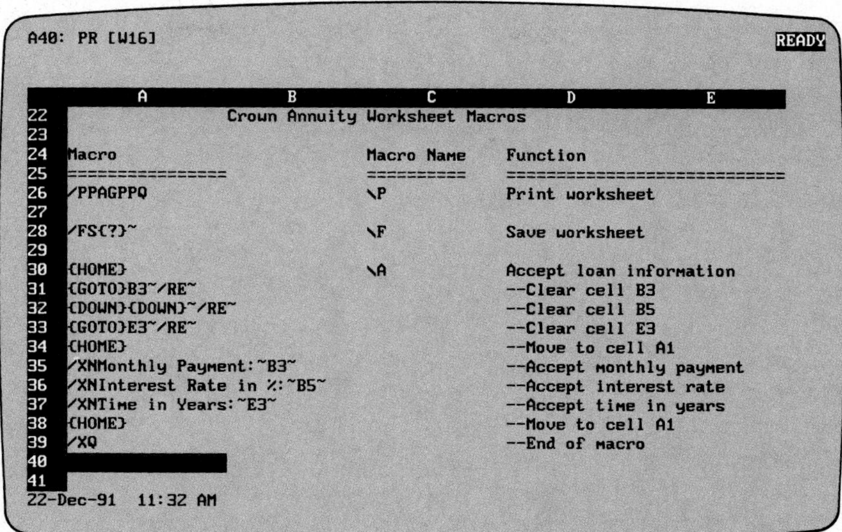

A40: PR [W16]
READY
A B C D E
22 Crown Annuity Worksheet Macros
23
24 Macro | Macro Name | Function
25 ================ | ========== | ============================
26 /PPAGPPQ | \P | Print worksheet
27
28 /FS{?}~ | \F | Save worksheet
29
30 {HOME} | \A | Accept loan information
31 {GOTO}B3~/RE~ | --Clear cell B3
32 {DOWN}{DOWN}~/RE~ | --Clear cell B5
33 {GOTO}E3~/RE~ | --Clear cell E3
34 {HOME} | --Move to cell A1
35 /XNMonthly Payment:~B3~ | --Accept monthly payment
36 /XNInterest Rate in %:~B5~ | --Accept interest rate
37 /XNTime in Years:~E3~ | --Accept time in years
38 {HOME} | --Move to cell A1
39 /XQ | --End of macro
40
41
22-Dec-91 11:32 AM


**FIGURE 4-32**
**Student Assignment 10**

3. Change the printer range to A1..E19.
4. Use the STEP mode to test each macro. For the \F macro, use the file name STUS4-10. For the \A macro, use the following data: monthly payment, 350; rate of interest, 8%; time in years, 7.
5. Enable cell protection for the worksheet. Unprotect cells B3, B5, E3, and the range F7..H20.
6. Press function key F8 to recalculate the data table.
7. Use the \F command to save the worksheet a second time.
8. Print the complete worksheet (A1..H39) with the future value for the data described in step 4.

## STUDENT ASSIGNMENT 11: Building Macros for the Weekly Payroll Worksheet

**Instructions:** Load 1-2-3 and perform the following tasks.

1. Load STUS4-7, the weekly payroll worksheet, which was created in Student Assignment 7. This worksheet is illustrated in Figure 4-29.
2. Disable cell protection and add macros that will do the following:

   a. Save the worksheet under the file name entered by the user (\S).
   b. Print the range A1..H16 (\P).
   c. Erase the current hours worked and accept the new hours worked (\A).

3. Enable cell protection for the worksheet. Cells C6..C11 should be left unprotected.
4. Use the STEP mode to test each macro. For the save macro, use the file name STUS4-11. For the accept hours worked macro, enter the following hours worked: Col, Joan—36.5; Fiel, Don—42.5; Dit, Lisa—53.5; Snow, Joe—40; Hi, Frank—40; Bri, Edie—61.5.
5. Use the save macro to save the worksheet a second time. Use the file name STUS4-11.
6. Print the worksheet (A1..H16) for the data described in step 4.

# PROJECT 5

## Graphing with 1-2-3

### Objectives

You will have mastered the material in this project when you can:

- Create a pie chart.
- Create a line graph.
- Create a multiple-line graph.
- Create a scatter graph.
- Create a simple bar graph.
- Create a side-by-side bar graph.
- Create a stacked-bar graph.
- Create an XY graph.
- Assign multiple graphs to the same worksheet.
- Dress up a graph by adding titles and legends.
- Save a graph as a PIC file.
- Save a worksheet with the graph specifications.
- Print a graph.
- View the current graph and graphs saved on disk.

As we have seen in the previous four projects, a worksheet is a powerful tool for analyzing data. Sometimes, however, the message you are trying to convey gets lost in the rows and columns of numbers. This is where the graphics capability of 1-2-3 comes in handy. With only a little effort, you can have 1-2-3 create, display, and print a graph of the data in your worksheet and get your message across in a dramatic pictorial fashion. With the Graph command, you can select a pie chart, a line graph, a variety of bar graphs, an XY graph, or a scatter graph. We will study these types of graphs in this project.

We will use the year-end sales analysis worksheet shown in Figure 5-1 to illustrate all the graphs except the XY graph. The worksheet in Figure 5-1 includes the quarter sales for each of six cities in which King's Computer Outlet has a store. Total sales for each quarter and the year are displayed in row 13. The total sales for each of the six cities are displayed in column F.

A1: [W12] READY

| | A | B | C | D | E | F |
|---|---|---|---|---|---|---|
| 1 | | | King's Computer Outlet | | | 12/22/91 |
| 2 | | | Year-End Sales Analysis | | | |
| 3 | | | | | | Total |
| 4 | City | Quarter 1 | Quarter 2 | Quarter 3 | Quarter 4 | Sales |
| 5 | ============ | ============ | ============ | ============ | ============ | ============ |
| 6 | Chicago | 40,135 | 52,345 | 38,764 | 22,908 | 154,152 |
| 7 | Tampa | 48,812 | 42,761 | 34,499 | 56,123 | 182,195 |
| 8 | Atlanta | 12,769 | 15,278 | 19,265 | 17,326 | 64,638 |
| 9 | Dallas | 38,713 | 29,023 | 34,786 | 23,417 | 125,939 |
| 10 | Boston | 34,215 | 42,864 | 38,142 | 45,375 | 160,596 |
| 11 | Oakland | 52,912 | 63,182 | 57,505 | 55,832 | 229,431 |
| 12 | ------------ | ------------ | ------------ | ------------ | ------------ | ------------ |
| 13 | Total | 227,556 | 245,453 | 222,961 | 220,981 | 916,951 |
| 14 | | | | | | |
| 15 | | | | | | |

**FIGURE 5-1**
**The year-end sales analysis report we will use to illustrate graphing with 1-2-3.**

Before going any further, let's build the worksheet shown in Figure 5-1. As a guide, we will follow the first 23 steps in the list of keystrokes given in the Project Summary section at the end of this project.

## THE GRAPH COMMAND

With the worksheet in Figure 5-1 in main computer memory, the first step in drawing a graph is to enter the command /Graph (/G). The **Graph menu** displays at the top of the screen in the control panel as shown in Figure 5-2. The functions of the commands listed in the Graph menu are described in Table 5-1.

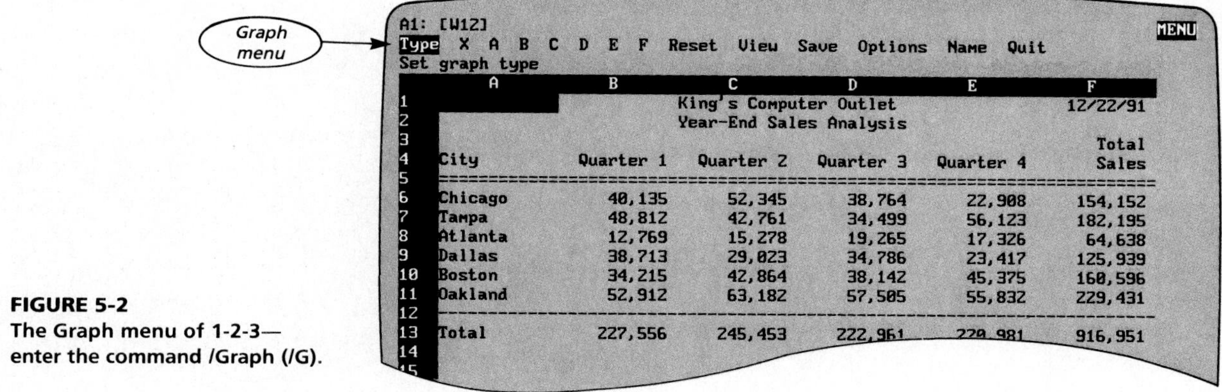


**FIGURE 5-2**
The Graph menu of 1-2-3—enter the command /Graph (/G).

**TABLE 5-1** Commands Available in the Graph Menu

| COMMAND | FUNCTION |
|---|---|
| Type | Allows you to select the type of graph you want to display—Line, Bar, XY, Stacked-bar, Pie. |
| X | Defines a range of labels for the X axis for a line or bar graph. Defines a range of labels to describe each piece of a pie chart. In an XY graph the X range is assigned the X coordinates. |
| ABCDEF | Allows you to define up to six Y-axis data ranges. For example, in a multiple-line graph each data range is represented by a line. |
| Reset | Clears the current graph specifications. |
| View | Displays the current graph. |
| Save | Saves the current graph to disk. 1-2-3 automatically adds the extension .PIC to the graph file. |
| Options | Allows you to define titles or labels for the X and Y axes and for the top of the graph. |
| Name | Allows you to save a set of graph specifications by name. In this way you can have several different graphs associated with the same worksheet. |
| Quit | Quits the Graph command. |

# PIE CHARTS

A **pie chart** is used to show how 100% of an amount is divided. Let's create the pie chart in Figure 5-3. This pie chart shows the percentage of total annual sales for each of the six cities where King's Computer Outlet has a store. The total annual sales for each of the six stores are in the range F6..F11 of the worksheet in Figure 5-4.

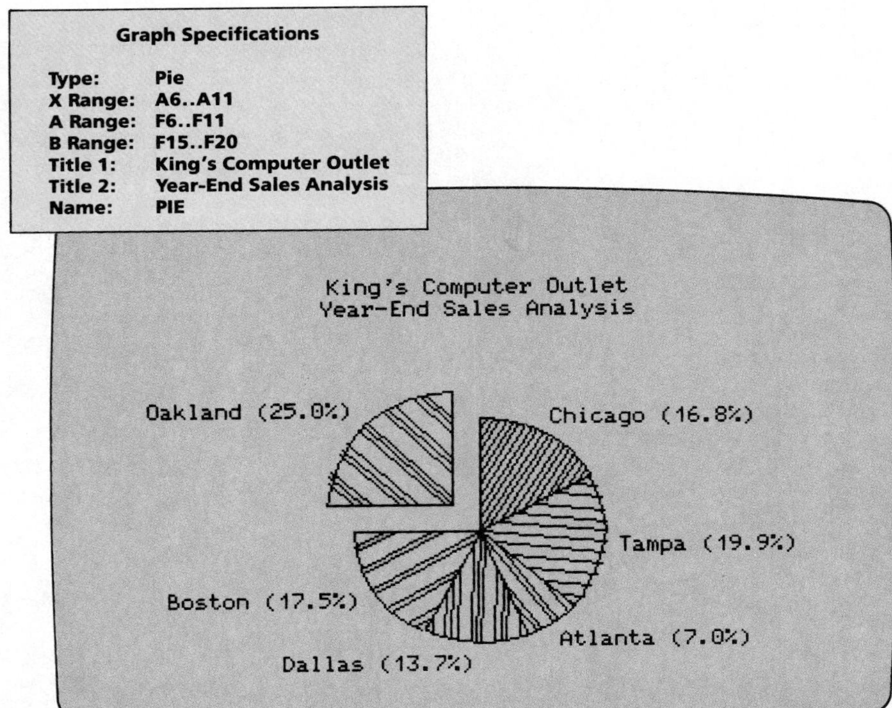


**FIGURE 5-3**
**Pie graph with titles, shading, and "exploded" segment showing the annual sales for each of the six cities in the worksheet in Figure 5-4.**

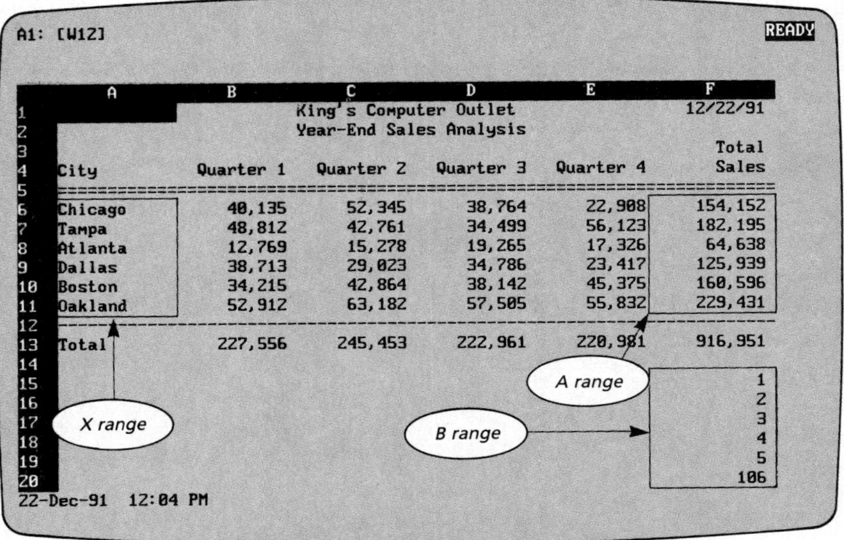


| | A | B | C | D | E | F |
|---|---|---|---|---|---|---|
| 1 | | | King's Computer Outlet | | | 12/22/91 |
| 2 | | | Year-End Sales Analysis | | | |
| 3 | | | | | | Total |
| 4 | City | Quarter 1 | Quarter 2 | Quarter 3 | Quarter 4 | Sales |
| 5 | ========== | ========== | ========== | ========== | ========== | ========== |
| 6 | Chicago | 40,135 | 52,345 | 38,764 | 22,908 | 154,152 |
| 7 | Tampa | 48,812 | 42,761 | 34,499 | 56,123 | 182,195 |
| 8 | Atlanta | 12,769 | 15,278 | 19,265 | 17,326 | 64,638 |
| 9 | Dallas | 38,713 | 29,023 | 34,786 | 23,417 | 125,939 |
| 10 | Boston | 34,215 | 42,864 | 38,142 | 45,375 | 160,596 |
| 11 | Oakland | 52,912 | 63,182 | 57,505 | 55,832 | 229,431 |
| 12 | ---------- | ---------- | ---------- | ---------- | ---------- | ---------- |
| 13 | Total | 227,556 | 245,453 | 222,961 | 220,981 | 916,951 |
| 14 | | | | | | |
| 15 | | | | | | 1 |
| 16 | | | | | | 2 |
| 17 | | | | | | 3 |
| 18 | | | | | | 4 |
| 19 | | | | | | 5 |
| 20 | | | | | | 106 |

**FIGURE 5-4**
**Ranges specified in the worksheet for the pie graph in Figure 5-3.**

To create any graph using 1-2-3, we need to enter the type of graph, the ranges in the worksheet to graph, graph titles, and graph options. Collectively, these are called the **graph specifications**.

With the Graph menu on the screen (see Figure 5-2), enter the command **T**ype **P**ie (TP). This command tells 1-2-3 that we want to create a pie chart as the current graph. The **current graph** is the one that displays when we enter the command /**G**raph **V**iew (/GV).

## Selecting the A Range

After we type the letter P for Pie, the command cursor returns to the Graph menu, the menu that begins with the command Type in Figure 5-2. For a pie chart, we can select only one data range to graph, and it must be assigned as the A range. As shown in Figure 5-4, assign the annual sales for each city (F6..F11) as the A range. Type the letter A. 1-2-3 responds by displaying the prompt message "Enter first data range: A1" on the input line. Enter the range F6..F11 and press the Enter key.

## Selecting the X Range

The X range is used to identify each "slice" or segment of the pie. We must select a range that can identify the cells in the A range. Since the A range is equal to the annual sales for each of the six cities, select the names of the cities (A6..A11) to identify each segment of the pie. With the command cursor in the Graph menu, type the letter X. 1-2-3 responds by displaying the prompt message "Enter X axis range: A1" on the input line. Enter the range A6..A11 and press the Enter key.

After we define the A range and X range, 1-2-3 has enough information to draw a *primitive* pie chart, one that shows the characteristics assigned thus far. With the command cursor in the Graph menu, type the letter V for View and the primitive pie chart in Figure 5-5 displays on the screen. After viewing it, press any key on the keyboard to return to the Graph menu. Once a range has been assigned you may view the pie chart at any time and make changes if you feel the pie chart is not being drawn the way you want it.

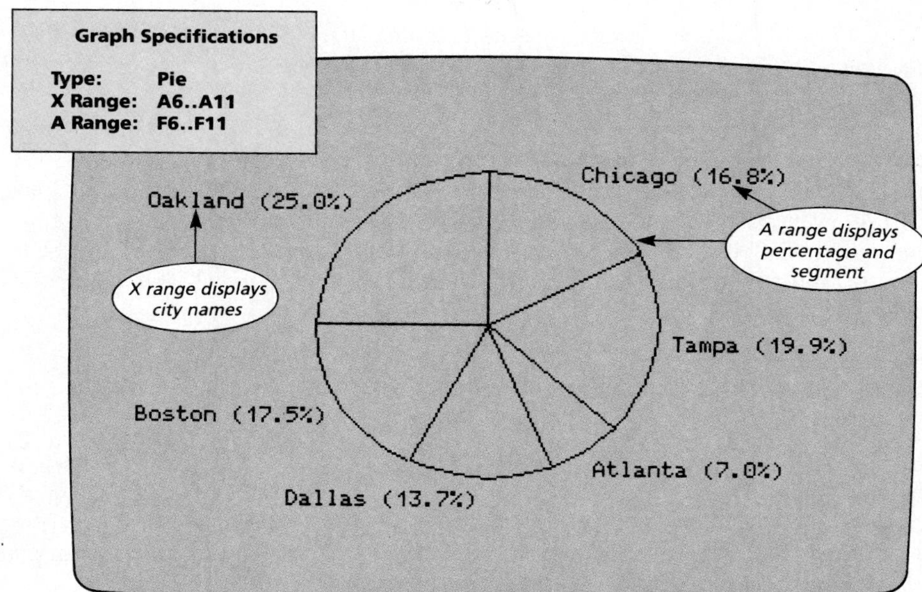


**FIGURE 5-5**
**Primitive pie chart with no titles or shading. Shows the proportion of annual sales contributed by each city in the form of a "slice of the pie".**

It is the A range that causes the pie in Figure 5-5 to be divided into segments. Each segment is proportionate to the annual sales for each city. The A range is also responsible for the percentage value displayed within parentheses outside each segment. The city names outside each segment of the pie are the labels assigned as the X range.

In certain instances, you may want to assign the same group of cells to both the A and X ranges. When both ranges are assigned the same group of cells, the values in the A range that determine the size of each segment of the pie are also used to identify (label) each segment.

## Selecting the B Range

The B range is used to "dress up" the pie chart and make it more presentable and easier to read. Through the use of the B range, you can create segment shading and "explode" a pie chart. An **exploded pie chart** is one in which one or more segments are offset or slightly removed from the main portion of the pie so that they stand out (see Figure 5-3).

The B range is usually set up off to the side or below the worksheet. To shade and explode the pie chart in Figure 5-5 so that it looks more like Figure 5-3, we need to choose six adjacent cells for the B range, one for each pie segment. In each cell, enter a code number between 0 and 7. Each code represents a different type of shading. A code of zero instructs 1-2-3 to leave the corresponding segment of the pie chart unshaded.

Let's use the range F15..F20 to enter the code numbers. The first of the six cells, F15, will refer to the first entry in the A range, Chicago. The last of the six cells will refer to the last entry in the A range, Oakland.

To enter the shading codes, first quit the Graph menu by typing the letter Q. Use function key F5 to move the cell pointer to F15. Enter the shading codes 1 through 5 in the range F15..F19. To explode one or more segments of the pie chart, add 100 to the shading values. Explode the segment representing Oakland by entering the number 106, rather than 6, in cell F20. The six shading codes are shown in the range F15..F20 in Figure 5-4.

Select the range F15..F20 by entering the command /**G**raph **B** (/GB). Enter the range F15..F20 and press the Enter key. Press the V key to view the pie chart. The pie chart (without titles) displays as shown in Figure 5-3. The pie chart is complete. However, we still have to add graph titles. After viewing the pie chart, press any key to redisplay the Graph menu.

## Adding a Title to the Pie Chart

To add the graph titles above the pie chart in Figure 5-3, type the letter O for Options. This causes the **Graph Options menu** to display. With the Graph Options menu on the screen, type the letter T for Titles. We are allowed two title lines—First Line and Second Line—of up to 39 characters each. Type the letter F for First Line. Enter the title—King's Computer Outlet—and press the Enter key. Type the letters T for Titles and S for Second Line. Enter the second line of the title—Year-End Sales Analysis—and press the Enter key.

To quit the Graph Options menu, type the letter Q for Quit. 1-2-3 returns to the Graph menu. The graph specifications for the pie chart in Figure 5-3 are complete. Type the letter V for View and 1-2-3 displays the pie chart with titles as shown in Figure 5-3. To terminate the View command, press any key on the keyboard and the Graph menu redisplays on the screen.

If the title you plan to use for a graph is identical to one in the worksheet, you can press the Backslash (\) key followed by the cell address in place of the title. For example, we could have entered \C1 for the first title and \C2 for the second title, since the titles are identical to the worksheet titles in cells C1 and C2 (see Figure 5-4).

## Naming the Pie Chart

With the command cursor in the Graph menu and the pie chart complete, our next step is to name the graph specifications. That way we can develop a new graph from the same worksheet and still have the pie chart specifications stored away to view and modify at a later time. To assign a name to the graph specifications, type the letter N for Name. The **Graph Name menu** displays at the top of the screen as shown in Figure 5-6. Type the letter C for Create. 1-2-3 displays the prompt message "Enter graph name:" on the input line. Enter the name PIE for pie chart and press the Enter key. After assigning the name, 1-2-3 returns control to the Graph menu.

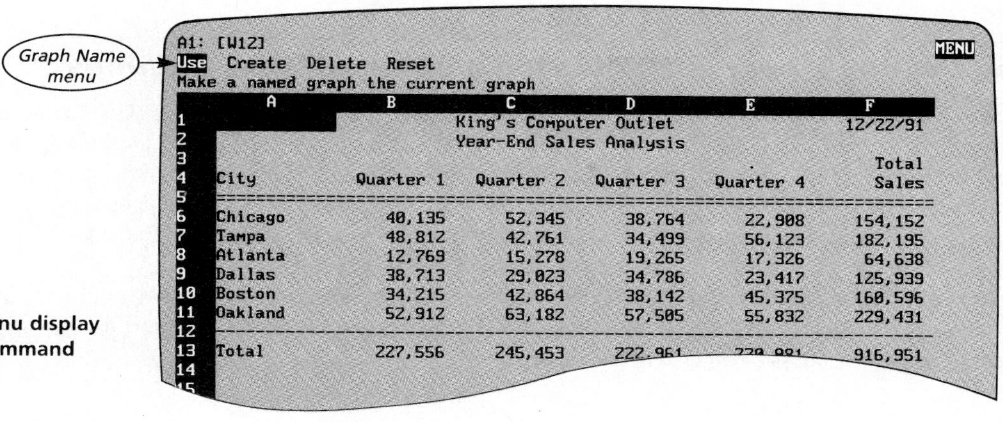

Graph Name menu

```
A1: [W12]                                                              MENU
Use  Create  Delete  Reset
Make a named graph the current graph
        A            B           C            D            E            F
1                            King's Computer Outlet                   12/22/91
2                            Year-End Sales Analysis
3                                                                       Total
4  City           Quarter 1   Quarter 2   Quarter 3   Quarter 4        Sales
5  ===========================================================================
6  Chicago           40,135      52,345      38,764      22,908      154,152
7  Tampa             48,812      42,761      34,499      56,123      182,195
8  Atlanta           12,769      15,278      19,265      17,326       64,638
9  Dallas            38,713      29,023      34,786      23,417      125,939
10 Boston            34,215      42,864      38,142      45,375      160,596
11 Oakland           52,912      63,182      57,505      55,832      229,431
12 ---------------------------------------------------------------------------
13 Total            227,556     245,453     222,961     [illegible]  916,951
14
15
```

**FIGURE 5-6**
**The Graph Name menu display after entering the command /Graph Name (/GN).**

The graph specifications for the pie chart are now stored under the name PIE. Graph names, like PIE, can be up to 14 characters long and should be as descriptive as possible. Table 5-2 summarizes the commands available in the Graph Name menu.

**TABLE 5-2 Summary of the Graph Name Commands**

| COMMAND | KEYSTROKES | FUNCTION |
|---|---|---|
| Use | /GNU | Lists the directory of graph names associated with the current worksheet. Assigns the selected named set of graph specifications as the current graph and displays the graph. |
| Create | /GNC | Saves the current graph specifications as a part of the worksheet so that another graph can be built. This command does not save the graph specifications to disk. |
| Delete | /GND | Deletes the named set of graph specifications. |
| Reset | /GNR | Deletes all graph names and their specifications. |

## The Effect of What-If Analyses on the Pie Chart

Once you have assigned the pie chart specifications to the worksheet, any values changed in the worksheet will show up in the pie chart the next time it is drawn. For example, quit the Graph menu and change the sales amount for Quarter 1 for Chicago in cell B6 from 40,135 to 45,550.

With the worksheet on the screen, press Function key F10 to view the pie chart. When the worksheet is displayed on the screen, it is quicker to press the F10 key to display the current graph than it is to enter the command /GV. Compare the displayed pie chart to the one in Figure 5-3. Note that the segments representing all six cities have changed because of the change in the first quarter sales for Chicago. After viewing the pie chart, press any key on the keyboard to return to the worksheet. Before continuing with this project, change the sales amount for Chicago in cell B6 back to 40,135.

## Saving the Worksheet with the Pie Chart Graph Specifications

When you assign a name, like PIE, to the current set of graph specifications using the /GNC command, they are not saved on disk. To save the named graph specifications you must save the worksheet itself using the File Save command. When the /FS command is used, both the current graph settings and any named graph specifications are saved with the worksheet. To complete the save, first type the letter Q to quit the Graph menu. When the worksheet reappears on the screen, enter the command /**F**ile **S**ave (/FS). When the file name PROJS-5A appears on the input line, press the Enter key. Finally, type the letter R for Replace.

Later, when you retrieve the worksheet, the pie chart specifications will be available and you can display or print the pie chart at any time. If you retrieve the worksheet and decide to change any of the pie chart specifications, you must save the worksheet again or the latest changes will be lost.

## Printing the Pie Chart

Printing a graph is a three-step process: first, save the graph to disk using the command /**G**raph **S**ave (/GS); second, quit 1-2-3; and third, load the PrintGraph program (PGRAPH) into main computer memory and print the graph. The PrintGraph program allows you to print graphs that have been saved with the /**G**raph **S**ave (/GS) command.

Let's print the pie chart by following the three steps described above. With 1-2-3 in the READY mode, enter the command /**G**raph **S**ave (/GS). In response to the prompt message on the input line, enter the file name PIE-5A and press the Enter key. The pie chart (not the worksheet) is saved to disk under the name PIE-5A with an extension of .PIC (picture). We call a graph file, like PIE-5A.PIC, a **PIC file**. With the graph saved, quit the Graph menu and quit 1-2-3.

Our next step is to load the PrintGraph program into main computer memory. If you have a computer with a fixed disk, then at the DOS prompt enter PGRAPH and press the Enter key. If you have a computer with two floppy disks and no fixed disk, replace the 1-2-3 system disk in the A drive with the PrintGraph disk and make sure the disk with PIE-5A.PIC is in the B drive. At the DOS prompt, enter PGRAPH and press the Enter key. After several seconds the **PrintGraph menu** displays on the screen (see Figure 5-7). Table 5-3 describes the commands available in the PrintGraph menu.

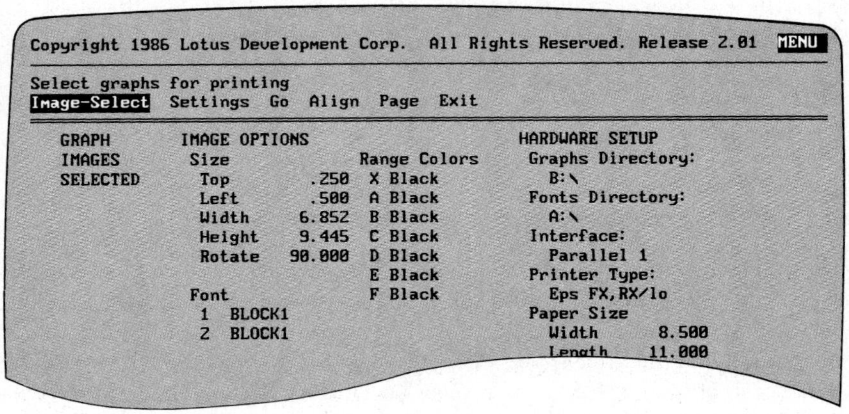

```
Copyright 1986 Lotus Development Corp.  All Rights Reserved. Release 2.01  MENU
Select graphs for printing
Image-Select  Settings  Go  Align  Page  Exit
  GRAPH       IMAGE OPTIONS                          HARDWARE SETUP
  IMAGES        Size                 Range Colors      Graphs Directory:
  SELECTED       Top        .250   X Black               B:\
                 Left       .500   A Black             Fonts Directory:
                 Width     6.852   B Black               A:\
                 Height    9.445   C Black             Interface:
                 Rotate   90.000   D Black               Parallel 1
                                   E Black             Printer Type:
                Font               F Black               Eps FX,RX/lo
                 1  BLOCK1                             Paper Size
                 2  BLOCK1                               Width      8.500
                                                         Length    11.000
```

**FIGURE 5-7**
The PrintGraph menu.

**TABLE 5-3 Summary of PrintGraph Commands**

| COMMAND | FUNCTION |
|---|---|
| Image-Select | Allows you to specify the graph to print. |
| Settings | Lets you set the default drive; adjust the size of the graph; select colors, fonts, and the hardware. |
| Go | Starts printing the graph. |
| Align | Resets the PrintGraph line counter. |
| Page | Ejects the paper in the printer to the top of the next page. |
| Exit | Ends the PrintGraph session. |

With the PrintGraph menu on the screen, type the letter I for Image-Select. PrintGraph displays the **Image-Select menu** (see Figure 5-8). This menu includes a list of all the PIC files on the default drive. Use the Up Arrow and Down Arrow keys to highlight the one to print. In our case, there is only one PIC file and it is highlighted. Press the Enter key to select PIE-5A. The PrintGraph menu shown in Figure 5-7 redisplays on the screen.

Check the printer to be sure it is in the READY mode. Type the letter A for Align and G for Go. The pie chart prints on the printer. Type the letter P for Page to advance the paper to the top of the next page. If the graph fails to print properly, see Lotus's *Getting Started Manual* for a description of the requirements for your hardware.

To the right of the list of PIC files in the Image-Select menu in Figure 5-8 are instructions explaining how to select a graph from the list. Two keys in the instructions that need additional explanation are the [SPACE] and [GRAPH]. [SPACE] represents the Space Bar. This key is used to mark or unmark the highlighted graph in the list. A graph name that is marked has a number sign (#) displayed to the left of the name. All marked graph names print when you use the Go command in the PrintGraph menu. Hence, when you print a second graph, you should unmark the previous one or it will print also.

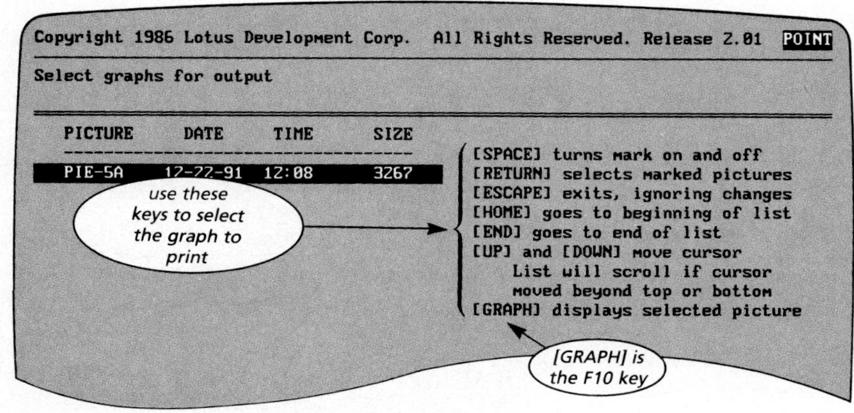


**FIGURE 5-8**
**The Image-Select menu.**

The [GRAPH] key is the function key F10. You may press this key to display the highlighted graph on the screen. When you are finished viewing the graph, press any key to return to the Image-Select menu.

To quit PrintGraph, type the letter E for Exit and Y for Yes to confirm your exit from the PrintGraph program. At the DOS prompt, type 123 to reenter the spreadsheet program.

## LINE GRAPHS

Line graphs are used to show changes in data over time. For example, a line graph can show pictorially whether sales increased or decreased during quarters of the year. The lines are drawn on X and Y axes. You can have from one to six lines in the graph. Each line represents a different data range in the worksheet. We will create two line graphs, one with a single data range and another with six data ranges.

First we will create a line graph with a single data range that shows the trend of the total sales for the four quarters (see Figure 5-9). Begin by resetting the current graph specifications associated with PROJS-5A. That is, clear the pie chart—the current graph—to begin the line graph because the specifications are different. With the Graph menu on the screen, type the letter R for Reset. The **Graph Reset menu** displays at the top of the screen as shown in Figure 5-10. Note that the graph specifications can be reset on an individual basis (X, A, B, C, D, E, F) or for the entire graph (Graph). In this case, reset all the graph specifications. With the command cursor in the Graph Reset menu, type the letter G for Graph. The pie chart is no longer the current graph. Remember, however, that the pie chart specifications are stored under the name PIE and can be accessed at any time using the Graph Name Use command (see Table 5-2).

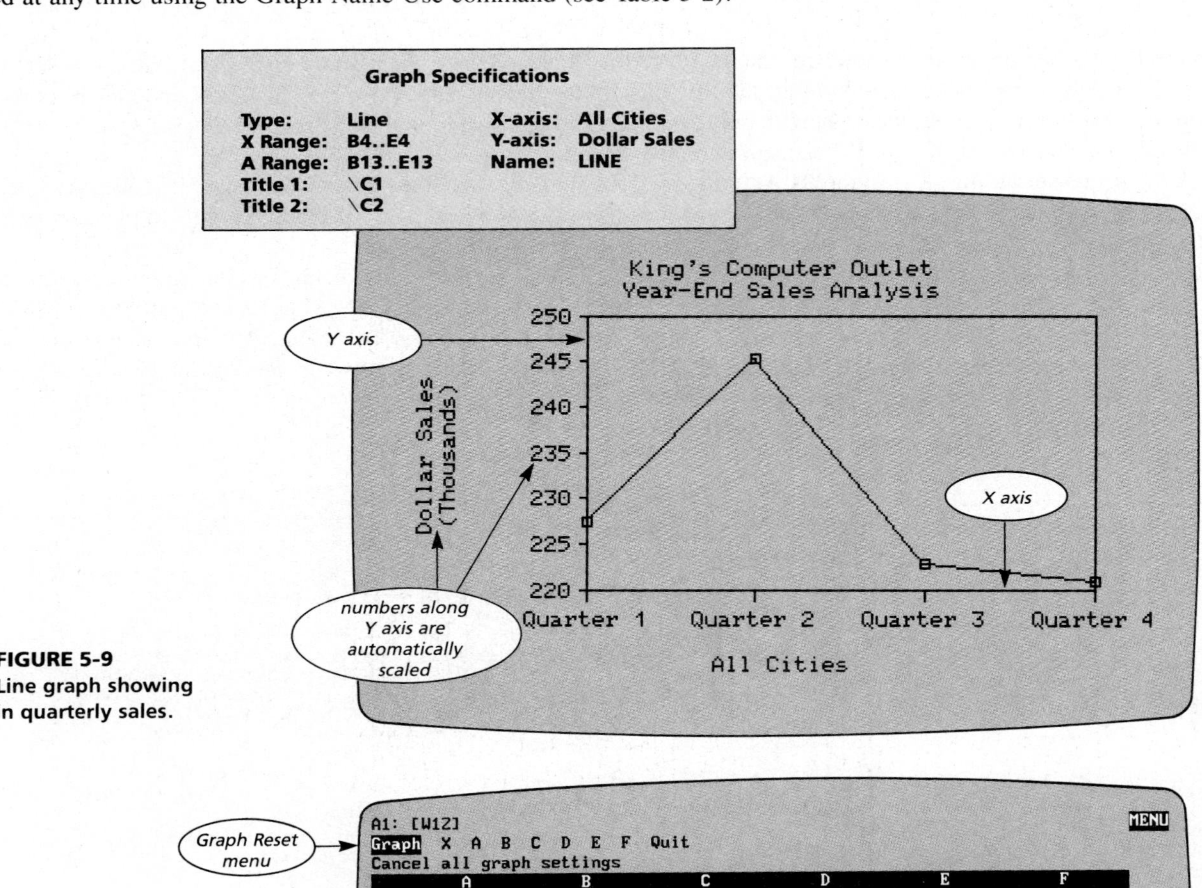


**FIGURE 5-9**
**Line graph showing in quarterly sales.**

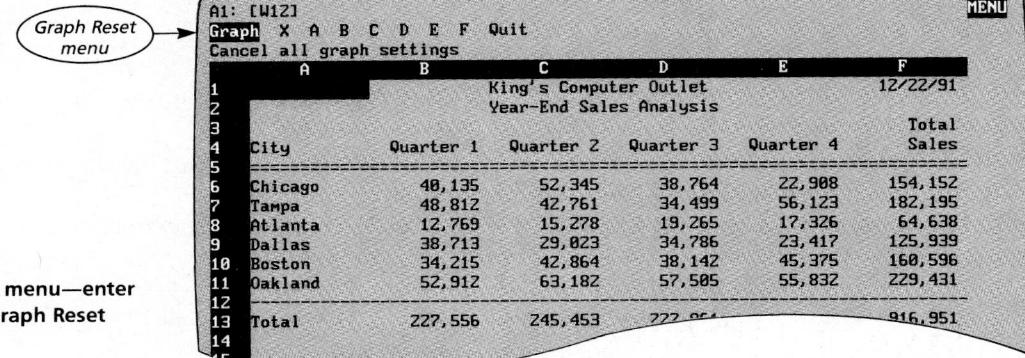


**FIGURE 5-10**
**The Graph Reset menu—enter the command /Graph Reset (/GR).**

The command cursor returns to the Graph menu after resetting the graph specifications. We can now proceed to build the line graph in Figure 5-9. There are four steps involved:

1. With the Graph menu on the screen, enter the command **T**ype **L**ine (TL).
2. Define the X range—the cells that contain the desired labels for the X axis.
3. Define the A range—the cells that include the values that the line graph will represent.
4. Enter the title of the line graph and titles for the X and Y axes.

## Selecting the X Range

With the command cursor in the Graph menu, type the letter X and assign the range B4..E4 to the X range. As shown in Figure 5-11, cells B4 through E4 contain the labels Quarter 1, Quarter 2, Quarter 3, and Quarter 4. These labels display along the X axis in the line graph (see Figure 5-9).

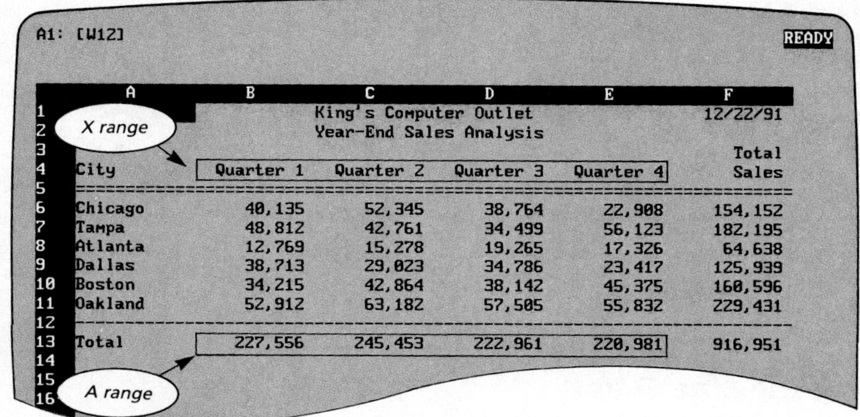


| | A | B | C | D | E | F |
|---|---|---|---|---|---|---|
| 1 | | | King's Computer Outlet | | | 12/22/91 |
| 2 | | | Year-End Sales Analysis | | | |
| 3 | | | | | | Total |
| 4 | City | Quarter 1 | Quarter 2 | Quarter 3 | Quarter 4 | Sales |
| 5 | ========== | ========== | ========== | ========== | ========== | ========== |
| 6 | Chicago | 40,135 | 52,345 | 38,764 | 22,908 | 154,152 |
| 7 | Tampa | 48,812 | 42,761 | 34,499 | 56,123 | 182,195 |
| 8 | Atlanta | 12,769 | 15,278 | 19,265 | 17,326 | 64,638 |
| 9 | Dallas | 38,713 | 29,023 | 34,786 | 23,417 | 125,939 |
| 10 | Boston | 34,215 | 42,864 | 38,142 | 45,375 | 160,596 |
| 11 | Oakland | 52,912 | 63,182 | 57,505 | 55,832 | 229,431 |
| 12 | ---------- | ---------- | ---------- | ---------- | ---------- | ---------- |
| 13 | Total | 227,556 | 245,453 | 222,961 | 220,981 | 916,951 |
| 14 | | | | | | |
| 15 | | | | | | |
| 16 | | | | | | |

**FIGURE 5-11**
**Range specifications for line graph in Figure 5-9.**

## Selecting the A Range

The next step is to select the A range. Assign to the A range the cells that include the values we want the line graph to represent. This is also called the **Y-axis data range**. With the command cursor in the Graph menu, type the letter A and enter the range B13..E13. The desired A range is shown in the worksheet in Figure 5-11.

## Adding Titles to the Line Graph

We can add three different titles to the line graph: (1) line graph title (we are allowed two of these); (2) X-axis title; (3) Y-axis title. Let's add the same line graph title used for the pie chart. For the X axis use the title "All Cities". For the Y axis use the title "Dollar Sales".

To add these titles, type the letter O for Options while the Graph menu is on the screen. The Graph Options menu shown in Figure 5-12 displays. Type the letters T for Titles and F for First. Enter \C1 and press the Enter key. \C1 instructs 1-2-3 to use the label assigned to cell C1 in the worksheet as the first title. Next, type the letters T and S to enter the second title. Enter \C2 and the Enter key. The label in cell C2 serves as the second title.

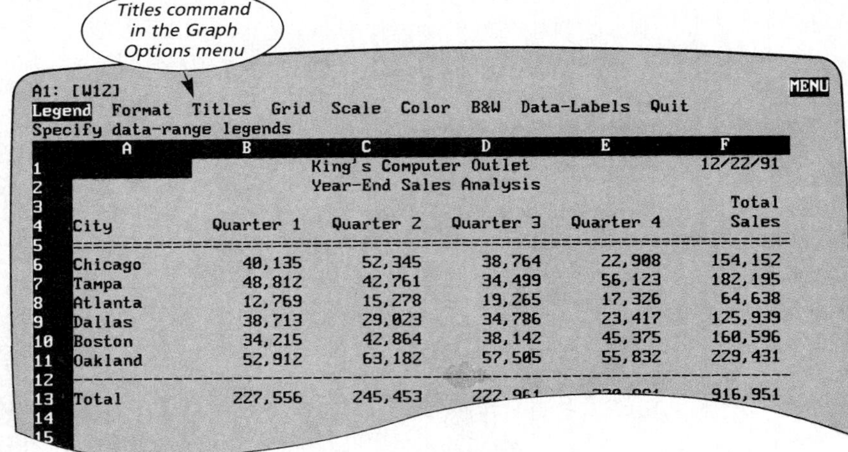


**FIGURE 5-12**
**Graph Options menu allows you to enter a title for the line graph and titles for the X and Y axis.**

Enter the X-axis title by typing the letters T and X and the label "All Cities". Press the Enter key. Enter the Y-axis title by typing the letters T and Y and the label "Dollar Sales". Press the Enter key. Finally, type the letter Q to quit the Graph Options menu.

## Viewing the Line Graph

With the command cursor in the Graph menu, type the letter V for View. The line graph in Figure 5-9 displays. Note that 1-2-3 automatically scales the numeric labels along the Y axis on the basis of the numbers in the A range. The small squares that the line graph passes through represent the points whose coordinates are the corresponding values in the X and A ranges.

You can see from Figure 5-9 that the line graph is useful for showing a trend. The line graph clearly shows that sales for King's Computer Outlet increased significantly during the second quarter and then fell sharply in the third quarter. Finally, there was a slight drop in sales during the fourth quarter. Here again, if we change any numeric values in the worksheet, the line graph will show the latest values the next time we invoke the View command.

After viewing the graph, press any key to redisplay the Graph menu.

## Naming the Line Graph

With the line graph complete and the command cursor active in the Graph menu, type the letters N for Name and C for Create. When 1-2-3 requests the graph name, enter the name LINE and press the Enter key. The line graph specifications are stored under the name LINE.

## Saving and Printing the Line Graph

To save the named graph specifications (LINE) with the worksheet to disk, type the letter Q to quit the Graph menu. Enter the command /**F**ile **S**ave (/FS). Press the Enter key when the file name PROJS-5A appears on the input line. Type the letter R for Replace to rewrite the file to disk. Now there are two sets of graph specifications associated with PROJS-5A—PIE and LINE. The line graph continues to be the current graph.

Make a hard copy of the line graph in the same manner described for the pie chart. That is, with the command cursor in the Graph menu, type the letter S for Save and name the graph LINE-5A. Quit the Graph menu and quit 1-2-3. At the DOS prompt, enter PGRAPH. When the PrintGraph menu displays (see Figure 5-7), type I for Image-Select and select the PIC file LINE-5A. Turn the printer on, type A for Align, G for Go, and P for Page. When the printing activity is complete, quit PrintGraph, load 1-2-3, and retrieve PROJS-5A.

## Multiple-Line Graphs

1-2-3 allows up to six Y-axis data ranges (A–F) and the range of corresponding labels (X) to be assigned to a line graph. When more than one data range is assigned to a line graph, it is called a **multiple-line graph**. The multiple-line graph in Figure 5-13 includes six lines, each representing the four quarterly sales for one of the six cities in the worksheet. Multiple-line graphs like this one are used not only to show trends, but also to compare one range of data to another.

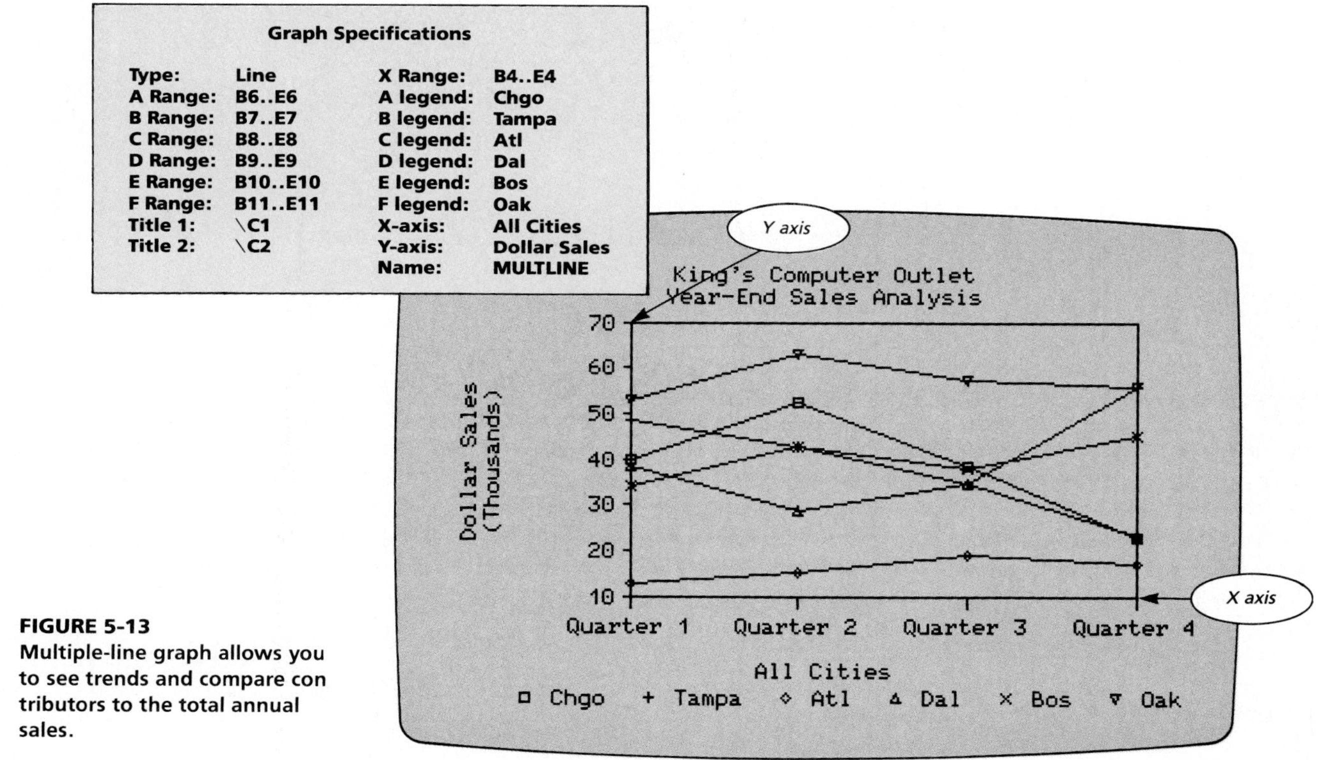


**FIGURE 5-13**
**Multiple-line graph allows you to see trends and compare con tributors to the total annual sales.**

The multiple-line graph in Figure 5-13 uses the same titles, X range, and graph type as the line graph in Figure 5-9, the current graph associated with the worksheet. Therefore, rather than resetting the current graph specifications, modify them.

With the command cursor active in the Graph menu, assign to the six data ranges A through F the quarterly sales of the six cities shown in Figure 5-14. Type the letter A for the A range. Enter the range B6..E6 and press the Enter key. Follow the same procedure for the other five ranges—assign the B range B7..E7, the C range B8..E8, the D range B9..E9, the E range B10..E10, and the F range B11..E11.

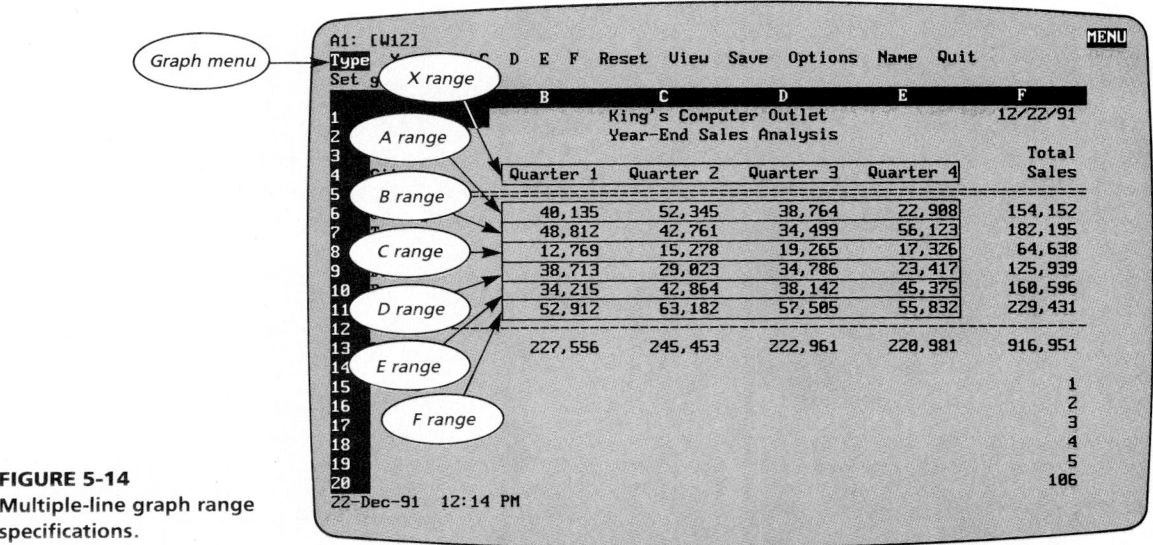


**FIGURE 5-14**
Multiple-line graph range specifications.

## Assigning Legends to the Data Ranges

Before quiting the Graph menu, we need to enter **legends** that help identify each of the six lines that are drawn in the multiple-line graph. Without legends, the multiple-line graph is useless because we cannot identify the lines.

To enter the legend that identifies the A range, type the letters O for Options, L for Legend, and A for A range. From Figure 5-14 we can determine that the A range was assigned the quarterly sales for Chicago (B6..E6). Therefore, enter the label Chgo in response to the prompt message "Enter legend for A range:" on the input line. Assign the abbreviated city names as the legends for the B through F ranges as described at the top of Figure 5-13.

## Viewing the Multiple-Line Graph

Next, type the letter V for View and the multiple-line graph illustrated in Figure 5-13 displays on the screen. The six lines in the graph show the trend in quarterly sales for each of the six cities. The graph also allows us to compare the sales for the six cities. To identify the line that represents a particular city, scan the legends at the bottom of the graph in Figure 5-13. Before each abbreviated city name is a special character called a **symbol**, like the square for Chicago. The line that passes through the square in the graph represents Chicago's four quarterly sales. After viewing the multiple-line graph, press any key to return control to the Graph menu.

## Naming the Multiple-Line Graph

To assign a name to the multiple-line graph specifications, type the letters N for Name and C for Create. When 1-2-3 requests the graph name, enter the name MULTLINE and press the Enter key. The multiple-line graph specifications are stored under the name MULTLINE.

There are now three graphs associated with the worksheet—PIE, LINE, and MULTLINE. However, there is only one current graph. At this point, the current graph is the multiple-line graph, because it was the last one created.

## Saving and Printing the Multiple-Line Graph

Type Q to quit the Graph menu. The worksheet in Figure 5-1 reappears on the screen. Save the worksheet. This ensures that the graph specifications under the name MULTLINE are saved with the worksheet on disk. Enter the command /**F**ile **S**ave (/FS). When the file name PROJS-5A appears on the input line, press the Enter key. Type the letter R to replace the old version of PROJS-5A with the new one.

After saving the worksheet, enter the command /**G**raph **S**ave (/GS) to save the multiple-line graph as a PIC file using the name MLINE-5A. Quit the graph menu and quit 1-2-3. At the DOS prompt enter PGRAPH. Follow the steps for printing a graph outlined earlier.

## Scatter Graphs

A **scatter graph** displays the points (symbols) in a graph without any connecting lines. Sometimes a scatter graph is better able to illustrate what a multiple-line graph is attempting to show. To create the scatter graph shown in Figure 5-15, we need only instruct 1-2-3 not to connect the symbols with lines in the multiple-line graph. Remember, the multiple-line graph is still the current graph.

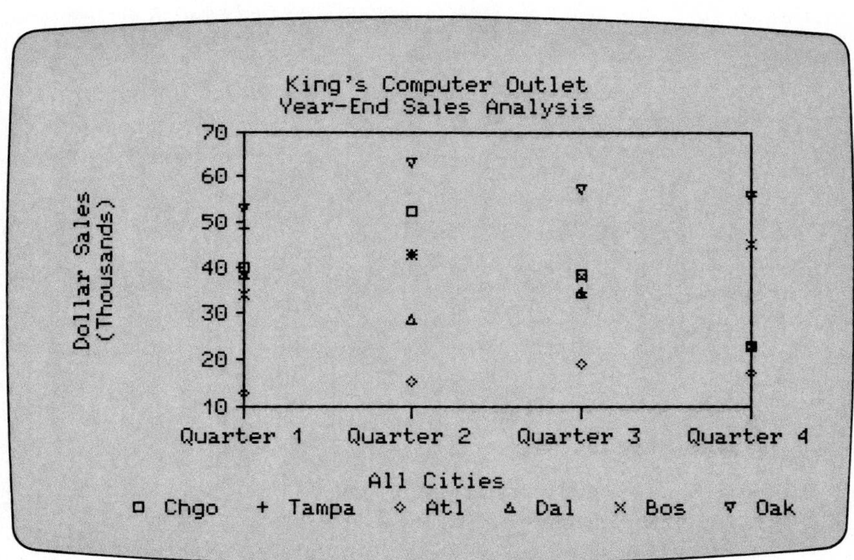


**FIGURE 5-15**
**The scatter graph is an alternative to the multiple-line graph.**

**Changing the Multiple-Line Graph to a Scatter Graph** With the Graph menu on the screen, type the letter O for Options, F for Format, and G for Graph. The default setting for the Format Graph command is Both. This means that both lines and symbols are displayed for the current multiple-line graph. Change this to Symbols so that only the symbols are displayed. Type the letter S for Symbols. Finally, type the letter Q twice, once to quit the Format section of the Graph Options menu and once to quit the Graph Options menu.

**Viewing the Scatter Graph** Type the letter V and the original multiple-line graph (see Figure 5-13) displays as a scatter graph (see Figure 5-15). Here again, the symbols are identified by the legends displayed below the scatter graph. Press any key to redisplay the Graph menu.

**Naming, Saving, and Printing the Scatter Graph** To assign a name to the scatter graph specifications, type the letters N for Name and C for Create. When 1-2-3 requests the graph name, enter the name SCATTER and press the Enter key. Type the letter Q to quit the Graph menu and save the worksheet to disk using the File Save command. Now there are four graphs associated with the worksheet—PIE, LINE, MULTLINE, and SCATTER.

To print the scatter graph, first save it as a PIC file using the /Graph Save (/GS) command and the filename SCAT-5A. Next, quit 1-2-3 and use PGRAPH to print the PIC file SCAT-5A.

## BAR GRAPHS

The **bar graph** is the most popular business graphic. It is used to show trends and comparisons. The bar graph is similar to a line graph, except that a bar rather than a point on a line represents the Y-axis value for each X-axis value. Unlike the line graph that shows a continuous transition from one point to the next, the bar graph emphasizes the magnitude of the value it represents.

We will discuss three types of bar graphs: simple bar graphs, side-by-side bar graphs, and stacked-bar graphs. The following examples change the preceding line graphs to bar graphs. The range settings, titles, and legends remain the same.

### Simple Bar Graphs

A **simple bar graph** has a single bar for each value in the X range. The graph specifications for a bar graph are similar to those for a line graph. Let's create the bar graph in Figure 5-16. It is a bar graph of the same data used earlier for the line graph shown in Figure 5-9. Recall that the line graph showed the trend in total sales for the four quarters.

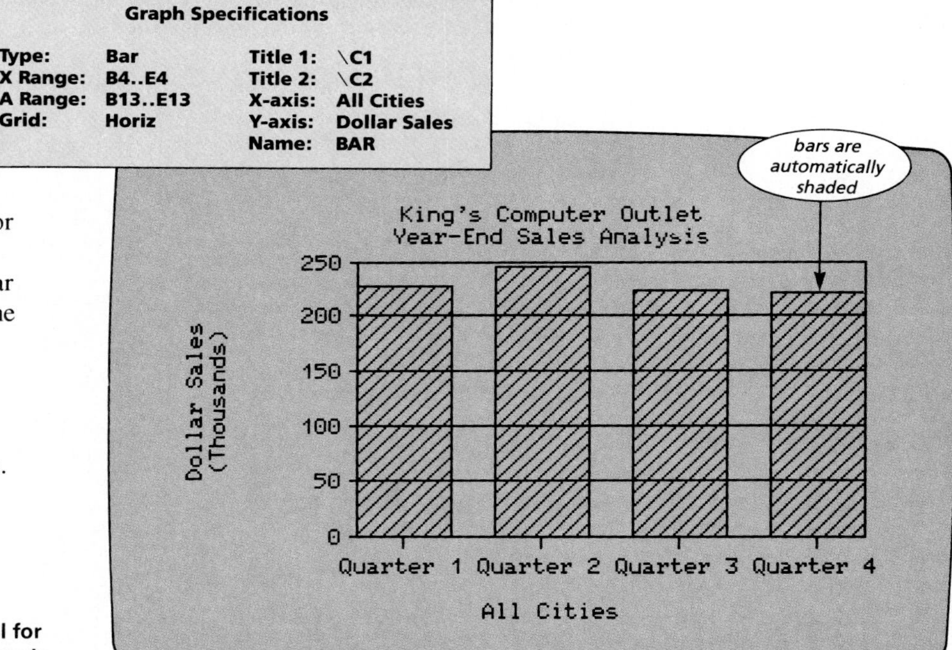


**FIGURE 5-16**
**A simple bar chart is useful for comparing and showing trends.**

**Using a Named Graph** The first step in creating the bar graph is to assign the line graph specifications stored under the graph name LINE as the current graph. Therefore, with the Graph menu on the screen, type the letters N for Name and U for Use. 1-2-3 displays an alphabetized list of all the graph names associated with worksheet PROJS-5A—LINE, MULTLINE, PIE, and SCATTER. With the command cursor on the name LINE, press the Enter key. The line graph in Figure 5-9 immediately displays on the screen. Press any key on the keyboard and the Graph menu reappears. The graph specifications for the line graph (LINE) now represent the current graph.

**Changing the Line Graph to a Bar Graph** With the Graph menu on the screen, type the letters T for Type and B for Bar. The current graph is now a bar graph, rather than a line graph. To improve the appearance of the bar graph and make it easier to read, add a horizontal grid. Type the letter O for Options. With the Graph Options menu displayed, type the letters G for Grid and H for Horizontal. Quit the Graph Options menu by typing the letter Q for Quit.

**Viewing the Simple Bar Graph** Type the letter V for View. The simple bar graph shown in Figure 5-16 displays on the screen. Note that it gives a more static view of the total sales for each quarter as compared to the line graph in Figure 5-9. The horizontal grid in the simple bar graph makes it easier to recognize the magnitude of the bars that are not adjacent to the Y axis. When you are finished viewing the graph, press any key on the keyboard. The Graph menu reappears on the screen.

**Naming, Saving, and Printing the Simple Bar Graph** To name the simple bar graph, type the letters N for Name and C for Create. Enter the graph name BAR and press the Enter key. Type the letter Q to quit the Graph menu. Use the command /**F**ile **S**ave (/FS) to save the worksheet to disk. Press the Enter key when the file name PROJS-5A appears on the input line. Next, press the letter R to replace PROJS-5A on disk with the latest version. Now there are five graphs associated with the worksheet—PIE, LINE, MULTLINE, SCATTER, and BAR.

Save the simple bar graph as a PIC file by entering the command /**G**raph **S**ave (/GS). When 1-2-3 requests a file name, enter BAR-5A and press the Enter key. Use PrintGraph to print the bar graph.

## Side-by-Side Bar Graphs

Like a line graph, a bar graph can have from one to six independent bars (data ranges) for each value in the X range. When a bar graph has more than one bar per X value, we call it a **side-by-side bar graph** (see Figure 5-17). This type of graph is primarily used to compare data. For example, you might want to compare the sales in each quarter for Oakland to the sales of the rest of the cities.

**Graph Specifications**

| | | | |
|---|---|---|---|
| Type: | Bar | A legend: | Chgo |
| X Range: | B4..E4 | B legend: | Tampa |
| A Range: | B6..E6 | C legend: | Atl |
| B Range: | B7..E7 | D legend: | Dal |
| C Range: | B8..E8 | E legend: | Bos |
| D Range: | B9..E9 | F legend: | Oak |
| E Range: | B10..E10 | X-axis: | All Cities |
| F Range: | B11..E11 | Y-axis: | Dollar Sales |
| Grid: | Horiz | Name: | SIDEBAR |
| Title 1: | \C1 | | |
| Title 2: | \C2 | | |

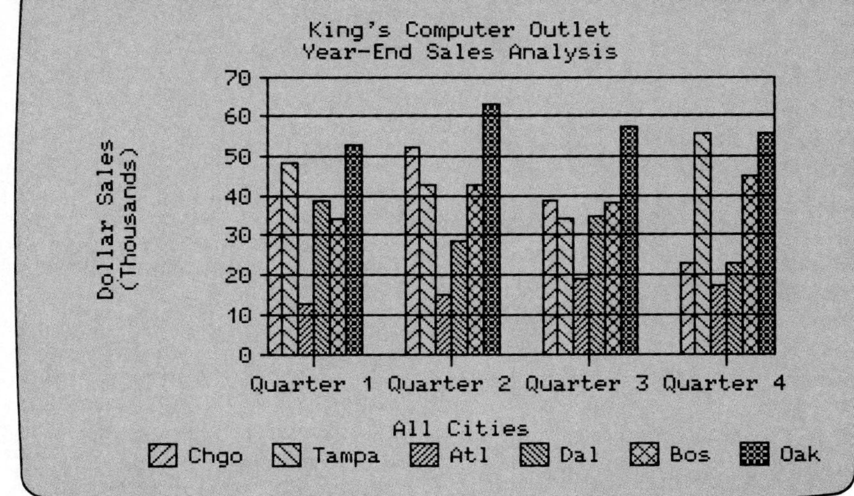


**FIGURE 5-17**
**A side-by-side bar graph allows you to compare the sales in each city on a quarterly basis.**

**Using a Named Graph** To create a side-by-side bar graph, let's assign the graph name MULTLINE as the current graph. With the command cursor in the Graph menu, type the letters N for Name and U for Use. When the list of named graphs display on the screen, select the name MULTLINE and press the Enter key. The multiple-line graph in Figure 5-13 displays on the screen and is assigned to the worksheet as the current graph. Press any key to redisplay the Graph menu.

**Changing the Multiple-Line Graph to a Side-by-Side Bar Graph** Change the current graph from a multiple-line graph to a side-by-side bar graph by typing the letters T for Type and B for Bar. All the other graph specifications (A–F ranges, titles, and legends) remain the same. Add the horizontal grid, as we did earlier with the simple bar graph, by typing the letters O for Options, G for Grid, and H for Horizontal. Quit the Graph Options menu by typing the letter Q.

**Viewing the Side-by-Side Bar Graph** Type the letter V for View. The side-by-side bar graph shown in Figure 5-17 displays on the screen. The different shading that you see for each bar (data range) is automatically done by 1-2-3. The legends below the graph indicate which shaded bar corresponds to which city. Compare Figure 5-17 to Figure 5-13. The side-by-side bar graph is much easier to interpret than the multiple-line graph. For example, it is clear that Oakland had the greatest sales during the first three quarters. For the fourth quarter, Oakland had about the same sales as Tampa. After viewing the graph, press any key to redisplay the Graph menu.

**Naming, Saving, and Printing the Side-by-Side Bar Graph** With the Graph menu on the screen, type the letters N for Name and C for Create to name the side-by-side bar graph. Enter the graph name SIDEBAR and press the Enter key. Next, type the letter Q to quit the Graph menu.

Use the command /**F**ile **S**ave (/FS) to save the worksheet to disk. Press the Enter key when the file name PROJS-5A appears on the input line. Finally, type the letter R for Replace. Now there are six graphs associated with the worksheet—PIE, LINE, MULTLINE, SCATTER, BAR, and SIDEBAR.

With the worksheet on the screen, enter the command /**G**raph **S**ave (/GS) to save the side-by-side bar graph as a PIC file. Use the file name MBAR-5A. Quit 1-2-3 and load PrintGraph into main computer memory. Type the letter I for Image-Select and highlight MBAR-5A. Press the Enter key and the PrintGraph menu redisplays. Type the letters A for Align and G for Go. The side-by-side bar graph shown in Figure 5-17 prints on the printer.

**Graph Specifications**

| | | | |
|---|---|---|---|
| **Type:** | **Stacked-bar** | **A legend:** | **Chgo** |
| **X Range:** | **B4..E4** | **B legend:** | **Tampa** |
| **A Range:** | **B6..E6** | **C legend:** | **Atl** |
| **B Range:** | **B7..E7** | **D legend:** | **Dal** |
| **C Range:** | **B8..E8** | **E legend:** | **Bos** |
| **D Range:** | **B9..E9** | **F legend:** | **Oak** |
| **E Range:** | **B10..E10** | **X-axis:** | **All Cities** |
| **F Range:** | **B11..E11** | **Y-axis:** | **Dollar Sales** |
| **Grid:** | **Horiz** | **Name:** | **STACKED** |
| **Title 1:** | **\C1** | | |
| **Title 2:** | **\C2** | | |

## Stacked-Bar Graphs

One of the problems with the side-by-side bar graph in Figure 5-17 is that it does not show the combined total sales for the six cities for any quarter. An alternative graph to consider is the stacked-bar graph. A **stacked-bar graph** has a single bar for every value in the X range (see Figure 5-18). Each bar is made up of shaded segments. Each segment or piece of the total bar represents an element (city) as a distinct contributor. Together, the stacked segments make up a single bar that shows the cumulative amount (total quarterly sales) of all elements for each value in the X range (quarter).

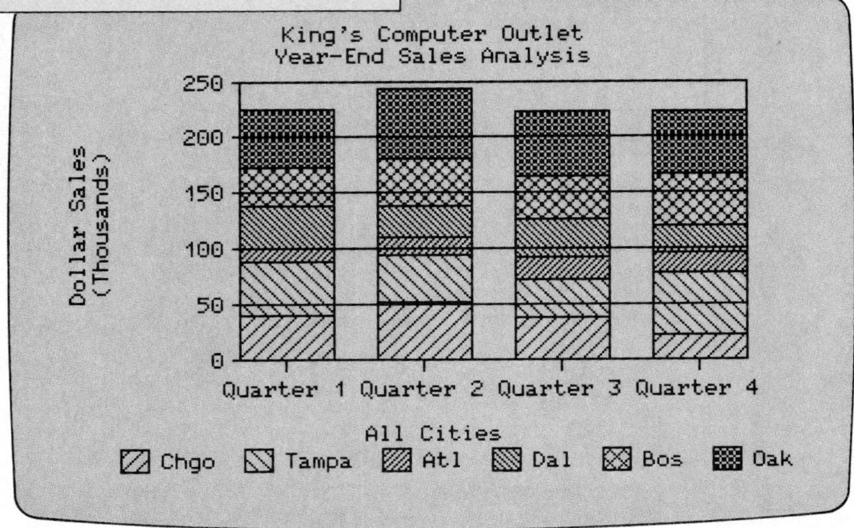


**FIGURE 5-18 A stacked-bar graph allows you to compare the sales in each city on a quarterly basis. It also shows the total sales for each quarter.**

**Changing the Side-by-Side Bar Graph to a Stacked-Bar Graph** The side-by-side bar graph is still the current graph associated with the worksheet. Therefore, let's modify it to display the stacked-bar graph shown in Figure 5-18. With the Graph menu on the screen, enter the command **T**ype **S**tacked-bar (TS). This command changes the side-by-side graph to a stacked-bar graph. All the other graph specifications (A-F ranges, titles, horizontal grid, and legends) remain the same.

**Viewing the Stacked-Bar Graph** Type the letter V for View. The stacked-bar graph shown in Figure 5-18 displays on the screen. Compare Figure 5-18 to Figure 5-17. Notice how the stacked-bar graph shows both the quarterly contributions of each city and the total sales for each quarter. The stacked-bar graph is an effective way of showing trends and contributions from all segments, while still showing a total for each quarter.

**Naming, Saving, and Printing the Stacked-Bar Graph** With the stacked-bar graph still on the screen, press any key to redisplay the Graph menu. Type the letters N for Name and C for Create to name the stacked-bar graph. Enter the graph name STACKED and press the Enter key. Quit the Graph menu by typing the letter Q.

Save the worksheet to disk. Enter the command /**F**ile **S**ave. Press the Enter key when the file name PROJS-5A appears on the input line. Press the letter R for Replace. Now there are seven graphs associated with the worksheet—PIE, LINE, MULTLINE, SCATTER, BAR, SIDEBAR, and STACKED.

Save the stacked-bar graph as a PIC file by entering the command /**G**raph **S**ave (/GS). Use the file name SBAR-5A. Finally, use PrintGraph to print the stacked-bar graph.

## ADDITIONAL GRAPH OPTIONS

Three graph options that we did not cover in this project are the Data-Labels, Scale, and Color/B&W commands.

### Data-Labels

Data-labels are used to explicitly label a bar or a point in a graph. Select the actual values in the range that the bar or point represents. 1-2-3 then positions the labels near the corresponding points or bars in the graph (see Figure 5-19).

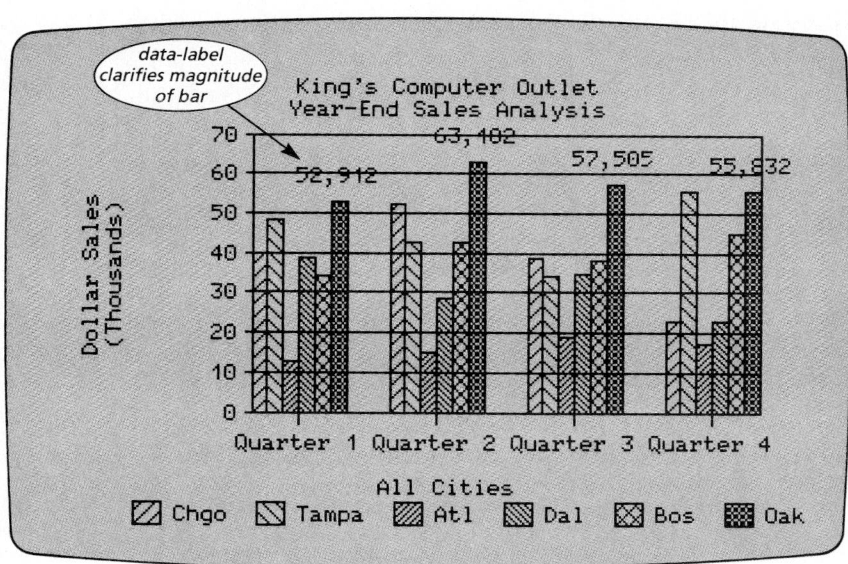


**FIGURE 5-19**
**Data-labels are useful for clarifying and emphasizing various segments of the graph.**

To illustrate the use of data-labels, make the SIDEBAR graph specifications the current graph by entering the command /**G**raph **N**ame **U**se (/GNU). When the alphabetized list of named graphs display on the screen (see Figure 5-20), use the Down Arrow key to select SIDEBAR and press the Enter key. 1-2-3 immediately displays the side-by-side bar graph shown in Figure 5-17. Press any key on the keyboard and the Graph menu reappears on the screen.

*alphabetized listing of the graphs associated with PROJS-5A*

```
A1: [W12]                                                              NAMES
Enter name of graph to make current:
BAR             LINE            MULTLINE        PIE             SCATTER
            A           B           C           D           E           F
1                            King's Computer Outlet                 12/22/91
2                            Year-End Sales Analysis
3                                                                      Total
4   City          Quarter 1   Quarter 2   Quarter 3   Quarter 4        Sales
5   ========================================================================
6   Chicago          40,135      52,345      38,764      22,908      154,152
7   Tampa            48,812      42,761      34,499      56,123      182,195
8   Atlanta          12,769      15,278      19,265      17,326       64,638
9   Dallas           38,713      29,023      34,786      23,417      125,939
10  Boston           34,215      42,864      38,142      45,375      160,596
11  Oakland          52,912      63,182      57,505      55,832      229,431
12  ------------------------------------------------------------------------
13  Total           227,556     245,453     222,961     220,981      916,951
14
15
```

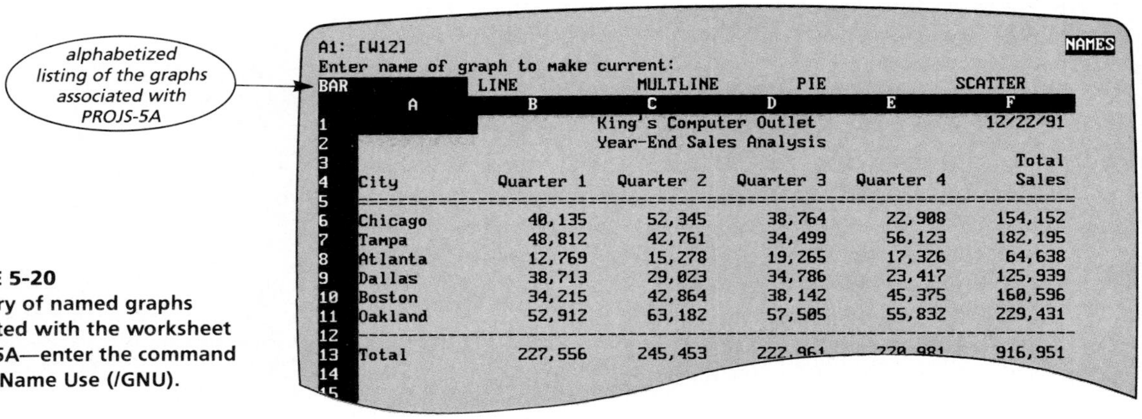

**FIGURE 5-20**
**Directory of named graphs associated with the worksheet PROJS-5A—enter the command /Graph Name Use (/GNU).**

Let's emphasize the four bars in Figure 5-17 that represent the quarterly sales for Oakland by displaying the actual quarterly sales above each corresponding bar. Enter the command **O**ptions **D**ata-Labels (OD). This command causes the **Data Labels menu** to display.

Type the letter F to select the F range because it was assigned the range representing the four quarterly sales for Oakland. The worksheet reappears on the screen and 1-2-3 responds with the prompt message "Enter data label for F range data: A1". Type the range B11..E11 and press the Enter key. The range B11..E11 contains the four quarterly sales for Oakland. Therefore, we are selecting the same range for the F data-label that we selected earlier for the F range.

After we press the Enter key, 1-2-3 prompts us to enter the desired position of the data-labels in the graph. A response to this prompt is only possible for line and XY graphs. For simple and side-by-side bar graphs, 1-2-3 automatically positions data-labels above each bar. Hence, press the Enter key. Next, type the letter Q twice, once to quit the Data-Labels section of the Graph Options menu and once to quit the Graph Options menu. Finally, type the letter V for View. The modified side-by-side bar graph in Figure 5-19 displays on the screen. Notice how the data-labels above the four bars representing Oakland emphasize and clarify them in the graph.

Press any key to redisplay the Graph menu. Type the letter Q to quit the Graph menu. The worksheet in Figure 5-20 displays on the screen.

## Scale Command

When you build a graph, 1-2-3 automatically adjusts the graph to include all points in each data range. The Scale command in the Graph Options menu may be used to override 1-2-3 and manually set the scale on the X or Y axis or both. This command may also be used to specify the display of labels on the X axis and to format the numbers that mark the X and Y axis.

## Color/B&W Commands

If your monitor can display colors, the Color command in the Graph Options menu causes bars, lines and symbols to display in contrasting colors. Alternatively, the B&W command causes the bar and stacked-bar graphs to have crosshatched patterns. The B&W command is the default setting. The Color and B&W commands are mutually exclusive.

## XY GRAPHS

**Graph Specifications**

| | | | |
|---|---|---|---|
| **Type:** | **XY** | **Title 1:** | **Graph of *y* = *x*^2** |
| **X Range:** | **A5..A13** | **Title 2:** | **Between *x* = −2 and *x* = 2** |
| **A Range:** | **B5..B13** | **X-axis Title:** | **X axis** |
| | | **Y-axis Title:** | **Y axis** |

XY graphs differ from the graphs we have discussed thus far. Rather than graphing the magnitude of a value at a fixed point on the X axis, an XY graph plots points of the form (x,y), where x is the X-axis coordinate and y is the Y-axis coordinate. Adjacent points are connected by a line to form the graph (see Figure 5-21). The XY graph is the type of graph used to plot mathematical functions.

In an XY graph, both the X and Y axes are automatically scaled relative to the low and high values, so that all (x,y) points display and the graph fits on the screen. You can switch to manual scaling and scale either the X or Y axis yourself (use the Scale command).

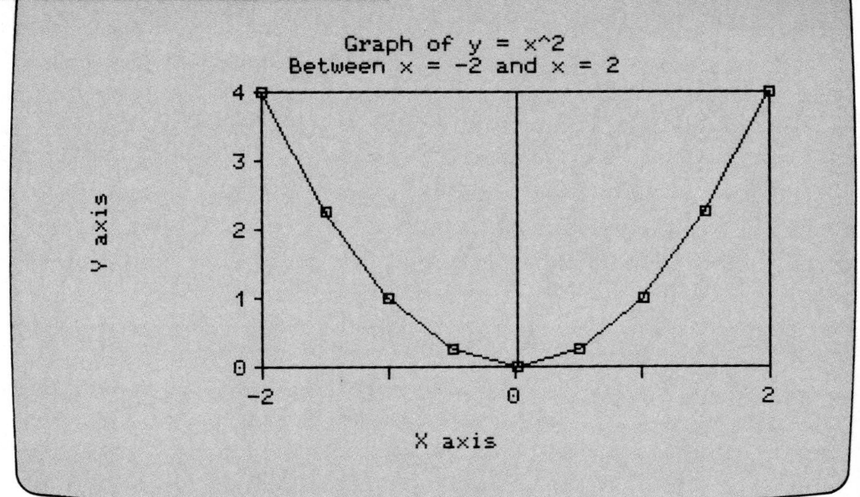


**FIGURE 5-21** The XY graph is useful for plotting mathematical functions.

To illustrate an XY graph, we will use the worksheet in Figure 5-22. As the title indicates, this worksheet includes a table of x and y coordinates for the function y = $x^2$. The x coordinates are in the range A5..A13. They begin at −2 and end at 2 in increments of 0.5. The x coordinates are formed in the worksheet by using the Data Fill command. The y coordinates are determined by assigning the formula +A5^2 to cell B5 and then copying B5 to the range B6..B13. Enter the worksheet in Figure 5-22 by following the first seven steps in the second list of keystrokes in the Project Summary section.

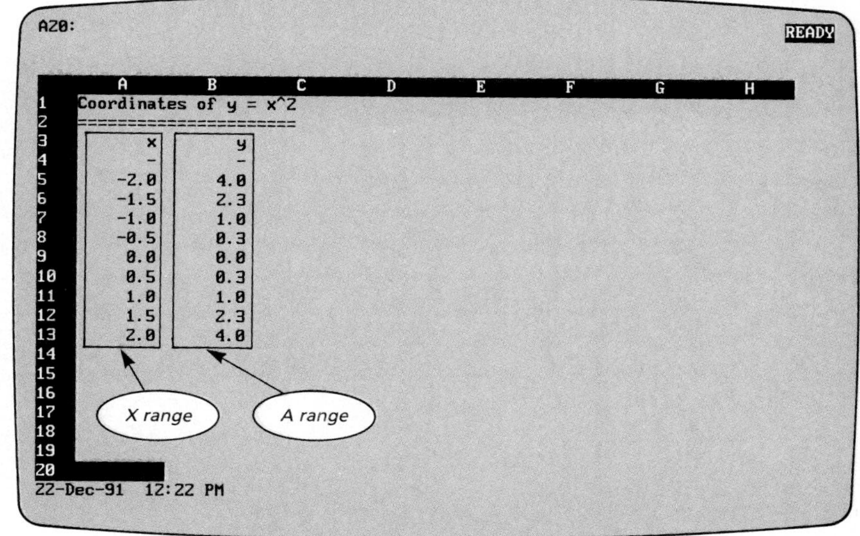


**FIGURE 5-22** The worksheet we will use to plot the function y = $x^2$.

To plot the function y = $x^2$ in the form of an XY graph, enter the command /**G**raph **T**ype **XY** (/GTX). Next, type the letter X to define the X range. Assign the X range the x coordinates (cells A5 through A13). Type the letter A to define the A range. Assign the A range the y coordinates (cells B5 through B13).

To complete the XY graph, let's dress it up using the Graph Options menu. Assign "Graph of y = x^2" to the first line of the title and assign "Between x = −2 and x = 2" to the second line. Label the X axis as "X axis" and the Y axis as "Y axis". Type the letter Q to quit the Graph Options menu.

With the command cursor in the Graph menu, type the letter V for View. The XY graph shown in Figure 5-21 displays on the screen. To return to the Graph menu after viewing the graph, press any key on the keyboard.

Finally, quit the Graph menu and save the worksheet shown in Figure 5-22 as PROJS-5B. Print the XY graph in Figure 5-21 by saving it as a PIC file. Use PrintGraph to print the XY graph.

# PROJECT SUMMARY

In this project, you created several graphs. Each of the steps required to build the worksheets and graphs is listed in the following two tables.

**SUMMARY OF KEYSTROKES—PROJS-5A (Figure 5-1 and Associated Graphs)**

| STEPS | KEY(S) PRESSED | STEPS | KEY(S) PRESSED |
|---|---|---|---|
| 1 | /WGC12↵ (Build worksheet) | 42 | V |
| 2 | →→King's Computer Outlet↓ | 43 | ↵NCLINE↵Q |
| 3 | Year-End Sales Analysis→→→↑ | 44 | /FS↵R |
| 4 | @NOW↵ | 45 | /GSLINE-5A↵ |
| 5 | /RFD1↵ | 46 | AB6.E6↵ (Build multiple-line graph) |
| 6 | ↓↓"Total↵ | 47 | BB7.E7↵ |
| 7 | F5 A4↵City→"Quarter 1→"Quarter 2→ | 48 | CB8.E8↵ |
| 8 | "Quarter 3→"Quarter 4→"Sales↵ | 49 | DB9.E9↵ |
| 9 | F5 A5↵\=↵/C↵.→→→→→↵ | 50 | EB10.E10↵ |
| 10 | ↓Chicago→40135→52345→38764→22908↵ | 51 | FB11.E11↵ |
| 11 | F5 A7↵Tampa→48812→42761→34499→56123↵ | 52 | OLAChgo↵LBTampa↵LCAtl↵ |
| 12 | F5 A8↵Atlanta→12769→15278→19265→17326↵ | 53 | LDDallas↵LEBos↵LFOak↵Q |
| 13 | F5 A9↵Dallas→38713→29023→34786→23417↵ | 54 | V |
| 14 | F5 A10↵Boston→34215→42864→38142→45375↵ | 55 | ↵NCMULTLINE↵Q |
| 15 | F5 A11↵Oakland→52912→63182→57505→ 55832↵ | 56 | /FS↵R |
| 16 | F5 A12↵\-↵/C↵.→→→→→↵ | 57 | /GSMLINE-5A↵ |
| 17 | F5 F6↵@SUM(B6.E6)↵ | 58 | OFGSQQ (Build scatter graph) |
| 18 | /C↵.↓↓↓↓↓↵ | 59 | V |
| 19 | F5 A13↵Total→ | 60 | ↵NCSCATTER↵Q |
| 20 | @SUM(B6.B11)↵ | 61 | /FS↵R |
| 21 | /C↵.→→→→↵ | 62 | /GSSCAT-5A↵ |
| 22 | /RF,0↵A6.F13↵ HOME | 63 | NU→↵ (Build simple bar graph) |
| 23 | /FSPROJS-5A↵ | 64 | ↵TB |
| 24 | /GTP (Build pie chart) | 65 | OGHQ |
| 25 | AF6.F11↵ | 66 | V |
| 26 | XA6.A11↵Q | 67 | ↵NCBAR↵Q |
| 27 | F5 F15↵1↓2↓3↓4↓5↓106↵ | 68 | /FS↵R |
| 28 | /GBF15.F20↵ | 69 | /GSBAR-5A↵ |
| 29 | OTFKing's Computer Outlet↵ | 70 | NUMULTLINE↵ (Build side-by-side bar graph) |
| 30 | TSYear-End Sales Analysis↵Q | 71 | ↵TB |
| 31 | V | 72 | OGHQ |
| 32 | ↵NCPIE↵Q | 73 | V |
| 33 | /FS↵R | 74 | ↵NCSIDEBAR↵Q |
| 34 | /GS | 75 | /FS↵R |
| 35 | PIE-5A↵ | 76 | /GSMBAR-5A↵ |
| 36 | RG (Build line graph) | 77 | TS (Build stacked-bar graph) |
| 37 | TL | 78 | V |
| 38 | XB4.E4↵ | 79 | ↵NCSTACKED↵Q |
| 39 | AB13.E13↵ | 80 | /FS↵R |
| 40 | OTF\C1↵TS\C2↵ | 81 | /GSSBAR-5A↵ |
| 41 | TXAll Cities↵TYDollar Sales↵Q | | |

**SUMMARY OF KEYSTROKES—PROJS-5B (Figures 5-21 and 5-22)**

| STEPS | KEY(S) PRESSED | STEPS | KEY(S) PRESSED |
|---|---|---|---|
| 1 | /WEY | 10 | AB5.B13↵ |
| 2 | Coordinates of y = x^2↓ | 11 | OTFGraph of y = x^2↵ |
| 3 | =======================↓ | 12 | TSBetween x = -2 and x = 2↵ |
| 4 | "x→"y↓"-←"-↓ | 13 | TXX axis↵ |
| 5 | /DFA5.A13↵-2↵0.5↵↵ | 14 | TYY axis↵Q |
| 6 | → +A5^2↵/C↵B6.B13↵ | 15 | V |
| 7 | /RFF1↵A5.B13↵ | 16 | ↵Q/FSPROJS-5B↵ |
| 8 | /GTX (Start XY graph) | 17 | /GSXY-5B↵ |
| 9 | XA5.A13↵ | 18 | Q/QY |

The following list summarizes the material covered in Project 5:

1. 1-2-3 allows you to create, display, and print a graph of the data in your worksheet and get your message across in a dramatic pictorial fashion.
2. The first step in drawing a graph is to enter the command /**G**raph (/G). This command activates the command cursor in the **Graph menu**.
3. A **pie chart** is used to show how 100% of an amount is divided.
4. With a pie chart, you are allowed only three ranges. The A range specifies the data that is used to segment the pie. The X range is assigned the range of labels that identify the segments. The B range is used to shade and explode segments of the pie chart.
5. Through the Graph Options menu, you can assign two title lines of 39 characters each to identify the graph. Except on the pie chart, you may also add titles of up to 39 characters each for the X axis and Y axis. Titles may be entered by keying in the title or by keying in a cell address preceded by a backslash (\).
6. When numbers are changed in a worksheet, the current graph will reflect the changes the next time it is displayed.
7. The command /**G**raph **N**ame **C**reate (/GNC) can be used to store the current graph specifications under a name. This allows you to have more than one set of graph specifications associated with a worksheet. To assign a named set of graph specifications as the current graph, use the command /**G**raph **N**ame **U**se (/GNU).
8. To save any named graph specifications to disk, you must save the worksheet. Use the /**F**ile **S**ave (/FS) command.
9. The command /**G**raph **R**eset (/GR) allows you to reset all the current graph specifications or any individual ones.
10. Printing a graph is a three-step process: first, save the graph to disk as a PIC file; second, quit 1-2-3; and third, use the PrintGraph program (PGRAPH) to print the graph.
11. **Line graphs** are used to show trends. You may have from one to six lines drawn in the graph. Each line represents a different data range (A through F) in the worksheet.
12. In a line graph, assign the labels for the X axis to the X range and assign the data ranges to the A through F ranges.
13. When more than one line is assigned to a line graph, it is called a **multiple-line graph**. Multiple-line graphs are used to show trends and comparisons.
14. To identify the lines in a multiple-line graph, use the Legends command in the Graph Options menu.
15. A **scatter graph** displays the points in a graph without any connecting lines.
16. To create a scatter graph, follow the steps for a multiple-line graph. Next, through the Graph Options menu, use the Format Graph Symbols command to draw the symbols and delete the connecting lines.
17. A **bar graph** is used to show trends and comparisons.
18. A **simple bar graph** has a single bar (A range) for each value in the X range.
19. To add a horizontal grid to a graph, display the Graph Options menu and type the letters G for Grid and H for Horizontal.
20. A **side-by-side bar graph** is used to compare multiple data ranges. A side-by-side bar graph may have up to six bars per X range value.

### Project Summary (continued)

21. A **stacked-bar** graph shows one bar per X range value. However, the bar shows both the sum of the parts and the individual contributors.
22. 1-2-3 automatically scales the Y axis for bar and line graphs and the X and Y axes for XY graphs. If you prefer to set the scales manually, use the Scale command in the Graph Options menu.
23. The Color and B&W commands in the Graph Options menu are used to display graphs in color or in black and white.
24. Data-labels are used to explicitly label a bar or point in a graph. You may label any of the six data ranges A through F.
25. **XY graphs** are used to plot mathematical functions. In an XY graph the X range is assigned the X-axis values and the A range is assigned the Y-axis values.

# STUDENT ASSIGNMENTS

## STUDENT ASSIGNMENT 1: True/False

**Instructions:** Circle T if the statement is true or F if the statement is false.

T F 1. A pie chart is used to show a trend.
T F 2. The Save command in the Graph Options menu saves the worksheet.
T F 3. A PIC file contains a worksheet.
T F 4. The Print Graph program is used to print PIC files.
T F 5. A pie chart can have from one to six data ranges.
T F 6. The B range is used to shade the segments of a pie chart.
T F 7. A line graph can have from one to six lines.
T F 8. To store the graph specifications assigned to a worksheet under a name, save the worksheet using the Save command in the Graph menu.
T F 9. Multiple-line graphs are used to show trends and comparisons.
T F 10. If the title for a graph is the same as a label in a cell of the corresponding worksheet, enter the cell address preceded by a circumflex (^) for the title.
T F 11. Legends are used to identify the bars and lines in a graph.
T F 12. Data-labels are used to clarify a bar or a point in a graph.
T F 13. A scatter graph shows a random sample of points in the graph.
T F 14. Side-by-side bar graphs are used to compare data ranges for the same period.
T F 15. A stacked-bar graph differs from a side-by-side bar graph in that it shows the combined total of the contributors.
T F 16. 1-2-3 automatically scales the axes in a graph unless you use the Scale command in the Graph Options menu.
T F 17. The XY command in the Graph Type menu is used to display a bar graph.
T F 18. The Reset command in the Graph Options menu allows you to reset individual graph specifications, like the ranges A through F.
T F 19. There can be only one current graph assigned to a worksheet.
T F 20. The Graph Retrieve command is used to assign a named graph as the current graph.

## STUDENT ASSIGNMENT 2: Multiple Choice

**Instructions:** Circle the correct response.

1. Which of the following types of graphs can you draw with 1-2-3?
   a. line b. bar c. pie d. XY e. all of these
2. Which of the following ranges are meaningless for a pie chart?
   a. X b. A c. B d. C through F

3. A pie chart is used to show __________ .
   a. how 100% of an amount is divided
   b. trends
   c. how two or more data ranges compare
   d. none of these
4. A side-by-side bar graph can have up to __________ bars per value in the X range.
   a. 3 b. 5 c. 6 d. 8
5. Data-labels are used to ______________ .
   a. assign a title to the graph
   b. define which bar or line belongs to which data range
   c. clarify points and bars in a graph
   d. scale the X and Y axes
6. To explode a segment of a pie chart, add __________ to the corresponding cell in the ______________ range.
   a. 10, C b. 100, B c. 1000, A d. none of these
7. In a stacked-bar graph each bar shows __________ .
   a. the total amount for a label in the X range
   b. the contribution of each participant
   c. none of these
   d. both a and b
8. Which one of the following commands in the Graph menu displays the current graph?
   a. View b. Type c. Save d. both a and b

## STUDENT ASSIGNMENT 3: Understanding Graph Commands

**Instructions:** Describe the function of each of the following commands.

a. /G ________________
b. /GRG ________________
c. /GNU ________________
d. /GO ________________
e. /GTB ________________
f. /GTP ________________
g. /GOTF ________________
h. /GRXQ ________________
i. /GS ________________
j. /GV ________________
k. /GQ ________________
l. /GND ________________
m. /GTS ________________
n. /GNC ________________
o. /GOL ________________
p. /GOD ________________

## STUDENT ASSIGNMENT 4: Understanding the Graph Options

**Instructions:** Describe the purpose of the following titled sections in the Graph Options menu.

a. DATA-LABELS

   Purpose: ________________________________________

b. TITLES

   Purpose: ________________________________________

c. LEGEND

   Purpose: ________________________________________

d. SCALE

   Purpose: ________________________________________

e. FORMAT

   Purpose: ________________________________________

**Student Assignment 4 (continued)**

f. GRID

Purpose: ______________________________

g. COLOR

Purpose: ______________________________

h. B&W

Purpose: ______________________________

i. QUIT

Purpose: ______________________________

## STUDENT ASSIGNMENT 5: Drawing a Pie Chart

**Instructions:** Load 1-2-3. Retrieve the worksheet PROJS-2 built in Project 2 (see Figure 2-2).

Draw a pie chart that shows the revenue contribution for each month to the total quarterly revenue in the first quarter sales report. The pie chart should resemble the one shown in Figure 5-23. Use the following graph specifications:

| | | |
|---|---|---|
| Type = Pie | A range = B4..D4 | Title 1 = \B1 |
| X range = B2..D2 | B range = E4..E6 (explode the February revenue) | Title 2 = TOTAL REVENUE |

Save the worksheet with the graph specifications as STUS5-5. Save the graph as STUSP5-5.PIC. Use PrintGraph to print the pie chart.

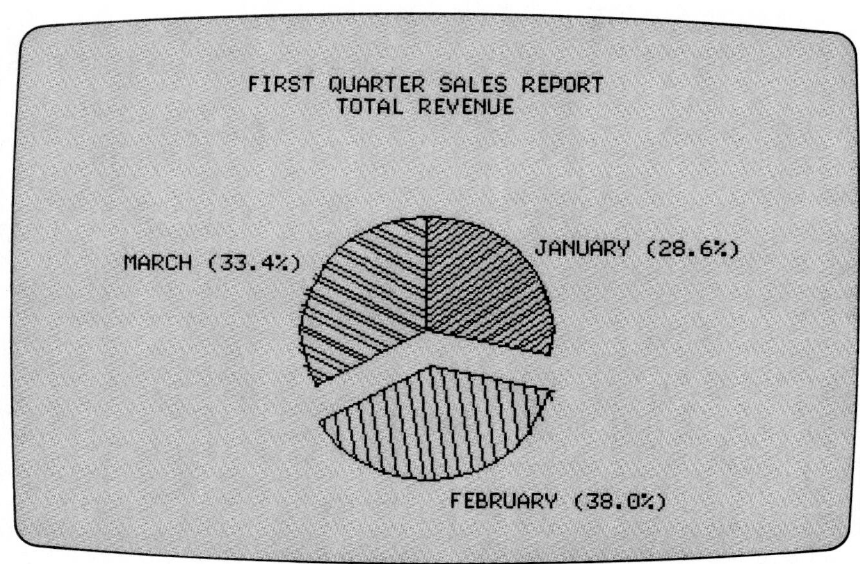


**FIGURE 5-23**
**Student Assignment 5**

## STUDENT ASSIGNMENT 6: Drawing a Multiple-Line Graph and Side-by-Side Bar Graph

**Instructions:** Load 1-2-3. Retrieve the worksheet PROJS-2 built in Project 2 (see Figure 2-2).

Draw a multiple-line graph and a side-by-side bar graph that show the trends in the revenue, costs, and profit of the first quarter sales report. The multiple-line graph should resemble the one shown in Figure 5-24. The side-by-side bar graph should resemble the one shown in Figure 5-25. Name the multiple-line graph MULTLINE and the side-by-side bar graph SIDEBAR.

Use the following graph specifications:

Type = Line
X range = B2..D2
A range = B4..D4
B range = B5..D5
C range = B6..D6
Title 1 = \B1
Y axis title = Dollars
A legend = \A4
B legend = \A5
C legend = \A6

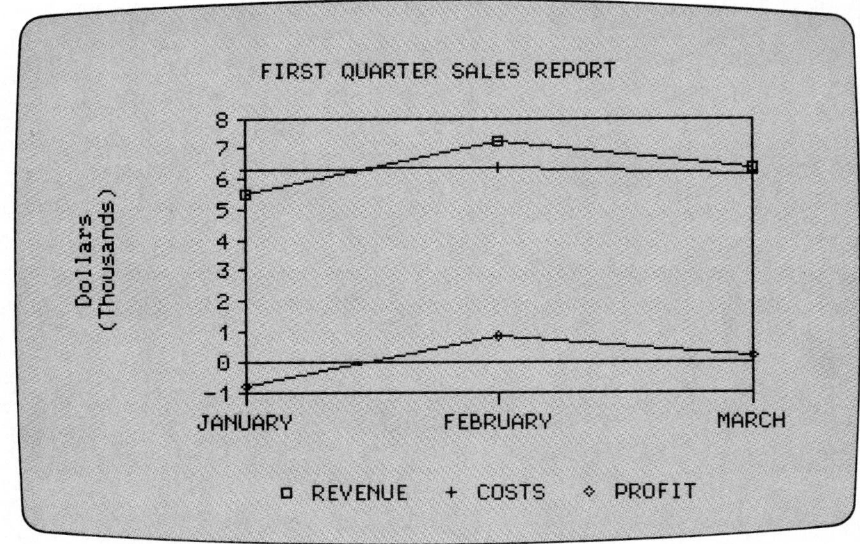


**FIGURE 5-24**
**Student Assignment 6A**

For the side-by-side bar graph, change the Type to Bar. Save the worksheet as STUS5-6. Save the multiple-line graph as STUSM5-6.PIC and the side-by-side bar graph as STUSS5-6.PIC. Use PrintGraph to print both graphs.

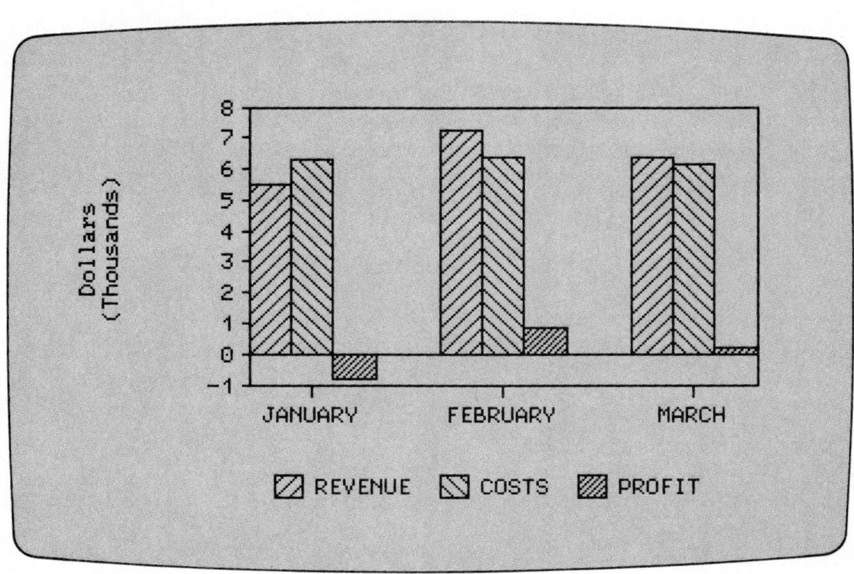


**FIGURE 5-25**
**Student Assignment 6B**

## STUDENT ASSIGNMENT 7: Drawing a Stacked-Bar Graph

**Instructions:** Load 1-2-3. Retrieve the worksheet PROJS-3 built in Project 3 (see Figure 3-1).

Draw a stacked-bar graph that shows the individual contributions of each expense category and the total estimated expenses for each of the three months. The stacked-bar graph should resemble the one shown in Figure 5-26.

Use the following graph specifications:

Type = Stacked-bar
X range = B5..D5
A range = B15..D15
B range = B16..D16
C range = B17..D17
D range = B18..D18
E range = B19..D19
Title 1 = \A1

Title 2 = Estimated Expenses
Y axis title = Dollars
A legend = Mfg.
B legend = Res.
C legend = Mktg.
D legend = Adm.
E legend = Fulfill.
Grid = Horizontal

Save the worksheet with the stacked-bar graph specifications as STUS5-7. Save the stacked-bar graph as STUSS5-7.PIC. Use PrintGraph to print the stacked-bar graph.

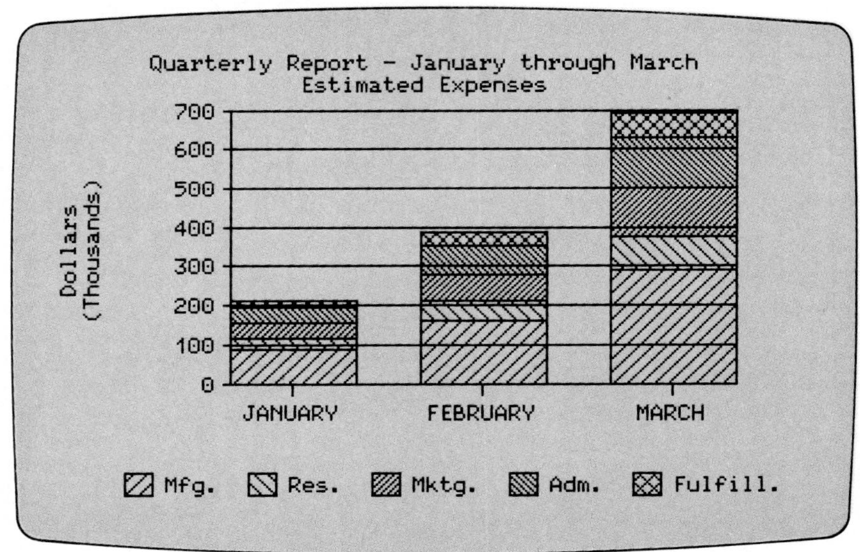


**FIGURE 5-26**
**Student Assignment 7**

## STUDENT ASSIGNMENT 8: Building a Table of Coordinates and Drawing the Corresponding XY Graph

**Instructions:** Load 1-2-3. Build the table of coordinates for the function $y = 2x^3 + 6x^2 - 18x + 6$ shown in Figure 5-27 and draw the corresponding XY graph shown in Figure 5-28.

For the worksheet, use the Data Fill command to build the column of X coordinates in the range A6..A20. Start with –5, increment by 0.5, and stop at 8191. Assign the formula 2*A6^3+6*A6^2–18*A6+6 to B6. Copy B6 to the range B7..B20. Format the range A6..B20 to the Fixed type with 1 decimal position.

For the XY graph (see Figure 5-28), use the following graph specifications:

Type = XY
X range = A6..A20
A range = B6..B20
Title 1 = Graph of y = 2x^3 + 6x^2 − 18x + 6
X axis title = X axis
Y axis title = Y axis

Save the worksheet with XY graph specifications as STUS5-8. Save the graph as STUSX5-8.PIC. Use PrintGraph to print the XY graph.

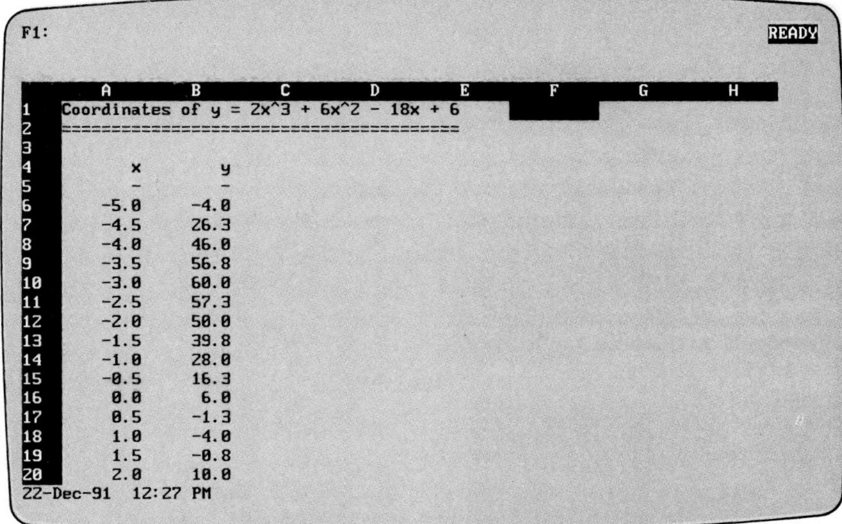


**FIGURE 5-27**
**Student Assignment 8 worksheet**

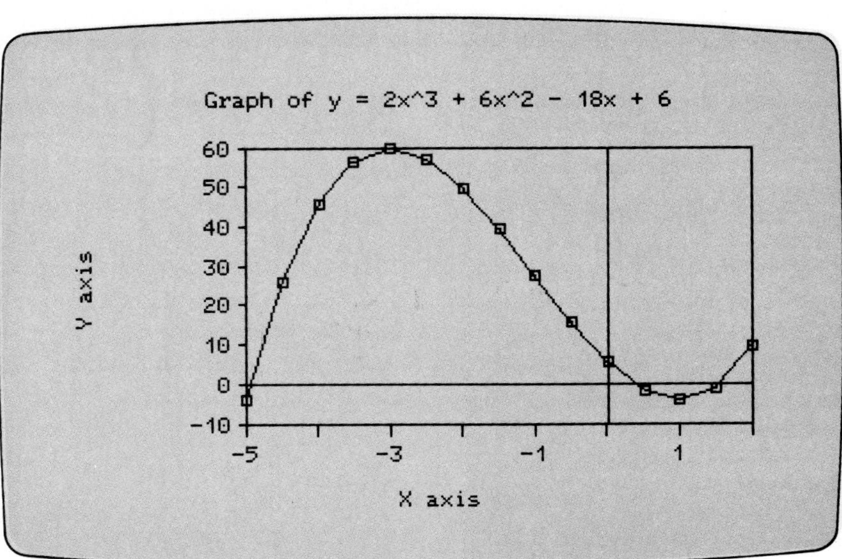


**FIGURE 5-28**
**Student Assignment 8 XY graph**

# PROJECT 6

## Sorting and Querying a Worksheet Database

### Objectives

You will have mastered the material in this project when you can:

- Define the terms database, DBMS, field, field name, and record.
- Differentiate between records in ascending and descending sequence.
- Sort a database on the basis of a primary key.
- Sort a database on the basis of both primary and secondary keys.
- Establish criteria for selecting records in a database.
- Find records in a database that match specified criteria.
- Extract records from a database that match specified criteria.
- Apply the database functions to generate information about the database.
- Utilize the lookup functions to select values from a list or a table.

In this project we will discuss some of the database capabilities of 1-2-3. A **database** is an organized collection of data. For example, a telephone book, a grade book, and a list of company employees are databases. In these cases, the data related to a person is called a **record**, and the data items that make up a record are called **fields**. In a telephone book database, the fields are name, address, and telephone number.

A worksheet's row and column structure can easily be used to organize and store a database (see Figure 6-1). Each row of a worksheet can be used to store a record and each column can store a field. Furthermore, a row of column headings at the top of the worksheet can be used as **field names** to identify each field.

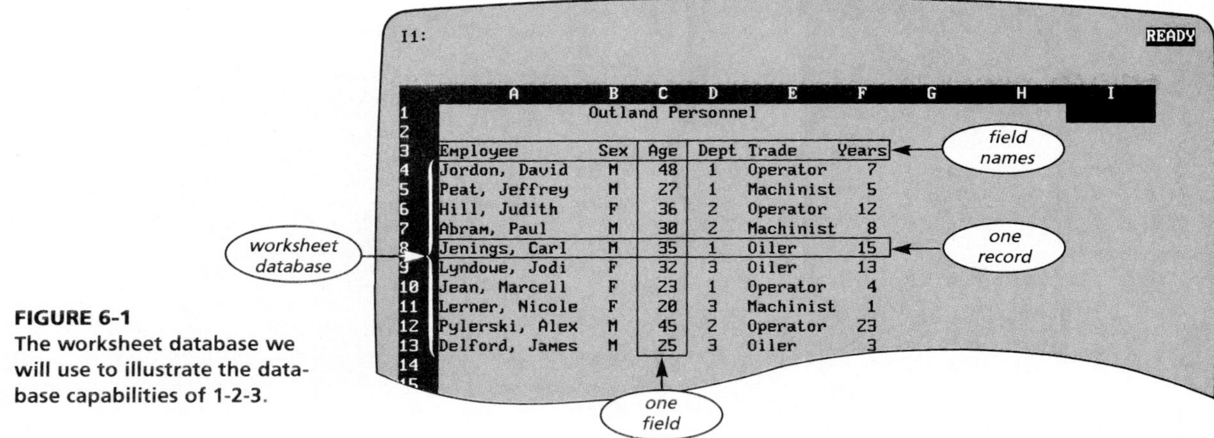


**FIGURE 6-1**
**The worksheet database we will use to illustrate the database capabilities of 1-2-3.**

A **database management system (DBMS)** is a software package that is used to create a database and store, access, sort, and make additions, deletions, and changes to that database. Although somewhat limited by the number of records that can be stored, 1-2-3 is capable of carrying out all the DBMS functions. In many ways, we have already used 1-2-3 as a database management system when we built, formatted, and enhanced our worksheets in the earlier projects.

In this project, we will focus on the two functions of a DBMS that we have not yet discussed—sorting and accessing records. We also discuss the special database and table lookup functions available with 1-2-3. For the remainder of this project, the term database will mean worksheet database.

The database for this project is illustrated in Figure 6-1. It consists of 10 personnel records. Each record represents an employee for the Outland Company. The names, columns, types, and sizes of the fields are described in Table 6-1. Since the database is visible on the screen, it is important that it be readable. Therefore, most of the field sizes (column widths) in Table 6-1 are determined from the column headings (field names) and not the maximum length of the data as is the case with most database management systems. For example, column E represents the Trade field, which has a width of nine characters because the longest trade designation is machinist (nine characters). Column F, which represents the years of seniority, is five characters wide because the field name Years is five letters long. The column headings in the row immediately above the first record (row 3) play an important role in the database commands issued to 1-2-3.

**TABLE 6-1 Field Descriptions for the Outland Personnel Database**

| FIELD NAME | COLUMN | TYPE OF DATA | SIZE |
|---|---|---|---|
| Employee | A | Label | 16 |
| Sex | B | Label | 5 |
| Age | C | Numeric | 5 |
| Dept | D | Label | 6 |
| Trade | E | Label | 9 |
| Years | F | Numeric | 5 |

Build the database shown in Figure 6-1 by following the steps listed in the first table of the Project Summary section at the end of this project.

## SORTING A DATABASE

The information in a database is easier to work with and more meaningful if the records are arranged in sequence on the basis of one or more fields. Arranging the records in sequence is called **sorting**. Figure 6-2 illustrates the difference between unsorted data and the same data in ascending and descending sequence. Data that is in sequence from lowest to highest in value is in **ascending sequence**. Data that is in sequence from highest to lowest in value is in **descending sequence**.

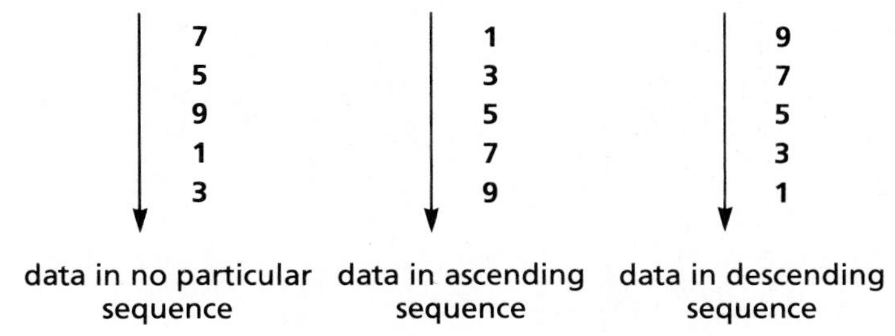


**FIGURE 6-2** Data in various sequences.

## The Sort Menu

To sort a database, enter the command /**D**ata **S**ort (/DS). The **Sort menu** displays in the control panel at the top of the screen (see Figure 6-3). The commands available in the Sort menu are described in Table 6-2.

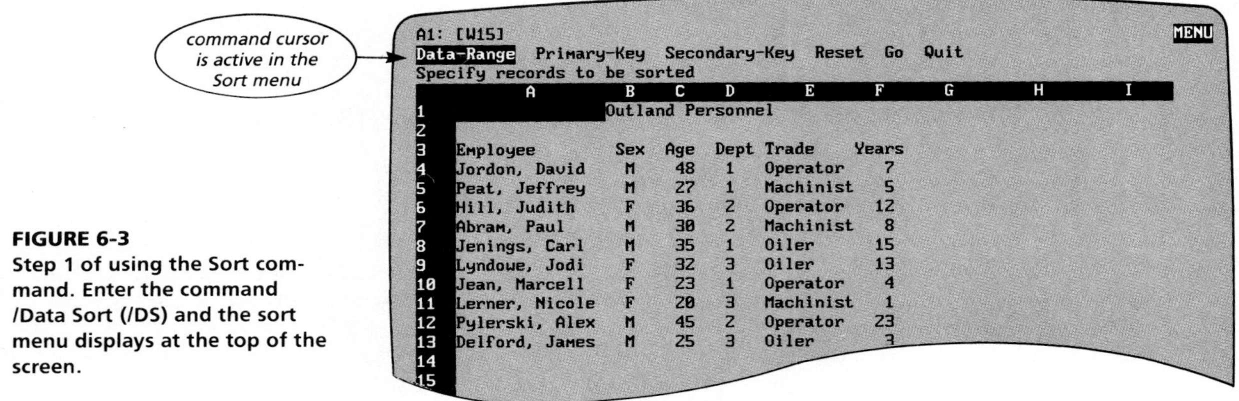


**FIGURE 6-3**
**Step 1 of using the Sort command. Enter the command /Data Sort (/DS) and the sort menu displays at the top of the screen.**

**TABLE 6-2 Commands Available in the Sort Menu**

| COMMAND | FUNCTION |
|---|---|
| Data-range | Prompts you to specify the range of the database to sort. |
| Primary-key | Prompts you to enter the field (column) you wish to sort the records on and the sequence. |
| Secondary-key | Prompts you to enter a second field (column) you wish to sort on within the primary-key field, and the sequence for the secondary-key field. Used to "break ties" on the primary-key field. |
| Reset | Clears all sort settings. |
| Go | Causes the database to be sorted on the basis of the sort settings. |
| Quit | Quits the Data command and returns control to READY mode. |

To illustrate the use of the Data Sort command, we will first sort the database in Figure 6-1 into ascending sequence on the basis of the employee name field (column A). Next, we will sort the same database on years of seniority (column F) within the sex code (column B). That is, the sex code will be the primary-key field and years of seniority will be the secondary-key field.

## Sorting the Records by Employee Name

With the command cursor active in the Sort menu (see Figure 6-3), do the following:

1. Enter the data range.
2. Enter the primary-key field.
3. Enter the Go command.

To enter the data range, type the letter D for Data-range. The **data range** defines the fields and records to be sorted in the database. The data range almost always encompasses *all* the fields in *all* the records below the column headings, although it can be made up of fewer records or fewer fields. Be aware, however, that if you do not select all the fields (columns) in the database, the unselected fields will not remain with the records they belong to and the data will get mixed up.

When you type the letter D for Data-range, 1-2-3 responds by displaying the "Enter Data-Range: A1" prompt message on the input line. Use the arrow keys and Period key to select the range A4..F13 as shown in Figure 6-4. Press the Enter key and the Sort menu shown at the top of the screen in Figure 6-3 reappears on the screen.

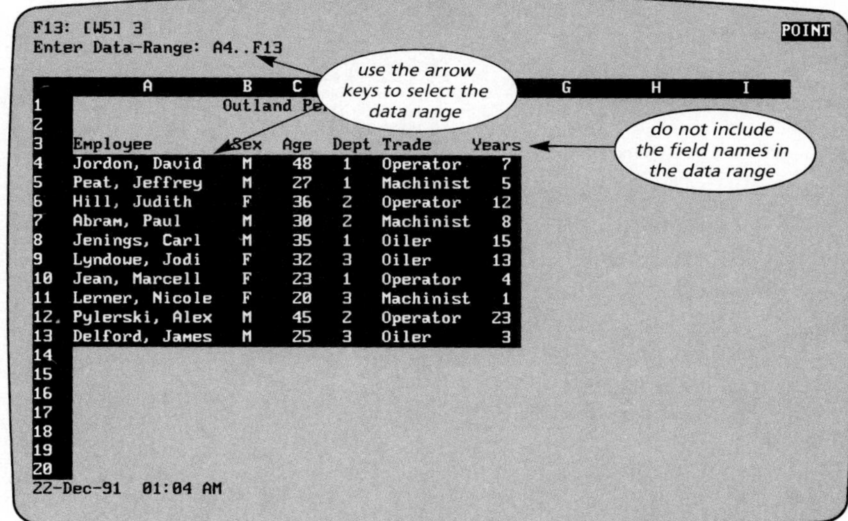


**FIGURE 6-4**
**Step 2 of using the Sort command. Enter the Data range. The Data range usually encompasses all the fields in all the records of the database.**

The next step is to enter the primary-key field. With the Sort menu on the screen and the cell pointer at A4, type the letter P for Primary key. 1-2-3 responds by displaying the prompt message "Primary sort key: A4" on the input line. Since column A is the employee name field and the cell pointer is in column A, press the Enter key. As shown in Figure 6-5, 1-2-3 responds with a second prompt message requesting the desired sequence of the sort. Type the letter A for ascending sequence and press the Enter key.

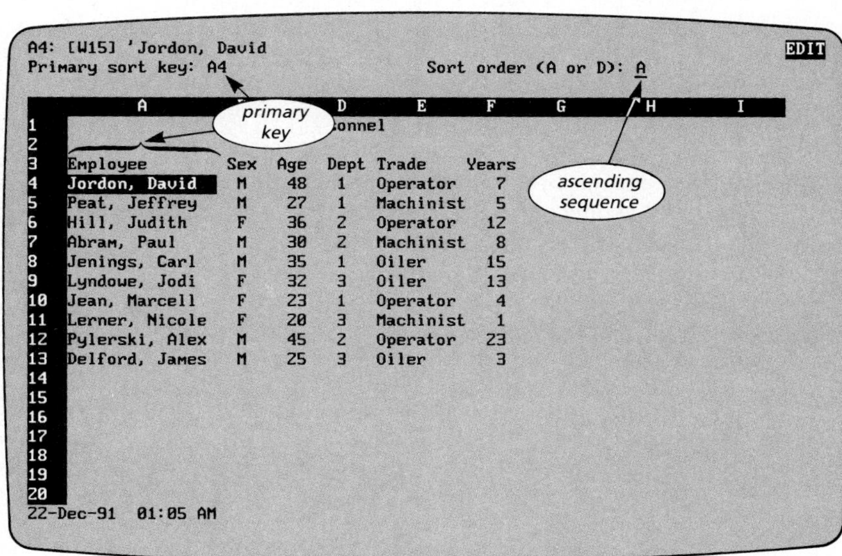


**FIGURE 6-5**
**Step 3 of using the Sort command. Enter the primary key and desired sequence for sorting the database by employee name.**

To complete the sort, type the letter G for Go. 1-2-3 sorts the records and displays them in ascending sequence according to employee name. Following the completion of the Go command, control returns to READY mode as shown in Figure 6-6. Whereas the records in Figure 6-1 are in no particular sequence, the same records in Figure 6-6 are now in ascending sequence by employee name.

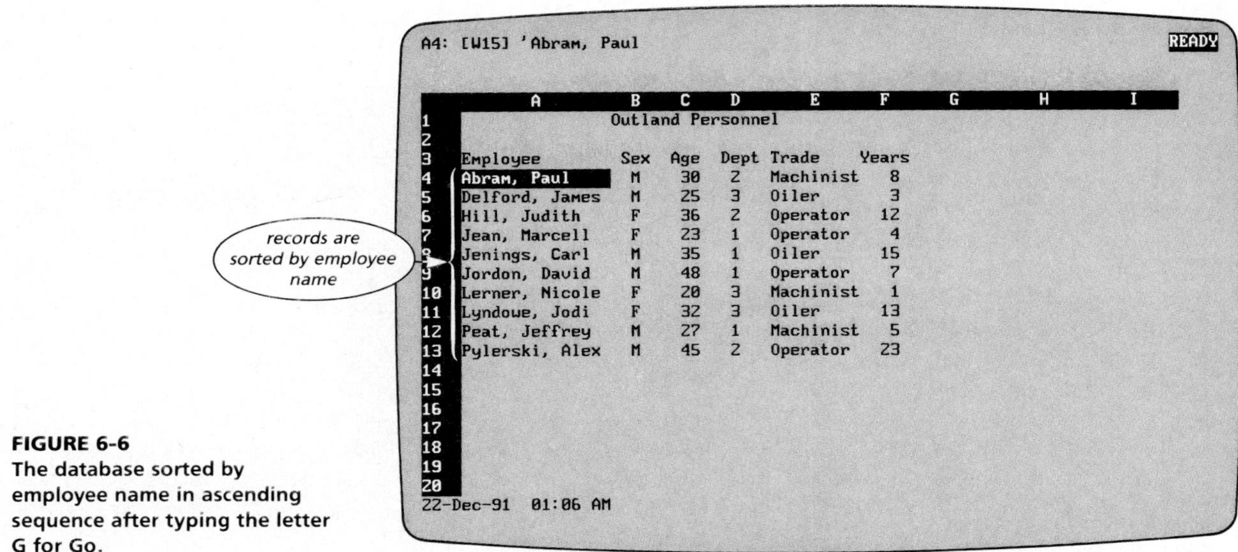


**FIGURE 6-6**
**The database sorted by employee name in ascending sequence after typing the letter G for Go.**

To complete this portion of the project, save and print a hard copy of the sorted database. Save the database using the file name PROJS-6A. Print the database using the same procedures we used in the previous projects.

## Sorting the Records by Years of Seniority within Sex Code

In this example, we will use two sort keys. Our goal is to order the records so that the secondary-key field, years of seniority (column F), is ordered in descending sequence within the primary-key field, sex code (column B). We will sort the primary-key field into ascending sequence. Therefore, the female with the most years of seniority will be at the top of the list, and the male with the least seniority will be at the bottom of the list. This nested sorting always assumes that the primary-key field contains duplicate values.

To start this portion of the project, load the original database PROJS-6 (see Figure 6-1) into main computer memory and enter the command /**D**ata **S**ort (/DS). With the command cursor active in the Sort menu (see Figure 6-3), type the letter D for Data-range. Next, select all the records in the database (A4..F13) as shown in Figure 6-4. Press the Enter key and the Sort menu shown in Figure 6-3 reappears on the screen.

After the data range is set, enter the primary-key field. To accomplish this, type the letter P for Primary key. Move the cell pointer to column B (sex code) and press the Enter key. Type the letter A for ascending sequence. The primary-key field selections are shown on the input line in Figure 6-7. Press the Enter key to finalize the primary-key selections.

Type the letter S for Secondary key. 1-2-3 responds by displaying a prompt message on the input line requesting the secondary key. Move the cell pointer to column F, the one that contains the years of seniority, and press the Enter key. In response to the second prompt message on the input line, leave the D for descending sequence. The secondary-key field selections are shown in Figure 6-8. Press the Enter key.

To complete the sort, type the letter G for Go. 1-2-3 sorts the records and places them in ascending sequence according to the sex-code field in column B. Within the sex code, the records are in descending sequence according to the years of seniority in column F. This is shown in Figure 6-9. Following the completion of the Go command, 1-2-3 displays the sorted records and returns to READY mode.

Save and print a hard copy of the sorted database. Use the file name PROJS-6B.

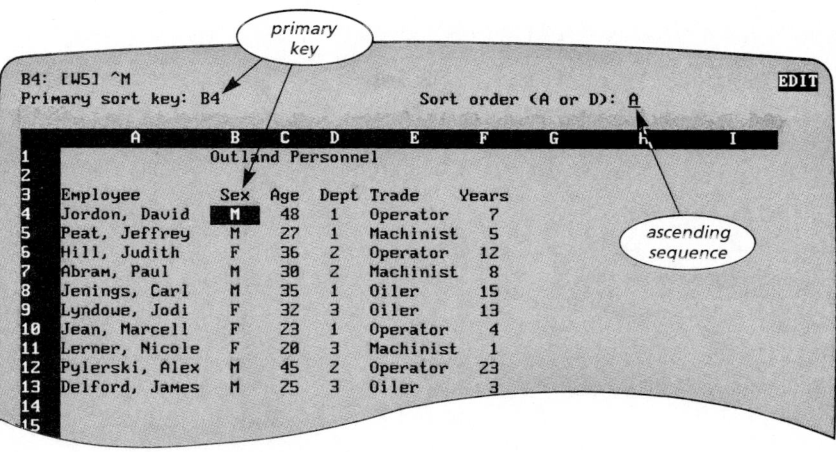


**FIGURE 6-7** Entering the primary key and desired sequence for sorting the database by years of seniority within sex code.

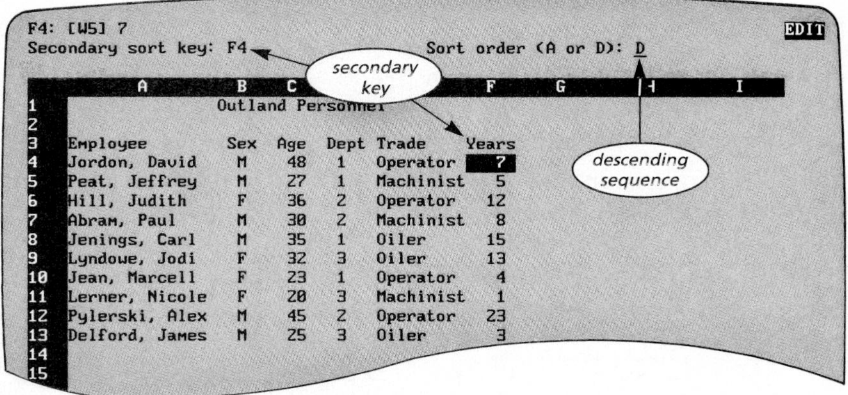


**FIGURE 6-8**
**Entering the secondary key and desired sequence for sorting the database by years of seniority within sex code.**

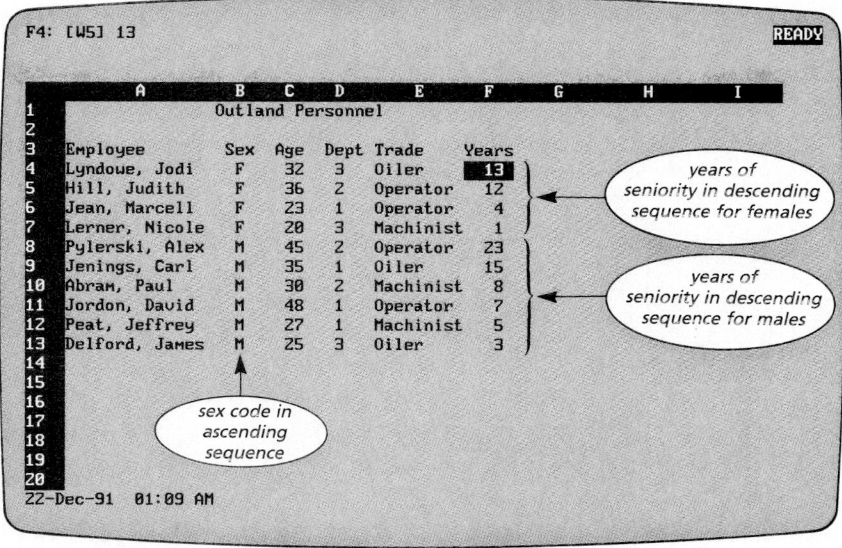


**FIGURE 6-9**
**The database sorted by years of seniority within sex code.**

# QUERYING A DATABASE

One of the most powerful aspects of a DBMS is its ability to select records from a database that match specified criteria. This activity is called **querying a database**. Records that match the criteria can be highlighted, copied to another part of the worksheet, or deleted.

## The Query Menu

To query a database, enter the command /**D**ata **Q**uery (/DQ). The **Query menu** displays in the control panel at the top of the screen (see Figure 6-10). The function of each of the Query commands is described in Table 6-3.

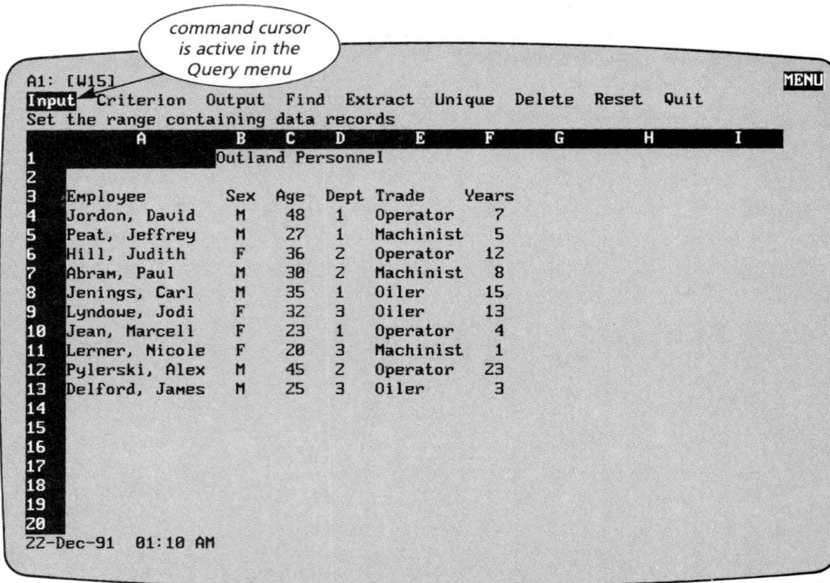


**FIGURE 6-10**
**The Query menu displays when you enter the command /Data Query (/DQ).**

**TABLE 6-3 Commands Available in the Query Menu**

| COMMAND | FUNCTION |
|---|---|
| Input | Prompts you to enter the range of the database to be queried. Usually the entire database is selected. |
| Criterion | Prompts you to enter the range of cells that includes the conditions for record selection. The conditions are entered into the worksheet off to the side or below the database. |
| Output | Prompts you to enter a range of cells to which records can be copied. The Output range is defined in the worksheet off to the side or below the database. |
| Find | Moves the cell pointer to the first record in the database that passes the test. The cell pointer moves one record at a time as you press the Up Arrow or Down Arrow keys. When you invoke the Find command, the cell pointer extends to include the entire record. Pressing the Esc key or Enter key cancels the search. |
| Extract | Copies all selected records from the database to the Output range. The records that pass the test are selected from the database. Records that flunk the test are not copied to the Output range. |
| Unique | Same as the Extract command, except that it copies only the first of any duplicate records. |
| Delete | Deletes all records from the database that pass the test. |
| Reset | Resets the Input, Output, and Criterion settings. |
| Quit | Quits the Data command and returns control to READY mode. |

## The Find Command

The Find command is used to search for records in the database that meet certain criteria. The command highlights the first record in the database that passes the test and continues to highlight records that pass the test as you press the Up and Down Arrow keys. If no more records pass the test in the direction you are searching, the computer beeps at you and the last record meeting the criteria remains highlighted.

With the database (PROJS-6) in Figure 6-10 in main computer memory, let's search for records representing males who work in department 2 (Sex = M AND Dept = 2). To complete the search, do the following:

1. Choose an unused area off to the side of the database and set up the criteria.
2. Type the command /**D**ata **Q**uery (/DQ) and enter the Input range.
3. Enter the Criterion range.
4. Type the letter F for Find.

The first step in setting up the Criterion range is to select an unused area of the worksheet. Let's begin the Criterion range at cell H3. Next, copy the names of those fields (column headings) that we are basing the search on to this area. That is, copy cell B3 (Sex) to cell H3 and cell D3 (Dept) to cell I3. You can bypass the Copy command and enter the field names through the keyboard, but the field names in the Criterion range must agree with the field names in the database, or the search won't work properly. To ensure that they are the same, it's best to use the Copy command.

An alternative to using the Copy command to set up the field names in the Criterion range is to assign cell H3 the formula +B3 and cell I3 the formula +D3. However, be aware that when you use formulas to assign a label to a cell, you lose right-justification and centering. Even so, the labels are considered to be identical. A positive result of using the formula method instead of the Copy command is that if you change a field name in the database, the corresponding field name in the Criterion range will change automatically.

Under each field name in the Criterion range, enter the value for which you want to search. In our example, we want to search for males who work in department 2. Therefore, enter the letter M in cell H4. (1-2-3 considers lowercase m and uppercase M to be the same in a Criterion range). In cell I4, enter the label 2 (^2 or "2 or '2). These entries for the Criterion range are shown in Figure 6-11. Note that the Criterion range must contain at least two rows—the field names in the first row and the criteria in the second row.

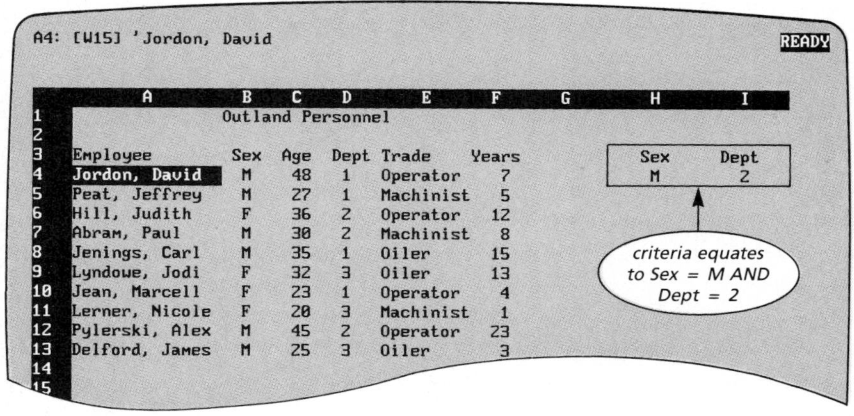


**FIGURE 6-11**
**Step 1 of using the Find command. Enter the criteria in unused cells off to the side of the database before issuing the Data Query command.**

After building the Criterion range, enter the command /**D**ata **Q**uery (/DQ). The Query menu displays as shown in Figure 6-10. Type the letter I for Input and use the arrow keys to select the entire database (A3..F13). This is shown in Figure 6-12. Note that the field names in row 3 must be included in the Input range. Press the Enter key.

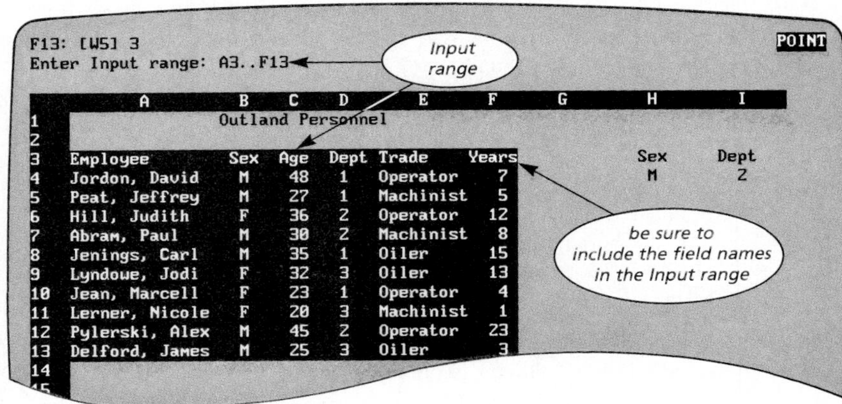


**FIGURE 6-12**
**Step 2 of using the Find command—enter the command /Data Query Input (/DQI). Enter the Input range, which should encompass all the fields in all the records of the database, including the field names at the top.**

Earlier, we set up the Criterion range (H3..I4). Now we must select it. Therefore, type the letter C for Criterion. Select the range H3..I4 as illustrated in Figure 6-13 and press the Enter key.

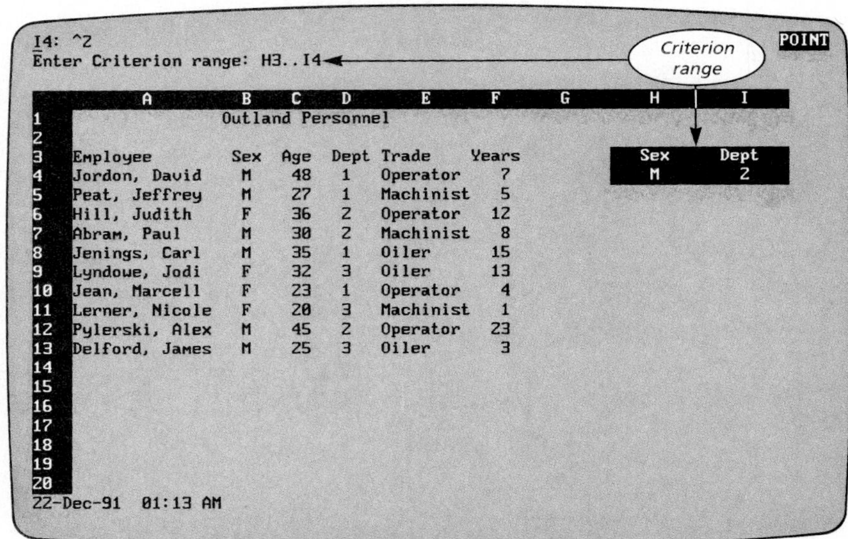


**FIGURE 6-13**
**Step 3 of using the Find command—select the Criterion range.**

Next, type the letter F for Find. As shown in the top screen of Figure 6-14, the first record that passes the test (Sex = M AND Dept = 2) is highlighted. Press the Down Arrow key and the next record that passes the test is highlighted. This is shown in the lower screen in Figure 6-14. If we press the Down Arrow key again, the computer will beep at us because there are no more records that pass the test below the highlighted one. If we press the Up Arrow key, the previous record that passed the test is highlighted again.

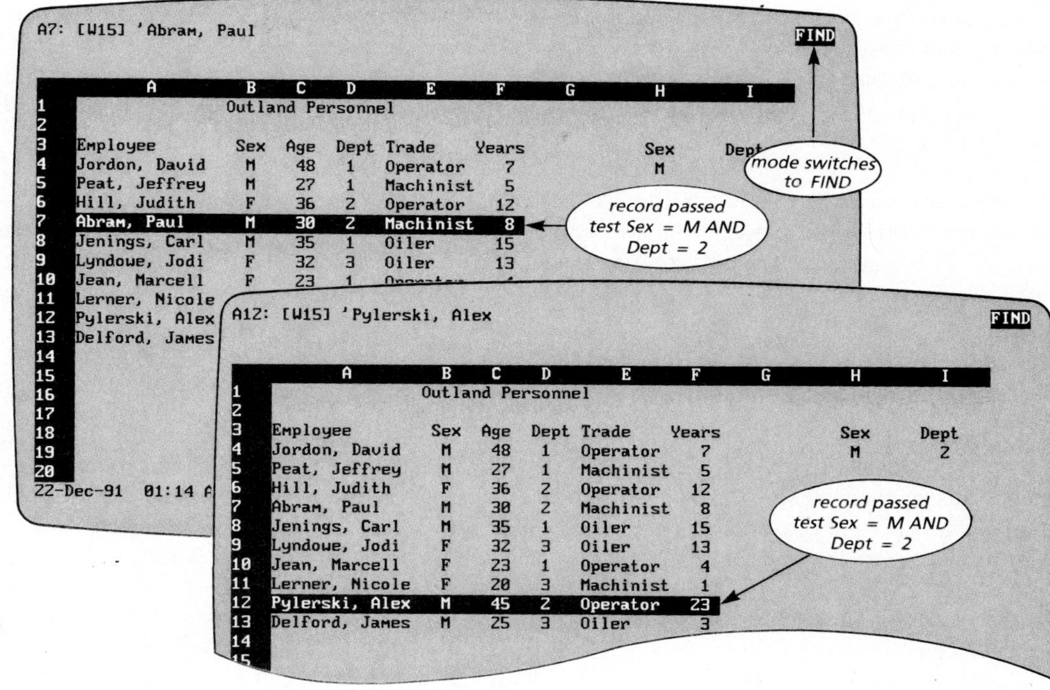


**FIGURE 6-14**
**Step 4 of using the Find command—use the Up and Down Arrow keys to highlight the next record that passes the criteria.**

After typing the letter F to invoke the Find command, we can move the elongated cursor to the very first record by pressing the Home key. We can move it to the last record by pressing the End key. These two keys allow us to start the search at the top or the bottom of the database. To terminate the Find command, press the Enter key or the Esc key to return to the Data Query menu.

While the Find command is still active, we can edit the record that is highlighted. Use the Right Arrow and Left Arrow keys to move from one field to another. Because the entire record is highlighted, the cell pointer does not move to the different fields when we use the arrow keys. However, we can determine the field location of the cell pointer because the cell address displays at the top of the screen on the status line. The blinking underline cursor that is active in the current cell also indicates the location of the cell pointer. When the cell address of the field we want to change displays on the status line, we can retype the contents or use function key F2 to edit them. If we decide the original values were correct before pressing the Enter key to complete the change, we can press the Esc key to discard the change.

To complete this portion of this project, save and print the database and criteria. Use the file name PROJS-6C.

## More About the Criterion Range

The way you set up the Criterion range determines which records pass the test when you use the Find command. The following paragraphs describe several different examples of valid field names and logical expressions within a Criterion range.

**No Conditions** If the Criterion range contains no values below the field names, all the records pass the test. For example, if you use the Criterion range at the right, then all the records in the Input range pass the test and the Find command highlights every record in the Input range, one at a time.

| Sex | Trade |
|---|---|
| | |

**Conditions with Labels** The values below the field names in the Criterion range can be labels, numbers, or formulas. For example, if you want to select all the records in the database that represent employees who are operators, use the criteria at the right. In this example Operator is a label. If you use the Find command, this Criterion range causes 1-2-3 to use the condition Trade = Operator to evaluate each record. If the condition is true, the record passes the test and it is highlighted. If Trade does not equal Operator, the record fails the test and it is bypassed.

| Trade |
| --- |
| Operator |

More than one type of trade can be listed in the Criterion range. For example, if you want to select records that represent employees who are operators or employees who are oilers (Trade = Operator OR Trade = Oiler), you can set up a Criterion range with the entries at the right. In this example, the Criterion range is three rows long.

| Trade |
| --- |
| Operator |
| Oiler |

The global characters question mark (?) and asterisk (*) can be used within labels. The asterisk (*) means "any characters at this position and all remaining positions." The question mark (?) means "any character at this position." These global characters are also called **wild-card characters**. For example, the Criterion range at the right causes all records whose trade begins with the letter O to be selected. In our database, records with the trade of oiler or operator pass the test. The remaining records fail the test.

| Trade |
| --- |
| O* |

The Criterion range at the right causes all records to be selected that represent employees whose trade is five characters long, begins with the letter O, and ends with the letters er. With regard to the placement of wild-card characters in a label, the question mark (?) can be used in any character position. The asterisk (*) can only be used at the end of a label.

| Trade |
| --- |
| O??er |

Labels can also be preceded by the tilde (˜) to exclude a match. To select the records representing employees that work in any department other than department 3, you may use the criteria at the right. Note that the department numbers in our database are labels, not numbers. The tilde (˜) can only precede labels. Table 6-4 summarizes the special symbols that may be used with labels in a Criterion range.

| Dept |
| --- |
| ˜3 |

**TABLE 6-4 Summary of Special Symbols That Can Be Used with Labels in a Criterion Range**

| SYMBOL | MEANING | EXAMPLE |
| --- | --- | --- |
| * | Any characters at this position and all remaining positions | Tr* |
| ? | Any character at this position | M??T |
| ˜ | Not | ˜F |

**Conditions with Numbers** If you want to select records that represent employees who are 30 years old, enter the criteria in the entry at the right. In this example, 1-2-3 uses the expression Age = 30 to determine if each record passes the test when the Find command is used. It is invalid to begin a number with any of the special characters described earlier for labels, like *, ?, and ˜.

| Age |
| --- |
| 30 |

**Conditions with Formulas** Formula criteria are entered into the Criterion range beginning with a plus sign ( + ). The plus sign is followed by the address of the cell of the first record immediately below the specified field name in the Input range. The cell address is followed by a relational operator and the value to which to compare the field name. (See Table 4-3 in Project 4 for a list of the valid relational operators.) If you want to select all records that represent employees who are older than 25, use the criteria at the right.

| Age |
|---|
| +C4>25 |

The cell address C4 is the first cell in the database below the field name Age (see Figure 6-15 on the following page). Since C4 is a relative cell address, 1-2-3 adjusts the row as it goes through the database, passing and flunking records. Hence, when you invoke the Find command, cell address C4 is only used to evaluate the first record. Thereafter, the 4 in C4 is adjusted to 5, 6, and so on, as each record in the database is evaluated.

In the previous example, the formula +C4>25 was shown in the cell below the field name Age. Actually, when a condition containing a formula is assigned to the cell, 0 or 1 displays. The number displayed in the cell assigned the formula +C4>25 depends on the value in cell C4. If it is greater than 25, then 1 (true) displays. If C4 contains a value less than or equal to 25, then 0 (false) displays. You can use the command /**R**ange **F**ormat **T**ext (/RFT) to display the formula in the Criterion range, rather than the numeric value 0 or 1.

Compound conditions may be formed by using the logical operators #AND#, #OR#, and #NOT#. (See Table 4-4 in Project 4 for an explanation of their meaning.) In the following example, all records are selected that meet the criteria Age < 37 AND Years ≥ 10.

| Age |
|---|
| +C4<37#AND#+F4> =10 |

Note that the compound condition may include fields that are not directly under the field name. In this case, C4 refers to the Age field and F4 refers to the Years field.

**Mixing Conditions with Formulas and Labels** If the criteria require both a label and a formula, use multiple field names. For example, if you wanted to find all records in the employee database that represent operators with more than 10 years of seniority (Trade = Operator AND Years > 10), use the criteria at the right.

| Trade | Years |
|---|---|
| Operator | +F4>10 |

To select records that meet the criteria Trade = Operator OR Years > 10, use the entry at the right. Because the expressions Operator and +F4>10 are in different rows, 1-2-3 selects records that represent employees who are operators or have more than 10 years of seniority.

| Trade | Years |
|---|---|
| Operator | |
| | +F4>10 |

## The Extract Command

The Extract command copies data from the records that pass the test to the designated fields in the Output range. The Output range is a group of cells off to the side or below the database. The first row of the Output range includes duplicates of the field names in the Input range that you want to extract. This command is very powerful because it allows you to build a database that is a subset of the original one. The subset database can be printed, saved as a new database, or queried like any other database.

Again, consider the employee database in Figure 6-1. Assume that your manager wants you to generate a list of all those employees who meet the following criteria:

Age ≥ 27 AND NOT(Dept = 3) AND Years < 10

In the list, include the employee name, department, and sex code of all the records that pass the test.

To complete the extract, do the following:

1. Choose an area off to the side of the database and set up the criteria.
2. Choose an area below the database and set up an area to receive the extracted results.
3. Invoke the command /**D**ata **Q**uery (/DQ) and enter the Input range.
4. Enter the Criterion range.
5. Enter the Output range.
6. Type the letter E for Extract.

The criteria for this query involve three fields—Age, Dept, and Years. Use the cells in the range G3 through I4 for the Criterion range. Copy the three field names Age, Dept, and Years from the database in row 3 to cells G3, H3, and I3. The first condition in the previously stated criteria is Age ≥ 27. Therefore, in cell G4, enter the formula +C4> =27. This is shown in Figure 6-15. (Cells G4 through I4 have been formatted to the Text type so that the formulas display, rather than the numeric values 0 or 1.) The second condition is NOT(Dept = 3). Therefore, in cell H4, enter ~3. The condition for the third field is Years < 10. In cell I4, enter +F4<10.

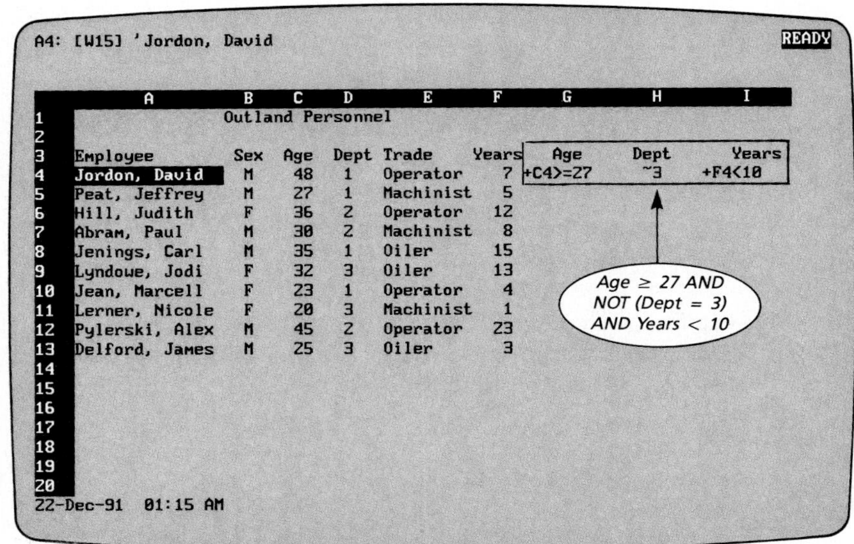


**FIGURE 6-15**
**Step 1 of using the Extract command—enter the criteria in unused cells off to the side of the database.**

The next step is to set up the Output range. This involves copying the names of the fields at the top of the database (row 3) to an area below the database. Since we want to extract the employee name, department, and sex code, copy the three field names to row 16 as illustrated in Figure 6-16.

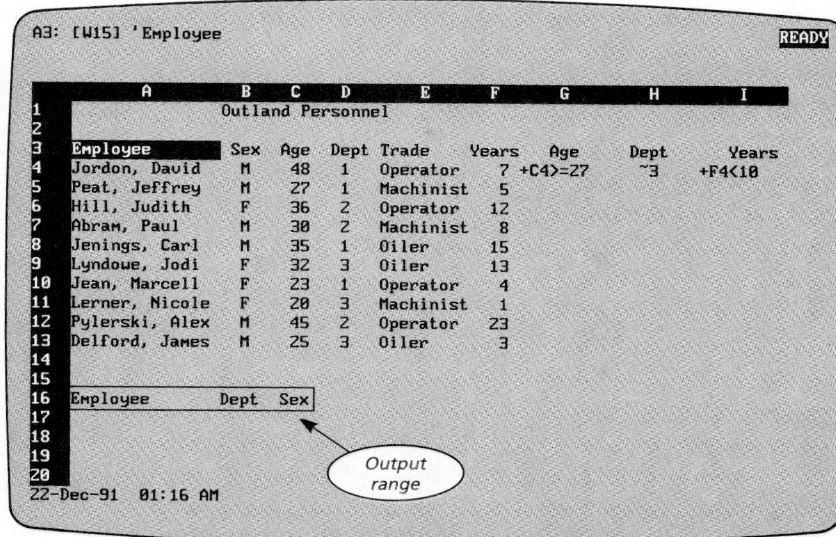


**FIGURE 6-16**
**Step 2 of using the Extract command—copy the field names for the Output range below the database.**

Enter the command /**D**ata **Q**uery (/DQ). The Query menu shown at the top of the screen in Figure 6-10 displays. Type the letter I for Input. Use the arrow keys to select the entire database, including the field names in row 3 (A3..F13). The Input range is shown in Figure 6-17. Press the Enter key.

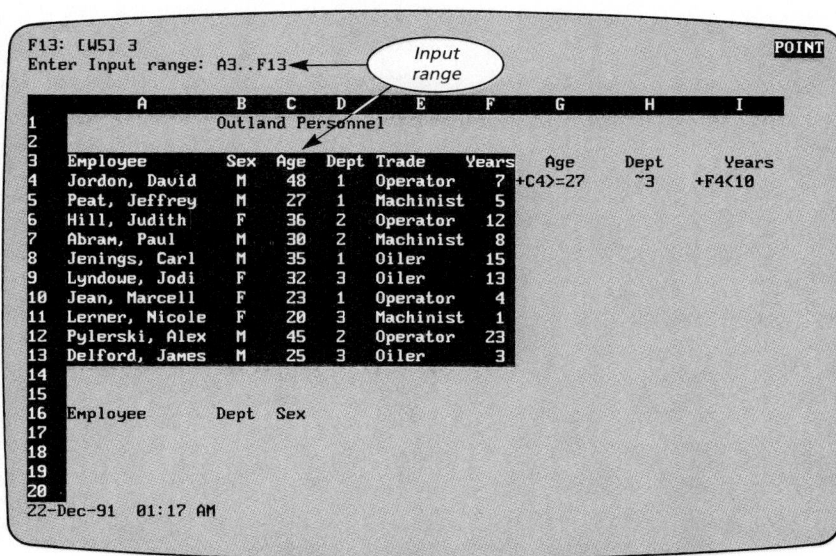


**FIGURE 6-17**
**Step 3 of using the Extract command—enter the command /Data Query (/DQ) and enter the Input range. The Input range usually encompasses all the fields in all the records of the database, including the field names.**

With the command cursor in the Query menu, type the letter C for Criterion. Select the Criterion range G3..I4 as shown in Figure 6-18. Press the Enter key. Now type the letter O for Output. Select the range A16..C16 (see Figure 6-19). Press the Enter key.

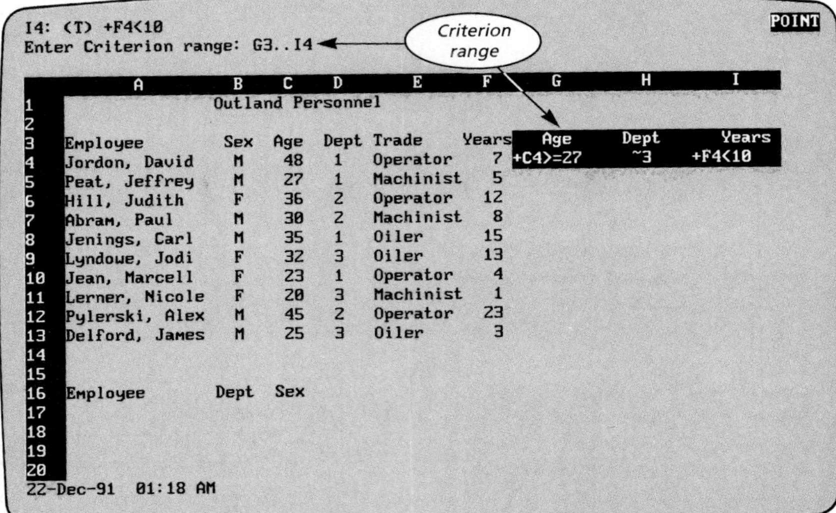


**FIGURE 6-18**
**Step 4 of using the Extract command—enter the Criterion range.**

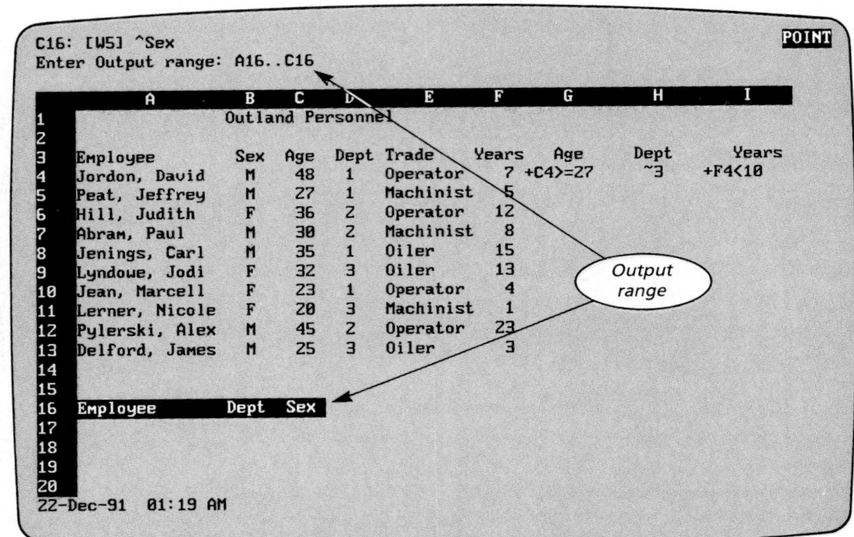


**FIGURE 6-19**
**Step 5 of using the Extract command—enter the Output range.**

After the Input, Criterion, and Output ranges are set, type the letter E for Extract. This causes 1-2-3 to select the records that meet the criteria specified in the range A3..I4. For each record selected, it copies the employee name, department, and sex code to the next available row beneath the field names in the Output range. Type the letter Q to Quit the Data Query command. The results of the extract display below the database as shown in Figure 6-20. Save and print the database, criteria, and records extracted. To save the database, use the file name PROJS-6D.

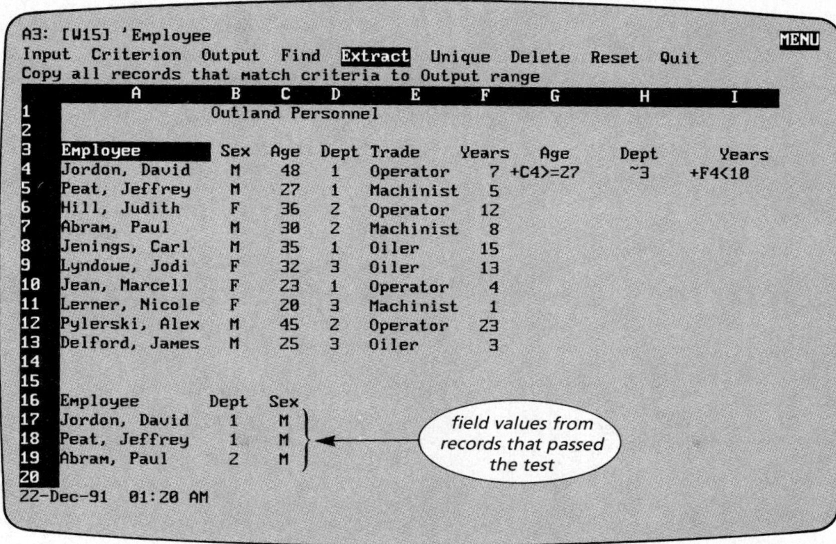


**FIGURE 6-20**
**Step 6 of using the Extract command—invoke the Extract command. Specified fields are displayed in the Output range from the records that pass the test Age > = 27 AND NOT(Dept = 3) AND Years > 10.**

In the previous example, we defined the Output range to be the row containing the field names (A16..C16). When the Output range is defined in this fashion, any number of records can be extracted from the database. The alternative is to define a rectangular Output range. In this case, if more records are extracted than rows in the Output range, 1-2-3 displays the diagnostic message "Too many records for Output range."

## THE DATABASE FUNCTIONS

-2-3 has seven functions for evaluating numeric data in the database. The functions, which are similar to the statistical functions discussed in Project 4, are described in Table 6-5.

**TABLE 6-5 Database Statistical Functions**

| FUNCTION | FUNCTION VALUE |
|---|---|
| DAVG(I,O,C) | Returns the average of the numbers in the Offset column (O) of the Input range (I) that meet the criterion (C). |
| DCOUNT(I,O,C) | Returns the number of nonempty cells in the Offset column (O) of the Input range (I) that meet the criterion (C). |
| DMAX(I,O,C) | Returns the largest number in the Offset column (O) of the Input range (I) that meet the criterion (C). |
| DMIN(I,O,C) | Returns the smallest number in the Offset column (O) of the Input range (I) that meet the criterion (C). |
| DSTD(I,O,C) | Returns the standard deviation of the numbers in the Offset column (O) of the Input range (I) that meet the criterion (C). |
| DSUM(I,O,C) | Returns the sum of the numbers in the Offset column (O) of the Input range (I) that meet the criterion (C). |
| DVAR(I,O,C) | Returns the variance of the numbers in the Offset column (O) of the Input range (I) that meet the criterion (C). |

The purpose of these functions is to return a statistic, like the average, on the values in the column of the records that meet the specified criteria. For example, with the database in Figure 6-1 in main computer memory, let's compute the average age of the male employees and the average age of the female employees.

The first step is to set up the criteria for each average. For the average age of females, use the criteria shown in cells H3 and H4 in Figure 6-21. Likewise, for the average age of males, use the criteria shown in cells I3 and I4. Next, enter the labels that identify the averages. This is shown in cells A16 and A17 in Figure 6-21.

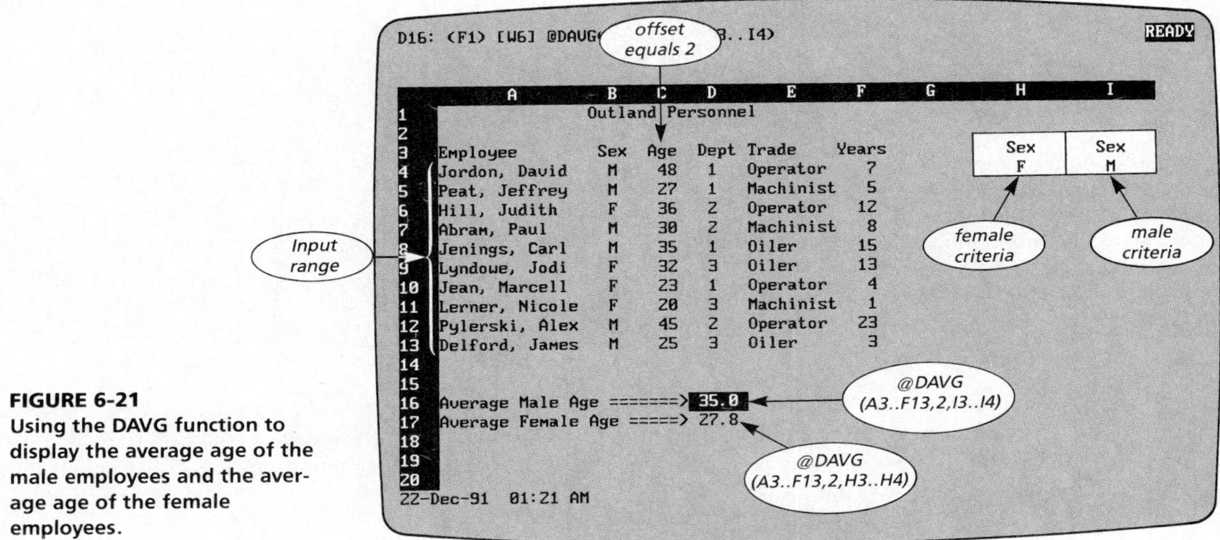


**FIGURE 6-21**
**Using the DAVG function to display the average age of the male employees and the average age of the female employees.**

We can now assign the DAVG function to cells D16 and D17. This function has three arguments—Input range, offset, and Criterion range. Since the arguments in the function define the ranges, this function does not require that the ranges be defined through the Data Query command.

Set the Input range to the entire database (A3..F13). The **offset** argument defines the field in the database to be used in the computation. The offset of the leftmost field (Employee) is 0. The offset of the Sex field is 1. The offset of the Age field is 2, and so on. Hence, use the value 2 for the offset argument in the DAVG function. The third argument is the range of cells that make up the criteria—H3..H4 for females and I3..I4 for the males.

With the cell pointer at D16, enter the function @DAVG(A3..F13,2,I3..I4). This causes the average age of the male employees to display in cell D16. Press the Down Arrow key and enter the function @DAVG(A3..F13,2,H3..H4). This function causes the average age of the female employees to display in cell D17. Format cells D16 and D17 to the Fixed type with one decimal position. The effect of entering these two functions and formatting the results is shown in Figure 6-21. To complete this portion of the project, save and print the database, criteria, and averages. Save the database using the file name PROJS-6E.

## THE LOOKUP FUNCTIONS

Three functions that we have not discussed are the CHOOSE, VLOOKUP, and HLOOKUP functions. These three functions are called **lookup functions** because they allow you to look up values in a list or a table that is part of the worksheet.

## The CHOOSE Function

The CHOOSE function selects a value from a list on the basis of an index. The general form of the CHOOSE function is @CHOOSE(x,y0,y1,y2,...,yn), where the value of x determines the value in the list (y0, y1, y2, ..., yn) to store in the cell. If x equals 0, the first value (y0) is stored in the cell. If x equals 1, the second value (y1) is stored in the cell, and so on. The list can contain values, quoted strings, cell addresses, formulas, range names, or a combination of these.

Consider the partial worksheet in Figure 6-22. The table in the range E1..E7 contains costs. B1 is assigned the index that determines the value in the list that the function returns. The CHOOSE function is assigned to cell B3. It is entered as follows: @CHOOSE(B1,0,E2,E3,E4,E5 + .02,E6*.95,E7,.46). Since B1 is equal to 3, the CHOOSE function returns the fourth value in the list—the value of cell E4.

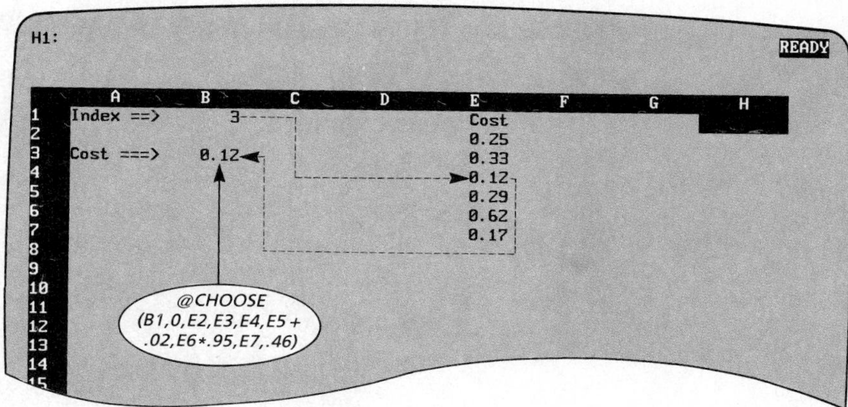


**FIGURE 6-22**
**Using the CHOOSE function to select a value from the list of arguments following the index.**

If we change the value of B1 to some other number between 0 and 7, the function will store a different value in B3. If the value in B1 exceeds the number of items in the list, the diagnostic message ERR is assigned to B3. Note that an index value of zero in cell B1 causes the CHOOSE function to assign zero to B3. If cell B1 is assigned a value of 7, the function returns the value .46 from the list and stores it in cell B3.

## The VLOOKUP and HLOOKUP Functions

The VLOOKUP and HLOOKUP functions are useful for looking up values in tables, like tax tables, discount tables, and part tables. The general form of the VLOOKUP function is @VLOOKUP(x,range,offset). The first argument, x, is called the **search argument**. It is compared to values in the leftmost column of the multiple-column table defined by the second argument, range. The leftmost column of the range is called the **range column**. Offset defines the column from which a value is returned when a hit is made in the range column. A **hit** occurs when a value is found in the range column that is closest to but not greater than the search argument x.

The offset in the VLOOKUP function can be zero or positive. The offset value of the range column is zero. A positive offset causes a value to be selected from a column to the right of the range column.

While the VLOOKUP function looks up values in a table arranged vertically, the HLOOKUP function looks up values in a table arranged horizontally. Vertical tables are used more often than horizontal tables.

Consider the top screen in Figure 6-23. Column B contains a list of student test scores. A grade scale table is in the range F5..G9. Look up the corresponding letter grade in the grade scale table for each student test score and assign it to the appropriate cell in column D. For example, a test score of 78 returns the letter grade C; a test score of 99 returns the letter grade A. To look up the letter grades for the student test scores, enter the function @VLOOKUP(B5,$F$5..$G$9,1) in cell D5, the location of the letter grade for student number 1035.

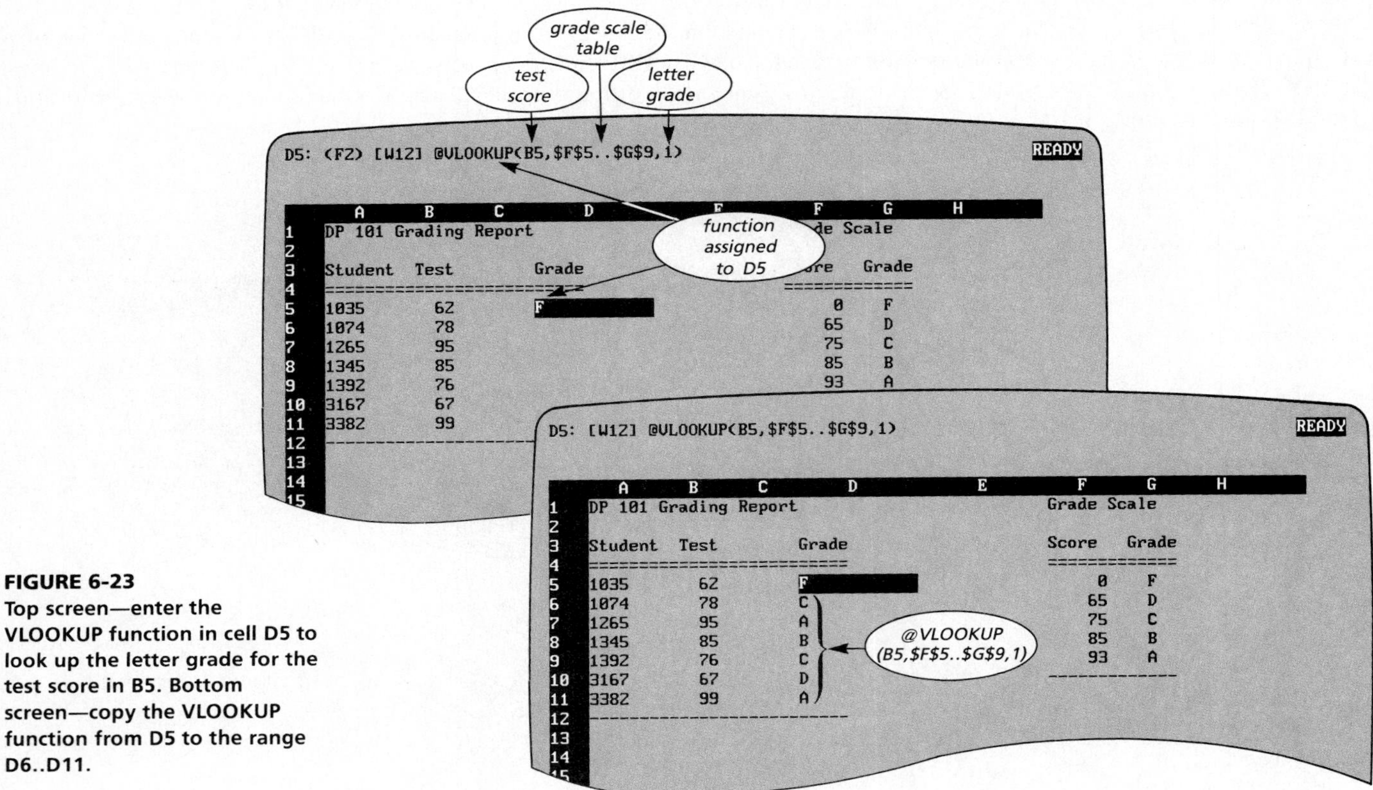


**FIGURE 6-23** Top screen—enter the VLOOKUP function in cell D5 to look up the letter grade for the test score in B5. Bottom screen—copy the VLOOKUP function from D5 to the range D6..D11.

The first argument in the VLOOKUP function is cell B5, the test score for student number 1035. The second argument, $F$5..$G$9, defines the grade scale table. The third argument, 1, is the offset. It instructs 1-2-3 to assign the corresponding value in the grade scale table that is located one column to the right of the range column—column F.

Copy the VLOOKUP function in cell D5 to the range D6..D11. As the copy takes place, the first argument in the VLOOKUP function, B5, is adjusted to B6, B7, B8, and so on. The result of copying the VLOOKUP function is shown in the lower screen in Figure 6-23. In this case, the VLOOKUP function in cells D5 through D11 returns the letter grades that correspond to the student test scores.

## PROJECT SUMMARY

In this project you learned how to sort and query a worksheet database. You sorted the database in two different ways, first by employee name and then by years of seniority within sex code.

Querying a database involves searching for records that meet a specified criteria. The selected records can be highlighted, extracted, or deleted.

Powerful database functions can be used to generate information about the database. In this project you were introduced to the lookup functions. These functions are used to return a value from a list or table.

Each of the steps required to build and manipulate the worksheet database presented in Project 6 is listed in the following tables.

**SUMMARY OF KEYSTROKES—PROJS-6 (Figure 6-1)**

| STEPS | KEY(S) PRESSED | STEPS | KEY(S) PRESSED |
|---|---|---|---|
| 1 | /WCS16← | 13 | F5 A4←Jordon, David→ ^M→48→ ^1→Operator→7← |
| 2 | →/WCS5← | 14 | F5 A5←Peat, Jeffrey→ ^M→27→ ^1→Machinist→5← |
| 3 | →/WCS5← | 15 | F5 A6←Hill, Judith→ ^F→36→ ^2→Operator→12← |
| 4 | →/WCS6← | 16 | F5 A7←Abram, Paul→ ^M→30→ ^2→Machinist→8← |
| 5 | →→/WCS5← | 17 | F5 A8←Jenings, Carl→ ^M→35→ ^1→Oiler→15← |
| 6 | F5 B1←Outland Personnel↓ | 18 | F5 A9←Lyndowe, Jodi→ ^F→32→ ^3→Oiler→13← |
| 7 | ↓←Employee→ | 19 | F5 A10←Jean, Marcell→ ^F→23→ ^1→Operator→4← |
| 8 | ^Sex→ | 20 | F5 A11←Lerner, Nicole→ ^F→20→ ^3→Machinist→1← |
| 9 | "Age→ | 21 | F5 A12←Pylerski, Alex→ ^M→45→ ^2→Operator→23← |
| 10 | ^Dept→ | 22 | F5 A13←Delford, James→ ^M→25→ ^3→Oiler→3← |
| 11 | Trade→ | 23 | Home |
| 12 | "Years← | 24 | /FSPROJS-6← |

**SUMMARY OF KEYSTROKES**
**Sorting PROJS-6 by Employee Name (Figure 6-6)**

| STEPS | KEY(S) PRESSED |
|---|---|
| 1 | /FRPROJS-6← |
| 2 | /DS |
| 3 | DA4.F13← |
| 4 | PA4←A← |
| 5 | G |
| 6 | /PPRA1.F13←AGPPQ |
| 7 | /FSPROJS-6A← |

**SUMMARY OF KEYSTROKES**
**Sorting PROJS-6 by Years of Seniority within Sex Code (Figure 6-9)**

| STEPS | KEY(S) PRESSED |
|---|---|
| 1 | /FRPROJS-6← |
| 2 | /DS |
| 3 | DA4.F13← |
| 4 | PB4←A← |
| 5 | SF4←← |
| 6 | G |
| 7 | /PPRA1.F13←AGPPQ |
| 8 | /FSPROJS-6B← |

## Project Summary (continued)

**SUMMARY OF KEYSTROKES**
**Finding Records That Meet the Criteria Sex = M AND Dept = 2 (Figure 6-14)**

| STEPS | KEY(S) PRESSED | STEPS | KEY(S) PRESSED |
|---|---|---|---|
| 1 | /FRPROJS-6↵ | 7 | CH3.I4↵ |
| 2 | F5 B3↵/C↵H3↵ | 8 | F↓↓ |
| 3 | F5 D3↵/C↵I3↵ | 9 | Esc |
| 4 | F5 H4↵^M→^2↵ | 10 | /PPRA1.I13↵OMR77↵QAGPPQ |
| 5 | /DQ | 11 | /FSPROJS-6C↵ |
| 6 | IA3.F13↵ | | |

**SUMMARY OF KEYSTROKES**
**Extracting Records That Meet the Criteria Age > = 27 AND NOT (Dept = 3) AND Years < 10 (Figure 6-20)**

| STEPS | KEY(S) PRESSED | STEPS | KEY(S) PRESSED |
|---|---|---|---|
| 1 | /FRPROJS-6↵ | 9 | F5 B3↵/C↵C16↵ |
| 2 | F5 C3↵/C↵G3↵ | 10 | /DQ |
| 3 | →/C↵H3↵ | 11 | IA3.F13↵ |
| 4 | →→/C↵I3↵ | 12 | CG3.I4↵ |
| 5 | →↓+C4> =27→^~3→+F4<10↵ | 13 | OA16.C16↵ |
| 6 | /RFT←←↵ | 14 | EQ |
| 7 | F5 A3↵/C↵A16↵ | 15 | /PPRA1.I20↵OMR77↵QAGPPQ |
| 8 | F5 D3↵/C↵B16↵ | 16 | /FSPROJS-6D↵ |

**SUMMARY OF KEYSTROKES**
**Using the Database Function DAVG (Figure 6-21)**

| STEPS | KEY(S) PRESSED |
|---|---|
| 1 | /FRPROJS-6↵ |
| 2 | F5 B3↵/C↵H3.I3↵ |
| 3 | F5 H4↵^F→^M↵ |
| 4 | F5 A16↵Average Male Age =======>↓ |
| 5 | Average Female Age =====>↵ |
| 6 | F5 D16↵@DAVG(A3.F13,2,I3.I4)↓ |
| 7 | @DAVG(A3.F13,2,H3.H4)↑ |
| 8 | /RFF1↵↓↵ |
| 9 | /FSPROJS-6E↵ |
| 10 | /PPRA1.I17↵AGPPQ |

The following list summarizes the material covered in Project 6:

1. A **database** is an organized collection of data.
2. The data related to a person, place, or thing is called a **record**.
3. The data items that make up a record are called **fields**.
4. Each row in a worksheet can be used to store a record.
5. Each column in a worksheet can be used to store a field.
6. The row immediately above the first record contains the field names.
7. A **database management system (DBMS)** is a software package that is used to create a database and store, access, sort, and make additions, deletions, and changes to that database.
8. **Sorting** rearranges the records in a database in a particular sequence on the basis of one or more fields.
9. Data that is in sequence from lowest to highest is in **ascending sequence**.
10. Data that is in sequence from highest to lowest is in **descending sequence**.
11. To sort a database, enter the command /**D**ata **S**ort (/DS). Enter the data range and the sort keys. To complete the sort, enter the Go command.
12. The data range for a sort is usually all the records in the database. Never include the field names in the data range.
13. A sort key, like the primary key, is assigned a column and a sort sequence.
14. Selecting records in a database on the basis of a specified criteria is called **querying a database**. Records that match the criteria can be highlighted, copied to another part of the worksheet, or deleted.
15. To query a database, enter the command /**D**ata **Q**uery (/DQ).
16. Before you enter the Data Query command, the criteria should be present in the worksheet. If you use an Output range, the field names for the Output range should also be present in the worksheet.
17. The Find command highlights records that pass the criteria.
18. To apply the Find command to a database, use the Data Query command to define the Input range and Criterion range. Finally, type the letter F for Find.
19. The criteria used to pass records include the field names and the values that the field names are compared to. Field names can be compared to labels, numbers, and formulas.
20. Global or wild-card characters are allowed in labels in the criteria. The two valid wild-card characters are the asterisk (*), which means "any characters in this position and all remaining positions," and the question mark (?), which means "any character at this position." The question mark (?) can be used anywhere in the label. The asterisk (*) can only be used at the end of a label.
21. A label preceded by a tilde (~) in the criterion range negates the condition.
22. The criteria can include the logical operators AND, OR, and NOT.
23. The Extract command is used to copy selected records from the database to the Output range.
24. 1-2-3 includes database statistical functions to generate information about the database.
25. The lookup functions, CHOOSE, VLOOKUP, and HLOOKUP allow you to look up values in a list or table that is part of the worksheet.

# STUDENT ASSIGNMENTS

## STUDENT ASSIGNMENT 1: True/False

**Instructions:** Circle T if the statement is true or F if the statement is false.

T F 1. A database is an organized collection of data.
T F 2. A database management system is a worksheet.
T F 3. The series of numbers 1, 3, 4, 5, 6 is in descending sequence.
T F 4. The Reset command in the Sort menu resets the database back to its original sequence.
T F 5. In a sort operation, the secondary-key field has a lower priority than the primary-key field.
T F 6. A sort key is identified by any cell in the column containing the field you wish to sort by.
T F 7. To query a database, you must first select unused cells off to the side or below the database and set up the criteria.
T F 8. The Find command copies selected records to the Output range.
T F 9. The Criterion range must contain at least two rows and two columns.
T F 10. A Criterion range consisting of field names and empty cells below the field names will cause all the records in the database to be selected.
T F 11. The wild-card character asterisk (*) may only be used at the front of a label that is part of the criteria.
T F 12. The tilde (~) is used to negate a condition in the Criterion range.
T F 13. It is not required that the field names in the Output range be the same as the field names in the Input range.
T F 14. The database functions require that you define the Input range and Criterion range by invoking the Data Query command.
T F 15. The Offset column is relative to the rightmost field in the Input range.
T F 16. The DAVG function returns the average number of records in the database.
T F 17. The Offset column in the VLOOKUP function cannot be negative.
T F 18. An Offset column value of zero causes the VLOOKUP function to return the value in the range column that is closest to but not greater than the search argument.
T F 19. The VLOOKUP and HLOOKUP functions are the same, except that VLOOKUP verifies the search of the table and HLOOKUP does not.
T F 20. The CHOOSE function is used to select a value from a list on the basis of an index.

## STUDENT ASSIGNMENT 2: Multiple Choice

**Instructions:** Circle the correct response.

1. Which one of the following series of numbers is in descending sequence?
   a. 1, 2, 3, 4, 5 b. 5, 4, 3, 2, 1 c. 1, 3, 5, 3, 1 d. none of these
2. Which one of the following commands in the Query menu is used to highlight records?
   a. Find b. Extract c. Unique d. Criterion
3. To properly execute the Find command, the ______________ and ______________ range must be set.
   a. Input, Output b. Input, Criterion c. Data-range, Output d. Data-range, Criterion
4. Which one of the following characters represent "any character in this position?"
   a. tilde (~) b. number sign (#) c. asterisk (*) d. question mark (?)
5. To copy all records that satisfy the criteria to the Output range, use the ______________ command.
   a. Find b. Extract c. Delete d. Output
6. Which one of the following database functions returns the number of nonempty cells in the Offset column (O) of the records in the Input range (I) that meet the Criterion range (C)?
   a. DMAX(I,O,C) b. DAVG(I,O,C) c. DCOUNT(I,O,C) d. DVAR(I,O,C)
7. If a database has four fields, the rightmost column has an Offset value of __________ .
   a. 0 b. 3 c. 4 d. 5
8. Which one of the following functions is used to search a columnar table?
   a. CHOOSE b. VLOOKUP c. HLOOKUP d. both b and c

## STUDENT ASSIGNMENT 3: Understanding Sorting

**Instructions:** Rewrite the order of the seven records in the database listed below on the basis of the problems that follow. Treat each problem independently.

1. Sort the database into descending sequence by division.
2. Sort the database by district within division. Both sort keys are to be in ascending sequence.
3. Sort the database by department within district within division. All three sort keys are to be in ascending sequence.
4. Sort the database into descending sequence by cost.
5. Sort the database by department within district within division. All three sort keys are to be in descending sequence.

| DIVISION | DISTRICT | DEPARTMENT | COST |
|---|---|---|---|
| 2 | 1 | 2 | 1.21 |
| 1 | 2 | 2 | 2.22 |
| 2 | 1 | 3 | 1.57 |
| 1 | 2 | 1 | 3.56 |
| 1 | 1 | 1 | 1.11 |
| 2 | 1 | 1 | 1.45 |
| 1 | 2 | 3 | 2.10 |

## STUDENT ASSIGNMENT 4: Understanding Criteria

**Instructions:** Write the criteria required to select records from the database in Figure 6-1 according to the problems listed below. So that you can better understand what is required for this assignment, we have answered the first problem.

1. Select records that represent male employees who are less than 25 years old.

Criteria:

| Sex | Age |
|---|---|
| M | +C4<25 |

2. Select records that represent employees whose trade is machinist or oiler.

Criteria:

| |
|---|
| |
| |

3. Select records that represent employees whose last names begin with P or who work in department 2.

Criteria:

| | | |
|---|---|---|
| | | |

4. Select records that represent female employees who are at least 30 years old and have at least 10 years of seniority.

Criteria:

| | |
|---|---|
| | |
| | |

5. Select records that represent male employees or employees who are at least 30 years old.

Criteria:

| | |
|---|---|
| | |
| | |

6. Select records that represent male machinist employees who are at least 28 years old and whose last names begin with P.

Criteria:

| | | | |
|---|---|---|---|
| | | | |

## STUDENT ASSIGNMENT 5: Understanding Database and Lookup Functions

**Instructions:** Load 1-2-3 and perform the following tasks.

1. Consider Figure 6-21. Write a database function and the criteria that will assign to the current cell the number of years of seniority for the female employee with the maximum years of seniority. Use a Criterion range of I3..I4.
2. Consider Figure 6-21. Write a database function and the criteria that will assign to the current cell the average years of seniority of the male employees. Use a Criterion range of I3..I4.
3. Consider Figure 6-21. Write a database function and the criteria that will assign to the current cell the sum of the ages of the female employees. Use a Criterion range of I3..I4.
4. Consider Figure 6-21. Write a database function and the criteria that will assign to the current cell the average years of seniority for both the male and female employees. Use a Criterion range of I3..I4.
5. Consider Figure 6-22. Use the CHOOSE function to assign cell B3 twelve times the cost in column E. Select the cost in column E on the basis of the index value in cell B1.
6. Consider Figure 6-23. Consider the VLOOKUP function in the upper screen in Figure 6-23. Complete the following problems independently and write down the results displayed in column D:
   a. Decrease all test scores in column B by 10 points.
   b. Increase all test scores in column B by 10 points.
   c. Reset the test scores in column B to their original values and change the offset argument in the VLOOKUP function to zero.

## STUDENT ASSIGNMENT 6: Building and Sorting a Database of Prospective Programmers

**Instructions:** Load 1-2-3 and perform the following tasks.

1. Build the database illustrated in Figure 6-24. Use the field sizes listed in Table 6-6.
2. Save and print the database. Use the file name STUS6-6.
3. Sort the records in the database into ascending sequence by name. Print the sorted version.
4. Sort the records in the database by age within sex. Select descending sequence for the sex code and ascending sequence for the age. Print the sorted version.

**TABLE 6-6 Field Descriptions for the Prospective Programmer Database**

| FIELD NAME | COLUMN | TYPE OF DATA | SIZE |
|---|---|---|---|
| Name | A | Label | 16 |
| Sex | B | Label | 5 |
| Age | C | Numeric | 5 |
| Years | D | Numeric | 7 |
| BASIC | E | Label | 7 |
| COBOL | F | Label | 7 |
| C | G | Label | 5 |
| RPG | H | Label | 5 |
| 123 | I | Label | 5 |
| DBASE | J | Label | 7 |

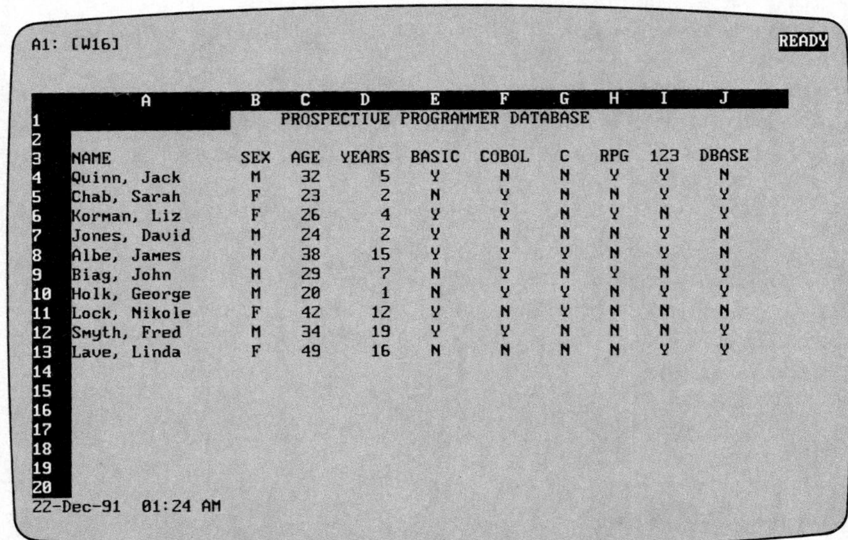
A1: [W16] READY

PROSPECTIVE PROGRAMMER DATABASE

| NAME | SEX | AGE | YEARS | BASIC | COBOL | C | RPG | 123 | DBASE |
|---|---|---|---|---|---|---|---|---|---|
| Quinn, Jack | M | 32 | 5 | Y | N | N | Y | Y | N |
| Chab, Sarah | F | 23 | 2 | N | Y | N | N | Y | Y |
| Korman, Liz | F | 26 | 4 | Y | Y | N | Y | N | Y |
| Jones, David | M | 24 | 2 | Y | N | N | N | Y | N |
| Albe, James | M | 38 | 15 | Y | Y | Y | N | Y | N |
| Biag, John | M | 29 | 7 | N | Y | N | Y | N | Y |
| Holk, George | M | 20 | 1 | N | Y | Y | N | Y | Y |
| Lock, Nikole | F | 42 | 12 | Y | N | Y | N | N | N |
| Smyth, Fred | M | 34 | 19 | Y | Y | N | N | N | Y |
| Lave, Linda | F | 49 | 16 | N | N | N | N | Y | Y |

22-Dec-91 01:24 AM

**FIGURE 6-24** Student Assignment 6

## STUDENT ASSIGNMENT 7: Finding Records in the Prospective Programmer Database

**Instructions:** Load 1-2-3 and perform the following tasks.

1. Load the database created in Student Assignment 6 (STUS6-6). This worksheet is illustrated in Figure 6-24.
2. For the Criterion range, copy row 3 (A3..J3) to row 15 (A15..J15).
3. In columns E through J of the database, the letter Y indicates that a prospective programmer knows the language or software package identified by the field name. The letter N indicates no experience with the language or software package. Find records that meet the following criteria. Treat each set of criteria in problems a through e separately.
   a. Find all records that represent prospective programmers who are female and can program in COBOL.
   b. Find all records that represent prospective programmers who can program in BASIC and RPG and use 123.
   c. Find all records that represent prospective male programmers who are at least 26 years old and can use dBASE.
   d. Find all records that represent prospective programmers who know COBOL and dBASE.
   e. Find all records that represent prospective programmers who know at least one programming language and can use 123 or dBASE.
   f. All prospective programmers who did not know dBASE were sent to a seminar on the software package. Use the Find command to locate the records of these programmers and change the entries from the letter N to the letter Y under the field name dBASE. Save and print the database and the accompanying Criterion range. Use the file name STUS6-7.

## STUDENT ASSIGNMENT 8: Extracting Records from the Prospective Programmer Database

**Instructions:** Load 1-2-3 and perform the following tasks.

1. Load the database created in Student Assignment 6 (STUS6-6). This worksheet is illustrated in Figure 6-24.
2. For the Criterion range, copy row 3 (A3..J3) to row 15 (A15..J15). For the Output range, copy the field names NAME, SEX, and AGE (A3..C3) to K3..M3. Change the widths of column K to 16, column L to 5, and column M to 5. Extract the three fields from the records that meet the criteria in problems a through e. Treat each extraction in problems a through e separately. Print the worksheet after each extraction.
   a. Extract from records that represent prospective programmers who are female.
   b. Extract from records that represent prospective programmers who can program in COBOL and RPG.
   c. Extract from records that represent prospective male programmers who are at least 24 years old and can use 123.
   d. Extract from records that represent prospective programmers who know COBOL and dBASE.
   e. Extract from records that represent prospective programmers who do not know how to use any programming language.
3. Save the database with the Criterion range specified in 2e. Use the file name STUS6-8.

## STUDENT ASSIGNMENT 9: Property Tax Rate Table Lookup

**Instructions:** Load 1-2-3 and perform the following tasks to build the worksheet shown in Figure 6-25. This worksheet uses the VLOOKUP function in cell C5 to look up the tax rate in the tax table in columns F and G. The VLOOKUP function employs cell C3 as the search argument. From the tax rate, the tax amount due in cell C7 can be determined.

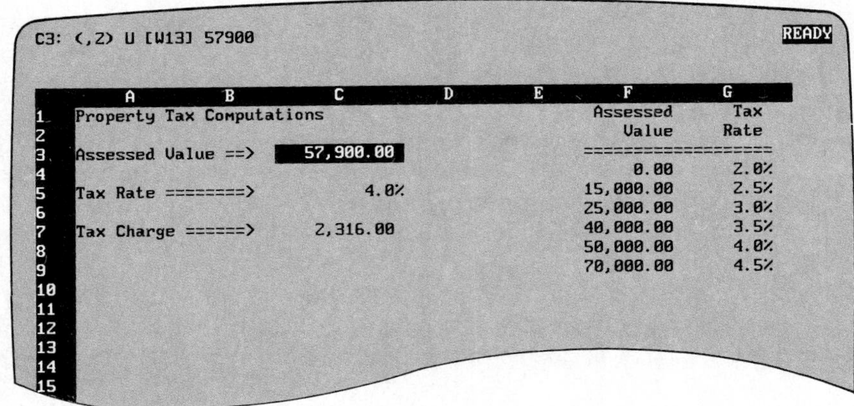


**FIGURE 6-25**
**Student Assignment 9**

1. Change the widths of column A to 11, column C to 13, and column F to 10. Leave the widths of the remaining columns at 9 characters.
2. Enter the title, column headings, and row identifiers.
3. Format cells C3 and C7 and range F4..F9 to the Comma (,) type with two decimal positions. Format cell C5 and range G4..G9 to the Percent type with one decimal position.
4. Enter the table values in the range F4..G9.
5. Assign the function @VLOOKUP(C3,F4..G9,1) to cell C5.
6. Assign the formula +C3*C5 to cell C7. This cell displays the tax amount due.
7. Test the worksheet to ensure that the VLOOKUP function is working properly.
8. Use the command /**W**orksheet **G**lobal **P**rotection **E**nable (/WGPE) to enable (turn on) cell protection. Unprotect cell C3.
9. Save the worksheet. Use the file name STUS6-9.
10. Determine the tax rate and tax charge for the following assessed valuations: $10,980.00; $25,000.00; $350,450.00; $48,560.00; and $57,900.00. Remember that commas (,) are not allowed in a numeric entry. Print the worksheet for each assessed valuation.

# Lotus 1-2-3 Index

# Database Management Using dBASE III PLUS



Creating, storing, sorting, and retrieving data are important tasks. In their personal lives, most people keep data in a variety of records such as the names, addresses, and telephone numbers of friends and business associates, records of investments, and records of expenses for income tax purposes. These records must be arranged so that the data can be accessed easily when required. In business, information must also be stored and accessed quickly and easily. Personnel and inventory records must be kept; payroll information and other types of data must be accumulated and periodically updated. Like personal records, business records must be organized so that the information they contain can be retrieved easily and rapidly.

The term **database** describes a collection of data organized in a manner that allows access, retrieval, and use of that data. A database is a structure that can hold data concerning many different types of objects (technically called **entities**) as well as relationships between these objects. For example, a company's database might hold data on such objects as sales reps and customers. In addition, the database would include the relationship between sales reps and customers; that is, we could use the data in the database to determine the sales rep who represents any particular customer, and to determine all the customers who are represented by any given sales rep.

Figure 1 gives a sample of such a database. It consists of two tables: SLSREP and CUSTOMER. The columns in the SLSREP table include the sales rep number, name, address, total commission, and commission rate. For example, the name of sales rep 3 is Mary Jones. She lives at 123 Main St. in Grant, Michigan. Her total commission is $2,150.00 and her commission rate is 5 percent.

| SLSREP_ NUMBER | SLSREP_NAME | SLSREP_ADDRESS | TOTAL_ COMMISSION | COMMISSION_ RATE |
|---|---|---|---|---|
| 3 | Mary Jones | 123 Main,Grant,MI | 2150.00 | .05 |
| 6 | William Smith | 102 Raymond,Ada,MI | 4912.50 | .07 |
| 12 | Sam Brown | 419 Harper,Lansing,MI | 2150.00 | .05 |



| CUSTOMER_ NUMBER | NAME | ADDRESS | CURRENT_ BALANCE | CREDIT_ LIMIT | SLSREP_ NUMBER |
|---|---|---|---|---|---|
| 124 | Sally Adams | 481 Oak,Lansing,MI | 418.75 | 500 | 3 |
| 256 | Ann Samuels | 215 Pete,Grant,MI | 10.75 | 800 | 6 |
| 311 | Don Charles | 48 College,Ira,MI | 200.10 | 300 | 12 |
| 315 | Tom Daniels | 914 Cherry,Kent,MI | 320.75 | 300 | 6 |
| 405 | Al Williams | 519 Watson,Grant,MI | 201.75 | 800 | 12 |
| 412 | Susan Lin | 16 Elm,Lansing,MI | 908.75 | 1000 | 3 |
| 522 | Mary Nelson | 108 Pine,Ada,MI | 49.50 | 800 | 12 |
| 567 | Joe Baker | 808 Ridge,Harper,MI | 201.20 | 300 | 6 |
| 587 | Judy Roberts | 512 Pine,Ada,MI | 57.75 | 500 | 6 |
| 622 | Dan Martin | 419 Chip,Grant,MI | 575.50 | 500 | 3 |



**FIGURE 1** Sample Database of Sales Reps and Customers

The first five columns in the customer table include the customer number, name, address, current balance, and credit limit. The name of customer 622 is Dan Martin. He lives at 419 Chip St. in Grant, Michigan. His current balance is $575.50, which happens to exceed his $500 credit limit.

The last column in the customer table, SLSREP_NUMBER, serves a special purpose. It *relates* customers and sales reps. Using this column, we can see that Dan Martin's sales rep is sales rep 3 (Mary Jones). Likewise, we can see that Mary Jones also represents customers 124 (Sally Adams) and 412 (Susan Lin). We do this by first looking up Mary's number in the SLSREP table and then looking for all rows in the CUSTOMER table that contain this number in the column labeled SLSREP_NUMBER.

In a sense, the tables shown in Figure 1 form a database even if they are simply kept on paper. But for easy and rapid access, they should be kept on a computer. All that is needed to do this is a tool that will assist users in accessing such a database. The term database management system describes this tool. A **database management system** or **DBMS** is a software product that can be used easily to create a database; make additions, deletions, and changes to data in the database; sort the data in the database; and retrieve data from the database in a variety of ways.

The most widely used DBMS available for personal computers is dBASE III PLUS, developed by Ashton-Tate. dBASE III PLUS is a powerful DBMS. Its commands let users easily create and manage databases for either personal or business needs. dBASE III PLUS is one of a general category of database management systems called **relational**. In simplest terms, this means that the data in the database can be visualized in exactly the fashion you saw in Figure 1, that is, as a collection of tables, each consisting of a series of rows and columns, which relate different pieces of data.

The dBASE III PLUS software package used in this book is an educational version of dBASE III PLUS. This version contains all the features of the original product except that the number of rows in each table is limited to 31. From this point on we will refer to dBASE III PLUS as simply dBASE.

In the first five projects, you will use a dBASE feature called the ASSISTANT. The **ASSISTANT** is a collection of menus that assist you in processing the data in a database. The menus and choices covered in this text are shown in Figure 2. Don't worry about the specifics of these options now. They will become clear as you work your way through the material in these projects. In Project 6, you will learn to type commands to access the database. The commands you will use are shown in Figure 3 on the next page. Again, don't worry about the specifics at this point.

| OPTION | PURPOSE |
|---|---|
| Set Up | Activate a |
| Database file | database file |
| View | view |
| Quit dBASE III PLUS | leave dBASE III PLUS |
| Create | Create a |
| Database file | database file (extension DBF) |
| View | view (extension VUE) |
| Report | report (extension FRM) |
| Update | Change a database file by |
| Append | adding records at the end |
| Edit | changing records viewing one at a time |
| Browse | changing records viewing several at a time |
| Replace | changing the data in all records that satisfy some condition |
| Delete | deleting records |
| Recall | undeleting records |
| Pack | physically removing deleted records |
| Position | Move the record pointer by |
| Seek | finding a match using an index |
| Locate | finding the first record that satisfies some condition |
| Goto Record | specifying a record number |
| Retrieve | Retrieve data from a database file |
| List | show desired fields and records on the screen or printer |
| Display | like "List" (differences between the two are covered in the text) |
| Report | print a report |
| Sum | calculate a total |
| Average | calculate an average |
| Count | count the number of records |
| Organize | |
| Index | create an index (extension NDX) |
| Sort | sort a database file |
| Modify | Change an existing |
| Database file | database file |
| Report | report file |
| Tools | |
| List structure | show the structure of the active database file |

**FIGURE 2** Menus and Options within the dBASE ASSISTANT

| COMMAND | PURPOSE |
|---|---|
| APPEND | Add records to a database file |
| AVERAGE | Calculate an Average |
| CLEAR | Clear the screen |
| COUNT | Count the number of records |
| DISPLAY | Show desired fields and records |
| DO | Run a command file (program) |
| EJECT | Force the printer to advance to the top of the next page |
| MODIFY COMMAND | Create a command file (program) (extension PRG) |
| SET VIEW TO | Activate a view |
| SORT | Sort a database file |
| SUM | Calculate a total |
| USE | Activate a database file |

**FIGURE 3**
**dBASE Commands**

Each project ends with four minicases. Minicase 1 in each project involves a database of personal checks. Minicase 2 involves a music library database. Minicase 3 deals with a database for a software store. The database for Minicase 4 contains information on homes for sale. You should work on the same minicase in each project. Your instructor will probably assign you a specific minicase. If not, you can choose any of the four. Just make sure you select the same one in each project.

The material in the minicases is cumulative. That is, the assignment for Minicase 1 in Project 2 builds on the assignment for Minicase 1 from Project 1. It is very important that you work through the minicase completely before proceeding to the next project. If not, you will encounter serious difficulties later on.

As you work through these projects, you will create a number of files and select a name for each one. dBASE will automatically add a period and three characters to the name you have chosen to indicate the type of file created. This is called the file extension. It need not concern you, but if you examine the files on your disk, you will see these extensions. In the first project, for example, you will create a database file and name it EMPLOYEE. Since dBASE uses the extension DBF for database files, the file on your diskette will actually be called EMPLOYEE.DBF. You can see the file types used in these projects and their extensions in Figure 4.

| FILE TYPE | EXTENSION |
|---|---|
| Database file | DBF |
| Index file | NDX |
| Report file | FRM |
| View file | VUE |
| Command file (program) | PRG |

**FIGURE 4**
**dBASE File Types and Extensions**

# PROJECT 1

## Creating and Displaying a Database

### Objectives

You will have mastered the material in this project when you can:

- Plan a database
- Load and use dBASE
- Choose menus and options using the dBASE ASSISTANT
- Create a database file
- Add records to a database file
- Correct errors in a database file
- Display a list of all records in a database file

In Project 1, you will learn how to create a database using dBASE. You will use the menus and options in the ASSISTANT that are indicated in Figure 1-1. To illustrate the process, we will work through a sample problem about creating and accessing a company's employee records.

| OPTION | PURPOSE |
|---|---|
| Set Up | Activate a |
| Database file | database file |
| View | view |
| Quit dBASE III PLUS | leave dBASE III PLUS |
| Create | Create a |
| Database file | database file (extension DBF) |
| View | view (extension VUE) |
| Report | report (extension FRM) |
| Update | Change a database file by |
| Append | adding records at the end |
| Edit | changing records viewing one at a time |
| Browse | changing records viewing several at a time |
| Replace | changing the data in all records that satisfy some condition |
| Delete | deleting records |
| Recall | undeleting records |
| Pack | physically removing deleted records |
| Position | Move the record pointer by |
| Seek | finding a match using an index |
| Locate | finding the first record that satisfies some condition |
| Goto Record | specifying a record number |
| Retrieve | Retrieve data from a database file |
| List | show desired fields and records on the screen or printer |
| Display | like "List" (differences between the two are covered in the text) |
| Report | print a report |
| Sum | calculate a total |
| Average | calculate an average |
| Count | count the number of records |
| Organize | |
| Index | create an index (extension NDX) |
| Sort | sort a database file |
| Modify | Change an existing |
| Database file | database file |
| Report | report file |
| Tools | |
| List structure | show the structure of the active database file |

**FIGURE 1-1**
Menus and Options within the dBASE ASSISTANT

The employee record form (see Figure 1-2) is the basis of the database. Each record contains an employee number, the employee name, the date hired, a department name, the employee's pay rate, and an entry indicating whether the employee is a member of the union. The forms taken as a whole comprise a **file**. Each form that contains information about a single employee is called a **record**, and the individual units of information within each record are called **fields**. In this example the date hired is a field. All the information about Anthony P. Rapoza is a record. And Anthony Rapoza's record along with the records of all the other employees in the company make up the file.

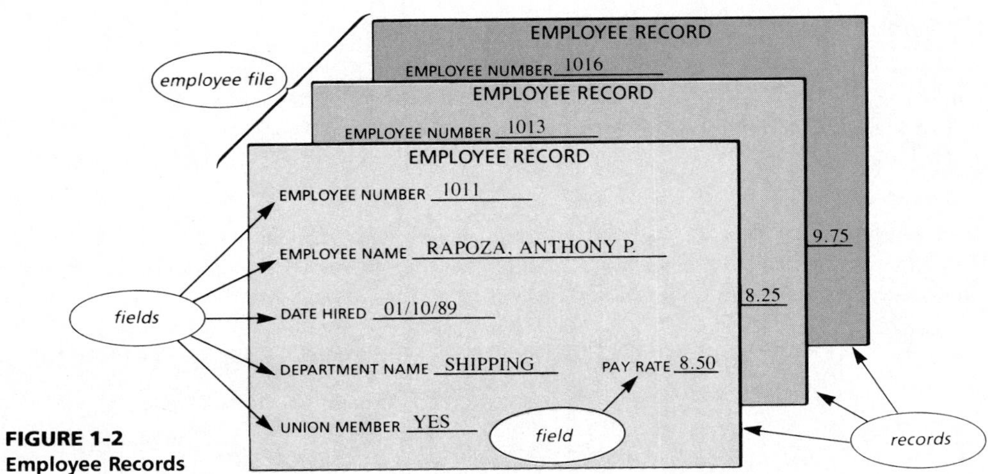


**FIGURE 1-2**
**Employee Records**

Now look at the sample table shown in Figure 1-3. Notice that it contains the same data shown in Figure 1-2, but the data is represented in a more concise fashion. The rows in this table are the records, the columns are the fields, and the whole table is a file.

| EMPLOYEE NUMBER | EMPLOYEE NAME | DATE HIRED | DEPARTMENT NAME | PAY RATE | UNION MEMBER |
|---|---|---|---|---|---|
| 1011 | Rapoza, Anthony P. | 01/10/89 | Shipping | 8.50 | Y |
| 1013 | McCormack, Nigel L. | 01/15/89 | Shipping | 8.25 | Y |
| 1016 | Ackerman, David R. | 02/04/89 | Accounting | 9.75 | N |
| 1017 | Doi, Chan J. | 02/05/89 | Production | 6.00 | Y |
| 1020 | Castle, Mark C. | 03/04/89 | Shipping | 7.50 | Y |
| 1022 | Dunning, Lisa A. | 03/12/89 | Marketing | 9.10 | N |
| 1025 | Chaney, Joseph R. | 03/23/89 | Accounting | 8.00 | N |
| 1026 | Bender, Helen O. | 04/12/89 | Production | 6.75 | Y |
| 1029 | Anderson, Mariane L. | 04/18/89 | Shipping | 9.00 | Y |
| 1030 | Edwards, Kenneth J. | 04/23/89 | Production | 8.60 | Y |
| 1037 | Baxter, Charles W. | 05/05/89 | Accounting | 11.00 | N |
| 1041 | Evans, John T. | 05/19/89 | Marketing | 6.00 | N |
| 1056 | Andrews, Robert M. | 06/03/89 | Marketing | 9.00 | N |
| 1057 | Dugan, Mary L. | 06/10/89 | Production | 8.75 | Y |
| 1066 | Castleworth, Mary T. | 07/05/89 | Production | 8.75 | Y |

records

fields

**FIGURE 1-3**
**Employee Table**

Rather than the term "file," however, dBASE uses the term "database file." Thus, in dBASE, a **database file** is a single table. Recall from the introduction that a relational database can be a single table or a collection of tables. In dBASE terminology, this means that a database is a collection of database *files*. (You don't have to worry about the distinction at this point, however. In the examples discussed in the first four projects, each database will consist of a single database file (a single table). In Project 5, you will encounter databases that contain more than one database file.

Other database management systems use the terms **table** (for file), **row** (for record), and **column** (for field). We use the dBASE terminology throughout this text.

## PLANNING A DATABASE FILE

Before using dBASE to create a database file, you must perform four steps. These steps are:

1. Select a name for the database file.
2. Define the structure of the database file. This means determining the fields that will be part of the file.
3. Name the fields.
4. Determine the type and width of each field.

### Naming a Database File

When using dBASE, you must assign a name to each database file. The rules for forming a name are:

1. The name can be up to eight characters long.
2. The first character must be a letter of the alphabet.
3. The remaining characters can be letters, numbers, or the underscore (_).
4. Blank spaces are not allowed.

You should select names that are as meaningful as possible. This will make it easier to identify the database file later. In the sample problem, let's use the name EMPLOYEE.

### Defining the Structure of a Database File

To define the structure of the database file, you must determine the fields that will make up the file. The fields you want to include must be based upon the type of information you want to extract from the database. We have determined that we will require access to each of the fields contained on the employee form in Figure 1-2, that is, the employee number field, the employee name field, the date hired field, the department name field, the pay rate field, and the field that tells whether or not the employee is a member of the union. In dBASE, you can have a maximum of 128 fields in a record and records can be a maximum of 4000 characters long.

### Naming the Fields

You must assign a unique name to each field in the database.

1. A field name can contain up to 10 characters.
2. The first character must be alphabetic.
3. The remaining characters can consist of letters of the alphabet, numbers, or the underscore (_).
4. No blank spaces are allowed.

The chart in Figure 1-4 illustrates the field names that will be used in the sample database file.

| FIELD DESCRIPTION | FIELD NAME |
|---|---|
| EMPLOYEE NUMBER | NUMBER |
| EMPLOYEE NAME | NAME |
| DATE HIRED | DATE |
| DEPARTMENT NAME | DEPARTMENT |
| PAY RATE | PAY_RATE |
| UNION MEMBER | UNION |

**FIGURE 1-4**
**Fields in Employee File**

You should select meaningful field names that are closely related to the contents of the field. Note that the field name for the pay rate field is PAY_RATE. We often use the underscore to join words together to improve readability, because blanks are not allowed within field names.

## Defining Field Types

Next, you must determine the type of each field in the database. There are five field types in dBASE. They are:

1. **Character fields** These fields may be used to store any printable characters that can be entered from the keyboard. This includes letters of the alphabet, numbers, special characters, and blanks. A maximum of 254 characters may be included in a character field.
2. **Data fields** Date fields are used to store dates. Unless otherwise specified, the date is stored in the form MM/DD/YY (month/day/year). The field width is always eight characters.
3. **Numeric fields** These fields are used to store integer or decimal numbers. Integer numbers are numbers that do not contain a decimal point. Numeric fields may contain a plus (+) or minus (-) sign. Accuracy is to 15 digits. A field must be defined as numeric if it will be used in a calculation.
4. **Logical fields** Logical fields consist of a single value representing a true or false condition. The entry must be T (true), F (false), Y (yes), or N (no). Lowercase letters of the alphabet can also be used. The field width is always one character.
5. **Memo fields** Memo fields are used to store large blocks of text such as words or sentences. Memo fields may be up to 4000 characters long.

Figure 1-5 illustrates the field type for the various fields used in the sample problem. Note that the employee number is specified as a character field. A field that contains all numbers but is not involved in calculations should normally be defined as a character field. The name field is defined as a character field, the date hired field as a date field, the department name field as a character field, the pay rate field as a numeric field, and the union code field as a logical field.

| FIELD DESCRIPTION | FIELD NAME | FIELD TYPE | WIDTH | DECIMAL POSITIONS |
|---|---|---|---|---|
| EMPLOYEE NUMBER | NUMBER | CHARACTER | 4 | |
| EMPLOYEE NAME | NAME | CHARACTER | 20 | |
| DATE HIRED | DATE | DATE | 8 | |
| DEPARTMENT NAME | DEPARTMENT | CHARACTER | 10 | |
| PAY RATE | PAY_RATE | NUMERIC | 5 | 2 |
| UNION MEMBER | UNION | LOGICAL | 1 | |

*decimal positions only necessary for numeric fields*

**FIGURE 1-5**
**Field Characteristics for Employee File**

### Indicating Width and Decimal Position

The width of the field indicates the maximum number of characters that will be contained in the field. Date fields always have width 8 and logical fields always have width 1. For other types of fields, you must specify the width. In addition, for numeric fields, you must specify the decimal position, or the location of the decimal point. For example, a decimal position of 2 indicates that there are two positions to the right of the decimal point.

In Figure 1-5 the PAY_RATE field is defined as having a width of five characters. This means that the maximum value that can be stored in the PAY_RATE field is 99.99. In a numeric field, count the decimal point when specifying the field width.

## USING dBASE

### Loading dBASE

To create a database file, you must load dBASE into main memory. First, load the operating system and enter the current date and time. You should see the A> prompt displayed on the screen. Place your first dBASE disk in drive A. Then type the word dbase in either uppercase or lowercase letters. The example in Figure 1-6 uses lowercase letters. (If you have dBASE on a hard disk drive, make that the default disk before typing the word dbase.)

**FIGURE 1-6** Loading dBASE

After typing the word dbase, press the Enter key (also called the Return key). After you have done this, dBASE will be loaded into main computer memory and the display in Figure 1-7 will appear on the screen.

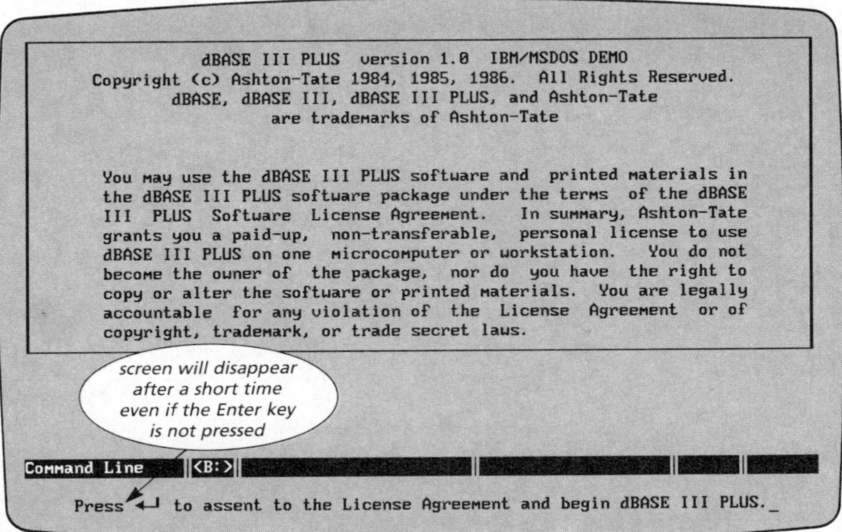


**FIGURE 1-7**
**The License Screen for dBASE III PLUS**

The paragraph displayed in Figure 1-7 describes the licensing agreement and related information. The line at the bottom of the screen tells you to press the Enter key to begin working with dBASE. Once you have done this, the display will change. (If you wait a few seconds without pressing the Enter key, the display will change automatically.) The display will change to the screen shown in Figure 1-8 unless you are using dBASE on a hard disk, in which case you will immediately proceed to the display shown in Figure 1-9.

The message at the bottom of the display in Figure 1-8 tells you to place the second dBASE disk in drive A and a data disk in drive B. Initially, this data disk will be empty. As you create files using dBASE, you will put them on this disk. Once these diskettes have been inserted in the correct drives, press the Enter key. (If you are using dBASE on a hard disk, you should still place your data disk in drive B unless your instructor indicates differently.)

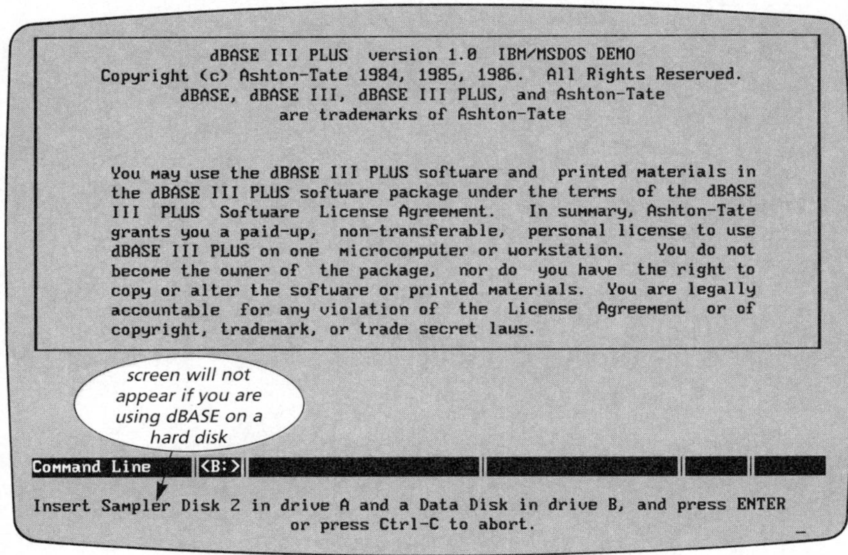


**FIGURE 1-8**
**Ready to Insert Disks**

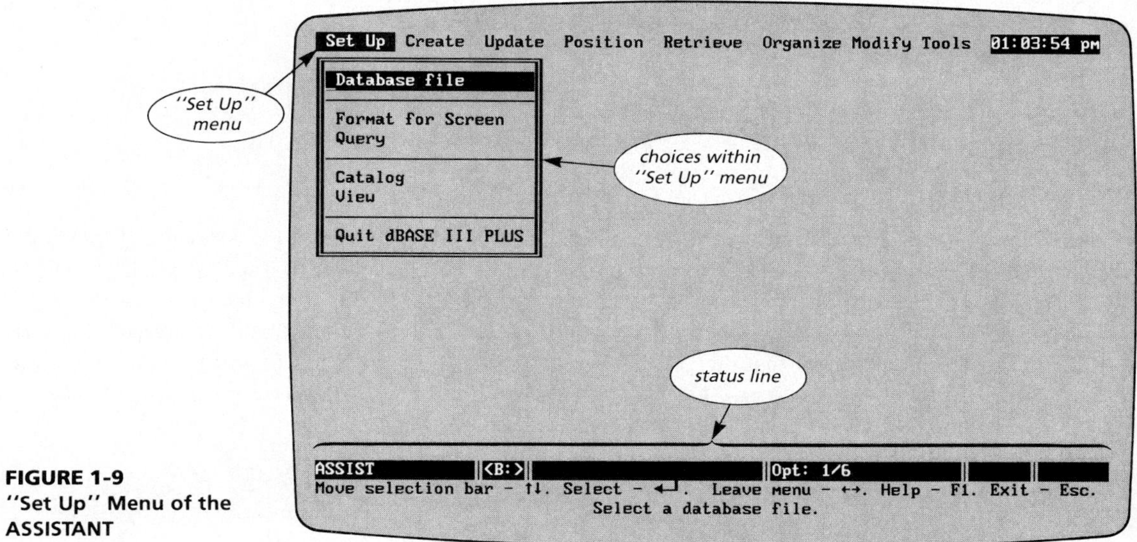


**FIGURE 1-9**
**"Set Up" Menu of the ASSISTANT**

## The ASSISTANT

At this point, the display will look like the one shown in Figure 1-9. This screen is part of the dBASE ASSISTANT. The **ASSISTANT** is a collection of menus that assist you in processing the data in a database. When you use the menus, you are in **ASSIST** mode. The names of the various menus are displayed across the top of the screen. They are "Set Up," "Create," "Update," "Position," "Retrieve," "Organize," "Modify," and "Tools." Notice that the name of one of the menus is highlighted on the screen. The highlight indicates the currently selected menu. Thus, at this point, the "Set Up" menu is the one from which you can choose. Press the Right Arrow key a few times. Notice how the highlight and the box move to the menus immediately to the right of the current menu. Press the Left Arrow key a few times and notice how the highlight and the box move to the menus immediately to the left. Notice also how the choices within the selected menu are displayed in a box on the screen.

To indicate your choice, you would use the Up or Down Arrow keys to move the highlight within the box to the desired selection and then press Enter. Try this with the choices in the "Set Up" menu. Move the highlight to your selection. Do not press Enter yet, however.

The line shown at the bottom of the screen is called the **status line** or **status bar**. This line gives information about the current status of dBASE. In Figure 1-9, for example, the status line indicates that:

1. You are currently in ASSIST mode; that is, you are using the ASSISTANT but have not yet begun to take any special action.
2. The default drive for data files is B.
3. No database file is currently active (if one were active, its name would appear in the next portion of the screen).
4. The option currently highlighted is option 1 out of 6.

Compare the status line in Figure 1-9 to the one shown in Figure 1-10 which indicates that:

1. Data in a database file is being EDITed (changed).
2. The file is located in drive B.
3. The file name is EMPLOYEE.
4. The current position in the file is record 1.
5. There are 15 records altogether.
6. The insert mode is on (Ins).

If insert mode is on, a character that you type will be inserted into a string of characters rather than replacing an existing character. Press the Ins key several times and watch the insert portion of the status line. You will see that pressing Ins when insert mode is off turns it on. Pressing Ins when insert mode is on turns it off.

Two other lines, beneath the status line, give important information. The first line indicates the effect of special keys. In Figure 1-9, for example, this line indicates that the Up and Down Arrow keys are used to move the status bar, the Enter key is used to make a selection, the Right or Left Arrow keys are used to leave this menu (and move to another), and so on. The second line under the status line gives a brief description of the current option.

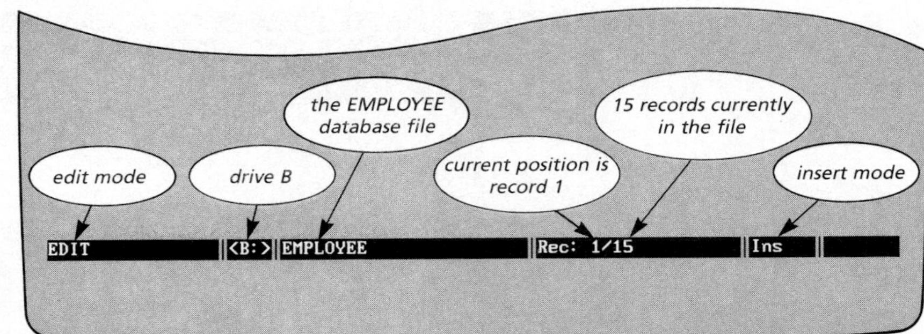


**FIGURE 1-10**
**Status Line**

## The Dot Prompt

Press the Esc key with the ASSISTANT menu on the screen. Your display will change to the one shown in Figure 1-11. The period near the lower left-hand corner of the screen is called the **dot prompt** in dBASE. It puts you into the **dot prompt mode**. (In the student version, the dot is preceded by the word DEMO.)

The dot prompt indicates that dBASE is ready to accept a command. A **dBASE command** is a word or collection of words that will cause some function to be performed by dBASE, such as displaying data or calculating a total. Following the dot prompt is a blinking underscore character called a cursor. The **cursor** indicates where the characters you enter at the keyboard will be displayed.

In Project 6, you will have a chance to type commands at this dot prompt. In the rest of the projects, however, your work will be done through the ASSISTANT in what is termed the **ASSIST mode**. Even though you will be working in the ASSIST mode, you need to be aware of the dot prompt because if you press the Esc key, you may find yourself in this dot prompt mode. Fortunately, there is an easy way to return to the ASSIST mode. Simply press F2 (function key 2). The ASSISTANT menu will return to the screen and you will be back in ASSIST mode.

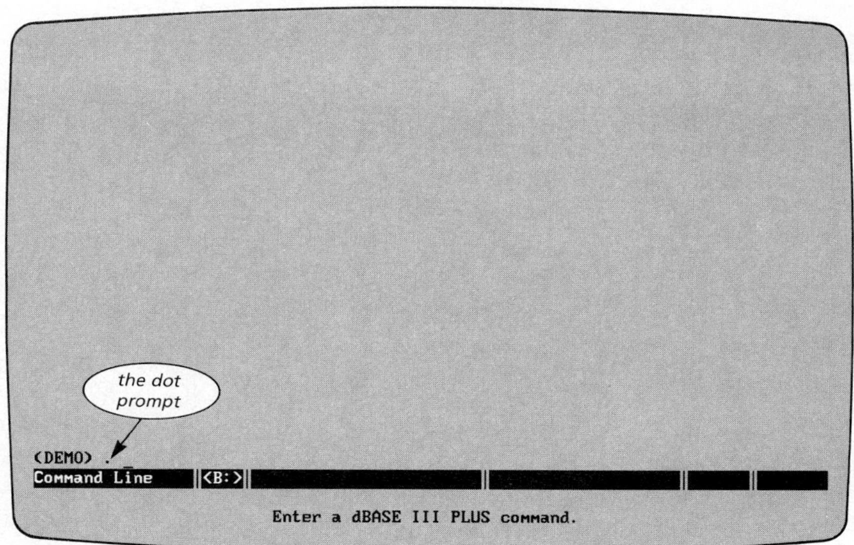


**FIGURE 1-11**
**The Dot Prompt Screen**

When you use the ASSISTANT, dBASE actually constructs the commands for you. These are the same commands that you could type at the dot prompt. They are shown immediately above the status line. As you work through the examples in the first five projects, watch these commands as they are being constructed. This will help you when you get to Project 6 and start constructing these commands on your own.

## Escaping from Problems

When using the ASSISTANT, you might find that you have selected an option that you did not want and you might not be sure how to leave the option. Even if you have selected the correct option, there may be times when you are not sure how to proceed. In other cases, you may discover that you simply don't have enough time to complete the task you started. For these reasons, you will occasionally want to *escape* from a task.

Normally the Right or Left Arrow keys will allow you to leave a task. If they don't, however, there is another way to escape. Repeatedly press the Esc key. Eventually, this will bring you to the dot prompt (Figure 1-11). Once you see the dot prompt, press F2 and you will return to the "Set Up" menu of the ASSISTANT.

## Quitting

You stop using dBASE by returning to the "Set Up" menu (Figure 1-12) and selecting "Quit dBASE III PLUS." First, choose the "Set Up" menu by using the Right or Left Arrow keys. Then move the highlight to "Quit dBASE III PLUS" using the Down Arrow key. After that, press the Enter key. Control will return to the operating system. Practice this now. Then restart dBASE in the same manner as before.

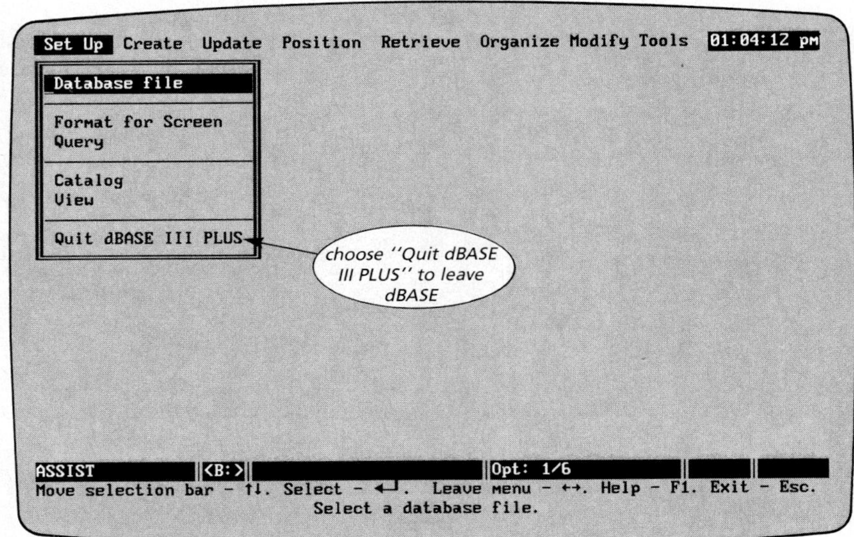


**FIGURE 1-12**
**"Set Up" Menu**

## Getting Help

If you need additional information about dBASE, you can use the help feature. As indicated on the screen (Figure 1-12), press the F1 key for help. When you press this key, you will see information concerning the menu choice that is currently highlighted on the screen. Pressing the F1 key while the highlight is on the "Database file" option within the "Set Up" menu, for example (see Figure 1-13a), would display the screen shown in Figure 1-13b. Once you have viewed this information, simply press any key and the display will return to its original state.

## Practicing

At this point, it's a good idea for you to practice moving through the menus. As you do, note the effect on the last two lines on the screen. Try getting help. Try pressing the Esc key to move to the dot prompt and then pressing F2 to get back to the ASSISTANT. Do this until you are comfortable moving around the menu structure.

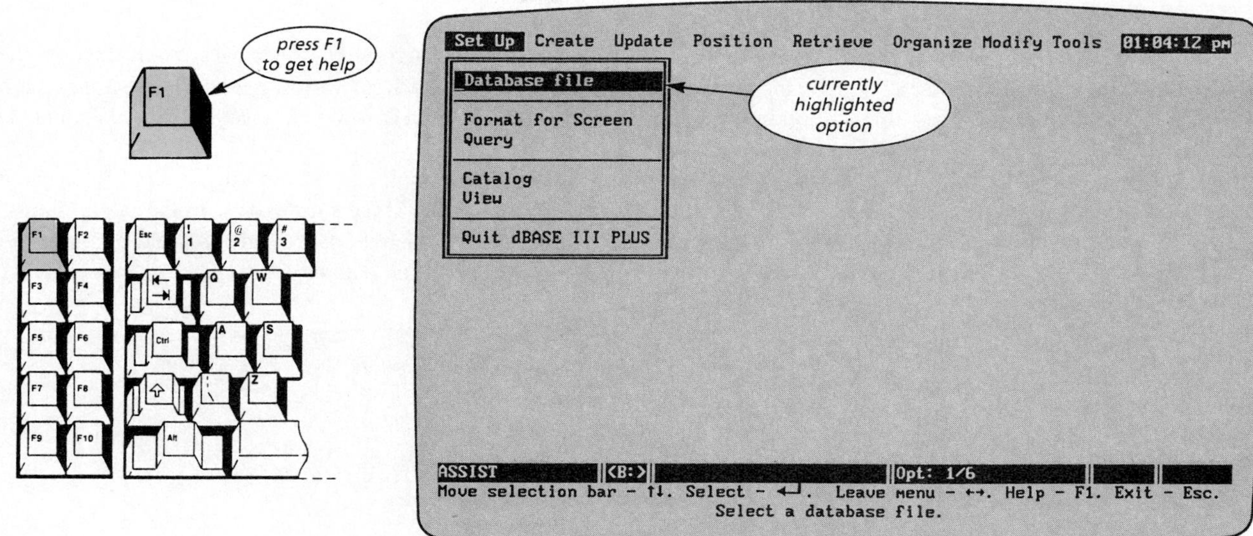


**FIGURE 1-13a** Getting Help

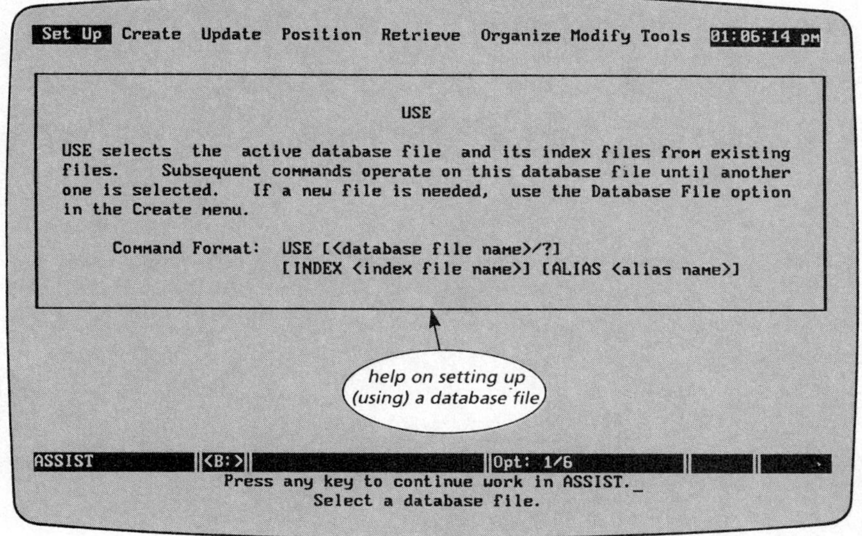


**FIGURE 1-13b** Sample Help Screen

## CREATING THE DATABASE

To create the database, move to the "Create" menu using the Right or Left Arrow keys. If you are currently on the "Set Up" menu, you only have to press the Right Arrow key once. The highlight within the box will already be on "Database file," which is the correct option, so you will not need the Up or Down Arrow keys. Press the Enter key to indicate that "Database file" is your choice.

The display should now look like the one shown in Figure 1-14. (Note: Your display may have only A: and B: in the box. It may also have additional options besides A:, B:, and C:. Don't worry about this.) Make sure that B: in the box is highlighted. If it isn't, use the Up or Down Arrow keys to move the highlight to it, because the file created should be placed on the diskette in drive B. Then press the Enter key. It is now time to indicate the name of the database file.

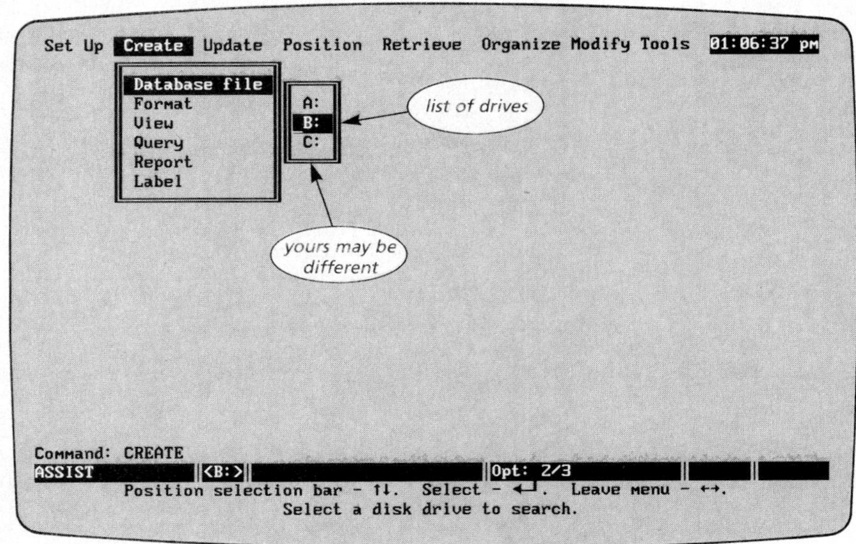


**FIGURE 1-14**
Creating a Database File

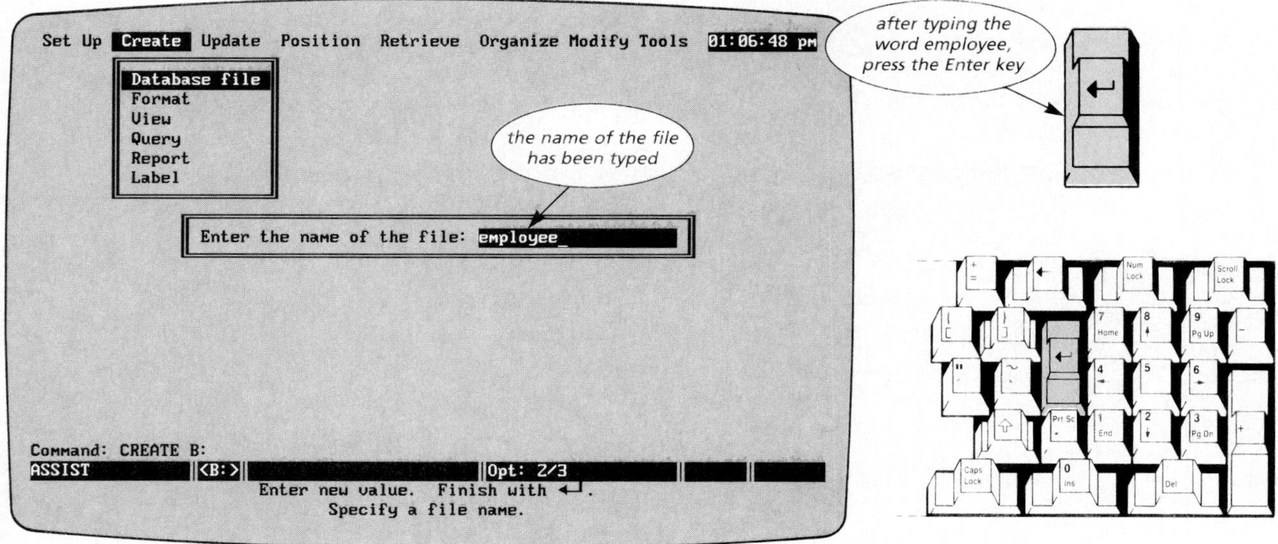


**FIGURE 1-15**
Entering the Name of the File

As shown in Figure 1-15, type the word employee (in either uppercase or lowercase) and press the Enter key. The screen used to define the structure of the database will appear, as shown in Figure 1-16.

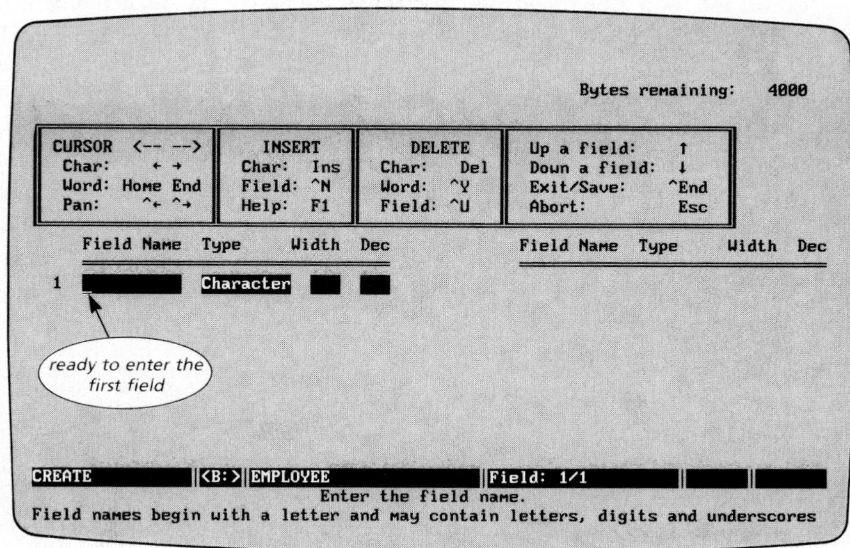


**FIGURE 1-16**
**Entering the First Field**

Next, define the structure of the database by specifying the following information for each field: field name, field type, field width, and decimal places (if appropriate). The screen in Figure 1-16 assists you in entering this information. Near the bottom of the screen you will see the file name EMPLOYEE. In the upper right-hand portion of the screen, information specifies the bytes remaining in the record. A *byte* is a single position of main computer memory, the amount of main memory required to store a single character. Thus, you can think of "byte" and "character" as being synonymous. In dBASE, a record can contain a maximum of 4000 bytes or characters, so the number 4000 appears. Underneath the byte display is a box indicating the effect of some of the special keys.

Beneath this box are screen headings for field name, type, width, and dec (decimal position). There are two sets of these entries, one set at the left of the screen and the other set at the right. Beneath the headings at the left of the screen are reverse video blocks. These indicate where you will enter the field name, select the field type, and enter the field width and decimal positions for numeric fields. The cursor is in the first position of the area where you enter the field name. The number 1 to the left of the cursor merely indicates that this is the area in which you will define the first field.

The entry at the bottom of the screen provides information to assist you in making the appropriate entry in the field name portion of the display. This message will change as the cursor moves from one portion of the screen to the next.

Begin by typing the name of the first field you wish to define. In the example, the first field is the employee number field. Recall from Figure 1-5 that the field name is NUMBER. Therefore, enter the word NUMBER as the first field name (Figure 1-17).

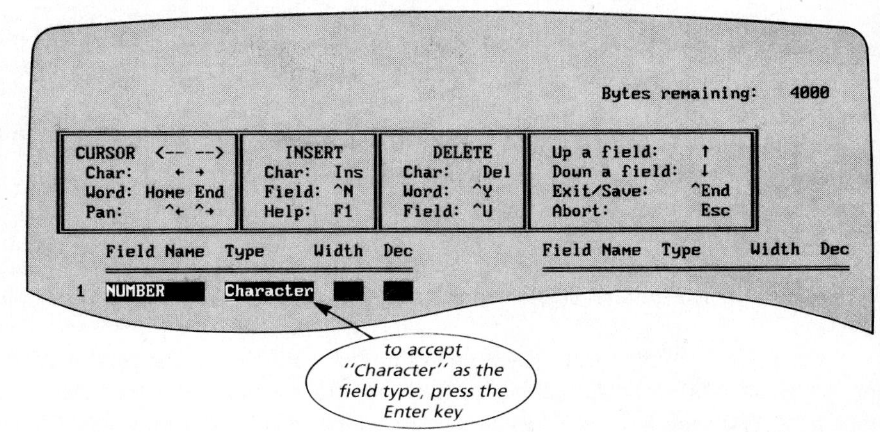


**FIGURE 1-17**
**Selecting Field Type**

If the entry in the field name portion of the screen has less than 10 characters, you must press the Enter key to move the cursor to the next area on the screen. Since the word NUMBER contains only six characters, press the Enter key. When you have done so, the cursor will move to the type column on the screen. Under the type column is the word "Character" within the reverse video block (Figure 1-17).

Next you will specify the type of field being defined. To do this, simply press the space bar until the desired field type is displayed. Do this a few times. After you have pressed it once, the entry in the type column will change to the word "Numeric." A second time changes it to "Date." The next time, it changes to "Logical," and one more time changes it to "Memo." Pressing the space bar again changes it back to "Character," at which point the whole sequence would start all over again.

Because the employee number field is not used in calculations, the field should be defined as a character field. To specify that NUMBER is a character field, make sure the word "Character" is displayed on the screen and press the Enter key. The cursor will then advance to the width column (Figure 1-18).

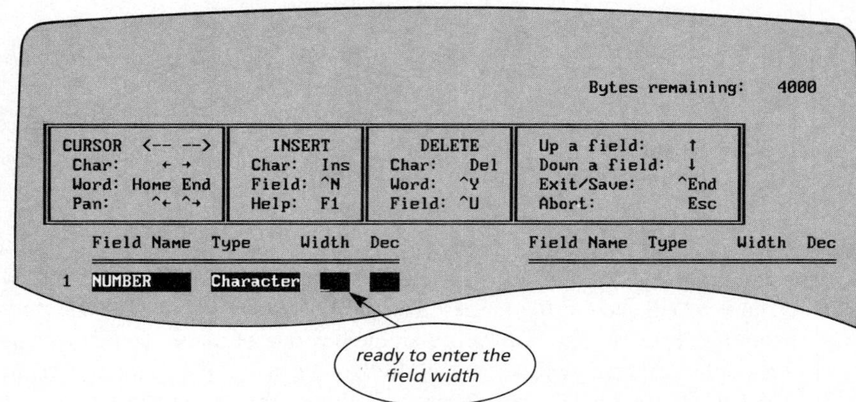


**FIGURE 1-18**
**Entering Field Width**

Now you must type the width of the field. In the example, there are a maximum of four digits in the employee number field (see Figure 1-5). Therefore, type the number 4 and press the Enter key, producing the display shown in Figure 1-19. There can be no decimal entries for a character field, so the entries for the NUMBER field are complete once you indicate the width. Thus, the cursor and the reverse video display move to the next line. Look at the upper right corner of Figure 1-19. You will see that 3996 bytes remain for this record.

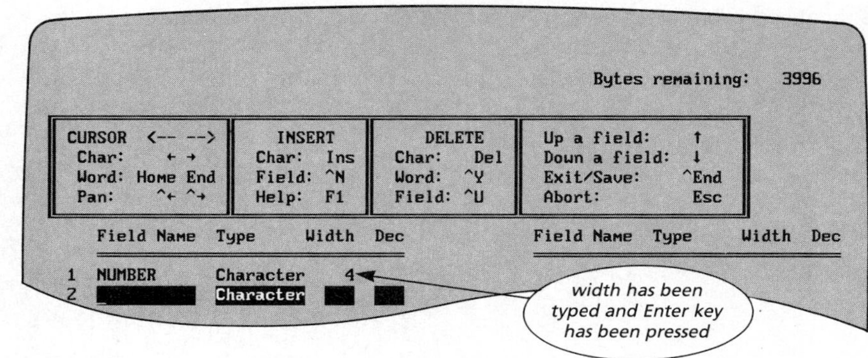


**FIGURE 1-19**
**Ready to Enter Another Field**

The entries for the NAME field are illustrated in Figure 1-20. Make these entries in the same fashion as for the NUMBER field. Figure 1-20 also shows the name of the DATE field. You should make the same entry now and then press Enter.

When you press the Enter key after typing the word DATE, the cursor will move to the type column. Because DATE is to be treated as a date field, press the space bar repeatedly until the word "Date" appears in the type column (Figure 1-21) and then press the Enter key. dBASE will automatically specify the width as 8. (Remember that the slashes in a date count as positions in the field.)

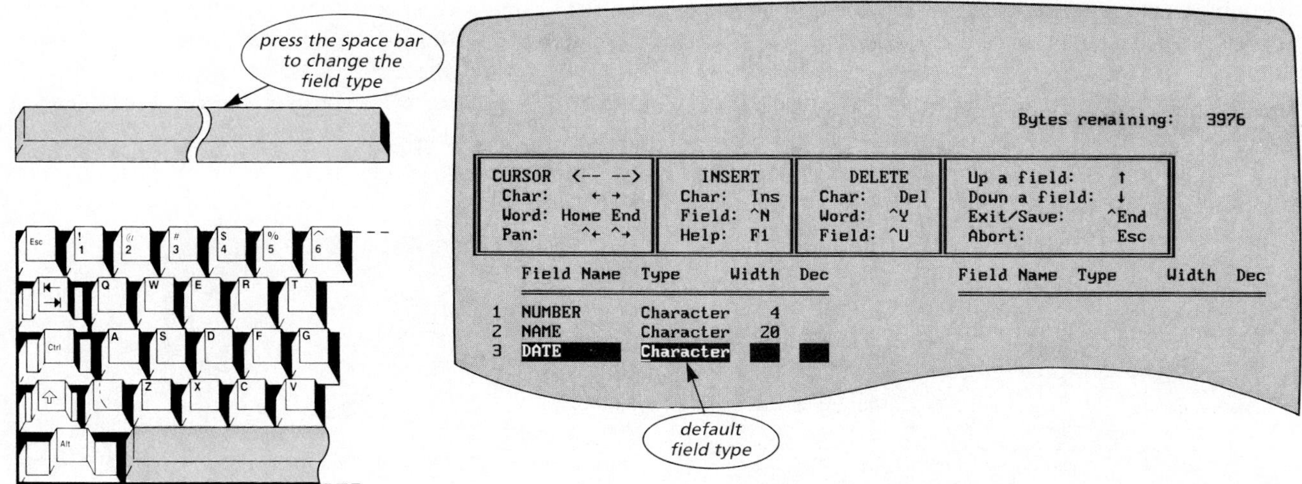


**FIGURE 1-20** Changing the Type

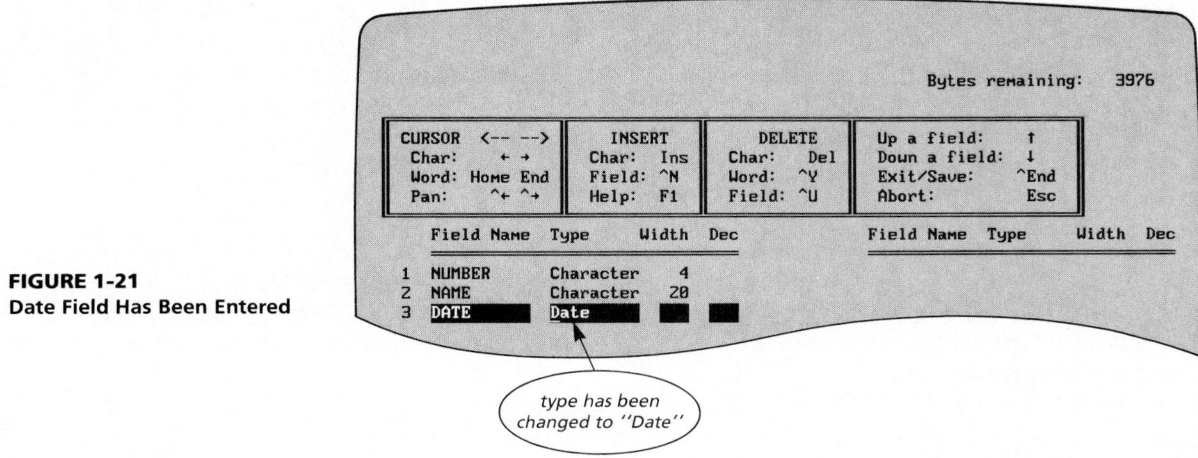


**FIGURE 1-21**
**Date Field Has Been Entered**

Make the remaining entries as shown in Figure 1-22.

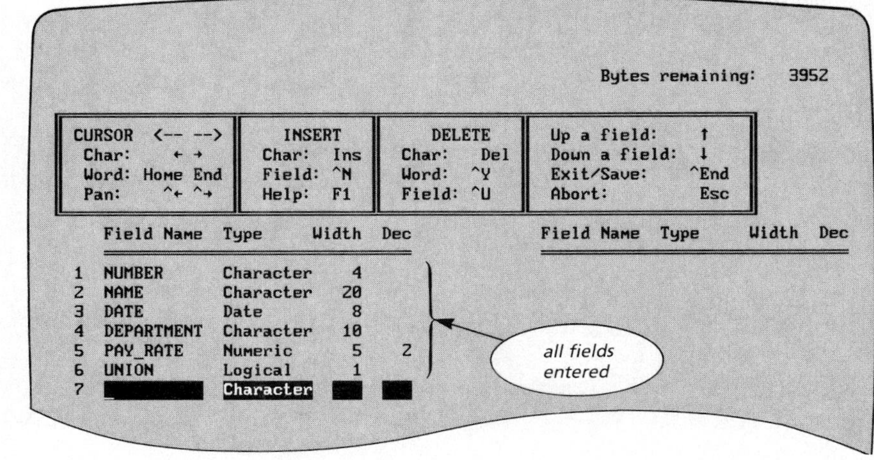


**FIGURE 1-22**
**All Fields Have Been Entered**

Because the name DEPARTMENT occupies all positions in the field name portion of the display, when you type the last character (the last T in DEPARTMENT), a beep will sound and the cursor will automatically advance to the next column.

You have now defined all the fields in the database. Press the Enter key while the cursor is in the first position of the blank row (Figure 1-23). A message will appear at the bottom of the screen directing you to press Enter to confirm that you are done or any other key to resume. Press the Enter key again.

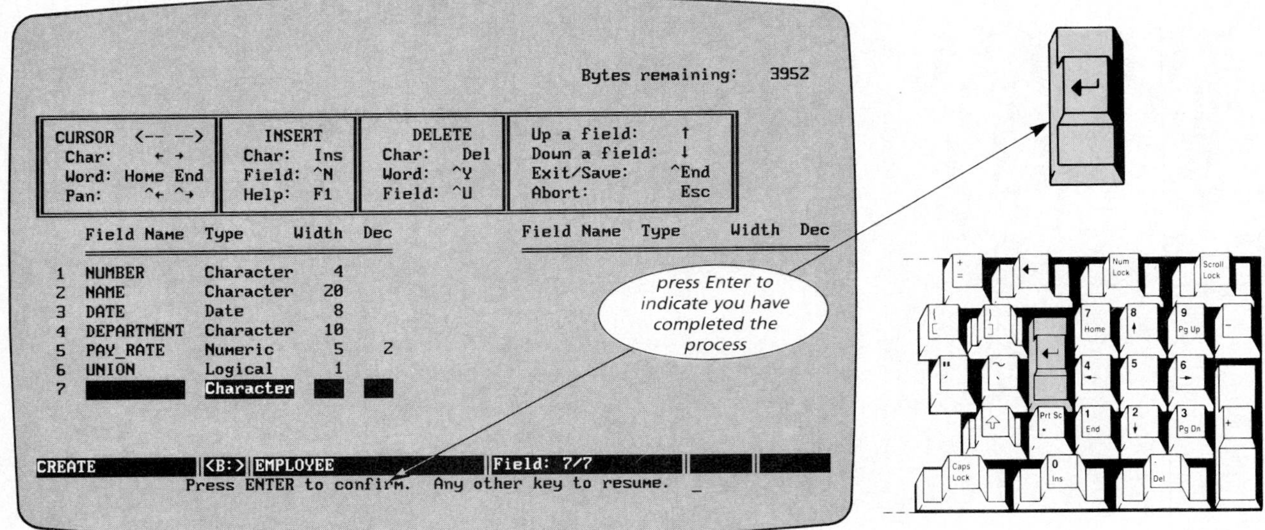


**FIGURE 1-23 Completing the Creation Process**

At this point, dBASE will ask if records are to be added now. If you answer with the letter Y (yes), you could begin entering records immediately. This is a special shortcut that dBASE provides for adding records. It only works immediately after you create a file. We will use the normal method for adding records, one that is appropriate whether or not the file has just been created. Type the letter N (no) to indicate that you will not use this feature to add any records. The ASSISTANT menu screen will reappear.

# ENTERING DATA

## Adding Data

Move the highlight to the "Update" menu (see Figure 1-24). To add records, choose the "Append" option. Make sure the word "Append" is highlighted (it should already be) and press Enter, producing the screen shown in Figure 1-25.

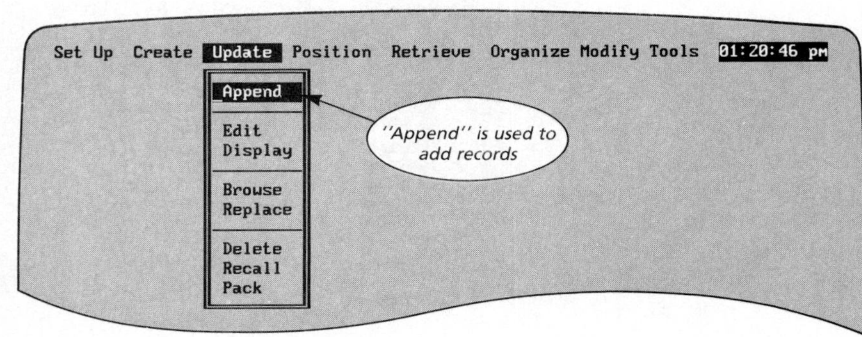


**FIGURE 1-24**
**The "Update" Menu**

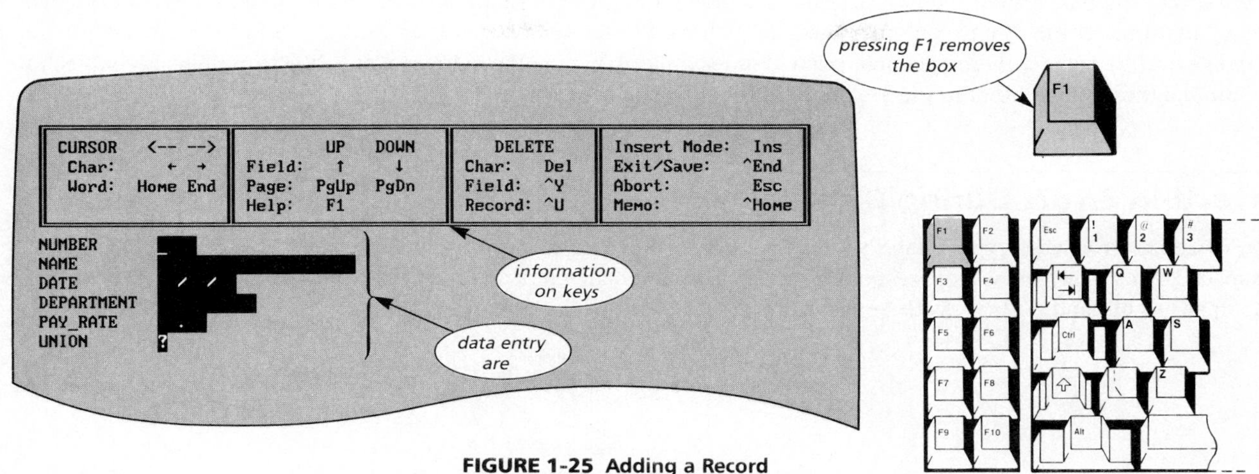


**FIGURE 1-25 Adding a Record**

At the top of the screen in Figure 1-25 is a box that describes various keys used during the data entry process. Pressing F1 removes the box from the screen. Pressing F1 a second time will return the box to the display. A common practice is to remove it from the screen and then bring it back whenever you need to see any of the information it contains.

The next portion of the screen is the area where you will enter data. It consists of the field names from your database file followed by reverse video blocks representing the maximum number of characters that can be entered in each field. Notice that the DATE field contains slashes. When you enter the date, type a two-digit month, a two-digit day, and a two-digit year. The date will be positioned correctly around the slashes. The PAY_RATE field contains a decimal point in the screen display because it was defined as a field with a width of 5 and two positions to the right of the decimal place. The UNION field, defined as a logical field, contains a question mark because all logical fields have a question mark in the area where you enter the letter Y, N, T, or F.

When you enter a value for UNION, it's a good idea to restrict yourself to just T (true) or F (false), even though dBASE allows you to enter Y (yes) or N (no). It is easy to get confused if you use T or F some of the time and Y or N other times. Further, when dBASE displays this data, it will display only T or F. So even if you enter the letter Y, it will be displayed as T. If you enter N, it will be displayed as F. For these reasons, it makes sense to use only T or F.

Enter the data up to the union code, as shown in Figure 1-26. Note that the name Rapoza, Anthony P. is to be entered incorrectly as Rappozi, Athony P. This will give you a chance to experiment with making corrections.

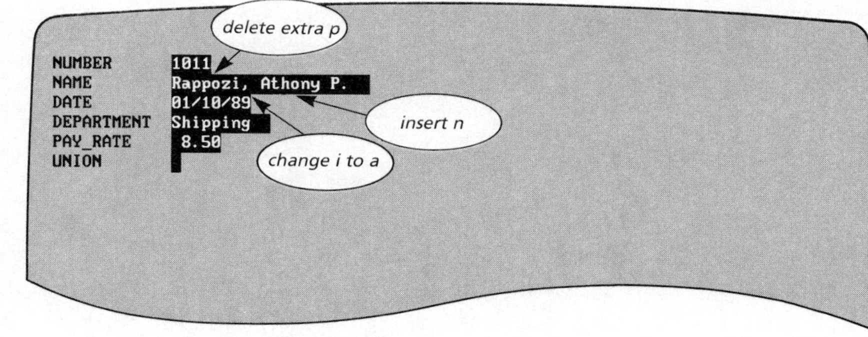


**FIGURE 1-26**
**Incorrectly Entered Name—**
**Must Be Fixed**

Enter the data one field at a time. The cursor will automatically move to the next line if the data entered occupies the entire width of the field. If not, you must press the Enter key after you have entered the data for a field. When entering the pay rate, you enter the value with the decimal point. For example, you type the amount 8.50. dBASE will properly position the value around the decimal point in the area reserved for the pay rate.

## Correcting Errors During Data Entry

If you make an error when typing data, you can correct it, provided you have not yet pressed the Enter key. Merely press the Backspace key as many times as necessary to delete unwanted characters and then retype the data. The Backspace key is found in the upper right-hand portion of the keyboard (Figure 1-27).

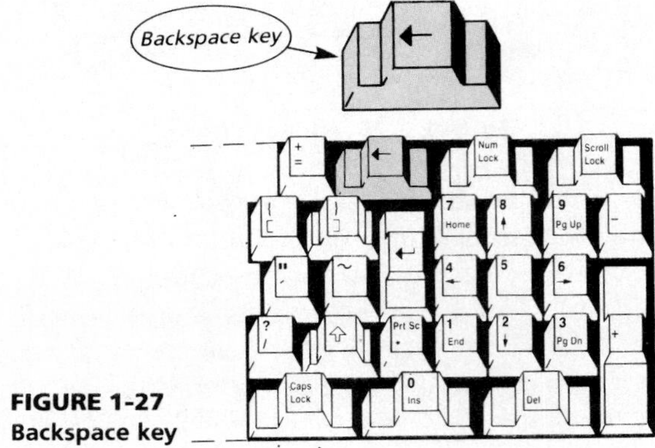


**FIGURE 1-27**
**Backspace key**

dBASE has very powerful editing capabilities for correcting errors made *after* you have pressed the Enter key. These editing capabilities are useful both when entering data on the screen that defines the field name, type, width, and decimal position, and when entering data directly into the database.

For example, let's suppose that after you entered the data for PAY_RATE in the first record, you discover that you spelled the name Rapoza, Anthony P. incorrectly as Rappozi, Athony P. (Figure 1-26).

Three errors are apparent. First, there is an extra p in the last name. Second, the last character in the last name should be a instead of i; and third, n should be inserted after the first character in the first name.

You can use the Up, Down, Right, and Left Arrow keys to move the cursor to the location where you want to make a correction. You could simply retype the whole name, this time making sure you do it correctly. Often a quicker alternative is to use the Delete and Insert keys to delete and insert data. Figure 1-28 illustrates the keys that are used for moving the cursor and inserting and deleting data. Let's correct the name by using these keys.

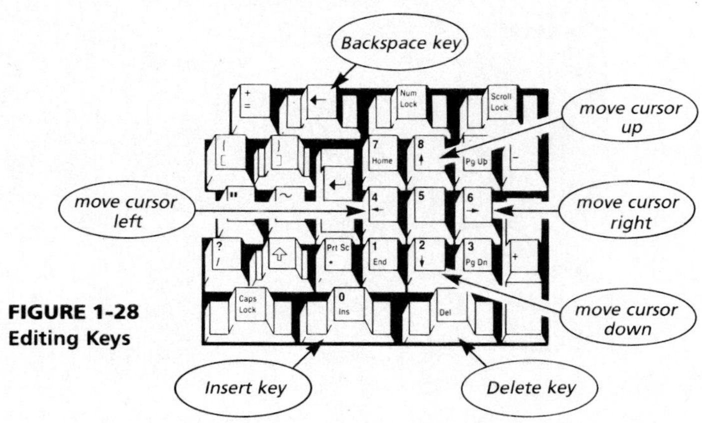


**FIGURE 1-28**
**Editing Keys**

First, use the Up and Right Arrow keys to move the cursor so that it is under the extra p in Rappozi. Once the cursor is in position, press the Delete key, found in the lower right-hand portion of the keyboard, to produce the display shown in Figure 1-29. When you press the Delete key, the extra p will be deleted. The field now reads "Rapozi, Athony P." The cursor is positioned under the letter o.

**FIGURE 1-29 Deleting a Letter**

To change the last character in the name Rapozi from i to a, position the cursor under the i by pressing the Right Arrow key two times. Then, with the cursor positioned under the incorrect character, type the correct letter (a). The results are shown in Figure 1-30. When you type the letter a, it replaces the i and the cursor will move one position to the right. The name now reads "Rapoza, Athony P."

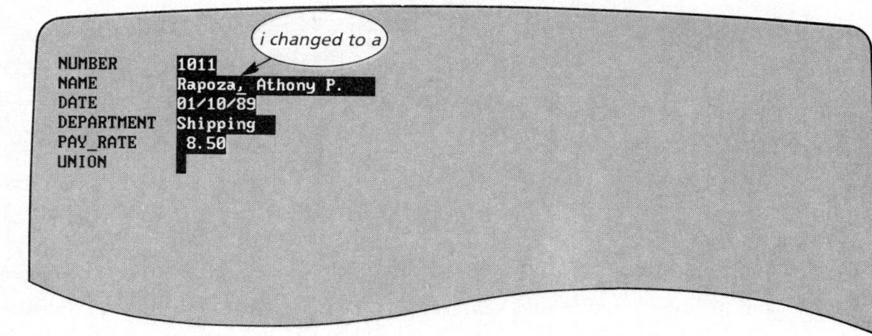


**FIGURE 1-30**
**Letter Has Been Corrected**

The next step is to insert an n before the letter t in the name Athony. Do this by pressing the Right Arrow key three times to place it under the letter t, pressing the Insert key to enter the insert mode (see the result in Figure 1-31), and then typing the letter n (see the result in Figure 1-32).

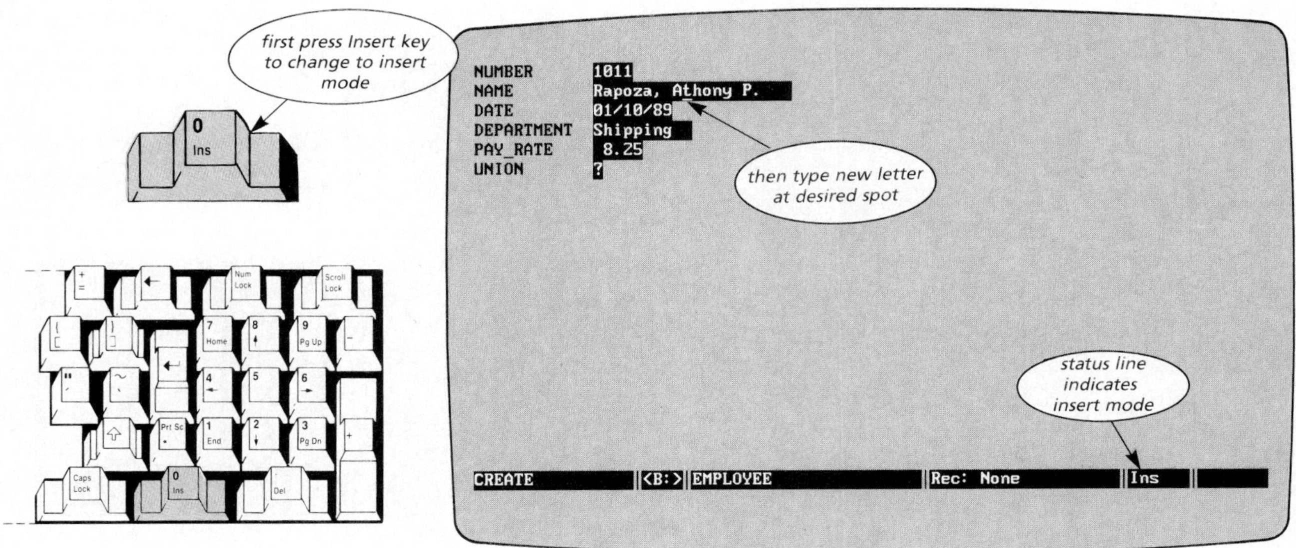


**FIGURE 1-31** Inserting a Letter

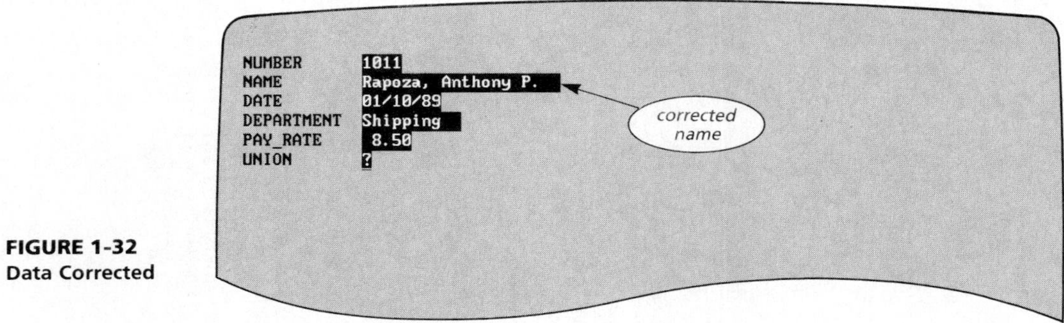


**FIGURE 1-32**
**Data Corrected**

When you press the Insert key, the letters "Ins" appear in the lower portion of the screen, indicating that the insert mode is in effect. While you are in this mode, each character you type will be inserted at the location of the cursor. The character at the cursor location and all characters to the right of it will move one position to the right. When you typed the letter n, it was inserted at the location of the cursor and the characters "thony P." were all shifted one position to the right.

After completing the insertion, press the Insert key again to exit from the insert mode. The letters "Ins" will no longer appear on the screen.

Once you have made the corrections to the name, you can resume normal data entry.

## Resuming Normal Data Entry

Now enter the union code. dBASE allows you to type either T or F (true or false) or Y or N (yes or no). As mentioned earlier, it is a good idea to restrict yourself to T or F. Therefore, enter the letter T for those employees with Y in the UNION column and the letter F for those employees with N. When you have entered the union code (the letter T in this case), a new screen will appear automatically. It contains the field names and blank reverse video blocks so that you may enter the data for record 2.

Make the entries for record 2 and record 3 as illustrated in Figures 1-33 and 1-34. Note that you are to make some mistakes in the data for record 2. They will be used to illustrate how to correct errors after records have already been added to the database file. Once you have entered these records, terminate the data entry process by pressing the Enter key when the cursor is in the first position of the first field on the screen. Another way to do this is to hold down the Ctrl key and press the key labeled End. At this point, the ASSISTANT menu screen will reappear. The data you have entered is automatically saved, so there is no need for a special save step, which you often encounter when using word processors or spreadsheet programs.

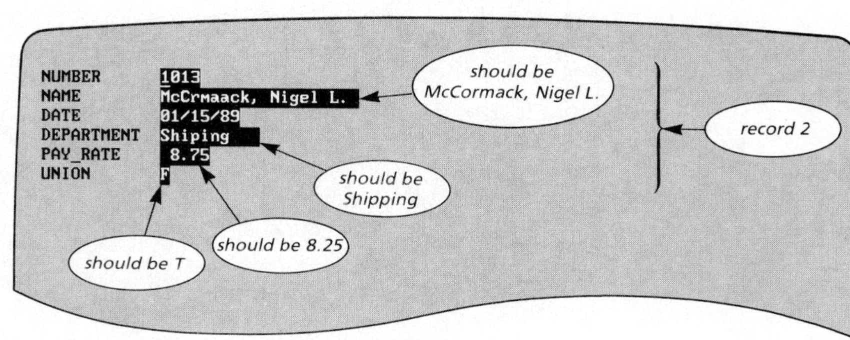


**FIGURE 1-33**
**Second Record (Entered Incorrectly)**

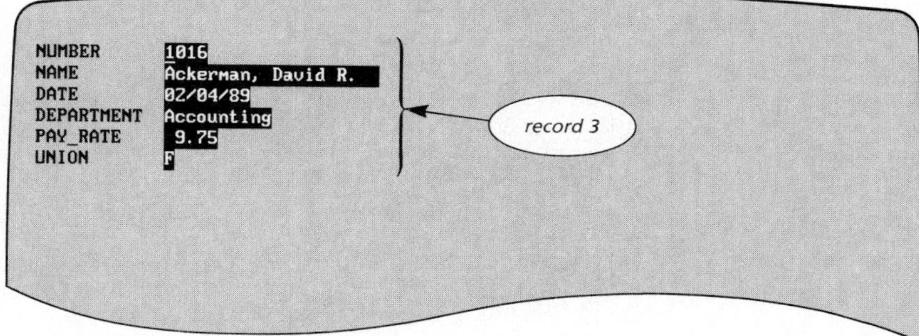


**FIGURE 1-34**
**Third Record Entered**

## Activating a Database File

As long as you continue working on the EMPLOYEE database file, it remains active. If you leave dBASE, however, EMPLOYEE is no longer active. Thus, if you don't have time to add all the records in a single sitting, you must be able to reactivate the EMPLOYEE database file the next time you start dBASE.

You accomplish this with "Database file" option of the "Set Up" menu (Figure 1-35). Use the Right or Left Arrow keys to move to this menu. (If you had just started dBASE you would already be on this menu.) Make sure the highlight is on "Database file." If it isn't, use the Up or Down Arrow keys to move the highlight to this selection. Then press Enter. Your display should look like the one shown in Figure 1-36.

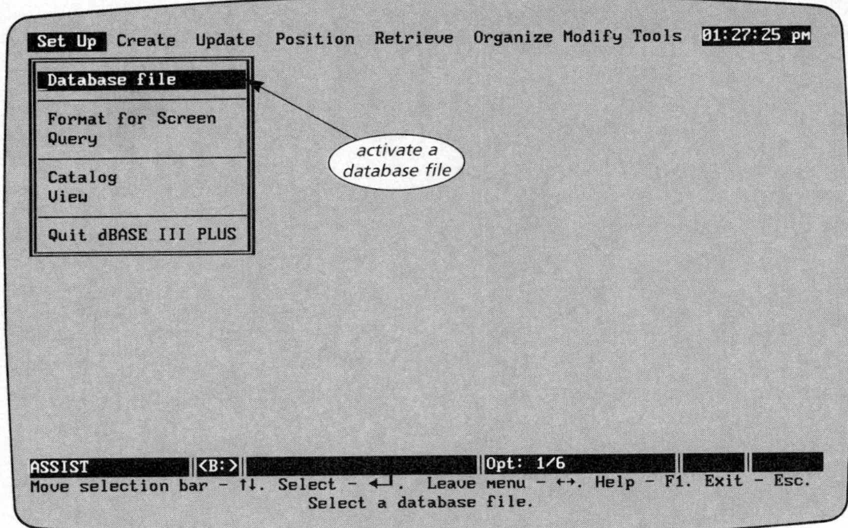


**FIGURE 1-35**
"Set Up" Menu

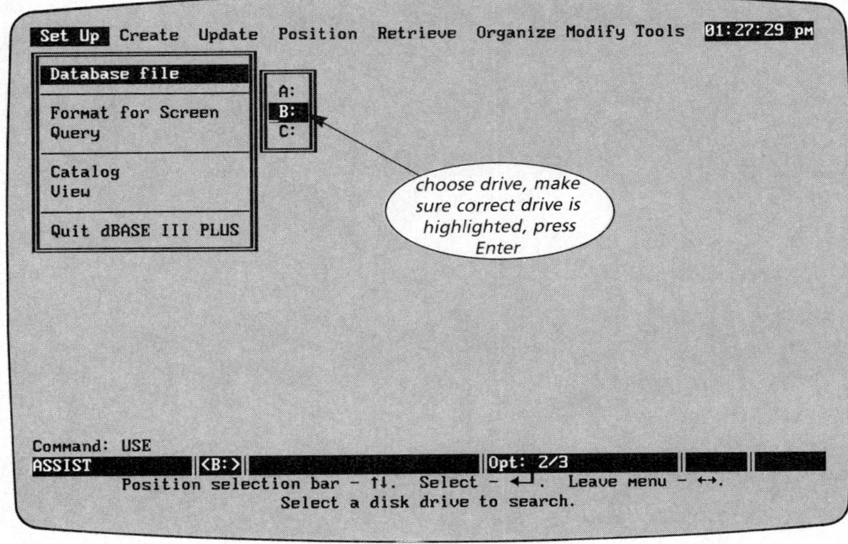


**FIGURE 1-36**
Selecting a Drive

This display allows you to indicate the drive on which the desired database file is located. Highlight B: and press the Enter key. This will display a list of all database files on the diskette (see Figure 1-37).

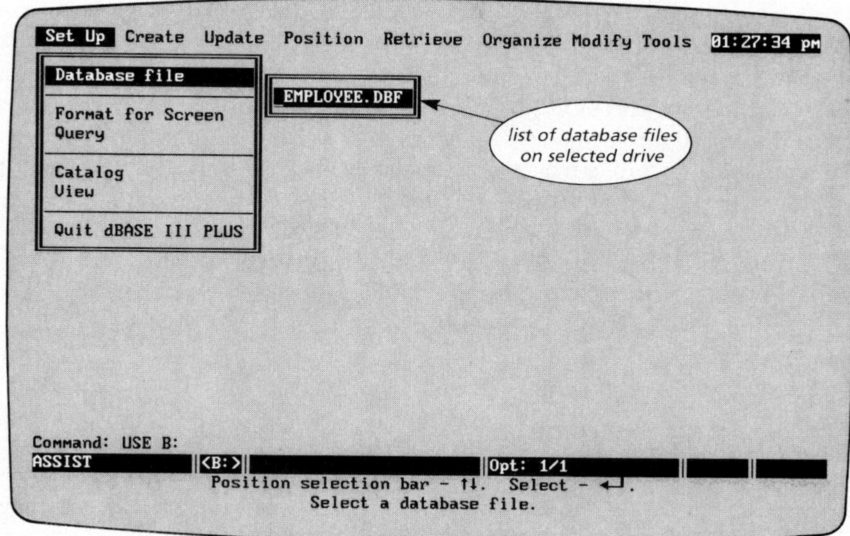


**FIGURE 1-37**
**Selecting a Database File**

At the present time, there is only one file, EMPLOYEE.DBF (remember that dBASE automatically assigns the extension DBF to database files). Because there is only one, you can simply press the Enter key. If there is more than one file, you must highlight the one you want before you press the Enter key. The final screen in this process is shown in Figure 1-38. dBASE is asking whether the file is indexed or not. At this point, no files are indexed, so you can type the letter N, which stands for no. Alternatively, you can simply press the Enter key, in which case dBASE will assume that the answer is no.

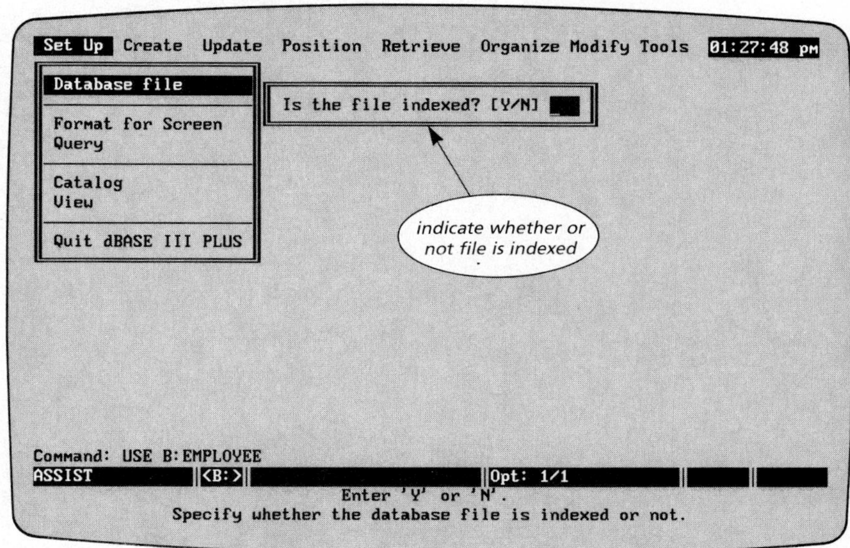


**FIGURE 1-38**
**Is File Indexed?**

## Changing Existing Records

You will now correct the errors made when you entered the data for record 2. Press the Right Arrow key twice to move to the "Update" menu and press the Down Arrow key once to move to the "Edit" option (see Figure 1-39). This option is used to correct errors that you discover after you entered the data. The file containing the error must be the active file. If it is not, activate it by using the technique described in the previous section.

Once you have chosen the "Edit" option, the same data entry screen you used to enter the data will appear. In addition, data will be displayed for the record identified by the record number that appears in the status line. You can change any of the data in this record in exactly the same way you corrected the name Rappozi, Athony P. earlier.

The record you want to correct must be on the screen. If it isn't, use the PgUp and PgDn keys to bring it to the screen. Pressing PgUp moves you to the previous record and pressing PgDn moves you to the next record. By pressing PgUp or PgDn enough times, you can bring the record you want to the screen. In this case, record 1 is on the screen but you want to correct record 2, so press the PgDn key once. Then make the necessary corrections. Change the name to McCormack, Nigel L., the department to Shipping, the pay rate to 8.25, and the union to T. Once you are done, hold the Ctrl key down and press the End key.

## Adding Additional Records

At this point, you should add the remaining records shown in Figure 1-3. To do so, choose the "Append" option of the "Update" menu (see Figure 1-39). If you make any mistakes, you can correct them using the same techniques you used to correct the errors in the first two records. It is not necessary to add all the records in one sitting. Just remember that if you leave dBASE, when you return you will have to reactivate the EMPLOYEE file (using the "Database file" option of the "Set Up" menu) and then choose the "Append" option of the "Update" menu to continue adding records.

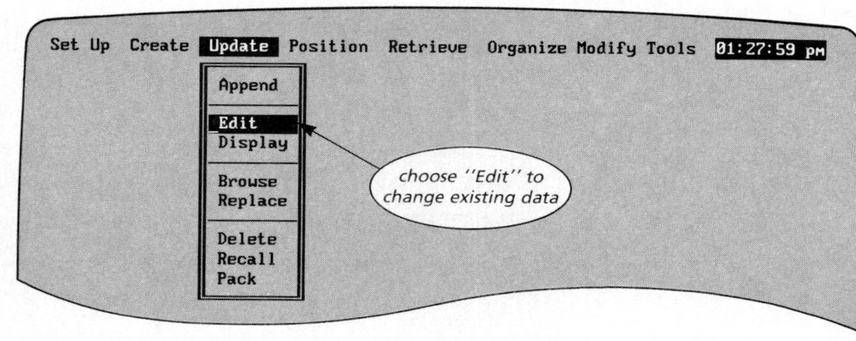


**FIGURE 1-39**
**Changing Existing Data**

# DISPLAYING DATA

After you have created a database, you have a variety of ways to display its contents. We discuss one way here, the "List" option of the "Retrieve" menu.

Move to the "Retrieve" menu using the Right or Left Arrow keys. Once you have done so, your display should look like the one shown in Figure 1-40. Since "List" is already highlighted, press the Enter key, producing the screen shown in Figure 1-41. Select "Execute the command." Since this option is already highlighted, press the Enter key. Your display should now look like the one shown in Figure 1-42. If you want to print the results, type the letter Y. If not, either type the letter N or press the Enter key. The results are shown in Figure 1-43 on page dB 30.

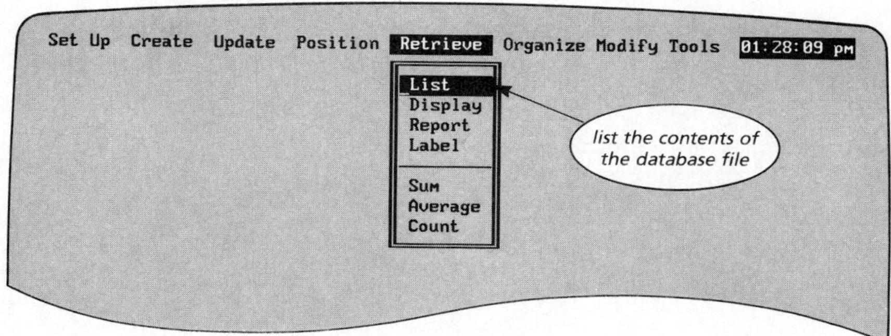


**FIGURE 1-40**
Retrieve Menu

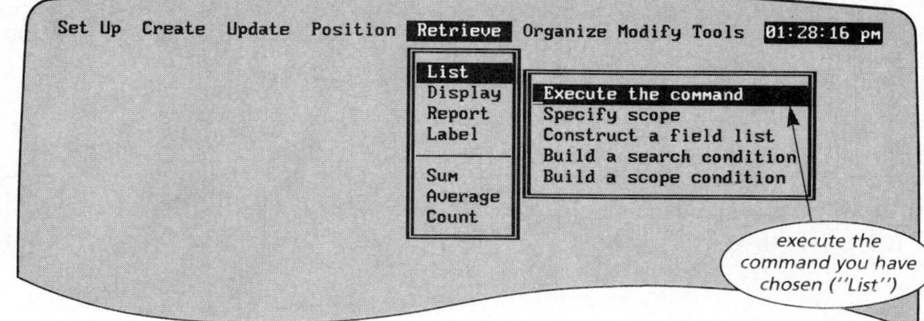


**FIGURE 1-41**
Option Box for Commands on the Retrieve Menu

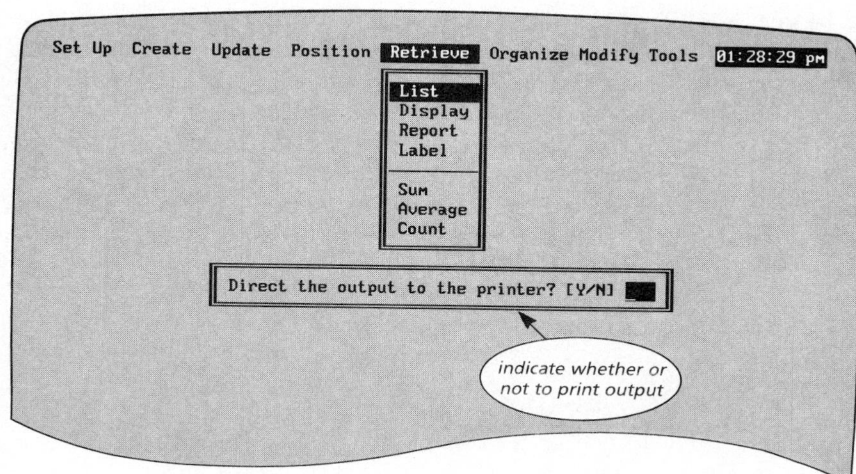


**FIGURE 1-42**
Output to the Printer?

```
Set Up  Create  Update  Position  Retrieve  Organize Modify Tools  01:29:15 pm

record numbers

Record#  NUMBER NAME                  DATE     DEPARTMENT PAY_RATE UNION
      1  1011   Rapoza, Anthony P.    01/10/89 Shipping       8.50 .T.
      2  1013   McCormack, Nigel L.   01/15/89 Shipping       8.25 .T.
      3  1016   Ackerman, David R.    02/04/89 Accounting     9.75 .F.
      4  1017   Doi, Chang J.         02/05/89 Production     6.00 .T.
      5  1020   Castle, Mark C.       03/04/89 Shipping       7.50 .T.
      6  1022   Dunning, Lisa A.      03/12/89 Marketing      9.10 .F.
      7  1025   Chaney, Joseph R.     03/23/89 Accounting     8.00 .F.
      8  1026   Bender, Helen O.      04/12/89 Production     6.75 .T.
      9  1029   Anderson, Mariane L.  04/18/89 Shipping       9.00 .T.
     10  1030   Edwards, Kenneth J.   04/23/89 Production     8.60 .T.
     11  1037   Baxter, Charles W.    05/05/89 Accounting    11.00 .F.
     12  1041   Evans, John T.        05/19/89 Marketing      6.00 .F.
     13  1056   Andrews, Robert M.    06/03/89 Marketing      9.00 .F.
     14  1057   Dugan, Mary L.        06/10/89 Production     8.75 .T.
     15  1066   Castleworth, Mary T.  07/05/89 Production     8.75 .T.
ASSIST          <B:> EMPLOYEE
                Press any key
```

**FIGURE 1-43**
**Results of "List" Option**

In the display in Figure 1-43, the leftmost column contains a record number that was created by dBASE based on the sequence in which the records were entered. The fields are displayed with the field names that you already defined. Note that in the UNION field there is a period before and after the letters T and F. This is the way dBASE displays logical fields.

## BACKING UP YOUR DATABASE FILES

To be safe, it is a good idea to periodically make a copy of your database files. This copy is called a **backup** copy and the database file itself is called the **live** copy. If you discover a problem with a database file, you can then copy the backup version over the live one. This effectively returns the database file to its original state.

While dBASE contains facilities to make such copies, there are some special issues involved in using them. You don't need to worry about them, however, since you can simply use the DOS COPY command after you have exited dBASE. For example, to copy the database file EMPLOYEE.DBF located on drive B to a backup copy named EMPLOYEE.BCK also located on drive B, you can use the command shown in Figure 1-44. The name EMPLOYEE.BCK is arbitrary. You can choose whatever name you wish. Just make sure it is something that is easy for you to recognize.

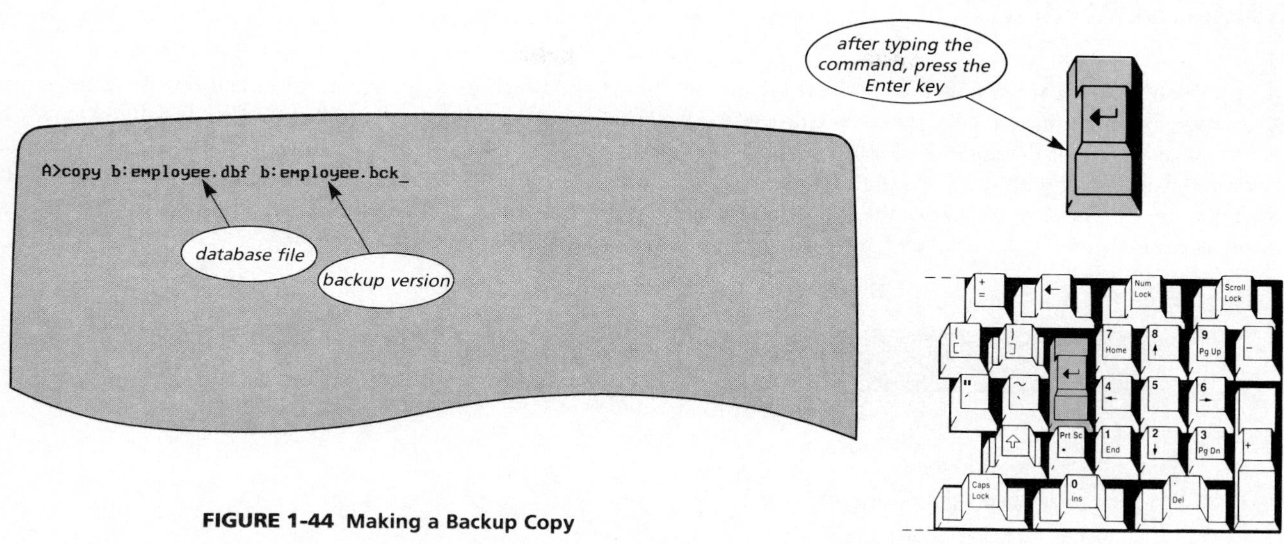


**FIGURE 1-44** Making a Backup Copy

If you discover a problem, you can restore EMPLOYEE.DBF to the state it was in when the backup was made by typing the command shown in Figure 1-45.

You may wish to place the backup copy on a separate diskette. Place the other diskette in drive A and change the letter B that precedes EMPLOYEE.BCK in the command to the letter A.

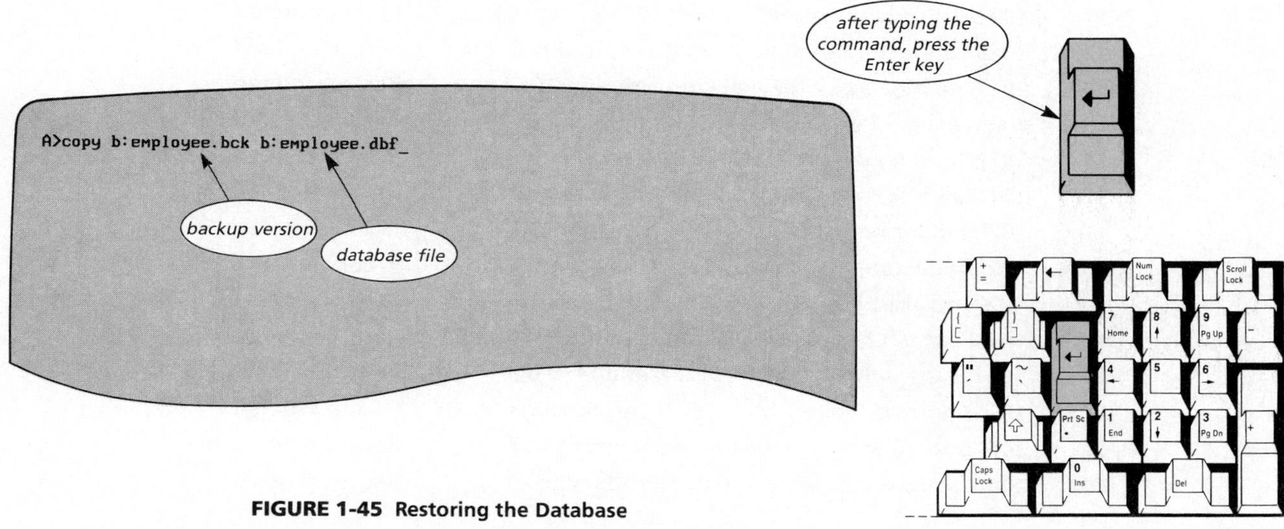


**FIGURE 1-45** Restoring the Database

## PROJECT SUMMARY

In Project 1 you learned how to create a database file, how to add records to a database file, and how to correct any errors you might have made. You also learned one way to display the contents of a database file. Finally, you saw how to make a copy of the database file for backup purposes.

If you followed along with the steps in this project, you have created the EMPLOYEE database file. If you did not, but wish to create this file now, you can use the following keystroke sequence. Start dBASE as described in the project but do not choose any options when the ASSISTANT menu appears on the screen. Instead, type the following:

**SUMMARY OF KEYSTROKES—Project 1**

| STEPS | KEY(S) PRESSED | RESULTS |
|---|---|---|
| 1 | → ↵ ↵ | Create database file |
| 2 | employee ↵ | |
| 3 | NUMBER ↵ ↵ 4 ↵ | |
| 4 | NAME ↵ ↵ 20 ↵ | |
| 5 | DATE ↵ SPACE SPACE ↵ | |
| 6 | DEPARTMENT ↵ 10 ↵ | |
| 7 | PAY_RATE ↵ SPACE ↵ 5 ↵ 2 ↵ | |
| 8 | UNION ↵ SPACE SPACE SPACE ↵ | |
| 9 | ↵ ↵ Y | Fields specified |
| 10 | 1011Rapoza, Anthony P. ↵ 011089Shipping ↵ 8.50T | Record entered |
| 11 | 1013McCormack, Nigel L. ↵ 011589Shipping ↵ 8.25T | Record entered |
| 12 | 1016Ackerman, David R. ↵ 020489Accounting9.75F | Record entered |
| 13 | 1017Doi, Chang J. ↵ 020589Production6.00T | Record entered |
| 14 | 1020Castle, Mark C. ↵ 030489Shipping ↵ 7.50T | Record entered |
| 15 | 1022Dunning, Lisa A. ↵ 031289Marketing ↵ 9.10F | Record entered |
| 16 | 1025Chaney, Joseph R. ↵ 032389Accounting8.00F | Record entered |
| 17 | 1026Bender, Helen O. ↵ 041289Production6.75T | Record entered |
| 18 | 1029Anderson, Mariane L.041889Shipping ↵ 9.00T | Record entered |
| 19 | 1030Edwards, Kenneth J. ↵ 042389Production8.60T | Record entered |
| 20 | 1037Baxter, Charles W. ↵ 050589Accounting11.00F | Record entered |
| 21 | 1041Evans, John T. ↵ 051989Marketing ↵ 6.00F | Record entered |
| 22 | 1056Andrews, Robert M. ↵ 060389Marketing ↵ 9.00F | Record entered |
| 23 | 1057Dugan, Mary L. ↵ 061089Production8.75T | Record entered |
| 24 | 1066Castleworth, Mary T.070589Production8.75T | Record entered |
| 25 | ↵ | |

The following list summarizes the material covered in Project 1:

1. An individual unit of information, such as an employee number or name, is called a **field**. A group of related fields is called a **record**. A collection of records is called a **file**. Sometimes, the words **table**, **row**, and **column** are used in place of file, record, and field, respectively.
2. In dBASE, each individual file (table) is called a **database file**. Thus, in dBASE, a database can actually be a collection of database files. (Throughout the first four projects, each database consists of a single database file.)
3. **Character fields** may be used to store any printable character. **Date fields** can only be used to store dates. **Numeric fields** can only be used to store numbers. Arithmetic operations can only be applied to numeric fields. **Logical fields**

consist of a single value representing a true or false condition. They can hold only T (true), F (false), Y (yes), or N (no). **Memo fields** may be used to store large blocks of text such as words or sentences.
4. The **ASSISTANT** is a collection of menus to assist you in accessing databases. When you use these menus, you are said to be working in **ASSIST mode** .
5. The **status line** or **status bar** is a line that appears near the bottom of the screen. It gives information about the current status of dBASE, including which database file is active and the current position within the file.
6. To select a different menu in the ASSISTANT, use the Right or Left Arrow keys.
7. To select an option within a menu, move the highlight to that option using the Up or Down Arrow keys and press the Enter key.
8. A **dBASE command** is a word or collection of words that will cause some function to be performed by dBASE.
9. The **dot prompt mode** is a mode of operating with dBASE in which a single dot, called the **dot prompt** appears on the screen. It prompts the user to type commands directly, rather than with the help of the menu structure of the ASSISTANT. It is followed by the blinking underscore or **cursor**, which shows where the characters you enter will be displayed. To change from the ASSISTANT to the dot prompt mode, use the Esc key. To change from the dot prompt mode to the ASSISTANT, use the F2 key.
10. To leave dBASE, select "Quit dBASE III PLUS" from the "Set Up" menu.
11. To get help, use the F1 key.
12. To create a database file, select "Database file" from the "Create" menu, then describe each of the fields that comprise the database file. After that, you will have a chance to begin entering data if you wish.
13. To add additional records, select the "Append" option of the "Update" menu. To activate a database file, select the "Database file" option of the "Set Up" menu, indicate the drive on which the desired database file is located, and then select the desired file from the list presented to you by dBASE.
14. To change records, select the "Edit" option of the "Update" menu.
15. To move between records when entering or editing data, use the PgUp and PgDn keys.
16. To display all data, select the "List" option of the "Retrieve" menu. Then select "Execute the command" and indicate whether or not the output is to be directed to the printer.
17. A **backup** copy of a database file is a copy that is made and stored as a safety measure. If problems occur in the active or **live** database file, copying the backup version over the live version returns the database file to the state it was in when the backup was made.
18. Make a backup copy of a database file by using the DOS COPY command after you have exited dBASE. In the event of a problem, you can copy the backup copy over the live version with the same COPY command.

# STUDENT ASSIGNMENTS

## STUDENT ASSIGNMENT 1: True/False

**Instructions:** Circle T if the statement is true and F if the statement is false.

T F 1. The term database is used to describe a collection of data organized in a manner that allows access, retrieval, and use of that data.
T F 2. A database can contain only a single table.
T F 3. In dBASE, there can be at most 10 fields in a record.
T F 4. In dBASE, a field name can contain a maximum of eight characters.
T F 5. WEEKLY_PAY is a valid field name.
T F 6. A field used in a calculation must be defined as a numeric field.
T F 7. A date field can be used in calculations.
T F 8. A logical field must contain either T, F, 0, or 1.
T F 9. Individual units of information within each record are called files.
T F 10. A numeric field that contains a value such as 99.99 is considered to have a width of 4.

### Student Assignment 1 (continued)

T F 11. In dBASE, a file name can be up to eight characters long.
T F 12. To load dBASE into memory, type the word DBASE in either uppercase or lowercase letters when the A> prompt appears.
T F 13. To create a database file, choose the option "Database file" from the "Set Up" menu.
T F 14. The option "List" of the "Retrieve" menu can be used to list all records of a database file on the screen.
T F 15. To move back one record while adding data, press the PgDn key.
T F 16. The line on the screen that indicates the name of the database file being accessed is called the database line.

## STUDENT ASSIGNMENT 2: Multiple Choice

**Instructions:** Circle the correct response.

1. A field that contains numbers but is not involved in calculations should normally be defined as a
   a. character field.
   b. numeric field.
   c. logical field.
   d. memo field.
2. The full name of a database file called EMPLOYEE and stored on drive B is
   a. B>EMPLOYEE
   b. EMPLOYEE
   c. B:EMPLOYEE.DBF
   d. EMPLOYEE:DBF
3. After you enter the data for all records, you can terminate the data entry process by
   a. pressing the Enter key when the cursor is in the last position of the last field entered.
   b. pressing the Esc key.
   c. pressing the Enter key when the cursor is in the first position of the first field on the screen where no entries have been made.
   d. pressing the Enter key while holding down the End key.
4. If you find an error in one of the records after entering the data and storing it on disk,
   a. you cannot correct the data.
   b. you can use the "Edit" option of the "Update" menu to correct the error.
   c. pressing F1 will allow you to correct the error.
   d. pressing Esc will allow you to correct the error.
5. To exit dBASE and return to the operating system,
   a. press Esc.
   b. choose the last option on the "Set Up" menu.
   c. choose the last option on the "Tools" menu.
   d. type the words exit dBASE.
6. "Edit" is an option on
   a. the "Set Up" menu.
   b. the "Create" menu.
   c. the "Update" menu.
   d. the "Retrieve" menu.

## STUDENT ASSIGNMENT 3: Understanding dBASE Options

**Instructions:** Explain what will happen after you perform each of the following actions.

Problem 1. Type the word dBASE at the A> prompt and press the Enter key.

Explanation: ______________________________________________

Problem 2. Choose the "Database file" option of the "Create" menu.

Explanation: ______________________________________________

Problem 3. Choose the "List" option of the "Retrieve" menu.

Explanation: ______________________________________________

Problem 4. Choose the "Edit" option of the "Update" menu.

Explanation: ______________________________________________

## STUDENT ASSIGNMENT 4: Using dBASE

**Instructions:** Explain how to accomplish each of the following tasks using dBASE.

Problem 1. Load dBASE into main computer memory.

Explanation: ______________________________________________

Problem 2. Create a database file.

Explanation: ______________________________________________

Problem 3. Move back to a previous record while adding data.

Explanation: ______________________________________________

**Student Assignment 4 (continued)**

Problem 4. Indicate that a given field is a numeric field.

Explanation: ______________________________

Problem 5. List the contents of a database file.

Explanation: ______________________________

Problem 6. Add records to an already existing database file.

Explanation: ______________________________

## STUDENT ASSIGNMENT 5: Recovering from Problems

**Instructions:** In each of the following cases, a problem occurred. Explain the cause of the problem and how it can be corrected.

Problem 1: The dot prompt appears on the screen.

Cause of Problem: ______________________________

Method of Correction: ______________________________

Problem 2: You find yourself looking at a display that you don't recognize and that definitely does not correspond to the option you thought you selected.

Cause of Problem: ______________________________

Method of Correction: ______________________________

Problem 3: You intended to print a list of all data in a database file on your printer. The list appeared on the screen, but not on the printer. You checked your printer and it is on.

Cause of Problem: ______________________________

Method of Correction: ______________________________

# MINICASES:

## Creating and Displaying a Database

Each project ends with four minicases. Minicase 1 in each project involves a database of personal checks. Minicase 2 involves a music library database. Minicase 3 deals with a database for a software store. The database for Minicase 4 contains information on homes for sale. You should work on the same minicase in each project. Your instructor will probably assign you a specific minicase. If not, you can choose any of the four. Just make sure you select the same one in each project.

The material in the minicases is cumulative. That is, the assignment for Minicase 1 in Project 2 builds on the assignment for Minicase 1 from Project 1. It is very important that you work through the minicase completely before proceeding to the next project. If not, you will encounter serious difficulties later on.

### Minicase 1: Personal Checks

**Instructions:** Design and create a database file to store a list of personal checks and related information on disk using dBASE. The data and field characteristics are illustrated below.

| CHECK NUMBER | DATE | PAYEE | CHECK AMOUNT | EXPENSE TYPE | TAX DEDUCTIBLE |
|---|---|---|---|---|---|
| 109 | 01/19/90 | Oak Apartments | 750.00 | Household | Y |
| 102 | 01/05/90 | Sav-Mor Groceries | 85.00 | Food | N |
| 111 | 01/19/90 | Edison Company | 55.25 | Household | N |
| 106 | 01/12/90 | Performing Arts | 25.00 | Charity | Y |
| 105 | 01/12/90 | Union Oil | 22.75 | Automobile | Y |
| 101 | 01/05/90 | American Express | 45.30 | Entertainment | Y |
| 107 | 01/19/90 | Sav-Mor Groceries | 64.95 | Food | N |
| 108 | 01/19/90 | Amber Inn | 22.45 | Entertainment | Y |
| 104 | 01/12/90 | Brady's Shoes | 69.50 | Personal | N |
| 110 | 01/19/90 | Standard Oil | 33.16 | Automobile | Y |
| 103 | 01/05/90 | Pacific Telephone | 23.72 | Household | N |

| FIELD DESCRIPTION | FIELD NAME | FIELD TYPE | WIDTH | DECIMAL POSITIONS |
|---|---|---|---|---|
| CHECK NUMBER | CHECKNUM | CHARACTER | 4 | |
| DATE | DATE | DATE | 8 | |
| PAYEE | PAYEE | CHARACTER | 18 | |
| CHECK AMOUNT | AMOUNT | NUMERIC | 6 | 2 |
| EXPENSE | EXPENSE | CHARACTER | 14 | |
| TAX DEDUCTIBLE | TAXDED | LOGICAL | 1 | |

### Minicase 1 (continued)

Perform the following tasks:

1. Load dBASE and insert your data disk in drive B.
2. Create the database file and enter the above data. Use the name CHECK for the database file.
3. After creating the database file and loading the data, use the "List" option of the "Retrieve" menu to display all the data.
4. Leave the database file that you created on this disk for use with assignments in later projects.

## Minicase 2: Music Library

**Instructions:** Design and create a database file to store information about a music library on disk using dBASE. The music is stored on either cassette tape (CS), long-playing records (LP), or compact disk (CD), as indicated by the entry under the heading Type. The data and field characteristics are illustrated below. The date field represents the date the music was obtained.

| DATE | MUSIC NAME | ARTIST | TYPE | COST | CATEGORY |
|---|---|---|---|---|---|
| 02/22/90 | Greatest Hits | Panache, Milo | LP | 8.95 | Classical |
| 02/15/90 | America | Judd, Mary | CS | 5.95 | Vocal |
| 01/02/90 | Rio Rio | Duran, Ralph | LP | 8.95 | Rock |
| 02/15/90 | Passione | Panache, Milo | LP | 6.99 | Classical |
| 01/02/90 | Country Hills | Lager, Ricky | CD | 11.95 | Country |
| 02/22/90 | Rockin' | Brady, Susan | CS | 5.95 | Rock |
| 02/22/90 | Pardners | Hudson, Randy | CS | 5.95 | Country |
| 01/02/90 | Private Love | Toner, Arlene | CD | 11.95 | Vocal |
| 02/22/90 | Moods | Silver, Sandy | CD | 11.95 | Rock |

| FIELD DESCRIPTION | FIELD NAME | FIELD TYPE | WIDTH | DECIMAL POSITIONS |
|---|---|---|---|---|
| DATE | DATE | DATE | 8 | |
| MUSIC NAME | NAME | CHARACTER | 14 | |
| ARTIST | ARTIST | CHARACTER | 14 | |
| TYPE | TYPE | CHARACTER | 2 | |
| COST | COST | NUMERIC | 5 | 2 |
| CATEGORY | CATEGORY | CHARACTER | 9 | |

Perform the following tasks:

1. Load dBASE and insert your data disk in drive B.
2. Create the database file and enter the above data. Use the name MUSIC for the database file.
3. After creating the database file and loading the data, use the "List" option of the "Retrieve" menu to display all the data.
4. Leave the database file that you created on this disk for use with assignments in later projects.

## Minicase 3: Computer Software Store

**Instructions:** Design and create a database file to store information about the inventory of a company that sells computer software. Fields in the database consist of the name of the software, the name of the company that sells the software, the software category, an entry Y (yes) or N (no) to indicate if the software is compatible with MS-DOS, the quantity of software on hand, and the cost of the software. A list of software products in inventory is illustrated in the chart below.

| SOFTWARE NAME | COMPANY | CATEGORY | MS_DOS | QUANTITY | COST |
|---|---|---|---|---|---|
| Databurst | Electric Software | Database | Y | 5 | 299.95 |
| Type Ease | Edusoft Inc. | WP | N | 22 | 29.95 |
| Image Fonts | Graph Tech Inc. | WP | Y | 12 | 49.95 |
| Data Filer | Anchor Software | Database | Y | 18 | 149.95 |
| Master | Edusoft Inc. | Education | N | 20 | 49.95 |
| Math Tester | Learnit Software | Education | N | 10 | 49.95 |
| PC-Writer | Anchor Software | WP | Y | 30 | 129.95 |
| Print File | Graph Tech Inc. | Database | Y | 16 | 99.95 |
| Learning Calc | Edusoft Inc. | Spreadsheet | Y | 34 | 69.95 |
| Number Crunch | Anchor Software | Spreadsheet | Y | 8 | 279.95 |

| FIELD DESCRIPTION | FIELD NAME | FIELD TYPE | WIDTH | DECIMAL POSITIONS |
|---|---|---|---|---|
| SOFTWARE NAME | NAME | CHARACTER | 14 | |
| COMPANY | COMPANY | CHARACTER | 17 | |
| CATEGORY | CATEGORY | CHARACTER | 12 | |
| MS_DOS | MS_DOS | LOGICAL | 1 | |
| QUANTITY | QUANTITY | NUMERIC | 6 | 0 |
| COST | COST | NUMERIC | 6 | 2 |

Perform the following tasks:

1. Load dBASE and insert your data disk in drive B.
2. Create the database file and enter the above data. Use the name SOFTWARE for the database file.
3. After creating the database file and loading the data, use the "List" option of the "Retrieve" menu to display all the data.
4. Leave the database file that you created on this disk for use with assignments in later projects.

## Minicase 4: Home Sales

**Instructions:** Design and create a database file to store information about homes for sale. The records contain the date the home was listed, its address, city, zip code, number of bedrooms, number of bathrooms, an entry Y (yes) or N (no) to indicate if the home has a pool, and the selling price of the home. A list of the homes in the database is illustrated below:

| DATE | ADDRESS | CITY | ZIP | BDRM | BATH | POOL | PRICE |
|---|---|---|---|---|---|---|---|
| 09/15/90 | 9661 King Pl. | Anaheim | 92644 | 4 | 2 | Y | 185000.00 |
| 09/19/90 | 1625 Brook St. | Fullerton | 92633 | 3 | 1 | N | 95000.00 |
| 10/02/90 | 182 Oak Ave. | Fullerton | 92634 | 4 | 2 | Y | 92000.00 |
| 10/09/90 | 145 Oak Ave. | Garden Grove | 92641 | 5 | 3 | Y | 145000.00 |
| 10/15/90 | 124 Lark St. | Anaheim | 92644 | 3 | 2 | N | 119000.00 |
| 10/22/90 | 926 Pine Ln. | Garden Grove | 92641 | 3 | 1 | N | 92500.00 |
| 11/20/90 | 453 Adams Ave. | Costa Mesa | 92688 | 5 | 3 | Y | 185000.00 |
| 11/23/90 | 1456 Kern St. | Costa Mesa | 92688 | 4 | 2 | Y | 163900.00 |
| 12/10/90 | 862 Stanley St. | Garden Grove | 92641 | 4 | 2 | Y | 189995.00 |
| 12/13/90 | 1552 Weldon Pl. | Garden Grove | 92641 | 3 | 2 | N | 169500.00 |

| FIELD DESCRIPTION | FIELD NAME | FIELD TYPE | WIDTH | DECIMAL POSITIONS |
|---|---|---|---|---|
| DATE | DATE | DATE | 8 | |
| ADDRESS | ADDRESS | CHARACTER | 16 | |
| CITY | CITY | CHARACTER | 12 | |
| ZIP | ZIP | CHARACTER | 5 | |
| BEDRMS | BDRM | NUMERIC | 2 | 0 |
| BATHRMS | BATH | NUMERIC | 2 | 0 |
| POOL | POOL | LOGICAL | 1 | |
| PRICE | PRICE | NUMERIC | 9 | 2 |

Perform the following tasks:

1. Load dBASE and insert your data disk in drive B.
2. Create the database file and enter the data above. Use the name HOME for the database file.
3. After creating the database file and loading the data, use the "List" option of the "Retrieve" menu to display all the data.
4. Leave the database file that you created on this disk for use with assignments in later projects.

# PROJECT 2

## Displaying Records in a Database

### Objectives

You will have mastered the material in this project when you can:

- Activate a previously created database file
- Display the structure of a database file
- Change the current active record
- Display a single record
- Display all records and all fields
- Display only selected fields
- Display only records meeting a given condition
- Use both simple and compound conditions
- Count the number of records satisfying a given condition
- Calculate sums and averages

A major benefit of a database management system is that once you have created a database, you can rapidly access its records and fields and easily display them. For example, after accessing the employee database file illustrated in Project 1, you can use dBASE options to display a single employee record or specific collections of records, such as the records of employees who work in the accounting department or the records of those who are members of the union.

As we work through this project, we explain the dBASE options that are used to display records and fields within records. We explain the options for counting various types of records and those for calculating totals and averages. You will use the menus and options within the ASSISTANT that are listed in Figure 2-1.

| OPTION | PURPOSE |
|---|---|
| Set Up | Activate a |
| Database file | database file |
| View | view |
| Quit dBASE III PLUS | leave dBASE III PLUS |
| Create | Create a |
| Database file | database file (extension DBF) |
| View | view (extension VUE) |
| Report | report (extension FRM) |
| Update | Change a database file by |
| Append | adding records at the end |
| Edit | changing records viewing one at a time |
| Browse | changing records viewing several at a time |
| Replace | changing the data in all records that satisfy some condition |
| Delete | deleting records |
| Recall | undeleting records |
| Pack | physically remove deleted records |
| Position | Move the record pointer by |
| Seek | finding a match using an index |
| Locate | finding the first record that satisfies some condition |
| Goto Record | specifying a record number |
| Retrieve | Retrieve data from a database file |
| List | show desired fields and records on the screen or printer |
| Display | like "List" (differences between the two are covered in the text) |
| Report | print a report |
| Sum | calculate a total |
| Average | calculate an average |
| Count | count the number of records |
| Organize | |
| Index | create an index (extension NDX) |
| Sort | sort a database file |
| Modify | Change an existing |
| Database file | database file |
| Report | report file |
| Tools | |
| List structure | show the structure of the active database file |

**FIGURE 2-1**
**Menus and Options within the dBASE ASSISTANT**

## ACTIVATING THE DATABASE

After you have loaded dBASE into main computer memory, you must activate a database file on disk so that you can access it. Recall that you do this with the "Database file" option of the "Set Up" menu (Figure 2-2).

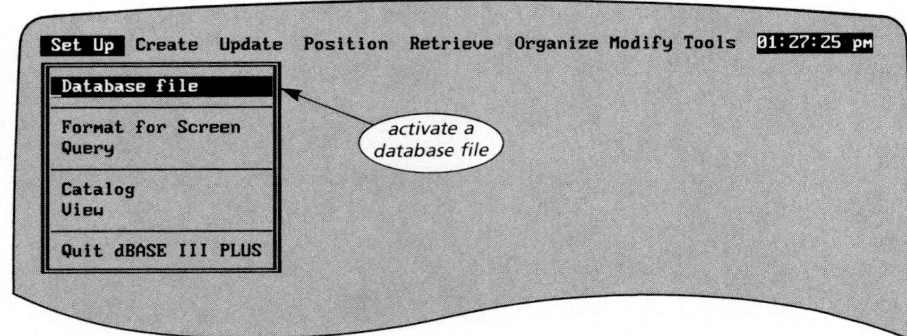


**FIGURE 2-2**
**The "Set Up" Menu**

Press Enter when the highlight is on "Database file" to produce the display shown in Figure 2-3. Make sure B: is highlighted and press the Enter key again to display a list of all database files on the diskette (see Figure 2-4). With EMPLOYEE.DBF highlighted, press the Enter key. At this point, dBASE will ask you if the file is indexed. Either type the letter N or just press the Enter key to indicate that the file is not indexed.

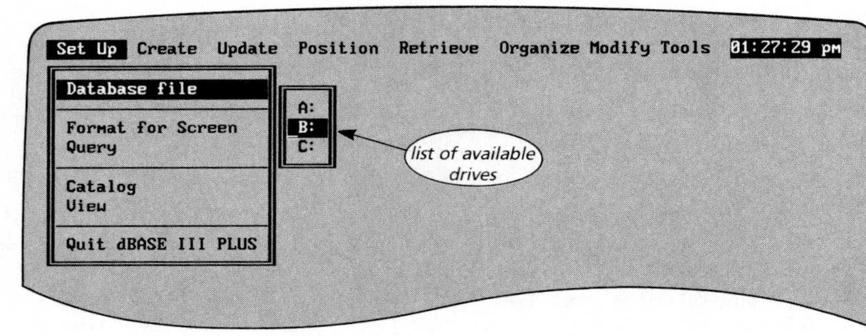


**FIGURE 2-3**
**Selecting a Drive**

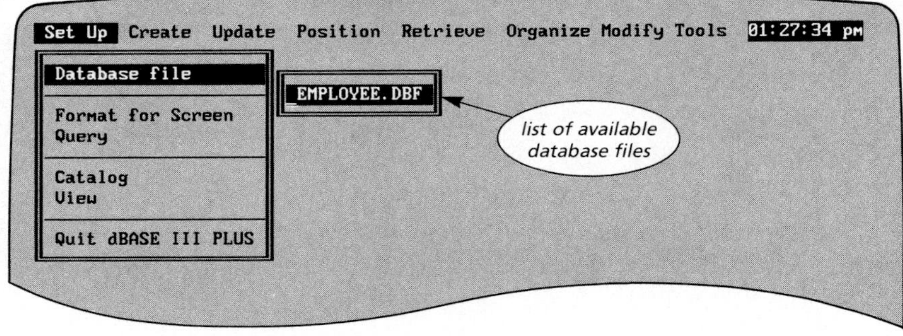


**FIGURE 2-4**
**Selecting a Database File**

In the following examples, we assume that the file with the name EMPLOYEE.DBF is the active database file.

## DISPLAYING THE DATABASE STRUCTURE

Sometimes you might not know the precise field names and characteristics of a database file. Perhaps you don't remember the specific names you used. You have probably written this information down somewhere, but maybe you don't have it with you. It may be that the database file was created by someone else. Fortunately, there is an easy way to obtain this information. Use the "List structure" option within the "Tools" menu to review the structure of a database, that is, to review the field names and related information. Select the "Tools" menu, move the highlight to "List structure" (Figure 2-5), and press the Enter key. At this point, dBASE asks whether or not you want to print the results (see Figure 2-6). If you do, you would type the letter Y. But let's assume you don't want the results printed. Simply type the letter N or press the Enter key. Figure 2-7, on the next page, shows the results of choosing the "List structure" option.

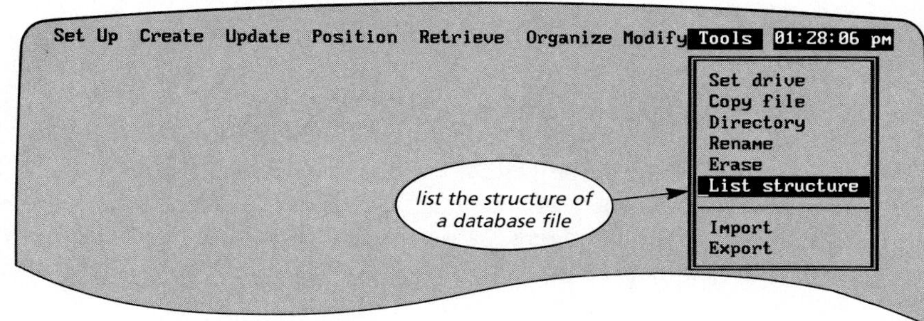


**FIGURE 2-5**
**The "Tools" Menu**

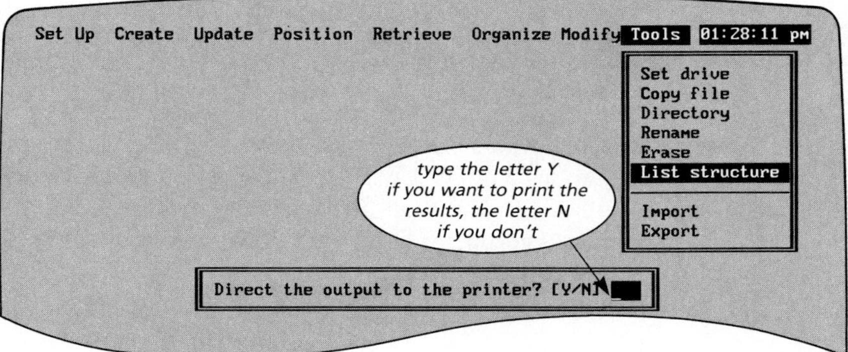


**FIGURE 2-6**
**Print the Results?**

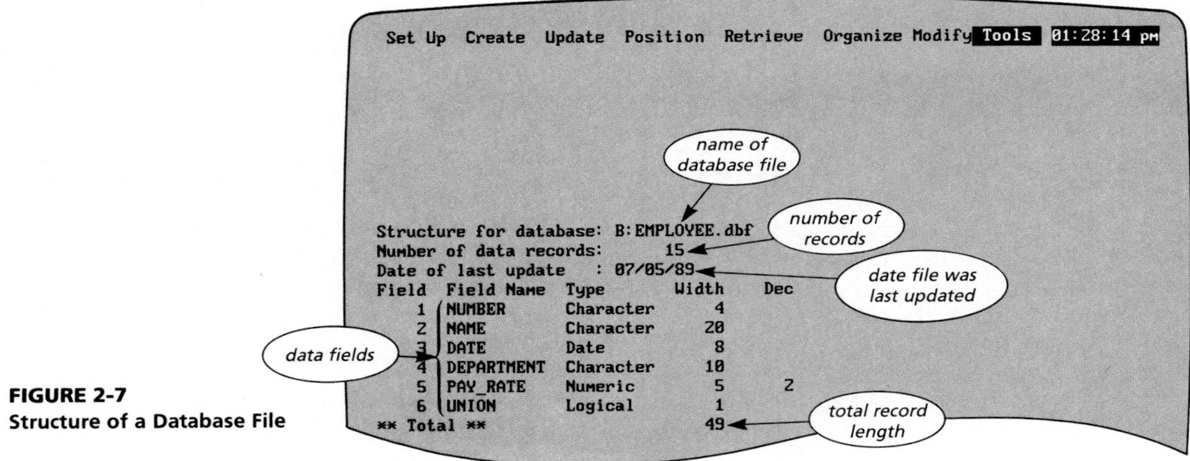


**FIGURE 2-7**
**Structure of a Database File**

In the figure, the first line of output gives the name of the active database file. It is identified by the entry B:EMPLOYEE .DBF. The next line displays the number of records in the file, and the third line gives the date of the last update. Following lines show the field number, field name, type, width, and decimal positions of any numeric fields in the database.

The last line contains the word "Total" and the total number of characters in the records in the file. If you add the field widths together the total will be 48. In the figure, however, the total number of charactures is specified as 49. This is because one position field is automatically attached to the beginning of each record. dBASE uses this field for its own internal purposes.

In this screen, as well as those throughout the remainder of the project, dBASE reminds you that you can press the Enter key as soon as you are finished with the display. This will return you to the ASSISTANT and allow you to take another action.

## DISPLAY

You saw in Project 1 that the "List" option within the "Retrieve" menu can be used to display the contents of a database file. The "Display" option within the same menu can also be used for the same purpose. The two options are very similar, but there are two main differences. First, if the data to be displayed does not fit on a single screen, the "Display" option will pause whenever the screen is full, but the "List" option will not. If you use the "List" option, the data seems to fly by, right before your eyes. Second, if you use the "List" option you will be given the chance to send the report to the printer, but with the "Display" option, you will not.

### Changing the Current Active Record

dBASE continually maintains a position within the active database file. The current position is indicated on the status line following the word Rec:. For example, Rec: 4/15 on the status line means that the current position is the fourth record of the fifteen records currently contained in the file. The number of the current position is called the **record pointer** and the record indicated by the record pointer is called the **current active record**.

For some operations, it doesn't matter which record is the current active record. If, for example, you want to display all the records in a database file, it makes no difference whether the current active record is record 4 or record 8 or anything else. There are some operations, however, such as displaying a single record, in which it is crucial that the current active record be the one that you want. Thus, there must be a way to change the current active record or, in other words, to change the record pointer.

Actually, there are two ways. One is to use PgUp and/or PgDn during data entry. Recall that when you used these keys in Project 1, the number following Rec: changed appropriately. This approach, while handy for moving a few records one way or the other, can be very time consuming, especially if the file contains many records. Fortunately, there is an alternative.

The alternative uses the "Position" menu. Select the "Position" menu using the Right or Left Arrow keys. You should see the screen shown in Figure 2-8. The only option that you want at this time is "Goto Record," so use the Down Arrow key to move the highlight to this option. Then press the Enter key, producing the screen shown in Figure 2-9. The three possibilities are "TOP," which will move the record pointer to the first record in the file; "BOTTOM," which will move it to the last record; and "RECORD." Select "RECORD" by moving the highlight to it and pressing the Enter key. You are now asked to supply a numeric value. The record pointer will then change to this value. Enter the number 3 (see Figure 2-10) and press the Enter key. The record pointer will change to 3; that is, the third record will become the current active record (shown in Figure 2-11).

Repeat the process, but this time choose "TOP" rather than "RECORD." This will make record 1 the current active record.

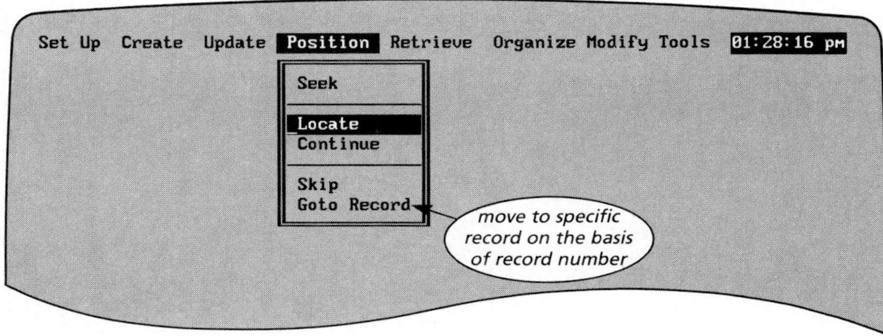


**FIGURE 2-8** The "Position" Menu

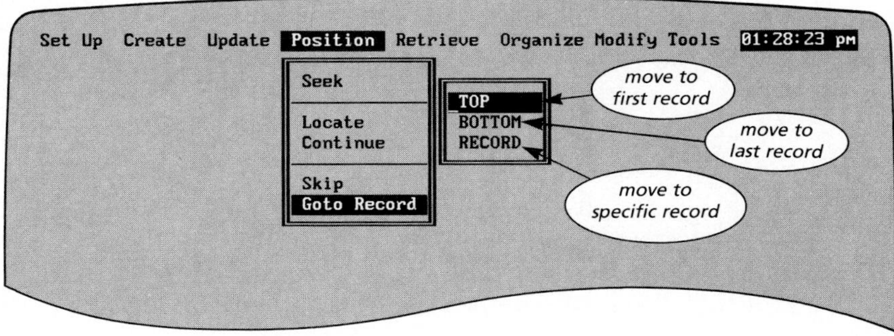


**FIGURE 2-9** Indicating Record

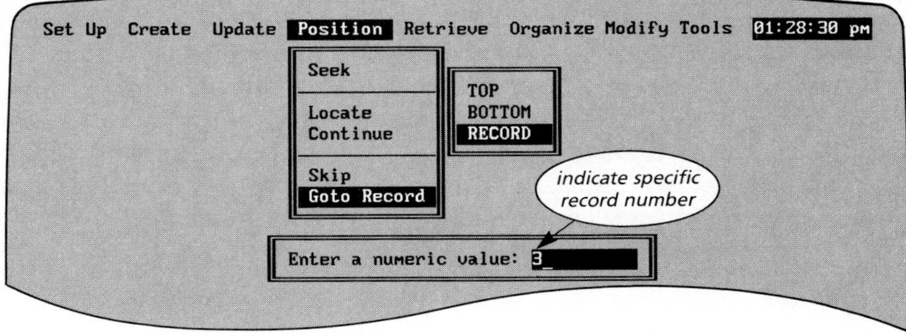


**FIGURE 2-10** Giving Record Number

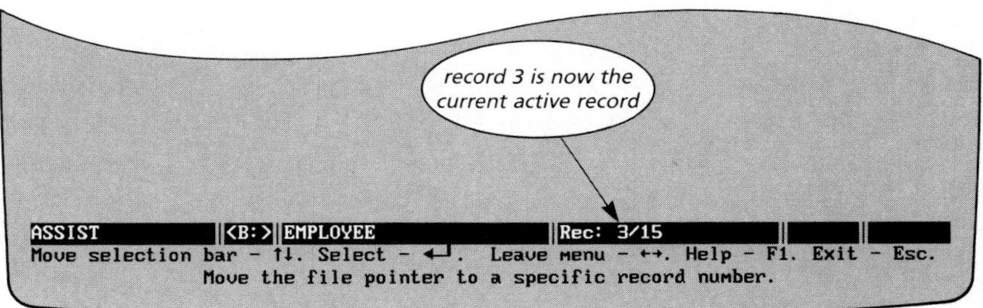


**FIGURE 2-11** Record Pointer Has Been Changed

## Displaying a Single Record

To display a single record, select the "Display" option from the "Retrieve" menu. To do so, use the Right and Left Arrow keys to move to the "Retrieve" menu, then the Down Arrow key to highlight the "Display" option. Once you have done so, press the Enter key. Your display should look like the one shown in Figure 2-12.

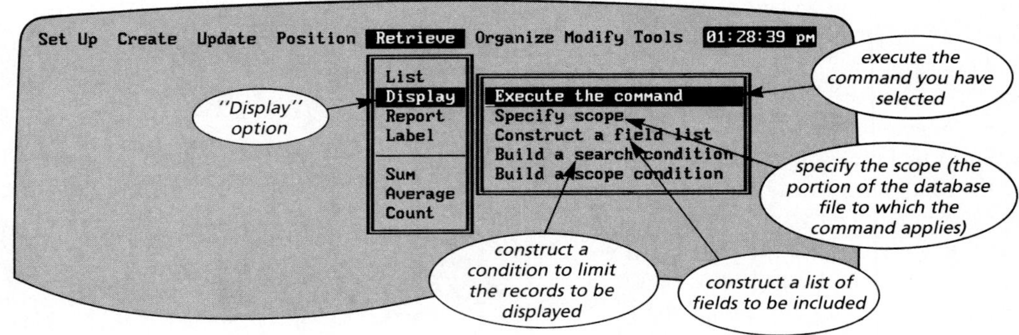


**FIGURE 2-12**
**Using the "Display" Option**

We use the right-hand box on the screen to specify precise details concerning the data we want displayed. The first choice, "Execute the command," is used once we have specified all other details concerning the fields and records we want included. To understand the second option, "Specify scope," you need to understand what dBASE means by scope. The **scope** is the portion of the database file to which the option (in this case, "Display") applies. The normal scope of the "Display" option is only a single record, namely the current active record. This means that unless special action is taken, only the current active record will be displayed. In this case, that is precisely what we want. If it is not, we use the "Specify scope" option to change it.

Normally, dBASE will display all fields. If this is not appropriate, we use the third option, "Construct a field list," to specify precisely the fields that we want. Sometimes we only want to list records that satisfy some condition (for example, all employees whose pay rate is $6.00). The fourth option, "Build a search condition," is used for this. (The fifth option, "Build a scope condition," is not often used and we will not cover it in this text.)

Since the normal scope of the "Display" option is a single record, the current active record, and dBASE normally displays all fields, you don't need to use any special options. Thus, you are ready to "Execute the command." That option is already highlighted, so you can simply press the Enter key. The results of this operation are shown in Figure 2-13. Note that only a single record was displayed. In this case it is record 1, because that is the current active record. If you wanted to display another record instead, such as record 3, you would first use the techniques of the previous section to make record 3 the current active record, then select the "Display" option.

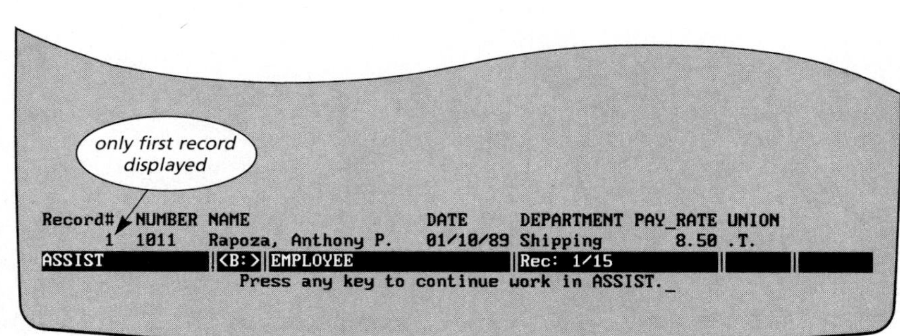


**FIGURE 2-13**
**Results of the "Display" Option**

## Displaying All Records

The normal scope, often referred to as the *default scope*, is not appropriate for displaying all records using the "Display" option, because it will only display one record. It must be changed, and fortunately this is easy to do. Select the "Display" option of the "Retrieve" menu as you did previously: Right or Left Arrow keys to move to the "Retrieve" menu, Down Arrow key to move to "Display," and then the Enter key. This time, however, don't immediately choose "Execute the command." Instead, move the highlight down to "Specify scope" (see Figure 2-14). Then press the Enter key, producing the display shown in Figure 2-15.

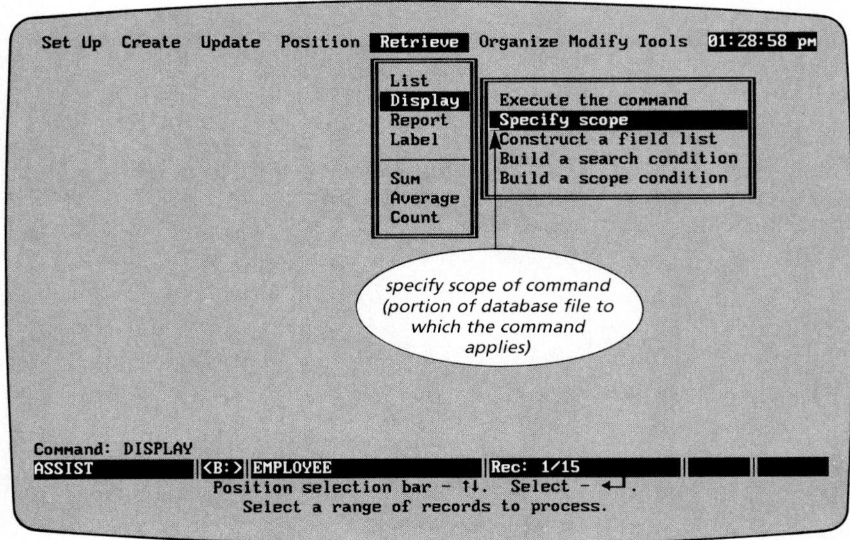


**FIGURE 2-14**
**Specifying Scope**

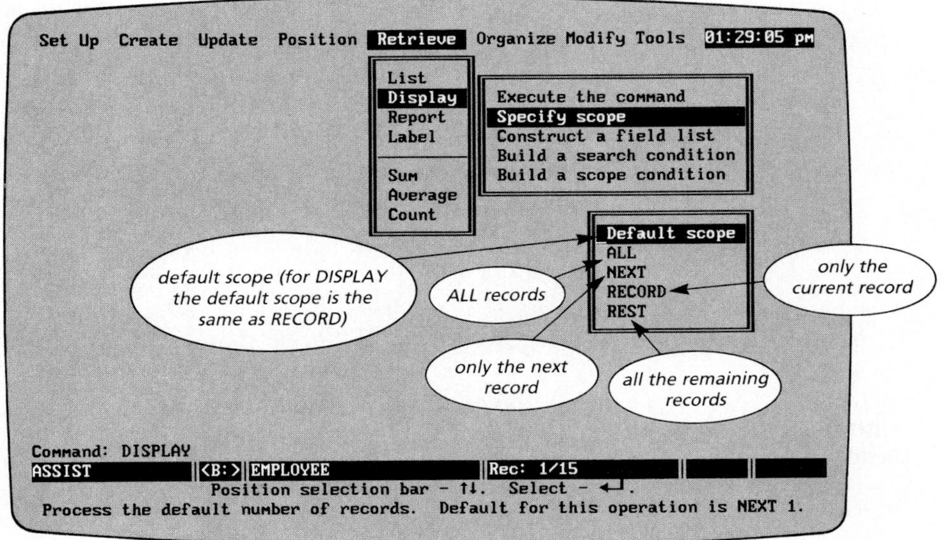


**FIGURE 2-15**
**Selecting a Scope**

The new box that has appeared contains the various possibilities of the scope. The "Default scope" for the "Display" option, as we saw earlier, is only the current active record. The second possibility, "ALL," means that the option applies to *all* records. "NEXT" means that the option only applies to the record *following* the current active record. "RECORD" means the option only applies to the current active record. Thus, for the "Display" option, "Default scope" and "RECORD" are the same. Finally, "REST" means that the option pertains to all the records from the current active record to the end of the file, but none of the earlier records.

Instead of the default scope, you want "ALL." Move the highlight to it using the Down Arrow key. Then press the Enter key, producing the display shown in Figure 2-16. Now you can use the Up Arrow key to move the highlight to "Execute the command" and then press the Enter key. The result is shown in Figure 2-17. Note that all records are indeed included.

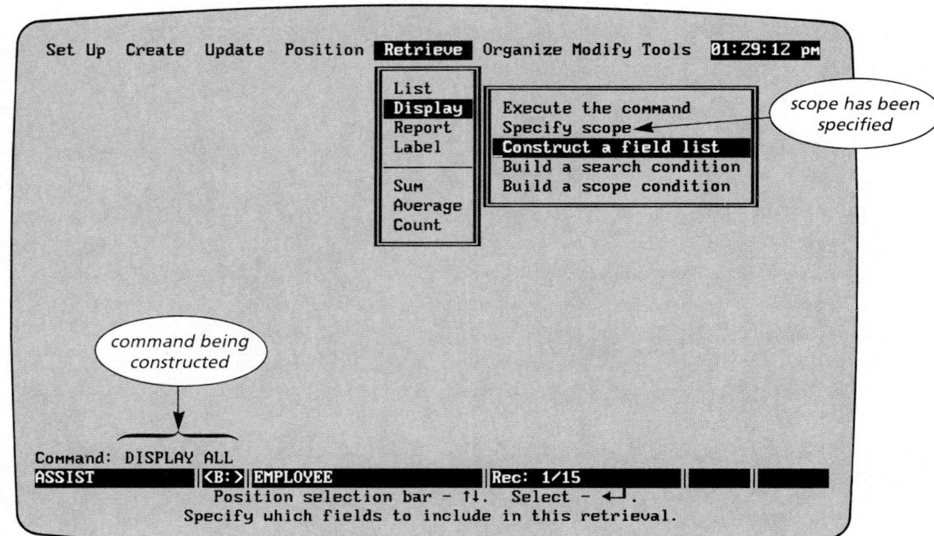


**FIGURE 2-16**
**Scope Has Been Specified**

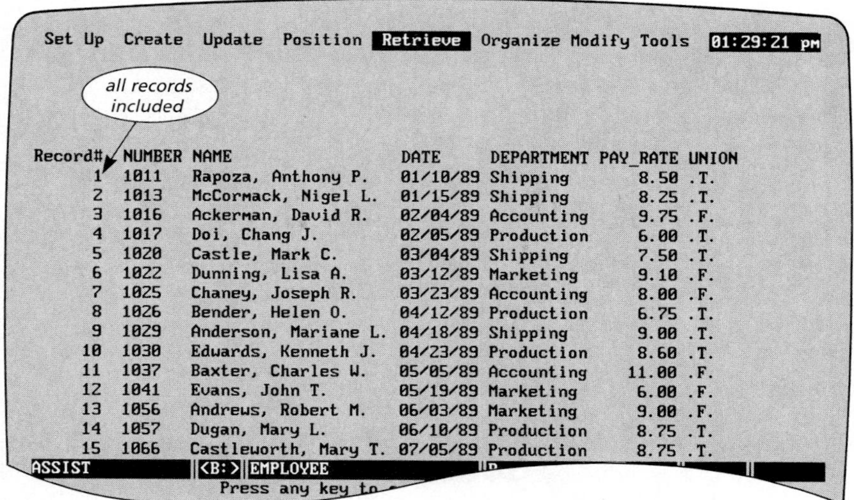


**FIGURE 2-17**
**Results of Display**

## Displaying Selected Fields

Often you only care about certain fields. For example, you may only be interested in each employee's name, department, and pay rate. Fortunately, it is not necessary to view all the fields in a record. You can display selected fields using the "Display" option. To do so, begin in exactly the same fashion as before. Select "Display" from the "Retrieve" menu and change the scope to "ALL," but do not choose "Execute the command" yet. Instead, highlight "Construct a field list" (shown in Figure 2-18), and press the Enter key, producing the display in Figure 2-19.

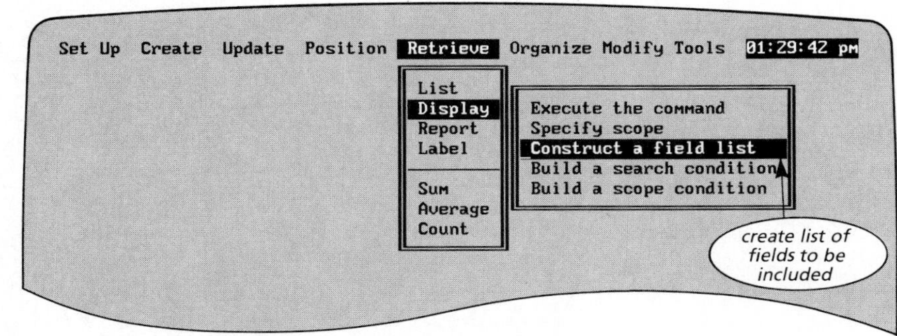


**FIGURE 2-18**
**Selecting Fields**

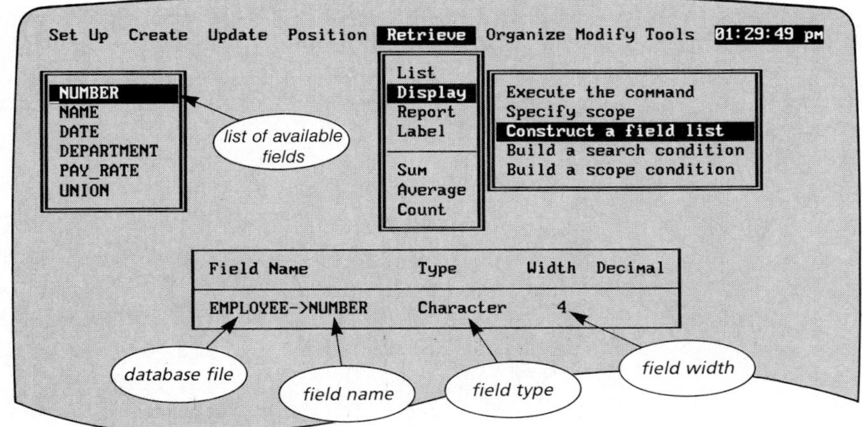


**FIGURE 2-19**
**Selecting Fields**

The box in the display gives the characteristics of the highlighted field. Within the box is an expression that may seem strange to you, EMPLOYEE->NUMBER. This is the notation used in dBASE to indicate that the NUMBER field is part of the EMPLOYEE database file. You may not see why this notation is important. After all, you are only working with a single database file at this point, so it is obvious that any field that appears on the screen must be part of the EMPLOYEE file. Later, however, when you work with more than one database file, you will find this notation to be very useful.

At this point, you can specify precisely those fields you wish to include in the display. In this case, you only want to included NAME, DEPARTMENT, and PAY_RATE. Move the highlight to the first field you want, NAME, using the Down Arrow key, and press the Enter key. Your display should now look like the one in Figure 2-20. Note that NAME is not as bright as the rest of the fields in the box. This means that it has been selected for the display. Note also that the command at the bottom now reads "DISPLAY ALL NAME," which also indicates that the NAME field has been selected.

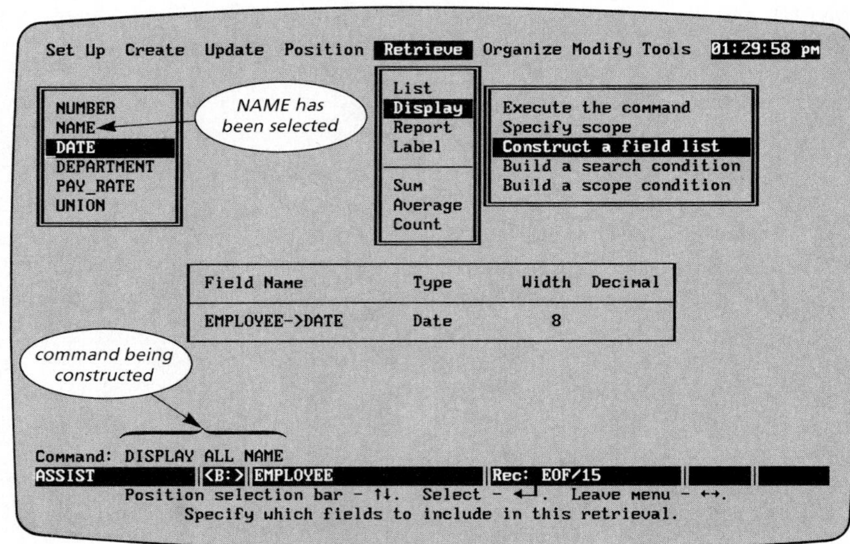


**FIGURE 2-20**
**One Field Has Been Selected**

Next move the highlight to DEPARTMENT and press the Enter key, producing the display shown in Figure 2-21. Now both NAME and DEPARTMENT are less bright than the other fields. In addition, the command at the bottom now reads "DISPLAY ALL NAME, DEPARTMENT." The highlight should now be on the PAY_RATE field, so you can simply press the Enter key to select it. After that, press the Right Arrow key to leave this menu. Your display should now look like the one in Figure 2-22. The command that dBASE has constructed for you, "DISPLAY ALL NAME, DEPARTMENT, PAY_RATE," is shown at the bottom.

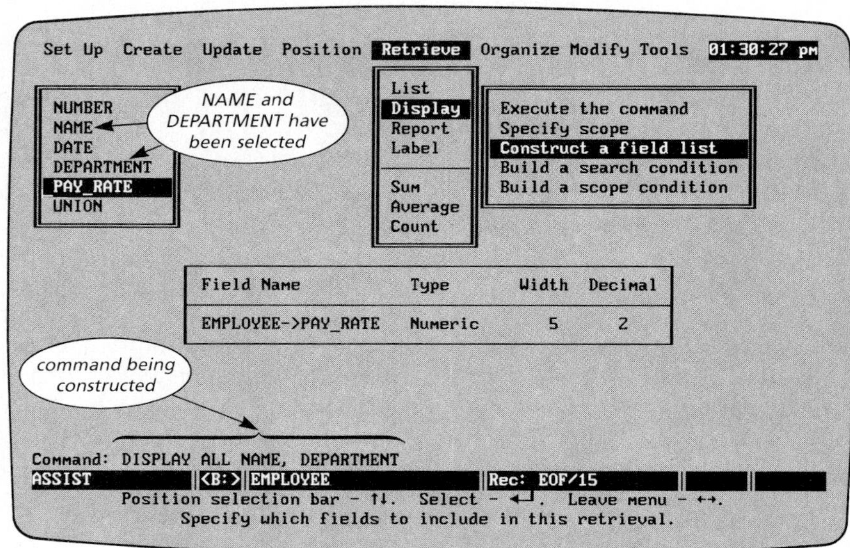


**FIGURE 2-21**
**Two Fields Have Been Selected**

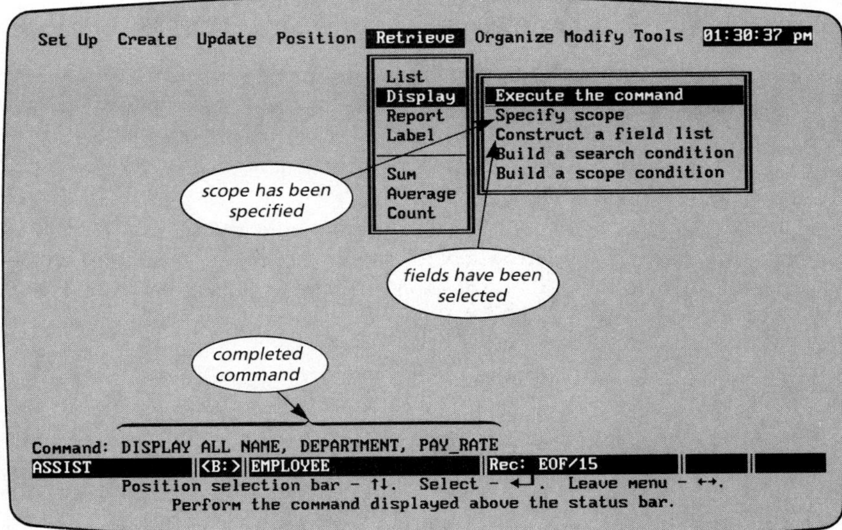


**FIGURE 2-22**
**Desired Fields Have Been Selected**

You are now ready to choose "Execute the command," so move the highlight to it and press the Enter key. The display produced is shown in Figure 2-23. Only the fields you selected have been included.

The order in which you select the columns is the order in which they will appear. Thus, to create a display with the same three columns in a different order, say DEPARTMENT, NAME, PAY_RATE, make sure you select them in this order. First move the highlight to DEPARTMENT and press the Enter key, then to NAME and press the Enter key, and then to PAY_RATE and press the Enter key. Then press the Right Arrow key to leave. When you choose "Execute the command," the columns will be displayed in the desired order.

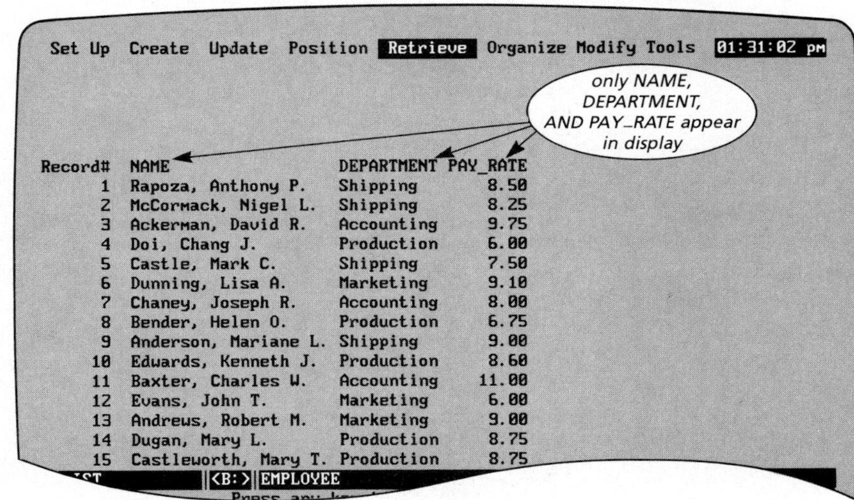


**FIGURE 2-23**
**Results of Display**

## Using Conditions

One very nice feature of dBASE is its ability to display records and fields based upon certain conditions. A **condition** is an expression that evaluates to either true or false. Suppose that you only wanted information about employee 1030. You don't want to see a report of all employees and have to scan through it looking for this employee. What you really want is to display only the information about the employee for whom the condition "number is equal to 1030" is true.

Select the "Display" option from the "Retrieve" menu in the usual manner: Right or Left Arrows to move to the "Retrieve" menu, Down Arrow key to move to "Display," then press Enter. This time move the highlight in the box to "Build a search condition" (Figure 2-24) and press the Enter key. Your display should look like the one shown in Figure 2-25.

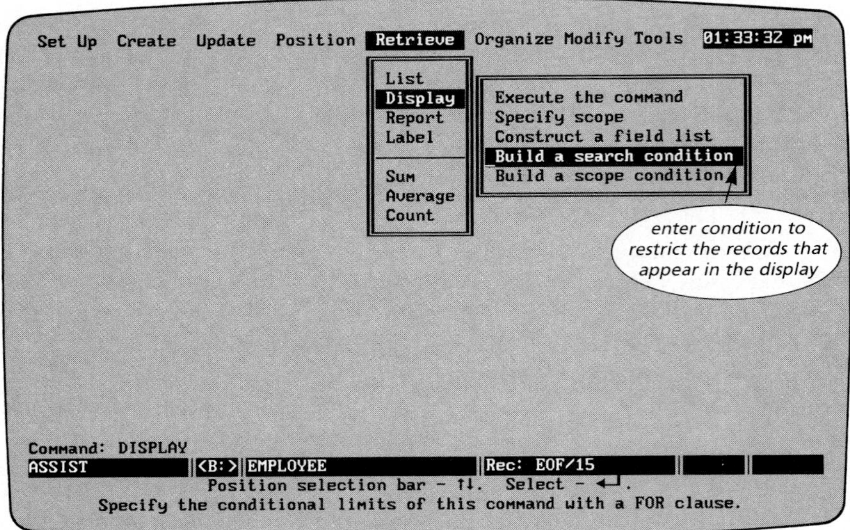


**FIGURE 2-24** Building a Condition

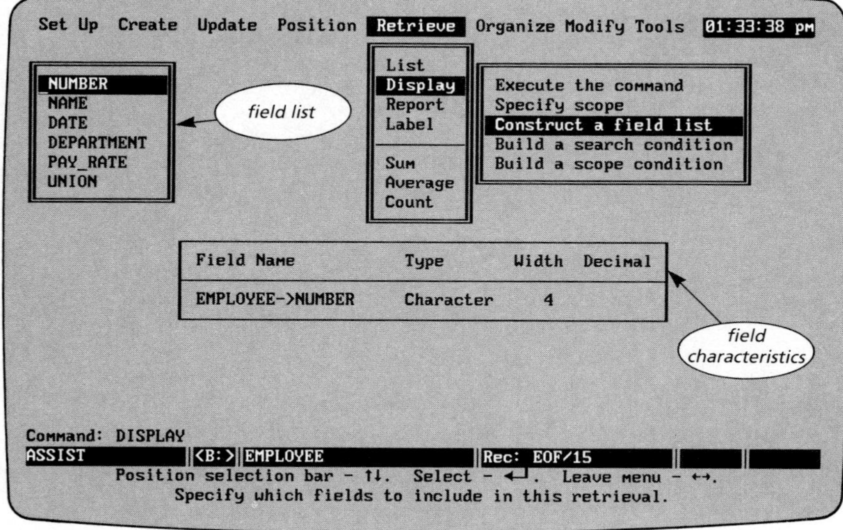


**FIGURE 2-25** Selecting a Field for the Condition

At this point, move the highlight to the field that will be used in the condition. In this case the field is NUMBER, which is already highlighted, so just press the Enter key. Your display now looks like the one shown in Figure 2-26.

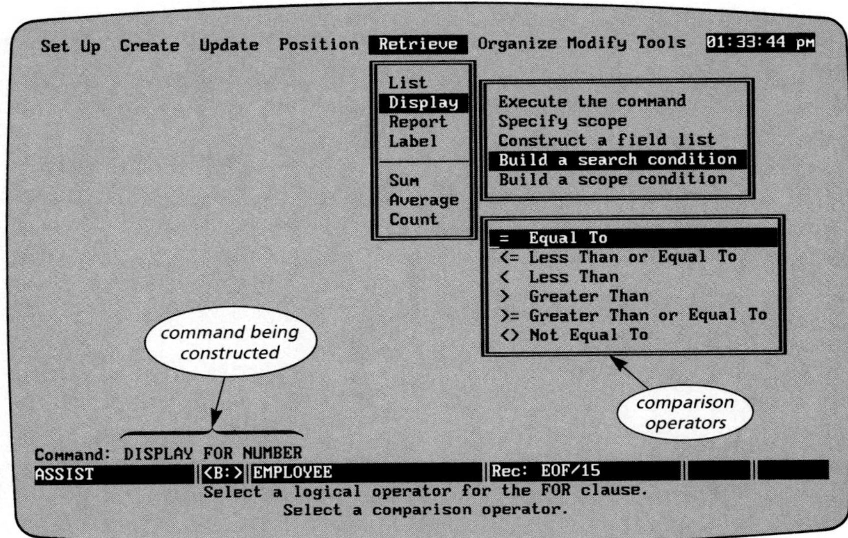


**FIGURE 2-26** Selecting a Comparison Operator

You are being asked to select a comparison operator. The possibilities are shown in the box on the screen. You want NUMBER to be *equal to* 1030, so you must highlight the "Equal To" line. Since it already is highlighted, press the Enter key. To choose a different operator, you would first move the highlight to your selection using the Down Arrow key and then press the Enter key.

You are now asked to enter a character string (Figure 2-27). Enter the number 1030 and the display will look like the one shown in Figure 2-28. At this point, if you had additional conditions, you would choose either "Combine with .AND." or "Combine with .OR." But since there are no other conditions, indicate this by pressing the Enter key (the line labeled "No more conditions" is already highlighted).

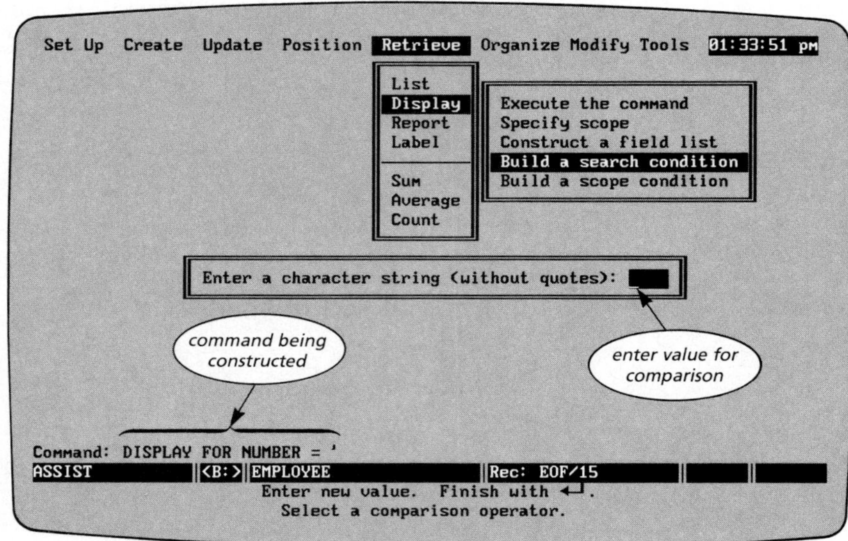


**FIGURE 2-27**
**Completing the Condition**

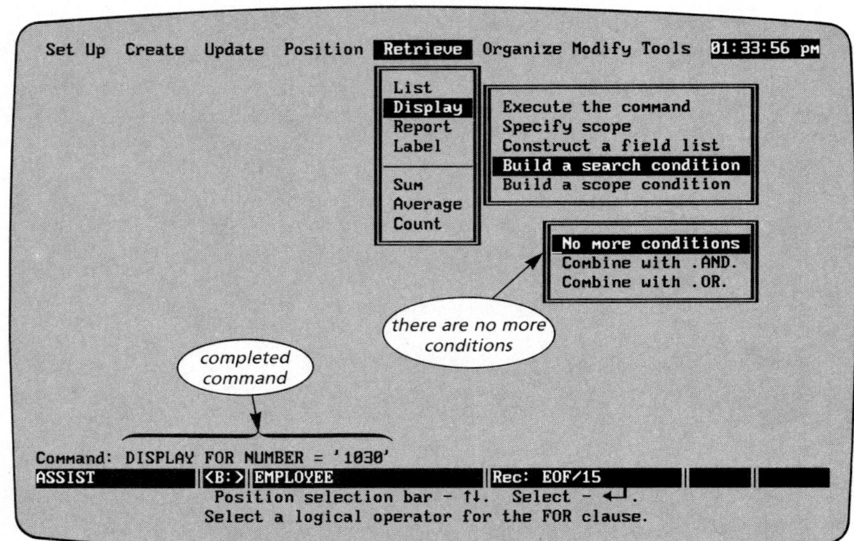


**FIGURE 2-28**
**Completing the Search Condition**

Move the highlight to "Execute the command" (Figure 2-29) and press the Enter key. The results are shown in Figure 2-30. The screen displays only information about employee 1030.

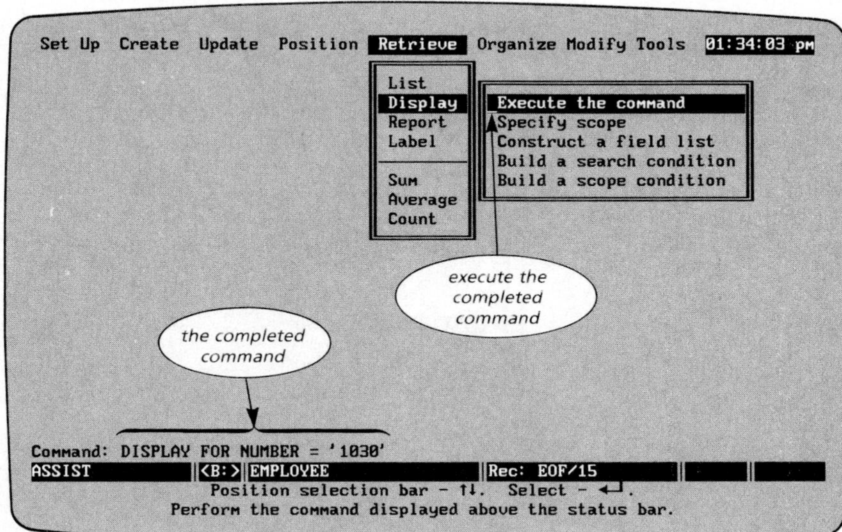


**FIGURE 2-29**
**Executing the Command**

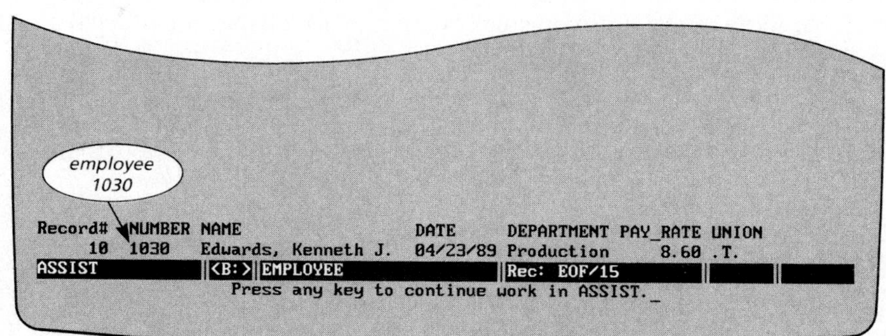


**FIGURE 2-30**
**Results of the Display**

You may have noticed that here, unlike the previous examples, you didn't specify a scope. This is because dBASE automatically uses the scope of "ALL" whenever you employ search conditions. It would not have been wrong to specify such a scope, however.

Try to produce a list of all employees whose pay rate is $6.00. You will have to select PAY_RATE instead of NUMBER when you are building a search condition. In addition, when you are entering a value, you should type the amount 6.00. Since this value does not completely fill the allocated space on the screen, you will have to press the Enter key to proceed. The correct results are shown in Figure 2-31.

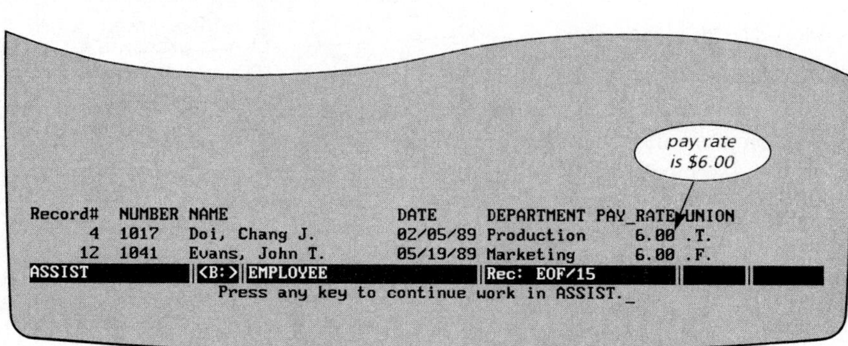


**FIGURE 2-31**
**Employees Whose Pay Rate Is $6.00**

Next try to produce a list of all employees whose pay rate is greater than $9.00. This time you will need to select "Greater Than" rather than "Equal To" as the comparison operator. The correct results are shown in Figure 2-32.

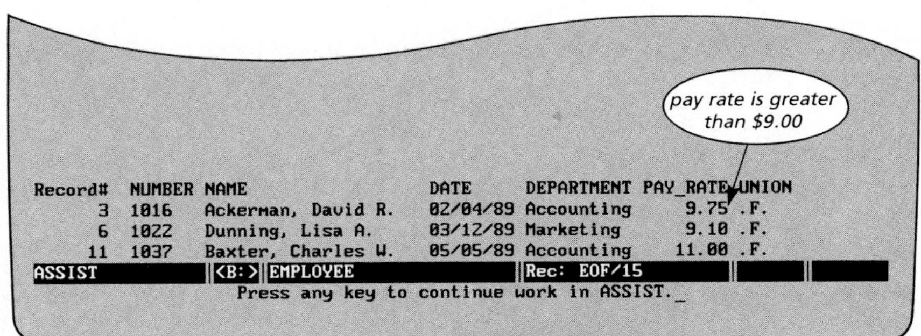


**FIGURE 2-32**
**Employees Whose Pay Rate Is Greater Than $9.00**

Now try to list the name, department, and pay rate for those employees in the shipping department. In this case, first construct a field list consisting of NAME, DEPARTMENT, and PAY_RATE in the same manner as before. Next, build a search condition that requires DEPARTMENT to be equal to Shipping. When you type the word Shipping it is important to type an uppercase S followed by lowercase hipping, because this is the way the information was entered into the database file. If you type SHIPPING, for example, no records will be found since dBASE considers SHIPPING to be different from Shipping. The correct results are shown in Figure 2-33.

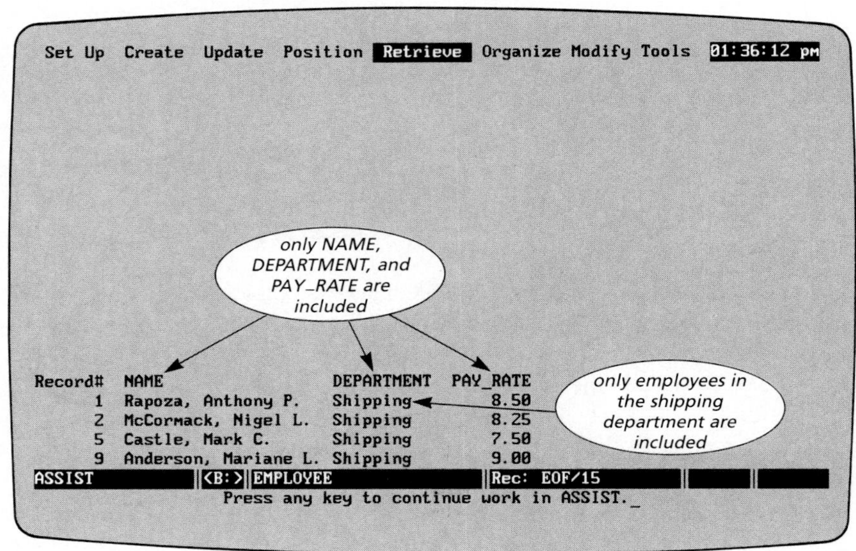


**FIGURE 2-33**
**Restricting Fields and Records**

Finally, try to produce a list of all employees whose name is the single letter A. This time the field in the condition will be NAME, the comparison operator will be "Equal To," and the character string will consist of a single uppercase A. This must seem strange. No employee has the name A. Try this anyhow. The results may surprise you.

The results are shown in Figure 2-34. Three employees are listed, none of whose names are A. Each name, however, *begins* with the letter A. This is, the way dBASE handles these comparisons. If the value in the field is equal to the character string entered as far as it goes, the two are considered to be the same. If the value had been An, for example, then Ackerman would not have been listed, but Anderson and Andrews would.

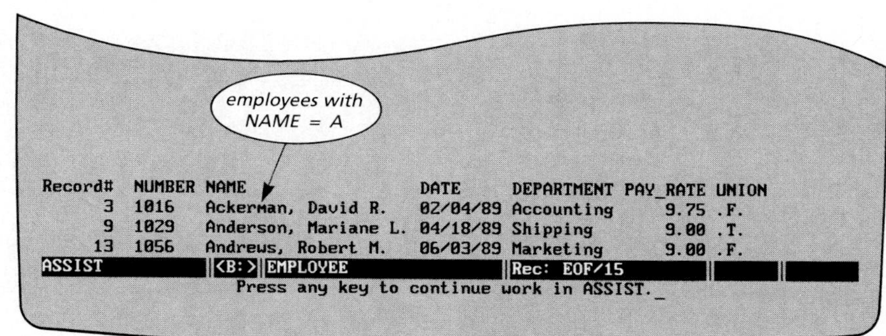


**FIGURE 2-34**
**Results of Display**

## Using Logical Fields in Conditions

Choose the "Display" option of the "Retrieve" menu as you have now done many times and then choose "Build a search condition." This time choose the UNION field (Figure 2-35). Notice that you are not asked to enter a comparison operator. Why?

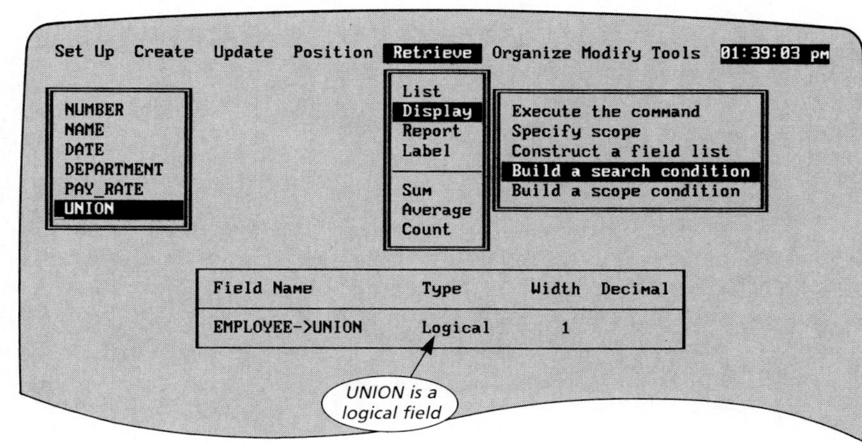


**FIGURE 2-35**
**Building a Search Condition**

Remember that a condition is simply an expression that can be either true or false. The condition "PAY_RATE = 6.00," for example, is true for some records and false for others. A logical field like UNION is either true or false *by itself*. It does not need to be compared with some value.

If you now choose "No more conditions" and "Execute the command," you will see the screen in Figure 2-36. Note that the employees listed are all those for whom the value of UNION is true (.T.).

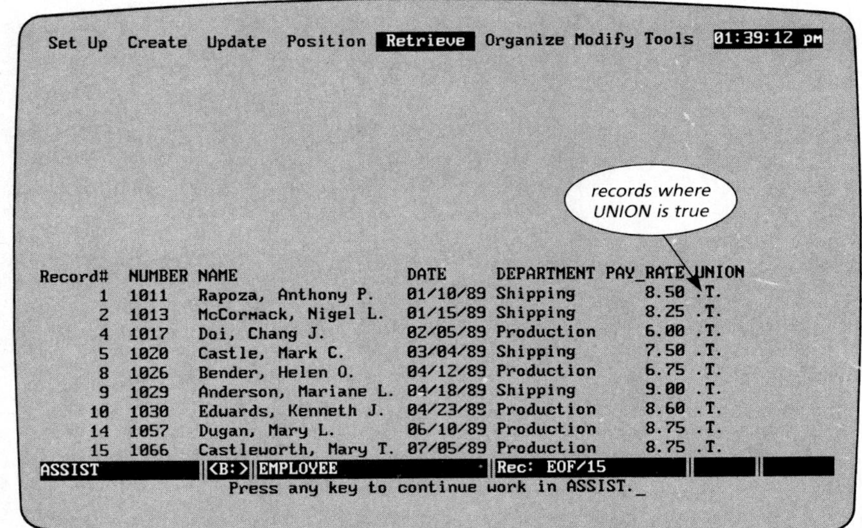


**FIGURE 2-36**
**Results of Display**

## Using Compound Conditions

The conditions you have used so far are called **simple conditions**. They consist of a single field, a comparison operator, and a value. (In the special case of logical fields, they consist solely of a single field.) Simple conditions can be combined using AND or OR to form **compound conditions**.

Suppose you want to list all employees in the accounting department whose pay rate is $11.00. That is, you want all employees for whom DEPARTMENT equals Accounting *and* pay rate equals 11.00.

Begin the process as before by selecting the "Display" option of the "Retrieve" menu. Start building a search condition. Choose DEPARTMENT, "Equal to," and then enter the word Accounting. This time, choose "Combine with .AND." by moving the highlight to it and pressing the Enter key. You can now build another condition. For this condition, choose PAY_RATE, "Equal to," and then enter the amount 11.00. Note the command that dBASE has created at the bottom of the screen (in Figure 2-37). This time, choose "No more conditions" and then "Execute the command." The results are shown in Figure 2-38.

```
Set Up  Create  Update  Position  Retrieve  Organize Modify Tools  01:40:37 pm

                                  List
                                  Display      Execute the command
                                  Report       Specify scope
                                  Label        Construct a field list
                                               Build a search condition
                                  Sum          Build a scope condition
                                  Average
                                  Count
                                                  No more conditions
                                                  Combine with .AND.
                                                  Combine with .OR.

                        constructed command
                                       compound condition

Command: DISPLAY FOR DEPARTMENT = 'Accounting' .AND. PAY_RATE = 11.00
ASSIST          <B:> EMPLOYEE             Rec: EOF/15
            Position selection bar - ↑↓.  Select - ←┘.
           Select a logical operator for the FOR clause.
```

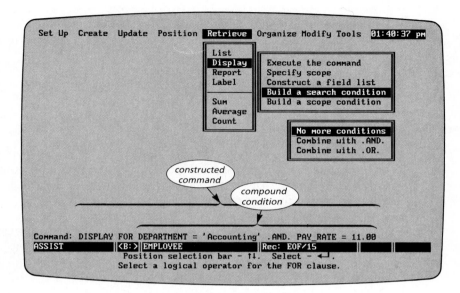

**FIGURE 2-37**
**Display with Compound Condition**

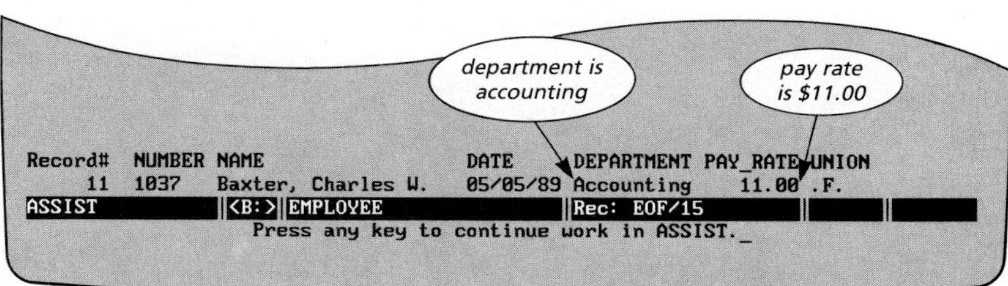


**FIGURE 2-38**
**Result of Display**

Now suppose you want to list all employees who are in the accounting department or who belong to a union (or both). Start just as you did in the previous example. This time, however, select "Combine with .OR." after you have finished the first condition. For the second condition, select the UNION field. Since this is a logical field, you need take no further action in building the condition. Choose "No more conditions" and then "Execute the command." The results are shown in Figure 2-39.

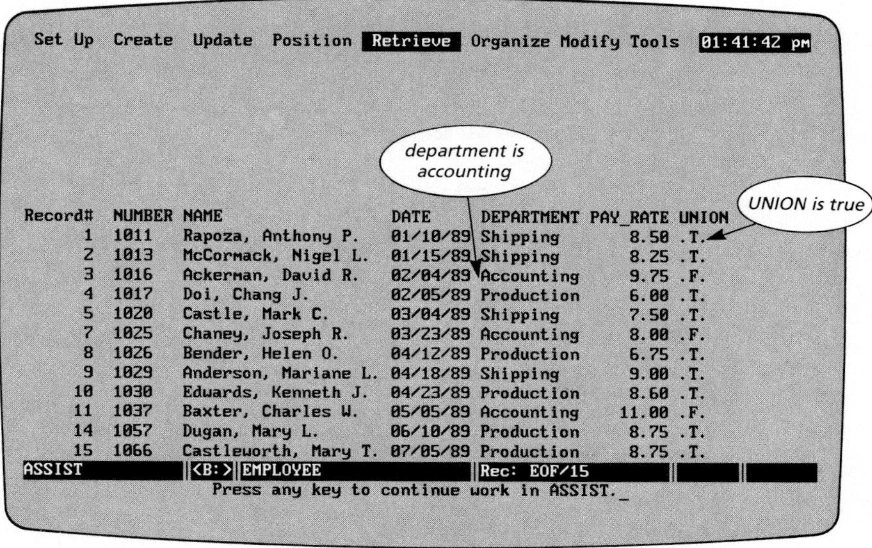


**FIGURE 2-39**
**Results of Display**

# CALCULATIONS

ou can perform three types of computations in dBASE: count, sum, and average. Select the appropriate option from the "Retrieve" menu exactly as you selected "Display." We use these options in a way that is very similar to the way we use the "Display" option.

## "Count"

To count the number of records in a database file that satisfy a certain condition, select the "Count" option from the "Retrieve" menu in the usual manner (see Figure 2-40). If you immediately choose "Execute the command," dBASE will count the number of records in the entire database file. Optionally, you could build a search condition, in which case dBASE will count only the records that satisfy the condition.

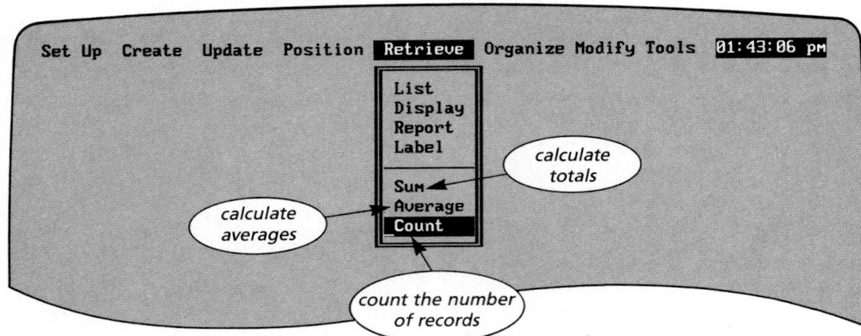


**FIGURE 2-40**
**Counting Records**

To count the number of employees in the accounting department, for example, select "Build a search condition," pick the DEPARTMENT field and the comparison operator "Equal to," and then enter "Accounting." Do this in exactly the same fashion as limiting the record to be displayed using the "Display" option. In the process dBASE creates a COUNT command for you (see Figure 2-41). Choose "Execute the command" to have the command executed and the count displayed (Figure 2-42).

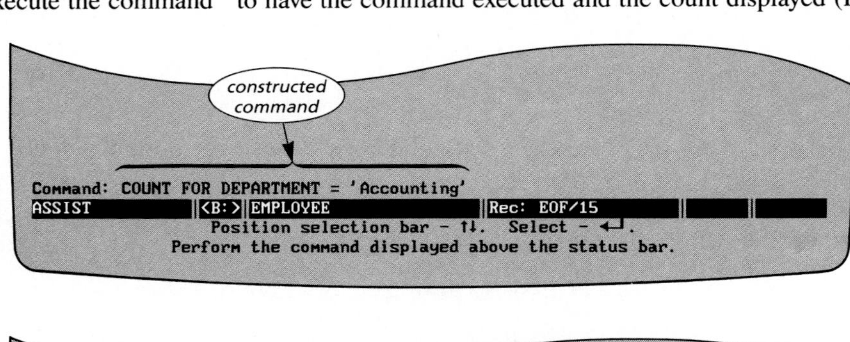


**FIGURE 2-41**
**Counting Records**

**FIGURE 2-42**
**Results of Count**

## "Sum"

To calculate a sum, choose the "Sum" option from the "Retrieve" menu. Next select "Construct a field list" just as you did with the "Display" option. In this case, you will indicate the fields for which you want a sum to be calculated. Only numeric fields may be summed.

Suppose you want to calculate the sum of all the pay rates. After you choose "Construct a field list" the highlight will be on PAY_RATE (Figure 2-43), so press the Enter key. Then choose "Execute the command." The results are shown in Figure 2-44. As you see, the sum is 124.95. Note that the screen also shows the number of records summed. Thus, if you needed to know the number of employees and the total of their pay rates, you could do it all with the "Sum" option. You would not have to use *both* the "Count" *and* the "Sum" options to produce the desired results.

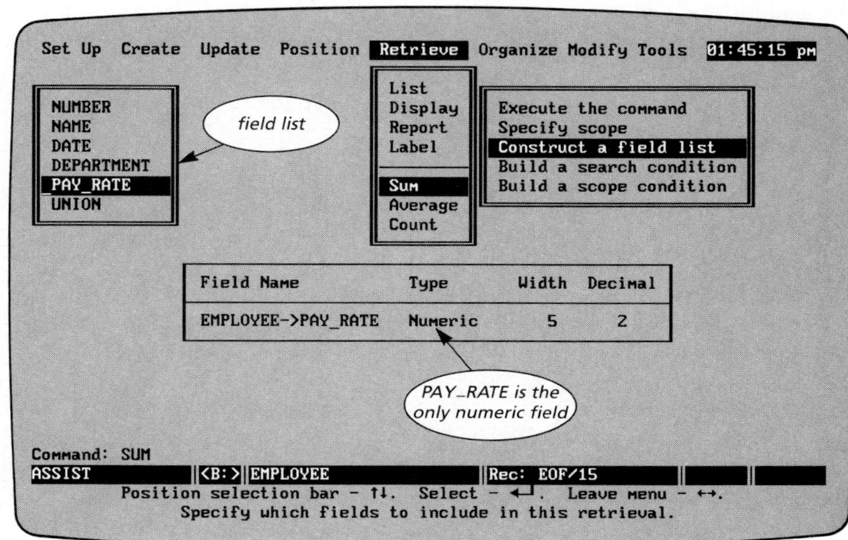


**FIGURE 2-43**
**Calculating a Total**

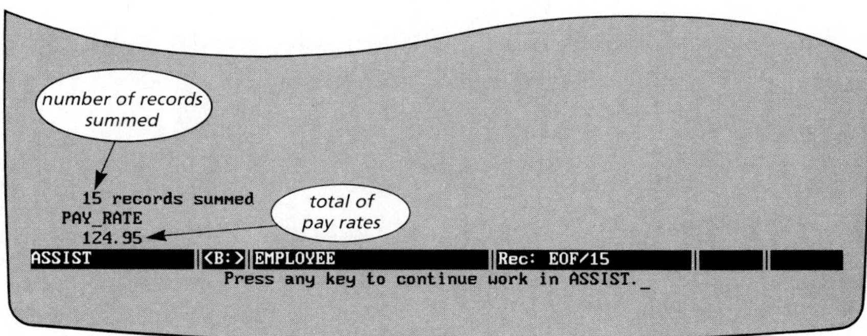


**FIGURE 2-44**
**Results of "Sum" Option**

It is also possible to employ search conditions so that only records that satisfy the conditions will be included in the total. Build these search conditions exactly as you did with the "Display" option. Try to calculate the total of the pay rates for the employees in the accounting department. If you have done it correctly, the answer should be three records summed and a total pay rate of $28.75.

### "Average"

The "Average" option within the "Retrieve" menu is employed in *exactly* the same fashion as the Sum option. The only difference is that dBASE will compute an average rather than a sum. Try to calculate the average pay rate of all employees. If you have done it correctly, dBASE will indicate that 15 records were averaged and the average pay rate is $8.33. Now try to calculate the average pay rate of all the employees in the accounting department. If you have done this correctly, dBASE will indicate three records averaged with the average pay rate being $9.58.

## PROJECT SUMMARY

In Project 2 you learned how to display the structure of a database file, how to use the "Display" option to list various fields and records within a database file, and how to use the "Count," "Sum," and "Average" options of the "Retrieve" menu to count records, calculate totals, and calculate averages.

If you followed along with the steps in this project, you have created a variety of displays. If you did not but wish to see the results now, you can use the following keystroke sequence. Start dBASE as described in the project and activate the EMPLOYEE database file. Then type the following:

**SUMMARY OF KEYSTROKES—Project 2**

| STEPS | KEY(S) PRESSED | RESULTS |
|---|---|---|
| 1 | → → → → → → → | |
| 2 | ↓↓↓↓↓ ↵ ↵ ↵ | Show database structure |
| 3 | ← ← ← ← ↓↓ ↵ | |
| 4 | ↓↓ ↵ 3 ↵ | Change record pointer |
| 5 | ↵ ↵ | Change record pointer |
| 6 | → ↓ ↵ ↵ ↵ | Display |
| 7 | ↵ ↓ ↵ ↓ ↵ ↑ ↵ ↵ | Display |
| 8 | ↵ ↓ ↵ ↓ ↵ ↵ ↓ ↵ | |
| 9 | ↓ ↵ ↵ → ↑ ↵ ↵ | Display |
| 10 | ↵ ↓↓↓ ↵ ↵ ↵ 1030 ↵ | |
| 11 | ↑↑↑ ↵ ↵ | Display |
| 12 | ↵ ↓↓↓ ↵ ↓↓↓↓ | |
| 13 | ↓ ↵ ↵ ↑↑↑ ↵ ↵ | Display |
| 14 | ↵ ↓↓↓ ↵ ↓↓↓ ↵ | |
| 15 | ↵ Accounting ↓ ↵ ↓↓↓↓ | |
| 16 | ↵ ↵ 11.00 ↵ | |
| 17 | ↑↑↑ ↵ ↵ | Display |
| 18 | ↵ ↓↓↓ ↵ ↓↓↓ ↵ | |
| 19 | ↵ Accounting ↓↓ ↵ ↓↓↓ | |
| 20 | ↓↓ ↵ ↵ ↑↑↑ | |
| 21 | ↵ ↵ | Display |
| 22 | ↓↓↓↓↓ ↵ ↵ ↵ | Count |
| 23 | ↵ ↓↓ ↵ ↓↓↓ ↵ ↵ | |
| 24 | Accounting ↵ ↑↑ ↵ ↵ | Count |
| 25 | ↑↑ ↵ ↓↓ ↵ ↵ | |
| 26 | ↑↑ ↵ ↵ | Count |

The following list summarizes the material covered in Project 2:

1. To display the structure of a database, use the "List structure" option within the "Tools" menu.
2. dBASE continually maintains a position within a database file. The number used to indicate this position is called the **record pointer**. The record indicated by the record pointer is called the **current active record**.
3. To change the current active record, you can use the "Goto Record" option of the "Position" menu.
4. The **scope** is the portion of a database file to which a given command or option applies. A scope of "ALL," for example, indicates the command or option is to apply to all records in the file.
5. To display the current active record, you can use the "Display" option of the "Retrieve" menu. Simply select "Execute the command" without specifying anything else and the current active record will be displayed.
6. To display all records, you can use the "Display" option of the "Retrieve" menu. Using the "Specify scope" option, change the scope to "ALL." Then select "Execute the command."
7. To display selected fields, you can use the "Display" option of the "Retrieve" menu. Using "Construct a field list," select the desired fields. Then select "Execute the command."
8. A **condition** is an expression that evaluates to either true or false. A **simple condition** consists of a single field followed by a comparison operator and a value. (The value could be replaced by another field.) A simple condition could also consist solely of a single field, if the field is a logical field. A **compound condition** is one or more simple conditions combined with .AND. or .OR.
9. To display only records meeting a certain condition, you can use the "Display" option of the "Retrieve" menu. Use the "Build a search condition" option to construct the appropriate condition. Then select "Execute the command."
10. To count the number of records, use the "Count" option of the "Retrieve" menu.
11. To calculate totals, use the "Sum" option of the "Retrieve" menu.
12. To calculate averages, use the "Average" option of the "Retrieve" menu.

# STUDENT ASSIGNMENTS

## STUDENT ASSIGNMENT 1: True/False

**Instructions:** Circle T if the statement is true and F if the statement is false.

T F 1. When you use the "Database file" option of the "Set Up" menu, dBASE will display a list of all the database files on the default drive.

T F 2. When you choose the "Database file" option of the "Set Up" menu and then request the EMPLOYEE database file, the contents of the database file are automatically displayed.

T F 3. To review field names and related information, use the "List structure" option of the "Tools" menu.

T F 4. Both the "List" and "Display" options of the "Retrieve" menu give you a chance to decide whether or not the output is to be directed to the printer.

T F 5. Selecting the "Display" option from the "Retrieve" menu followed by "Execute the command" causes all records of the database file to be displayed.

T F 6. To display the contents of record 6, select "Display" and then choose the "Record number" option.

T F 7. To change the record pointer to a specific number, use the "Goto Record" option of the "Position" menu.

T F 8. To change the record pointer to the last record in the file, select the "Goto Record" option of the "Position" menu, then choose "LAST."

T F 9. In order to select all records in a database file meeting a certain condition, use the option called "Build a search condition."

T F 10. If you have built a search condition while using the "Display" option and you want the scope to be "ALL," you don't have to use the "Specify scope" option.

T F 11. When building a search condition involving a character field, the character string must be enclosed in quotes.

T F 12. To specify a search condition to find those employees who are in a union, select "UNION," then "Equal to," and then type the letter T.

T F 13. To count the number of records, use the "Sum" option of the "Retrieve" menu.

**Student Assignment 1 (continued)**

T F 14. If you use the "Average" option of the "Retrieve" menu, you must build a search condition.

T F 15. You could build a search condition by choosing "NAME" and then "Equal to." Then you type the single letter B and press the Enter key. When the command is executed, the display will include any employees whose name begins with the letter B.

T F 16. The "Count" option can only be selected for numeric fields.

## STUDENT ASSIGNMENT 2: Multiple Choice

**Instructions:** Circle the correct response.

1. dBASE will display a list of all database files on the current directory when you select
   a. the "Database file" option of the "Set Up" menu.
   b. the "Database file" option of the "Create" menu.
   c. the "Database file" option of the "Retrieve" menu.
   d. the "Display" option of the "Retrieve" menu.
2. You first select the "List" option within the "Retrieve" menu and then choose "Execute the command." Then you select the "Display" option within the "Retrieve" menu and choose "Execute the command." Which of the following would be true in both situations?
   a. all records would be displayed.
   b. the display would pause every time the screen was filled.
   c. record numbers would be displayed.
   d. you would be asked whether or not the display was to be sent to the printer.
3. You have selected the "Display" option within the "Retrieve" menu and built the search condition "PAY_RATE = 6.00." When you execute this command, dBASE will
   a. display the first record in which the pay rate field contains a value equal to $6.00.
   b. display all the records in which the pay rate field contains a value equal to $6.00.
   c. display an error message because the value $6.00 was not enclosed in quotation marks.
   d. display the active record if the value in the pay rate field is $6.00.
4. Which of the following expressions is used by dBASE to indicate the field called NUMBER that is part of the database file called EMPLOYEE?
   a. EMPLOYEE.NUMBER
   b. NUMBER IN EMPLOYEE
   c. NUMBER->EMPLOYEE
   d. EMPLOYEE->NUMBER
5. Which option can be used to change the record pointer?
   a. the "Goto record" option of the "Position" menu.
   b. the "Change pointer" option of the "Position" menu.
   c. the "Change" option of the "Update" menu.
   d. the "Change" option of the "Retrieve" menu.
6. Which calculation cannot be made using the "Retrieve" menu?
   a. the sum of all the pay rates.
   b. the largest pay rate.
   c. the average of all the pay rates.
   d. the number of employees whose pay rate is greater than $6.00.

## STUDENT ASSIGNMENT 3: Understanding dBASE Options

**Instructions:** Explain what will happen after you perform each of the following actions.

Problem 1. Choose the "Database file" option of the "Set Up" menu.

Explanation: ______________________________

Problem 2. Choose the "Display" option of the "Retrieve" menu.

Explanation: ______________________________

Problem 3. Select the "Goto record" option of the "Position" menu.

Explanation: ______________________________

Problem 4. Select "Build a search condition."

Explanation: ______________________________

## STUDENT ASSIGNMENT 4: Using dBASE

**Instructions:** Explain how to accomplish each of the following tasks using dBASE.

Problem 1. Activate the database file called EMPLOYEE.

Explanation: ______________________________

Problem 2. Make record 3 the current active record.

Explanation: ______________________________

Problem 3. Display record 6.

Explanation: ______________________________

### Student Assignment 4 (continued)

Problem 4. Display the NAME and DEPARTMENT fields for all records.

Explanation: ______________________________

Problem 5. Display the records for those employees whose last name begins with the letter M.

Explanation: ______________________________

Problem 6. Count the number of employees in the union.

Explanation: ______________________________

## STUDENT ASSIGNMENT 5: Recovering from Problems

**Instructions:** In each of the following cases, a problem occurred. Explain the cause of the problem and how it can be corrected.

Problem 1: You chose the "Display" option to list all the records in the active database file. Only one record was displayed.

Cause of Problem: ______________________________

Method of Correction: ______________________________

Problem 2: You wanted to display all fields for those employees in a union. You selected UNION when a box containing all fields was displayed. The display that was produced contained all records, but only the UNION field.

Cause of Problem: ______________________________

Method of Correction: ______________________________

Problem 3: You attempted to choose the "Display" option from the "Retrieve" menu and were unable to do so since there was no highlight in the box to move to "Display."

Cause of Problem: ______________________________

Method of Correction: ______________________________

# MINICASES:

## Displaying Records in a Database

### Minicase 1: Personal Checks

**Instructions:** In Project 1 you created a database of personal checks. Now use this database and dBASE options to accomplish the following tasks. Obtain a printed copy of the output displayed after each command is executed. Do this by holding down the Shift key and pressing the PrtSc key. Write the step(s) to produce the output requested. Record the step(s) in the space provided and then execute them on the computer.

1. Activate the database file so you can access it.

STEPS: ______________________________

2. Display the structure of the database file.

STEPS: ______________________________

3. Display all the records in the database file.

STEPS: ______________________________

4. Display the CHECK NUMBER, DATE, PAYEE, and CHECK AMOUNT fields.

STEPS: ______________________________

5. Display the DATE field, then the CHECK NUMBER field, the PAYEE field, and the CHECK AMOUNT field.

STEPS: ______________________________

6. Use the "Position" menu to position the record pointer at the first record. Display the first record.

STEPS: ______________________________

## Minicase 1 (continued)

7. Use the "Position" menu to position the record pointer at the last record in the file. Display the last record.

STEPS: ______________________________

8. Display record 4.

STEPS: ______________________________

9. Display the record for check 108.

STEPS: ______________________________

10. Display the record that contains the check written for the amount of $69.50.

STEPS: ______________________________

11. Display the records for all checks written for entertainment. Include the CHECK NUMBER, PAYEE, CHECK AMOUNT, and EXPENSE fields.

STEPS: ______________________________

12. Display the records for all checks written to Sav-Mor Groceries.

STEPS: ______________________________

13. Display the records for all checks written that are tax deductible.

STEPS: ______________________________

14. Display the records of all checks written for entertainment for an amount of more than $25.00.

STEPS: ______________________________

15. Display the records for all checks written for household expenses or checks for food expenses.

STEPS:

16. Count the number of records in the database file.

STEPS:

17. Sum the amount of checks written.

STEPS:

18. Sum the amounts of the checks written for household expenses.

STEPS:

19. Average the amount of all checks written.

STEPS:

20. Average the amount of all checks written for entertainment.

STEPS:

## Minicase 2: Music Library

**Instructions:** In Project 1 you created a database of music library information. Now use this database and dBASE options to accomplish the following tasks. Obtain a printed copy of the output displayed after each command is executed. Do this by holding down the Shift key and pressing the PrtSc key. Write the step(s) to produce the output requested. Record the step(s) in the space provided and then execute them on the computer.

1. Activate the database file so that it can be accessed.

STEPS:

## Minicase 2 (continued)

2. Display the structure of the database file.

STEPS: ______________________________________________

3. Display all the records.

STEPS: ______________________________________________

4. Display the MUSIC NAME, ARTIST, TYPE, and COST fields.

STEPS: ______________________________________________

5. Display the CATEGORY first and then the other fields in the record.

STEPS: ______________________________________________

6. Use the "Position" menu to position the record pointer at the first record in the file. Display the first record.

STEPS: ______________________________________________

7. Use the "Position" menu to position the record pointer at the last record in the file. Display the last record.

STEPS: ______________________________________________

8. Display record 8.

STEPS: ______________________________________________

9. Display the records for the classical music.

STEPS: ______________________________________________

10. Display the records for all the music that costs $5.95.

STEPS: ______________________________

11. Display the records for all music on cassette tape (CS).

STEPS: ______________________________

12. Display the records for all music on compact disk (CD). Include the TYPE, MUSIC NAME, ARTIST, and COST fields.

STEPS: ______________________________

13. Display the records for all the music by Milo Panache.

STEPS: ______________________________

14. Display the records for all classical music that costs less than $8.95.

STEPS: ______________________________

15. Display the records for all rock music that costs less than $8.95.

STEPS: ______________________________

16. Display the ARTIST and MUSIC NAME for all rock music that is unavailable on cassette tape.

STEPS: ______________________________

17. Count the number of records in the database file.

STEPS: ______________________________

## Minicase 2 (continued)

18. Count the number of music selections in the vocal category.

STEPS: ______________________________

19. Sum the total cost of all types of music.

STEPS: ______________________________

20. Sum the total cost of the music in the country category.

STEPS: ______________________________

21. Determine the average cost for all types of music.

STEPS: ______________________________

## Minicase 3: Computer Software Store

**Instructions:** In Project 1 you created a database of software information. Now use this database and dBASE options to accomplish the following tasks. Obtain a printed copy of the output displayed after each command is executed. Do this by holding down the Shift key and pressing the PrtSc key. Write the step(s) to produce the output requested. Record the step(s) in the space provided and then execute them on the computer.

1. Activate the database file so that it can be accessed

STEPS: ______________________________

2. Display the structure of the database file.

STEPS: ______________________________

3. Display all the records.

STEPS: ______________________________

4. Display the SOFTWARE NAME field, the CATEGORY field, the MS_DOS field, the QUANTITY field, and the COST field for all records in the database.

STEPS: ______________________________

5. Display the CATEGORY field, the SOFTWARE NAME field, and the COST field for all records in the database.

STEPS: ______________________________

6. Use the "Position" menu to position the record pointer at the first record in the file. Display the first record.

STEPS: ______________________________

7. Use the "Position" menu to position the record pointer at the last record in the file. Display the last record.

STEPS: ______________________________

8. Display record 8.

STEPS: ______________________________

9. Display the record for the software called Image Fonts.

STEPS: ______________________________

10. Display all software produced by the company Anchor Software.

STEPS: ______________________________

11. Display all software in the education category.

STEPS: ______________________________

**Minicase 3 (continued)**

12. Display all software that is MS-DOS compatible (the entry .T. in the MS_DOS field).

STEPS: ______________________________

13. Display all records with a quantity less than 10.

STEPS: ______________________________

14. Display all records with a quantity greater than 25.

STEPS: ______________________________

15. Display all word processing software (WP in the CATEGORY field) that costs less than $50.00.

STEPS: ______________________________

16. Display all records in the database or spreadsheet categories.

STEPS: ______________________________

17. Count the number of records in the database file.

STEPS: ______________________________

18. Sum the QUANTITY field to determine the number of products on hand.

STEPS: ______________________________

19. Average the COST field to determine the average cost of the software.

STEPS: ______________________________

20. Average the cost of the software in the education category.

STEPS: ______________________________

## Minicase 4: Home Sales

**Instructions:** In Project 1 you created a database of information about homes for sale. Now use this database and dBASE options to accomplish the following tasks. Obtain a printed copy of the output displayed after each command is executed. Do this by holding down the Shift key and pressing the PrtSc key. Write the step(s) to produce the output requested. Record the step(s) in the space provided and then execute them on the computer.

1. Activate the database file so that it can be accessed.

STEPS: ______________________________

2. Display the structure of the database file.

STEPS: ______________________________

3. Display all the records.

STEPS: ______________________________

4. Display the ADDRESS field, the CITY field, and the PRICE field for all records in the database.

STEPS: ______________________________

5. Display the PRICE field, the ADDRESS field, the CITY field, and the ZIP field for all records in the database.

STEPS: ______________________________

6. Use the "Position" menu to position the record pointer at the first record in the file. Display the first record.

STEPS: ______________________________

## Minicase 4 (continued)

7. Use the "Position" menu to position the record pointer at the last record in the file. Display the last record.

STEPS: ______

8. Display record 8.

STEPS: ______

9. Display the record that has 10/22/90 in the DATE field.

STEPS: ______

10. Display information about the house at 145 Oak Ave.

STEPS: ______

11. Display the records for all houses listed in the city of Anaheim.

STEPS: ______

12. Display the records for all houses in the 92641 zip code.

STEPS: ______

13. Display the records for all houses with a pool (the entry Y in the POOL field).

STEPS: ______

14. Display the records for all houses that cost less than $125,000.00.

STEPS: ______

15. Display the records for all houses that cost more than $150,000.00.

STEPS: ______________________________

16. Display the records for all houses with four bedrooms that cost less than $100,000.00.

STEPS: ______________________________

17. Count the number of records in the database file.

STEPS: ______________________________

18. Find the average cost of a house in Anaheim.

STEPS: ______________________________

19. Find the average cost of a four-bedroom house.

STEPS: ______________________________

20. Find the average cost of a three-bedroom house in Garden Grove.

STEPS: ______________________________

# PROJECT 3

## Sorting and Report Preparation

### Objectives

You will have mastered the material in this project when you can:

- Sort the records in a database file
- Display the sorted records
- Understand the sequence in which records will be sorted
- Sort on multiple fields
- Create a report file using dBASE
- Print a report using a report file you have created
- Print a report containing only selected records
- Implement subtotals in a report

The records in a database file are initially arranged in the order in which you entered the data when you created the database file. Thus, when you use the "Display" or "List" options, the records will be displayed in the order they were entered.

For some applications, you may want to rearrange the records into a different sequence. For example, you may want to list the employees alphabetically by name. You can accomplish this by sorting the records in the database file. **Sorting** simply means rearranging the records so that they are in some desired order.

In Project 1, we entered the employee records in a date-hired sequence (see Figure 3-1). But there are additional ways in which to arrange the records to display the data in a useful form. For example, we could arrange them in alphabetical order by last name, in ascending or descending order by pay rate, or in alphabetical order within various departments. If you need a list of employees in alphabetical order by last name, for example, you must sort the records in the database file using the employee name field as the basis of the sorting operation (Figure 3-2). A field used as the basis of a sorting operation is called a **key field**. Figure 3-3 illustrates a display of records that have been sorted by pay rate. In this case, the PAY_RATE field was the key field.

*records are in sequence by date hired field*

| NUMBER | NAME | DATE | DEPARTMENT | PAY_RATE | UNION |
|---|---|---|---|---|---|
| 1011 | Rapoza, Anthony P. | 01/10/89 | Shipping | 8.50 | .T. |
| 1013 | McCormack, Nigel L. | 01/15/89 | Shipping | 8.25 | .T. |
| 1016 | Ackerman, David R. | 02/04/89 | Accounting | 9.75 | .F. |
| 1017 | Doi, Chang J. | 02/05/89 | Production | 6.00 | .T. |
| 1020 | Castle, Mark C. | 03/04/89 | Shipping | 7.50 | .T. |
| 1022 | Dunning, Lisa A. | 03/12/89 | Marketing | 9.10 | .F. |
| 1025 | Chaney, Joseph R. | 03/23/89 | Accounting | 8.00 | .F. |
| 1026 | Bender, Helen O. | 04/12/89 | Production | 6.75 | .T. |
| 1029 | Anderson, Mariane L. | 04/18/89 | Shipping | 9.00 | .T. |
| 1030 | Edwards, Kenneth J. | 04/23/89 | Production | 8.60 | .T. |
| 1037 | Baxter, Charles W. | 05/05/89 | Accounting | 11.00 | .F. |
| 1041 | Evans, John T. | 05/19/89 | Marketing | 6.00 | .F. |
| 1056 | Andrews, Robert M. | 06/03/89 | Marketing | 9.00 | .F. |
| 1057 | Dugan, Mary L. | 06/10/89 | Production | 8.75 | .T. |
| 1066 | Castleworth, Mary T. | 07/05/89 | Production | 8.75 | .T. |

**FIGURE 3-1**
**Records Sorted by Date**

records are in alphabetical order by last name

| NUMBER | NAME | DATE | DEPARTMENT | PAY_RATE | UNION |
|---|---|---|---|---|---|
| 1016 | Ackerman, David R. | 02/04/89 | Accounting | 9.75 | .F. |
| 1029 | Anderson, Mariane L. | 04/18/89 | Shipping | 9.00 | .T. |
| 1056 | Andrews, Robert M. | 06/03/89 | Marketing | 9.00 | .F. |
| 1037 | Baxter, Charles W. | 05/05/89 | Accounting | 11.00 | .F. |
| 1026 | Bender, Helen O. | 04/12/89 | Production | 6.75 | .T. |
| 1075 | Caine, William J. | 08/16/89 | Marketing | 9.25 | .F. |
| 1020 | Castle, Mark C. | 03/04/89 | Shipping | 7.50 | .T. |
| 1066 | Castleworth, Mary T. | 07/05/89 | Production | 8.75 | .T. |
| 1025 | Chaney, Joseph R. | 03/23/89 | Accounting | 8.00 | .F. |
| 1017 | Doi, Chang J. | 02/05/89 | Production | 6.00 | .T. |
| 1057 | Dugan, Mary L. | 06/10/89 | Production | 8.75 | .T. |
| 1022 | Dunning, Lisa A. | 03/12/89 | Marketing | 9.10 | .F. |
| 1030 | Edwards, Kenneth J. | 04/23/89 | Production | 8.60 | .T. |
| 1041 | Evans, John T. | 05/19/89 | Marketing | 6.00 | .F. |
| 1070 | Fisher, Ella C. | 07/15/89 | Accounting | 8.00 | .F. |
| 1013 | McCormack, Nigel L. | 01/15/89 | Shipping | 8.25 | .T. |
| 1011 | Rapoza, Anthony P. | 01/10/89 | Shipping | 8.50 | .T. |

**FIGURE 3-2**
**Records Sorted by Name**

records are sorted by pay rate

| NUMBER | NAME | DATE | DEPARTMENT | PAY_RATE | UNION |
|---|---|---|---|---|---|
| 1041 | Evans, John T. | 05/19/89 | Marketing | 6.00 | .F. |
| 1017 | Doi, Chang J. | 02/05/89 | Production | 6.00 | .T. |
| 1026 | Bender, Helen O. | 04/12/89 | Production | 6.75 | .T. |
| 1020 | Castle, Mark C. | 03/04/89 | Shipping | 7.50 | .T. |
| 1025 | Chaney, Joseph R. | 03/23/89 | Accounting | 8.00 | .F. |
| 1013 | McCormack, Nigel L. | 01/15/89 | Shipping | 8.25 | .T. |
| 1011 | Rapoza, Anthony P. | 01/10/89 | Shipping | 8.50 | .T. |
| 1030 | Edwards, Kenneth J. | 04/23/89 | Production | 8.60 | .T. |
| 1066 | Castleworth, Mary T. | 07/05/89 | Production | 8.75 | .T. |
| 1057 | Dugan, Mary L. | 06/10/89 | Production | 8.75 | .T. |
| 1029 | Anderson, Mariane L. | 04/18/89 | Shipping | 9.00 | .T. |
| 1056 | Andrews, Robert M. | 06/03/89 | Marketing | 9.00 | .F. |
| 1022 | Dunning, Lisa A. | 03/12/89 | Marketing | 9.10 | .F. |
| 1016 | Ackerman, David R. | 02/04/89 | Accounting | 9.75 | .F. |
| 1037 | Baxter, Charles W. | 05/05/89 | Accounting | 11.00 | .F. |

**FIGURE 3-3**
**Records Sorted by Pay Rate**

You may often need to sort on more than one field. For example, you may want to prepare a list of employees in alphabetical order by last name within departments. Figure 3-4 illustrates output from a sorting operation of this type. Note that the names are in alphabetical order within each department.

records are sorted by name within each department

| NUMBER | NAME | DATE | DEPARTMENT | PAY_RATE | UNION |
|---|---|---|---|---|---|
| 1016 | Ackerman, David R. | 02/04/89 | Accounting | 9.75 | .F. |
| 1037 | Baxter, Charles W. | 05/05/89 | Accounting | 11.00 | .F. |
| 1025 | Chaney, Joseph R. | 03/23/89 | Accounting | 8.00 | .F. |
| 1070 | Fisher, Ella C. | 07/15/89 | Accounting | 8.00 | .F. |
| 1056 | Andrews, Robert M. | 06/03/89 | Marketing | 9.00 | .F. |
| 1075 | Caine, William J. | 08/16/89 | Marketing | 9.25 | .F. |
| 1022 | Dunning, Lisa A. | 03/12/89 | Marketing | 9.10 | .F. |
| 1041 | Evans, John T. | 05/19/89 | Marketing | 6.00 | .F. |
| 1026 | Bender, Helen O. | 04/12/89 | Production | 6.75 | .T. |
| 1066 | Castleworth, Mary T. | 07/05/89 | Production | 8.75 | .T. |
| 1017 | Doi, Chang J. | 02/05/89 | Production | 6.00 | .T. |
| 1057 | Dugan, Mary L. | 06/10/89 | Production | 8.75 | .T. |
| 1030 | Edwards, Kenneth J. | 04/23/89 | Production | 8.60 | .T. |
| 1029 | Anderson, Mariane L. | 04/18/89 | Shipping | 9.00 | .T. |
| 1020 | Castle, Mark C. | 03/04/89 | Shipping | 7.50 | .T. |
| 1013 | McCormack, Nigel L. | 01/15/89 | Shipping | 8.25 | .T. |
| 1011 | Rapoza, Anthony P. | 01/10/89 | Shipping | 8.50 | .T. |

**FIGURE 3-4** Records Sorted on Two Fields

dBASE provides an option that can be used to perform sorting operations. In addition, dBASE provides an option for preparing report and column headings, space control, and totaling for numeric fields. We discuss sorting and report preparation in this project. You will use the menus and options within the ASSISTANT that are listed in Figure 3-5.

| OPTION | PURPOSE |
|---|---|
| Set Up | Activate a |
| Database file | database file |
| View | view |
| Quit dBASE III PLUS | leave dBASE III PLUS |
| Create | Create a |
| Database file | database file (extension DBF) |
| View | view (extension VUE) |
| Report | report (extension FRM) |
| Update | Change a database file by |
| Append | adding records at the end |
| Edit | changing records viewing one at a time |
| Browse | changing records viewing several at a time |
| Replace | changing the data in all records that satisfy some condition |
| Delete | deleting records |
| Recall | undeleting records |
| Pack | physically remove deleted records |
| Position | Move the record pointer by |
| Seek | finding a match using an index |
| Locate | finding the first record that satisfies some condition |
| Goto Record | specifying a record number |
| Retrieve | Retrieve data from a database file |
| List | show desired fields and records on the screen or printer |
| Display | like "List" (differences between the two are covered in the text) |
| Report | print a report |
| Sum | calculate a total |
| Average | calculate an average |
| Count | count the number of records |
| Organize | |
| Index | create an index (extension NDX) |
| Sort | sort a database file |
| Modify | Change an existing |
| Database file | database file |
| Report | report file |
| Tools | |
| List structure | show the structure of the active database file |

**FIGURE 3-5** Menus and Options within the dBASE ASSISTANT

## SORTING

Figure 3-6 illustrates the sorting process of the records in the EMPLOYEE file. First, the records in the EMPLOYEE file are read into main computer memory. Second, the records are sorted in main computer memory. Third, the sorted records are stored on the disk. In this example, the new sorted file is stored on disk with the file name SORTFLE1. After the sorting operation is completed, there are two separate files stored on disk: the original file (EMPLOYEE) and the sorted file (SORTFLE1).

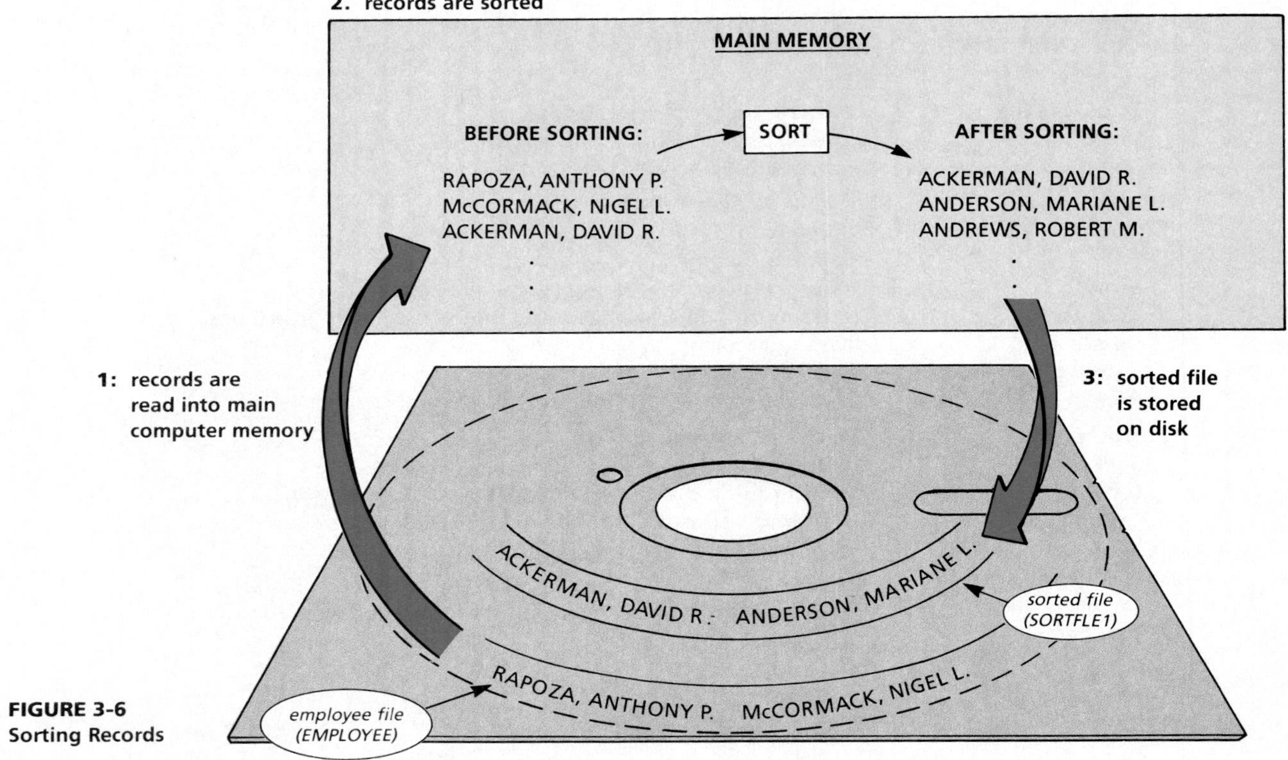


**FIGURE 3-6**
Sorting Records

## The "Sort" Option

Before you can sort, you must load dBASE into main computer memory and activate the file to be sorted using the "Database file" option of the "Set Up" menu. You will use EMPLOYEE, the same file used in Projects 1 and 2, to learn how to sort, so this is the file you should activate.

This file is currently in sequence by date hired, but now you want the records to be sorted in alphabetical order by last name. This requires sorting using the NAME field as the key field. Character fields, numeric fields, and date fields can be sorted, but logical fields and memo fields cannot be sorted. Since NAME is a character field, there is no problem using it as the key field.

To sort records in this file, choose the "Sort" option of the "Organize" menu (Figure 3-7). Use the Right Arrow key to move to the "Organize" menu. Then press the Down Arrow key once to move the highlight to "Sort" and press the Enter key.

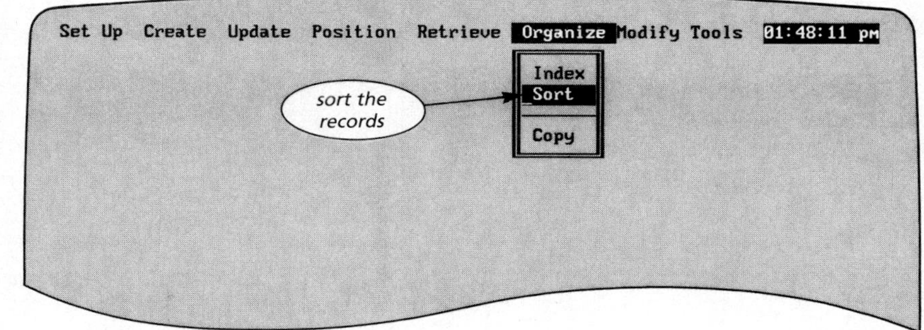


**FIGURE 3-7**
**The Organize Menu**

Next, dBASE will prompt you to indicate the key field. Note that all the fields are listed in a box on the left of the screen (Figure 3-8). Since we want to sort using NAME as the key field, move the highlight to the word NAME (in the figure, this has already been done) by pressing the Down Arrow key once. To indicate that this is the key field, press the Enter key. Then press the Right Arrow key to indicate that there are no other key fields. The display should now look like the one in Figure 3-9.

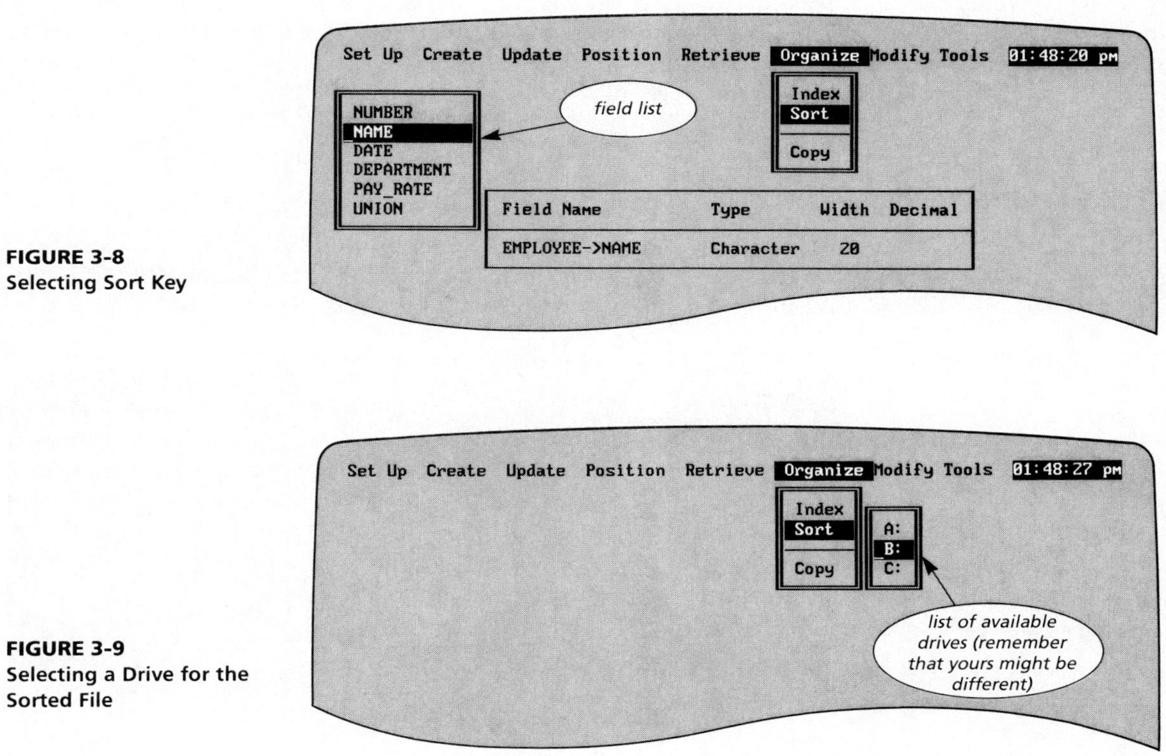


**FIGURE 3-8**
**Selecting Sort Key**

**FIGURE 3-9**
**Selecting a Drive for the Sorted File**

At this point, you must indicate the drive on which you want to place the sorted file. To do this, make sure the B: is highlighted and press the Enter key.

The display shown in Figure 3-10 will appear. It requests you to enter a file name. Any legitimate file name is allowed, except that you cannot sort a file onto itself. Thus, you can't use EMPLOYEE as the file name. In this example, pick the file name SORTFLE1.

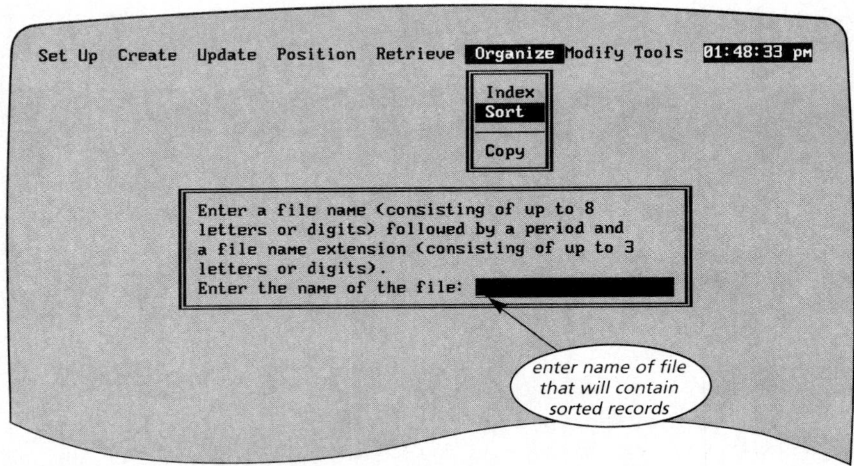


**FIGURE 3-10** Entering Name of Sorted File

Once you have typed the file name, press the Enter key. At this point, the sort will take place. During the sort operation, dBASE provides messages on the screen indicating the percentage of the file that has been sorted. Once the message says that the file has been 100% sorted, the sort is done. The number of records sorted will also be displayed. Your new sorted file, named SORTFLE1, is now stored on the disk in disk drive B.

## Displaying a Sorted File

You created SORTFLE1, but EMPLOYEE is still considered to be the active database file as stated in the status line in Figure 3-11. Therefore, any option you select, such as "List" or "Display," will operate on the records in EMPLOYEE. To use the sorted version, you must first activate it. Return to the "Set Up" menu and choose "Database file" as before.

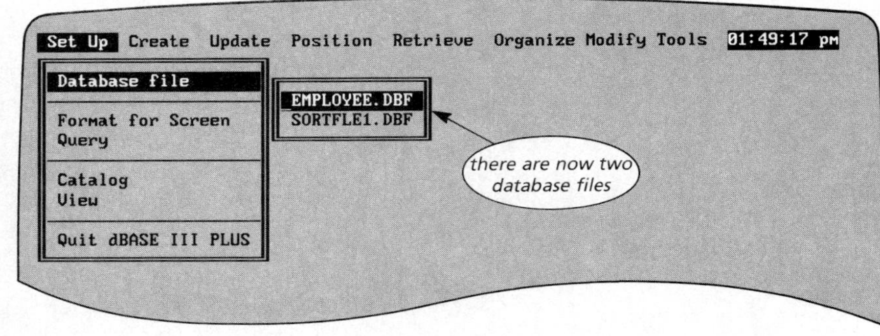


**FIGURE 3-11**
**Selecting a Database File**

Now SORTFLE1.DBF will be one of the files displayed (Figure 3-11). Activate it by moving the highlight to it and pressing the Enter key. Respond to the question "Is file indexed?" by typing the letter N. Then choose the "Display" option from the "Retrieve" menu, change the scope to "ALL," and choose "Execute the command." The results are shown in Figure 3-12. You can see that the records are now sorted alphabetically by name. Note the status line, which indicates that SORTFLE1 is the active database file. After displaying the records, SORTFLE1 is still considered the active file. If you now wanted to work on the EMPLOYEE file, you would have to reactivate it using the "Database file" option of the "Set Up" menu.

records have been sorted by NAME

```
Record#  NUMBER NAME                 DATE     DEPARTMENT PAY_RATE UNION
      1  1016   Ackerman, David R.   02/04/89 Accounting     9.75 .F.
      2  1029   Anderson, Mariane L. 04/18/89 Shipping       9.00 .T.
      3  1056   Andrews, Robert M.   06/03/89 Marketing      9.00 .F.
      4  1037   Baxter, Charles W.   05/05/89 Accounting    11.00 .F.
      5  1026   Bender, Helen O.     04/12/89 Production     6.75 .T.
      6  1020   Castle, Mark C.      03/04/89 Shipping       7.50 .T.
      7  1066   Castleworth, Mary T. 07/05/89 Production     8.75 .T.
      8  1025   Chaney, Joseph R.    03/23/89 Accounting     8.00 .F.
      9  1017   Doi, Chang J.        02/05/89 Production     6.00 .T.
     10  1057   Dugan, Mary L.       06/10/89 Production     8.75 .T.
     11  1022   Dunning, Lisa A.     03/12/89 Marketing      9.10 .F.
     12  1030   Edwards, Kenneth J.  04/23/89 Production     8.60 .T.
     13  1041   Evans, John T.       05/19/89 Marketing      6.00 .F.
     14  1013   McCormack, Nigel L.  01/15/89 Shipping       8.25 .T.
     15  1011   Rapoza, Anthony P.   01/10/89 Shipping       8.50 .T.
ASSIST          ||<B:>||SORTFLE1          ||Rec: 1/15
            Press any key to continue work in ASSIST._
```

SORTFLE1 is the active file

**FIGURE 3-12**
**Results of Sort**

**Sort Sequence** The data in numeric fields are sorted based on algebraic values. For example, if three records in a temperature field contain the values +10, –25, and +90 and the records are sorted in ascending sequence, the values would be arranged as follows: –25, +10, +90.

Character data are sorted in a sequence based on the **American Standard Code for Information Interchange**, called the **ASCII code**. This code is used when storing data. Figure 3-13 illustrates a segment of a chart of ASCII code.

| ASCII VALUE | CHARACTER | ASCII VALUE | CHARACTER | ASCII VALUE | CHARACTER | ASCII VALUE | CHARACTER | ASCII VALUE | CHARACTER |
|---|---|---|---|---|---|---|---|---|---|
| 032 | Space | 051 | 3 | 070 | F | 089 | Y | 108 | l |
| 033 | ! | 052 | 4 | 071 | G | 090 | Z | 109 | m |
| 034 | '' | 053 | 5 | 072 | H | 091 | [ | 110 | n |
| 035 | # | 054 | 6 | 073 | I | 092 | \ | 111 | o |
| 036 | $ | 055 | 7 | 074 | J | 093 | ] | 112 | p |
| 037 | % | 056 | 8 | 075 | K | 094 | ^ | 113 | q |
| 038 | & | 057 | 9 | 076 | L | 095 | — | 114 | r |
| 039 | ' | 058 | : | 077 | M | 096 | ` | 115 | s |
| 040 | ( | 059 | ; | 078 | N | 097 | a | 116 | t |
| 041 | ) | 060 | < | 079 | O | 098 | b | 117 | u |
| 042 | * | 061 | = | 080 | P | 099 | c | 118 | v |
| 043 | + | 062 | > | 081 | Q | 100 | d | 119 | w |
| 044 | , | 063 | ? | 082 | R | 101 | e | 120 | x |
| 045 | - | 064 | @ | 083 | S | 102 | f | 121 | y |
| 046 | . | 065 | A | 084 | T | 103 | g | 122 | z |
| 047 | / | 066 | B | 085 | U | 104 | h | | |
| 048 | 0 | 067 | C | 086 | V | 105 | i | | |
| 049 | 1 | 068 | D | 087 | W | 106 | j | | |
| 050 | 2 | 069 | E | 088 | X | 107 | k | | |

lowest value

highest value

**FIGURE 3-13** ASCII Codes

It is important to understand that numbers are lower in the ASCII sequence than uppercase letters of the alphabet, and uppercase letters of the alphabet are lower than lowercase letters of the alphabet. For example, in an auto supply store a part number field contains part numbers A33, 333, and a33. When these part numbers are sorted in ascending sequence, the fields would be sorted as 333, A33, a33. Number 333 would be first, because it does not begin with a letter, followed by A33, because it begins with capital A, and then a33, because it begins with lowercase a.

**Sorting on Multiple Fields** Records can be sorted on the basis of more than one field. Figure 3-4, for example, illustrated records sorted in alphabetical order by name within department.

Let's try another example and sort on more than one field. First, reactivate the EMPLOYEE database file in the usual manner, using the "Database file" option of the "Set Up" menu. Next sort the file as before. Select both key fields the same way you selected NAME in the previous example. The only special consideration is that the most significant field must be selected first. In this example, records are sorted by name *within* department; therefore, the most significant field is the DEPARTMENT field and you must select it first. After you select both fields, press the Right Arrow key. The remainder of the process is identical to the previous example, except that this time use the name SORTFLE2 for the sorted file (Figure 3-14).

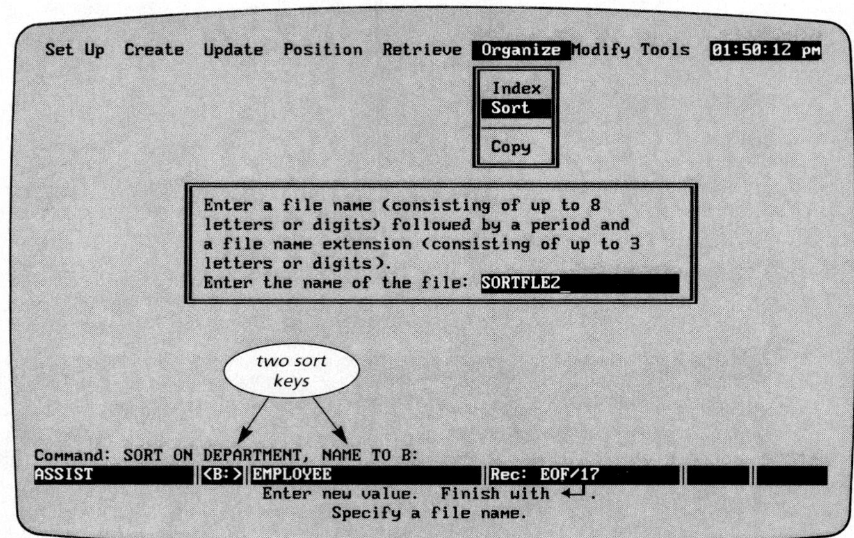


**FIGURE 3-14**
**Sorting with Two Keys**

Once the sort has been completed, activate SORTFLE2 and use "Display" to display all records. This produces the report shown in Figure 3-15. (Don't forget to specify a scope of "ALL.")

*data sorted by NAME within DEPARTMENT*

| Record# | NUMBER | NAME | DATE | DEPARTMENT | PAY_RATE | UNION |
|---|---|---|---|---|---|---|
| 1 | 1016 | Ackerman, David R. | 02/04/89 | Accounting | 9.75 | .F. |
| 2 | 1037 | Baxter, Charles W. | 05/05/89 | Accounting | 11.00 | .F. |
| 3 | 1025 | Chaney, Joseph R. | 03/23/89 | Accounting | 8.00 | .F. |
| 4 | 1056 | Andrews, Robert M. | 06/03/89 | Marketing | 9.00 | .F. |
| 5 | 1022 | Dunning, Lisa A. | 03/12/89 | Marketing | 9.10 | .F. |
| 6 | 1041 | Evans, John T. | 05/19/89 | Marketing | 6.00 | .F. |
| 7 | 1026 | Bender, Helen O. | 04/12/89 | Production | 6.75 | .T. |
| 8 | 1066 | Castleworth, Mary T. | 07/05/89 | Production | 8.75 | .T. |
| 9 | 1017 | Doi, Chang J. | 02/05/89 | Production | 6.00 | .T. |
| 10 | 1057 | Dugan, Mary L. | 06/10/89 | Production | 8.75 | .T. |
| 11 | 1030 | Edwards, Kenneth J. | 04/23/89 | Production | 8.60 | .T. |
| 12 | 1029 | Anderson, Mariane L. | 04/18/89 | Shipping | 9.00 | .T. |
| 13 | 1020 | Castle, Mark C. | 03/04/89 | Shipping | 7.50 | .T. |
| 14 | 1013 | McCormack, Nigel L. | 01/15/89 | Shipping | 8.25 | .T. |
| 15 | 1011 | Rapoza, Anthony P. | 01/10/89 | Shipping | 8.50 | .T. |

ASSIST <B:> SORTFLE2 Rec: 1/15
Press any key to continue work in ASSIST._

*SORTFLE2 is the active file*

**FIGURE 3-15**
**Results of Sort**

# REPORTS

In previous examples, we used the "Display" option to produce output that could be displayed on the screen or the printer. The format of this output was very restricted, listing only the field headings and one or more fields in a record or records.

You can also use dBASE to produce reports suitable for business purposes. These reports can contain such items as page numbers, dates, report and column headings, and totals. The reports may be formatted to give a professional appearance. dBASE's report-generating feature displays a series of screens prompting you in the steps necessary to produce the desired output. We explain this technique in the following paragraphs.

## Designing the Output

Design your report carefully *before* entering any information into dBASE. It helps to lay out the form of the output on graph paper or on a special form such as a printer spacing chart, illustrated in Figure 3-16a. Figure 3-16b, on the next page, shows a weekly payroll report, which we will design together. Printer spacing charts are readily available. You could take a blank chart and make the entries as we go along.

As you begin thinking about your report, you decide that you want to include employee name, department name, pay rate, and weekly pay. Weekly pay is calculated by multiplying the value in the pay rate field by 40. You want the report to contain page and column headings. You also want a final total to be accumulated and printed for the weekly pay, but you do not want to include the total of all the pay rates.

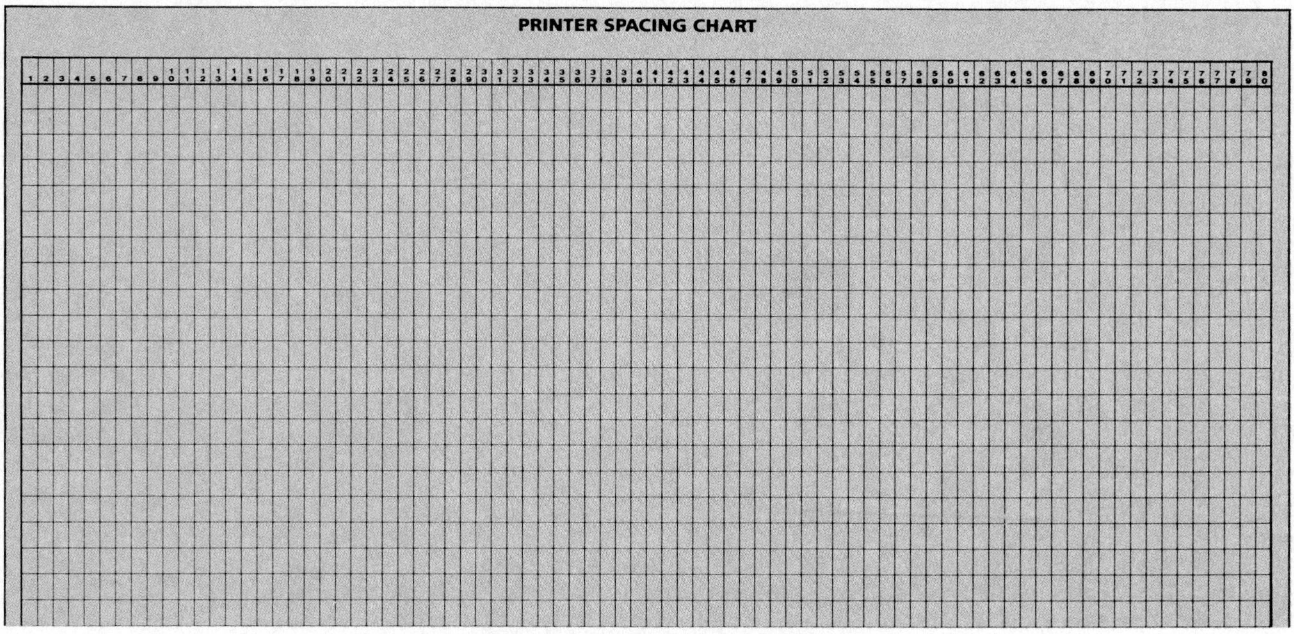


**FIGURE 3-16a** Printer Spacing Chart

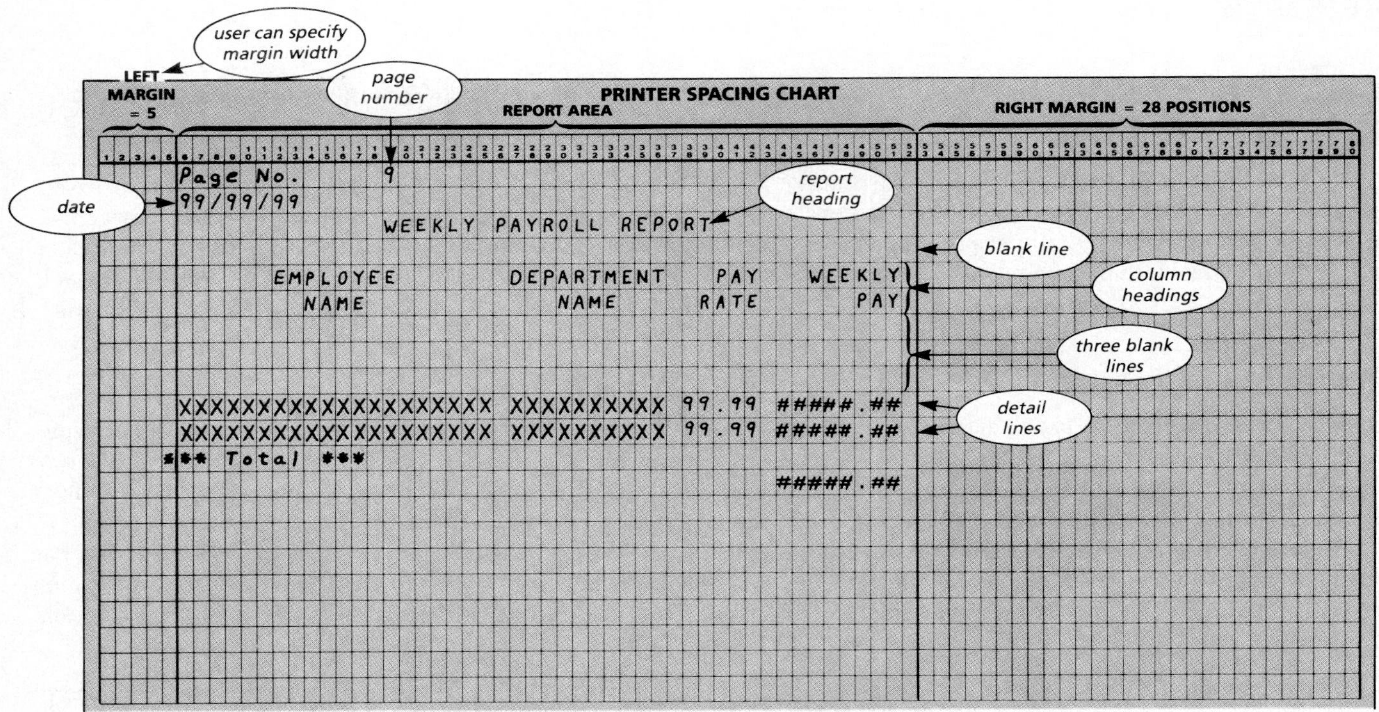


**FIGURE 3-16b** Report Layout

Before starting to lay out the report, let's examine the printer spacing chart in a little more detail. As you can see from Figure 3-16b, the numbers 1 to 80 are printed across the top of the form. These numbers represent the standard number of printing positions used by dBASE. Within the grid on the form you will record the location and the type of information that is to appear on the report.

The first thing to do is to specify the left margin of the report. We decide the left margin should be five and indicate this as shown in the figure.

Next, determine the report area, that is, the area occupied by the data that will appear on the report. Indicate where to place the data in this area by using the letter X for character fields, the number 9 for numeric fields for which no total will be calculated, or the symbol # for numeric fields for which a total is to be calculated. For numeric fields, place a decimal point where you want it to appear. Enter the appropriate symbols on the tenth line of the report as shown in Figure 3-16. The first data field, the employee's name, is represented by 20 X's, indicating that it is a character field 20 positions long. The second data field, the department, is represented by 10 X's. The third, pay rate, is represented by 99.99. This means that it is a numeric field occupying five positions, with the decimal point at the third position, and no total will be calculated for the field. The final field, weekly pay, is represented by #####.##. This means that it is a numeric field of eight positions, with the decimal point at the sixth position, and a total will be calculated for the field.

The unused right portion of the form, from one space past the end of the last field out to position 80, is considered to be the right margin. In this report the right margin is 28. It's important to specify the left margin, the report area, and the right margin, because dBASE will automatically center the page heading in the report area.

Now construct the top portion of the form. On the first line, place the words Page No. followed by the number 9. This does not mean page number 9. Rather, it indicates that a numeric value will be displayed in that space. The report-generating feature of dBASE will always produce the words Page No. and the actual page number on the first line of a report in the location you have indicated.

On the next line, place the entry 99/99/99, which shows where the date will be displayed. The date will always appear on the second line when you use the report-generating feature of dBASE. It is displayed in the MM/DD/YY format.

On the third line place the page heading, centered over the data fields. In our example the page heading is WEEKLY PAYROLL REPORT. Enter it as shown in Figure 3-16. Note that it is centered over the data. dBASE automatically centers this heading for you when you construct the report, but the main reason you center it here is to make sure that what you write on the printer spacing chart is an accurate reflection of the way the final report will look. Below the heading, leave a blank line and then write the column headings. Make sure the column headings are centered over the appropriate data fields.

There should be three blank lines between the column headings and the lines showing the data fields. dBASE puts these in automatically. If you have not left enough room on the chart for three blank lines, simply erase and redraw the bottom portion of the report.

You should always include two lines of the X's, 9's, and #'s to describe the vertical spacing of the report. The fact that there is no blank line between the two lines shows that the report is to be single spaced (no blank spaces between lines). To construct a double-spaced report, leave a single blank line between the two lines.

At the bottom of the display, place the entry *** Total *** on the left, and on the next line, underneath the weekly pay column at the right, place #####.##. This indicates where the total of the weekly pay amounts will appear. dBASE automatically generates the entry *** Total *** when a final total is taken. In addition, when you specify a left margin of one or more characters, dBASE places the leftmost asterisk of *** Total *** in the left margin. dBASE also controls the position of the total.

It is important to understand that dBASE automatically positions the page number, the date, the three blank lines after the column headings, the single blank space between each field, the entry *** Total ***, and the actual total at the bottom of the report. Whenever you design another report to implement in dBASE, make sure these sections of the new report are in the same positions as in this example.

## Beginning the Report Creation Process

After designing the report, make sure the database file that will furnish the data for the report is the active database file. Select the file SORTFLE1, since it will furnish the data, using the "Database file" option of the "Set Up" menu. Then use the "Report" option of the "Create" menu to call the screens that allow a report to be created.

Once you have chosen the "Report" option (Figure 3-17), indicate the drive on which to place the file that contains the report description. You are probably using a data disk in drive B. If so, select B: as you have done before. If not, select the correct drive by moving the highlight to it and pressing the Enter key. The display should now look like the one in Figure 3-18. Enter the name REPORT1 for the name of the report as shown in the figure and press the Enter key. dBASE will automatically add .FRM as an extension, so the file that is created will actually be called REPORT1.FRM.

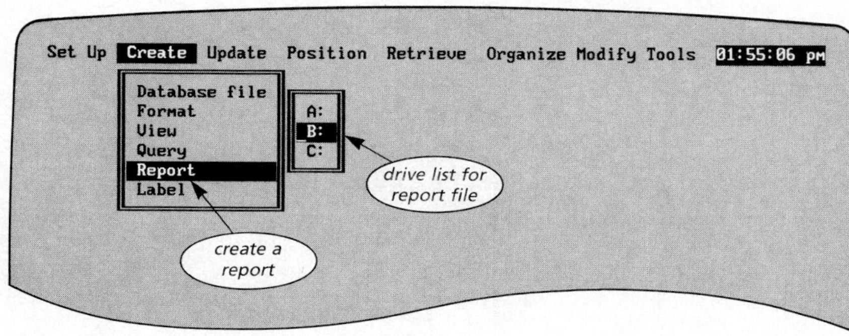


**FIGURE 3-17**
**Creating a Report**

**FIGURE 3-18**
**Entering the Name of a Report**

## Entering Basic Report Information

Once you have pressed the Enter key, you will see a screen on which you enter the page heading and define the page width, left and right margins, number of lines per page, and double or single spacing (Figure 3-19).

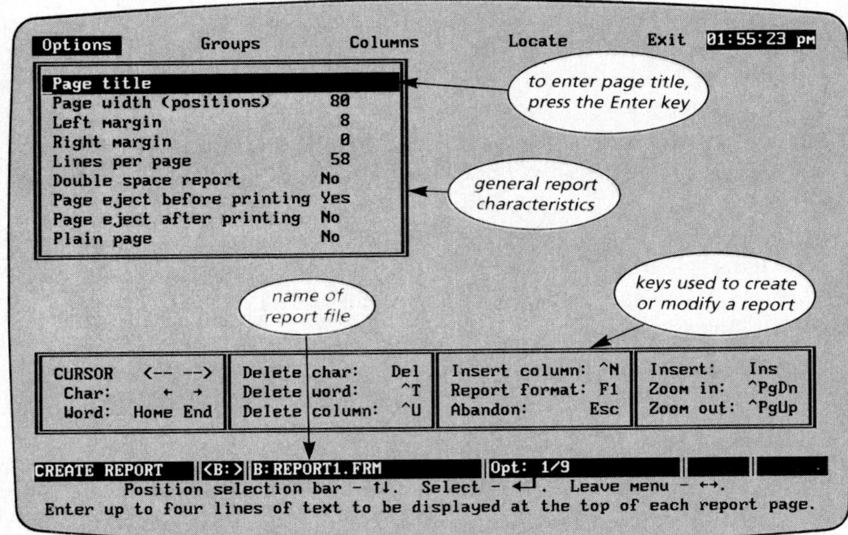


**FIGURE 3-19**
**Entering General Report Characteristics**

At the bottom of the screen appears the name of the input file. The box near the bottom of the screen describes some of the key combinations that you can us when creating or modifying a report. The box at the top of the screen indicates the various items that you can enter or change at this point.

The first step is to enter the heading, WEEKLY PAYROLL REPORT. To do so, highlight "Page title" and press the Enter key. The page heading area now appears (Figure 3-20).

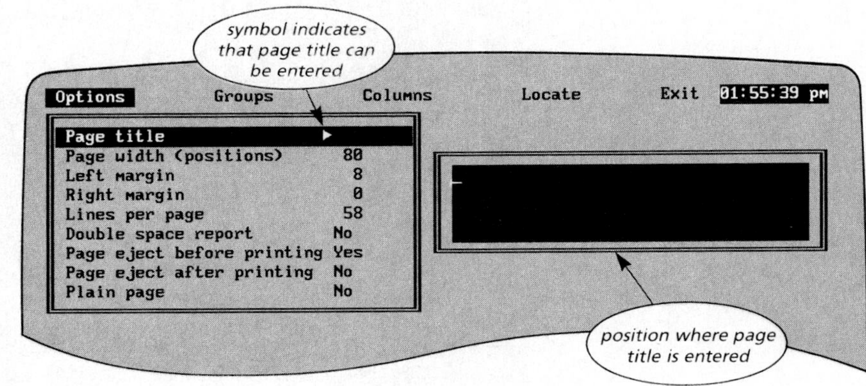


**FIGURE 3-20**
**Entering a Page Title**

Type the words WEEKLY PAYROLL REPORT in this page heading area (Figure 3-21). After you have typed the heading, press the Enter key. The cursor will move to the first position on the second line of the page heading area. There is room for four lines of headings in the page heading area. For example, the name of the company could be printed on the next line, followed by the city and state, and then the phone number. Because there are no additional headings in the example, hold the Ctrl key down and press the End key. The display now looks like the one shown in Figure 3-22. Note that a small portion of the title appears on the "Page title" line within the box.

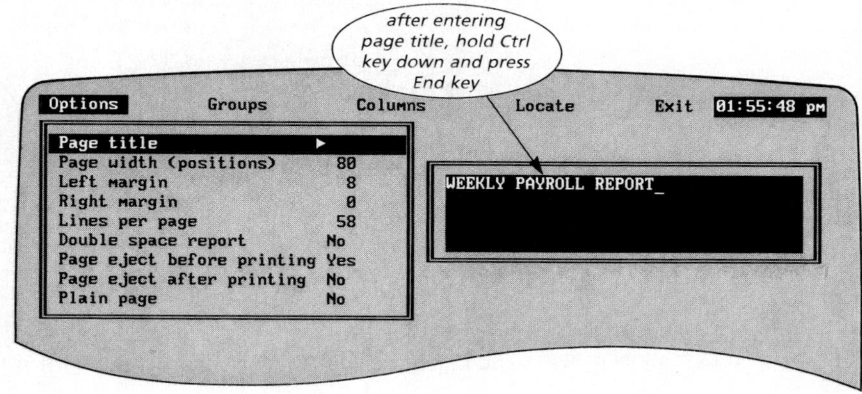


**FIGURE 3-21**
**Page Title Is Being Entered**

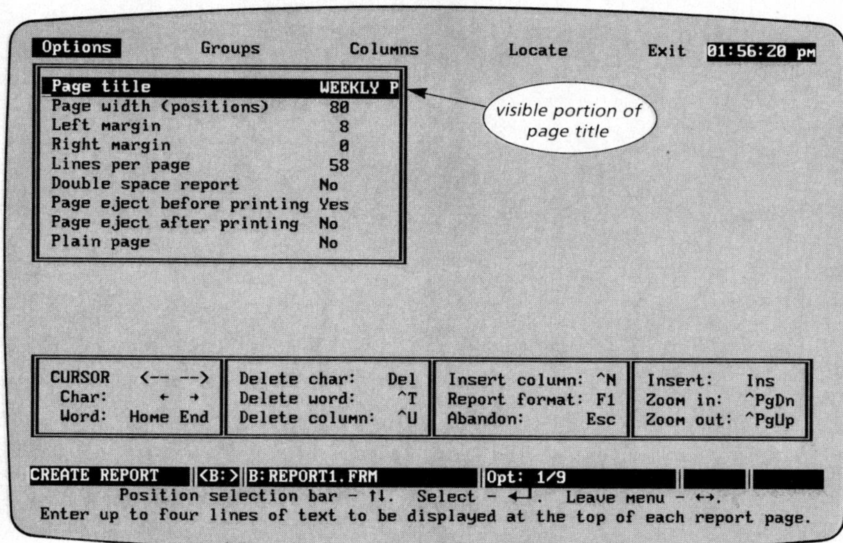


**FIGURE 3-22**
**Page Title Has Been Entered**

Move the cursor to the "Page width" line. A width of 80 is acceptable, so you don't have to take any action. Move the cursor again to the "Left margin" line. The default value for the left margin is 8, but in the example, the left margin is to be 5. To make the change, first press the Enter key, producing the screen shown in Figure 3-23. Note that a small triangle appears. This symbol acts as a prompt, indicating that you are to enter data.

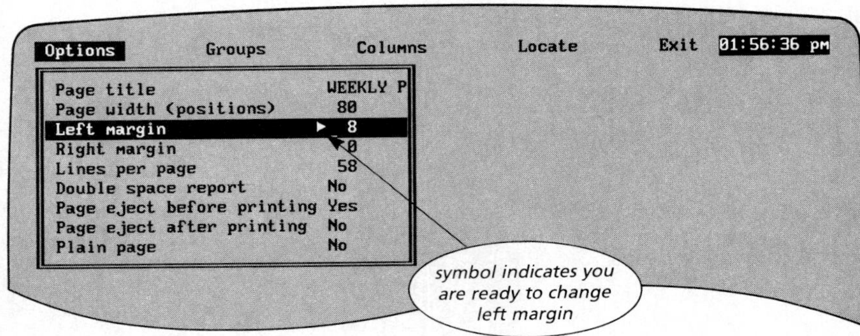


**FIGURE 3-23**
**Changing the Left Margin**

Now type the number 5 at the prompt (Figure 3-24). The 5 will be aligned to the left but the default value of 8 will still show on the screen. Press the Enter key. The number 5 will be right justified, and dBASE will now use a left margin of 5 (Figure 3-25).

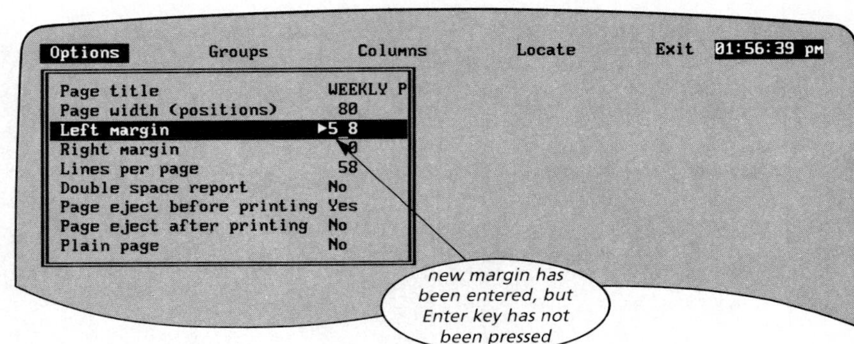


**FIGURE 3-24**
**Changing the Left Margin**

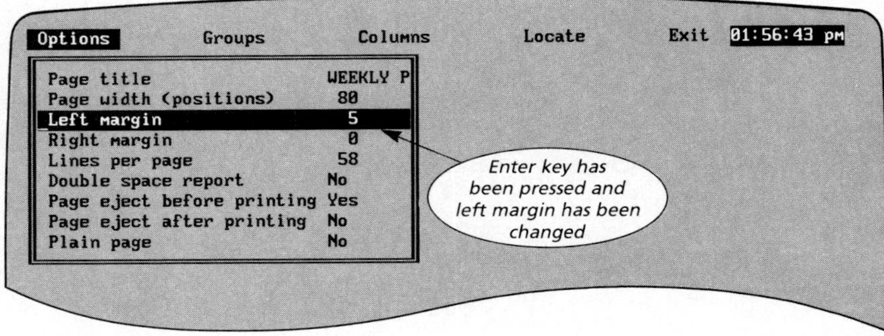


**FIGURE 3-25**
**Left Margin Has Been Changed**

Now change the right margin to 28 in exactly the same fashion. All the other values on this screen can be left as they are, so you are ready to move to the next step. To do so, press the Right Arrow key to move from "Options" to "Groups." The display will now look like the one shown in Figure 3-26.

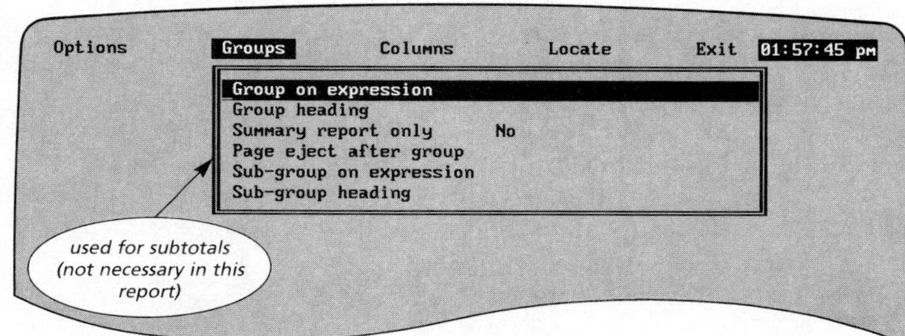


**FIGURE 3-26**
**Specifying Groups**

The box you see in the figure is used if any subtotals are required in a report. Since this report does not have subtotals, you will not use any of the options in this box. Press the Right Arrow key a second time and the display will look like Figure 3-27. This box is used to describe the body of the report.

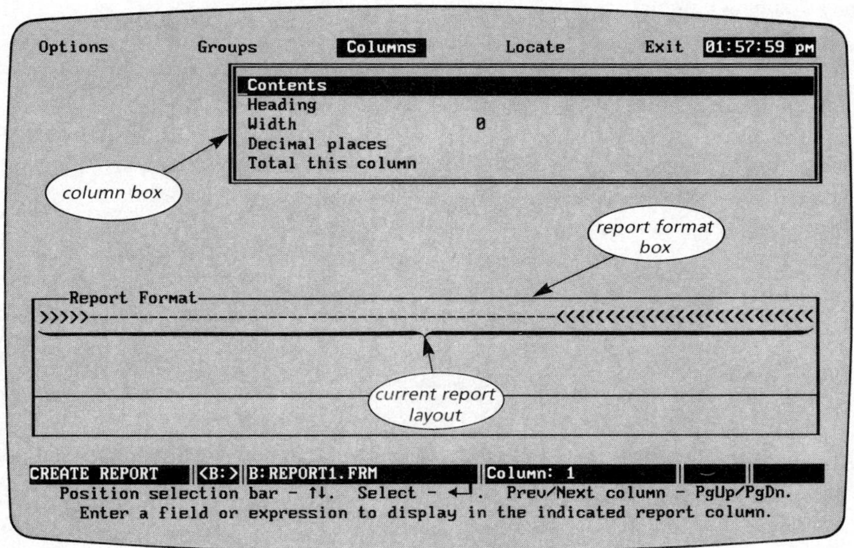


**FIGURE 3-27**
**Specifying Columns**

## Entering Column Information

You must make an entry on the screen illustrated in Figure 3-27 for each column in the report. The box near the top of the screen is used to describe the required information for the columns. The box near the bottom, called the report format box, continually displays the current layout of the report. The display > > > > > refers to the five spaces specified for the left margin area. The dashes (----) represent the area where the format of the report will be displayed. Later, as we describe the fields, the fields and headings will also be displayed in this box.

It is now time to describe each of the columns. Checking back with Figure 3-16, our report design, note that the first column to appear on the report is the employee name. To define this column, make sure the highlight is on "Contents" and press the Enter key. This produces the screen shown in Figure 3-28. Notice the small triangle that appears after "Contents," which indicates that you are to enter the field or expression for this portion of the report.

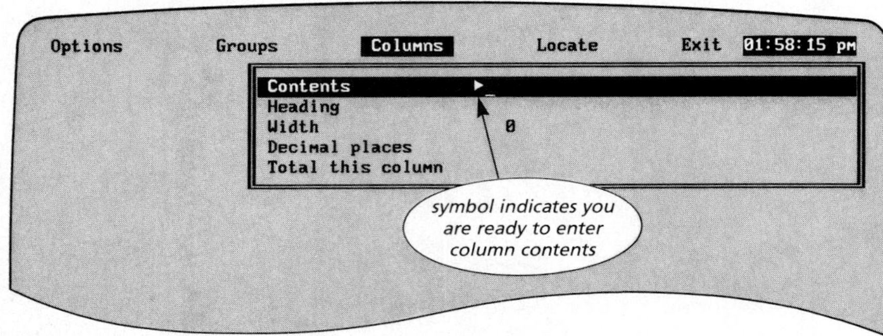


**FIGURE 3-28**
**Specifying Column Contents**

One way to specify the field is to type its name. In this case, you could type the word NAME and press the Enter key. If you know the exact name of the field, this is probably the simplest approach to take. But there are times when you might not remember the exact name. In such cases, you would like to see a list of the available fields. Fortunately, there is an easy way to do so. Press the F10 key and a field list will appear (Figure 3-29).

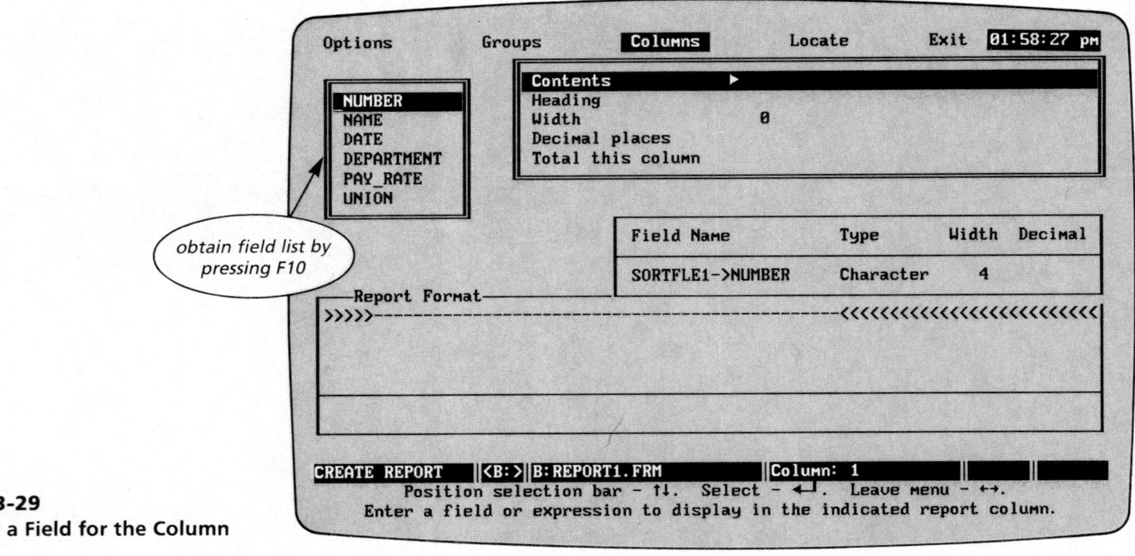


**FIGURE 3-29**
**Selecting a Field for the Column**

Use the Down Arrow key to move the highlight to the field you desire and press the Enter key. Select NAME. Your display should look like Figure 3-30. Press the Enter key again to remove the triangle symbol.

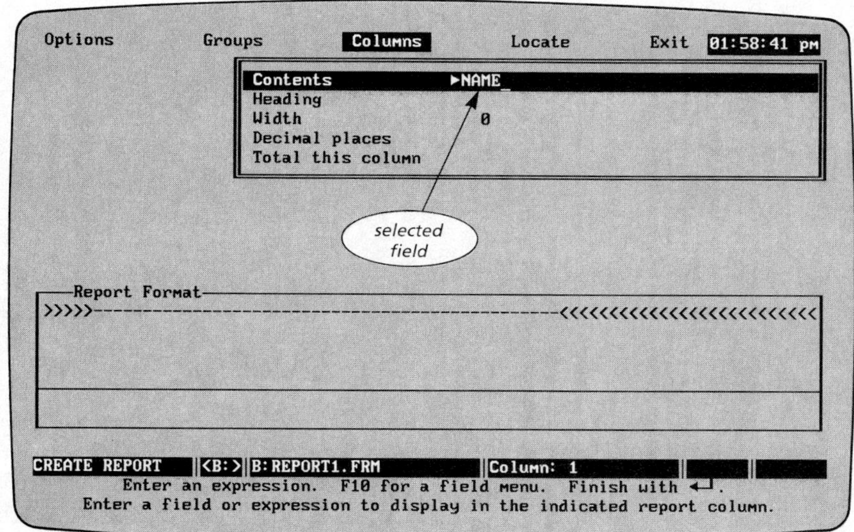


**FIGURE 3-30**
**Field Has Been Selected**

Now enter the heading that will be placed over the field. First move the highlight down to "Heading" and then press the Enter key. This produces the display shown in Figure 3-31. Note the box that is used to enter the heading. Also note the line of X's that have appeared in the report format box. These indicate the position of the first field, the NAME field, on the report.

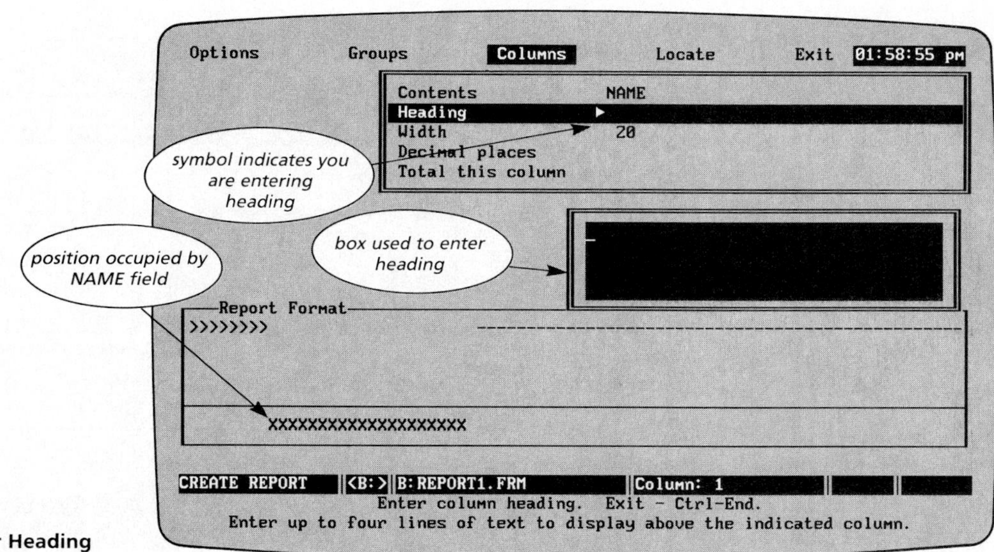


**FIGURE 3-31**
**Ready to Enter Heading**

Referring to your report design (Figure 3-16), remember that the first column heading consists of the words "EMPLOYEE NAME," which are indented and displayed on two lines. The first part of the column heading should be entered on the first available line. To accomplish this, press the space bar six times to indent and then type the word EMPLOYEE. After you have done so, press the Enter key, causing the cursor to move to the next line. Press the space bar eight times to properly position the cursor in the area where NAME must be typed, that is, to center it, and then type the word NAME (Figure 3-32).

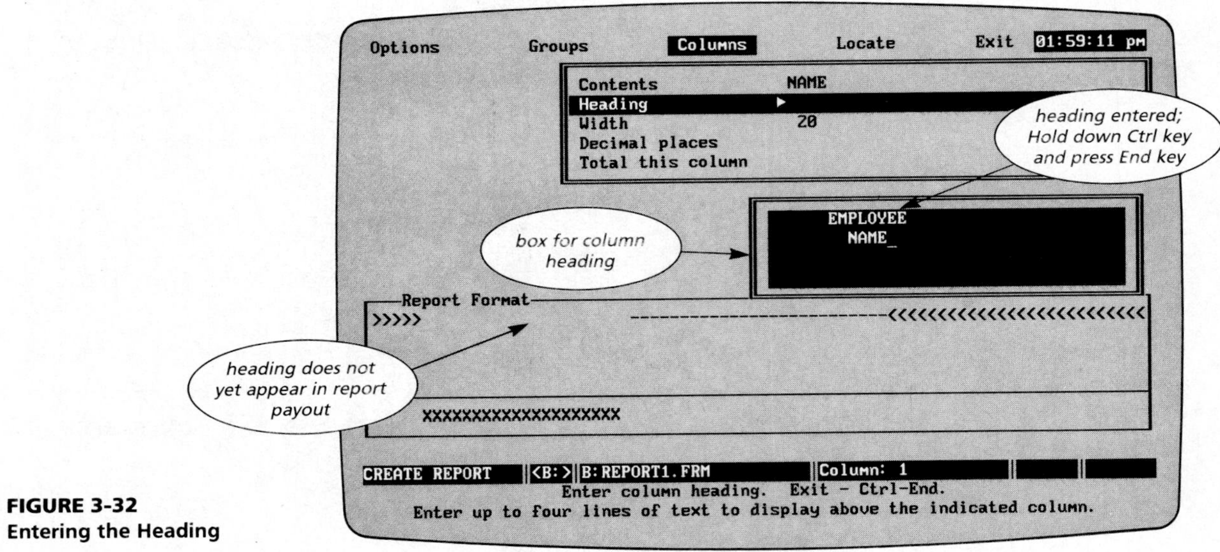


**FIGURE 3-32**
**Entering the Heading**

To complete the process, again hold down the Ctrl key and press the End key, or else repeatedly press the Enter key until you have returned to the "Heading" line in the box at the top of the screen. Now the display should look like the one in Figure 3-33. The heading is displayed in the report format box.

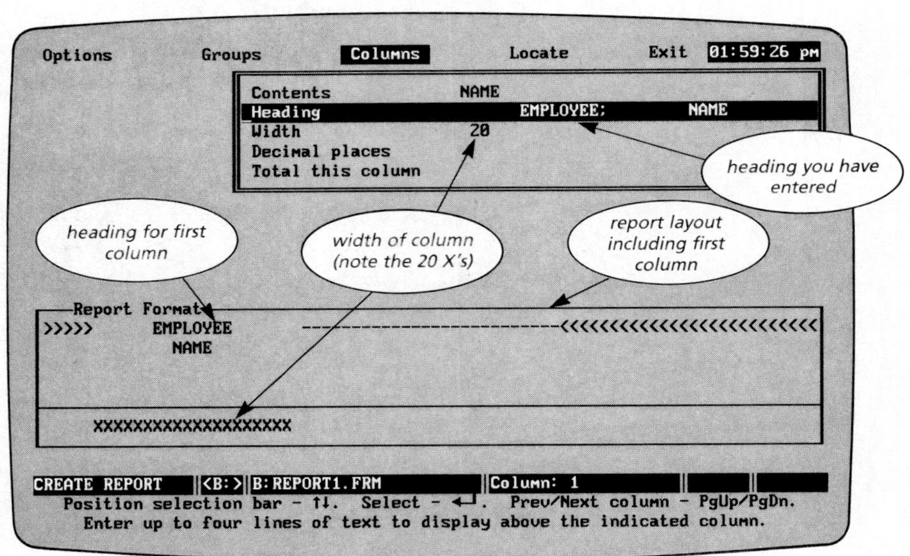


**FIGURE 3-33**
**Heading Has Been Entered**

The entry called "Width" indicates the width of the field. Initially dBASE sets this equal to the width of the NAME field. You can change it if you feel the width should be different. The other lines, "Decimal places" and "Total this column," do not apply to character fields like NAME.

Now, you are ready to proceed to the next column. Press the PgDn key, which is used to move to the next column in the report. (The PgUp key is used to move back to the previous column in the report.)

The next step is to enter the information for the second column. In the heading box, type the word DEPARTMENT, press the Enter key, press the space bar three times, type the word NAME, and then hold down the Ctrl key while pressing the End key. The results are shown in Figure 3-34.

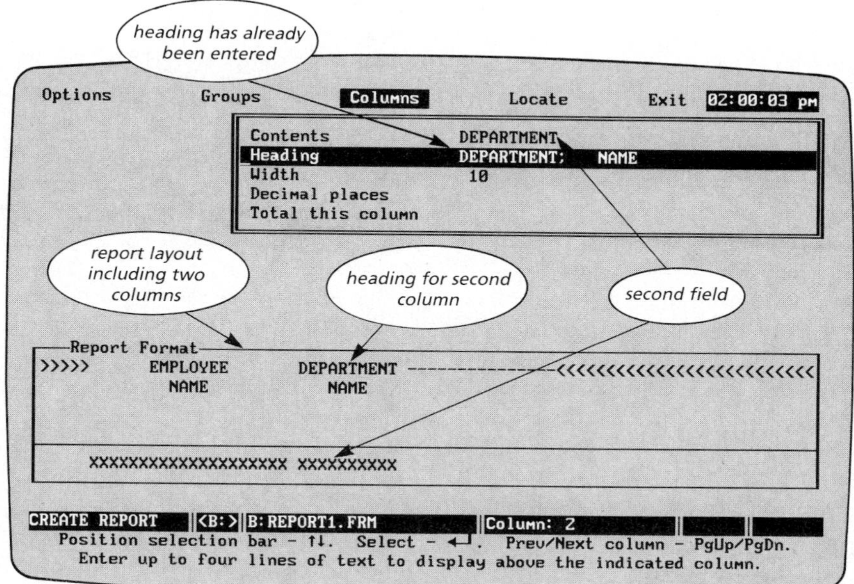


**FIGURE 3-34**
**Second Column Has Been Entered**

To create the third column, press PgDn and enter the information for PAY_RATE in the same way. In the heading box, press the space bar once, type the word PAY, press the Enter key, type the word RATE, and then hold down the Ctrl key while pressing the End key. This produces the screen shown in Figure 3-35. Do not move to the next column yet, however.

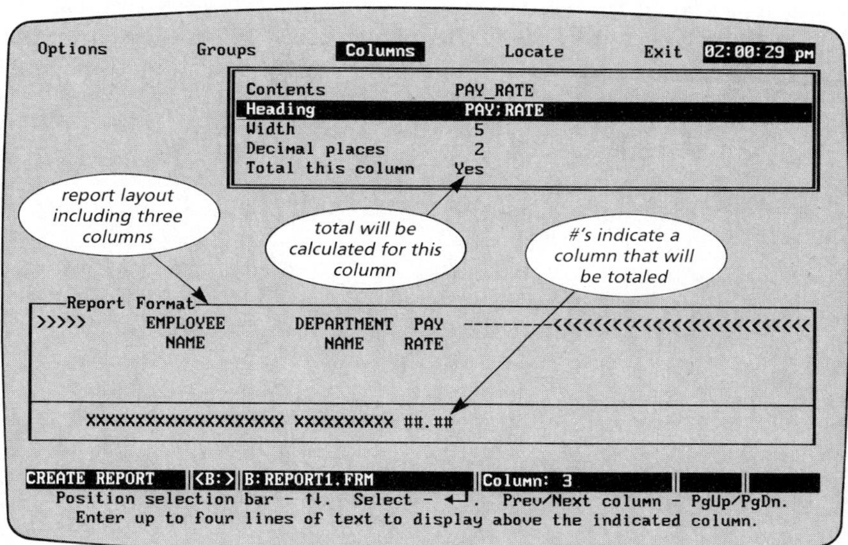


**FIGURE 3-35**
**Specifying Totaling**

This is the first numeric field that we have encountered. Two special things happen in numeric fields. First, the number of decimal places is filled in. There is no problem here, since dBASE automatically set the number of decimal places to 2 and that is exactly right. Second, there is an entry on the line labeled "Total this column." The value dBASE placed in this column is "Yes," meaning a total will be displayed automatically on the report. Since the report does not call for a total of all the pay rates, we must change this. Move the highlight to "Total this column" and press the Enter key. The word "Yes" will change to the word "No" (Figure 3-36). (Press the Enter key a few times and you will see the word change from "Yes" to "No" and back.) Note that the characters under PAY_RATE in the report format box changed from ##.##, which indicates a field that will be totaled, to 99.99, which indicates a field that will not be totaled. When this is done, press PgDn to move to the next field.

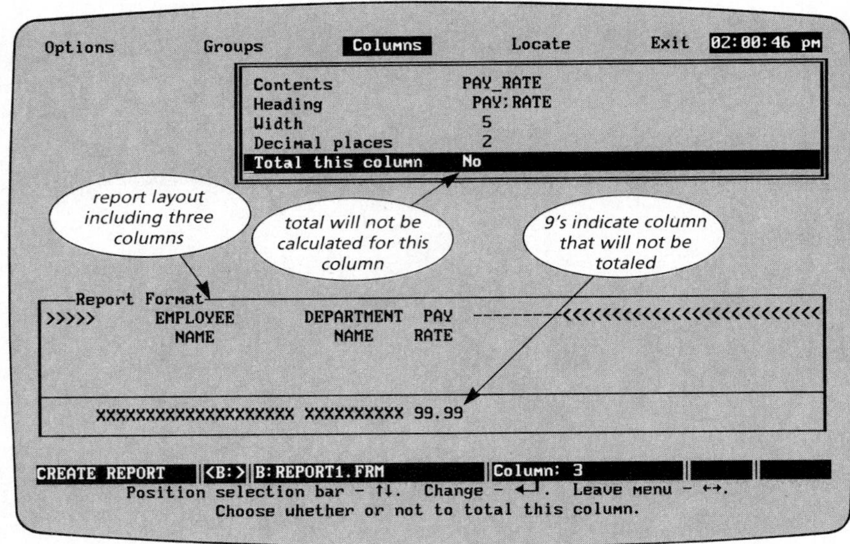


**FIGURE 3-36**
**Column Will Not Be Totaled**

The next field to be included on the report is the weekly pay field. This field is not contained in the records in the database. dBASE allows calculations to be specified as field contents, in which case the results of the calculations will be displayed on the report. To calculate the weekly pay, enter the numeric expression PAY_RATE * 40 in the contents row as shown in Figure 3-37. (Recall that you have to press the Enter key first to be able to enter the contents.) The asterisk, called an arithmetic operator, is used to specify multiplication. Other basic arithmetic operators include addition (+), subtraction (–), and division (/).

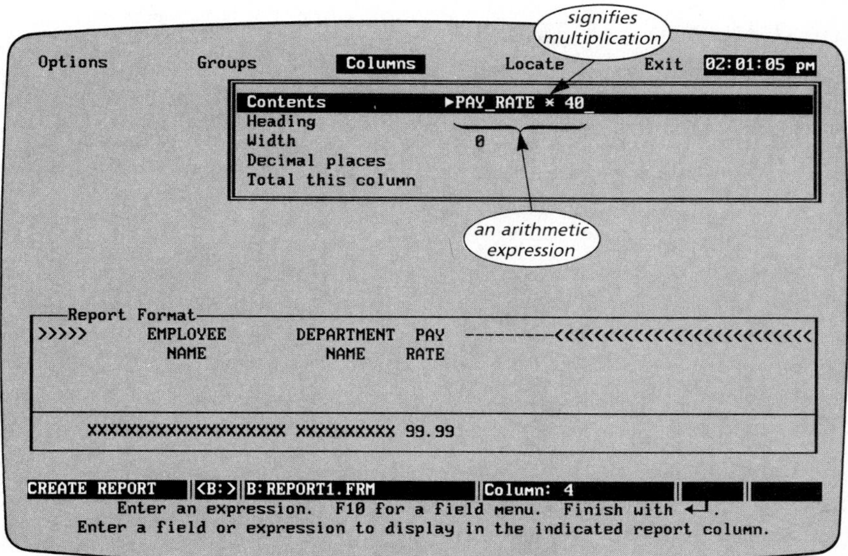


**FIGURE 3-37**
**Using an Expression**

After entering the calculation to be performed, press the Enter key. You can then enter the heading as shown in Figure 3-38. Press Enter to get the heading box. Then, in the heading box, press the space bar twice, type the word WEEKLY, press the Enter key, press the space bar five times, type the word PAY, and then hold down the Ctrl key while pressing the End key.

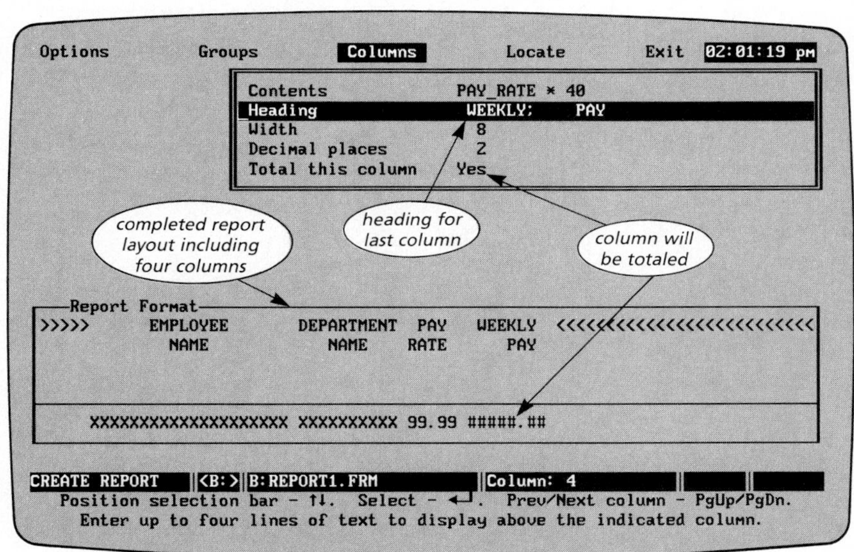


**FIGURE 3-38**
**Last Column Specified**

Because the entries for "Width," "Decimal places," and "Total this column" are appropriate (the total is to be of the weekly pay figures), you are done with this entry and, consequently, done with the report. The entire report format has been displayed in the report format box. Review it for accuracy. Any mistakes can be corrected by using the PgUp and PgDn keys to move to the column that is in error (PgUp moves you to the previous column and PgDn to the next). Then change the incorrect data in exactly the same fashion as you first entered the data.

## Saving the Report

Once you have determined that the report is correct, press the Right Arrow key, producing the display shown in Figure 3-39. The box shown in this figure can be used to rapidly move to any particular column on a report. Actually, unless a report has a large number of columns, it is just as easy to use PgUp and PgDn to move through the columns, so this feature is rarely used. The only reason we present it here is that we need to pass through it to get to the next option, the one that will allow us to finish the operation. Move to the next option now by pressing the Right Arrow key. The display will look like the one shown in Figure 3-40.

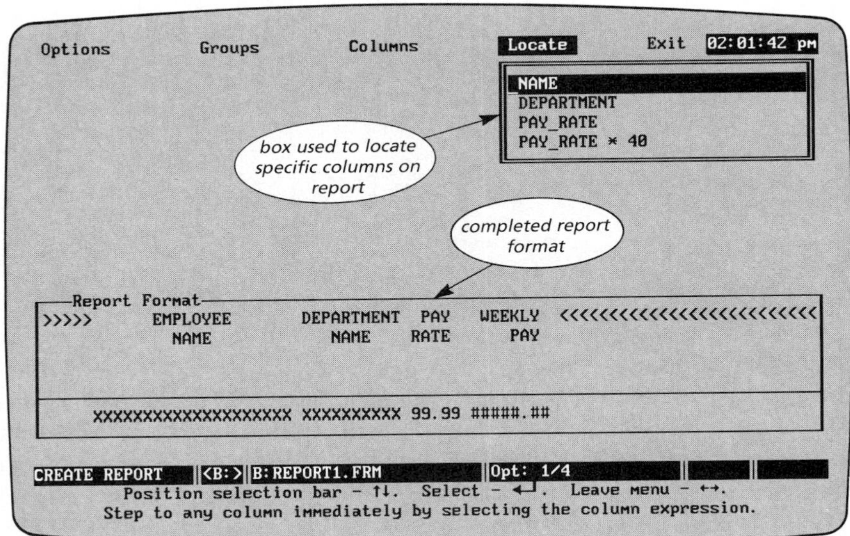


**FIGURE 3-39**
**The "Locate" Menu**

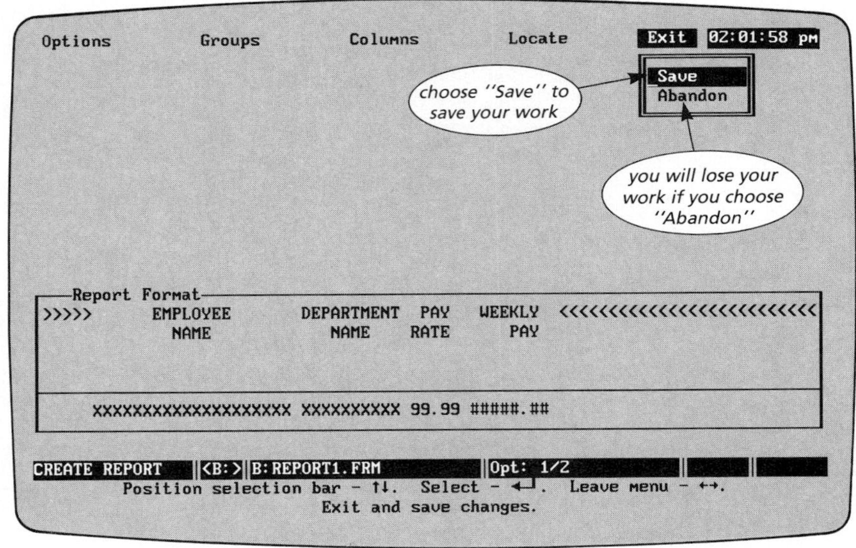


**FIGURE 3-40**
**The "Exit" Menu**

The two choices in this box are "Save" and "Abandon." "Save" is used to make the report description permanent. Assuming you like the report layout, select "Save" at this point. Make sure it is the highlighted choice and then press the Enter key. That will save the report on disk and you will return to the ASSISTANT menu.

In the event the report is not correct, you can use the Left Arrow key to return to one of the previous boxes, make the necessary corrections, and then return to this box to save your work. If you simply want to abandon the operation and start over again at some other time, choose "Abandon." Move the highlight to it and press Enter. dBASE will ask if you are sure you want to abandon the operation. If you type the letter Y (for yes) you will be returned to the ASSISTANT menu. Remember, if you choose "Abandon," none of your work will be saved.

## Printing a Report

To print a report, use the "Report" option of the "Retrieve" menu (Figure 3-41). Once you have pressed the Enter key, dBASE will ask you to indicate the drive on which the report is located. Make sure the highlight is on the correct drive (B:) and press the Enter key.

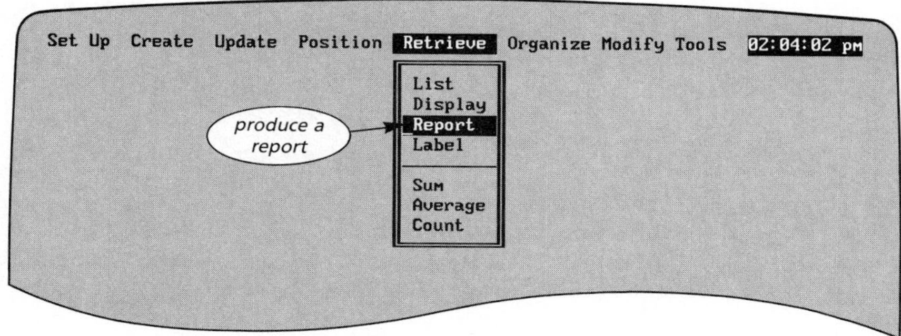


**FIGURE 3-41**
**The "Report" Option of the "Retrieve" Menu**

dBASE will now present a list of all reports on the indicated drive (Figure 3-42). In this case there is only one, so the right choice is automatically highlighted. If there were more than one, you would need to move the highlight to the correct report. Once this has been done, press the Enter key and the familiar box (the one that contains "Execute the command," "Specify scope," and so on) will appear.

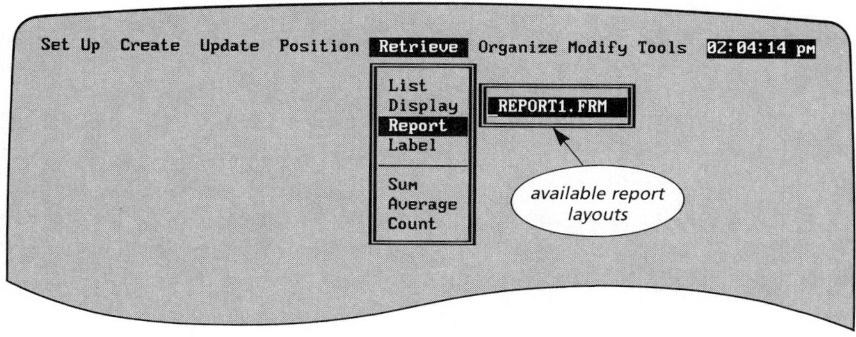


**FIGURE 3-42**
**Selecting a Report**

Assuming you simply want to produce the report and not impose any special search conditions, put the highlight on "Execute the command" and press the Enter key. dBASE will then ask if you want the report directed to the printer. If so, type the letter Y. If not, either type the letter N or press the Enter key. The report you just produced is shown in Figure 3-43.

column has not been totaled

column has been totaled

**Page No. 1**
**12/19/89**

**WEEKLY PAYROLL REPORT**

| EMPLOYEE NAME | DEPARTMENT NAME | PAY RATE | WEEKLY PAY |
|---|---|---|---|
| Ackerman, David R. | Accounting | 9.75 | 390.00 |
| Anderson, Mariane L. | Shipping | 9.00 | 360.00 |
| Andrews, Robert M. | Marketing | 9.00 | 360.00 |
| Baxter, Charles W. | Accounting | 11.00 | 440.00 |
| Bender, Helen O. | Production | 6.75 | 270.00 |
| Castle, Mark C. | Shipping | 7.50 | 300.00 |
| Castleworth, Mary T. | Production | 8.75 | 350.00 |
| Chaney, Joseph R. | Accounting | 8.00 | 320.00 |
| Doi, Chang J. | Production | 6.00 | 240.00 |
| Dugan, Mary L. | Production | 8.75 | 350.00 |
| Dunning, Lisa A. | Marketing | 9.10 | 364.00 |
| Edwards, Kenneth J. | Production | 8.60 | 344.00 |
| Evans, John T. | Marketing | 6.00 | 240.00 |
| McCormack, Nigel L. | Shipping | 8.25 | 330.00 |
| Rapoza, Anthony P. | Shipping | 8.50 | 340.00 |
| *** Total *** | | | |
| | | | 4998.00 |

**FIGURE 3-43**
**Weekly Payroll Report**

## Reporting Only Selected Records

You can use the REPORT1 format to display selected records from a file. For example, you want a weekly payroll report that contains information only about those individuals working in the shipping department. The report must be alphabetical by employee name. Since a file exists with the records sorted in alphabetical sequence by name and the REPORT1 file contains the format for a weekly payroll report, we can use existing files to produce this output. In fact, the only difference between producing this report and the previous one is that before choosing "Execute the command" you must choose "Build a search condition," in exactly the same fashion as before. In this case, you will select the field called DEPARTMENT and the comparison operator "Equal to," and then enter the word Shipping.

## Reports with Subtotals

It is also possible to produce reports with subtotals. The report in Figure 3-44 contains subtotals based on a change in department name. When the department name changes, a total is displayed.

**Page No. 1**
**12/19/89**

**WEEKLY PAYROLL REPORT**

| EMPLOYEE NAME | DEPARTMENT NAME | PAY RATE | WEEKLY PAY |
|---|---|---|---|
| ** Accounting | | | |
| Ackerman, David R. | Accounting | 9.75 | 390.00 |
| Baxter, Charles W. | Accounting | 11.00 | 440.00 |
| Chaney, Joseph R. | Accounting | 8.00 | 320.00 |
| ** Subtotal ** | | | |
| | | | 1150.00 |
| ** Marketing | | | |
| Andrews, Robert M. | Marketing | 9.00 | 360.00 |
| Dunning, Lisa A. | Marketing | 9.10 | 364.00 |
| Evans, John T. | Marketing | 6.00 | 240.00 |
| ** Subtotal ** | | | |
| | | | 964.00 |
| ** Production | | | |
| Bender, Helen O. | Production | 6.75 | 270.00 |
| Castleworth, Mary T. | Production | 8.75 | 350.00 |
| Doi, Chang J. | Production | 6.00 | 240.00 |
| Dugan, Mary L. | Production | 8.75 | 350.00 |
| Edwards, Kenneth J. | Production | 8.60 | 344.00 |
| ** Subtotal ** | | | |
| | | | 1554.00 |
| ** Shipping | | | |
| Anderson, Mariane L. | Shipping | 9.00 | 360.00 |
| Castle, Mark C. | Shipping | 7.50 | 300.00 |
| McCormack, Nigel L. | Shipping | 8.25 | 330.00 |
| Rapoza, Anthony P. | Shipping | 8.50 | 340.00 |
| ** Subtotal ** | | | |
| | | | 1330.00 |
| *** Total *** | | | |
| | | | 4998.00 |

**FIGURE 3-44** Report with Subtotals

Two approaches can be used to produce such a report. The first approach is to create another report format called, perhaps, REPORT2. This involves calling up the report generation screens provided by dBASE and making the appropriate entries.

The second approach is to modify the REPORTl format. If the report represents a permanent modification of the original report format, we can modify the original report format. To modify the report format for REPORT 1, choose the "Report" option from the "Modify" menu. This is illustrated in Figure 3-45.

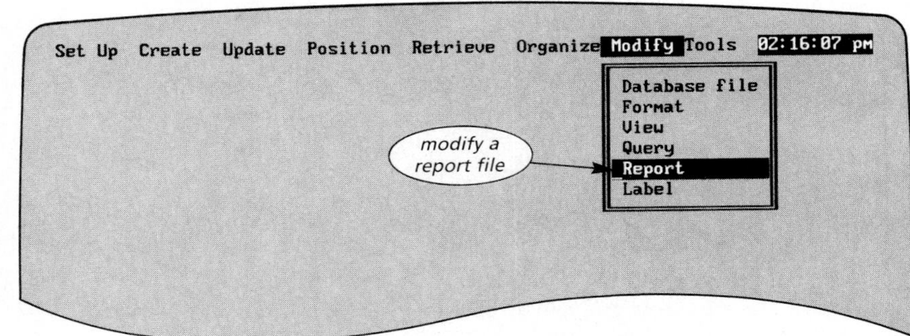


**FIGURE 3-45**
**The "Modify" Menu**

After indicating the drive on which the report file is located, you will see a list of all report files on the drive. Move the highlight to the desired report (in this case there is only one, so no movement is required) and press the Enter key. The display now looks like the screen in Figure 3-46.

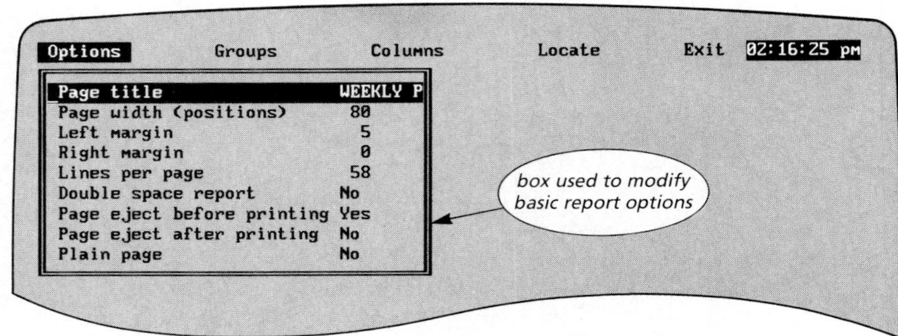


**FIGURE 3-46**
**Modifying a Report**

The process of modifying a report is similar to the process of creating a report. Just as you described the report initially, you can change the page title, margins, fields, column headings, and so on. In this case, the only change that needs to be made is to indicate the grouping that is to take place. Records are to be grouped by department.

To make this change, press the Right Arrow key to move to "Groups" (Figure 3-47). Press the Enter key and you will be able to enter the expression on which records are to be grouped. At this point, you could simply type the word DEPARTMENT. As before, you could also press F10 to get a field list (Figure 3-48), then move the highlight to DEPARTMENT and press the Enter key. In either case, the word DEPARTMENT will appear on the line labeled "Group on expression." Press Enter to complete this process. The screen should now look like the one in Figure 3-49. No further entries need be made, so press the Right Arrow key three times to move to the "Exit" box and choose "Save" in the same manner as before.

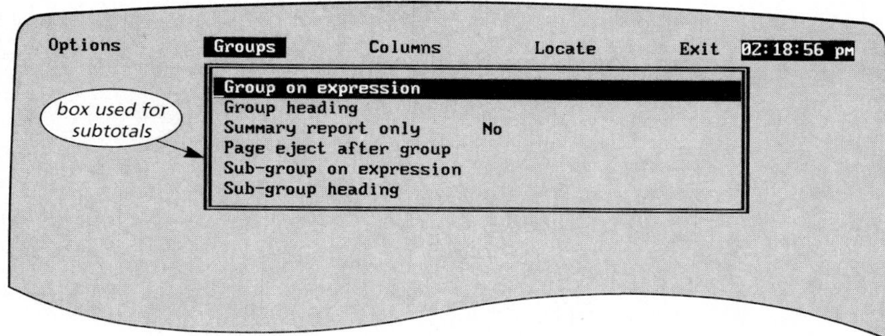


**FIGURE 3-47**
**Indicating Subtotals**

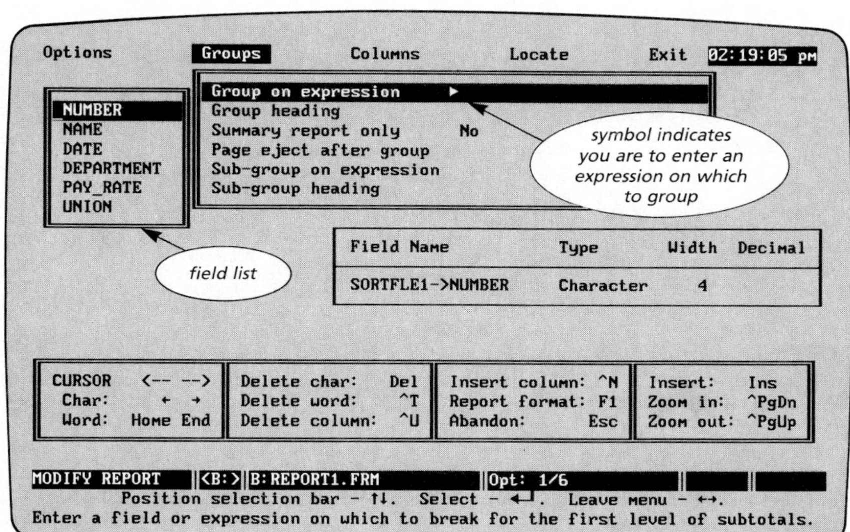


**FIGURE 3-48**
**Entering an Expression for Grouping**

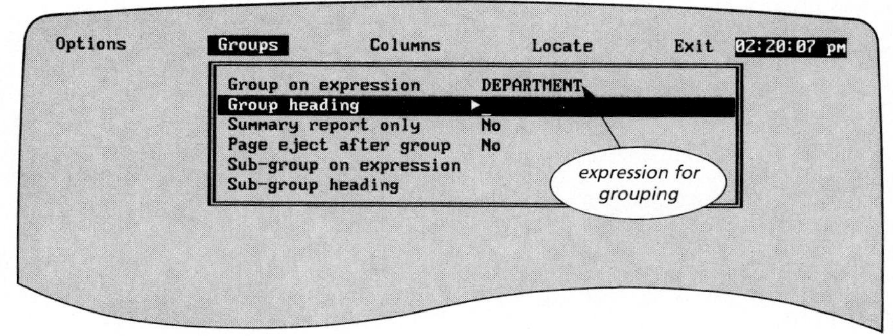


**FIGURE 3-49**
**Expression for Grouping Has Been Entered**

If you now produce the report just as you did before, you will see something interesting. Look at Figure 3-50 (to see the complete report, you should send it to the printer; it does not all fit on the screen). There is a group for accounting, followed by a group for shipping, one for marketing, and then *another* one for accounting. What's wrong? The problem is that the records are not sorted correctly. All the records for a given department must be together. This is not the case in SORTFLE1.

Page No. 1
12/19/89

WEEKLY PAYROLL REPORT

| EMPLOYEE NAME | DEPARTMENT NAME | PAY RATE | WEEKLY PAY |
|---|---|---|---|
| ** Accounting | | | |
| Ackerman, David R. | Accounting | 9.75 | 390.00 |
| ** Subtotal ** | | | |
| | | | 390.00 |
| ** Shipping | | | |
| Anderson, Mariane L. | Shipping | 9.00 | 360.00 |
| ** Subtotal ** | | | |
| | | | 360.00 |
| ** Marketing | | | |
| Andrews, Robert M. | Marketing | 9.00 | 360.00 |
| ** Subtotal ** | | | |
| | | | 360.00 |
| ** Accounting | | | |
| Baxter, Charles W. | Accounting | 11.00 | 440.00 |
| ** Subtotal ** | | | |
| | | | 440.00 |
| ** Production | | | |
| Bender, Helen O. | Production | 6.75 | 270.00 |
| ** Subtotal ** | | | |
| | | | 270.00 |

both are in accounting

**FIGURE 3-50**
**Weekly Payroll Report with Subtotals (Incorrect)**

Fortunately, another file that you have already created, SORTFLE2, contains records that were sorted by NAME within DEPARTMENT, which is precisely the correct order. Activate this file in the usual manner (using the "Database file" option of the "Set Up" menu). Then produce the report again and you will see that it looks like the one shown in Figure 3-44, which you were trying to get.

What if SORTFLE2 did not exist? All you would have to do now would be to create it, in exactly the fashion described earlier in this project.

## PROJECT SUMMARY

In Project 3 you learned how to sort a database file, producing a file containing the same records in a different order. You also learned how to design a report and use the dBASE report facility to create a report file containing the report layout. You used this report file to produced a report with the desired layout. Finally, you saw how to use subtotals in reports.

If you followed along with the steps in this chapter, you have created two sorted database files and a report. You have also modified the report. If you did not do this but you want to do so now, you can use the following keystroke sequence. Start dBASE as described in the project and activate the EMPLOYEE database file. Then type the following:

**SUMMARY OF KEYSTROKES—Project 3**

| STEPS | KEY(S) PRESSED | RESULTS |
|---|---|---|
| 1 | → → → → → ↓ ↵ ↓ | |
| 2 | ↵ → ↵ SORTFLE1 ↵ ↵ | File sorted |
| 3 | ← ← ← ← ← ↵ ↵ ↓ ↵ ↵ | |
| 4 | → → → → ↓ ↵ ↓ ↵ ↓ | |
| 5 | ↵ ↑ ↵ ↵ | Sorted file displayed |
| | (Make sure SORTFLE1 is active database file)<br>(Note: The following assumes you are at the "Set Up" Menu) | |
| 6 | → ↓ ↓ ↓ ↓ ↵ ↵ | |
| 7 | REPORT1 ↵ | Report creation begun |
| 8 | ↵ WEEKLY PAYROLL REPORT ↵ Ctrl-End | |
| 9 | ↓ ↓ ↵ 5 ↵ ↓ ↵ 28 ↵ | Basic report information entered |
| 10 | → → ↵ <F10> ↓ ↵ ↓ ↵ ↓ ↵ | |
| 11 | SPACE SPACE SPACE SPACE SPACE SPACE EMPLOYEE ↵ | |
| 12 | SPACE SPACE SPACE SPACE SPACE SPACE SPACE SPACE | |
| 13 | NAME ↵ Ctrl-End PgDn | First column entered |
| 14 | ↵ <F10> ↓ ↓ ↓ ↵ ↵ ↓ ↵ | |
| 15 | DEPARTMENT ↵ SPACE SPACE SPACE NAME ↵ Ctrl-End | |
| 16 | PgDn | Second column entered |
| 17 | ↵ <F10> ↓ ↓ ↓ ↓ ↵ ↵ ↓ ↵ | |
| 18 | SPACE PAY ↵ <RATE> Ctrl-End ↓ ↓ ↓ ↵ | |
| 19 | PgDn | Third column entered |
| 20 | ↵ PAY_RATE * 40 ↵ ↓ ↵ SPACE SPACE WEEKLY | |
| 21 | ↵ SPACE SPACE SPACE SPACE SPACE PAY ↵ | |
| 22 | Ctrl-End | Fourth column entered |
| 23 | → → ↵ | Report saved |
| 24 | → → → ↓ ↓ ↵ ↵ ↵ ↵ | |
| 25 | ↵ ↵ | Report printed |
| 26 | → → ↓ ↓ ↓ ↓ ↵ ↵ ↵ | |
| 27 | → ↵ DEPARTMENT ↵ → → → ↵ | Report modified |

The following list summarizes the material covered in Project 3:

1. A **key field** is a field that is used as the basis of a sorting operation.
2. To sort the records in a database file, producing a new database file, use the "Sort" option of the "Organize" menu.
3. To sort on multiple keys, select the keys in order of importance.
4. To display the records in a sorted file, first activate the file using the "Database file" option of the "Set Up" menu.
5. The **American Standard Code for Information Interchange**, usually called simply the **ASCII code**, is used for storing data.
6. Numeric fields are sorted on the basis of their algebraic values. Character data are sorted on the basis of the ASCII code.
7. To create a report, use the "Report" option of the "Create" menu.
8. When creating a report, to specify such things as page title, page width, margins, and so on, use the "Options" menu.
9. To indicate the fields and column headings on a report, use the "Columns" menu.
10. To terminate the report creation process, choose either "Save" (to save your work) or "Abandon" (to exit without saving your work) from the "Exit" menu.
11. To print a report, use the "Report" option of the "Retrieve" menu.
12. To change the layout of an existing report, choose the "Report" option of the "Modify" menu.
13. To specify grouping on a report, use the "Groups" option.

# STUDENT ASSIGNMENTS

## STUDENT ASSIGNMENT 1: True/False Questions

**Instructions:** Circle T if the statement is true and F if the statement is false.

T F 1. A field used as the basis of a sorting operation is called a key field.
T F 2. Before a file can be sorted, it must be made active.
T F 3. The file created as a result of the "Sort" option is automatically active.
T F 4. After choosing the "Sort" option of the "Organize" menu, you must type the names of each of the key fields.
T F 5. When sorting on more than one key field, the more important key must be specified last.
T F 6. A key field must be of a character field.
T F 7. In the ASCII code, letters of the alphabet are lower in the sorting sequence than numbers.
T F 8. Within the "Sort" option it is possible to build a search condition so that only records meeting the condition will be sorted.
T F 9. The "Report" option in the "Set Up" menu is used to call the screens that allow a report to be created.
T F 10. In the report creation feature of dBASE, the first screen is the screen for changing the page heading, page width, margins, and so on.
T F 11. To change the current entry for left margin, place the highlight on the "Left margin" line, press the Enter key, enter the new value, and press the Enter key a second time.
T F 12. When specifying the fields to include on a report, you can obtain a field menu by pressing F1.
T F 13. When specifying the fields to include on a report, you can use PgUp to move back to the previous field.
T F 14. When defining the contents of a field on a report, you may use expressions.
T F 15. To print a report, use the "Report" option of the "Retrieve" menu and then select the name of the desired report from the list of possibilities presented by dBASE.
T F 16. To change the layout of a report, use the "Report" option of the "Modify" menu.

## STUDENT ASSIGNMENT 2: Multiple Choice

**Instructions:** Circle the correct response.

1. To sort by name within department:
   a. First select the "Sort" option and choose the NAME field. After the sort has been completed, select the "Sort" option again and choose the DEPARTMENT field.
   b. First select the "Sort" option and choose the DEPARTMENT field. After the sort has been completed, select the "Sort" option again and choose the NAME field.
   c. First select the "Sort" option and choose the NAME field. Immediately after you have chosen the NAME field, choose the DEPARTMENT field.
   d. First select the "Sort" option and choose the DEPARTMENT field. Immediately after you have chosen the DEPARTMENT field, choose the NAME field.
2. You activated the EMPLOYEE database file, selected the "Sort" option, and chose the NAME field from the list of possible fields. You then pressed the Right Arrow key, typed the word DEPARTMENT, and pressed the Enter key. Which of the following will occur?
   a. The records within EMPLOYEE will be sorted by NAME within DEPARTMENT.
   b. The EMPLOYEE records will be sorted by NAME and the result will be placed in a file called DEPARTMENT.
   c. The EMPLOYEE records will be sorted by NAME and the result will be placed in a file called DEPARTMENT.DBF.
   d. An error will occur, since DEPARTMENT is a field within the EMPLOYEE file and thus cannot be used as the name of a file.
3. The values A99, 999, and a99 are to be sorted in ascending sequence. After sorting the sequence will be:
   a. 999, A99, a99
   b. a99, A99, 999
   c. A99, a99, 999
   d. 999, a99, A99
4. When you choose the "Report" option of the "Create" menu, the first thing you must do is
   a. specify the page heading.
   b. indicate a name for the report.
   c. indicate the page width for the report.
   d. indicate if any totals are to be calculated.
5. To print a report,
   a. select the "Report" option of the "Set Up" menu.
   b. select the "Report" option of the "Create" menu.
   c. select the "Report" option of the "Retrieve" menu.
   d. select the "Report" option of the "Modify" menu.
6. The "Report" option of the "Modify" menu will
   a. cause the output from a report to be displayed on the screen so that it can be modified from the keyboard.
   b. cause the report generation screen used for entering page headings and related information to appear.
   c. cause a new report file, which can be changed, to be created on disk.
   d. cause the current report format to be deleted.

## STUDENT ASSIGNMENT 3: Understanding dBASE Options

**Instructions:** Explain what will happen after you perform each of the following actions.

Problem 1. Select the "Sort" option of the "Organize" menu.

Explanation: ______________________________

Problem 2. Select the "Report" option of the "Create" menu.

Explanation: ______________________________

Problem 3. Choose the "Report" option of the "Retrieve" menu.

Explanation: ______________________________

Problem 4. Choose the "Report" option of the "Modify" menu.

Explanation: ______________________________

## STUDENT ASSIGNMENT 4: Using dBASE

**Instructions:** Explain how to accomplish each of the following tasks using dBASE.

Problem 1. Sort the EMPLOYEE file by pay rate within department, producing a file called SORTFL.

Explanation: ______________________________

Problem 2. After sorting EMPLOYEE and producing SORTFL, display all records in SORTFL.

Explanation: ______________________________

Problem 3. Create a report called REPT1.

Explanation: ______________________________

Problem 4. Specify a three-line page heading for REPT1.

Explanation: ______________________________

Problem 5. Cause totals to be calculated for a numeric field in a report.

Explanation: ______________________________

Problem 6. Make a change to the layout of the report called REPT1.

Explanation: ______________________________

## STUDENT ASSIGNMENT 5: Recovering from Problems

**Instructions:** In each of the following cases, a problem occurred. Explain the cause of the problem and how it can be corrected.

Problem 1: You are using the "Sort" option. When you specified a name for the sorted file, dBASE rejected the name you entered.

Cause of Problem: ______________________________

Method of Correction: ______________________________

Problem 2: You described a complete report layout, exited the report creation process, and later found that the report you specified does not exist.

Cause of Problem: ______________________________

Method of Correction: ______________________________

Problem 3: You specified a report using the "Report" option of the "Create" menu. The report involved a database called STUDENT, containing student data. In the report, you indicated that records were to be grouped by MAJOR, one of the fields in each student's record. After printing the report, you notice that it starts with a group of two students in biology, then one student in physics, followed by two students in math and then another student in biology.

Cause of Problem: ______________________________

Method of Correction: ______________________________

# MINICASES

## Sorting Records and Report Preparation

### Minicase 1: Personal Checks

**Instructions:** Use the personal checks database that you created in Project 1. These problems require sorting the database and preparing reports from it.

Problem 1: Sorting Records

a. Sort the records stored in the personal checks database that you created in Project 1 in ascending order by CHECK NUMBER. Use CKFLE1 as the file name for the sorted file. Record the steps you followed in the space provided below.

Steps: ______________________________

______________________________

______________________________

b. After sorting the records, display the CHECK NUMBER, DATE, PAYEE, and CHECK AMOUNT fields using the "Display" option. Record the steps you followed in the space provided below.

Steps: ______________________________

______________________________

______________________________

Problem 2: Sorting Records on Multiple Fields

a. Sort the records in the personal checks database file in alphabetical order by PAYEE within EXPENSE type. Use CKFLE2 as the file name for the sorted file. Record the steps you followed in the space provided below.

Steps: ______________________________

______________________________

______________________________

b. After sorting the records, display the EXPENSE, PAYEE, CHECK AMOUNT, DATE, and CHECK NUMBER fields. Record the steps you followed in the space provided below.

Steps: ______________________________

______________________________

______________________________

Problem 3: Creating a Report

a. Design the report using a printer spacing chart or graph paper. The report should contain a page number, date, and report and column headings. Include these fields: CHECK NUMBER, DATE, PAYEE, CHECK AMOUNT, and EXPENSE. Display a final total of the CHECK AMOUNT field.

b. After designing the report, enter the dBASE steps to create the report format.

c. After creating the report format and saving it on disk, enter the steps to print a report. Use the data contained in CKFLE1 to prepare the report.

d. Modify the report format so that a subtotal is taken when there is a change in EXPENSE. Enter the steps to display the output on the printer. Use the data contained in CKFLE2 to prepare the report.

## Minicase 2: Music Library

**Instructions:** Use the music library database that you created in Project 1. These problems require sorting the database and preparing reports from it.

Problem 1: Sorting Records

a. Sort the records stored in the music library database that you created in Project 1 in alphabetical order by ARTIST. Use MSCFL1 as the file name for the sorted file. Record the steps you followed in the space provided below.

Steps: ______________________________

______________________________

______________________________

b. After sorting the records, display the ARTIST, MUSIC NAME, TYPE, COST, and CATEGORY fields using the "Display" option. Record the steps you followed in the space provided below.

Steps: ______________________________

______________________________

______________________________

Problem 2: Sorting Records on Multiple Fields

a. Sort the records in the music library database file in alphabetical order by MUSIC NAME within CATEGORY. Use MSCFL2 as the file name of the sorted file. Record the steps you followed in the space provided below.

Steps: ______________________________

______________________________

______________________________

b. After sorting the records, display the MUSIC NAME, ARTIST, TYPE, COST, and CATEGORY fields. Record the steps you followed in the space provided below.

Steps: ______________________________

______________________________

______________________________

Problem 3: Creating a Report

a. Design the report using a printer spacing chart or graph paper. The report should contain a page number, date, and report and column headings. Include these fields: CATEGORY, MUSIC NAME, ARTIST, TYPE, and COST. Display a final total of the COST field.

b. After designing the report, enter the dBASE steps to create the report format.

c. After creating the report format and saving it on disk, enter the steps to print a report. Use the data contained in MSCFL2 to prepare the report.

d. Modify the report format so that a subtotal is taken when there is a change in CATEGORY. Enter the steps to display the output on the printer. Use the data contained in the file named MSCFL2 to prepare the report.

## Minicase 3: Computer Software Store

**Instructions:** Use the software inventory database that you created in Project 1. These problems require sorting the database and preparing reports from the database.

Problem 1: Sorting Records

a. Sort the records stored in the software inventory database that you created in Project 1 in ascending order by SOFTWARE NAME. Use SOFTFLE1 as the file name for the sorted file. Record the steps you followed in the space provided below.

Steps: ______________________________

______________________________

______________________________

b. After the records have been sorted, display the SOFTWARE NAME, CATEGORY, QUANTITY, and COST fields using the "Display" option. Record the steps you followed in the space provided below.

Steps: ______________________________

______________________________

______________________________

Problem 2: Sorting Records on Multiple Fields

a. Sort the records in the software inventory file in alphabetical order by SOFTWARE NAME within CATEGORY. Use SOFTFLE2 as the file name of the sorted file. Record the steps you followed in the space provided below.

Steps: ______________________________

______________________________

______________________________

b. After sorting the records, display the CATEGORY, SOFTWARE NAME, COMPANY, QUANTITY, and COST fields. Record the steps you followed in the space provided below.

Steps: ______________________________

______________________________

______________________________

Problem 3: Creating a Report

a. Design the report using a printer spacing chart or graph paper. The report should contain a page number, date, and report and column headings. Include these fields: SOFTWARE NAME, CATEGORY, COMPANY, QUANTITY, COST, and TOTAL INVENTORY VALUE. Calculate TOTAL INVENTORY VALUE by multiplying COST by QUANTITY. Display a final total of the TOTAL INVENTORY VALUE.

b. After designing the report, enter the dBASE steps to create the report format.

c. After creating the report format and saving it on disk, enter the steps to print a report. Use the data contained in SOFTFLE1 to prepare the report.

d. Modify the report format so that a subtotal is taken for TOTAL INVENTORY VALUE when there is a change in CATEGORY. Enter the steps to display the output on the printer. Use the data contained in the file named SOFTFLE2 to prepare the report.

## Minicase 4: Home Sales

**Instructions:** Use the database of houses for sale that you created in Project 1. These problems require sorting the database and preparing reports from the database.

Problem 1: Sorting Records

a. Sort the records stored in the home sales database that you created in Project 1 in ascending order by PRICE. Use HSFLE1 as the file name for the sorted file. Record the steps you followed in the space provided below.

Steps: ______________________________________________

______________________________________________

______________________________________________

b. After sorting the records, display the ADDRESS, CITY, ZIP, and PRICE fields using the "Display" option. Record the steps you followed in the space provided below.

Steps: ______________________________________________

______________________________________________

______________________________________________

Problem 2: Sorting Records on Multiple Fields

a. Sort the records in the home sales database file by PRICE within CITY. Use HSFLE2 as the file name of the sorted file. Record the steps you followed in the space provided below.

Steps: ______________________________________________

______________________________________________

______________________________________________

b. After sorting the records, display the ADDRESS, CITY, and PRICE fields. Record the steps you followed in the space provided below.

Steps: ______________________________________________

______________________________________________

______________________________________________

Problem 3: Creating a Report

a. Design the report using a printer spacing chart or graph paper. The report should contain a page number, date, and report and column headings. Include these fields: ADDRESS, CITY, ZIP, and PRICE. Display a final total of the prices of all houses. This total lists the total value of all houses for sale in an area.

b. After designing the report, enter the dBASE steps to create the report format.

c. After creating the report format and saving it on disk, enter the steps to print a report. Use the data contained in HSFLE1 to prepare the report.

d. Modify the report format so that a subtotal is taken when there is a change in CITY. Enter the steps to display the output on the printer. Use the data contained in the file named HSFLE2 to prepare the report.

# PROJECT 4

## Adding, Changing, and Deleting

### Objectives

You will have mastered the material in this project when you can:

- Add records to a previously created database file using "Append"
- Change records in a database file using "Edit"
- Position the record pointer using "Locate"
- Change records using "Replace"
- Change records using "Browse"
- Delete records using "Edit"
- Delete records using "Browse"
- Delete records using "Delete"
- Undelete records using "Recall"
- Physically remove deleted records using "Pack"

The examples in Projects 1, 2, and 3 illustrated many dBASE functions. You created a database file, displayed various records in the file, sorted the file, and prepared reports using the data in the file.

For your database file to be useful, however, you must keep the information in it up to date. New employees are hired; existing employees may leave the company; when employees are given pay raises, their pay rates must be changed; and so on. Thus, you must be able to perform three basic functions: add records to the file; delete records from the file; and make changes to the records in the file. In this project we explain the dBASE options that you can use to perform these functions. You will use the menus and options within the ASSISTANT that are listed in Figure 4-1.

| OPTION | PURPOSE |
|---|---|
| Set Up | Activate a |
| Database file | database file |
| View | view |
| Quit dBASE III PLUS | leave dBASE III PLUS |
| Create | Create a |
| Database file | database file (extension DBF) |
| View | view (extension VUE) |
| Report | report (extension FRM) |
| Update | Change a database file by |
| Append | adding records at the end |
| Edit | changing records viewing one at a time |
| Browse | changing records viewing several at a time |
| Replace | changing the data in all records that satisfy some condition |
| Delete | deleting records |
| Recall | undeleting records |
| Pack | physically remove deleted records |
| Position | Move the record pointer by |
| Seek | finding a match using an index |
| Locate | finding the first record that satisfies some condition |
| Goto Record | specifying a record number |
| Retrieve | Retrieve data from a database file |
| List | show desired fields and records on the screen or printer |
| Display | like "List" (differences between the two are covered in the text) |
| Report | print a report |
| Sum | calculate a total |
| Average | calculate an average |
| Count | count the number of records |
| Organize | |
| Index | create an index (extension NDX) |
| Sort | sort a database file |
| Modify | Change an existing |
| Database file | database file |
| Report | report file |
| Tools | |
| List structure | show the structure of the active database file |

**FIGURE 4-1**
Menus and Options within the dBASE ASSISTANT

## ADDING RECORDS

To study the commands for adding records to a file, let's use the EMPLOYEE database file created in Project 1 and assume that two new employes have been hired. The file is shown in Figure 4-2.

| RECORD# | NUMBER | NAME | DATE | DEPARTMENT | PAY_ RATE | UNION |
|---|---|---|---|---|---|---|
| 1 | 1011 | Rapoza, Anthony P. | 01/10/89 | Shipping | 8.50 | .T. |
| 2 | 1013 | McCormack, Nigel L. | 01/15/89 | Shipping | 8.25 | .T. |
| 3 | 1016 | Ackerman, David R. | 02/04/89 | Accounting | 9.75 | .F. |
| 4 | 1017 | Doi, Chang J. | 02/05/89 | Production | 6.00 | .T. |
| 5 | 1020 | Castle, Mark C. | 03/04/89 | Shipping | 7.50 | .T. |
| 6 | 1022 | Dunning, Lisa A. | 03/12/89 | Marketing | 9.10 | .F. |
| 7 | 1025 | Chaney, Joseph R. | 03/23/89 | Accounting | 8.00 | .F. |
| 8 | 1026 | Bender, Helen O. | 04/12/89 | Production | 6.75 | .T. |
| 9 | 1029 | Anderson, Mariane L. | 04/18/89 | Shipping | 9.00 | .T. |
| 10 | 1030 | Edwards, Kenneth J. | 04/23/89 | Production | 8.60 | .T. |
| 11 | 1037 | Baxter, Charles W. | 05/05/89 | Accounting | 11.00 | .F. |
| 12 | 1041 | Evans, John T. | 05/19/89 | Marketing | 6.00 | .F. |
| 13 | 1056 | Andrews, Robert M. | 06/03/89 | Marketing | 9.00 | .F. |
| 14 | 1057 | Dugan, Mary L. | 06/10/89 | Production | 8.75 | .T. |
| 15 | 1066 | Castleworth, Mary T. | 07/05/89 | Production | 8.75 | .T. |

**FIGURE 4-2**
**Employee Data**

You will add the two additional employees to the EMPLOYEE file. To add records, use the "Append" option of the "Update" menu. After you have loaded dBASE, activate the EMPLOYEE file as you have done before. Choose the "Database file" option of the "Set Up" menu, select drive B and the database file named EMPLOYEE.DBF, then indicate that the file is not indexed.

After that, choose the "Append" option within the "Update" menu (Figure 4-3). Once you have done this, the display shown in Figure 4-4 (on the next page) will appear. Note that this is the same display you saw when you first created the file. You are currently positioned at the end of the file. This is indicated by the fact that the current record (Rec:) is listed as EOF/15 (EOF is an abbreviation for end of file). Recall that pressing F1 will remove the box from the top of the screen.

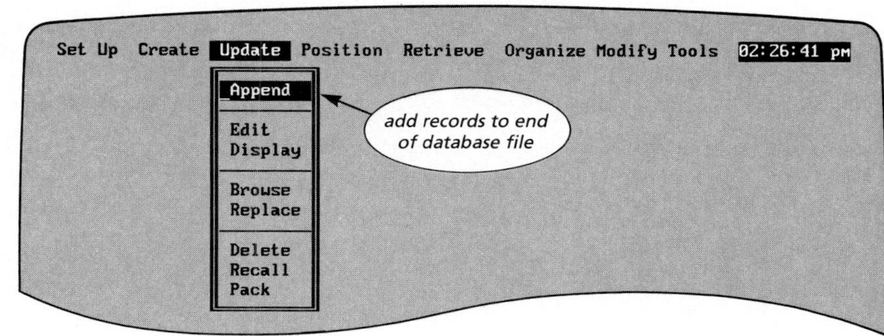


**FIGURE 4-3**
**Adding New Records**

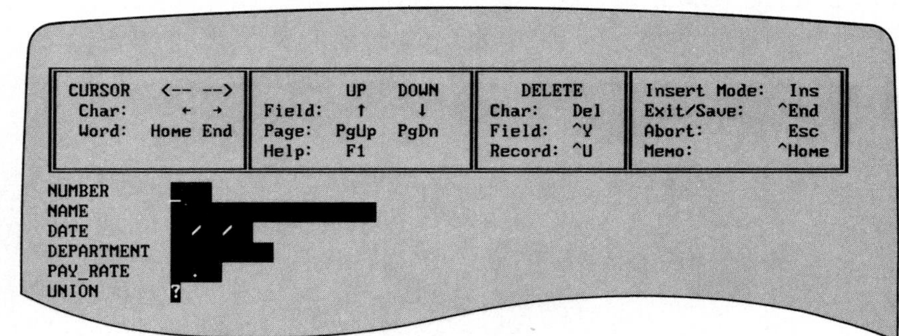


**FIGURE 4-4**
**Form for Adding Records**

After you have entered the information for the first additional record (Figure 4-5), another screen will appear and you can enter the information for the second (Figure 4-6). After you have entered the data for the second, a screen for a third additional record will appear. Because there are no more records to be added to the file, press the Enter key. The new additions will have been added to the end of the EMPLOYEE file, and you will be returned to the ASSISTANT menu screen.

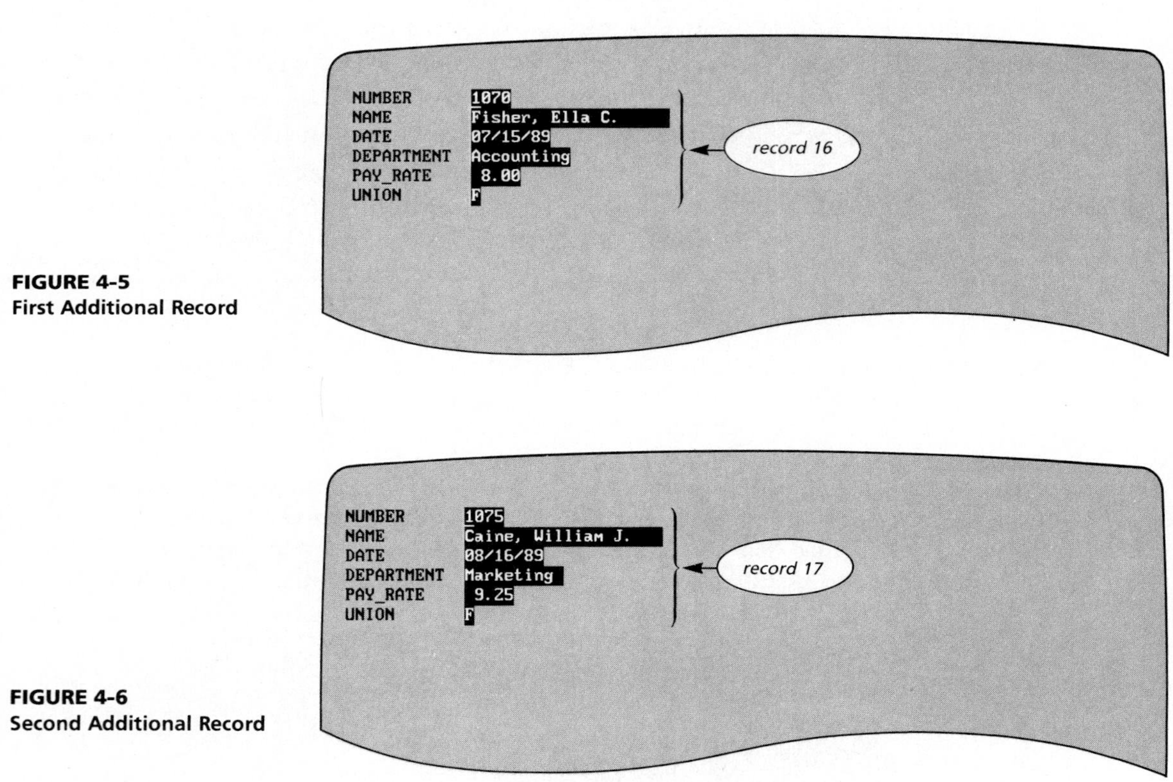


**FIGURE 4-5**
**First Additional Record**

**FIGURE 4-6**
**Second Additional Record**

Figure 4-7 illustrates the use of the "Display" option of the "Retrieve" menu to list all the records in the EMPLOYEE file after the two records have been added. Note that records 16 and 17 have indeed been added to the file.

| RECORD# | NUMBER | NAME | DATE | DEPARTMENT | PAY_ RATE | UNION |
|---|---|---|---|---|---|---|
| 1 | 1011 | Rapoza, Anthony P. | 01/10/89 | Shipping | 8.50 | .T. |
| 2 | 1013 | McCormack, Nigel L. | 01/15/89 | Shipping | 8.25 | .T. |
| 3 | 1016 | Ackerman, David R. | 02/04/89 | Accounting | 9.75 | .F. |
| 4 | 1017 | Doi, Chang J. | 02/05/89 | Production | 6.00 | .T. |
| 5 | 1020 | Castle, Mark C. | 03/04/89 | Shipping | 7.50 | .T. |
| 6 | 1022 | Dunning, Lisa A. | 03/12/89 | Marketing | 9.10 | .F. |
| 7 | 1025 | Chaney, Joseph R. | 03/23/89 | Accounting | 8.00 | .F. |
| 8 | 1026 | Bender, Helen O. | 04/12/89 | Production | 6.75 | .T. |
| 9 | 1029 | Anderson, Mariane L. | 04/18/89 | Shipping | 9.00 | .T. |
| 10 | 1030 | Edwards, Kenneth J. | 04/23/89 | Production | 8.60 | .T. |
| 11 | 1037 | Baxter, Charles W. | 05/05/89 | Accounting | 11.00 | .F. |
| 12 | 1041 | Evans, John T. | 05/19/89 | Marketing | 6.00 | .F. |
| 13 | 1056 | Andrews, Robert M. | 06/03/89 | Marketing | 9.00 | .F. |
| 14 | 1057 | Dugan, Mary L. | 06/10/89 | Production | 8.75 | .T. |
| 15 | 1066 | Castleworth, Mary T. | 07/05/89 | Production | 8.75 | .T. |
| 16 | 1070 | Fisher, Ella C. | 07/15/89 | Accounting | 8.00 | .F. |
| 17 | 1075 | Caine, William J. | 08/16/89 | Marketing | 9.25 | .F. |

*new records have been added*

**FIGURE 4-7 Updated Employee Data**

## CHANGING RECORDS

In most database files, the data in one or more fields must be changed periodically. In the EMPLOYEE database file, for example, pay rates may need to be changed. There are three options within the "Update" menu that you can use to make changes to the records in a file. These options are "Edit," "Browse," and "Replace."

## Using "Edit"

Assume that employee 1016 received a pay increase from $9.75 to $10.00 per hour. This pay rate change should be made to the PAY_RATE field in the database file. To accomplish this, choose the "Edit" option from the "Update" menu (Figure 4-8). The current active record will be displayed on the screen in the form that should now be very familiar to you (Figure 4-9). If the box describing the various keystrokes is on your screen, press F1 to remove it. Your screen will then look like the one shown in Figure 4-9.

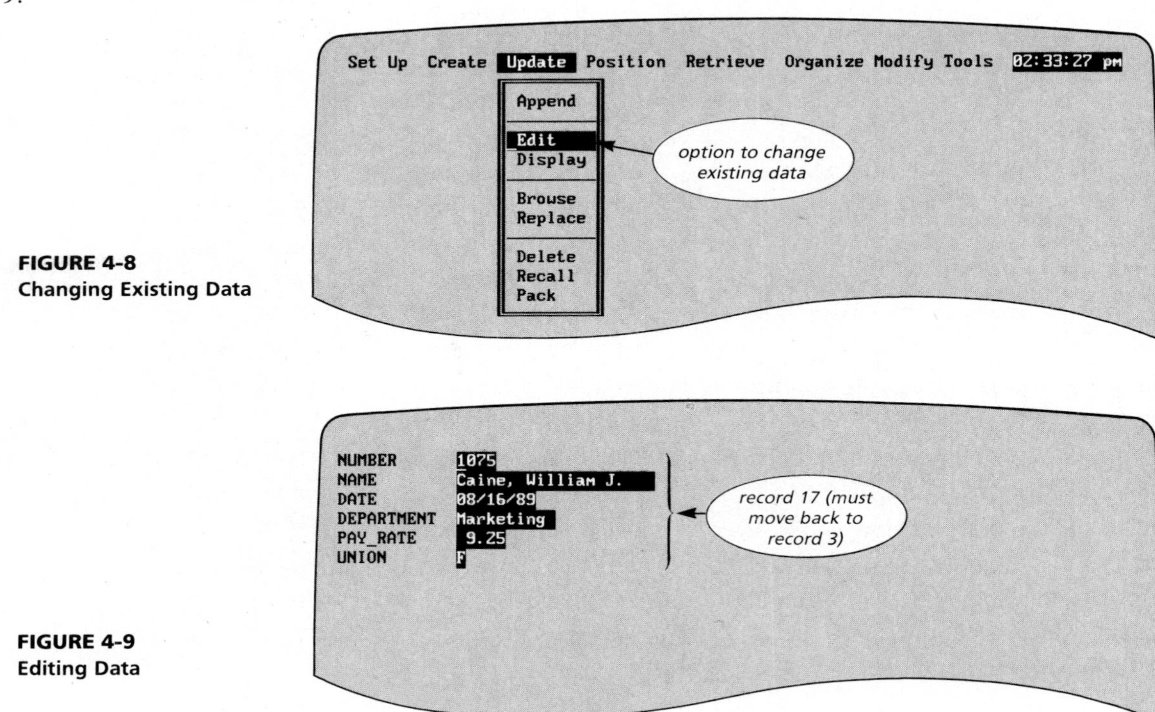


**FIGURE 4-8**
**Changing Existing Data**

**FIGURE 4-9**
**Editing Data**

If the record you want to update happens to be the one displayed on the screen, you could simply begin the updating process. In this case, it is not. So the first order of business is to bring the desired record to the screen. In a small file like this one, you can repeatedly press PgUp (to move to the previous record) or PgDn (to move to the next record) until you find the correct one.

Initially, the cursor is in the first position of the first field. Press the Down Arrow key four times to position the cursor in the PAY_RATE field (see Figure 4-10.) Then you can type the new pay rate. Type the amount 10.00. Since this is the only change, finish the process by holding down the Ctrl key while pressing the End key. The change will be saved and you will be returned to the ASSISTANT menu. Figure 4-11 shows the EMPLOYEE file with the pay rate change.

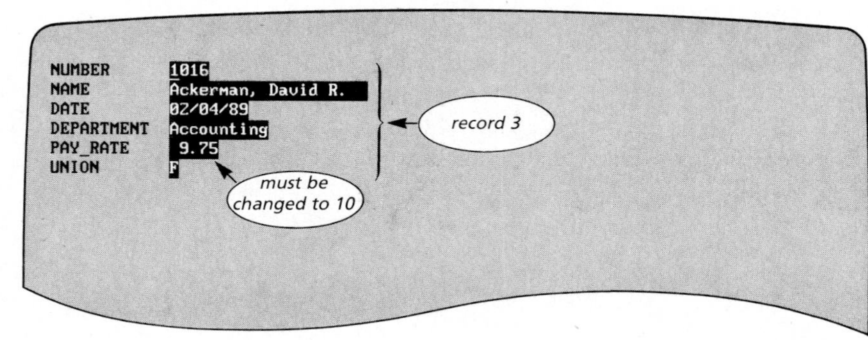


**FIGURE 4-10**
**Editing Data**

| RECORD# | NUMBER | NAME | DATE | DEPARTMENT | PAY_ RATE | UNION |
|---|---|---|---|---|---|---|
| 1 | 1011 | Rapoza, Anthony P. | 01/10/89 | Shipping | 8.50 | .T. |
| 2 | 1013 | McCormack, Nigel L. | 01/15/89 | Shipping | 8.25 | .T. |
| 3 | 1016 | Ackerman, David R. | 02/04/89 | Accounting | 10.00 | .F. |
| 4 | 1017 | Doi, Chang J. | 02/05/89 | Production | 6.00 | .T. |
| 5 | 1020 | Castle, Mark C. | 03/04/89 | Shipping | 7.50 | .T. |
| 6 | 1022 | Dunning, Lisa A. | 03/12/89 | Marketing | 9.10 | .F. |
| 7 | 1025 | Chaney, Joseph R. | 03/23/89 | Accounting | 8.00 | .F. |
| 8 | 1026 | Bender, Helen O. | 04/12/89 | Production | 6.75 | .T. |
| 9 | 1029 | Anderson, Mariane L. | 04/18/89 | Shipping | 9.00 | .T. |
| 10 | 1030 | Edwards, Kenneth J. | 04/23/89 | Production | 8.60 | .T. |
| 11 | 1037 | Baxter, Charles W. | 05/05/89 | Accounting | 11.00 | .F. |
| 12 | 1041 | Evans, John T. | 05/19/89 | Marketing | 6.00 | .F. |
| 13 | 1056 | Andrews, Robert M. | 06/03/89 | Marketing | 9.00 | .F. |
| 14 | 1057 | Dugan, Mary L. | 06/10/89 | Production | 8.75 | .T. |
| 15 | 1066 | Castleworth, Mary T. | 07/05/89 | Production | 8.75 | .T. |
| 16 | 1070 | Fisher, Ella C. | 07/15/89 | Accounting | 8.00 | .F. |
| 17 | 1075 | Caine, William J. | 08/16/89 | Marketing | 9.25 | .F. |

*pay rate has been changed*

**FIGURE 4-11** Updated Employee Data

## More on Positioning the Record Pointer

Earlier, you learned how to change the record pointer using the "Position" menu. You could move it to the first record in the file or the last record in the file. You could also move it to some specific record provided you knew the number of the record. But what if you don't know the number? What if you want to move the pointer to the record for employee 1016 and you don't happen to know where in the file this employee is located? It would be cumbersome to have to move through the file one record at a time looking for this employee. Fortunately, there is an easy way to move directly to this record.

In the discussion that follows, the current record pointer is assumed to be 1; that is, the first record is the current active record. If your current record pointer is not 1, you should change it at this time. Recall that you do this by selecting the "Goto" option of the "Position" menu and then selecting "TOP."

The option that will allow you to locate employee 1016 is the "Locate" option of the "Position" menu. Use the Right or Left Arrow key to move to the "Position" menu and the Down Arrow key to move to "Locate" (Figure 4-12). Then press the Enter key. Your screen should look like the one shown in Figure 4-13. Does the box on the right look familiar? It should. You have encountered it several times already.

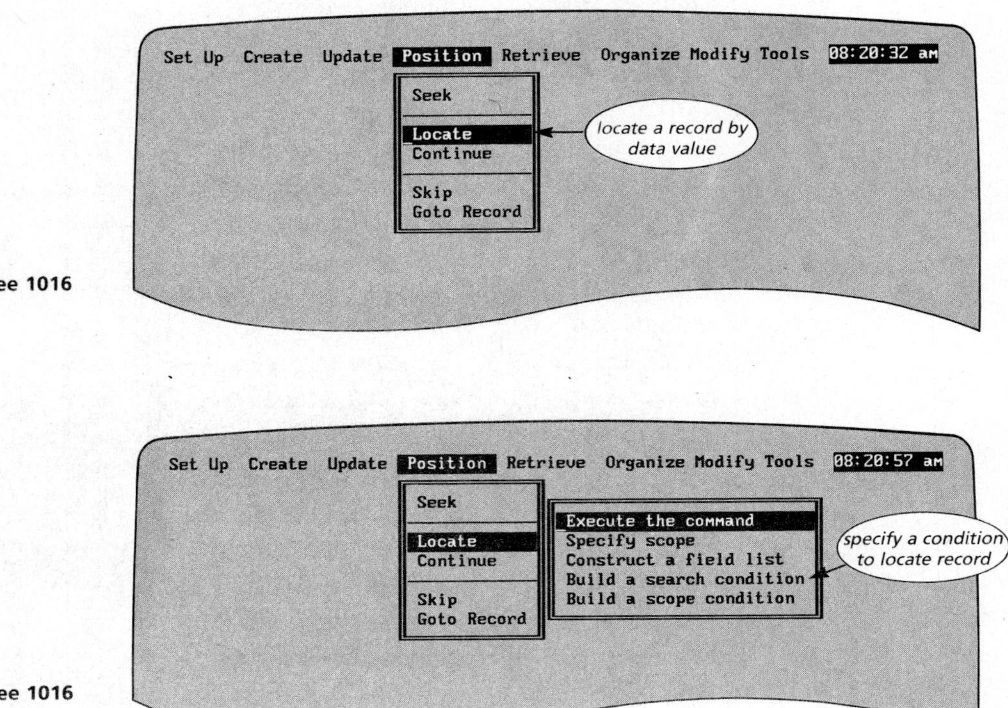


**FIGURE 4-12**
**Finding Employee 1016**

**FIGURE 4-13**
**Finding Employee 1016**

Next, build a search condition to identify the record you are looking for. In this case, select the field called NUMBER and the comparison operator "Equal to," and then enter the value 1016. Indicate that there are "No more conditions."

Notice the command that dBASE has constructed for you (see Figure 4.14). Move the highlight to "Execute the command" and press Enter. Your screen will now look like the one shown in Figure 4-15. Note that dBASE has identified the record for you, but the record pointer has not yet changed.

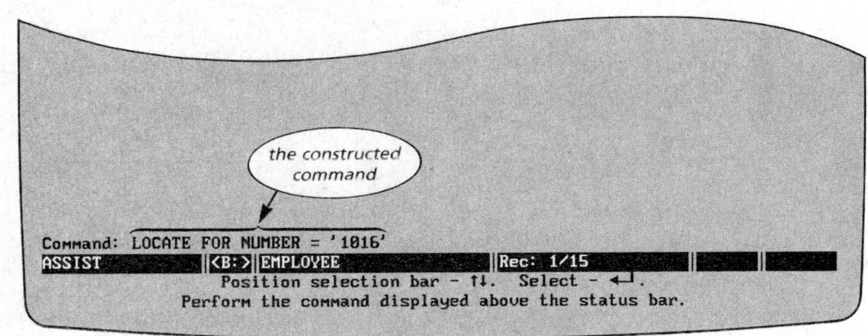


**FIGURE 4-14**
**Finding Employee 1016**

**FIGURE 4-15**
**Finding Employee 1016**

You are instructed to press any key to continue. Do so now and the screen shown in Figure 4-16 will appear. If you look at the record number in the status line, you will find that dBASE has indeed moved to the correct record.

**FIGURE 4-16**
**Finding Employee 1016**

## Using "Replace"

Another option that can be used to change data is the "Replace" option of the "Update" menu. Suppose you want to change the pay rate of employee 1016 from $10.00 back to $9.75, reversing the change you made earlier.

Select the option in the usual manner. Once you have done so, you will see a box containing all the field names. Move the highlight to PAY_RATE (Figure 4-17) and press the Enter key. Your display will now look like the one shown in Figure 4-18 on the next page. You are being asked to give the new value for PAY_RATE.

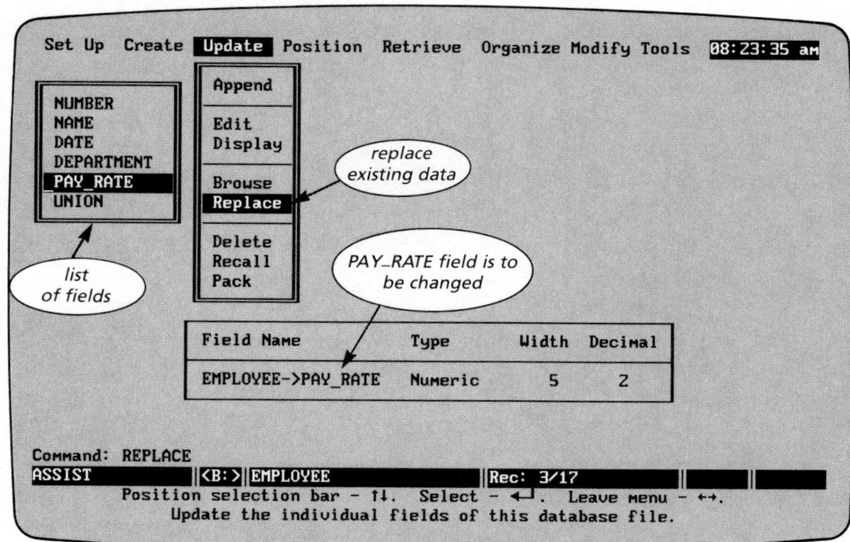


**FIGURE 4-17**
**Replacing Data**

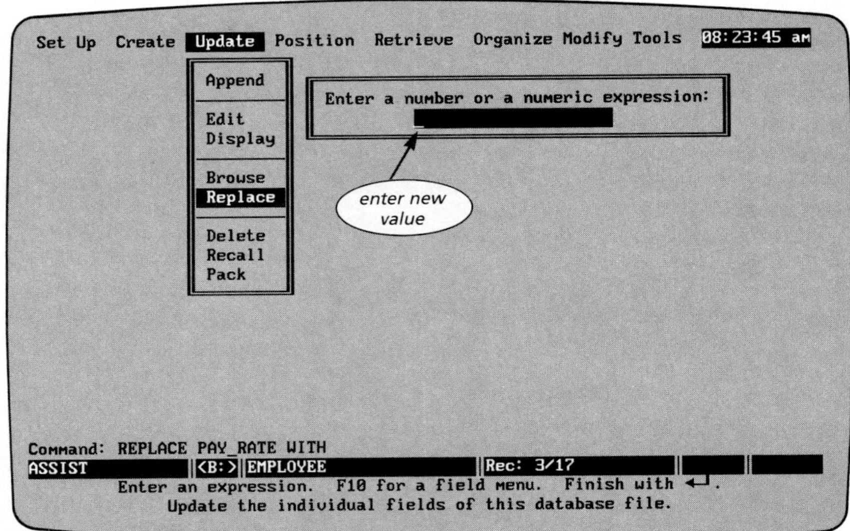


**FIGURE 4-18**
**Entering Replacement Value**

Enter the amount 9.75 and press the Enter key. The field menu reappears (Figure 4-19) and you could choose to make some other replacement, for example, changing the department to production. Since the change is only to the pay rate, press the Right Arrow key to leave this menu.

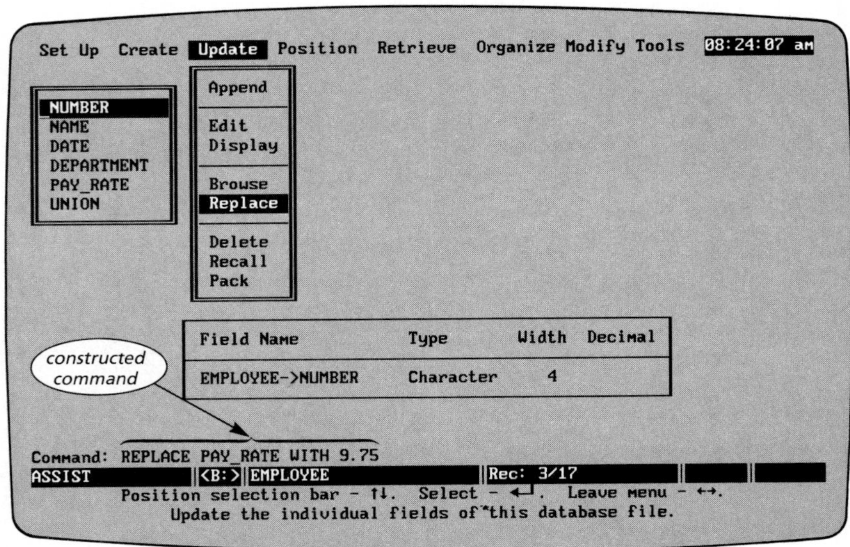


**FIGURE 4-19**
**Replacement Value Has Been Entered**

The familiar box will appear. It is now time to build a search condition to identify the record or records on which the change is to take place. For this condition, select the field NUMBER and the comparison operator "Equal to," and enter the number 1016. Indicate that there are no more conditions.

Your display should now look like the one shown in Figure 4-20. Note the command that has been constructed for you. At this point, choose "Execute the command." dBASE will make the change and display the message "1 record replaced." After you have read the message, press any key.

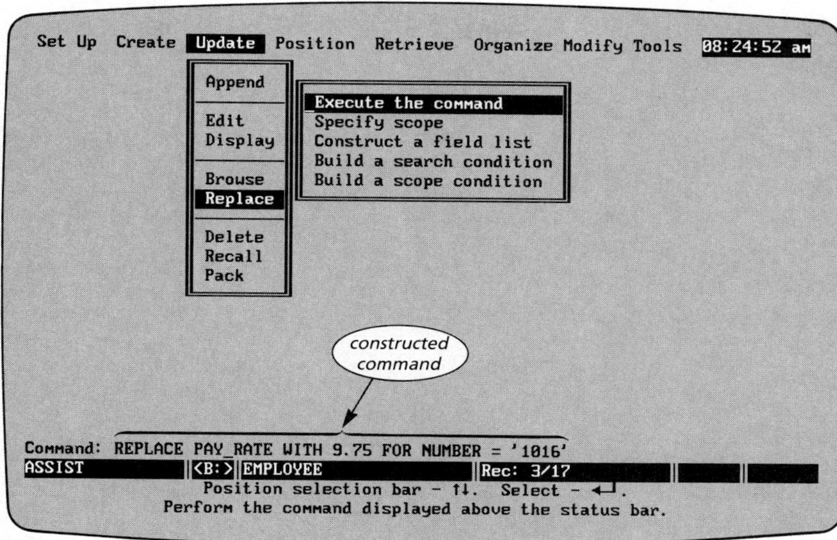


**FIGURE 4-20**
**Completed REPLACE Command**

This is a very powerful facility. You can change many records at the same time by entering a condition that will identify several records rather than just one (like DEPARTMENT, "Equal to," and Marketing). The change can also involve a computation. To give employee 1016 a 5% raise, for example, type the numeric expression PAY_RATE * 1.05 in the position where you typed the amount 9.75.

## Using "Browse"

The "Browse" option of the "Update" menu furnishes yet another method of making changes to records in a database. The "Browse" option will display up to 17 records on the screen at one time and as many fields as will fit horizontally on the screen. This option displays records beginning with the current active record and moving toward the end of the file. To begin with the first record, you should make sure it is the current active record. If not, use the techniques you have learned to make it the current active record. After that, select "Browse" from the "Update" menu as shown in Figure 4-21.

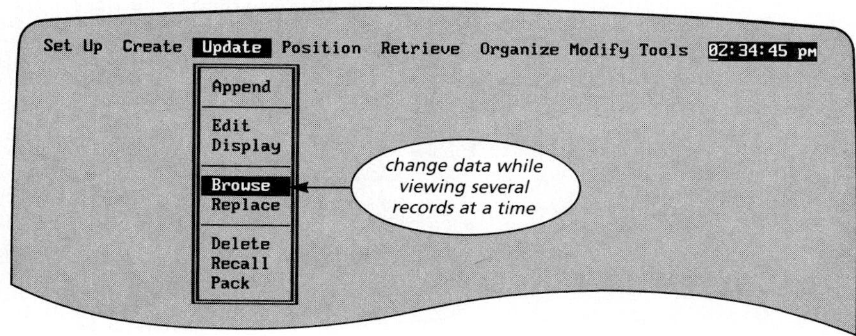


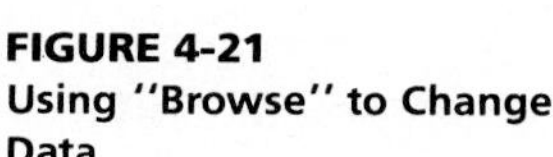

**FIGURE 4-21**
**Using "Browse" to Change Data**

The screen illustrated in Figure 4-22, will be displayed with the current active record highlighted. You can move the highlight to any other record by pressing the Down Arrow key or the Up Arrow key.

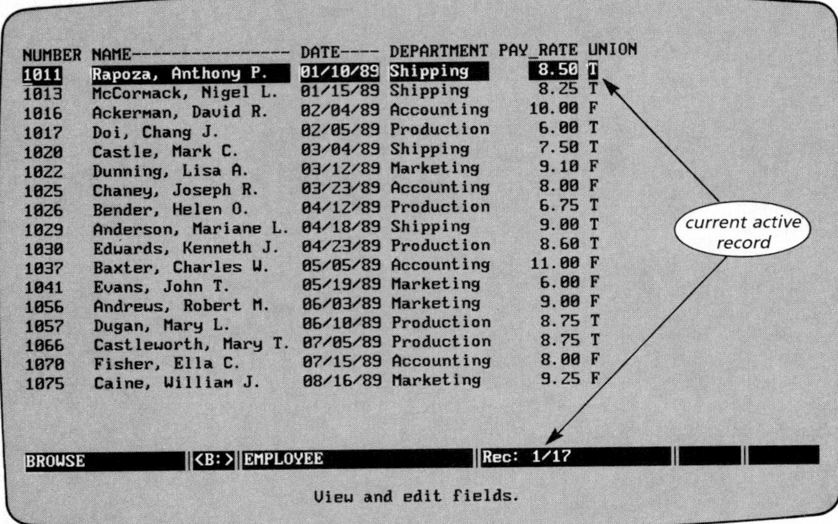

| NUMBER | NAME---------------- | DATE---- | DEPARTMENT | PAY_RATE | UNION |
|---|---|---|---|---|---|
| 1011 | Rapoza, Anthony P. | 01/10/89 | Shipping | 8.50 | T |
| 1013 | McCormack, Nigel L. | 01/15/89 | Shipping | 8.25 | T |
| 1016 | Ackerman, David R. | 02/04/89 | Accounting | 10.00 | F |
| 1017 | Doi, Chang J. | 02/05/89 | Production | 6.00 | T |
| 1020 | Castle, Mark C. | 03/04/89 | Shipping | 7.50 | T |
| 1022 | Dunning, Lisa A. | 03/12/89 | Marketing | 9.10 | F |
| 1025 | Chaney, Joseph R. | 03/23/89 | Accounting | 8.00 | F |
| 1026 | Bender, Helen O. | 04/12/89 | Production | 6.75 | T |
| 1029 | Anderson, Mariane L. | 04/18/89 | Shipping | 9.00 | T |
| 1030 | Edwards, Kenneth J. | 04/23/89 | Production | 8.60 | T |
| 1037 | Baxter, Charles W. | 05/05/89 | Accounting | 11.00 | F |
| 1041 | Evans, John T. | 05/19/89 | Marketing | 6.00 | F |
| 1056 | Andrews, Robert M. | 06/03/89 | Marketing | 9.00 | F |
| 1057 | Dugan, Mary L. | 06/10/89 | Production | 8.75 | T |
| 1066 | Castleworth, Mary T. | 07/05/89 | Production | 8.75 | T |
| 1070 | Fisher, Ella C. | 07/15/89 | Accounting | 8.00 | F |
| 1075 | Caine, William J. | 08/16/89 | Marketing | 9.25 | F |



**FIGURE 4-22**
**Using "Browse" to Edit Records**

To change a field in a record, you must highlight the record to be changed. For example, to change Helen Bender's pay rate from $6.75 to $7.00, move the highlight to record 8 by pressing the Down Arrow key seven times (Figure 4-23).

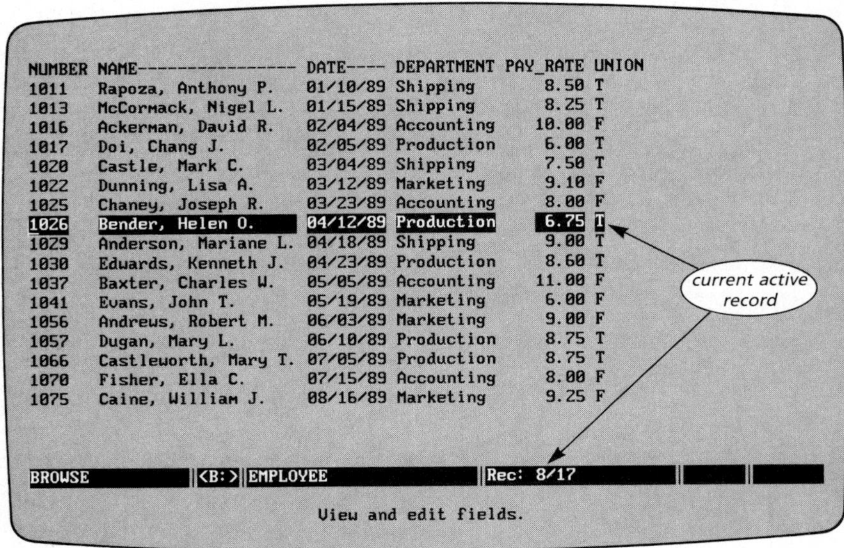

| NUMBER | NAME---------------- | DATE---- | DEPARTMENT | PAY_RATE | UNION |
|---|---|---|---|---|---|
| 1011 | Rapoza, Anthony P. | 01/10/89 | Shipping | 8.50 | T |
| 1013 | McCormack, Nigel L. | 01/15/89 | Shipping | 8.25 | T |
| 1016 | Ackerman, David R. | 02/04/89 | Accounting | 10.00 | F |
| 1017 | Doi, Chang J. | 02/05/89 | Production | 6.00 | T |
| 1020 | Castle, Mark C. | 03/04/89 | Shipping | 7.50 | T |
| 1022 | Dunning, Lisa A. | 03/12/89 | Marketing | 9.10 | F |
| 1025 | Chaney, Joseph R. | 03/23/89 | Accounting | 8.00 | F |
| 1026 | Bender, Helen O. | 04/12/89 | Production | 6.75 | T |
| 1029 | Anderson, Mariane L. | 04/18/89 | Shipping | 9.00 | T |
| 1030 | Edwards, Kenneth J. | 04/23/89 | Production | 8.60 | T |
| 1037 | Baxter, Charles W. | 05/05/89 | Accounting | 11.00 | F |
| 1041 | Evans, John T. | 05/19/89 | Marketing | 6.00 | F |
| 1056 | Andrews, Robert M. | 06/03/89 | Marketing | 9.00 | F |
| 1057 | Dugan, Mary L. | 06/10/89 | Production | 8.75 | T |
| 1066 | Castleworth, Mary T. | 07/05/89 | Production | 8.75 | T |
| 1070 | Fisher, Ella C. | 07/15/89 | Accounting | 8.00 | F |
| 1075 | Caine, William J. | 08/16/89 | Marketing | 9.25 | F |



**FIGURE 4-23**
**Using "Browse" to Edit Records**

You can use the Right Arrow key to move the cursor to the PAY_RATE field (Figure 4-24) and then type the new pay rate, 7.00. (see Figure 4-25). But pressing the End key is a faster way to move the cursor from one field to the next. Pressing the End key will move the cursor one field at a time to the right. Pressing the Home key will move the cursor one field at a time to the left. The End and Home keys can be very useful with the "Browse" option.

If you only want to change Helen Bender's pay rate, hold the Ctrl key down and press the End key. The change will be saved and you will return to the ASSISTANT menu. If you want to make changes to several records, make all of them before holding down Ctrl and pressing End.

You can also add records to a file using the "Browse" option by moving the reverse video block highlighting each record past the last data record. The message "Add new record? (Y/N)" will appear on the screen. If you choose Y, spaces will be displayed at the bottom of the screen so that you can enter a new record. If you select N, the highlight will remain on the bottom row. The most common method of adding records, however, is with the "Append" option.

```
NUMBER NAME---------------- DATE---- DEPARTMENT PAY_RATE UNION
1011   Rapoza, Anthony P.   01/10/89 Shipping       8.50 T
1013   McCormack, Nigel L.  01/15/89 Shipping       8.25 T
1016   Ackerman, David R.   02/04/89 Accounting    10.00 F
1017   Doi, Chang J.        02/05/89 Production     6.00 T
1020   Castle, Mark C.      03/04/89 Shipping       7.50 T
1022   Dunning, Lisa A.     03/12/89 Marketing      9.10 F
1025   Chaney, Joseph R.    03/23/89 Accounting     8.00 F
1026   Bender, Helen O.     04/12/89 Production     6.75 T
1029   Anderson, Mariane L. 04/18/89 Shipping       9.00 T
1030   Edwards, Kenneth J.  04/23/89 Production     8.60 T
1037   Baxter, Charles W.   05/05/89 Accounting    11.00 F
1041   Evans, John T.       05/19/89 Marketing      6.00 F
1056   Andrews, Robert M.   06/03/89 Marketing      9.00 F
1057   Dugan, Mary L.       06/10/89 Production     8.75 T
1066   Castleworth, Mary T. 07/05/89 Production     8.75 T
1070   Fisher, Ella C.      07/15/89 Accounting     8.00 F
1075   Caine, William J.    08/16/89 Marketing      9.25 F

BROWSE        <B:> EMPLOYEE          Rec: 8/17
                    View and edit fields.
```

field to be changed

**FIGURE 4-24**
**Using "Browse" to Edit Records**

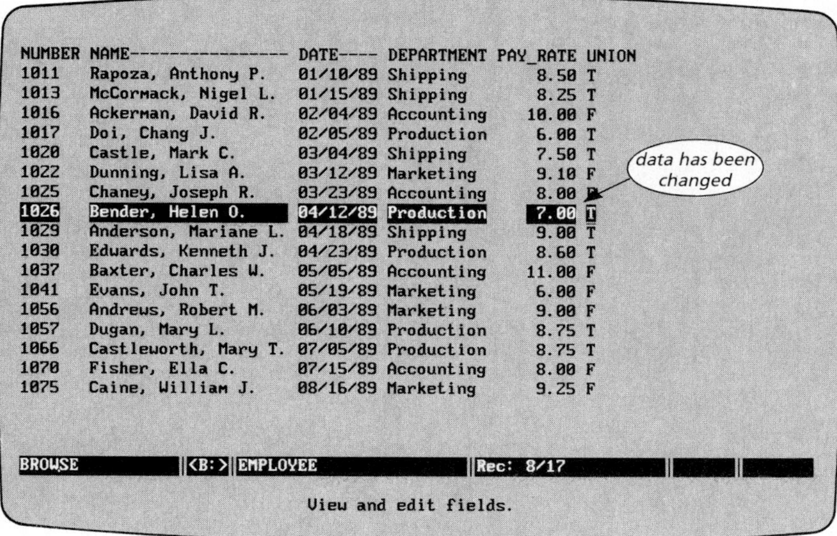

```
NUMBER NAME---------------- DATE---- DEPARTMENT PAY_RATE UNION
1011   Rapoza, Anthony P.   01/10/89 Shipping       8.50 T
1013   McCormack, Nigel L.  01/15/89 Shipping       8.25 T
1016   Ackerman, David R.   02/04/89 Accounting    10.00 F
1017   Doi, Chang J.        02/05/89 Production     6.00 T
1020   Castle, Mark C.      03/04/89 Shipping       7.50 T
1022   Dunning, Lisa A.     03/12/89 Marketing      9.10 F
1025   Chaney, Joseph R.    03/23/89 Accounting     8.00 F
1026   Bender, Helen O.     04/12/89 Production     7.00 T
1029   Anderson, Mariane L. 04/18/89 Shipping       9.00 T
1030   Edwards, Kenneth J.  04/23/89 Production     8.60 T
1037   Baxter, Charles W.   05/05/89 Accounting    11.00 F
1041   Evans, John T.       05/19/89 Marketing      6.00 F
1056   Andrews, Robert M.   06/03/89 Marketing      9.00 F
1057   Dugan, Mary L.       06/10/89 Production     8.75 T
1066   Castleworth, Mary T. 07/05/89 Production     8.75 T
1070   Fisher, Ella C.      07/15/89 Accounting     8.00 F
1075   Caine, William J.    08/16/89 Marketing      9.25 F

BROWSE        <B:> EMPLOYEE          Rec: 8/17
                    View and edit fields.
```



**FIGURE 4-25**
**Using "Browse" to Edit Records**

# DELETING RECORDS

It may be necessary to delete records from a file. For example, if an employee no longer works for the company, his or her record should be removed (deleted) from the EMPLOYEE file. This can be accomplished with the "Edit," "Browse," or "Delete" options of the "Update" menu.

When you delete records from a database file using any of these options, the records are not actually removed from the file. Instead, dBASE merely marks them with an asterisk as being deleted. It is the "Pack" option that physically removes the records from the file. Until such an operation is performed, the records are still in the file. dBASE will, however, indicate which records have been so marked. When a collection of records is displayed, an asterisk will be placed immediately before the first field of any deleted records. When records are being edited and the current active record happens to be one that has been marked for deletion, the letters "Del" will appear near the right-hand end of the status line.

Since records are only marked for deletion, dBASE provides another option, "Recall," that allows you to remove this deletion mark, that is, to "undelete" these records. This can come in handy if you ever delete the wrong records. Choosing the "Pack" option, however, physically removes such records and the "Recall" option can no longer bring them back. Always be very careful, both when choosing to delete records in the first place and also when deciding to pack your database files.

## Deleting Records with "Edit"

The "Edit" option is normally used to change data in one or more records in a database file. It can also be used to delete records, however. To delete a record, simply bring it to the screen using any of the methods we discussed. When the record is on the screen, hold the Ctrl key down and type the letter U. The record will be marked for deletion and the characters "Del" will appear near the lower right-hand corner of the screen. The same process can be used to recall a record. If a deleted record is on the screen, holding the Ctrl key down and typing the letter U will recall it. The record becomes an active record in the file and the letters "Del" will disappear from the screen.

## Deleting Records with "Browse"

Records can be deleted using the "Browse" option. Position the reverse video block over the record to be deleted and hold down the Ctrl key while typing the letter U. The record will be marked for deletion.

## Deleting Records with "Delete"

The "Delete" option within the "Update" menu is used to delete either individual records or groups of all records satisfying certain conditions. When you choose this option, the familiar box appears (Figure 4-26). Typically, you would then specify a search condition that will be used to identify the records to be deleted. If you immediately select "Execute the command," only the current active record would be deleted. This usually is not what you want.

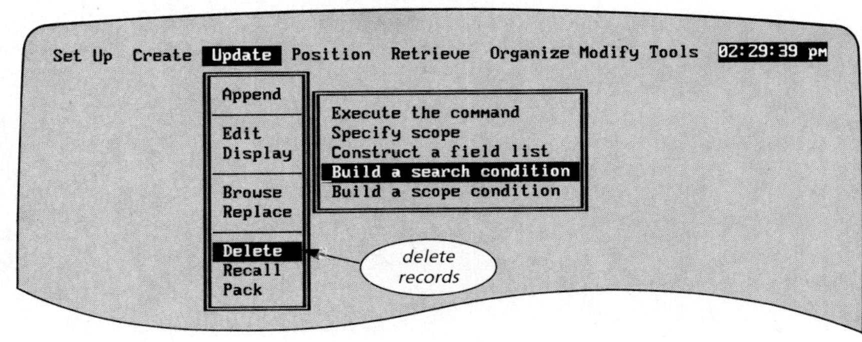


**FIGURE 4-26**
Using "Delete" to Delete Records

Search conditions are specified in exactly the same fashion as the "Display" option on the "Retrieve" menu. To delete the records for the employee whose name is Andrews, Robert M., for example, move the highlight to "Build a search condition" and press the Enter key. Then move the highlight to NAME (Figure 4-27) and press the Enter key. Select "Equal to" and type the name Andrews, Robert M. Press Enter and then select "No more conditions." Once this has been done, move the highlight to "Execute the command." Before pressing Enter, check the command that dBASE has constructed (DELETE FOR NAME = 'Andrews, Robert M.') to make sure you have typed everything correctly (see Figure 4-28). If so, press the Enter key. If not, press Esc and begin again.

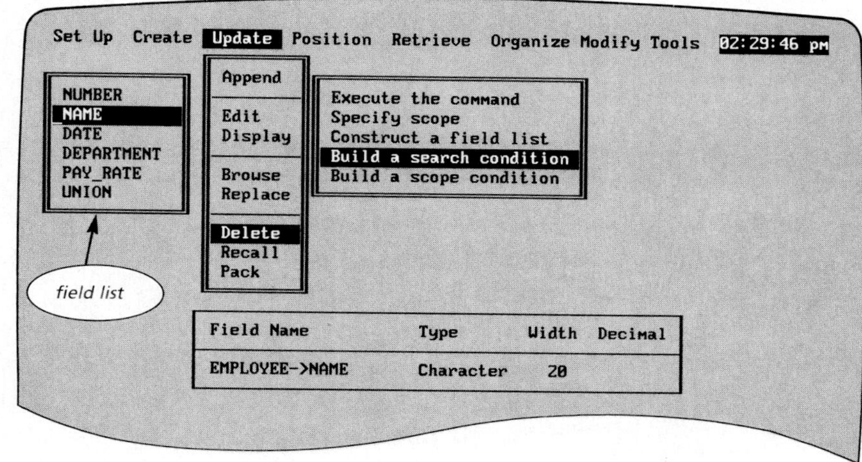


**FIGURE 4-27**
**Using "Delete" to Delete Records**

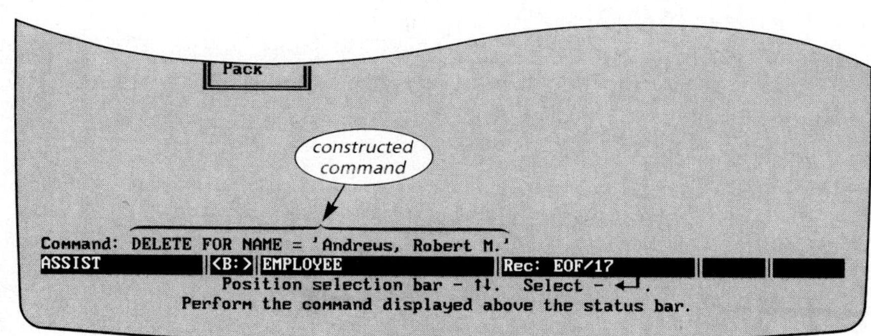


**FIGURE 4-28**
**Using "Delete" to Delete Records**

This record will now be marked for deletion. In the display of all employee records shown in Figure 4-29, it is marked with an asterisk. If we were to use "Edit" or "Browse," the letters "Del" would appear on the screen whenever this record was the current active record.

| RECORD# | NUMBER | NAME | DATE | DEPARTMENT | PAY_ RATE | UNION |
|---|---|---|---|---|---|---|
| 1 | 1011 | Rapoza, Anthony P. | 01/10/89 | Shipping | 8.50 | .T. |
| 2 | 1013 | McCormack, Nigel L. | 01/15/89 | Shipping | 8.25 | .T. |
| 3 | 1016 | Ackerman, David R. | 02/04/89 | Accounting | 10.00 | .F. |
| 4 | 1017 | Doi, Chang J. | 02/05/89 | Production | 6.00 | .T. |
| 5 | 1020 | Castle, Mark C. | 03/04/89 | Shipping | 7.50 | .T. |
| 6 | 1022 | Dunning, Lisa A. | 03/12/89 | Marketing | 9.10 | .F. |
| 7 | 1025 | Chaney, Joseph R. | 03/23/89 | Accounting | 8.00 | .F. |
| 8 | 1026 | Bender, Helen O. | 04/12/89 | Production | 7.00 | .T. |
| 9 | 1029 | Anderson, Mariane L. | 04/18/89 | Shipping | 9.00 | .T. |
| 10 | 1030 | Edwards, Kenneth J. | 04/23/89 | Production | 8.60 | .T. |
| 11 | 1037 | Baxter, Charles W. | 05/05/89 | Accounting | 11.00 | .F. |
| 12 | 1041 | Evans, John T. | 05/19/89 | Marketing | 6.00 | .F. |
| 13 | *1056 | Andrews, Robert M. | 06/03/89 | Marketing | 9.00 | .F. |
| 14 | 1057 | Dugan, Mary L. | 06/10/89 | Production | 8.75 | .T. |
| 15 | 1066 | Castleworth, Mary T. | 07/05/89 | Production | 8.75 | .T. |
| 16 | 1070 | Fisher, Ella C. | 07/15/89 | Accounting | 8.00 | .F. |
| 17 | 1075 | Caine, William J. | 08/16/89 | Marketing | 9.25 | .F. |

*indicates deleted record*

**FIGURE 4-29** **Current Employee Data**

## Using "Recall"

If you want to return a record or collection of records marked for deletion to the EMPLOYEE file once again, use the "Recall" option of the "Update" menu to reinstate the record. This option works in the same fashion as the "Delete" option except for one obvious difference. Instead of deleting records, this option *un*deletes (recalls) records. The manner in which the two options are used, however, is identical. To recall the record for Andrews, Robert M., follow the same steps as with the "Delete" option to produce the command shown in Figure 4-30. Then move the highlight to "Execute the command" and press the Enter key. Once this has been done, the record will no longer be deleted.

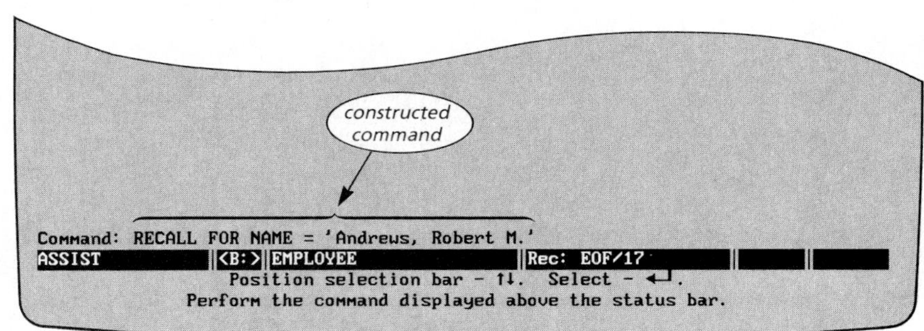


**FIGURE 4-30**
**Using "Recall" to Undelete Records**

## Using "Pack"

To permanently remove a record from a file, choose the "Pack" option of the "Update" menu. There are no choices to make once you have selected this option. "Pack" removes records that are marked for deletion from the active database file. These records are *permanently* removed from the file. You will no longer be able to recall any of them. Thus, it is a good idea to review the contents of the file before you choose this option to make sure that you have marked the correct records for deletion.

# PROJECT SUMMARY

In Project 4 you learned how to change the data in a database file, how to add records using the "Append" option of the "Update" menu, and how to change data using the "Edit," "Browse," and "Replace" options of that menu. You also learned how to delete records using the "Edit," "Browse," and "Delete" options; how to recall records using the "Recall" option; and how to physically remove deleted records using the "Pack" option.

If you followed along with the steps in this chapter, you have made a number of updates to the EMPLOYEE database file. If you did not but wish to make these updates now, you can use the following keystroke sequence. Start dBASE as described in the project and activate the EMPLOYEE database file. Then type the following:

**SUMMARY OF KEYSTROKES—Project 4**

| STEPS | KEY(S) PRESSED | RESULTS |
|---|---|---|
| 1 | → → ↵ | |
| 2 | 1070Fisher, Ella C. ↵ 071589 | |
| 3 | Accounting8.00F | |
| 4 | 1075Caine, William J. ↵ 081689 | |
| 5 | Marketing ↵ 9.25F ↵ | Records added |
| 6 | ← ← ↓ ↵ PgUp PgUp PgUp (Enough times to make record 3 the current active record) | |
| 7 | ↓ ↓ ↓ ↓ 10.00[Ctrl-End] | Records changed with "Edit" |
| 8 | → ↓ ↓ ↵ ↵ | Current active record is 1 |
| 9 | ↑ ↑ ↵ ↓ ↓ ↵ ↵ ↵ 1016 ↵ | |
| 10 | ↑ ↑ ↵ ↵ | Employee 1016 located |
| 11 | ← ↓ ↓ ↓ ↓ ↵ ↓ ↓ ↓ ↓ | |
| 12 | ↵ 9.75 ↵ → ↓ ↓ ↵ ↵ ↵ | |
| 13 | 1016 ↵ ↑ ↑ ↵ ↵ | Records changed |
| 14 | → ↓ ↓ ↓ ↵ ↵ | Current active record is 1 |
| 15 | ← ↓ ↓ ↓ ↵ ↓ ↓ ↓ ↓ ↓ | |
| 16 | ↓ ↓ End End End End 7.00 Ctrl-End | Records changed with "Browse" |
| 17 | ↓ ↓ ↵ ↓ ↓ ↵ ↓ ↵ ↵ | |
| 18 | Andrews, Robert M. ↵ ↵ ↑ | |
| 19 | ↑ ↵ ↵ | Record deleted |
| 20 | ↓ ↵ ↓ ↓ ↵ ↓ ↵ ↵ | |
| 21 | Andrews, Robert M. ↵ ↵ ↑ | |
| 22 | ↑ ↵ ↵ | Record recalled |
| 23 | ↓ ↵ ↵ | Database file packed |

The following list summarizes the material covered in Project 4:

1. To add records, use the "Append" option of the "Update" menu.
2. To change records while viewing one record at a time, use the "Edit" option of the "Update" menu.
3. To position the record pointer to a record containing a certain value, use the "Locate" option of the "Position" menu.
4. To make the same change to all records satisfying a certain condition, use the "Replace" option of the "Update" menu.
5. To change records while viewing several records at a time, use the "Browse" option of the "Update" menu.
6. Deleting records does not remove them from a database file. Rather, such records are marked for deletion. To physically remove such records from the file, use the "Pack" option of the "Update" menu.
7. To delete records, use the "Edit" or the "Browse" options of the "Update" menu. In either case, move to the record to be deleted, hold the Ctrl key down, and type the letter U. (The letters "Del" on the status line indicate that the current active record has been deleted.)
8. To recall records, use the "Edit" or the "Browse" options of the "Update" menu. In either case, move to the deleted record, hold the Ctrl key down, and type the letter U. The letters "Del" will disappear from the screen.
9. To delete all records satisfying a certain condition, use the "Delete" option of the "Update" menu.
10. To recall all records satisfying a certain condition, use the "Recall" option of the "Update" menu.

# STUDENT ASSIGNMENTS:

## STUDENT ASSIGNMENT 1: True/False

**Instructions:** Circle T if the statement is true and F if the statement is false.

T F 1. Three basic functions which must be performed to keep a database file up to date are making additions, deletions, and changes to the database.

T F 2. Use the "Append" option of the "Update" menu to add records at the beginning of a database file.

T F 3. When you choose the "Append" option of the "Update" menu, a screen will appear asking you to define the names of the fields to be used.

T F 4. When you are done adding records using the "Append" option, press the End key.

T F 5. When you use the "Edit" option of the "Update" menu, one record at a time is displayed on the screen.

T F 6. You can delete records using the "Edit" option of the "Update" menu.

T F 7. Use the "Locate" option of the "Position" menu to find the record for employee 1234.

T F 8. To make the same change to all records satisfying a given condition, use the "Change" option of the "Update" menu.

T F 9. To change a record using the "Browse" option of the "Update" menu, highlight the record.

T F 10. Records cannot be deleted using the "Browse" option of the "Update" menu.

T F 11. The "Browse" option is used to view data in a database but should not be used to make additions, deletions, or changes to the data.

T F 12. Records marked for deletion are physically removed from the file through the "Remove" option of the "Update" menu.

T F 13. Records may be undeleted using the "Edit" option of the "Update" menu.

T F 14. Records marked for deletion will not appear on a listing of all the data in the database file.

T F 15. The "Recall" option of the "Update" menu can be used to display deleted records.

T F 16. When you edit records with the "Edit" option of the "Update" menu, holding Ctrl down while typing the letter U always deletes the current active record.

## STUDENT ASSIGNMENT 2: Multiple Choice

**Instructions:** Circle the correct response.

1. The option to add records at the end of a database file is
   a. "Append" c. "Add"
   b. "Insert" d. "Change"
2. To change data while viewing several records at a time, the option is
   a. "View" c. "Edit"
   b. "Browse" d. "Replace"
3. Which of the following cannot be used to delete records?
   a. "Edit" c. "Delete"
   b. "Browse" d. "Remove"
4. Which of the following is not an option on the "Update" menu?
   a. "Append" c. "Locate"
   b. "Recall" d. "Replace"
5. Immediately after you select the "Browse" option of the "Update" menu, the first record shown on the screen
   a. will always be the first record in the file. c. cannot be updated.
   b. will always be the current active record. d. is always the last record in the file.
6. To physically remove records that have been marked for deletion, the option is
   a. "Remove" c. "Pack"
   b. "Delete" d. "Compress"

## STUDENT ASSIGNMENT 3: Understanding dBASE Options

**Instructions:** Explain what will happen after you perform each of the following actions.

Problem 1. Select the "Append" option of the "Update" menu.

Explanation: ______________________________________________

______________________________________________

______________________________________________

Problem 2. Select the "Edit" option of the "Update" menu.

Explanation: ______________________________________________

______________________________________________

______________________________________________

Problem 3. Select the "Browse" option of the "Update" menu.

Explanation: ______________________________________________

______________________________________________

______________________________________________

Problem 4. Select the "Pack" option of the "Update" menu.

Explanation: ______________________________________________

______________________________________________

______________________________________________

## STUDENT ASSIGNMENT 4: Using dBASE

**Instructions:** Explain how to accomplish each of the following tasks using dBASE.

Problem 1. Add a single record at the end of the active database file.

Explanation: ______

Problem 2. Use the "Edit" option to make a change to a field on the fourth record of the active database file.

Explanation: ______

Problem 3. Use the "Browse" option to make a change to a field on the fourth record of the active database file.

Explanation: ______

Problem 4. Add $1.00 to the pay rate for all employees in the shipping department.

Explanation: ______

Problem 5. Mark for deletion the records for all members of the marketing department.

Explanation: ______

Problem 6. Physically remove all records that have been marked for deletion.

Explanation: ______

## STUDENT ASSIGNMENT 5: Recovering from Problems

**Instructions:** In each of the following cases, a problem occurred. Explain the cause of the problem and how it can be corrected.

Problem 1: You were certain you made a change using the "Edit" option and yet, when you later examined the data, you found that the change was not made.

Cause of Problem: ______

Method of Correction: ______

Problem 2: You used the "Delete" option to delete employee 1016 and yet, when you later examined the data, you found that you had deleted all employees whose numbers were greater than 1016.

Cause of Problem: ____________________

____________________

Method of Correction: ____________________

____________________

Problem 3: You deleted a number of records incorrectly. Before discovering this, however, you chose the "Pack" option.

Cause of Problem: ____________________

____________________

Method of Correction: ____________________

____________________

# MINICASES:

## Adding, Deleting, and Changing Records

### Minicase 1: Personal Checks

**Instructions:** Use the personal checks database that you created in Project 1 for the following problems. These problems require adding, deleting, and changing records in the database.

Problem 1: Adding Records to a Database File

a. Using the "Append" option, add the checks listed in the table below to the personal checks database file created in Project 1. Record the steps you followed in the space provided.

| CHECK NUMBER | DATE | PAYEE | CHECK AMOUNT | EXPENSE TYPE | TAX DEDUCTIBLE |
|---|---|---|---|---|---|
| 113 | 02/19/90 | Oak Apartments | 750.00 | Household | N |
| 114 | 02/19/90 | Edison Company | 45.95 | Household | N |
| 115 | 02/21/90 | Pacific Telephone | 29.85 | Household | N |
| 116 | 02/21/90 | Standard Oil | 33.98 | Automobile | Y |
| 117 | 02/21/90 | Cable Television | 45.00 | Household | N |

STEPS: ____________________

____________________

____________________

b. After adding the records to the database file, obtain a listing of the records using the "Display" option. Record the steps you followed in the space provided below.

STEPS: ____________________

____________________

____________________

## Minicase 1 (continued)

Problem 2: Deleting Records from a Database File

a. Using the "Delete" option, delete the last record in the file, the record for check 117. Record the steps you followed in the space provided below.

STEPS: ______________________________

b. Display the records in the file. Record the steps you followed in the space provided below.

STEPS: ______________________________

c. The record for check 117 should remain in the file. Enter the steps that will make the record for check 117 part of the original file again and no longer marked for deletion. Record the steps you followed in the space provided below.

STEPS: ______________________________

Problem 3: Changing the Records in a Database File

a. Using the "Replace" option, change the DATE field for check 115 from 02/21/90 to 02/19/90. Record the steps you followed in the space provided below.

STEPS: ______________________________

b. Using the "Edit" option, change the CHECK AMOUNT field for check 116 from $33.98 to $39.98. Record the steps you followed in the space provided below.

STEPS: ______________________________

c. Obtain a listing of the records in the file. Record the steps you followed in the space provided below.

STEPS: ______________________________

Problem 4: The "Browse" Option

a. Delete and pack records with check numbers 113, 114, 115, 116, and 117.

b. Return to Problems 1, 2, and 3 of this minicase and use the "Browse" option to add, delete, and change records as specified.

## Minicase 2: Music Library

**Instructions:** Use the music library database that you created in Project 1 for the following problems. These problems require adding, deleting, and changing records in the database.

Problem 1: Adding Records to a Database File

a. Using the "Append" option, add the following records to the music library database file created in Project 1. Record the steps you followed in the space provided below.

| DATE | MUSIC NAME | ARTIST | TYPE | COST | CATEGORY |
|---|---|---|---|---|---|
| 02/26/90 | Summer Roses | Davis, Eva | CD | 11.95 | Vocal |
| 03/02/90 | What a Time | Logo, Tom | CS | 8.95 | Vocal |
| 03/02/90 | Camille | Rudin, Lana | LP | 8.95 | Classical |
| 03/02/90 | You Told Me | Lager, Ricky | CD | 11.95 | Country |
| 03/05/90 | Not Tomorrow | Baker, Ted | CS | 5.95 | Rock |

STEPS: ______________________________________________

______________________________________________

______________________________________________

b. After adding the records to the database file, obtain a listing of the records using the "Display" option. Record the steps you followed in the space provided below.

STEPS: ______________________________________________

______________________________________________

______________________________________________

Problem 2: Deleting Records from a Database File

a. Using the "Delete" option, delete the record of the music called "Not Tomorrow." Record the steps you followed in the space provided below.

STEPS: ______________________________________________

______________________________________________

______________________________________________

b. Display the records in the file. Record the steps you followed in the space provided below.

STEPS: ______________________________________________

______________________________________________

______________________________________________

c. You decided that this record should remain in the file. Enter the steps that will make the record part of the original file and no longer marked for deletion. Record the steps you followed in the space provided below.

STEPS: ______________________________________________

______________________________________________

______________________________________________

**Minicase 2 (continued)**

Problem 3: Changing the Records in a Database File

a. Using the "Replace" option, change the TYPE field for the record of the music called "America" from CS to LP. Record the steps you followed in the space provided below.

STEPS: ______________________________

b. Using the "Edit" option, change the music called "Camille" to "Carmen," the TYPE from LP to CD, and the cost from $8.95 to $11.95. Record the steps you followed in the space provided below.

STEPS: ______________________________

c. Obtain a listing of the records in the file. Record the steps you followed in the space provided below.

STEPS: ______________________________

Problem 4: The "Browse" Option

a. Delete and pack the five records added to the database file in Problem 1. Change the TYPE field in record 2 back to CS from LP.

b. Return to Problems 1, 2, and 3 of this minicase and use the "Browse" option to add, delete, and change records.

## Minicase 3: Computer Software Store

**Instructions:** Use the software inventory database that you created in Project 1 for the following problems. These problems require adding, deleting, and changing records in the database.

Problem 1: Adding Records to a Database File

a. Using the "Append" option, add the following records to the software inventory database file created in Project 1. Record the steps you followed in the space provided below.

| SOFTWARE NAME | COMPANY | CATEGORY | MS_DOS | QUANTITY | COST |
|---|---|---|---|---|---|
| Quick File | Electric Software | Database | Y | 10 | 99.95 |
| Math Drill | Edusoft Inc. | Education | N | 12 | 29.95 |
| Script Print | Graph Tech Inc. | WP | Y | 6 | 49.95 |
| Laser Print | Graph Tech Inc. | WP | N | 5 | 199.95 |
| Speed Calc | Anchor Software | Spreadsheet | Y | 20 | 49.95 |

STEPS: ______________________________

b. After adding the records to the database file, obtain a listing of the records using the "Display" option. Record the steps you followed in the space provided below.

STEPS: ______________________________________________

______________________________________________

______________________________________________

Problem 2: Deleting Records from a Database File

a. Using the "Delete" option, delete the Speed Calc record. Record the steps you followed in the space provided below.

STEPS: ______________________________________________

______________________________________________

______________________________________________

b. Display the records in the file. Record the steps you followed in the space provided below.

STEPS: ______________________________________________

______________________________________________

______________________________________________

c. You decided that this record should remain in the file. Enter the steps that will make the record part of the original file and no longer marked for deletion. Record the steps you followed in the space provided below.

STEPS: ______________________________________________

______________________________________________

______________________________________________

Problem 3: Changing the Records in a Database File

a. Using the "Replace" option, change the QUANTITY field for Databurst software from 5 to 4, the QUANTITY field for Image Fonts from 12 to 10, and the QUANTITY field for Print File from 16 to 10. Record the steps you followed in the space provided below.

STEPS: ______________________________________________

______________________________________________

______________________________________________

b. Using the "Edit" option, change the name of Type Ease software to Type Ease 1.0. Record the steps you followed in the space provided below.

STEPS: ______________________________________________

______________________________________________

______________________________________________

c. Obtain a listing of the records in the file. Record the steps you followed in the space provided below.

STEPS: ______________________________________________

______________________________________________

______________________________________________

**Minicase 3 (continued)**

Problem 4: The "Browse" Option

a. Delete and pack the records that you added to the database in Problem 1. Change the QUANTITY field for Databurst software back to 5, the QUANTITY field for Image Fonts to 12, and the QUANTITY field for Print File to 16. Also change the NAME field for Type Ease 1.0. back to Type Ease.

b. Return to Problems 1, 2, and 3 of this minicase. Use the "Browse" option to add, delete, and change records.

## Minicase 4: Home Sales

**Instructions:** Use the database of houses for sale that you created in Project 1 for the following problems. These problems require adding, deleting, and changing records in the database.

Problem 1: Adding Records to a Database File

a. Using the "Append" option, add the following checks to the home sales database file created in Project 1. Record the steps you followed in the space provided below.

| DATE | ADDRESS | CITY | ZIP | BDRM | BATH | POOL | PRICE |
|---|---|---|---|---|---|---|---|
| 12/15/90 | 321 Flora St. | Fullerton | 92633 | 4 | 2 | Y | 125000.00 |
| 12/15/90 | 499 Lake St. | Anaheim | 92644 | 3 | 1 | N | 98000.00 |
| 12/18/90 | 512 Sun Ave. | Fullerton | 92633 | 4 | 2 | N | 134900.00 |
| 12/18/90 | 221 Daisy Ln. | Garden Grove | 92641 | 3 | 2 | N | 110000.00 |

STEPS: ____________________

b. After adding the records to the database file, obtain a listing of the records using the "Display" option. Record the steps you followed in the space provided below.

STEPS: ____________________

Problem 2: Deleting Records from a Database File

a. Using the "Delete" option, delete the record of the house at 221 Daisy Ln. Record the steps you followed in the space provided below.

STEPS: ____________________

b. Display the records in the file. Record the steps you followed in the space provided below.

STEPS: ______________________________

c. You decided that this record should remain in the file. Enter the steps that will make the record part of the original file again and no longer marked for deletion. Record the steps you followed in the space provided below.

STEPS: ______________________________

Problem 3: Changing the Records in a Database File

a. Using the "Replace" option, change the PRICE field for the house at 182 Oak Ave. from $92,000.00 to $85,000.00. Record the steps you followed in the space provided below.

STEPS: ______________________________

b. Using the "Edit" option, change the address of the house at 926 Pine Ln. to 962 Pine St. Record the steps you followed in the space provided below.

STEPS: ______________________________

c. Obtain a listing of the records in the file. Record the steps you followed in the space provided below.

STEPS: ______________________________

Problem 4: The "Browse" Option

a. Delete and pack the records that were added in Problem 1. Change the PRICE field for the house at 182 Oak Ave. back to $92,000.00 and the address in Record 6 back to 926 Pine Ln.

b. Return to Problems 1, 2, and 3 of this minicase. Use the "Browse" option to add, delete, and change records.

# PROJECT 5

## Additional Topics

### Objectives

You will have mastered the material in this project when you can

- Change the characteristics of fields in a database file
- Add new fields to a database file
- Delete existing fields from a database file
- Create indexes for database files
- Use indexes in place of sorting
- Use indexes for rapid retrieval
- Create a view relating two database files
- Use a view for retrieving data from two database files

| OPTION | PURPOSE |
|---|---|
| Set Up | Activate a |
| Database file | database file |
| View | view |
| Quit dBASE III PLUS | leave dBASE III PLUS |
| Create | Create a |
| Database file | database file (extension DBF) |
| View | view (extension VUE) |
| Report | report (extension FRM) |
| Update | Change a database file by |
| Append | adding records at the end |
| Edit | changing records viewing one at a time |
| Browse | changing records viewing several at a time |
| Replace | changing the data in all records that satisfy some condition |
| Delete | deleting records |
| Recall | undeleting records |
| Pack | physically remove deleted records |
| Position | Move the record pointer by |
| Seek | finding a match using an index |
| Locate | finding the first record that satisfies some condition |
| Goto Record | specifying a record number |
| Retrieve | Retrieve data from a database file |
| List | show desired fields and records on the screen or printer |
| Display | like "List" (differences between the two are covered in the text) |
| Report | print a report |
| Sum | calculate a total |
| Average | calculate an average |
| Count | count the number of records |
| Organize | |
| Index | create an index (extension NDX) |
| Sort | sort a database file |
| Modify | Change an existing |
| Database file | database file |
| Report | report file |
| Tools | |
| List structure | show the structure of the active database file |

**FIGURE 5-1**
Menus and Options within the dBASE ASSISTANT

In this project, you will learn how to make changes to the structure of a database. You will be able to change the characteristics of existing fields, add additional fields, and delete fields. You will also learn about indexes and how they increase the efficiency of retrieval. Finally, you will learn about views and how they allow easy access to more than a single database file. You will use the menus and options within the ASSISTANT that are listed in Figure 5-1.

Before beginning the material in this project, start dBASE and activate the EMPLOYEE database file exactly as you have done before.

## CHANGING THE DATABASE STRUCTURE

### Why Change the Structure?

There are a variety of reasons why you might want to change the structure of a database file. Changes in users' needs might require additional fields. For example, if it is important to store the number of hours an employee has worked, we need to add such a field to the EMPLOYEE file, because it is not there already.

We might have to change the characteristics of a given field. It so happens that Mary Castleworth's name is stored incorrectly in the database. Rather than Castleworth, Mary T. it should be Castleworth, Marianne K. There is no problem changing the middle initial, but there is a big problem changing the first name from Mary to Marianne, because there isn't enough room in the NAME field to hold the correct name! To accommodate this change, we must increase the width of the NAME field.

It may turn out that a field in the database file is no longer necessary. If no one ever uses the DEPARTMENT field, for example, there is no point in having it in the database file. It is occupying space but serving no useful purpose. It would be nice to remove it.

Sometimes you discover that the structure you specified has some inherent problems. For example, you had to type a complete department name when entering each employee. Wouldn't it be easier to simply type a code number? This would make the data entry process simpler. It would also save space in the database, since storing a one- or two-character code number does not take as much space as storing a 10-character department name. Finally, it will cut down on errors during data entry. If you only have to type the number 01 rather than the name Accounting, you will be much less likely to make mistakes that can have serious consequences. If you inadvertently enter Accouning as the department for an employee, that employee will be *omitted* from any list of employees whose department is Accounting.

Thus, you might want to store the code number rather than the department number. What do you do, however, if you are supposed to print the department *name* on some crucial reports? The answer is that you create a separate table containing department numbers and names. This would mean that rather than the single table that you have been using (Figure 5-2), there will be two (Figure 5-3). Notice that the first table has no DEPARTMENT column but instead has a column for code numbers (DEPT_NUMB). The second table also has a DEPT_NUMB column as well as a column that contains the department name. Using these two tables still allows you to list the name of the department for each employee. To find the department name for Anthony Rapoza, you would first look in the DEPT_NUMB column in his row and find that he works in department 04. Then you would look for the row in the second table that contained 04 in the DEPT_NUMB column. Once you found it, you would look in the next column on the same row and see that department 04 is "Shipping." Thus, Anthony Rapoza works in the shipping department.



| EMPLOYEE NUMBER | EMPLOYEE NAME | DATE HIRED | DEPARTMENT NAME | PAY RATE | UNION MEMBER |
|---|---|---|---|---|---|
| 1011 | Rapoza, Anthony P. | 01/10/89 | Shipping | 8.50 | Y |
| 1013 | McCormack, Nigel L. | 01/15/89 | Shipping | 8.25 | Y |
| 1016 | Ackerman, David R. | 02/04/89 | Accounting | 9.75 | N |
| 1017 | Doi, Chang J. | 02/05/89 | Production | 6.00 | Y |
| 1020 | Castle, Mark C. | 03/04/89 | Shipping | 7.50 | Y |
| 1022 | Dunning, Lisa A. | 03/12/89 | Marketing | 9.10 | N |
| 1025 | Chaney, Joseph R. | 03/23/89 | Accounting | 8.00 | N |
| 1026 | Bender, Helen O. | 04/12/89 | Production | 7.00 | Y |
| 1029 | Anderson, Mariane L. | 04/18/89 | Shipping | 9.00 | Y |
| 1030 | Edwards, Kenneth J. | 04/23/89 | Production | 8.60 | Y |
| 1037 | Baxter, Charles W. | 05/05/89 | Accounting | 11.00 | N |
| 1041 | Evans, John T. | 05/19/89 | Marketing | 6.00 | N |
| 1056 | Andrews, Robert M. | 06/03/89 | Marketing | 9.00 | N |
| 1057 | Dugan, Mary L. | 06/10/89 | Production | 8.75 | Y |
| 1066 | Castleworth, Mary T. | 07/05/89 | Production | 8.75 | Y |
| 1070 | Fisher, Ella C. | 07/15/89 | Accounting | 8.00 | N |
| 1075 | Caine, William J. | 08/16/89 | Marketing | 9.25 | N |

**FIGURE 5-2** Employee Data in a Single File

Suppose that you also need to maintain some other information for each department, such as the department's office location, phone number, annual budget, and so on. With the approach that you have been using so far (Figure 5-2), you would have to add additional columns to the employee table: a column for location, a column for phone number, a column for annual budget, and so on. The location, phone number, and annual budget of the shipping department would appear on the first, second, fifth, and ninth rows in the employee table, since each of those rows contains employees in the shipping department. Doesn't this seem cumbersome? With the new approach (Figure 5-3), the new information would be added to the department table. In this case, the location, phone number, and annual budget of the shipping department would only appear on the fourth row, since that is the only row on which "Shipping" occurs. In this project you will focus on the two columns, DEPT_NUMB and DEPARTMENT NAME, as shown in Figure 5-3.

| EMPLOYEE NUMBER | EMPLOYEE NAME | DATE HIRED | PAY RATE | UNION MEMBER | DEPT NUMB |
|---|---|---|---|---|---|
| 1011 | Rapoza, Anthony P. | 01/10/89 | 8.50 | Y | 04 |
| 1013 | McCormack, Nigel L. | 01/15/89 | 8.25 | Y | 04 |
| 1016 | Ackerman, David R. | 02/04/89 | 9.75 | N | 01 |
| 1017 | Doi, Chang J. | 02/05/89 | 6.00 | Y | 03 |
| 1020 | Castle, Mark C. | 03/04/89 | 7.50 | Y | 04 |
| 1022 | Dunning, Lisa A. | 03/12/89 | 9.10 | N | 02 |
| 1025 | Chaney, Joseph R. | 03/23/89 | 8.00 | N | 01 |
| 1026 | Bender, Helen O. | 04/12/89 | 7.00 | Y | 03 |
| 1029 | Anderson, Mariane L. | 04/18/89 | 9.00 | Y | 04 |
| 1030 | Edwards, Kenneth J. | 04/23/89 | 8.60 | Y | 03 |
| 1037 | Baxter, Charles W. | 05/05/89 | 11.00 | N | 01 |
| 1041 | Evans, John T. | 05/19/89 | 6.00 | N | 02 |
| 1056 | Andrews, Robert M. | 06/03/89 | 9.00 | N | 02 |
| 1057 | Dugan, Mary L. | 06/10/89 | 8.75 | Y | 03 |
| 1066 | Castleworth, Marianne K. | 07/05/89 | 8.75 | Y | 03 |
| 1070 | Fisher, Ella C. | 07/15/89 | 8.00 | N | 01 |
| 1075 | Caine, William J. | 08/16/89 | 9.25 | N | 02 |

| DEPT NUMB | DEPARTMENT NAME |
|---|---|
| 01 | Accounting |
| 02 | Marketing |
| 03 | Production |
| 04 | Shipping |



**FIGURE 5-3** Employee Data Stored in Two Files

You now have a database that consists of more than one table or, in dBASE jargon, more than one database file. You will need a way of relating the two tables, that is, of using information from both. This is done by using what is called a view. You will see this a little later in this project. Before you can look at views, however, you must change the structure of the database from the one represented in Figure 5-2 to the one represented in Figure 5-3. You must also look at an important concept called an index.

To change the structure, you will:

1. Create and fill in the department database file (called DEPT).
2. Change the length of the NAME field in the EMPLOYEE database file to 24.
3. Add the DEPT_NUMB field to the EMPLOYEE file.
4. Fill in the DEPT_NUMB field with appropriate values.
5. Delete the DEPARTMENT field from the EMPLOYEE database file.

## Creating Additional Files

Before making changes to the EMPLOYEE file, create the file of departments mentioned in the previous section. Select "Database file" from the "Create" menu, choose drive B, and then enter the word DEPT as the name of the file. Describe the two fields shown in Figure 5-4 and then press the Enter key. Press the Enter key a second time to confirm that the information is correct.

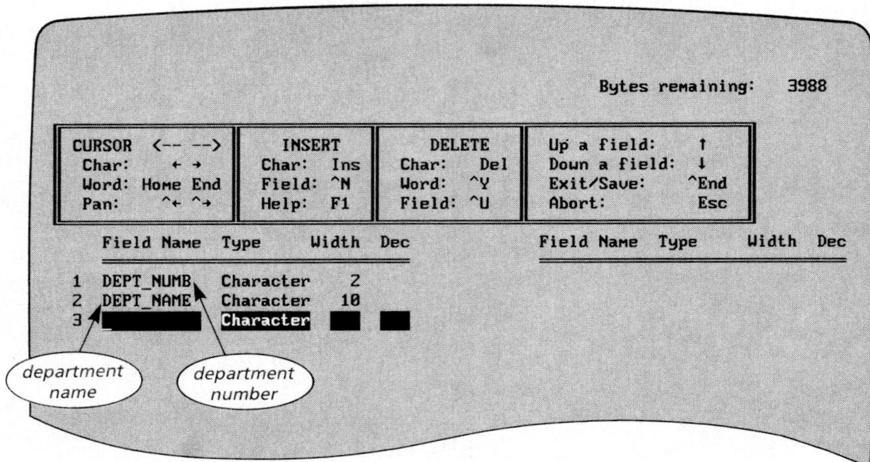


**FIGURE 5-4**
**Creating the DEPT Database File**

When asked if you wish to add data now, type the letter Y and then enter the data shown in Figure 5-5. The first record has 01 for the department number and Accounting for the department name. The second record has 02 for the number and Marketing for the name, and so on. Make sure to enter the zeros in the department number field. When you have added these four records, press Enter to complete the process.

| Record# | DEPT_NUMB | DEPT_NAME |
|---|---|---|
| 1 | 01 | Accounting |
| 2 | 02 | Marketing |
| 3 | 03 | Production |
| 4 | 04 | Shipping |

**FIGURE 5-5** Data for DEPT Database File

## Activating the Database File To Be Changed

The database file whose structure is to be changed must be activated. Activate the EMPLOYEE file now, using the "Database file" option of the "Set Up" menu.

To change the structure of the active database file, choose "Database file" from the "Modify" menu (Figure 5-6). The same screen you used to create the file in the first place is displayed along with all the current fields (Figure 5-7).

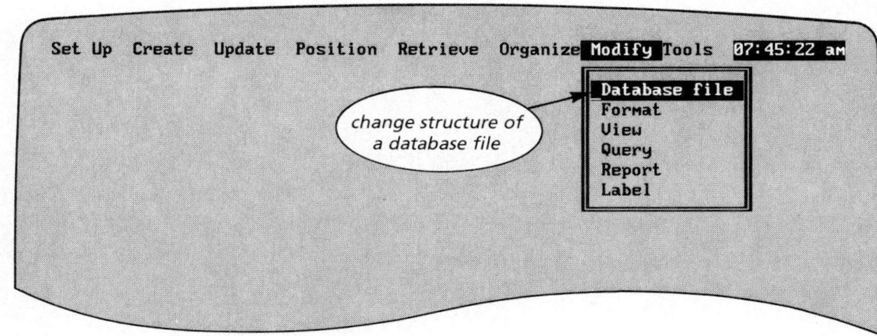


**FIGURE 5-6**
**Changing the Structure of a Database File**

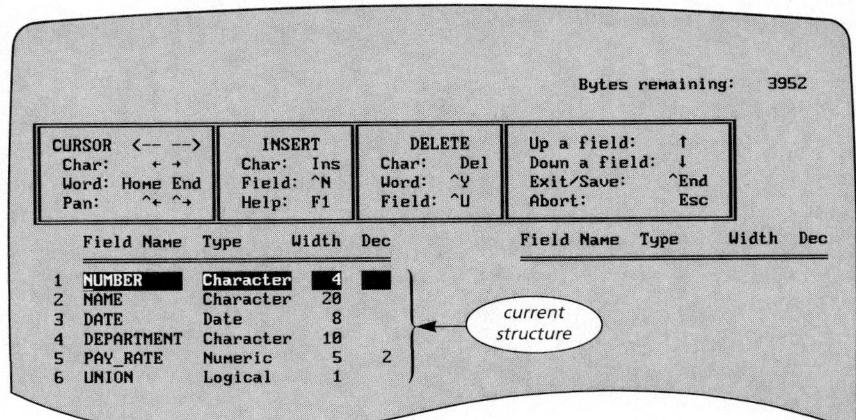


**FIGURE 5-7**
**Change Structure of a Database File**

## Changing the Characteristics of Fields

To change the characteristics of any field, repeatedly press the Enter key until the data to be changed is highlighted. In this case, move the highlight to the width column in the second row, type the number 24 (the new width for the NAME field), and press the Enter key.

## Adding New Fields

Keep pressing the Enter key until you have arrived at the bottom of the current list of fields. A new line will be created for you.

Type the words DEPT_NUMB as the name of the new field, choose Character for the type and enter the number 2 as the width, as shown in Figure 5-8. Another new line has been created for you. Since there are no other fields to add, simply press the Enter key.

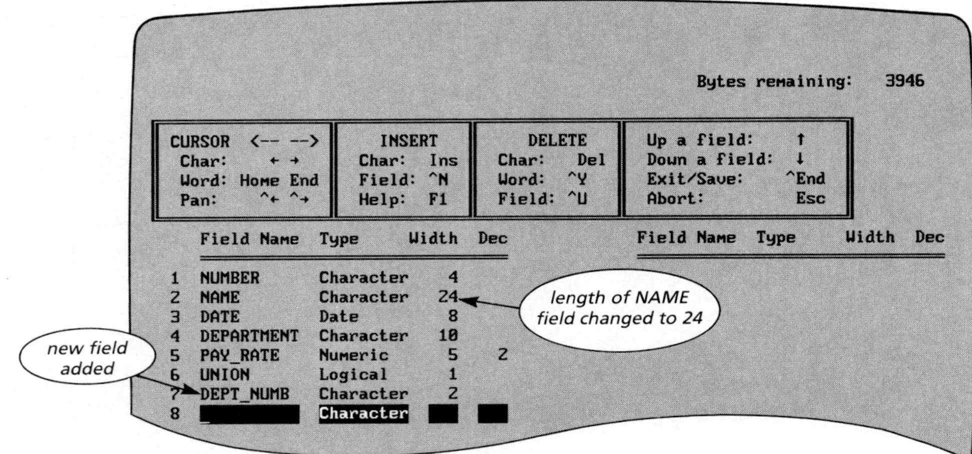


**FIGURE 5-8**
**Change Structure of a Database File**

Press the Enter key again as dBASE instructs you to and the changes will be made. The line at the bottom of your screen will state: "Database records will be APPENDED from backup fields of the same name only!!" This simply means that if you changed the name of any field, dBASE would not be able to keep the current data. Since you did not do so, there is no problem.

Once the process is complete, display all records and fields to see the screen shown in Figure 5-9. Note the new field, DEPT_NUMB, on the right. Since the headings do not fit on one line, dBASE wraps them around to the next. This is why the characters "DEPT" appear at the end of one line and "_NUMB" at the beginning of the next line. No entries have yet been filled in for DEPT_NUMB. Note also that the NAME field is wider than it was before.

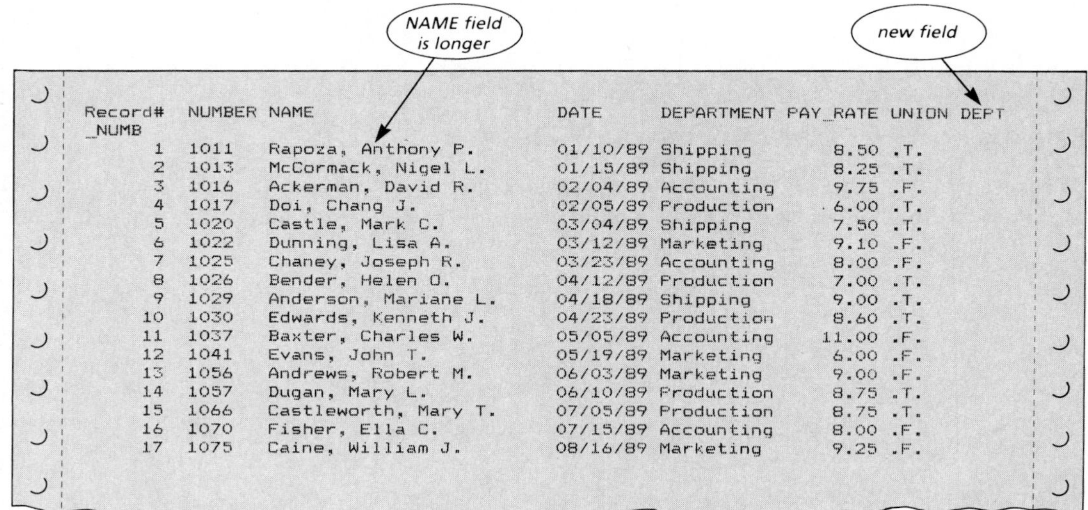


| Record# | NUMBER | NAME | DATE | DEPARTMENT | PAY_RATE | UNION | DEPT _NUMB |
|---|---|---|---|---|---|---|---|
| 1 | 1011 | Rapoza, Anthony P. | 01/10/89 | Shipping | 8.50 | .T. | |
| 2 | 1013 | McCormack, Nigel L. | 01/15/89 | Shipping | 8.25 | .T. | |
| 3 | 1016 | Ackerman, David R. | 02/04/89 | Accounting | 9.75 | .F. | |
| 4 | 1017 | Doi, Chang J. | 02/05/89 | Production | 6.00 | .T. | |
| 5 | 1020 | Castle, Mark C. | 03/04/89 | Shipping | 7.50 | .T. | |
| 6 | 1022 | Dunning, Lisa A. | 03/12/89 | Marketing | 9.10 | .F. | |
| 7 | 1025 | Chaney, Joseph R. | 03/23/89 | Accounting | 8.00 | .F. | |
| 8 | 1026 | Bender, Helen O. | 04/12/89 | Production | 7.00 | .T. | |
| 9 | 1029 | Anderson, Mariane L. | 04/18/89 | Shipping | 9.00 | .T. | |
| 10 | 1030 | Edwards, Kenneth J. | 04/23/89 | Production | 8.60 | .T. | |
| 11 | 1037 | Baxter, Charles W. | 05/05/89 | Accounting | 11.00 | .F. | |
| 12 | 1041 | Evans, John T. | 05/19/89 | Marketing | 6.00 | .F. | |
| 13 | 1056 | Andrews, Robert M. | 06/03/89 | Marketing | 9.00 | .F. | |
| 14 | 1057 | Dugan, Mary L. | 06/10/89 | Production | 8.75 | .T. | |
| 15 | 1066 | Castleworth, Mary T. | 07/05/89 | Production | 8.75 | .T. | |
| 16 | 1070 | Fisher, Ella C. | 07/15/89 | Accounting | 8.00 | .F. | |
| 17 | 1075 | Caine, William J. | 08/16/89 | Marketing | 9.25 | .F. | |

**FIGURE 5-9**
**Database File with New Structure**

## Making Entries for New Fields

To fill in the entries for DEPT_NUMB, you could use either "Edit" or "Browse" and simply proceed through each record. Whenever you encounter a record on which the value for DEPARTMENT is Accounting, set DEPT_NUMB to "01". If the value is "Marketing," set DEPT_NUMB to "02", and so on. Does this approach seem tedious to you? Even though there are only 17 records, it probably seems like a lot of busy work. What if there were several thousand records? It would take a long time to make these changes, with many chances to make errors. There must be an easier way.

Recall that the "Replace" option of the "Update" menu allowed you to make the same change to all records in a file that satisfy a given condition. This is exactly what you need. To use this option, choose "Replace" from the "Update" menu (Figure 5-10).

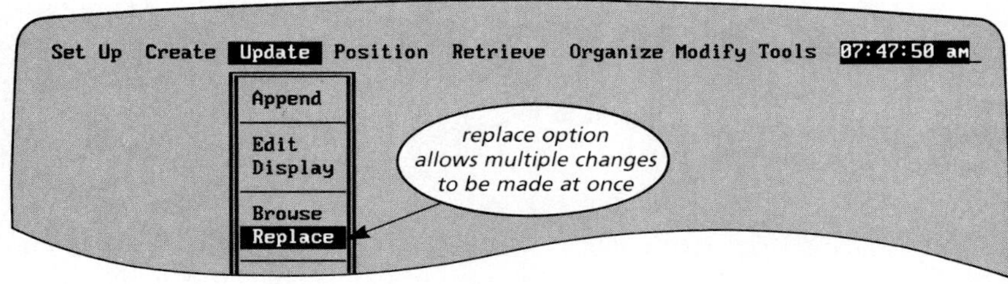


**FIGURE 5-10**
**Changing Data Using Replace**

Choose DEPT_NUMB from the field list that will be displayed by moving the cursor to it (Figure 5-11) and pressing the Enter key. You will next be asked for a character string (Figure 5-12). Enter the numbers 01. You can now choose other fields to replace. Press the Right Arrow key since this is the only field is to be changed.

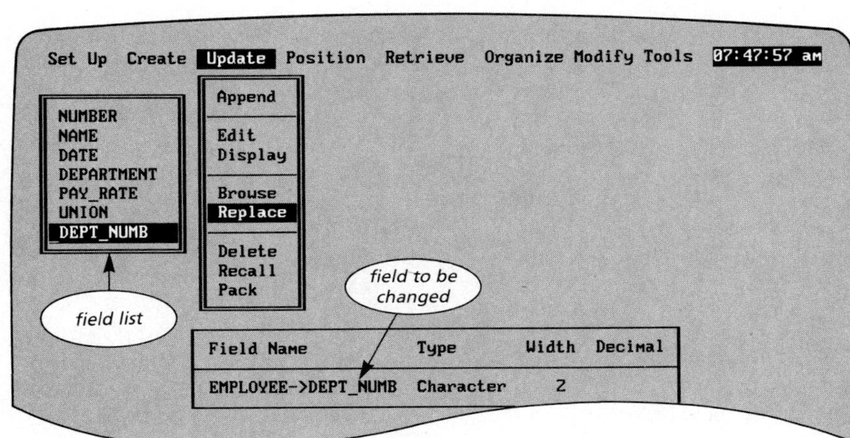


**FIGURE 5-11**
**Changing Data Using Replace**

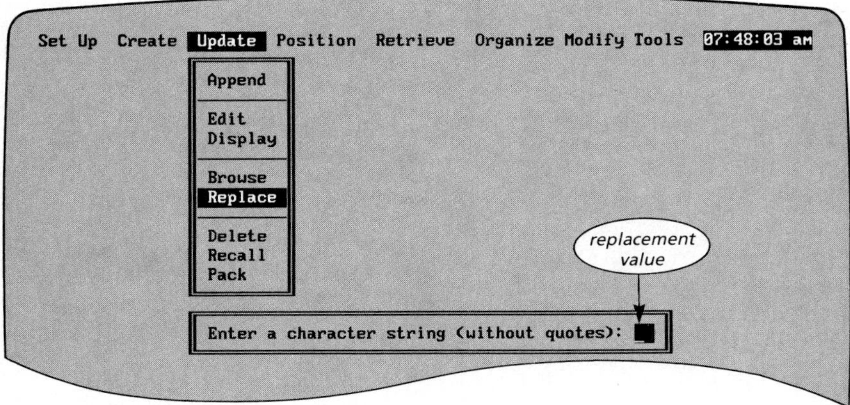


**FIGURE 5-12**
**Changing Data with Replace**

Next, select "Build a search condition" from the familiar box. Select the DEPARTMENT field in the usual manner, and then "Equal to." Enter the word Accounting as the character string and then choose "No more conditions."

Note the command dBASE has constructed for you (see Figure 5-13). Select "Execute the command." dBASE will replace the current value of DEPT_NUMB with 01 for all records in which DEPARTMENT is "Accounting." When this is done a message will appear on the screen indicating the number of records that were replaced (4).

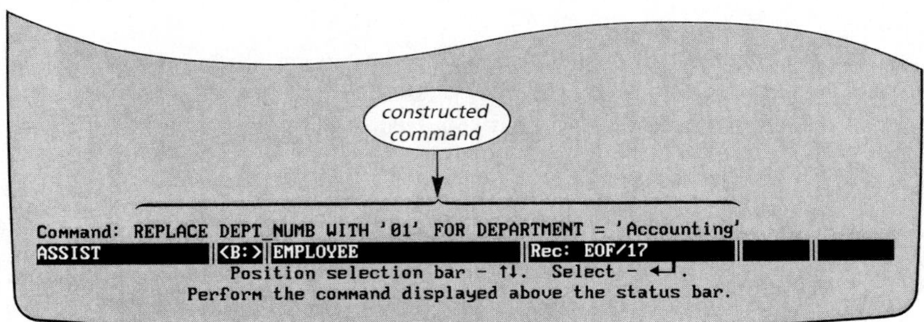


**FIGURE 5-13**
**Changing Data with Replace**

In exactly the same fashion, change the value for DEPT_NUMB to 02 for all records in which DEPARTMENT is "Marketing," 03 for all records in which DEPARTMENT is "Production," and 04 for all records in which DEPARTMENT is "Shipping." The changes are now complete and all records now contain an appropriate value in the DEPT_NUMB field.

## Making Other Corrections

Next, choose "Edit" from the "Update" menu and move to record 15 (Figure 5-14). Change the name from Castleworth, Mary T. to Castleworth, Marianne K. (Figure 5-15). If you have correctly changed the length of the NAME field, there should be sufficient room to make this change. Hold down the Ctrl key and press the End key to indicate that you are done.

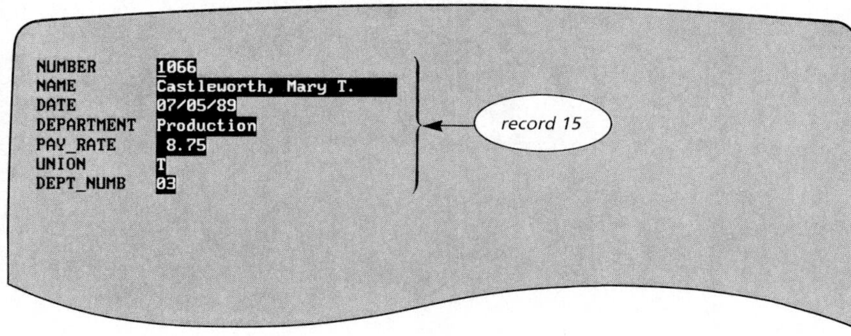


**FIGURE 5-14**
**Old Data for Record 15**

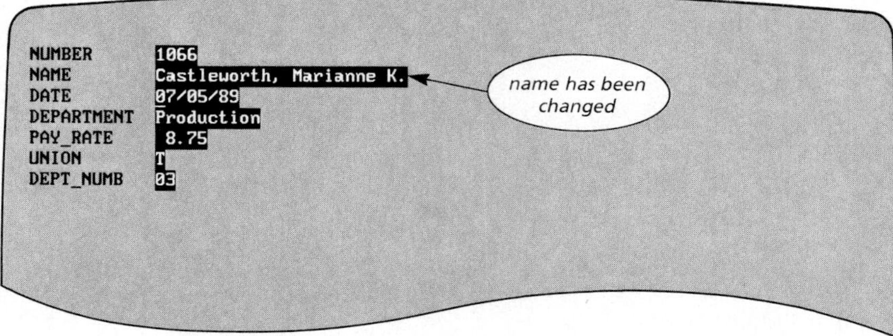


**FIGURE 5-15**
**New Data for Record 15**

At this point, display all records to produce the screen shown in Figure 5-16. Note that the DEPT_NUMB column contains the correct values and that the name of Marianne K. Castleworth is now correct.

| Record# | NUMBER | NAME | DATE | DEPARTMENT | PAY_RATE | UNION | DEPT _NUMB |
|---|---|---|---|---|---|---|---|
| 1 | 1011 | Rapoza, Anthony P. | 01/10/89 | Shipping | 8.50 | .T. | 04 |
| 2 | 1013 | McCormack, Nigel L. | 01/15/89 | Shipping | 8.25 | .T. | 04 |
| 3 | 1016 | Ackerman, David R. | 02/04/89 | Accounting | 9.75 | .F. | 01 |
| 4 | 1017 | Doi, Chang J. | 02/05/89 | Production | 6.00 | .T. | 03 |
| 5 | 1020 | Castle, Mark C. | 03/04/89 | Shipping | 7.50 | .T. | 04 |
| 6 | 1022 | Dunning, Lisa A. | 03/12/89 | Marketing | 9.10 | .F. | 02 |
| 7 | 1025 | Chaney, Joseph R. | 03/23/89 | Accounting | 8.00 | .F. | 01 |
| 8 | 1026 | Bender, Helen O. | 04/12/89 | Production | 7.00 | .T. | 03 |
| 9 | 1029 | Anderson, Mariane L. | 04/18/89 | Shipping | 9.00 | .T. | 04 |
| 10 | 1030 | Edwards, Kenneth J. | 04/23/89 | Production | 8.60 | .T. | 03 |
| 11 | 1037 | Baxter, Charles W. | 05/05/89 | Accounting | 11.00 | .F. | 01 |
| 12 | 1041 | Evans, John T. | 05/19/89 | Marketing | 6.00 | .F. | 02 |
| 13 | 1056 | Andrews, Robert M. | 06/03/89 | Marketing | 9.00 | .F. | 02 |
| 14 | 1057 | Dugan, Mary L. | 06/10/89 | Production | 8.75 | .T. | 03 |
| 15 | 1066 | Castleworth, Marianne K. | 07/05/89 | Production | 8.75 | .T. | 03 |
| 16 | 1070 | Fisher, Ella C. | 07/15/89 | Accounting | 8.00 | .F. | 01 |
| 17 | 1075 | Caine, William J. | 08/16/89 | Marketing | 9.25 | .F. | 02 |

*name has been lengthened*

*department numbers have been filled in*

**FIGURE 5-16 Changes Have Been Made**

## Deleting Fields

The DEPARTMENT field is no longer required so let's delete it. Choose "Database file" from the "Modify" menu, producing the display shown in Figure 5-17. Press the Enter key enough times to move the highlight to the fourth row (DEPARTMENT). Hold the Ctrl key down and type the letter U. Does this seem familiar to you? It is exactly the same way you delete records when using "Edit" or "Browse." Once this has been done, the field will disappear (Figure 5-18 on the next page). Since this is the only change you want to make, hold the Ctrl key down and press the End key. Press the Enter key to confirm that you want this change made.

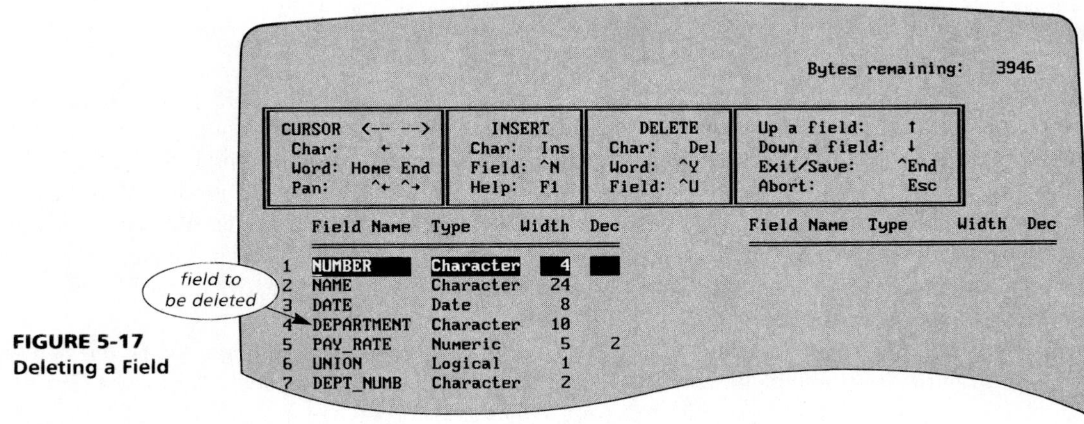


**FIGURE 5-17**
**Deleting a Field**

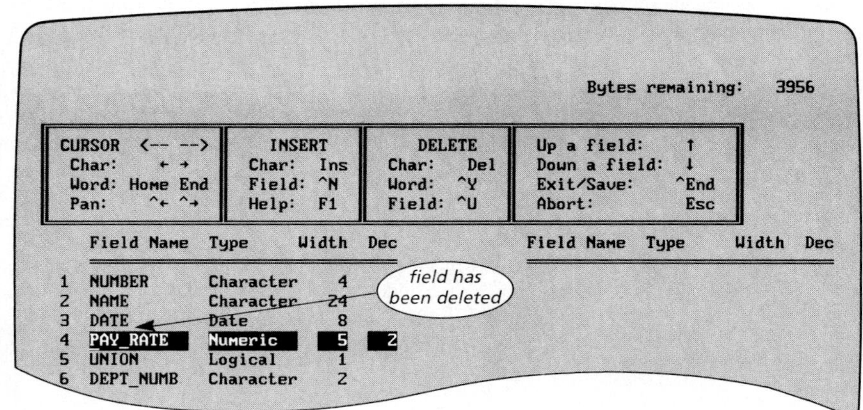


**FIGURE 5-18**
**Deleting a Field**

Now displaying all records produces the screen shown in Figure 5-19. Note that there is no DEPARTMENT column.

no DEPARTMENT field

| Record# | NUMBER | NAME | DATE | PAY_RATE | UNION | DEPT_NUMB |
|---|---|---|---|---|---|---|
| 1 | 1011 | Rapoza, Anthony P. | 01/10/89 | 8.50 | .T. | 04 |
| 2 | 1013 | McCormack, Nigel L. | 01/15/89 | 8.25 | .T. | 04 |
| 3 | 1016 | Ackerman, David R. | 02/04/89 | 9.75 | .F. | 01 |
| 4 | 1017 | Doi, Chang J. | 02/05/89 | 6.00 | .T. | 03 |
| 5 | 1020 | Castle, Mark C. | 03/04/89 | 7.50 | .T. | 04 |
| 6 | 1022 | Dunning, Lisa A. | 03/12/89 | 9.10 | .F. | 02 |
| 7 | 1025 | Chaney, Joseph R. | 03/23/89 | 8.00 | .F. | 01 |
| 8 | 1026 | Bender, Helen O. | 04/12/89 | 7.00 | .T. | 03 |
| 9 | 1029 | Anderson, Mariane L. | 04/18/89 | 9.00 | .T. | 04 |
| 10 | 1030 | Edwards, Kenneth J. | 04/23/89 | 8.60 | .T. | 03 |
| 11 | 1037 | Baxter, Charles W. | 05/05/89 | 11.00 | .F. | 01 |
| 12 | 1041 | Evans, John T. | 05/19/89 | 6.00 | .F. | 02 |
| 13 | 1056 | Andrews, Robert M. | 06/03/89 | 9.00 | .F. | 02 |
| 14 | 1057 | Dugan, Mary L. | 06/10/89 | 8.75 | .T. | 03 |
| 15 | 1066 | Castleworth, Marianne K. | 07/05/89 | 8.75 | .T. | 03 |
| 16 | 1070 | Fisher, Ella C. | 07/15/89 | 8.00 | .F. | 01 |
| 17 | 1075 | Caine, William J. | 08/16/89 | 9.25 | .F. | 02 |

**FIGURE 5-19**
**Field Has Been Deleted**

# INDEXES

## What Is an Index?

You are already familiar with the concept of an index. The index in the back of a book contains important words or phrases together with a list of pages on which the words or phrases can be found. An index for a database file is similar. Figure 5-20 shows the EMPLOYEE database file along with an index built on employee names. In this case, the items of interest are employee names rather than key words or phrases. Each employee name is listed along with the number of the record on which the employee name is found. If you were to use this index to find Helen Bender, for example, you would find her name in the index, look at the corresponding record number (8) and then go immediately to record 8 in the EMPLOYEE file. This is faster than looking at each employee name in turn. It is precisely what dBASE will do when using an index. Thus, indexes make the retrieval process much more efficient.

There is another benefit to indexes. They provide an efficient alternative to sorting. Look at the record numbers in the index. Suppose you need these to list all employees. That is, you simply follow down the record number column, listing the corresponding employees as you go. In this example, you would first list the employee on record 3 (David Ackerman), then the employee on record 9 (Mariane Anderson), then the employee on record 13 (Robert Andrews), and so on. You will be listing the employees in alphabetical order *without sorting the file*.

| REC NUM | EMPLOYEE NUMBER | EMPLOYEE NAME | DATE HIRED | PAY RATE | UNION MEMBER | DEPT NUMB |
|---|---|---|---|---|---|---|
| 1 | 1011 | Rapoza, Anthony P. | 01/10/89 | 8.50 | Y | 04 |
| 2 | 1013 | McCormack, Nigel L. | 01/15/89 | 8.25 | Y | 04 |
| 3 | 1016 | Ackerman, David R. | 02/04/89 | 9.75 | N | 01 |
| 4 | 1017 | Doi, Chang J. | 02/05/89 | 6.00 | Y | 03 |
| 5 | 1020 | Castle, Mark C. | 03/04/89 | 7.50 | Y | 04 |
| 6 | 1022 | Dunning, Lisa A. | 03/12/89 | 9.10 | N | 02 |
| 7 | 1025 | Chaney, Joseph R. | 03/23/89 | 8.00 | N | 01 |
| 8 | 1026 | Bender, Helen O. | 04/12/89 | 7.00 | Y | 03 |
| 9 | 1029 | Anderson, Mariane L. | 04/18/89 | 9.00 | Y | 04 |
| 10 | 1030 | Edwards, Kenneth J. | 04/23/89 | 8.60 | Y | 03 |
| 11 | 1037 | Baxter, Charles W. | 05/05/89 | 11.00 | N | 01 |
| 12 | 1041 | Evans, John T. | 05/19/89 | 6.00 | N | 02 |
| 13 | 1056 | Andrews, Robert M. | 06/03/89 | 9.00 | N | 02 |
| 14 | 1057 | Dugan, Mary L. | 06/10/89 | 8.75 | Y | 03 |
| 15 | 1066 | Castleworth, Mary T. | 07/05/89 | 8.75 | Y | 03 |
| 16 | 1070 | Fisher, Ella C. | 07/15/89 | 8.00 | N | 01 |
| 17 | 1075 | Caine, William J. | 08/16/89 | 9.25 | N | 02 |

**INDEX ON NAME**

| EMPLOYEE NAME | REC NUM |
|---|---|
| Ackerman, David R. | 3 |
| Anderson, Mariane L. | 9 |
| Andrews, Robert M. | 13 |
| Baxter, Charles W. | 11 |
| Bender, Helen O. | 8 |
| Castle, Mark C. | 5 |
| Castleworth, Mary T. | 15 |
| Chaney, Joseph R. | 7 |
| Doi, Chang J. | 4 |
| Dugan, Mary L. | 14 |
| Dunning, Lisa A. | 6 |
| Edwards, Kenneth J. | 10 |
| Evans, John T. | 12 |
| McCormack, Nigel L. | 2 |
| Rapoza, Anthony P. | 1 |

**FIGURE 5-20** Use of an Index

## Creating Indexes

To create an index, choose the "Index" option of the "Organize" menu (Figure 5-21). The next step is to define the **index key**, that is, the field or fields on which the index will be built (Figure 5-22).

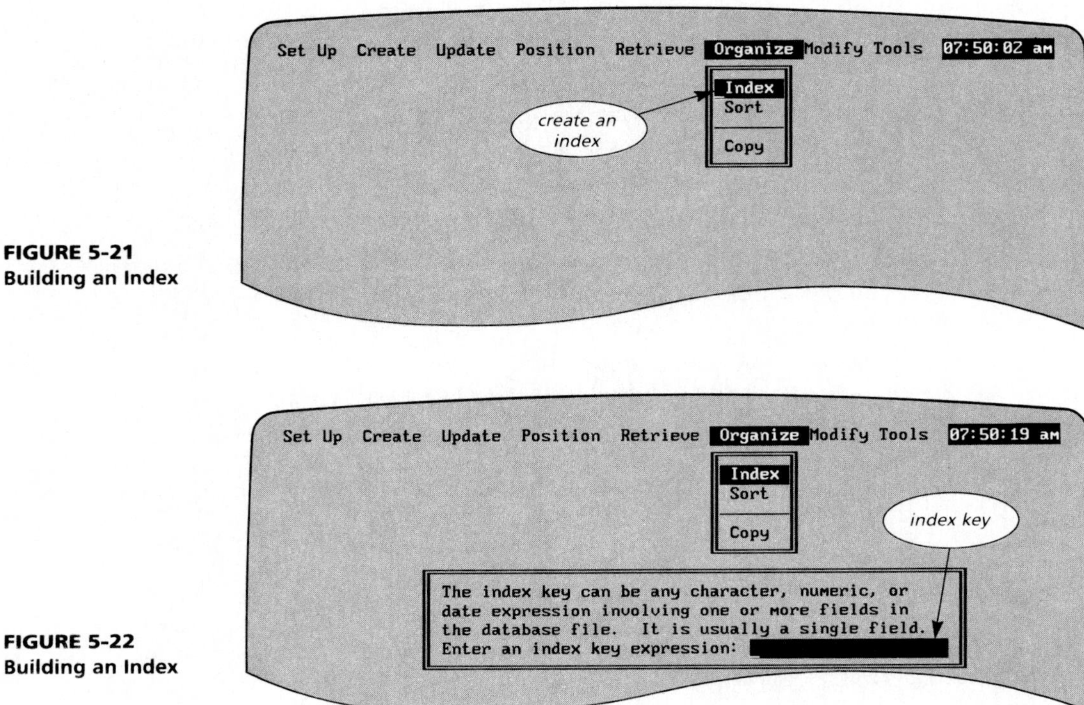


**FIGURE 5-21**
**Building an Index**

**FIGURE 5-22**
**Building an Index**

**Indexing on a Single Field** You can define the index key by simply typing the name of the field. Alternatively, you could press F10 to get a field list. Once you have done this, your display will look like the one shown in Figure 5-23. In this figure, the highlight has already been moved to NAME, the field on which the index is to be built.

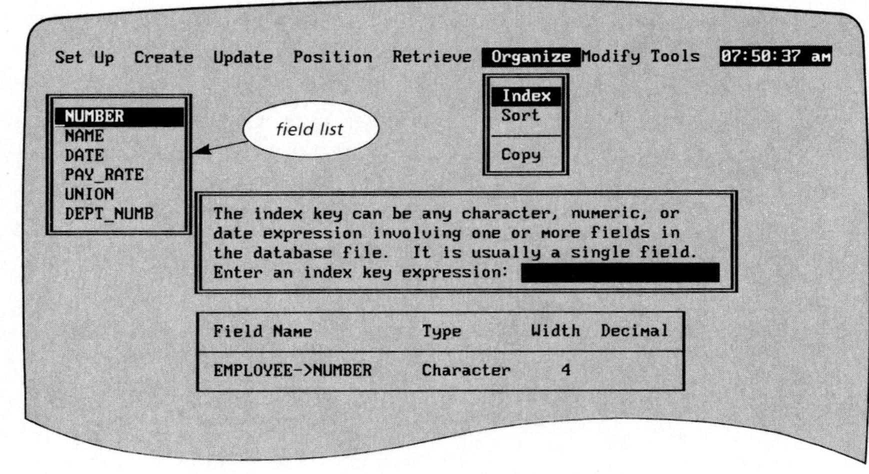


**FIGURE 5-23**
**Building an Index**

Next, press the Enter key, producing the display shown in Figure 5-24. You could specify additional fields at this point. In this case, however, the index key is only the NAME field, so press the Enter key.

Next, you must indicate the drive on which the index file is to be placed. Make sure the B: is highlighted and press the Enter key. The final step is to enter the name of the index file. Enter the word empind1 and press the Enter key. The index will be created. When the process is complete, you will see a message indicating that the file is 100% indexed and that 17 records were indexed. At this point, press any key to continue.

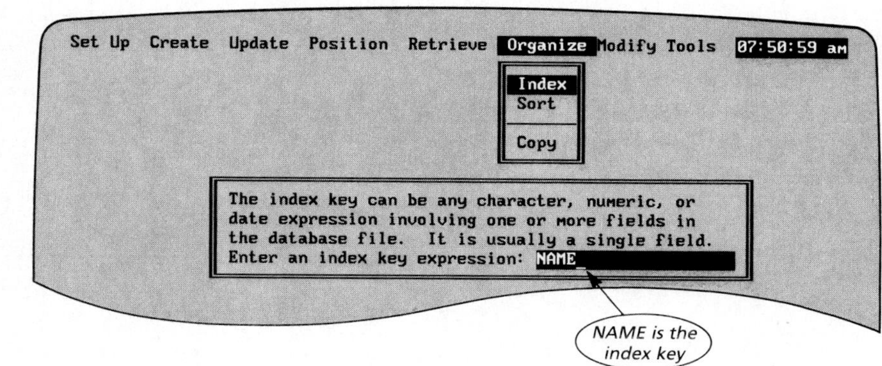


**FIGURE 5-24**
**Building an Index**

If you now display all the records, you will see the results shown in Figure 5-25. Note that the records appear to be sorted by name, even though the file itself has not been sorted.

*file appears to be sorted by NAME*

| Record# | NUMBER | NAME | DATE | PAY_RATE | UNION | DEPT_NUMB |
|---|---|---|---|---|---|---|
| 3 | 1016 | Ackerman, David R. | 02/04/89 | 9.75 | .F. | 01 |
| 9 | 1029 | Anderson, Mariane L. | 04/18/89 | 9.00 | .T. | 04 |
| 13 | 1056 | Andrews, Robert M. | 06/03/89 | 9.00 | .F. | 02 |
| 11 | 1037 | Baxter, Charles W. | 05/05/89 | 11.00 | .F. | 01 |
| 8 | 1026 | Bender, Helen O. | 04/12/89 | 7.00 | .T. | 03 |
| 17 | 1075 | Caine, William J. | 08/16/89 | 9.25 | .F. | 02 |
| 5 | 1020 | Castle, Mark C. | 03/04/89 | 7.50 | .T. | 04 |
| 15 | 1066 | Castleworth, Marianne K. | 07/05/89 | 8.75 | .T. | 03 |
| 7 | 1025 | Chaney, Joseph R. | 03/23/89 | 8.00 | .F. | 01 |
| 4 | 1017 | Doi, Chang J. | 02/05/89 | 6.00 | .T. | 03 |
| 14 | 1057 | Dugan, Mary L. | 06/10/89 | 8.75 | .T. | 03 |
| 6 | 1022 | Dunning, Lisa A. | 03/12/89 | 9.10 | .F. | 02 |
| 10 | 1030 | Edwards, Kenneth J. | 04/23/89 | 8.60 | .T. | 03 |
| 12 | 1041 | Evans, John T. | 05/19/89 | 6.00 | .F. | 02 |
| 16 | 1070 | Fisher, Ella C. | 07/15/89 | 8.00 | .F. | 01 |
| 2 | 1013 | McCormack, Nigel L. | 01/15/89 | 8.25 | .T. | 04 |
| 1 | 1011 | Rapoza, Anthony P. | 01/10/89 | 8.50 | .T. | 04 |

**FIGURE 5-25 Employee Data Using Index**

**Indexing on Multiple Fields** It is possible to build an index on a combination of fields. The process is almost identical to that for building an index on a single field. To build an index on the combination of DEPT_NUMB and NAME, for example, the only difference is that you define the index key to be DEPT_NUMB + NAME. You could simply type this expression directly. Alternatively, you could press F10 for a field menu, choose DEPT_NUMB, type the symbol +, press F10 for another field menu, and choose NAME.

In either case, once you have entered the expression, press the Enter key, choose drive B, and then type the word empind2 as the name of this index file. Now, if you display all the records, you will see the display shown in Figure 5-26. Note that the records appear to be sorted by name *within* department.

file appears to be sorted by NAME within DEPT_NUMB

| Record# | NUMBER | NAME | DATE | PAY_RATE | UNION | DEPT_NUMB |
|---|---|---|---|---|---|---|
| 3 | 1016 | Ackerman, David R. | 02/04/89 | 9.75 | .F. | 01 |
| 11 | 1037 | Baxter, Charles W. | 05/05/89 | 11.00 | .F. | 01 |
| 7 | 1025 | Chaney, Joseph R. | 03/23/89 | 8.00 | .F. | 01 |
| 16 | 1070 | Fisher, Ella C. | 07/15/89 | 8.00 | .F. | 01 |
| 13 | 1056 | Andrews, Robert M. | 06/03/89 | 9.00 | .F. | 02 |
| 17 | 1075 | Caine, William J. | 08/16/89 | 9.25 | .F. | 02 |
| 6 | 1022 | Dunning, Lisa A. | 03/12/89 | 9.10 | .F. | 02 |
| 12 | 1041 | Evans, John T. | 05/19/89 | 6.00 | .F. | 02 |
| 8 | 1026 | Bender, Helen O. | 04/12/89 | 7.00 | .T. | 03 |
| 15 | 1066 | Castleworth, Marianne K. | 07/05/89 | 8.75 | .T. | 03 |
| 4 | 1017 | Doi, Chang J. | 02/05/89 | 6.00 | .T. | 03 |
| 14 | 1057 | Dugan, Mary L. | 06/10/89 | 8.75 | .T. | 03 |
| 10 | 1030 | Edwards, Kenneth J. | 04/23/89 | 8.60 | .T. | 03 |
| 9 | 1029 | Anderson, Mariane L. | 04/18/89 | 9.00 | .T. | 04 |
| 5 | 1020 | Castle, Mark C. | 03/04/89 | 7.50 | .T. | 04 |
| 2 | 1013 | McCormack, Nigel L. | 01/15/89 | 8.25 | .T. | 04 |
| 1 | 1011 | Rapoza, Anthony P. | 01/10/89 | 8.50 | .T. | 04 |

**FIGURE 5-26 Employee Data Using Index**

Unfortunately, to build an index on a combination of fields, both fields must be of character type. This means that you couldn't use the same technique to build an index on the combination of DEPARTMENT and PAY_RATE, for example. There are ways around this problem, but they are beyond the scope of this text. Fortunately, you usually won't need to do this. If you ever find yourself in such a situation, consult the dBASE manual.

## Using Indexes

One use for indexes is as an alternative to sorting. The index on the NAME field caused the database file to *appear* to be in name order. The index on the combination of the DEPARTMENT and NAME fields caused it to appear to be sorted by name within department.

The other use for indexes is to allow you to rapidly find records. Build an index on the NUMBER field and call it empind3. Use the "Index" option of the "Organize" menu, select NUMBER as the index key, press the Enter key, choose drive B, and enter the word empind3 as name of the file. If you were to list the records now, they would appear to be sorted by employee number.

Now let's suppose that you to find employee 1037. Choose "Seek" from the "Position" menu (Figure 5-27). You will then be asked to enter an expression. Enter the number 1037 as shown Figure 5-28. The quote marks are crucial, since the NUMBER field is of character type. Without them, dBASE would indicate that there is a "Data type mismatch." Once you have entered the number, press the Enter key. If there were no such employee, dBASE would display the message "No find." If, as is the case here, there is such an employee, this employee's record will become the current active record. Displaying a single record would cause the data for employee 1037 to be displayed as shown in Figure 5-29.

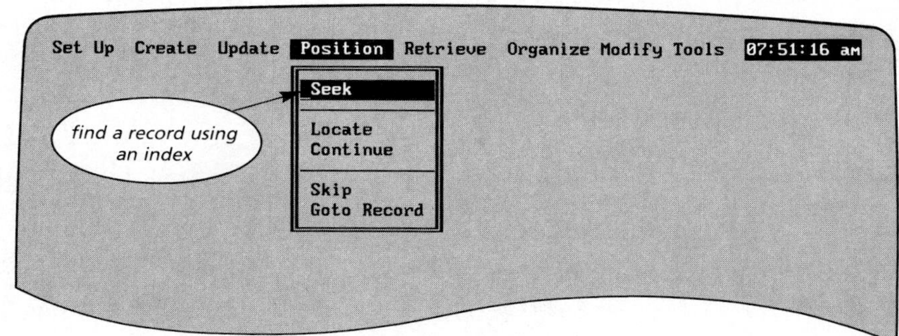


**FIGURE 5-27**
**Using "Seek" to Find a Record**

**FIGURE 5-28**
**Using "Seek" to Find a Record**

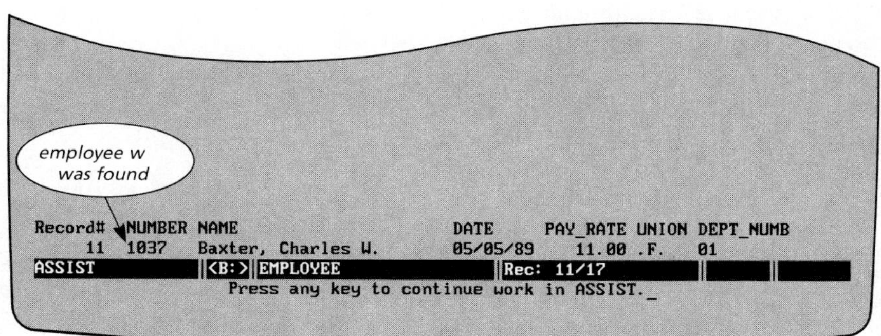


**FIGURE 5-29**
**Desired Record**

At this point, you might wonder what value this option has. You may recall that you used the "Locate" option to accomplish the same task back in Project 2. Why is this "Seek" option necessary?

The answer is that the "Seek" option, which only works if you are using an index, is *much* more efficient than the "Locate" option. The "Seek" option will use the index to go directly to the desired record. The "Locate" option steps through every record looking for one that will match the condition. In the case of a file with only a handful of records, this doesn't make much difference. But imagine a file with 50,000 records in which the record that you want happens to be record 40,176. Think about the time it will take if dBASE has to look at the first 40,175 records before finding the one you want. In such a case, the difference between "Seek" and "Locate" will be dramatic.

**Activating Indexes** To activate an index, simply type the letter Y in response to the question "Is the file indexed?" dBASE will present you with a list of possible indexes (Figure 5-30). Note that each index contains the extension NDX, which was added automatically by dBASE.

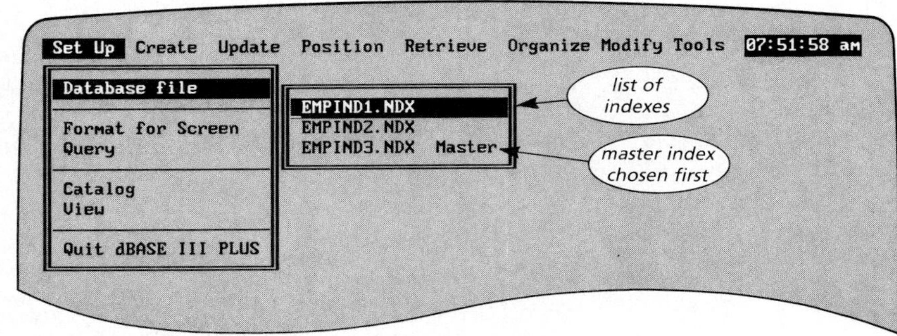


**FIGURE 5-30**
**Activating Indexes**

Simply move the highlight to the desired index and press Enter (in the figure this has already been done). In this example, EMPIND3 was chosen. Recall that this is the index built on employee number. Thus, dBASE can rapidly retrieve employees on the basis of their numbers. Also, a list of employees will automatically appear in numbered order. If you wanted one of the other orders, such as name, you would pick a different index.

You can pick more than one index. The other indexes will not affect the order. The only reason to select additional indexes is that any index selected will be kept current by dBASE; that is, if you make a change to the database that requires changing the index, dBASE will do so. Adding additional employees, for example, requires changes to all indexes. Changing the name of an employee would require a change to the index that was built on NAME but not to any others. Any index not selected will not be kept current.

To select additional indexes, simply move the highlight to them and press Enter. dBASE will indicate that these indexes have been selected by placing numbers (02, 03, and so on) after these indexes. Once all indexes have been selected, press the Left Arrow key to indicate that you are done with this step.

**Keeping Indexes Current** As long as you activate all indexes associated with a database file whenever you activate the file, the indexes will be kept current. But what if you forget? If an index does not match the actual data in the database it is useless. How can you fix an index that is no longer current? The answer is simple. The "Pack" option of the "Update" menu not only physically removes records marked for deletion, it also recreates the data in all indexes that are active. If you activate a database file and all its indexes and then choose "Pack," all indexes will be valid when you are done.

## VIEWS

### What Is a View?

To access data from more than one database file in dBASE, you use a view. A **view** is a pseudotable or pseudodatabase file that can combine two or more existing database files. Calling it a pseudodatabase file simply means it appears to the user to be a database file. The data doesn't really exist in this fashion, however. Instead, dBASE will assemble the data for you at the time you use the view.

To see how it works, consider the two database files shown in Figure 5-31, EMPLOYEE and DEPT. There is a special kind of relationship, called a **one-to-many relationship**, between these two files. In this case *one* department is associated with *many* employees, but each employee is associated with *one* department. Department 01, for example, is associated with employees 1016, 1025, 1037, and 1070. Employee 1016, on the other hand, is associated with *only* department 01. DEPT is called the "one" database file and EMPLOYEE is called the "many" database file in this relationship.

When two database files are related in this fashion, they can become part of a view. In such a case, you work with the "many" database file and dBASE automatically keeps track of which record in the "one" file is associated with the current active in the "many" file. For example, if record 1 (employee 1011) is the current active record, dBASE knows that the related record in the DEPT file is record 4 (department 04) since the department numbers match (see the arrow in Figure 5-31). dBASE will allow you to use not only fields in the EMPLOYEE file but also any fields in the DEPT file. Thus, if you list the department name for employee 1011, you will get "Shipping," since it is the name on the related record in the DEPT file.

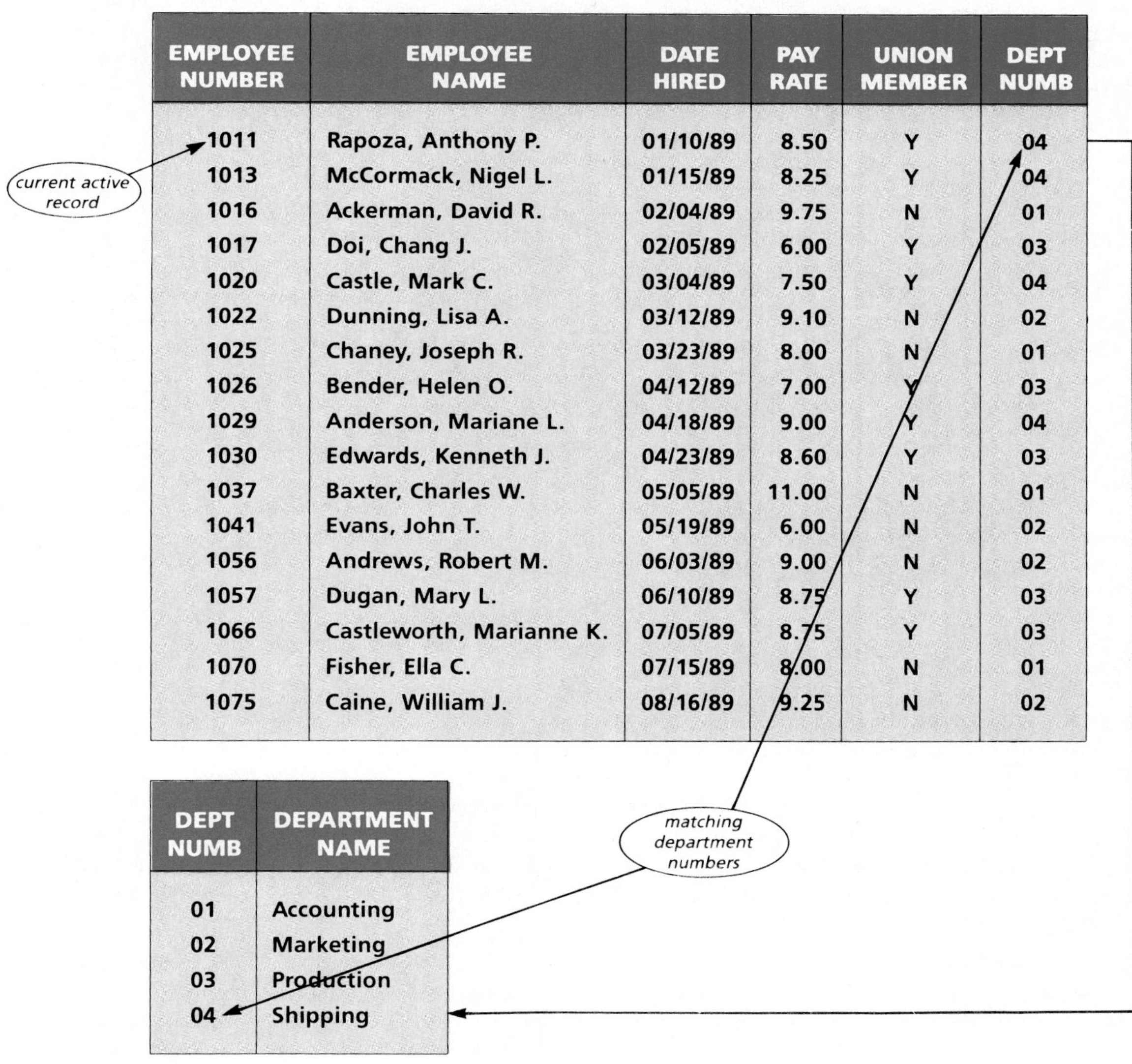

| EMPLOYEE NUMBER | EMPLOYEE NAME | DATE HIRED | PAY RATE | UNION MEMBER | DEPT NUMB |
|---|---|---|---|---|---|
| 1011 | Rapoza, Anthony P. | 01/10/89 | 8.50 | Y | 04 |
| 1013 | McCormack, Nigel L. | 01/15/89 | 8.25 | Y | 04 |
| 1016 | Ackerman, David R. | 02/04/89 | 9.75 | N | 01 |
| 1017 | Doi, Chang J. | 02/05/89 | 6.00 | Y | 03 |
| 1020 | Castle, Mark C. | 03/04/89 | 7.50 | Y | 04 |
| 1022 | Dunning, Lisa A. | 03/12/89 | 9.10 | N | 02 |
| 1025 | Chaney, Joseph R. | 03/23/89 | 8.00 | N | 01 |
| 1026 | Bender, Helen O. | 04/12/89 | 7.00 | Y | 03 |
| 1029 | Anderson, Mariane L. | 04/18/89 | 9.00 | Y | 04 |
| 1030 | Edwards, Kenneth J. | 04/23/89 | 8.60 | Y | 03 |
| 1037 | Baxter, Charles W. | 05/05/89 | 11.00 | N | 01 |
| 1041 | Evans, John T. | 05/19/89 | 6.00 | N | 02 |
| 1056 | Andrews, Robert M. | 06/03/89 | 9.00 | N | 02 |
| 1057 | Dugan, Mary L. | 06/10/89 | 8.75 | Y | 03 |
| 1066 | Castleworth, Marianne K. | 07/05/89 | 8.75 | Y | 03 |
| 1070 | Fisher, Ella C. | 07/15/89 | 8.00 | N | 01 |
| 1075 | Caine, William J. | 08/16/89 | 9.25 | N | 02 |

| DEPT NUMB | DEPARTMENT NAME |
|---|---|
| 01 | Accounting |
| 02 | Marketing |
| 03 | Production |
| 04 | Shipping |



**FIGURE 5-31** Relating Database Files

Suppose you make record 3 the current active record (Figure 5-32). Then the corresponding record in the DEPT file is record 1 (department 01). If you list the department name for this employee, you will get "Accounting."



| EMPLOYEE NUMBER | EMPLOYEE NAME | DATE HIRED | PAY RATE | UNION MEMBER | DEPT NUMB |
|---|---|---|---|---|---|
| 1011 | Rapoza, Anthony P. | 01/10/89 | 8.50 | Y | 04 |
| 1013 | McCormack, Nigel L. | 01/15/89 | 8.25 | Y | 04 |
| 1016 | Ackerman, David R. | 02/04/89 | 9.75 | N | 01 |
| 1017 | Doi, Chang J. | 02/05/89 | 6.00 | Y | 03 |
| 1020 | Castle, Mark C. | 03/04/89 | 7.50 | Y | 04 |
| 1022 | Dunning, Lisa A. | 03/12/89 | 9.10 | N | 02 |
| 1025 | Chaney, Joseph R. | 03/23/89 | 8.00 | N | 01 |
| 1026 | Bender, Helen O. | 04/12/89 | 7.00 | Y | 03 |
| 1029 | Anderson, Mariane L. | 04/18/89 | 9.00 | Y | 04 |
| 1030 | Edwards, Kenneth J. | 04/23/89 | 8.60 | Y | 03 |
| 1037 | Baxter, Charles W. | 05/05/89 | 11.00 | N | 01 |
| 1041 | Evans, John T. | 05/19/89 | 6.00 | N | 02 |
| 1056 | Andrews, Robert M. | 06/03/89 | 9.00 | N | 02 |
| 1057 | Dugan, Mary L. | 06/10/89 | 8.75 | Y | 03 |
| 1066 | Castleworth, Marianne K. | 07/05/89 | 8.75 | Y | 03 |
| 1070 | Fisher, Ella C. | 07/15/89 | 8.00 | N | 01 |
| 1075 | Caine, William J. | 08/16/89 | 9.25 | N | 02 |

| DEPT NUMB | DEPARTMENT NAME |
|---|---|
| 01 | Accounting |
| 02 | Marketing |
| 03 | Production |
| 04 | Shipping |

**FIGURE 5-32** **Relating Database Files**

When accessing such a view, you don't have to be aware of these details. dBASE will handle them automatically. Simply indicate that you wish the department name included on a display or report and dBASE will ensure that it is the correct name.

## Creating Views

Before beginning the process of creating the view, activate the DEPT database file and build an index on DEPT_NUMB. Call the index DEPTIND1. Once you have finished this process, activate the EMPLOYEE file in the usual manner, without indexes. Then, choose "View" from the "Create" menu (Figure 5-33). Indicate that the view will be created on drive B and that the name of the view file will be "empdept."

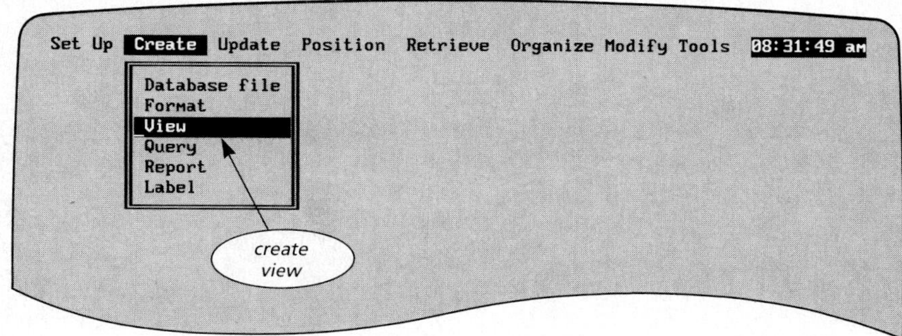


**FIGURE 5-33**
**Creating a View**

**Selecting Database Files** You are now asked to select the database files that will be represented in the view (Figure 5-34). When you select one, a special mark will appear in front of its name in the list. Note that there already is such a mark in front of EMPLOYEE, the active database file. dBASE assumes that you will want to choose this one. To choose any other, move the highlight to it and press the Enter key. A similar mark will appear in front of the database file you have selected. You can remove the mark (that is, *de*select a previously selected file) by moving the highlight to it and pressing the Enter key. If you don't want the active database file included in the view, it is a simple matter to remove the mark.

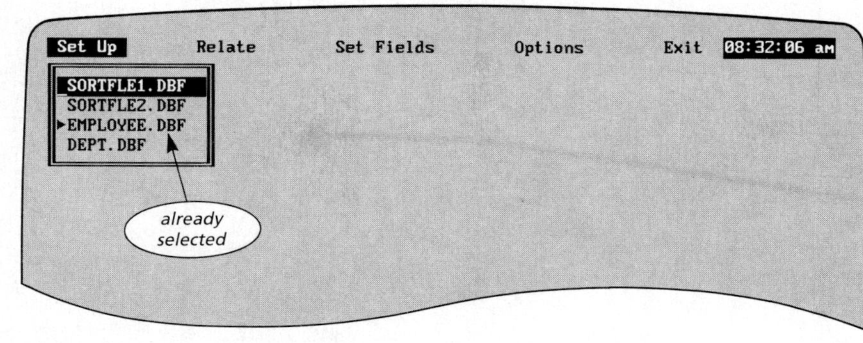


**FIGURE 5-34**
**Selecting Database Files for a View**

In your case, you want EMPLOYEE.DBF, which is already selected, and DEPT.DBF, which is not. Highlight DEPT.DBF and press the Enter key. When you do so, the display shown in Figure 5-35 will appear. You are asked to select an index file for DEPT.DBF. It is essential that you select an index built on the field that will be used to match records with EMPLOYEE.DBF. In this case, this field is DEPT_NUMB. Fortunately, such an index already exists. It is called DEPTIND1.NDX. If it did not exist, you would have to create it using the method discussed earlier. Select this index by moving the highlight to it and pressing the Enter key. There are no other indexes to select, so use the Left Arrow key to leave this process.

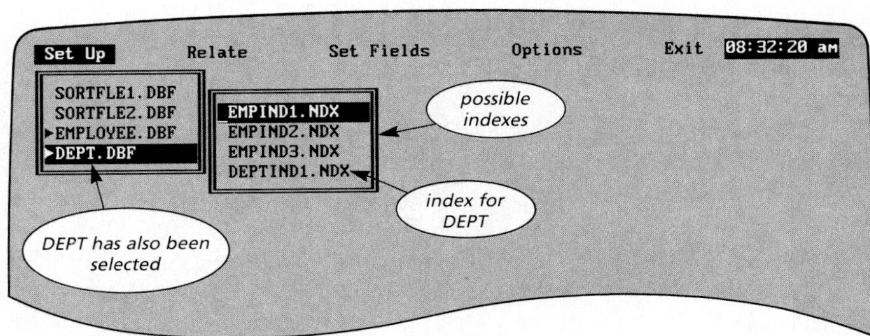


**FIGURE 5-35**
**Selecting Database Files for a View**

**Relating Database Files** Next, use the Right Arrow key to move to "Relate." This option (Figure 5-36) is used to indicate the relationship between the database files. You must first select the database file that represents the "many" part of the relationship, in this case, EMPLOYEE.DBF. With the highlight on EMPLOYEE.DBF, the "many" part of the relationship, press the Enter key, producing the display shown in Figure 5-37.

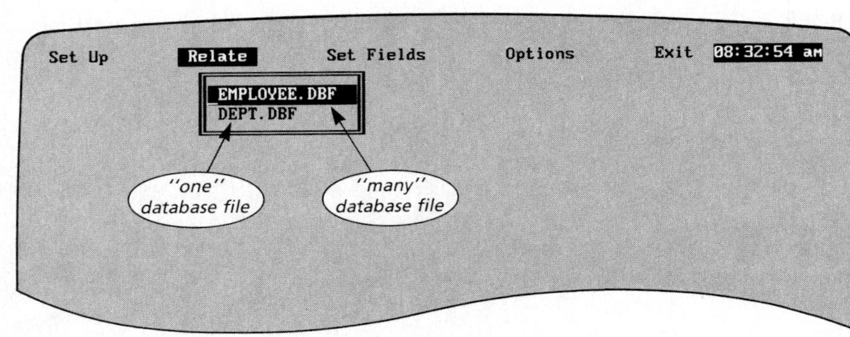


**FIGURE 5-36**
**Relating Database Files**

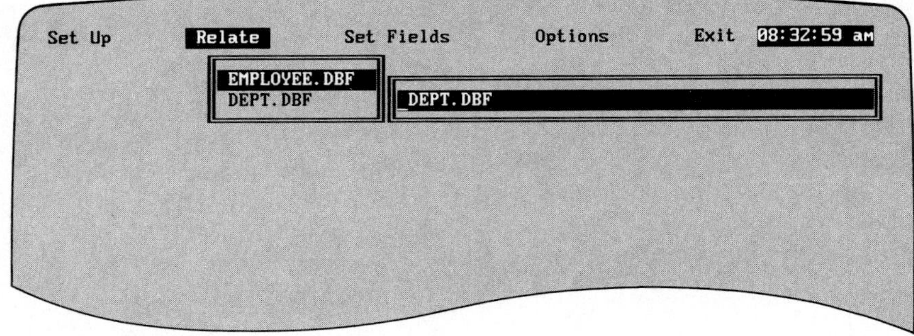


**FIGURE 5-37**
**How Database Files Are Related**

In the right-hand box, you must indicate the database file that represents the "one" part of the relationship. It might seem strange that you have to do this. It should be obvious that it must be the only other database file, namely DEPT.DBF. The reason that it must be specified is that dBASE permits more than two database files to be included in a view. In general, this step would indicate which of the other database files forms this part of the relationship.

Next you must indicate how the two files are to be related, that is, which fields in the two files must match. In the database file that is the "one" part of the relationship, dBASE automatically assumes that the field is the one on which the index was built. In your case, that means dBASE will assume that the field within the DEPT.DBF database file is DEPT_NUMB. So you only need to identify the matching field within EMPLOYEE.DBF. To do so, press the Enter key, producing the display shown in Figure 5-38. The mark that follows DEPT.DBF indicates that you must make an entry, namely, the matching field in the other database file, EMPLOYEE.DBF.

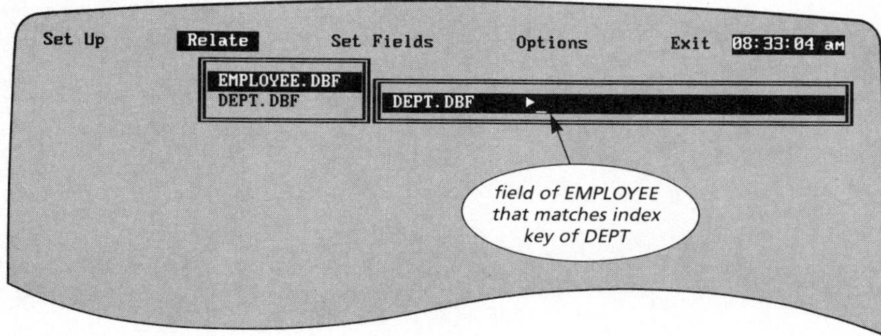


**FIGURE 5-38**
**How Database Files Are Related**

You can type the name of the field directly. Alternatively, you can press F10 to get a field menu, move the highlight to DEPT_NUMB, and press the Enter key. In either case, you produce the screen shown in Figure 5-39. Press the Enter key a final time and then the Left Arrow key to indicate you are done. The mark will be removed.

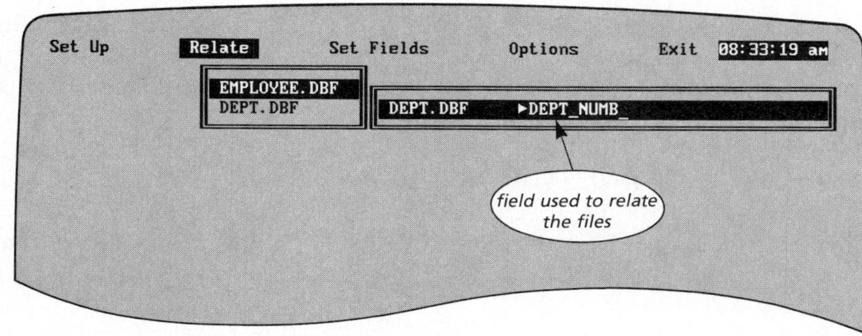


**FIGURE 5-39**
**How Database Files Are Related**

**Selecting Fields** The final part of the process is to indicate which fields from both tables are to be included in the view. To do so, press the Right Arrow key to move to "Set fields" (Figure 5-40). To indicate which of the fields from EMPLOYEE.DBF you want to include, press the Enter key while the highlight is on EMPLOYEE.DBF, producing the display shown in Figure 5-41.

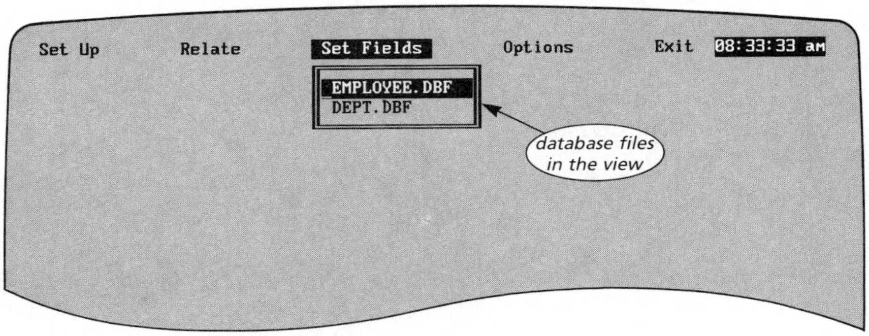

**FIGURE 5-40**
**Selecting Fields To Be Included**

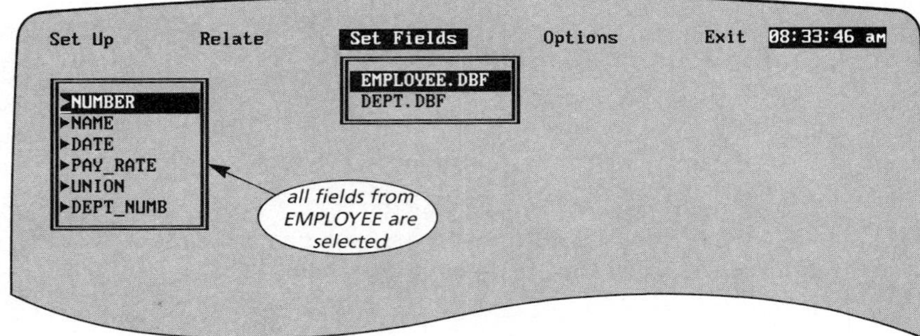


**FIGURE 5-41**
**Selecting Fields To Be Included**

All fields are listed within the box at the left. The mark in front of a field signifies that it is currently selected, or currently considered to be part of the view. You can "deselect" a field by moving the highlight to it and pressing the Enter key, in which case the mark will disappear. In this case you want all of these fields included, so just press the Right Arrow key to remove this box from the screen.

Next, move the highlight to DEPT.DBF and press the Enter key. The fields from DEPT.DBF are displayed (Figure 5-42). You have chosen to include the field DEPT_NUMB from the EMPLOYEE.DBF file, so there is no need to include DEPT_NUMB from the DEPT.DBF file (remember that the two must match). Press the Enter key with the highlight on DEPT_NUMB to deselect this field. Next, press the Right Arrow key to remove the box from the screen.

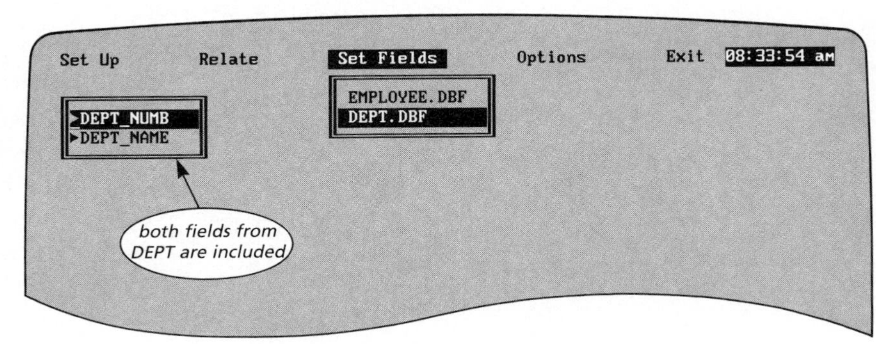


**FIGURE 5-42**
**Selecting Fields To Be Included in the View**

Press the Right Arrow key a second time to move to "Options." You will not use these options, so press the Right arrow key again to move to "Exit." With the highlight on "Save," press the Enter key to save your work.

## Using Views

The display of all records shown in Figure 5-43 could be produced using either "List" or "Display." This particular one has been printed. If you display it on your screen, you will see only one screen full at a time. If you want to print it, use the "List" option and answer Y when dBASE asks you if the result is to be sent to the printer. Note that the department names listed for each employee are exactly what they should be.

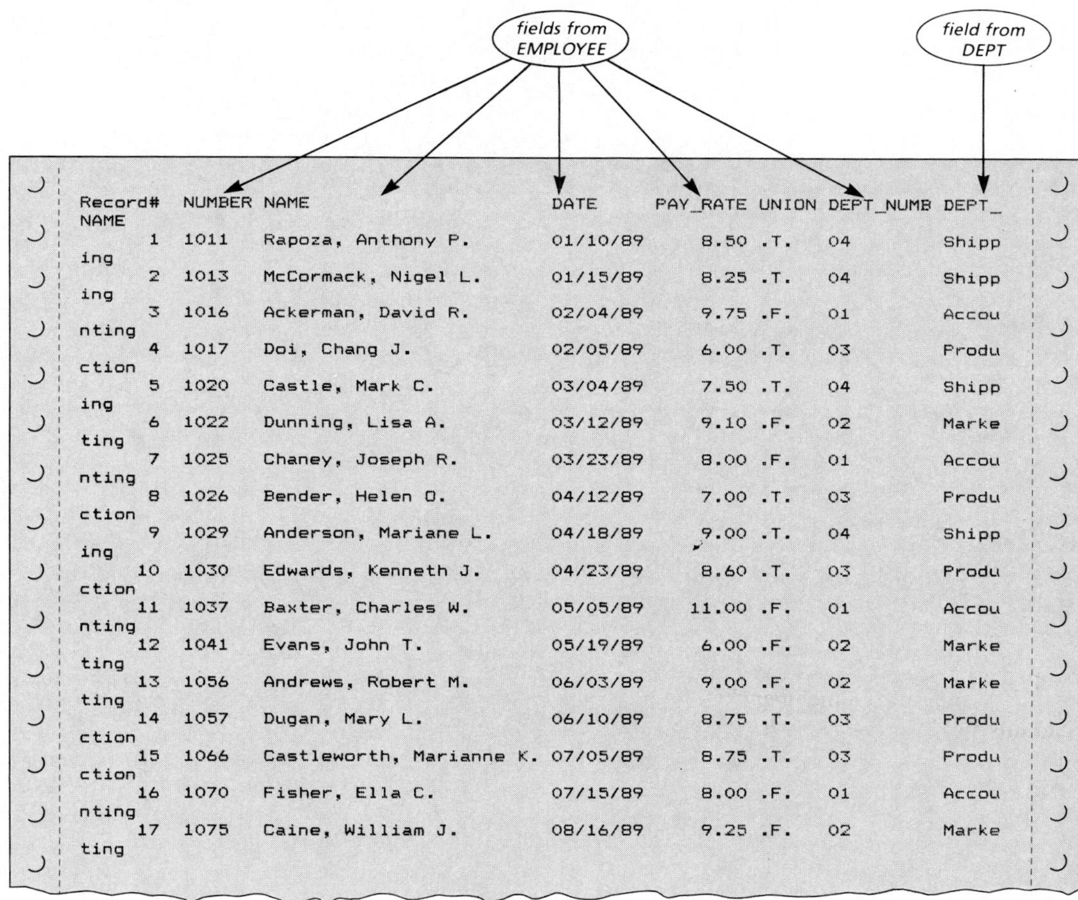


```
Record#  NUMBER NAME                      DATE       PAY_RATE UNION DEPT_NUMB DEPT_
NAME
      1  1011   Rapoza, Anthony P.        01/10/89       8.50 .T.   04        Shipp
ing
      2  1013   McCormack, Nigel L.       01/15/89       8.25 .T.   04        Shipp
ing
      3  1016   Ackerman, David R.        02/04/89       9.75 .F.   01        Accou
nting
      4  1017   Doi, Chang J.             02/05/89       6.00 .T.   03        Produ
ction
      5  1020   Castle, Mark C.           03/04/89       7.50 .T.   04        Shipp
ing
      6  1022   Dunning, Lisa A.          03/12/89       9.10 .F.   02        Marke
ting
      7  1025   Chaney, Joseph R.         03/23/89       8.00 .F.   01        Accou
nting
      8  1026   Bender, Helen O.          04/12/89       7.00 .T.   03        Produ
ction
      9  1029   Anderson, Mariane L.      04/18/89       9.00 .T.   04        Shipp
ing
     10  1030   Edwards, Kenneth J.       04/23/89       8.60 .T.   03        Produ
ction
     11  1037   Baxter, Charles W.        05/05/89      11.00 .F.   01        Accou
nting
     12  1041   Evans, John T.            05/19/89       6.00 .F.   02        Marke
ting
     13  1056   Andrews, Robert M.        06/03/89       9.00 .F.   02        Marke
ting
     14  1057   Dugan, Mary L.            06/10/89       8.75 .T.   03        Produ
ction
     15  1066   Castleworth, Marianne K.  07/05/89       8.75 .T.   03        Produ
ction
     16  1070   Fisher, Ella C.           07/15/89       8.00 .F.   01        Accou
nting
     17  1075   Caine, William J.         08/16/89       9.25 .F.   02        Marke
ting
```

**FIGURE 5-43** Data in the View

Next, use the "Display" option again, choose a scope of "ALL," and then choose "Construct a field list." In the list of fields displayed on the screen (Figure 5-44), you will see all the fields in the view, the fields from EMPLOYEE.DBF as well as those from DEPT.DBF. Simply select the ones you want in exactly the same manner as before. In this case, select NUMBER, NAME, and DEPT_NAME. When you are done, choose "Execute the command" and you will see the results shown in Figure 5-45.

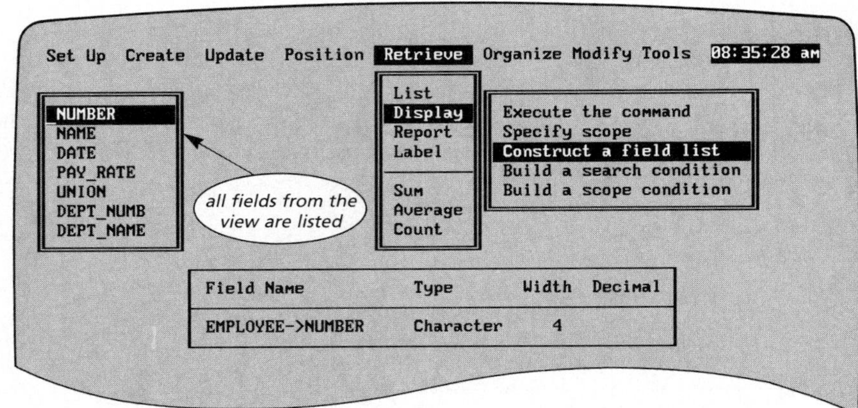


**FIGURE 5-44**
**Selecting Fields from the View**

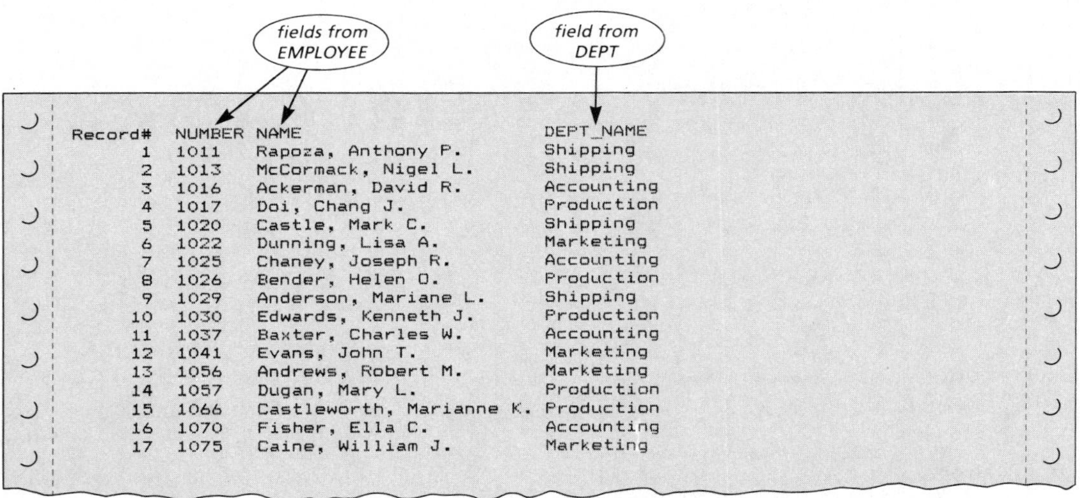


**FIGURE 5-45 Selecting Fields from the View**

Since you just constructed this view, it is considered to be active. Once you leave dBASE, however, it will no longer be active. To use it again, you must activate it by choosing "View" from the "Set Up" menu, indicating the drive on which the view is found, and then selecting the view from the list that is displayed (Figure 5-46). You do this *instead of* selecting a database file. Once this has been done, you can use the view exactly as you did before. You can use all the options on the "Retrieve" menu with views. You can create reports for views. You can sort views producing database files containing the sorted data. The only thing you really should not do with the view is update the data. That should be done by updating the individual database files that are part of the view.

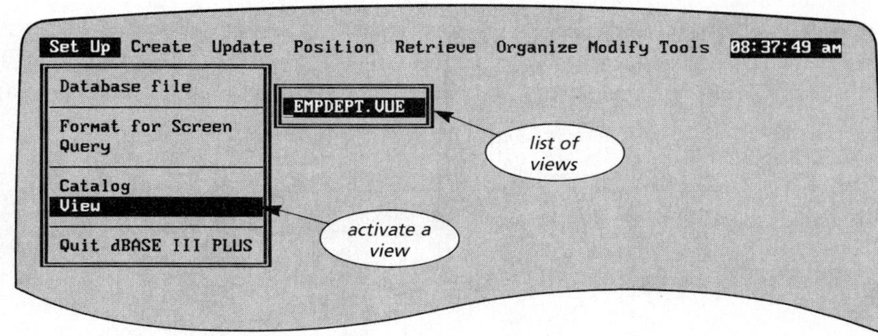


**FIGURE 5-46**
**Activating a View**

## Special Considerations

There are some special considerations concerning views:

1. When you have activated a view, only the "many" database file (in the example, the EMPLOYEE database file) is displayed in the status bar. Don't worry about this. You can access all the fields that you selected for the view regardless of which database file they are in.
2. To update any of the data, update the appropriate database file. For example, to add a new employee, activate the EMPLOYEE database file and use the "Append" option of the "Update" menu to add the employee. To change the name of an employee, activate the EMPLOYEE database file and use the "Edit" option. To add a new department, though, activate the DEPT database file before using the "Append" option.
3. The data never exists in the form represented in a view. Rather, dBASE draws data from the underlying database files and assembles it in the form defined for the view *at the time you access the view*. No special action is taken beforehand. The nice thing about this arrangement is that, whenever changes are made to any of the database files included in the view, you will automatically see the results of these changes the next time you use the view. You don't need to recreate the view to access the current data.

# PROJECT SUMMARY

In Project 5 you learned how to change the structure of a database file using the "Database file" option of the "Modify" menu. You saw how to add new fields, change the characteristics of existing fields, and delete fields. You also learned how to create indexes, using the "Index" option of the "Organize" menu. You can use these indexes in place of sorting as well as to increase retrieval efficiency. You learned how to create a view encompassing data from two database files, using the "View" option of the "Retrieve" menu. You also saw that data could be retrieved from a view in the same manner as from an individual database file.

If you followed along with the steps in this chapter, you have changed the structure of your database file, created an additional database file, created some indexes, and created a view. If you did not do these things but wish to do so at this time, you can use the following keystroke sequence. Start dBASE in the usual manner. Then type the following:

**SUMMARY OF KEYSTROKES—Project 5**

| STEPS | KEY(S) PRESSED | RESULTS | STEPS | KEY(S) PRESSED | RESULTS |
|---|---|---|---|---|---|
| 1 | → ↵ ↵dept↵ | | 20 | Ctrl-End | Name changed |
| 2 | DEPT_NUMB↵ ↵2↵ | | 21 | (Move to the "Modify" menu, then do the following) | |
| 3 | DEPT_NAME↵ ↵12↵ ↵ ↵Y | | 22 | ↵ ↵ ↵ ↵ ↵ ↵ ↵ ↵ ↵ Ctrl-U Ctrl-End ↵ | DEPARTMENT field deleted |
| 4 | 01Accounting↵ | | 23 | (Move to the "Organize" menu, then do the following) | |
| 5 | 02Marketing↵ | | 24 | ↵ F10 ↓ ↵ ↵ ↵ | |
| 6 | 03Production↵ | | 25 | empind1↵ ↵ | Index built |
| 7 | 04Shipping↵ ↵ | DEPT file created | 26 | ↵DEPT_NUMB + NAME↵ ↵ | |
| 8 | ← ↵ ↵ ↵ ↵ | EMPLOYEE file activated | 27 | empind2↵ ↵ | Second index built |
| 9 | → → → → → → ↵ | | 28 | ↵NUMBER↵ ↵empind3↵ ↵ | Third index built |
| 10 | ↵ ↵ ↵ ↵ ↵24↵ | | 29 | ↵'1037'↵ ↵ | Employee found |
| 11 | ↵ ↵ ↵ ↵ ↵ ↵ ↵ ↵ ↵ ↵ ↵ | | 30 | (Activate DEPT using the "Database file" option of the "Set Up" menu, then do the following) | |
| 12 | DEPT_NUMB↵ ↵2↵ ↵ ↵ | EMPLOYEE file structure modified | 31 | → → → → → ↵DEPT_NUMB↵ ↵deptind1 ↵ ↵ | Index built for DEPT |
| 13 | (Move to the "Update" menu, then do the following)↓↓↓↓↵ | | 32 | Activate the EMPLOYEE file without any indexes using the "Database file" option of the "Set Up" menu, then do the following) | |
| 14 | ↓↓↓↓↓↓↵01→↓↓ ↵↓↓↓↵↵Accounting ↵↑↑↵↵ | | 33 | →↓↓↵↵empdept↵ | |
| 15 | ↵↓↓↓↓↓↓↵02→↓↓ ↵↓↓↓↵↵Marketing ↵↵↑↑↵↵ | | 34 | ↓↓↓↵ (Note: Make sure DEPT.DBF is highlighted before pressing ENTER) | |
| 16 | ↵↓↓↓↓↓↓↵03→↓↓ ↵↓↓↓↵↵Production ↵↑↑↵↵ | | 35 | ↓↓↓↵ (Note: Make sure DEPTIND1.NDX is highlighted before pressing ENTER) | |
| 17 | ↵↓↓↓↓↓↓↵04→↓↓ ↵↓↓↓↵↵Shipping↵ ↵↑↑↵↵ | Values entered for DEPT_NUMB | 36 | ← → ↵ ↵ F10 ↓↓↓↓↓ ↵ ↵ ← → | |
| 18 | ↑↑↑↵ | | 37 | ↓ ↵ ↵ → → → ↵ | View created |
| 19 | PgUp PgUp ↵Castleworth, Marianne K. | | | | |

The following list summarizes the material covered in Project 5:

1. To change the structure of a database file, activate the database file in the usual way, then choose the "Database file" option from the "Modify" menu.
2. To change the characteristics of a field, move the highlight to the data to be changed and enter the new value.
3. To add a field, move the highlight to the beginning of the first row past all the existing fields, then type in the name and characteristics of the new field.
4. To make mass changes to the new field, use the "Replace" option of the "Update" menu.
5. To delete a field, use the "Database file" option from the "Modify" menu, move the highlight to the field to be deleted, hold the Ctrl key down, and type the letter U.
6. An **index key** is the field or combination of fields on which an index is built.
7. To build an index, use the "Index" option of the "Modify" menu. Specify the index key and the name of the file to hold the index.
8. To build an index on multiple fields, the fields should be character fields. Enter the names of the fields separated by plus signs.
9. If an index is active, records in a database file appear to be sorted in the order of the index key.
10. An index may be used to allow rapid retrieval of individual records on the basis of the index key.
11. Indexes are activated when they are created. They can be activated later using the "Database file" option of the "Set Up" menu by indicating that the file is indexed and then selecting the appropriate indexes from the list presented on the screen. The first index selected is the master or controlling index. The other selected indexes will be kept up to date when changes are made to data in the database.
12. If indexes are out of date, they can be made current by activating them and then choosing "Pack" from the "Update" menu.
13. A **view** is a pseudotable or pseudodatabase file.
14. A **one-to-many** relationship between two database files occurs when one record in one of the files is related to many records in the second but each record in the second is related to only one record in the first. The first database file is called the "one" database file and the second is called the "many" database file.
15. To create a view, use the "View" option of the "Create" menu. Specify the database files to be included in the view, the relationship between these database files, and the fields from the database files that are to be included.
16. To activate a view, use the "View" option of the "Set Up" menu. The database files that comprise the view are then activated automatically.
17. Once activated, a view may be used in displays and reports just as though it were a database file. It may also be sorted, producing a database file.
18. To update any of the data in a view, update the appropriate database file.

## STUDENT ASSIGNMENTS

### STUDENT ASSIGNMENT 1: True/False

**Instructions:** Circle T if the statement is true and F if the statement is false.

T F 1. To change the structure of a database file, use the "Database file" option of the "Update" menu.
T F 2. You can change the length of an existing field in a database file.
T F 3. You can add new fields to a database file, but you can't delete existing fields.
T F 4. If you add a character field to a database file, initially the field will be blank on all records.
T F 5. The simplest way to change a given field to a specific value for all records meeting some condition is by using the "Browse" option.
T F 6. An index may be used in place of sorting.
T F 7. The field on which an index is built is called an index key.
T F 8. An index key can only be a single field.

**Student Assignment 1 (continued)**

T F 9. A plus sign ( + ) between two field names in an index key expression means that the fields are to be added together to produce the index key.

T F 10. When an index is created it is automatically active.

T F 11. Any out-of-date indexes may be brought up to date using the "Reindex" option of the "Update" menu.

T F 12. A view can involve more than one database file.

T F 13. Database files in a view need not have any relationship with each other.

T F 14. To say there is a one-to-many relationship between database file A and database file B means that each record in file A is related to many records in file B but each record in file B is related to only one record in file A.

T F 15. To indicate a relationship between two database files when creating a view, first select the "one" database file, then the "many."

T F 16. When creating a view, if you don't take special action, all fields from both database files will be included in the view.

## STUDENT ASSIGNMENT 2: Multiple Choice

**Instructions:** Circle the correct response.

1. To change the structure of a database file, use the
   a. "Database file" option of the "Set Up" menu.
   b. "Database file" option of the "Create" menu.
   c. "Database file" option of the "Update" menu.
   d. "Database file" option of the "Modify" menu.
2. What kind of changes to the structure of a database file are possible?
   a. adding new fields.
   b. changing the characteristics of existing fields.
   c. deleting fields.
   d. all of the above.
3. The simplest way to change the value of DEPT_NUMB to "02" for all records on which DEPARTMENT = "Marketing" is to use the
   a. "Edit" option.
   b. "Browse" option.
   c. "Replace" option.
   d. "Update" option.
4. Which of the following statements about creating indexes is not true?
   a. The file on which the index is created must be active.
   b. The index that is created will automatically be active.
   c. The index key can be more than one field.
   d. The file on which the index is created cannot have any other indexes.
5. Which of the following statements is not true?
   a. The "Index" option of the "Tools" menu is used to create an index.
   b. Indexes give an alternative to sorting.
   c. Any time a change is made in a database file, dBASE automatically makes changes in corresponding indexes.
   d. Indexes may be brought up to date by using the "Pack" option.
6. To activate an existing view, use the "View" option of the
   a. "Set Up" menu.
   b. "Create" menu.
   c. "Update" menu.
   d. "Modify" menu.
7. Which of the following is true concerning the way two database files involved in a view are related?
   a. There need be no relationship between the files.
   b. There must be fields that have the same name in both files.
   c. A field in one file must match the value in the index key of the second file.
   d. The index key of one file must match the index key in the second.
8. Views can be used just as if they were database files when using the
   a. "Display" option.
   b. "Edit" option.
   c. "Report" option.
   d. "Sort" option.

## STUDENT ASSIGNMENT 3: Understanding dBASE Options

**Instructions:** Explain what will happen after you perform each of the following actions.

Problem 1. Choose the "Database file" option of the "Modify" menu.

Explanation: ____________________

Problem 2. Choose the "Replace" option of the "Update" menu.

Explanation: ____________________

Problem 3. Choose the "Index" option of the "Tools" menu.

Explanation: ____________________

Problem 4. Choose the "View" option of the "Create" menu.

Explanation: ____________________

## STUDENT ASSIGNMENT 4: Using dBASE

**Instructions:** Explain how to accomplish each of the following tasks using dBASE.

Problem 1. Change the length of a field in an existing database file.

Explanation: ____________________

Problem 2. Add a new field to an existing database file.

Explanation: ____________________

Problem 3. Delete a field from an existing database file.

Explanation: ____________________

### Student Assignment 4 (continued)

Problem 4. Create an index.

Explanation: ______________________________________________

______________________________________________

______________________________________________

Problem 5. Use an index instead of sorting.

Explanation: ______________________________________________

______________________________________________

______________________________________________

Problem 6. Create a view.

Explanation: ______________________________________________

______________________________________________

______________________________________________

## STUDENT ASSIGNMENT 5: Recovering from Problems

**Instructions:** In each of the following cases, a problem occurred. Explain the cause of the problem and how it can be corrected.

Problem 1: You were changing the structure of a database file, intending to delete the fourth field. You looked up at your display and found you deleted the third field instead.

Cause of Problem: ______________________________________________

______________________________________________

Method of Correction: ______________________________________________

______________________________________________

Problem 2: You attempted to find a record using the "Seek" option of the "Position" menu and were told there was a data type mismatch.

Cause of Problem: ______________________________________________

______________________________________________

Method of Correction: ______________________________________________

______________________________________________

Problem 3: When you display the data in a view, the data seems totally wrong. None of the data from the "many" database file matches anything from the "one" database file.

Cause of Problem: ______________________________________________

______________________________________________

Method of Correction: ______________________________________________

______________________________________________

# MINICASES:

## Changing the Structure of a Database

### Minicase 1: Personal Checks

**Instructions:** Modify the structure of the personal check database called CHECK that you created in Project 1. Change the structure from:

| CHECK NUMBER | DATE | PAYEE | CHECK AMOUNT | EXPENSE | TAX DEDUCTIBLE |
|---|---|---|---|---|---|
| 109 | 01/19/90 | Oak Apartments | 750.00 | Household | Y |
| 102 | 01/05/90 | Sav-Mor Groceries | 85.00 | Food | N |
| 111 | 01/19/90 | Edison Company | 55.25 | Household | N |
| 106 | 01/12/90 | Performing Arts | 25.00 | Charity | Y |
| | | . | | | |
| | | . | | | |
| | | . | | | |

to:

| CHECK NUMBER | DATE | PAYEE | CHECK AMOUNT | TAX DEDUCTIBLE | EXP_ CODE |
|---|---|---|---|---|---|
| 109 | 01/19/90 | Oak Apartments | 750.00 | Y | HH |
| 102 | 01/05/90 | Sav-Mor Groceries | 85.00 | N | FD |
| 111 | 01/19/90 | Edison Electric Company | 55.25 | N | HH |
| 106 | 01/12/90 | Performing Arts | 25.00 | Y | CH |
| | | . | | | |
| | | . | | | |
| | | . | | | |

| EXP_ CODE | EXPENSE DESCRIPTION |
|---|---|
| HH | Household |
| FD | Food |
| CH | Charity |
| AU | Automobile |
| EN | Entertainment |
| PR | Personal |

Make the following changes:

1. Expand the length of the PAYEE field to accommodate the name Edison Electric Company, the new name for the Edison Company.
2. Add a second database file. This file contains two fields, EXP_CODE and EXP_DESC, used to relate expense codes to the corresponding descriptions (for example, HH stands for household).
3. Remove the EXPENSE field from the original database file.
4. Add a new field, EXP_CODE.
5. Fill in the correct codes for each check.

To make these changes, perform the following tasks:

1. Create the new database file. Use the name EXPCATS for this file.
2. Add the indicated expense codes and descriptions to this database file.
3. Create an index on the EXP_CODE field for the EXPCATS database file. Call the index EXPIND1. Use it to list the data in the database file.

## Minicase 1 (continued)

4. Change the length of the PAYEE field in the CHECK database file to accommodate the name Edison Electric Company. Change the names.
5. Add the EXP_CODE field to the CHECK database.
6. Fill in the EXP_CODE field in the CHECK database with appropriate data (HH for records where EXPENSE is household, FD for records where EXPENSE is food, and so on).
7. Delete the EXPENSE field from the CHECK database.
8. Create an index called CHECKIN1 on the Payee field in the CHECK database. Use it to list the records in CHECK in PAYEE order.
9. Create an index called CHECKIN2 on the combination of the EXP_CODE and PAYEE fields in the CHECK database. Use it to list the records in CHECK ordered by PAYEE within EMP_CODE.
10. Create an index called CHECKIN3 on the CHECK NUMBER field in the CHECK database. Use this index and the "Seek" option to locate the record containing check 107. Display the record.
11. Create a view called EXPVIEW that contains both the EXPCATS and CHECK database files. The EXP_CODE field in both files should be used to relate the two. Include all fields from the CHECK database and the EXP_DESC field from the EXPCATS database in this view. List all the data in the view.
12. Using this view, display the CHECK NUMBER, DATE, PAYEE and AMOUNT for all checks whose description is Household.
13. What do you think about the change that was made? Is it a good idea? What are the advantages? What are the disadvantages?

## Minicase 2: Music Library

**Instructions** Modify the structure of the database called MUSIC, that you created in Project 1. Change the structure from:

| DATE | MUSIC NAME | ARTIST | TYPE | COST | CATEGORY |
|---|---|---|---|---|---|
| 02/22/90 | Greatest Hits | Panache, Milo | LP | 8.95 | Classical |
| 02/15/90 | America | Judd, Mary | CS | 5.95 | Vocal |
| 01/02/90 | Rio Rio | Duran, Ralph | LP | 8.95 | Rock |
| 02/15/90 | Passione | Panache, Milo | LP | 6.99 | Classical |
| | | . | | | |
| | | . | | | |
| | | . | | | |

to:

| DATE | MUSIC NAME | ARTIST | TYPE | COST | CAT_ CODE |
|---|---|---|---|---|---|
| 02/22/90 | Greatest Hits #1 | Panache, Milo | LP | 8.95 | CL |
| 02/15/90 | America | Judd, Mary | CS | 5.95 | VO |
| 01/02/90 | Rio Rio | Duran, Ralph | LP | 8.95 | RK |
| 02/15/90 | Passione | Panache, Milo | LP | 6.99 | CL |
| | | . | | | |
| | | . | | | |
| | | . | | | |

| CAT_ CODE | CATEGORY DESCRIPTION |
|---|---|
| CL | Classical |
| CO | Country |
| VO | Vocal |
| RK | Rock |

Make the following changes:

1. Expand the length of the MUSIC NAME field to accommodate the name "Greatest Hits #1," the correct name for the "Greatest Hits" album by Milo Panache.
2. Add a second database file. This file contains two fields, CAT_CODE and CAT_DESC, used to relate category codes to corresponding descriptions (for example, CL stands for classical).
3. Remove the CATEGORY field from the original database file.
4. Add a new field, CAT_CODE.
5. Fill in the correct codes for each record.

To make these changes, perform the following tasks:

1. Create the new database file. Use the name MUSCATS for this file.
2. Add the indicated category codes and descriptions to this database file.
3. Create an index on the CAT_CODE field for the MUSCATS database file. Call the index CATIND1. Use it to list the data in the database file.
4. Change the length of the MUSIC NAME field in the MUSIC database file to accommodate the name "Greatest Hits #1." Change the name.
5. Add the CAT_CODE field to the MUSIC database.
6. Fill in the CAT_CODE field in the MUSIC database with appropriate data (CL for records where CATEGORY is classical, CO for records where CATEGORY is country, and so on).
7. Delete the CATEGORY field from the MUSIC database.
8. Create an index called MUSICIN1 on the TYPE field in the MUSIC database. Use it to list the records in MUSIC in TYPE order.
9. Create an index called MUSICIN2 on the combination of the ARTIST and MUSIC NAME fields in the MUSIC database. Use it to list the records in MUSIC ordered by MUSIC NAME within ARTIST.
10. Create an index called MUSICIN3 on the MUSIC NAME field. Use this index and the "Seek" option to locate the record on which the music name is "Rio Rio." Display the record.
11. Create a view called MUSVIEW. This view should contain both the MUSCATS and MUSIC database files. The CAT_CODE field in both files should be used to relate the two. Include all fields from the MUSIC database and the category description field from the MUSCATS database in this view. Display the data in the view.
12. Using this view, display the DATE, MUSIC NAME, ARTIST, and COST for all classical records.
13. What do you think about the change that was made? Is it a good idea? What are the advantages? What are the disadvantages?

## Minicase 3: Computer Software Store

**Instructions:** Modify the structure of the database called SOFTWARE that you created in Project 1. Change the structure from:

| SOFTWARE NAME | COMPANY | CATEGORY | MS_DOS | QUANTITY | COST |
|---|---|---|---|---|---|
| Databurst | Electric Software | Database | Y | 5 | 299.95 |
| Type Ease | Edusoft Inc. | WP | N | 22 | 29.95 |
| Image Fonts | Graph Tech Inc. | WP | Y | 12 | 49.95 |
| Data Filer | Anchor Software | Database | Y | 18 | 149.95 |
| Master | Edusoft Inc. | Education | N | 10 | 49.95 |
| | . | | | | |
| | . | | | | |
| | . | | | | |

## Minicase 3 (continued)

to:

| SOFTWARE NAME | CATEGORY | MS_DOS | QUANTITY | COST | CMP_ CODE |
|---|---|---|---|---|---|
| Databurst | Database | Y | 5 | 299.95 | 01 |
| Type Ease | WP | N | 22 | 29.95 | 05 |
| Image Fonts | WP | Y | 12 | 49.95 | 04 |
| Data File Manager | Database | Y | 18 | 149.95 | 02 |
| Master | Education | N | 10 | 49.95 | 05 |
| | . | | | | |
| | . | | | | |
| | . | | | | |

| CMP_ CODE | COMPANY NAME |
|---|---|
| 01 | Electric Software |
| 02 | Anchor Software |
| 03 | Learnit Software |
| 04 | Graph Tech Inc. |
| 05 | Edusoft Inc. |

Make the following changes:

1. Expand the length of the NAME field to accommodate the name Data File Manager, the new name for Data Filer.
2. Add a second database file. This file contains two fields, CMP_CODE and CMP_NAME, used to relate company codes to corresponding names (for example, 01 is the code for Electric Software).
3. Remove the COMPANY field from the original database file.
4. Add a new field, CMP_CODE.
5. Fill in the correct codes for each record.

To make these changes, perform the following tasks:

1. Create the new database file. Use the name SOFTCATS for this file.
2. Add the indicated company codes and names to this database file.
3. Create an index on the CMP_CODE field for the SOFTCATS database file. Call the index CMPIND1. Use it to list the data in the database file.
4. Change the length of the NAME field in the SOFTWARE database file to accommodate the name Data File Manager. Change the name.
5. Add the CMP_CODE field to the SOFTWARE database.
6. Fill in the CMP_CODE field in the SOFTWARE database with appropriate data (01 for records where COMPANY is Electric Software, 02 for records where COMPANY is Anchor Software, and so on).
7. Delete the COMPANY field from the SOFTWARE database.
8. Create an index called SOFTWIN1 on the CATEGORY field in the SOFTWARE database. Use it to list the records in SOFTWARE in CATEGORY order.
9. Create an index called SOFTWIN2 on the combination of the CATEGORY and NAME fields in the SOFTWARE database. Use it to list the records in SOFTWARE ordered by NAME within CATEGORY.
10. Create an index called SOFTWIN3 on the NAME field in the SOFTWARE database. Use this index and the "Seek" option to locate the record containing Image Fonts. Display the record.
11. Create a view called SOFTVIEW. This view should contain both the SOFTCATS and SOFTWARE database files. The CMP_CODE field in both files should be used to relate the two. Include all fields from the SOFTWARE database and the CMP_NAME field from the SOFTCATS database in this view. Display the data in the view.
12. Using this view, display the NAME, CATEGORY, and COST for all software produced by Electric Software.
13. What do you think about the change that was made? Is it a good idea? What are the advantages? What are the disadvantages?

## Minicase 4: Home Sales

**Instructions:** Max, the user of the HOMES database file that you created in Project 1, decided to make a change. Max realized that there were only a few zip codes in which the homes for sale were likely to be located. Further, since each of these zip codes uniquely identified a city, Max decided to remove CITY from the HOMES file and create a separate database file called ZIPCODE, relating zip codes and cities. In particular, the structure is to be changed from:

| DATE | ADDRESS | CITY | ZIP | BDRM | BATH | POOL | PRICE |
|---|---|---|---|---|---|---|---|
| 09/15/90 | 9661 King Pl. | Anaheim | 92644 | 4 | 2 | Y | 185000.00 |
| 09/19/90 | 1625 Brook St. | Fullerton | 92633 | 3 | 1 | N | 95000.00 |
| 10/02/90 | 182 Oak Ave. | Fullerton | 92634 | 4 | 2 | Y | 92000.00 |
| 10/09/90 | 145 Oak Ave. | Garden Grove | 92641 | 5 | 3 | Y | 145000.00 |
| 10/15/90 | 124 Lark St. | Anaheim | 92644 | 3 | 2 | N | 119000.00 |
| 10/22/90 | 926 Pine Ln. | Garden Grove | 92641 | 3 | 1 | N | 92500.00 |
| | | . | | | | | |
| | | . | | | | | |
| | | . | | | | | |

to:

| DATE | ADDRESS | ZIP | BDRM | BATH | POOL | PRICE |
|---|---|---|---|---|---|---|
| 09/15/90 | 9661 King Pl. | 92644 | 4 | 2 | Y | 185000.00 |
| 09/19/90 | 1625 Brook St. | 92633 | 3 | 1 | N | 95000.00 |
| 10/02/90 | 182 Oak Ave. | 92634 | 4 | 2 | Y | 92000.00 |
| 10/09/90 | 145 Oak Ave. | 92641 | 5 | 3 | Y | 145000.00 |
| 10/15/90 | 124 Lark St. | 92644 | 3 | 2 | N | 119000.00 |
| 10/22/90 | 926 Pine Ln. | 92641 | 3 | 1 | N | 92500.00 |
| | | . | | | | |
| | | . | | | | |
| | | . | | | | |

| ZIP | CITY |
|---|---|
| 92644 | Anaheim |
| 92641 | Garden Grove |
| 92688 | Costa Mesa |
| 92633 | Fullerton |
| 92634 | Fullerton |

Perform the following tasks:

1. Create the new database file. Use the name ZIPCODE for this file.
2. Add the indicated zip codes and cities to this database file.
3. Create an index on the ZIP field for the ZIPCODE database file. Call the index ZIPIND1. Use it to list the data in the database file.
4. Delete the CITY field from the HOMES database.
5. Create an index called HOMESIND on the ADDRESS field in the HOMES database. Use this index and the "Seek" option to locate the record for the house at 145 Oak Ave. Display the record.
6. Create a view called ZIPVIEW. This view should contain both the ZIPCODE and HOMES database files. The ZIP field in both files should be used to relate the two. Include all fields from the HOMES database and the CITY field from the ZIPCODE database in this view. Display the data in the view.
7. Using this view, display the DATE , ADDRESS, CITY, ZIP, and PRICE for all homes in Fullerton.
8. What do you think about the change that was made? Is it a good idea? What are the advantages? What are the disadvantages?

# PROJECT 6

## The Dot Prompt

### Objectives

You will have mastered the material in this project when you can accomplish the following from the dot prompt:

- Activate a database file
- Clear the screen
- Correct errors in commands
- Send the results of DISPLAY commands to the printer
- Display individual records
- Display all records
- Display selected fields
- Display computed fields
- Use conditions
- Calculate counts, sums, and averages
- Sort database files on multiple keys, using descending order if desired
- Display the contents of a view
- Create programs (command files) and execute the programs from the dot prompt

In this project, you will learn to use the commands shown in Figure 6-1 at the dot prompt. By now, you should have become comfortable with the ASSISTANT and the way it helps you access your database files. You might wonder why you would ever need to type commands at the dot prompt. There are two reasons.

| COMMAND | PURPOSE |
|---|---|
| APPEND | Add records to a database file |
| AVERAGE | Calculate an average |
| CLEAR | Clear the screen |
| COUNT | Count the number of records |
| DISPLAY | Show desired fields and records |
| DO | Run a command file (program) |
| EJECT | Force the printer to advance to the top of the next page |
| MODIFY COMMAND | Create a command file (program) (extension PRG) |
| SET VIEW TO | Activate a view |
| SORT | Sort a database file |
| SUM | Calculate a total |
| USE | Activate a database file |

**FIGURE 6-1**
**dBASE commands**

First, if you know a particular command, you can often type it more quickly than you can go through the appropriate menus of the ASSISTANT. Second, and more important, there are some things that can be accomplished through commands at the dot prompt that *cannot* be accomplished through the ASSISTANT. You will see examples of these operations in this project. For both of these reasons, it is important to know how to enter and use commands at the dot prompt.

To begin, press Esc to change to dot prompt mode. With the dot prompt on the screen, type the words USE EMPLOYEE. This activates the EMPLOYEE database file. It is like using the "Database file" option of the "Set Up" menu and then choosing the EMPLOYEE database file.

## USEFUL TIPS

Before we examine the commands, we will look at two special tips that can be helpful. The first is how to clear the screen and the second involves correcting errors in commands.

### Clearing the Screen

There are various times when you might wish to clear the screen. To do so, simply type the word CLEAR at the dot prompt. All the material other than the dot prompt and the status line will disappear.

### Correcting Errors in Commands

Occasionally, you may make a mistake when you type a command. You might, for example, type the word DSPLAY instead of DISPLAY. In such cases, dBASE responds with an error message as shown in Figure 6-2, and asks whether or not you want help. To receive help, type the letter Y. Otherwise, type the letter N or simply press the Enter key. Sometimes the information dBASE provides is indeed helpful. Usually, however, you can discover the problem yourself by carefully comparing the line you typed with examples you have used before. If you want help on a specific command, you can type the word HELP followed by the command at the dot prompt. Typing the words HELP DISPLAY, for example, would produce the screen shown in Figure 6-3.

command entered

error message

```
(DEMO) . DSPLAY ALL
*** Unrecognized command verb.
          ?
DSPLAY ALL
Command Line  <B:> EMPLOYEE          Rec: 1/17
                 Do you want some help? (Y/N)
                Enter a dBASE III PLUS command.
```

**FIGURE 6-2**
**Incorrectly Entered Command**

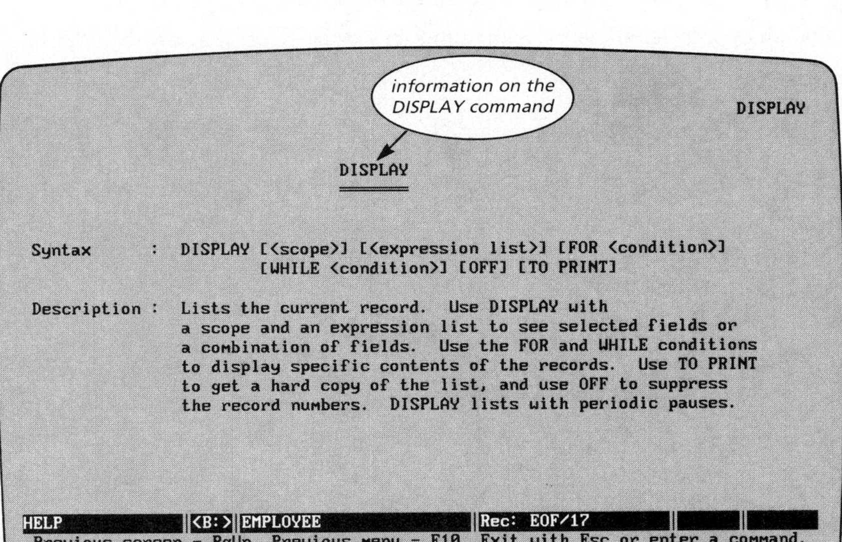


**FIGURE 6-3**
**Help Screen**

Once you have discovered the problem, you could simply retype the entire command correctly. There is a shortcut, however. If you press the Up Arrow key, the command containing the mistake will be displayed on the screen (Figure 6-4). At this point, use the Right and Left Arrow keys to move the cursor to the mistake, make the necessary corrections (Figure 6-5) and press the Enter key. In this example, the problem is that the letter I in DISPLAY was omitted. To correct the problem, you would move the cursor to the letter S in DSPLAY, press the Ins key to change to insert mode, type the letter I, and then press the Ins key again to leave insert mode.

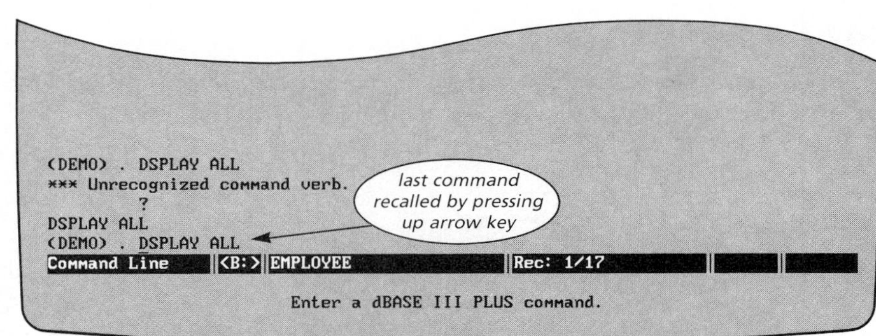


**FIGURE 6-4**
**Displaying Incorrect Command**

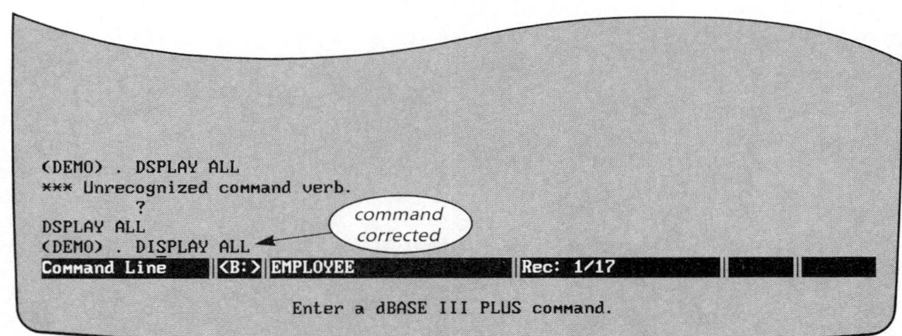


**FIGURE 6-5**
**Command Has Been Corrected**

Once you have corrected the problem and pressed the Enter key, dBASE will display the results (Figure 6-6).

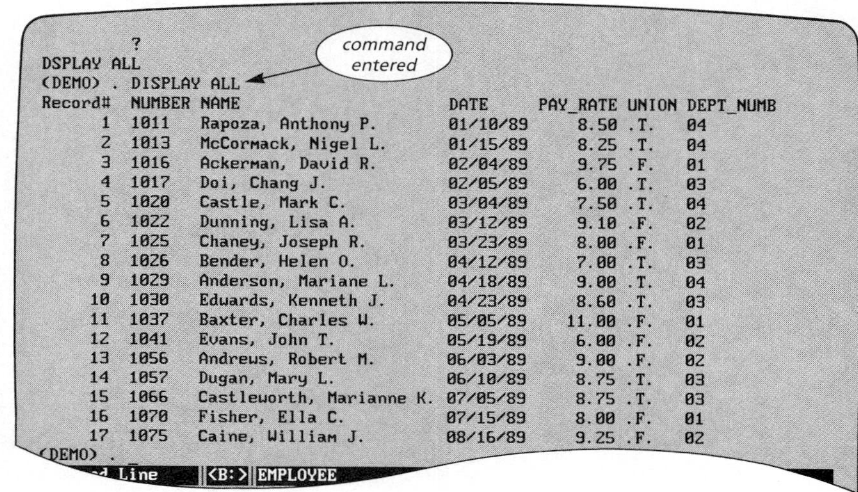


| Record# | NUMBER | NAME | DATE | PAY_RATE | UNION | DEPT_NUMB |
|---|---|---|---|---|---|---|
| 1 | 1011 | Rapoza, Anthony P. | 01/10/89 | 8.50 | .T. | 04 |
| 2 | 1013 | McCormack, Nigel L. | 01/15/89 | 8.25 | .T. | 04 |
| 3 | 1016 | Ackerman, David R. | 02/04/89 | 9.75 | .F. | 01 |
| 4 | 1017 | Doi, Chang J. | 02/05/89 | 6.00 | .T. | 03 |
| 5 | 1020 | Castle, Mark C. | 03/04/89 | 7.50 | .T. | 04 |
| 6 | 1022 | Dunning, Lisa A. | 03/12/89 | 9.10 | .F. | 02 |
| 7 | 1025 | Chaney, Joseph R. | 03/23/89 | 8.00 | .F. | 01 |
| 8 | 1026 | Bender, Helen O. | 04/12/89 | 7.00 | .T. | 03 |
| 9 | 1029 | Anderson, Mariane L. | 04/18/89 | 9.00 | .T. | 04 |
| 10 | 1030 | Edwards, Kenneth J. | 04/23/89 | 8.60 | .T. | 03 |
| 11 | 1037 | Baxter, Charles W. | 05/05/89 | 11.00 | .F. | 01 |
| 12 | 1041 | Evans, John T. | 05/19/89 | 6.00 | .F. | 02 |
| 13 | 1056 | Andrews, Robert M. | 06/03/89 | 9.00 | .F. | 02 |
| 14 | 1057 | Dugan, Mary L. | 06/10/89 | 8.75 | .T. | 03 |
| 15 | 1066 | Castleworth, Marianne K. | 07/05/89 | 8.75 | .T. | 03 |
| 16 | 1070 | Fisher, Ella C. | 07/15/89 | 8.00 | .F. | 01 |
| 17 | 1075 | Caine, William J. | 08/16/89 | 9.25 | .F. | 02 |



**FIGURE 6-6**
**Results of Corrected Command**

# DISPLAY COMMAND

## Sending the Results to the Printer

To print the results of any DISPLAY command, end the command with the words TO PRINT. We will not do so in the examples in this project, however. Make sure your printer is on before you execute a command containing this clause!

## Displaying the Current Active Record

The simplest form of the DISPLAY command is just the word DISPLAY. As shown in Figure 6-7, this command will display a single record, the current active record. If the current active record does not happen to be the one you want, you can type the word GOTO followed by the number of the desired record at the dot prompt. The command GOTO 1, for example would make the first record the current active record. Once you have done this, type the DISPLAY command as shown in the figure.

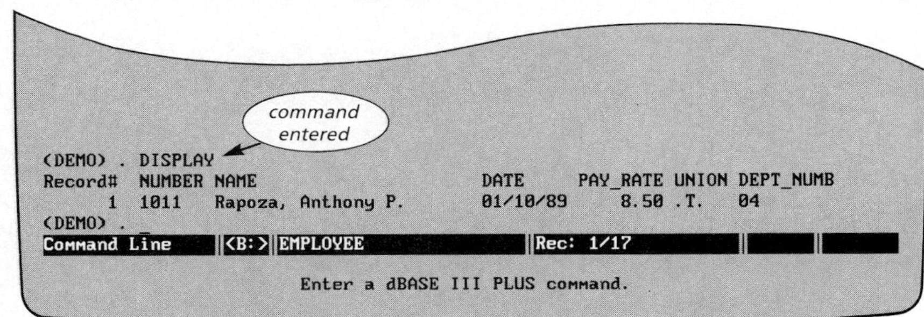


**FIGURE 6-7**
**Displaying a Single Record**

## Displaying All Records

To display all the records, you need some way of changing the scope to "ALL" (remember the "Specify scope" option). You do this by including the word ALL in the DISPLAY command (shown in Figure 6-6).

## Omitting Record Numbers

With the ASSISTANT, there was no way to request that record numbers *not* be displayed. This is easily accomplished at the dot prompt by including the word OFF in the DISPLAY command (Figure 6-8).

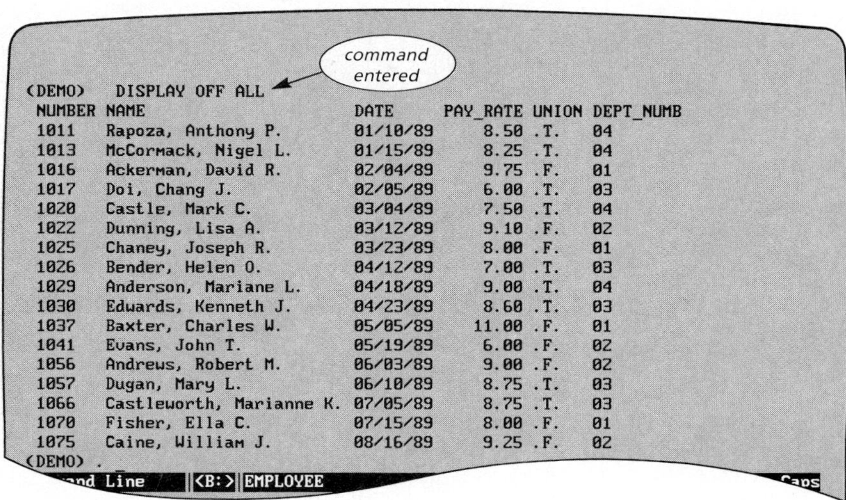


**FIGURE 6-8**
**Omitting Record Numbers**

## Displaying Selected Fields

To specify a particular collection of fields to display, list the fields in the command (Figure 6-9).

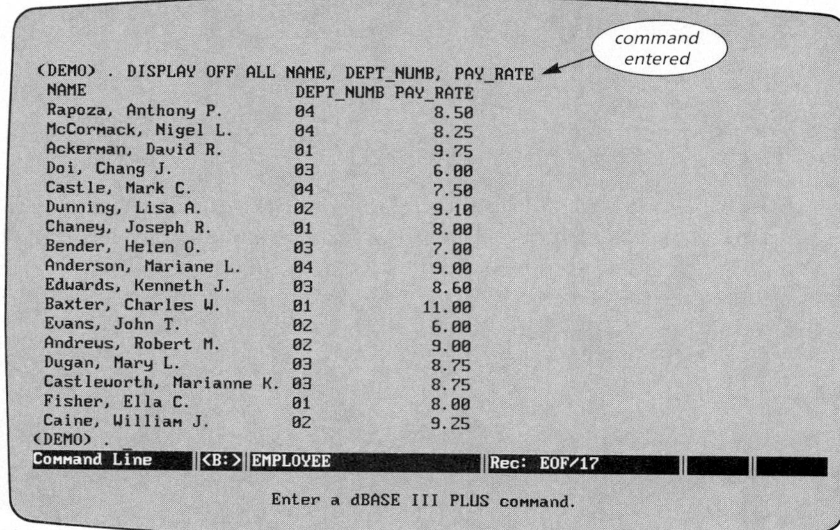


**FIGURE 6-9**
**Displaying Selected Fields**

## Making Computations

Suppose you want to list the number, name, pay rate, and weekly pay (pay rate times 40) for all employees. Further, you do not wish to include record numbers. You can do so by the DISPLAY command shown in Figure 6-10.

```
(DEMO) . DISPLAY OFF ALL NUMBER, NAME, PAY_RATE, PAY_RATE * 40
 NUMBER NAME                         PAY_RATE PAY_RATE * 40
 1011   Rapoza, Anthony P.               8.50        340.00
 1013   McCormack, Nigel L.              8.25        330.00
 1016   Ackerman, David R.               9.75        390.00
 1017   Doi, Chang J.                    6.00        240.00
 1020   Castle, Mark C.                  7.50        300.00
 1022   Dunning, Lisa A.                 9.10        364.00
 1025   Chaney, Joseph R.                8.00        320.00
 1026   Bender, Helen O.                 7.00        280.00
 1029   Anderson, Mariane L.             9.00        360.00
 1030   Edwards, Kenneth J.              8.60        344.00
 1037   Baxter, Charles W.              11.00        440.00
 1041   Evans, John T.                   6.00        240.00
 1056   Andrews, Robert M.               9.00        360.00
 1057   Dugan, Mary L.                   8.75        350.00
 1066   Castleworth, Marianne K.         8.75        350.00
 1070   Fisher, Ella C.                  8.00        320.00
 1075   Caine, William J.                9.25        370.00
(DEMO) .
Command Line  <B:> EMPLOYEE          Rec: EOF/17          Caps
                 Enter a dBASE III PLUS command.
```

command entered

**FIGURE 6-10**
**Making Computations**

## Displaying a Specific Record

You have already seen how to change the current active record using GOTO and how to display the current active record. You can accomplish both tasks in a single step by listing the desired record number in the DISPLAY command as shown in Figure 6-11, where the desired record number is 6. This command will display record 6 and also make record 6 the current active record.

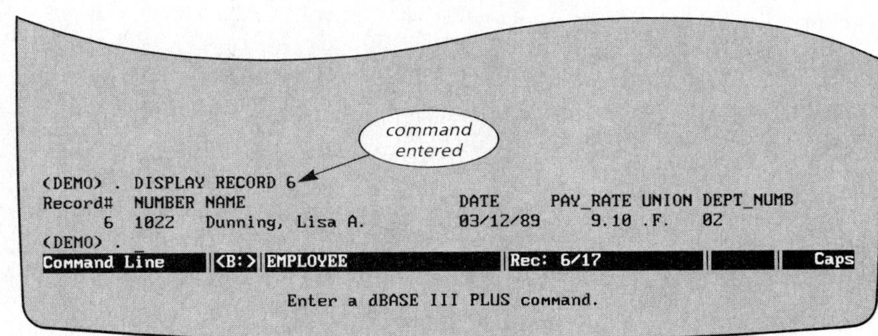


**FIGURE 6-11**
**Displaying a Single Record**

## Using Conditions

Search conditions are indicated in a DISPLAY command through the FOR clause. To display the data for employee 1030, for example, you can use the DISPLAY command shown in Figure 6-12. When you used the ASSISTANT, you didn't need to enter the quote marks around the number 1030. But they are essential when you enter DISPLAY commands at the dot prompt. Whenever you are making a comparison involving a character field, you *must* use quote marks, either double quote marks (") or single quote marks (') around the character string.

You may have noticed that the command does not include the word ALL. The word is not required if a FOR clause is used. Including the word ALL would not be wrong, however.

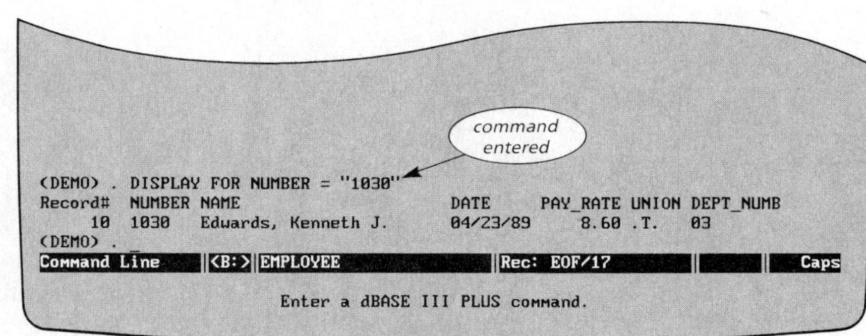


**FIGURE 6-12**
**Using Conditions**

The DISPLAY command shown in Figure 6-13 will display all employees whose pay rate is $6.00. Since PAY_RATE is a numeric field, the 6.00 *must not* be enclosed in quotes.

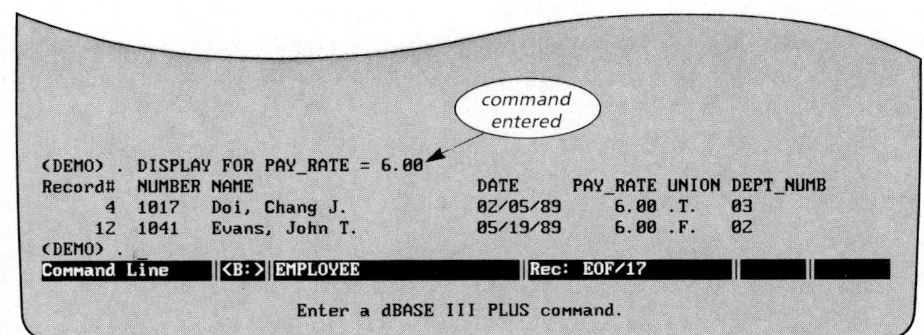


**FIGURE 6-13**
**Using Conditions**

Comparisons need not involve equality. You can use any of the normal comparison operators (=, >, <, > =, < =) as well as > < (NOT EQUAL). The DISPLAY command in Figure 6-14, for example, lists all employees whose pay rate is more than $9.00.

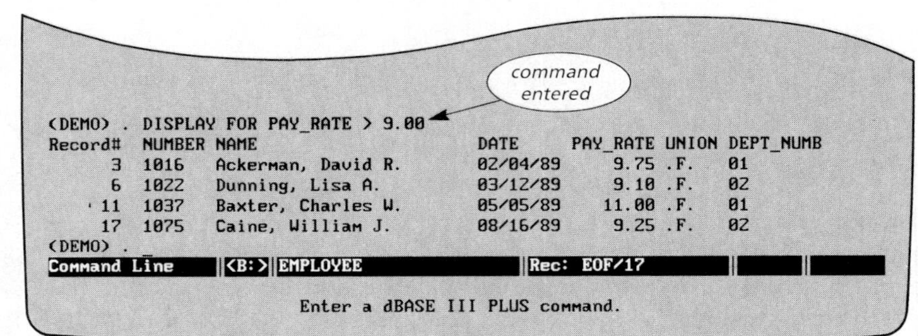


**FIGURE 6-14**
**Using Conditions**

To restrict the display to certain columns and rows meeting a given condition, list the desired columns in the DISPLAY command and include an appropriate condition. The DISPLAY command in Figure 6-15 lists the name, department number, and pay rate for all employees in department 04.

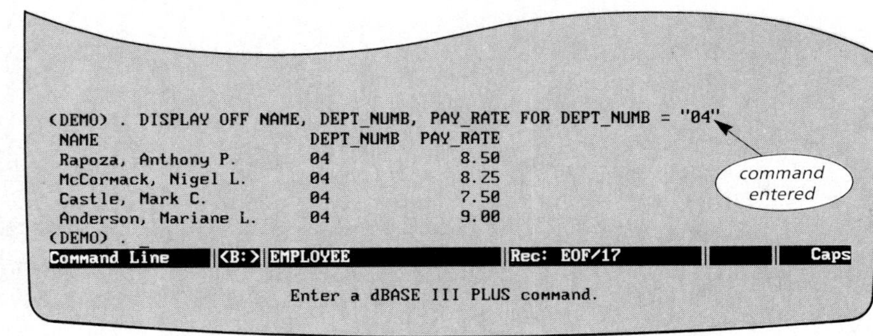


**FIGURE 6-15**
**Using Conditions**

## Searching for a Name

Recall that when you search for a name, you must type the letters the same way they occur in the database. The DISPLAY command shown in Figure 6-16 would find Charles Baxter, but the DISPLAY command shown in Figure 6-17 would not, since the letters are all uppercase and that is not the way the name was entered into the database.

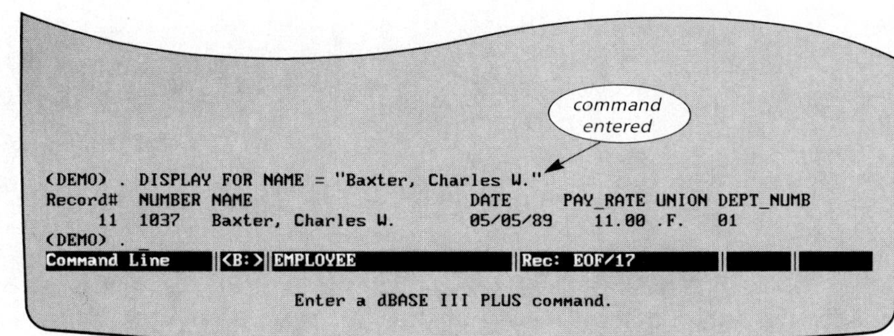


**FIGURE 6-16**
**Searching for a Name**

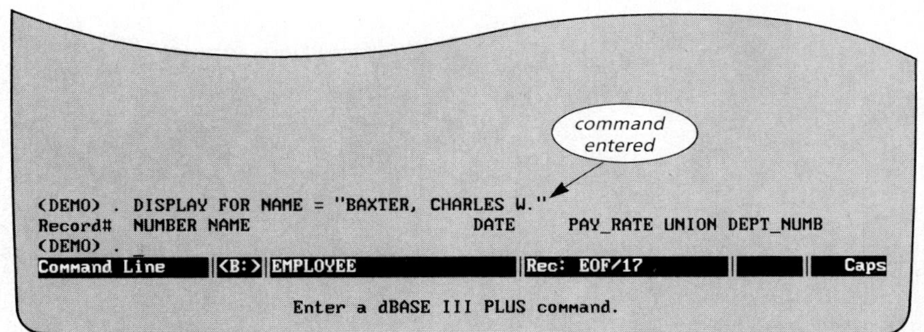


**FIGURE 6-17**
**Searching for a Name**

Fortunately, when using the DISPLAY command, there is a simple way around this problem. You use a special dBASE function called UPPER, as shown in Figure 6-18. The expression UPPER(NAME) represents the same letters that are in NAME, converted to upper case. Thus, if NAME is Baxter, Charles W., UPPER(NAME) would be BAXTER, CHARLES W. and the condition would be true.

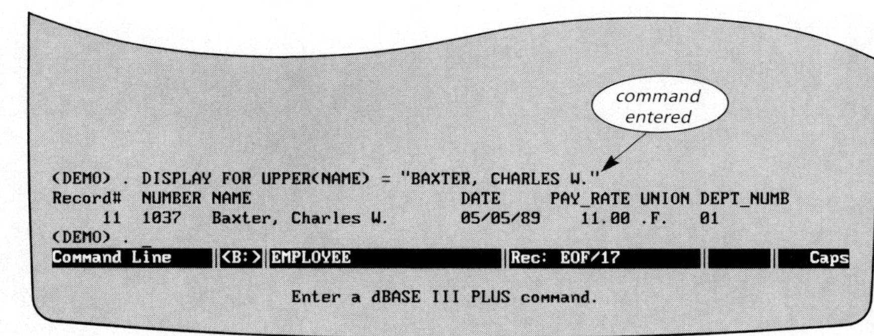


**FIGURE 6-18**
**Using the UPPER Function**

As with the ASSISTANT, if you enter the single letter A in the comparison, you will find all employees whose name *begins with* the letter A (Figure 6-19).

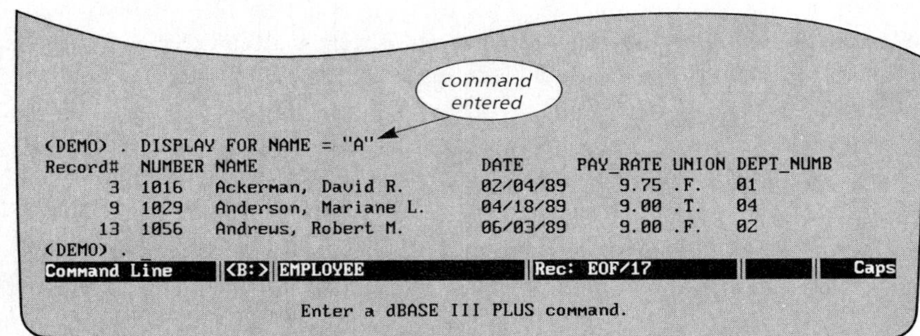


**FIGURE 6-19**
**Searching for Names That Begin with A**

With the ASSISTANT, there would be no way to find all the employees having a given first name. This can easily be done in the DISPLAY command, using the $ function, technically called the substring function. It is used to determine whether one string of characters is contained in (a "substring" of) another. Thus, to find all employees whose names contain the characters David, you could use a DISPLAY command like the one shown in Figure 6-20.

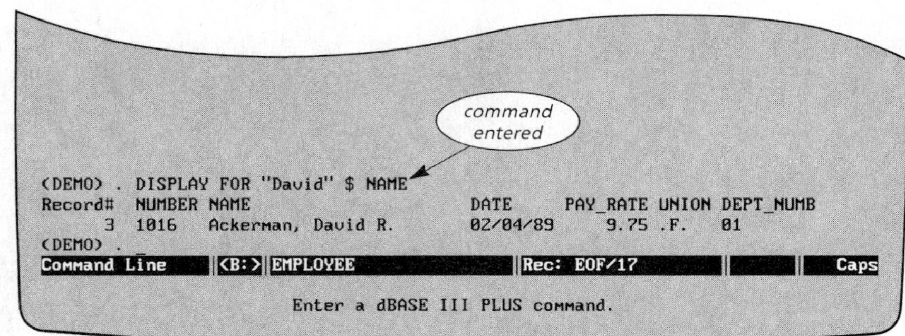


**FIGURE 6-20**
**Searching for Names That Contain David**

## Using Logical Fields in Conditions

As with the ASSISTANT, you can use logical fields in comparisons by themselves. The DISPLAY command shown in Figure 6-21 is used to display all employees for whom UNION is true.

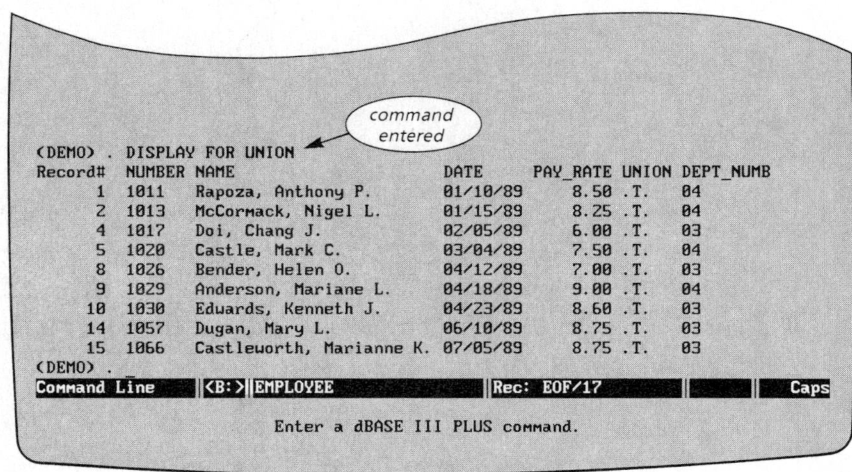


**FIGURE 6-21**
**Using Logical Fields**

One of the things you cannot do with the ASSISTANT is to DISPLAY all employees for whom UNION is false. This is easily accomplished through a DISPLAY command by preceding the word UNION with the word NOT as shown in Figure 6-22. Any condition can be preceded with the word NOT. Doing so simply reverses the truth or falsity of the condition. If UNION is true, NOT UNION is false. Likewise, if UNION is false, NOT UNION is true. When you use the word NOT, you must put periods on both sides of the word as shown in the figure.

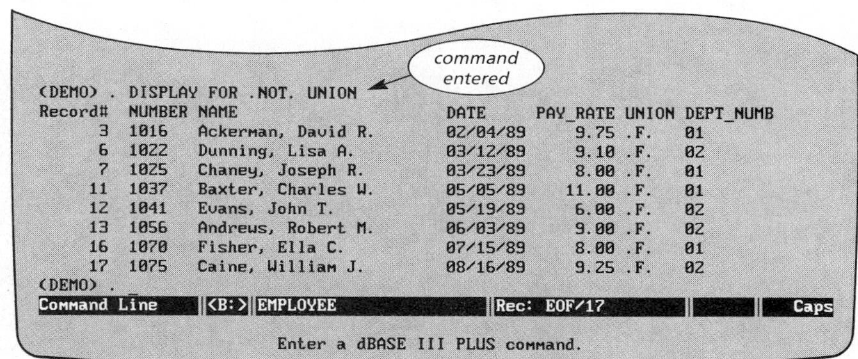


**FIGURE 6-22**
**Using Logical Fields**

## Using Dates in Conditions

Date fields may be used in conditions. Dates must be entered using a special dBASE function called CTOD (it stands for convert characters to a date.) The proper way to enter 01/15/89, for example, is CTOD("01/15/89"). A FOR clause to find employees who were hired on 1/15/89 would be FOR DATE = CTOD("01/15/89") as in Figure 6-23. A FOR clause to find employees who were hired after 3/1/89 would be FOR DATE > CTOD("03/01/89") as in Figure 6-24.

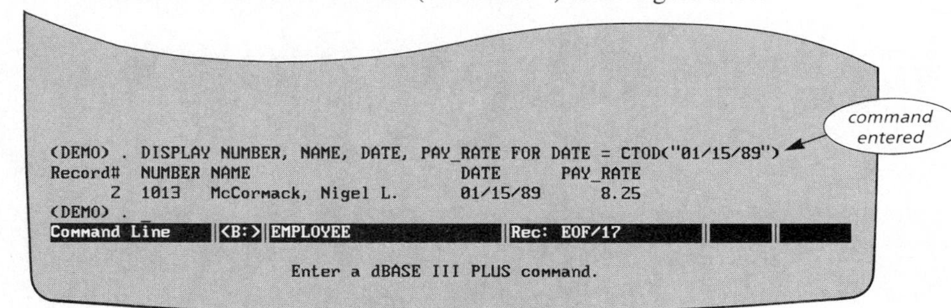


**FIGURE 6-23**
**Using a Date**

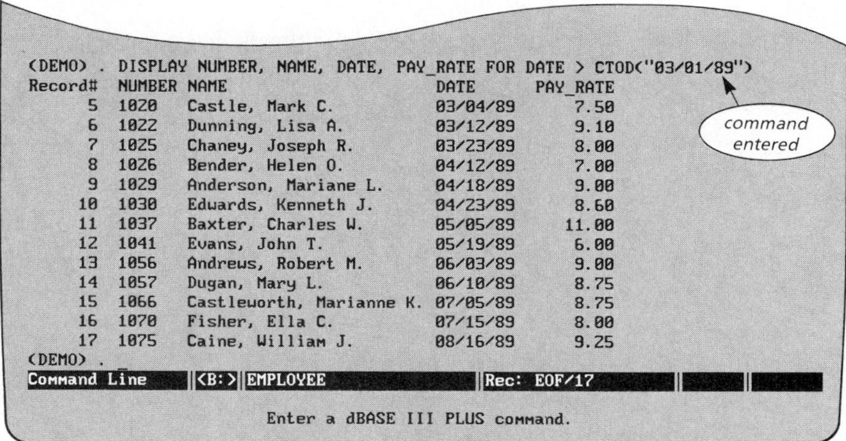


**FIGURE 6-24**
**Using a Date**

## Using Compound Conditions

You can create compound conditions. To find all employees who are in department 01 and have a pay rate of $11.00, for example, you can use a condition like the one shown in Figure 6-25. Note that like the word NOT, the word AND must have periods on both sides.

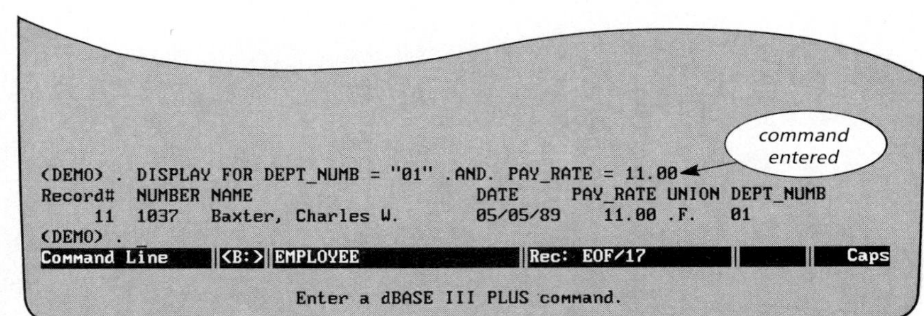


**FIGURE 6-25**
**Using AND**

You can also use conditions involving the word OR. The DISPLAY command shown in Figure 6-26, lists all employees who are in department 01 or who belong to the union.

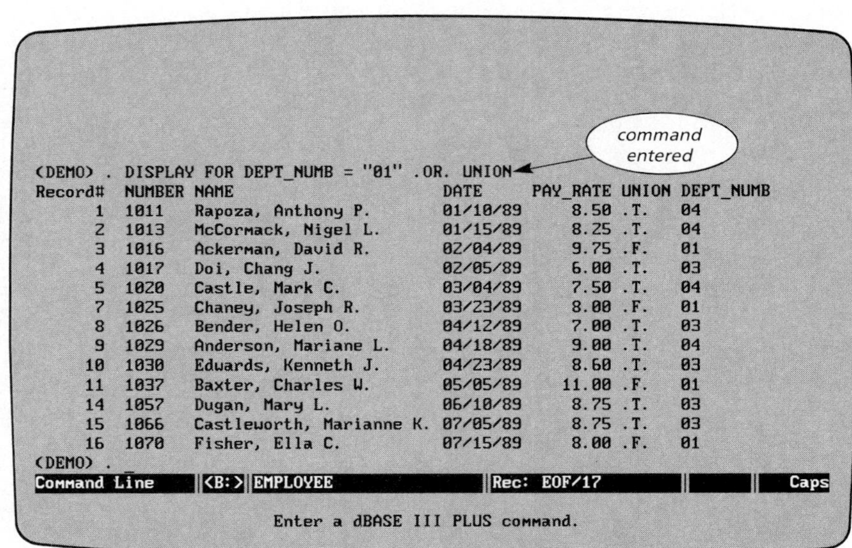


**FIGURE 6-26**
**Using OR**

# CALCULATIONS

Within the ASSISTANT, you can count records and calculate sums and averages. The same calculations are available from the dot prompt using the COUNT, SUM, and AVERAGE commands.

## COUNT

To count all the records in a database file, the command is simply COUNT, as shown in Figure 6-27.

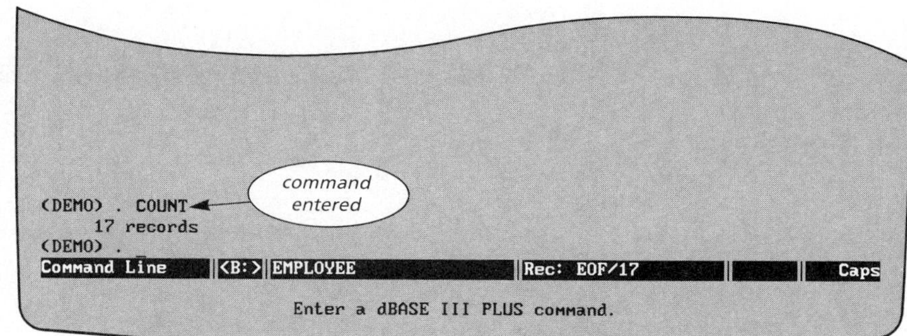


**FIGURE 6-27**
**Counting All Records**

To count all the records satisfying some condition, include an appropriate FOR clause after the word COUNT. To count the number of employees in department 01, for example, you would use the command shown in Figure 6-28.

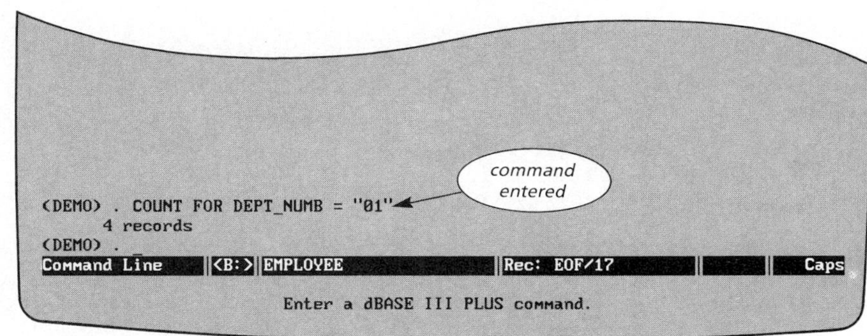


**FIGURE 6-28**
**Counting Records with Conditions**

Like conditions within the DISPLAY command, the condition could involve a logical field. The command shown in Figure 6-29 produces a count of the number of employees who are in the union.

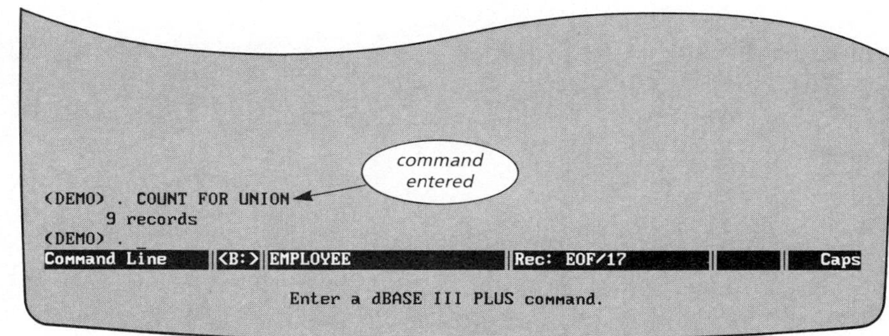


**FIGURE 6-29**
**Counting Records with Conditions**

## SUM

The SUM command is used to obtain totals. The word SUM is followed by a list of the fields to be totaled. To calculate the total pay rate, for example, use the command shown in Figure 6-30.

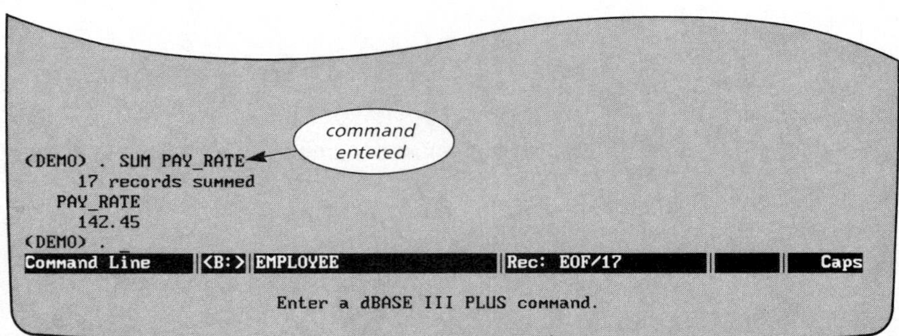


**FIGURE 6-30**
**Calculating a Total**

The command shown in Figure 6-31 calculates the total pay rate for all employees in department 01.

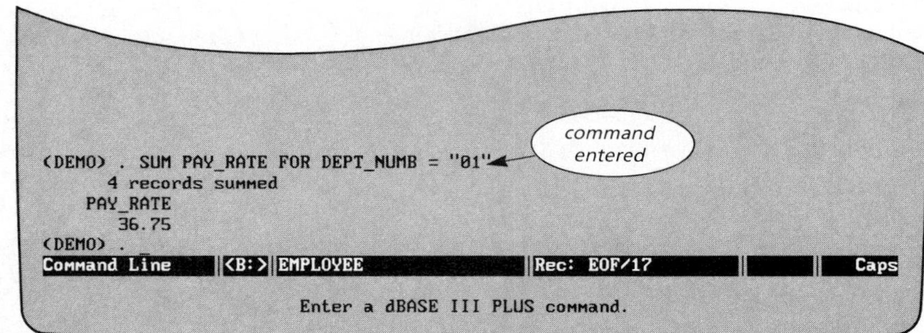


**FIGURE 6-31**
**Calculating a Total with Conditions**

The command shown in Figure 6-32 calculates the total pay rate for all employees in the union.

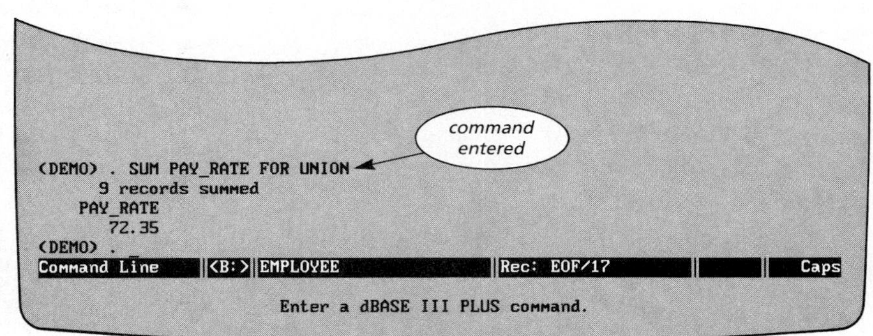


**FIGURE 6-32**
**Calculating a Total with Conditions**

## AVERAGE

The AVERAGE command is almost identical to the SUM command. The only difference is that it produces an average rather than a total. The word AVERAGE is followed by a list of the fields to be averaged. To calculate the average pay rate, for example, use the command shown in Figure 6-33.

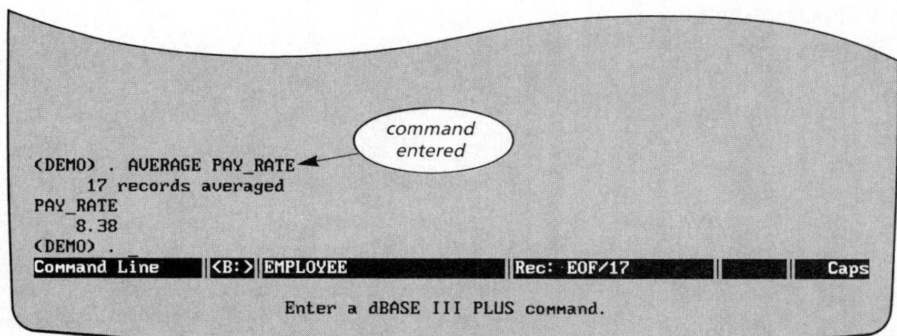


**FIGURE 6-33**
**Calculating an Average**

The command shown in Figure 6-34 calculates the average pay rate for all employees in department 01.

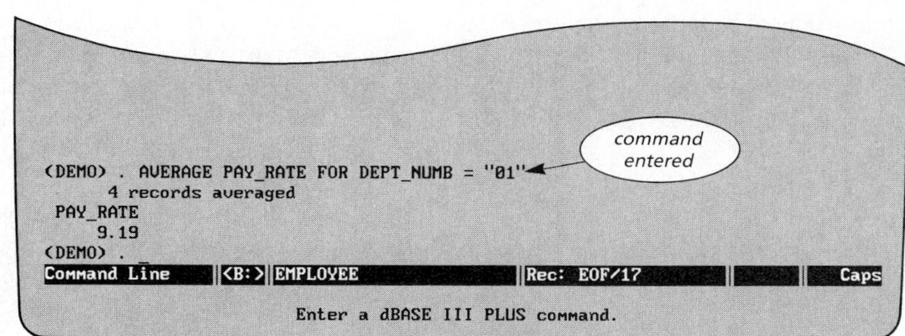


**FIGURE 6-34**
**Calculating an Average with Conditions**

The command shown in Figure 6-35 calculates the average pay rate for all employees in the union.

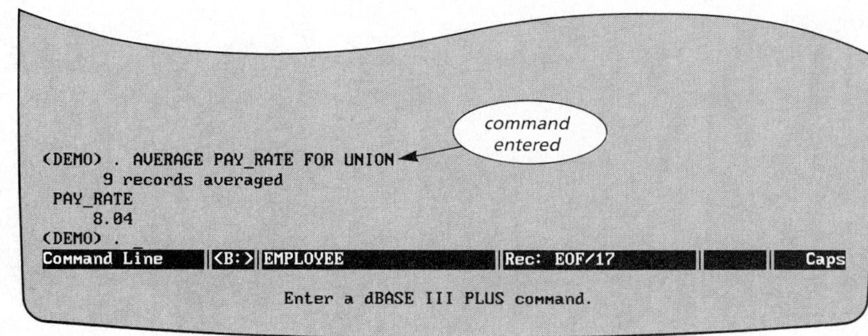


**FIGURE 6-35**
**Calculating an Average with Conditions**

## ENTERING LONG COMMANDS

Suppose you want to type this DISPLAY command: DISPLAY OFF NUMBER, NAME, DATE, PAY_RATE, DEPT_NUMB FOR DEPT_NUMB = "01" .AND. PAY_RATE > 9.00. Clearly there won't be enough room to fit this command on a single line. How can you type this line?

It turns out that dBASE handles this situation in an interesting way. Start typing the command and stop when you get to the position shown in Figure 6-36.

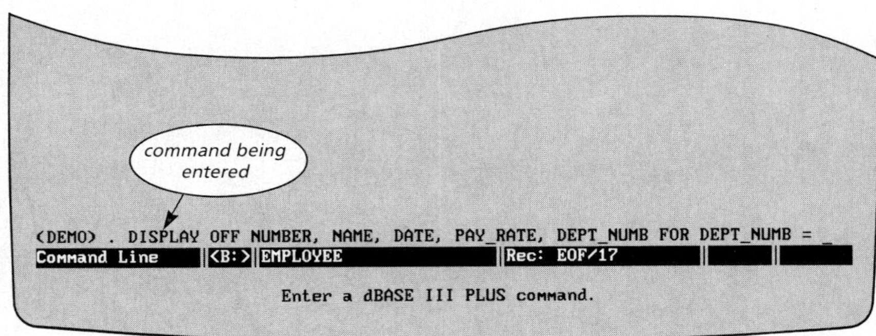


**FIGURE 6-36**
**Typing a Long Command**

Continue typing. You will see the portion you have typed move to the left to allow you to continue with the command (Figure 6-37). By the time you have completed the command, your screen will look like the one shown in Figure 6-38. If you need to corect a portion of the line that has disappeared from the screen, simply press the left arrow key enough times to move back to the desired position. As you do, dBASE will return the portion that has disappeared back to the screen.

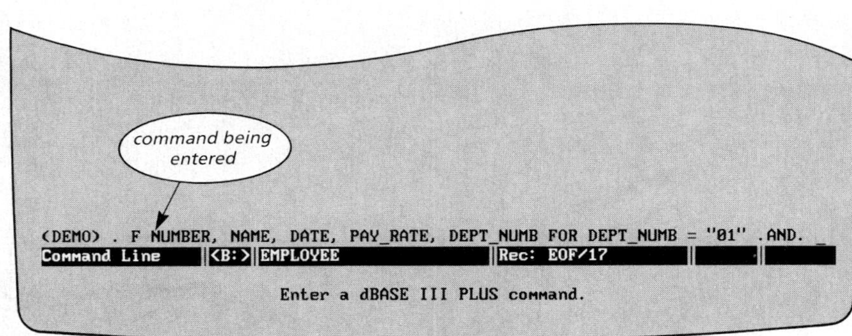


**FIGURE 6-37**
**Typing a Long Command**

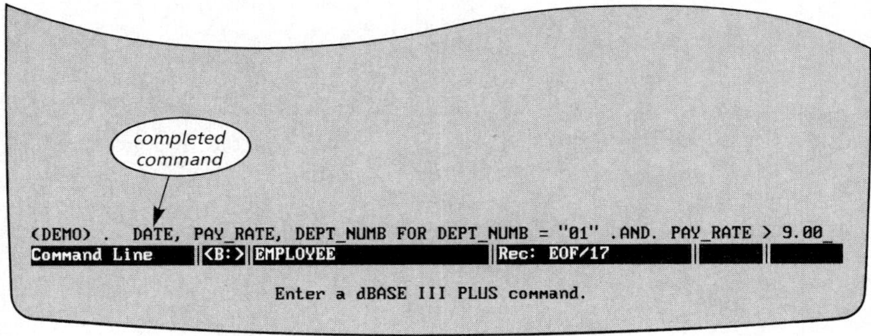


**FIGURE 6-38**
**Command Has Been Completed**

Once the command is complete, press the Enter key. The results are shown in Figure 6-39.

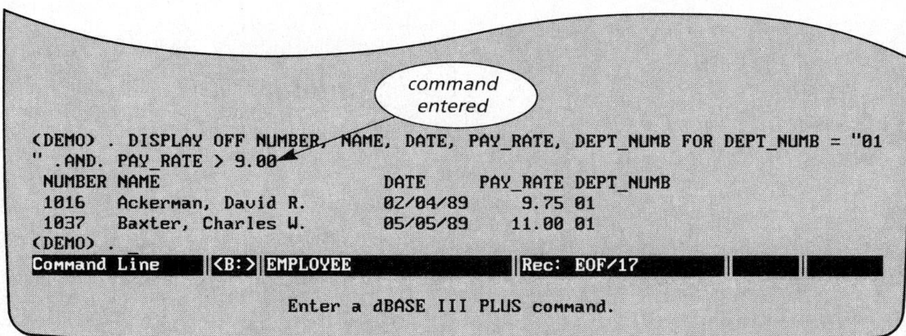


**FIGURE 6-39**
**Results of Command**

## SORT

You can use the SORT command to sort a database file. The command in Figure 6-40, sorts the active database file (EMPLOYEE) on the NAME field, producing a file called SORT1 (actually SORT1.DBF). Because it is simple enough to sort using the ASSISTANT, it might seem that you would never need this command.

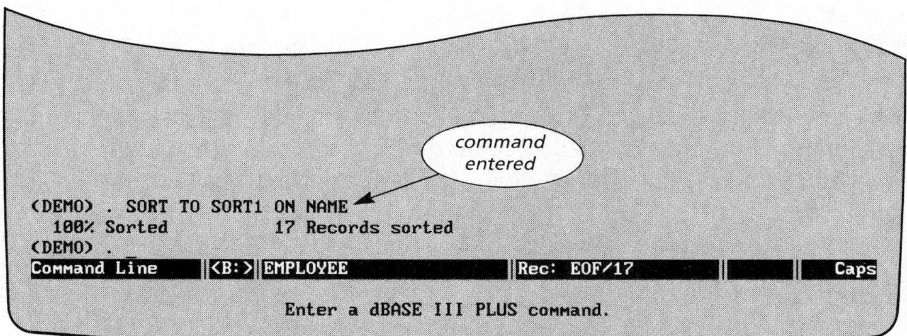


**FIGURE 6-40**
**Sorting**

There is one difficulty about sorting within the ASSISTANT, however. There is no way to sort in reverse (usually called *descending*) order. Fortunately, there is an easy way to do so using the SORT command. Simply follow the name of the key with a slash and the letter D, as shown in Figure 6-41. If there were multiple sort fields, they would all be listed after the word TO and separated by commas. Any sort field for which you want descending order would be followed by the slash and the letter D.

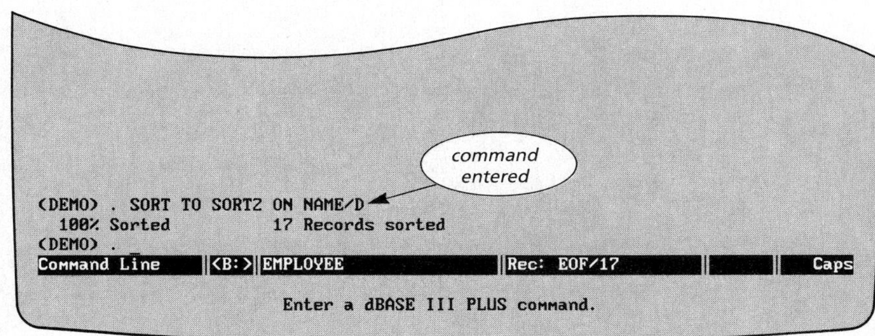


**FIGURE 6-41**
**Sorting in Descending Order**

To see the results of the sort in Figure 6-41, you could activate the file called SORT2 and then display all the records. Activating the file can be accomplished through the "Database file" option of the "Set Up" menu within the ASSISTANT. It can also be activated from the dot prompt. Type the word USE followed by the name of the file. Thus, to activate SORT2 and display all the records, you could use the commands shown in Figure 6-42. Note that the records displayed are in *reverse* alphabetical order.

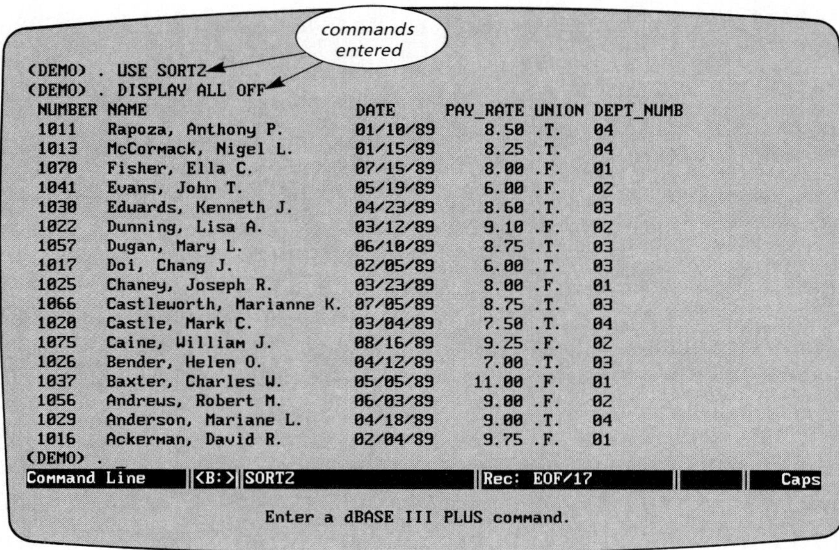


**FIGURE 6-42** Results of the Sort

# USING VIEWS

## Activating a View

Views can be used in DISPLAY commands. Activate the view before executing any of the commands. This can be accomplished through the "View" option of the "Set Up" menu within the ASSISTANT, or from the dot prompt by typing the words SET VIEW TO followed by the name of the view.

## Displaying Data in a View

To display all the data in the EMPDEPT view, for example, type the two commands shown in Figure 6-43.

Once you have activated the view you will not need to keep typing the SET VIEW TO command. From this point on, each DISPLAY command will access the data in the EMPDEPT view.

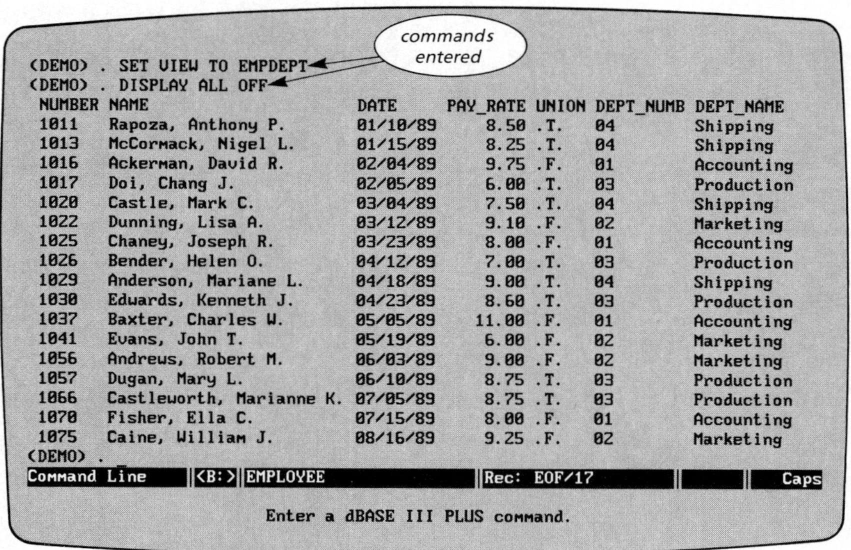


**FIGURE 6-43** Using a View

## PROGRAMMING

Using the ASSISTANT or typing commands at the dot prompt are both relatively simple actions once you have become comfortable with the various options. Sometimes, however, you may find that there is a command or series of commands that you use frequently. For example, once a week you may enter a DISPLAY command to display the employee number, name, hire date, pay rate, and pay amount (pay rate times 40). You have to enter a separate command for each department, one to print just the employees in department 01, another for department 02, and so on. You also need to calculate the average pay rate for the employees in the department and the total pay amount.

If you find yourself in such a situation, you will undoubtedly wish that there were a simple way to type the commands once and be able to use them from that point on. Fortunately, there is an easy way to do this. You simply create a file containing these commands. Such a file is called a **command file** or **program**. Programs can be created using a word processor that is capable of producing ASCII files or through the dBASE text editor. We will create some sample command files using the dBASE editor.

Let's create a program that will: (1) activate the EMPLOYEE database file; (2) produce a display of the employee number, name, hire date, pay rate, and pay amount for all employees in department 01; (3) calculate the average pay rate of all employees in department 01; and (4) calculate the total pay amount for all employees in department 01.

To start the dBASE editor, type the words MODIFY COMMAND followed by the name of the program. Let's call this program LISTEMP1. Then the appropriate command is MODIFY COMMAND LISTEMP1. Once this command has been executed you will see the screen shown in Figure 6-44. At the top of the screen is the name of the program. Note that dBASE has automatically added the extension "prg" to the name you entered. If you look for this file on your disk, it will appear as LISTEMP1.PRG.

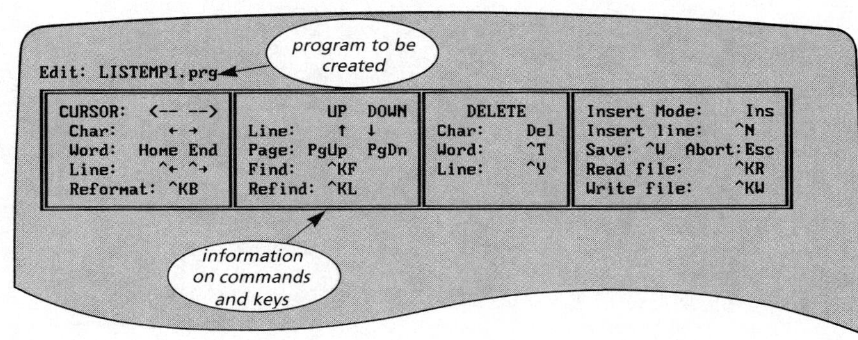


**FIGURE 6-44**
**The dBASE Editor**

The box on the screen shows the various things you can do as you create a program. The first part of the box indicates that the Left and Right Arrows will move the cursor one character to the left or right. The Home key will move the cursor one word to the left, and the End key will move it one word to the right. Holding the Ctrl key down while pressing the Left or Right Arrow key will move the cursor to the left or right end of a line. Holding the Ctrl key down and pressing the letters K and B will reformat a paragraph. (This type of reformatting, while useful for creating documents, is not used to create programs.)

The second part of the box indicates that the upward and downward arrows are used to move up or down one line, respectively. The PgUp and PgDn keys are used to move up or down a whole page. When you hold down the Ctrl key and press the letters K or F, dBASE will ask you for a string of characters to find and will then locate this string in the file. If you want to locate the next occurrence of the string of characters you just found, you can use ∧KL instead of ∧KF.

The next part of the box indicates that the Del key is used to delete a single character. Ctrl plus the letter T is used to delete a whole word. Ctrl plus the letter Y is used to delete a whole line.

The final part of the box indicates that the Ins key is used to change from insert mode to overwrite mode and back. In insert mode, typed characters are inserted into the file at the position of the cursor. In overwrite mode, typed characters at the position of the cursor replace those characters previously in the file. To insert a new line, use Ctrl plus the letter N. To save the file and terminate editing, use Ctrl plus the letter W. To terminate editing the file *but not save the changes you have made*, use Esc. (As a safety feature, dBASE will ask whether you are sure you don't want to save the changes.) To insert the contents of another file at the position of the cursor, hold down the CTRL key and type the letters KR. dBASE will request the name of the file to read. Finally, to write the contents of the current file to a different file, hold the Ctrl key down and type the letters KW. dBASE will ask you for the name of the file to write.

To create the first program, type the commands as shown in Figure 6-45. These commands accomplish the specified tasks. You should recognize the commands from the work you have done earlier in this project. There are only two new things. First, in a program, you can continue a command from one line to another by ending the line with a semicolon. Thus, the DISPLAY command is spread over three lines. Second, note the word EJECT. This is used to make the printer advance to the top of a new page. Technically, this is called a *page eject*.

If you wanted to access the EMPDEPT view rather than the single EMPLOYEE database file, the USE EMPLOYEE command would be replaced with SET VIEW TO EMPDEPT. This was not necessary here, however, since all the required data is contained within the EMPLOYEE file.

To save this program, hold the Ctrl key down and type the letter W. You can execute the commands in a program by typing the word DO followed by the name of the program at the dot prompt. Thus you may execute the commands you created by typing the words DO LISTEMP1. Try this now.

Figure 6-46 shows another useful program called ADDEMP. This program will activate the EMPLOYEE file and then put you into Append mode to allow you to add additional records to the EMPLOYEE file—the same as selecting the "Append" option from the "Update" menu of the ASSISTANT. Once you make all the additions and exit the APPEND process, the CLEAR command will clear the screen.

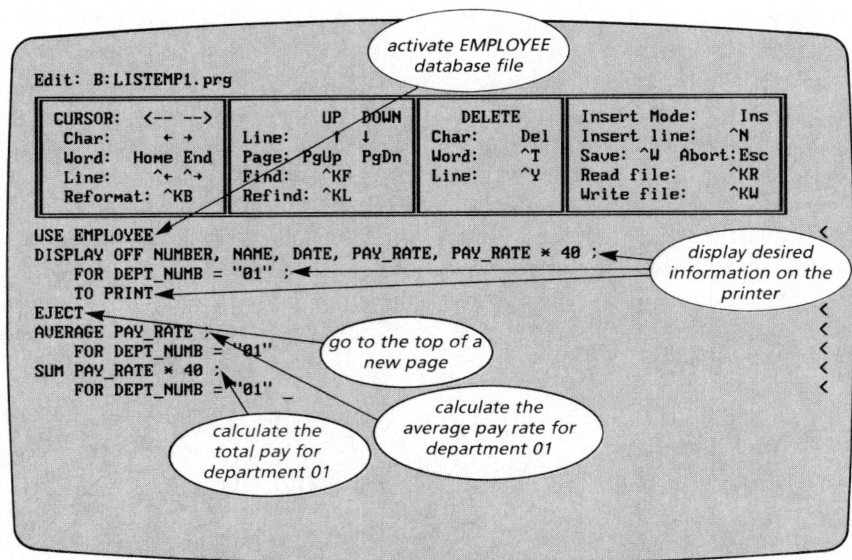


**FIGURE 6-45** Program LISTEMP1

With this program in place, if you want to add records, you don't have to go through the options of the ASSISTANT or the commands at the dot prompt. You can simply type the words DO ADDEMP. You could create a similar program called EDITEMP that replaces the word APPEND with the word EDIT. This program could be used when you want to change existing records rather than add new ones.

This is as far as we will go with programming in dBASE in this text. dBASE does have a complete programming language. There are many textbooks about dBASE programing to consult if you are interested in pursuing this study further.

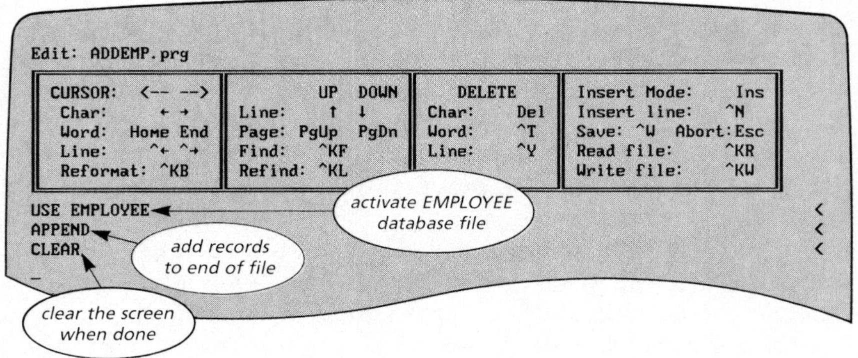


**FIGURE 6-46** Program ADDEMP

## PROJECT SUMMARY

In Project 6 you learned how to use the DISPLAY command to display data from the dot prompt. You also learned how to use the COUNT, SUM, and AVERAGE commands to calculate statistics. You learned that you can sort from the dot prompt. You activated a view and displayed data in the view from the dot prompt. Finally, you saw how to place dBASE commands in a program (also called a command file) and how to execute the commands in these programs.

If you followed along with the steps in this chapter, you have created a variety of displays. If you did not but wish to see the results now , you can use the following keystroke sequence. Start dBASE and press Esc to change to the dot prompt mode. Then type the following:

### SUMMARY OF KEYSTROKES—Project 6

| STEPS | KEY(S) PRESSED | STEPS | KEY(S) PRESSED |
|---|---|---|---|
| 1 | USE EMPLOYEE ↵ | 32 | SUM PAY_RATE FOR DEPT_NUMB = "01" ↵ |
| 2 | DISPLAY ↵ | 33 | SUM PAY_RATE FOR UNION ↵ |
| 3 | DISPLAY ALL ↵ | 34 | AVERAGE PAY_RATE ↵ |
| 4 | DISPLAY OFF ALL ↵ | 35 | AVERAGE PAY_RATE FOR DEPT_NUMB = "01" ↵ |
| 5 | DISPLAY ALL NAME, DEPT_NUMB, PAY_RATE ↵ | 36 | AVERAGE PAY_RATE FOR UNION ↵ |
| 6 | DISPLAY OFF ALL NUMBER, NAME, PAY_RATE, | 37 | DISPLAY OFF NUMBER, NAME, DATE, PAY_RATE, DEPT_NUMB |
| 7 | PAY_RATE * 40 ↵ | 38 | FOR DEPT_NUMB = "01" .AND. PAY_RATE > 9.00 ↵ |
| 8 | DISPLAY RECORD 6 ↵ | 39 | SORT TO SORT1 ON NAME ↵ |
| 9 | DISPLAY FOR NUMBER = "1030" ↵ | 40 | SORT TO SORT2 ON NAME/D ↵ |
| 10 | DISPLAY FOR PAY_RATE = 6.00 ↵ | 41 | USE SORT2 ↵ |
| 11 | DISPLAY FOR PAY_RATE > 9.00 ↵ | 42 | DISPLAY ALL OFF ↵ |
| 12 | DISPLAY OFF NAME, DEPT_NUMB, PAY_RATE FOR | 43 | SET VIEW TO EMPDEPT ↵ |
| 13 | DEPT_NUMB = "04" ↵ | 44 | DISPLAY ALL OFF ↵ |
| 14 | DISPLAY FOR NAME = "Baxter, Charles W." ↵ | 45 | DISPLAY NUMBER, NAME, PAY_RATE, DEPT_NAME FOR |
| 15 | DISPLAY FOR NAME = "BAXTER, CHARLES W." ↵ | 46 | DEPT_NAME = "Accounting" ↵ |
| 16 | DISPLAY FOR UPPER(NAME) = "BAXTER, CHARLES W." ↵ | 47 | MODIFY COMMAND LISTEMP1 ↵ |
| 17 | DISPLAY FOR NAME = "A" ↵ | 48 | USE EMPLOYEE ↵ |
| 18 | DISPLAY FOR "David" $ NAME ↵ | 49 | DISPLAY OFF NUMBER, NAME, DATE, PAY_RATE, |
| 19 | DISPLAY FOR UNION ↵ | 50 | PAY_RATE * 40 ; ↵ |
| 20 | DISPLAY FOR .NOT. UNION ↵ | 51 | SPACE SPACE SPACE SPACE FOR DEPT_NUMB = "01" ; ↵ |
| 21 | DISPLAY NUMBER, NAME, DATE, PAY_RATE FOR DATE = | 52 | SPACE SPACE SPACE SPACE TO PRINT ↵ |
| 22 | CTOD("01/15/89") ↵ | 53 | EJECT ↵ |
| 23 | DISPLAY NUMBER, NAME, DATE, PAY_RATE FOR DATE > | 54 | AVERAGE PAY_RATE ; ↵ |
| 24 | CTOD("03/01/89") ↵ | 55 | SPACE SPACE SPACE SPACE FOR DEPT_NUMB = "01" ↵ |
| 25 | DISPLAY FOR DEPT_NUMB = "01" .AND. | 56 | SUM PAY_RATE * 40 ; ↵ |
| 26 | PAY_RATE = 11.00 ↵ | 57 | SPACE SPACE SPACE SPACE FOR DEPT_NUMB = "01" Ctrl-W |
| 27 | DISPLAY FOR DEPT_NUMB = "01" .OR. UNION ↵ | 58 | DO LISTEMP1 ↵ |
| 28 | COUNT ↵ | 59 | MODIFY COMMAND ADDEMP ↵ |
| 29 | COUNT FOR DEPT_NUMB = "01" ↵ | 60 | USE EMPLOYEE ↵ |
| 30 | COUNT FOR UNION ↵ | 61 | APPEND ↵ SPACE SPACE SPACE SPACE |
| 31 | SUM PAY_RATE ↵ | 62 | CLEAR Ctrl-W |

### Project Summary (continued)

6. To suppress the printing of record numbers, use the word OFF in the DISPLAY command.
7. To display only selected fields, list the fields in the desired order in the DISPLAY command.
8. To display a single record other than the current active record, use DISPLAY RECORD followed by the number of the desired record.
9. To restrict the display to those records meeting a condition, use a FOR clause in the DISPLAY command.
10. To avoid having to worry about uppercase and lowercase letters when searching for a name, use the UPPER function.
11. To search for a name containing a given string of characters, use the substring function, $.
12. To use a date field in a condition, use the CTOD function.
13. To count the number of records satisfying a given condition, use the COUNT command.
14. To calculate totals, use the SUM command.
15. To calculate averages, use the AVERAGE command.
16. To sort the records in a database file, producing another database file, use the SORT command. To sort in descending order, follow the name of the sort key with /D.
17. To activate a view, use the SET VIEW TO command. (The view could also be activated through the ASSISTANT using the "View" option of the "Set Up" menu.)
18. To enter a command that is too long to fit on the screen, simply type the command. Once you have reached the right-hand edge of the screen, dBASE will begin pushing the command to the left to allow more room for you to type.
19. A file containing dBASE commands is called a **command file** or **program**. To execute the commands in the file, type the word DO followed by the name of the program at the dot prompt. dBASE automatically assigns such files the extension "PRG."
20. The EJECT command causes the printer to advance to the top of the next page.
21. The APPEND command can be used to add records to a database file.
22. The EDIT command can be used to change records in a database file.

## STUDENT ASSIGNMENTS

### STUDENT ASSIGNMENT 1: True/False

**Instructions:** Circle T if the statement is true and F if the statement is false.

T F 1. While working at the dot prompt, pressing the up arrow key will recall the most recently entered command.
T F 2. To clear the screen from the dot prompt, type the word CLEAR.
T F 3. If no scope is entered in a DISPLAY command, a scope of "ALL" is assumed.
T F 4. To send the results of a DISPLAY command to the printer, include the clause TO PRINT in the command.
T F 5. To suppress the printing of record numbers, include the clause NOREC in a DISPLAY command.
T F 6. To display a single record, the record must be the current active record before the DISPLAY command is executed.
T F 7. To restrict the display to records meeting a certain condition, use a FOR clause.
T F 8. The command DISPLAY FOR NUMBER = "1030" is invalid because 1030 cannot be enclosed in quotes.
T F 9. The command DISPLAY PAY_RATE > 9.00 will display all records that contain a pay rate greater than 9.00.
T F 10. If the UNION field is a logical field, the command DISPLAY FOR UNION could be used to display all records for which the UNION field is true.
T F 11. The SUM command could be used to count the number of records in a database file.
T F 12. To list each employee whose name contains the characters "R.", an appropriate FOR clause would be "R." $ NAME.
T F 13. The command SORT TO XXX ON YYY will create a file called YYY.DBF.
T F 14. To sort in descending order, follow the name of the sort key with a slash and the letter D (/D).
T F 15. A DISPLAY command can be used to display data in a view.
T F 16. To execute the commands stored in the command file XXX.PRG, type the expression DO XXX at the dot prompt.

## STUDENT ASSIGNMENT 2: Multiple Choice

**Instructions:** Circle the correct response.

1. The command DISPLAY OFF ALL will display
   a. all records but the record number will not be displayed.
   b. all records on the screen but the printer will be turned off.
   c. all records on the printer but the screen display will be turned off.
   d. only the first record in the file.
2. The command DISPLAY FOR PAY_RATE = 6.00, when the PAY_RATE field is a numeric field, will display
   a. the first record in the database file where the pay rate field contains a value equal to 6.00.
   b. all the records in the database file where the pay rate field contains a value equal to 6.00.
   c. the current active record if the value of the pay rate field on that record is equal to 6.00. If not, no records will be displayed.
   d. an error message, since 6.00 is not enclosed in quotes.
3. The command DISPLAY FOR UPPER(NAME) = "BAXTER, CHARLES W." will display
   a. all names in uppercase letters of the alphabet.
   b. the name Baxter, Charles W. if it is in the NAME field of the active record in uppercase letters of the alphabet.
   c. all records in the database containing the name following the equal sign regardless of whether the characters were entered in uppercase or lowercase letters of the alphabet.
   d. all records in the database containing the name Baxter, Charles W. in uppercase letters of the alphabet.
4. Which of the following commands can be used to display all records in a logical field called UNION that contain the entry .F.?
   a. DISPLAY FOR UNION
   b. DISPLAY FOR UNION = F
   c. DISPLAY FOR .NOT. UNION
   d. DISPLAY FOR NOT UNION
5. The command to count all the records in a file is:
   a. SUM
   b. SUM ALL RECORDS
   c. COUNT ALL RECORDS
   d. COUNT
6. The clause that can be used to test whether the characters "Mary" are contained within the NAME field is:
   a. NAME CONTAINS "Mary"
   b. "MARY" $ NAME
   c. "MARY" ISIN NAME
   d. NAME $ "MARY"
7. The command to sort the EMPLOYEE file by descending pay rate, producing the file called SORTEMP, is:
   a. SORT TO SORTEMP on PAY_RATE/D
   b. SORT TO SORTEMP ON DESCENDING PAY_RATE
   c. SORT ON SORTEMP, PAY_RATE/D
   d. SORT DESCENDING PAY_RATE TO SORTEMP
8. When typing a command at the dot prompt that is too long to fit on a single line,
   a. type what will fit on one line, press Enter, and continue typing.
   b. type what will fit on one line, type an ampersand (&), press Enter, and then continue typing.
   c. just keep typing.
   d. such a command cannot be entered from the dot prompt. You must use the ASSISTANT.

## STUDENT ASSIGNMENT 3: Understanding dBASE Options

**Instructions:** Explain what will happen after you have typed each of the following lines at the dot prompt and pressed the Enter key.

Problem 1. DISPLAAY

Explanation: ____________________

Problem 2. DISPLAY OFF ALL TO PRINT

Explanation: ____________________

### Student Assignment 3 (continued)

Problem 3. DISPLAY FOR UNION

Explanation: ____________________

Problem 4. SORT TO DEPARTMENT ON NAME

Explanation: ____________________

## STUDENT ASSIGNMENT 4: Using dBASE

**Instructions:** Explain how to accomplish each of the following tasks using dBASE.

Problem 1. Recall the most recently entered command.

Explanation: ____________________

Problem 2. Display all records without record numbers.

Explanation: ____________________

Problem 3. Send the results of a DISPLAY command to the printer.

Explanation: ____________________

Problem 4. Find all employees with a first name of Mary.

Explanation: ____________________

Problem 5. Find the average pay rate for those employees who are not in the union.

Explanation: ____________________

Problem 6. Sort the EMPLOYEE file by descending pay rate within department, producing a file called SORTPAY.

Explanation: ____________________

## STUDENT ASSIGNMENT 5: Recovering from Problems

**Instructions:** In each of the following cases, a problem occurred. Explain the cause of the problem and how it can be corrected.

Problem 1: You type the expression DISPLAY FOR NUMBER = 1030 and dBASE responds with the message "Data type mismatch."

Cause of Problem: ____________________

Method of Correction: ____________________

Problem 2: You attempt to display all data for members of the union by typing the words DISPLAY ALL UNION. Instead, you see a column of T's and F's.

Cause of Problem: ____________________

Method of Correction: ____________________

Problem 3: You attempt to display the record for an employee with a specific name. No record is displayed even though you know such an employee exists in the database.

Cause of Problem: ____________________

Method of Correction: ____________________

# MINICASES

## Working from the Dot Prompt

### Minicase 1: Personal Checks

**Instructions:** Use the database of personal checks that you created in Minicase 1 of Project 1 and modified in Minicase 1 of Project 5. You should use the view, EXPVIEW, that you created in Project 5. Activate the view by typing the words SET VIEW TO EXPVIEW at the dot prompt. Once you have done this, use dBASE commands to accomplish the following tasks.

For each problem, write the command that you use to accomplish the task in the space provided. Execute the command on the computer. Obtain a printed copy of the output by holding down the Shift key and pressing the PrtSc key, or by ending the command with the clause TO PRINT.

1. Display the first record.

   COMMAND: ______________________________

2. Display all the records.

   COMMAND: ______________________________

3. Display all the records but do not include record numbers.

   COMMAND: ______________________________

4. Display the CHECK NUMBER, DATE, PAYEE, CHECK AMOUNT, and EXPENSE code fields for all records.

   COMMAND: ______________________________

5. Display the sixth record.

   COMMAND: ______________________________

6. Display the record for check number 108.

   COMMAND: ______________________________

7. Display any record on which the check amount is $25.00.

   COMMAND: ______________________________

8. Display any record on which the check amount is greater than $50.00.

   COMMAND: ______________________________

9. Display the records for all checks written for entertainment. Include the CHECK NUMBER, PAYEE, CHECK AMOUNT, and EXPENSE DESCRIPTION fields.

   COMMAND: ______________________________

10. Display the records for all checks written to Sav-Mor Groceries. Use the UPPER function in your DISPLAY command.

    COMMAND: ______________________________

11. Display the records for all checks on which the name of the payee contains the word "Groceries."

    COMMAND: ______________________________

12. Display the records for all checks written that are tax deductible.

    COMMAND: ______________________________

### Minicase 1 (continued)

13. Display the records for all checks written that are not tax deductible.

    COMMAND: ______________________________

14. Display the records for all checks written on January 19, 1990. (Remember that you have to use the CTOD function. In this case, you would use CTOD("01/19/90") rather than simply 01/19/90 in your FOR clause.)

    COMMAND: ______________________________

15. Display the records for all checks written on or after January 12, 1990.

    COMMAND: ______________________________

16. Display the records of all checks written for entertainment with a check amount above $25.00.

    COMMAND: ______________________________

17. Display the records for all checks written for household expenses or for food expenses.

    COMMAND: ______________________________

18. Count the number of checks in the database file.

    COMMAND: ______________________________

19. Count the number of checks on which the expense is charity.

    COMMAND: ______________________________

20. Count the number of tax-deductible checks.

    COMMAND: ______________________________

21. Sum the amount of checks written.

    COMMAND: ______________________________

22. Sum the amounts of the checks written for household expenses.

    COMMAND: ______________________________

23. Average the CHECK AMOUNT for all checks written.

    COMMAND: ______________________________

24. Average the CHECK AMOUNT for all checks written for entertainment.

    COMMAND: ______________________________

25. Sort the data in the view on descending CHECK AMOUNT within EXPENSE CODE, producing SORTEXP1. Activate SORTEXP1. List the records in SORTEXP1.

    COMMAND: ______________________________

26. Create a program called CHKLIST1. This program should (a) activate the CHECK database file; (b) display the check number, date, payee, and check amount for all expenses with the expense code HH; (c) calculate the total of the check amounts for all expenses with the expense code HH which are tax deductible; and (d) calculate the total of the check amounts for all expenses with the expense code HH which are not tax deductible. Once you have done this, execute the program. Enter the commands in your program in the space below.

    COMMANDS: ______________________________

    ______________________________

    ______________________________

## Minicase 2: Music Library

**Instructions:** Use the music library database that you created in Minicase 2 of Project 1 and modified in Minicase 2 of Project 5. You should use the view, MUSVIEW, that you created in Project 5. Activate the view by typing the words SET VIEW TO MUSVIEW at the dot prompt. Once you have done this, use dBASE commands to accomplish the following tasks.

For each problem, write the command that you use to accomplish the task in the space provided. Execute the command on the computer. Obtain a printed copy of the output by holding down the Shift key and pressing the PrtSc key, or by ending the command with the clause TO PRINT.

1. Display the first record. COMMAND: ______________________
2. Display all the records. COMMAND: ______________________
3. Display all the records but don't include record numbers.

   COMMAND: ______________________
4. Display the MUSIC NAME, ARTIST, TYPE, and COST for all records.

   COMMAND: ______________________
5. Display the sixth record. COMMAND: ______________________
6. Display the record on which the Music Name is "America."

   COMMAND: ______________________
7. Display the records for the music with the category of classical.

   COMMAND: ______________________
8. Display any record on which the cost is greater than $7.00.

   COMMAND: ______________________
9. Display the records for all music on compact disk (CD). Include the TYPE, MUSIC NAME, ARTIST, and COST.

   COMMAND: ______________________
10. Display the records on which the artist is "Judd, Mary." Use the UPPER function in your DISPLAY command.

    COMMAND: ______________________
11. Display the records on which the name of the artist contains "Ralph."

    COMMAND: ______________________
12. Display the records for all music that is on LP.

    COMMAND: ______________________
13. Display the records for all music that is not on LP.

    COMMAND: ______________________
14. Display the records for all music on which the date is February 15, 1990. (Remember that you have to use the CTOD function. In this case, you would use CTOD("02/15/90") rather than simply 02/15/90 in your FOR clause.)

    COMMAND: ______________________
15. Display the records for all music on which the date is after February 1, 1990.

    COMMAND: ______________________
16. Display the records for all classical music that costs less than $8.95.

    COMMAND: ______________________

**Minicase 2 (continued)**

17. Display the records for all music that is either classical or vocal.

    COMMAND: ____________________

18. Count the number of records in the database file.

    COMMAND: ____________________

19. Count the number of music selections in the vocal category.

    COMMAND: ____________________

20. Sum the total cost of all types of music.

    COMMAND: ____________________

21. Sum the total cost of the music in the country category.

    COMMAND: ____________________

22. Determine the average cost for all types of music.

    COMMAND: ____________________

23. Determine the average cost of music in the classical category.

    COMMAND: ____________________

24. Sort the data in the view on descending COST within CATEGORY, producing SORTMUS1. Activate SORTMUS1. List the records in SORTMUS1.

    COMMAND: ____________________

25. Create a program called MUSLIST1. This program should (a) activate the MUSIC database file; (b) display the date, music name, artist, category code, and cost for all records whose type is LP; (c) calculate the average cost for all records whose category code is CL; and (d) calculate the average cost for all records whose category code is RK. Once you have done this, execute the program. Enter the commands in your program in the space below.

    COMMANDS: ____________________

## Minicase 3: Computer Software Store

**Instructions:** Use the database of computer software that you created in Minicase 3 of Project 1 and modified in Minicase 3 of Project 5. Use the view, SOFTVIEW, that you created in Project 5. Activate the view by typing the words SET VIEW TO SOFTVIEW at the dot prompt. Once you have done this, use dBASE commands to accomplish the following tasks.

For each problem, write the command that you use to accomplish the task in the space provided. Execute the command on the computer. Obtain a printed copy of the output by holding down the Shift key and pressing the PrtSc key, or by ending the command with the clause TO PRINT.

1. Display the first record.

   COMMAND: ____________________

2. Display all the records.

   COMMAND: ____________________

3. Display all the records but don't include record numbers.

   COMMAND: ______________________________

4. Display the SOFTWARE NAME field, the CATEGORY field, the MS_DOS field, the QUANTITY field, and the COST field for all records in the database.

   COMMAND: ______________________________

5. Display the sixth record.

   COMMAND: ______________________________

6. Display the record on which the software name is Image Fonts.

   COMMAND: ______________________________

7. Display any record on which the cost is $49.95.

   COMMAND: ______________________________

8. Display any record on which the cost is less than $50.00.

   COMMAND: ______________________________

9. Display the records for all software produced by Electric Software. Include the software name, category, quantity, and cost.

   COMMAND: ______________________________

10. Display the records for all software on which the category is "Database." Use the UPPER function in your DISPLAY command.

    COMMAND: ______________________________

11. Display the records for all software whose name contains "Data."

    COMMAND: ______________________________

12. Display all software that is MS-DOS compatible (the MS_DOS field is true).

    COMMAND: ______________________________

13. Display all software that is not MS-DOS compatible.

    COMMAND: ______________________________

14. Display all records with a quantity less than 10.

    COMMAND: ______________________________

15. Display all records with a quantity greater than 25.

    COMMAND: ______________________________

16. Display all word processing software (WP in CATEGORY field) that costs less than $50.00.

    COMMAND: ______________________________

17. Display all records with a category of database or spreadsheet.

    COMMAND: ______________________________

18. Count the number of records in the database file.

    COMMAND: ______________________________

### Minicase 3 (continued)

19. Sum the QUANTITY field to determine the number of products on hand.

    COMMAND: ______________________________

20. Average the COST field to determine the average cost of the software.

    COMMAND: ______________________________

21. Average the cost of the software with the category of Education.

    COMMAND: ______________________________

22. Sort the data in the view on descending COST within CATEGORY, producing SORTSFT1. Activate SORTSFT1. List the records in SORTSFT1.

    COMMAND: ______________________________

23. Create a program called SRTLIST1. This program should (a) activate the SOFTWARE database file; (b) display the software name, category, quantity, cost, and on-hand value (quantity times cost) for all software produced by the company whose code is 05; (c) calculate the average cost of all the software for which the company code is 05 and that is MS-DOS compatible; and (d) calculate the average cost of all the software for which the company code is 05 and that is not MS-DOS compatible. Once you have done this, execute the program. Enter the commands in your program in the space below.

    COMMANDS: ______________________________

    ______________________________

    ______________________________

## Minicase 4: Home Sales

**Instructions:** Use the database of homes for sale that you created in Minicase 4 of Project 1 and modified in Minicase 4 of Project 5. Use the view, ZIPVIEW, that you created in Project 5. Activate the view by typing the words SET VIEW TO ZIPVIEW at the dot prompt. Once you have done this, use dBASE commands to accomplish the following tasks.

For each problem, write the command that you use to accomplish the task in the space provided. Execute the command on the computer. Obtain a printed copy of the output by holding down the Shift key and pressing the PrtSc key, or by ending the command with the clause TO PRINT.

1. Display the first record.

   COMMAND: ______________________________

2. Display all the records.

   COMMAND: ______________________________

3. Display all the records but do not include record numbers.

   COMMAND: ______________________________

4. Display the PRICE field, the ADDRESS field, the CITY field, and the ZIP field for all records in the database.

   COMMAND: ______________________________

5. Display the sixth record.

   COMMAND: ______________________________

6. Display the record that has 10/22/90 in the DATE field. (Remember that you have to use the CTOD function. In this case, you would use CTOD("10/22/90") rather than simply 10/22/90 in your FOR clause.)

   COMMAND: ______________________________

7. Display information about the house at 145 Oak Ave.

   COMMAND: ______________________________

8. Display the records for all houses listed in the city of Anaheim.

   COMMAND: ______________________________

9. Display the records for all houses in the 92641 zip code area.

   COMMAND: ______________________________

10. Display the records for all houses with a pool (the POOL field is true).

    COMMAND: ______________________________

11. Display the records for all houses that do not have a pool.

    COMMAND: ______________________________

12. Display the records for all houses with a price of less than $125,000.00.

    COMMAND: ______________________________

13. Display the records for all houses with a price greater than $150,000.00.

    COMMAND: ______________________________

14. Display the records for all four-bedroom houses that cost less than $100,000.00.

    COMMAND: ______________________________

15. Count the number of records in the database file.

    COMMAND: ______________________________

16. Find the average cost of a house in Anaheim.

    COMMAND: ______________________________

17. Find the average cost of a four-bedroom house.

    COMMAND: ______________________________

18. Find the average cost of a three-bedroom house in Garden Grove.

    COMMAND: ______________________________

19. Sort the data in the view on descending PRICE within ZIP, producing SORTHSE1. Activate SORTHSE1. List the records in SORTHSE1.

    COMMAND: ______________________________

20. Create a program called HMSLIST1. This program should (a) activate the HOMES database file; (b) display the date, address, zip, number of bedrooms, number of bathrooms, and price for all homes with a pool; (c) calculate the average price for homes with a pool; d) calculate the average price for homes that do not have a pool. Once you have done this, execute the program. Enter the commands in your program in the space below.

    COMMANDS: ______________________________

    ______________________________

# dBASE Index

# Photo Credits

**Chapter 1**

**Page 1.1** H. Armstrong Roberts/Camerique / **1-1** Photo Network/Michael Manheim / **1-2, 1-3** International Business Machines Corp. / **1-4** Wyse Technology / **1-8** (a) Compaq Computer Corp.; (b) NCR Corp.; (c) International Business Machines Corp.; (d) Cray Research, Inc.; (e) Paul Shambroom / **1-10** Curtis Fukuda / **1-15** Hewlett-Packard Co. / **1-16** Honeywell Bull, Inc. / **1-17** Modular Computer Systems, Inc. / **1-18** Hewlett-Packard Company / **1-19** Coin Financial Systems / **1-20** Control Data Corp. / **1-21** Racal-Milgo / **1-22** McDonnell Douglas Automation Co. / **1-23** Intertec Diversified Systems / **1-24** Racal-Milgo / **1-25** Management Science America / **Page 1.25** Top: United Press International; Bottom: (left) Carl Howard; (center) Iowa State University; (right) Princeton University / **Page 1.26** Top: U.S. Department of the Navy; Bottom: (both) / International Business Machines Corp. / **Page 1.27** Top: (left) International Business Machines Corp.; (right both) Intel Corp.; Bottom: (left) Dartmouth College News Service; (right) Digital Equipment Corp. / **Page 1.28** Top: (left both) International Business Machines Corp.; (right) Ira Wyman; Bottom: (left) The Computer Museum, Boston; (right) Apple Computer, Inc. / **Page 1.29** Top: (left) Microsoft Corp.; (right both) Lotus Development Corp.; Bottom: International Business Machines Corp. / **Page 1.30** Top: International Business Machines Corp.; Bottom: Compaq Computer Corp.

**Chapter 2**

**Page 2.1** P. Skrivan/H. Armstrong Roberts / **2-1** (a,b,d) Curtis Fukuda; (c) Ashton-Tate / **2-2** (left) Curtis Fukuda; (right) Hewlett-Packard Co. / **2-12** (left) Curtis Fukuda; (right) Lotus Development Corp. / **2-14** International Business Machines Corp. / **2-21** Curtis Fukuda / **2-29** Compaq Computer Corp. / **2-30** Radio Shack, A Division of Tandy Corp. / **2-31** Electrohome Ltd. / **2-32** Aldus Corp. / **2-33** Claris Corp. / **2-34** Curtis Fukuda / **2-35** (top both, bottom left) Curtis Fukuda; (bottom right) TDA, Inc. / **Page 2.20** MicroPro International Corp. / **Page 2.21** (both) Ashton-Tate / **Page 2.22** Polaroid Corp.

**Chapter 3**

**Page 3.1** Gary Gladstone/Image Bank

**Chapter 4**

**Page 4.1** Texas Instruments, Inc. / **4-2** Curtis Fukuda / **4-3** (left) Wyse Technology; (right) Apollo Computer, Inc. / **4-4** Wyse Technology / **4-5** International Business Machines Corp. / **4-6** (top) Logitech, Inc.; (bottom) Curtis Fukuda / **4-7** Logitech, Inc. / **4-8** Compaq Computer Corp. / **4-9** Diebold, Inc. / **4-10** Adage, Inc. / **4-11** Lear Siegler, Inc. / **4-12** CalComp / **4-13** Computervision Corp. / **4-14** Texas Instruments, Inc. / **4-16** NCR Corp. / **4-17** Soricon Corp. / **4-20** Caere Corp. / **4-21** (both) Spectra Physics / **4-22** AST Research, Inc. / **4-23** Wang Laboratories, Inc. / **4-24** LXE Division of Electromagnetic Sciences, Inc. / **4-25** Motorola, Inc. / **4-33** Curtis Fukuda / **4-37** Mohawk Data Sciences Corp. / **4-44** Acme Visible Records

**Chapter 5**

**Page 5.1** Micron Technology, Inc. / **5-18** Intel Corp. / **5-20** NCR Comten, Inc. / **Page 5.17** (1), (2), (3) Intel Corp. / **Page 5.18** (4), (5) Siltec Corp.; (6), (7), (8) Intel Corp. / **Page 5.19** (9) Intel Corp.; (10) National Semiconductor Corp.; (11) International Business Machines Corp.; (12) AT&T Bell Laboratories; (13) 3M Company

**Chapter 6**

**Page 6.1** Eastman Kodak Co. / **6-1** Xerox Corp. / **6-6** Micrografx, Inc. / **6-7** International Business Machine Corp.; / **6-8** Micrografx, Inc. / **6-11** (left) Storage Technology Corp.; (right) Atchison, Topeka and Santa Fe Railway Co. / **6-12** Epson America, Inc. / **6-13** (both) Printronix / **6-14** DataProducts Corp. / **6-18** Okidata / **6-19** Beagle Bros. / **6-20** Radio Shack, A Division of Tandy Corp. / **6-22** International Business Machines Corp. / **6-24** Hewlett-Packard Co. / **6-26** McDonnell Douglas Automation Co. / **6-27** Dataproducts Corp. / **6-28** Xerox Corp. / **6-29** Beehive International / **6-32** Toshiba America, Inc. / **6-33** Radio Shack, A Division of Tandy Corp. / **6-36** (left) Applicon, Inc.; (right) Evans & Sutherland / **6-38** Hewlett-Packard Co. / **6-39** (both) CalComp

**Chapter 7**

**Page 7.1** Michael Salas/Image Bank / **7-2, 7-3** Curtis Fukuda / **7-5** Kao Corp. of America / **7-12** Hewlett-Packard Co. / **7-13** (both) Plus Development Corp. / **7-14** Seagate Technology / **7-16** Plus Development Corp. / **7-17** Curtis Fukuda / **7-18** Everex Systems, Inc. / **7-19** NNC Electronics / **7-20** International Business Machines Corp. / **7-21** Lockheed Corp. / **7-24** (top) Hewlett-Packard Co.; (bottom) Curtis Fukuda / **7-27** Hewlett-Packard Co. / **7-28** Curtis Fukuda / **7-32** (left) 3M Company; (right) Drexler Technology Corp. / **7-33** Hitachi America Ltd. / **7-34, 7-35** Storage Technology Corp.

**Chapter 8**

Page 8.1 © Brett Froomer 1988 / **8-17** Hewlett-Packard Co.

**Chapter 9**

**Page 9.1** Lou Jones/Image Bank / **9-2** BR Intec Corp. / **9-3** Corning Glass Works / **9-4** Siecor Corp. of America / **9-5** Gregory Heisler/Image Bank / **9-6** Hewlett-Packard Co. / **9-7** NASA / **9-16, 9-17** Hayes Microcomputer Products, Inc. / **9-18** Panasonic Industrial Co. / **9-20** International Business Machines Corp. / **9-21** Hayes Microcomputer Products, Inc. / **9-25** Bank of America

**Chapter 10**

**Page 10.1** AT&T Archives / **10-9** UIS, Inc. / **10-11** International Business Machines Corp. / **10-12** Apple Computer, Inc.

**Chapter 11**

**Page 11.1** American Software / **11-2** (c) Adobe Systems, Inc. All rights reserved. / **11-3** T/Maker Co. / **11-4** WordPerfect Corp. / **11-5** TOPS, A Division of Sun Microsystems, Inc. / **11-6** Computer Associates / **11-7** Ziff-Davis Publishing Co. / **11-11** InfoWorld Publishing, Inc. / **11-12—11-14** Curtis Fukuda

**Chapter 12**

**Page 12.1** Kay Chernush/Image Bank / **12-1** Internal Revenue Service / **12-2** Hewlett-Packard Co. / **12-3** Integrated Software Systems Corp. / **12-4** Neuron Data, Inc. / **12-18** Curtis Fukuda / **12-19** American Software / **12-20** Walter Bibikow/Image Bank / **12-21** Curtis Fukuda

**Chapter 13**

**Page 13.1** Curtis Fukuda / **13-12** U.S. Department of the Navy / **13-26, 13-27** Oracle Corp.

**Chapter 14**

**Page 14.1** Compaq Computer Corp. / **14-1** Radio Shack, A Division of Tandy Corp. / **14-2** © 1988 Christopher Springmann / **14-4** ComputerLand / **14-5** Radio Shack, A Division of Tandy Corp. / **14-6** Cullinet Software / **14-12** Interface Group, Inc. /

**Chapter 15**

**Page 15.1** Don Carroll/Image Bank / **15-1** (top to bottom) Radio Shack, A Division of Tandy Corp.; Claris Corp.; Lotus Development Corp.; Compaq Computer Corp.; Hewlett-Packard Co. / **15-2** Canon USA, Inc. / **15-3** NEC America, Inc. / **15-4** Apollo Computer, Inc. / **15-5** NASA / **15-6** General Motors Corp. / **15-8** (both) Broderbund Software, Inc. / **15-9** Electronic Arts / **15-11** Quicksoft, Inc.

**Cover**: Art direction and design by Alexander Atkins Design / **Photo(s)**: Tim Davis Photography.

# Computer Concepts Index

*See also:*
Introduction to DOS Index, page DOS 32
WordPerfect Index, page WP 175
Lotus 1-2-3 Index, page L 239
dBASE III PLUS Index, page dB 240

**Access arms**: Mechanical arms that hold one or more read/write heads; used in hard disk drives.
and hard disk storage, 7.9
**Access time**: The time required to access and retrieve data on a floppy disk.
defined, 5.15, 7.7–8
Actuator (See Access arms)
Adding records, 8.7–8.8
**Ada**: A language used by the Department of Defense that is designed to be portable (usable on different computers) and easy to maintain; named after Augusta Ada Byron.
Alpha numeric, 3.4
**American National Standards Institute (ANSI)** and program flowcharts, 13.6
American Standard Code for Information Interchange (See ASCII)
**Analog signal**: A signal used on communications lines that consists of a single, continuous electrical wave. Compare with digital signal.
and data communications, 9.9
**Analysis**: In information system development, the separation of a system into its parts to determine how the system works, combined with the development of a proposed solution to system problems.
defined, 12.6 detailed system, 12.7–9
example of, 12.10
feasibility study, 12.9–10
preliminary investigation, 12.7
ANSI (See American National Standards Institute)
**Application generators**: Programs that produce other programs based on input, output, and processing specifications from the user.
and program development, 13.18
**Application software package**: Computer programs that perform common business or personal tasks; purchased from software vendors or stores, 1.10
commercial, 11.2
example of, 1.12–15
general, 11.3–6
microcomputer, 1.10–15, 15.11
operating system and, 10.4
purchasing guidelines, 2.18
system software vs., 10.2
types of, 1.11
**Arithmetic/logic unit**: The part of the CPU that performs arithmetic and logic operations.
CPU and, 5.3
instruction execution and, 5.10
**Arithmetic operations**: Numeric calculations such as addition, subtraction, multiplication, and division.
in CPU, 5.3
defined, 1.7
example of, 3.9–10
Arrow keys, 4.5
**Artificial intelligence**: Methods of simulating aspects of human reasoning with computers.
and expert systems, 12.4
**ASCII (American Standard Code for Information Interchange)**: The most widely used computer code for representing characters.
data representation and, 5.5–6
floppy disk storage and, 7.7
**Assembly language**: Similar to machine language, but uses abbreviations for machine instructions called mnemonics or symbolic operation codes that are easier for humans to work with.
defined, 13.12–13
**Asynchronous transmission mode**: Data communication method in which individual characters (made up of bits) are transmitted at irregular intervals, for instance as they are entered by a user.
defined, 9.10
**Attribute**: A field in a relational database.
defined, 8.13
**Automated office**: Describes the use of computers, facsimile machines, and electronic communications to make office work more efficient.
information processing trends and, 15.2
summary of, 15.5
**Auxiliary storage**: Stores programs and data when they are not being processed; similar to a filing cabinet.
defined, 7.2
direct-access storage devices, 7.12
disk cartridges, 7.10
file organization methods, 8.3–7
floppy disks, 7.4–8
hard card, 7.9
hard disks, 1.7, 7.8–10
in information processing cycle, 3.3
magnetic disks, 7.12–14
magnetic tape, 7.14–17
mass storage devices, 7.18
on microcomputers, 7.4–12
on medium and large computers, 7.12–17
networks and, 9.15
optical, 7.17–18
solid-state devices, 7.18
types of, 1.17–18, 7.19
user needs and, 7.3
**Auxiliary storage unit**: Computer hardware used to store instructions and data when they are not being used in the main memory of the computer.
defined, 1.7 (See also Auxiliary storage)

Backup of data files, 3.6
disks and, 7.11–12
magnetic tape and, 1.17, 7.15
reasons for, 7.9, 7.21
sequential files and, 8.4
**Bandwidth**: The range of frequencies that a communications channel can carry.
and transmission rates, 9.11
Banking, and data processing, 4.10
**Bar chart**: A common form of graphical display of information in which data is represented by vertical or horizontal bars.
advantages of, 6.4
graphics and, 2.14
**Baseband**: A type of coaxial cable that carries only one signal at a time, 9.4
**BASIC (Beginner's All-purpose Symbolic Instructional Code)**: A commonly used high-level programming language.
described, 13.15
**Batch control**: The technique of balancing numeric data to a predetermined total to check the accuracy of data input.
and batch processing, 4.24
**Batch processing**: Data is collected and at some later time, all the data that has been gathered is processed as a group or batch.
applications for, 3.16
batch control and, 4.24
combined with interactive processing, 3.18
compared with interactive processing, 3.16
data entry for, 4.23–24
defined, 3.16
example of, 3.16–17
offline data entry and, 4.24
source documents and, 4.24
**Baud rate**: The number of times per second that a data communications signal changes; with each change, one or more bits can be transmitted.
and data transmission, 9.12
**Benchmark test**: A test that measures the time it takes for particular software or hardware to process a set of transactions.
and software evaluation, 11.10
**Bidirectional printing**: A form of printing in which the print head can print both when moving left to right and when moving right to left.
and printer features, 6.8
Binary number system bit
representation and, 5.5
described, 5.8–9
**Bit**: An element of a byte that can represent either of two values, "on" or "off".
defined, 5.5
**Bit-mapped display**: A type of screen used for graphics in which the number of addressable locations corresponds to the number of dots (pixels) that can be illuminated. Also called dot-addressable display.
and display methods, 6.17
**Bits per inch (bpi)**: A measure of the recording density of a disk.
and floppy disk storage, 7.7
**Bits per second (bps)**: A measure of the speed of data transmission; the number of bits transmitted in one second.
and transmission rate, 9.12
**Blocked records**: A method of organizing records on magnetic tape into groups called blocks for easier access.
and storage, 7.16
**Bold**: Bold characters are displayed on a screen with greater brightness than the surrounding text.
defined, 6.15
**Booting**: The process of loading the operating system into main memory of the computer.
described, 10.3–4
**Bottom-up design**: Design approach that focuses on the data, particularly the output, of a system.
and information system development, 12.11
**Broadband**: Describes coaxial cable that can carry multiple signals at one time.
defined, 9.4
**Bucket**: The location where a record is stored in a direct file.
and direct file organization, 8.6
**Buffer**: A reserved area of memory that the operating system uses to temporarily store data that has just been read or is about to be output.
and memory management, 10.7
**Bugs**: A name for programming errors.
and program testing, 13.10
**Bulletin board systems (BBS)**: Computer systems that allow users to communicate with each other and share data.
data communications and, 9.18
entertainment and, 15.10
**Bus**: A path along which bits are transmitted from one part of the computer to another.
and processor speeds, 5.12
**Bus network**: A network in which all devices share and are connected to a single cable.
advantages of, 9.17
Byron, Augusta Ada, 13.17